ORAL
ROBERTS

AN AMERICAN LIFE

David Edwin Harrell, Jr.

*Indiana
University
Press*

BLOOMINGTON

Manufactured in the United States of America

Library of Congress Cataloging in Publication Data

Harrell, David Edwin.
   Oral Roberts : an American life.
      Bibliography: p.
   Includes index.
      1. Roberts, Oral.   2. Methodist Church—United States—
Clergy—Biography.   3. United Methodist Church (U.S.)—
Clergy—Biography. 4. Pentecostals—United States—
Biography.   I. Title.
BX8495.R528H37   1985   269'.2'0924   [B]   84–48484
ISBN 0-253-15844-3
1 2 3 4 5 89 88 87 86 85

CONTENTS

Preface / vii   *Acknowledgments / xiii*

PART ONE: THE MOLD, 1918–1947

Prologue: Ada, Oklahoma, July 1935

I.	Roots	8
II.	The Mold	25
III.	Evangelist	35
IV.	Pastor	55

PART TWO: MIRACLES, 1947–1960

Prologue: Australia, January 20–February 10, 1956

V.	Healing Revivalism	80
VI.	Ministry	111
VII.	The Price of Glory	146
VIII.	Private Side	183

PART THREE: MAINSTREAM, 1960–1975

Prologue: Berlin, October 26–November 4, 1966

IX.	Oral Roberts University	207
X.	Beyond the Tent	253
XI.	Mainstream	287
XII.	Private Side	312

v

PART FOUR: MAELSTROM, 1975–1985

Prologue: Tulsa and Palm Springs, February 1977

XIII. Maelstrom   336
XIV. Completing the Healing Vision   358
 XV. Tightening the Family   397

PART FIVE: MEANINGS

  XVI. The Message   439
 XVII. The Man   469
XVIII. The Ministry   485

Epilogue / *497*   *Bibliographical Essay* / *499*
          Notes / *505*   *Index* / *615*

PREFACE

Oral Roberts has been one of the most influential religious leaders in the world in the twentieth century. I did not set out to prove that point; I finished this book convinced that it was true. Of course, such judgments are risky and subjective at best, depending as much on the future as on the past, but it is altogether fitting that this remarkable story—filled with unlikely and startling turns—begin with the assertion that Roberts has influenced the course of modern Christianity as profoundly as any American religious leader.

That judgment rests on three roles Roberts has played. First, and probably most important, are the leadership and publicity he has given to the pentecostal and charismatic movements since World War II. Pentecostal religion, with its joyful worship and emphasis on the miraculous, surged around the world in the decades after the war; the charismatic movement, pentecostalism's glamorous offspring, has had a profound impact on both mainstream Protestantism and Roman Catholicism. While such claims must be taken guardedly, a pentecostal spokesman in the 1980s claimed that fifty million people throughout the world had received the baptism of the Holy Spirit and predicted that by the end of the century, half of the world's Protestants would be pentecostal.

Of course, the pentecostal and charismatic movements were not the creations of Oral Roberts. The pentecostal churches, the Full Gospel Business Men's Fellowship International, and, among individuals, David du Plessis played catalytic roles in the spread of spirit-filled religion. But Roberts stands nearer the head of the amorphous movement than any other man, commanding respect throughout it. He was the leader of the generation of dynamic revivalists who took the pentecostal message of healing and deliverance around the world in the years after 1947. He sensed the far-reaching significance of the charismatic stirring in the mainline churches in the early sixties and brought traditional pentecostals and charismatics together in a series of dynamic conferences to explore the theology of the Holy Spirit. In the mid-1980s he stood as a figure uniquely honored and listened to in the fragmented pentecostal and charismatic world.

In his nearly four decades of healing revivalism, Oral Roberts has personally touched over a million human beings; several million more have answered his call to "accept Christ"; tens of millions more have heard him preach and pray on radio, television, and in films; hundreds of millions of pieces of literature have been mailed to every corner of the globe from his headquarters in Tulsa, Oklahoma. He has ministered to, and sometimes influenced, an astonishing variety of celebrities, leading many into the baptism of the Holy Spirit and

vii

speaking in tongues. A generation of students has been trained at Oral Roberts University. Cumulatively, the impact has been staggering. In those expectant areas of South America, Africa, and Asia, where zealous Christians are seeking an abundant life while still clinging to a miraculous God that does the impossible, Oral Roberts's name is spoken, and revered, and young men fervently pray that God will give them a touch like that granted Brother Roberts.

Roberts's second major influence on modern Christian history stems from his innovative use of the media, particularly television. His decision to film his healing crusades for television in the mid-1950s was a huge financial risk. His programs shocked and outraged many Americans; they piqued the curiosity of millions more. Perhaps even more important was Oral's return to television in 1969 in a series of slickly produced prime-time specials. He literally took his healing message to Hollywood, escaped the Sunday morning religious ghetto, discarded the traditional preaching format, and prepared the way for the modern electronic church.

Finally, Roberts, as well as others, has often noted that his name has become inextricably linked with religious healing. It was healing that launched his ministry in 1947, and it is healing that is the foundation of the controversial City of Faith complex rising high over the Tulsa skyline. In the 1950s, Oral shamed the mainstream Christian community into thinking again about the relationship of Christian faith and physical healing. In the 1960s and 1970s, he searched—in ways not to be expected of a pentecostal revivalist—for the meaning of human wholeness. He stood ready both to listen and to lecture in a world increasingly aware of the limits of medical science and the intimidating compartmentalization of modern thought. At the end of the 1970s, Roberts launched the most audacious undertaking of his ministry, the building of a medical school and the City of Faith hospital and research center, which would combine medicine and prayer. By the time others had come to believe in wholeness, Oral had set out to find it. He believed that at the end of his quest lay major victories, including the conquest of that dread destroyer, cancer.

Why, one must ask, have this extraordinary man and his ministry received so little notice from serious students of American religion and culture? Of course, Roberts is widely known by the public; his name is only slightly less recognized than that of Billy Graham. Roberts and his wife have written best-selling books about themselves, but those accounts are, of course, uncritical stories read mostly by supporters. Several exposés have been written about Roberts by former employees. They vary in quality and accuracy, but none attempts to deal comprehensively with his life and influence. Countless journalists have written about him, occasionally accurately and perceptively, but usually with reprehensible carelessness and bias. In all, there is an astonishing void.

Perhaps most surprising is the lack of knowledge about Roberts in the scholarly community. No serious and objective book has been written about him; almost no articles have appeared in scholarly journals. Sydney E. Ahlstrom, in his justly celebrated 1,100-page *A Religious History of the American People,* named Roberts one time in a sentence which erroneously reported his joining the Methodist church in 1965.

Two reasons for this neglect seem apparent. The first has to do with the pervasive condescension of academics and intellectuals. It is hard to entertain the thought that an "Okie Holy Roller" should be taken seriously. Furthermore, in spite of his astonishing success, Roberts remained outside the pale of respectability, an artifact from the dusty past of brush arbors and camp meetings. God still talked to him; he had personally beheld Jesus, and he believed in miracles. To some he seemed dangerous, to others absurd, or comical. Even were he all of those, his omission from history is inexcusable.

Roberts has contributed to the unbalanced public perception of him. He has often made himself inaccessible to reporters, and he has an abiding distrust of all popular writers. Like other celebrities, he has occasionally fallen totally mute. Oral's wariness has not been without reason; his lifelong struggle with bad publicity is a recurrent theme in the pages that follow.

This book is a serious effort to overcome both of those prejudices and to place Roberts in perspective in the development of modern Christianity. I am not pentecostal or charismatic, though I have been intimately acquainted with both movements. I had kinfolks who were pentecostals, and I well remember attending a Roberts tent crusade in Jacksonville, Florida when just a teenager. The whole pentecostal subculture left me with an enduring incredulity and curiosity. It was that curiosity, partly, which led me in 1975 to write *All Things Are Possible,* a book about the independent pentecostal preachers who took their healing message to the nation and the world in the years after World War II. By the time I finished that study, I was convinced that Oral Roberts was a consummately important religious figure. I continued to do research on Roberts and slowly and tediously became acquainted with people in his organization and, finally, with Oral and his family.

While discussing biases and judgments, I offer forthrightly several others which should help place into context what follows. First, I judge Oral Roberts to be a sincere and honorable man. I would not make such a sweeping statement about many of the religious leaders I have studied. My judgment does not imply that Roberts's methods have always been above question; they frequently are marked by an ingenious and inexorable pragmatism. But his faults, if faults they be, are rooted not in chicanery but in calling; he is motivated not by greed but by God, as he hears Him. Nonetheless, I suspect that some readers will be troubled by an objective biography of Roberts which does not conclude with a harangue against religious quacks and profiteers. The facts simply will not bend to such a clear and moral interpretation.

I acknowledge the propensity of biographers to take on the causes of their subjects. Oral Roberts is charismatic in the broadest sense of that word; it would be easy to be captured by him. Those close to Oral repeatedly told me of his unpracticed power in private conversation to encompass and surround one, to rivet his attention on his interviewer and take him captive. Furthermore, it would be difficult to follow Oral's dogged upward climb and not admire his tenacity, his skills as a communicator, and the raw courage behind some of his decisions. That admiration, frankly admitted, surely shows through in the pages that follow.

Fortunately, two reservations have helped me keep Roberts in perspective and, hopefully, have contributed to a balanced treatment. First, he is not entirely likable. He is human, earthy, visceral, volcanic. He swings from Himalayan peaks to pitch-black deeps. Those who love him best have seen him at his worst. No one knows better than Oral the human frailties with which he has struggled, and he has confessed to faults profound enough to make him eminently human, though not bloodthirsty enough to satisfy his critics.

My second reservation is personal and well confessed at the outset. I do not accept Roberts's theology. Nor am I convinced by the empirical evidence which I have seen. I regard the question of God's miracle-working power as a distinctly theological one, a question that has to do with one's reading of the Bible and one's faith. As we shall see, I believe that Roberts sees the question in the same way, and I have attempted to outline the major arguments for and against his beliefs. I have generally stated those beliefs in the words of the participants. Though I have not littered the text with *allegedly* every time I present the testimony of Roberts or some other believer, the reader should understand that such reports must be judged on their own merits.

While it is well to get such biases before us in the beginning, I hope that none of them, positive or negative, will be apparent as one reads this story. This book is an effort to tell Oral Roberts's story, who he is, what he has done, and what he believes. That story did and does raise countless questions as to why some have regarded him as a charlatan and false teacher and others as God's man to bring healing to his generation. In keeping with my understanding of good historical writing, this book is an effort not so much to settle those questions as to fairly raise and explore them.

When I wrote to Roberts in 1981 that I was about to embark on a "detached" assessment of his ministry, he replied that if I accomplished that feat it would be "something new relative to attempts made to comment on this ministry." If Oral has been surprised that someone would write objectively about him, I have been shocked by his cooperative spirit in dealing with me. He opened the doors for me to talk with everyone within his organization and his family. In an early interview, he told me: "Dr. Harrell, you're free to ask our people or me anything in the world." Furthermore, many of the interviews I conducted with people outside the Roberts organization could have been obtained only with his consent and, on occasion, with letters of introduction from him. Most important, I worked for nearly five months in the archives at Oral Roberts University amidst mountains of tapes and other materials. I was given free access to hundreds of thousands of pages of transcripts of Roberts's sermons, speeches, and lectures. In addition, I read transcripts of hundreds of public and private meetings in the various ministry organizations dating from the 1950s. The documentary record of the development of the ministry in the archives is varied and comprehensive.

I have not had access to two types of materials, financial reports and healing case histories. In neither case did I consider that lack a major liability; this book is not an effort to verify claims in either area. There is much public information on both questions. While the press has been obsessed with Roberts's private finances, and Roberts has probably been overly defensive on that question, there are clearly no closets filled with skeletons of financial abuses. As the pages that will follow show, Roberts is not wealthy, though he lives extremely well. He spoke to me freely about his private finances. As noted earlier, I regard the validity of healing testimonials largely as a theological question. The ministry's case histories, many of which are public, are a record mainly of the faith of the subjects and a measure of the commitment and sophistication of the organization in verification. They certainly "prove" nothing pro or con.

Perhaps the most serious difficulty in researching this book has been finding useful materials about Roberts from outside the ministry. Of course, there are thousands of newspaper stories and a few books and articles written by critics; but most of the critical assessments of the ministry are superficial and are based on little research. Many of Oral's bitterest critics know little about him; their objections are largely philosophical and theological. In many ways the most astute observers of Roberts have been his Tulsa friends who admire him but do not share his religious beliefs. They have been close enough to Oral and his organization to know its workings, while feeling free to criticize when they felt it was appropriate. But, at many crucial stages in this story, particularly in the portions about the early life of Roberts, I have been forced to lean heavily on the memories of Oral and his family and friends. The book includes notes, and the reader may make his own judgment about the reliability of the sources.

Roberts's cooperation with my research has been so thorough that many inside the organization came to identify my book as his "authorized" biography. That, of course, is not the case; from the outset Roberts has understood my intentions to write an objective account. Nonetheless, I was startled during a conversation when Oral, after agreeing to arrange several interviews for me with his friends, cautioned me, "I think you should talk to people that don't believe in us. . . . You have to get the whole story." That statement comes from a mature and slightly mellowed Oral Roberts, a man hardened and sharpened by a life of controversy and struggle but one turned introspective and reflective in the autumn of his life. The "whole story" needs to be told.

The whole story, it turns out, is two stories. The ministry and the man cannot be separated. A part of this book, the largest part, is about the ministry. The ministry is now bigger than the man, though it has not always been, and it will survive him. But it is permeated by him, it reflects him, it depends on him, and how well it will survive him is a question much on the minds of all interested parties. That is one story.

But this book is also about a man and his family. The Roberts clan staked a claim in Indian Territory, survived the Oklahoma depression, and rose to worldwide fame. When the City of Faith opened in 1981, Tulsa publisher Jenkin Lloyd Jones, Sr. called the hospital "a new monument to the peculiarly American spirit of can-do." On more than one occasion, Oral has expressed the same wonder at his rags-to-riches journey: "Only in America could a little stuttering boy, born in the Indian territory of Pontotoc County, Oklahoma, the son of a poor preacher, . . . amount to anything, could start a school from scratch and build a university." Quintessentially, his is "an American life."

The history of the Roberts family has been as turbulent as that of Oral's public ministry. Oral and Evelyn have been tenderly devoted to one another, and they have been fiercely loyal to their children. Their life together has been filled with incredible fulfillment and achievement and agonizing tragedy and defeat. Every member of the family inescapably became a part of the drama which surrounded Oral's call. While it is true that it has paid Oral Roberts (and his family) to follow the leadings which arose from deep inside him, it has also cost an excruciating price.

ACKNOWLEDGMENTS

In a work of this magnitude, the author is inevitably indebted to many people. Scores of individuals discussed freely with me their knowledge of Oral Roberts and his ministry. The list of taped interviews in the bibliographical essay lists only the most formal of those conversations. Those discussions have allowed me to view Roberts from a wide variety of perspectives.

Most important to me was the cooperation I received from Roberts himself. I taped about six hours of interviews with him, including one session at the beginning of my research and two after it was completed. Roberts intentionally did not talk with me while the book was in progress, because, he told me, he did not want to try to influence the finished product. I assured him that he would not, that I was a professional historian and intended to write the story as I saw it. But his decision was probably a wise one. We can both truthfully say at this point that Roberts freely answered questions and gave aid, but never made any suggestions about the interpretative content of the book. It may be that I did not ask him the right questions or that my judgments are naive or misguided, but, whatever the case, the responsibility rests on me and not on Roberts.

Evelyn Roberts was my most useful contact with the Roberts family. I talked with her on a number of occasions while I was writing, and she read the manuscript as it progressed. She made a number of factual corrections which have improved the accuracy of the book and on only two or three occasions asked that I listen to a further explanation of some incident I had discussed. I also talked for several hours with Richard Roberts and Roberta Roberts Potts and found both of them to be open and cooperative.

The person most responsible for facilitating my research at Oral Roberts University was James Buskirk, who, until mid-1984, was the vice-provost for spiritual affairs. His administrative assistant, Margie Shields, spent many hours arranging appointments for me. I am also indebted to William Jernigan for opening the ORU library to me. The staff of the Oral Roberts University Archives, headed by Lannae Graham, became my valued friends in my months of work in their basement hideaway. I owe special thanks to Jim Dulebohn of the archives staff and to student worker Kendra Getter. As in the past, Karen Robinson and the staff of the Holy Spirit Room in the ORU library offered ready assistance. I am also indebted to the photograph library of the Oral Roberts Evangelistic Association, headed by Karen Jermyn. Her assistant, Christy Helms, selected and identified many of the photographs in the book.

Many people helped in the preparation of the manuscript. I am deeply indebted to Suzanne Maberry, a doctoral candidate at the University of Arkansas, who not only typed much of the manuscript but also did much of the work in assimilating the notes and aided in countless other ways. Edrene Montgomery, another product of the Arkansas history department, prepared large portions of the manuscript. Nancy Gould did much of the early work on the manuscript, Terry Garrity helped in the final stages, and Kim Scott helped with the notes. I also acknowledge the assistance of my wife, Adelia, and my daughter, Marilyn Lee, for typing thousands of notes during my research.

In the past I have received grants to do research on Roberts from the University of Alabama in Birmingham, the Center for the Study of American Catholicism, and the Institute for Ecumenical and Cultural Research. In addition, the University of Arkansas has generously supported and encouraged my work during the past three years. I am particularly indebted to History Department Chairman Timothy Donovan; Jack C. Guilds, Dean of the Fulbright College of Arts and Sciences; and Chancellor Willard B. Gatewood. Professor Gatewood's assistance was that of a colleague and friend; he read much of the manuscript while it was in preparation and offered many helpful suggestions.

When I began the final stages of research for this volume, before I discovered that the Oral Roberts University Archives had an extensive collection of newspaper clippings, I wrote to a number of friends and colleagues asking for their help in locating newspaper articles. Many of them sent articles which I otherwise might not have found, and I wish to express my thanks to Don Alexander, Cecil Belcher, O. C. Birdwell, Jr., Jack Bise, Jr., Floyd Chappalear, Wilson Copeland, Ken Dart, Samuel G. Dawson, George R. Dickson, Bill Fairchild, Jerry Fite, Bill Fling, Elden Givens, Leon Goff, Bill Hall, Sewell Hall, Ricky Dowdy, Berry Kercheville, Gary Kerr, Daniel H. King, Phil Morr, David J. Ormerod, Dale Pennock, Randy Pickup, Norman E. Sewell, Dale Smelser, L. A. Stauffer, James Trigg, and Steve Wolfgang.

Finally, I am indebted to Indiana University Press. I especially thank my friend John Gallman, director of Indiana University Press, for his encouragement and support.

I also wish to express appreciation to Oral Roberts for permission to quote from the following titles:

Evelyn Roberts, *His Darling Wife, Evelyn*
Oral Roberts, *My Story*
E.M. and Claudius Roberts, *Our Ministry and Our Son Oral*
Oral Roberts, *The Holy Spirit in the Now*

ORAL

ROBERTS

PART ONE

THE MOLD

1918–1947

PROLOGUE

Ada, Oklahoma, July 1935

THE EIGHTEEN MILES leading from Stratford to Ada wound through the still-young farmland of western Pontotoc County toward the rolling hills that lay to the east. The landscape was luxuriant green after a summer blessed with abundant rainfall. Oklahoma Highway 19, reported the map, had escaped the state's road improvement campaign; it remained "earth, maintained but not standard grade." Laboriously it bridged Brook Creek both before and after reaching Center and then, just before reaching Ada, crossed over Sandy Creek, a favored spot for baptizing.[1] Now lined by pastures, prosperous Quarter horse ranches, and producing oil wells, in 1935 the road passed by monotonous cotton fields and scattered wildcat drilling rigs that heralded a modest oil boom which fanned local hopes in the 1930s.[2]

Oral Roberts's fateful journey to Ada in late July 1935 began abruptly. His older brother, Elmer, burst into their parents' small parsonage in Stratford and announced that he had come to take Oral to a tent revival to be healed. Elmer, the oldest son in the family of Ellis and Claudius Roberts, was "not a Christian"; his act of faith surprised the other family members. Twelve years older than Oral, Elmer had never felt close to his younger brother; he had, in fact, often predicted that Oral would "never amount to a hill of beans."[3] But all of the Roberts children, held together by fierce clan loyalties, had been deeply moved by the spectral appearance of their baby brother, whose illness had been diagnosed as tuberculosis.

Elmer's wife, Ora, persuaded her husband to attend a tent campaign that was stirring the summer dust and pentecostal fervor in Ada, and Elmer, who had stoically witnessed and resisted many an exhibition of heavenly ecstasy, was impressed. He determined that he must get Oral to the meeting. That was not easy. Elmer and Ora were struggling through the Depression, thankful for his laborer's job at the flour mill. On this July evening, Elmer borrowed a neighbor's Model T, spent his last thirty-five cents on gasoline, and set out for Stratford to get Oral.[4]

When Elmer reached his parents' home, he insisted that Oral get dressed immediately, impatiently explaining his mission. "I can't get dressed," Oral protested. Elmer "literally dressed" him. Ellis and Claudius "began to cry and rejoice"; the air was charged with excitement and anticipation. As Elmer helped Oral dress, he confessed his own faith: "I believe if I take him there the Lord will heal him."[5] Oral felt too weak to walk, his six-foot frame having shriveled to a skeletal 120 pounds, so Elmer picked him up, along with the feather mattress on which he had rested for almost five months, and placed him in the rear of the borrowed car.

Elmer, Ellis, and Claudius talked excitedly in the front seat, and Oral listened intently as Elmer described the miraculous healings he had seen. Oral knew that "Elmer is not the kind of man you can fool easily."[6] Then, their voices became distant, and Oral's mind sank into an acutely alert but tranquil reverie. He sensed that cosmic forces were focused on him. He was prepared to be healed. A few days earlier his sister Jewel had wept when she visited him but had erupted with seven long-remembered words: "Oral, God is going to heal you." Jewel's words had pierced Oral's psyche; he had clung to them; they had begun to challenge the despondency that had gripped him for months. A few days earlier he had been "saved and sanctified" and had begun to hope for healing. He had written earnestly to the *Pentecostal Holiness Advocate,* his church's small magazine, requesting the prayers of his fellow Christians.

Stratford, Okla.

I am happy and free because I have just been saved and sanctified. It is so glorious I want everyone to know it. Surely I have a right to be happy. . . .

I have been bedfast for 130 days, and I praise God for it. During this time I have been saved and sanctified. I have had several doctors, medical and chiropractic, but they seem of no avail. It seems that God is the only one that knows my condition. He has been dealing with me for a long time, and I have now awakened to the realization that I must obey Him. I feel the call to preach very definitely, but before I recover and enter into the work I must have the abiding Comforter, the Holy Ghost, to comfort me and help me to overcome my infirmities.

Dear readers, if you ever prayed an earnest prayer, please do so for me. The field is so broad, and the workers are few, I feel I must hurry and enter it. As I lie in bed thinking it grieves my heart that so many are unsaved and others are falling away because the cross is so great.

Yours for the lost,
Oral Roberts[7]

In the midst of this reverie came a private existential experience that Oral was to recount thousands of times to millions of people. "Suddenly I was aware of God's presence," he recalled,

> God spoke to me. . . . Audibly! Every fragment of my consciousness tingled and I was in sacred conversation with a divine Presence. His existence was so vibrant that I can only describe Him as God. . . . I was conscious of the car and the presence of others with me, but I was remote from them. . . . I was alone with God, His words were clear and unmistakable. "Son, I am going to heal you and you are going to take My healing power to your generation."[8]

The event and the message, awesome and far-reaching as they were, were accepted at face value by the seventeen-year-old. "It was no big, earth-shaking affair," he later remembered. "I grew up with a father and mother who believed in continuing revelation of the word, . . . that God still speaks. That angels still work. And it was normal. . . . I just heard it and believed it and that was it."[9] In the short run, the experience prepared Oral completely for his personal drama that evening: "Even before the evangelist prayed for me that night, I knew I would be healed."[10] But God's message to Oral was laden with meanings which would continue to appear in the decades ahead.[11]

Elmer's destination was a big tent pitched near the center of Ada where large crowds had been assembling in the torrid and sweaty June nights. God's man of the hour was "Geo. W. Moncey—evangelist, divine healer."[12] Moncey remains an elusive and shadowy figure, one of that generation of roving revivalists who continued to fight the devil in the depths of the Depression after such stalwarts of the 1920s as Aimee Semple McPherson, Charles Price, B. B. Bosworth, and Raymond T. Richey had retired to the shelter of local churches. Working out of an Oklahoma City Post Office box, Moncey was one of those will-of-the-wisp characters who fit many of the popular stereotypes of "Holy Roller" preachers. Local pentecostals had never heard of Moncey before the meeting, nor did he return to the city again; rumor persisted that he left town under a cloud.[13]

Whatever Moncey's reputation and future behavior, he came to Ada preaching a message of grim determination and supernatural power that spoke powerfully to the physical and spiritual needs of the poor of Pontotoc County. His theme song was "Hold On":

> Mary had a chosen son
> Jews and Romans had him hung
> Keep your hands on the plow hold on.
> They led him away to Calvary
> There they nailed him to a tree
> Keep your hands on the plow hold on.
>
> CHORUS
> Hold on, hold on
> Keep your hands on the plow hold on.

Jesus was so humble and sweet
He stooped and wash his disciples' feet
Keep your hands on the plow hold on.
Peter was so nice and neat
He wouldn't let Jesus wash his feet
Keep your hands on the plow hold on.

Jesus said if I wash them not
With me you'll have no part or lot
Keep your hands to the plow hold on.
Peter took the towel and said
Not my feet only but my hands and head
Keep your hands to the plow hold on.

Paul and Silas were put in jail
No one there to go their bail
Keep your hands to the plow hold on.
Midnight came and they began to shout
The angels came and turned them out
Keep your hands to the plow hold on.[14]

The tent was crowded when the Roberts family arrived, but Elmer had brought a rocking chair for Oral and placed it in an aisle. Oral's parents carefully placed pillows around him because "my body was so sore I could hardly bear for anything to touch me."[15] The weather had turned exceptionally cool for July, breaking a punishing heat wave; many in the audience wore "coats and shawls."[16] Elmer left to sit with his wife; Mama and Papa Roberts stayed with Oral.

Oral had never witnessed anything to compare with the flamboyant Moncey's service, though he had attended hundreds of ecstatic services in the small pentecostal churches and camp meetings of eastern Oklahoma. He listened intently as Moncey preached for about an hour. Oral was "touched"; he felt that he "was in the presence of a man that I felt *knew* God."[17] Then Moncey formed a healing line, a technique Oral later perfected but never recalled seeing before that evening. Witnesses later reported that the line was exceptionally long that evening, and Moncey individually prayed for perhaps two hundred persons. There were spurts of enthusiasm, but by eleven o'clock the service was dragging to a close. Many "were beginning to get heavy-eyed," and "a great deal of interest had died down," recollected a visiting minister.[18] But Oral's eyes followed Moncey like a hawk. Through his mind rushed all the faith-building experiences that had brought him this far; he knew "I'm going to be healed."[19]

Finally, when the entire healing line had passed by Moncey, the evangelist approached Oral's chair. He had been told that Oral would be there to seek healing. Moncey strode toward the youth and spoke: "Son, there was a boy here last night who was 17, who was an Indian boy and God healed him of tuberculosis."[20] He knew that Oral was part Indian and seventeen, and with that preparation he commanded Oral to stand up. Mama and Papa helped Oral to his feet while Moncey prayed. Claudius remembered that Oral sat down after the prayer and that Moncey started to leave him when suddenly he turned and prayed again. When he did he found a ready subject, though one unprepared for the vehemence of Moncey's words. In 1982, Oral described, as he has literally thousands of times, that powerful moment:

> Brother Moncey said words that I think I can quote . . . pretty accurately . . . because they were so different and they were so penetrating. He did not pray, "O Lord, heal this boy." . . . He spoke to another power and he said, "You foul tormenting disease, I command you in the name of Jesus Christ of Nazareth, come out of this boy. Loose him and let him go free!" Now, you see, nobody was praying prayers like that.[21]

As Moncey prayed, Oral recalled, "a blinding flash of light of God swept over my face and eyes and spirit."[22] Oral has tried to describe the sensation of that moment many times:

> I felt the healing power of the Lord. It was like your hand striking me, like electricity going through me. It went into my lungs, went into my tongue, and all at once I could breathe. I could breathe all the way down. Before that when I tried to breathe all the way down I would hemorrhage.[23]

Again, in 1982, he recollected feeling

> the presence of God, which my parents believed . . . was always something you could feel and they had taught that . . . to all their children, starting in at my feet. And it started coming up my legs. It was like, it was sort of like an electric current. . . . On the other hand, it was like a kind of warm liquid feeling that came up and came all the way up my lungs and when it got to my lungs, my lungs opened up. . . . I breathed, I got that *deep* breath, and I was clear.[24]

A rumble spread through the audience, giving way to shouts of "Glory" and "Hallelujah." "Mr. Roberts' son has been healed," someone shouted.[25] Moncey thrust the microphone toward Oral and said, "Son, tell the people what the Lord has done for you." Many in the audience knew Oral and were praising God for healing him, but they fell silent when he was told to speak, because he stuttered when under pressure.[26] Oral jumped up on the platform, shouting, "I'm healed! I'm healed!" For several minutes he ran back and forth across the stage, his baggy clothes sagging on his thin body, "testifying of what Christ had done for me and for the first time my tongue was free and the words came pouring out."[27] The audience was amazed at Oral's eloquence; he recalled that the "words rolled out of my mouth that night."[28] The family left the tent rejoicing; Oral was convinced that "my lungs were open and a whole new world lay out ahead of me."[29]

CHAPTER

I

Roots

REFLECTING ON HIS healing experience many years later, Roberts perceptively mused: "My upbringing had prepared me for this moment."[1] It was indeed a moment continuous with his past, not a disjuncture; its explanation could be taken as both miraculous and ordinary, divine and natural. Oral's experience harked back to the restless search for place begun by his Celtic forebears in Indian Territory, America's last frontier. It drew consciously on their reckless, brash pentecostal faith and their consuming hunger for personal meaning in the midst of the grapes of wrath.

Oral's recollections of his "upbringing" began with his grandfather Amos Pleasant Roberts, who migrated to Indian Territory in 1894 "Uncle Pleas," as he was called, was Welsh, a part of that adventuresome, uprooted band of Celts who pioneered the South and West in the nineteenth century. According to family tradition, Amos Pleasant began his trek west as a young man just turned twenty, moving from Alabama, where he had been a slave overseer, to Conway County, Arkansas, where he established the town of Robertsville. Along with him came his bride, Mary Jane Maddox.[2] In those verdant foothills of the Ozarks, Pleasant and his brother Ed began their families and made lasting friendships with their neighbors who had founded the town of Morrilton and other aspiring villages with sounding names such as Scotland, Jerusalem, Sardis, and Old Hickory.[3]

The 1890s were turbulent years in the South and Midwest. The decade was marked by profound changes in race relationships, by changing patterns of land ownership in the South, by the rapid spread of tenant farming and the crop lien system, and by the rise of political populism. This economic and political uncertainty was accompanied by unsettling shifts of population in the region. All of these pressures were at work in Conway County. A pioneer settler of Pontotoc County, Oklahoma recalled the sequence of events which led to the settlement of that area:

> The Roberts Brothers, Edd, and "Uncle Plez" as everyone called him, heard about the wonderful Indian country to the west of Arkansas, where they lived, and decided to move there which they did in 1893. They wrote to the Sloans, Stevensons and Medlocks in Texas, whom they had known in Arkansas, about this wonderful Chickasaw Nation where land could now be rented or leased from the Indians, and so in the fall of 1894 the Stevensons and Sloans moved from Mexia, Texas to Center, Indian Territory.[4]

Actually, the Roberts brothers most likely moved to Texas themselves in 1890 before going on into the Indian Territory, having made several trips into the area to locate a lease before moving.[5]

At any rate, the Roberts brothers were among the leaders of the pioneer vanguard into the Chickasaw Nation, settling in northwest Pontotoc County, a name brought from Mississippi by the Indians meaning "cattails growing on the prairie."[6] Ed Roberts, who built "what would have been called at that time a big house" in the community of Center, once again pulled up roots in 1900 and headed west. An early settler recalled the day when "the Roberts clan loaded their three wagons, drove their cattle behind them and started out on what was considered at that time as a long journey—they were moving to Wetumka."[7] Like generations of Celtic migrants before them, they piled their earthly possessions into wagons and drove their herds toward the setting sun. But Pleasant stayed behind, having settled a few miles to the north near Bebee, a community which was given a federal post office in 1896 and was named for Frank Bebee, the postal official who toured the Indian Territory establishing the mail system.[8]

Amos Pleasant Roberts was an esteemed citizen of early Pontotoc County. In 1895 he, Hugh Stevenson, and "Mr. Hobgood organized the first Sunday School at Center." It was a "Union" Sunday school, and Uncle Pleas was elected the first "superintendent." The Sunday school continued to meet for fifty years, drawing officers and teachers from all of the denominations of the community. Some thought it had a lasting impact on the moral and religious life of the community.[9] An early settler recalled that the area around Center attracted "good people" because of the religious tone of the community.[10] Roberts himself was a Methodist, a lifelong steward in the church; on occasion he "conducted services" in the absence of a minister.[11]

According to family tradition, Uncle Pleas was a justice of the peace and was President Theodore Roosevelt's choice as a federal judge in the Indian Territory, but he lacked the needed educational qualifications.[12] He was known as "Judge" Roberts in the community and was a frequent witness in the nineteenth century in the Sixth District County Court, which met in Center in the Indian Territory.[13] Without a doubt the Roberts brothers were pillars of respectability. Ed Roberts was one of the deputies in the posse which found and killed Bill Dalton near Ardmore, Oklahoma in June 1894.[14]

Amos Pleasant Roberts died in 1930. In later years Oral remembered visiting his grandfather and being completely captivated by his reputation and his presence. "He was a big, striking figure of a man, above six feet tall, weighing about 240 pounds." He had a "booming voice"; his grandchildren would sit enthralled listening to Bible stories mixed with reminiscences from a life that spanned the southern frontier.[15]

The country where Amos Pleasant Roberts settled was in the midst of the red, sandstone hills of southeastern Oklahoma. To the east were the Ouachita Mountains spilling over from Arkansas and to the west the Arbuckle Mountains, a rugged badlands that sheltered a generation of outlaws in the late nineteenth century. The gently rolling hills were covered with blackjack thickets and stately trees; after tne land was cleared it proved to be extremely vulnerable to erosion, and deep gullies soon marred the landscape.[16] Generally blessed with adequate rainfall, southeastern Oklahoma was not a part of the Dust Bowl, though the region did suffer during the intense droughts that have scorched Oklahoma in three cycles since the coming of whites, most severely in the 1930s.[17]

The white migration into this virgin land came largely from the South. From the Red River Valley of Texas, a steady stream of settlers from Arkansas, Mississippi, Alabama, and Georgia poured into the Indian Territory in the decade after 1890. The Red River Valley itself, a former coastal plain, stretched for thirty miles north of the clay-filled river, and from there its tributaries reached tentacles into the fine sandstone hills. When Oklahoma became a state in 1907, its population was perhaps more varied ethnically than that of any other state in the union. Its late development had attracted diverse fortune seekers, but the southeastern quarter remained strongly southern, long bearing the nickname "Little Dixie."[18]

Indian Territory was already a land in transition when white settlers began to arrive.[19] Present-day Oklahomans are only one generation removed from the frontier and only a century and a half removed from Tonkawas, Caddoes, Comanches, Kiowas, and Shawnee migrating as they had done for centuries past.[20] When Arkansas became a state in 1836, the western half of that territory was reorganized as Indian Territory. Already the rapidly expanding settlement of the Southeast had begun to force the removal of the major tribes of that region—the Cherokee, Creeks, Chickasaw, Choctaw, and Seminole—into Indian Territory at a tremendous price in human suffering and life.

Those proud and powerful tribes that established themselves in the eastern half of Indian Territory were cultures in transition. They brought with them from the East not only methods of agriculture and open-range ranching they had learned from the white settlers but also slaveholding.[21] The Civil War devastated the political power of the relocated Indian Nations. In all of the tribes, major elements sided with the Confederacy, and by the 1870s their territories and rights had been further constricted. In 1876 the Chickasaw Nation, which included Pontotoc County, organized politically and began the practice of leasing land to white settlers who wished to establish businesses or farms.

By the 1890s, the Indians had become thoroughly alarmed by the growing population of whites in Indian Territory, but it was too late to reverse the tide.

The Chickasaw Nation was the most unbalanced. In 1890 it reported less than 4,000 Indians within its boundaries—far fewer than the Cherokee, Choctaw, and Creek—and nearly 50,000 whites.[22] By the time the major tribes came to seek the expulsion of whites from their nations, their own rights were about to be changed. In 1889 the great rush had been made into the unassigned lands in the territory, renamed Oklahoma Territory. Furthermore, in 1887 the Dawes Severalty Act had allowed for the division of all Indian territories into private holdings, and strong pressure to adopt individual ownership came with the establishment of the Dawes Commission in 1893. The transition to private ownership and the demise of the old Indian Nations were completed in 1907, when the Oklahoma and Indian territories were combined to form the state of Oklahoma.

These transitional years in Indian Territory were turbulent and lawless, the authentic Wild West. The children of these late-nineteenth-century frontiersmen were often awed by the sight of bands of Indians in full regalia.[23] Furthermore, the territory was a magnet for desperadoes. Fugitives from the East mingled freely with drifters, cowboys, and Indians in a frontier melting pot. The Corner Saloon, at the Corner Crossing of the South Canadian River twelve miles northwest of Ada and not far from Bebee, was one of the most notorious watering holes in the West. As late as 1907, the deputy U.S. marshal in Ada "reported 223 cases of intoxication involving whiskey, 30 murder cases—killing under the influence, 52 assaults to kill, and three rapes, all under the influence of whiskey. Most of the cases come from the infamous Corner Saloon."[24] Hiram Brooks built the first store in Bebee in 1897; older residents remembered "how frightened the children were when drunken men came through Bebee from the old Corner Saloon. . . . They would stop at one of the stores across the street and eat."[25] By 1900, the citizens of Maxwell Township, which included Bebee, had incorporated and drafted an ordinance warning rowdies to stay away:

> If any person shall willfully or maliciously disturb the peace and quiet of the Incorporated town of Maxwell or Neighborhood, or family by loud or unusual noise or by abusive violent obscene or profane language whether addressed to the party so disturbed or some other person or by threatening to fight[,] fighting or shooting off any fire arms or brandishing the same or by running any horse at unusual speed along the street or alley, he or they shall be deemed guilty of a misdemeanor And on conviction in Mayors Court shall be fined in any sum not more than $200.00 (Two Hundred Dollars), or be imprisoned not more than SIX MONTHS or both at discretion of the Mayor trying the case.[26]

For the most part, life was more sedate for the early settlers. They followed the patterns learned through two centuries of frontier subsistence agriculture, clearing the forests, hunting the abundant game of the region, tending their herds of animals, and raising enough food for themselves and their livestock.[27] Little towns soon began to dot the countryside. Some, like Bebee, would eventually vanish. Center, so named because of its central location in Indian Territory, remained small.[28] It was Ada, founded in 1891 by William Jeff Reed, a cowboy who helped the Daggs brothers drive their cattle through the area and stayed to build a store, that was to become the most flourishing urban center of southeast Oklahoma.[29]

Already in 1896 schools had been established in the small communities of the county, including one in Bebee. Pontotoc County seemed to have a bright future. Although cotton was the early backbone of its economy, the area never depended on "just one resource."[30] As early as 1897 there were oil leases in the county, and in the early 1920s the very substantial Bebee field was discovered in the area where Pleasant Roberts had settled. In the 1930s an even larger discovery, the Fitts field, was made in south Pontotoc County, and that strike helped to blunt the worst of the Depression in southeastern Oklahoma. By 1937 Pontotoc County had become the second-richest oil county in Oklahoma. Ada had grown to a population of over 8,000 by 1920, and by 1935 it had an estimated population of 13,000.[31] While local residents conceded that Tulsa was the "oil capital of the world," Ada was the "recognized oil capital of southern Oklahoma."[32] Nonetheless, the residents of Pontotoc County suffered through the 1930s as did other Okies. Even staunch Oklahoma boosters admitted there was a "modicum of truth in Grapes of Wrath," as mechanized farming "decreased the rural populations" and set adrift thousands of former tenant farmers.[33] Well over half the farmers in the state were tenants in the 1930s.[34]

Ellis Melvin Roberts grew from a teenager to a young man in this rambunctious environment. Born in 1881 in Arkansas, Ellis grew up in Bebee, Maxwell Township, acquiring a farm in the same area as his father and brothers, John and J. Willis Roberts. He was an inconspicuous part of the turbulent landscape, a gentle, unambitious farmer.[35]

By 1900, Ellis had grown into a tall and slim teenager, when chance brought to his attention Claudius Irwin, the fourteen-year-old daughter of a migrant farming family which had just moved to Maxwell Township. The Irwins were a part of that same pattern of Celtic migration which had brought the Roberts brothers into Indian Territory. Claudius and Ellis were born no more than fifteen miles apart in Arkansas; the families followed the same trail from Arkansas to the Red River Valley in Texas and then on to Indian Territory. Claudius's father was a sharecropper, and she had lifelong recollections of long, sultry, hazy days in cotton fields, of the merchant Lige Jackson, who kept them trapped in debt, of fantasies of escape. "I despised my country life," she later recalled. "From as far back as I can remember I always said, 'When I grow up I'll marry a preacher. I'll never marry a farmer.' "[36] But Ellis was tall and slim and handsome, and Claudius was vivacious and blessed with the beauty of her full-blooded Indian grandmother. They courted for a year, and on February 17, 1901, they drove Ellis's buggy to Hart, where a minister married them in the noonday sun as they sat in the buggy. Ellis was nineteen, and Claudius was fifteen.[37] The union cemented a racial mixture typical of Oklahoma; Welsh and English names like Roberts, Irwin, Maddox, and Holden mingled with a proud but nameless Cherokee heritage.[38]

Claudius remembered that in the years after their marriage they were "a poor family when it came to this world's goods, but we were a happy family."[39]

But clouds soon darkened the young couple's life. They had two children quickly. Velma, the oldest daughter, was born in 1902, and Elmer, the oldest son, was born in 1906. Velma soon became the controlling force in their family life. Claudius remembered her as a "precious baby" who loved to sing. She would frequently "get up before the congregation in church and sing. Her little life was a song until she was six years old." Then Velma began having "epileptic seizures." They became worse and worse, apparently wrecking her health and contributing to her early death at the age of nineteen.[40]

Velma's illness cast a pall over the household; it left permanent marks. The family felt ostracized because Velma "wasn't normal like other children." Ellis recalled, "We couldn't go anywhere unless a neighbor came in and stayed with her or until Elmer got big enough to take care of her." One Sunday morning Ellis walked dejectedly to the "back of my little farm" and emptied himself to God: "Lord, why was I ever born into the world. I am deprived of all privileges. I can't go to church. I can't get out with my friends on account of my afflicted child."[41] The future seemed dark indeed.

The gloom did not begin to lift from the Roberts home until 1914, when Ellis and Claudius began another pioneer pilgrimage, this time a religious one. That journey would lead them out of their personal despair, through frightful physical hardships, into their promised land of spiritual hope and peace.

New neighbors brought light back into the despondent Roberts home. J. P. and Martha Pryor moved into the community and one evening drove their wagon by lantern light to "bear witness to them of their experience with Jesus Christ."[42] A little later the Dryden family moved into nearby Stratford—"big, raw-boned people, plain and God-fearing—and began 'setting the woods afire' with old time revival meetings." The Drydens had received "the light on the Baptism of the Holy Ghost," and when they preached and sang, "people came for miles to hear them, to find God and get healed."[43]

In 1914, pentecostal evangelists shook Pontotoc County. The three Dryden brothers, Luther, Bill, and Dewey, were joined in an old-fashioned brush arbor meeting by Dan and Dolly York, who had received their baptism in the Spirit in 1908.[44] The whole country was being stirred, or so it seemed to Ellis and Claudius. One evening Claudius's mother came to sit with Velma and Elmer, and Ellis and Claudius visited the brush arbor. Claudius described the scene:

> Tree trunk poles holding up the freshly cut brush formed an arbor. Lanterns swinging with the night breeze cast light and shadow across a huge crowd of people. It looked as if all of Pontotoc County was attending the revival meeting. The people singing around the folding pump organ sounded heavenly as their voices resounded across the hills.[45]

"It was a sight to hear them sing and testify and preach," recalled Ellis.[46] Dan York was one of the pioneers of pentecost in the West. Called to preach as a seventeen-year-old Methodist in Texas and later expelled from the church because of his belief in "instant sanctification," he had preached holiness and Holy Spirit baptism since he was nineteen, once walking eighty miles to preach with feet bloodied by the journey and a stomach filled with wild berries.[47] In 1929, a church leader reported that when

> Dan York begins to talk, all of us get quiet and lean forward to listen. . . . The stories that man can tell can command my ear any time. . . . They are stories of the real pioneer, stories of fighting snow storms and blizzards, fording swollen streams with wagon and ponies, going into darkened streets in dreary hours of the night to rescue some unfortunate sinner from the clutches of the devil, stories of threatened starvation, loss of property and final victory over all opposition.[48]

Dan and Dolly York sang "Open the Pearly Gates," Dan pumping the organ and singing the lead, and Dolly, also an ordained minister, singing alto "like a mockingbird."[49]

The effect of the service on the young Roberts couple was electric. Ellis was soon standing up close to the organ, captivated by the sights and sounds. But it was Claudius who first realized that "these people had the kind of salvation I wanted." When a neighbor told Ellis that Claudius was about to get "shouting religion," Ellis turned to his wife and abruptly commanded, "Wife, let's go home. I've seen all I want to see and I'm not coming back."[50]

A year passed before the Drydens and Yorks once again teamed up to conduct a big brush arbor meeting, this time fifteen miles northwest of Ada in a remote area on Buck Horn Creek. In the meantime, both Ellis and Claudius had been pondering their spiritual condition. They had always been religious, but Velma's illness kept them from attending church. After their experience in 1914, they became increasingly morose about their predicament. Privately, Ellis came to feel a call to preach; he remembered that as a boy he had tried to imitate the preacher who held services in his father's Methodist church. But the way seemed closed.

The couple attended the revival on Buck Horn regularly, taking Velma with them when they could find no one to stay with her, alternately going under the arbor while the other stayed with Velma. Night after night they went to the altar to seek salvation. One evening Claudius, moved by a sermon by "brother Dryden," "prayed through" and happily arrived home "a new woman." Ellis was disappointed that he had been unsuccessful in having an "experience" in spite of his seeking. The meeting was drawing to a close, and Ellis brooded over his failure.

On the evening that Claudius received her experience, Ellis also knelt at the altar to pray and was joined by one of his neighbors, Bud Holiday, who had recently become a preacher. As they prayed that evening, Holiday imploring God on his neighbor's behalf, Ellis became aware that his conscience was burdened. He remembered that several years before, he had killed a hog belonging to Holiday because it had repeatedly broken into his corn field. The act was accidental, but he had hidden it and had carried a feeling of guilt ever since. He remembered the incident as they returned home after Claudius's happy experience; the next morning he ate no breakfast. He bolted from the house, shouting to Claudius that he was on his way to the brush arbor for the morning service and that he would not return until he had received his salvation. He went first to Holiday and confessed his wrongdoing and then rushed through his father's house to tell Pleasant that he was on his way to seek salvation, waiting for no answer. His brother-in-law, Ernest Sutton, asked Ellis about his haste, and Ellis shouted back, "I'm on my way to get saved." When he returned home that evening, the work was done.[51]

"God called Ellis to preach the day he was saved," Claudius later wrote, but it was not until a year later that he answered "the call."[52] Claudius exhorted Ellis to sell their small farm and to "start out to evangelize and pioneer new churches for the Master." Ellis tried to be "practical"; he was hesitant to abandon his farm that had provided a decent if marginal living for the family.[53] The obstacles were formidable: Ellis was thirty-three years old, with no formal education, no experience preaching, and no assets except his land. He felt, with some reason, that he "never had had a chance in life."[54] But, in 1916, he cut his moorings and launched out to preach salvation and holiness to "the goodhearted, rough country people" of southeastern Oklahoma.[55] He sold his farm, paid off his debts, and purchased a Bible, a buggy, and a portable organ, the tools of his new trade. Shortly after Ellis sold his farm, the Bebee oil field began to produce; he missed the modest wealth that accrued to his family and neighbors. But Ellis declared that he never regretted his decision. The years that followed were a "period of great happiness."[56]

Ellis and Claudius Roberts were now a part of a tightly-knit, young, expansive pentecostal subculture in its formative stages. Pentecostalism was little more than a decade old when Ellis and Claudius received the baptism of the Holy Spirit. The new religion spread like wildfire across the nation after the heralded Azusa Street meeting in Los Angeles in 1906. For several decades prior to that historic meeting, leaders on the most fervent fringe of American evangelical religion had been seeking deeper religious experiences and particularly had been preoccupied with a fuller understanding of the baptism with the Holy Spirit. This search signaled that many of the mainstream American evangelical churches, particularly the Methodists, were beset by growing theological and cultural tensions reflecting class antagonisms. The holiness movement in the Methodist church had isolated the most fervent and emotional Methodists (and usually the poorest) into associations and churches of their own. This loose community of expectant saints was stirred when, in 1900, students at Charles G. Parham's school in Topeka began speaking in tongues and interpreted their experience as evidence of the baptism with the Holy Spirit. Parham became the earliest important spokesman of the new movement, but the real explosion came in 1906, when for months a revival continued at the Azusa Street Mission, attracting people from across the country. Loose, amorphous, but white-hot, pentecostalism spread through a network of ubiquitous religious papers, influential individuals, and camp meetings, and by word of mouth.[57]

The central doctrine of the new pentecostal "full-gospel" revival was that the New Testament baptism with the Holy Spirit, as experienced in Acts the second chapter, on the day of Pentecost, was available as an additional experience for Christians and that it was accompanied by (or the "initial evidence" of it was) the gift of speaking in tongues (*glossolalia*). In the earliest days of the rapturous movement, tongues speaking was widely assumed to be *xenoglossy,* the miraculous ability to speak a foreign language, although that assumption was not universal and soon was questioned by many pentecostals. In addition to their belief in glossolalia, early pentecostals were strongly millennialistic and emphasized the miraculous, particularly divine healing.[58]

In many places pentecostalism was simply imposed on the already existing network of holiness churches and camp meetings.[59] While the full-gospel message of speaking in tongues was new, the fervent, free-flowing pentecostal worship was like that of the frontier churches of the early nineteenth century. The Methodism that Ellis Roberts was reared in, the Methodism of the Indian Territory, was "shouting Methodism," the strain that made one "as limber as an acrobat" and felled hardened sinners with its power.[60] When Amos Pleasant Roberts, during his declining years, came to hear his son Ellis preach, the old Methodist steward approved of what he heard and bore witness that "God is in my boy's life."[61]

By the time Ellis joined the pentecostal movement in 1915, it had fragmented into dozens of small, frequently erratic sects. For the next three decades it continued to splinter over doctrinal eccentricities and personality cults. By the 1930s, the most important pentecostal churches were the Assemblies of God, a loosely united group of congregations headquartered in Springfield, Missouri; the Churches of God, a centrally organized denomination dominated for a generation by A. J. Tomlinson in Cleveland, Tennessee; the Foursquare Gospel church, which grew out of the work of Aimee Semple McPherson, by far the most visible pentecostal leader during the 1920s and 1930s; and the Pentecostal Holiness church, a group with strong holiness connections that had centers of strength in the Carolinas and Georgia and in Oklahoma and Texas.

It was to this latter small church that Ellis and Claudius were attracted by the Drydens and the Yorks. The church was the outgrowth of the "fire-baptized" movement among holiness Methodists in the Midwest which was begun by B. H. Irwin, an enigmatic and elusive figure whose unconventionalities removed him from visibility by 1900.[62] In the religious census of 1916, the church members numbered 5,353.[63] By 1936 the membership had reached 16,513.[64]

While the center of strength of the small church was in the East, it very early established a foothold in Oklahoma.[65] The Fire-Baptized Holiness Association made some headway in Oklahoma around the turn of the century, and when the pentecostal outpouring came in 1906, many were anxious to seek the new experience.[66] Joseph H. King, a Methodist minister, conducted a holiness revival in Snyder, Oklahoma Territory, in 1905, and when the pentecostal outpouring came to the state two years later, many of King's acquaintances united with the Pentecostal Holiness church. In the summer of 1907, a revival held in the Blue Front Saloon Mission resulted in scores of persons from throughout the area being baptized in the Holy Spirit, and Pentecostal Holiness congregations were begun in over twenty places as a result, including at Stratford in the

Indian Territory.[67] The Pentecostal Holiness congregations in Oklahoma became something of a western branch in the small church. For many years there
were two bishops, one in the East and one in the West.[68]

By the 1930s, most people in polite religious circles were aware of the
pentecostal subculture; after all, the "barbaric rhythm of their music and the
declaiming in 'unknown tongues' can be heard for blocks." In 1949, Angie
Debo, sensitive observer of Oklahoma's history, pointed out that the enthusiasts
were there, out where "the cities thin out into modest suburbs or the plains
tangle up into blackjack hills," but she was at a loss to account for them.[69] To
outsiders, they were the "Holy Rollers," a generic form of religious madness
that was "against the vices of infidelity, evolutionism, sexual recreation, the use
of gin, and fallen Methodism. They are against plain prayer without orgies as
much as they are against dancing, liquor and tobacco. They are against faith
without a personal Devil as much as they are against jewelry, tea and coffee,
transparent female garments, polygamy and theological liberalism."[70] Such condescending and undiscriminating accounts of pentecostalism infuriated leaders
of the growing movement. There were, of course, vast variations in the pentecostal sects—differences they were keenly aware of but which few others understood a generation later.

The Pentecostal Holiness church was probably the most rational of all the
new pentecostal churches. J. H. King was one of the few early pentecostal leaders actually ordained in the Methodist ministry before becoming pentecostal.[71]
The church's paper, the *Pentecostal Holiness Advocate*, was written in a thoroughly
rational tone. When G. H. Montgomery became editor of the paper in 1937,
the church acquired the services of one of the better pentecostal journalists of
his generation. While most of the church's early preachers were uneducated
men, such as Ellis Roberts, there was also an early emphasis on education and
the founding of schools. In 1933 the church organized a junior college, Emmanuel, in Franklin Springs, Georgia. The group's moderate stance resulted in
strong support for the establishment of interdenominational organizations in the
1940s, including the National Association of Evangelicals and the Pentecostal
Fellowship of North America. In both organizations, Pentecostal Holiness leaders were active and prominent.[72]

Doctrinally, the Pentecostal Holiness church occupied a middle ground
among the pentecostals. In 1938, G. H. Montgomery warned that "many harm-
ful, embarrassing, and degrading ideas had their birth amongst so-called Pentecostal people, but the Holy Ghost is not responsible for them. His coming
into the world has not produced the many delusions and wild fires that have
broken out in his name."[73] The more radical element in the Pentecostal Holiness movement, which "stressed the theory of leaving off neckties, not drinking
tea, . . . what was called worldliness in women's dress, and . . . made . . . the use
of hog meat an offense," left the church to form the Fire-Baptized Pentecostal
Holiness church in 1919.[74] To some, the church's aversion to fanaticism gave
the appearance that its leaders had "backed off" the early pentecostal emphasis
on the miraculous.[75] In short, by the 1920s the Pentecostal Holiness church had
sloughed off its most radical elements and had established a stable denomina-

tional organization. While most of its ministers and leaders were still uneducated men, the church had tried to rid itself of the "sensational evangelist with
his shady tactics," the "religious clown," and the stereotypic "Holy Roller"
preacher.[76]

Of course, painted in its most somber tones, the Pentecostal Holiness
church, in doctrine and practice, appeared to be a madhouse to more traditional
Christians. Pentecostals knew well that they were outside the "recognized denominations," ostracized because of their beliefs and the "emotionalism" of
their worship. They regretted their isolation, wrote G. H. Montgomery in 1938,
but "Christ is outside those churches; the Holy Ghost is out and the revival is
out."[77]

Primarily, pentecostalism was separated from mainstream Protestantism by
its distinctive doctrines, doctrines that were, indeed, at variance with traditional
orthodoxy at important points. Most crucial was the pentecostal belief in speaking in tongues as the "initial evidence" of the baptism of the Holy Spirit. That
belief was succinctly stated in the Pentecostal Holiness *Discipline*:

> We believe also that the Pentecostal Baptism of the Holy Ghost and fire is
> obtainable by a definite act of appropriating faith on the part of the fully
> cleansed believer, and that the initial evidence of the reception of this experi-
> ence is speaking in tongues as the Spirit gives utterance (Luke 11:13; Acts 1:5;
> 2:1–4; 8:17; 10:44–46; 19:6).[78]

A second tenet which set pentecostals apart from other evangelicals was
their belief in divine healing: "We believe also in divine healing as in the
atonement (Isa. 53:4, 5; Matthew 8:16, 17; Mark 16:14–18; Jas. 5:14–16; Ex.
15:26)."[79] While there was general agreement among pentecostals about
speaking in tongues, divine healing was a more divisive doctrine. Nor was the
pentecostal emphasis on healing a complete departure from the evangelical
mainstream. Pentecostal beliefs about healing were akin to and drew upon the
views of Christian and Missionary Alliance leaders, as well as a historic stream
of orthodox theologians.[80]

The most vexing question about divine healing for early pentecostals was
whether or not God's provision in the atonement ruled out the use of natural
means of healing. From its beginning, the Pentecostal Holiness church allowed
diverse views on that subject. While the discipline clearly stated that the church
believed in divine healing, it also made clear that "a person who fails to appropriate it is not counted as unworthy of membership among us. We do not therefore hold that it is a sin to use remedies, nor do we dismiss anyone for using
them."[81] Thus, contrary to the practice of the more frenzied pentecostal sects,
the Pentecostal Holiness church tolerated the use of medicine, albeit reluctantly
on the part of many.[82]

A third doctrinal pillar of the Pentecostal Holiness church was "entire
sanctification." The discipline stated: "We believe also that entire sanctification
is an instantaneous, definite, second work of grace, obtainable by faith on the
part of the fully justified believer (John 15:2; Acts 26:18)."[83] This doctrine most

strongly connected the Pentecostal Holiness church to its Methodist roots and separated it from the "single work" pentecostals, who believed that the baptism of the Holy Spirit and sanctification were simultaneous experiences. Remote and trivial as the distinction appeared to outsiders, the issue has remained an important one to many pentecostals. Not only did the "one work" doctrine violate the personal experience of many former holiness people (they could point to discrete moments when they had been saved, sanctified, and baptized with the Spirit), but also many felt that "the only firmly organized Pentecostal denominations with a strong central government which proposes to establish the same rules of conduct for all its people everywhere, are those denominations that hold the doctrine of instantaneous and definite sanctification."[84]

A fourth distinctive Pentecostal Holiness belief, and one the church shared with the militant fundamentalist movement of the early twentieth century, was dispensational premillennialism: "We believe in the imminent, personal, premillennial second coming of our Lord Jesus Christ (1 Thessalonians 4:15–18; Titus 3:13; 2 Peter 3:1–4; Matthew 24:29–44; and we love and wait for His appearing—2 Timothy 4:8)."[85] While pentecostals were never preoccupied with prophecy to the extent that the modern fundamentalist movement has been, and while they contributed little to the growing body of literature defining dispensational premillennialism, the theory was nonetheless an ever-present assumption, and it was frequently discussed by preachers and editors.[86]

Historian Vinson Synan has described pentecostal theology as the product of an "instantaneous" mind set. It was Protestantism's "crisis" mentality taken to its logical extreme. Not only was salvation an instantaneous experience, so was sanctification, the baptism of the Holy Spirit, healing, and the second coming of Christ. Nothing came gradually; every Christian experience was precipitous and cataclysmic.[87]

In addition to these theological distinctives, Pentecostal Holiness people were constantly and factiously attentive to questions of personal morality. In its earliest days the church forbade "outward adorning, such as jewelry, gold, feathers, flowers, costly apparel, or ornamentation of any kind," though in later years members were simply "forbidden to follow immodest and extravagant styles in dressing, or to wear needless ornamentation."[88] Still, as late as 1939, a preacher just returned from the East Oklahoma camp meeting observed that "the quartet that sang last night was not made up of Pentecostal Holiness singers, I am sure; for the ladies wore short sleeves and finger rings; and Pentecostal Holiness ladies do not wear short sleeves in East Oklahoma . . . and as for rings—well, they just aren't worn by our women out here in this conference."[89] Church members were constantly advised about the dangers of "moving picture shows, baseball games, picnics, circuses, dancing halls, county and state fairs" and other "worldly amusement," although this prohibition specifically exempted "any Sunday School or church outing for recreation."[90] Whether divorced persons could under any circumstances be church members was the cause of an early division in the group and long continued to be a source of debate and contention.[91] The use of tobacco was prohibited, as well as its sale or growth, but the church was required to make some concessions through the years because of its strength in the North Carolina tobacco belt. In the 1930s the discipline added the explanation that the word *growth* did not apply to "hired help, or wives, and children who are required to work for tenants or landlords."[92] In the early years, church members were banned from joining unions, though, again, by the 1930s the discipline permitted a member's "consistent association with a legal effort on the part of labor to prevent oppression and injustice from capitalism."[93]

The moral and ethical problems which the church struggled with, and which often divided the pentecostal subculture, were real issues in the world of tenant farms and mill town slums. The church's moral code was a strenuous guidebook for lifting oneself from squalor. Sanctification meant that "all our members are required to be patterns of frugality, diligence, faith and charity, taking up the cross daily, and true to the abiding baptism of the Holy Ghost."[94] If some of the regulations of the church seemed stringent, they were demanded by the ferocity of the battle. Pentecostalism was bred in a society in which moral lapses and sexual promiscuity constantly threatened to undermine the family; Steinbeck's Jim Casey was a figure well known to pentecostals. Most pentecostals knew the pleasures of sin as well as the ecstasy of salvation, and they knew the Devil must be tightly bound.[95] In 1935, the superintendent of the Oklahoma Conference, Dan Muse, surveyed the fate of the 6,628 people who had come into the church in that conference since its inception. Only fifty-three percent remained in the church. Forty-five percent had either withdrawn or been expelled. Nearly half of the congregations established in the church's first quarter-century had vanished.[96]

It was, of course, among the rejects and derelicts of society that the church had its birth and made its early gains. The pioneer Oklahoma pentecostals who began meeting in the Blue Front Saloon made frequent pastoral visits to the jails and the homes for "fallen women."[97] While early pentecostal preachers believed their converts came from the "great middle class," "the common people," they were, in fact, those who aspired to those labels, or tenaciously clung to the bottom sides of them.[98] It is not strange that Oklahoma pentecostals frequently found themselves competing for souls with the Socialist Party which flourished in the state in the 1920s and 1930s.[99]

The Pentecostal Holiness clergy reflected this class status. While the church's leaders commended education, they also refused "to make a difference between those who are educated and those who are uneducated."[100] In general, the church's clergy fit the model constructed by historian Robert Anderson: 1. They were rural by birth but frequently had moved to the city and become part of the marginal work force. 2. They were poor. 3. Their educational level was about the national average but much below that of clergymen in the mainstream churches. 4. They often had a history of physical ailments. 5. Their lives were often beset by personal tragedy. 6. They came from religious families.[101] In addition, like most new sects, the Pentecostal Holiness church had a vast oversupply of ministers. One of the attractions of such groups is that they provide an avenue for advancement and professional status outside traditional institutional channels. In 1934, according to the statistics gathered by Dan Muse in the

Oklahoma Conference, one out of every ten members of the Pentecostal Holiness church was either a minister or a mission worker.[102] Ordination opened the door of service for the talented, the devout, and the aggressive. But ahead lay a thorny path. Many ministers, perhaps most, continued to work with their hands all their lives.

The Brush Creek experience placed Ellis Roberts in this stream of "rugged ministerial stock." Claudius had to push him into a final commitment. After a year of waiting, she finally told him: "Well, I'm going to ask God if you won't preach the gospel to call me." "Why," Ellis replied, "if the Lord was to call you, you'd go through anything to do it," and then he hesitantly agreed, "I'm going to preach it myself." Shortly thereafter, he climbed aboard his "little mule" and rode off to preach, leaving Claudius behind to stay with Velma, "shouting, praising God because he was obeying God."[103] He traded "our old family organ for a little portable organ, reserved the nearby Woostel School House and held his first revival." It turned into a "landslide for God."[104]

Ellis studied hard, but in the early days he had only a few sermons, and after a few days' preaching he would return home to study some more. "When he felt that his soul was refreshed and some new sermons had been added to his ministry, then out he would go again and preach the Word."[105] Claudius was not "called to preach," but she was "called to pray for the sick," and people sought her out from "far and near." "I would preach people to the altar," recalled Ellis, and "she would pray them through."[106]

Through those early years Claudius was the dynamo. Frequently Ellis felt that he was unprepared to preach, but Claudius sent him on his way, telling him to "just go on, the Lord will send the message."[107] It was Claudius who buoyed Ellis's spirit when he preached in "hard neighborhoods" where it was "hard to even get an Amen." "I'd say," he later recalled, "now wife you'll have to break the ice the first night."[108] And it was Claudius who got them ejected from a meeting in a nonpentecostal church one evening when she became "so far gone in the Lord" that she "preached the best sermon that they ever heard" in the church yard.[109]

They were a team. Ellis was "loving and kind." "I don't think I ever heard him raise his voice at any one," Evelyn Roberts remembered in later years.[110] He was honest, kind to his children, sympathetic with those suffering adversity, more interested in the "fruits of the spirit" than in the "gifts of the spirit," ever sweet in spirit.[111] But he nonetheless was remembered as a powerful preacher. He preached in the classic pentecostal style—"if the Lord didn't anoint and inspire him, he didn't have a message." Under his ministry, thousands came to the altar and scores of young men felt the call to preach.[112] Claudius, on the other hand, supplied the faith and the pluck. She "rebuked the Devil when something went wrong at home, she prodded Ellis to be faithful to his call, she neither wallowed in self-pity nor passed out sympathy to others when hardships abounded."[113]

In his early years Ellis was an itinerant evangelist, renting school houses, stores, and other abandoned buildings for his meetings, or building brush arbors in the countryside. Only the more experienced pentecostal preachers were assigned pastorates; the rest were placed on the evangelistic list, the conference "dumping grounds."[114] He did some tenant farming, and he and his family worked in the fields of his neighbors. Claudius frequently went with Ellis once Elmer was old enough to stay with Velma. It was a simple but satisfying experience. After a successful revival, the unambitious Ellis would return home to "rest until the groceries ran out and the rent was due."[115]

When Velma died in 1921, the pattern of life changed slightly. Up until that time the family continued to live on Pleasant Roberts's farm, and Ellis's travel had been restricted by the need to care for Velma. Through the 1920s and 1930s, Ellis sometimes pastored small churches around the area and sometimes did evangelistic work; his growing family itinerated with him. Most often they lived in Ada, and that came to be the hometown of the Roberts children.[116]

For year after grinding year, Ellis happily set out to his meetings, often walking to a school house or a brush arbor that had been built in some remote community. "I've walked as high as fourteen miles to preach at my appointments in order to save my offerings to support my family," he later recollected.[117] In his later life he reflected on the advantages he gained from his burdens:

> I'd start 100 miles to hold a meeting afoot. Get up there and hold it, and they'd forget to take the offering, and I'd have to walk back. . . . But I didn't fall out with them. . . . But here's the secret to it. . . . Before I'd get there . . . I'd seek a grove and I'd get down on my knees, and call upon God. I'd get a hearin' from heaven. Brother, when I got there I had something to tell 'em. I forgot to write it down on a paper. I had it in my heart. . . . And brother we had one revival meeting right after another.[118]

In later years, after Velma was gone, the whole family frequently set out on foot to one of Ellis's meetings, hoping that a wagon or car would pick them up. Even when school was in session, the children went along; sometimes they stayed for as long as three weeks, watching Papa preach and Mama pray.[119]

Not only did the children attend the revivals, they often contributed to the support of the family by working in the fields during the day. "The whole Roberts family spent the daylight hours in the field picking cotton," recalled Claudius. "The cotton money provided us with a few groceries."[120] Sometimes the family hoed corn. Once Ellis borrowed a cow from a local farmer to provide milk for the children. The support was never adequate. Oral's most frequently quoted recollection of his youth was of the pentecostal belief that "if God would keep Rev. E. M. Roberts humble, they'd keep him poor."[121] As they moved from "one revival to another—from one cotton field to another," they generally lived in the homes of the "Christian folk who had invited us for the revival." Each evening the children would speculate about whether they would spend that night on a pallet, on a corn shuck mattress, or in a warm and clean bed. Most welcome was the smell of chicken frying early in the morning, signaling "a good substantial breakfast for . . . Preacher Roberts and his family."[122]

Often the struggles were monumental. When Ellis decided to conduct a revival in nearby Center, he found the town's church building abandoned and weeds growing tall around it. The building had been used as a "gambling place" by the "rough cowboys" and the oil "roustabouts," and "blood was splattered three feet high on the walls—the aftermath of their drunken brawls." The Roberts family scrubbed, cleaned, cut weeds, repaired the building, picked cotton in the daytime, preached and prayed at night. There seemed to be little interest. Then, one glorious night, "nineteen people were saved," and the "whole community" was stirred. Before the revival closed, "sixty men and women had given their hearts to the Lord," including a seventeen-year-old lad named Raymond O. Corvin, whose life thereafter closely intertwined with the Roberts family. When the revival offering turned out to be four dollars, it "liked to have tickled Ellis to death." The money was a godsend; Ellis had walked to the meeting each evening with "cardboard soles" carefully cut out to fit inside his shoes to keep him from "walking on the ground even with shoes on."[123]

In the midst of the adversities, there were times when heaven seemed to open and the glory poured through. "Many times," recalled Claudius "the altar would be full of people who were seeking a blessing from the Lord. I prayed for them until they were either satisfied or gave up and went home—even if it took all night." There was an evening in Ada when Ellis's preaching "stirred up a nest of gamblers." Five of them "came to the altar and were gloriously saved," and all five eventually became "preachers of the gospel."[124] And whatever the discouragement, Claudius would not be defeated. "We started out to be faithful to the end," she reminisced, "so even though the hindrances hurt us, they didn't stop us from preaching the gospel."[125] They had no regrets. Shortly before his death, Ellis Roberts gave his testimony to a group of ministers on the Oral Roberts University campus: "I've spent 49 years traveling for Jesus, and if I had a thousand years to live I would invest it in holiness tonight."[126]

Like many pentecostal ministers, Ellis moved easily back and forth between the roles of evangelist and pastor. Some years the conference stationed him at one of the small Pentecostal Holiness congregations in the East Oklahoma Conference. Evangelizing was a precarious living, but pastoring a little flock of ten to twenty people was little better. Ellis's first pastoral assignment was in Sulphur, where the church "consisted of a few chairs placed in rows beneath some willow trees in the yard of one of the church members." The stationing committee offered the post to several ministers who did not feel called to accept, but Ellis told them, "I'll be glad to go." And so, off he went, walking and hitchhiking to Sulphur. Feeling sick the first Sunday he was to preach at his new station, he nonetheless set out walking. Walking in the hot sun and failing in his effort to hitchhike, he began to wonder "if he would make it." In keeping with his character, "he sat down under a tree to rest for a while" and began to talk to God: "Lord, I am on my way to Sulphur to preach. I'm trying to get there and I am sick in body. It seems I cannot make it. But if you will please send someone along in a car to help me get there, I will preach tonight."[127] Pretty soon a Model T came along and picked him up. In the years between the two world wars, Ellis pastored a number of the small congregations of the East Oklahoma Conference, helping to build half a dozen new church buildings in the process.[128]

The three younger Roberts children were reared in this environment. Jewel was born in 1909 and was eight years old when Ellis made his decision to preach. She traveled with her parents and played the portable organ "by ear," though her feet could barely reach the pedals. In 1916 Vaden was born, the first of two boys who were to be fast friends and companions through their years of growing up poor, pentecostal, and preacher's kids.

Velma was remembered only vaguely by the younger children. Her condition continued to deteriorate. Once, recalled Ellis Roberts, she was "almost completely healed" when "the Lord put it on Bill Dryden to fast and pray for three days and on the third night she would be healed." On the second evening when they gathered together to pray, Velma suddenly seemed "perfectly normal," and they all rejoiced, believing that she had been healed. Dryden did not return the third evening "for some reason," and "that was the last touch of healing that Velma ever had."[129]

While Velma's death freed the family to travel, and in many ways lifted a burden from them, it had a withering psychological effect. Elmer, who frequently stayed home with his sister, was "hurt badly."[130] Elmer drifted away from the family; he was a teenager by the time Velma died. He never traveled in his father's ministry, and he never had a "born again" experience. "He'd always want to stay at home and work," recalled Claudius in 1963, "and I remember how we'd leave him sitting there and it'd nearly break my heart. But I put him on the altar to God, and tonight he's still on God's altar. I'll never take him up."[131]

Velma's death devastated Claudius. The family spent all the money they had on doctors and "prayed for the Lord to spare her life." When Velma died, it made Claudius "wonder about divine healing." She continued to work with her husband and to pray for sinners at the altar, but she prayed for the sick less frequently. "The great faith she had had way back there when we first got saved had seemed to die down," recalled Ellis.[132]

CHAPTER

II

The Mold

IN HINDSIGHT, the most portentous event in the Roberts family history came with the birth of Ellis and Claudius's third son and final child, Granville Oral Roberts, on January 24, 1918. Oral was born in an isolated log house near Bebee on Grandpa Pleasant Roberts's farm. It was a good year in Pontotoc County; the economy was booming, and the population was growing, although a flu epidemic wasted the county in the fall, causing the closing of all schools, theaters, and churches.[1] Ellis was preaching and Claudius was praying for the sick, and there was a warm glow in the family.

In later years Claudius related several events surrounding the birth of Oral that were to become part of his ministry's hagiography. A few months before Oral was to be born, she was called to the home of some pentecostal neighbors, Charlie and Mattie Engle, to pray for nine-year-old Francis Engle, who had fallen desperately ill. Mrs. Engle believed that God had spoken to her, revealing that if Francis were not healed that evening he would die. When his little brother, Marvin, came running to the Roberts house to get Claudius, she wondered why they had not called the Drydens, who had "lots of Faith in God," but Ellis agreed to stay with Velma, and she set out walking to the Engle house. She came to a gate that was stuck, and when she could not open it, she had to crawl through a barbed wire fence. Suddenly, she "felt the Spirit of the Lord hovering near," and she sensed that the child "I carried was a special child that would have God's anointing upon him." She promised God that if He would heal the Engles' son, she would give her child to Him. Claudius later retraced what happened when she arrived: "I was sitting there and holding that child's hand, but when he raised up the Holy Ghost fell all over the house and fell on Brother Charlie and he danced in the spirit. And I looked around, and there was little Francis sitting up in bed, and he said, 'Mother, I'm healed.' " She returned home convinced that God had promised her a "little preacher."[2]

When Oral was about a month old, his parents took him to a service at a school house which had been christened "Paris Chapel," where Bill Dryden was pastoring a small church. There were several visiting ministers present, and Claudius told them the story of her experience prior to Oral's birth. At the conclusion of the service, Ellis and Claudius carried the baby to the front of the building and "laid him on the altar." Dryden was joined by the visiting ministers, S. E. Stark, Dan York, and Dan T. Muse, as they laid their hands on the baby and "prayed a prayer of dedication."[3] Periodically during his childhood, Oral was reminded of the special religious call that had been placed on his life.[4]

Before Oral was born, Claudius, like most mothers, mused about the child she carried. She was "happy . . . over Brother Roberts' preaching, and we were just having a good time in the Lord." She made up her mind that she wanted a blue-eyed boy who looked like an Indian, proud as she was of her own Indian heritage. "The thought came to me," she recalled, " 'Why don't you ask God.' " So, she did: "I said, 'God, I want a little black-headed boy, and I want him to look like a full-blooded Indian, and I want him to have blue eyes.' "[5] And, sure enough, the baby was born dark, black-haired, and blue-eyed. "My little black boy I called him," said Claudius, until "I had to quit . . . because I got to saying little black boy in place of his name."[6]

Curiously, Claudius had not given much thought to naming the baby when he arrived. It was Cousin Minnie Lewis, eldest daughter of Willis Roberts and the oldest grandchild in the Roberts clan, who customarily named Roberts babies. Minnie "enjoyed the standing honor of washing and dressing all the new babies that came to the five families of the clan." She named them, "if she could think of a suitable name."[7] Minnie arrived in time to give Oral his second bath, and Claudius asked if she had thought of a name. After reflection, Minnie replied: "Auntie, his name is Granville Oral and we will call him Oral."[8] Claudius was pleased with this "pretty name." Granville was a Roberts family name; Oral was simply Minnie's creation. Friends of the family remembered several "O" names in the Roberts family, including Oris, Otis, and Ora, in addition to Oral.[9] In later years, reporters were fascinated by the theatrical sound of Oral's name, but cousin Minnie had no such designs. When asked in the 1950s if she knew the meaning of Oral's name, she replied, "So far as I know, I had never even heard the word before."[10]

Oral's earliest recollections of his childhood included images of his parents' humble religious devotion. Immediately after their conversions Ellis and Claudius established "a family altar in our home" and taught their children "to pray and to love God."[11] Like most country people they awakened early in the mornings, and the children could hear them praying, though not ritualistically; it was more like a "conversation with Jesus." "I actually thought," Oral recalled, "that Christ lived in our house, was a member of our family."[12] All through his life Ellis retained a simple, childlike faith in prayer. In 1966 he testified that "the most completest healing" he ever witnessed came when he laid his own hands on his wife as she lay ill in a motel: "I walked the floor. I said, 'Lord, . . . I don't know anybody. . . . I'm going to ask you while she is so sick to lay the nail-scarred hand upon her forehead.' And I just walked over. I said, 'Jesus, I've got to have you. You never did let me down.' . . . Five minutes, she was sound asleep."[13]

Vaden and Oral were "buddies," only fifteen months apart in age and "almost raised like twins."[14] Vaden was a stocky and strong youngster; Oral grew tall and slim, almost frail. They were a lively pair. Claudius painfully remembered the weekly ordeal of scrubbing and dressing the boys for Sunday services and finding her efforts wrecked before the family left home by their wrestling in the yard.[15] Oral later acknowledged that "people said that Vaden and I were the meanest children in the county."[16] Through the years Oral told countless stories about Vaden's mischief. Once Vaden, on a dare from Oral, nailed his brother's hand to a stump, and one evening during a camp meeting, Vaden whipped out his knife and began to cut off the ear of a youngster who was pestering him and Oral on their pallet.[17] While Oral remembered that Vaden was "strong" and he was "shy," some of his earliest friends recalled that Vaden was relatively quiet and that Oral was mischievous and lively. It was Oral who delighted in ruining the girls' sand castles with his feet; it was Oral who arranged the hide-and-seek games and managed to secret himself with pretty Boyce Carson;[18] and it was Oral who, a little later, "cared nothing in the world for anything except playing ball."[19] When Vaden threatened the youngster at camp meeting, it was Oral who held him for his brother.

The Roberts family continued to live on the farm for several years after Oral had begun grade school at the small community school in Bebee. Along with the other children, he pulled corn and picked cotton in his father's fields and rode in the wagon taking the cotton to the gin owned by Bob Kerr's father in Ada.[20] After the family moved to Ada, Oral generally traveled with his father and mother to meetings, and he continued to labor in the fields, but he more and more identified Ada as his home.[21] Until he became a teenager, Oral's strongest associations were with other pentecostal youngsters—"sleeping on the same pallet at brush arbor meetings, eating at the same table, . . . wearing the deacons' kids' hand-me-down clothes."[22]

The image of Oral Roberts as a youngster, or Obadee, as he was called by friends, is curiously blurred, filled with those anomalies that betray a sensitive, creative mind. Oral was shy and a leader; he was self-conscious and an extrovert; he was poor and pentecostal, and he aspired to respectability. As a small overalled boy, his sharp eyes peered out at a world that had passed the Roberts family by; yet in his fertile mind danced dreams of grandeur.

There are glimpses of these tensions scattered through Oral's childhood. Uncle Willis, like brother Elmer, always considered Oral "the most unpromising boy I had ever seen in my life." He told Ellis, and he told Oral, "That boy ain't worth a dime. He will never amount to a hill of beans."[23] Uncle Willis knew Oral. His nephew frequently stayed with him while Ellis and Claudius were away preaching, and he complained that "Oral was awkward at working with his hands and didn't pick as much cotton or chop wood as well as some of the others."[24] Oral never forgot the harsh judgment of his uncle: "I was never able to shake off what my kinfolks said about me when I was growing up. They never believed in me nor took time with me. They tantalized and tormented me. Perhaps they didn't mean any harm by it but it left an awful mark upon my life."[25] As a child, Oral often stood pensively on the weathered porch of his father's farm house, his hands "in my back pockets of my overalls," looking out on the red Oklahoma horizon wondering whether he would ever "amount to anything," whether he would "ever see what was on the other side of those hills."[26]

Oral's earliest memories of self-consciousness came because he stuttered. While his speech impediment had its "lighter moments," it could also be humiliating.[27] Grandpa Pleasant Roberts loved to hear Oral stammer, but his good-natured amusement never bothered Oral. However, some of the Robertses' neighbors and relatives, particularly Uncle Willis, "tantalized" Oral. He would hide from them when they visited. Cousin Minnie recalled that Oral would "come here to the door to tell me something, and he couldn't get it out to save his life. . . . We would often whisper to Aunt Claudius and Uncle Ellis that it was too bad about the poor little fellow but they would just shake their heads and say Oral would make his mark some day."[28]

Later, when the family moved to Ada, Oral was pursued home from school one day by a group of taunting boys "because I stammered so badly and I didn't want to be mocked." Claudius pulled the distraught lad onto her lap and told him: "Oral, . . . I gave you to God when you were a baby. You're God's property. . . . Someday He's going to heal your tongue, and you will talk. Son, you will preach the gospel."[29] But the stigma remained. When he was in the seventh grade, Oral was asked by his teacher to recite the "multiplication tables forwards and backwards out loud." He knew them, and could always win contests when the class wrote them, but when he stood before the class "the stuttering hit me so hard I could not talk. I burst into tears." "When I sat down," he later avowed, "you could have bought me for a penny."[30]

As Oral grew older, he increasingly felt the sting of being poor and pentecostal. All of the Roberts children knew the malaise of abject poverty. Vaden once asked his father for a dime so he could buy a tablet for school, but Ellis was about to depart for a revival and had not one penny to leave behind. He had to "leave the little fellow standing there without even a tablet so he could go to school."[31] In later years Oral sold papers "in the rain and snow to earn a few pennies to buy his pencils and paper for school." Even as a lad in junior high school, Oral still had only "one pair of overalls"; Claudius would "wash them at night in order to have them fresh and clean for him the next morning."[32] Sometimes the Roberts family experienced hunger. More than once relatives and neighbors anonymously left groceries behind their door because they knew that Ellis was away preaching and that the family had nothing to eat.[33]

Of course, in the 1930s poverty was endemic in Pontotoc County; many of Oral's friends were little better off than the Robertses. But one public mortification burned deeply into Oral's memory—and in the minds of his childhood friends. When he graduated from elementary school, Oral was elected "King of his Class." He saved his money from selling papers to buy new overalls to wear at his coronation ceremony.[34] When Oral arrived at the school to escort the queen, Mary Lou White, the "daughter of a rich family," he discovered her dressed in a "beautiful white satin evening gown." His teacher told the young-ster that he still had time to go home and put on his good clothes, but Oral replied that he was wearing his best. To his friends Oral appeared unperturbed, but the incident scarred him; it awakened him to the debasing stench of poverty.

And yet, inside the psyche of this poor, shy, stuttering youngster was a bright, irrepressible spirit. Oral was always one of the brightest students in his class, quick to memorize, nimble witted. Vaden struggled through his classes, complaining that Oral never had to study; but, reminisced Jewel, "Oral just knew it."[35] Oral later called to mind having an "insatiable curiosity" as a child, being particularly "awakened" by teachers in the third, seventh, and ninth grades.[36] And, in spite of his traumatic memories, Oral was popular as well as bright. Ironically, in spite of his speech defect, he usually played the leading role in school plays, apparently performing flawlessly under the pressure.[37] He was "a born leader and organizer."[38]

Oral's ingenuity and drive are clear to see in hindsight. He was a consum-mate salesman. Uncle John Roberts told Claudius one day: "Oral is up there on the street selling newspapers. The other boys just as well go home. Oral is the only one selling any papers. He's quite a talker!"[39] His mind was restless and inventive. During the years he sold papers, he also helped a nearby farmer deliver milk in return for a quart of milk to drink for breakfast.[40] One summer while still a teenager, Oral announced that he was going to hitchhike to California, joining the Okie migration. Claudius implored him to remain in Ada and attend summer school. Oral agreed, got a job in a store where Vaden worked, and made enough money to pay his tuition and buy his meals during summer school.[41] In all, his mother found him "strong willed" and "harder to deal with than the other children."[42]

Above all, Oral was an optimist. "Oral always had faith—even from a small child," remembered Claudius. When problems arose, "Oral would always say to me, 'Everything will be all right.' " No matter how "trying" the times, "Oral was the one who had faith. When we were running low on food, Oral was the one who reminded us that the Lord would provide for us."[43]

Whatever other traits lurked in the spirit of the Oklahoma youngster, they were to be subsumed under a supernaturalistic world view. The Roberts chil-dren lived their parents' faith, including a belief in "the fact of healing through faith in God." "Whenever they got sick," they asked their parents to call for the Drydens to come pray for them.[44] In Oral's case, there was an additional assur-ance that God had called him for a special purpose. In later years Oral recalled that his father told him: "Son, when you are grown you will conduct revivals in the largest auditoriums in the nation and men will go in front of you to make the arrangements and you will go and minister to the people. You will have the greatest revivals of your time."[45] Oral frequently put such prophesies out of his mind, but there remained "layers of things my family had put in me, and without my knowing it, those layers were there."[46] "Something in me told me that I was a child of destiny," said Oral in retrospect, "and from earliest childhood I was dubbed 'preacher' by my playmates."[47]

This subterranean religious proclivity became less and less apparent as Oral entered adolescence. He had been a good student in Sunday school as a child, as he had been in school, but his interest waned as he grew older.[48] When he was fourteen or fifteen, Oral joined the Methodist church in Stratford, but his decision was a response to peer pressure rather than an act of religious faith. Thinking back on the incident, he wrote: "I'm ashamed of that episode in my life, but it was not all my fault."[49] Increasingly, Oral's mind was preoccupied with "this big dream inside me." "I was bursting to amount to something, but everything was thrown across my path."[50] Claudius grew concerned about Oral: "He was strong-willed, highly inquisitive and seemed, in spite of all we could do, to be drawn to worldly things. He was popular among his schoolmates and . . . indifferent to the things of the Lord. It was clear to me that Satan was making a high bid for Oral's life, for it was evident that he had outstanding talents. He chose to associate with friends not affiliated with the church."[51]

By the time he entered high school, Oral had grown tall and agile and was considered a good athlete. Baseball was his passion, and he played on a local Ada team which included future major-league pitcher Harry (The Cat) Brecheen.[52] Dark and strikingly handsome, Oral was coolly conscious that his presence quickened the pulses of high school girls. While the moral sensibilities of Ada's parents in the 1930s were doubtless archaic by modern standards, Oral soon developed a reputation of being "too fast" to date the daughters of the more careful.[53] Oral chose to attend Byng High School six miles north of Ada, apparently because of the school's outstanding athletic record in the state. He finished his sophomore year agog with dreams of athletic fame, of university study, a law degree, and a political career. He was riding one of those euphoric highs which would periodically reappear throughout his life.[54] Dramatic changes were closing in.

In the fall of 1934, Oral's junior high school history teacher, Herman Hamilton, accepted a job coaching basketball in Atoka, a town about fifty miles southeast of Ada, deep in the coal-mining district of "Little Dixie." Atoka was an old town, founded in 1868; it was, appropriately in Oral's story, named for Captain Atoka, "a Choctaw ball player."[55] In what amounted to a recruiting raid still remembered by a Byng High School coach, Hamilton persuaded Oral to accompany him to Atoka to play basketball.[56]

When Oral went home to tell his parents that he was leaving, they were heartbroken. Ellis threatened to send the police after him if he left, but the defiant teenager replied: "No matter how many times they bring me back, I will run away again."[57] His parents relented. The six-foot fifteen-year-old was beyond their control. Claudius tearfully told him: "You will never be able to go beyond our prayers. Each day we will pray and ask God to send you home." Papa and Mama asked Oral to kneel with them and pray. Oral later reframed their words: "Oh, Lord, this is our baby boy. You gave him to us, and we have given him back to you. He is leaving us to go on his own. Now we commit his young life into Your loving hands. Watch over him and bring him back to us. In Jesus' name, Amen."[58] Oral shivered. He almost changed his mind, but he left. But he did not forget; it was as if his parents had "branded me with a hot iron."[59]

In later years, and probably at the time, Oral was conscious that his leaving home was triggered by deep discontents, not so much against his parents as against the way of life they represented. He was "sick and tired of being poor," of living in "a little three-room shotgun house" with nothing but a "monkey heater" to warm by in the winter.[60] The "strong ambition" building inside him could find no release in his parents' home.[61] He would never be "interested in a trade like my brothers"; his dreams soared higher than others could see.[62]

Both implicitly and explicitly, Oral came to recognize that his parents' religion was a roadblock to his ambitions. He came to resent the fact that his parents had forced him to attend Sunday school and church; he recoiled from being a "preacher's boy": "I got to where I hated it."[63] All of Christianity seemed repressive and confining. "I felt," recalled Oral, "that I didn't have a prayer if I became a Christian, because they taught you so much that you are to deny yourself and all of that."[64] Oral rebelled against self-denial; he was not "concerned about going to heaven," so "he ran away to get away from the Lord."[65]

Oral's act of rebellion was repeated by thousands of young pentecostals. In his own family, Elmer never joined a church, and Vaden "hated the church" because "they liked to have starved us to death."[66] Wayne Robinson, a perceptive observer who later became Oral's close confidant during his own personal journey out of pentecostalism, graphically described his family's disintegration. The poverty of his family, often combined with a callous disregard on the part of the church members who supported his preacher father, permanently "scarred" him by the time he was a teenager. Robinson painfully remembered being identified as a "Holy Roller" by his classmates, and being banned from attending movies, as his sisters were from wearing makeup. "I hated being poor, Pentecosal, and a preacher's son," he wrote, "and, in my late teens, my actions were loud disclaimers."[67] Of course, such revolt carried with it the pangs of guilt—"feelings of wrongdoing."[68]

Scrupulous Christians have always had to pay a price to prove they had overcome the world; the cost for pentecostals was very high. "Anybody who would have embraced the pentecostal message in the twenties and thirties," reminisced Assembly of God leader Thomas Zimmerman, invited "ridicule" and "derision."[69] Early pentecostals were "put out of buildings and pastorates and expelled from missionary societies; were generally ostracized, and branded by some quite spiritual believers as 'of the devil.' "[70] Their children endured the "jeers of classmates and teachers."[71]

While Oral carried away with him these internal broodings, his move to Atoka began as a sparkling success. According to his memory, he was elected class president, probably "mostly because I was a stranger."[72] He also was an honor student, editor of the school paper, a cheerleader for the football team, and a member of the basketball squad.[73] Oral "loved to study," and he set firm "goals" for himself. With a singleminded zeal that was to resurface again and again in his life, he set out to "make something of myself."[74]

In addition to his activities at school, the fifteen-year-old also "held down three part-time jobs and completely supported myself." He lived in the home of a local "judge," building fires and doing chores in return for his room and board. He also "worked in a store on Saturdays and . . . became a reporter for my home-town paper, the *Ada Evening News*."[75] Oral also indulged his appetite for the law. While living in the judge's home, he studied whenever possible in the law library, and when he left he carried with him some of the judge's books, a matter that was later to trouble his conscience until he could return them.[76] When court was in session, he went to "listen and watch," visualizing himself as "Governor of this state, even though I stammered."[77] His character was in place—a voracious appetite for work, an impatient urge to explore, and a capacity to dream the unimaginable.

In the midst of this bustle of activity, Oral also found time to fall "deeper and deeper into sin."[78] Actually, he continued to be a nominal Christian, attended church, and taught a young boys' Sunday school class. A high school athlete, he taught the kids how to play ball, but "I didn't teach them anything about Jesus because I couldn't teach somebody I didn't have."[79] And more and more he fell in with the "wrong kind of crowd."[80] His father had never allowed him to drive; he now learned and "drove fast," heading at "breakneck speed to partake in the sinful things of the world."[81] He began to learn "to drink" and to be "an immoral person," a pentecostal lad enchanted by the allurements of painted lips.[82]

These were busy months; his was a "demanding schedule." "Many times," Oral remembered, "I didn't have enough to eat or the right place to sleep."[83] He was a young man possessed, throwing his body recklessly into the battle to escape. It was not the last time Oral fought with such abandon, but it was one of the rare encounters he was to lose. The end came swiftly.

Oral later recalled the prelude to his collapse. "During the months previous to that," he said, "I had noticed myself being weak, and when I wakened in the morning it was like I hadn't slept. I'd waken with bed sweats. Of course, being a boy, I didn't attach any significance to that."[84] At any rate, collapse he did, in February 1935, by his recollection in the "final game of the Southern Oklahoma basketball tournament" while "dribbling toward the basket to make the jump-shot that would win the game." He "felt life going out of my lungs" and rose from the floor with "blood running from my mouth."[85] His coach, Herman Hamilton, drove him to his family's home in Ada. Oral's teenage rebellion had come to an abrupt and disquieting end.[86]

Ellis and Claudius were shaken; friends who visited Oral in the weeks that followed were shocked by his emaciated appearance.[87] Although he appeared optimistic to visitors, he increasingly settled into a mood of sullen despair, "bitter and unresponsive over my sickness."[88] For day after day he lay in bed, coughing and spitting, sometimes so violently that the walls were spattered with blood.[89] He ate little and became "irritable and hard to get along with."[90] "Lying there," he recalled, "every dream I had was swept away."[91]

During Oral's illness, Ellis accepted a call to pastor in Stratford and moved the family there. The "extra expense" of Oral's illness drained the family, and Ellis "began selling Bibles in order to help."[92] Although doctors were not "plentiful," and many of their pentecostal friends objected to their use, Ellis had Oral examined by Dr. Craig and Dr. King, their "family doctors," and later by Dr. Shy, "a dear friend."[93] Oral recalled that the doctors examined "my blood, my spittle, my lungs" and rendered the unanimous verdict that he had tuberculosis.[94] They gave the family little hope that Oral would recover; Papa, "his chin quivering," relayed their diagnosis to his son: "tuberculosis in both lungs and in the final stages."[95]

A pall of death settled around the house. The family was haunted by the knowledge that Claudius's father and two older sisters had died of tuberculosis. Oral's doctors requested his admittance to the state TB hospital in Talihina. The youngster remained confined to his bed for week after week, continuing to lose weight until his tall frame held only 120 pounds. His old friend Vaden Noble walked a mile each day to bring Oral a diet of raw eggs and milk, the "unpalatable" prescription for TB sufferers in the 1930s.[96]

Oral's whole family was "broken hearted." His brother Vaden broke down sobbing, threw himself across Oral's body, and cried, "God, put this sickness on me. He's never been strong, and I am."[97] Ellis was a constant source of comfort, and he and others stayed by Oral's side much of the time, talking and reading the Bible to him. Papa had telephoned or written "everyone he knew who knew how to pray, particularly for healing," and Oral's name was frequently called in the little churches of the area.[98] And Claudius's faith was indomitable. When confronted with the pessimism of the doctors, she felt welling up within her a message from God that "I'm going to heal him and leave him down here to bless the whole world."[99] Oral knew that his family, Mama and Papa Roberts especially, was pleading his case with God, but he had lost his own faith.[100]

Negative reinforcement of the doctors' verdict came from a variety of sources. Oral was "a captive audience to the various friends who came to visit my father and mother and me and whatever they had to say, I had to hear it." Oral was told that God had "tracked him down." Such talk infuriated Claudius, who assured Oral that God had nothing to do with his illness. "The devil afflicted you, son," she retorted, "he is trying to destroy your life."[101] But the gloom nonetheless overspread the household. Oral frequently thought back on the dispiriting effect of a visit from his "pastor," a "beloved man" who was minister at the small Methodist church in Stratford where Oral had joined with his friends before going to Atoka. The preacher prayed tentatively and unpersuasively and offered consolation: "Son, you will have to be patient with this affliction."[102] Oral felt he was surrounded by the comforters of Job—faithless and powerless at best and false accusers of God at worst. "I dreaded Sunday afternoon," he recalled; "I was captive and had to listen to my visitors. Invariably my room would be filled, and as usual they began discussing the moral and religious aspects of my illness."[103]

Then, after months of suffering and mental anguish, after hundreds of visits and countless prayers, wallowing through the hot summer on his sweaty mattress, the sequence began which was to lead Oral dramatically, though slowly, to a new life out beyond the hills of Pontotoc County. First, he experienced a classical, though existentially unique, salvation experience. Four months into Oral's illness, Mama and Papa Roberts stayed home from church services one evening, asking the deacons to take charge, and together with Oral's "nurse" they circled the sick youngster's bed and told him, "The time has come for you to get saved." For all his religious instruction and childhood experiences, Oral protested that he did not know how. Claudius instructed him to "open your heart and tell God how you feel."[104] But it was Papa who provided the spark that hot evening. Sweet and mild, he could preach and pray with fervent power; he could speak "like a command." The three adults began to pray surrounding Oral's bed, led by Papa—on his knees at the foot of the bed, "a big and powerful man with a large booming voice ... the tears ... streaming down his face"—fervently talking to God.[105] Oral's mind "drifted," and when his attention once again returned, Mama and the nurse were sitting in chairs with their heads in their hands, and Papa was still praying at the foot of the bed. Oral later described his experience: "Lying there listening to Papa's earnest prayer and knowing he was praying because he loved me, I felt a warmth flow into my body. For some reason I raised my head and looked at Papa. His eyes were closed and tears were wetting his cheeks and running off onto the floor. As I looked, Papa's countenance changed in my sight. A bright light seemed to envelop him and suddenly the likeness of Jesus appeared in his face. ... I fell back on the pillow sobbing and crying, 'Jesus, save me!" Jesus, save me!' "[106] In later years Oral would try to understand and explain the personal appearances of Jesus to him. For the moment, he was certain only that he felt "the presence of God go through me from my head to my feet," and he and his family began "crying, laughing and praising God."[107]

He was not, however, healed. He later came to believe that "saving faith" and "healing faith" are not the same.[108] But his faith began to grow; it was expressed fervently in the expectant letter he wrote to the *Pentecostal Holiness Advocate*. And then hope leaped in him when his sister, Jewel, spoke the words "Oral, God is going to heal you." Jewel's visit was unplanned; she had driven from Ada "on the spur of the moment," but she supplied the seed of enlightenment which grew into Oral's healing.[109] Oral had heard divine healing taught all his life, but it had not penetrated; Ellis and Claudius had encouraged him for months and finally led him through a conversion experience, but they had "never been able to reach me."[110] In all probability Oral had repeatedly been told the very words spoken by Jewel, but he had not been ready; "I hadn't heard."[111] Now, the time was ripe. "A wonderful sensation of hope surged through me," Oral recalled, "suddenly I realized that I was somebody. ... I was going to stand up, and I was going to be a human being."[112] The way was prepared for Elmer's visit and the journey to Brother Moncey's tent.

CHAPTER

III

Evangelist

ORAL ROBERTS was convinced, and has remained convinced, that he was healed of tuberculosis on that memorable evening in Ada. Afterward, his parents took him to the Sugg Clinic in Ada to be "fluoroscoped by Dr. Morey," and his lungs were found to be "absolutely perfect."[1] Years later, Oral testified that "I carry on my lungs now some scars and when our family physician xrays me, which he does every year, he and I talk about those old scars. The proof is in my lungs that I had TB and the proof is there that I am healed."[2]

Sudden and awesome as was Oral's healing, his recovery was slow and onerous. Oral's faith wavered. Those buoyed by the Spirit have always faced the dilemma of how to get the mountaintop experiences which explode under the tents to endure through the valleys that lie beyond. The morning after his healing, Oral was back on his mattress, weak and wondering. He soon became openly discouraged. "I couldn't understand why after I presumably had been healed I didn't have all my strength back," he later recalled.[3] Some of the family's relatives and friends openly derided their "foolish hopes" that Oral would recover, because he remained so "weak and looked thin and pale."[4] Through these burdensome days, it was once again the faith of Claudius that sustained the family. She held on tightly to the "glorious victory" and gently nudged Oral's faith. "Every time you feel like it, Oral, sit up," she counseled, "and little by little you will gain your strength."[5] Claudius's faith was as practical as it was indomitable. "Oral," she told her son, "it's all right to go in and lie down some during the day and rest while you're getting your strength back, but, son, don't put on your pajamas and get under the covers."[6]

The family made plans for Ellis to leave his pastorate in the fall to begin an evangelistic ministry, with Oral joining him to form a father and son revivalistic team. Immediately after his healing, however, Oral spent the summer preaching with some other Pentecostal Holiness youngsters from the area. Oral "received his call to preach the night he was healed," although he had clearly given the matter serious thought since his conversion experience.[7] Several of the young men from Pontotoc County had been attending Holmes Bible School, a quasi-official seminary for the Pentecostal Holiness church, and were home for the summer months. One of the youngsters was Raymond O. Corvin, whose family lived near Center and who had been converted under the preaching of Ellis Roberts. The youngsters paired off to hold revivals. Oral teamed with Simpson Merritt, and the two of them began preaching at the Homer school, "a little bitty schoolhouse in the country" four miles east of Ada. Oral practiced his first sermon preaching to the trees, and when he delivered it "two people were saved."[8] After two weeks of preaching, the aspiring revivalists took an offering, which netted them eighty-three cents each.[9]

When the other young men returned to school in the fall, Oral joined his father in holding meetings.[10] His reputation soon spread through the local pentecostal community. He was baptized in Sandy Creek that fall along with a group of other young people. The minister baptized Oral first, and then he allowed him to assist in the immersion of others.[11] Many who came to hear him "marveled at the wonderful healing wrought in his life."[12] A childhood friend remembered traveling to Roff to hear Oral preach in a rented store building when he was still too weak to stand and had to deliver his sermon from a rocking chair.[13] His early sermons were adequate but not singular. Sister Jewel remembered that Oral's first sermon "came out of his heart," but it was also brief.[14] His efforts were obviously still those of a beginner; Uncle Willis was not "much impressed with his preaching ability."[15]

Oral and Ellis took to the field in the fall; by December they had more calls for revivals than they could accept.[16] Their first joint effort was in Fox, Oklahoma, a small community where Claudius had lived as a child. At first, Ellis preached most evenings. Ellis was a powerful preacher "in the old-fashioned way," and he remained Oral's "hero in the ministry."[17] In 1936, a small-town Oklahoma pastor reported that Ellis had just concluded their "first successful revival held in several years," adding that "God's blessings are flowing freely and the church has taken on new life."[18] Another local pastor commended Ellis as a "man of God" and reported that eighteen had "joined the church" in Durant during a revival.[19]

Oral clearly rode his father's coattails in those early months. He recalled that the only thing he could do well was "preach short, eight to ten minutes." But Ellis gently and tenderly led Oral along. Oral later reflected about his feelings during these months of apprenticeship: "Papa could get up and open the Bible and just turn loose and preach and I'd sit back and say, 'Oh, I wonder if I'll ever be able to do that?' And my self-worth would plummet on the one hand, but . . . I watched him and noticed how he loved me and encouraged me and finally asked me to preach every other night as we traveled."[20] And

Claudius was there to prod. When Oral complained that he was out of sermons, Claudius retorted: "Well, go into the bedroom, get your Bible, study it and pray, and the Lord will give you another sermon." Slowly Oral improved. Elmer came to hear him one evening and "went forward but somehow was not quite ready to believe God to save me."[21] The slim, handsome young man had one gift that Ellis could not match. In one meeting "seventeen young girls came to the altar to accept the Lord, and one old man and one old woman!"[22] Oral soon learned that "Papa could outpreach me, but I could win more souls."[23]

Oral also became the leader of the Pentecostal Young People's Society in the East Oklahoma Conference of his church. In June 1936 he was elected secretary of that organization and held that position for three years. He was a frequent speaker at the young people's meetings.[24] In the summer of 1937, the young preacher, ordained less than a year, wrote a fiery article for the *Pentecostal Holiness Advocate* decrying the "formality" of the young people's meetings. "Oh, how we need Spirit-filled young men and women in our ranks today," he exhorted.[25] Lukewarm Christians had heard their first salvo from an uncompromising foe.

Between the time of his healing and the East Oklahoma Conference camp meeting which was held in Sulphur in August 1936, Oral preached, recovered, and impatiently waited for the camp meeting. It was at the Sulphur camp meeting that Oral was first licensed as a minister in the Pentecostal Holiness church, a memorable moment for him, although he had already spent nearly a year preaching.[26] Even more important, Oral set his sights on the camp meeting to receive the baptism of the Holy Spirit and to speak in tongues. For nearly a year he had chafed while preaching to others about the power of the Holy Spirit, having not received the pentecostal baptism himself.[27] He set his sights on Sulphur with an uncanny tunnel vision which made him oblivious to all else around him. By brute determination he did receive his baptism in Sulphur; he missed the meaning of other pregnant events which occurred there.

Pentecostal camp meeting time was a physical and spiritual feast—pleasant, peaceful, recuperative days and white-hot, incandescent, ecstatic nights. Camp meeting came in the midst of the fiercely hot Oklahoma summer, but there was always "plenty of shade," and tents were available to rent for only three dollars.[28] The faithful came from miles around, sometimes as many as three thousand, arriving in cars, on the train, and in wagons. Claudius recalled hitching up a "good team" and loading the bedding, cooking utensils, and children into a wagon when the family was young: "We jostled along the dirt roads, happy in the Lord and looking forward to ten wonderful days of Christian fellowship."[29] The day began with a "prayer service" at half past six in the morning. That was followed by a "testimony" service at ten and a sermon by the main camp meeting speaker at eleven. At three in the afternoon one of the visiting preachers was invited to speak; at five there was a "children's service," at six a young people's meeting, at 7:30 "another song and praise service," and then at 8:30 the main preaching service.[30] The evening meeting rarely ended before midnight, and sometimes the "power of God fell" so "abundantly upon" the assembly that the shouting and praying lasted until nearly dawn. "I cannot estimate the time that this sustained shower of blessing fell upon us," wrote one of the leaders of the East Oklahoma camp meeting in 1940, "for when a soul is enraptured by the presence of Jesus, time doesn't count, he simply loses all consciousness of the time element. However, even after the first great outpouring of the Spirit somewhat subsided, the Holy Ghost continued to work in a very gracious manner, and the meeting continued till around three o'clock the next morning, with souls praying through on all lines."[31] The sultry evening air was filled with songs of grim determination:

OLD CAMP MEETING DAYS

I'd like to be a boy again
    In old camp meeting times,
To hear old-fashioned people sing
    Their Hallelujah rhymes;
To see the mourners at the bench
    The pilgrims kneeling round,
Awaiting for the Holy Ghost
    To show the Savior found!

I'd like to see that preacher's face
    Above the bench again,
A smiling through his happy tears
    Like sunshine in the rain;
To hear his "Glory to God!"
    His wonderful "Amen!"
When half a dozen anxious souls
    Were truly born again.

Oh for one day of those past years,
    And of that day one hour,
When good old mother filled with God,
    Was shouting with the power;
And men and women laughed and cried
    As she went down the aisle,
A shaking hands and blessing all
    In old camp meeting style.

Well, praise the Lord: I am glad to see
    We're coming back again.
The Holy Ghost is here today,
    So let us say, Amen!
New-fashioned ways we don't approve,
    Tho' some may call us slow;
We like the good old-fashioned ways
    Of forty years ago![32]

Sulphur was a favored place for pentecostal camp meetings. Hundreds of tents were spread in Platt National Park surrounding the artesian sulphur springs which gave the town both its name and a pungent odor. The meetings there were noted for their spiritual ferocity. "It is impossible to describe the enthusiasm with which these Westerners worship God," wrote G. H. Montgomery after preaching in Sulphur in 1937. "Holy laughter rings out from the great congregation. Triumphant testimonies, sometimes as many as six at once, set the camp aflame, running, leaping, shouting and dancing are common occurrences in the services."[33] And so, in Sulphur, in August 1936, Oral "knelt in the shavings and poured out my soul to God," and "He baptized me with this mighty experience."[34] He spoke in tongues, though he later confessed that he had little understanding of what he had experienced and had sought the experience because his parents and others had told him that he "needed the baptism of the Holy Spirit."[35]

Important as Oral's baptism in the Spirit was to his understanding of his own Christian status, and important as it was to his future career in the church, it was probably less significant than a personal encounter he almost ignored. Considering the tightly knit subculture of which he was now a part, the encounter seems almost as inevitable as his baptism with the Spirit. It came at the young people's meeting at six o'clock on the first evening of the camp meeting. Oral took a seat on the platform to play in the band. At the last moment a young girl rushed in to take the empty seat beside him with her guitar in hand. "Well," said Oral, "haven't seen you around here before. Where are you from?" "From Westville," she replied. "What do you do?" asked Oral. "Well, I've taught a year of school." "Oh, a schoolmarm, huh?" replied the apparently impressed young preacher. Oral asked if his hair was combed, and she, slightly flustered, replied that he looked fine. The two played their guitars in adjoining chairs throughout the camp meeting and exchanged polite conversation. But, uncharacteristically, Oral was not interested in girls; he was "really seeking" the baptism of the Holy Spirit. He later had vague memories of the girl who sat beside him, but it took another set of circumstances to excite his interest.[36]

Evelyn Lutman Fahnestock had much stronger feelings and more vivid memories of the encounter. When she saw the tall, slim, black-haired young man, her "heart began to pound." When she returned to her tent that evening, she scribbled in her diary: "I sat by my future husband tonight."[37] She showed her prediction to her mother and sister, and they guffawed. Her premonition could remain only private. Oral was "too super spiritual . . . to think of girls," and convention would not allow her to speak boldly to him.[38] So, she waited until time and circumstances once again brought them to the attention of one another.

Because both families were core members of the Oklahoma Pentecostal Holiness subculture, the chances of another encounter were good. Ira A. Fahnestock was Evelyn's stepfather, having married her divorced mother when Evelyn was five years old. As a youngster, Evelyn was sensitive because she did not know her father, but it was her stepfather who was to guide her directly to Oral Roberts. Evelyn's natural father, whose name, Lutman, she consistently wore as an adult, was one of that band of German immigrants who had settled in the Ozark area of southern Missouri. At least from her perception, he turned out to be a "plain drunk," and when Evelyn was four and a half years old her mother was granted a divorce. Evelyn and her sister, Ruth, were given into the custody of her maternal grandparents. When her mother remarried two years later, Evelyn returned to live with the Fahnestocks.[39]

Fahnestock was "not a Christian" at the time of his marriage, but he was from a "good Christian background," apparently from a pious German Methodist family. He soon combined the drudgery of farming in the Missouri Ozarks with the excitement of a quest for Holy Ghost religion.[40] When he heard that "something had happened that was unusual, out of the ordinary" at a small church near Coffeyville, Kansas, where the pentecostal message scorched the prairie landscape in the 1920s, he pulled up roots and moved his family for a year. During that year he received his baptism in the Holy Spirit and became one of the pentecostal vanguard in the Midwest. Ruth and Evelyn had reached school age, and Fahnestock set out to find a Christian school for his children to attend. He discovered a small Pentecostal Holiness school in Checotah, Oklahoma, housed in an abandoned public school building. The Fahnestocks sold their farm and moved to Checotah. Evelyn's mother became a dormitory supervisor, and her stepfather preached and worked as a laborer.[41]

The little school in Checotah collapsed after a year, a victim of the endemic poverty and personal instability within the pentecostal subculture. A part of the faculty moved to Monte Ne, Arkansas, a serene village nestled in the Ozarks. The Fahnestocks followed the school to Monte Ne, and the children again enrolled in the little will-of-the-wisp institution. Evelyn remembered fondly her experiences in the makeshift school: "I got Bible classes every day, and I wouldn't take anything in the world for the Bible that I learned in that school."[42] The Monte Ne school survived five years before it floundered financially and disbanded. Fahnestock could not locate another pentecostal school, and so he settled on the best compromise he could think of, "a place where there's a good spiritual church and where they have good schools."[43] Once again the family moved, this time to Westville, Oklahoma, just across the line from Arkansas. There the children finished their schooling, and Westville became their home town.

Fahnestock was typical of the generation of marginal, itinerant farmer-laborer-preachers populating the fringes of the pentecostal movement in the first half of the twentieth century. He apparently always aspired to be a minister, was ordained in 1919, and preached occasionally in Pentecostal Holiness churches. During the Depression he tried his luck at itinerate evangelism. Evelyn and Ruth traveled with him; Ruth played the violin, Evelyn played the guitar, and Fahnestock preached. But the compensation was scanty, usually just a little food.[44] Fahnestock never was assigned a pastorate by the conference; he always made his living farming or working as a laborer. In the midst of the Depression, much to the embarrassment of Evelyn, he was forced to take a job with the WPA. In later years he operated a barber shop in Westville and more or less "retired" from preaching.[45]

In all, Evelyn's childhood was filled with grinding, humiliating poverty. Only the spiritual insulation her parents provided had shielded her. She resented the poverty, but, she later recalled, "the Spirit of Jesus in our home far outweighed the 'riches' of many other families."[46] Whatever her stepfather's shortcomings, "he knew Jesus and he knew how to have family prayer and how to read the Bible to us, and how to do it in an atmosphere where Jesus was."[47]

And the family exodus to Coffeyville, Checotah, and Monte Ne exposed her to a constant stream of pentecostal evangelists. In fact, she later recalled, "It seemed I was always in church or at a religious meeting."[48] In one of these meetings in Monte Ne, at age twelve, Evelyn "found Jesus Christ as my Savior."[49] Whatever his own abilities as a preacher, Fahnestock's "remarkable determination to keep the family in a spiritual environment prepared Evelyn someday to meet Oral."[50] In fact, his determination made their meeting inevitable; it was Fahnestock who ordered the family to "can everything you can find," pile into the car, and head for Sulphur for the camp meeting in August 1936.[51]

By 1936 Evelyn had finished high school and two semesters of college at nearby Northeast State Teachers College in Tahlequah. At the age of eighteen she had secured a teaching certificate and had taught for a year in a one-room school house in the country near Westville. She earned forty dollars per month in the depth of the Depression, paid her parents' room and board, and tried to continue her college classes on Saturdays. Evelyn yearned for respectability; she wanted to graduate from college; she resented the poverty that surrounded her. Fahnestock's determination had brought her this far, the restricted confines of the Pentecostal Holiness church had seated her next to Oral Roberts; ahead lay months of youthful uncertainty and anxiety before her life's work was sealed.

For the moment, Oral returned to his evangelistic career with a new vigor and determination. He preached more and more regularly and more effectively. For two years Ellis and Oral preached together, until a traumatic meeting in the summer of 1937 broke up the partnership. In the midst of a revival, a local pastor approached Ellis and told him that Oral's preaching was unacceptable and that Ellis should conduct the remaining services. Ellis tried to diplomatically preempt Oral each evening, but Oral learned the truth. He was crushed and indignant and announced he was leaving. Claudius and Ellis smoothed over the hurt, and restored Oral's turn in the preaching rotation, but the incident sealed his decision to strike out on his own.

Actually, Oral had already gained some fame, and his conference superintendent had suggested that he and Ellis needed to separate.[52] When the two preached in Holdenville in 1937, the local paper featured Oral: "a 19-year-old boy so prominent in his church's activities that he has been named a delegate to the world's conference of Pentecostal churches."[53] Oral immediately conducted a "small meeting" with some success and began to book revival appointments.[54]

In the months that followed, Oral sporadically preached in eastern Oklahoma, learning the pitfalls and perils of the profession he had chosen. He hitchhiked or walked to his meetings and frequently received little pay, his compensation coming on a "free will offering basis."[55] Roberts family tradition identified a post in Sulphur which was a "landmark" of these austere days: "It gave Oral the support he needed one day when he could walk no farther. He had walked for miles in order to get there to preach. He was so tired and weak that he held on to that post in order to stand. Every time we pass that corner and that post, it is a reminder of the determination to fulfill God's call at any price."[56] Oral later told of another evening during those months "when I had no place to sleep and nothing to eat and was a visitor in a town in sub-zero weather, . . . wandering about . . . wondering if I would freeze to death before the morning."[57] But through it all Oral remained optimistic. He later recalled a conversation with his father while the two were "standing at a railway station in a small Oklahoma town when I was only 19 years old." Ellis turned to him and said, "Oral, if you will be obedient, some day God will give you the largest ministry of your day." "Papa, how can this be?" answered the incredulous youngster. "You'll live to see the day that God will do it through you if you obey Him," replied his father, speaking, his son believed, in "the spirit of prophecy."[58]

One distraction still danced on the periphery of Oral's mind. He was still drawn to politics. Between the ages of seventeen and twenty-one he vacillated about whether "to preach or be a lawyer." He packed law books around with him as he traveled to evangelize, and in 1938 he threw himself wholeheartedly into the campaign to elect Leon C. (Red) Phillips governor of Oklahoma. Young Bob Kerr, later to be governor and senator from Oklahoma, had long known the Roberts family and was the leader of the Phillips campaign. Oral recollected that Bob's brother, Aubry, offered him a job in state government after the campaign and that the Kerrs encouraged him to run for office as soon as he was twenty-two. While his political future may not have been so promising as it loomed in his own mind, one could hardly doubt that Oral had a flair for oratory and persuasion. He was intrigued, but by the time the political temptation arose in 1938, his ministerial career was expanding so rapidly that it demanded his full attention.[59]

Oral's metamorphosis as an evangelist between the fall of 1937 and the spring of 1938 was remarkable. Bright and aggressive, he had become both well known and effective by the time he turned twenty in January 1938. He began a revival in Sand Springs in February which lasted five weeks and ended with "fifty-two saved, nine sanctified, four received the Holy Ghost, nine baptized in water, twenty-six united with the church, and forty babies dedicated to God." "His messages," reported the pastor, "born out of sincere study and prayer, were certainly inspirational, interesting and convincing. The crowds that nightly overflowed the church were seemingly held spellbound, hungry for the Word of God, as it fell from the lips of this fine young man."[60] Oral's Sand Springs revival caught the attention of the national leaders of the church. G. H. Montgomery commended him in the *Pentecostal Holiness Advocate* as "a promising young evangelist. . . . Studious, zealous, and fervent, he can be mightily used of God, and we believe that he will be."[61]

By the fall of 1938, Oral was much in demand, and his reports were glowing. He held a three-week meeting in Okmulgee that netted "twenty-five conversions" and "eighteen received into the church." In Konawa, where his father had gone to pastor, he preached for three and a half weeks and reported twenty-six saved and fourteen received into the church. By the end of the year, there was an air of confidence, even cockiness, in Oral's reports. The crowds were too large for the small buildings in which he was preaching. He bought a "public address system," which he used "to advertize the revival by day over the town." He usually conducted "street services in these revivals," and they were "a boon to our success." "Using our Loud Speaker and securing the best of singers," he reported, "we put on a good Pentecostal Holiness program. . . . By this method we came in contact with those who never go to church or hear the gospel. This also was good advertizing for our revivals and always increased our crowds."[62]

During these successful revivals, the young evangelist put special emphasis on getting converts to join the church. Whenever one goes fishing, quipped Oral, he always "strings the fish." "So as we are 'fishers of men' it is a good and sound policy to 'string' our 'catch' of converts. . . . My goal for the year is 100 new members."[63] Such constructive zeal "impressed" and "highly pleased" the small denomination's leaders and once again brought Oral national publicity.[64]

Thus, by 1938 Oral had already become visible throughout his church. His aptness as a student and his writing experience served well in a movement where preachers were often marginally literate. Oral began to write articles for publication in the *Pentecostal Holiness Advocate* in the fall of 1937. In August 1937, just after he returned from preaching in the East Oklahoma camp meeting, editor G. H. Montgomery published an article by Oral entitled "Character Building." In it Oral reminded young people that their "good character" was "the most precious earthly treasure a youth can have" and exhorted them not to be "haughty and rebellious in this period of life."[65]

Oral quickly submitted articles on other such safe topics as tithing and praying.[66] In spite (or perhaps because) of his youth and inexperience, he offered broad critiques of others' shortcomings, generally parroting tried and true pentecostal shibboleths. He condemned "the clergy" for an attitude "little short of infidel spirit." "When a young man goes off to these modern colleges and seminaries to be educated for the ministry, what is he taught?" asked the young high school dropout. "Is he taught the fundamentals of the Word of God, that God is on the lookout for men of prayer, full of the Holy Ghost; that the real sermon is made in the closet, that the man, the preacher, the pastor, is made in the closet of prayer? Nay!"[67] In the spring of 1938 he wrote an article outlining the proper relationship of pastors and evangelists, an undertaking some of the older heads in his own church considered presumptuous.[68]

In retrospect, it is easy to see that there was something special about this young man. He was perpetually looking for new methods to arouse old enthusiasms. He was openly critical of "pessimistic" pastors, living on "the dark side of life," defeating the glorious work they should be building.[69] At age twenty he was already trying to goad his church into revival: "Oh how this old world needs a new outpouring of the Holy Ghost, a truly God-sent revival that will bring new life from God to the ministry, the church and the world. The need is clear. When then shall we do it? Pray! Pray! until the Spirit comes and God revives His people."[70]

In early 1938, Oral's first book was published, a small pamphlet entitled *Salvation by the Blood.* Printed by the Pentecostal Holiness church publishing house, the slender volume was "lovingly dedicated to my parents who have so faithfully lived for Christ and taught me to love and fear God."[71] G. H. Montgomery wrote a benign introduction, noting that the "little pamphlet" contained a "message full of vital gospel truth." Particularly commendable, he concluded, was the author's "sincerity of purpose" and his "righteous desire to lead men to a better understanding of the gracious truth of atonement for sin."[72]

The atoning blood of Christ was a safe enough theme for the pen of a rising young preacher; pentecostal audiences no doubt received well his admonition never to "line up with any church until that church accepts this blood stained label. For no matter how fine the church, how high the steeple, how elaborate the furnishings, how eloquent the preacher, if the blood is denied it is not the church of Jesus Christ."[73] Oral's style was florid and sophomoric, but it was a commendable effort for a pentecostal lad who had not finished high school. If the pamphlet was not erudite, it did reflect a scattered reading of Wesley and Moody as well as some history. At any rate, it was heady business for a novice preacher to see his twenty-cent pamphlet listed among the "books that are available written by members of the Pentecostal Holiness Church" and recommended as a "sermon worthy of wide distribution."[74]

One of the more propitious side effects of the publication of *Salvation by the Blood* was the author's decision to send an autographed copy to Evelyn Lutman on her twenty-first birthday. The act was calculated and disconcertingly unromantic. Oral had decided to get married, and he had begun practically and singlemindedly to address that problem. Finding a wife was serious business.

Oral's meteoric success as an evangelist had opened the way for thoughts of marriage. While pentecostal revivalism was by no means a lucrative business, by the spring of 1938 Oral had saved enough money for a down payment on a new 1938 Chevrolet coupe. He cut a dashing figure.[75] As might be expected, he was constantly beset with "girl friend troubles."[76] Oral learned vicariously "all of the temptations that a young man goes through, sexual and everything else," and though he "never yielded," the struggle grew more desperate. One of the church members in Westville, where Ellis had moved to pastor, planted a seed in his mind: "Oral, you need a wife." Oral agreed, and his advisor continued: "I'll tell you who's for you. And that's Evelyn." Oral later reconstructed the description that followed: "She was consistent, steady. She was not a changeable person. She was a person who respected people, respected their opinions. She was a very attractive person. She was intelligent. She was well educated. She was a good cook, a neat housekeeper, willing to endure hardship and was also a good pianist." Oral listened; he remembered the young schoolmarm in Sulphur; "everytime he tolled the bell, I heard it ring."[77]

Evelyn's life since she had met Oral nearly two years earlier had strayed slightly from her pentecostal past. Evelyn "wanted to be a teacher so bad," but she seemed trapped in Westville.[78] After teaching for a year there, her mother's parents invited her to live with them in San Bonita, Texas, in the Rio Grande Valley. They promised to help Evelyn find a job and assist her in finishing college, something she felt she would never accomplish in Westville.

After Evelyn moved to Texas, she still remembered the "tall, handsome, Indian young man" who had knowingly captured her heart the year before, but she could imagine "no way in the world for me ever to see this young man again." As her memories of Oral grew dimmer, she "proceeded to get involved in the community where I was and just kind of left the church out of my life."[79]

Evelyn's compromise with the world consisted of attending movies and dances, minor lapses even by pentecostal standards, but her conscience troubled her sufficiently that she "sent a letter home and said to take my name off the church book because I was no longer good enough to be on it."[80]

In this slightly backslidden state, Evelyn opened her small package from Westville on her twenty-first birthday, thinking it to be a gift from home. Inside the little book she found an inscription from the author: "Congratulations on your 21st birthday. Please accept this little book from me. I trust it will bless your soul." It was "like a bomb shell dropped out of heaven"; Evelyn "dropped everything and read the book through before I stopped."[81] She immediately wrote Oral thanking him. Oral recalled: "Back came a letter. Oh, this is an outstanding book. I knew she was smart now. And I wrote her back. And she wrote and I wrote."[82]

Oral's interest accelerated through the spring. He dated Evelyn's younger sister, Ruth, but apparently spent most of his time discussing Evelyn, whose picture in the Fahnestock home had captured his fancy.[83] But the correspondence was the magic that produced the romance. "At first," recalled Evelyn, "Oral's letters were only friendly, describing his ministry. He was an evangelist. He told me all about his family, about his hobbies, etc." Then the letters became more serious; Oral sometimes would send "an entire sermon which he intended to preach," and Evelyn "would write back with her praises and criticisms. Not until she gave her opinion would he preach the sermon."[84] Oral respected education and efficiency; he had found in Evelyn's warm good sense a balance that would anchor him for life.

Then, one hot summer day, Evelyn received "a never to be forgotten letter." Near its end Oral had written: "Who knows, we may spend the next fifty years of our lives together." Evelyn's heart and thoughts raced.[85] Was this not what she had yearned for? Was this not where the correspondence had been leading? And yet, surging to the surface came all the resentments she had harbored for years, her own pentecostal bitterness against the squalor and indignity of her childhood. It was escape that had given her the ambition to be a teacher; it was ambition that had brought her to Texas. Whatever the charm of the young Indian preacher, a proposal to share a lifetime of free-will offerings and poverty was a dream-shattering thought. Evelyn wrote back hastily and hostilely. Oral later summarized her reply: "If you think I'm going to marry a preacher and have a house full of children, and be dragged from pillar to post as a preacher's wife, you have another thought coming."[86]

Oral was crushed, even more deeply than most jilted suitors. Throughout his life he has been scrupulously careful to avoid rejection—he has never wanted to intrude where he was not wanted. Evelyn slammed the door and "caught his nose."[87] Oral quickly wrote retracting his hypothetical offer and closing the correspondence. His letter crossed a second written by Evelyn and mailed shortly after her first reply. She had quickly thought over the matter and regretted her first reaction. She asked Oral to disregard her letter of rejection. Oral was soothed and soon wrote asking if he could come visit her. Evelyn encouraged him to come.

So, in September 1938, Oral packed his new Chevrolet coupe and headed for the Rio Grande Valley. A part of his load was Claudius; her role was partly sightseer, partly chaperon, and partly inspector to see that Oral got the "right girl."[88] Claudius probably knew, as Evelyn did not, that Oral meant business: he had done his research on Evelyn, and "when Oral finds what he wants and he is sure the Lord wants him to have it, he doesn't tarry, he doesn't even hesitate, he goes after it with full speed ahead."[89] They had only a long weekend together, but Oral had time to spare.

Oral and Claudius arrived at Evelyn's school on Thursday afternoon during a recess just forty-five minutes before classes were to dismiss for the long weekend. Oral remembered Evelyn as a "beautiful young woman," coyly embarrassed when her students ran into the school yard shouting: "Oh, Miss Evelyn, your boy friend is here."[90] For her part, Evelyn was devastated by Oral's radiant good looks: "He had on a light grey suit, which made him even more handsome. I shall never forget that suit, nor the smile he had on his face. . . . He just took my breath away." Both struggled to keep their poise. They "shook hands," Oral introduced Evelyn to Claudius, she taught another period (completely flustered and quivering inside), and then the three of them went to her grandparents' home.[91]

The weekend was crammed full—picnicking, boat riding, sightseeing, and fishing. Friday the couple went fishing in the Gulf of Mexico, and at the end of the day, on a sandbar in the gulf, Oral blurted out his carefully prepared proposal:

> My huge, happy, hilarious heart is throbbing tumultuously, tremendously, triumphantly with a lingering, lasting, long-lived love for you. As I gaze into your bewildering, beauteous, bounteous, beaming eyes, I am literally lonesomely lost in a dazzling, daring, delightful dream in which your fair, felicitous, fanciful face is ever present like a colossal, comprehensive constellation. Will you be my sweet, smiling, soulful, satisfied spouse?

Evelyn replied, "Listen, here, boy, if you are trying to propose to me, talk in the English language."[92] He did, and she did. From the beach they drove to the country school house where Evelyn taught, and there, as Oral held the flashlight, she played the piano for him. "Old practical Oral," recalled Evelyn, "he was not going to marry somebody who could not play the piano."[93]

The audition successfully completed, the young couple talked excitedly about their plans and hopes. Evelyn told Oral about her anxiety over her own spiritual condition, and he replied confidently that "the Lord could fix that."[94] Saturday evening they visited an "old time camp meeting." Evelyn later described its conclusion: "When the minister gave the altar call, Oral was standing beside me. He didn't say, 'Won't you come and give your heart to the Lord.' He just stepped out and waited for me to go. What could I do? He didn't say 'Come on,' he just stepped out and just stepped aside and I went just as naturally as could be and it took me just about that long to get back to where I used to be."[95]

The engagement was announced, and the wedding was set for the next June. Evelyn's teaching contract required that she remain unmarried, and an earlier date seemed impossible. But Oral had no sooner returned home than he began pressing for a Christmas wedding. Evelyn was to learn that he "gets in a hurry often," and he usually gets his way. In November, Evelyn asked the school board for permission to marry, and it was granted on the condition that she agree to finish teaching that school year.[96] Plans were hastily made for a Christmas wedding.

The weeks between the September engagement and the December wedding were filled with natural anxieties. Evelyn's mother and stepfather were delighted by the prospects (although Evelyn's mother had initially resisted moving to Oklahoma because she feared her daughter might marry an Indian), but her grandmother was disappointed, feeling that she was "settling for a lot less than she would have liked for me to." Grandmother had hoped Evelyn could "marry some big businessman and get up high in the world society."[97] For three months the bride-to-be fretted, "lonely," "with no full gospel church within reach and the boy I was going to marry far away," still frightened at the prospect of being a "poor preacher's wife."[98]

Oral returned to the revival circuit and began to wrestle with the financial obligations of marriage. He drove down to Okmulgee to discuss his economic prospects with Oscar Moore, one of the most respected Pentecostal Holiness ministers in the state and a longtime friend of both the Roberts and Fahnestock families. Oral had held a successful revival in Moore's church just a few weeks earlier; he now asked Moore to help him negotiate a loan with his Okmulgee banker. The older minister agreed to cosign Oral's note, and the two successfully secured a twenty-dollar loan. The bank deducted two dollars for interest, Oral subsequently paid Moore five dollars to perform the wedding ceremony, he bought three dollars worth of flowers, and he started his married life on the other ten dollars.[99]

The couple was married "in Papa's church in Westville with the church filled with her friends and mine" on Christmas Day 1938.[100] It was the first time a wedding had been conducted in the humble little frame church in Westville; Oral and Evelyn were far more radiant than their surroundings. But the occasion was elegant to them. Oral's cousin, Lona Roberts, sang "I Love You Truly," and Oscar conducted a "beautiful ceremony."[101] It was a fitting beginning for an enduring love story, "for we did love each other," recalled Evelyn.[102] They have never changed their minds since that Christmas Day, or probably seriously entertained an idea that they could or should.

The four months that followed were "terrible, terrible days and weeks."[103] Evelyn returned to Texas to finish the school year, and Oral continued his evangelistic work. They saw each other only once, "although we were newlyweds and madly in love."[104] It was, Evelyn later imagined, as if she were a war bride whose husband had left for battle.[105]

Once they were reunited, Oral and Evelyn lived with his parents, in Konawa, where Ellis accepted a pastorate in August 1939.[106] They spent most of their time away conducting revivals, mostly in eastern Oklahoma but occasionally straying as far from home as Memphis. In February 1939, for the first time, Oral's revival schedule was listed in the *Pentecostal Holiness Advocate*.[107]

The high point of their first year of marriage came on December 16, 1939, when Rebecca Ann Roberts was born in Papa and Mama Roberts's home in Konawa.

In May 1940, Oral, Evelyn, and Rebecca headed east to Georgia for Oral's first revival in the eastern stronghold of the Pentecostal Holiness church. For three weeks he preached in Athens in the congregation of Pastor Jesse Lee Jordan; he reported to the *Advocate* that "the church began to fill up until on Sunday night we had to secure forty extra chairs from the local Funeral Homes to accommodate the crowds."[108] Never one for understatement, Oral continued: "Shouts of victory could be heard through-out the building and prayer rooms, as hungry Christians and sin-laden sinners knelt before Christ in prayer. The people were very responsive to the messages, and each night the prayer rooms were filled with seekers."[109] His "only regret," reported Oral, was that he must return to Oklahoma to preach in "previously scheduled meetings."[110]

Oral and Evelyn remained in Oklahoma until after the camp meeting in August, and then they once again headed east "with a full year's work ahead of us." He spoke to a P.Y.P.S. meeting in Leaksville, North Carolina, and then worked his way north to a revival in South Norfolk, Virginia. The "revival tide ran high," except for a few "rainy nights," and Oral closed that meeting at the end of September and set out for Canada, where he had been invited by the Ontario Conference to conduct four revivals. Oral's spirit was soaring: "Well, here we are on our way to Canada and a series of revivals and happy on our way and in the Lord's harvest fields."[111] Everything was rosy. In Oklahoma, he was already recognized as "one of the outstanding young ministers in the church."[112] The *Pentecostal Holiness Advocate* offered its readers a laudatory sketch of the team:

> Brother Roberts joined the East Oklahoma Conference in 1936. He is the son of a P. H. minister; "was reared in the church"; spent one year with his father in evangelistic work, after which he took to the field alone. Has conducted revivals in almost every church in his Conference, besides preaching in Texas, Arkansas, Tennessee, Virginia, Georgia, North Carolina and Canada. He now travels with his wife and baby. Mrs. Roberts is a talented worker and a great help to her husband's evangelistic efforts. They both sing, and have considerable experience on radio.[113]

The winter trip to Canada chilled momentarily some of Oral's warmest expectations. Two of his four meetings in Canada were canceled "without very much notice"; such commitments were casually struck and loosely honored. He and Evelyn skidded out of Canada in subzero weather, delinquent on a car payment, with twenty dollars in cash and nowhere to go.[114] Oral's "full slate," it turned out, excepted open dates "from the last of December until the last of March, also part of May."[115] They drove south to Washington, D.C., where an old family friend, A. E. Robinson, took them in for a few days, giving Oral time to try to drum up some business.[116]

The disappointments were short-lived; 1941 proved to be a busy and productive year. From Washington, Oral and Evelyn drove south to Greensboro, North Carolina, where G. H. Montgomery was conducting a revival. In a magnanimous gesture, the influential Montgomery invited Oral to preach, and the local minister, C. D. Burchell, "asked other pastors to give him a few services."[117] Oral's talent did the rest. By January his schedule was filled with meetings in North Carolina, Virginia, and Georgia in some of the best churches in the East. He soon had regained his jaunty confidence. In February, he reported that "we have had to turn down calls from six states in the last five weeks because of a filled slate." He also asked the *Advocate*'s readers to pray "that our physical strength will hold up under the great strain of evangelism." His schedule was, without a doubt, "taxing to physical strength, especially the nerves."[118]

Oral's talent and energy as an evangelist were growing. Within the confines of his little church, his accomplishments were impressive. In April 1941 he conducted a meeting in the important church in Washington, D.C. which was pastored by Hubert T. Spence, later a bishop in the church (and a bitter critic of Oral's healing ministry). One of the members reported that the congregation had had "other good preachers and evangelists . . . but there seemed to be more than usual providential intervention in the arrangements for this meeting." The church had experienced "a shower of the latter rain"; even Spence noted that Oral's sermons on prophecy "were up to those of our older and more experienced preachers."[119] G. H. Montgomery visited the meeting one evening and reported that he could hardly find a seat. He wrote: "After an hour of preliminaries, Brother Roberts preached a stirring sermon, and gave the altar call, and although it was fully 9:30 P.M. when the altar call was made, there must have been at least a dozen people who knelt for prayer. They tell us that, in the week that the meeting has been in progress, about fourteen experiences have been received, and God is blessing gloriously."[120]

In June, Oral was elected by the East Oklahoma Conference as a clerical delegate to the General Conference of the Pentecostal Holiness church, which met at Franklin Springs, Georgia, and Evelyn was elected a lay delegate.[121] In July, he was invited to be the speaker at the Mt. Gap, Georgia camp meeting. W. Ralph McBroom, the camp meeting manager, reported: "Large crowds, beautiful singing, blessed fellowship, spiritual services and dynamic preaching characterized the thirty-first annual session of the Mt. Gap, Georgia Camp Meeting. . . . The Camp Meeting was conducted by the Rev. Oral Roberts, Evangelist Extraordinary, from Oklahoma, assisted by his wife at the piano and his mother and father, the latter doing some of the morning preaching."[122] Oral's evangelistic career was snowballing. He went to Oklahoma for camp meeting in August and then returned east for revivals in North Carolina and Virginia. Then, suddenly, in November 1941, he accepted a call to pastor a church in Fuquay Springs, North Carolina, signaling a sharp change in career aims and lifestyle.

Oral and Evelyn's two and a half years in itinerant evangelistic work were both exhilarating and exhausting. Oral later wrote:

> Scores have been the nights when I have preached, sung, prayed, wept, worked in the altar until I was so physically and mentally exhausted that when I went to bed I could not sleep until near morning; and some nights I have not

shut my eyes in sleep thirty minutes. Repeat this process, night after night, revival after revival, year after year, and the evangelist is near a physical breakdown, if not completely so.[123]

The pay was never adequate, and was always dependent on the good will of the brethren. If misfortune struck, as it did in the midst of Oral's successful Washington, D.C. meeting when a burglar broke into his car and stole his "guitar, typewriter, portable radio," and "almost all" of the family's clothes, they were totally dependent on the mercy of friends.[124] In between meetings in 1941, Oral earned five dollars a day helping Pastor L. C. Synan of Hopewell, Virginia hang wallpaper in his home.[125] "Those were great days," Oral later recalled, but days "I don't want to live over."[126]

The unsung heroines of these evangelistic years were Evelyn and Rebecca. Oral's second book, published in 1941, was "lovingly dedicated to my faithful wife who has been my constant companion and co-laborer in the evangelistic work both in the States and in Canada."[127] While Oral preached, Evelyn played the piano, sang, and tried hard to make a home for the family as they lived in a tumultuous collage of homes. They were sometimes welcome and comfortable; they were frequently treated as intruders. For three weeks the three of them might be confined to one bedroom and one bed. Sometimes the hostess refused to cook for them, and Evelyn tried to fend for herself in a strange kitchen. There were homes, reflected Evelyn, where the "dishes were dirty, the floors were dirty, the bedroom was dirty. I've had to clean the bathroom before I could take a bath. I have had to turn the light on at night to keep the mice out of our bed."[128] Oral later reminisced about an unheated room they occupied in subzero temperatures. Each evening he and Evelyn would put Rebecca "between us so we could keep her warm."[129] Nonetheless, Evelyn could always look back with warm nostalgia on those years and the "beautiful people" they suffered with.[130] Oral judged both the times and the people who inhabited them more harshly.[131]

But Oral learned and gained invaluable experience. He not only preached hundreds of sermons, he also frequently preached on the radio.[132] He began to build a reputation as an expert on prophecy, the subject of his second book, *The Drama of the End-Time*. One can wonder, with Oral, how he found "the time and energy to give justice to the writing of this little book" in the midst of his evangelistic work, but it was an engrossing subject. The beginning of World War II had "made the study of prophecy doubly interesting," and Oral noted that his sermons on the subject had attracted "large crowds" and "unusual interest." "Almost in every church," he wrote, "there has been a demand for these studies to be printed."[133] The book reflected a general though not profound understanding of dispensational premillennialism, a prophetic theory rampant in fundamentalist circles. Oral long remained interested in premillennial themes, and his Scofield Reference Bibles were filled with notes of prophetic import.[134]

Oral and Evelyn also gained experience as performers. They played their guitars and sang, both in their services and over the radio. In 1941 they recorded "two of our songs."[135] Oral also composed a song, "Empty Tomb in Jerusalem":

There's an empty tomb in Jerusalem to-day,
    Where our dear Savior once lay,
Oh! It saddens my heart to think of the time,
    When they led dear Jesus away.
As He climbed up old Golgatha,
    His heavy cross bending Him low,
He fell under the load, not able to rise,
    I can hear Him sing, soft and low.

They beat Him with stripes and mocked Him to scorn,
    But He ne'er returned them a word.
He was humbly born, but was brutally killed
    When the blows of the hammer were heard.
When His awful death was over
    Joseph came and took Him away.
And laid Him to rest in a newly made tomb,
    There to wait to arise the third day.

There's an empty tomb in Jerusalem to-day,
    Where our dear Savior once lay.
Death could not keep Him there and the grave had no power,
    When Jesus came forth that day.
And to think He counts us worthy
    To be redeemed and made whiter than snow.
He sits on His throne, in the city of love,
    He has gone where all righteous go.[136]

While Oral continued to sing in the early days of his independent ministry, his musical talents obviously never rivaled his preaching ability.

Perhaps the most important lessons Oral learned during these years had to do with the political nuances within his denomination. He began to make his aggressive presence felt. In later years, Oral admitted with some remorse that he had been completely caught up in the "politics" of the "kingdom of God."[137] It was a thinly veiled and tough political world in which dexterous revivalists and tenacious organizers struggled for position within their tiny universe. Shut off from positions in mainstream Christianity, those in power doggedly defended their status against young interlopers. The ministerial rank was freely given, but denominational standing was won in battle. Pentecostal superintendents and bishops were Christian warlords jealously protecting their small and ever-vulnerable financial and spiritual fiefdoms. In short, in the midst of the ecstasy and free flow of the spirit there was an undercurrent of peasant cunning and political common sense.[138]

By the 1940s the Pentecostal Holiness church was a relatively stable institution, having survived numerous internal coups and schisms in its short history. The church had developed an orderly and entrenched hierarchy modeled on Methodism. It was not the place for a young man in a hurry; one must work his way up slowly, tediously, and deferentially. "Rugged individualism is soundly out of place in organized religion," warned the editor of the *Pentecostal Holiness Advocate* in 1943; one must be loyal to his church.[139]

Young Oral Roberts soon learned to watch for the political undercurrents within his church. He immediately ran afoul of the seething jealousy between pastors and evangelists. Traditionally, the more entrenched ministers were assigned as pastors to the little churches, where they were assured skimpy but steady salaries.[140] By the time Oral began evangelizing, denominational leaders were trying to upgrade the evangelistic image, and sometimes protective pastors and ambitious revivalists had difficulty balancing their interests, particularly in the "greenback phase of the program."[141] It was this clash of interests which stimulated Oral to write his practical and sensible series of articles on the relations of pasters and evangelists.

Oral's path was blocked largely by his age and limited experience. By the 1940s the leaders of the Pentecostal Holiness church were one to two decades older than Oral; they were veterans in preaching the pentecostal message, and they had built the denomination. G. H. Montgomery, who became editor of the *Pentecostal Holiness Advocate* in 1938, had an eye for talent and frequently encouraged young preachers, including Oral, through the church's paper. In 1939, Montgomery published a remonstrance he had received which probably reflected the feeling of many older ministers: "I want to drop a word of warning about the way you are playing up our young preachers. I am afraid that you are going a step too far in this direction. We have always been led to believe that to boost a young minister is the surest way to ruin him. . . . This never has been done in our church, and I don't think it ought to be done now."[142] Oral very early learned to chafe and fidget under the restraints imposed by older heads who had no intention of being led by children.

The church's internal politics were also geographic and connectional. When Oral went east in 1940, he had already established his place as a rising star in the East Oklahoma Conference. In 1940, he served as chairman of the Conference Committee on Education and Publication, and in 1941 he was on the important Finance Committee.[143] His election as a delegate to the church's General Conference in 1941 was an additional feather in his cap. But he remained an outsider in the eastern segment of the church, cordially received but not a part of the insiders' clique of mutual friendships and kinships.

Oral's outsider status in the East was exacerbated by his lack of education, particularly because he had attended neither Emmanuel College, the church's small, unaccredited junior college in Franklin Springs, Georgia, nor Holmes Bible Institute. Oral instinctively perceived these deficiencies and tried, as he always would try, to compensate for his weaknesses. As the chairman of the Education and Publication Committee, he sponsored a special fund-raising service for Emmanuel College at the East Oklahoma camp meeting.[144] While in the East in 1940, Oral reported that he had visited Emmanuel: "I have preached there, I have met members of the faculty, I have mingled with the students, I have felt the heavenly atmosphere." While he had been "deprived of the privilege" of attending the school, his "heart was with Emmanuel College." "Some weeks ago," he reported from one of his revivals, "the Lord impressed me to raise $70 with which to furnish a dormitory room in the new building there." A politically astute act, Oral's support of Emmanuel College was an early expression of his life-long desire to support an educational institution in which students could "receive a Christian education in a college where each teacher is baptized with the Holy Ghost and fire."[145]

Oral's early identification with Emmanuel, like much of his other activity, was at least partly an effort to ingratiate himself to the church he had inherited and through which he hoped to rise to a place of usefulness. In later years, he judged himself harshly for his willingness to conform: "I could give a decent presentation of the Gospel. But I made the mistake most young preachers make, still make, I became too much a part of my denomination. I began to be like them. I began to love the doctrine. . . . I did not count my success in terms of the souls I led to Christ or the healings of the people, but the fact that I had really told them what the Bible teaches."[146] And, indeed, the young Oral was a bastion of pentecostal orthodoxy, defending "the great doctrine of atonement," sanctification, and the "wonderful outpouring of the Latter Rain" of the Holy Ghost.[147] He wrote passionately but safely rebuking sin: "Oh sin! How long wilt thou wreck and ruin lives?"[148] His preaching was filled with tough-talking exhortation: "We need the same old-fashioned, Holy Ghost, straight-from-the-shoulder preaching in this modern day. May God have saving mercy upon these cold-storage preachers of today that speak like they have bunions on their tongues and give out a soft-pedal gospel." He castigated those "Pharisees" who wanted the services closed by nine o'clock but the next night "go to the theatre or to the dance or the social, and . . . stay until midnight, being the life of the show."[149] His antenna identified the rising preachers within the church, such as J. A. Synan, and he quoted them.[150] In fact, Oral admitted, he came to parrot them: "I had a way about me, if I heard another preacher preach, the first thing I knew I was emphasizing things as he was. And I would almost mimic him so that if you heard me after you had heard him, you didn't know which one you were hearing."[151]

Oral's dedication and loyalty brought rewards. Lesser young men would have been thrilled by his progress. G. H. Montgomery had befriended Oral, and other church leaders noticed him. "Rev. Roberts," wrote Bishop Dan T. Muse in his "Introduction" to Oral's second book, "is a young man of sterling qualities, an apt student at the foot of the Cross, ever aspiring to a clearer and more thorough understanding of the Word of God, and intimately associated with his Bible in the all-absorbing study of prophecy. He is a fluent speaker and understandable writer. God has signally blessed Rev. Roberts with a successful evangelistic ministry."[152]

But Oral's gift and curse—that probing, innovative, creative, restless spirit which attracts the masses and makes queasy less-talented men—boiled precariously near the surface. It sometimes spilt out as an innocent brashness, made innocuous by his toothy smile and open friendliness. He was, after all, from Oklahoma, where everyone "looked with disfavor at anything that had stood in the same place for ten years." Oral was a "Sooner."[153] Harold Paul, an old friend and preaching contemporary of Oral's, recalled his first encounter with the young preacher, at a camp meeting in 1940 in which G. H. Montgomery and O. E. Sproull were the featured speakers. Oral burst into the apartment where Paul was talking to the older preachers: "I noted that Oral was not bash-ful. He told of the revivals he was having. . . . He wanted to know how much they were paying these preachers. . . . He asked, 'Well, how much do they pay you here?' "[154] When he appeared at the General Conference in 1941, Oral arrived early for each session, hurried to take the front seat, and unabashedly spoke his mind.[155]

In spite of his growing political awareness, Oral's audacity sometimes turned doctrinal and unorthodox. The view he and Ellis held on the use of medicine branded them as liberals in the minds of some, but Oral also decried other archaic pentecostal teachings. He denounced the lingering ban on wed-ding bands, believing it unnecessarily injured his evangelistic efforts. In the 1941 General Conference, Oral entered a motion than an entire section be struck from the church's discipline. "Antinomianism," he asked, "what is that?" In the long run, Oral's ecumenical leanings and impatience with theological jar-gon were to have an impact, but for the moment his impertinence seemed ridiculous. His friend G. H. Montgomery turned Oral's suggestion away lightly: "Mr. Chairman, I've got a book on that subject. I'll loan it to the young brother."[156]

As long as his church could take Oral in good humor, he was safe inside. But he was never entirely at ease. He early sensed that he was "a maverick within the church. I was coming up with intellectual ideas that were not looked upon with favor inside the church. I was growing intellectually through those years."[157] That growth was to continue, and the uneasiness would eventually become unbearable.

CHAPTER

IV

Pastor

F OR THE TIME being, a major change in lifestyle proved sufficient to keep Oral occupied for several years. In November 1941 he accepted his first pastorate, in Fuquay Springs, North Carolina. His new position was lucrative by pentecostal standards and presented him with some unique challenges which kept him busy for almost a year.[1]

Oral met the founder of the Fuquay Springs church, J. M. Pope, at the Falcon camp meeting in 1941, and Pope persuaded the dynamic young minister to become the church's first pastor. Pope was "a prominent and successful businessman in Fuquay Springs, . . . the owner and operator of the Pope 5¢ to $5 Stores, seven of them in that vicinity." The son of a Pentecostal Holiness minister, Pope felt "impressed" by God "to build a concrete block tabernacle" in his village at a cost of $4,500. When Oral arrived in November 1941, the church was being operated as an independent congregation under the name the Full Gospel Tabernacle.[2] While the congregation was "inter-denominational," Oral and other Pentecostal Holiness leaders were led to believe that the group would become a Pentecostal Holiness church at the "proper time."[3]

Oral's first pastorate was eminently successful; Fuquay Springs residents remembered him as "handsome, charming, full of energy and on fire with the desire to reach everyone with the Gospel of Jesus Christ."[4] He was bursting with ideas and energy. He and Evelyn conducted a religious census of the community, going from door to door to meet the people. He wrote an article for the local newspaper reporting his findings, rejoicing that "so many of our people are church-minded and trying to live up to the laws of their respective creeds."

After Pope had taken him on a tour of the town's businesses to meet the village fathers, Oral wrote another article, pronouncing his blessing:

> I like it here. I am enjoying my work. I am looking forward to that time when every church in this community shall be filled with people to worship the King of Glory, Christ Jesus our Lord. And I sincerely believe that when in the future, progressive minded people step forward with programs designed to improve the community, that there shall be a wholehearted response and support by Fuquay and Varina.[5]

Somewhat obliquely, the confident twenty-three-year-old was probably offering his leadership to Fuquay Springs, as he was to do in Tulsa in later years, but Oral's vision was too grand for small-town North Carolina.

"He was so full of energy," recalled Mrs. Pope, "he couldn't be still. And he put his heart in what he was doing. He tried to build the church and he did."[6] He preached everywhere he could, including on street corners: "He sometimes put a loudspeaker on top of his car, drove to a good main street location, playing records to attract attention. When a crowd gathered, he preached to them."[7] And he hosted a sequence of revivals—Joe E. Campbell, noted North Carolina evangelist, came in late 1941, followed in 1942 by Oral's friends from Oklahoma, Mildred Wicks, "great woman preacher of the West," and Oscar Moore. Oral gave a detailed report of the "preliminary work" he did before the Mildred Wicks revival:

> I constructed and had painted over twenty signs and placed them at conspicuous places both in town and country cross roads, advertising the Tabernacle and its work. We ran a half-page ad in the town paper with pictures of the revival workers. We also had 1000 large circulars printed and distributed in town and the three small towns located near Fuquay Springs. Then we sent several of them to other Pentecostal Holiness Churches over the district. Added to this was our radio work. On my regular Sunday morning broadcast over WRAL, Raleigh, I gave much publicity to the meeting. Radio time was secured over this station Monday through Friday the first week of the revival. When the workers finally arrived and the first service began, all things were in readiness. The last sermon I preached before the starting of the revival was "How to have a successful revival." . . . In short, people knew about the revival when it began, had been invited several times through the press, radio and personal contact.[8]

When Oscar Moore concluded his revival, Oral not only praised his old friend as "one of the finest, cleanest, most spiritual and effective preachers in the entire Pentecostal Holiness Church," he also reported that the congregation was making "good progress" and that he aimed to make it a "beehive of spiritual activity."[9]

That hope did not materialize. In July 1942, Oral decided to return to Oklahoma to accept a call to pastor the church in Shawnee in the East Oklahoma Conference. Apparently, the most important reason was Pope's unwillingness to affiliate the independent congregation with the Pentecostal Holiness church. Oral, and probably others, felt that the "proper time" had come. Oral was a staunch church man, still committed to a career within the organization; he could not permanently remain with an independent church.[10] And, too, Oral and Evelyn were homesick for Oklahoma. Mama and Papa Roberts had just been to visit them in Fuquay Springs; the church in Shawnee, though small, was one of the better ones in the conference; it seemed a good time to leave.[11] They parted friends with the folks in North Carolina; they were remembered "very kindly."[12]

Upon his return to Oklahoma, Oral began the longest pastorate of his preaching career, remaining in Shawnee for three full years. The church in Shawnee was small, and Oral made "quite a financial sacrifice" to accept the call, "starting out at less than half what they were receiving." But he returned to an Oklahoma revitalized by a wartime boom and alive with new economic hope.[13] By the time he left Shawnee three years later, the church's membership had grown from forty-two to ninety-five and its yearly revenues from $1,700 to $8,700. When he arrived, Oral immediately began broadcasting over two radio stations, in Shawnee and in Ada, assuming the financial obligation for the broadcasts himself. His program was called "The Gospel of the Cross" and featured the "Shelton Brothers, famous Stamps-Baxter Trio." Oral became, to at least one listener, "the best radio preacher I have ever heard."[14]

At the end of his pastorate, the secretary-treasurer of the church summarized the congregation's accomplishments under Oral's leadership:

> During these three years there were 119 saved, 50 sanctified and 32 received the Holy Ghost. There were also many things accomplished. . . . First, on Nov. 5, 1942, we purchased a Neon sign for the church at a cost of about $90, including a time clock to automatically turn the sign on and off, and in February, 1943, we purchased a parsonage at a cost of $2,500, which has now been paid down to $600. In June, 1943, we purchased new pews at a cost of $575.00, also rubber matting for the aisle. In September, 1943, we also installed two floor furnaces in the church at a cost of $175, which solved the heating problem we had faced for several years. We then completed the church basement, by cementing the floor, building two modern rest rooms and seven Sunday school rooms, also a drinking fountain, all at a cost of approximately $1,000, and in Sept. 1944 we installed a large air circulating fan in the church auditorium at a cost of $150.00. All of the above improvements were paid for as they were completed, and a balance on the church loan of $838.28 was also paid off.[15]

Oral had clearly already discovered the secret of keeping goals before the people which they could accomplish together. And he unselfishly gave himself to the task. In 1943 he reported preaching 208 sermons, making 850 "pastor's visits," and traveling 10,000 miles in his ministry.[16] By 1945, he was being paid $2,633 per year, the largest salary in the East Oklahoma Conference.[17]

As World War II drew to an end in the spring of 1945, Oral and Evelyn had spent nearly four years in relatively stable pastorates. Their record was unsullied; their relationships with their congregations had been constructive and loving. Oral was "neat and debonair," but he was also "folksy," capable of relating to anyone and perfectly comfortable "raiding the refrigerator" in some parishioner's home.[18] He was impulsive and impatient, nowhere more than with Evelyn and the children. If the whole family was not in the car on Sunday morning in time to arrive at services early, "he would go sit in the car and honk the horn" until they scurried out.[19] He had become a fine preacher by pentecostal standards; "he preached loudly, dramatically, compellingly."[20] And he was an indefatigable worker, never asking more of others than he gave of himself. Most impressive was his "creative energy." "He had more ideas than fifty average people," recalled Evelyn. Some worked and some did not. Some he could not test because he could not raise the money. Sometimes, much to the irritation of Evelyn, he would use the "grocery money" to "accomplish some pet project for God."[21] Such talent and dedication were not commonplace in the pentecostal ministry, and perceptive church members knew that Oral was exceptional. But others acknowledged his success grudgingly, and he was quickly outrunning the capacity of his church to reward him.

Perhaps Oral's greatest asset was his family. He was careful to keep his own "reputation above reproach." He refused to visit a woman at home unless Evelyn was with him; when the young girls from the church rode in his car, they were never permitted to ride "in the front seat with Oral."[22] And Evelyn was more than "practical Oral" could have calculated. She canvassed, she played the piano, she was "a wonderful Sunday school teacher," she raised a garden in Fuquay Springs.[23] "Only once," Oral recalled, "did she threaten to go home to her mother." The first six months they lived in Enid, the church had no parsonage, and they were forced to live "in the home of some church people." Evelyn felt the church could do better and told Oral she was leaving until they did. Oral got the message; the church board acted, and within two weeks "had purchased a very nice parsonage and we moved in."[24] Evelyn could assert herself; but Evelyn had no critics.

The family grew. In Fuquay Springs Evelyn had a miscarriage, perhaps "because of working in the garden."[25] But she was soon pregnant again, and in Shawnee, Ronald David was born on October 22, 1943. Every Sunday was a challenge for Evelyn, determined as she was, and as Oral was, that their family be an "example." "Our children were on the front seat," she remembered. "I kept one of them, our oldest, on the piano bench right by me, when she was so tiny she could hardly sit up, because she wouldn't sit with anybody else. And so she had to sit on the piano bench with me. And she sat there very straight and precise until I was through with the piano and then she went back and sat down. . . . When my children were little . . . they were well behaved."[26]

Oral also worked ambitiously in denominational causes during these years. He regularly served on the Education and Publication Committee of the East Oklahoma Conference and was a fountain of suggestions and new ideas. He inaugurated a conference "lending library for the benefit of young preachers" and continued to champion Emmanuel College.[27] In 1943 he was elected to the influential Conference Stationing Committee and the following year was elected as an alternate to the General Conference.[28] In 1943, the twenty-five-year-old pastor proposed the establishment of a "preacher's magazine" and the convening of "semi-annual preachers' meetings." Both projects, he urged, would be supported by the "up-and-coming preachers" in the church: "I was born in a Pentecostal Holiness home. And for twenty-five years that is about all I have known. But as a member of the younger group in our movement I do not want to rest upon the achievements of the past or sail along on the victories of yesterday. My blood craves action! I desire advancement! My spirit calls for progress! Thank God for all the glory of the past! But let's do better tomorrow!"[29] By 1944, he was editor of the *Conference News,* and he was one of the featured speakers at the first minister's conference in the region, along with such prominent and older preachers as G. H. Montgomery, Oscar Moore, and M. L. Dryden.[30] If his ideas were rejected, he turned to something else; if the task was assigned to him to carry out, he did it.

While Oral's projects continued to strike even his friends such as Oscar Moore as "presumptuous," his personal conduct and his doctrine were above question.[31] His little book on dispensational premillennialism was hawked for forty cents per copy by the church publishing house; Pastor Byon A. Jones of Portsmouth, Virginia assured that "from first to last one's soul is gripped and stirred by the dramatic picturization [*sic*] of the great events just ahead."[32] In preparation of the book, Oral and "a minister friend" conducted an interview "with the head of the Zionist Organization of America" and came away as reputed experts on the thrilling subject of the end-time.[33] While he avoided specific predictions, Oral's general conclusion was the expected: "Hallelujah! I believe the rapture is near. Get ready for that day."[34]

Otherwise, Oral's public pronouncements were usually orthodox and often innocuous. He heralded the baptism with the Holy Ghost and scolded the mainstream churches for tolerating sinners but not those "who have the Holy Ghost and speak with tongues." He chided timid pentecostals who wanted to "by-pass the Holy Ghost" because they "don't want the persecution and opposition."[35] His sermons ranged from advice to parents to the "Risks of Death-Bed Repentance" to an examination of John 3:16, "The Greatest Text in the Bible."[36] His advice to other pastors was eminently sound: do not "think too highly" of one's self, do not be "too bookish and stale in the pulpit," avoid being "chummy" with "special friends" in the congregation, never be "jealous" of other ministers, "make friends with the business leaders," and avoid "formalism." In a gem of wisdom likely to soothe church leaders, Oral urged that young ministers be "conference-minded."[37]

By the mid-1940s, Oral had chosen a new field of expertise, religious education. He came to view himself as a Sunday school expert. Beginning in November 1945, he wrote a series of articles for the *Pentecostal Holiness Advocate* on the Sunday school, "our sleeping giant."[38] His articles reeked of the conventional wisdom he had acquired in religious education classes at Oklahoma Baptist University in Shawnee. While one did not need "a college degree" to be a good Sunday school teacher, Oral advised, the job did require "some knowledge of psychology of a child's life."[39] But his advice on how to handle problems was typical Roberts common sense: "1. Spend much time in prayer. 2.

Bring the problem up at your monthly officers' and teachers' meeting if it's not too personal. 3. Don't take it too hard. 4. Cultivate the fine art of smiling. 5. Talk quietly, pleasantly. 6. Pay little attention to criticism."[40] And he brought to his new interest his usual exuberance. When his friend Harold Paul asked the name of the best book on religious education, Oral cited the text he had studied, with the qualification: "That's the best until the best is written. I'm going to write it."[41]

Oral's new interest in religious education was related to another cause which captured his attention for several years, beginning in 1943—the establishment of a Pentecostal Holiness college in Oklahoma. The initial impetus for a school grew out of that old familiar culture clash between pentecostals and the world. Oral reported that the need was felt in Shawnee because "the local school has been compelling our high school girls to dress immodestly (in shorts or slacks) while taking gym, while young men look on, in order for the girls to receive their credits in other subjects."[42] The agitation for a school began in the "Shawnee-Seminole area"; it spread through the East Oklahoma Conference and the Oklahoma Conference, and then "the entire western section of the Church."[43] In February 1944 the "Official Boards of the East Oklahoma and Oklahoma Conferences met in joint session in the Shawnee Pentecostal Holiness Church . . . for the purpose of coordinating their efforts and laying plans for the establishment of a Pentecostal Holiness School in the West." R. O. Corvin accepted the presidency, and Oral and L. E. Turpin were commissioned to "present the matter to the churches." They set out immediately on a fund-raising tour. Oral reported almost immediately that he had raised $1,300 in Shawnee and continued his tour until the end of 1944.[44] The idea of a competing college in the West probably did not sit well with the supporters of struggling Emmanuel College, although Oral quickly assured that "our efforts are NOT independent of our general set-up, but in fullest harmony with our general work. The above program, if and when launched, will be done under the auspices of the entire P. H. Church."[45]

The prospects of the new school loomed large in Oral's mind for the next two years and partly explained his resignation as pastor in Shawnee and a sharp reevaluation of his career objectives. He decided to go to college and began taking classes at Oklahoma Baptist University—secretly at first, for fear his "church board" would fire him.[46] He felt a resurgence of his "thirst for education" and resolved to "go on and get a doctor's degree." In this endeavor, as in others, he "wanted to go to the very top."[47] Education, perhaps, was to be his new pathway up in his church, taking him beyond the confinement of small-town pastorates. If necessary, he would, by main force, build a college, and finance it, and teach in it. It was a tall order for a high school dropout, but by 1945 he had seized the challenge, and he would never completely lay it aside.

This disruption in his career objectives led to a period of instability for the Roberts family which lasted two years and ended with one final, bold turn. When Oral resigned his pastorate in Shawnee, he apparently intended to hold revivals in that area and attend Oklahoma Baptist. But in the late summer of 1945, while preaching in a North Carolina camp meeting, Oral was asked by

Robert E. "Daddy" Lee of Toccoa, Georgia to consider becoming pastor of his small, eighty-member congregation in North Georgia. Oral suggested that they "pray about it" and, unexpectedly, decided to accept. He, Evelyn, and the children moved in the fall. Housing was hard to find in these postwar months, and they were forced to live in a boarding house. Oral was, once again, a singular success; local residents remembered him as "a deep thinker" and "just full of preach." They feared that he would not stay long, because "Toccoa's too small for this man." And, indeed, by the end of the year Oral had moved, though not apparently by choice. He had run afoul of denominational politics; "the Georgia conference frowned on having a minister from outside its conference as pastor."[48] By January the Roberts family was back in Shawnee, and Oral had reenrolled at the university.

The Toccoa detour, short though it was, had a lasting impact on the family. It was there that Rebecca, then five years old, met her future husband, Marshall, for the first time. Marshall's father, W. J. Nash, was the superintendent of the Georgia Conference.[49] More important in the short run were two incidents of healing which occurred in Toccoa. Oral would later look back on these events as his "first realization" that "I was approaching 'my hour.' "[50]

One day Oral received an "urgent phone call" telling him that Clyde Lawson, one of the deacons in the church, "had dropped a heavy motor on his foot and was painfully injured." When Oral arrived and saw Lawson in pain, "a feeling of compassion swept over me which was indescribable," and he bent over, touched Lawson's foot, and said, "Jesus, heal!" Lawson stopped his writhing and asked: "Oral, what did you do to me?" "Nothing, Clyde, except pray," Oral replied. They both stood amazed as Lawson "rose up and stamped his foot several times." Bill Lee, another deacon, asked as they drove away, "Oral, can you do that very often?" "Good night, no," Oral retorted. "If you could," said Lee, "you could bring revival to the church."[51] In the weeks that followed, Lee's prophetic words began to take root in Oral's mind. And the news of the healing spread. Shortly after the incident, a local mother interrupted a meeting Oral was conducting with a group of Sunday school teachers, requesting that he pray for her sick child. The baby "was restless with a high fever." Oral prayed, and then, reported those present, "the baby looked up and smiled at him."[52] A legend was waiting to be born.

For the moment, Oral, Evelyn, and the two children returned to Shawnee, and he enrolled as an "unclassified student."[53] They struggled to survive. Oral preached in "weekend revivals" wherever he could to support his family. He no longer owned an automobile, so he had to "highway it" to his meetings, hitchhiking to Okmulgee, Muskogee, and other nearby towns. He later calculated that he earned an average of sixteen dollars a week during these months, out of which he fed his family and paid tuition.[54] And many of his pentecostal friends were distraught by his new interest in education—"they thought it would make me disbelieve the Bible or weaken my witness."[55] One church member nearly "lost her religion" when she discovered that Oral had enrolled at a Baptist institution, declaring that he now "even walked like a Baptist."[56] Of course, some church leaders supported Oral's new objectives. When J. A. Synan visited

Shawnee in the spring of 1946 to conduct a revival, he was pleased and impressed that Oral arranged for him to speak before the university student body.[57]

The economic crunch in Shawnee was intolerable, however, and when pastorates were assigned in the fall of 1946, Oral accepted an assignment in the Oklahoma Conference at Enid. Oral's call to the Enid church was once again a step up; it was a singular honor for a twenty-eight-year-old minister. The congregation had "the finest and best equipped church edifice in the Oklahoma Conference," built, noted the *Pentecostal Holiness Advocate,* "on 'this side' of the railroad tracks."[58] Oral's salary was set at $55 per week in a conference which averaged paying its pastors $1,406.72 per year (his own East Oklahoma Conference averaged $942.76); he was now one of the three highest-paid ministers in the state of Oklahoma in his church.[59] He once again threw himself wholeheartedly into building the church. Enid was soon flooded with "Let's Get Acquainted" cards featuring the pastor's smiling picture and the greeting: "Welcome Neighbor to Our Services." Among other things, visitors were promised "dynamic youth services" and "live-wire preaching."[60]

"Aside from official positions" in the denomination, which he could hardly expect for a few years yet, noted G. H. Montgomery, Oral had reached "the top."[61] But "official positions" seemed on the horizon in 1946 because the campaign for a western school finally came to fruition, largely as a result of Oral's influence and efforts. Oral was appointed secretary of the Southwestern Board of Education in 1946, and he united his efforts with those of his old friend from Center, Raymond O. Corvin, to get a school in operation by the end of the year. Corvin had now completed an M.A. degree at the University of South Carolina and B.D. degree at Lutheran Southern Theological Seminary and was appointed chairman of the education board and named president of the college.[62] Corvin was the church's rising educational star and had also been made the secretary of the General Board of Education.[63] In the spring and summer, the Southwestern board investigated about forty proposed sites for the school before purchasing Abe Hale's Night Club in Oklahoma City for $37,500 in July.[64] On July 5, Oral began "a tour of the Kansas Conference" to raise funds for the college, and by October the school had opened with ninety-three students. While the project was clearly under Corvin's control, Oral remained its strongest supporter, digging the first shovel of dirt for Falcon Music Hall in September and serving as director of religious education on the first faculty.[65]

All in all, Oral's stature within his denomination continued to grow rapidly. He was one of the featured speakers at the Fourth Annual Preachers' Convention held in Oklahoma City in early 1947 and was added to the regular "Church News Staff" by the *Pentecostal Holiness Advocate.*[66] Evelyn penned a rare article in 1947 for the church paper, lauding the "loyal women of the P. H. Church in the West."[67] From all appearances, Oral's "head was scraping the ceiling."[68]

The young minister also continued his college study at Phillips University, a Disciples of Christ school founded in Enid in 1907. He enrolled as a sophomore in September 1946 and completed fourteen semester hours during the academic year, fighting for "every moment I studied." In retrospect, he believed that his education taught him to "think for myself," and it gave him glimpses of a world larger than the pentecostal subculture which had consumed his thought.[69] Each Tuesday evening the young pastor-student-educator drove to Oklahoma City to teach a class in "Sunday School administration" for preachers at Southwestern College.[70] With patience, he could become an educational leader in his church.

In the meantime, the Roberts family's life in Enid was sheer bedlam, a round of eighteen-hour days that drained even the irrepressible Oral.[71] His physical fatigue from his grinding schedule probably did something to suppress his volcanic restlessness. But it also fed a growing depression, that mood of desperation which forewarned of a creative outburst. In this state of exhaustion and anxiety, Oral turned broodingly introspective. To his friends it seemed that this should be a time for a quiet savoring of triumphs; within Oral a thunderhead was billowing up in preparation for a cloudburst.

Looking back, Oral has often said that he was discontented during the entire twelve years of his ministry in the Pentecostal Holiness church. Partly, that discontent was the natural fruit of second-generation pentecostalism—the feeling that the power was gone, the great truths dimmed, the momentum lost because of selfish human distractions. It was precisely that broad, subterranean malaise (which Oral shared with his entire subculture) that formed the base for the impending pentecostal revival. In 1941, G. H. Montgomery had pondered the question of "why revival doesn't last" in the churches and had laid the blame squarely on the "church itself." Pentecostalism had become "stiff and sophisticated"; the only fire left was in the young evangelists, and their converts were "frequently lost because turning them over to the church for spiritual life is too often like laying a newborn babe on a dead mother's breast for nourishment."[72] By 1947, no one felt the need for a pentecostal revival more keenly, or expressed it more passionately, than young Oral Roberts. In a radio sermon in early 1947, he pleaded: "The supreme need of the Church today is to throw off its lethargy, shake loose from complacency, rid itself of luke-warmness and become stirred to the uttermost over a lost generation. . . . When a church examines its record and discovers that it has failed to win one soul in one year . . . it is high time that another Elijah appeared on the scene to bring about a revival."[73]

Oral had long questioned some of the most divisive beliefs of the Pentecostal Holiness church. He increasingly resented the "fanatical" legalism of his church and became "concerned about myself . . . just thinking I felt it."[74] Complementing the legalism was an absence of "feeling on the part of the people for signs and wonders."[75] He approached "one of the leaders" of the church to discuss his discontent and was told, "Son, you have one of the best churches in this Conference, you had better go home and be satisfied with it." He asked his father why there were so few miracles when they preached, and "he didn't have any answer."[76] Some of the church's leaders warned Oral that his "restlessness was a sign of instability and they told me plainly I should settle down and be content."[77] But it was to be war, not peace, both for Oral and for the leaders of his denomination.

If Oral's angst in 1947 was partly pentecostal, shared by many others within that hot movement grown cool, it was partly personal, rooted in the experience of his immediate past. Oral had dealt constructively with the drive of youth, funneling his boundless energies into constructive denominational channels. He had tried to "do the things which made him acceptable to his denomination." He had learned "the lessons of discipline and experience."[78] He even "patterned the style of my preaching after theirs and conducted my service according to the pattern set by my church"; he had been an "echo," instead of being "true to himself."[79] He now judged his preaching to be "mediocre," and his preaching was his life.[80]

Nearing thirty, Oral had reached an age to look back. "I don't think a man ever really gets a grasp of life until he's 30," he would later surmise.[81] His father, Ellis, had made his decision to enter the ministry at about that age, and his son Richard would later feel his call to become an evangelist at the same age; both Oral and Richard have reflected on the fact that it was at age thirty that the son of a Jewish carpenter took up his public ministry nearly two thousand years earlier.[82]

At age thirty, Oral also reached a plateau; he had achieved too many of his goals. Being repeatedly reminded that he was at the top of his church, Oral was forced to look realistically at the view from the top. There were other minor elevations to climb, a place in the educational hierarchy and perhaps someday in the church's political organization, but those hills were far on the horizon. The view from the pinnacle in Enid was unsatisfactory; it was, in fact, dismal. While Oral's salary of fifty-five dollars per week was "the highest salary they had ever paid any preacher," the Roberts family lived precariously from pay check to pay check.[83] When Oral asked for a raise, he was required to submit a list of necessities that demanded more money, including "two haircuts a month." He grew increasingly "resentful" and embarrassed by his poverty.[84] The family owned perhaps three hundred dollars' worth of furniture, including a table that "leaned so bad . . . it would almost fall over"; they could hardly meet the payments on their "old car"; Oral rode the bus to his classes because he could not afford gasoline; on more than one occasion at the supermarket checkout counter "we'd have to take out some of the groceries and put them back on the shelves."[85]

This personal squalor—which was, after all, the world Oral and Evelyn were accustomed to, and a way of life they shared with most of their church members—was highlighted by Oral's growing awareness of the world around him. His entire life, except for his foray to Atoka and his dickering with politics, had been lived within the confines of pentecostalism. During the previous three years he had attended college classes and had encountered "three professors in the three years . . . who awakened me to the world."[86] They encouraged him to read "other books about the world," and, unexpectedly, they urged him to take pride in his own beliefs. He increasingly began to sense "that the Kingdom of God was bigger than the church of which I was proud to be a member."[87]

The immediate circumstance that triggered Oral's call to an independent ministry was his dissatisfaction with his congregation in Enid. Most of them were "good people," he later recollected, but they were "satisfied to attend church, contribute, pray and give their pastor a 'fair hearing.' "[88] Oral could not get them excited: "They didn't care whether souls were saved or not. . . . I'd get stirred up and preach and get them stirred up and it would last one week. Come back the next Sunday, they would just look at you. What's that guy so excited about?"[89] He tried to get the church to "take a Sunday School canvass," and the deacons voted him down.[90] Oral would "duck his head and pray," only to return to be "turned down again."[91] The congregation's leaders were not "concerned about the power of God," and as Oral's mind began more and more to dwell on the miracle-working power of God, his relations with the church began to sour. Even though the people "really loved me," he recalled, they began to "turn against me." Evelyn did not feel the estrangement so keenly, but Oral did, and he was puzzled by it.[92] He did not think he had changed. But he had. He had gone through a virtual personality transformation and had emerged a prophet possessed. Prophets possessed are impatient, intimidating, and discomforting.

The metamorphosis of 1947 was painful, halting at first, and finally cataclysmic. Oral was to plumb the depths before he soared to his peaks. He was "so miserable, and the people about me so miserable," he later recalled, that something had to give.[93] "What's wrong with you?" Evelyn repeatedly asked. "Nothing is wrong." "Yes, something is wrong because you're praying every night after I've gone to bed." "I don't know," Oral replied.[94] And he probably did not know—his resentments had "smoldered in me for years." Pounding inside was a "feeling of destiny," but no one else felt it and there was no place to go.[95] According to Evelyn, Oral's trauma drove him to "his knees" and to his Bible, the two sources of solace he had known from his youth, the only spiritual reservoirs he had. Oral later testified: "The Lord impressed me that the only original knowledge in the world, about Christ, is in these five books of our New Testament. Matthew, Mark, Luke, John and Acts. . . . And while on my knees I would read, sometimes I would laugh. Sometimes I would cry. Sometimes I would be shaken to the depths of my soul. I felt so little, so low."[96] He threatened God, warning that if He "didn't meet me and put His power in my life I was going to walk out."[97] "I came to the point of giving up the whole church," he recalled, "of giving up my salvation. Right at this point, I would not accept part of the Bible and reject the rest."[98] He was wrestling his own personal devils, looking God square in the face, testing, as all children of faith must do, his own innermost confidence in the Creator. Sickened by the specter of nominal commitment in an ecstatic religious movement, he had come to demand either-or. On this spiritual battlefield of prayer and meditation, Oral would win a final victory over ontological and cosmic doubts which plague less-resolute men throughout their lives. It is not true, as some of his critics would later imply, that Oral has never considered the deeper meaning of Christian faith. He thought deeply about his own belief in God. Perhaps not profoundly, certainly not systematically or in the language of theologians, but he faced intimately those ultimate questions raised by experiential religion and left them ever behind in the pastor's study in Enid. One can fault him for the simplicity and clarity of his decision, but it was precisely that which freed him to ponder other questions—such as wholeness and healing—and, above all, to act.

Out of this period of spiritual trauma came a sequence of instantaneous insights, revelations as Oral viewed them. The first occurred one morning as he read III John 2: "I wish above all things that thou mayest prosper and be in health, even as thy soul prospereth." Oral had rushed out of his house one morning to catch the bus to class when he realized he had not read his Bible as was his custom. He returned, hastily grabbed his Bible, opened it "at random," and read III John 2. He had read his New Testament, he reported, at least a hundred times, but this verse seemed brand-new. He called Evelyn and read it to her. "That is not in the Bible," she challenged. "It is," Oral replied, "I just read it."[99] "Evelyn," he said, "we have been wrong. I haven't been preaching that God is good. And Evelyn, if this verse is right, God is a good God." The idea seemed revolutionary, liberating. They had been nurtured in a belief system that insisted "you had to be poor to be a Christian." Perhaps it was not so. They talked excitedly about the verse's implications. Did it mean they could have a "new car," a "new house," a "brand-new ministry?"[100] In later years, Evelyn looked back on that morning as the point of embarkation: "I really believe that that very morning was the beginning of this worldwide ministry that he has had, because it opened up his thinking."[101]

Oral's new-found insight was soon put to a practical test. The agent was a Mr. Gustavus, a neighbor who owned the Buick automobile dealership in Enid. Mr. Gus liked Oral, and, although he was a "nonreligious" man, he listened to his neighbor's preaching occasionally and liked his emphasis on the "here and now."[102] One morning Mr. Gus noted that Oral's old car looked "pretty bad" and suggested that he buy a new one. It seemed a preposterous idea. Cars were still "practically unobtainable" in these postwar months, and there was no slack in the Robertses' tight budget. But Mr. Gus showed them a way; he sold their old car for the "highest ceiling" price and acquired a new Buick for Oral at "dealer's cost." Mr. Gus, Oral, and Evelyn drove together to Detroit to pick up the car. As they drove back to Enid in their "brand new . . . long, green, slick Buick," Oral and Evelyn pondered the significance of this seemingly impossible turn. Evelyn asked Oral to stop: "We have just got to hold hands and praise the Lord for this car."[103] For Oral, the "new car became a symbol to me of what a man could do if he would believe God." Nor was Mr. Gus through. He kept egging Oral on. "Son, the message you are preaching is too big for one town," he told Oral, "the country is waiting for it. . . . Preach it, son. And you will stir this generation."[104]

Far-reaching as was this new insight into the joys of prosperity and the power of human capabilities, a more dramatic revelation was just ahead. The first understanding had come dramatically, had been realized through Mr. Gus, and had produced a new car. The next new leading came from a higher source and would produce a new life.

The beginning of Oral's acute spiritual crisis came in the midst of a sociology class at Phillips. The professor was "a brilliant man," and Oral was "fascinated" by the subject. Unexpectedly one morning, the teacher began to ridicule the idea that Eve was made from Adam's rib. Oral was "shocked, amazed," and deeply disappointed by such a lack of faith in a religious school. He was moved to protest, but instead his mind wandered until "it seemed I was alone in the presence of God." He then heard "the same voice I had heard in 1935." This time the voice said: "Son, don't be like other men. Don't be like other preachers. . . . Be like my Son, Jesus Christ, and bring healing to the people as he did."[105]

It was that experience which triggered Oral's month-long period of praying and study of the gospels and Acts. Toward the end of the month he began to fast and increasingly sought solitude. "One morning," he recalled, "I told Evelyn I was going to the church alone, and I would remain there in prayer until the Lord revealed himself to me." Evelyn smiled and replied that she would be praying at home. Oral went to the church study, stretched "myself out upon the floor, face down, hands clasped together," and "told the Lord I had come to the end of myself and that I would not leave Him until He spoke to me."[106] It was another of those mystical, private, existential moments: "I was just with the Lord. Was no longer aware of anything physical. It was like He took eternity and held it and stopped it. Like everything was suspended. I felt like I wasn't touching anything."[107] Suddenly, Oral recalled, he once again heard an "audible voice" speaking like a "military commander, words of crisp command, clear and strong." "Stand upon your feet," the voice said. "Go and get in your car." Oral obediently walked to his car. "Then God said, 'Drive one block and turn right,'" starting him back toward his parsonage. As he drove toward his home, the message was completed: "From this hour your ministry of healing will begin. You will have my power to pray for the sick and to cast out devils."[108]

Oral "burst in the door," hugged Evelyn, and told her to cook. She knew that the "Lord had spoken to him." "So she cooked and we ate and laughed and cried and talked and planned."[109] It was a healing ministry that God was calling him to. For the first time he revealed to Evelyn that God had spoken to him on the evening he was healed. He remembered the words of Bill Lee in Toccoa about the potential of healing to bring revival. He told Evelyn of a recent encounter with one of his teachers at the university, who had told him that she believed that "faith can heal disease." "You have a keen, analytical mind," she had assured Oral, "I think you're on the right track. . . . People must be shown how to recapture their faith. I think you will be one of the men God uses to give faith back to the people."[110]

One final incident centered Oral's mind on healing. Enid had been visited by a healing revivalist holding union services. Like Moncey twelve years earlier, he was one of those nameless, tarnished warriors known to all pentecostals. Oral had been fascinated by the services. Always generous in his evaluation of other ministers, Oral judged him to be an "outstanding preacher," and sensed that he "had a feeling for other people." But there was something awry which sapped the "power in his prayers." He placed an "undue emphasis upon money," the fatal Achilles heel of such clumsy entrepreneurs, sometimes spending a full hour to take his "offering." Even then, recalled Oral, "he didn't get very much money," and he left behind "an odor in the room that you didn't like."[111] Most local pentecostals were repulsed by the meeting because of the minister's excesses, but Oral saw the people's hunger for miracles. If one could only avoid the abuses. Before he began his ministry, he made a pledge to avoid financial chicanery, and whatever his critics may have perceived, his efforts to be honest set him apart from many of the healing evangelists who vied for public acclaim after World War II.

In April, Oral began holding Sunday afternoon healing services at the church in Enid and preaching messages on divine healing on his radio program. He reported this new departure in the *Pentecostal Holiness Advocate,* making clear that "this is the work of the Church. It was not done in a corner back there, it was for everybody."[112] "The Pentecostal Holiness Church fully embraces divine healing," he reminded, and assured that "there is no show, nothing spectacular, no ostentations" in his services. The church, he added, was "benefiting from the healing services," and attendance was at an "all-time high."[113]

Oral's early reports were, as always, wildly enthusiastic, but they were also guarded, even slightly nervous. He wrote proudly that some of "the leading doctors and professional men of Enid have sent us congratulations," but that he had received "no support from the pastors of the city." Most likely, he added, that was because he would not "compromise" his pentecostal message and convictions. By the end of May he reported he had received calls from other places to conduct healing services and was "sending out a considerable supply of anointed handkerchiefs."[114] Oral knew that many considered his new departure "unorthodox and sensational."[115] But he implored his church to go with him down the uncharted path to Bible miracles: "So many are afraid . . . but the only thing we have to fear is fear itself."[116]

On May 25, Oral took a giant step, moving his healing service out of the church building into the large Education Building in downtown Enid. It was a calculated risk. Some advised him to keep his service in the church building, where it had been strikingly successful; others urged him to leave town if he intended to hold a "union" service, since he was too well known in Enid. But he rented the building, obligating himself for the $160 rental fee, and scheduled the service. He did so with trepidation. "Do you suppose I really heard God?" he asked Evelyn.[117] He told his wife that he was putting out "three fleeces" which would give him the answer to his question. First, he wanted a crowd of 1,000 people, though his Sunday morning audience at his own church rarely exceeded 200. Second, he wanted expenses to be met "without fuss or bother." Third, he demanded that "enough people . . . be healed beyond any question that they and I would know that I was called."[118]

On Sunday afternoon at 2:00 P.M. the count of the audience revealed about twelve hundred people present. An offering was taken, "without pressure," and Oral was handed a slip showing that the expenses had been met and that there was a "small sum left over." At that point Oral was bursting to preach. He delivered his sermon: "If You Need Healing—Do These Things!" It would soon be published to be read by millions. "The anointing of the Holy Spirit," he later recalled, "was so strong upon me that my flesh quivered." He spoke with "vibrancy" and "authority."[119] Gilbert "Gib" Bond, who led singing at the service, remembered that Oral "grabbed the microphone and preached heaven down on that crowd." When he finished his sermon, Oral invited those wishing prayer for healing to come to the front. According to Bond, "the people charged to the front. I'd never seen anything like it. He jumped down from the stage and met the people and started praying for them. It was like the world exploded."[120] Very early Oral prayed for "a German woman . . . who had had a crippled, crooked and stiff hand for thirty-eight years." She began to scream "at the top of her voice, I am healed. I am healed, and she began to show it and people ran around."[121] Pandemonium broke loose. The service continued until six o'clock; over one hundred sick were prayed for, and eight "hard men" who had long rejected conversion "came over to Oral and wanted him to pray for them to get saved."[122]

At six o'clock Oral walked out of the building, "wet to my hide," having prayed for the last supplicant. The emotional and physical drain of such a session was, as he was to learn better than any other human, an enfeebling catharsis. But as he walked out that evening, there was no self-pity, no second-guessing: "I looked at the world and inside me and I said, 'Look out, I'm coming. I'm coming your way.'"[123] He wrote to the *Pentecostal Holiness Advocate*: "We can say that this has been the greatest PENTECOST DAY service we have ever seen and believe that 'greater things' than these are ahead."[124]

In a sense, the last element in Oral's crucial decision, the determination to leave Enid and once again begin independent evangelistic work (this time with a healing emphasis), was a foregone conclusion. In fact, Oral had fallen "out of love with the denominational system." And just as surely many within his denomination, including the leaders of the church in Enid, were falling out of love with him. Oral was "dealing with dynamite" in his healing services.[125] Many doubted his sincerity. Two of his friends in the Enid church, including his song leader, "Gib" Bond, were convinced Oral "had found a way to make a quick buck" and asked to be cut in on the "racket."[126] Oral was venturing into unknown territory. His former friends could not judge his motives; nor could they go so far so fast.[127]

Furthermore, the door was opening and the world was beckoning. In June, Oral announced that he had received invitations from eight states as a result of his successful meetings.[128] As invitations came in, Oral naturally thought once again of becoming an evangelist. The move was a financial risk, but they had little to lose; they had "started our marriage with borrowed money and had never been out of debt very long at a time."[129] The chief risk was his healing message, which took him "out from the established pattern of the ministry." Oral talked with Bishop Dan T. Muse, explaining his plans to him. "It was a great encouragement to Oral when Bishop Muse replied, 'I believe you are in God's will — the *high* will of God for you!'"[130]

Oral resigned his pastorate, and he and Evelyn once again excitedly faced an unknown future. One June morning she drove Oral from Enid to Tulsa to catch a plane to the East, where he had been invited to hold healing services. Neither of them had ever ridden an airplane. Evelyn remembered: "He kissed me goodbye, walked up the steps and disappeared. . . . Pretty soon I saw him at the window; he was waving to me. Tears came to my eyes. I had the feeling I would be doing this during all the years of our youth — years we both wanted to be together."[131] It was to be so.

PART TWO

MIRACLES

1947–1960

PROLOGUE

Australia, January 20-February 10, 1956

THE DECISION to strike the big tent in Melbourne three days before the scheduled end of the healing campaign was the "greatest crisis" encountered in the first decade of Oral Roberts's independent ministry.[1] It was made after an anxious evening of meetings between Oral's team and local sponsors and was based on a genuine fear that lives were in danger. The crusade had degenerated into a sorry, dangerous confrontation. The Australian debacle triggered in Oral a period of personal examination and soul searching.

Oral was slow to take his healing campaigns outside the United States, though other evangelists had been spectacularly successful holding such crusades around the world. The "full gospel" churches of Australia planned and negotiated for nearly two years to persuade Oral to come. Australian pentecostal interest had been aroused by the healing of Shirley Jones (born Shirley Surtees in Cairns, Australia) in a 1954 Roberts meeting in Rocky Mount, North Carolina, where she was living with her ex-serviceman husband. Mrs. Jones had spent months in a wheelchair, suffering from a "nervous collapse," before rising to walk away from Roberts's healing line.[2] A more important stimulus, however, was the expansion of Oral's radio network to include several Australian stations by the early 1950s.

By 1956, Oral was intent on developing a visible overseas ministry. He was, however, a fastidious planner and insisted that preparations be thorough. For several years he had expressed an interest in conducting foreign crusades but complained that the "full gospel brethren overseas" moved "entirely too slowly in securing auditoriums and pertinent information about entering and leaving their countries."[3] But the 1956 venture had been carefully planned and generously funded. A year earlier Oral had conducted his first overseas campaign in South Africa; its success caused his staff to "change their entire thinking about preaching the gospel." By the next year Oral had launched a new "World Outreach" program, built around the trip to Australia.[4] Australian pentecostals first contacted Oral in 1954, and immediately after his South African campaign in January 1955, he dispatched his friend and advisor Lee Braxton to make the necessary arrangements. The Australians were ecstatic after talking with Braxton: "Such a visit should mean a time of great visitation of God's power in this land. This is something to pray and prepare for!"[5]

For the first (and only) time the big tent, expanded by two extra sections to accommodate 18,000 people, along with thousands of folding chairs and other equipment was loaded on a freighter in New Orleans headed for Sydney. Oral considered renting auditoriums, but the Australian sponsors "urged him to bring the tent equipment," and no one loved the atmosphere of the big tent more than he did. The team stopped in the Philippines for a crusade before journeying on to Australia; they predicted that the entire junket would win "100,000 souls."[6] The cost of shipping the tent was around $40,000; the estimated total expense of the campaign was over $100,000, but confidence ran high that the meetings in Sydney and Melbourne would be striking successes. Advertisements in Sydney newspapers announced the coming of "America's Healing Evangelist."[7]

Upon his arrival in Sydney, Oral was greeted by a fierce and unprecedented barrage from the Australian press, "ten times worse than we had ever had in America."[8] A few relatively benign descriptions of his ministry appeared, but most of the accounts of his arrival and of his early meetings were extremely inflammatory. Roberts and his team were convinced that there was a conspiracy to smear him. Hart R. Armstrong, Roberts's public relations secretary, later speculated that the "public press of both Sydney and Melbourne were prejudiced against us before we landed in Australia." He spoke to reporters on the telephone before arriving and found them openly "antagonistic." When the members of the team arrived in Sydney, they were bombarded with "belligerent questions."[9] Roberts did grant several interviews to reporters in Sydney and Melbourne, who told him they were "very favorably" impressed. The Roberts team's conspiracy interpretation seemed confirmed when these reporters' stories failed to appear.[10] Bob DeWeese, Oral's assistant minister, has remained convinced that "it had to be some kind of conspiracy" and recalled that several reporters admitted, "We're acting on orders from above."[11]

That was not Oral's first, or his last, encounter with a hostile press, but it was the most coordinated and belligerent attack. The opposition apparently was planned and, to some degree, organized. Prior to Oral's arrival, thousands of copies of a tract attacking his ministry, "The Modern Tongues and Healing Movement," written by American Presbyterian minister Carroll Stegall, Jr., had been circulated to the Australian press and ministers.[12] A Billy Graham aide who visited Australia in preparation for a Graham campaign in 1957 reported that "one of Australia's leading businessmen" had "spent considerable time and money" to see that Oral was ejected from the country a year earlier.[13]

When Oral's Sydney meeting opened, the best treatment he got was a good-humored ribbing by the *Sydney Bulletin's* entertainment critic, who rated the evening service "of its kind . . . all quite good stuff—'hot gospelling' . . . until he got too long." He also noted, however, that Oral arrived "looking rather like an immaculate high-pressure salesman," while his crowd was "a sad and earnest gathering, with but an infrequent spot of youth and beauty among them."[14] Others were less gentle. An article in the *Sydney Sun* dubbed Oral's crusade a "circus" of "rapid-fire, razzle dazzle religion, ecstatic ravings, mass hysteria and high pressure, super-sold, soul-saving 'cures.' "[15] Sydney newsmen discovered that Oral was staying under an assumed name in the city's leading hotel, the Glen Ascham, in a twenty-dollar-a-day room, and they hammered relentlessly on Oral's financial good fortunes.[16]

Nonetheless, the Sydney campaign was declared by the Roberts team to be the "greatest religious campaign" ever held in the city.[17] Seventy-five thousand attended the services, and "perfect order" had been maintained by crusade workers and the police. Oral and his team were stung by the press treatment and refused interviews when they arrived in Melbourne, but they moved on anticipating a good crusade there.[18]

The Melbourne crusade began on Sunday, February 5, and was scheduled to last eight days. The Sunday service was well attended, and about four hundred answered the altar call.[19] Then, recalled Oral, "the next morning (Monday), the Melbourne newspapers launched an all-out attack against me personally and the crusade. The articles were anti-God, anti-Bible and anti-American."[26] On Monday evening the crowd was still large, but only "250 dared to come forward," and there was open heckling, which turned into "loud yelling" when the healing line started. At this point Oral was convinced that the meeting was headed for a "crisis."[21] By Wednesday evening, the heckling had become organized and widespread, and there was open intimidation of those who answered the altar call. Only about sixty came forward by Wednesday, but, recalled Oral, "what heroes they were."[22] The number of hecklers had grown to several hundred, and when the services ended on Wednesday there were several ugly confrontations outside and a few scuffles. The *Argus,* perhaps the most hostile of the Melbourne papers, announced, with apparent approbation, that "American hot-gospeller, Oral Roberts, was chased and abused by a big crowd after his 'faith-healing' meeting last night." "As he roared away in a big, modern, American sedan," continued the article, "men and women shouted, 'You ought to be tarred and feathered. We aren't a mob of hill-billies.' " Oral was "smuggled out of the tent" while crowds surrounded a "decoy car."[23]

By Thursday, the situation had grown ominous. The harshness of the press coverage and the anger of the Roberts team rose each day. "In view of the attitude of the press," the Roberts organization "informed reporters and photographers that they could not roam at will in the services, but would have to be seated in the congregation." The press interpreted this ban as "suppression"; some reported that they were "roughed up and otherwise hindered from getting news." When Collins Steele, Oral's equipment manager, found a photographer perched on a box trying to photograph the offering, he "drawled with his good-natured Alabama accent, 'You'd better be careful. You might fall and break a leg.' " However intended, the warning was taken by the reporter to be a threat.[24] By Thursday evening the antagonistic press coverage had emboldened the harassers, and the services were disturbed by the throwing of stink bombs, catcalls during Oral's sermon, and, allegedly, by a reporter trying to pour beer into Oral's water glass.[25] More foreboding was a telephone call to the police threatening that "a hand grenade would be thrown at Roberts."[26]

Oral's crusade team had often encountered problems in maintaining order, but never such a massive disruption. Most serious, however, was the lack of cooperation they received from the Melbourne police. In America, the police readily aided in the suppression of religious hecklers. In Melbourne, the police, while present at every service of the crusade, refused to interfere as long as the disruptors committed no act of violence.[27]

The Roberts team's efforts to control the meeting were fruitless. Oral discussed the difficulties with the American vice-consul, and while he was "cooperative and understanding," Oral left knowing, without being told, that "what he could do was limited."[28] In America, team members and ushers would have ejected the protesters themselves. Collins Steele asked a police officer in Melbourne: "Suppose I just grab that guy and throw him out of the tent?" "I'd have to arrest you," replied the officer. The soft-spoken Alabamian dejectedly observed: "That's a little different than I'm accustomed to."[29] Bob DeWeese, who more than anyone else was responsible for the maintenance of order during services, was infuriated by the taunting of the hecklers. He called the Australian pentecostal pastors together, "rolled up his sleeves, and said, 'Pastors, if you'll go with me we'll clean that bunch out.' "[30] DeWeese was disappointed that "the pentecostal people would not address themselves to the problem"; they seemed "intimidated" and "scared for their lives."[31] The "good ministers" were "terribly embarrassed," but they would not act. And, in spite of the posturing by Steele and DeWeese, the Roberts organization issued printed instructions to all "ushers and personal workers" instructing them "not to resort to violence" lest a riot ensue and they be held responsible.[32]

On Thursday evening the confrontation climaxed. City Councilman W. J. Brens, former Lord Mayor of Melbourne and then chairman of Melbourne Parks and Gardens, requested an interview with Oral, because the city had been criticized for allowing the use of Yarra Park for the crusade. Brens was invited to question Oral after the evening service, and a crowd of over 10,000 assembled, including many agitators. Oral preached "a calm, dispassionate sermon on 'A Man's Life,' " and, commented one Australian reporter, "the main body of people . . . listened and were impressed with what they saw and heard." While he did not care for "this type religious service nor the American pronunciation of sacred names," the reporter continued, "no decent-minded man or woman could deny the sincerity of the various men who took part in the proceedings."[33] When Oral extended the altar call, 40 responded—"the bravest men and women I have ever seen," wrote G. H. Montgomery.[34] At the close of the service Councilor Brens came forward for the "unenviable task" of asking Roberts the "blunt questions" supplied to him by the press. Brens was cheered by the audience when he began his task, "including by the interjectors," but he proceeded with dignity and respect, and the hecklers soon taunted him with calls of "What's your cut, Brens?"[35] Oral "was as dignified and well-poised as the Councilor," and "amid hoots and jeers," he answered the questions "without a falter or a hesitation."[36] Brens "expressed himself satisfied with Mr. Roberts' replies," and the meeting was dismissed amidst a considerable uproar.[37]

It was the scene that followed the Thursday evening service which convinced the Roberts team and the crusade committee that the campaign must be ended prematurely. Oral was again whisked away secretively, but agitators continued to mill around the tent area, angered by the proceedings of the evening. A group rushed to the car in which Evelyn was riding and rocked it threateningly before it was able to break away. Other team members were cursed and threatened.[38] Most alarming, a fire broke out in one of the party's trailer trucks, causing only minor damage but raising new fears. The *Argus* reported that the "mysterious fire" appeared to be a "deliberate attempt" to destroy the Tent Cathedral and added, the Roberts team felt with a hint of approval: "Earlier *The Argus* has been told by an official source: 'We have heard that an attempt may be made to set fire to the big tent tonight.' "[39]

During the evening, Oral's team huddled and decided to urge the closing of the campaign. Oral recollected that he retired and that the decision was made by Bob DeWeese.[40] The team feared that continuing would endanger Oral's life and the lives of others. They also felt that there was a real risk that the equipment would be destroyed. Oral issued a statement the following day outlining the concerns of his team and likened his situation to that of the apostle Paul, whose friends insisted that he not speak when his life was threatened: "Like the friends of Paul who refused to permit him to come before the mob, so my disciples have insisted that I must not speak again in Melbourne."[41] Hasty arrangements were made, and Oral departed on Saturday, sullen and silent. The Australian press dutifully noted his "secret and nervous departure," "wearing white trousers, blue embroidered shirt and gray jacket," and trailed by "five of his 16 'disciples,' including two bodyguards," twenty pieces of luggage, and "40,000 down."[42]

The *Sydney Sunday Truth* greeted Oral's departure with the headline "Good Riddance"; an apt summary of the Americans' feelings as well.[43] Bob DeWeese issued an acid retort, charging that the crusade had not been afforded police protection. "Mr. Roberts and his team are unlikely ever to set foot in the country again," said DeWeese, expressing "bitter disappointment" in finding Australia "so sinful and faithless."[44] "Louts and hooligans defiled my consecrated tent," was Oral's parting shot.[45]

Oral, and most of his team, believed that the leaders of the disturbance were Communist agitators. Speaking to the Tulsa Chamber of Commerce shortly after his return to the city, Oral charged that "communist led mobs were responsible for breaking up his evangelical meetings in Melbourne."[46] G. H. Montgomery reported that most of the troublemakers were "youngsters" but that the outbursts were kept alive by "sharp-faced men, with cockeyes and a cigarette dangling from the corner of their mouth, moving purposefully from one to another. The cell members were doing their dirty work trying to whip these fine young people into a killing frenzy, to mold them in the Kremlin's own image."[47] Oral later surmised that his persecution brought "to light the power of the Communist minority in Australia," and helped to expose the fact that "true religious liberty was not known there."[48]

It is difficult to account fully for the explosive Australian confrontation. Norman Banks, one of Melbourne's most influential news commentators, gave probably the fairest appraisal of the events immediately after the Roberts party left. Most of the people at the meeting, he reported, were orderly and supportive. Banks judged that news accounts which estimated there were a thousand demonstrators were "the grossest exaggeration." Most of the milling crowd, he believed, had simply come to see the action:

> These so-called demonstrators, a total not exceeding fifty at most, consisted in the main of curious people who were looking for entertainment. The actual disruptionists could be numbered on two hands. THIS element embraced three COMMUNISTS who I've seen on the Yarra bank and at recent election meetings, particularly at the anti-Communist meetings—a couple of vulgar exhibitionists who played to a small gallery of 'widgy' and 'bodgy' types, several semi-drunken smart alecks, and a remnant of hooligans most anxious to find out who takes the collections.[49]

In short, there appeared to be no conspiracy, but rather an unhappy collection of negative circumstances fanned to intense heat by the press. Yarra Park, where the tent was located, was Melbourne's Hyde Park, and heckling was considered fair play. Collins Steele recalled that Australian "longshoremen were on strike and there were a lot of people milling around that had nothing to do and some of them were from an element of society that would tend to generate problems."[50] Taken together, these forces blended into the ugly scene which ended the crusade.

Upon reflection, many responsible Australians were ashamed of the incident. Some apologies came immediately. Commentator Banks's critique of the incident was the most vigorous attack on the "silly inane questions" of the disruptionists and on their questionable character. But there were other quick condemnations. Dr. C. Irving Benson, a Melbourne Presbyterian minister, issued a statement to the press announcing he was "ashamed" of the "intolerance and persecution shown toward this visiting preacher."[51] Several religious organizations, including nonpentecostal churches, denounced the incident and demanded that authorities offer assurances that future religious meetings would be protected.[52] Several expressed concern that Billy Graham might receive similar treatment when he came to Australia the next year. Six months after the episode, Gordon Powell, religious editor of the *Sydney Morning Herald,* reflected on the Roberts debacle in an article entitled "The Boomerang." While some still took "considerable satisfaction" over Roberts's expulsion, Powell noted, "more responsible people . . . saw the dangerous implications in what had happened." The Presbyterian church in Victoria passed a resolution condemning "this intrusion into religious liberty" and requesting "more effective safeguards" against rowdyism. Powell reported that Australian Anglican and

Methodist leaders had taken up the cause of protecting "pentecostal rights." It also appeared that the Australian incident had not detracted from Roberts's influence in America, where his campaigns were bigger and more bountifully funded than ever before. All in all, concluded Powell, "from what has happened since, it is evident that these events stirred sympathy in the thousands who were previously luke-warm towards Oral Roberts."[53]

The vanquished evangelist could see no positive derivatives from the experience in 1956; his return home was humiliating. "When we got off the plane in San Francisco," recalled Evelyn, "the angry press stories had already reached America. We couldn't seem to leave that ugly experience behind us."[54] Even the Tulsa papers were filled with unfriendly accounts from abroad, and national news magazines reported the difficulties of the "natty faith healer" with apparent relish.[55] Some of the stories were vicious. One labeled Oral "an oily hypocrite who has racked up a fortune by his pious howling over radio and television."[56] In the months ahead, reporters covering Oral's campaigns would demand repetitious explanations of the Australian episode.[57]

Oral and Evelyn arrived home in Tulsa on Monday, February 13, and, reported the *Tulsa Tribune,* "went directly to their Robin Hood farm near Bixby where Mr. Roberts will relax until his next religious campaign."[58] There Oral and Evelyn contemplated the "greatest hurt" they had yet experienced; for "many months" after the incident Oral settled into "deep soul searching."[59] Evelyn scribbled in her diary: "What do you do when you've given your life to God's work, left your children, and done everything you know to do for the Lord, and then are misrepresented?" "When something like Australia . . . happens," she reflected in later years, "I think it's our nature . . . to search our souls and search the Bible. Oral and I did a lot of praying and discussing in those days after Australia."[60] Evelyn felt that God "had let us down," and Oral's "period of bitterness" lasted for nearly a year.[61] In an interview in June 1957, Evelyn discussed their struggle: "Things bore down on Oral more than even I care to admit. One night he said to me, 'Honey, come in here and sit down. We are going to have this thing out with God once and for all. . . . Evelyn, what am I going to do? The newspapers have tried to crucify us. How are these things going to affect my ministry here in America?' "[62]

Australia came at the end of almost ten years of clawing and climbing, a decade of uninterrupted growth and recognition. There had been countless problems along the way, but the triumphs had bred euphoria. The Australian debacle was a clublike blow which drew Oral's attention—to the world outside and to himself. The result was not a sharp discontinuity, but in 1957 a Los Angeles journalist noted that the experience seemed to have a "sobering, maturing effect on Roberts, reflected in the literature, sermons and general evangelism approach that marks him today."[63] Oral felt that he had seen the death angel. One does mature under such circumstances.

CHAPTER

V

Healing Revivalism

IN JULY 1947, Oral, Evelyn, Rebecca, and Ronnie moved to Tulsa. They were expectant newcomers in a vibrant city. The Tulsa to which the family had come was a young city, still directed by the urban pioneers who "laid out the streets, organized the churches, and established industry in Tulsa."[1] Located where the ancient transcontinental transportation routes crossed the Arkansas River, Tulsey Town was first settled as a Creek village in the 1840s; the Creeks named the spot for a more ancient Alabama village which was visited by De Soto in 1540. In post-Civil War years, the Indian village careened from trading post, to cow town, to oil-boom town, to World War II industrial center.[2] The population of Tulsa rose from 7,298 in 1907 to 72,075 in 1920 and to over 140,000 in 1940. Postwar Tulsa tingled with the excitement of early adolescence. Ambitious and bold young Tulsans would accumulate some of the most colossal fortunes in the nation in the postwar generation. Tulsa was a place to dream big; it was a place where men were judged by their accomplishments and not by their pedigree, where one must stand not on what he had done but on what he was doing.

Oral chose Tulsa, he later revealed, because it was "centrally located in the United States" and because it had "excellent travel facilities."[3] Just after he moved to the city, the local newspaper proclaimed Tulsa the "air crossroads of the nation," pointing out that the city was served by four major airlines—American, Braniff, Continental, and Mid-Continent.[4] But more than the airlines drew Oral to Tulsa; in hindsight his choice seemed predestined. He was and has remained an Oklahoma press agent, and after millions of miles of travel, he still judged Tulsa to be "the most beautiful city I have ever seen."[5] In 1949 he wrote: "Tulsa is my home until Jesus calls or comes for us."[6] But, more basic, Oral somehow sensed the exuberance of the city, its Wild West individualism. Here was a place where new ideas could find room to soar, a city that was "progressive," where bold experimentation "can be nurtured and great ideas can be had and great movements can be launched."[7] Somehow, intuitively, or, as he would believe, with divine "guidance," Oral had found the place to build and, to some extent, to be appreciated.[8]

Of course, no grand vistas loomed close on the horizon in June 1947, when the Roberts family pulled into town with heads full of dreams and pockets devoid of cash. Two months earlier they had come to Tulsa to find a place to live and had spent an evening with Oscar Moore, who was now superintendent of the East Oklahoma Conference. Oscar had been working as an evangelist but had accepted a call to replace Oral as pastor of the church in Enid. The Moores had put their little home located on North Main Street up for sale for $6,000 and had a prospective buyer, but they welcomed Oral and Evelyn to stay with them until they found a place to live. Housing was scarce in postwar Tulsa, and Oral and Evelyn could find nothing to lease which they could afford. They wanted to buy Oscar Moore's home, but it was committed and they had no down payment. The problem solved itself. The prospective buyer failed to appear, and Oscar offered his home to Oral. Oral accepted, though he had only $25 in his pocket. Fortunately, Oscar had already decided that he needed no down payment; when told, the relieved Oral tried to receive the news nonchalantly. He asked Moore to sell him a "little desk over in a corner." The price was $12. "So I paid him $12," Oral recalled, "and I had $13 left. And we started our ministry on the dining room table and on that little $12 desk."[9]

The new shape of Oral's healing ministry had begun to take form before his move to Tulsa. In May and June he had made a series of visits to small Oklahoma churches, conducting healing services.[10] Everywhere the crowds were "outstanding," and Oral boldly experimented with his new craft. In Seminole he had the "cockiness" knocked out of him when an epileptic in his healing line went into convulsions standing in front of him: "All my cockiness disappeared and I stood before the desperation of the human being. . . . I had nothing to draw on. I couldn't get advice from anyone. And I leaned over and prayed for her and nothing happened. I stood back. I wanted to run." That incident closed triumphantly when the woman "leaped up," but evening after evening Oral discovered both the power and the precariousness of prayer.[11] In June he visited Georgia, conducting two healing services in Athens amid "the largest crowds in the history of the church" before moving on to Newnan.[12] In Newnan Oral preached in the municipal auditorium in a Sunday afternoon healing service, and "about 200 people were in the healing line in that one service. The high and low, rich and poor, the saved and lost mingled together and many of them found perfect deliverance."[13] In the Georgia revivals Oral was assisted by his old friend Mildred Wicks and by George Stephenson; the three hoped to "conduct healing revivals in different parts of the nation as the Lord led." By the end of June, Oral was broadcasting his "Healing Waters" program over radio stations in Oklahoma City and Enid and had announced his plan to acquire a tent as well as expand his radio work.[14]

During their house-hunting visit, Oral and Evelyn, along with the Moores, attended a revival being sponsored by a local Pentecostal Holiness pastor, Steve Pringle, in a tent at 615 North Main Street. Pringle had pitched a second-hand tent, which seated over 1,000 people, in the early spring and had been preaching in it himself.[15] In early July Pringle invited the "Bridgeman Evangelistic Party" to continue the revival, and they boasted in their advertisements that "cancers and other diseases have been healed by faith and prayers."[16]

When Oral showed up at Pringle's tent in May, he was invited to preach for a few nights. After completing his move in July, he began preaching in the tent, and it was a badly needed opening for Oral's new career. The first two nights the crowds were "very small" because of driving rains. The big tent swallowed the audience of less than two hundred people. "I wasn't even known," Oral reminisced, but "I preached and when I had my line for people to come up who had a need, there were seven or eight people who were definitely helped."[17] The crowds increased, and the results grew more impressive; each night, Oral recalled, "something happened of a miraculous nature."[18] One evening a "blind man who had been brought from Kansas" bolted from the healing line shouting, "I can see! I can see!"[19] By the end of the week the tent was filled, and Pringle insisted that Oral continue. For nine weeks the healing revival flourished. Word spread through the midwestern pentecostal subculture like prairie fire. From all across eastern Oklahoma, and from bordering states, pentecostals came to see Oral in his new calling. Carl Hamilton, later provost of Oral Roberts University, remembered riding with his parents from Bartlesville to hear Oral, who was "wearing a maroon sport coat and white trousers and black and white wing tip shoes, preaching Samson and Delilah." On the way home his father offered the suspended judgment felt by many pentecostals, "If it is of God, it will endure. If it is not of God, it will not. No one need to worry about what Oral Roberts is doing."[20] But by August many judged the tent meeting to be Tulsa's "greatest healing revival since 1922 when Raymond T. Richey had stirred the city."[21]

One warm August evening, an incident occurred which Oral believed triggered national interest in his ministry. He later told the story many times of a bullet that "plowed through the canvas about 18 inches above my head" while he was preaching. Actually, no one realized the shot had been fired until the next day.[22] As it unraveled, the shooting incident grew out of a neighborhood protest against the tent meeting. On August 2, the *Tulsa Daily World* reported, "Torrid nights, fervent tent revival meetings and a blaring public address system are most upsetting to residents of the 600 block N. Main St."[23] A group of neighbors complained to the city council about the noisy meetings which frequently lasted past midnight and the traffic congestion caused by the huge crowds. They received no help from the city council, and four nights later cab driver Bill Doyle fired four shots into the tent because the revival was disturbing his ill wife.[24] The parties met and reconciled their differences a few days later, and criminal charges against Doyle were dismissed.[25]

Oral's later recollections of the Doyle case were imprecise in detail and were colored by the dramatic impact the event had on those attending the revival.[26] Oral and others also recalled that the AP and UP wire services carried accounts of the shooting, although it seems likely that the small stories in the Tulsa papers were the limit of news coverage of the event.[27] But if the significance and visibility of the shooting were not so grand as Tulsa pentecostals imagined, the story undoubtedly did sweep through American pentecostalism. "How they found out," Oral wondered in 1967, "I don't know."[28] But "letters started pouring in from all over the country. Also telegrams and telephone calls."[29] Others recalled that the incident "made him known nationally overnight."[30] However the news had spread, Oral's name had been raised to celebrity status. He made the most of Mr. Doyle's angry protest against pentecostal noise, wearing the label "controversial evangelist" as a badge of honor.[31]

The Tulsa interlude in Steve Pringle's tent set the stage for a busy fall in some of the nation's largest pentecostal churches as Oral was "thronged with invitations from all over America."[32] As his fame spread, "people offered to pay my plane fare if I would fly to their side or that of their loved ones and pray for them."[33] Just as important, the Tulsa meeting opened Oral's eyes to the need to reach beyond the local church. Under the tent he saw a "unity among the people"; he began "to see what this ministry could do to bring people together. It blotted out all denominational barriers, color lines and disunity."[34]

In August Oral flew to Alton, Illinois to conduct healing services in the First Assemblies of God church, his first major campaign outside his own denomination. He was still learning. In Alton, he got "a little careless" in his healing line because, he believed, of a "lack of experience." He told a woman on crutches to cast them aside and walk: "Her hands went up and people leaped to their feet rejoicing and I was standing there thrilled from head to toe." Then, suddenly, "like a bird had been shot, she just wilted and went down." Oral managed to get her to her feet again and the people "rejoiced somewhat," but their faith had weakened. "The Lord was trying to say something to me and He did," recalled Oral later. "I became very, very careful from that point on."[35]

In September, Oral conducted a three-week revival in the Masonic Temple Auditorium in Muskogee, sponsored by the three major pentecostal denominations of the city. The sponsoring pastors were ecstatic about the "mighty miracles" which they witnessed. Among the "definite miracles" was the healing of thirteen-year-old Aline Green, who had been stricken by polio the year before. Oral sometimes referred to her case as his first "major healing." He "rebuked the disease in Jesus' Name," and "she took off the brace before all the people and could walk normally again after 10 years."[36]

After meetings in churches in Granite City, Illinois and East St. Louis, in November Oral scheduled a revival in an auditorium in Chanute, Kansas. It turned out to be a "serious mistake."[37] Chanute Memorial Hall seated approximately 2,300 people, and as the weather turned cold in November, the crowds dropped to a thousand or less. Oral, keenly attuned to his audiences, felt that the people "did not respond."[38] Worse yet, the contributions fell far short of paying the rent on the auditorium. "Several times," recalled Oral, "I had almost quit, but Evelyn talked me out of it." At the beginning of one service, when the

collection plates came back nearly bare, Oral dejectedly walked off the platform. He later recalled:

> I said to my wife and to my brother Vaden who was with me at that time, "I'm
> going to give it up." And she said, "What in the world do you mean you are
> going to give it up?" "Well," I said, "If I can't trust God for finance, I have no
> right to preach." And I meant it. And my brother Vaden, who wasn't even
> saved, said, "Oral, you can't do this." "Well," I said, "I am doing it." Evelyn
> said, "You get back on that stage." And I just marched right back on the stage.
> . . . I believe that was a command of faith.[39]

For the only time she could remember, Evelyn went on stage with Oral and
took the microphone: "People, you don't know Oral like I do. He's not here for
the money. He's here for the Gospel. . . . My husband's about to give up this
ministry and I know he will do it. . . . I think you people should understand it
and do something about it." One of the women in the audience rose and castigated the crowd, commandeered her husband's hat, and called for a new collection. Evelyn passed the "black hat with the big western brim" through the
crowd, "and brother," reported Oral, "she brought the tent money in."[40] The
Chanute experience once again brought Oral down to earth, and it made him
"thoroughly ashamed of himself." And, more than anything else, "it proved to
me again that God had given me a helpmate."[41]

In spite of his disappointment in Chanute, Oral began 1948 full of optimism. It proved to be another year of transition and learning; by the time it
ended, his crusade ministry had taken the shape it was to retain for nearly two
decades. He began the year holding auditorium campaigns in Oklahoma City,
sponsored by five Pentecostal Holiness congregations, and in Tulsa Convention
Hall with the cooperation of the city's three major pentecostal denominations,[42]
and then conducted a two-week crusade in the Wings of Healing Temple in
Portland, Oregon, the famous church of pioneer pentecostal healer and radio
broadcaster Thomas Wyatt. In the spring he toured some of the largest pentecostal churches in the nation, including the Fremont Temple in Minneapolis,
the First Assembly of God in Kansas City, and the Moline Gospel Tabernacle in
Illinois. In a typical report, Pastor Russell H. Olsen of the Fremont tabernacle
pronounced Oral's crusade the "most glorious revival" in the church's history.[43]

In mid-1948, Oral made two major changes in his ministry. First, he announced that he would no longer hold revivals in local churches, insisting that
all future campaigns "be conducted on a city-wide, inter-Pentecostal basis."[44]
Oral received his "final touch that caused me no longer to go to a local church"
in late 1947 in St. Louis. He recalled that just before he began his first sermon
in that meeting, the church's minister, a well-known pentecostal pastor, "leaned
over and said, 'Rev. Roberts, are your miracles real?'" Oral was stunned; he
"struggled for a week, day after day, night after night" until the faithless pastor's
"people rose up against him." Although the doubting pastor later became fully
convinced himself, proclaiming Roberts "the greatest healing evangelist of our
times," Oral left convinced "that this kind of ministry could not be controlled
by one minister, or local church. So I began to develop faith to get into auditoriums and ultimately to get a big tent."[45]

In a second dramatic move in mid-1948, Oral purchased a huge tent. He had decided at least six months earlier that he needed a tent because of difficulties in securing adequate auditoriums and because the tent symbolized his independence from domineering sponsoring pastors. In the January 1948 issue of his newly begun magazine *Healing Waters*, Oral announced that he had ordered a tent capable of seating 2,000. The cost was $21,000, and he was forced to borrow $15,000; but he hoped to pay off the debt during the summer's campaigning.[46] Actually, Oral's first challenge was to borrow enough for a down payment. When he explained his dream to his banker, Oral recalled, he "looked at me like I was a man from Mars." "What do you want with a tent? What do you want with a truck and trailer?" asked the loan officer. Oral reminisced: "Well it was crazy to say I wanted to win souls because he didn't understand what I meant by winning souls. But . . . they loaned $9,000."[47] Through the spring Oral's vision grew. In the back of his Bible he scribbled his revised calculations:

[210?]	$53,700 cost
180' long	
90' wide	

18,900 square feet
2000 Steel folding chairs
2 Trucks-Trailers
Hammond Electric Organ
Portable Platform
Steinway Piano
26,000 watts elc. power
10,000 song books[48]

By April he had committed himself to a 210-foot "orange-trimmed tent" which would seat 3,000 people. It was a "daring step," but by the time he placed the order, he had raised half the money in his campaigns.[49] In May, while conducting a crusade in Duluth, Minnesota, Oral purchased a "'Cathedral Toned' Hammond organ and Steinway grand piano" in "the Grand and Organ Salon of the Miles Music Company, Duluth's largest and oldest music dealer."[50] On the eve of his first tent crusade in Durham, North Carolina, *Healing Waters* proudly announced: "The tent is fireproof. . . . This fine gospel equipment cost nearly $60,000.00, a mere fraction of the worth of one soul being saved or one body being healed. Brother Roberts is taking God's best to the people of this generation."[51]

Oral would later remember the Durham campaign as "the greatest meeting I've ever had, maybe not in size, but it was the first one."[52] It began inauspiciously. When the tent arrived in Durham, Oral and a swarn of volunteers from the local pentecostal churches struggled in vain to hoist it; the opening service had to be canceled. The next day Oral secured professional assistance, and the meeting opened on June 4 with a disappointing crowd of 700 people scattered under the big tent.[53] But interest grew each evening, and in the concluding service on June 29 the estimates of the crowd ranged from 7,000 to

9,000. One observer wrote: "When 7:45 P.M. starting time opened the meeting the tent and grounds were literally human-stacked. Seats had been secured to seat an additional thousand people around the tent for this service, but standing room was at a premium within 100 feet of the tent."[54] People came to the tent from "hundreds and thousands of miles"; the Durham police department provided special officers to direct the "heavy traffic"; one of the sponsoring ministers reported the "greatest out-pouring of God's healing power we have ever seen." He described his view from the platform: "I stood by Bro. Roberts as he prayed for the sick and the afflicted. With my own eyes and ears I saw the deaf healed and heard them speak, I saw crippled people throw their crutches away and walk unaided as well as I could, I saw little children walk without braces, I saw people get up from stretchers and walk again. Cancers melted, tumors went, eyes opened, deaf ears heard, dumb tongues spoke." The meeting had been filled with the extraordinary, even by pentecostal standards. One evening, about eleven o'clock, as Oral sat "weary and exhausted" as the last of the healing line passed before him, "suddenly he announced that there was a wave of God's healing power coming":

> As he was talking this power struck like a bolt from the blue; he leaped off the platform with the strength of a lion, people started running toward the platform from all directions. Cripples were hobbling as fast as possible, the blind were groping their way, mothers with little babies were crying for God's touch on their afflicted bodies, the deaf were brought and while Bro. Roberts touched them or they touched him God's sovereign power swept in healing streams over the mass of surging, praying, believing people. As soon as the crippled were touched they threw their crutches away, deaf ears snapped open, people leaped off stretchers. Next morning crutches were lying all around the tent where they had been left. The power lasted for 30 minutes.[55]

The Durham tent campaign had a profound impact on the ministers of the area. It began with two sponsors and ended with between forty and fifty.[56] More important, many of them went away with renewed enthusiasm and a rekindled belief in the miracle-working power of God.[57] But the profoundest impressions of the Durham crusade were made on the man at the center of the pandemonium, Oral Roberts. Years later he could still vividly describe what he saw on those psychedelic nights. Oral always knew the role he played in the healing drama, he was never naive, but when the power began to move under the tent, in the minds and bodies of expectant believers, Oral could be as awestruck as any pentecostal minister.[58] If Oral ever had any doubt about his $60,000 investment, Durham dispelled it.

The big tent moved flawlessly through the summer of 1948, to Granite City, Illinois in July, Minneapolis in August, and Ada, Oklahoma in September. The massive, noisy meetings almost escaped public attention in these early months, but the pentecostal world was exploding, and it became increasingly difficult for outsiders to ignore the phenomenon. In Minneapolis an incredulous reporter visited the big "Ringling-Brothers-size tent" and found 4,000 believers overflowing its borders. The bumper-to-bumper traffic, he noted, included cars from "all the states throughout the Upper Midwest."[59]

Taking the big tent to Ada in September 1948 was a moment of personal triumph which Oral quite fittingly savored. It was a Roberts family celebration. Vaden, who had become Oral's equipment manager, pitched the tent. Oral stayed during the two-week revival in the home of Elmer and Orie.[60] The local press ignored the revival, but it attracted "people from twenty states," and, according to a local pastor, "the whole state of Oklahoma was touched."[61] Uncle Willis, Oral recalled, came to the meeting and "couldn't get a seat." Oral preached "my sermon on the 'Fourth Man' and God really annointed" him; Uncle Willis "got so carried away his mouth fell open."[62] Oral's pentecostal friends were stunned by his transformation. Oscar Moore wrote to the *Pentecostal Holiness Advocate*:

> I've known Oral Roberts ever since he entered the Ministry thirteen years ago, and have had him in my pulpit many times, he has lived in my home, . . . but the man who preached that night was not the Oral Roberts I have known for 13 years. He was no more the same than if he were not Oral Roberts at all. . . . His ministry and methods have passed through changes that have greatly improved them.[63]

Two other 1948 meetings left Oral with permanent memories. From Ada he went to Denver for a two-and-a-half-week revival in the Municipal Auditorium. While there, he formed a lasting and important friendship with Charles Blair, minister then of the Central Assembly of God church in Denver and later of one of the largest independent charismatic churches in the world.[64] In addition, Oral experienced a "second call" while in his motel room preparing to go to the crusade one evening. God "spoke to my heart and showed me that I would be the John the Baptist to my time in the sense that I would help prepare the way . . . for a great healing to come to the body of Christ."[65] With characteristic impulsiveness, Oral "just got up and announced it to everybody."[66] He later regretted it: "I should have kept my mouth shut. They said, 'Well, where does that leave us, if you are going to . . . be a forerunner, where does that leave our ministry?' And I . . . said 'I don't know.' There are some things God tells you, you should keep your mouth shut about, and I was talking when I should have been listening."[67] Oral subsequently treated the Denver revelation more discreetly, but he harbored it through the decade that followed, and its meaning slowly became clearer to him with the eruption of the charismatic movement.

While Oral was in the Denver Municipal Auditorium, the big tent was pitched in Dallas for a two-week revival. As that meeting neared its end, the sponsoring pastors begged Oral to continue another week. Oral refused but agreed to consider extending the crusade for three nights, until Wednesday, November 10. There was a problem, however; he needed to clear the change with Evelyn in Tulsa. The third Roberts child was scheduled to arrive on November 10. Oral telephoned to ask Evelyn's approval. She demurred. "The pastors," Oral urged, "estimated nine hundred more souls would be saved in those three nights." Finally, Evelyn answered, "Well, let's pray." So they prayed over the telephone. Then Oral proposed, "I'll tell you what let's do. Let's trust the Lord, let's postpone this baby's birth. For two days. No, . . . let's do it for one day, for Thursday." Evelyn replied, "Well, if you come on Thursday you will be tired. . . . Let's postpone it until Friday night."[68] Richard Lee Roberts arrived on Oral and Evelyn's schedule, on the evening of November 12, 1948.

By 1949 Oral had established a pattern of campaigning which was to remain generally intact for a decade. In 1949 the "country's largest fireproof tent" moved from Miami in January through Tampa, Jacksonville, Tallahassee, Norfolk, Ft. Worth, Denver, Tacoma, Bakersfield, Houston, and Mobile before Oral closed the year with a December crusade in a B-29 hangar at Seymour Field in Goldsboro, North Carolina. Typically, the crusades lasted seventeen or eighteen days, though a few were scheduled for only two weeks. For several years Oral would begin his seasons with a series of meetings in Florida, where the pentecostal churches were particularly supportive and where vacationing northerners supplied a diverse audience.[69] It was a year of unbroken successes; over 15,000 conversions were reported during his Florida meetings from January through April, and in his closing thirteen days in Goldsboro, around 85,000 people attended and over 5,500 were "converted from sin."[70] Oral's spirit was soaring. "I know I will be immortal until my work is done," he told a reporter in Houston in October 1949, revealing that he planned to preach all over the world in the next few years.[71]

These early months remained a time of learning for Oral. "As I began to preach in 1947," he later recalled, "I had to develop all new sermons. I still have the old outlines and not a one of them would work in my new thinking."[72] And from the beginning, Oral's crusades featured his preaching; they were devoid of special music or other frills often used to draw crowds. In 1949, a California pastor reported: "Brother Roberts has no entertainment in the services. There are no specials, just a part of two songs, prayer and sermon. He preaches for about 1 to 1½ hours each service."[73] In Oral's earliest meetings, the introductory, warmup activities were handled by a local pastor. First the audience would be offered copies of the "Healing Waters Hymnal" for twenty-five cents and urged to subscribe to *Healing Waters* magazine for one dollar per year. Then, one of the sponsoring pastors, or, later, a member of Oral's team, would give a brief exhortation before taking a collection.[74] In these early years, Oral would likely begin his appearance with a raspy rendition of his favorite song, "When He Reached Down His Hand for Me":

> Once my soul was afar
>   From the Heavenly way
> I was wretched and blind as could be
> But my Savior in love
>   Turned my darkness to day
> When He reached down His hand for me.
>
> CHORUS
> When my Savior reached down for me
>   When He reached down His hand for me
> I was lost and undone
>   Without God or His Son
> When He reached down His hand for me.

I was near to despair
　　When the Lord found me there
And He told me that I could be free
Then He lifted my soul
　　Out of Satan's dark snare
When He reached down His hand for me.

　Now my heart does rejoice
　　Since I made the Lord my choice
In the tempest to Him I can flee
There to lean on His arm
　　Safe, secure from all harm
Since He reached down His hand for me.[75]

However austere Oral's meetings appeared in comparison to those of other independent evangelists, and no matter how much emphasis he placed on his sermons, excitement rippled through the pentecostal audience when the time came to heal the sick. First, a few of the chronically ill straggled to the front for Oral's touch, and he prayed, slowly and deliberately, for each of them. Then, they began to come by the hundreds, and, finally, by 1949, by the thousands, tapping into Oral's incredible spiritual and physical strength. The crowds sat enthralled, amazed at the miracle of Oral Roberts. Pastor Jake Till reported from Tallahassee in May 1949: "Even the miracle of strength to Brother Roberts' body was witnessed many nights as the people stood behind him with their prayers, especially the last Sunday night of the revival, when he prayed for around 2,000 to be healed. He had to stop and rest but as the people prayed, the strength returned and many more were healed as they passed by for Brother Roberts to pray for them."[76]

Oral's healing-line technique went through a number of refinements during these early months. Perhaps the most important came after Oral once again "heard the voice of God as though He were standing beside me" while holding a one-night healing service in Nowata, Oklahoma in the spring of 1948. The voice said: "Son, you have been faithful up to this hour, and now you will feel My presence in your right hand. Through My presence, you will be able to detect the presence of demons. You will know their number and name, and through My power they will be cast out."[77] That was Oral's first glimpse of what became one of his most important insights—the "point of contact." Two months later he reported that "from that hour until this practically everyone in the Healing Line has been made perfectly whole." Although Oral felt the power of God moving in his left hand "some," it was his right hand that was to become the point of contact with millions of sufferers. Also, from this moment Oral realized that "most forms of human affliction are caused by demons" and that those "demons recognize God's power in my life."[78]

In May 1947, Oral published the first edition of his little book *If You Need Healing—Do These Things!* The first printing of 3,000 was followed by a second of 10,000 in September. The early editions of the book consisted of five of Roberts's favorite sermons on healing and an appeal for "partners." But the book was also a step-by-step instruction manual for those seeking healing in the campaigns. Oral wrote: "I always ask people who are sick and afflicted to read this book before they come to me to be anointed for healing." It would help to clear one's mind of "hindrances and questions" and would "tell you when I expect you to believe, what I expect you to do and how to lay hold on God during your needs."[79] The book went through six printings before 1950, with only slight revisions, and by that time there were nearly 100,000 copies in circulation.

While the outlines of the later crusade techniques were clearly visible during this transition period, the early meetings were also marked by a mood of experimentation and pentecostal exuberance, which would slowly regress. The crowds under the tent sometimes erupted into mass demonstrations as Oral sensed the power of God moving in exceptional ways. Oral frequently "discerned" what was about to happen; in Goldsboro he said that "God definitely told him that three would-be suicides were in the congregation," and he urged them to repent before the act was consummated.[80] In Durham one evening he revealed that "there are exactly seventy-one people in this audience who are rejecting God." He gravely warned the sinners of the consequences if they should refuse to answer his altar call: "Only two people have ever refused to come when the Lord spoke to me to call them out. I told them they would dig their own graves if they did not come, and they did. One became a raving maniac in a matter of hours, and the other one died violently the following day."[81] "He was bold," recalled Steve Pringle of these early months, "he didn't care if people liked what he said."[82]

Of course, these early campaigns were essentially pentecostal crusades, even though Oral's earliest advertisements emphasized that they were "for all people of all churches."[83] But, Oral recollected, "hard core Pentecostals were the backbone, they were the ones who had the anointing, they were the ones who believed in the power of God above all others."[84] These earliest meetings had a stronger aura of the marvelous than those in later years. People "danced and shouted without restraint"; sometimes they were fanned into a "frenzy."[85] Evelyn remembered that "many people told me that they've seen Jesus standing beside Oral while he's preaching, and some have seen the Lord's hand on his when he prays for the sick. I do not doubt any of this."[86] And Oral himself felt a powerful miraculous presence under the tent: "Angels walk the grounds, the Lord walks the aisles, people feel the Holy Ghost and fire under the tent. Many people have said, 'Brother Roberts, when I walk on the grounds I feel the presence of God.'"[87]

Oral's pentecostal constituency kept him from straying too far away from the main tenets of pentecostal orthodoxy. For instance, in his early meetings he began to place increasing emphasis on demon possession. "I discovered that the word demon meant tormenter," he later wrote, and since all of the sick who approached him seemed tormented, "I began to call everything they had, thou demon." A group of pentecostal ministers "lowered the boom on him," and Oral agreed that "theologically I was incorrect." Frequently he felt that such criticisms were not well intended, but he learned from them and adjusted his teachings and his methods.[88]

By far the most significant change in his early meeting format was the addition of an altar call during the Duluth, Minnesota crusade in May 1948. In his early meetings, Oral simply issued a call at the end of his sermon for all to come forward who "had a need." In this mass, he recalled, "would be Christians who were sick, sinners who didn't know the way to God, backsliders, and I'd deal with each one according to his need." But, among other things, this method left no place for "personal workers" to counsel the converts, and it did not "bring them into the church." In Duluth, at the insistence of local pastors, Oral began issuing an altar call at the end of his sermon before he called for the healing line. In later years he became ambivalent about the technique. Oral always felt that the pastors were "partially right," but he also became increasingly disillusioned with the sectarian maneuvering that pervaded the prayer tent where the converts were counseled. "For example," he recalled, "the trained counsellors would just naturally after they led a soul to Christ, urge him to come join their church. It turned out to be a real battle of denomination."[89] But whatever the shortcomings of the system, by 1950 it was firmly established, and, in fact, was to become the most publicized feature of the ministry.

BY 1950, the Oral Roberts crusades had become more or less standardized in the form they would maintain for the rest of the decade. The team began 1950, as it had 1949, with a seventeen-day crusade in Miami. But the campaign was conducted in a new tent, the "largest ever constructed for the gospel ministry," which would seat over 7,000.[90] When that tent was destroyed in the summer by a violent storm in Amarillo, Texas, it was replaced by a new one that would seat 10,000; in 1952 Oral ordered a tent seating 12,500 and costing $200,000; in the late 1950s, crowds of over 15,000 frequently spilled outside the tents.[91]

In 1957, G. H. Montgomery, editor of Oral's magazine, summarized a decade's work. Roberts had conducted 147 campaigns, "stood before (on his own platform) an aggregate of more than 8½ million people," preached 1,706 sermons, prayed for the healing of about 500,000, preached over 78,000 sermons on radio and 31,200 on television, and "led to Christ for salvation" nearly 3,000,000.[92] And the grandest was yet ahead. The years from 1957 to 1960 witnessed the largest crusade crowds in Oral's ministry; Roberts was conscious by the end of the decade that his had become "one of the most popular ministries that this country has ever known."[93] In 1950 he was a rambunctious, ambitious healing revivalist with a tent, a small headquarters building housing about twenty employees, a modest radio network of about seventy stations, and a large but controversial reputation in the pentecostal subculture. He ended the decade a slightly mellowed and introspective evangelist with huge radio and television networks, a spectacular seven-story headquarters building in Tulsa, and a national reputation as the number two evangelist in the United States.

The Oral Roberts that captured the imagination of the American public in the decade of the fifties was a tent preacher. He was perceived as the nation's "faith healer," though he always rejected that label as inaccurate and pejorative. Throughout the decade, Oral swept from one end of the nation to the other, averaging one crusade a month, most under the big tent but a few each year in large city auditoriums. The average campaign lasted seventeen days in 1950, but in 1954 the average length was reduced to ten days.[94] Although Florida, North Carolina, and the South in general remained favorite spots for crusades, no major city in the country was left untouched—New York, Los Angeles, Oakland, Seattle, Philadelphia, Washington, D.C., Baltimore, Minneapolis, Boston, Detroit, Chicago, St. Louis, San Diego, Milwaukee, Denver. Nor were the audiences thinner or less responsive in Spokane than in Pensacola, in Dayton than in Charlotte. By 1952 Oral's itinerary had picked up Canadian cities; in 1955 he made his first overseas trip to South Africa; in 1956 he went to the Philippines and Australia; in 1957 he returned to South Africa; and in 1958 he visited Puerto Rico. Probably the largest nightly attendance in the history of Oral's American campaigns came during a crusade in Hempstead, New York, just outside New York City, in March 1958.[95] But frequently Oral attracted "audiences . . . greater than any that had ever before attended a public event" in the cities he visited.[96]

Oral's organization expanded and diversified in a variety of ways in the 1950s, but the crusades remained the heartbeat of the ministry. They exposed millions of nonpentecostal people to healing revivalism; they were witnessed by an entourage of curious reporters; and they gave Oral personal contact with the growing body of Americans who knew him as a media celebrity. The ten years of campaigns touched thousands of lives; they defy generalization and capsulization. The big tent was an imaginative and unpredictable laboratory. Oral later recollected:

> When you get desperate people, you are going to get some kooks. You are going to get some people who are far out. Some of them would yell out while I was preaching. I never had anyone to yell out in my dignified church services in twelve years. . . . But I found at these revivals that right in the middle of a sermon some maniac or demon possessed person would scream and scare us half out of our wits. What do you do when someone like that yells out? You do the best you can and go on.[97]

But there were patterns which remained constant through the years, trademarks of a Roberts campaign, and there were some patterns of change which flowed consistently through the decade. First, Oral's crusades were marked by a cordial and carefully cultivated relationship with "sponsoring pastors." Oral received literally thousands of invitations in the 1950s; he systematically insisted that his meetings be sponsored by a unified group of "full gospel" ministers, generally by the regional pentecostal fellowship. Oral's associate evangelist, after 1951 Bob DeWeese, visited the area about six months in advance of the crusade and negotiated with the sponsoring churches, including "what the financial arrangements would be." While the preparations for Oral's campaigns never rivaled the efficiency of a Billy Graham crusade, by pentecostal standards his meetings were "highly organized."[98] In the early days a crusade might begin with no more than three or four sponsoring pastors, but by the mid-1950s his meetings often attracted over a hundred.

The incentives for the sponsoring pastors were evident. Many were pastors of weak, struggling pentecostal churches, and the opportunity to bask in the limelight with Oral, sitting on the platform before the huge audience, was reward enough. When the praying started and the spirit moved, the local preachers were frequently the most enthusiastic seekers. But there were more concrete rewards. Once during the campaign, Oral hosted a "minister's banquet," treating the sponsoring pastors and their spouses to a meal and a special inspirational address.[99] And, perhaps most important, one evening during the campaign a contribution was taken to be divided among the sponsoring pastors, a precaution taken to guard against the potential reduction in local church collections during the campaign. In addition, if the campaign collections exceeded the announced expenses of the crusade, which was not usual, the overage was left with the sponsoring pastors.

In return for these advantages, the sponsoring pastors furnished a number of services. Most important, they encouraged their congregations to attend, providing the supporting cast for the drama. Generally, sponsoring churches canceled all services during the campaign except for one Sunday morning meeting.[100] In addition, the local churches supplied most of the workers for the campaign, including in the early years the labor to raise and lower the tent. Volunteer ushers and personal workers were assembled just before the campaign and told by DeWeese "how the meeting would work"; they became the primary labor force during the crusade.[101] The personal workers who counseled those answering the altar call used the campaign as a means of building their own congregations, even though they were instructed "not to argue or dictate, but to contribute a pentecostal counsel."[102]

Oral was singularly successful in the 1950s in maintaining good relations with sponsoring pastors, even though he had serious troubles with the leaders of his denomination. Many of the independent pentecostal revivalists abandoned local sponsorship during these years, disgusted by the doctrinal and financial bickering which often accompanied the negotiations. Oral's continued success rested partly on the size of his operation; by 1950 his ministry was so popular that he could set the terms for his campaigns. In addition, his hold on the people was so strong that even balky pastors were compelled to back his campaigns. But the continued support of pentecostal pastors was also a tribute to Oral's consummate skill as a preacher's preacher, since sponsoring pastors repeatedly testified that his sermons "stirred our souls and stimulated our faith."[103] "Whatever else one may say about Oral Roberts," wrote a pastor who attended a 1950 service, "no one can possibly say that he is insincere."[104]

Probably most important to local pastors were Oral's moderation and responsibility. Not only were the campaigns "well organized," recalled his associate Bob DeWeese, there also was a "reasonableness" about them.[105] Oral was financially responsible in an environment which was, Evelyn recalled, filled with "people going up and down . . . saying they were going to do things in raising money . . . [who] went off with the people's money. And the people never saw them again." Local pastors had confidence in the Roberts team, Evelyn believed, because "we have never broken faith with them. We have always done what we said we were going to do."[106] Oral's reputation for honesty also extended to the community; he repeatedly instructed Collins Steele to leave a clean record behind: "Every bill had to be paid. We had to live up to the letter of the law in every area. . . . If we made an agreement with a city or a fire authority . . . you didn't just pass that off lightly."[107]

Not only was Oral responsible, there also was an orderliness and rationality about his services which made him less objectionable to organized pentecostalism. Reporters frequently compared Oral's meetings—which were punctuated by "Amens" from the audience and occasional "Hallelujahs"—with those of Billy Graham, and some imagined that the Roberts tent was the lunatic fringe of American revivalism. Ignorant of the more exuberant species of pentecostal revivalism thriving under countless smaller tents, most outsiders did not recognize the restraint of a Roberts service. Oral discouraged tongues speaking, and he would "not tolerate hysteria." In 1958, in a typical incident in Charleston, South Carolina, when a member of the audience "became overly 'happy in the Lord' the evangelist interrupted his sermon with a businesslike 'please keep control of yourselves.'"[108] "I'm growing more wary of emotions," Oral told a Colorado reporter in the same year, "faith is a tremendous thing when let loose but it can happen inside a person."[109] All pentecostal evangelists ran the risk of having their services interrupted, even hijacked, by would-be prophets emboldened by their own private leadings. Oral would not tolerate such outbursts. In Indianapolis in 1956, a newsman reported that "an unidentified young man in a brown suit hurtled past two ushers, leaped a rope over the ramp and stormed up on the stage during Roberts' sermon." Oral turned to the audience and asked: "Do you want to listen to this man?" "No," shouted the audience. "It took six ushers to get the young man off the stage and out a rear door," but the unperturbed evangelist "led the audience in prayer for the young man" and then continued the sermon.[110]

Bob DeWeese, Collins Steele, and the team of ushers maintained order in the meetings. During a particularly unruly campaign in Los Angeles, DeWeese convened a special meeting of the volunteer workers:

> I just sat down with the ushers and I said, "Listen, we can't have this." I said, "Tonight I am going to make an explanation of why we cannot have it. . . . And I'm going to be defied. . . . I don't want you to walk, I want you to run and grab that person and put them out of this place instantly." So I got up and I made my little talk . . . and up jumps a lady, "Thus saith the Lord," and I said, "There's the first one, put her out." And boy, they ran, and they grabbed her and they put her out. . . . From then on the meetings were beautiful.[111]

Sometimes the team employed off-duty policemen to help maintain order, but generally Steele and his crew of ushers required no additional assistance.[112]

Collins Steele also made the physical arrangements for the crusades. He generally began a year in advance to locate a suitable site for the tent. His work was frequently made difficult by opposition from local authorities; sometimes the team was refused permits at the urging of local ministerial associations or groups of churches.[113] "Many of the communities did not welcome us," recalled Steele; often they were forced to rent fields from farmers on the outskirts of town.[114] But the team never failed to be ready for a crusade opening in the

1950s, rolling the eight semi trucks of canvas cathedral across the nation on a backbreaking schedule.

The atmosphere under the big tent varied in the eyes of the beholder. Bob DeWeese recalled that from "the first time I was with Oral I just felt an authority, a spiritual authority, that I'd never had before in my life. . . . It was uncanny."[115] Many of the reporters who came to view the spectacle for the first time were also captured by the intensity of the drama: "Under the spreading canvas, under the fierce lights, in the heat and the sweat, the music of the organ and the hymn-singing, given confidence by the steady voice of the evangelist and the strong grip of his hands and arms about their heads, many, many people seem to find the faith and hope they seek."[116] On the other hand, other observers saw only a "professionally planned show, dominated by deception."[117]

The order of an Oral Roberts meeting was firmly established in 1950, and the ritual was profusely described by both friend and foe in the course of the decade. Bob DeWeese arrived at the tent promptly at 7:15 in the evening and made an appearance to sell songbooks. He then disappeared beneath the platform, where he led a brief prayer service with the sponsoring pastors. DeWeese and the ministers then mounted the platform, where he, or someone selected by him, led the audience in a spirited singing of such "old gospel standards" as "Leaning on the Everlasting Arms" and "Blessed Assurance"; the tent provided a remarkably fine acoustical setting.[118] A distinguished visitor would then lead a prayer, which was followed by announcements, including detailed reports on the campaign's finances. One of Oral's books would be offered for sale, and then DeWeese, or one of the sponsoring pastors, would make an appeal before the evening's offering. At five minutes before eight, Oral mounted the platform, ready to be introduced by DeWeese. Oral launched immediately into his sermon, perhaps prefaced by a song or some casual banter with the audience. In his early years he often preached for an hour, or even longer, but by the end of the decade most of his sermons lasted only about thirty minutes. At the end of his sermon, he asked sinners to come stand before the platform. After receiving brief instructions from Oral, these penitents were led away to a "prayer tent," where they were counseled by volunteer workers from the sponsoring churches. Those remaining in the tent sang hymns and chatted as the organ played, and Oral moved swiftly to the "invalid" section of the tent, where the seriously ill were waiting in isolation. Each evening he prayed for each of the thirty-odd people admitted to that section. By the time Oral returned to the main tent, Bob DeWeese had organized the prayer line, usually between thirty and sixty people who would pass across the platform in front of Oral to receive his touch and prayer. The entire service lasted from two and a half to four hours, generally ending between nine-thirty and eleven in the evening. The weary Oral was then whisked off to his hotel as the heavy-eyed faithful slowly filed out of the huge tent into an evening traffic jam.[119]

Before this evening drama began, one other preliminary had been accomplished. Each afternoon at two o'clock, Bob DeWeese conducted a "faith building" service. In the early 1950s he preached in one of the sponsoring churches, but later, as the crowds grew, he preached in the main tent. In the afternoon service, DeWeese explained to those seeking healing how the meetings were managed and how they could secure a place in the healing line. Before entering the healing line, one had to secure a card and sign a release which acknowledged that entry into the prayer line did not "guarantee healing" and authorized the Roberts organization to publish the results of the healing if it so desired. The "prayer cards" were coded by colors and letters which determined the sequence in which they would be called during the campaign. Although some exceptions were made, and Oral always reserved "the right to pray for any person at any time, as God leads him," according to Bob DeWeese, the cards were distributed on "a first come, first serve basis."[120]

Outsiders were particularly suspicious of the card system, viewing it as a means of screening out the most seriously ill. Indeed, the Roberts organization never denied some selectivity in its procedures. An instruction booklet given to supplicants explained: "Sometimes a person whose healing might be especially helpful to encourage the faith of others may be prayed for first." Roberts frequently chose special cases to highlight in order "to inspire faith in the audience." In addition, all prayer cards had to be "validated" before one could enter the line. The validation process required an interview with one of the local sponsoring pastors, who would "ask you some questions, . . . check to see that your card is correctly filled out and signed, and then . . . stamp your card with the validating stamp."[121] "The purpose of the counselling," explained an aide, was "to make clear to the applicant that only God can heal, that they must have faith through prayer and realize that healing occurs when it is God's will."[122] The seriously ill were given white cards, which gave them entry into the "invalid room." There were occasional rumors that those seeking healing were asked for contributions, but the organization's literature emphasized that "no charge is made for the prayer cards," and on more than one occasion careless newsmen were forced to publish retractions of such charges.[123]

Whatever other purposes they may have served, the prayer cards were considered necessary to preserve order. By the 1950s, the number of people seeking admission to the healing line during a campaign usually ran into the thousands; many came from great distances to seek Oral's touch. The seekers were repeatedly warned not to expect personal attention: "Brother Roberts cannot grant personal interviews at the campaigns. Time and physical strength will not permit it." Those coming from far away were instructed to "make preparations to stay several days or until your card is called. . . . Do not come expecting to be prayed for the same day you arrive. If you can stay for a day or two only, we advise you not to come, for in all likelihood you will have to wait several days or possibly until the closing day of the crusade." Oral "promised to pray for all" who would stay until the end of the campaign, but he could not predict the number who would pass through the line on a given evening. Those who had to leave a campaign before their turn in the healing line had to settle for the prayers of DeWeese and the local pastors.[124]

The logistical problems in handling the prayer line became more complicated when the services began to be televised in the mid-1950s. The healing line slowed markedly under the glare of the television lights as Oral deliberately prayed and chatted with those on camera. Oral had been able to pass several hundred people through the line in an evening, but in a televised service, the total number prayed for was likely to fall to fifty or fewer. Although Oral repeatedly explained that the slow and personal technique he used during filming was only a strategy to produce faith in the television audience, others came to expect the same kind of treatment. The line moved rapidly under Oral's touch when the cameras were not on, and supplicants were urged not to "expect long prayers or special attention in the prayer line, but make the laying on of Brother Roberts' hand their point of contact for the release of their faith." "If I pray quickly with you," wrote Oral in an instruction manual, it is because "I am quick by nature in the use of my faith." In fact, he tried to persuade the thousands of seekers that they did not need to be in the line at all: "You can be healed in the audience before I touch you—or if I never touch you. If you touch God by your faith, you may be healed wherever you are."[125]

The day service, with its explanation of the healing routine, was also a part of the faith-building preparation. Oral was keenly aware of the role that faith played in the success or failure of the prayer line, and he believed that those seeking healing should attend several services before entering the line "so that their faith can be built up through the preaching of God's Word." He knew that the healings people experienced were tied strongly to the atmosphere under the tent. "The several nights you may have to wait until your card is called," read an instruction pamphlet, "will permit you to watch others as they are prayed for, and better learn how to release your faith."[126] Whatever theological underpinning Oral might give to divine healing in his sermons, the most powerful stimulus to the seeker's faith was witnessing the powerful spiritual aura when the thousands of believers under the tent touched their metal chairs as a point of contact and prayed with Oral for a healing touch from God.

To many pentecostals, the most distinctive feature of a Roberts crusade remained Oral's preaching. In 1951, Demos Shakarian, who later founded the Full Gospel Business Men's Fellowship International, judged that "without any reservation, Oral Roberts is today the world's most powerful preacher."[127] Many of the reporters who ventured under the big tent in the 1950s were similarly impressed by Oral's ability to move his audiences. A South Carolina newsman wrote: "Not an actor, for his sincere faith is obvious, Mr. Roberts is however a talented showman. Whether he is striding about the platform, clutching the microphone as if it were a broom sweeping sin from the tent, or making three-syllable words of 'God' and 'soul,' the audience is in complete harmony with him."[128] The chemistry between Oral and his audiences ignited them both. The evangelist later recalled his feeling as he mounted the platform before the huge crowds: "I felt like a Niagara of power about to be released. I felt the power of God in my soul. I could scarcely wait to reach the people."[129] Oral's rapport with his audiences was also friendly and relaxed. When opening a campaign in Milwaukee in 1958, he began by ordering the audience "to smile, remarking that last time here it took him three days to get them relaxed." "There are lots of good smiling folks down South," Oral ribbed the northerners, "they're no better than you are, but they smile better."[130]

During the 1950s, Oral's preaching techniques changed considerably. A reporter covering a 1948 meeting reported that Oral "jumped about" as "he shouted and exhorted the audience. . . . He hopped. He seemed to do a kind of frenzied shuffling dance, moving from one end of the platform to the other."[131] Nearly a decade later, another newsman reported that Roberts "resembled an aggressive football coach exhorting his team to 'get out and win' as he paced the platform, clutching the microphone in both hands."[132] But, in fact, Oral's sermons diminished in exuberance as they shortened in length.[133] The changes were partly concessions to exhaustion, but they also reflected changes in Oral's audiences and a maturing of his theology and his self-perception.

The content of Oral's sermons also changed perceptibly during the decade. During his first few years, he preached on healing almost exclusively, but by 1951 he spoke only once during a campaign directly on healing, although many of his sermons touched on the subject. He preached increasing numbers of "teaching sermons," lessons which emphasized such traditional virtues as "the importance of reading the Bible, of teaching children to say grace before meals, of tithing to the church of a family's choice."[134] By the end of the decade, a Miami reporter described Oral's preaching as "quiet" and "businesslike."[135]

The altar call which followed Oral's sermon was identical to that of the hundreds of other itinerant evangelists in American history who have urged the sinners in their audiences who were touched by remorse during the evening's message to raise their hands, stand to their feet, and walk forward to the platform to join with the evangelist in prayer. Roberts frequently ended his sermon with an impassioned prayer:

> Oh my God, tonight I know that first things come first, and the most important thing of all is that men and women and young people surrender their lives to Christ, that they be saved from their sins, that Christ may come into their hearts. God don't let a mother's boy who heard me preach tonight go to hell. Don't let a mother's girl who heard me preach tonight go to hell. Don't let a daddy or a mother who heard me preach tonight go to hell. Save them, Jesus, save them tonight from all their sins and may they be born again by Thy Spirit, washed in the blood and saved through and through, without the loss of any, I pray. Amen.[136]

Visitors, including newsmen, were usually impressed by "the great number of persons confessing and repenting their sins" in the campaigns; in the late 1950s, the organization came to emphasize soul saving as the major aim of the ministry.[137]

Oral sometimes closed his altar call with impromptu interviews with those who had come forward. His homey, personal banter with those in the healing line became a Roberts trademark, but he frequently lapsed into similar chats with those who had answered the altar call. For instance, this exchange followed his prayer in Erie, Pennsylvania in June 1956:

> ROBERTS: Well, that's wonderful. I'd just like to know—Sir, did you get saved tonight? You believe you did. How about you—you believe you did. Sir, do you feel that you received Christ? How about you, Sir? Don't think

you quite made it yet, but you came up and made a stand didn't you—for that reason we have a prayer tent—we are going to pray with all of you further. I know some of you though really were saved while you were praying that prayer. How about you sister—you know you were. How about you—you what? You got to be. Brother DeWeese, would you come down here and assist me please—I want to talk to some of the folks tonight. I haven't been able to do this, but I feel like many of these people have made a decision for Christ. Brother DeWeese, I would like to know who this lady is right here. Who are you, please?

LADY: Margie Norris.

ROBERTS: Where are you from Margie?

LADY: 321 German Street.

ROBERTS: Here in Erie?

LADY: Yes, sir.

ROBERTS: Did you receive Christ?

LADY: Yes, sir.

ROBERTS: How does it make you feel to receive him?

LADY: Wonderful. Light as a feather.

ROBERTS: Light as a feather. Have you been wanting to do this?

LADY: Yes.

ROBERTS: Yes. Have you been thinking about it for some time?

LADY: Oh, a long time.

ROBERTS: And did the campaign here help you to make your decision?

LADY: Tremendously.

ROBERTS: Now, then, tell me what you intend to do about this.

LADY: Well, I go to a Catholic church, but I've been just going back—you know what I mean, not attending and, well, you know how a person is.

ROBERTS: Are you going to really serve God?

LADY: Oh, God, yes.

ROBERTS: You are really going to serve Him?

LADY: I sure am.

ROBERTS: And do the right thing?

LADY: Absolutely.

ROBERTS: Well, Amen. We are so proud you came tonight.[138]

After this exchange, Oral gave a charge and further instructions:

If you feel that you have surrendered your life to Christ, if you have made a decision I would like for you to write me: Oral Roberts, Tulsa, Oklahoma. Say, "Brother Roberts, I did surrender to Christ" or if you did not—if you want my prayers write me: Oral Roberts, Tulsa, Oklahoma. I will be happy to send you a little booklet entitled: "How You May Know You Are Saved" free and post-paid just ask for it: Oral Roberts, Tulsa, Oklahoma. . . . Now, I want you, friends, to get to the prayer room—get on your knees and pray until you know you are saved and then I will come back in a few minutes and pray for the sick.[139]

Inside the prayer tent the converts were entrusted into the hands of the local ministers and counselors, and what ensued was an old-fashioned pentecostal prayer service. A newsman who visited the smaller tent in 1950 reported that the "emotions really run wild." "It seems to be mass hysteria. With more than 400 in the prayer tent, there is shouting, talking in tongues, screaming, promises of reformation, young and old clinging to each other, seeking to comfort one another. Ministers and others talk to some."[140] Although local workers received some instructions from the Roberts organization, the proceedings in the prayer tent were the portion of the campaign least under the control of the crusade team.

Frequently at this point in the evening, as everyone returned to the tent to await the healing line, the offering was taken, usually by DeWeese. In contrast to the more radical pentecostal revivalists of the 1950s, Oral did not regard the crusades as a major source of income, and he avoided the "hard pulls" which often characterized such meetings. Before a campaign began, the Roberts team and the local committee established an expense budget that in the 1950s averaged between $15,000 and $35,000.[141] The two contributions taken each day were set aside for expenses, and the audiences were given regular accounts of the amount received. If the budget was exceeded, the excess was left with the sponsoring churches; if a deficit was incurred, it was met by the Roberts organization. In the early years Oral received two "love offerings" for his personal use, but by the early 1950s he received only one during a campaign, usually the last Saturday evening's collection. One "generous offering" during the campaign was given to the sponsoring pastors.[142] The organization generally made public the size of expense offerings (they averaged about 25¢ per person), but the size of the "love offerings" was a carefully protected secret. Oral's "love offering" from the appreciative audiences was usually the most generous of the campaigns; an Oklahoma reporter in 1958 estimated they averaged $5,000.[143] In addition to the regular contributions, Oral sometimes asked his audiences for help with special projects, ranging from the purchasing of tent equipment to sponsoring television, generally with remarkable success.[144] But fund raising did not divert attention from the main business at hand—saving souls and healing the sick. Oral used his meetings not to fleece the audiences for short-range financial advantage, but rather to impress them with the worth of his ministry. And he carefully built lasting relationships with thousands of individuals who felt a personal debt to Oral Roberts, Tulsa, Oklahoma.

Finally came the climax for which so many had assembled. Oral strode back to the platform and seated himself in a chair before the microphone, having removed his coat and rolled up his shirt sleeves. Bob DeWeese called for those holding certain prayer cards to form a line leading from Oral's left up a ramp to the spot before his chair. The audience was braced to join with the evangelist in prayer, to witness the miraculous moving of God. "You will be permitted to watch the miracles tonight, with the exception of cases of demon possession and when I pray for little children," Oral instructed them. In those particularly tense moments he would order every head bowed and every eye closed.[145]

Actually, Oral had begun the healing service before the line formed, having already toured the invalid section. Critical reporters often charged that the Roberts team intentionally hid the most desperately ill from the eyes of the audience. In 1958, a United Press story about Oral's Long Island campaign re-

ported: "Ambulances pulled up to the doors to discharge children with gro-
tesquely twisted arms and legs, hollow-eyed victims of palsy, of cancer, of
rheumatic fever and polio. The saddest cases were brought into a ward-like
special room safe from the eyes of others."[146] Years later, Oral still had vivid
memories of the invalid tent, where every evening he encountered "ambulance
cases . . . or demon possessed that were tied to poles because they were dangerous."[147] And he confessed that he sometimes felt his own faith sinking in the
presence of the severely handicapped; but his tour of the invalid tent night after
night in city after city was a grim test of his own integrity. Bob DeWeese remembered that some evangelists avoided contact with the most severely ill: "We
felt at least that they should have gone and knelt beside each one and touched
them."[148] In 1963, Oral gave to the regents of his new university a glimpse of
his experiences going "to the ends of the earth. . . . I remember laying my hands
on them when my flesh crawled, and I wondered if I would catch it and the Lord
protected me. I remember one thing tonight, that in sixteen and one-half years
of laying my hands upon hundreds of thousands of the most miserably ill people
on earth, that God has let none of their diseases come upon me, and that is a
testimony of His being with us."[149] Whatever Oral's aversion to the hopelessly
ill, he did pray for them, and he touched them—the filthiest, most cadaverous of
the world's human refuse. He did not linger there, but he passed by; he saw and
smelled the suffering and he never forgot the feel of it.[150]

If the invalid tent was somewhat grim, the calling of the healing line in the
big tent generated "an electrifying tension in the air, penetrating every corner of
the immense hall."[151] Even though Oral and others in the late 1950s broadened
their preaching to include more than healing, that was the magnet that drew the
people.[152] Oral took his seat above the ramp with an air of authority; frequently
before the procession of sick began to pass before him, he ordered, "Devil, take
your hands off God's property." That command invariably had a "profound effect upon the audience" which was as much a part of the atmosphere of faith as
were the supplicants and their intercessor.[153] "Never," wrote an impressed visitor, "have we heard a man speak with authority and power that held men and
women spellbound like him."[154] Oral and his audience became a team. A Los
Angeles reporter observed: "From time to time, Mr. Roberts halted the line and
bellowed to the thousands: 'Who is the healer?' 'God!' they shouted. And he
asked them again and again to pray with him. Everyone prayed."[155] On thousands of expectant evenings weathered and gnarled hands reached forward to
touch the seat in front of them as a point of contact as the members of the vast
audience joined their minds and faith with the distant forms under the spotlight.

"You were quite an actor," surmised Evelyn in later years after watching a
film of an early crusade, "because you kept those people happy at the same time
they were watching a healing that they really didn't know what was going on in
your mind." While Oral agreed that "you have to have enough results to inspire
people in the audience, let them see that God is actually healing someone" and
also establish "a credibility that the television audience will grasp," he insisted
that "acting" was not a fitting label. Rather, he reflected, he was a "participant":
"I'm actually a part of the action. I'm in the arena of human suffering. I'm there

with the success and failure." And though he suffered through many an evening with a lukewarm audience, he instinctively felt their response and craved their support. "I feel every mood they have," recalled Oral, "I know what's going on all over the crowd. I can feel faith coming from this section, opposition coming from this section and I have to tie it together. I don't know how I do it, I just do it."[156]

The parade of humanity which passed across the healing ramp laid claim to virtually every illness known to medical science, ranging from organic illnesses such as cancer, goiters, and diabetes to psychological disorders ranging from "depression" to "psychoses." "I'd pray for anybody," Oral recalled, "I never segregated my healing line. . . . You saw them healed or not healed. I took everybody."[157] Oral's friend John Wellons recalled an occasion when Oral agreed to visit the automobile of a close friend to pray for her "relative." The sick woman was "mean and hateful and hostile," shouting at Oral, "You're a fake and I don't want you praying for me." But Oral "ignored her hostility," placed his "hand on her forehead and proceeded with one of the most impressive and dynamic prayers" Wellons had ever heard.[158] While the most severely ill were relegated to the invalid section, some very sick people passed under Oral's touch; some were so ill that they died shortly after the experience. In short, while there was some selection of candidates on the basis of their faith in God's healing power, none were barred because of the severity of their illnesses. Nor were the supplicants easily categorized by religious affiliation. In the earliest months, most were pentecostals, but by 1951 *Healing Waters* reported that in the recent Tampa crusade "over one-half of those in the healing line were Methodists and Baptists, Presbyterians and Episcopalians, Lutherans and Catholics." One of those "gloriously healed" was "a prominent member of the famous Riverside Church in New York City."[159] The denominational diversity in the healing line increased greatly in the late 1950s after Roberts's television program roused the curiosity of many nonpentecostal Christians.

If Oral's success was built partly on superior preaching, his handling of the healing line became a model for a generation of revivalists who felt a call to heal. In this one-on-one confrontation, Oral brought the full intensity of his powerful personality and his power of concentration on the subject before him. Seated above the ramp, Roberts displayed the full range of his moods—sometimes he was charming and soothing, sometimes jocular and persuasive, sometimes irritable and commanding.

When rested and relaxed, particularly when performing before the grinding television cameras, Oral often turned lighthearted and witty. "It was a different Mr. Roberts on the prayer line than in the pulpit," noted a Louisville reporter: "He was open, affectionate, warmly concerned."[160] He was always "particularly gentle with children"; a reporter at an early meeting noted that "children seem to respond to him immediately."[161] From the beginning, Oral's handling of the healing line was marked by an "interesting, running line of comment . . . carried on with those for whom he prayed."[162] When a seventy-five-year-old woman in Louisville told Oral that she wanted a "general overhaul," he cracked: "You want to be 16 again? . . . Well, the Lord may not make you 16, but He may make you a young 75."[163] Typical was this warm exchange with a confessed alcoholic in Long Beach, California in 1956:

ROBERTS: And now do you honestly feel He can deliver you from the appetite for this thing?
MAN: Yes, sir.
ROBERTS: And take alcoholism out of your system?
MAN: Yes, sir.
ROBERTS: Why do you think you can do it, Mr. McLinden?
MAN: Because I tried everything else and I can't do it any other way.
ROBERTS: Now then it is up to God.
MAN: It is up to God.
ROBERTS: Are you ready for me to pray for you?
MAN: Yes, sir.
ROBERTS: Audience, are you ready?
AUDIENCE: Yes.
ROBERTS: Good. Oh, Father, we come into Thy presence tonight not in our name or strength but in His mighty name. We ask that this man be delivered from alcoholism. Oh, God smite this appetite . . . destroy it by the spirit of God, and heal him through and through including his heart. Make him a new creature in Christ. What did you say?
MAN: Wonderful, wonderful feeling.
ROBERTS: Did it come then?
MAN: Yes, sir, I believe.
ROBERTS: What did it feel like?
MAN: It was a certain lifting up.
ROBERTS: You felt a lifting up.[164]

If Oral was sometimes warm, relaxed, and compassionate in the healing line, at other times he was rough, authoritarian, and irritable. The grasp of his right hand was always vigorous, but sometimes it became vicelike and violent, roughly shaking the heads of the seekers.[165] In later years Oral and Evelyn reflected about the fact that to many he seemed "cold and hard" in the healing line. "I know he has hit people so hard that it's been terrible sometimes," recalled Evelyn; "in the crusades they wondered why does Brother Roberts hit us so hard." Evelyn accounted for Oral's vehemence partly on the grounds that he hated the "disease in this person and he hates the devil and he hates the devil for putting this on people." But she thought it was also clinical, just as a "cold and businesslike" doctor was often more effective, so Oral sometimes felt that if one was "too sympathetic you can't help a person."[166] Oral acknowledged that his powerful grip was calculated to stimulate healing faith. "Well," he recalled, "it looked like more pressure than there was. . . . But if I could touch you and then give a little pressure . . . it seems like that my faith would be released better. And I was utterly unconscious of what people thought anyway. . . . I was concerned about that little girl and I wanted her healed and if it took my hands feeling pressure, why O.K."[167] Oral's manner also turned harsh sometimes because he sensed a lack of faith in the supplicant or in the audience. In 1957 he told a crusade audience in Pensacola: "Now I admit it irritates me when someone does something that defeats them and me. I was irritated last night because I left with the thought, 'I probably haven't helped this woman at all, and she'll wonder what it's all about after it's all over.' . . . Really, people, when we come to Him we should have our minds on this one, idea, 'I will believe God right now.' "[168]

There is no tally of the tales hatched in those magic moments in the center of the ramp, instants when, Oral and his supporters believed, "all manner of diseases and all conditions were healed."[169] Braces and hearing aids were hurled into the air, believers saw goiters vanish before their eyes of faith, cancers were pronounced healed. Joining the parade of derelicts and maimed who passed under Oral's grasp were occasional celebrities of sorts. For instance, there was the wife of Bill McKechnie, "former major-league baseball manager," who announced herself "rapturously" healed of "nervous depression," and, in a more general vein, the "night club singer" who was "delivered of cigarettes" and "demon possession" and began immediately to use her "talent for the Lord."[170]

The ever-present demons lurking inside the afflicted were, according to the testimony of those possessed, dispatched nightly at Oral's command. A New York newsman recorded Oral's confrontation with a confessed alcoholic in 1958: "Roberts grabbed the man's head and said 'Demons, come out!' " The crowd froze in anticipation, then, " 'They came out,' said the Californian, and walked happily off the rostrum."[171] Sometimes such encounters turned violent. In 1949 Oral prayed for a "demon possessed" woman in Denver:

This woman was so powerfully possessed that they even had to strike her to keep her captive behind the platform until I finished preaching. . . . When she came in my presence I never thought much about it—I knew she was demon possessed, but when I reached out to touch her with my hand she wouldn't let me. The most extraordinary strength I've ever encountered in a fellow human being was in her. When I reached forth my hand, sitting there on the platform and she was standing in front of me, she just reached up and got me by the front of the coat and she just ripped that coat and the buttons flew off. She jerked me off the platform, on to the ramp, just like I was a little child. I stood there—fortunately, since 1947, I have had no fear of demon-possessed people. And I used to have a very great fear, because my father-minister taught me never to pray for a demon-possessed person unless I was sure I had God's power, because when the demon comes out he strives to enter another. And he always tries to get back in the same person . . . and that's why when we're successful in prayer and the demon comes out, we ask God to forbid the demon to come back. . . . Well anyway, I reached forth my hand toward her to touch her head, because I knew if I could get my hand on her head I'd have a very fine chance of praying the prayer of faith. And she would just take me and shove me back, or pitch me back like that. . . . And I began to move my hand like this and she was using her hands to capture my hand, and I shot my hand through her arms and got it on her forehead. When I did the Spirit of God came upon me, and I always feel it in my hand. . . . So when I touched her I felt the warmth, the sensation of Christ, and I discerned her. I forget, it was some forty or fifty demons she had. I discerned the number of years she had them. It just opened up as I had my hand upon her, and she would lunge and try to strike me, but something invisible held her hands. From the moment I touched her with my hand she could not strike my body. When those demons came out they shook her body as though she had a chill. And suddenly, as they left her, she screamed a blood-curdling yell, and then she was as quiet and calm as you are. And she looked about and cried, "I am free!" I don't know, but that may be the greatest miracle I've ever seen in my life.[172]

The healing-line experience was probably the most concentrated dose of medical psychology ever encountered by a human. In 1983, Oral speculated that "I've probably had more people in our meetings for prayer in front of me than most doctors have in their whole life." The collage of memories from those meetings under the tents burned deeply into Oral's psyche: "I've dealt with lots of people. I've been closer to them . . . than most anybody in the country. I live with the sick and the demon possessed. I've heard them scream. I've seen their white faces. I've seen their terrified attitude. I've seen their twisted bodies."[173]

Of course, it was a fortunate minority who received Oral's personal attention. Most passed briskly across the ramp, receiving a quick touch accompanied by a crisp request that God heal them. "In stretches," wrote a Milwaukee reporter, "he swam along the line using a modified sidestroke, touching one person with his left, the next with his right."[174] Over and over Oral explained that he could not linger over each case: "Some people say, 'Brother Roberts, pray a long time for me. I'm really sick.' I don't pray hours for one person. There are millions of people whom I want to reach. I don't want to spend all my time with one person. I'm trying to reach the masses for Christ. . . . I can't heal you. Only God can save and heal. I am to help you release your faith."[175] And he repeatedly told crusade audiences why their experience would differ from what they saw on television:

> I do take more time on the television nights; not because I require it or even the person requires it, but because people at home, who don't know anything about this, will not believe it unless there is some conversation. They want to know who the man is and they'd like to know what church he's from, and they like to hear a little conversation to make it more believable. If I just touched them and they moved on people at home would say, 'Well, what's this?' But I don't do that for myself.[176]

Most who received Oral's touch did so as a part of the "long line," or, as some evangelists called it, the fast line, in the closing service of the campaign. All those with uncalled healing cards formed the long line, which passed rapidly across the ramp. The technique was never popular, but Roberts really had no alternative. "If I could touch a thousand people at one time I would be much happier," Oral told his audiences, but he pleaded for understanding.[177] He instructed an audience in 1957: "I'll be praying for most of you tomorrow in a long line, and I can hear some of you saying, 'Yes, there'll be so many, what will I do?' I'll tell you what you will do. You'll do one of two things. You'll say, 'Well, my faith is in Oral Roberts,' or 'My faith is in God.' You'll do one of the two."[178]

The physical limitation of the healing line was sometimes overcome when spontaneous healing broke out in the audience. In 1951, Bob DeWeese reported that "over 300 stood and said they had been healed during Bro. Roberts' special prayer for them" without going through the healing line. "God has been leading Bro. Roberts out on this way of delivering those we cannot pray for in the line," announced DeWeese.[179] Then there was an evening in Jacksonville "when the little boy who was born without a hip socket came for prayer." Oral recalled the scene:

> The miracle started and all of a sudden I cried out that my right hand was like it was on fire. My hand was hurting like you were sticking it with a thousand pins. . . . Suddenly I jumped to my feet. I didn't say anything and the crowd jumped up and here they came and completely engulfed the platform and me. People were pushed up in wheelchairs. They came out of the wheelchairs and just kept right on walking. . . . Collins, the next day you fellows picked up armloads of crutches and eyeglasses and hearing aids. . . . It started and stopped in five minutes.[180]

The confinement of the healing-line technique probably contributed to Oral's early hopes for a "mass miracle," an idea which has recurred in his thought throughout his life. In 1957, he told a crusade audience in Columbus, Ohio, "One of the reasons we have these big television cameras in the tent is the hope that one night in the meeting God will heal this whole audience. And if the nation tuned in to this program can see you healed, . . . it just might set off a chain reaction of healing from border to border and ocean to ocean that can leap over into other nations and set the world on fire for Jesus of Nazareth."[181]

But other methods could not replace the prayer line. It was Oral's touch that the people came to receive. In his early years, he frequently prayed for 200 in an evening, sometimes pausing to "conserve his strength," often ducking under the platform to drink some chocolate milk. Later, when the long line passed in front of him, he would place his hands on thousands of heads. One evening in Columbia, South Carolina, 9,300 passed through the line. "For three days and nights I was numb," Oral recalled, "I scarcely knew who I was." And he remembered another meeting when "a dust storm came up" but the people "still wanted to be prayed for": "We formed a healing line, over three thousand came through it. We were caked with this dust and mud. Our whole bodies, our eyes, our hands, and I had prayed until my arm literally ached."[182] Many times Collins Steele "held him up to get to the car he would be so exhausted. . . . When he got through there wouldn't be a dry thread on him."[183] It was a draining, exhausting experience that left Oral spiritually depleted and physically spent.

IF ORAL's crusades fell into a predictable pattern by the 1950s, there were, nonetheless, countless nights laden with special meaning. Some were times for savoring, such as those October evenings in 1950 when, in the aftermath of a storm in Amarillo, Texas which had destroyed his tent, Oral returned to Shawnee and Enid for three-day meetings in the small Oklahoma towns where he had formerly pastored churches. In the closing service in the Shawnee Municipal Auditorium, 4,500 people crammed into an auditorium designed to seat 3,000, far surpassing Shawnee's record turnout a year earlier to hear Eleanor Roosevelt. In "the greatest spiritual awakening Enid has ever known," hundreds were turned away from the town's convention hall.[184] And there was an evening in Syracuse, New York when 6,000 "waded through mud" to "see and hear him"; an afternoon in Huntington, West Virginia when 8,000 stood in the snow to gain entrance to the tent; and an afternoon service in Columbus, Ohio when "20,000 to 25,000 persons . . . braved almost unbearable heat in his huge cathedral tent at the State Fairgrounds."[185] A September 1957 evening in the Hollywood Bowl climaxed in an altar call that lasted twenty-three minutes.[186] Years later, Bob DeWeese still remembered vividly an evening in Los Angeles when "a kid got to ramming around out on the lot with some kind of cutdown Ford . . . and he ran into one of these big cables that went up to the top of one of these big tent poles. . . . It just pulled that big tent pole over . . . and then let it go and that whole tent went whomp, whomp . . . right in the middle of a sermon." The startled audience, recalled DeWeese, "thought the rapture had happened."[187]

But, save for the debacle in Australia, no single evening in Oral Roberts's crusading career left deeper memories than the evening of Sunday, September 10, 1950, in Amarillo, Texas. The crusade had begun promisingly, attracting crowds of between 5,000 and 7,000 in Oral's new "four-master tent advertised as the largest fireproof gospel tent in the world."[188] The local press seemed friendly; one reporter described Oral as "a personable young man with extremely black hair and a wide and engaging smile."[189] But, in hindsight, there were some ominous signals. The Texas Panhandle was receiving its late summer rains, not in the form of pleasant and refreshing showers, but with the fury and exaggeration of all High Plains weather. While the forecast predicted only "scattered showers" as Oral's crusade began, every local resident knew that an Amarillo "shower" could swell high and black into the stratosphere and leave havoc in its wake.[190]

Warning came on Friday evening, September 8. Huge thunderstorms, filled with wind and hail, swept across the plains area.[191] About two-thirds of the way through the tent service that evening, ten "tent pegs at the southeast side of the tent pulled loose from the soggy soil," and "one side of the tent ballooned in a sudden gust of wind." One of the main poles started to rise from the ground, but several men seated nearby held it down. Oral asked the audience to rise and leave the tent in an orderly fashion; they filed out singing "'Tis So Sweet to Trust in Jesus." The evacuation was followed by a horrendous traffic jam, "the worst," reported an ambulance driver called to the scene, "ever seen in Amarillo." And tragedy struck when sixty-four-year-old Robert E. Jones of Lubbock, who had been "in ill health several years" and had attended the meeting "in the hope that it would benefit" him, died on the grounds shortly after running through the storm to his car.[192]

Showers were predicted again for Sunday, though the forecast indicated that "the Texas Panhandle is in the edge of the wet belt."[193] On Sunday evening, September 10, the tent was once again filled to its capacity of about 7,000. Four hundred people had just answered the altar call when a rumbling, hail-filled thunderstorm suddenly engulfed the tent. Oral had already "announced that anyone was free to leave if he desired," but few had departed. After the incident on Friday evening, the Roberts crew had "double-staked the tent completely around it" and had posted "two men to steady each border pole and eight men to each quarter pole." When the heavy rain began, Oral came to the center of the platform, took the microphone, and began leading the congregation in songs, thinking that the winds would calm once the rain subsided. Instead the torrential rain turned to hail, and the winds grew in intensity. As the crowd sang "When the Saints Go Marching In," the light suddenly faded out, and the tent lifted toward the sky like a kite, pulling the huge aluminum poles aloft. The tent then began to rip and settled slowly down on the audience, gently lowering the thousand-pound poles so that they did relatively little harm. Oral recalled that there was "absolutely no panic"; another witness remembered that "some people were screaming, some crying, some singing and some praying."[194]

People slowly crawled out of the maze of twisted chairs which lay under the canvas; the confusion lasted late into the night. Many were separated from their families. The prayer tent was still standing, and Oral rushed there in search of Evelyn and Richard Lee, but met Vaden, who told him they were safe under the platform. After caring for Evelyn and Richard, Oral wandered among the dazed crowd, many of whom held folding chairs over their heads for protection from the continuing hail. Oral remembered praying for several of those who had suffered "minor injuries." When officers from the fire and police departments assured him that no one was seriously injured (one officer told him: "This is the most miraculous thing I have ever seen"),[195] the evangelist went to his hotel room.

By midnight, news reports confirmed that about fifty people had been hospitalized. Only a few were seriously injured, although forty remained in local hospitals the next day.[196] Oral issued a statement the next morning that "the real miracle, as I see it, was that out of 7,000 people crowded under that tent less than 50 persons were hurt." "It was," he concluded, "the greatest miracle I ever saw."[197] The meeting, of course, was closed, since no suitable auditorium could be secured in which to continue, although Oral did conduct a concluding healing service in the First Assembly of God auditorium for those who had received healing cards.[198]

The Amarillo disaster prompted a variety of public reactions. Some of Oral's critics made the most of it. V. E. Howard, widely known Church of Christ radio speaker, taunted:

Why were the injured rushed to the hospitals? . . . Mr. Roberts was performing before his audience of some 7,000 people claiming that great 'miracles' and 'healings' were being performed. This would have been a most opportune time to really prove himself. . . . But, my friends, this was the real thing; no fake about the broken limbs and crushed ribs. That medium sized Texas 'norther' put him out of the 'healing' business right on the spot. He pulled out of Amarillo, Texas and left the Doctors and Nurses to 'heal' the injured in the hospitals.[199]

On the other hand, *Amarillo Daily News* editor Wes Izzard saw a positive lesson in the tragedy. He compared the Roberts tent disaster to a circus tent fire in Hartford, Connecticut six years earlier in which over 100 people died. The remarkable thing about the Amarillo incident, wrote Izzard, was not that it was a "miracle," but rather that the faith of the people had protected them from panic and had kept anyone from being trampled to death. He wrote: "The important thing is that most of the people in that tent were thinking about God, each in his own way, when disaster struck. And there was enough trust in God manifested there to prevent deadly panic."[200]

Oral was shaken. He remembered looking at the scattered debris and wondering, "Am I finished? Is this the end?"[201] He was forced to cancel tent campaigns in California scheduled for October and November. William Branham, the nation's other premier healing evangelist, called to offer Oral the use of his tent for his California crusades, but Roberts declined and rather persuaded Branham to substitute for him in those meetings. He confided to the readers of his magazine that he needed "to rest but have had little opportunity"; he felt as though he had been through the "valley of the Shadow of Death."[202]

On the other hand, it was not so easy to quash the ebullient Roberts spirit in 1950, nor could the trauma caused by this natural disaster compare with the anguish which had followed his persecution in Australia. Oral was soon back on his feet. He revised his schedule, setting up meetings in auditoriums in Oklahoma; Gary, Indiana; Philadelphia; Augusta, Georgia; and in Saint Nicholas Arena in New York City. Soon Oral was chafing under the inconveniences of his new auditorium schedule, complaining that his hastily arranged crusades had been interrupted by previously scheduled wrestling matches and other events which left a "godless atmosphere" in the auditoriums.[203]

Oral yearned to return to the "sweet spirit of the 'Tent Cathedral' " and in November announced that he had ordered a "fine new tent with a seating capacity of 10,000 people." He and Vaden visited the United States Tent Company in Chicago, where Oral gave special instructions for "triple reinforcement throughout the canvas." In addition, he ordered a "circus-type stake driver from the Lewis Diesel Equipment Company in Memphis" which was "identical to the one used by Ringling Bros. Circus," having "learned that the secret in holding a tent during a storm is in the tent construction and the staking." "All this takes money, large money," Oral told the readers of *Healing Waters,* "but what is money compared to the saving of a human soul and the healing of a human body?" In March 1951 in Tampa, Florida, the new triple-reinforced, double-staked tent made its debut—crammed full and paid for.[204]

The hundreds of thousands who filled the tents between 1947 and 1960 fit into a pattern nearly as neatly as did the format of the meetings. They came early to reserve chairs near the front; many "ate their suppers at a refreshment stand outside of the tent in order to be sure of having a seat before the tent filled."[205] Although an enthusiastic pentecostal observer noted in a 1950 audience "lawyers, some university professors, and some business men," almost everyone under the tent appeared to come from "untutored laboring classes."[206] The hard-handed men wore work shirts or sat stiff and "uncomfortable in their best suits." They were accompanied by plain women without makeup, "white-haired and unpretentious in their dress."[207] Some observers found the audiences graceless and depressing, a collection of "the economically and socially unaccomplished."[208] "The great majority of the followers of the healers," wrote one critic, "are old people, frustrated people, neurotic people, shallow people—people cast aside by society."[209] But some seasoned reporters were touched by the "timid warmth" of the "plain people" who came to turn their faith loose and to participate in a divine drama.[210] Whatever their reactions, outsiders who ventured under the tent knew that they had stumbled upon the religious ritual of the underside of American society.

Although Oral's partners in the 1950s did include a smattering of upwardly mobile businessmen and professionals, he knew that the majority of his supporters were those who had "fallen upon hard times or are desperately ill or have terrible family or business problems." "The rich pay very little attention to us," he readily acknowledged.[211] Oral began his ministry in 1947 with the conviction that "God has always dared to bless the world through insignificant men and women," and he was to retain an identification with the downtrodden throughout his life.[212] His audiences were the poor, and those who, by hard work and moral habits, were one generation removed from society's bottom rung. He was of them, he knew their hungers; and they recognized him as the best of their boys.

However, Oral's audiences did slowly change in the years before 1960. In his early crusades his crowds were almost entirely pentecostal, but by the early 1950s that uniformity broke down. First, Oral and the other deliverance evangelists noted that their healing lines included more and more members of the mainstream denominations.[213] Then, increasingly, Oral became aware that his ministry was attracting "large numbers of the unchurched and the unconverted." The "irresistible excitement" of the "miracles of deliverance" had attracted them, he believed, and he became fascinated by his potential to reach such people.[214] In 1958, he told a New York reporter that the "fundamental difference" between him and Billy Graham was his ministry to the "unchurched," those who most of all needed a God of "love and compassion."[215] Oral could read his audiences instinctively; he knew who they were. And increasingly he saw that they were not just pentecostals, nor were they only the ill; they were simply people with needs. "I look on the members of the audiences as persons in need," Oral told a reporter in 1958 "and my sermons are designed to help them."[216] In reaching out to all those who were hurt and damaged, Oral was to have a dramatic impact on American religion in the 1960s and 1970s.

CHAPTER

VI

Ministry

T HE GROWTH OF Oral Roberts's crusades was accompanied by a parallel expansion in the size and scope of his organization. At the same time that Oral's energies were being consumed by sermon preparation, preaching before huge audiences, and the emotionally exhausting ritual of praying for the sick, he was forced to become a business executive and to try to construct a rational organization to support his crusade team. In the long run, it was his skills in this area—his ability to manage, to recruit talented assistants, and to share responsibility—that most clearly set him apart from the other deliverance evangelists of his generation.

"The summer of the first year" of campaigning, Evelyn later recalled, "was the most hectic." Oral began receiving letters in May, and the number increased dramatically after his nine weeks in Steve Pringle's tent in Tulsa. "Our lives changed overnight," Evelyn wrote. "In a few short weeks our house was changed from a docile little domain to a miniature Grand Central Station."[1] Oral was thrilled when he began to receive written requests for prayer, and he carefully dictated answers to his volunteer secretarial helpers.[2] One memorable day in July he received 8 letters; the number rapidly grew as word of the ministry spread. For several months Oral's office was the little $12 desk he had purchased from Oscar Moore and placed in his dining room, but before the end of the year a makeshift work area had been built in the garage.[3] In the first six months of 1948, Oral's workers answered 25,000 letters, mailed out 30,000 "anointed handkerchiefs," and distributed 15,000 books and 90,000 magazines.[4]

As the volume of mail grew, Oral depended on volunteer help from several young women who had attended the tent crusade in Tulsa. Each evening after work, they came to the Roberts home to type responses to letters. One of the young women was teenager Ruth Rooks, at the time employed as an attorney's secretary. The thought of working for Oral "scared her half to death," but at the same time she was intrigued and excited by Oral's ministry. She was to become the "only secretary Oral was ever to have," an institution in the Roberts organization, a woman, in Oral's estimation, of "magnificent Christian character."[5]

In the earliest months of the independent ministry, Evelyn carried a heavy load of responsibility. While Oral was away, Evelyn "conducted all the office business, performed all her household duties, and cared for her children."[6] When *Healing Waters* magazine was begun in November 1947, the burden increased dramatically. The magazine "was planned, written and laid out on our dining room table," Evelyn remembered, and when the first copies were received from the printer, Evelyn, with "the aid of three girls who volunteered to help, worked day and night, hand-addressing, sorting, stamping, bundling and mailing the magazine."[7]

Oral's decision to begin publishing a monthly magazine was a crucial step in linking him with his supporters. By 1950, *Healing Waters* was one of the "four major tasks" which the Roberts ministry had undertaken, along with the healing crusades, the "ministry of prayer cloths" sent through the mail, and regular radio broadcasts. *Healing Waters* was "the first of the healing magazines with national and international coverage"; it became a model for scores of later imitators.[8] The monthly magazine featured pictures and stories about the crusades, an endless series of healing testimonies, and samples of Oral's sermons. Most important, it became Roberts's communication lifeline with his partners, announcing his schedules, his plans, and his dreams. Oral never allowed the magazine to get far from his own personal supervision. When the first issue was printed there were only 500 subscribers, but Oral ordered a printing of 10,000. They were soon distributed, and by the end of 1949 the paper's circulation was approaching 5,000 per month.[9] The name of the magazine was taken from a Bible story in the fifth chapter of John or, more directly, from a song in Oral's early repertoire, "Where the Healing Waters Flow."[10] In 1969, Oral wrote that "through the years we've had different editors, all of whom gave us great help. Still it is difficult for anyone outside Evelyn and me to put into the magazine what we really feel from the Lord." The magazine, he believed, was "God in me talking to you."[11]

In July 1948, Oral organized his ministry as Healing Waters, Inc., a nonprofit religious organization. The trust agreement stipulated that in the event of Oral's death, the ministry's assets, including office and tent equipment, would be given to three churches—the Pentecostal Holiness church, the Assemblies of God, and the Church of God—"for the benefit of old-age ministers." The incorporation ensured that "no part of Healing Waters or any of its profits can accrue to Brother Roberts or members of his family."[12]

In the hectic early months, Oral constantly shuffled his team, both those who traveled in the crusades and his growing office staff. But by 1950 the organization began to stabilize, and Oral had employed several people who were to make lasting contributions to his work. Roberts sought talent wherever he could find it, and the two most important resources he used in his early career were his family and his church.

By the spring of 1948, the Healing Waters office staff consisted of Oral Roberts, "Founder and Director," "Mrs. Oral Roberts, Office Manager," "L. V. Roberts, Relations," and five stenographers.[13] Oral was organization-conscious and built with pride. In December 1948 he sponsored the "first Annual Healing Waters Banquet . . . at Michaels Cafeteria . . . in honor and thanksgiving for the completion of 18 months of ever-expanding service through the work of Healing Waters."[14]

Oral persuaded Vaden to travel with him in some of his earliest meetings, even though his brother protested, "Oral, I'm not even a Christian." Vaden later reported that he "did not develop much interest even though I saw some things that appeared to be miraculous," until, during a crusade in Tulsa in April 1948, he and his family "got saved." He immediately sold his restaurant business and joined Oral as his "equipment manager." For several years Vaden traveled with the team and made the physical arrangements for the meetings before family responsibilities forced him to retire.[15]

Evelyn remained ever present in the early months of the ministry. She not only managed the office but sometimes traveled with the team, occasionally joining Oral on the platform.[16] The other members of the earliest crusade team were the Millards—Geneva on the organ and her aunt Roberta on the piano.[17]

Oral stepped outside his family for the first time when Reg G. Hanson joined him as manager of the campaigns. Hanson was "a leading businessman from Kansas City" (a public relations consultant) who had been active in promoting "inter-pentecostal meetings." Hanson began helping in the crusades during the summer of 1948, taking charge of the day services, preaching faith-building lessons, and supervising the arrangements for the evening services. He also was master of ceremonies for the "preliminaries of the great night services" and "handled the Healing Line and stood by Brother Roberts while the people are healed." Hanson remained in that role for only a few months, and never relinquished his own business interests, but Oral remembered him as a "humble, praying man of God with a compassion for lost and suffering humanity."[18]

By 1950, the organization had begun to stabilize and take the form it would retain for a decade. The officers of Healing Waters, Inc. were Oral, "Founder and President"; Evelyn, "Secretary-Treasurer"; and A. G. Stanfield, CPA. W. B. Lee, a member of the Pentecostal Holiness congregation Oral had pastored in Toccoa, Georgia, was listed as the general manager of the Healing Waters Office, and Manford Engel as assistant manager. The Oral Roberts campaigns were led by Oral Roberts, Minister; Reg G. Hanson, Manager; Dr. O. E. Sproull, Associate Manager; and L. V. Roberts, Manager of Equipment.[19] Particularly important were the 1949 additions of Engel and Sproull to the team. While Lee and Hanson soon departed, Engel and Sproull made lasting contributions.

Engel remained in an important administrative role in the Roberts organization until the mid-1970s. He joined Roberts in September 1949, and soon became the Healing Waters "office manager." Engel was from Enid; his wife was the pianist in the Pentecostal Holiness church, and he was a deacon and its treasurer. In the 1960s he became executive vice-president of the Oral Roberts Evangelistic Association. Oral had implicit faith in Engel, considering him "one of the most loyal men I have ever known." The evangelist felt "a rapport that is far more than human" with his former church treasurer. Others in the Roberts organization felt that Engel was "a good balance-wheel" for Oral. While Oral was "impetuous and quick," Engel was a "staunch, stable person" and often acted as an intermediary between the evangelist and his staff. Engel had that perfect combination of loyalty and pentecostal mind set which was so crucial in putting Oral's plans into action.[20]

In the short range, Oral's acquisition of O. E. Sproull as his associate crusade evangelist was by far his most impressive organizational coup. *Healing Waters* proudly announced the appointment in January 1949: "Dr. Sproull is one of the most powerful, spirit-filled preachers of this generation, having wide acceptance among the full gospel people and is in demand as a camp meeting speaker everywhere. . . . Dr. Sproull has cancelled his schedule to join with Brother Roberts in spreading the message of Bible deliverance."[21] In later years, Oral still considered Sproull's willingness to become his associate "one of the greatest honors I've ever received."[22] Only a few years earlier, Oral had been a skinny youngster on his way to Canada to hold a few meetings in the conference where Sproull reigned supreme, preaching in Toronto at one of the most dynamic Pentecostal Holiness churches in the world. At the time Sproull accepted Oral's invitation, he was pastor of the Ebenezer Pentecostal Holiness Church in Tampa and was probably the most visible preacher in his denomination. But by 1949, Oral's ministry offered more than the Pentecostal Holiness church—in more ways than one. When asked by an acquaintance why he had joined Oral, Sproull replied: "Do you know what he's paying me? . . . You take what the bishops are getting and then double it and then double some more."[23] Oral had learned that the right man was worth his price.

In addition to his visibility in the pentecostal community, Sproull brought a number of other talents to the organization. He was a "fiery speaker" and added a zest to the day services which Hanson had not provided. Furthermore, Sproull took "some of the heat off Oral" in confrontations with his critics. He was feisty, "would tackle a buzz saw"; he was a perfect buffer between Oral and bickering local pastors and church leaders and an increasingly inquisitive press. In addition, Sproull had always "had a vision beyond" the Pentecostal Holiness church, reaching out in his own ministry to the mainline churches, and he both appreciated and encouraged Oral's ecumenical temperament. Hanson and Sproull had been "close friends for many years," and they worked together for several months before Hanson turned over his managerial role to Sproull.[24]

In the long run, the most important new member of the Roberts team, though he did not become a full-time employee until 1960, was S. Lee Braxton. Braxton, the son of a North Carolina village blacksmith, worked his way through Holmes Bible School in Greenville, South Carolina and then moved to Whiteville, North Carolina in 1926 to begin working as an automobile mechanic. Braxton "determined to be the best mechanic in town"; he saved part of his thirty-dollar-a-week salary and began accumulating property. By the outbreak of World War II he was a rising businessman in the small community. Braxton's businesses blossomed during the war, and by 1950 he owned a wholesale auto parts store and "was president or an official in twenty-two different companies." A millionaire, and later elected mayor of Whiteville, Braxton was probably the wealthiest and most visible layman in the Pentecostal Holiness church at the end of World War II.[25]

Braxton learned about Oral's new ministry during the Falcon camp meeting in the summer of 1948. Someone told him about Oral's Durham tent meeting and gave him a copy of *If You Need Healing—Do These Things!* Braxton was "fascinated" by the book and perceived that he "had been using the same kind of faith to get the things I wanted" but that he had been unable to articulate it. Braxton had long known Sproull, and he wrote to him asking for an appointment with Oral. In January 1949, Braxton flew to Miami to attend Oral's tent crusade. He reported to the readers of *Healing Waters* that he "received something in that meeting that I don't believe I will ever get over."[26]

Oral was also greatly impressed by Braxton. He and Braxton met for a day and talked excitedly about Oral's growing ministry. Braxton was "carried away with his vision and plans for reaching lost humanity on a world-wide scale." On his part, Oral asked "scores of questions on business matters" and seemed to appreciate any advice Braxton offered. Oral recalled: "I just asked every conceivable question like, 'What do you do in this kind of business? How do you handle books? How do you publish literature? How do you build buildings? How do you see that all bills are paid?' "[27] Braxton later reflected on the same conversation: "He seemed to be the most anxious person I ever saw to conduct his affairs in the proper manner."[28]

The meeting of Braxton and Roberts was more than a chance encounter between two opportunists eager to use one another; it was a genuine meshing of complementary minds. Long before he met Oral, Braxton was immersed in "positive thinking"; Dale Carnegie's *How to Win Friends and Influence People* was "the book that really put me in business."[29] The ebullient businessman scissored the word *impossible* out of his dictionary and throughout his life collected a library of books on success and possibility thinking which he shared with Oral.[30] In fact, at their first meeting he presented Oral with a copy of a booklet entitled "How I Raised Myself from Failure to Success in Selling." Oral absorbed the book, and, speaking at Braxton's funeral in 1982, he revealed that he had read it "every year since 1949."[31] Braxton had found in Oral someone who could place this positive-thinking emphasis in a spiritual context that promised boundless blessings to those who would turn their faith loose.

Braxton influenced the two most important physical developments in the Roberts organization prior to 1950—the construction of a new headquarters building and the expansion of the Healing Waters radio network. The first time the two met, Braxton challenged Oral to expand his radio ministry. Oral's answer was, "Lee, I don't have the money."[32] But Braxton immediately began sponsoring the program of the station in Whiteville, and by the end of 1949 he had accepted the title of director of the Healing Waters broadcast. For several years he worked in that capacity as a nonsalaried employee, and under his leadership the radio network expanded rapidly.[33]

Perhaps Oral's proudest achievement prior to 1950 was the completion of the Healing Waters headquarters building on South Boulder Street in the fall of 1949. When the building opened, the *Tulsa World* reported that it "houses the business offices of Healing Waters, Inc., and a well-equipped printing plant used in publication of the magazine, for religious tracts, a book, . . . and a songbook containing 79 religious hymns." The total outlay represented an investment of perhaps $250,000 and was the fulfillment of Oral's "dream far beyond expectations."[34] The front of the building featured a "big neon sign" flashing the message:

> Turn Your Faith Loose
> HEALING
> WATERS
> MAGAZINE
> Oral Roberts—Founder[35]

The walls were lined with pictures from the campaigns and a bizarre "sort of trophy case full of crutches and braces and ear pieces"; the building became a tourist mecca for proud visiting pentecostals.[36]

As with most of Oral's achievements, his first building did not come easily. But by the end of 1949 the Healing Waters organization had expanded to nearly thirty employees, and it was very inadequately housed in the former Roberts residence on North Main Street. Oral began searching and found "the perfect site" on South Boulder Street near downtown Tulsa. The lot was for sale for $11,000, but he could muster less than half that amount. In his financial pinch, Oral contacted one of his old church friends from North Carolina, a man he would call on many times in the future, John Wellons, requesting a loan. Oral asked for $7,000, but Wellons misunderstood and sent the entire $11,000. When Oral informed him that he had sent too much, Wellons told his friend to "go ahead and use the money for God's work."[37] Wellons's support, like that of Braxton, was an early indication of Oral's ability to form close and lasting friendships with pentecostal businessmen.

Once Oral had acquired his lot, he still faced the problem of financing the construction of a new building. It was Braxton who supplied the business acumen to solve that problem. Oral had asked Braxton to visit Tulsa during their first meeting, and the North Carolina businessman came in the early spring of 1949 and toured Oral's operation. Among other things, Braxton advised Oral to "build an office and do this work in a businesslike way instead of piecemeal like you're having to do here."[38] Oral was anxious to comply, but he had been unable to negotiate a loan with a Tulsa bank. Braxton introduced Oral to the art of negotiation. After the two of them had been coolly received by several Tulsa institutions, Braxton instructed Oral to return to the bank which had been handling his business and tell the loan officer that Braxton had agreed to secure the necessary funds in North Carolina. Apparently the strategy worked; the

Tulsa institution supplied the large construction loan. Years later, Oral remembered that financial transaction as one of the most important in his career: "It has helped me in much larger ones since."[39]

The new building was an important symbol of Oral's effort to find the most efficient way to handle the exploding public response to the ministry. Almost as important as the crusades in promoting that response was the growing Healing Waters radio network. Oral began the broadcast on KCRC in Enid at the same time he started holding healing services in 1947. He had been "conducting a church broadcast" while "struggling to preach my first deliverance sermons, trying to get a foothold in my own thinking," when the "Lord directed" him to use as a theme song the old hymn "Where the Healing Waters Flow."

> Oh the joy of sins forgiven,
> Oh the bliss the blood-washed know,
> Oh the peace akin the Heaven,
> Where the Healing Waters flow.
>
> Where the Healing Waters flow,
> There the joy celestial glow,
> Oh there's peace and rest and love,
> Where the Healing Waters flow.

Five years later, Oral reported that "this name has caught the imagination of the people and everywhere they love to sing it."[40] By the fall of 1947, Oral's broadcast was heard on stations in Enid, Tulsa, Oklahoma City, and Durham, North Carolina, and the number grew slowly through 1948.[41]

By 1949, the format of the radio program had become set, and its impact was growing. The program was broadcast thirty minutes a day, addressed to "all people of all churches." Announcer Jerry Jones introduced each session:

> We present the "Healing Waters" broadcast, the nationwide radio healing ministry of Reverend Oral Roberts. Each week at this time Brother Roberts ministers healing through the power of God to all people of all churches. Each Healing Waters broadcast brings release, peace, and God's healing to thousands of people from coast to coast. Healing Waters is produced and transcribed under Brother Roberts' personal supervision at his national headquarters in Tulsa, Oklahoma. And now, here's Oral Roberts, the man with the heart and faith for suffering humanity.

Then, in his broad Oklahoma brogue, Oral spoke:

> Thank you, Jerry. And hello, neighbors. This is Oral Roberts, your partner for deliverance. God marked me in my mother's womb and chose me to bring His healing power to lost and suffering humanity. God has spoken to me three times. I was told God's healing power would be felt in my right hand. The Lord is healing thousands through my humble prayers. Neighbor, I am sent of God today to bring God's healing power into your life by faith. So believe and turn your faith loose, and God will set you free in soul, mind, and body during the Healing Waters broadcast today.

A musical interlude followed, usually featuring Oral Roberts and the Healing Waters Trio of Harry Correll, Doyle Zachary, and Paul Taylor singing selections from the "souvenir Healing Waters Song Book." Next came "Testimony Time," with Evelyn reading selections from the "hundreds of testimonies on file in Tulsa." Jerry Jones offered Oral's book and *Healing Waters* magazine, each at a cost of one dollar, and then Oral preached a short sermon—generally dealing with healing. Last came the climax of the broadcast, the healing prayer. Oral placed his own hand on the microphone in the studio and instructed his listeners:

> Now, neighbors, reach out and lay your hands on your radio cabinets. If you can't do that, lift your heart to God wherever you are. God told me His healing power would be felt in my right hand, and I lay my hand over this microphone, and, lo, I am laying it upon you there in your home. Now, Father, I come to Thee in the name of Thy son, Jesus of Nazareth. Grant me this miracle according to Thy will in heaven. And now, Father, I meet sickness and disease. I meet sin and despair, and fear and demon oppression through the authority of God. And I charge you, Satan, to loose suffering humanity. I command thee to let them go free today. Let Thy healing virtue surge into every fiber of their body, oh God. Heal those little children. Heal those dads and mothers, and these precious ones who are gathering around their radios now. In Jesus' name, I command their diseases to go! Now, neighbor, rise and be made whole by the power of God. Only believe.[42]

Oral early recognized the importance of his radio program; from the beginning, a large percentage of his healing testimonials came from radio listeners. Pete White, owner of White Advertising Agency in Tulsa, produced and distributed the radio program, persuading scores of reluctant stations to air the unconventional message. But it was Braxton who furnished the major impetus for growth. Braxton proposed to Oral a plan that would place the program on 100 radio stations all over the nation. Braxton's scheme was to secure individuals or churches as sponsors for the program in their area for several months in hopes that the local audience would then make the program self-supporting. In September, Oral instructed the readers of *Healing Waters:* "If you can see your local radio station, secure time on Sunday between 8:00 and 9:00 A.M. or 12:00 to 2:00 P.M. and if you are willing to pay for the station time only for the first three months, then we will sign the contract for one year and trust that others will hear the program and will contribute regularly to its support so we may remain on the station indefinitely."[43] In June 1949, Oral named Braxton national radio director. By the summer of 1949, the radio network had expanded to 25 stations, and by the end of the year the energetic Braxton was working to secure sponsors for 100 stations, though they were still well short of that number by 1950.[44]

The financial underpinnings of the growing Roberts organization were also firmly in place by 1950. While the heartbeat of the ministry was the crusades, the partner system was its life blood. The limited financial goals of the crusades, the avoidance of the "pulls" and "drives" characteristic of other evangelists, won Oral widespread good will.[45] Growing thousands of those touched by the crusades became permanent "partners for deliverance." Evelyn later recalled that "the very first partners we ever had were those people who took a little tiny brown envelope in one of our very first meetings in an auditorium and said I will take this envelope and I will pledge $10 a month to help you get on radio."[46]

Entrepreneurial pentecostal evangelists had long funded their radio programs and other projects by recruiting regular supporters. The first issue of *Healing Waters* magazine called for "warriors" who would volunteer to labor, fast, pray, and "make an investment in human deliverance."[47] Early subscribers to *Healing Waters* were offered a variety of articles to purchase, including a record album of Oral singing "all the songs he sings in the Roberts campaigns."[48] *If You Need Healing—Do These Things!* included an appeal for financial support from those who were being helped by the ministry. "When you serve with me as my PARTNER FOR DELIVERANCE," wrote Oral, "you will have a part in every soul being saved, every captive being delivered from sickness, affliction or demon-possession, in every preacher getting the vision to be a 'Bible' preacher, in every Church being revived and in every constructive effort made during these times of great need."[49]

The other important activity which helped Oral gain new partners was sending "anointed cloths" to all who requested his prayers. The use of such cloths for healing was a well-established practice in the pentecostal subculture, based on an incident recorded in Acts 19:11–12. By the summer of 1948, thousands were being mailed each month, with instructions and the assurance that Oral "prays over each cloth separately and individually and then as our requests come into the office, even while he is away in a campaign of deliverance, the handkerchief is mailed to you. You need not send a piece of cloth or handkerchief since our cloths are of uniform size and fit nicely into a letter. Also, if you insist on using your own handkerchief it might arrive while Brother Roberts is away and there will be a delay in getting the cloth back to you."[50] As the requests multiplied, Evelyn solicited help from "Ladies Missionary Societies and individuals" to "cut squares of cloth 2½ inches by 5." "Use old sheets (white)," she instructed, "and be careful to cut them only with pinking shears to prevent raveling, also be sure to keep them in uniform size."[51] The early prayer cloths were imprinted with a simple message:

> I prayed over this cloth for God to deliver you—use as a point of contact (Acts 19: 11–12). Oral Roberts, Tulsa 2, Oklahoma. It is not necessary to wear the cloth unless you feel you should. It can be used more than once or for more than one person. If you wish to request more, I will be glad to send them to you. The important thing is to use the cloth as a point of contact for the release of your faith in God, so that when you pray and put the cloth on your body, you will believe the Lord will heal you at that moment. I have prayed over this cloth in the name of Jesus of Nazareth and asked Him to heal you when you apply it to your body.[52]

The prayer cloth ministry expanded rapidly; by 1949 the number mailed out had climbed to nearly 100,000 a year.[53] While the cloths were sent without charge, Reg Hanson reminded those requesting them that "some of our dear friends remember the great expense of the office where four full-time stenographers and secretaries and two part-time office clerks work five days a week, helping in this wonderful work of mercy and love. Sometimes they send a free-will offering to help pay some of this great expense."[54]

On this solid organizational base, Oral built his huge, diversified ministry in the decades of the 1950s. It grew steadily in size and vision—sometimes the growth came in breathtaking spurts. Through most of the 1950s, the ministry published periodic box scores of its accomplishments, although in the middle of the decade the counting came to center almost entirely on soul saving. The ministry tally for 1950 included nine "full scale meetings" and four shorter campaigns; 52,211 "souls saved"; 1,327,550 people in attendance at the campaigns; 83,783 healing cards issued; 3,849 Healing Waters radio broadcasts with an estimated 19,000,000 listeners; 66,000 subscribers to *Healing Waters* magazine; 53,674 copies sold of *If You Need Healing—Do These Things!*; 700,000 tracts distributed; over 148,000 letters received and 96,173 prayer cloths mailed.[55] In 1954, the report listed eleven tent and nine auditorium campaigns with a total attendance of 1,430,000; 35,764 conversions; and a total of 72,500 passing through the healing line. But while the campaigns had more or less stabilized in size, other phases of the ministry had ballooned. The number of radio stations broadcasting Oral's sermons had increased to 215, and the estimated listening audience was "over 100,000,000." The organization placed the number of conversions among the radio audiences at 175,147. The subscription list of *Healing Waters* had expanded to 355,000; the office had mailed out over 155,000 "blest cloths," and the incoming mail during the year had reached nearly 800,000 pieces.[56]

The 1954 report included a calculation of "total conversions" from "all phases of work," 268,113.[57] It was this figure which increasingly was used as the annual measure of the effectiveness of Oral's efforts, a fact reflecting two important shifts in the ministry. First, it signaled a growing emphasis on the evangelistic rather than the healing role of the ministry, a philosophical drift which was clear in Oral's preaching as well. Second, the conversion count emphasized the growing complexity of the organization and, though it was not so perceived in the 1950s, highlighted the diminishing importance of the crusades. In July 1953, Oral announced that he had set a goal of converting a million people. In March 1959, Manford Engel, executive vice-president of the Oral Roberts Evangelistic Assn., Inc., announced that the "Fourth Million Soul Crusade has just been successfully completed," the last million souls being won in just twelve months. The "accounting department" broke down the sources of the conversions, and the list revealed much about the expansion and diversification of the ministry:

FOURTH MILLION SOUL REPORT
March 1959

	Total Souls Won in 12 Months
Crusade	47,057
Overseas	8,866
South Africa	7,500
Television Ministry	532,880
Radio Ministry	364,448
Bibles for Israel	1,156
Indian Crusades	1,600
Literature:	
Abudant Life	34,766
True Stories	3,913
Happiness and Healing	5,117
Books (English Editions)	1,453
Books (Foreign Translations)	1,245
Tracts (English)	954
Tracts (Foreign)	91
Films	4,282
Tapes	720
Prayer Group	279
Correspondence (Letters)	8,879
Total	1,025,206[58]

To some extent, Oral always had emphasized the evangelistic dimension of his crusades, at least since instituting the altar call during his early church meetings. A 1951 advertisement of his Oakland, California crusade heralded him as "America's leading soul-winner," whose 50,000 converts in 1950 included "many of the nation's outstanding business and civic leaders."[59] But from the time Oral announced his first million soul crusade in 1953, there was a growing emphasis on that theme. By 1955, he often summed up his mission in solely evangelistic terms. He told a crusade audience in Florence, South Carolina of a conversation with a newsman in which he had been pressed on the question of his "goal":

I said, "I want to win a million souls to Jesus Christ." He said, "That's good. Now what else?" I said, "That's it." "Well, don't you have another goal?" "No." "Don't you have a second desire?" "No. ... I want to win a million souls to Christ, and once we've won the first million I want to help win a million souls to Christ each year for ten years, if Jesus tarries. Now that's my goal—to win a million souls to Jesus Christ, my first, second, third and last goal—that's it. Besides that I have no other."[60]

When Associated Press religion writer George W. Cornell interviewed Oral in 1958, the evangelist denied vehemently that he was a "faith-healer" and insisted that "my main business, by far, is to win souls. ... If a man's soul is right, he'll go to heaven, whether he's sick or well." Oral conceded to Cornell, as he would to others later, "that in his early ministry, the stress was on faith-healing, mainly because most of his congregations already were Christians." But now, "with 60 per cent of his audiences unchurched, the picture was changed."[61]

Oral's initial million soul campaign was planned in February 1953, when he called in nine of his closest advisors and supporters in a "momentous meeting" which set a goal of a million reported conversions by July 1, 1956.[62] The specific goals of the plan were staggering—"500 radio stations broadcasting Bible deliverance as preached by Oral Roberts; 500,000 magazine subscriptions; 50 television stations carrying the message visually as well as audibly right into the homes of the people." Some wondered if such grand plans did not "clash with the truth of the imminent coming of our Lord Jesus Christ" but Roberts was certain that "this crusade is in harmony with God's plan for progress until the very instant of Christ's return."[63]

The first campaign for a million souls was completed by the end of 1954, far ahead of schedule. In January 1955, Oral issued a "second call to action," announcing that he was about to begin his quest for a second million conversions. In an impassioned appeal for support, Oral told his partners that "in a mysterious and fascinating way, the Lord is preparing the hearts of people everywhere to receive the gospel."[64] Fourteen months later, the magazine announced that "the task is finished"; television had surpassed radio for the first time as the major source of calculated conversions.[65] A third million soul crusade was completed in March 1958, and a fourth in April 1959.[66]

In 1959, the crusade for souls had been for six years the major public thrust of the Roberts organization. After six years and four million reported conversions, the theme seemed jaded, but in May 1959, Oral announced that the new major objective of his ministry would be "souls unlimited." The Souls Unlimited campaign called for winning "five million souls for Christ during the next 36 months." Oral solicited the support of his partners, noting that while others might announce grandiose plans, his organization was "tried and proved in winning three million souls in the past five years" and "big enough to win five million souls in the next three years!" It was, Oral felt, a grand scheme, one about which "the Lord has dealt with me personally and powerfully during the past weeks." He urged his partners to cement "a miracle partnership between you and me that will run for three years, perhaps for life!"[67]

The conversion counts of the 1950s were speculative, to say the least, although Manford Engel reported to Oral that "we have been very careful that the auditing is checked and rechecked in every detail—such were your instructions."[68] Nonetheless, all that the organization claimed was "reasonable accuracy" in estimating the "number of souls believed converted."[69] Even so, Al Bush, the young managerial wizard who was increasingly responsible for such matters, in the 1970s defended the counts:

> We tried to keep a tabulation of the number of people who were converted through our various outreaches. . . . People would write to us and we would actually tabulate the number of conversions they were reporting. Some were personal, some were other members in the family, but they would tell us and

we would actually try to count these. And then we had the same problem, that some people would never tell us, so we used to try to estimate, very conservatively. I ... think we were too conservative.[70]

Whatever the accuracy of the counts, conversion testimonials came to rival healing testimonials in the Roberts publications, including such newsworthy cases as that of flagpole sitter Tony Martin, who found "Christ as his Savior" on the fortieth day atop his pole in Miami, Florida, after reading a copy of "Oral Roberts' Life Story."[71]

The emphasis on soul saving particularly highlighted the importance of Oral's radio and television programs. The expansion of the radio network was steady in the early 1950s, from about 20 stations in mid-1949 to 70 in the spring of 1950. Lee Braxton's goal of 100 stations was finally reached in the summer of 1951. By the summer of 1953, the network carrying Oral's broadcasts, all independent stations, had reached 200, and the organization had set a goal of 500.[72] In October 1953, in a major breakthrough, Oral negotiated a contract to broadcast over the American Broadcasting Company network. The addition of ABC stations nearly doubled the number broadcasting Healing Waters and added greatly to the prestige of the ministry.[73] For the remainder of the decade, Oral's radio network fluctuated between 300 and 500 stations in the United States and Canada, and he remained on ABC throughout the period.[74] In January 1955, Roberts announced plans to acquire a "world network of 1,000 radio stations," but there was no serious effort to fulfill that goal as, increasingly, the radio program was overshadowed by the expanding television ministry.[75]

Radio probably remained Oral's most important foreign voice in the 1950s. In 1953, Radio Luxembourg, a powerful station which blanketed much of Europe, was added to the Healing Waters Radio Log as a "purely missionary venture." "The good people of these countries cannot send money to this country," Oral's partners were reminded.[76] By the end of 1956, the Healing Waters broadcast was being carried on over forty overseas radio stations in fifteen countries, some of them powerful short-wave stations, such as Radio Ceylon and Radio Luxembourg. The most extensive foreign network was in Australia, where twenty-five stations were listed by 1956.[77]

Oral apparently felt that a part of his missionary obligation could be filled by radio in the 1950s, and it was clear that some such projects captured the imagination of his American supporters. In January 1957 Roberts asked his partners to "help me win souls in Russia," informing them that the opportunity had presented itself to begin "immediately broadcasting our radio program to people held in Russian domination" through the Pan-American Broadcasting Company. The evangelist was pleased that the short-wave station had identified his work as "a positive ministry that can lift the people" out of the "tension, fear, and frustration" which gripped those behind the Iron Curtain. "This is the hour when I want to strike a blow for deliverance," he wrote his partners. "We can leap the Iron Curtain and they will hear my sermons in the Russian language."[78] The broadcasts began in April, when Oral signed a one-year contract with the Boston station.[79] By 1959, Oral was tinkering with the idea of building a number of short-wave stations "powerful enough to cover the entire earth." While he was currently broadcasting over several such stations, his representatives found it increasingly difficult to buy time because of the opposition of foreign governments and other "religious groups." Perhaps the answer, Oral proposed to his partners in 1959, was the construction of a series of stations "that we can control ourselves." He wrote: "The Lord actually gave me this plan as far back as 1948. Now he has told me the hour has arrived for it to be put into effect." He estimated that the project would cost $3,000,000 and urged his partners to be ready to pay the price.[80]

The building of the Healing Waters radio network required both skill in marketing the programs to radio stations and new techniques in systematic fund raising. The first of these problems was handled by Pete White and his advertising agency in Tulsa, and the second was orchestrated by Lee Braxton. White was crucial in designing the format of the program and in marketing it. "They know radio," wrote Oral in 1950, "what stations reach the most people and where we can make our radio offerings buy the most time to carry this message of Bible Deliverance to increasing thousands."[81] Oral early discovered "that the broadcast just couldn't be carried on without a good radio Agency back of it. Much prejudice has been broken down by our Agency which is thoroughly sold on the ministry of Brother Roberts."[82]

The other key to the growth of Oral's radio network was Lee Braxton, who seemed ever present in the 1950s, although he did not live in Tulsa. The "good judgment of Brother Braxton" was behind countless decisions. It was Braxton's "sponsorship" plan which went into operation in mid-1949 that provided the financial base for the expansion. Getting local people to support the program in an area for a stipulated length of time proved such a popular idea, wrote Braxton, that in "a short time there were so many good people interested in securing the program on a station in their area that my desk was covered with mail. Some of them were so insistent that I found myself working almost day and night."[83] Once the program had begun in an area, the organization kept careful tabs on which stations prompted "enough offerings to pay the full radio cost."[84] Braxton reached out in other innovative ways to find radio sponsors, including a call in 1951 for fifty "business and professional men to meet me in Tulsa in April" to discuss the future expansion of the Healing Waters network. The "summation of the meeting" was that "the radio is the best means of reaching the masses of people with this powerful message of Bible deliverance."[85] By the end of the decade, the radio program had declined in significance, but in 1959 Oral announced that the expansion of his radio network would still play a "big role" in his future plans.[86]

In addition to expanding his radio network, Oral was constantly probing for other ways to get his message before the public. One remarkably successful project was the production of a film entitled *Venture into Faith* in 1952. The film was produced by Pete White, who secured the services of Herb A. Lightman, "a director whose skill in motion picture production was equalled by his sincerity and understanding, his compassion and deep feeling for this great work." The film featured a professional cast in a story about a couple whose young son was stricken with tuberculosis. "What happens to the Collins family after they have attended two of the Roberts meetings furnishes the action for this powerful, gripping story which will be understood by everyone who has been faced with tragedy," announced producer Pete White.[87] More important than the story, the film featured Oral preaching and praying for the sick in his Birmingham, Alabama crusade in May 1952. The result, advertised *Healing Waters,* was not only "the world's first Bible Deliverance picture" but also "the most powerful religious film ever produced."[88]

The organization announced that the film could not be "shown in theaters, but only in auditoriums, churches, schools, etc."; a smashing success from the beginning, it was shown in pentecostal churches across the nation.[89] Early in 1953 Oral announced that the movie was "exceeding all expectations . . . being shown to packed audiences everywhere with many, many souls being saved." Whenever the film was shown, contributions were solicited to help pay its $80,000 production costs.[90] By 1954, thirty-five copies of the movie were in circulation, and it had been dubbed in German.[91] Widely circulated in the United States in the early 1950s, *Venture into Faith* continued to be used for years as a missionary tool, and was shown thousands of times throughout the world.[92] Its popularity probably peaked in 1954, when it was reportedly shown 2,131 times to audiences numbering nearly 500,000, resulting in 22,258 conversions.[93]

By the end of 1954, all other phases of the Roberts ministry began to diminish in significance because of Oral's decision to televise his campaigns. Early in the 1950s, Oral grasped the potential of television; he was impressed by Billy Graham's early use of the medium, but, of course, the costs were intimidating. At the beginning of 1952, in *Healing Waters,* he floated the idea of a program, noting that it would probably cost a million dollars to sponsor a broadcast on fifty stations for a year. Such a sum was staggering, but by the beginning of the next year, Oral announced that he was "working very hard" on starting a television series, having "consulted with the TV people both in New York City, Chicago, and Los Angeles." "The Lord is pressing me about TV," wrote Oral. "The devil must not steal this great medium from God's people." He urged his readers to "pray right now for Healing Waters to go on TV before the end of 1953."[94]

Oral did not quite make that deadline, but in the fall of 1953 he did go to Hollywood to film the first segments of a television series, which was shown for the first time on January 10, 1954. Oral and Evelyn worked arduously filming twenty-six thirty-minute programs entitled "Your Faith Is Power." The cost of the filming was $104,000, most of which was borrowed.[95] Oral was exhilarated "about this great move for God." "Evelyn and I have worked the hardest ever to get these programs made," he wrote, "but it was a joyous work. We do not regret one moment we spent under those powerful lights pouring out our souls for the glory of God."[96]

The format of the television program was much like that of the radio broadcast. Oral believed that the telecast was "more like my ministry in the tent campaigns than anything I have ever done."[97] G. H. Montgomery previewed the programs for *Healing Waters*: "You who know Brother Roberts, know that he strives for perfection in everything he undertakes. His television services will be no exception to this rule." Montgomery continued:

> The announcer briefly describes the service to follow, and then introduces Sister Roberts, who reads one or two testimonies from people who have been healed under Brother Roberts' ministry. Following the testimonies Brother Roberts is introduced and preaches for twenty-two minutes, one of the most dynamic sermons I have ever heard him preach. . . . Following the salvation prayer, Brother Roberts prays for the sick. He has the sick place their hands upon their chest over their heart and he prays for their deliverance. Then he commands the "tormenting disease" to come out. No one is left out of the prayer. He prays for "this man and that woman" as if he were right there with you. He remembers "this little child" and "that person in the wheel chair."[98]

After six months the program was scrapped. Montgomery later reported that "it was a good program and the results were encouraging, but Brother Roberts was not satisfied."[99] In fact, the format simply had not worked; looking back, Evelyn labeled it a "very stilted program."[100] The cancellation of the series did not mean Oral had lost his interest in television, however; he remained convinced that "more souls can be reached through TV than through any other means."[101] By June, Roberts was already hard at work recasting the program into a format which would arouse national interest and protest.

Oral understood from the beginning that he needed to reproduce as nearly as possible the atmosphere of the crusades. That was difficult, probably impossible, in a studio. No performer was ever more sensitive to his surroundings than Oral; he needed the presence of people.[102] The unsuccessful series was Oral's introduction to the importance of atmosphere—it was not to be his last. Nor was it the last time that he would boldly discard a method which did not meet his standards.

The man most responsible for the new television format was Oral's friend Rex Humbard. Humbard was the first of the modern television evangelists to perceive the importance of the new medium, and he had begun broadcasting the services of his church in Akron, Ohio in 1952.[103] As Oral prepared for a campaign in Akron in March 1954, Humbard urged his old friend to film the tent services for television. "The NBC people have told me that it can't be done," retorted Oral, but Humbard insisted: "Well it can be. Don't let them tell you no. Just do it."[104] Still rebuffed by NBC, Oral turned to Pathescope Productions of New York City, a production company which had been experimenting with a new fast film "so high powered that fast action pictures can be taken with but very little auxiliary lighting." Three pilot films were made in Akron at a cost of $42,000, and the result was so impressive that Oral immediately began revising his entire television concept. Not only were three sermons filmed, but "altar calls, healing lines, actual miracles, the coming and going of the great crowds, the reaction of the congregations—all these were put on film."[105] A medium had been discovered that was capable of introducing the nation to the remarkable phenomenon which had gripped the pentecostal subculture for nearly a decade.

The filming was expensive, but Oral was enthusiastic about the results. He delayed returning to television until February 6, 1955; by that time he had purchased nearly $500,000 worth of production equipment and had made a backlog of programs for distribution. He was convinced that he had found the way to reach out beyond the crusades. Oral recognized that in his campaigns "the saturation point is being reached." He fretted under the restraints: "God awakened me at night. He has led me to take long walks in the woods so he could talk to me." Now he had received the "blueprint and course of action"— he must take the "holy atmosphere" of the tent campaigns into the homes of America.[106]

The new Oral Roberts television programs probably came as close as was technically possible to doing just that, to catching on film the excitement and spiritual anticipation that pervaded the big tent. The program began as Oral "stepped to the front of the beautiful platform in his great tent cathedral and announced dramatically, 'My name is Oral Roberts. I am a minister of the gospel.'" In the early broadcasts, a curious ritual followed, in which a notarized document was presented, signed by a local judge, swearing that he had been present at the filming and that "the events and incidents to follow occurred on the spot in a meeting conducted in the great tent cathedral."[107] Oral was conscious that he was the television "pioneer" of healing revivalism, and "to initiate the first action we felt that we should have some sort of believability. . . . [The judges] watched the entire proceedings and then I could sit down before them and say to the public, this is unrehearsed, this is exactly as it is. And the judge then would put his name on it. I think it gave a word to the nation that this was not staged or pre-arranged in any manner."[108] Next Bob DeWeese introduced Oral, and he preached a brief message. The audience then saw the altar call, with "hundreds of people marching down the aisles of the great cathedral." Then came the televising of the healing line, featuring Oral's lively chatter, his fervent prayers, and his magnificently expressive face. The television audience "had what thousands of people, even among those who attend the campaigns, never have—a front row seat. They saw the evangelist in action, the line passing before him, the power of God in operation as sick and afflicted people turned their faith loose at the touch of Brother Roberts' hand and were instantly healed by God's power." Then, in a dramatic finale, Oral reappeared before the cameras to pray a "healing prayer" for those watching in their homes. Asking them to place their hands over their hearts or on their television sets, Oral extended his healing touch into the homes of millions.[109]

The televising of the tent crusades created practical and logistical problems which took time to solve. Not only was the pace of the service slowed by the grinding of the cameras, causing particularly the healing line to be shortened, but, perhaps more important, it was difficult to preserve the spiritual aura under the tent in the presence of the cameras. It was the "anointing of His Holy Spirit" which Oral felt under the tent that made him want to bring the cameras there. He told a crusade audience in 1957: "I tried to make television programs by going into a studio. There I had no audience . . . and the cameras turned on me and they said, 'Now we want you to do what you do in your tent.' Well, I tried and I couldn't do it. I just could not produce like that."[110] But once the cameras came to the tent, Oral had to persuade his audiences to "co-operate by being themselves and worshipping God as though the cameras were not there" so that the program would "capture on film the true spirit of the crusade." Never were his powers in controlling his audiences more apparent than in those crusades when Oral competed with the cameras for the attention of the people and captured for the world a glimpse of the expectation that pervaded the healing revival. It was, in Oral's words, one of his most successful "selling jobs."[111]

In addition, Oral had to convince his pentecostal followers that the films carried the same healing power as his live presence. The Roberts organization repeatedly assured that "the anointing will be projected into the homes of the people who see these services on their television screens."[112] But, in the long run, it was results that silenced the criticisms of insiders. Healing testimonials began to pour in as the television broadcast spread, including one of the most striking and well-publicized cases in the entire history of the Roberts ministry. On Monday, May 2, 1955, the newspapers in Wichita Falls, Texas carried a front-page story about a young air force sergeant's wife under the headline "Paralyzed, She Walks after Prayer." The story of Anna Williams was remarkable; it was picked up by the wire services, published across the country, and featured by ABC commentator Paul Harvey. The story was simple and powerful. Anna Williams had been crippled by a series of misfortunes: in 1951 she broke her leg in an automobile accident; twenty months later she was stricken by polio; and in 1953 she was "crippled by spinalitis." Since the onset of the last disease, she had been "paralyzed from the waist down" and had been confined to a wheelchair.[113] While watching Oral's telecast on Sunday, May 1, Anna placed her hand over her heart during the healing prayer and, after its conclusion, asked her husband to help her stand. She began walking, tentatively at first, then with more confidence, finally borrowing high heels from a friend to dance about the room. Anna Williams became a celebrity in Wichita Falls, one of the most powerful testimonials ever received by the Roberts ministry, and the premier validation of the early television ministry.[114] Oral was "stunned" when he read the story, and he was quick to take advantage of the publicity.[115]

The inauguration of the new television series was clearly the most important innovation by the Roberts ministry since Oral's decision to begin tent crusades. It was a frighteningly expensive undertaking, with regard to both production costs and the purchase of air time, and Oral began carefully and tentatively. In January 1955, Lee Braxton announced that time had been purchased on 31 stations, but the first projected schedule included no major markets.[116] By the time the first program was broadcast in February, however, the number of stations had reached 61, including New York City, Chicago, and Los Angeles.[117] As in the development of the radio network, the Roberts organization fought two battles simultaneously: first, persuading television stations to accept the controversial program, and second, urging Oral's partners to provide the necessary funds.[118] The initial cost for air time was $8,350.89 per week; by the middle of 1955, the television network had grown to 91 stations, costing $11,592.04 per week.[119] The network continued to grow through the decade; by the end of 1957, Oral's program was shown on 135 of the nation's 500 television stations, reaching, according to the ministry's calculations, "80 per cent of the television audience every week," and it was also broadcast in Canada and the Philippines.[120]

The initiation of the television program had a stunning impact on the Roberts ministry. Immediately after the first telecast, Lee Braxton announced that "letters by the thousands have poured into the Tulsa office from enthusiastic viewers, telling how God blessed the people through the television program. Some of them were saved, some of them were healed, as they sat in their living rooms."[121] G. H. Montgomery later recalled that the "mail in the Tulsa office shot up 66 per cent in thirty days," adding incredulously: "In Tulsa we live very close to the miraculous all the time. We become accustomed to the idea of people being healed by God's power. But the testimonies that began to pour in from the new TV audience threatened to tax even our credulity."[122] "The day we went on television," Oral told the Tulsa Kiwanis Club in 1956, "there was a great change in our whole organization."[123] Oral's program never rivaled "I Love Lucy" in the television ratings, but, wrote Bob Foresman of the *Tulsa Tribune*, "in many areas he is giving top programs serious competition."[124]

Oral struggled with the financial burden the television series imposed; the new medium proved to be the financial graveyard of many aspiring evangelists who tried to emulate his success. The early stations in his network were financed by adapting the sponsorship plan which had proven so successful in expanding the radio network. The ministry carefully outlined the cost of buying time in each city and asked for sponsors who would guarantee the first thirteen weeks "until the people have the opportunity to see and hear Brother Roberts on TV." In areas where the time was relatively cheap, such as Fresno and Amarillo, the price of $81 per week was quickly pledged.[125] More difficult were the major markets, such as WABC-TV in New York City, where Oral signed a fifty-two-week contract at a cost of $502 per Sunday.[126] While Roberts received a few substantial contributions, such as the $3,000 given by Mrs. Sadie R. McArdle to sponsor six weeks of the program in New York, most of the money to fund the television series came in small contributions.[127] But the sponsorship technique worked admirably to get the program started, and the massive mail response quickly turned television into a financial asset rather than a liability.

Probably more critical had been the task of raising the large production costs. Wrestling with that problem, Oral happened onto a fund-raising technique which was to have a lasting impact on his ministry. Burdened with the need for $42,000 for the initial pilot films during his tent crusade in Akron, Ohio, Oral suddenly challenged his crusade audience one evening to supply 420 donors of $100. In return for their gifts, Oral pledged to pray that the donors would receive their money back within twelve months, and, if they did not, his organization would refund the contribution. "No one had heard of that," recalled Oral later, "I certainly had not. But I felt it was from the Lord." It was the beginning of the "Blessing Pact" concept; in "minutes" 420 people in Akron accepted the challenge.[128] Oral soon expanded this technique, with slight modification, to raise $500,000 to purchase cameras and pay for the production of the first fifty-two segments of the program. He asked 5,000 of his partners to give $100 immediately to defray these costs and in return promised them ten-year subscriptions to his magazine, and, more important, pledged to enter into a "prayer-pact" with them asking "that God will especially prosper you in your job, or your business, or your profession."[129]

SUCCESSFUL as the Roberts radio and television programs were in expanding the ministry's influence, Oral's most crucial link with his partners remained his publications. His monthly magazine, which continued to feature the campaigns and an endless barrage of healing and conversion testimonials, was an amazing success story. In every campaign new subscribers were added; by 1950 the subscription list had reached 50,000, and in 1952 the circulation passed 100,000. Then, with the advent of the television series, the circulation exploded, to 355,000 in 1955 and 1,000,000 by the middle of 1956.[130] The circulation stabilized at that level for the remainder of the decade.

The organization also diversified its publications in the 1950s, beginning in 1956 with the publication of *Oral Roberts' True Stories* comic books, which featured Oral's own healing and stories from the campaigns.[131] Millions of comic books were printed before the series was discontinued in 1961. In 1959, Oral also began writing a weekly column for distribution to newspapers; it reportedly was printed by 674 newspapers. Modeled on Billy Graham's popular column, Oral's articles appeared mostly in small-town newspapers.[132] More successful was *Daily Blessing*, "a devotional magazine" which began publication in 1959 and proved to be a popular and enduring addition to the ministry's literature.[133]

Roberts's monthly magazine went through a significant series of name changes in the 1950s, changes that told much about the evolving goals and self-perceptions of the ministry. It continued to be issued under the name *Healing Waters* until September 1953, when the title was changed to *America's Healing Magazine*. That change was instigated by the naivete of many of Oral's supporters, who persisted in requesting samples of the "healing waters." "Many letters have had to be written in answer to inquiries about the matter," wrote G. H. Montgomery; he hoped the name change would "eliminate the confusion."[134] *America's Healing Magazine* seemed an adequate title until early 1956, when the expanding overseas emphasis of the ministry led to shortening the title to *Healing*. That name was used for only a few months before a final switch was made to *Abundant Life*. Oral believed that he had finally found "the right name" for this important link with his supporters, a title which properly expressed his current understanding of his ministry. The new name was a part of Oral's general effort in the late 1950s to rid himself of the single-dimensional "healer" image: "After going on television where I minister in millions of homes each week, we have discovered that many of the people have gotten the mistaken impression that our entire ministry consists of prayer for the healing of the sick. As people who attend our campaigns know, the winning of lost souls to Christ and helping them use their faith for the more abundant life offered by Jesus Christ is our main ministry."[135]

By far the most important influence on Oral's publications in the 1950s, and perhaps the most important addition to his staff during the decade, was G. H. Mongomery, who moved to Tulsa in 1951. Montgomery was regarded as one of the "greatest preachers" and "greatest writers" in the Pentecostal Holiness church; until October 1949 he edited the *Pentecostal Holiness Advocate*, resigning under pressure from denominational leaders who accused him of personal misconduct.[136] Oral either did not believe or chose to ignore the charges against Montgomery; the editor had been helpful to him in earlier years, and Oral admired his talent. With Montgomery's addition, Oral had secured the services of one of the finest writers and best editors in the pentecostal world. By May 1953, Montgomery was listed as "Managing Editor" of the magazine, and in 1958 he assumed the title of "Director of Publications." W. T. Jeffers, who assisted Montgomery for a number of years, noted that Roberts both "appreciated and respected" Montgomery and that he "leans more heavily upon this man than perhaps he himself realizes."[137] No other individual in the history of the ministry had the same independent control over Oral's publications as Montgomery. Montgomery understood Oral's beliefs and objectives, and he threw himself selflessly into building an effective publication program.

Montgomery was only one of the important new members of the Roberts team in the 1950s. Forced to make countless complicated business decisions in a time schedule seriously curtailed by his travel schedule, Oral desperately sought able executives. His talent pool remained limited; he could employ only those who understood and shared his vision. But he did increasingly reach out beyond the Pentecostal Holiness church into the wider pentecostal world that he came to know so well in the 1950s.

The most important changes in the Roberts organization in the 1950s came early in the decade with the replacement of two key members of the crusade team. In January 1951, the four chief officers in the organization were: Office Manager, Manford Engel; Manager of Roberts Meetings, O. E. Sproull; Manager of Equipment, L. V. Roberts; and Director of Healing Waters, Lee Braxton. Engel and Braxton were still important administrators at the end of the decade, but within a few months both Sproull and Vaden Roberts had retired and turned their jobs over to men who played key roles in the Roberts ministry into the 1980s. In March 1951, Sproull was succeeded as Oral's associate evangelist by Robert F. DeWeese; Collins Steele joined the team at about the same time, and in 1952, when Vaden decided he could no longer travel regularly with the team, Collins became the equipment manager. The two men became Oral's most loyal and trusted friends.

Sproull's departure from the team in 1951 was both a shock and a setback. G. H. Montgomery recalled that Oral and Sproull were "almost inseparable. It was difficult to think of one without the other."[138] Oral believed that Sproull "just wore himself out and had to have some rest," an explanation which clearly had some merit.[139] Others, on the contrary, felt that Sproull was "hale and hearty, but he thought he saw the apex of the ministry."[140] He "came along as far as his vision would permit him to go," surmised his friend Harold Paul.[141] As criticism of the healing evangelists grew in the early 1950s, many wondered if their organizations could survive; no one in 1951 could have predicted the dramatic impact that television would have on the Roberts ministry.[142]

When Sproull insisted that he was leaving, Oral asked him to recommend a replacement. Sproull urged Oral to contact Bob DeWeese, who had been the chairman of the sponsoring pastors in the Tacoma, Washington campaign in August 1949. DeWeese was in the midst of a revival of his own in Pasadena, California when Oral called him, but he accepted immediately and joined the team in the first meeting under the new 10,000-seat tent in Tampa. DeWeese was a minister in the small pentecostal Open Bible church, having been reared in the Foursquare Gospel church founded by Aimee Semple McPherson and converted under the ministry of Dr. Charles Price, one of the most respected of the first-generation pentecostal healing revivalists.[143] He brought to the ministry a broad and irenic understanding of pentecostalism and a wide circle of acquaintances, especially in the West.

The hiring of DeWeese was one of the most fortuitous appointments Oral ever made. "His life is an effervescent flow of enthusiasm," wrote G. H. Montgomery, "his work a dynamic force for good."[144] And he was all of that. Young, energetic, articulate, bubbling with good humor and wit, DeWeese was the perfect "warmup" man for Oral's evening service. He could coax an audience along, and he could quickly harness one that was unruly; he unobtrusively managed the entire service, leaving Oral free to preach and pray. Oral later recalled: "Bob DeWeese's presence, the sound of his voice, and the enthusiasm of his spirit had a way of capturing the people. His ability to ready the people for my message and the healing of the sick always amazed me."[145] By the mid-1950s, virtually the entire management of the campaigns fell on DeWeese, coordinating the sponsoring pastors, training the workers, and managing the services. Those who knew the business best considered his work "a masterpiece of generalship."[146]

Of course, DeWeese was also a preacher of considerable ability. He conducted morning services during the crusades, at first in a local church chosen by the sponsoring pastors, but by the mid-1950s his audiences had become so large that the services were conducted in the prayer tent which seated 3,000 people. "Frequently," wrote G. H. Montgomery, "the tent is packed and jammed with those who come to hear Bob DeWeese's sparkling sermons, to laugh at his witticisms and to take encouragement from his words of faith."[147]

The secret to the long and fruitful partnership between Oral and DeWeese lay in their personal relationship. It was close, candid, and yet deferential. "Of all the men who work with Oral Roberts," observed G. H. Montgomery, "none is closer to him than his campaign manager. Yet, never once in these four years has familiarity bred contempt. He calls him *Rev.* in private, but there is no lack of respect in the way he says the word." Some insiders were "puzzled" as to how DeWeese could submerge his own "dynamic personality" and "live in the shadow" of Oral Roberts. While Oral denied that DeWeese's role required such sublimation, to some extent that was the sacrifice required of everyone who worked for Oral—but especially of his associate evangelist.[148] For all his talent and energy, DeWeese never forgot whose charisma drew the crowds; he never ceased to marvel at the changes the telephone call from Oral had wrought in his own life—the challenges, excitement, and fulfillment it had brought to him—and, above all, and in spite of his intimate personal relationship with Oral, year after year he united with the audiences under the tent as they fell under the spell of Oral's ministry. Night after night he stood directly to the left of the man in the chair, and as much as anyone under the tent he stood in awe of him.[149]

The addition of Collins Steele to the crusade team was not so visible as that of DeWeese, but the quiet, soft-spoken Alabamian was to become, in a deferential sort of way, Oral's most intimate and loyal friend. Steele, a member of the Pentecostal Holiness church in Mobile, resigned his job with Alcoa in the spring of 1951, and he and his wife, Lois, began traveling with the crusade team. Partly because they remained childless, the Steeles for the next fifteen years lived the life of gypsies as they traveled from one crusade site to the next, making the local arrangements for the campaigns, securing the necessary permits, arranging for traffic control and security, training the ushers, supervising the transporting and erection of the huge tents, and solving any physical problems that arose during the crusade. While Lois managed the "Million Souls Stand" at the rear of the tent, securing subscriptions to *Healing Waters* and selling books, Collins roamed the tent, dealing with the traffic police, fire marshals, problems in the public address system, and the placement of television cameras, keeping order in the prayer line, and quashing any disturbance that might erupt.[150] In perhaps his most important role, Steele became the closest thing that Oral had to a bodyguard. Strong yet gentle, unswervingly loyal to Oral, it was Steele who would whisk Roberts away from the meetings in the evenings, sometimes supporting the exhausted evangelist, protecting him from the irrepressible mobs. He was Oral's "Johnathan," the solidest rock in the ministry's foundation.

The office staff remained stable through most of the 1950s. Manford Engel continued to provide adequate management in the office, and he was aided by a growing group of able assistants, such as public relations expert Hart R. Armstrong.[151] In 1949, Oscar Moore became a member of the Healing Waters board and moved to Tulsa in 1960 as "resident trustee," giving Oral a trusted friend in the home office. Lee Braxton became a fixture in the Tulsa office, although he did not move until 1960. These men provided stability and dependability during this period when Oral was almost constantly away from Tulsa. All three were figures from Oral's Pentecostal Holiness past; he could trust them, and they believed in the message he preached. All showed considerable capacity for growth, but by the end of the decade, the expansion of the Roberts organization increasingly called for new managerial techniques and skills.

Two far-reaching organizational changes were made in 1957, one apparent at the time, the other to have its impact a decade later. First was a reorganization in 1957 which changed Healing Waters, Inc., the original nonprofit religious corporation founded in 1948, into the Oral Roberts Evangelistic Association, Inc. The original trust was aimed at winning the loyalty of the pentecostal denominations with its provision of funds for retired ministers."[152] In the early

1950s, a parade of pentecostal leaders "whole-heartedly accepted the plan" as they were "called in to examine and approve the Trust from time to time."[153] By 1957, the change in Oral's crusades and his redefined goals had made the old trust archaic. His relations with the pentecostal denominations had sputtered through years of bitter recrimination, and the old arrangement simply was no longer reasonable. *Abundant Life* magazine explained that the "new name reflects the scope and nature of the Sevenfold World Outreach ministry of the organization spearheaded by Oral Roberts."[154] Like the change in the name of the magazine and the shifting emphasis in the campaigns, the new organization was the product of the thorough reappraisal which reshaped the Roberts ministry in the late 1950s.

The new Oral Roberts Evangelistic Association proved to be a permanent institution. Controlling the assets of the association was a six-person board, including Oral and Evelyn. The other charter trustees were four of Oral's most trusted friends and helpers—Oscar Moore; Demos Shakarian, influential Los Angeles dairyman; Dr. John Barton, a Connecticut dentist; and Nick Timko, a Detroit businessman and faithful Roberts contributor. Of course, Oral made all major decisions, but legally the organization was under the control of an independent and self-perpetuating board.[155]

In the long run, perhaps the most important organizational move made by Oral in the 1950s was the hiring of twenty-four-year-old Al Bush. Bush was a serious-minded, bright, articulate, and handsome youngster who had just worked his way through Drake University and graduated with a major in philosophy. Intense and thoughtful, fascinated by Alfred North Whitehead's philosophy, Bush had discovered that he had a propensity for management and was intent on finishing an MBA degree when he was contacted by Bob DeWeese about coming to Tulsa. Bush had grown up in a congregation where DeWeese had pastored in Iowa, and the never-ending hunger for talent in the Roberts organization brought him to Oral's attention. Al Bush turned down the first offer made to him by Roberts, but Oral persisted, as he always does when he knows what he wants, and ultimately persuaded Bush to move to Tulsa. The two established an immediate rapport. "He felt like he could mold me, I think," recalled Al Bush later, "and he was right." Oral saw in Bush those qualities which he instinctively knew he needed—brilliance, dedication, business acumen, and an unerring moral integrity. Oral told the young Bush, with an almost prophetic sense of judgment, "Ultimately I want you to run this."[156] It would be a while before that happened, but the time would come when Al Bush would be the most important non-Roberts ever to be associated with the ministry.

THE GROWTH of the Roberts organization, as well as its increasing sophistication, both allowed and encouraged further diversification. Beginning in January 1955, the ministry's programs were labeled the Seven World Outreaches, a term contributed by Braxton. Oral told the readers of his magazine that "while driving down a beautiful, scenic highway in Oregon a few weeks ago," God revealed the outreach program to him "in less than ten minutes." The Seven World Outreaches announced in 1955 included: first, continued tent crusades (with an increased number planned for the "foreign field"); second, the new television series; third, "a world radio network of 1,000 stations"; fourth, "a special work among the Jewish people"; fifth, "a special ministry among the American Indians"; sixth, "a very large and special work among the world's children"; and seventh, "a missionary venture in reverse," which would bring foreign nationals to America to learn of "Bible deliverance." The world outreach program marked, at least conceptually, the internationalizing of the Roberts ministry. Up to that time, Oral's crusades had been entirely American. By 1955, as the American revival began to perceptibly falter, the more marginal healing evangelists turned to foreign evangelism and the support of mission projects to raise funds. Fittingly, Oral was the last evangelist to appeal for support as a missionary, because his was the strongest of the domestic ministries. But by 1955, the time had come to broaden his appeal. He wrote: "Now my time has come. My ministry in America must not stop. Instead, it must be extended beyond our shores, leaping over boundary lines of other nations, reaching for the Jew first and the world of the Gentiles. . . . I must preach the gospel to the total population of this earth."[157]

The Seven World Outreach programs shifted from time to time. In 1956, Oral outlined his plans in more evangelistic terms; the seven outreaches were American campaigns, foreign campaigns, radio programs, television films, Bible and literature distribution, foreign circulation of films, and "special evangelistic committees" to be established in foreign countries.[158] In general, all of these projects remained visible through the remainder of the decade as instruments to achieve the soul-saving mission of the ministry.[159]

Some of Oral's projects never progressed far, which gave detractors cause to charge that they were no more than fund-raising ruses. Oral's "special burden" for the "children of the world" resulted only in a spate of publications aimed at children in the late 1950s. His "missionary-in-reverse project," designed to bring foreign nationals to America for training, did not bear fruit in the 1950s, but it was an idea that Oral never entirely abandoned. It would be revived in later years in a variety of forms as Oral continued to probe for ways to extend the message of God's goodness into the farthest reaches of the globe.

Oral's outreach to the American Indians was a natural outgrowth of his conscious pride in his Indian heritage. In August 1955, he scheduled a crusade in Billings, Montana, and in the midst of it he designated one evening "all Indian night." He was invited to preach on the Crow Indian reservation and afterwards was treated to a "buffalo barbecue held on the reservation."[160] These small attentions brought Oral strong support from the American Indian community, but the Roberts organization never formulated a substantial "outreach" to them. In 1957, Oral reported that "the main thing we have been doing is placing our television films and tape recordings of my sermons and prayers, along with our literature, in the hands of our partners who are going into the reservations and from home to home among the Indians."[161] Not until 1959 did Oral schedule another major Indian crusade, this time a three-day meeting in Window Rock, Arizona. Invited by the Navajo Tribal Council to conduct the All-Indian crusade, the campaign was touted to partners as a "missionary venture" because the Indians were "poor, and the meeting, although the largest of its kind ever conducted, did not nearly pay its expenses."[162]

More extensive, more visible, and more controversial was Oral's outreach to Israel. His interest in Israel was both old and, no doubt, sincere. Before they were married, Oral and Evelyn discussed his "vision to take the gospel to the Jews."[163] When Oral finally set foot in Israel for the first time, in 1953 (his first trip outside the United States), he avidly visited every important Christian shrine in the country with a seventeen-pound "specially made, battery powered portable recorder . . . slung over his shoulder" to record his impressions for his American partners. He gave minute descriptions of his feelings at every stop, solemnly confiding that his visit to the empty tomb was "the most sacred moment of my life."[164] When he returned to America, G. H. Montgomery described Oral as "a man transformed, endued, anointed."[165] Returning from a third visit in 1959, Oral announced that the nation had cast a "spell" over him: "There is a feeling akin to awe that sweeps over me when I step on the soil of Israel. My entire being seems to vibrate with the presence of God."[166] Oral was a devout premillennialist and believed he was walking not only in the midst of fulfilled prophecy but in the land where momentous happenings were about to begin, including the conversion of the Jewish nation to Christianity. By 1956, his plans for extending his work to Israel were given increased publicity. "I feel," he wrote, "that the success or failure of my ministry hinges on the Jewish work. . . . There is no revival among the Jews. The time has come for it, but it hasn't happened."[167]

The Roberts Jewish Outreach was shaped and guided by Myron Sackett, who joined the organization in mid-1955 and remained as director of the Jewish program until his death in 1967. Sackett was a pentecostal evangelist who early in his life had managed Aimee Semple McPherson's campaigns, but, beginning in 1945, he felt a call to "take the Gospel" to the Jewish people.[168] Between 1945 and 1949, Sackett made a number of trips to Israel trying to formulate a strategy for accomplishing that task, and concluded that the best hope was to get copies of the Bible into the hands of as many Jewish people as possible. In 1951 Sackett founded an organization, Christian Friends of Israel, Inc., with a fivefold purpose:

> 1. Distributing the Holy Scripture to Jewish people, and presenting the true scriptural interpretation of Jesus Christ, the Messiah. 2. To impress Gentile Christians of all denominations, of their biblical responsibility to assist in the work of interpreting Christ to the Jewish people. 3. To encourage a better understanding between Jews and Gentiles, and discourage anti-Semitism, wherever found. 4. To assist the many thousands of immigrants (refugees) now coming into Israel. . . . 5. To fulfill Jesus' command to preach the Gospel to every creature.[169]

Sackett was introduced to Oral by Bob DeWeese in January 1953 during a crusade in Phoenix, and Sackett explained to Oral his vision of distributing Bibles among the Jews. Oral told Sackett, "Doc, when I was a young man, the Lord impressed me about a ministry in the Holy Land." Oral loaned Sackett a copy of *Venture into Faith*, and he made German subtitles for the film before showing it during a tour of Europe and Israel.[170] Oral was delighted with Sackett's work; the friendship between the two grew, and in December Sackett served as Oral's guide in Israel when he made his first trip abroad.

In April 1954, Oral invited Sackett to integrate his work into the Roberts ministry as one of the World Outreaches, and Sackett gratefully accepted the offer. Sackett was delighted, believing that Oral had the "same vision and burden as I do to take the gospel to the Jewish people around the world" and recognizing that Oral's fund-raising abilities far exceeded his own.[171] Some believed that Sackett's vision was used by Roberts as a fund-raising gimmick, but the old warrior never seemed to think that was the case. He believed, probably correctly, that he could never have accomplished alone what he did as a part of the Roberts ministry.

More difficult to evaluate is the long-range impact of the highly publicized outreach to Israel. Depending on one's perspective, the accomplishments of the outreach seem both minimal and somewhat impressive. Sackett's plan was simply to distribute Hebrew Bibles to Jews all over the world, including in Israel. The Roberts ministry frequently solicited funds for printing the Bibles (which was done in Sweden), but the most difficult chore was to find ways to give them away. In 1957, Oral reported: "While we have distributed only a few hundred Bibles in the Hebrew language in the last year, we have been working with all the skill at our command to be ready to give more Bibles when the door opens."[172] It was a testimony to the ingenuity of Sackett that at the time of his death Oral estimated that the organization had "placed more than 150,000 Hebrew Bibles in Jewish homes in nearly 25 countries."[173]

To some extent, the Roberts organization even succeeded in distributing Bibles in Israel, including in school and public libraries.[174] During his 1959 trip to the Holy Land, Oral had a brief interview with Prime Minister David Ben-Gurion and left awestruck and elated. As he entered the prime minister's office, the diminutive, white-haired statesman "took my breath away by asking the first question": "Mr. Roberts, as a Christian evangelist, what are you trying to do with people? I don't mean what are you trying to get them to believe, but what are you trying to get them to be and to do?" Taken aback, Oral answered, "I am teaching people that they cannot love God without also loving their fellow man." Ben-Gurion "smiled," and the two chatted amicably about the need for practical religion and the importance of the Bible. Oral presented the prime minister with a copy of his organization's Hebrew Bible, "prayed with the Prime Minister and took my leave."[175] Oral's lack of dogmatism, his genuine respect and admiration for Israel and the Jewish community in America, and his warm cordiality toward those with whom he disagreed opened doors for him in Israel. But in spite of all that, the objectives of Oral's Israel outreach remained quite limited and only minimally successful. He certainly never approached the goal of putting "a Hebrew Bible in every Jewish home in Israel and the world, and to preach to them in Israel and elsewhere."[176]

Probably more important, though impossible to measure, was the impact of the outreach designed to circulate literature, tape recordings, and films throughout the world. The organization repeatedly unveiled ambitious plans for the free circulation of teaching materials in foreign countries. In 1957, Oral announced that he hoped "to print and distribute at least one piece of literature for every person in the world during the next 10 years."[177] While no such grand scheme was ever accomplished, much was done. In early 1957, the director of the "literature outreach program" made an "extensive tour of 20 Latin-American countries" to discuss with missionaries and ministers the distribution of free literature.[178] In 1959, the organization announced that "literature saturation crusades" had been completed in "several small countries in which we placed a piece of our Christ-centered literature in the homes of at least 90 per cent of the people."[179] By the end of the decade, the organization reported that a dozen publications had been translated into Spanish, Chinese, Japanese, Arabic, Swedish, Serbo-Croatian, Kanarese, Italian, Russian, and Indonesian and that plans were underway for translations into "many other languages."[180] The ministry had also begun wide distribution of the television films. According to Al Bush, "We had some 300 different films in 16 languages, which were circulated throughout Central and South America and Africa in various languages and dialects."[181]

While it is difficult to assess the effect of the overseas media blitz, it is clear that such projects, particularly when combined with his radio broadcasts, made Oral's name known around the world. When Oral held his first campaign in South Africa in 1955, he was stunned at the size of the crowds, most of whom knew of him because of his radio program. "I am told," he wrote in 1955, "by competent people our broadcast is the most listened to half-hour in South and Central Africa."[182] The literature and the broadcasts had attracted sufficient supporters by 1954 for Roberts to employ representatives in England, Northern Ireland, South Africa, Australia, and New Zealand, and overseas partners had begun to sustain many foreign broadcasts with their own contributions.[183] After visiting the Philippines in 1956, Oral returned home "amazed at the vast number of people who listen to our radio program."[184]

Oral's desire to extend his influence around the world, and the need to project an international image to his partners, demanded that he begin overseas crusading in the mid-1950s. Others, such as Tulsa evangelist T. L. Osborn, had turned to foreign crusades full-time and had built strong American support for their ministries. Before Oral ever ventured outside of the United States for a crusade, the most famous deliverance revival of the twentieth century had already been conducted by Tommy Hicks in Buenos Aires. For sixty-two days Hicks preached to crowds as large as 100,000 in the city's stadium, praying and laying hands on the sick. Oral publicized the Hicks meeting, as did most of the pentecostal world, and proudly announced that Hicks "got his bearings in an Oral Roberts meeting in Bakersfield, California, and launched out to preach deliverance to humanity."[185] The reports received from the evangelists holding overseas revivals were mind-boggling; no world-class deliverance evangelist could ignore that exciting theater forever.

As early as 1949, Oral stated an intent to take his crusades overseas, telling a Houston reporter that by 1951 he intended to tour South America, Europe, Africa, and parts of Asia.[186] But in 1952 he had still only "thought of" going overseas, insisting that his tent was such an integral part of his meetings that he wanted to take all his equipment with him when he did go. That, of course, presented major financial and logistical problems. Furthermore, Oral complained that the foreign "brethren . . . were a little slow" to satisfy his penchant for orderly planning.[187] A year later Oral issued a similar appeal for more thoughtful overseas invitations.[188]

By 1954 an overseas campaign seemed imperative, and in December Oral, Evelyn, and the team embarked on a long journey which took them from Tulsa to Israel, where they filmed two television programs in December, and then on to South Africa for a campaign in Johannesburg from January 1 to 8. The "boys from the office" came to the airport to see them off: "They were bright and cheery, for they said they feel this is the beginning of a new era for the Lord's work. 'All Nations and Every Creature' is our slogan."[189] The South African choice turned out to be a fortunate one; Oral's campaign broke "all attendance records" in Wembley Stadium. At the closing service the stadium was jammed beyond seating capacity, and Oral prayed "individually" with the 7,000 remaining persons who held prayer cards, bringing the total of those passing through the line to 11,400.[190] Roberts reported that 30,000 had been converted during the campaign.[191] The party was pretty rudely treated by the South African press, which featured such headlines as "20,000 Went and Prayed and Paid" and "Amen, Mr. Roberts, Now Please Get Out of South Africa," but the attendance and the financial support received raised everyone's spirits.[192] DeWeese judged the meeting a "fantastic success," and Oral, while exhausted, was exuberant.[193] "Whither now?" the charged evangelist asked. "Back to America for our 1955 schedule in the big tent. . . . Then next winter—overseas again!"[194] "God is stirring my nest in America," he told his campaign audiences. "He is leading me to go to the ends of the earth, because, I have heard the Macedonian call and the man in the vision has said, 'Come over and help us.' "[195]

It was in the afterglow of the successful South African campaign that Oral dispatched Lee Braxton on his whirlwind tour around the world to "help set the stage for my ministry to reach all nations and every creature."[196] On that trip Braxton made the arrangements for the fateful 1956 Australian venture, planning for the first and last time the shipping of the crusade equipment overseas.

In the aftermath of the Australian debacle, Oral's commitment to overseas crusading was clearly shaken. Nonetheless, his world outreach concept demanded continued overseas work. He was heartened by his reception in the Philippines prior to the Australian crusade, and, during a stop in Hong Kong between the Manila and Sydney campaigns, he received his seventh message from God, confirming his evangelistic commission to win ten million souls.[197] In short, his reception in Manila, where he had been invited to visit the president of the republic and had preached to nearly 100,000 people in eight days, did something to compensate for the Australian disappointment.[198]

Nonetheless, as the time approached for a second crusade in South Africa, in January 1957, Oral faced the trip with "great apprehension." Upon his return he told the workers at the evangelistic association: "This is one trip that I took . . . when I did not want to go; when I was burdened so much I could not control my emotions, and if there had been any way of backing out in any Christ-like manner I would not have made the trip." He was filled with "uncertainty," feeling that "the forces of evil would be concentrating their power against us."[199] But the second South African crusade was another resounding success; this time Oral preached in Durban and Salisbury, Rhodesia in addition to Johannesburg. He was again greeted by huge crowds, and was particularly pleased by the reception he received from the black Africans.[200] "The *awareness* of the natives in Africa to the reality of God is one of the most outstanding things I have ever seen," reported Oral on his return. "The natives have so little to unlearn that it is a pleasure to preach to them."[201]

But the second South African crusade also left some extremely negative memories. The Johannesburg papers again blistered Oral as a "hot-gospeller" conducting "a big, brassy, American-style meeting."[202] The trip ended with an incident that brought another spate of bad publicity. Oral purchased two diamond rings while in South Africa and, ignorant of customs procedures, failed to get the necessary bank permits for taking them out of the country. After considerable discussion, he was allowed by customs officials to depart with the rings since he had clear proof of purchase, but the incident was reported by the press in a most uncomplimentary story. A newsman present at the confrontation, "planted" there, Evelyn believed, wrote an article implying that Oral was searched and found to be carrying the rings after he had stated that he had no "dutiable articles to declare." Roberts vehemently denied the accusation, explained that he was a "victim of circumstances," and insisted that customs authorities had been satisfied before he left the country. But the incident left a bitter taste, and another flurry of public controversy followed the campaign in both South Africa and the United States.[203]

Oral's relatively unsatisfactory overseas ventures led to a lapse of foreign crusading for the rest of the decade. In 1958 he preached for a week in San Juan, Puerto Rico and held a short crusade in Canada; in 1959 he did not leave the United States. Oral did continue to discuss overseas invitations. In 1958, he told his partners of an invitation to hold a crusade in Japan and indicated he "already had plans for a crusade in Korea and several other foreign countries."[204] But nothing came of the Asian invitation. Even more dramatic was the announcement that he intended to "conduct a crusade in Russia" in 1959.[205] Responding to Oral's bold plan to preach behind the Iron Curtain, Demos Shakarian, his close friend and leader of the Full Gospel Business Men's Fellowship International, addressed a telegram to Deputy Premier Anastas Mikoyan, asking that Oral be allowed to proceed and offering "to come immediately to you for . . . discussion, bringing with me Evangelist Oral Roberts."[206]

Overseas campaigning was a financial drain on the organization. The South African campaigns paid their own way, but the Australian crusade had been a financial disaster.[207] In an area such as the Philippines, the organization had to "bear most of the heavy expenses of the campaign."[208] The collections taken in the overseas campaigns were used to defray the expenses of the meetings, but they rarely paid the full cost, and they contributed nothing to the maintenance of the ministry in America. But, as with Oral's other programs, World Outreach was a powerful fund-raising concept. Soul winning throughout the world was the most repetitious single motif in Oral's financial appeals in the late 1950s. "Because I have been gone representing you on the mission field where we have used all the funds available to win souls," wrote Oral in 1956, "I especially need your prayerful financial support at this time. Help me continue this great ministry of deliverance for all people by standing with me with your faithful prayers and means."[209]

PERHAPS in no area did the Roberts organization grow more in sophistication during the fifties than in the area of fund raising. Increasingly the ministry depended less and less on the collections from the crusades to fund its diverse operations. Rather, Oral targeted the growing list of those who subscribed to his magazine and wrote to his Tulsa office to support the expenses incurred in his million soul crusade. It was this huge direct-mail constituency which was to become the backbone of the organization. By 1959 the Roberts ministry was "the largest receiver and sender of first class mail in a city renowned for many large oil companies."[210]

This growing partner pool was kept constantly informed of the organization's needs. Generally speaking, soul saving was the common goal of Oral and his partners; in 1951 the association calculated that Oral could save souls "at a cost of only approximately five dollars per person." By 1953, with the start of the million soul crusade, the price had dropped to two dollars per person.[211] Radio and television, Oral reported to his followers, were particularly cost-efficient, giving "more conversions to Christ per dollar invested."[212] Of course, such ciphering encouraged imitators; radical deliverance evangelist A. A. Allen reported to his followers that his converts "cost only twenty-five cents each, or FOUR FOR A DOLLAR!"[213]

Throughout the decade, Oral drifted more and more toward targeting contributions, asking his partners to give to sponsor a radio or television program, to buy a piece of essential equipment, or to provide Bibles for Jewish families.[214] He also talked candidly with his partners when he had an "emergency." "We are in a crisis," he wrote in 1956. "The crisis is so severe that unless I get help immediately, we will fail. If we fail, God will hold us responsible for each soul we could have won if we had done our part."[215] Those who hitched their religious fortunes to the Oral Roberts ministry in the 1950s were kept informed about where God was leading them, but they also became accustomed to lurching from crisis to crisis.

Clearly the most innovative departure in the fund raising of the 1950s was the Blessing Pact concept, which was introduced in 1954. The idea that God wanted people to be prosperous had always been around in Oral's literature, but the emphasis on prosperity grew throughout the decade.[216] In the mid-1950s the message became much more specific. In an appeal for radio funds in 1954, Oral revealed that God had "impressed" him that his partners' gifts would be returned to them "seven times," "putting back into their hands every dollar their needs require."[217] When Oral proposed his "Blessing Pact" later in the year to raise the initial money for his television pilots, he took the prosperity theme a step further, promising, "I will use your gift to win souls; and because of this, I will earnestly pray that the Lord will return your gift in its entirety from a totally unexpected source."[218] "If at the end of the year," he continued, "this has not happened, you may write and tell me, and our Evangelistic Association will refund you the same amount immediately and no questions asked."[219] Oral offered the guarantee for only a brief time, although only a few people ever asked for their money back, but the Blessing Pact scheme became the backbone of the ministry's fund raising.[220] The readers of *Abundant Life* were repeatedly and meticulously instructed about the advantages of the Blessing Pact:

> THE BLESSING-PACT PLAN OFFERS A REGULAR SYSTEMATIC WAY TO WIN SOULS IN 154 MISSIONARY LANDS AND 75 DIFFERENT LANGUAGES, AS WELL AS THE OPPORTUNITY TO SHARE IN THE UNLIMITED PERSONAL BENEFITS THAT COME TO THOSE WHO ARE FAITH PARTNERS IN THE BLESSING PACT.
>
> Thousands of people, all over the world, have found that it has literally transformed their lives in a spiritual, physical and financial way. They are daily expecting and receiving God's blessings in good times and bad times.[221]

While they were never very important in raising revenue, countless minor promotions were used in the 1950s which smacked of Oral's pentecostal roots. Fourteen-carat "yellow gold filled Jesus Heals" pins were advertised through 1950, with the announcement that they were "sweeping the nation." The pins could be purchased for only one dollar or six for five dollars.[222] In the mid-1950s the organization ran a "new readers-new souls contest" to expand the circulation of *America's Healing Magazine.* The contest offered "$2500 in valuable merchandise prizes," including a fifty-two-piece sterling silver service, for the "authorized representatives" of the magazine who secured the most new subscriptions.[223]

Far more important was the evolution of a system of partner conferences. The first conference sponsored by the organization, the brainchild of Lee Braxton, was designed to expand the radio network. In March 1951, Braxton issued an appeal for "fifty individuals, business and professional men, to meet me in Tulsa" for a conference that "will go down in history as one of the most important meetings ever had for God's work."[224] The radio conference met in June 1951 at the Hotel Tulsa, was presided over by Braxton, and featured a series of testimonials praising the radio program. The visitors were expected to pay their own transportation costs to attend the meeting, but their expenses in Tulsa were paid by the Roberts organization. After dinner and breakfast meetings, the "visitors were taken on a tour through Healing Waters offices and printing plant."[225]

The use of conferences mushroomed in the mid-1950s with the beginning of the World Outreach program. The million soul crusade was launched at a conference in 1953, when Oral called nine of his closest supporters to Tulsa to unveil his plans. A year later, on August 9, 1954, a second conference was held in Tulsa, this time attracting "approximately 100 business men and women."

Oral "didn't ask for money"; he simply presented to these select partners a clear projection of his vision for soul saving.[226]

In the summer of 1955, the first World Outreach Conference was held in Tulsa. The meeting attracted "about 400 people, mostly Christian business laymen, who responded to Brother Roberts' invitation to come to Tulsa to help him plan his crusade to win a million souls a year." It was a surprisingly diverse collection of people, including "of course, just about every branch of the Full gospel movement," but also "Baptists, Brethren, Catholics, Christians, Episcopalians, Lutherans, Methodists, Amish Mennonites, Presbyterians, and a few with no church connections at all."[227] The World Outreach conferences continued to grow throughout the decade. In 1956, "nine hundred people from almost every state in the United States and Canada, the Philippines, Jerusalem, Germany, Sweden and Alaska" came to Tulsa for a three-day conference.[228] By 1957, the attendance was estimated at fourteen hundred, and the meeting was expanded to four days of speeches, panels, and tours.[229] By 1959, the growth demanded holding two conferences.[230]

The conferences, no doubt, were effective in tying more and more people of means to the Roberts ministry in a personal and systematic way. "The people returned to their homes renewed in spirit," wrote Yvonne Nance in *Abundant Life*, "with their faith revitalized, and with a greater determination to be powerful partners for deliverance in this Million Soul Crusade."[231] The conferences gave Oral's most important supporters the opportunity to have personal contact with him and other members of the party. They became, in a sense, a celebrity showcase. Evelyn remembered that the highlight of each conference was "a big barbecue" held at the Robertses' Robin Hood Farm. There the partners could play with the Roberts children, while Bob DeWeese and Oral dressed in cowboy hats and boots and spent the evening "just showing off." "The partners loved it," Evelyn remembered. "They just loved to come out there and they took pictures. There were cameras clicking everywhere. This just helped those partners to see that we were real people."[232]

The growth of the Roberts ministry was perhaps most clearly charted in the 1950s by the series of buildings it occupied. In the summer of 1953, Oral decided to expand the Healing Waters building. A new modern structure was built on the property on the corner of Sixteenth and South Boulder; the old building was razed to make room for the new one.[233] By August 1954, the new building had been completed at a cost of $400,000, providing work space for 125 workers in its three floors.[234]

In the aftermath of the television response, the ministry was soon pressed for space once again. In 1956, Roberts announced the acquisition of 175 acres on the corner of Forty-first Street and Memorial Drive in Tulsa along with plans to build a "City of Faith." A new headquarters building was projected which would include movie and television studios.[235]

The "City of Faith" project was dropped in the spring of 1957 in favor of a new plan to construct a building across the street from the existing headquarters, on the corner of Seventeenth and South Boulder. Governor Raymond Gary of Oklahoma spoke at the ground-breaking ceremonies, observing that "the fact that Oral Roberts has built this great organization in 10 years is a miracle in itself."[236] The seven-story building was designed by Tulsa architect Cecil Stanfield and provided 108,000 square feet of space, including an auditorium capable of seating fifteen hundred partners. Oral made a trip to Vermont to select the two-inch white marble which faced the windowless structure; marble quarried in France was used around the first floor entrance and in the foyer.[237] Oral's brother Elmer supervised the construction, which proceeded on schedule until the summer of 1958.[238]

In the winter of 1957–58, Oral faced the most serious financial crisis in the life of his young ministry, one of the most severe he would ever face. The building was funded on a "pay-as-you-go basis" until the skeleton had been completed; then Manford Engel informed Oral that construction would have to stop because of a shortage of funds. The nation was in a recession, and Oral's partners were clearly unable to pay for the building on a day-by-day basis.[239] Suddenly, in the midst of winter, construction stopped. Oral felt that he "faced absolute defeat."[240] The Tulsa papers publicized the crisis, rumoring that Oral was out of money, a statement which he challenged and which he feared would cripple his ability to negotiate a loan. Oral later described his depression: "I went down there one day and looked up at it. It was a skeleton, . . . and the devil whispered to me and said, 'That's going to be named Oral Roberts' folly. And people will pass it and shake their heads and say, "What a fool." ' "[241]

Oral had anticipated that a large loan might be necessary to complete the new headquarters, and before his crusade in Australia, he and Lee Braxton thought they had received a verbal commitment from a Tulsa bank to furnish a million dollars.[242] But in November 1957 the loan commitment turned "uncertain," and Oral faced the possibility of being unable "to borrow the large money it will take to complete the building."[243] He and Braxton hurried about, trying "to borrow money throughout the nation and were turned down right and left."[244] Finally, in the spring, the evangelist negotiated a loan of 1.25 million dollars from the First National Bank and Trust Company in Tulsa, the largest financial institution in the city, placing a mortgage on both the old and new buildings.[245] The affair was a harrowing one. When financial pressures mounted to find money to build the new Oral Roberts University in the early 1960s, Oral staunchly refused to mortgage the headquarters building again. "This is one building that must never be lost," he told his supporters. "It came from God. I didn't sweat blood, but it felt like blood, and others did too. I prayed enough prayers on this building and shed enough tears to swim in. That's a figurative statement, but it means a lot to me, and I have a holy horror of putting another mortgage on this building."[246] The crisis slowly abated. In April 1959, the old headquarters building was sold to Mid-Continent Casualty Co., and within a few years the debt on the new building had been retired.[247]

The Abundant Life building was, in the words of Vice-President W. E. Bender, Jr. of the First National Bank, "a beautiful new addition to the City of Tulsa."[248] The building received a final touch with the addition of a four-hundred-square-foot, three-dimensional mural, called the Redemptorama, which was located in the "Meditation Chapel" on the first floor. The work of art, which was later moved to the Prayer Tower on the Oral Roberts University campus, was constructed by Warren Straton, son of the noted fundamentalist pastor of New York's Calvary Baptist Church, John Roach Straton. Straton's mural portrayed "the universe centered by a rainbow and spangled with planets including a vial containing hands reaching up symbolizing the earth, with the hands of God reaching down to help mankind." "The hands of God the Father and the nail-scarred hand of God the Son depicted in the mural," explained Straton, "were modeled after photographs taken of the hands of Oral Roberts." Oral was captivated by the mural and "revealed that he himself had had a similar conception of the way the mural should be but lacked the ability to express it."[249]

The new Abundant Life building was "dedicated to the glory of God" in the spring of 1959. A gala banquet was held in the new building's auditorium, which was filled with "distinguished guests," including Tulsa mayor James Maxwell, Congressman Page Belcher, University of Tulsa president Ben Heneke, and countless other local dignitaries. Postmaster General Arthur E. Summerfield was to speak but was dispatched overseas by the president, and Governor J. Howard Edmondson gave the "main address" of the evening, praising the new structure as "not only a monument to Tulsa's beauty but to the efforts of a *man* who is contributing so much to the filling of that world-void with *faith* in the hearts and minds of men throughout the earth."[250]

The completion of the building was a great triumph for Oral—just twelve years removed from his decision to leave the pastorate of the Pentecostal Holiness church in Enid. Yvonne Nance, one of the organization's faithful staff reporters, was enthralled by the meaning of the nearing completion of the building. "Does sacred history repeat itself?" she asked, comparing the Abundant Life building with Solomon's Temple. She noted that both buildings had been begun in May; that the temple was built on Mt. Moriah and the Abundant Life building was "on the crest of a hill"; that thousands participated in the building of the temple, and thousands of partners had contributed to the financing of Roberts's building; and that both were of white stone. She was convinced that the Abundant Life building was "divinely conceived": "The parallelism between the two buildings erected to honor God is too startling to leave to coincidence."[251] An air of spiritual anticipation surrounded the occupation of the new building. It was a fitting end to an incredible decade of triumph and change; surely this was the place to listen to the voice of God as Oral waited for new directions in the 1960s.[252]

CHAPTER

VII

The Price of Glory

O RAL ROBERTS and his expanding ministry were simply the most visible part of the broad healing revival which erupted in 1947 and was carried throughout the world by an army of talented evangelists. Roberts was then, and has remained ever since, a loner, one responding directly to the voice of God speaking to him, content to mind his own business and to let others make their own contributions, but he nonetheless recognized that he was a part of a wider "moving of the Holy Spirit." Oral never aspired to be the general of the revivalist army (nor would its spirited evangelists have accepted any such authority), but he was its model soldier.[1]

While the pentecostal churches played a role in the groundswell after World War II, David J. du Plessis, premier leader of the charismatic movement, correctly diagnosed that the postwar revival was not the work of the denominations or of a "great leader," it was a movement arising from the people.[2] A new generation of pentecostal church members who hungered for association with other "spirit-filled" Christians began to support "citywide rallies" in the 1940s. As these rallies grew, they fired pentecostal enthusiasm and caught the attention of the world. When Southern California pentecostals packed over 20,000 young people into the Hollywood Bowl for a youth rally in September 1948, it became difficult to dismiss them as a marginal aberration.[3] Pentecostalism was an expectant religion, and many of its first-generation leaders had repeatedly prophesied that a great outpouring was about to begin.[4] The second-generation pentecostals who emerged from World War II with steady jobs and newly opened bank accounts were spiritually hungry. Oral wrote in 1953: "I just didn't know the hunger for Bible deliverance there is in the world today. People want something real, something they can feel, and Bible deliverance is God's answer."[5]

Throughout the 1930s, the divided state of pentecostalism would have made such union meetings unthinkable. But there was a growing craving for a more unified witness. In 1938, G. H. Montgomery, then editor of the *Pentecostal Holiness Advocate*, wrote: "One of the terrible tragedies that has befallen the Pentecostal movement is its divided condition. We are aware that some of these divisions are natural, having arisen in some distinctive schools of theology. . . . But for the most part, the divisions are both unnatural and unnecessary; and if a remedy for them can be found, we should look for it and apply it." Montgomery speculated that he would not "be permitted to live to see the day when all this evil will be undone," to see "the petty differences" dropped, but he was wrong. He did see, within a decade, a remarkable coming together among pentecostals.[6] By 1946 union rallies had become common throughout the nation.[7] In 1948 the youth rally in the Hollywood Bowl was sponsored by 800 pentecostal churches.[8] At the beginning of 1948, G. H. Montgomery wondered, along with many others, if pentecostalism was on the brink of the ecumenical revival "for which we have been waiting and praying for many years."[9]

Actually, by 1948 a pan-pentecostal movement was well under way at the denominational level. In 1943 a number of the largest pentecostal churches had become charter members of the National Association of Evangelicals, an organization which included many evangelical churches and replaced the moribund fundamentalist associations of the 1930s. The pentecostal leaders were "astonished" by the loving reception they received from the evangelicals, who had rudely rejected them in the 1930s, but just as important was the renewed association which they had with one another in the NAE.[10] In 1947, a world pentecostal rally was held in Zurich, which resulted in the formation of a fellowship of the major pentecostal denominations throughout the world. The spectacular success of that meeting paved the way for a convention of North American pentecostal churches in Des Moines, Iowa in October 1948. That meeting resulted in the formation of the Pentecostal Fellowship of North America, a union of eight of the major pentecostal groups in North America, including the Pentecostal Holiness church.[11]

Oral was invited to speak at the closing service of the conference, the "climax to this great occasion which we feel is one of the most important and significant steps ever taken in Pentecost and Christendom."[12] It was a singular honor for Oral, who had begun his healing ministry less than eighteen months earlier and had been on the verge of abandoning it less than a year before the convention. The *Pentecostal Holiness Advocate* noted with pride that "our brother Oral Roberts" had given the closing address.[13] In order to preach at the convention, Oral was forced to cancel an evening service in his Dallas crusade, but he explained that when he understood "the true meaning of this meeting . . . I felt in my heart that the least I could do was to close my little part down and come up and minister God's deliverance to you as God talked to my heart."[14] Oral preached a "good evangelistic sermon," extended an altar call, and conducted a healing line, just as he did in his meetings.

The Roberts service at the convention meeting was loaded with symbolic meaning. For better or worse, the healing revivalists were to be the key figures in the pan-pentecostal revival. It was prophetic that the denominational leaders in 1948 recognized that fact, though many very soon had second thoughts. A Des Moines minister summarized the feeling at the close of the convention: "As the many hundreds of ministers left this great convention there was in all of our hearts an assurance of closer fellowship and unity as we press on in this great age of revivals until Jesus comes."[15] Gordon Lindsay, the pentecostal leader who more than anyone else became the publicist of the healing revival, noted the evening with pride: "Beyond doubt the great ministry of healing manifested through such men as Brother Branham, Brother Freeman and Brother Roberts, has led the way for city-wide united efforts for the healing and conversion of thousands. It was significant and fitting that Brother Roberts should be the final speaker of the Convention, when four thousand attended, and at which a great number were saved and healed the same night."[16]

By 1948 the healing revivals had become the most visible sign of the "new spirit of cooperation among Pentecostals."[17] By 1949, Donald Gee, whose magazine, *Pentecost*, published in England, was the voice of world pentecostalism, had begun reporting the American healing campaigns and had identified Roberts as one of the leaders of the revival.[18] He wrote: "There is very noticeable renewed emphasis upon divine healing in connection with evangelism in the U.S.A. and Canada, and various preachers are conducting immense meetings on the lines that older friends will connect with such names as Mrs. Woodworth-Etter and others." Gee noted that one of the revivalists, a young man "partly Indian and partly Irish," claimed that God had spoken to him twice. The editor, who most likely heard Oral preach at the Des Moines convention, reported that "he surely preaches with unction, and he surely preaches 'Pentecost.'"[19] World pentecostal leaders kept a careful eye on the evangelists. In 1956 David J. du Plessis judged that the "sudden move towards mass evangelism" could be attributed only to "the spontaneous move of the Holy Spirit upon all flesh."[20]

From the beginning of his ministry, Oral identified himself as a part of this general revival. In the summer of 1948, *Healing Waters* reported that

> God has revealed to Brother Roberts that the Sign-Gift ministries are His means of Divine Deliverance to get the people ready for the coming of His Son, Jesus Christ. These ministries are to work hand-in-hand with the established Church where possible. It is an era of mass-evangelism. . . . No longer can we depend on our Church forms, our special music, our educated ministry, our fine church machinery to bring in the masses to God. We must have the "power and demonstration of the Holy Spirit."[21]

Oral was just as awed by the worldwide explosion of healing revivalism as were denominational leaders. "The spiritual revival," he wrote in the mid-1950s, "this tremendous resurgence of faith in the hearts of millions throughout the earth, can only mean that we are now seeing the literal and complete witnessing of Christ and for Christ to all nations and every creature."[22] His sermons in the first half of the 1950s were filled with allusions to the "new world-wide emphasis on healing and supernatural deliverance," which had been accompanied by "a visitation of men by angels as in Bible times."[23] Oral repeatedly expressed the "feeling" that the healing revival was a signal of the approaching end of time.[24]

Oral knew personally most of the other healing revivalists. He was delighted when old-time evangelist Fred F. Bosworth attended his crusade in Miami in 1949, and his magazine frequently featured stories about such pioneers.[25] Oral had a cordial, but somewhat distant, relationship with the dozens of other talented preachers who began healing ministries in the 1940s and 1950s. In 1949, the most successful of these evangelists—William Branham, William Freeman, Gayle Jackson, Jack Coe, T. L. Osborn, A. A. Allen, and a number of others—formed an umbrella organization under the leadership of Gordon Lindsay in Dallas, Texas. Lindsay began publishing a magazine, *The Voice of Healing*, only a few months after Oral had launched *Healing Waters*, and Lindsay's journal was, at least for a few years, the publicity organ for all of the other evangelists.[26]

Lindsay and Roberts met for the first time in 1948, when Oral attended a Branham crusade; they remained friends through the years, though their paths drifted slowly apart. But in the early 1950s the two worked out a cooperative agreement, whereby Lindsay publicized Oral's meetings, though he was not affiliated with the Voice of Healing organization, and *Healing Waters* noted the schedules and achievements of Lindsay's stable on an irregular basis.[27] In December 1951, when the Voice of Healing fellowship held its yearly convention in Tulsa, Oral was the featured speaker, and the visiting evangelists were taken on a tour of the Healing Waters office.[28]

Particularly significant was Oral's relationship with William Branham, the meek, mystical, independent Baptist preacher who sent the first shock waves through the pentecostal subculture with a series of revivals in the winter of 1946–1947 in Arkansas and Louisiana and on the West Coast, where he met Lindsay and persuaded him to become his manager. In retrospect, Branham's power over his audiences seems implausible. In almost every respect he was the opposite of Roberts—small and unimpressive in appearance, halting and rambling in his preaching, totally unprepared for his sudden rise to fame. Furthermore, Branham's background was not pentecostal. He had received the baptism of the Holy Spirit, but his informal links with the organized pentecostal movement were through the "Jesus Only" movement, the most heterodox and sectarian wing of pentecostalism. But Branham amazed his audiences with his gift of "discernment," telling apparent strangers their names, addresses, and other bits of personal information. An air of mystery and expectancy surrounded the early Branham meetings which was probably never equaled elsewhere in the healing revival. His acceptance by pentecostals and his meteoric rise were the preeminent signs of the craving within the pentecostal community for a new demonstration of God's power. By the end of 1947, Branham's name had swept through the pentecostal churches; thousands clamored for his attention. In the late 1950s his doctrinal eccentricities and his lack of business acumen weakened his influence, but in 1948, when Oral first met him, he stood atop the healing revival, with Oral as his nearest rival.[29]

Roberts's first meeting with Branham, in April 1948, came when Oral was conducting a healing revival at the First Assembly of God in Kansas City, Missouri and Branham was holding a crusade across the river in Kansas. On Saturday evening Oral attended the Branham campaign. He was introduced to Lindsay, who knew Oral's reputation as a "dynamic young man" already being "greatly used in the deliverance ministry."[30] Lindsay escorted Roberts backstage, where he met Branham and had his picture taken with the entire Branham team—Young Brown, Jack Moore, Gordon Lindsay, and Branham; apparently Oral had planned ahead to have a photographer present.[31] Oral sat engrossed through the Branham meeting; it, no doubt, solidified his resolve to schedule only citywide campaigns in the future. "I think he learned some things," mused Lindsay later, "he picked things up everwhere."[32] *Healing Waters* reported the encounter with pride: "Brother Branham is a very precious, humble and specially-called man of God, with the gift of healing working through his life. There is a striking similarity between the manner in which God's healing gifts work through Brother Branham and Brother Roberts. The power of healing works through Brother Roberts' right hand while it works through Brother Branham's left hand." As a result of their meeting, the "working agreement" was reached which provided that *Healing Waters* would publicize Branham's schedule and the *Voice of Healing* would announce Roberts's meetings.[33]

Oral's visit to the Branham campaign in 1948 was patly religious politics, a joint endorsement of one another by the revival's frontrunners. But it also illustrated how much the evangelists were both the truest believers in the revival and the architects of it. Over and over again in his life, Oral showed an unaffected appreciation for other ministers, a guileless faith in others' gifts. In later years, he reflected about his evening with William Branham:

> This preacher took me in the side door. I was standing there and here came this fellow about five foot six. They brought him in the door and he looked around and he didn't act like he knew where he was. The fellow with me . . . said, "Brother Branham this is Oral Roberts." And the little fellow almost cried. "Oh," he said, "God bless you. My, that you'd come to hear me." . . . And I said, "My goodness, I wouldn't have missed it." So they led him down the hall. . . . And somebody brought him up on the stage just like leading him. He preached just about eighteen or twenty minutes. Quiet. You had to listen. And prayed for about eight or ten people. He would say, "There's somebody here with such and such." Of course, I had never seen him. I wasn't dealt with in that particular way. So I was very interested. . . . I never knew Brother Branham closely but I knew God was with him.[34]

Oral was present not simply to steal trade secrets, or to build political alliances, he came to be blessed and to have his own faith in healing reinforced. He did not go away disappointed.

Oral continued to have a special, though detached, relationship with Branham for several years. In the summer of 1948, Branham complained of nervous exhaustion—a symptom both of the excruciating toll taken by healing revivalism and of his nonchalance about honoring commitments—and canceled all of his meetings. Oral called on the readers of *Healing Waters* to "immediately go to their knees, calling Brother Branham's name in prayer, that he may be restored to strength for the mighty work that still awaits his labors."[35] When Branham returned to the field the next year, he paid a visit to the Roberts campaign in Tampa, and the encounter was once again heralded as a summit meeting in the deliverance revival. "It was wonderful beyond words," wrote Reg Hanson, "to watch these two faithful men, both called of God, both having heard the voice of the same wonderful Savior, both commissioned of the Lord to deliver humanity, as they talked of the marvelous things of God."[36] Branham's stature as a "great and big man," wrote Gordon Lindsay, was magnified when he described the Roberts lesson of the evening as "the greatest sermon that he had heard in all his life."[37]

As the years passed, Branham's crusades waned as Oral's waxed stronger. Branham was a poor manager, careless of financial matters, and he increasingly preached controversial doctrines. Oral was the opposite; he developed into a skillful financier and executive, and he avoided doctrinal extremes. Oral and the other healing evangelists continued to honor Branham, even stand in awe of him, but it was Roberts who was to become the unquestioned leader of the revival.[38]

The genuine mutual respect between Branham and Roberts was repeated thousands of times over in the pentecostal ministry. No group was more deeply marked by the revival—they came seeking healing of their own bodies and bringing their loved ones in the full assurance of faith.[39] Many of those who came in faith received under the tents new calls to do grander works. No one inspired more to preach deliverance than Oral.

From the very beginning of his healing ministry in 1947, Oral encouraged others to stir up the gifts in them. After the Tulsa meeting in Steve Pringle's tent, Pringle "launched out into a healing ministry . . . and many other ministers did the same."[40] Oral frequently called ministers out of his audience to pray for them; in Minneapolis in 1948 he "commissioned about 150 preachers for the ministry of healing, in turn, these pastors, evangelists and missionaries are truly on fire for God."[41] Many of Oral's old friends in the Pentecostal Holiness church followed him into healing ministries. Mildred Wicks developed a "very large and fruitful ministry of Bible deliverance" and long continued to receive Oral's encouragement.[42] Doyle Zachary, who sponsored Oral's first tent crusade in Durham, felt called during that crusade and established a substantial independent ministry.[43] Others, such as L. E. Turpin, were less successful. Turpin drove 4,000 miles to Oral's Tampa crusade in 1949 to have his old friend "pray for me," and "the Lord wonderfully healed me of heart trouble." The experience, he wrote, had "given me a new spiritual life, new hopes, a new love, a real compassion for the lost and sick world, and a new anointing in my sermons." "The Lord burdened" Turpin to buy a "60 × 120 ft. fireproof Gospel tent to bring the full gospel message of Bible deliverance, for soul, mind, and body to thousands who otherwise would never hear the full gospel preached," but his ministry, like those of countless others, remained relatively unknown.[44]

Most of those who felt the call to enter worldwide healing ministries in the late 1940s and 1950s were destined to fail. But a few saw their calling confirmed. David Nunn first heard Roberts in the Dallas campaign of 1948 and felt a call that led him into the heart of the growing revival in the 1950s.[45] Another minister who first heard Oral in Dallas in 1948 was Kenneth Hagin. Although Hagin did not begin a healing ministry of his own for many years, he was deeply influenced by Roberts; in the 1980s he had come to be the leader of a healing movement which would have a powerful counterinfluence on Oral.[46] In the short run, Oral's most successful emulator was Asa Alonzo Allen, an Assembly of God minister from Corpus Christi who attended the Dallas campaign. By the early 1950s, Allen had established one of the largest and most controversial healing ministries in America.[47]

Many of Oral's fellow ministers sought his healing touch. Steve Pringle called Oral to the emergency room of a Tulsa hospital to pray for him after an accident in 1949 and reported that "immediately I felt His healing virtues going through my body."[48] Velmer Gardner, who had a large healing ministry before making a modest fortune in real estate investments, journeyed to Tampa in 1949 to have Oral pray for "two tumors on the side of my face." He testified that six weeks later "I went to wash my face and laying on my cheek were both of those tumors, God confirmed his work."[49] Gardner felt his call to enter the independent ministry later in that year during a Roberts crusade in Tacoma.[50] Rex Humbard of the "Humbard Musical Evangelistic Party" drove to a Roberts campaign in Mobile in November 1949, and later testified that his son, Rex Jr., was healed of "lung trouble."[51] During that meeting Humbard bought Oral's old tent for his own independent ministry—a ministry which was to have its own brand of Cinderella ending.[52]

By the middle of the 1950s, the sense of community among the independent evangelists began to break down. One reason was their busy schedules; each was consumed with building his own ministry. Oral was especially isolated because he did not belong to the Voice of Healing fellowship or regularly attend its conventions.[53] But the revivalists also began to employ divergent techniques in their efforts to sustain their expensive operations—some became increasingly crude and extreme; many openly attacked the pentecostal denominations. Daring, raucous Jack Coe challenged Oral for the leadership of the revival in the early 1950s. "His hold on the common man," judged Gordon Lindsay, "was greater than Oral Roberts'. . . . He had such a combination of spirituality and buffoonery." Coe "never learned ethics," Lindsay continued, and free-for-all tactics kept him in hot water.[54] But Oral respected Coe, as he did most other evangelists, and *Healing Waters* praised Coe's work when he held a crusade in Tulsa in 1950.[55] On more than one occasion Lee Braxton asked Oral how Coe's methods could succeed; Oral would reply, "Jack has faith."[56]

But Coe's tactics riled Oral on several occasions. In 1951, Coe attended a Roberts meeting, measured Oral's tent, had one constructed that was three feet longer, and then proudly announced that his was "by a slight margin the largest Gospel tent in the world."[57] Oral was perturbed; he wrote Lindsay a letter of protest. Lindsay agreed that "Jack had no business doing that," but he tried to soothe Oral: "You're too big a man to be bothered by that. . . . Your ministry is great, you don't need to worry." Nevertheless, Lindsay believed, "from that time on we didn't have the closeness that we had at the beginning."[58] Nor was Jack Coe finished. By 1956 he was back on the same theme with a vengeance. In an article entitled "Which Evangelist Has the World's Largest Gospel Tent?" Coe assured that he was "not in competition with others," but he insisted that "when evangelists make statements about the size of their tent, they could dispel much of the controversy by giving the actual length and width. Then people would not feel that someone was telling a lie or exaggerating." Coe insisted that he was not trying to "belittle or condemn some other evangelist"; his only interest was truth. If someone had a larger tent, he wrote, he would "praise God for it! If they will write me, telling me the size of their tent, . . . I will print this information in my magazine, admitting that mine is only the second or third largest."[59]

Although many of the evangelists resorted to increasingly sensational tactics, almost all of them tried to cling to Oral's coattails. In the mid-1950s, both Coe and A. A. Allen came under heavy fire from their denomination, the Assemblies of God, as well as from the secular press, and they frequently publicized attacks on Oral to establish common cause with him.[60] But despite such efforts, most insiders understood the growing differences in style and substance.

However, in 1951 another organization was formed, which both held the revival together and gave it impetus: the Full Gospel Business Men's Fellowship International. The time was ripe for the organizing of pentecostal businessmen with the emergence of a smattering of aggressive, largely young, entrepreneurs in the pentecostal churches. This new elite, a first-generation middle class, was loaded with farmers enriched by property appreciation and sturdy achievers in such service businesses as construction and auto sales. They were increasingly restless in the autocratic pentecostal denominations, which were ruled firmly by pastors and denominational leaders. The formation of the Full Gospel Business Men's Fellowship International was a layman's rebellion in pentecostal ranks as the emergence of the independent healing ministries had been an uprising in the ranks of the aspiring clergy.

The two parachurch movements began and grew in concert with one another. The early citywide crusades of the healing evangelists were frequently aided by ad hoc local committees of pentecostal businessmen. Demos Shakarian, the Los Angeles dairyman who was the architect of the FGBMFI, began sponsoring tent revivals as early as 1940, as did other businessmen. When Oral preached in Tacoma, Washington in 1949, seventy-five businessmen from the area met with Bob DeWeese to discuss the financing of the campaign.[61] The businessman-independent evangelist alliance was a natural one, but it was the vision of Shakarian and the backing of Oral Roberts that launched one of the most powerful parachurch organizations in modern history.

Shakarian served as chairman of the local committee sponsoring Oral's campaign in Los Angeles from September 28 to October 14, 1951. During the meeting, the Armenian dairyman told Oral of the "burden God put on my heart." He laid before the evangelist his plan to organize pentecostal businessmen: "The church is wonderful but it's not enough for the layman. They go to Rotary Club. . . . That's wonderful and some of them go to other clubs that's not so good. . . . They need spiritual encouragement from men of the business community, the same type men they are." Oral reacted quickly and enthusiastically: "He got excited. . . . 'Man, get going.' he said, 'I'll speak for you. I'll do anything to help you.' "[62]

Shakarian hastily invited his pentecostal business acquaintances from the Los Angeles area to meet with him at Clifton's Cafeteria for a Saturday luncheon, announcing that Oral would speak. He anticipated a crowd of several hundred "with a world-famous evangelist as an inducement" and was profoundly disappointed when only twenty-one people, including him and Oral, showed up for the meeting. Oral's irrepressible spirit was at its best when faced with potential disaster. He spoke briefly and thanked God for the small beginnings of an organization which would soon reach around the world in a thousand chapters. The little group began singing "Onward Christian Soldiers," joining hands and marching. "Spiritually," Shakarian later said, the FGBMFI "began when Oral Roberts shared his Dream of a Thousand and we all held hands like children and marched in place singing a battle song."[63]

A second meeting was convened in Fresno in November following Oral's crusade there. "Acting upon Brother Roberts' suggestion, a business meeting was held following Brother Roberts' address," and the "temporary name" Full Gospel Business Men's Fellowship of America was chosen.[64] Shakarian then followed Roberts to Phoenix, where the fellowship was formally organized as a nonprofit corporation in January 1952. Not only did Roberts encourage the fellowship from the beginning and nurture it in his campaigns, he also recruited some of its most important early supporters. The first vice-presidents of the FGBMFI were Lee Braxton and Binghampton, New York automobile dealer George Gardner, one of Oral's closest friends.[65] The friendship between Roberts and Shakarian remained close; Shakarian became a lifelong member of Oral's innermost circle of friends and advisors.

In its early months, the growth of the FGBMFI seemed slow to Shakarian, but by 1953 it began spreading very rapidly. All of the independent evangelists lent their influence to the establishment of new chapters during their campaigns. In 1953 the fellowship held its first international convention in Los Angeles, hosting thousands of businessmen and featuring a Who's Who of revivalist speakers such as Gordon Lindsay, Tommy Hicks, Raymond T. Richey, Jack Coe, and Oral Roberts.[66] The next year's international convention, in Washington, D.C., was highlighted by a visit by Vice-President Richard Nixon and evening speeches by A. C. Valdez, Jr., Jack Coe, William Branham, and, in the final climactic service, Oral Roberts.[67] While the FGBMFI was Shakarian's vision and was built by his tireless energy and unabashed optimism, he never questioned that Oral was the organization's spiritual father and guide.[68]

Lee Braxton later recalled that he and the other early leaders of the FGBMFI saw the fellowship as a tool to take the "full gospel" message into the mainstream denominations and to those who had "influence" and "money."[69] No one could have foreseen how successful they would be. In 1974, Oral judged the FGBMFI to be "the most powerful, effective tool to bring men and women into the Holy Spirit this world has ever known."[70] In 1982, according to Shakarian, the organization had chapters in eighty-one countries with nearly 800,000 members.[71] When the healing revival of the 1950s turned into the charismatic revival of the 1960s, the FGBMFI and Oral Roberts would be the two institutions most successful in making the transition from the first to the second revival.

While the FGBMFI was flourishing in the late 1950s, there was a growing anxiety about the waning of the healing revival. Oral, and the other healing revivalists, tried to discourage negative thinking. In 1957 Oral reported that "many people" had asked him if the revival was a "temporary" phenomenon, but he assured that "the present wave of healing power that's sweeping the world today is the most permanent thing that I know about in the world."[72] Again, in 1959, Oral assured his partners that he had not come to a "leveling-off place": "With what I feel in my soul now, it seems as though I have only begun."[73] But, in fact, deep down inside all of the healing evangelists knew that changes must come. The novelty was gone, the faithful had become sated on miracles, and the opposition without and within had grown formidable and organized.

The camaraderie the healing evangelists felt with one another and with the FGBMFI was partly a defense against the growing hostility of pentecostal denominational leaders. Shakarian knew that the healing evangelists supported his fellowship because they "saw danger" and were "frightened."[74] Pentecostal denominational leaders reacted slowly to the outbreak of the revival in 1947 and 1948, partly because its power was a surprise and partly because most did not attend a revival for several months. Furthermore, while the emphasis of the evangelists was somewhat novel, there was ample precedence for healing revivalism, and most preached orthodox pentecostal messages. Most important, pentecostal lay people and local pastors were swept away by the new wave; by 1948 the tide into the tents could hardly have been dammed up by denominational leaders.

Very soon, however, denominational leaders, particularly in the Assemblies of God, the largest of the pentecostal denominations and the mother church of most of the independent revivalists, began to try to contain the revival. In late 1949, Stanley H. Frodsham was removed as editor of that church's paper because he supported the revival, and in 1951 the General Presbytery of the Assemblies of God publicly asserted its authority to supervise all private corporations operated by the denomination's ministers. In an ugly and highly publicized confrontation in 1953, church leaders revoked Jack Coe's ministerial license.[75] Once church leaders had successfully disciplined Coe, lesser independent revivalists were forced to either withdraw from the church or submit their ministries to the regulation of the denominational hierarchy.

Responsible leaders on both sides tried to reconcile differences. As early as 1949, Gordon Lindsay, anticipating the dangers ahead, urged the evangelists to show "humility" and to "seek to work with local pastors." He warned them against "doctrinal hair splitting" and "fanaticism," and, perhaps most important, he urged avoidance of a "covetous spirit," else "this revival can be greatly retarded if there is a continual auctioneering for money in the campaigns."[76] Lindsay's warning touched on many of the sources of tension—pride and jealousy, the exaggerated claims of the evangelists, and, most important, "one word, 'm-o-n-e-y,' money."[77] In 1956, Donald Gee, still hoping for reconciliation, wrote an astute summary of the causes of the rupture:

> Such an upsurge of energy, frequently by independent evangelists, backed by all the techniques of modern propaganda, attracting generous financial support, and providing a glamorous contrast with more pedestrian ministries is bound to produce tensions. Hasty claims have been made that these many campaigns represent nothing less than a new Revival which now supersedes its parent Pentecostal Revival of the last half-century. There has been a tendency to dub established Pentecostal organizations and more conservative brethren, as hidebound, timid and backslidden in zeal and vision. . . .
>
> On the other hand, there have been cases of local pastors or officials who have allowed themselves to become sour in spirit about the whole business. They have seen and felt the inevitable temporary deflection of funds—for these campaigns are a costly business. They have become, perhaps unconsciously, envious of the healing-evangelists while they themselves have laboured faithfully for years with only moderate results. It has been easy for them to fasten on features open to criticism by those who want to criticize, such as exaggerated claims for numbers, the ephemeral nature of many of the boasted conversions or healings, or the final lack of lasting fruit in the building up of the local churches.[78]

While pentecostal people still overwhelmingly supported the revivals in the late 1950s, and some of the evangelists (most notably Oral Roberts) could still get the sponsorship of large numbers of local pastors, many of the healing evangelists openly labeled their former denominations as the "Plenty-Crossed churches."[79]

In spite of his prestige, Oral could not escape the battle between the evangelists and the churches. Most of the Pentecostal Holiness denominations's leaders had attended a Roberts crusade by the middle of 1948, and they almost uniformly endorsed the revival. Bishop Dan T. Muse of Oklahoma was one of Oral's strongest supporters. Just a few months before he died, the old bishop wrote to Oral: "The God of heaven give you strength and courage in your great ministry of blessing humanity. God alone knows how much I appreciate you and Evelyn and your great work for the Master, and the relief you are bringing to suffering mankind, and the thousands of souls that are being brought to a saving knowledge of the Saviour."[80] In 1950, the East Oklahoma Conference of the Pentecostal Holiness church passed a resolution of "appreciation for Brother Roberts and his great work by a rising vote of thanks."[81] In the early months of his ministry, Oral also received strong support from the eastern wing of his church. Bishops J. A. Synan and T. A. Melton attended meetings in 1948 and wrote Oral letters of commendation.[82] Even Hubert T. Spence, later editor of the *Pentecostal Holiness Advocate* and a bitter critic of Roberts, was impressed by a message Oral delivered in 1949 and joined in a "special prayer" in his behalf.[83] Some denominational leaders were rabid supporters. L. J. Oliver, the Pentecostal Holiness Florida Conference superintendent, wrote after Oral's 1951 crusade in Tampa: "This Latter-Rain Pentecostal revival may be the last great revival the world will ever see. I for one, have resolved not to be left 'high and dry' as it sweeps anew over the world."[84] Up to 1950 Oral was supported overwhelmingly, by both his own denominational leaders and those of other pentecostal churches.[85]

There seemed to be ample reasons for Oral's denomination to support him during the early months of the revival. Although the long-term results cannot be measured, local pastors were generally ecstatic about the immediate effect of the crusades on their congregations. After Oral's 1948 campaign in Ada, Oscar Moore reported his church had gained forty-four new members; a Jacksonville, Florida pastor wrote that the Roberts crusade had "revolutionized my church," adding over one hundred new Sunday school members; a steady stream of similar reports appeared in *Healing Waters*.[86] Doyle Zachary boasted that Oral's Durham tent meeting "put Pentecostal Holiness on the map," urging other pastors: "Brother Roberts had a real set-up to help the Pentecostal ministers that want to build their churches up."[87] It was true that Oral's early preaching was strongly pentecostal and that he tried to help the pastors. In his early years, he often suggested that a change in denominations might be advisable: "Get away from cold creeds. . . . I never ask a man to change churches. . . . But if you can't get healed where you are then you need to get out."[88]

Lee Braxton, along with many other pentecostals, believed that "the greatest opportunity of a lifetime has come to the Full Gospel Churches through the Oral Roberts Ministry."[89] In retrospect, his judgment seems correct; many became harshly critical of the churches as the opportunity slipped away in the 1950s. Some Pentecostal Holiness churches left the denomination when its leaders cooled toward the revival, but Oral never supported such actions. In a 1955 sermon, Oral openly addressed those disenchanted with the church: "I've had many preachers come to me and say, 'Brother Roberts, I'm discouraged. I haven't been treated right, I'm going to come out of the church.' I always say, 'No, brother, don't ever come out of the church because you have no other place to go. The gates of hell shall never prevail against the church. Don't ever leave the church!'"[90] Throughout the decade, Oral continued to tell those at his altar to "seek a spiritual church—a church that believes in the power of God," to tithe to that church, and to support their local pastor.[91] Even though his audiences were changing by the end of the decade, and even though he had been through a bitter fight within his denomination, Oral still remained a supporter of the local church at the end of the 1950s.

Oral also tried not to offend his denomination's doctrinal sensibilities. "By all means," he wrote in the *Pentecostal Holiness Advocate* in the fall of 1947, "those who want to be healed should listen to Full Gospel radio programs, attend Full Gospel services, read Full Gospel literature and accept the Full Gospel for their own lives."[92] Lee Braxton assured *Advocate* readers in 1949 that "Brother Roberts is preaching the message our Church stands for."[93] Particularly important to Pentecostal Holiness leaders, Roberts did not compromise his belief in sanctification as a second distinct work of grace, a doctrine which separated his church from other forms of pentecostalism. Reporting on the Tacoma campaign in 1949, J. M. MacLean wrote: "Another blessed fact was that the doctrine of holiness was not omitted. Twice, or more, there were calls for those seeking the Baptism of the Holy Ghost, but seekers were assured by Brother Roberts that they needed a clean heart before the Lord would baptize them."[94] As late as 1953 G. H. Montgomery reported that Oral "preaches the fundamentals of salvation, holiness and pentecost as zealously and as faithfully as any man I have ever heard."[95]

Oral had also learned his church politics well as a youngster, and he made several adroit efforts to keep peace with his church. The addition of Sproull to his team provided a buffer between him and the denomination's hierarchy, and his friendship with Braxton allied him with the church's leading layman. At the local level, Oral had the unfailing gift of convincing local pastors that he had their interests at heart. Into the early fifties Oral continued to send articles to the *Pentecostal Holiness Advocate,* and his campaign schedule was listed in the magazine.[96] He not only maintained his ministerial credentials in the church, he also found time in his busy schedule to attend the East Oklahoma camp meetings in 1948 and 1950 and regularly contributed his "ministerial tithes." In 1948 he reported "6,000 converted, 600 sanctified, and 425 baptized with the Holy Ghost under his ministry during the Conference year," and in 1950 his presence was greeted by a standing ovation from the attending ministers.[97] In 1952 Oral sent a thousand-dollar contribution to Emmanuel College, along with the assurance: "Believe me, Evelyn and I are standing for the church and what it teaches and believes. We are for our young people and the Bible Schools that open their doors to the finest young people in the land."[98]

Once O. E. Sproull left his team, Oral's most important liaison with denominational leaders was Lee Braxton. Braxton remained a strong supporter of the church's programs, and his backing of Oral carried considerable weight.[99] By far the most important single effort made by Roberts and Braxton to assuage the growing hostility within the Pentecostal Holiness denomination was a 1953 contribution of $50,000 to Southwestern College in Oklahoma City. The large donation (which came in the midst of Oral's most dangerous spat with denominational leaders) was a saving godsend for the small college which Oral had helped to establish and which was still presided over by his friend Raymond O. Corvin.[100] Oral's gift surely had several meanings. He had a personal interest in the school and apparently always had tucked away in his mind the vision of being a school builder, but there is no doubt that his $50,000 contribution was an effort to avoid open war with the leaders of his denomination.

In spite of the early positive signs, some ministers quickly disclaimed Oral's ministry. Oscar Moore remembered that "many church leaders" balked at Oral's new tack from the beginning, and to Evelyn it seemed that "Oral didn't get any encouragement from anybody in the world except his mother and his father and me."[101] The publication of *If You Need Healing—Do These Things!* in 1947 was greeted by the *Pentecostal Holiness Advocate* with the cool nonrecommendation: "The author has recently become an enthusiastic minister of healing after several years in pastoral and evangelistic work."[102] When evangelist Joseph E. Campbell published a history of the Pentecostal Holiness church in 1951, his brief notice of Oral reflected the denomination's growing ambivalence: "Although some have questioned the Scriptural validity of the new emphasis on healing, as well as the sincerity of its director, Mr. Roberts, continues to count hundreds who are converted, as well as healed, in his campaigns, and numbers friends by the thousands who are his loyal supporters. . . . [sic] This new type of ministry has caused many to look on with mingled wonder and suspicion."[103]

To the supporters of the revival the growing hostility within the church seemed motivated by petty jealousy. Looking back in later years, Lee Braxton labeled his denomination's leaders "little people" who were "educationally limited" and lacking in "vision."[104] An acquaintance of Bishop Muse remembered asking him shortly before the old preacher's death in 1950 why the opposition to Oral had arisen. "I don't know why it is," he replied, "but every time God seems to start blessing any of our men in an unusual way, the brethren seem to get jealous of him."[105] Clearly Oral had run rampant over the newly won and jealously guarded status prerogatives of his church's leaders. There was more than a touch of pride in the church's announcement in 1951 that it had acquired homes for bishops Melton and Synan in Memphis, noting that Synan's cost $18,000 and was "well located on one of the best residential streets" in the city.[106] It was difficult for such men to swallow magnanimously the huge growth in Oral's ministry, including the fact that he could offer a pastor such as Sproull a salary far surpassing those of the church's bishops. It was an unfortunate impasse, reflected Bob DeWeese many years later: "Oral could have been Mr. Pentecost to all of these denominations and have been a tremendous help to all of them," but "a hierarchy doesn't put its stamp of approval on anything it can't control."[107]

The growing schism between pentecostal leaders and the independent revivalists can only partly be explained by jealousy, however. There were many serious, perhaps irreconcilable, conflicts of interest between the two groups. Church leaders repeatedly asked honest and reasonable questions about the methods of the revivalists. In an article in the summer of 1948 in the *Pentecostal Holiness Advocate,* G. H. Montgomery, while not opposing the campaigns, clearly outlined a series of issues which would not go away. First, Montgomery warned, there were those "who dare to commercialize the holy doctrine" of healing "for no other purpose than to get rich." The problem of financial abuse was real, and it was often accompanied by a flagrant disregard for the well-being of local churches. In addition, warned Montgomery, the claims of the revivalists were often extravagant and misleading, sometimes contributing to "the calamity of a collapse of faith that always invariably follows an inflated healing campaign." "I feel under the most sacred obligation to tell you who are afflicted," wrote Montgomery, "that God can heal your body without fanfare or flourish, without great programs and mysterious incantations, without the aid of any man who claims to be a special apostle of divine healing, without a contribution from you of a sum of money which you may not be able to afford, and without any of the sensational and gaudy showmanship that we hear of so frequently in healing campaigns."[108] Some of the leaders of the Pentecostal Holiness church felt that Oral's tactics placed him in this unworthy class.[109] The influential Synan brothers grew disturbed when their mother died of cancer after being prayed for in Oral's healing line, and others grew increasingly skeptical of the healing-line technique.[110]

Finally, there was the question of denominational authority and responsibility. Oral was sometimes deferential to authority, but he sometimes urged local pastors "not to be afraid of your boards or ecclesiastical leaders, for nobody can put his thumbs on you if you're a man of God."[111] To many responsible denominational leaders, it seemed that the revivalists had rejected all authority and become dangerously individualistic. "There was a fine line," recalled Assembly of God leader Thomas Zimmerman, "between being spiritually motivated and ego propelled."[112] The Pentecostal Holiness church began to squeeze its healing revivalists in the summer of 1950. H. T. Spence replaced G. H. Montgomery as editor of the *Advocate,* and he refused to publish the campaign schedules of the healing evangelists. Spence warned that the healing evangelists were "unconsciously classifying themselves in the minds of many of our people as The Full Gospel preachers of The Pentecostal Holiness Church." But what about the "other 1600 faithful preachers of the Pentecostal Holiness Church?" Were they to be regarded as something less than "full gospel preachers?" Spence also noted that a "Divine Healing Convention" was about to be convened by some of the evangelists, an event he felt would highlight their elitist feelings and have a tendency to draw other pastors away from their churches.[113] Spence's editorial seemed to pose a question of whether one could be both a Pentecostal Holiness minister and a healing revivalist.

In 1953, at the same time that the Assembles of God expelled Jack Coe, there was a strong move by the Pentecostal Holiness church to revoke Oral's ministerial credentials. An effort to "summons" Oral before the church's executive board was defeated by a 3-2 vote. Oral's opponents were some of the most formidable leaders in the denomination; among the most vociferous were editor Hubert Spence and Virginia Conference superintendent L. C. Synan. But unquestionably Oral's most weighty critic was Bishop J. A. Synan—lovable, respected, the foremost leader in the denomination. Bishop Synan was not so vitriolic as his brother and Spence, but he was just as convinced that Oral's impact on the church had become negative and that discipline was needed.[114]

Oral escaped expulsion from his church for two reasons. First, he was protected by the conference organization of the denomination. Oral's ordination was granted by the East Oklahoma Conference, and in that jurisdiction he was a hero. Although his critics contended that Oral had become "more than just an ordained minister," technically his ordination was not controlled by the denomination's hierarchy. Second, Oral was protected by his powerful friends within the denomination, particularly Oscar Moore and Raymond O. Corvin. Both were members of the General Executive Board, and Moore was superintendent of the East Oklahoma Conference; together they defeated the campaign of Oral's opponents.

The struggle between Oral and his denomination's leaders climaxed in the

General Conference in 1953. The meeting was a political brawl, and Oral's supporters came away with an impressive victory. Corvin and Moore succeeded in putting Oral on the program to preach one evening. In addition, in a considerable upset, Moore was elected one of the church's two bishops, unseating an incumbent who had opposed Oral. In the wake of the conference some thought the denomination might divide into Roberts and anti-Roberts factions.[115]

During the tense four years in which Synan and Moore served as joint bishops, the issue was slowly defused. A large part of the credit belonged to Bishop Synan, who under "intense pressure" kept the "church from splitting."[116] Although Synan had sided with the anti-Roberts forces, his opposition never gave way to personal rancor; when Oral spoke at the 1953 convention, "Synan embraced him before everybody."[117] Synan and Moore maintained an uneasy working relationship for four years, and at the General Conference in 1957 the church was reorganized, with Synan becoming sole bishop. By that time the move to discipline Oral had lost its steam. In fact, after the mid-1950s, Oral and his denomination drifted apart on diverging paths. Oral continued to have a large following among Pentecostal Holiness pastors, and probably gained increasing respect from denominational leaders, but his ties to his church became less and less important to him.

Oral's struggle with his denomination was the dominant trauma of his early ministry. He paid little attention to the sniping of the press in his early years because "we were never in that world." "We were in the preacher world," recalled Oral, and "the preachers were the first judges of me."[118] He felt that he was being persecuted by his people, his friends. Although politically astute enough to protect himself, it seemed to Oral that his opponents were belittling spiritual success. He rarely criticized others, and he was hurt by the attacks on his work. The thought of leaving his church never occurred to Oral in the 1950s (nor was there any avenue open to him during those years), but the 1953 attack on him left open and festering wounds.

BY THE mid-1950s, Oral's success attracted a variety of other critics. At times the list seemed endless to Evelyn: "When God called my husband to take the healing power of Jesus Christ to his generation, it was a new thing. Pastors rebelled. People rebelled. The new media rebelled."[119] Oral's nonpentecostal critics brought with them a wide variety of intellectual assumptions, but they united in opposition to "faith healing."

Probably Oral's most acid and unrelenting critics were the historical enemies of pentecostal theology — fundamentalists and conservative sectarians such as the Churches of Christ. Fundamentalist opposition to pentecostalism dated from the early twentieth century, when most of the leaders of American evangelicalism rejected the pentecostal understanding of the baptism of the Holy Spirit and barred pentecostals from participation in the organized fundamentalist movement. Doctrinally, the fundamentalists' case was not rigid and clear-cut; they objected generally to the emphasis that pentecostals placed on the gifts of the spirit and miracles, rather than denying the validity of either. The classic fundamentalist doctrinal statement was written by Benjamin B.

Warfield in a book which branded modern healing claims "counterfeit."[120] Fundamentalist leaders were ever ready to offer negative briefs to the press; many reserved sermons on "So-Called Divine Healing Campaigns" for the arrival of a healing evangelist.[121]

More dogged and doctrinaire was the opposition of the Churches of Christ. Throughout the 1950s, the beginning of a Roberts crusade would likely elicit a series of newspaper advertisements by a local Church of Christ challenging Oral to debate and offering a $1,000 reward for documentary evidence that a miracle had occurred. A typical announcement in the *Sacramento Union* in 1955 read:

> We will give $1,000.000 reward, which is on deposit in a North Highlands bank, for acceptable evidence of one case of instantaneous and miraculous divine healing of cancer that has been pronounced in a state of malignancy by competent medical authority, active tuberculosis, withered limbs, or paralysis. Testimony of three reputable Sacramento County physicians upon whom we are mutually agreed, will be accepted as sufficient evidence. We stand ready to deny in public discussion that such power is given to men today.[122]

Sometimes the messages continued after the campaign closed. In 1955, the following advertisement appeared in a Jacksonville, Florida newspaper: "In view of the fact that a revival campaign has just concluded, in which claims were made both over the radio and through the mails that many had been healed of the above named diseases, the Churches of Christ felt compelled to take this means of bringing out the truth that NOT ONE SINGLE CASE OF MIRACULOUS DIVINE HEALING CAN BE PRODUCED.[123]

Churches of Christ opposition to Oral and other healers was based on a full-blown dispensational theology which held that the "miracles worked by the apostles were to confirm the word spoken by the apostles and their helpers" and that "miracles ceased with the death of the last apostle and the last person upon whom an apostle had laid his hands."[124] Actually scores of debates were conducted in the 1940s and 1950s between pentecostal and Churches of Christ ministers as the two fast-growing movements scoured the South recruiting new members among the section's working classes. While the battle raised substantial and fairly clear questions about Biblical teaching, it frequently degenerated into barroom tactics. Churches of Christ ministers labeled Oral a "fake healer," a "sham and a hoax," and a "professional religious racketeer."[125] He was repreatedly taunted about his failures — the Amarillo storm, the death of persons in his meetings, his admission that not all in his healing lines were helped — and challenged to deliver a miricle on demand.[126] In perhaps the harshest charge made against him, a widely distributed tract accused Oral of "payola":

> I offered to appear before the Senate Investigating Committee in Washington and present evidence that Oral Roberts was guilty of "payola" on his TV Healing program. Among other things, I had evidence to prove that a person had "performed" on the Robert's [*sic*] healing TV program, claiming that he was healed as a "cripple," but it was all a fake and he was paid by them to "fake" the healing. The person, who faked the healing, offered to testify.[127]

Oral systematically ignored the challenges of the Churches of Christ, but he was stung by their assault. He was quick to publish the occasional support he received from a member of the Church of Christ who did not "share the narrow views" of the church's leaders.[128] Years later, Evelyn still bristled at the treatment they had received: "They were always wanting him to debate the question. . . . The days of miracles are past, we want to prove it. We want to debate with you. But he would never debate with them because you either accept the Bible or you don't accept it."[129] While Oral refused a public confrontation with evangelists from the Churches of Christ, he by no means yielded to them on his own turf. Several Churches of Christ ministers during the 1950s reported being forcibly ejected from the Roberts tent when they became too inquisitive about the well-being of those who had just passed through the healing line.[130]

The clash between the healing evangelists and the Churches of Christ and fundamentalists was an extension of an old war pitting familiar adversaries. But Oral's growing fame in the 1950s increasingly brought him to the attention of mainstream Protestantism and American Catholicism. By the mid-1950s, most American ministers were prepared to speak a word about Oral. A Roberts crusade in town was likely to call forth a barrage of negative assessments from both the Protestant and Catholic clergymen. In 1959, a professor at Southern Baptist Theological Seminary in Louisville, Kentucky warned that an overemphasis on healing made one "an idolator"; the leading Presbyterian and Lutheran ministers in Charleston, West Virginia labeled Oral's meetings "offensive"; and a Lutheran minister in Sioux Falls, South Dakota denounced his methods as the "ultimate blasphemy."[131] When Oral visited Milwaukee in 1958, the local Catholic newspaper warned: "Let it be stated emphatically that no Catholic may attend faith healing services."[132] Another Catholic journal judged that "it would be gravely sinful for a Catholic to attend an Oral Roberts meeting or program."[133]

Probably the most damaging religious attack on Oral ever published appeared in the *Presbyterian Outlook* in 1955. The article, written by Carroll R. Stegall, Jr., pastor of the Pryor Street Presbyterian Church in Atlanta, Georgia, was later republished in a widely circulated tract. It was Stegall's tract which preceded Oral to Australia and fanned opposition to him. Stegall's curiosity was piqued by the March 1952 issue of *Healing Waters,* which featured a cover picture of "three great medical doctors congratulating Oral Roberts."[134] Stegall and Donald Grey Barnhouse, noted conservative Presbyterian pastor in Philadelphia, addressed an inquiry to the American Medical Association that "brought the answer from their bureau of investigation that not one of the men mentioned . . . could be identified as doctors of medicine. . . . One of the three men was found operating in Phoenix as a 'naturopathic physician.' No organization headed by 'Dr. J. H. Miller, outstanding medical doctor and president of a medical society of over 20,000 physicians,' was discovered."[135] Stegall later attended a number of campaigns, interviewed Oral, and did some follow-up interviews with those who had passed through the healing line. He concluded that Oral was not "as bad as some others in the miracle business," but found no basis to support his claims: "I have never seen a vestige of change. I challenge any honest investigator to follow my technique and see whether his findings do not agree with mine."[136] Stegall concluded: "So far from glorifying God with this, they [the healing evangelists] cause His name to be blasphemed by the world by their excesses. So far from curing, they often kill. Far from blessing, their arrival in a city is rather a curse, a misery, a racket, a destruction of faith in simple people."[137]

The mainstream Protestant and Catholic attacks on Oral presented a wide-ranging critique of his theology, his techniques, and his style. Most offensive to many theologians was his emphasis on the goodness of God, the supposed availability of miracles to all who seek them. Both Protestant and Catholic theologians branded such ideas "a travesty of Christian teaching," a rebirth of the heresy of Pelagianism.[138] Many dismissed Oral as "superficial"; even W. E. Mann, an Episcopalian clergyman who was one of Oral's more understanding critics in the 1950s, concluded in the *Christian Century:* "In general, he lacks any developed critical sense, either theologically or in respect to healing."[139] Critics repeatedly charged that Oral had no theology of suffering, that he ignored the message of Job, that his techniques were manipulative and degrading to God. "What we argue against," wrote a Presbyterian clergyman in 1956, "is the patent attempt to make God merely a means to our own goal, whether that goal be success, blooming health, or wealth. Such attempts are condemned as heresy and doomed to failure."[140] The *Christian Century* agreed that it was a "profound heresy" to believe that God "is susceptible to such pushing around by man."[141]

But if theologians were troubled by Oral's message, many Americans probably agreed with it; the public was more disturbed by attacks on the validity of the healing claims. Over and over again, critics asked for verification: "We have only the word of the Roberts organization that these victims are as ill as described, or later that they are as whole as they seem. No before-and-after verification is ever offered by an impartial medical board. No physicians are on hand to check the symptoms."[142] Oral was repeatedly described as "overeager" to confirm a healing, "pronouncing one healed with nothing more than the excited testimony of an individual that he felt better."[143] Stegall's negative assessment after his follow-up was bolstered by several other reports in the 1950s. Writer John Kobler interviewed two individuals recommended to him by Roberts as "the most striking instances of cures" and reported that while both believed themselves healed, one had never visited a physician, and the other had subsequently undergone surgery to remove a cancer.[144] W. E. Mann reported that a Toronto, Canada physician had examined thirty persons who passed through Oral's healing line and found no case of healing "that could not be explained, in terms of psychological shock or straight hysteria." At least one had died.[145] Oral's critics repeatedly charged that he "covered up his failures," particularly because the television tapes were edited to show only the most favorable cases.[146]

The negative assessments were exacerbated by the morbid fascination of the press with the periodic tragedies which struck the crusades. In 1951, an Alabama businessman died while attending a Roberts campaign in Atlanta.[147]

Such tragedies struck with some regularity during the 1950s and were generally accompanied by flurries of bad publicity. In 1955, the death of an elderly Indian, Jonas Rider, during Oral's campaign in Calgary, Canada occurred, according to the local press, "in the evangelist's tent surrounded by converts and followers of the cult." A "prominent Southern Alberta physician" condemned the campaign as "ridiculous," no more than "mass hypnotism."[148] The following January, Mary Ida Buddington Vonderscher, who had appeared the year before on Oral's television program in the healing line, returned to testify of her healing of cancer, but she died in her California home only twelve hours after her testimony was aired.[149] The year 1959 was particularly beset by tragedy. In January, a sixty-four-year-old California man died of a heart attack during a campaign in Oakland Auditorium.[150] Then, in May, death struck twice in a campaign in Fayetteville, North Carolina. First, a three-year-old girl died under the tent in her parents' arms while waiting for the service to begin.[151] Hart Armstrong issued a statement that "the unfortunate incident was one occurring when people bring their sick in a dying condition. We might point out that Mr. Roberts makes no promise to heal, but attempts to help people by praying for their illnesses."[152] The next evening an elderly Indian woman died on her way to the campaign, causing a local physician to issue a warning against "moving critically ill patients to a faith healer."[153] Finally, in July 1959, in a case which seemed to pose the most serious ethical questions about religious healing, a woman "threw away her insulin" in the belief that she had been healed in a Roberts campaign, and she died in a Detroit hospital.[154] The woman, Wanda Beach, had not gone through the healing line; she had acted totally on her own perception that she had been healed. Bob DeWeese decried the "tragic case" and reminded the press that "we constantly advise people never to do a thing like that. We advise them to go to their own doctor and get a medical examination and clearance before stopping medical treatment."[155] But such disclaimers could hardly repair the damage; *Newsweek* magazine advertised the incident nationally, though without "blaming" Oral for the death.[156]

The Catholic press was particularly intent on distancing its belief in the miracles of Lourdes from the claims of healing evangelists. "The whole matter is particularly confusing," wrote a Catholic journalist in 1957, "because we Catholics alone publicly acknowledge our belief in miracles."[157] "I do believe in divine healing," wrote a priest in 1956, "but I do not believe in Oral Roberts."[158] The National Catholic Welfare Conference noted that while "medical evidence from doctors is frequently included in the testimony of the cured" in Roberts's reports, there was "no effort on the part of the Roberts staff to gather extensive medical and psychiatric evidence." At Lourdes, the report continued, the picture "is totally different." Of the thousands of cases presented to the Medical Bureau of Lourdes, only a few had "passed the rigid tests of acceptance as miracles."[159]

The Roberts organization never satisfactorily came to grips with its critics on the verification issue, though it did feel compelled to address the question. In 1955, G. H. Montgomery explained why Roberts ignored the challenges of the Churches of Christ:

Suppose, for instance, Brother Roberts should take the time to answer those who offer $1,000 rewards for proof that one miracle has been performed in his meetings. The testimonies of the people who were healed would not be accepted by those making the challenge. The testimony of competent, believing physicians would not be accepted. Then where could an effort to satisfy the challengers end? Perhaps in a civil court to be dragged out with weeks of litigation that would do nobody any good. Meantime, the person who has been healed is still healed. He doesn't need proof.[160]

In a 1956 rebuttal, Oral estimated that "multiplied thousands" were being healed in the crusades. "I don't try to prove it," he protested, "I just say, 'There's the person. Let him tell you.' " While such unscientific evidence would hardly satisfy his critics, it was sufficient "to me and to the person."[161]

Oral correctly recognized also that the verification question was as much a theological issue as a medical one, and he refused to be drawn into a theological argument. "I don't argue religion with anybody," he insisted, "I don't force my religion on anybody. I do what I believe is right. If a person is healed, the evidence satisfied me and it satisfied them."[162] Over and over, Oral excused himself as too busy to debate: "I'm not quarreling with anybody. . . . I just promote my product."[163]

The Roberts organization was not completely silent on the verification question, partly because Oral's supporters frequently raised the issue themselves. In 1954, G. H. Montgomery wrote: "Many of our friends write us every month asking us to prove something to them so they can prove it to someone else. It is a little difficult to say without appearing to be brusque, but it is a fact, that we do not concern ourselves with the unbelief of people. Brother Roberts just cannot afford to spend his time trying to prove to people . . . that God is a good God."[164] Oral clearly saw the issue as a Catch-22. "I can't prove any person who ever came to me was healed," he told a reporter in 1959, "that is I can't prove it to the satisfaction of everyone."[165] It was difficult for Oral not to distrust the motives of his critics—as they did his. A supporter sent him a copy of a Catholic attack on him with the note scribbled on it: "These boys are a little jealous of you Oral. However, you keep up your good work."[166]

Partly, at least, the lack of verification of the healings was a product of the loose way in which the campaigns were organized and run. In 1981, Evelyn confessed: "We never even kept count of those who were healed. I have no idea of how many people were healed."[167] Not only were the healings not verified, the follow-up work in the revivals was sporadic and dubiously effective.[168] Recognizing the general problem, a pentecostal leader wrote in 1957: "Let us pray that we shall be able to find the solution to the follow-up work, that the Church shall be strong and that the Church shall harvest the great results from these marvelous campaigns."[169]

Of course, some efforts were made by the organization to verify healing testimonials from the beginning, and those efforts grew more elaborate through the years. Those passing through the healing line were always told to write to Oral telling him of their healing and offering medical evidence if possible. In a 1949 radio sermon, Oral announced that "many of these testimonies have been checked by many people," including a "newspaper man," who had found them to be true.[170] An occasional newsman did indeed report "many apparent recoveries attested by the afflicted themselves," but only rarely did one actually support the testimonies.[171] An important exception was Will Oursler, a respected religious journalist, who in 1957 investigated several cases of alleged healings and concluded that "Oral Roberts does appear to have something." "At least," he wrote, "I have talked to people who claim to have been cured by his touch and his prayer. And these cures, they say, have lasted for years."[172]

Of course, the Roberts ministry received testimonies by the thousands. An effort was made to select the most reliable ones for publication in *Healing Waters* and, after 1956, for presentation on television. "We have a young lady whose job is to see that what goes into the magazine is the truth," wrote G. H. Montgomery. "We check with neighbors, we check with preachers. When we can we check with doctors. We write everywhere, and, if necessary, we go see the people in that community to find out if it is the truth."[173] The television programs in the late 1950s often featured flashbacks showing a person in an earlier healing line and then returning for an interview. Typical was the case of Fred O'Dell, who first entered Oral's healing line in Jacksonville, Florida in 1955:

> ROBERTS: What's wrong with you, Fred?
> O'DELL: Well the doctors say I have incurable cancer on the lymph gland and it's all over my body. He says I've had it at the longest eight months time.
> ROBERTS: You know, a lot of people don't stop to realize that Almighty God is able to heal cancer. He's fully able to do it. We need to believe and to turn our faith loose. Fred, I'm going to pray for you now. I know this great audience will have compassion and pray with me. Oh God, I bring this young man, . . . to thee tonight, not in my name but in the name of Jesus of Nazareth, Son of the living God. Hear thy servant's prayer and heal him. Heal the lymph glands of cancer. Set him free of it, destroy the cancer that it shall leave his body, in the name of Jesus of Nazareth. Well, the power of God is so strong tonight I'm amazed. Fred, look up here for a minute, please. Why were you trembling so violently? Well, Fred, it is possible to feel the presence of God. People in Bible days felt that presence and they did exploits. You came here to be healed, didn't you?
> O'DELL: And I got it.

A little over a year later, O'Dell returned for another appearance with Oral:

> O'DELL: I have in my hands the first xrays and the series of xrays and the last xray that I had made showed that the cancer is completely gone.
> ROBERTS: How much weight have you gained?
> O'DELL: Well at the time the cancer came on me I weighed about 167. Within a matter of less than a month I lost down to 138 pounds. I now weigh 172.
> ROBERTS: How are you?
> O'DELL: I am in better health than I have been in my life. . . . I haven't missed a day's work because of illness since the night I was prayed for.[174]

Such testimonies, while they by no means silenced Oral's critics, represented the most strenuous effort of the Roberts organization to verify its healing claims.

Oral understood the desire of outsiders for better verification, and he toyed with the idea of doing more thorough follow-up investigations. When Episcopalian minister W. E. Mann interviewed Oral in 1956, he "pointed out that a battery of impartial doctors attempt to validate the miraculous cures at the famous shrine in Lourdes, France, and asked him why something similar could not be done at his meetings." Oral confessed that "this is worth thinking about," and Hart Armstrong hinted that "if medical men came and requested the chance to check up before and after, they might not be refused."[175] During the mid-1950s, the ministry did improve its method in collecting "records of miracles," claiming that all testimonies were "carefully investigatged, checked and recorded. The facts. The dates. The medical histories."[176] In 1957, Oral announced that the ministry was "preparing for publication a book, *Documented Healings of the Twentieth Century*," based on the testimonial files. "We believe," Oral wrote, "those healed by Christ have a definite responsibility to shed light upon the paths of others and give them the hope they have found in Christ. They should gather, wherever possible, definite medical evidence of the physical change in their bodies by Christ's healing touch." The planned volume was never published, though numerous accounts of individual healings were printed in book form. Even as Oral contemplated this effort to document his ministry's claims, he continued to recognize that "where religious prejudice has closed the mind, not even medical proof is accepted as valid evidence of God's healing power."[177]

More than any other healing evangelist, Oral grappled with the problem of failure. His healing philosophy left room for the inscrutable, as opposed to the rigid beliefs of some of the evangelists, and in later years he recognized that the spotlighting of his successful cases raised "legitimate questions."[178] In 1971 he explained to a group of Oral Roberts University students the rationale for his television editing:

> I was trying to establish in the minds of people the possibility that a healing can take place in this century. And that's why that I brought people who were. Now I admit there are disadvantages to this, but I had to weigh the advantages over the disadvantages and think of the viewer and his need. If I could inspire him to be healed and that often occurred. . . . The Bible tells how Jesus went to Nazareth and many were not healed. In fact, they could not be healed. A few were, and the Bible tells about the few who were. So I think my thinking could be best understood by my background of the knowledge of the Bible."[179]

While Oral's theology of divine healing raised serious questions in the minds of many Christian leaders, the attacks on him often had more to do with style than with his preaching or his results. At worst, his critics were both undiscriminating and condescending. As late as 1963, a Catholic writer noted that "few Catholics regard Pentecostals with more than amusement, if they take notice of their existence at all."[180] Another Catholic journal, noting that Oral was "born in the backwoods near Ada, Oklahoma," described him as "a combination of old John D. Rockefeller in business, Phineas Taylor Barnum in showmanship, ... and Will Rogers in looks."[181] Other outsiders left Oral's services feeling they had witnessed "a nauseating display of superstitious bad taste."[182] Although healing evangelists might seem perfectly rational outside the pulpit, warned a journalist, when they mounted the platform, they became "shriekers and arm-wavers ... generating a commotion which makes the late Billy Sunday seem restrained and scholarly, and Billy Graham a model of the spiritual."[183]

While some observers were shocked by the goings on under the tents simply because of their own cultural prejudice, others raised legitimate questions about the techniques of the revivalists. Serious critics questioned the emphasis on the spectacular—the apparent desire to "sell the product." W. E. Mann believed that Oral employed "methods taken over wholesale and uncritically from the advertising and selling world of America."[184] "The tremendous emphasis upon publicity" and "the hiring of both an advertising and public relations agency" seemed highly questionable to many mainstream churchmen.[185]

Nor were most outside observers comfortable with the pentecostal concepts of "calling" and "gifts," which concentrated so much attention on one individual. Visiting Oral's meeting, W. E. Mann felt "an unhealthy concentration of attention on him and his healing gift. Asked why he did not train others to assist him in his healing ministry he answered merely, 'This must be a call of God.'"[186] Stegall's analysis of the same problem was less gentle: "The ego of these men is enormous. They reign like kings over their tents and theaters full of subjects. They swell upon the admiration of the crowds. They're astute enough to make a great show of giving God glory, but one glimpse of their publicity will show what the main attraction is."[187] A Catholic spokesman noted that the cures of Lourdes were not credited to "any individual person": "Unanimously the cure is accredited to the Blessed Virgin. Oral Roberts and associates please take notice."[188]

Finally, of course, ever present was the conviction that Oral was enriching himself at the expense of his gullible audiences. The budget of the Roberts organization, reaching $3,000,000 a year by the mid-1950s, encouraged the belief that Oral had accepted "the huckster approach applied to the House of God."[189] Mainstream Protestant and Catholic clergymen were shocked by the reported opulence of Oral's lifestyle—allegedly sustained by an income of $100,000 a year. In 1956, a Presbyterian writer charged that Oral's financial appeals brought in "enough money to keep him in splendid garb that seems never to be worn a second time, in several expensive cars, and in a sizeable ranch where Black Angus cattle are bred as a hobby."[190] A Catholic spokesman dismissd Oral with the observation: "I can't see any connection between miracles and $40 shirts for faith healing preachers."[191]

The critique of Oral by religious leaders was paralleled by increased attention from the press. Not only did his meetings attract copious local coverage, but by the mid-1950s he had become a national media personality. Oral's relationship with the press was schizoid from the beginning. Much of his press coverage was condescending and degrading; some of it was vicious. And yet, attention from the national media made him a hero among pentecostals; it was a recognition of his leadership of the healing revival. Thus began a love-hate relationship which would last through the evangelist's life.

Oral earned the reputation of ducking "reporters' questions" in the 1950s. His crusade workers did receive printed instructions warning that "eager reporters of an unfriendly newspaper love to get hold of a talkative usher. . . . When you are approached by any person desiring information and you have reason to feel he is from the press, refuse to talk or give any statements. Say, 'I am only an usher here. I have no information about that. . . .' Then turn away and go about your work."[192] Oral frequently charged that the press had "defamed us and deliberately misunderstood our work and our mission," and he vacillated between trying to educate them or avoid them.[193] In 1957, shortly after the Australian debacle, Oral addressed an "open letter to magazine and newspaper editors" pleading for fairness. The letter was a dignified effort to explain his attitude about healing, his style, and his personal finances. All religion was "controversial," he concluded, but everyone should be given a respectful hearing.[194] But most of the team felt that they never did get a fair hearing from the press because of their belief in healing. "You know there's a scripture in Mark 2," reminded Bob DeWeese playfully in 1983, "that says the people couldn't come nigh to Jesus because of the press."[195]

Sometimes the local coverage of Oral's crusades was scathing. A Canadian reporter labeled Oral an "oily hypocrite" who had established a "continental suck system to bleed the gullible, ignorant and superstitious of North America."[196] A Pennsylvania editor classed Oral with "witch-doctors" and other "quacks" who "preyed on mass superstition and ignorance."[197] But more distressing to the Roberts organization than these malicious attacks—which were fairly rare—was the pervasive interest of the press in issues which Oral considered peripheral (such as his personal finances) and the inability or unwillingness of reporters to correctly represent his beliefs about healing.

Oral's first major media breakthrough came in May 1951, when he was featured in a *Life* magazine story which dubbed him "a rival of Billy Graham." The photographic essay on his Atlanta campaign pictured Oral as the "loudest and splashiest revivalist to appear since the advent of Billy Graham."[198] The article was superficial but, in fact, a relatively respectful notice. In July 1951, *Look* magazine featured Roberts, along with Billy Graham and healing evangelist Gayle Jackson, as one of "the nation's most powerful soul savers."[199] Oral was pleased by the attention; he alerted the readers of his magazine to the articles: "The press is carrying some very favorable accounts of Oral Roberts' ministry now. The Full Gospel is on the march to deliver the people in these trying times."[200] When the ministry published Oral's *Life Story* in 1952, the book chided the balky pentecostal press: "It is significant that secular magazines have been more interested in our meetings than some of the religious publications."[201]

These early notices were followed in 1954 by a second major photographic essay in *Look* magazine, which was one of the most penetrating assessments Oral received in the 1950s. Author Chester Morrison portrayed Oral as the psychiatrist of "country people." He made clear that Oral claimed no "divine power," and while acknowledging that "sometimes the cures may not last," he judged the "performance impressive." Clearly captured by the magnetism of the tent atmosphere, Morrison concluded: "Skeptics come to his meetings prepared for an exhibition of mass hysteria, and sometimes that is what they find. But many an unbeliever goes away wondering whether there may not be some cases in which simple faith can ease the mind, can wash away at least those illnesses that began in the mind and became real through long self-deception."[202]

It was not until 1955 that Oral began to be noticed by news magazines such as *Time* and *Newsweek,* and to attract the attention of major syndicated columnists. That attention was part of the largely unfavorable reaction to the beginning of his television ministry. Along with the sniping of local writers, and his catastrophic encounter with the overseas press, it was Oral's battle with the national media over his television rights which left him most scarred.

ORAL FACED a series of serious obstacles in the 1950s which could have stalled the growth of his ministry. In early 1950 he made a special trip to Washington to talk with postal officials who questioned his mailing permit; with the help of Senator Robert S. Kerr of Oklahoma, he satisfied the authorities.[203] Equally threatening were repeated rumors that legislation was about to be introduced prohibiting "any unauthorized person from praying for the healing of the sick."[204] In 1956, evangelist Jack Coe was arraigned in a Florida court for practicing medicine without a license, and although he was acquitted, the threat continued to hang over healing evangelists. Joseph Lewis, president of the Freethinkers of America, who had challenged Coe in the Florida suit, pursued Oral throughout 1959, allegedly hiring "private detectives" to sit in the audience in an effort to accumulate evidence for a suit.[205]

The most serious threat to Oral's ministry in the 1950s was the attack on his radio and television programs. In 1950, he was summoned to appear before the Federal Communications Commission to answer complaints about his radio program. He was "frightened out of my wits," certain that an unfavorable ruling "could have ended this ministry." Lee Braxton accompanied Oral to Washington, where the beleaguered young evangelist tried to explain the "point of contact" to the commission. The commissioners apparently remained theologically skeptical, but Roberts recalled the chairman's verdict: "I'm going to let you get by with it. I'm not going to take you off the air." Oral and Lee Braxton later savored that day as one of "the most crucial times" in the ministry's history.[206]

A far more important crisis arose in 1955 in reaction to the television program. For the first time, millions of Americans were exposed to the raw drama of the healing line. This first-hand witnessing of Oral's techniques, combined with the awesome potential of television itself, brought a rash of criticism in the summer of 1955. New York columnist John Crosby questioned the validity of the healing testimonies and concluded: "I suppose there is an audience for this sort of thing, but it definitely isn't me."[207] In a gentle putdown, *Variety* noted that the "show-wise bunch" in New York had been watching "Dr. Orval

Roberts" and had judged his "video showmanship" first rate.[208] Other articles were more threatening. Columnist Harriet Van Horne suggested that both Oral's radio and television programs raised questions about "how elastic the famous FCC licensing clause is—the one requiring a TV station to 'operate in the public interest.'" She challenged the right of television stations "to further confound the simple by broadcasting the work of this evangelical pitchman."[209]

Probably the most damaging critique of Oral in the 1950s was written on February 19, 1956, by columnist Jack Gould, radio and television critic of the *New York Times*. Gould argued that Oral's program posed "a matter of fundamental policy for the broadcasting industry." The columnist announced that he believed that faith could aid healing, but, he wrote, "it is quite another matter to have miracles on a weekly basis and to claim on the screen, without even the most rudimentary proof, permanent cure of an endless variety of ailments." Gould's judgment was sharp and clear-cut: "If Brother Roberts wishes to exploit hysteria and ignorance by putting up his hands and yelling 'Heal,' that is his affair. But it hardly seems within the public interest, convenience and necessity, for the TV industry to go along with him."[210]

The Roberts organization reacted to the Gould article with a circular letter to its partners charging that the editorial had been "entirely beyond the realm of unbiased criticism which is the true activity of a columnist." Oral's partners were asked to write immediately to the *New York Times* protesting the column, since "there is a definite possibility that the influence of such articles might in the none-too-distant future jeopardize our religious freedom in praying for the sick."[211] By March 4, 1956, the *Times* had received 1,450 letters of protest; a number of them were published by the paper.[212]

While Oral's partners flooded the *Times* with letters, some correspondents supported Gould, including Charles H. Schmitz, director of the Broadcast Training, Broadcasting, and Film Commission of the National Council of Churches of Christ.[213] The threat to Oral's television ministry was especially serious because of the political maneuvering of the National Council. In June 1955, the *Christian Century* warned that "the Oral Roberts sort of thing" could "do the cause of vital religion far more harm" than anything that had been aired in the past.[214] There was a concerted move to upgrade the quality of mainstream religious programming, but, also, in 1956 the National Council launched a campaign to ban the sale of air time for religious purposes. Supported by the Catholic church, which along with the National Council had been the chief recipient of free religious television exposure, the NCC lobbied throughout 1956 for regulatory legislation.[215] While the efforts of the National Council seemed self-serving, and were unsuccessful, at the local level those opposed to Oral's program sometimes won skirmishes. In 1957, a California group called the National Association for Better Radio and Television attacked several stations which refused to cancel Oral's program, seeking the revocation of their licenses by the FCC.[216]

Oral's television program had actually reopened an old struggle for the control of religious television—a conflict between liberals and evangelicals which had contributed to the formation of the National Association of Evangelicals in

1942 and the National Religious Broadcasters two years later.[217] Roberts had allies from the beginning, including Southern Baptist minister Warren G. Hultgren, who moved to Tulsa in 1957 and spoke strongly in defense of Oral's right to buy air time.[218] In 1974, when Hultgren gave the baccalaureate address at Oral Roberts University, Oral remembered that in "those days when we were having some of our most terrible struggles of being recognized as authentic people of God, Warren Hultgren stood up for us. . . . He will possibly never know how much that meant to us."[219] But it was a dark period; it was a constant struggle to keep the program on local stations. Oral fought for his rights. He made frequent trips to Washington to lobby; he told several senators that he might "organize a caravan and come to Washington for a public hearing."[220] Congress took no action, and the crisis slowly abated as the novelty of Oral's programs wore off. For his part, Oral increasingly entrusted his public image into the hands of advertising experts.

Oral's sensitivity to adverse press coverage was never simply a matter of an injured ego. As in the case of the television squabble, strongly negative attacks frequently led to legal problems for the ministry. A 1956 article in *American Magazine,* entitled "Oral Roberts: King of the Faith Healers," sparked an investigation of the ministry by the Internal Revenue Service, which required Oral and his tax attorney, Donald Moyers, to make frequent trips to Washington over a period of about six months. It was a harrowing experience; the IRS had accepted author John Kobler's assessment of Oral's personal fortune as "gospel" and was intent, Moyers believed, on "undoing us." While the ministry rallied sufficient evidence to protect its tax-exempt status, Oral was shaken by the experience. Shortly after the encounter, the "love offering" was abandoned as a means of Oral's support on the advice of his tax attorneys.[221]

ONE BYPRODUCT of Oral's growing visibility in the late 1950s was a resurgence of interest in the proper relationship of religion and health by the nation's clergymen and intellectuals. Several commissions were appointed which published reports on the subject. In 1956, a British medical commission, appointed by the Archbishop of Canterbury, reported: "We can find no evidence that there is any type of illness cured by spiritual healing alone which could not have been cured by medical treatment."[222] While recognizing "the power of faith on the individual mind as a factor that may affect the condition of sick people," the *Journal of the American Medical Association* in 1956 issued a warning against "faith healers." The *Journal* agreed that "in cases where no organic disease exists," healers could cause believers to feel that "they have had curative ministrations." But, the warning continued, the healing revivals were conducted with a "woeful ignorance of public health measures," allowing diseased people to mingle freely with others. And, most important, the healers could do harm to those who were seriously ill: "The further danger exists that persons whose physical condition demands prompt and adequate scientific medical attention may, by delay or abandonment of such care, contribute to their needless early death."[223] A Presbyterian report issued a few months later condemned "the desire to use 'faith' to manipulate God."[224]

While some of the reports in the mid-1950s were deprecatory, others begrudgingly viewed Oral as a prophet. The Protestant press abounded in introspective searchings about the meaning of Oral's popularity. "Finally . . . one may ask," wrote Wayne E. Gates in the *Review and Expositer* in a notice of *If You Need Healing—Do These Things!*, "if this phenomenon is not stark testimony against the established denominations who have been timid beyond the right which the Biblical record gives them in exploring the real and vital relationship between religion and health."[225] By the end of the decade, the United Lutheran church had also established a commission to explore "spiritual healing," and the Order of Saint Luke, the historic Episcopal healing order, had experienced a revitalization.[226] While many of the studies still "decried the likes of Roberts," few questioned that his "meteoric rise to national prominence" had triggered the "swelling tide of ecclesiastical interest in spiritual healing."[227] In 1959, the *Christian Century* conceded: "He must be given credit for spreading among the masses the new idea that Christianity involved healing of the body and the emotions as well as salvation of souls. . . . Anyway one looks at it Oral Roberts is a figure to reckon with in American religious life today."[228]

Episcopalian critic W. E. Mann recognized that Oral's ministry had convinced "thousands, if not millions, of people with the validity of clairvoyance and faith healing," and he himself was convinced "that Roberts has some kind of healing gift; there is a power in his right hand."[229] He urged that the "main churches" establish an "investigation commission and undertake a thorough study of all of his work." If such a study were conducted "sympathetically," it was possible that Oral could be given some "useful counsel."[230]

In the spring of 1956—in the most extensive published examination in the aftermath of Oral's television program—the semischolarly journal *Religion in Life* printed a forty-one-page symposium on "spiritual healing." The symposium revealed that many individuals and a number of church agencies had been interested in spiritual healing for several decades, but, as Presbyterian minister John Pitts pointed out, it was Oral who had forced American religious leaders to restudy "faith healing." "Today," he wrote, "interest in extramedical methods of healing men's minds and bodies is widespread and deep-seated, and the phenomena of Faith Healing can no longer be dismissed with a shrug of the shoulders, a snap judgment, and a clever phrase, either by the church or by the medical profession."[231] Pitts's own judgment, and that of other writers in the symposium, was that "there seems to be more than enough evidence to affirm that spiritual healing is a fact."[232]

THE HIGHLY visible attacks on Oral tended to obscure the considerable amount of good press that he received during the decade. A Memphis reporter in 1950 went away from the crusade "impressed by Roberts' efforts"; Bill Rose, religion editor of the *Oakland Tribune,* consistently spoke well of Oral; a Charleston, South Carolina reporter confessed that he found Oral's healing line "in some cases spectacular."[223] No doubt, many publishers shared the sentiment of the editor of the Danville, Virginia *Register,* who, beset by "irate" critics of Oral, declared: "We are not carrying any torch for Oral Roberts, nor are we deter-

mined to 'debunk' him. . . . We will leave it at that."[234] A Colorado paper declared its policy was "to report the work of all denominations—but not to pass
judgment on them" and published a long list of healing testimonies after a
crusade in Pueblo.[235] It was not uncommon for newspapers to publish objective
accounts of reported healings, often accompanied by follow-up interviews.[236]
Occasionally a local paper boldly advised Oral's critics to "be slow to hinder the
work by adverse criticism"; a few were disdainful of the challenges to the healing revivalists by Churches of Christ.[237] By the late 1950s, such treatment from
the press was likely to elicit a letter of appreciation from Hart R. Armstrong or
some other Roberts official for the "objective and straightforward reporting of
our meetings."[238]

In the late 1950s, Oral received several important boosts from friendly
journalists. Perhaps most important was a series of articles written by *Tulsa
Tribune* business writer Bob Foresman shortly after Oral's return from Australia
in 1956. Foresman had met Oral several years earlier; he liked him and had
written several articles about the local evangelist celebrity. Oral asked Foresman
to write an extensive article that could be used by a national journal. The article
was designed for the *Saturday Evening Post,* but when the magazine decided not
to publish it, the Roberts organization broke it into thirteen segments and distributed it to every newspaper in the country. Although the series was never
run in Tulsa it was widely published. Foresman was no sycophant, and he turned
down an offer to become circulation manager of *Healing Waters,* but his articles
were objective, and they helped Oral's image.

In February 1957, Will Oursler, Associated Press religion writer, published
an article on Oral in the *American Weekly* which was later included as a chapter
in his book *The Healing Power of Faith.*[240] Oursler began his investigation perfectly neutral, he reported, and came away convinced that Oral was honest and
effective. Oursler interviewed Oral, asking him "hard questions," and he was
impressed by the responses: "They were good answers. They were not in any
way evasive. They presented the picture of a man who has become—in a very
real sense to many thousands of people, a channel of healing."[241]

Even more supportive was the assessment of Emily Gardiner Neal, a widely
published journalist who in 1959 authored a book entitled *God Can Heal You
Now.*[242] Neal reputedly began her research with the intention of exposing
spiritual healing but became a believer instead. Her chapter on Oral, entitled "A
Simple Man Who Loves Jesus," argued that Oral's theology of healing was
squarely in the mainstream of Christian thought. Oral was euphoric after being
interviewed by Neal; he told the workers at the Oral Roberts Evangelistic
Association that such sympathetic journalists could signal a "breakthrough."
"She was just as hungry as a child," exuded Oral, "and she took this message
that we gave her."[243] Perhaps most pleasing was the news that Neal had asked
Episcopal bishop Austin Pardue of Pittsburgh about including Oral in her book,
and the bishop reportedly told her: "While I couldn't possibly work as does Mr.
Roberts, and temperamentally dislike his methods, I definitely *like* the fact that
he is helping so many."[244]

Pardue was in the vanguard of a growing group of mainstream clergymen who openly spoke well of Oral's ministry—forerunners of the charismatic revival which would surface just after the turn of the decade. Increasing numbers of clergymen agreed with the president of the Charleston, West Virginia ministerial association: "He has a right to appear. I don't agree with a lot of things which go on in the religious world, but I respect a person's right to his opinion. I'll champion that right."[245] Oral was aware of this rising undercurrent of support, and he did all he could to call attention to it.[246]

Another boding of better things to come was Oral's improving image in Tulsa. In March 1956, he was invited to address the Tulsa Chamber of Commerce, and in 1958 he spoke to the Tulsa Ministerial Alliance.[247] Oral charmed both audiences, deftly fielding questions; his performance in 1958 was before "the largest crowd in the history of the ministers' organization."[248] Oral's friend Bob Foresman arranged a meeting between the evangelist and editor Jenkin Lloyd Jones of the *Tulsa Tribune,* and the two had an immediate liking for one another. In May 1959, Jones wrote the first of what was to be a series of frank but supportive editorials about Oral under the title: "A Famous Tulsan." Roberts, he guessed, was "Tulsa's best known citizen"; he also had the "largest daily flow of mail" in the city and was an unquestioned economic asset. "You might not personally care for his brand of preaching," the editor concluded, "but you cannot deny that the Oral Roberts organization fills a human need." The time had come for Tulsans to recognize that he was an asset to the community.[249]

While Oral's improving image was partly the result of the growing interest of nonpentecostals in spiritual healing, it was also a tribute to his personal charisma and powers of persuasion. Few people who knew Oral personally disliked him. One of the first ministers to welcome him when he arrived in Tulsa was Forney Hutchinson, former minister of the prestigious Boston Avenue Methodist Church, who had been personally acquainted with Oral when they were both ministers in Shawnee.[250] Although Oral frequently felt betrayed when he gave interviews to the press, many reporters, even in the early years, found him to be a "man of charm."[251] He could disarm even antagonistic reporters with his friendly smile and greeting: "Ask whatever you like. I'll do my best to answer."[252]

Oral went through a period in the mid-1950s when he turned sulky because of the criticisms of his ministry, but by 1957 he began an intensive campaign to better his relations with the press, including commissioning a New York public relations agency to schedule interviews with influential writers. Associated Press religion writer George W. Cornell interviewed Roberts in New York City in March 1958 in a suite in the Plaza Hotel and found that while Oral might be "oratorical lightning in the pulpit," in a "sitting room conversation he is a relaxed, unaffected sort of person with an engaging warmth and friendliness."[253] Oral's personal magnetism made friends wherever he chose to turn it on. He charmed a "part-time elevator operator in Indianapolis" and prompted from a Charleston, South Carolina hotel waitress the exclamation: "Gee, it must be bad to be so good."[254] He captivated a young woman volunteer worker named Ruth Carter Stapleton in a campaign in North Carolina.[255]

1. Oral Roberts, 1918.

2. Amos Pleasant Roberts and Mary Jane Maddox Roberts, Oral's paternal grandparents.

3. Ellis Roberts, Oral's father, posing with the portable organ he used as an itinerate evangelist, Summer 1920.

4. Vaden and Oral, about 1924.

5. Oral and his bride, Evelyn, on their wedding day,
Westville, Oklahoma, December 25, 1938.

6. Oral, Evelyn, and two-year-old daughter Rebecca, 1942.

7. O. E. Sproull, Oral, and Reg G. Hanson, about 1950. Sproull and Hanson were Oral's first assistant evangelists.

8. Revival meeting tent in Amarillo, Texas, destroyed by a storm on September 10, 1950.

9. Florence, South Carolina, 1955.

10. Anna Williams and her husband, Air Force Sergeant Williams, after
her recovery. Confined to a wheelchair for several years, Anna walked
again after watching an Oral Roberts television program in May 1955.
Her testimony was publicized throughout the nation and gave Oral's
television campaign an important boost.

11. The Roberts family. From left to right: Ronnie, Oral, Richard, Roberta, Evelyn, and Rebecca at home on Robin Hood Ranch, about 1954.

12. Oral's family listens as Evelyn speaks to an audience in Trenton, New Jersey, 1957. Oral was pleased when his family could join him on a crusade. From left to right: Rebecca, Ronnie, Roberta, Oral, Richard, and Evelyn.

13. Pensacola, Florida, April 1957.

14. Detroit, Michigan, 1959.

15. A tent gathering in Marietta, Georgia, 1960.

16. The Roberts family. Fom left to right: Vaden, Jewel Roberts Faust,
Ellis, Claudius, Oral, and Elmer, about 1960.

17. Oral consults with Dr. Raymond O. Corvin in November 1962. Roberts and Corvin were boyhood friends in the Pentecostal Holiness Church. Oral leaned heavily on Corvin during the early years of building Oral Roberts University.

18. Oral receiving the Indian of the Year Award in Anadarka, Oklahoma, July 1963. He was proud of his Cherokee heritage.

19. San Jose, California, 1965.

20. Ministry leaders during a fund-raising campaign for Oral Roberts University, 1966. Left to right: Lee Braxton, John Messick, R. O. Corvin, Ron Smith, Oral, ? , Manford Engel, and Frank Wallace.

21. Ministry leaders holding building designs during the Oral Roberts University fund-raising campaign, 1966. From left to right: Oral, Lee Braxton, R. O. Corvin, John Messick.

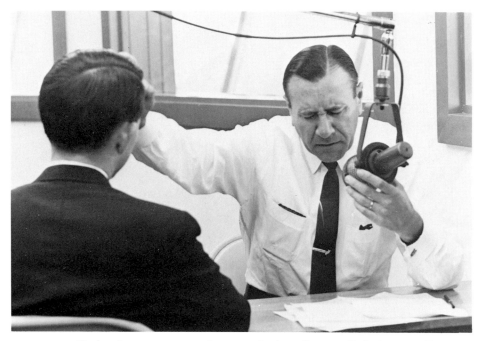

22. Oral using a team member as a "point of contact" during a radio broadcast, June 1967.

23. After the crusades ended in 1968, Oral placed one of the battered tent chairs in the Prayer Tower as a reminder of the thousands of evenings he spent preaching and praying.

24. The builders of Oral Roberts University. From left to right: John Messick, Oral, unidentified, and Carl Hamilton, December 1967.

25. Oral and Billy Graham at the dedication of Oral Roberts University, April 2, 1967.

Oral played golf with the religion editor of a Milwaukee newspaper, who then reported with confidence that "Oral Roberts is above board"; a Johnstown, Pennsylvania interviewer discovered that Oral looked like Cary Grant and "exuded friendliness."[256] In 1959, a North Carolina reporter summed up Oral's new image: "Sincerity—that key word stuck in this reporter's mind as the basic impression made by evangelist Oral Roberts during a personal interview."[257]

In short, by the end of the 1950s, Oral Roberts had survived a decade of criticism and had begun to win important friends. His circle of personal acquaintances and supporters had grown impressively broad. Almost from the beginning of the campaigns, an array of local politicians had crossed his platform to welcome him to their community in the presence of thousands of pleased voters. By the end of the decade, he counted among his acquaintances senators Herman Talmadge of Georgia, Kerr Scott of North Carolina, Henry Jackson of Washington, and Albert Gore of Tennessee, in addition to his closer friendships with Oklahoma senators Robert S. Kerr and Mike Monroney and Governor Raymond Gary.[258] When Oral returned from a 1957 visit to Washington, he reported to his partners that he "spent some time . . . in earnest discussion of world events in the light of Bible prophecy with several United States Senators and Congressmen."[259]

In his early years, Oral was as star-struck as any country boy on his way up; his name dropping seemed largely calculated to impress his pentecostal customers. After a visit to Hollywood, he wrote a widely distributed tract which told of his and Evelyn's visiting Hollywood and Vine and encountering a faded star named "Eddie" who "had made $180,000.00 and spent it all."[260] When one of his supporters sent a subscription to *Healing Waters* to Mamie Eisenhower in 1953, Oral announced to a South Carolina audience that the president's wife was "a subscriber to his healing magazine."[261] It was this overanxiousness to legitimatize his ministry that made Oral stretch, carelessly on occasion, to find support from the medical community.[262]

By the end of the decade, Oral and Evelyn did have a circle of celebrity friends. Roy Rogers and Dale Evans had introduced him to influential Henrietta Mears of Hollywood Presbyterian Church; General Mark Clark had invited him to speak at the Citadel; columnist Dr. George W. Crane, after a visit with the couple, compared the evangelist to "one of the 12 apostles."[263] In June 1958, the Robertses were houseguests in Washington in the home of Mr. and Mrs. Oliver Presbrey, prominent television producers whose credits included "Meet the Press." The guest list at the two dinner parties given in their honor included senators John McClellan of Arkansas, Clinton Anderson of New Mexico, Herman Talmadge of Georgia, and Barry Goldwater of Arizona as well as Postmaster General Arthur Summerfield and a smattering of other dignitaries.[264] A few months later, Oral and Evelyn spent several days in New York and were invited to conduct a Sunday morning service in the home of Hearst columnist Bob Montgomery. Oral prayed for each guest, and, reported Evelyn, "they all seemed so appreciative."[265] Oral discovered that the nation's elite were "common, everyday people who feel the need of God's help and who appreciate the power of prayer."[266] And Oral and Evelyn slowly awakened to the notion that they were celebrities. "This is what television has done for our ministry," an incredulous Evelyn wrote to their partners in December 1958.[267]

Oral's improving image was also linked to his success in separating himself from the less responsible forms of healing revivalism. As the revival turned more and more radical, he never criticized any individual, but he tried to distance himself from the extremists. When someone published a tract in 1957 "claiming that Oral Roberts is Jesus Christ returned to earth," the Roberts organization denounced it as "insidious, false and hurtful to Brother Roberts."[268] In a 1957 interview in Los Angeles, Oral pointed out that "the press and public used to compare me with every Tom, Dick and Harry who held a tent meeting, and I suffered for it," but fortunately, he continued, they now "accept me as an individual."[269] Fighting the "Holy Roller" stereotype, Oral became an ambassador for the pentecostal churches, repeatedly explaining to reporters that pentecostals were a recent offshoot of mainstream Protestant churches (and that his own grandfather had been a Methodist) and that "we have many of the same beliefs of the other Protestant churches."[270] Under his tutelage, a *New York Times* reporter learned that "Pentecostal adherents are not to be confused with 'Holy Rollers.' This term, now almost archaic, refers to groups in the ultra-fanatic fringe of religion that practices excesses and contortions."[271]

An association which helped Oral in the 1950s, and one which he encouraged, was identification with Billy Graham. As Billy catapulted to fame after his 1948 revival in Los Angeles, it became a common journalistic tactic to compare Roberts's crusades with those of Graham, especially if the two visited a community during the same year. When Graham and Roberts both preached in Columbia, South Carolina in 1950, a local reporter found a "definite similarity" in their techniques, though he noted that "the Oral Roberts meeting was entirely different in background, in sponsorship, in the way it was housed and in Mr. Roberts' practice of faith healing."[272] Some reporters were totally undiscriminating. A Canadian writer predicted that the "howling horror known as Billy Graham" was about to lose his revivalistic crown to Oral Roberts, "the Bible Beggar of the Airwaves."[273] But whatever the tone of the articles, it was a boost to Oral to be touted as the "flashiest revivalist since Billy Graham's advent."[274]

By the end of the decade, Oral was almost always described by the press as "next to the Rev. Dr. Billy Graham the widest-known evangelist in the country."[275] Many writers had come to understand the more substantial differences between the two, as well as their similarities. Bill Rose, religion editor for the *Oakland Tribune,* wrote a sophisticated comparison in 1959, noting that the primary differences were Graham's vastly superior organization and Oral's belief in healing. The most "striking similarity" was their "sense of dedication and mission and their desire to win souls for Christ."[276]

Oral was shamelessly flattered by the Graham comparisons; in fact, he often suggested them. His admiration of Graham was sincere and natural—as was his admiration of other preachers—and it was deepened by two brief personal encounters which made lasting impressions on Oral. The two met for the first time in 1950, shortly after Oral's tent had been destroyed in Amarillo. Oral and

Evelyn were visiting on the West Coast with friends, recuperating from the mishap, when an acquaintance encouraged them to come to Portland, where Graham was conducting a campaign. Oral recalled that "I didn't want to go," exhibiting his reluctance to push himself where he might not be wanted, but he and Evelyn were finally persuaded to attend.

As they left their Portland hotel to catch a taxi to the crusade, Billy was just leaving. The ever-gracious Graham grabbed Oral's hand and requested that he and Evelyn ride with him. Oral demurred, but Billy insisted; inside the taxi he told Oral that he expected him to sit on the platform and lead the evening prayer. Oral protested: "Billy you can't afford to have me pray." As they rode, Billy told Oral that he and Cliff Barrows had visited a Roberts campaign in Florida a few months before, slipping in and out unnoticed, and they had been "blessed" by it. He also revealed that his wife's sister had experienced a healing in a pentecostal setting; he was not ashamed to be identified with Oral Roberts. Oral offered the evening prayer, and that evening, after he and Evelyn returned to the hotel coffee shop, Billy and Ruth Graham insisted that they join them for a snack.[277]

The meeting had been brief, casual, and, mostly, unplanned. But for Oral it was loaded with meaning. His appearance on Graham's platform was unprecedented recognition for a pentecostal to receive from an evangelical minister—especially from Billy Graham. Graham's personal kindness, his glad and wholesome embrace of a fellow Christian, placed Oral momentarily in a larger, more respectable, world than he had ever imagined he could be a part of. He had glimpsed a vision which Graham would open to him more clearly sixteen years later.[278]

Oral's second and only other personal encounter with Graham in the 1950s came when he was deeply depressed, wrestling with the meaning of his Australian persecution. Billy had just returned from a successful crusade in Australia—a campaign which had probably been helped by the backlash against the harassment of Roberts. At least, Billy believed that Oral had paved the way for him, and he had written a letter from Australia thanking Roberts for the work he had done there.[279] In June 1957, the two were in the New York City area at the same time, and a mutual friend tried to persuade Oral to call on Billy. "I was really stinging and hurting," recalled Oral, "so I told him no." So Billy came knocking on Oral's hotel door, embraced him, called him "brother Oral," and told him a touching story of a blind man who had followed him in India thinking that he was Oral Roberts and the emptiness he had felt because he could not help. As Graham soothed Oral's hurt feelings, Oral recalled, "he just broke my spirit. All that sting that I had about Australia, he just killed it."[280]

Oral knew that Graham was vulnerable because of his kindness to him. "He has had a love for me that I've never been able to be grateful for enough," he told his students years later.[281] Actually, some pentecostals were criticized for associating with Graham, but by and large, the risks were overwhelmingly in the other direction.[282] When a Milwaukee reporter asked Roberts in 1958 if he knew Graham well, Oral proudly replied, "Well I have prayed at meetings with him. Yes, I know him pretty well." Hart Armstrong interjected that "you might say he doesn't know him intimately," but the fact remained that Oral's relationship with Billy was personal and something which he considered "priceless."[283]

Oral frequently used Graham to try to explain himself to reporters in the late 1950s. He took courage from Graham's climb to a position of "wider acceptance" and hoped that others would come to see that his ministry had also "been a blessing."[284] Oral defended himself against charges of financial irresponsibility by pointing out that his campaigns were inexpensive when compared with those of Graham and that he refused to take personal gifts, while Billy did accept them.[285] And Oral repeatedly pointed out that the preoccupation of the press with his healing ministry overlooked the underlying hopefulness of his theology as compared to Graham's thunderbolts. He and Billy were not in the "same field": "Graham is pricking the conscience of mankind with his hell fire and brimstone. I think he's doing a good job. But I'm in another realm, emphasizing the love and goodness of God."[286]

Oral's second meeting with Graham came in the midst of the personal reappraisal that had brought changes throughout his ministry. By 1956, he sensed that he was "entering into a new phase of my ministry." The "new phase," he felt at times, was populated by new "demon spirits—cunning, evil, destroying spirits, who would destroy my ministry, who would destroy the gospel, and who would destroy the human race."[287] As the attacks mounted in the 1950s—Australia, the challenges to his radio and television programs, the bitterly antagonistic press, the financial crisis of 1958—Oral first passed through a period of deep despair and then matured.[288] In a frank meeting with his workers in February 1957, he brooded over the persecution he was facing and warned that even at the peak of his "greatest popularity," his workers must be "prepared for the turning of the masses against us, and be able to take the suffering that comes our way." He was at a loss, he told his team, to know how to deal with the "fantastic distorted stories about our ministry," because he would not use the tactics of his detractors: "When we start fighting and they are more skilled in fighting as the world fights than we Christians are, because we don't know how to lie like they lie. We don't know how to distort things, we don't know how to be deceptive. We don't know how to come in and smile and pat you on the back and say, 'you are certainly a fine fellow,' and then go out at your back and do the opposite."[289] Actually, in these dark months, the nadir was passed.

It was in this siege setting that Oral hired public relations advice and began the effort to change his image with the media. By 1958, his $1,500,000 public relations account was big business, passing through several large agencies before settling with the firm of Swan and Mason Advertising, Inc., with partner Willard Mason locating in Oral's Tulsa office.[290] In February 1959, *New Yorker* magazine reported receiving a packet from a West Fifty-seventh Street public relations firm touting Oral as "The Man of God *Most* in the News."[291]

The primary thrust of the new public relations campaign, on the part of both Oral and his agencies, was to clarify what he felt was his constructive message. Over and over again, he explained to reporters, "My main business, by far, is to win souls. If a man's soul is right, he'll go to heaven, whether he's sick or well."[292] Although Oral felt that soul winning had always been a primary emphasis in his ministry, for several years the nation's reporters heralded the arrival of a "new" Oral Roberts who "will concentrate on healing the souls of men."[293] Just as repetitiously, Oral explained that he was not a "faith healer" and that he deeply resented the tag—as he did the epithet "Holy Roller."[294] His repeated denials that he was a "faith healer" prompted in the *National Enquirer* a feature story with the provocative, and true, heading: "I Don't Cure."[295]

By the late 1950s, Oral was working hard to explain his basic beliefs. He constantly stressed his support of medical science—"some of my best friends, my finest friends, are doctors."[296] Speaking to the Tulsa Kiwanis Club in 1956, he reduced his beliefs to an attractive formula: "What am I trying to do? . . . I'm preaching that God is a good God—in a world of violence, distrust, fear, and hatred. . . . The second thing I am preaching is divine intervention. That God divinely intervenes in human affairs. I believe in miracles, however, I'm not off on a tangent. I do not understand miracles to mean that we are not to do for ourselves. I believe in the creative genius of man."[297] Oral was a master popularizer of ideas, and he was recasting pentecostal theology in powerful new language. "One thing I have learned," he told a Los Angeles reporter in 1957, is that "words mean things to people and we are far more careful now what we say and how we say it than we were in the beginning."[298]

Oral's beliefs had also mellowed. By the late 1950s, he felt free to admit that "many 'cures' have been claimed by psychosomatic cases," and, in retrospect, he conceded that his early emphasis had been far too much on the healing of people's bodies.[299] In an interview with the religion editor of the *Miami Herald* in 1958, Oral confessed that he had been "guilty" of emphasizing healing too much in his early years, explaining that his pentecostal audiences had expected it.[300] He came to understand the cultural objections of mainstream Christians who were offended by his "methods." He tried not to be "offended" in return: "I just said, 'if you don't like mine, use your own, but don't stop God's healing power because you don't like a fellow's methods.' "[301] On the other hand, he instructed his own followers: "We who preach the total goodness of God have learned that healing is not an end in itself but a means to that infinitely greater miracle, the conversion of the soul. It leads people to understand that God is concerned about their whole being—the spiritual AND the physical."[302]

THE THIRTEEN years after Oral left the pastorate in Enid were crammed with spiritual lows and highs, battles fought and won, undreamed-of material rewards, and the creation of an American legend. In a sense, by 1957 Oral had once again conquered his small world. He had risen to the head of the pentecostal revival, he had led it to new heights, he had nullified the opposition within his own church, and he had exposed the outside world to the message of healing. His campaign audiences remained large in 1958 and 1959—although many of the deliverance revivalists experienced serious setbacks to their ministries— but the novelty was gone, and many publicly wondered what would come next. In 1959, Oral was asked if the time had come to "level off." "I do not believe in 'leveling off,' " he replied, "with what I feel in my soul now, it seems as though I have only begun."[303] And yet, how much more was there to do? How big could the tent become? And what if the seats began to empty? And how many more people could he touch?

As 1959 approached, Oral fidgeted; that old restlessness gripped his spirit. As early as 1957 he had declared that he had a "special feeling about 1959," the year his new building would be occupied. Perhaps, he thought, "the coming of Christ is much nearer than we realized."[304] When the year arrived, he still felt that something dramatic was about to happen, something that would spread "throughout the world" a "new awareness of the Lord Jesus Christ."[305] Oral's fertile mind and spirit were pressed with the question of why God had brought him this far. In May 1959, he spoke candidly to his partners: "Today as I write, I am only 41 years of age and at the peak of my physical, mental and spiritual powers. I am fired with new vision and faith for the salvation and healing of all people. The hand of the Lord is upon me."[306] Astute Oral Roberts watchers could perceive such language as a red flag signaling an explosion. But at the end of 1959, there had been no public intimations of the boiling torrent of new ideas which during the next fifteen years were to take Oral Roberts and his ministry in new directions and to unforeseen heights.

CHAPTER

VIII

Private Side

I N THE YEARS from 1947 to 1960, Oral Roberts's life was, to a remarkable degree, his crusade ministry. He spent about three-fourths of his time away from Tulsa—in out-of-the-way motels and the nation's plushest hotel suites— and when at home he was burdened with the growing complexities of his ministry. Much of his energy was publicly spent, drained in countless hours of ministering and orchestrating his growing empire. He threw his body recklessly into the battle, and he expected others (including his family) to willingly accept the sacrifice that went with his calling. In later years Oral had inklings of insight into how much he demanded of himself and others—in 1960 he was still too young, his ministry too demanding, his place in history still insecure.

Oral's routine on the road became as organized and structured as the meetings he conducted each evening. Everything pointed toward the two to three hours he would spend under the tent. In an isolation imposed on him by his growing celebrity status, he spent most of his time in his hotel room, reading, writing, praying, leaving behind a wreckage that caused one maid to explain: "Preachah, you just breaks mah heart."[1] While he sometimes "charmed" the waitresses and other hotel employees, he generally had little time for small talk.[2] At dinner time, especially, he was impatient: "He wants his meal immediately, if not sooner, so he can get back to his room."[3] No one could visit or call Oral's room without being cleared through the aides who accompanied him.[4]

Except for the coveted visits from Evelyn which Oral constantly pined for, he lived in a totally male world. His constant companions, who referred to him affectionately as "Rev," were Bob DeWeese, Collins Steele, and others who sometimes traveled with the team, including Manford Engel, Hart Armstrong, and Lee Braxton. Every morning during a crusade, the men relaxed together, usually swimming or horseback riding, and between crusades they sometimes went on hunting trips.[5] Although Oral grew slightly plump in the early 1950s, he was always a devotee of exercise, and by the late 1950s he had trimmed down and become an advocate of conditioning. He told a reporter in Pueblo, Colorado: "Notice how trim all my men are? We don't want any heart attacks among us."[6] Oral usually lost about five pounds during a campaign, eating only lightly in the evenings before preaching, and often performing in saunalike conditions.[7]

In the 1950s, Bob DeWeese introduced Oral to golf. Oral's athletic ability and his fierce competitiveness drew him relentlessly to the game. He took lessons and practiced, and, increasingly, he and DeWeese played regularly during the campaigns. Oral's skills grew rapidly; he soon passed his playing partner, and by the late 1950s he was impressing local newsmen with his "par-shattering" play.[8] Although he continued to hunt occasionally, golf became his passion. It served well to "break the strain" of the stream of long nights under the tent; and as the "most difficult game of all," it proved irresistible to Oral's perfectionist instincts.[9]

By three in the afternoon, Oral secluded himself in his room. He remained there, except for a quick and light dinner, until it was time for him to be delivered to the tent. During those hours he napped, rested, and prepared himself for the service, refusing to see anyone, "unless it was his wife or some very, very important person."[10] Working with a "portable writing board in his lap" and "a clock before him," Oral outlined his sermons, though he did not preach from notes.[11] It was this period of preparation, he felt, which "produced the high pitch which he feels before mounting the platform."[12] "The Lord builds in me like a coiled spring," he told a reporter, "by the time I'm ready to go on, my mind is razor-sharp. I know exactly what I'm going to say and I am feeling like a lion."[13]

Immediately after the service was over, Oral was whisked away by his aides back to the privacy of his room. Often wringing wet after an evening of preaching and praying, he would don a "sweater-vest" under his coat and wrap himself in a light trench coat to guard against catching colds.[14] Most of the team members would stop somewhere for refreshments after the service, but Oral usually hurried back to the hotel. If some special friends were in the audience, he might "pick a little out-of-the-way place" where he would not "be recognized" to have a snack before retiring. But even then, recalled his friend John Wellons, Oral was not given to "small-talk"; the conversation turned rather to "looking ahead" and "planning big."[15] Almost always, Oral made a beeline for his room, took a shower, climbed into his pajamas, and ordered a snack. When he returned to the hotel, still "high" from the evening's experience, he liked to have someone with him; if Evelyn was not along, one of his aides joined him. After some discursive talk and perhaps some reading, extending usually well past midnight, he retired.[16]

It was Evelyn that Oral wanted and needed by his side; she was his confidant, his "safety valve," his cheerleader, and his only true love. Without her he grew restless, lonely, and sometimes depressed. Evelyn recalled: "I often went and took the baby just to be with Oral because he couldn't stand to be alone. Oral was lonely through the day simply because he was not the kind of person that got out and talked with people all day long. . . . Everything in his life that day was geared to that meeting that night. . . . He didn't converse with anybody through the day."[17] Never a good traveler, uninterested in sightseeing, necessarily protected from the hordes of supplicants, he longed for Evelyn's companionship.

Oral felt inspired when Evelyn was in his audience: "It is a thrilling thing as I preach to look out and see her shining face. She loves to hear me preach and this inspires me to preach better."[18] When they returned to the hotel they would discuss the service until two or three o'clock in the morning. Evelyn was a diplomatic counselor; she never crushed Oral's spirit: "On nights when the Devil's power is strong and the sermon doesn't go over as Oral thinks it should, he goes to his room discouraged. . . . Those are times when I like to be with him and encourage him. If he had used bad English or made a mistake I do not tell him so, but try to get him to leave the results with God. Then when he feels on top of the world again I may mention a few mistakes."[19] For the first couple of years, Evelyn "didn't get to be in the meetings very much," but finally she found "a very dependable lady" to stay with the children.[20] However, when Rebecca and Ronnie became teenagers, it once again became increasingly difficult for Evelyn to be in the campaigns; sometimes she had to help Oral over the "rocky roads" over the telephone. She struggled to be both a good wife and a good mother. Sometimes she could not visit a campaign at all, but generally she tried to spend the first half of the crusade in Tulsa with the children and the second with Oral.[21]

Oral's time in Tulsa, particularly in the early years, was consumed by the hundreds of business and personnel decisions demanded by the growing organization. He really had no choice but to throw himself wholeheartedly into the ministry's business: "I did not choose to be a businessman. It was forced upon me by the growth of the ministry. I had to learn the principles of operating a business."[22] His insatiable curiosity served him well; he pumped every successful businessman he met, asking torrents of questions.[23] As early as 1951, Demos Shakarian saw in Oral a "keen practical sense of business acumen"; that reputation grew throughout the decade.[24] In 1956, Oral confessed to an impressed journalist: "I have a pretty fair business sense."[25] At the end of the decade the *Wall Street Journal* published a long feature story praising Oral's "executive ability" as the key to his startling success.[26]

In the early 1950s, Oral's hand was in almost every phase of the ministry—answering the mail, composing the magazine, making even minor policy decisions. As he added competent people to his staff, he tried to withdraw somewhat from the day-to-day problems of the office. "In recent years," reported the *Wall Street Journal* in 1959, "Rev. Roberts has spent less time running his organization, preferring to devote most of his time to revival meetings

... trips abroad and his sermons." "He has decentralized his authority," Manford Engel told the *Journal,* "to where he needs to spend only about two days a month making executive decisions."[27]

Necessarily, Oral's home life revolved around his demanding schedule of travel and office work. By the time the crusade ministry was five years old, he was fighting to preserve whatever privacy he could manage. He had "no certain days" to be in his office, and supporters were warned that they would not be able to see him in Tulsa.[28] Many years later, Evelyn recalled that when Oral returned from a three-week crusade, he was emotionally exhausted; all he "wanted the first few days was to be alone to rest and relax."[29] In 1953, Evelyn described Oral's regeneration during his week at home:

> Oral always looks so tired when he comes home at the end of a meeting. The lines on his face seem deeper each time. He is only 35 years old ... but he isn't the boy I married fourteen years ago. How long he will last at this awful pace is something I don't know. Sometimes I think 10 years—sometimes 20— then sometimes I say, surely he can't go on that many years without getting more rest between meetings. Every time I ask him to rest and quit working so hard, he promises me he will, but his body is strong and after staying on the farm a week, he is rested and ready to go again. At the end of his visit home, when it's just about time to leave again, the children and I watch him. The children say, "Mother, Daddy's body is here but his mind is not."[30]

In some ways Oral's time at home broke his routine and made him restless. "He's like a bird out of a cage," Evelyn told a Tulsa reporter.[31]

The fount to which Oral returned for succor was Evelyn. She met him at the airport, often with children jumping, waving, and running to the ramps as Oral deplaned.[32] Everything was prepared for his return home. "We cook and clean house and get so excited we can hardly wait," Evelyn told a reporter. The house came alive during those "wonderful days" when Oral was at home, and then, when he left, the family "feels like we have died."[33] In spite of his lengthy absences, the house remained Oral's home, and Evelyn meticulously prepared it for his return.

The smattering of reporters who interviewed Evelyn, the "quiet half of the team," were at least impressed and sometimes captivated. "Mrs. Roberts," wrote a Miami reporter, "is a pretty dark-haired woman with a soft, lovely voice. She doesn't wear lipstick, but her dark, expressive eyes are carefully made up and her clear complexion is subtly touched with rouge. A friendly and comfortable person, she smiles quickly and often."[34] Approaching forty, she remained an "attractive, petite brunette" with "sparkling green eyes and a youthful appearance."[35] But Evelyn was more than a pretty companion. She ran the Roberts household, handled their personal finances, and spent many a lonely evening, occasionally frightened, nurturing the children in a fatherless house.[36] Researchers who probed a bit found beneath Evelyn's "demure exterior" a "shrewd and forceful mind."[37]

Evelyn probably was Oral's closest advisor, having "counseled him at many a critical juncture of his rise to fame."[38] Contrary to many of those closest to him, she felt free to be "frank and honest in asserting my opinions about the ideas he has, and I feel not the slightest inhibitions about telling him if I think he is wrong." But primarily she was a "good listener," a helpmate to comfort Oral through his periods of "depression and defeat."[39] Evelyn's role as confidant hung on two main cords in their personal relationship. First, there was an absolute openness and honesty in sharing with one another. "We have never had secrets from each other," she told a Pennsylvania reporter in 1958. "We've always told each other our hearts; we still do. When he feels like saying, 'Evelyn, I love you,' he says it. If he doesn't like something I do, he is quick to tell me he thinks it's wrong. I do the same."[40] Second, Evelyn had an unerring and total faith in Oral's ministry. However frank she might be with her husband, she stood in "awe" of him when he mounted the pulpit and when he spoke with the assurance that the message came from God.[41] Oral recognized, and used, Evelyn's good sense, but he was revived by her faith in God—and in him.

Evelyn knew exactly her role—she accepted it, embraced it, and fulfilled it. In 1957, she described her "particular ambition": "First of all, my most important ambition is to be a Christian—to know I am saved. . . . Second, I want to be a good wife to Oral and a good mother to our four children. I want to help them have faith for their own lives. . . . When I was young I wanted very much to be a missionary. . . . Instead, he has given me a family to look after. If I fail to do the job he has given me, I fail in what I think is a woman's highest calling."[42] Evelyn's view of the home, and her role in it, was unabashedly old-fashioned: "In the New Testament the Lord set the order for the home. . . . The father is to be the head boss."[43] Oral's moodiness sometimes made her calling difficult. She recalled one of his arrivals when she and Rebecca had spent the day preparing a special dinner for him:

> He sat down to the dinner table, and, of course, when he is tired, he is very irritable, . . . and he was awfully tired. . . . He said, "My this tastes awful." And he passed it on and got something else, and he said, "What did you put in this?" And I said, "Well, honey . . . doesn't it taste good? It is your favorite dish." "No, it isn't my favorite dish." . . . Pretty soon he said, "Would you all mind to tell me why you never have me in mind when you prepare a meal around here in this house?" And Rebecca looked at me and she said, . . . "Mother, how can you stand it? How can you put up with it?"

Evelyn had a marvelous capacity to "put up with" Oral's bad humor, knowing that it would pass with the tiredness and be forgotten.[44]

And Oral could always charm Evelyn with a boyish playfulness that many women found irresistible. He once mailed Evelyn, with no note of explanation, four photographs taken in an arcade booth showing his head in both profiles and from the front and back. And, Evelyn recalled, there were occasions when "he used to come in the kitchen when I was cooking dinner and he would take up his trouser legs . . . and just kind of dance a little jig. And I'd say, 'What does that mean?' He'd say, 'Oh, I just feel good. Just want to tell you that I love you. Just no special deal. Just had to come in and dance a little jig.' "[45]

It was, no doubt, their unfeigned love which held Oral and Evelyn together so firmly through the strains of their unusual marriage. He repeatedly, fervently, and publicly confessed his devotion to her and his need for her. He told a crusade audience in Indianapolis in 1956: "There are times I've called Evelyn to fly across the country to my side. I needed her. . . . Because I become very lonely sometimes in my room, and I'm very much in love with my wife. I'm a one-woman man. I've only loved one woman in my life, except my mother, and that's my wife."[46] It was, sometimes, a possessive love which challenged Evelyn's ingenuity. Oral chided his wife during one of his visits home: "Evelyn, I want to tell you something. There is something wrong in our marriage." Evelyn was shocked and asked for an explanation. "Well, I don't know," replied Oral, "but when I come home, you don't pay enough attention to me. You are just around with the children all the time and I can do whatever I want to. You never even know I am in the house." Evelyn protested that the whole routine of the home was geared to Oral's needs and retorted: "Oral, I tell you, you are a problem. When you come home, you come home so seldom because you are out on the field, . . . that you don't even know what a normal marriage is supposed to be like." "I don't want a normal marriage," snapped her husband. "If it can't be more than normal, I don't want it. It has got to be above normal." Evelyn "almost laughed," but instead she "had to sit on his lap and . . . promise him . . . that I would go with him wherever he went." And so, during his visit home, Evelyn went with him when he got in the car, when he walked to the barn, "wherever he went," and Oral left "happy as a lark," satisfied with his "above normal" marriage.[47]

Both Oral and Evelyn struggled in their own ways with balancing family responsibilities with their own needs and the demands of the ministry. The births of Richard in 1948 and Roberta in 1950 completed the family. They were attractive youngsters; Rebecca, Ronnie, and Roberta, wrote Tulsa newsman Bob Foresman in 1958, resembled Evelyn in appearance, while Richard "looks much like his father."[48]

Oral betrayed an intense loyalty to his wife and children in countless ways, and he constantly brooded over the impact that his absence might have on his children. "We all love each other very much and miss being together," Oral wrote in his 1961 autobiography; "Evelyn and I both feel that it is perhaps harder on our children than on us." But they had agreed early in his ministry that Evelyn would "raise the children" while Oral preached, and they remained bound by that commitment.[49] In 1956, Oral told a crusade audience that he had "apologized to my children" because he had called Evelyn to join him even though she had to leave the children with a "stranger to babysit." In hindsight, he felt that "they needed her more than I did"; there would be no end to the questioning and self-doubts that such decisions left behind.[50] Oral "envied" Evelyn because she stayed home with the children, but he could not control the "burning urge in my soul that God put there."[51]

The Roberts children did, no doubt, carry extraordinary burdens. Rebecca and Ronnie finished high school during these busy years, quietly struggling in their own ways with Oral's higher calling. It was not easy to cope with their father's constant absence. Bob DeWeese remembered a conversation with his granddaughter, who missed him. When told that her grandfather was in South

Carolina because "Jesus sent me here to work for Him," the youngster replied: "Let me talk to Him."[52] The Roberts children tried to understand, but all later confessed to harboring some resentments about the absence of their father, and, sometimes, even more about Evelyn's trips to join him.[53] Years later, Oral recalled that a "close relative" callously told him: "Oral, I feel sorry for your children. I feel sorry for you, too, because you are gone so much; your children will never love you." Evelyn labeled such talk a "trick of the devil," but the thought of losing his family gnawed at Oral as the children grew into adulthood.[54]

Up to 1960, however, Oral remained confident—almost cocky sometimes—about the fate of his family. "I'm not afraid of the future for my children," he wrote in 1950. His children loved to hear him preach, he reported, and Rebecca and Ronnie already had manifested "a remarkable interest in faith and what it will do."[55] Seven years later, he told a crusade audience in Texas that both Rebecca and Ronnie had had a "definite experience with the Lord Jesus" and that the two younger children were learning about the "presence of God."[56]

Oral's relationship with his children was loving and caring, but it was also authoritarian. "They have always respected what I tell them," he wrote, "because they know I will do what I say I will do."[57] He gave "great attention" to "teaching them the Bible" and insisted that the children conform to the strict moral code which he had been taught as a pentecostal youngster and which he preached. In 1956, Oral told a reporter that he did not "go to dances, circuses, or fairs, nor permit his family to do so."[58] A year later he assured a South African journalist that his children were "deeply religious": "They don't dance or anything like that because they're too wrapped up in church affairs."[59] Oral also instructed his children in more mundane matters, insisting that they "articulate" correctly, remembering his own struggle to speak plainly.[60] On the other hand, he "rarely did baby sitting and once, after a particularly trying time, he swore off the job for good."[61]

Oral felt that his children had a quiet respect and affection for him: "They don't say much, but they show they desire to be near me." And there were upbeat, relaxed times when the family had a "wonderful time together."[62] Evelyn reported that "all four chilren have a hilarious time playing games with him on the rare . . . occasions when he can be home with them." Ronnie and Richard loved to "go fishing with their father," and, though Ronnie was not inclined to athletics, by 1960 Oral had already taught twelve-year-old Richard to play golf.[63]

The children frequently accompanied Evelyn to the campaigns when they were not in school, especially when they were young. Rebecca and Ronnie attended many of Oral's early meetings and, apparently, were good listeners, particularly enchanted by the healing line.[64] In 1958, Richard and Roberta told a Pennsylvania reporter that they loved listening to their father's "story" sermons.[65] On the other hand, Richard expressed a sentiment shared by all when "he said he was tired of going to the meetings because 'Daddy just studies and prays all the time.'"[66]

Evelyn felt that the children were progressing well at the end of the decade.

"I hear of other people's problems with their teen-agers," she wrote, "but I believe that Oral has instilled so much of the Lord in our children that they want to do right and, so far, I have not experienced any teen-age problems."[67] While Oral taught the children, it was Evelyn who got the four of them ready for Sunday school and church each week and saw that their lessons were prepared.[68] It was Evelyn who grew most solicitous when she was separated from the children for very long.[69] And it was Evelyn who tried to provide a normal home in a celebrity environment. She told a reporter in 1958 that her youngsters led "surprisingly normal" lives in spite of the notoriety of their father. "To the kids in the neighborhood," she said, "Ronnie is just Ronnie and he's like any other teen-ager."[70]

Aside from the absences of their father and mother, the lives of the Roberts children were much like those of their middle-class schoolmates. They attended public schools until 1952, when they moved to a farm just outside Tulsa. Evelyn was so disappointed in the public schools in Bixby that she enrolled the children in Holland Hall, a private Episcopalian school. Rebecca finished high school there; because its enrollment was limited to girls after the sixth grade, Ronnie attended Edison High School in Tulsa. The children "wanted to be like everybody else. They never wanted to be on display."[71] Evelyn believed they were "independent little things" who had learned the art of survival as Oral Roberts's children.[72]

No matter how much they wanted to be "like everybody else," Oral Roberts's children in the 1950s lived with two constant intimidating pressures; pressures felt particularly by Rebecca and Ronnie, who passed through adolescence during that tumultuous decade. First, the disbelief and hostility of the press filtered down through the minds of parents, teachers, and children, who would boldly ask: "Can your daddy really heal?" or, as Ron recalled, "Is your father a fake?"[73] To live with a constant sneering questioning of the integrity of one's father was no easy burden. "We know that Daddy is honest," the children told Evelyn, but "we are getting tired of people asking us questions all the time."[74] A child could pluckily assert that he was "not ashamed of Daddy or what he's doing," but underneath all of the children "resented the fact that their dad *needed* defending."[75] Second, and perhaps more important for Rebecca and Ronnie, the Roberts children were reared in the "pressure cooker" of pentecostal restraints while living in a middle-class environment. To Oral's children, as to many other pentecostal children of the 1950s, their heritage seemed a "religion of 'nos,'" an unreasoning and negative rejection of life. Richard Roberts surmised that during those years his father "was struggling and fighting with himself" against the taboos of pentecostal culture, restraints that he ultimately cast off with his church and never imposed on his younger children. But, Richard believed, that pentecostal repression "took its toll" on the two older children.[76] All of the Roberts children showed some signs of rebellion—mixed with intense family loyalty—but in the cases of the sons the rebellion was serious.

Rebecca Ann was seven years old when her father began his healing ministry in 1947, and she grew up working in the ministry, "folding magazines, sacking books, stamping envelopes." At age eight she confided that "her ambition was to be a teacher and musician, like her mother."[77] Rebecca's closest friends remained her childhood acquaintances in the Pentecostal Holiness church; she attended a church high school in Oklahoma City for one semester.[78] Rebecca remained close to the ministry, working for Oral's secretary Ruth Rooks and his good friend Lee Braxton at various times.[79] After graduating from Holland Hall High School, she entered Tulsa University to work toward a "secretarial certificate." While there she encountered for the first time "people who worship Mohammed instead of God and professors who don't believe in Bible miracles or present-day Christianity." The experience revealed Rebecca's genuine character; she marveled at the seeming emptiness of the lives of most of the students and thanked "God for the planned path he has for me and the goals he has put in my heart."[80]

Rebecca's straight course was sealed on June 1, 1959, when she married Marshall Everett Nash, son of the state superintendent of the Pentecostal Holiness church in Georgia. Marshall's brother, Bill, had moved to Tulsa to work for Oral and had introduced Rebecca to Marshall. About six months after they were married, Marshall took a job with the Roberts organization as a film editor and remained with the organization for a number of years. Rebecca's life seemed settled and serene by 1960. She and Marshall, a very able young man, were to have a rich and rewarding future together.[81]

Oral's singular pride and joy was Ronald David, "his father's little helper." In an early issue of *Healing Waters*, Oral boasted that "Ronnie knows thirty gospel choruses and frequently sings on the broadcast his father carries on." "Ronnie is heir to all my wealth (mostly spiritual riches, of course)," wrote the proud father.[82] Two years later, Oral acknowledged that "every crow thinks his little crow is the blackest," but he nonetheless boasted that first-grader Ronnie Roberts was particularly "nimble with his mind and tongue."[83]

Oral was at least partly correct in his assessment of his son; Ronnie did prove to be an outstanding student. He showed an early facility for languages and as early as his sophomore year in high school manifested an interest in learning Russian.[84] While in high school he spent one summer studying Chinese in the home of a Chinese minister in Taiwan, and another representing his school as an exchange student in Bonn, Germany. His high school record was outstanding, and in 1960 Ron enrolled in Stanford University, an accomplishment which made his parents "really proud."[85]

By 1960, Ronnie had only begun to show signs of the rebellion which would destroy his life. As a youngster he had followed closely in his "father's footsteps," "hanging on every word" during his visits to the campaigns.[86] But as he entered adolescence, he eschewed any relationship with his father's ministry.[87] Nonetheless, Oral and Evelyn continued to believe that Ronnie was to play a notable role in the ministry. In 1958, after an interview with Evelyn, a Miami reporter wrote: "Although she emphasized that they love all their children equally, she said 'We feel that the Lord has something special in mind for Ronnie. We feel that Ronnie will follow in the footsteps of his daddy.'"[88] Everyone in the family felt that Ronnie had a gift similar to Oral's. When Oral was away and his mother became ill, she called for Ronnie to pray for her:

"When he placed his hand on my head to pray," Claudius wrote, "it seemed like Oral praying. The power of God came into that room and Ronnie said, 'Granny, you're healed!'"[89]

The two younger Roberts children, Richard Lee and Roberta Jean, were children of the ministry, born in November 1948 and December 1950, in Tulsa. Although both remembered the taunts of their school companions, they were largely untouched by the controversies of the 1950s; they were the children of the success of the 1960s. But they had developed their basic personalities by 1960—Richard was "impish," "athletic," and "courteous" and had strong aversions to study and other forms of work.[90] At age ten, Richard was an "accomplished" skeet shooter and had "the build of a young fullback."[91] Naturally left-handed, his father began to teach him to play golf right-handed at age six, and he soon was a formidable competitor.[92] Roberta, on the other hand, was strong-willed, "independent," and devoutly religious—turning to God in the absence of her parents.[93]

Next to Oral's absence from home, the thing that most dramatically changed the Robertses' personal lives in the years from 1947 to 1960 was his modest accumulation of wealth. A young man suddenly favored with an income beyond his dreams, Oral quickly became accustomed to a lifestyle which would have been difficult for some of his followers to understand. In 1953, Evelyn reported that some people criticized Oral "for riding planes home"; they could hardly have been expected to approve of his more expensive tastes.[94] In many ways Oral was, and remained, an Oklahoma farm boy made good, fascinated by wealth and its symbols. "Signs of wealth and power in others greatly impress Roberts," wrote a journalist in 1956: "'A very important person,' is a phrase frequently on his tongue, and it denotes high social approval."[95] At the end of the decade, the *Wall Street Journal* summarized the "material rewards" accumulated by the evangelist: "membership in the swank Tulsa Country Club; election by the Tulsa Chamber of Commerce to its list of 50 top executives in the area; a private twin-engine plane (donated by followers) and ownership of a 10-room, ranch-style house centered in five acres of tree-studded lawn in one of the more expensive suburban areas of Tulsa."[96]

Oral shared his new prosperity. In 1948, he presented Ellis and Claudius with a "new Ford car" and moved his parents to Tulsa, where he helped them build a home with "the first money I earned in 1947."[97] He considered it "my privilege to provide for Papa and Mamma in their sunset years."[98] Oral also encouraged Evelyn's parents, the Fahnestocks, to move to Tulsa, where he and Evelyn could help them.[99]

The most visible symbol of Oral's growing prosperity was the sequence of homes he acquired. The family lived for only about two years in the small house on North Main Street before the expansion of the ministry forced them to move; they bought a home on Thirty-fifth Place in the fashionable Brookside section of Tulsa. Then, in 1951 Oral purchased a 240-acre ranch southeast of Tulsa, near Bixby, and began stocking it with purebred Aberdeen Angus cows. At first he intended to build only a cabin on the ranch where the family could spend weekends, but by 1952 he had completed a rambling ten-room ranch house built of redwood and crab-orchard stone, and the family moved to the ranch.[100]

The Robin Hood Ranch (named for one of Oral's childhood heroes) was the Roberts home from 1952 to 1958; "some of the best years of our lives," recalled Evelyn.[101] For Oral it was a refuge from the pressure of the campaigns. When he bought the ranch he was "on the verge of a breakdown"; he told a Tulsa reporter: "I was cracking up. I wouldn't be here today if it weren't for this."[102] The children "loved" the ranch and abandoned it with their parents reluctantly in 1958.

Having become a gentleman rancher, Oral threw himself into the project wholeheartedly. In partnership with a wealthy Chicago insurance man, Paul L. Temple, he set out to build the finest Aberdeen Angus herd in the nation, buying the "royalty of the breed." His Chicago friend purchased a $25,000 bull to sire the herd; by 1953, Oral had forty cows on the ranch and his partner twenty. Oral operated the ranch under the slogan "The Lord Owns Our Cattle."[103] Although he frequently declared that he did not expect to make money in the cattle business, he probably had some early illusions. He told a Tulsa reporter in 1953 that should Robin Hood "develop into one of the nation's top Angus breeding establishments," he would contribute the profits to Southwestern Bible College.[104] In fact, the ranch developed into a serious financial liability—one of the few times when Oral was seriously injured by his insistence on going first class. Evelyn recalled: "We weren't making any money. Because when Oral goes into something, he has to go into it with all he's got. . . . He can't buy a mediocre cow. He's got to buy the best one. . . . So he just nearly lost his shirt on that farm."[105]

But the ranch was probably worth the investment. Oral loved to show his cattle, and he was rejuvenated by the serenity of the country. "I am in this for the rest and relaxation," he told Bob Foresman. "I love those big black cattle."[106] And the ranch was the perfect spot to host the big barbecues that gave Oral's partners a chance to meet his family.

It was not the financial liability of the ranch which finally led to the Robertses' decision to move in 1958. The most immediate reason was Evelyn's dissatisfaction. Increasingly, the children's activities pulled them toward Tulsa, and Evelyn "ran my legs off with all those children." She insisted that they admit they had made a "big mistake" and return to the city.[107] "I am gone about three-fourths of the time, and it has become increasingly difficult for Mrs. Roberts to take the children to the different schools they attend," Oral explained. "It is with regret that I am leaving the farm but I am happy to move to Tulsa which is the city I love."[108] The sale of the ranch also removed one of the most persistent sources of outside criticism. Over and over Oral was forced to offer the public explanation that a 240-acre ranch was considered small in Oklahoma.[109] In 1959, Manford Engel candidly told a reporter: "We were glad to see that go. It brought nothing but misunderstanding."[110]

Early in 1958, the family moved into the John D. Mayo home, which was located on five acres on East Thirty-eighth Street in Tulsa. That home, which featured a "ribbed-pole" room built by Indian settlers as its "show piece," was completely remodeled in 1958 and sold to the Oral Roberts Evangelistic Association.[111] A distinguished house, it served as the Roberts residence until 1962, when changes in the family and ministry dictated one final move.

Less well known than the Roberts family's moves in Tulsa was the fact that Oral also purchased an "expensive" home in Corona Del Mar in California in 1958. Given to harsh attacks of hay fever in the fall in Oklahoma, he early discovered he could find relief on the West Coast. The California home, while an eminently sensible investment, was not widely publicized.[112]

Oral's income and his accumulation of personal wealth were the single issue which made him most defensive. His sensitivity seemingly kindled the curiosity of the press; their probing increased his uneasiness. Of course, there was room for honest differences of opinion about the level of personal support a national evangelist should receive—Oral and his critics repeatedly explored the issue in the 1950s. In 1956, he curtly "terminated" an interview with writer John Kobler when the reporter indicated that he intended to highlight the evangelist's private finances.[113]

Oral frequently expressed "dismay" at the dogged curiosity of the press about his personal income and persistently refused to satisfy their curiosity.[114] He refused to divulge his income on the grounds that "the Pentecostal policy is never to reveal the amount" of love offerings. but he also knew that his income might be used against him. "There are so many poor," he told a reporter, "that no matter how much it was, it would be offensive."[115] Furthermore, argued the evangelist, his income was no one else's business: "I'm not going to tell you how much I make from a love offering because that's nobody's business but my own. Is this not a personal matter? And do not the top ministers of big churches receive good salaries?"[116] It was not, Roberts insisted, as if he were robbing the evangelistic association for personal gain; he received income only from his "love offerings" and from book royalties. In fact, it was he who supported Healing Waters, rather than the reverse.[117] Although critics charged that Oral profited personally from praying for sick people, and wealthy supporters such as Paul Temple did aid his private ventures, he and his organization repeatedly denied that he took personal contributions.[118]

In fact, Oral did become modestly wealthy during the 1950s. By the end of the decade, the organization estimated his "love offerings" at "not far from the $27,000-a-year mark." Less visible to the public were Oral's earnings on book royalties. In 1959, the *Wall Street Journal* estimated that those had ranged between $50,000 and $80,000 during the decade.[119] On the other hand, another reporter judged that Oral's income was "around $1 million annually for three consecutive years."[120] Roberts simply replied that he did not "think my income is too big," adding that he had never believed that the possession of wealth was evil.[121] But, he protested, "I'm a million miles from ever being rich."[122]

Of course, the primary indication of Oral's escalating income was his changed lifestyle. Even so, his accumulation of property was not necessarily considered outrageous, at least not in oil-rich Tulsa. If Robin Hood Ranch was not, as Oral told Dr. George Crane, "a 240-acre strip in the dust bowl," it was entirely correct that such a spread in Oklahoma was "not considered very big, even when not mortgaged."[123] An Oklahoma reporter who visited the farm judged that the Roberts family lived "in very modest circumstances."[124] Another journalist described their new home in 1958 as "a modest ranch style house on the edge of Tulsa."[125] Of course, other reporters regarded the Robertses' lifestyle as nearly criminal. The *Wall Street Journal*, noting that the average salary of Protestant ministers in the nation was under $5,500 per year, reported that many ministers considered "Rev. Roberts' way of life extravagant," and that his executives often found it "embarrassing."[126]

In a sense, both estimates were true. Oral had attained an undreamed-of financial prosperity and was learning to live like a successful executive. His new prosperity was probably resented less by those who contributed to Oral's "love offerings" than by the middle-class reporters who suspected that the whole drama was a fraud. Actually, some evangelists paraded their new wealth; Oral did not. He was, in fact, overly scrupulous to avoid offense—so scrupulous that he seemed to many to be evasive and deceptive. On the other hand, Oral could truthfully protest that little of the massive income passing through his growing organization was diverted to his personal use. He could have been a wealthy individual by 1960. He was not.

PERHAPS nothing told more about the evolution of Oral Roberts's ministry than the changes in Oral himself. In the early 1950s he looked like a pentecostal preacher. Not only did he speak with a "broad Okie drawl" which lent itself to caricature, he loved to play the role of cowboy, complete with western boots and ten-gallon hats.[127] He dressed gaudily, having a "flair for sporty two-toned outfits."[128] Oral later explained:

> I had been reared informally, out in Oklahoma. And I really had got wild on clothes and didn't know it. . . . No one had ever told me. Lee Braxton and I went into a store and bought two white coats. And two pairs of maroon trousers. And when I met Bob DeWeese the first time in Tacoma, Washington, . . . half the time I preached in that white coat and those maroon trousers. It never dawned on me that I shouldn't dress like that as a minister of the Gospel in the pulpit.[129]

In manner, wrote one reporter, he had "the meticulous air of a dandy, or one constantly worried about his appearance"; he "continually combed his hair and wiped perspiration from his face as he spoke."[130]

By the end of the decade, Oral's personal appearance had changed dramatically. His flamboyant clothes had given way to an "expertly tailored grey herringbone" suit, or "a dark business suit creating a dignified background for his black hair and dark, penetrating eyes."[131] "His dress," wrote Tulsa reporter Bob Foresman in 1957, "is always impeccable and his taste in clothing is conservative."[132] By 1959, he had not only changed his attire, he had discarded his "fancy red Bible" and many of the "oratorical flourishes" characteristic of earlier times.[133]

Once again, Oral had been a ready learner. His new taste in dress began with a conversation with his first television producer. When asked why he wore such colorful attire, Oral retorted, "I do?" "I know your people don't mind it," his producer instructed. "I've watched them in the audiences and they don't mind it, but I'd like to ask you, do you expect to reach the nation?" Oral was ready to listen. "How should I dress?" he asked. Told he should wear "conservative clothes," Oral changed his wardrobe: "So I did it. And I knew it was right. So I came back to my office and I announced the news to my men and they got the hint too."[134] His employees got more than a hint; in fact, they got a lecture on "endeavoring to appear well-groomed for the Lord's sake."[135]

Over a dozen years of travel and constant encounters with the press and other public figures had introduced Oral Roberts's observant and curious mind to a whole new nonpentecostal cosmos. He was reshaped by that exposure, and, consciously and unconsciously, he educated himself to be able to influence that new world. Oral was still a stranger to mainstream America and its religion in 1960—he knew few of that world's inhabitants—but he had seen it, and he now knew that his potential universe was vastly larger than his present vision. Oral had reached the limits of deliverance revivalism. He had thoroughly explored and exploited its possibilities. By 1960, he had arrived once again at a personal impasse remarkably like the one that had gripped him in Enid. Were there no other worlds for Oral Roberts to conquer? Was this all?

In another way Oral's mental state in 1960 approached that of his crisis period in Enid twelve years earlier. Not only had his career reached a bottleneck, he also was physically exhausted—bone weary in body and emptied in spirit. For year after weary year, Oral had returned home from the campaigns, having lost from five to fifteen pounds, to eat Evelyn's "biscuits and sorghum molasses" and revive his spirit.[136] But now recovery came slower. "I grew tired," Oral later recalled. "Over a period of months I grew desperately tired. I was tired in my soul. I was tired of living with these people."[137] He was settling into one of those moods of exhaustion, depression, and self-examination which made him a conduit for the voice of God.

PART THREE

MAINSTREAM

1960–1975

PROLOGUE

Berlin, October 26-November 4, 1966

THE WORLD CONGRESS on Evangelism, sponsored by *Christianity Today* magazine with Billy Graham serving as honorary chairman, attracted over 1,100 evangelical clergymen to Berlin in hopes of "breathing new life into contemporary churches." It was an august gathering in evangelical circles, featuring among its main speakers, in addition to Graham, congress chairman and editor of *Christianity Today* Carl F. H. Henry, Emperor Haile Selassie of Ethiopia, and Rev. John Stott, Anglican rector from London and chaplain to the queen. The delegates came from diverse backgrounds—including, noted the United Press announcement of the conference, "such diverse figures as evangelist-faith healer Oral Roberts from Tulsa, Okla. and Anglican Bishop Chandu Ray of Pakistan."[1] They had assembled for a "council of war," announced chairman Henry; the conference won press coverage throughout the world, marking "a major breakthrough for evangelicals in news-media exposure."[2]

It was predictable that Oral would be invited along with most other evangelists who had major radio and television ministries. Besides, in 1965 Oral Roberts University had opened, pushing further into the background the faith healer image of the 1950s. Carl F. H. Henry wrote Oral a "letter of congratulations" at the time, along with the note: "Billy Graham and I are hopeful that you will be at the World Congress on Evangelism in Berlin, . . . and I know that an invitation will be forthcoming in the months ahead." Of course, reservations remained in the minds of most evangelicals about keeping company with the likes of Oral Roberts. Henry reminded Oral of them in his letter: "I suppose my points of reservation are predictable—glossolalia and healing, if these are made to be central and indispensable facets of normative Christian experience."[3]

199

More surprising than the invitation was Oral's decision to accept. Although he valued Graham as a "warm friend" and had been given the minor honor of chairing a panel session on healing, he was reluctant to go. Whittling ten days out of his busy schedule was a "great sacrifice," and he accepted the invitation only because of Billy's "personal request."[4] But time was not the chief deterrent—it was Oral's tender ego. Upon his return home, he recalled:

> Perhaps any reluctance on our part was that our ministry of evangelism and healing have been considered by some to be on the periphery of the great stream of evangelical Christianity. We felt a deep love and appreciation for these dedicated men for their sacrificial labors to win souls. However, since the healing ministry had not been understood to be an integral part of the mainstream of the Gospel, we were not sure how our ministry would be accepted or what our contribution could be to the Congress.[5]

Oral struggled with his inferiority complex, with his phobia against intruding where he was not wanted. His friend Warren Hultgren, pastor of the First Baptist Church in Tulsa, pressed him: "Oral, you need to listen. You're always talking. . . . This is the cream of the mainstream of Christ."[6] Despite such assurances, Oral departed tentatively, with foreboding. Speaking to his staff just a few days before leaving, he said: "As yet I have not seen the way that God would use us there. This is something that we seldom ever do. We usually go about our work, carrying on our ministry through the world and let such events like this be conducted in their own way. And we usually do not attend.This will be our first time to attend such a world program as this. My prayer is that God will help us to give and to be a part of the blessing that God would give."[7]

When Oral arrived in Berlin, he went into his "usual hiding act."[8] He and R. O. Corvin, the dean of his theology school, who accompanied him, ate their meals in their room, sensing a "hostility" which his friend Warren Hultgren insisted was not there.[9] But Oral's presence had "spooked" the conference to some extent; everyone recognized him but did not know what to do with him. R. O. Corvin recalled: "When we first arrived . . . we didn't know what to expect. . . . It reminded me of when I was a boy. When we brought a new animal to our farm, the other farm animals would 'eye' him. . . . When Brother Roberts entered the convention, people watched him. They observed him as he walked through the lines and . . . sat at tables with others. A large segment knew of his ministry; but, for many, this was their first personal encounter with him."[10]

The ombudsman who introduced Oral Roberts to mainstream Christianity was Calvin Thielman, an open, warm Texan who pastored the Presbyterian church in Montreat, North Carolina, the home congregation of Ruth Graham, where Billy often attended. Thielman had been a college roommate and best friend of Graham's brother-in-law, Leighton Ford, and he had access not only to Graham but also to the other evangelical leaders at the conference. Calvin was quartered at the Berlin Hilton, as was Oral, and he noted how "people were sort of walking in a big circle around him. They were afraid to speak to him." Not Calvin. He approached Oral, gave him a Texas handshake, and invited him for a cup of coffee. Oral joined him, though he did not drink coffee. They had a frank discussion in which, Thielman recalled, "he was very kind to me when I was very rude to him." Oral disarmed his new friend, accepting Calvin's "testimony" that he had the Holy Spirit even though he did not speak in tongues. Calvin was impressed: "Look, I like you and there are a lot of people around here that would probably like to talk to you that are scared of you." "You better stay away from me," Oral replied, "or people won't speak to you." "I don't take much to that way of thinking," retorted Thielman. Calvin then made a proposal: "I'm going to ask some of them to come and eat with you. And you're gonna have to pay for it because I don't have any money." Oral remained "low key," but he agreed to cooperate with any plans Calvin could arrange.[11]

Calvin became Oral's social secretary. He sought out the Bishop of London, the pastor of the First Presbyterian Church in Pittsburgh, and several other influential delegates: "Why don't you ask this guy all these questions that are bothering you. And let him answer for himself. . . . I think you'll be surprised. He'll answer honestly and you'll like him." A luncheon was arranged, the guests asked Oral "tough questions," and they liked his answers. That was the "ice-breaker," though not everyone was convinced. Leighton Ford hailed Calvin in the hotel lobby and asked: "What in the world are you doing hanging around Oral Roberts?" Calvin replied, "Leighton, would Jesus do that?" Ford assured his friend that he had heard reports from Australia which raised serious questions about Oral's ministry, but Calvin knew he liked him. Oral and Calvin became inseparable, sharing taxis to the sessions and eating their meals together.[12]

Calvin's attentiveness to Oral was soon reported to Billy Graham, who sent a note summoning Thielman to his room. When Calvin got there, the evangelist had already retired; he peered over his glasses and said: "T. W. tells me that you're getting together everywhere to eat with Oral Roberts." Calvin began defensively, "Well, Billy, we invited him here and he is being avoided by people. . . . They treat him like an honorary leper." Graham interrupted, tears welling up in his eyes: "God bless you for that. . . . I can remember when I was preaching on the street corners in Florida. . . . You tell Oral that I want him to eat with me." Then, Billy asked a bolder question: "What would you think about me having him speak at the Congress Hall?" Calvin supported the idea, noting that the conference included many pentecostals from South America who looked upon Oral as a hero. "All right. We'll do it," Billy said. It was an audacious decision that would bring immediate attacks from fundamentalist and conservative evangelical critics.[13]

Oral was coy but "tickled as a little kid" to be invited to dine with Billy and a circle of conference dignitaries. As the dinner closed, Billy told Oral that he wanted him to lead prayer before one of the plenary sessions of the congress, and Oral "quietly declined." As Billy greeted each guest as he left, he asked Oral, "Oral, when are you going to invite me to speak to your campus?" Oral, seizing the opportunity, replied, "How would you like to come to the campus not only to speak but to dedicate the University?" "I'd be honored to do it," replied Graham, making a commitment which placed his own ministry in some jeopardy.[14]

Oral's panel on "Twentieth Century Evangelism" did not take place until Wednesday, November 2. It had been scheduled in the largest available room, but the crowds flooded outside the doors and windows. Oral presented a brief paper calling for a renewed emphasis on the gifts of the spirit and then was joined in a discussion by Dr. Harold Ockenga, Boston Congregationalist minister, former president of Fuller Theological Seminary, and long considered Billy Graham's resident intellectual, and two other panelists. The official report noted "a remarkable measure of agreement among panelists. All recognized the reality of divine healing, acknowledged that it is but one part of the gospel presentation, and openly repudiated the errors and excesses so often connected with it in popular campaigns."[15]

The panel was, in fact, the most explosive session in the congress. Oral was nervous, knowing that the meeting would be crowded with professional theologians and Graham's personal friends; on the way to the meeting room, he implored Calvin, "Don't forsake me now."[16] Thielman remembered that the room was filled with "very sharp people" loaded with "very sharp questions." Oral felt keenly that "he wasn't any match for these theologians."[17] But he was disarmingly candid and direct; he relieved some pent-up tension in a folksy exchange with the first questioner. Anglican bishop R. O. C. King of Jamaica rose and began to speak instead of asking a question. Oral, on strict instructions to limit comments from the floor, quipped: "Hold on, brother, do you have a question, or are you making a talk?" "Well, I was trying to say," replied the bishop, "that I have 3,500 members in my church in Jamaica, and many of them have been healed as a result of your radio and television work." Roberts quickly retorted: "Oh, that's all right, brother. Just take all the time you want!"[18] King ended his comments with a declaration of faith: "So I would say to all brethren here, in the Name of God the Father, God the Son, and God the Holy Spirit, let us approach the question of healing in prayer and in faith and in humility."[19]

The questions did become increasingly pointed, however. "Why is it that Christ and the Apostles had no failures in healing?" Oral knew that question well: "I do not believe that Christ had no failures. I read the Word where, in Nazareth He *could* not—he didn't say He *did* not—it said He *could* not, because of their unbelief." "Isn't it a part of superstition if we sent out prayer cloths as were taken from Paul's body . . . if we have people touch us, or the wireless—radio—and say by that: 'You are healed?'" "I agree," replied Oral, "according to the phrasing of your question, if we say, 'You are healed by this.' But I don't know anyone who says they are healed. Those I know, use a point of contact for the releasing of faith to help people use their faith in Jesus Christ." And, finally, "If we put emphasis on healing, isn't that taking a risk of not stressing the whole Gospel?" "I agree," replied Oral again, adding a penetrating self-appraisal that opened up the congress to him and was widely publicized by the press:

> I believe that healing or any other thing can be stressed too much. . . . I think this is a warning to us, that we should be balanced and, above all, preach the Word of God. . . . I would like to say I think that in the early part of my ministry I made mistakes. I had to learn the hard way. . . . For example, now in

our ads we simply announce an Abundant Life Crusade. In the early part of our work, however, we stressed far more than that. I suppose it was the eagerness that we felt in our hearts.[20]

While Oral scored points with such answers, Ockenga repeatedly came to his aid. Some framed their questions in theological jargon that left Oral groping, "deliberately trying to embarrass him," Thielman thought. Ockenga "did one of the most chivalrous things I ever saw anyone do," recalled Thielman: "He reached right over and he got the microphone away from Oral before he attempted to answer and he said, 'Brother Roberts, let me answer this question.' "[21] Ockenga offered his own personal testimony that "there have been three times I have been healed through prayer in a very definite and permanent way."[22] Oral came away unscarred and with his spirit soaring: "From then on," Corvin reported, "we felt we were one with these delegates."[23]

Another incident had put Oral's name before the conference delegates. During an "informal gathering" between sessions, he was accosted by an Indian pastor who told him: "Brother Roberts, I have not been accustomed to the healing ministry, but sometime ago there was a family that brought their little boy dying with tetanus and they thrust him into my hands and said pray for him. And before I realized I had touched him and asked God to heal him." The sick child recovered, but the pastor was criticized for his act. He asked Oral, "Did I do right in praying for the little boy?" Oral paused, and answered, "Why don't you ask the little boy?" The phrase "Ask the little boy" spread through the delegates and was accepted by many as a common-sense defense of the healing ministry.[24]

The World Congress on Evangelism ignited, and Oral Roberts went through a metamorphosis on Wednesday evening at the plenary session. Billy sent word to Oral that he was going to ask him to come forward to give a greeting and lead the assembly in prayer. Calvin Thielman remembered that Oral was again "scared" by the prospect of appearing before the main assembly, but Billy Graham's introduction was warm and fraternal:

Our prayer is going to be led by a man that I have come to love and appreciate in the ministry of evangelism. He has just built, and is in the process of building, a great university. He is known throughout the world through his radio and television work, and millions of people listen to him. They read what he writes and they thank God for his ministry. I am speaking of Dr. Oral Roberts, and I'm going to ask him to say a word of greeting to us before he leads the prayer.[25]

Oral rose and was "startled" that he was "applauded rather enthusiastically" by the large contingent of South American pentecostals.[26]

Oral's rapport with the audience was magical—he spoke, recalled Thielman, a "real inspired word."[27] He confessed with obvious humility what the experience had meant to him:

If there is a phrase that characterizes this Congress to me, it is: "We have been conquered by love." I could not conceive in advance what God would do in my heart as I found that men of diverse backgrounds, religious persuasions, and beliefs could not only sit together, but could learn to understand each other.

I don't know if Dr. Graham and Dr. Henry realize the significance of this Congress and the way God has used them to call delegates from more than one hundred nations, and cause us to sit down together in the warmth of real Bible, Christlike fellowship.

I shall always be glad that I came. When I left I was tense—tense from the problems of a growing ministry. I needed to sit down and listen to someone else for a change. I have found there are men here that can preach better than I can, and that has been a great awakening for me. (Laughter) When you begin to believe your own press notices and all your wife tells you about your preaching, you'd better look out. Since coming to the Congress, I realize that I have been out-preached, out-prayed, and out-organized. (Laughter)

I thank you, Billy, and Dr. Henry, for helping to open my eyes to the main stream of Christianity, and to bring me a little closer to my Lord.

I have come to see the Holy Spirit in men who are here today. Yesterday I even had lunch with a Bishop. (laughter) Can you imagine a Pentecostal evangelist eating with a Bishop of London? (Applause). . . .

. . . . We have talked of the glories of Pentecost in our denomination, but I wonder if we have thought enough of the unity of Pentecost. I think we Pentecostals owe a debt to the historic churches, and you might owe a small debt to us for we have held on to Pentecost. We have learned new dimensions about it, and I thank God, Billy, and all of you for that.[28]

It was an electric moment. When the applause began, "pandemonium broke loose. They jumped up from every angle and applauded and applauded."[29]

But it was the prayer that followed that fired the audience. Warren Hultgren considered it the "unconscious turning point" in the conference and in Oral's life. R. O. Corvin described it as an "unusual prayer," worded as though "he were praying in the crusades."[30] Most of the assembled dignitaries were more accustomed to liturgical formulas than to tent petitions. But praying was, after all, Oral's specialty:

We come to you, our Heavenly Father, not in our name, not in our strength, but in the incomparable name of Your Son, Jesus Christ of Nazareth. We know that You scooped out the bed for the oceans, flung the stars from Your fingertips, sculptured the mountains and hung the earth on nothing. But that didn't save us. That didn't meet our needs. It was Your shed blood—Your death, Your breaking asunder the bonds of death, Your standing there where the stone was rolled away, and looking over the world and saying to Your people. "Because I live, ye shall live also."

We think of when You vaulted into space and rode on the wings of the morning star in Your ascension. We are grateful that when You arrived, You prayed the Father and He sent us the Paraclete, the Holy Ghost.

We are thankful that You called the Apostles, and they went forth in Your tradition—men of faith, men of compassion, men of miracles. But not only did You do it for them, but You did it for us. We have felt a response this week and, we pray that we shall not lose it, but that we will find it increasing and multiplying by Your hands on us even as You multiplied the loaves and the fishes.

God, be merciful to us and help us for we need You and want You, and we are determined that we shall have You.

God, bless the wives who are back home and our children and the people we represent.

And God, bless Billy and protect him. Satan, we adjure you in the name of Jesus Christ, whose we are and whom we serve, you shall not touch this man, God's servant. And we ask You, Lord, to anoint him as he has never known it before, but that he shall speak with a new force, a new power, a new vision, to this whole generation.

Bless his team, this dedicated group of men, and let them feel our love and appreciation.

May tonight, and tomorrow, and the closing service on Friday, be for Your glory, the glory of Your only begotten Son because He will invade this place and He will speak to us and we will say, "Speak, Lord, for Thy servant heareth Thee." We ask in the name of Christ. Amen.[31]

Oral's prayer, many felt, "moved the entire Congress."[32] Leighton Ford tracked down Calvin Thielman and asked for an introduction to Oral; others clamored to meet him. As the delegates returned home, many filtered through Montreat to talk with Billy, and Calvin reported that "every word I heard about Oral Roberts was one of great commendation. People deeply appreciated the contribution which he made to the Congress. He made an impression on all of us that was good."[33] The *Christianity Today* report on the conference emphasized the good will Oral had won in the evangelical community:

Evangelist Oral Roberts won a significant measure of new respect through the congress. He made a host of friends among delegates who were openly impressed with his candor and humility. When a panel got around to discussing over-emphasis on healing, Roberts readily acknowledged that he made "some mistakes" in the past. He indicated to a plenary session that he wanted to be identified more with mainstream Christianity.[34]

It was Oral who had been most deeply changed by the congress. "What it did, in effect," surmised Calvin Thielman, "was to open a new . . . circle of friends to him."[35] Oral came away convinced that "God is going to give a great revival in these last days"; his mind was racing for clues on how best to "capitalize upon our acceptance in Berlin."[36] Oral dispatched Lee Braxton to Montreat to fly Calvin to Tulsa to advise him on how to "widen the circle" of his influence among his new-found friends. At Calvin's suggestion, he invited a series of evangelical speakers, including Leighton Ford and Ockenga, to Oral Roberts University to speak.[37] There were other immediate aftereffects of the congress. The Chilean pentecostal delegation insisted that Oral schedule a crusade in Chile, and London pentecostals—who had heretofore snubbed the deliverance evangelists—joined with the English evangelicals in inviting Oral to London.[38]

More important than any specific result of the congress was the personal impact on Oral. He was deeply touched by Billy Graham's display of affection: "I knew that Billy loved me, . . . but I don't think the public knew it."[39] But it was the total experience which had shaken him. Evelyn told a reporter several years later: "All these years Oral has been a loner. He didn't necessarily want it this way but he just didn't know how others felt about him. At Berlin he was absolutely overwhelmed by the love he felt."[40] He went through a near-conversion experience. When Oral thanked Graham for opening his eyes to the mainstream, his friend Warren Hultgren, seated in the assembly, said to himself: "This guy is going to make a change." "That was when he got his feet wet," Hultgren believed, "and found that the world was bigger than a tent."[41] When Thielman came to Tulsa immediately after the congress, Oral not only pumped him for practical suggestions, he spoke quietly and incredulously of his gratitude. "You don't realize what happened out there," he told his new friend. "Those kind of people never spoke to me before. They have avoided me and there was no way I could ever break through it until now. . . . This is bigger than you understand. Because you've lived in these circles all your life and I haven't. I've been on the outside looking in."[42]

CHAPTER

IX

Oral Roberts University

IN JUNE 1960, while having dinner with Pat Robertson in Richmond, Virginia, Oral began to write on his napkin. He has repeated the message thousands of times since, rhythmically, as if reciting poetry:

> Raise up your students to hear My voice,
>   to go where My light is dim,
> Where My voice is small and
>   My healing power is not known.
> To go even to the uttermost bounds
>   of the earth.
> Their work will exceed yours
>   And in this I am well pleased.[1]

These were not, Oral was convinced, his words; he had received another charge from God.[2]

Whatever the source of the message, it spoke to a question much on the minds of Oral and the other members of his organization in 1960—what would God do next? By 1960, almost everyone would acknowledge, privately at least, that the healing revival was aging and fading and that Oral must take some concrete step to "perpetuate his ministry." The two most obvious ways to accomplish that end were to form a "new denomination" (an idea which Oral early rejected) or to establish a school.[3] Oral Roberts University was the answer; it would, Oral told a Houston reporter in 1962, "perpetuate my ministry and multiply it thousands of times, a ministry that otherwise would die."[4]

The idea of building a university had apparently long lurked on the periphery of Oral's mind, obscured by the long shadow of his mushrooming crusade ministry. He associated his new understanding with his earlier work to establish Southwestern Bible College in collaboration with Raymond O. Corvin.[5] Glimpses of the idea did surface from time to time in Oral's conversations and then disappear—forgotten by all except him. In the early 1950s, he told his family that he would build a university, and he mentioned the idea to Lee Braxton "several years before ORU was formally announced."[6] Between 1958 and 1960, Evelyn knew that "Oral began seriously to consider building a Bible school for foreign students."[7] "I have known all the time that we would build a university some day," he told his staff in the summer of 1962. "I knew that we would have to get it into the minds of the youth."[8]

Nonetheless, Oral's announcement in 1961 that he would build a school "kind of slipped up on his team."[9] In July 1961, he called his staff together and informed them: "I came to some decisive actions for the future of my ministry. One is that I definitely now am committing myself to the institute and bringing foreign people over to America. . . . Then I have come nearer to my decision to establish an institute in the strictest sense of the word which will ultimately become a college."[10] Initially, most of Roberts's seasoned team members dismissed the idea lightly; many other projects had come stillborn from Oral's fertile brain. "Well, of course, everybody laughed at that," recalled DeWeese, "and everybody said to him, you can't do it."[11] It was a lonely and discouraging time for Oral: "I talked to my friends but I usually ended up for the worse. My wife who was standing with me only because she was married to me and believed in me, when I finally found the key that unlocked my mind, she finally had to say that I had gone off the deep end."[12]

Oral's first plan in 1961 was to build a "boot camp" for training foreign evangelists. The crusade team thought the boot camp idea was no "big deal," basically because it seemed in harmony with the evangelistic ministry which had brought Roberts fame and fortune.[13] By August 1961, his plans for such a school were clearly in place, and he had called his staff from California asking that they "pray earnestly for God to give us the land to build the 'boot camp' on."[14]

The acquisition of the property on the corner of Eighty-first Street and South Lewis where Oral Roberts University is now located was regarded by Roberts's supporters as another of those providential miracles which confirmed the ministry. Oral later remembered driving by the property many times, as early as 1952, and stopping to pray with his family: "I pointed it out to them that this was where the university would be built some day, and we all bowed our heads and prayed that God would hold the land, and He did."[15] As he increasingly felt pressed about building the school in the summer of 1961, Oral called his lawyer, Saul Yager, and instructed him to make an offer on the property, although it was owned by a "very wealthy oil family" and was not for sale.[16] Yager protested that "builders have tried to buy this farm and they've always turned them down," but he agreed to try. When contacted, the owners revealed that they had just decided the day before to put the land on the market. Roberts purchased the 160-acre farm at a bargain price of about $1,850 per acre. The association quickly purchased an adjoining 20 acres, giving an initial holding of 180 acres on which to build the new school.[17]

While the purchase of the property was being negotiated, Oral's vision went through a series of escalations. His first idea, described to his staff in detail in a telephone conversation from California in August 1961, was to build a series of "little cottages," initially conceived as "little log cabins," to house visiting ministers. He excitedly described his plan to his team:

> We will build a "boot camp" outside of Tulsa. I plan to bring about 40 students from overseas this spring. These will be more trained than the others— important men and women—cream of the crop—already in this work. Train them two or three months and send them home. Then in the fall of 1962, start a regular term like a school term. . . . Start with 100 students this fall and hope within ten years to have 1,000 per year coming for training.

"Note that term . . . 'boot camp,'" insisted Oral; the accommodations were to be spartan and the regime strict. Bill Roberts estimated that the cottages could be constructed for about $7,500 each, and the only other facilities needed were a dining hall and classroom building. Oral was prepared to present the scheme to his partners.[18]

The property acquisition was not completed until December 1961, and by that time Oral's plans had reached a second stage.[19] He had commissioned Cecil Stanfield, architect for the Abundant Life building, to design three buildings for an Oral Roberts University of Evangelism. The three buildings, each "contemporary in design and built of native stone and large expanses of glass," included an administration and classroom building and two dormitories capable of housing a total of 320 students. By February 1962, construction had begun on the three buildings and a program had been designed and announced.[20]

The "objectives and plans" for the University of Evangelism were to "train each year 1,000 or more young foreign national ministers and American ministers and workers." Attendance would be by "invitation only," and there would be "no charge for tuition, board or room." The students were to be trained in "soul winning on a personal level and mass scale"; "healing of the sick throughout the world through faith"; the "Abundant Life Concept"; and the use of "radio, television, films and other modern methods to win souls." By returning these "young foreign national ministers to their own countries to conduct evangelistic crusades, pray for the sick, win souls and bring Bible deliverance to their people," the university would "perpetuate the Oral Roberts ministry of winning souls and ministering healing to the sick."[21] Oral assured his partners that "between our regular crusades, I will spend my time with the students," and while he was away, "my faithful staff" would teach them.[22]

A "Board of Directors" was appointed for the new University of Evangelism, and Oral was elected president.[23] He informed his partners that "there is nothing like it in the world" and urged them to support his drive to build the new facilities "debt free." "When you make a gift of $10.00 or more toward our training program," he wrote to his partners in January 1962, "your name will be sealed, along with mine, in the cornerstone of the Assembly Hall where the teaching will be done. The inscription will read: 'Dedicated to the fulfillment of THE GREAT COMMISSION of preaching the gospel to every creature.'"[24]

Long before the three buildings for the University of Evangelism had been completed, Oral had made the decision to build an accredited university. He had alerted his staff as early as July 1961 that his thoughts were moving in that direction: "When we build a school, by the help of God, we'll build one whose academic standing will be high enough that it will have a great appeal to young people who want to have a real high academic education. This is possibly several years off, but I want you to know what my thinking is."[25] The beginning of the University of Evangelism more or less pushed the larger idea into the background, but in Oral's mind the seed continued to germinate, and in the summer of 1962, he committed himself to establishing a university. In a July meeting he told his administrative staff: "When it came to us, it was small, it was little in its implication, now it is growing; it's getting big."[26] The transformation in his thinking, Oral believed, was the result of his opening his mind to God's leading:

> I began to see all this . . . without having any human being teach it to me. And through the intervention of the Holy Spirit upon my intellect, my intellect could see the university. It could see the buildings. It could see the type of faculty. It could see that it should become a very highly rated academic institution. That it would have to operate in a way that it would not be classified as a mere Bible school although the Bible itself would always be the number one Book, and without apology of course.[27]

To Oral's closest advisors, his growing vision seemed a nightmare. The Roberts empire had been built on his evangelistic ministry. While a University of Evangelism made some sense, building a full-scale university seemed a diversion from his call and mission. By the summer of 1962, everyone had glimpsed the astronomical costs involved—Oral envisioned that $25,000,000 would be needed to build the university.[28] The leaders of the Evangelistic Association—Lee Braxton, Manford Engel, Bob DeWeese, and several others—held a private meeting to coordinate their unanimous objections to the project and steeled themselves for a showdown conference with Oral. They told him forthrightly that they opposed the university on the grounds that it would preempt his evangelistic ministry and urged that the idea be dropped. All of them would subsequently remember the confrontation well. Oral recalled that it nearly brought a "dissolution of my office and of the team," because he had been unable to "communicate" the vision that "God put in my heart."[29] But in this meeting he got his point across. The message was: "I started this ministry without you, I will continue to obey God without you."[30] Oral described the meeting's conclusion: "When I finished I was on my feet. I was churning inside and I was reaching out to these beloved men. Manford let out a gurgling sound and burst into tears. Lee Braxton sat with tears streaming down his cheeks. Bob DeWeese was broken up. . . . I don't know how it happened, but in moments 12 men were on their feet and we were embracing each other and praising God!"[31] A university it would be, by 1965. All that was left was some notion of how to bring it about and how to pay for it.

While Oral's decision to begin a "strong academic university" no doubt had deep roots and bears no simple explanation, a part of his haste to begin grew out of concern for his son Ronnie, who enrolled in Stanford in 1962. Oral told his pentecostal friends that he wanted to send Ronnie to a "Bible School but it was impossible because Ronnie wishes to major in Foreign Languages." In fact, Oral and Evelyn were proud of their son's academic achievements. However, they soon became increasingly concerned about his spiritual welfare in the Stanford environment. In 1962, Oral explained to his workers his haste to build the university: "I get this fighting instinct to get this school going sooner than we intend because it has come home; it's in my family. This is affecting my family. My son got his balance but when will they hit him again?"[32] Pentecostals had a general problem, Oral believed; "many thousands" of young people were being "lost to the Full Gospel movement by virtue of going to these other universities where God was not supreme." The only answer, he concluded, was "to build a major, Class 'A', academic university in addition to the University of Evangelism."[33]

Oral Roberts realized, and frequently confessed, that he had not the slightest inkling about how to build a university. "I have carried as far as my part's concerned this University about as far as I can," he told a group of advisors, but then "God began to send men in here."[34] First, and most important in the formative months of the university, was Oral's old friend from Pontotoc County and the Pentecostal Holiness church, Raymond O. Corvin. Corvin had remained as president of Southwestern Bible College since 1946, taking courses in a variety of institutions before earning a doctorate in religious education from Southwestern Baptist Seminary in 1956. When he joined Oral Roberts in 1962, Corvin reportedly had completed "427 hours of undergraduate and post-graduate university work"; while in Tulsa he completed a Ph.D. in education at the University of Oklahoma.[35]

Oral called Corvin to Tulsa in March 1962 and invited him to "head up the Oral Roberts University from an academic standpoint." During that meeting, Roberts and Corvin reminisced, as they did many times subsequently, about conversing as youths "under an oak tree" in front of the Corvin home, pledging themselves to make their respective marks as an evangelist and a Christian educator. "I am now ready to fulfill our pact," Oral told his old friend, proposing that they combine their efforts in "the greatest soul-winning venture of this age." Oral still believed that his "calling was to preach the gospel," but now, "through Dr. Corvin and the university, we have God's way of continuing this ministry permanently." Corvin moved to Tulsa in June and was named chancellor of the university, and he and Oral began to plan for the opening of the school in 1965.[36] By August, the two had conceived a twenty-five-year plan which would result in a university with 3,000 students fired with a vision for worldwide evangelism.[37] The cost of the vision had risen to $50,000,000.[38]

Oral's alliance with Raymond Corvin was predictable and, in some ways, fortunate. Corvin was a gifted teacher and a man of unquestioned spirituality. Furthermore, he was a dreamer—a partner fit to share in Oral's visions, to incite and stimulate them. More questionable were Corvin's academic credentials. He was an academic vagabond, collecting a smattering of degrees in education. Although Oral heralded him as "one of the limited number upon whom a doctorate of religious education has been bestowed," he did not earn a Ph.D. until 1967. Corvin's administrative experience had been entirely in a Bible school atmosphere. When faced with the concrete problems of constructing an academic program, many of his contemporaries found him to be unsure and hesitant.[39] Almost immediately, however, Corvin made contacts with several consultants whom Oral instinctively understood were competent to design a university.

Oral Roberts University was formally established on November 27, 1962, with the appointment of a board of regents headed by Lee Braxton and the election of Oral as president and Corvin as chancellor. Oral summoned to Tulsa thirty of his oldest and most loyal friends for a meeting with him and the trustees of the Oral Roberts Evangelistic Association. The board of regents was an honor roll of tried and true friends—John Wellons, Dunn, North Carolina candy manufacturer; Velmer Gardner, Orange, California motel owner; Frank Foglio, Fontana, California real estate man; Mike and Nick Cardone, Philadelphia automotive products dealers; Carl Williams, Scottsdale, Arizona well driller; and former ministerial associates Byon Jones of Ocala, Florida and Vep Ellis of Fontana, California.[40] The regents and trustees met for three days in the new buildings of the University of Evangelism, feasting on hearty worship and drinking in the vision of Oral and R. O. Corvin. On November 26, Monday morning, Oral taught "the first class conducted in the university," instructing the trustees and regents on "The Baptism with the Holy Spirit."[41] Then he and Corvin outlined the plan—a $50,000,000 university ($25,000,000 in physical expenditure and an equal amount in endowment funds), enrollment of 3,000 students who would win 2,000,000 souls each year, seven academic colleges, the establishment of four graduate schools by 1980, a faculty with sixty percent holding doctoral degrees, rapid accreditation, and immediate plans to build four more buildings. Before the regents arrived, much of the campus had been graded in preparation for construction, including, as an act of faith, "digging a hole for the building of a library which was to be the center of the campus."[42]

From its inception, Oral Roberts University was viewed as "an outreach of Oral Roberts Evangelistic Association, Inc." It was "built primarily by the prayers and sacrificial gifts of Christian people who are partners of the ministry that brought it into existence."[43] The regents of the university were appointed by the trustees board of Oral Roberts Evangelistic Association, and the two boards were effectively tied together. The relationship of the university to the evangelistic association was a matter of much discussion during accreditation proceedings in later years, but the fundamental ties remained intact. While the Oral Roberts University board of regents was an independent body with authority over the school, it served at the will of the board of trustees of the evangelistic association.[44] The regents were assured that they would not be mere "figure heads," but Oral also announced: "I'm running for president here, and if I get elected president in the morning I hope I get to be a regent too."[45] The board of regents ultimately grew to include forty-one members, all men and women "of integrity, of spiritual insight, and filled with God's Holy Spirit."[46]

An additional issue which faced the charter board in its first meeting was naming the new university. In hindsight it seems inevitable that the university would bear Oral's name, although at the time several other possibilities were apparently considered. But Oral's name was a "symbol . . . of the image that has been built up over these years," argued Lee Braxton, and the regents agreed that it must be attached to the university.[47] Carl Hamilton believed that Oral knew the use of his name would hinder the academic development of the institution for a "full generation." "He knew what derision, what ridicule, some would put up initially." But there was another, more powerful, practical reason for calling it Oral Roberts University: "What became apparent to everyone was that . . . if it is not named Oral Roberts University we will not be able to get the support from the partners within the time frame necessary to establish the university in a quality way. . . . It was a matter of that being the most effective way to carry out God's call."[48]

As Oral's plans for the university matured and grew, he kept in close touch with his partners, outlining his latest plans and explaining in detail the costs. He set out to build the first three buildings on a "pay-as-you-go basis" in an effort to avoid "high interest rates." In February 1962, Oral dispatched a detailed progress report to his partners: "I intend to keep you informed as the construction progresses. You will want to live it with me. In the meantime, I invite you to write me concerning anything that is on your heart or any of your needs. I love to pray for you. May I hear from you today?"[49] In July, Roberts reported to his staff that his letter had brought in $400,000 and that total pledges for the university had reached $1,000,000.[50]

As Oral's plans mushroomed, it became increasingly apparent that he would not be able to construct the major university buildings without a loan. In December 1962, he was forced to borrow $150,000 to complete the University of Evangelism buildings and then began seeking a large loan to begin construction of the university library building.[51] Oral had vivid memories of his meeting with his bank board, facing "the power structure of Tulsa sitting around that table." "Well, men," he told them, "I want to build a university right out here on South Lewis." His listeners sat zombielike: "If one of them had died and they came to embalm him they'd got the whole bunch. And I'm standing there and I'm telling my story and I'm hurting. I'm not crying outwardly, but inside I'm crying buckets of tears." Oral left, convinced that his plea had fallen on deaf ears, but he had, in fact, become an important Tulsa industry. The next morning the bank's president called: "Oral Roberts, I should have my head examined, but the three million dollar check is waiting."[52] On the basis of that loan, construction began on Oral Roberts University; its academic program was to begin in the fall of 1965.

Preoccupied with the hubbub of fund raising and keeping his partners informed, Oral recognized that someone would have to design the academic program for the school. In the summer of 1962, Lee Braxton persuaded his old friend John D. Messick, former president of East Carolina College, to visit Tulsa as a consultant. Oral knew he had his man. He told his staff: "We brought out to Tulsa . . . a man who is almost without peer in the educational circles in the United States. . . . He has a Ph.D. from New York University. He has the baptism of the Holy Spirit. . . . If we get Dr. Messick, we have a great deal of our program won."[53] Oral sensed that Messick could give the university instant credibility, and he immediately offered him the position of dean of academics. Messick turned the job down, but Oral persisted, and at the November regents meeting he gave his star consultant a stirring introduction: "I want you to meet Dr. Messick. We love this man. We admire this man. This man stands tall in this nation. He served with the President of our country. He's had some high positions in this nation, head of great institutions and he's been willing to help us and guide us. This man is one of the keys."[54] In January 1963, Messick accepted the position as dean; his wife had demurred about the move, but when they both attended a conference in the spring in Tulsa, she found the participants "cultured, likeable and sincere Christians" and agreed to the move.[55] When Messick arrived on the prospective campus in July 1963, the university finally had a cornerstone upon which to build. Oral beamed: "This man . . . is probably the only man in the whole world that could put the campus together and God had him ready for us."[56]

While not, perhaps, all that Oral had imagined him to be in 1963, John Messick was at the end of a solid and distinguished career as a university administrator. After completing an undergraduate degree at Elon College, a small Congregational school, in 1922, he served as a principal and county superintendent in North Carolina public schools. In 1934 he completed a Ph.D. in education at New York University, taught briefly at Asheville College, and then returned to Elon as the head of the school's education department and dean of administration. He served for three years as dean of Montclair State Teachers College in New Jersey before returning to North Carolina in 1947 to be president of East Carolina College, a small teacher's institution which grew rapidly during his term as president. After his retirement from that post in 1959, he worked briefly as a research specialist for the House of Representatives Committee on Education and Labor and then accepted a job as dean of instruction at Lyndon State College in Vermont.[57] Messick was an insider in the nation's educational establishment, with many friends in Washington, D.C. In 1983 he reminisced: "During my presidency at East Carolina College . . . I invited a goodly number of people from Washington to make addresses. . . . I invited these people for help at East Carolina, not knowing that they would mean so very much to me later elsewhere."[58] Messick's reputation also greatly aided the Roberts image in Tulsa. He immediately was elected to the board of the prestigious Boston Avenue Methodist Church and was welcomed by the city's civic and social elite.

Messick's religious qualifications to head the new university's programs were less clear. News accounts labeled him a "Methodist educator," and that was clearly the image that he cultivated.[59] Like many youngsters with pentecostal roots, Messick had distanced himself from his religious past. In his youth he had been a member of the Pentecostal Holiness church, and apparently held ministerial credentials in the denomination, having graduated from Falcon Holiness School.[60] He remained a friend of G. H. Montgomery and contributed occasional articles to the *Pentecostal Holiness Advocate* while Montgomery edited that journal.[61] He knew Lee Braxton well but was only casually acquainted with Oral and R. O. Corvin when he came to Tulsa for the first time, and he never fully shared Oral's religious vision of the university.[62] But Messick was intrigued by the concept of a quality university under "the leadership of consecrated Holiness-centered people," and his decision to accept the offer "was based entirely on my faith in God" and a belief that it was "God's will" for him to move to Tulsa.[63]

When Messick arrived in July 1963, Oral was away in a crusade and Corvin was out of the country recruiting foreign religious leaders for a seminar in Tulsa. Nothing had been done to get the university off the ground. Oral's architect, Frank Wallace, and his head of construction, Bill Roberts, were waiting for Messick to instruct them about the design of the first building. The newly arrived dean asked for an hour to collect his thoughts and then began a series of conferences which would last for two years and result in the creation of Oral Roberts University. Not only did Messick receive aid from a capable team of experts from the region, but he, Wallace, Bill Roberts, and others made scores of visits to leading universities throughout the world to discuss innovative designs and programs. But Messick was the creative catalyst. He "wrote the first catalog, faculty handbook, advised the salary schedule, retirement pay, etc." He used his contacts in the Office of Education to have the new school's curriculum critiqued as it was drafted. The "heart of the liberal arts program" designed by Messick was an innovative thirty-two-semester-hour Western civilization course which required each student to complete a wide range of core courses in humanities, social studies, literature, philosophy, and fine arts. In addition, the initial students faced rigid requirements in English, sciences, languages, and religion. Each student also participated weekly in a "colloquium" designed to give a broad view of some foreign culture.[64] Of course, all of Messick's work was done with "the approval of President Roberts." The new dean's office was next door to Oral's, and Messick found the president "very cooperative and understanding."[65]

It was an exciting challenge for a professional educator to be able to build a new institution; Messick was a creative thinker, and he wanted to make the most of the opportunity. He took Oral's commitment to quality seriously and believed that they could create a university which would rival Davidson or the University of the South in academic standards.[66] At first, Messick proposed entrance requirements of four years of high school math and four years of a foreign language, but under pressure from Oral the standard was reduced to two years of each.[67] "I actually had to ask Dr. Messick to cut back on some of the stringent requirements," recalled Oral in 1983. "He had so taken my charge of 'excellence' to heart that had we followed his plan, we might have graduated only a dozen students a year!" Among Messick's enduring contributions to the academic program, however, were the school's leadership in the area of "educational technology" and "a core curriculum of general arts and science courses that requires some fifty semester hours—far more than many schools and certainly more than the majority of schools in the 1960s."[68]

The emergence of John D. Messick as the academic architect of the new school led to a shuffling of titles that redefined R. O. Corvin's role. The initial university *Bulletin* listed Corvin as chancellor and dean of the Graduate School of Theology and Messick as provost and dean of instruction.[69] By 1967, the titles more clearly reflected the roles that each played; Messick had been named executive vice-president, and Corvin was dean of the Graduate School of Theology.[70] Corvin apparently accepted the change in duties gracefully, understanding that Messick was capable of managing the university which he and Oral had conceived.

Actually, by the time Messick arrived, Corvin's role had already been narrowed to that of theological leader. In January 1963, Oral announced that a "theological seminary" would soon be added to the liberal arts program. "Frankly we are interested in assisting in the producing of the world's greatest theologians. It takes thirty years to produce a theologian," Oral told a group of visiting ministers.[71] When the university opened in 1965, Corvin was the head of a Graduate School of Theology with twenty-nine students, which he described as "a seminary solidly anchored in Jesus Christ. . . . A citadel in which the doctrines of the Word of God implemented by the charismatic operations of the Holy Spirit are expressed as well as theory. . . . A Graduate School of Theology insisting upon the highest academic excellence."[72]

More important, in the long run, Corvin became the coordinator of a series of seminars and conferences beginning in 1963 which were looked upon as the forerunners of Oral Roberts University. Thousands of ministers, laymen, and young people were invited to the campus for conferences which explored pentecostal theology in new and creative ways and introduced the vision of Oral Roberts University to a diverse audience. The conferences were important stimuli to the budding charismatic movement, although their more immediate purpose was to promote the founding of a charismatic university.

The first ministers' seminar sponsored by the Oral Roberts University of Evangelism lasted from January 16 to January 22, 1963; about 350 ministers and their wives were housed in the University of Evangelism dormitories. The group represented eleven different denominations, though it was solidly pentecostal. Among the delegates were such notable ministers as David du Plessis, Ralph Wilkerson, Charles Blair, and Rex Humbard. The conference featured Oral teaching on "the manifestations of the Holy Spirit and the nine gifts of the Spirit" and R. O. Corvin delivering a series of lessons entitled "Christology of the Epistles to the Hebrews," and another on "Agape Love." A series of panel discussions addressed questions about the role that Oral Roberts University would play in the pentecostal world—revealing serious tensions just beneath the surface. The first seminar drew heavily on Oral's and Corvin's Pentecostal Holiness connections; Tulsa pastor Dan Beller was elected the first class president. All in all, it was a grand pentecostal meeting; the "students" in this "first class" were given "graduation certificates," and Oral noted that there "have not been many graduations where people broke into ecstatic praise and into speaking in other tongues as they talked to God and told Him how they felt."[73]

A second ministers' seminar followed in April. It once again was heavily pentecostal, but the list of speakers also included Baptist pastor Howard M.

Ervin, a rising leader in the charismatic movement. "Several received the baptism," reported *Abundant Life,* "including people of the Baptist and Church of Christ churches who were present in the seminar."[74] Three more seminars were held during 1963, in addition to the regular conferences with partners. In June, 450 young people participated in a youth seminar, coming from forty states, three countries, and ten denominations.[75] In November, the association sponsored an international seminar, bringing to Tulsa over two hundred delegates from fifty-six countries for "twelve days of heart-shaking, soul-stirring experiences together."[76] Finally, in December, a laymen's seminar assembled a variety of potential supporters on the campus. The seminars were expensive, but they were the fruition of Oral's plans for a University of Evangelism. Oral was elated about the conferences and believed that even after the academic phase of the university began, "the very heartthrob of this ministry will be in these three buildings."[77]

The conference schedule continued with little abatement through the 1960s. In 1970, Oral reported that the seminars were still "our largest outreach in terms of numbers of people personally ministered to. More than 20,000 have attended seminars since the first three buildings opened in 1963. . . . We believe the seminars should be continually expanded to include many more types of people who are not in a position to enroll in our academic program."[78] The most notable change in the conference format was the growing dominance of nonpentecostals in the meetings. Increasingly the reports on the meetings featured the presence of mainstream ministers; it became clear that these mainstream charismatics had given the university its friendliest welcome.[79] In a laymen's conference in the spring of 1968, the organization listed in the "record-breaking crowd" people from "more than thirty-five denominations."[80]

The change in the composition of the seminars was a barometer of the difficulties Roberts was once again encountering with his pentecostal brethren. While Oral's breach with the leaders of his own denomination had nearly healed by 1963, his vision to build an accredited charismatic university posed a new set of divisive issues for pentecostals. Some of the issues were old ones. The university exposed the historic antiintellectualism in pentecostalism, a prejudice which had encouraged the founding of unaccredited Bible colleges. The "older people," recalled Evelyn, "couldn't quite understand what had happened to Brother Roberts. Why is he leaving the healing ministry and going into education?"[81] And pentecostal theological wrangling made it difficult to conceive of an ecumenical charismatic institution. During the early ministers' seminars, Oral tried to tiptoe through the minefield of pentecostal sectarian theology, avoiding such controversial questions as "sanctification" and "holiness."[82] But in a variety of ways he offended old-time pentecostals. After the school opened, many were shocked that the girls wore makeup and by the generally modish appearance of the students.[83]

By far the most serious obstacle in gaining pentecostal support was the threat the university posed to the small pentecostal colleges which littered the countryside. By 1950, pentecostals operated over fifty Bible colleges, and several had hopes for accreditation as junior colleges. The most important pentecostal educational institution was Evangel College, a liberal arts school established in Springfield, Missouri by the Assemblies of God in 1955. When Oral announced his university, Evangel was struggling toward accreditation and aspired to be the premier educational institution in pentecostal ranks. Oral assured the pentecostal ministers who visited his campus in 1963 that he had no intention of detracting from the "excellent full gospel schools." "This school was not raised up to be competitive. . . . There are several million young people who are going to get an education. . . . Now as far as I know and if I'm wrong, I certainly wish to be corrected because I hope I'm wrong, I do not know of a single full gospel institution that is a major four year college, that is fully accredited by the Regional Associations."[84]

The assurances of Oral and Corvin satisfied some pentecostal ministers, particularly those from the smaller denominations which had no competitive institutions.[85] Even those churches sponsoring junior colleges did not feel threatened by the new university. J. Floyd Williams, executive director of education in the Pentecostal Holiness church, saw "no conflict" and hoped his church's junior colleges would "dove-tail our curriculum so that we can send our students . . . here to the university to complete their education."[86] But Assemblies of God leaders bristled. Lee Braxton recalled that "they went so far as to say, 'We forbid you to build a university.' "[87] Years later, Al Bush remembered a trip he made to Springfield, Missouri for a "toe to toe and chin to chin" confrontation with Assemblies of God general superintendent Thomas Zimmerman. According to Bush, Zimmerman vowed to suspend the ministerial license of any Assemblies of God clergyman who became associated with the new university.[88] Oral's new project had run afoul of the most powerful pentecostal organization in the nation.

The renewed hostility of organized pentecostalism no doubt hastened the drift of Oral Roberts University toward the charismatic movement in the traditional churches. Even in the early ministers' conferences, which had been strongly pentecostal in makeup, tone, and teaching, Oral made it clear that the university would not be denominationalized: "I'd like for every faculty member to be 100% in harmony with what I'm preaching. I don't mean to say that he has to be a member of the same church, or he might even be a member of the Presbyterian church, but he'll have to have the experience of the Holy Ghost and be in harmony with this ministry. I think that we will make a very serious mistake if we demand that every teacher will have Pentecostal credentials because there's a great move on today."[89] The early university bulletins included a statement of "spiritual ecumenicity":

> ORU exists to serve the whole body of Christ, worldwide. It is not concerned with changing the church allegiance of its students; rather, it seeks to bring each student into a more personal, vital relationship with Christ, to acquaint him more fully with the charismatic power of the Holy Spirit, to give him a clearer understanding of the principles of Christian living and to send him back to his own church as a committed witness of the Lord.[90]

By the time Oral Roberts University opened in the fall of 1965, its basic mission had been fully articulated and disseminated. The stated goals of the university have changed little in its two decades of existence, though there have been changes in the methods used to achieve those ends. In 1964, Oral summarized the "eight major goals" of the university: "educational excellence," "a climate of positive faith in God," "an atmosphere of the Holy Spirit," "spiritual and moral purity," "a search for truth," "a permanent projection of the healing ministry," "in-residence exposure," and "no worthy student denied for lack of finances."[91]

The mission of the university was more succinctly stated as a "quest for the whole man." In his opening address to the first students at the university in 1965, Oral explained his idea of educating mind, body, and spirit—a "daring new concept in higher education." "Education for your mind," Oral told the students, was a widely understood objective of universities, but at Oral Roberts University students would encounter innovative methods and be given personal attention. The concept of educating the body was not fully developed in Oral's early thinking, but from the beginning students were required to participate in intramural sports, and both students and faculty were required to participate in a "healthful walking program." Dr. James C. Spalding, a charismatic Methodist physician, was charged with the development of the university's fitness program, which included "a clinic for examination and individual instruction." Third, Oral Roberts University would provide "a unique opportunity for the education or development of the inner man, for the most important part of you is your spirit." "Toward this end," Oral announced, "every professor at ORU is qualified to help you develop in the inner man. He is available to counsel and pray with you."[92] The spiritual program of the school was the responsibility of the university chaplain, Tommy Tyson, a charismatic Methodist evangelist.[93]

To Oral and his supporters, the "whole man" concept was both Biblical and full of promise. It was a matter of developing as "Jesus did as a youth"—"And Jesus increased in wisdom (intellectually) and stature (physically) and in favor with God (spiritually) and man (socially). (Luke 2:52)."[94] Charismatic physician William Standish Reed believed the concept offered an opportunity to "produce a new type of person. . . . In medicine, there is what we called a potential space."[95] The idea of whole-man education has remained central at the university, but in 1970 Oral confessed that its implementation was "the hardest thing I've ever tried to accomplish." Building buildings and recruiting students and faculty were hard chores, reported Oral, "but that's not nearly as difficult as it is to really offer a whole man type education. . . . When you get serious about that you run up against his pre-education, that in his mind education is concerned more with knowledge than it is with wisdom or character-building."[96]

The quest for academic excellence was largely John Messick's concern, but it was a goal often stated and honestly pursued. Oral and Corvin sometimes talked unrealistically about their academic aspirations. Charles Farah, a charismatic Presbyterian with a Ph.D. from Edinburgh University, remembered that in the early days of planning there were frequent comparisons to Harvard, allusions which he regarded as "pretentious and impossible."[97] But Messick's academic plans were impressive; he hoped to build a "collegiate Utopia" where "earnest students, seeking a place where scholarship is paramount and where a complete collegiate education in a Christian atmosphere is the ultimate goal," would find a haven.[98] Whatever the university's ultimate academic stature, it began on a level far above previous pentecostal efforts; and it did win instant credibility in the eyes of outsiders. It was a source of academic pride for those who, like Rex Humbard, had risen from the pentecostal religious ghetto to positions of importance: "I've tried many times to explain to people that Rev. Oral Roberts has a very high academic college here, a university that . . . is going to meet the standards of any other university or any other college."[99]

But while academic credibility was necessary, it was the spiritual purpose of the university which motivated Oral: and it was that quality that he fought a constant battle to protect. Oral reiterated it over and over: "ORU was never intended to be purely an educational institution, but a tool, an instrument, for the higher purposes of our calling."[100] He told a faculty assembly in 1974:

> We are not built on the philosophers of the ages, I wouldn't give you a dime for all of them rolled into one. Unless we take Jesus Christ and put Him at the center and put His healing of persons, soul and body and mind right at the heart of it all, I don't believe they're worth the paper their words are written on. . . . They bring us into the area of the rational, that's as cold as ice and can turn out a bunch of students who are no longer human beings, who don't have a feeling.[101]

The distinctive quality of ORU, wrote charismatic Baptist Howard M. Ervin, was that this spiritual "vision permeates the entire structure of the institution."[102] Or, as black Bishop Patterson of the Church of God in Christ put it, students at ORU had the "opportunity to get your learning and at the same time keep your burning."[103] Knowledge without spiritual wisdom, Oral warned, had loosed on the world a generation of "educated monsters."[104]

Nothing turned Oral Roberts hostile more quickly than suggestions that the spiritual vision of the university should be changed. Reaffirming those principles in 1970, he warned, "Our commitment to God and our founding purposes cannot change." As the university improved in quality, he often was piqued by suggestions that the school should model itself on some distinguished university. "I could care less about what that guy does or what that school does," he told the student newspaper, "because we aren't raised up to be like 'other schools.' "[105] Preserving the "founding goals and principles" of the university was constantly on the minds of the board of regents and the president during the university's early years. In 1971, Oral announced that "for the first time since ORU's inception, I'm beginning to feel pressure to destroy us." But challengers found themselves facing an iron will. "I'm here as a servant of God, as your president, representing the Board of Regents," Oral wrote in 1970, "to tell one and all that our founding purpose is not debatable. It cannot be changed; it can only be reaffirmed."[106]

Theologically, the central tenet on which the university was built was a belief in the charismatic working of the Holy Spirit. Oral always envisioned that there would be diversity of beliefs on the campus, but they would be united on one issue: "We have to be broad enough for diversity. But that diversity must never be at the point in which the University had its birth. And that point of birth is the Holy Spirit."[107] At the initial convening of the board of regents in November 1962, Oral charged them: "This university has to be because God told me to build it. Now it has got to have the Holy Ghost at the center of it."[108]

The university catalog stated in unequivocal terms that "ORU is a Christian institution with the distinctive charismatic dimension of the baptism with the Holy Spirit and the gifts of the Spirit." A long section in the catalog summarized Oral's theology of the Holy Spirit and explained that the "particular emphasis" placed on that subject was intended to "enable faculty and students to reach toward their fullest potential."[109] The unabashed association of the campus with the Holy Spirit was captured in the school's fight song, written by Vep Ellis:

> Oh ORU
> Oh ORU
> Oh OR University
> Holy Spirit blessed,
> Seeking out the best
> Of the human trinity.
>
> Oh ORU
> Oh ORU
> Ordained for holy destiny
> May your torch still burn
> At the Lord's return
> And count for eternity.

In 1972, when Sir Arthur Rank, noted British motion picture producer, funded the first endowed chair at Oral Roberts University, Oral was given the appointment to teach a course on "The Holy Spirit in the Now." It was the first and only time that Oral taught a course at the university. The course enrolled over 1,200 students during its first year, and video tapes of the class became a permanent part of the school's curriculum.[110] Whatever tensions might develop in the future, it would be difficult to break the identification of ORU with the Holy Spirit.

The university projected an inaugural freshman class of 600, but began on September 7, 1965 with a class of 312, including 29 students in the Graduate School of Theology. The small student body included young people from forty-five states, twenty-four countries, and thirty religious denominations.[111] Most of the students knew why they were there; they had come with a sense of spiritual mission. The campus was bedlam as the students arrived, lugging their suitcases to newly completed dormitories through the mud of the unfinished construction. There was a camaraderie known only to those embarking on a pioneer venture. Arriving students were greeted by the university's faculty and staff; young Patti Holcombe was flabbergasted that the man who lugged her suitcase to the dormitory turned out to be Oral Roberts. "Everyone was so excited about being there," she recalled, "we all had such a sense of purpose. It wasn't anything like going to college. It was more like founding a country."[112] Oral fired the students on in his speech at the opening session of the university: "I think you can emerge as the world's most-wanted graduates. Why not? A healthy body that you know how to take care of, a trained and disciplined mind that never settles for less than excellence, governed by an invincible spirit of integrity, inspired by a personal relationship with a living God, and driven by an irresistible desire to be a whole man to make a troubled world whole again! Yes, you will be in demand."[113] They had come to the end of two hectic years of building, recruiting faculty and students, and fund raising. It was the beginning of a decade of change and growth that would leave Oral Roberts University a firmly established, accredited, and reputable liberal arts undergraduate college.

Roberts, Messick, and Corvin had scurried about trying to find competent faculty members who were sympathetic with the goals of the new university. The initial catalog outlined the dual goals for faculty recruitment: "It is the desire of the University administration, including the Board of Regents, that a faculty may be secured who are dedicated, Spirit-filled individuals. They should be aware of what is happening in the world, what new ideas are being projected, . . . and what uses can best be made of all available resources in educational media."[114] Most of the early faculty was recruited from the pentecostal denominations, people known by Oral, Messick, or Corvin. However, from the beginning, the institution was open to charismatics from the mainstream denominations, and a number of important additions were made from nonpentecostal sources by 1966. To a remarkable degree, however, the original faculty was pentecostal; in fact, it was heavily Pentecostal Holiness. Oral once again raided the talent pools that he knew best, and Emmanuel College and Southwestern Bible College contributed heavily to the early faculty.[115]

The search for qualified academicians who had experienced the baptism with the Holy Spirit was difficult. Oral recognized from the beginning that he might have to educate his own faculty; as soon as the idea of the university was firmly in his mind, he began encouraging the brightest of his young associates to return to graduate school. The ministry provided approximately $50,000 a year in grants to graduate students, including one to young Carl Hamilton, who left his editorial work in the evangelistic association to complete a Ph.D. in English at the University of Arkansas.[116] Of the twenty-six full-time faculty during the school's first year of operation, twelve held doctorates of some type; Messick pronounced the faculty "better than anticipated" and noted that a disproportionate number were young people just completing their graduate degrees.[117]

While the original faculty was strongly pentecostal in background, and the inner core of the administration is still dominated by such individuals, the university's recruiting policies soon broadened to allow hiring faculty members who had not undergone a charismatic experience but who professed themselves "open to it." In the late 1960s and early 1970s, the religious complexion of the faculty changed dramatically, coming to include representatives of numerous denominations and a majority who had not spoken in tongues.[118] The growing diversity of the faculty symbolized the broadening academic aspirations of the university and was a constant concern to its architect and head, Oral Roberts.

Recruiting students for the new university followed much the same pattern as did faculty recruitment. During the first five years, the student body was predominantly pentecostal; in 1968 nearly one-third was from the Assemblies of God. The student body grew steadily in number and diversity during the school's first decade. In 1968, the 865 students enrolled included representatives from twelve foreign countries.[119] By 1975, the student body had passed 2,500, and its religious composition had changed radically. A 1972 estimate reported that "classical pentecostals comprise only about 50 percent of the student body," and a 1974 religious survey found that Methodists had become the largest group on campus and Baptists second.[120]

The changing religious composition of the student body was symptomatic of the changes within the Oral Roberts ministry. The original students were attracted largely through advertising in *Abundant Life* magazine and alerting the partners to "keep young people in full gospel churches and when advisable those in other churches acquainted with the University offerings."[121] "Church banquets" were held throughout the country, encouraging youngsters to attend the university. As the ministry evolved in the early 1970s, so did the methods of attracting students. The university did "extensive advertising in magazines such as *Life, Look, Seventeen,* and *Sports Illustrated.*" And, after Oral returned to television in his new upbeat format in 1969, "the TV ministry [became] an overwhelming factor in drawing students to ORU."[122]

The maturation of the university was most visibly symbolized by the erection of a series of spectacular buildings. The central gem of the campus was the Learning Resources Center, a six-story structure with over four acres of floor space. It was designed to house a library of 500,000 volumes (although only 45,000 books were on hand when the university opened), and it also provided most of the university's classroom and office facilities. The building was designed by architect Frank Wallace in collaboration with Bill Roberts, Oral's nephew, who supervised the construction of the campus, and John Messick. After months of planning and consultation, construction on the projected $3,000,000 building was begun in April 1964.[123]

The interior design of the Learning Resources Center "brought national and international attention to ORU." For months, Messick, along with Wallace and Roberts, visited universities in the United States and abroad, seeking innovative designs which would aid the experimental curriculum he was designing. Messick particularly wanted to use the "electronic media." He invited Ernest Hollis, chairman of the United States Department of Higher Education, to campus to meet Oral and discuss the plans. As a result of the visit, the university was given a $500,000 grant to turn the projected library into a model learning laboratory.[124] The experiment was so successful that the Ford Foundation named the center "the most innovative facility of its kind."[125] The building's lecture rooms were equipped with unprecedented audio-visual capabilities, all orchestrated from a central media core in the center of the building. The centerpiece of the Learning Resources Center was a $500,000 RCA-designed "dial access information retrieval system" (DAIRS). A parade of envious educators from around the world visited the campus to study the system. DAIRS allowed students to individually view films and video tapes at 130 stations in the learning center. While the system was initially envisioned as an "enrichment tool," under the leadership of Paul I. McClendon, the first director of the center, and William Jernigan, the director of the library, its uses were expanded to include core curriculum lectures, allowing faculty members to meet students in small seminar sessions. Professors were rewarded for "media innovativeness," and DAIRS has continued to play a major role in the university's educational program.[126]

By the time the university opened in the fall of 1965, several other buildings had been completed. The University of Evangelism buildings, renamed Timko-Barton Hall, were used for classrooms, offices, and a dining area, and to house the School of Theology. A health resources center had also been built, containing a gymnasium, swimming pool, and additional classroom space, and a seven-story dormitory capable of housing six hundred students had been completed. In keeping with the university's innovative design and curriculum, a remarkable "gas turbine total energy system" was built to provide for the total energy of the school.[127]

The most spectacular and controversial of the buildings constructed during the university's first phase of construction was the 200-foot-tall Prayer Tower, located in a sunken garden in the heart of the campus. The tower was a bold architectural design of steel and glass, looking remarkably like a giant cross, and was topped by a gas flame lighting the evening sky. It quickly became a Tulsa landmark and tourist attraction and housed in its base a visitor's center. The circular observation deck of the Prayer Tower included facilities for the Abundant Life Prayer Group, and, later, for a radio station.[128]

The idea of having a prayer tower in the center of the campus, symbolizing the university's unique goals, appeared very early in Oral's planning. At the first ministers' seminar in 1963, Oral announced that the "prayer tower should be the center of the entire campus and the whole thinking of the school."[129] But as the academic plans for the university matured, there was growing resistance to tying the university so closely to Oral's evangelistic image. Oral wavered and considered abandoning the project. He gave Lee Braxton credit for holding him to his commitment: "We might never have had a Prayer Tower, but old Lee Braxton got up on his high horse and said, 'We are going to have a Prayer Tower.' And he blew around and yelled around and threw his weight around . . . and we got that Prayer Tower built."[130] Construction began in 1966, and the tower was finished in April 1967.

In 1966, long before the Prayer Tower had been completed, the university announced a sweeping master plan to construct an additional $10,000,000 in buildings. By 1975, a series of high-rise dormitories had been completed, raising to over 2,000 the number of students who could be housed on campus, and a spectacular student activities center and dining commons building had been constructed.[131] But the most impressive additions to the campus were three buildings completed after 1970: a special events center, a chapel, and the aerobics center.

The building of the special events center, a magnificent arena capable of seating over 10,500 spectators for basketball games, was a special tribute to the personal faith of Oral Roberts. In 1970, Oral sprang the idea of the $5,000,000 project during a meeting with eleven close associates, persuading them to begin the project by giving what they had in their wallets at the time. They collected $257, and Oral announced that the arena would be built. The special events center was an important addition to the Tulsa community. After receiving a $1,000,000 gift from the John Mabee Foundation of Tulsa, Roberts named the building the Mabee Center. Architect Frank Wallace designed a beautiful, compact arena, in which the seating placed specators unusually close to the basketball court. In addition, the building was suitable for artistic performances and could be used as a television studio for the production of the Roberts specials. The building's interior design was extremely sophisticated and complicated, and the final cost of the structure soared to $11,000,000.[132]

The construction of the Mabee Center was in part an acknowledgment of the growing importance of the university's basketball program. The arena became a showplace for a nationally prominent team. But the building also tied the university to the city of Tulsa in an unprecedented way. Not only did local donors contribute in a major way to the cost of the arena, but Oral announced that he hoped the Mabee Center would be an "interim building" for the community until the city had adequate facilities for the performing arts. In recognition of the building's community functions, the university announced that the campus ban on smoking would be relaxed in Mabee Center as an accommodation to the general public.[133] Oral was euphoric as the arena neared completion. There was, he told his faculty, "nothing like it in the state and few like it in the country. And we'uns is the ones that's got it."[134]

In the spring of 1971, plans also were made to build Christ's Chapel, a building capable of seating the entire faculty and student body for chapel services. Aided by a large anonymous donation, the project got underway in 1972. The chapel was later expanded to accommodate 4,000 people in the main sanctuary and also included a small "communion chapel" and the offices of the Spiritual Life Department of the university. Its completed cost was around $4,000,000.[135]

In the fall of 1974, the university added one of the most sophisticated health and physical education facilities in the nation. Named the Kenneth H. Cooper Aerobics Center, the $2,000,000 building was dedicated by the popularizer of the aerobics fitness system. Oral had become a fervent convert to Cooper's program. The building housed not only the finest athletic facilities but also a sophisticated human performance laboratory capable of designing individual health programs for all of the students and faculty members.[136]

The physical accomplishments by 1975 were impressive, even staggering. An article in the *Chronicle of Higher Education* noted: "The campus itself is an impressive, $60-million collection of futuristic buildings in one of Tulsa's classiest suburbs. It ranks as one of the city's most popular tourist attractions."[137] Oral believed that the accomplishments could be accounted for only by "the gift of working of miracles." He told an audience in 1974: "I believe that without this gift from time to time in my ministry, we never would have had the Oral Roberts University, which we had to start *with* nothing and *from* nothing."[138] The metamorphosis of the campus was not only implausible, Oral believed, it was impossible to explain except as a work of God. "I didn't dream up this school," he told a group of students in 1971, "God told me to build it. Nobody in his right mind will say, I have the ability to build these buildings. Only God can do them. And I built them the way God said and the beauty, the harmony, the commodiousness of the buildings, all these things are in harmony with God."[139]

The creative genius employed by Oral Roberts to design the extraordinary buildings was architect Frank Wallace. Between 1963 and 1968, Wallace maintained an office on the campus and worked full-time on university construction. He has designed every major building constructed by the Roberts Organization since the University of Evangelism was completed in 1963. During the years when the university was under construction, Wallace worked closely with Oral—drafting sketches, incorporating Oral's ideas, offering constant revisions for his approval. Frequently, Oral had quite precise ideas about what type building he wanted; his preferences dictated the contrasting light and dark color patterns used on the university buildings and the widespread use of gold-tinted glass and trim.[140]

It was Wallace's "ultramodern," "futuristic" architecture which was to make Oral Roberts University the leading tourist attraction in Tulsa. His invitation to design the campus came when Cecil Stanfield, architect for the Abundant Life building and the University of Evangelism, rejected Oral's offer to work full-time on the project. Wallace had assisted in drafting the Abundant Life building, he had worked closely with Bill Roberts, and he related well to Oral, and so he received the appointment. Wallace was a country boy from Afton, Oklahoma; his speech and manners betrayed his humble origins. Introducing him in 1974, Oral kidded: "How anybody could come from Afton, Oklahoma and look like that and have so much architectural genius as he has is something that my nephew Bill has never figured out."[141] Wallace was a high school dropout who, after a term in the service, went to work on a railroad gang. He wanted to be an artist but was hindered because he was partially colorblind. He had never heard the word *architecture* until he was twenty-four years old, when his wife began to tell him about the studies of the husband of one of her fellow workers. Wallace become convinced that architecture was his calling, and he enrolled first in the Oklahoma junior college using his veteran's benefits, and later transferred to the University of Arkansas.[142]

At the University of Arkansas, Wallace was trained in a school dominated by Ed Stone, a nationally prominent disciple and friend of Frank Lloyd Wright. Wallace struggled, "studying night and day to get through." He failed the university's junior English exam and graduated only after taking a remedial English course. But he finally made it, another Oklahoma success story, filled with the native ability of a sculptor and a desire "to be Frank Lloyd Wright."[143]

Wallace's buildings can hardly be identified with any architectural school— they were, in his words, "my thing." "They don't teach this at Arkansas," Wallace conceded: "It's the opportunity you have to present yourself. . . . [Roberts] is a very progressive person and he's wanting progressive ideas." Frank Wallace fell heir to an Oklahoma architect's dream—to sculpt a multimillion-dollar vision on the Tulsa landscape. Out of the earth rose gleaming monuments to the hopes and aspirations of two poor sons of the Oklahoma soil. Wallace has received other minor commissions since leaving the campus in 1968—mostly churches and vocational-technical schools—but Oral Roberts University remains by far his most significant architectural achievement.[144]

The buildings on the campus were loaded with symbolic meaning to Roberts supporters—although most of it was not intended by the architect.[145] Three-sided buildings were considered representative of the Trinity; the Prayer Tower appeared to be a cross with a "crown of thorns" around it; "the school colors of blue and gold symbolize divinity, while the white color of some of the buildings stands for purity."[146] The ultramodern design of the buildings has drawn a variety of comments, ranging from Congressman Carl Albert's judgment that it was "the finest modern architecture of any university in the world," to the jibes of local pundits who dubbed the campus "Six Flags over Jesus."[147] But whatever one's assessment of the architecture, there was a touch of genius in its choice. One might deem it "kooky," noted Tulsa business mogul John Williams "but it gets talked about."[148] Oral Roberts University needed visibility, and architect Frank Wallace helped provide it.

While the design of the buildings was the cooperative creation of Oral and Frank Wallace, the construction was supervised by Bill Roberts, Elmer's son and a graduate in engineering from the University of Oklahoma. Oral's penchant for changing buildings once they were under construction, combined with Wallace's unorthodox designs, made it imperative that the organization do its own contracting. Furthermore, when money was not available to continue work on a project, as was sometimes the case, the organization could slow or speed construction to fit its cash flow. Bill Roberts and Wallace worked together with extraordinary success through the years, tackling unusual new demands in each building and delivering at remarkably low costs per square foot.[149] As the dramatic buildings began to appear on the campus, some of Oral's partners questioned the financial advisability of building such flamboyant structures.[150] But few insiders ever questioned the ability of Wallace and Bill Roberts to deliver at bargain prices. Oral never compromised on quality, but, on the other hand, contributors clearly got their money's worth in the building of the university campus.

The construction of Oral Roberts University with the accumulation of relatively little capital debt was something of a financial miracle. Of course, the university remained primarily a financial project of the Oral Roberts Evangelistic Association. In 1972 it paid sixty percent of the university's $4,600,000 operating budget and contributed "nearly all of its capital funds"; the subsidy generally exceeded fifty percent.[151] The university had begun with a commitment to keep tuition costs reasonably low—the estimated student cost per year rose from $1,800 to $2,700 between 1965 and 1975—with the understanding that the evangelistic association would provide a permanent subsidy.[152] Two major loans financed the early building of the university. The first $3,000,000 was secured by Oral locally, and a second loan of $3,500,000, at a very low interest rate, was granted by the United States Office of Education through the good offices of Ernest Hollis. John Messick and the university's new business manager, Bob Eskridge, successfully overcame considerable opposition within the federal bureaucracy to obtain the crucial loan.[153]

After the early loans, most of the money for the expansion of the university and its maintenance was contributed by Oral's partners. The evangelistic association continued to depend on small contributors, but most of the major buildings on campus attracted large donations. In addition, in the late 1960s the university effectively tapped the Tulsa financial community. The university's 1966–67 expansion drive was launched with an elaborate appeal to Tulsa businessmen, netting nearly $1,500,000 in contributions. Oral Roberts University felt it could rightly press its claims on Tulsa support: "The University is good for Tulsa business, good for Tulsa's children, good for Tulsa's future. We think that aiding the growth of this great University, largely financed thus far from sources outside our city, now properly becomes an obligation of Tulsa."[154] When Oral announced his intention to build the special events center, and pointed out its implications for the community, a local fund-raising committee was established, headed by F. G. McClintock, chairman of the board of First National Bank and Trust Company of Tulsa, and John H. Williams—two of the wealthiest and most respected businessmen in the city.[155]

TWO MOMENTS during the university's first decade were particularly poignant. On April 2, 1967, the university was formally dedicated and Oral was invested as its president. The significance of the occasion was profoundly altered when Billy Graham accepted Oral's invitation to deliver the dedication address.

When Oral returned from the Berlin conference, the most important bounty he brought back with him was a verbal commitment from Graham to come to Tulsa to speak at the dedication. Calvin Thielman had brokered the deal, getting the word from Graham that he would be amenable to an invitation and passing it along to Oral. It was a ticklish decision for Billy; he made it, according to Warren Hultgren, "against the unanimous advice of his people."[156] Graham's supporters feared he would be irreparably damaged by such a close association with Oral; his office in Minneapolis was flooded with letters warning him of the risk.[157] Oral was ecstatic when he returned, announcing Graham's promise to the press almost immediately, praising Billy as a "real revolutionary" who "has come to the point where he is ready and willing to say exactly what he believes."[158] Oral was keenly aware that Graham's decision "cost him something," and he was genuinely humbled by Billy's acceptance.[159]

When Oral announced that Graham would speak at the dedication ceremony, he speculated that the occasion might draw a crowd of over 4,000. When the day arrived, over 20,000 invitations had been issued, and about 18,000 people flooded the campus, after braving a horrendous traffic jam. Cameramen scurried about snapping pictures of the assembled dignitaries, including Senator Mike Monroney, representatives Page Belcher and Ed Edmondson, Governor Dewey Bartlett, Mayor J. M. Hewgley, Jr., and a covey of Oklahoma educational leaders. But the particular targets were Billy and Oral, who brought up the rear of the processional. A photographer hovered overhead in a helicopter until he was waved off for causing interference in the public address system. It was a festive, colorful, ebullient assemblage, come to share in a triumph of faith. In the spirit of understatement, Bob Foresman summarized the occasion: "It was a great day for evangelist Oral Roberts. He was invested as president of his school, and presented a gold medallion. One hundred and twenty colleges and universities, among them the largest in the land, sent official delegates to join the procession."[160]

When the program began at 2:30 in the afternoon, it was a stroll down memory lane. Bob DeWeese was introduced, Bishop Joseph A. Synan of the Pentecostal Holiness church read a scripture, John D. Messick presided, R. O. Corvin delivered a greeting from the faculty, and Warren Hultgren gave the invocation. Then, after the political dignitaries had been recognized, Lee Braxton introduced Oral, whose "dream of a truly great Christian university smoldered in his breast . . . all these years."[161] "What you see and feel here today has not come about without effort," said Oral's old friend. "Fear has knocked at this man's door many times but faith has always answered, 'No one is here.' "[162]

Oral responded with a speech outlining his philosophy of educating the whole man and stressing the desperate need for such education in a society torn by war in Vietnam and internal dissension at home. His speech was entitled "God Is Not Done with Man"; it affirmed his confidence in the destiny of the new university. In a more personal vein, Oral stated how "deeply honored" he was by the presence of Billy Graham and the other dignitaries. Finally, his voice cracking with emotion, his mind swept back to his humble origins: "This honor is not for me, but for my father, 86, a sainted minister of the Gospel who inspired me, but who is not able to be here today. It is for my mother, 82 years young and a firebrand who would still fly to the ends of the earth with me if it meant the winning of a soul and who taught me to be little in my own eyes."[163] It was a touching moment, filled with nostalgia, as Oral signaled Claudius to rise to be recognized by the huge throng come to honor her son. Finally, Oral offered his thanksgiving for "the sacrificial gifts and prayers of thousands of dedicated people throughout the world."[164]

Billy Graham spoke on "Why I Believe in Christian Education." He decried the failure of the great universities to meet the spiritual and personal needs of students. He had just visited a major university campus where "they have some of the most brilliant minds in the world. But their spirits had been neglected, and they had ten psychiatrists full time on the campus to take care of the problems of the students." He thanked God that "here at Oral Roberts University these young people are being taught not only how to make a living, but how to live." Finally, he warned that other evangelists in the past—Edwards, Finney, and Moody—had established educational institutions, but history had proven how difficult it was to keep such institutions true to the goals of the founders. "Somewhere along the line," Billy warned, "they became more and more secularistic, and humanistic, searching for truth without reference to God."[165] Billy charged Oral to remember the university's founding, to savor it, and to protect it.

The gala dedication, featuring the appearance of Graham, was a major public relations triumph for the university. Graham was adored in Tulsa; community leaders had repeatedly tried to persuade him to hold a crusade in the city.[166] Graham's endorsement had been magnanimous and unequivocal. "I think that Mr. Roberts is on the right track in making the university deeply spiritual and Biblical, but at the same time the very highest in academics," he told Bob Foresman. "I think the combination is going to meet a great need in this country."[167] Graham's commendation, wrote the editor of the *Tulsa World*, came "as a kind of second-stage rocket for the educational flight of Tulsa's Oral Roberts University." "A number of Tulsa individuals and businesses—including the Tulsa *Daily World*—already have contributed financially to the future of Oral Roberts U.," continued the editor. "Now is the time for others to step up and climb aboard."[168] Editor Jenkin Lloyd Jones of the *Tulsa Tribune* expressed delight that the city now had "an unashamed school for squares." Jones praised Oral as a "can do" man with a set of objectives that sounded good to him. "We hope he gets away with it," wrote the conservative editor. "Lord, how it is needed!"[169]

Dedication day was another giant step toward mainstream American Christianity, calling the attention of the outside world to the new image of Oral Roberts. For the thousands of pentecostals and charismatics who roamed the campus, it was a time for savoring the taste of respectability. Bishop J. A. Synan belived that the new institution offered great hope for "presenting the full Gospel of Christ to our world." Young Pat Robertson told an interviewer that it was "one of the great days of Evangelical history." Kenneth Hagin saw the dedication as a signal that "the Charismatic Revival is gaining momentum and others in all religious groups are actually looking this way." Rex Humbard, exultant that the "two leading soul winners in our world" were on the same platform, predicted "a great future ahead."[170] Unrecorded were the hosannas of those thousands of partners who trod as if on holy ground, who had come to see their partner and leader honored by the king of the outside world, who gazed awestruck at the grandiose monuments which had risen from Oral's vision. Together with Oral they had done it; this day resounded Amen.

The dedication of the university was a celebration, a declaration of common cause with the wider Christian world. The academic accreditation which was gained in 1971 was a more somber and challenging accomplishment. One does not proclaim academic credibility; it is a license to be earned.

The process of gaining accreditation from the North Central Association of Colleges and Secondary Schools was a slow and tedious business, filled with self-studies and site visits by representatives of the association. The university made its first major breakthrough in January 1967, when the Oklahoma Board of Regents for Higher Education accredited ORU, allowing its students to transfer credits to other institutions in the state.[171] After the necessary years as a candidate institution, Oral Roberts University applied for full accreditation in 1970 and was visited by an examining team in November. On March 31, 1971, the association granted accreditation. It was the end of a remarkably successful campaign, shortening the usual period of candidate status by several years. The fact that the university was granted full accreditation and was not required to go through a usual probationary period indicated the extraordinary progress made in the school's first six years of existence.[172]

The swift march of Oral Roberts University to accredited status obscured the wrenching struggles that filled those years. As the stream of academic consultants and North Central Association examiners paraded through the campus, they repeatedly challenged the basic goals of the university. They told Oral that a true university could exist only where there was a diversity of purpose and urged him not to seek administrators who parroted his views. Oral was told his students should be "mavericks," not conformists, and some visitors directly challenged Roberts's position in the university. In a 1967 chapel service, Oral told the students of a confrontation with a group of visiting professors: "They were in my office and they were trying to say something to me that would not offend me. They were trying to say, 'You dumb faith healer, what in the world are you doing connected with a great school like this?' That's not the way they said it. But I got the point real good."[173]

Oral was successively frustrated, angered, and shaken during the accreditation fight. After one heated meeting, he came away with a view of higher education that he "wanted to spit and vomit out." He sometimes bristled, telling visiting consultants that "ORU is a horse of a different color."[174] But he sometimes wavered, "struggling personally on occasions until I was almost physically ill because I knew what God wanted."[175]

Most serious was the repeated demand that the university board of regents be independent of the evangelistic association.[176] Not only did outside consultants press Oral on this point, but some insiders were "academically ashamed" of the relationship. In later years, Oral confessed that his own commitment would "swing back and forth, I'd get negative and positive about it."[177] "I found out early," quipped Oral, "that the higher the educator the less evangelism he wanted."[178] But Lee Braxton, Don Moyers, and, curiously, Roberts's Jewish lawyer Saul Yager insisted that the evangelistic association remain in control, because "the safest thing in the United States in a non-taxable charter is not a university, it is religion." Besides, they argued, if Oral succeeded in building a university that did not "carry with it the evangelistic thrust that you created in the world, with the healing ministry, what will you have?" Oral turned the matter over to his lawyers, who established "autonomous boards" but vested ultimate authority in the evangelistic association. Oral triumphantly announced: "Now I was smart enough not to ask any questions . . . but I will stake my life on the fact that no educator can ever separate Oral Roberts University from the Oral Roberts Evangelistic Association." The preservation of that relationship during the accreditation fight Oral considered a victory of "eternal magnitude."[179]

If the struggle was harsh, the victory was sweet. On the morning that the university was notified it had received accreditation, Oral spoke in chapel: "I looked out the bedroom window last night at the Prayer Tower with the flame typical of the Holy Spirit and I told God I didn't know what I would do if we did not get it. . . . But God gave it to us and it's a miracle."[180] Oral announced to the press that the university had entered a "new era." "I can't tell you how happy I am for ORU, for its future, for the student body, for the faculty and all the friends of the university who have made it possible," the president bubbled. "We designed ORU to be accredited. We worked for it. We've done just about everything in our power."[181] Among the advantages that followed accreditation was the right of the university to apply for admission to the National Collegiate Athletic Association and begin building the major sports program which Oral very much coveted.

In the wake of accreditation, Oral and the university once again basked in the warm good graces of Tulsa. The recognition, editorialized the *Tulsa World*, meant that the school was "moving up from the bush leagues to the majors." Many had remained suspicious that the university was just a "Bible college" in disguise, but accreditation should squelch the skeptics: "It also will make new believers in ROBERTS himself. When he talks now about bringing a national basketball championship to Tulsa in a few years, it sounds far-fetched and even presumptuous—but those who are quick to snicker should know that he is a specialist at making scoffers eat their words."[182] Jenkin Lloyd Jones happily noted that "something good happened to Oral Roberts Wednesday." Jones had long since become convinced that the conservative, God-centered education being dispensed by Oral Roberts University would "in some happier times be fashionable in this great nation."[183]

EARLY IN 1968, long before accreditation was gained, the university weathered two administrative upheavals resulting in the exit of both John D. Messick and Raymond O. Corvin. Their departures marked the end of the infant, formative stage of the university. Both men had contributed much to the early development of the school, but by 1968 they no longer fit neatly into Oral's vision. Oral had always been in uncontested control of the university, but both Corvin and Messick had carved spheres of influence within the institution. Their departures, while not the result of simple power struggles, left Oral with no real challenger as policy maker. The shakeup also brought to the leadership of the university a young man whose quiet talents made him Oral's most valuable single lieutenant in the next decade and a half.

John Messick's retirement in February 1968 was, on the surface, quite routine. He himself wrote the *Faculty Handbook*, which required mandatory retirement at age seventy, but it was under pressure that he resigned. He and Oral agreed to appoint Carl Hamilton assistant dean and Messick's potential successor.[184] Messick told the press that his years in Tulsa had been the "happiest and most beneficial years of my life"; on the other hand, Oral praised Messick as the academic architect of the university, with whom he had "worked heart to heart, walked side by side, gone hand in hand."[185] The learning resources center which the vice-president had creatively designed was named the John D. Messick Learning Resources Center; in 1969 he returned to the campus to deliver the baccalaureate address.[186] In later years, Messick spoke only with the profoundest respect for Oral and Evelyn, and Oral has never neglected to give proper credit to John Messick as ORU's academic architect.

The mutual respect between the two men was apparently genuine, and it held their partnership together through rough seas. Messick was a man of some academic stature and was highly respected in Tulsa—he clearly challenged Oral as the leader of the university. It was sometimes difficult to mesh the visions of the two men. Messick was enchanted by the possibility of building an innovative liberal arts university, although he shared much of Oral's spiritual vision. But the balance was never the same in the minds of the two men. Carl Hamilton recalled: "He and Oral came to agree toward the end of his time here that Dr. John's commitment to the academic world *per se* was greater than his commitment to Oral's ministry."[187] To others, the differences seemed sharper. "Messick couldn't abide the ministry," surmised Ron Smith.[188]

Messick wielded accreditation as a club. In 1983, he wrote: "I can recall when we had the first chapel. The time ran over for about half an hour. That was the time I had to step in and with the idea that such would not be approved by the accrediting agency."[189] Oral resented such intimidation. He wanted a strong university; he knew that was his call, but he found many of the academic people he met offensive.[190] He sensed their superiority complexes; he listened to the their pontifications about how he should build his university and spend the money he had raised; he deciphered the scorn in their voices. It was no surprise that many of Oral's closest associates welcomed the departure of John Messick.[191] What is amazing is that Roberts and Messick remained in harness together for so long, that they did so much, and that they parted with public grace and genuine admiration.

The appointment of Carl Hamilton as Messick's successor was one of the most fortuitous choices Oral Roberts ever made. More than any other individual, perhaps even more than Oral himself, Carl Hamilton understood and was personally engrossed in creating a reputable academic institution that would be true to the vision of Oral Roberts. "Carl understands both," said ministry leader Ron Smith, "and so the university survived."[192]

It was as if Carl Hamilton had been born for the job he assumed at age thirty-three. He grew up in Bartlesville, Oklahoma, the son of a farming family who were faithful members of the local Pentecostal Holiness church. He attended Oral's 1947 meeting in Tulsa while still a child. As a youngster he had stuttered, like Oral, and had experienced, he believed, a miraculous religious healing.[193] His roots reached deep into the same cultural and spiritual soil which produced Oral Roberts, and, more than any other person at the university, Carl Hamilton viscerally understood the Roberts ministry.

Hamilton attended Southwestern Bible College in Oklahoma City, presuming that he would enter the Pentecostal Holiness ministry. But he was an exceptional student; after transferring to Oklahoma City University, he earned a B.A. degree and graduated as valedictorian of his class. He returned to Southwestern to teach for three years before Oral coaxed him into joining the *Abundant Life* editorial department in 1960. Hamilton earned an M.A. in English from the University of Tulsa while working in the Oral Roberts Evangelistic Association, and when Oral's plans to build a university became firm, he "signed the first ORU faculty contract."[194] Accepting a subsidy from the evangelistic association, Hamilton entered a Ph.D. program in English at the University of

Arkansas. He joined the ORU faculty in 1966 and completed his Ph.D. degree in 1968, the same year he was named academic dean and John D. Messick's successor.[195]

At first appearance, the appointment of the thirty-three-year-old Hamilton seemed incredible; *Tulsa Tribune* education writer Kyle Goddard reported that "the state's academic world was rocked by the promotion."[196] But the succession went without a hitch. While it was apparent that Hamilton was Oral's choice, it also became clear that he had the endorsement of John Messick.[197] Messick told the press that not only was Hamilton "compatible" with the distinctive spiritual emphasis of the university, he also had the universal respect of his "peers." Messick and Roberts agreed that "Carl will have to live a few years" before he would have the academic clout that Messick brought to the school, but Messick felt that his successor would learn, and Oral announced that he was committing at least "half of his time" to university business.[198]

Reserved, soft-spoken but articulate, exuding a quiet integrity, Hamilton became "'Mr. Inside' for the president."[199] He won the universal respect of the university's faculty and became an impressive representative for the school in academic circles. Oral paid him public tribute after the university had gained accreditation:

> When we met the final executive committee . . . I've never seen a man that was more anointed than Dr. Hamilton. I was a little strained, I was so close to it that I don't think I was at my best. . . . But everytime Carl opened his mouth it seemed like they were words of power and once when I was on the wrong track in answering, Carl just put his hand on me and said, "President Roberts, that's not quite accurate." . . . Other things like that happened and he seemed to be charged with the spirit of God. He had the grasp of this whole academic program. He had it on his fingertips and I just had to stop after it was over and thank God that God had raised him up for such a task.[200]

At times, particularly when Oral became obsessed with building a national basketball power in the early 1970s, Hamilton's independence irritated Oral and strained their relationship.[201] But whatever their disagreements, there could never be a question about Hamilton's commitment to the spiritual objectives of the total ministry and his desire to make the university a part of the whole. His first loyalty was to the vision of Oral Roberts, and he became the invaluable ministry representative, negotiator, and interpreter in the midst of an academic community increasingly distanced from its origins and source.

The public confrontation between Raymond O. Corvin and Roberts in March 1968 which resulted in the closing of the School of Theology was more melodramatic and troublesome. Symbolically, the exit of Corvin was just as important a landmark in the changing of the university as the departure of Messick, although Corvin's influence had already declined markedly. By the time he left, Corvin had become the emblem of an earlier age, and the School of Theology was at best irrelevant and at worst an embarrassment.

The announcement on March 19, 1968 that Corvin had been removed as dean of the School of Theology came as a shock to outsiders, but it was the culmination of an escalating feud between Corvin and Oral. "If I had been R. O. Corvin," said Oscar Moore, "I would have left Oral years ago and if I had been Oral Roberts, I would have fired Corvin. . . . Their viewpoints led them to clash after clash."[202] Their differences became heated in the summer of 1967, and, after a series of conferences among Oral, Corvin, and Associate Dean of the School of Theology Howard M. Ervin failed to reconcile the issues, the faculty of the theology school, including Corvin, signed an agreement making Ervin acting dean. The compromise provided that at the end of one year the faculty would elect a new dean, "by secret ballot," for a two-year term.[203] Three days after the compromise was reached, the policy dispute became public when Corvin told the press, "I was fired." According to Corvin, Oral told the theology school faculty, "Either he is removed as dean or I will close the school of theology." Corvin labeled the dispute another fight over academic integrity: "Since the university's founding, it has been very difficult to resolve the question of whether ORU is to be a 'clear-cut academic institution' or a 'clear-cut evangelistic association' or whether the two 'can be fused' into one." Messick, Corvin told reporters, "said the two roles should not be meshed and I do not see how they can be." But Corvin discovered, as Messick had, that "Roberts' presidency of the Oral Roberts Evangelistic Association gives him 'power' to nominate regents of university [sic] and in effect 'control' of the ORU board of regents."[204]

While the removal of Corvin did indeed lay bare the power source at Oral Roberts University, it was not so clearly a struggle between academic excellence and religious mission as had been the tiff between Roberts and Messick. The rupture between Oral and his old friend and fellow dreamer had to do with diverging religious visions. It was exacerbated by personality conflicts and a series of misunderstandings that made rapprochement impossible.

The immediate source of friction between Oral and Corvin was a conflicting view of the School of Theology. Oral and many of the other leaders of the university came to view Corvin as an inflexible Pentecostal Holiness churchman, uneasy in the increasingly volatile environment of the charismatic revival. Corvin "preached church theology the whole time," recalled Lee Braxton: "He couldn't grow into a broader spectrum. . . . We didn't want him here to build a church school."[205] Carl Hamilton believed that "R. O. perceived the Graduate School of Theology as a seminary for the Pentecostal Holiness church and slanted everything that way."[206] Oral, on the other hand, was growing, and he had always been oriented to the "historic Christian church." The tensions became intolerable. Oral became convinced that "R. O. had a private dream" and that "all he wanted from Oral was the money to operate it." He discovered, as others had and would, that "Oral has no interest in anybody's private dream."[207]

The removal of Corvin coincided with the announcement that Oral was leaving the Pentecostal Holiness church to become a minister in the Methodist church. "A spokesman for ORU" assured the press that Corvin's removal "has no relation to Dr. Oral Roberts, ORU president, joining the Boston Avenue Methodist Church," and in a formal sense, that was true.[208] The breach between the two was already irreparable. But Oral's meaning-laden change of denominations, combined with Corvin's fierce church loyalties, was in another sense the whole story. In a symbolic act which he called to public attention, R. O. Corvin attended the Tulsa Evangelistic Center (a Pentecostal Holiness congregation) on the Sunday morning that Oral and Evelyn joined the Boston Avenue Methodist Church, and publicly read the Articles of Faith of the Pentecostal Holiness church, "reaffirming his faith in the Pentecostal faith in general and the pentecostal church in particular."[209]

After his removal, Corvin charged that Oral was flirting with existential philosophy and neoorthodox theology. He told reporters that he had written a "five-point protest" against Oral's theological views, including a charge that "Roberts leaned toward Christian existentialism and had read some 50 volumes written by such men as Soren Kierkegaard, Rudolph Bultmann, Albert Camus and Jean Paul Sartre."[210] Others believed that Corvin's theological charges were "blue smoke and mirrors." "It is true that Oral did some reading in some existential philosophers and theologians," recalled Carl Hamilton, but "the only residual there is of that is his interest in being in the now. . . . There never were any theological differences."[211] "Oral will take something that he likes out of something like existentialism," explained James Buskirk, later the university's dean of theology, "he's such an eclectic, and almost redefine it for his purposes."[212]

But the theological differences seemed real to Corvin. Oral had added to his inner circle of advisors bright young Wayne Robinson, a recent graduate in theology at Southern Methodist University, and Robinson had informally tutored Oral in Christian existentialism. In November 1967, Oral told a group of students: "I've just finished a very extensive and exhaustive study of some books on contemporary theology. It was rather brutal upon my spirit to stay with it, because there were so many points where I most violently disagreed. . . . I have just finished Barth's book on the *Epistle to the Romans*, and about thirty books in other areas. I'm not afraid to expose myself, for I might find some truth."[213] Wayne Robinson recalled: "He was greatly intrigued by the existentialists. . . . He used to ask me, 'All right, Wayne, explain existentialism to me again.' . . . In the process he could pick up that language and the motif and begin to articulate it, even though he would read and . . . say, 'I couldn't understand a word that he said.' But on the other hand, he picked it up."[214] Corvin wanted Robinson fired, but Oral defended and protected him. Corvin's removal became inevitable once Oral became convinced he was too rigid to fairly accommodate the truth in contemporary theology.[215]

In another sense, the Roberts-Corvin confrontation was not theological, it was practical and tactical. Oral clearly believed that no Christian "could accept existentialism *per se*."[216] He was simply fascinated, noted Charles Farah of the School of Theology faculty, by the "nowness and passion of faith," and he was "reacting against the staticism of fundamentalism and the great Princeton theology."[217] Corvin interrupted Oral while he was giving a lecture on existentialism in November 1967 to point out that Oral's lecture should not be taken as an endorsement of the "philosophical concept." "But that doesn't keep me from studying it," retorted Oral "and doesn't keep me from examining any truth I run across. Maybe there's something in there, and there usually is a point or two that you can take."[218] "R. O. never . . . grasped the fact that Oral's nature was so dynamic that changes were inevitable," reflected Howard Ervin many years later.[219]

A curios fiasco which began in 1967 probably did more to explain the Corvin-Roberts schism than all of the discussion of their theological differences. Immediately after the two returned from the Berlin congress, Corvin was dispatched to Chile to begin negotiations with pentecostals there about a campaign the following year. All that occurred is not clear, but it is evident that Corvin's commitments far outstripped what Oral was willing to honor. Oral had a vague, sometimes articulated, dream in the mid-1960s of establishing extensions of ORU outside the United States. Such an idea was discussed generally with the Chilean pentecostal leaders. But, during Corvin's 1966 visit to Chile, the idea blossomed into concrete, imposing promises. Egged on by John Nichols, who was allegedly a "national representative for the WCC in Chile" and a "consultant for the Evangelical Church Council of Chile," an organization of Chilean pentecostals, Corvin fanned Chilean expectations.[220] Young Vinson Synan, who accompanied Corvin as a representative of the Pentecostal Holiness church, remembered "sitting with President Eduardo Montalva and Corvin showing him pictures of Oral Roberts University and telling the president of Chile . . . that Oral Roberts was going to build a university for 10,000 students that would cost a hundred million dollars. . . . I kept asking R. O., 'Are you sure Oral approved that?'"[221] In May 1967, the Chilean minister of education visited Tulsa to discuss the project, and when Corvin returned to Chile in December to prepare for the Roberts crusade there, he announced to the press that an evangelical university "is expected to be the outgrowth of a visit this month by Oral Roberts." Through all of the hullabaloo, Oral had remained noncommittal, issuing a statement that his "attitude . . . would be that this is an exploratory operation as far as the educational program is concerned."[222] The crusade turned sour, recalled Charles Farah, when it became clear that Corvin had gotten "out on a limb and began promising things that Oral in no way . . . could deliver."[223]

Partly, the Chilean fiasco developed because of Corvin's staunch denominationalism in a ministry that was becoming increasingly ecumenical. On each of his visits to Chile, Corvin had taken along representatives of the Pentecostal Holiness church to arrange denominational alliances. Vinson Synan sensed that Oral believed Corvin had taken "unfair advantage of Oral's reputation to push the interests of his church."[224] To many, it seemed that Corvin's grand plan was no more than an effort to extend the power of his small denomination in Chile.[225]

The Chilean debacle, many believed, betrayed a deeper flaw in Corvin's nature—and probably the ultimate reason for his rift with Oral. R. O. Corvin was a dreamer who lived in a world of grand and airy schemes. Oral, for all his vision, was an intensely practical man. "His dreams seemed to become facts before they were realities," said Oscar Moore of his old friend Corvin. "Often his ladder doesn't touch earth or heaven."[226] Carl Hamilton described the same qualities:

R. O. Corvin was a man who might have been. . . . R. O. was a superb Bible teacher. . . . He was a conceptualist who could never quite make the connection between what he could see and the reality of it. There was always a gulf fixed between what he had dreamed and hoped to do, much of which was excellent, and actually getting it done. He was still conceptualizing after it was time to begin to get concrete things functioning. And he would have been conceptualizing five years after the university started.[227]

He "did what he could," in the judgment of Harold Paul, Corvin's long-time friend and colleague at Southwestern and at Oral Roberts University, but "he wasn't qualified to build a university."[228] Messick had bailed Corvin out in the building of the university, but Corvin was never able to comprehend that the vision had outrun him and become a fact. After his removal as dean, he reminded reporters that he was the "first professional educator" to be associated with the university: "I was here thirteen months before John D. Messick came. He, Oral Roberts and I structured the university."[229]

Neither Oral nor anyone else at the university ever tried to belittle the role that Corvin had played in its conception. Oral offered him a permanent sinecure if he would retire as dean.[230] "Oral and I are good friends," Corvin concluded as they parted, returning home to become assistant general superintendent of the Pentecostal Holiness church.[231] At the meeting of the university board of regents in February 1969, the decision was made to close the School of Theology, integrating its faculty into an undergraduate department of theology.[232] Oral never publicly reacted to the theological charges made against him. Thus ended the dream of the two pentecostal youths from Pontotoc County. "It was two good men," reminisced Oscar Moore, "that cared about each other, but because of their relationship when they were young, they dreamed big dreams and they shared those dreams . . . and at a late time in life they tried to merge them. They didn't fit. . . . When they finally tried it, they had traveled separate roads too long."[233]

The departures of R. O. Corvin and John D. Messick in February and March 1968 were administrative changes of the first magnitude. The result was an immensely simplified chain of command. The road was open for Carl Hamilton to become an indispensably important figure. But, for the moment, President Oral Roberts wielded total authority. In retrospect, it is clear that it never had been otherwise. Whatever ambitions and perceptions of power the other founders may have had, it was Oral Roberts University. After the spring of 1968, no one would have presumed to question that fact.

The changes at the university in 1968 were related to, and to some extent made possible, other dramatic innovations in the Roberts ministry. For the first time since the university had been conceived, Oral felt he did not have to fight for control of it. Evelyn wrote: "For the past three years Oral has felt that he has had to stay close to the ORU campus because the Lord said, 'I have not given you this baby to neglect.' But now Oral feels that the University is in the competent hands of Spirit-filled men and women. He feels that we have turned a corner and can give more time to crusades and our overseas ministry."[234] Carl Hamilton could be trusted. Oral could now turn his attention to the burning imperative he felt to return to television.

The administrative reshuffling of 1968 meant that there would be no tampering with the philosophical underpinnings of the university. It was God's school—under Oral's guidance—and that preeminent commitment would not be offered on the altars of academic excellence or denominational loyalty. The university would be conformed to the vision God gave to Oral Roberts, or there would be no university. Oral loved John D. Messick and R. O. Corvin, but it was him that God had called to build a university.

It was the pursuit of those spiritual goals and the integration of Oral Roberts University into the total vision of Oral Roberts's ministry which gave the institution distinctive meaning. The essence of the university, its leaders believed, was its "lifestyle." That lifestyle included rules—often interpreted rigidly and enforced stringently—but it was perceived as a more recondite spiritual quality. Oral Roberts University has remained an intensely religious campus in the midst of great denominational diversity and wide theological permissiveness—united by a mystical devotion to a "lifestyle."

In the first conference held on campus, in January 1963, Oral tried to explain to the visiting pentecostal ministers his vision of a campus made spiritual not by the teaching of religion or the convening of chapel services (though both of those would take place on campus) but by a "religious emphasis pervading the whole atmosphere. . . . The worship center will be in every teacher's heart and every student's heart."[235] In 1983, Carl Hamilton, then provost of the university, summed up that atmosphere:

> I see Oral Roberts University as a lifestyle which includes quality academic and professional programs. And also as the logical outgrowth of Oral's evangelistic ministry. Evangelism is still the white hot heart of all that Oral Roberts University is or ever will be. I don't think anyone here questions my commitment to academic excellence or my knowledge of what is involved, but I joined Oral when I joined his ministry. And I'm here because it is the ministry. . . . When push comes to shove . . . my basic commitment is to the same call that drives Oral's life.[236]

The contractual basis of the university's lifestyle was the "Code of Honor" which was signed by every student and faculty member.

THE CODE OF HONOR PLEDGE

Recognizing that our Lord and Savior, Jesus Christ, is the Whole Man, it is my aim to follow in His footsteps and to develop in the same ways in which He did: "And Jesus increased in wisdom and stature, and in favour with God and man." (Luke 2:52)

I pledge, by the help of God to work diligently toward the ideal of the "whole man."

I will apply myself to my studies and endeavor to develop the full powers of my mind.

I will practice good health habits and regularly participate in wholesome physical activities.

I will endeavor to seek the Will of God for my life and to exemplify Christ-like character, through my daily personal prayer life and study of the Word of God, and through faithful group worship on and off campus.

I will yield my personality to the healing and maturing power of the Holy Spirit and earnestly strive to manifest God's love toward my fellowman by following Christ's example to "do unto others as I would have them do unto me."

I will conform to and abide by the rules and regulations which I believe exist for the best interests of the students.

Please study the above statements carefully and prayerfully. Your signature is your acceptance of the entire Code of Honor and is a contract between you and Oral Roberts University. This pledge will become a part of your permanent file.

Signature: _____[237]

The honor code has remained essentially unchanged through the years. The 1981–83 university catalog opened with a two-sentence statement: "When a student enrolls at ORU, he voluntarily accepts a unique way of life that seeks to provide development of his spirit and body on the same high level as that of his intellect. He is expected to maintain the highest standards of behavior and performance while attending ORU, both on and off the campus."[238]

As the university matured and grew, the honor code and its defense sometimes became a near-obsession to Oral. The code, he told a group of students in 1971, was designed to "help save your life and save your soul."[239] He bristled when he heard faculty murmuring about the rigidity of the code. In a banquet speech in 1972, Oral put the matter squarely in perspective: "Now the honor code is a matter of life and death. It is a matter of this school being opened or closed. The honor code is not debatable. You buy it or you don't buy it. And if you don't buy it, you don't live here. Nobody has to keep it but if he lives here he has to keep it. He has to go somewhere else if he doesn't."[240]

While not conceived of as a legal system, the Oral Roberts University lifestyle was most visibly expressed in a code of personal conduct. To outsiders that code often seemed archaic and its enforcement brutal, but to its architects it was fair, wholesome, and a legitimate test of one's commitment to the goals of the university. If one was to be a soldier in the army, he would have to pass muster.

The rules spelled out in the early student handbooks were sweeping and clear. "Although the inappropriateness of the following activities should be taken for granted," read the 1967–68 *Handbook,* "it is stated for the record that they are *not* permitted at Oral Roberts University: (a) profanity, (b) smoking, (c) gambling, (d) cheating, (e) drinking alcoholic beverages of any kind, and (f) immorality." Students were also instructed to "avoid excessive public displays of affection which to onlookers often appear cheap and unbecoming." In addition to these moral restraints, each student was to "make every effort to be *where* he is expected to be *when* he is expected, and to respect established boundaries," a general rule which meant students were required to attend all classes, chapel meetings, and Sunday morning worship at some church.[241]

The most controversial of the lifestyle regulations were probably the student dress codes. In the first *Students Handbook,* the rules were announced:

Basic Christian standards imply that everything you wear will be in harmony with the spiritual atmosphere at ORU. Women may wear blouses, skirts and sweaters or simple dresses for classroom and casual wear. Dressy clothes for church and social events. Semi-formals for Friday night dinners and special events. Slacks, pedal pushers or bermudas for sports wear. (No short shorts, please.) Men will wear ties and coats, or sweaters when in the classrooms, cafeteria and chapel.[242]

Through the years, the dress code has undergone slight modifications; the requirement of coats for men was relaxed after one year, and there was a gradual acceptance of casual wear during weekends and in the evenings. But, basically, the original concept has simply been refined; the university has issued endless clarifications and definitions in an effort to retain the code's integrity. By 1967, the women's dress code specifically banned "midriff outfits, muu-muu's, pin curls, rollers, boudoir bonnets and *mini skirts more than two (2) inches above the top of the knee* . . . in the lounges or outside the private living areas of the residence hall."[243] Later directives raised the hemline to three inches above the knee, but added bans on such variants as "culottes, gauchos, sundresses with spaghetti straps, halter or backless sundresses, low necklines or plunging lace-up tops, midriff outfits, short pant dresses . . . and tube tops." Men's regulations came to include detailed instructions about hair length, requiring that "half the ear be showing on the sides." Beards were not permitted, and moustaches, if worn, "should extend no lower than the mouth line and be kept neat and trimmed."[244]

Like all legal systems designed to protect grand concepts, the university's codes sometimes seemed trivial and legalistic. In the early years an "elaborate judicial system" enforced the regulations, but "it became a farce," admitted Dean Robert G. Voight—students proudly lined their walls with "citations" for PDAs (Public Displays of Affection).[245] Enforcement became more discriminating and flexible in later years—but there remained no room for flagrant dissent. "Nobody can come here to seek knowledge and disregard behavior and wisdom," warned Oral in 1970, "because I will separate you from this student body. I'll have you off this campus in less than 12 hours and I mean it."[246]

Oral repeatedly defended the university's honor code and lifestyle on two grounds. First, they were voluntary. No one had to attend Oral Roberts University. No one had to sign the honor code. He told a group of students in 1972: "If you can honestly say, this is not for me, I would never criticize you. I would expect you to be honest and not try by that attitude of not doing it to destroy what we are building up here."[247] He made the same appeal to the faculty:

This honor code, you should study it. If you have private reservations, come to me directly or to the deans directly. If they are not really serious, perhaps we can reconcile them. If they are deadly serious and you cannot buy it and you will not stand for it, please have the honesty to resign and don't take our money. . . . I'm not trying to blame anybody if he says, "I can't buy this, and this is serious with me." I'm going to say, "Fine, God may bless you somewhere else, but don't destroy what I'm trying to do unto God."[248]

Oral Roberts University was a city set on a hill broadcasting a message with no uncertain sound. No one had to enter the city, but if one did, he obeyed the laws.

In the second place, the university lifestyle was not repressive and punitive, its supporters insisted, it was liberating and protective. "Any student coming here with the right attitude," declared Evelyn in 1971, "really wanting to stand tall in the inner man," would find the honor code no "hardship."[249] The rules "won't affect you," Oral assured the student body in 1970, "if you really love Jesus." Law is onerous only to the rebellious.[250] In fact, discipline has never been a major problem at the university; to a remarkable degree, the faculty and student body extol the lifestyle.

Nonetheless, the sentiment has surfaced periodically through the years that the lifestyle was a remnant of older, outmoded pentecostal moral values. As both the faculty and student body became predominantly mainstream Protestant in the 1970s, the rules against smoking and drinking and the dress code seemed less clearly related to spirituality. A growing ambivalence was captured in a graffiti litany penned on a toilet wall at the university:

> We must go as a light to the nations!
> Help stamp out smoking!
> I'll drink to that!!!
> Smoking is not a sin but it is a *hindrance* in your walk with Jesus.
> Please explain.

Carl Hamilton insisted there were no "proof texts" in the honor code.[251] "These things can be changed and need to evolve and need to be relevant," he told a group of students in 1971, "but always in terms of what will contribute the most to the Christian witness of the university."[252]

The university's emphasis on physical education is best understood as a part of its lifestyle concerns. That emphasis, present from the beginning of the school, became more controversial in 1972, when Oral became a devotee of Kenneth Cooper's aerobics program. After Oral met Cooper, he was so excited that he dispatched Hamilton to Dallas immediately to discuss the physician's fitness program. Hamilton discovered that aerobics "provided an excellent methodology . . . into what was already a goal."[253] By 1975, when the university's modern aerobics center was completed, all students, faculty, and administrators had been placed on compulsory, computerized aerobics programs. Students judged to be physically unfit were placed on "physical probation"; the university provided "special foods to persons interested in losing weight." Failure to meet the physical requirements could lead to expulsion.[254]

Oral insisted that the lifestyle was reasonable and served a useful purpose. It was not a question of "whether it's wrong or it's right" to drink, smoke, and dance, he told a faculty gathering: "I am saying that God raised us up in a different way and for our witness, which is the only reason this campus came into existence, for our witness for Christ, that is not behavior."[255] However one felt about the Biblical basis of the rules, Oral believed they gave cohesion to the campus. He explained the significance of the dress code to the faculty at the beginning of the 1971 academic year:

A little thing like a tie or like hair being too long is nothing within itself. As far as I'm concerned he can wear it to his hips. . . . But in the context of our ministry in this nation, he's going to wear a tie, he's going to cut his hair, and I want you to stand up with me on it. . . . I've dealt with scores of kids last year on the hair question. I have yet to deal with one boy about his hair who didn't have other problems that were more serious and the hair was symbolic and in his heart he wanted to pull this thing down. . . . When we had finals and let the boys pull off their ties do you know the kids on this campus fell apart. Never again will that happen. There's behavior on this campus directly attributable to the little tie and the fact that they knew school was going to be out and they kept growing their hair down and it was symbolic of something else.[256]

The lifestyle was an outward declaration that the faculty and students shared the spiritual vision of Oral Roberts.

The second acid test of spirituality on campus, at least in Oral's mind, was chapel. Twice a week the entire university community assembled in an expression of spiritual unity. The services were directed by the university chaplain, first Tommy Tyson and later Robert J. Stamps, but Oral sometimes preached his old campaign sermons and ended the chapels with healing prayers.[257] Chapel attendance was an important symbol to Oral: "I'm not saying the chapel is the only thing that puts God first, I'm saying it's the symbol of putting God first." Chapel attendance was carefully monitored, and nothing was more likely to spring Oral's hair-triggered temper than a flagrant disregard for its importance. On his way to chapel one morning he noted the baseball team practicing for a one o'clock game. "It was like a knife in my heart because they had to play at 1:00," he told the assembled audience when he arrived: "Why don't they play at 2:00? What's wrong with coming to chapel? Maybe you wouldn't lose so many games. You think I'm not serious, brother, I'm serious. Maybe you'd get some spiritual fortification and athletics is not all physical."[258] Oral candidly lectured the faculty in 1971:

Chapel attendance is a very important matter on this campus, and some of you have been neglecting it. . . . You know in the final analysis this university will rise or fall on the chapel. . . . And I'll tell you this. When it comes to contract time, if I felt a faculty member has no interest in our chapels by his failure to attend, I don't want to renew the contract. And if it's tenure, then we are going to have trouble. I don't know the outcome, but I know one thing, I'll stand up for the commitment you made here and that chapel is important. . . . This campus will disappear without it because once you give up the chapel then you are going to give up something else.[259]

The Oral Roberts lifestyle did, indeed, contain a message, and it was one that many conservative Americans were thrilled to hear during the decade of campus discontent from 1965 to 1975. The clean, courteous, neatly dressed students became the best advertisement the university could muster. When Oral told the initial student body, "The world doesn't need more college students to wave flags, carry placards, halt traffic, and riot against law and order," he found his speech heading the editorial page of the *Tulsa Tribune*.[260] Senator Jennings Randolph of West Virginia visited the campus in 1969 to deliver the commencement address; he returned to Washington so impressed that he inserted a description of a campus prayer service into the *Congressional Record*.[261] In 1974, Oral related to his faculty a conversation he had just had with one of Tulsa's newspaper editors: "He thought ORU was in perfect time, that it was right where it should be, and that this was our moment more than it is the moment of any other school in America because we came along at the time when that ugly rebellious spirit was at its height and now it's beginning to taper off. And the rules and regulations we have here begin to make sense now because they give strength."[262] "It is too early to tell," Jenkin Lloyd Jones wrote in 1967, "whether the neatly-jacketed and primly-skirted, non-drinking, non-smoking students at Oral Roberts University represent a wave of the future that is still below the horizon. But Man has gone on binges of hedonism and license before and always he has awakened with a vomiting hangover."[263]

Lifestyle was not an advertising technique, however; it was the heartbeat of the university. "In the beginning God told Oral that he was going to raise up a university to carry on the ministry as he began it," Evelyn told a class in 1971, "and if these great concepts can get into the minds of our faculty members and our students, then it can be like little ministries going all over the world."[264] To Carl Hamilton, the university was "the logical outgrowth of God's call upon President Roberts' life to take the message of God's saving and healing power to his generation and to bring wholeness to the body of Christ."[265] To encourage religious work by students while they were on campus, the Christian Service Council was formed in October 1968.[266] The broader involvement of students in the evangelistic ministry was a goal constantly explored throughout the institution's history. It has been an elusive objective—but building spiritual leaders has remained the central aim of Oral Roberts University.[267]

UNDERSTANDING the university as an arm of Oral Roberts's ministry best explains the most successful and controversial of the university's programs—its nationally ranked basketball team. The school's first basketball coach was Bill White, hired from the Pentecostal Holiness church's Emmanuel College. In its early years, the school played other small colleges in the region, but in the 1970s the program mushroomed. In April 1969, Ken Trickey, a highly successful coach at Middle Tennessee State University, was hired to build a first-class team.[268] During the 1970–71 academic year, Trickey had an outstanding team, finishing with a record of 21–5, including a victory over Hofstra in Madison Square Garden. Trickey's team featured a future All-American in high-scoring guard Richard Fuqua.[269] In 1971–72, the school's first year as a member of the NCAA, the team finished with a fine 25–1 record and was rewarded with an invitation to the National Invitational Tournament in Madison Square Garden. Fuqua finished the season as the nation's second-leading scorer and was named to the United States Basketball Writers' Association All-American team.[270] The Titans capped another fine year in the spring of 1973 with a second appearance in the National Invitational Tournament, and the following year they reached the peak of their basketball success by advancing to the quarterfinal round of the NCAA basketball tournament.

The meteoric rise of the Oral Roberts University basketball program owed much to the brilliance of Trickey, but it was also the calculated result of Oral Roberts's recruiting efforts. Oral was an uninhibited fan. He related openly to newsmen his hopes to win a national championship by 1975: "We should be a national competitor and be consistently in the top ten and by 1975 possibly win a national championship."[271] He was intimately involved in the program. When the team played in Madison Square Garden in 1971, the evangelistic association mailed over 55,000 letters to partners in the New York City area urging them to attend and support the team.[272] When Mabee Center was dedicated the next year, Oral urged the workers at the evangelistic association to "get your families there Monday night."[273] In the heat of battle, Oral sometimes prayed for the healing of injured players: "When one of our boys was injured and carried off the court, God miraculously healed him after prayer. In two minutes he was back in the game, causing the coach of the other team to say, 'We can battle your basketball team, but a miracle we can't contend with.' "[274] And it was hard for him not to seek direct assistance. "I try not to pray for us to win," he told a group of Methodists in 1975, "but it's awful hard not to pray that way."[275]

But Oral was not merely a fan; he made more direct contributions to the success of the program. He used his influence to try to get major colleges to schedule the upstart Titans. While taping a television special in southern California in January 1972, he called Ken Trickey to join him "to meet with UCLA and USC and to see if they were any nearer considering our little country school on their schedule." When one of the coaches chided Oral for being in such a hurry to attain national eminence, Oral replied, "Well, I know what you mean, but we have a president that doesn't have a lot of time left. . . . We've got to do it now."[276]

Oral's most controversial relationship to the program had to do with recruiting. The university emphasized national recruiting from its inception, and, without a national alumni base to aid its efforts, Oral's name and personality were its strongest appeals.[277] Ken Trickey told the press that Oral "is the biggest plus we have in recruiting. People who don't even know we have a school know Oral Roberts. And he will help us recruit a player any time his busy schedule allows him to. Anytime we have boys for a visit, if the President is on campus, he wants to visit with them."[278] In 1972, *Sports Illustrated* reported that ORU won a recruiting battle for seven-foot David Vaughn of Memphis because Oral preached in his father's church. The affair riled Memphis State coach Gene Bartow, who had earlier gotten a commitment from Vaughn, but Oral was jubilant: "Now, it wasn't wrong for me to go over there and preach for David's dad, was it? And take up a nice offering for his church? Nothing in the rules against that, is there?"[279]

Oral's recruiting zeal inevitably led to tensions within and without the university. In his faculty orientation speech in August 1971, he apprised the faculty of the significance of the athletic program, making suggestions which surely ruffled feathers:

> We've got a tool here. We've got an instrument that God can use. . . . You can talk about losing all you want to, but I'm not for it. And you've got to have

the horses. . . . You should understand unless you think athletics is an adjunct here and it's like other schools. It's not like other schools. It's part of the calling. It's part of how we are going to help reach this nation. . . . Now, here's this boy who can barely read and write, being practical about it, I mean. His comprehension ability has not been developed because nobody in his family has ever wanted this boy to go to school. . . . Because for hundreds of years our black people have gone to inferior schools. . . . But this boy is here so you are going to flunk him out, but he's made more progress than that boy has. . . . I am concerned about the minority people in this country. . . . Some way you've got to find a way to judge the boy on where he came from, or shut your doors and say we will admit no more. . . . Ah, you want me to cheat, you want me to give him a D or a C when he deserves an F. Who is the judge? Well, you are the judge. I understand that. But let's talk about the calling of the university. . . . I hope you don't misunderstand me, but if you say I'm trying to get you to cheat then I'm going to ask you who has been cheating these people. . . . Because we will never be able to graduate over one out of ten of them if we don't help them. . . . I know that higher education from which you sprang is against everything I'm saying, and [if] you are not careful you will be a product of it and you will ignore that this boy has ability in other areas. How would you like to give your final examination before 3,000 people? Everytime this year we'll be playing a basketball game we will probably be packed out. . . . I don't want you to cheat. If that boy refused to come to class and refused to work, you have got to give him an F. . . . But if he will try and will come to class, . . . you've got him now at a point where it can go either way, a D or an F, a C or a D, which way are you going? Academia will say, "Give him the lowest grade." I'll tell you it's not God. . . . You've got to help him. And then if we have to flunk him out in the second year, he takes something home with him.[280]

Oral appealed to the faculty to "grade them spiritually."[281] According to Wayne Robinson, the confrontation between Oral and his faculty became so heated in 1971 that Carl Hamilton asked Robinson to "help him find a job." Hamilton "suffered severe consequences" because of his opposition to some of the recruiting tactics, losing a good deal of his administrative power.[282]

The most embarrassing incident in the school's recruiting history came in 1974 as a result of a visit Oral made to the home of Moses Malone in Petersburg, Virginia. *Sports Illustrated* published an article about the legendary recruiting war waged to lure Malone which included the paragraph: "Perhaps the strangest of these episodes occurred when Oral Roberts showed up at Malone's home in Petersburg, Va. and offered to cure his mother of her bleeding ulcers. Roberts left the Malones in no doubt that his university would be a fine place for Moses to play basketball. What kind of stuff is that?"[283] The article apparently was distorted. Oral had visited the Malone home for about fifteen minutes and had led a prayer before leaving, but he and Mrs. Malone denied both the specifics and the implications in the article. Mrs. Malone considered meeting Roberts "the most exciting thing that ever happened to me" and was distressed by the tone of the story. Actually, by the time the Malone story surfaced, Oral's activities in recruiting had slackened; he insisted that "I don't believe in personally doing much recruiting."[284] And Oral became increasingly disenchanted with the pampering that seemed essential for a successful athletic program. When he announced the decision to build an athletic dormitory in 1974, he told the faculty:

> We feel it must be done since I have to have athletics. I have to have it because God told me to, and I cannot be in disobedience to God. And it is the toughest assignment that I've ever undertaken because these students . . . for the most part do not choose ORU. We recruit them. The other students choose us. They're much easier dealt with. But when you recruit someone . . . that a hundred other schools want, then you have a boy that can be spoiled rotten before he gets here.[285]

The motive behind the frantic and divisive emphasis on basketball in the first decade of Oral Roberts University was clearly evangelical. Although he obviously enjoyed the sport, Oral repeatedly denied that his interest in the program was personal. "I saw athletics as an instrumentality," he told the faculty in 1971, "and I had to select the one thing we could live with."[286] If the school could become a "national power" in basketball, it would offer a "positive Christian witness" and call attention to the entire ministry.[287] "The basketball team," he told association workers in 1972, "has done more to change the feeling of the entire nation and the media toward us" than anything he had ever done.[288] His judgment was probably correct. The basketball team probably got more newspaper copy than all of the other facets of the ministry combined in the 1970s. Frequently stories about the university's "high scorers for the Gospel" turned into full-scale reports on the activities and aspirations of Oral Roberts. "Roberts and the team mix sports appeal and spiritual message much as corporations blend sports and hard sell," wrote an impressed Los Angeles reporter in 1972.[289] Though it was not always clear in the early 1970s whether Oral had become the servant of his basketball team or the team a part of Oral's ministry, in hindsight it appears that the latter was the case.

Oral Roberts University's basketball program peaked in 1974 with the appearance of the team in the NCAA tournament. Before the tournament, Ken Trickey resigned, though he was reinstated until the end of the season. The immediate cause of the resignation was Trickey's citation on charges of driving while intoxicated. But the parting reflected deeper tensions, which had been aggravated by the intensity of the building program. Trickey and Oral had become close, almost inseparable, personal friends, and the pressure of representing the ministry had weighed heavily on the coach. "Say I want to go have a beer," he told a reporter shortly after announcing his decision to leave. "Well, I have to look over my shoulder, to be sure who's watching me. The old man has got people everywhere who write to him." And there was the intense pressure of working as if it were for God; there was no room for failure and little credit for victory. "Yeah," volunteered assistant coach Dwayne Roe, "the Lord has won 117 games—and we've lost 22."[290]

Trickey's leaving was nonetheless "very friendly."[291] He was replaced by young, clean-cut Jerry Hale, who once again led the Titans to the National

Invitational Tournament in 1975. But the heyday had passed. There was no national championship, though many felt that save for the unfortunate and disruptive lapse by Coach Trickey there might have been. It had been a brave effort.

THE SPIRITUAL mission of Oral Roberts University, made binding by the school's legal relationship with the evangelistic association, was the source of countless practical problems. Some of the skirmishes were trivial in the long run, but others implicated the university's survival. Solving these problems occupied much of the time and energy of Oral Roberts in the years from 1960 to 1975.

Both the university and the Roberts family lived under increasing security protection in the 1970s, a security that sometimes seemed arbitrary to outsiders and embarrassing to insiders. But Oral's celebrity status made the university a target for cranks; the school sometimes received threats which extended to "our student body and various buildings." "We have the right to admit on this campus who we wish and we have the right to expel who we wish," Oral told a group of students, "and there's safety in that."[292] In 1974, a "former mental patient" was shot and wounded in the Prayer Tower after threatening to "blow up the Prayer Tower and Mabee Center."[293]

More important were the constant internal struggles which resurrected the academic-spiritual tensions inherent in the campus. Every brush fire was ignited by the same spark—whether the construction of the Prayer Tower, the retirement of John Messick, the removal of Raymond O. Corvin, the recruiting of a basketball team—every issue, at least in the mind of Oral Roberts, came back to understanding the mission of the university, that it was not an entity in its own right. There was a pervasive fear in the minds of the university's builders that "its philosophy is not clearly understood by all who fill responsible positions of leadership."[294]

In the early 1970s, Oral seemed constantly to be sparring with the faculty. He fretted because many seemed unconcerned about speaking in tongues: "The Spirit keeps reminding me, 'I didn't call you to raise up this school to not emphasize the Holy Spirit.' We have men and women on this campus who don't speak in tongues that are dependable but they are missing something. . . . The basis of fellowship is not tongues, but belief in Jesus Christ. But saying that does not cancel out the ability to edify oneself by praying in the Spirit."[295] In the spring of 1972, Oral's concern boiled over in a faculty meeting. He challenged those faculty members who had declared themselves "open to the Holy Spirit" but had not exercised the gift of tongues: "He told me to build it on the Holy Spirit. . . . Well, do you think we can do it if people say they're open to it and the openness means nothing? It scares me. . . . I'm going to start teaching on this in the Chapels and I'm asking you to pray for me that I will not sound coercive because I realize how devastating coerciveness can be."[296]

Oral took to heart Billy Graham's charge that ORU not follow the long list of other religious schools which had left their founding principles. He was constantly reminded that "the people uptown" believed that "within ten to twenty years Oral Roberts University will become like any other university that was founded by a religious leader."[297] The only way to stop such drifting, Oral believed, was through "spiritual growth in the Holy Spirit." Faculty members had an "instinctive feeling to be academic," warned Oral, and there was little need to "prod" them toward academic excellence, but they neglected their spiritual growth.[298]

The specific issues which seemed to Oral most directly to threaten the delicate spiritual equilibrium of the university were freedom of speech and academic tenure. There has always been an undercurrent of student discontent on the campus—occasionally it has erupted into public criticism. A student editorial in 1968 stretched the limits of free expression far beyond acceptable bounds:

> For more than three years a prevailing attitude has built among the majority of the student body that the administration of this university is not ready to listen to—and discuss—pertinent complaints and honest questions. I suggest we make another try at the question and answer sessions at the all-school assemblies on Thursday. This time, though, when we have an open discussion let's really make it open. If someone is brave enough to ask about fraternities, dancing, censorship, the security force, or smoking . . . he should be able to expect an answer in public, immediately from an authoritative source.[299]

Such public criticism was rare; it simply was not allowed. When a student in 1983 complained that the campus newspaper had censored negative contributions, Carl Hamilton called attention to the paper's statement of aims: "The *Oracle* shall strive to maintain objectivity, clarity, precision, and truthfulness in a constructive effort toward building harmony, rapport and understanding among students and faculty, and between students and administrators. The *Oracle* shall strive for fairness, objectivity and contain no material whch significantly interferes with school integrity and which might disregard the aims of the university."[300]

Academic freedom at Oral Roberts University existed only in the context of the ministry. "There is no limitation on freedom of teaching," stated a report the university submitted to the North Central Association in 1967, "so long as it is compatible with the philosophy of the university. Doctrines which are contrary to the accepted way of life in American society would not be tolerated, nor would doctrines opposing principles which are considered fundamental and Biblical theism be permitted."[301] Fifteen years later Vice-Provost for Academic Affairs Robert G. Voight expressed the same view: "There is no place in the world you have the academic freedom you have here. . . . We present all sides of the issue and then show how Christianity, Jesus Christ, makes a difference."[302]

Academic tenure posed an even more serious potential threat to the spiritual focus of the school. From the very beginning, Oral recognized that tenure raised peculiar problems for a religious institution. Speaking to the President's Advisory Cabinet in 1965, he said:

> On tenure, great care must be exercised. On those rare occasions when a faculty member on tenure is not meeting the standards of the institution, I must

bear the ultimate burden of decision. . . . Once a professor has been here a specified number of years and has been accepted as a person who fits into the program, he is given what is called in academic circles, tenure. That is he can only be released for cause. And the cause, is very clearly, quite clearly defined so that if that were breached, one could lose accreditation of the university. So, we expect to give our men tenure at the proper time. And therefore we say that care must be exercised that we may know we have God's man and God's woman. We're in a very delicate area here.[303]

But as time went on, Oral chafed under the restraints of tenure. He was frustrated by what seemed to him an unethical undermining of the school's philosophy by faculty members who refused to honor his invitation to leave. In April 1972, he belligerently confronted the faculty over what he perceived as a disregard for chapel attendance:

If you faculty people don't think this chapel is worth your attendance, I'm going to suspend you two weeks. I'll take your pay away from you and if you keep on, I'll try to break your contract, even if you are on tenure, because you are breaking the philosophy of this institution, and I had a deal with the accrediting people that if you break the philosophies of this institution I can go to the mat with you. The Holy Spirit has talked to me and says "Oral Roberts, you close this hole up and you close it up today." . . . I'll shut this thing down. I shut a seminary down on this campus. . . . Ten years from now or a little later they might run it without me, but they can't run it without me now because they can't get the money. Now that's telling it straight and like it is.[304]

Speaking to a faculty meeting a few days later, Oral was slightly less belligerent but just as emphatic:

If you honestly don't think that this is right, . . . I frankly don't want you here. . . . I know there are legal problems in what I am saying. Higher education is so organized against God and against the Bible, . . . rules and regulations, some of what I'm saying may come to a legal thing. Somebody here may challenge me on it. But I promise you I'll go to the mat with you. You may win it, but I'll fight until the last breath in my body.[305]

Carl Hamilton, in a genuinely brilliant maneuver in the spring of 1972 (a move which other top advisors believed replaced him in Roberts's favor), guided through the faculty a policy change which essentially abolished tenure at Oral Roberts University.[306] The new policy, "devised by the faculty," retained the standard provision for the granting of tenure no later than the seventh year of a professor's employment, but it also made possible "dismissal of a teacher whose incompetence is judged serious but not critical enough to justify firing under the standard tenure policy." The policy provided that all tenured faculty would be signed to three-year contracts each year, protecting them against sudden termination, but allowing dismissal of tenured faculty "for causes detrimental to the spiritual, academic or physical goals of the university." Grounds for dismissal, explained Hamilton, included "academic incompetence, moral turpitude or willful opposition to the ministry and lifestyle of ORU."[307] The change was "a Herculean task in an academic setting," commented Ron Smith, and Hamilton won Oral's gratitude and respect for managing the compromise.[308]

Nothing stirred Oral's wrath more quickly than a display of flagrant ingratitude on the part of students or faculty. He berated students who complained about the quality of the meals they were served, even though "I have to raise nearly $3,000 for every student who enrolls here above what he pays."[309] Oral became incensed when students arrived late for chapel—or slept or studied during the service. He once estimated that only "about 8% of the students on this campus are completely tuning out," but he over and over reiterated his willingness to take the consequences of enforcing the honor code.[310] If enforcement means that "the enrollment next fall is one half what it is now," he would do it; if it meant the school would be denied accreditation, the university would stand for "an eternal principle."[311]

The point, which Oral never dodged, was that Oral Roberts University was a "semitheocracy." In 1963, Oral assured his supporters that "my spirit will be strong in the institution and the concept of this ministry will be the concept of the university."[312] The final authority on the campus was Oral Roberts. "I want to state right here," he told a chapel assembly in 1970, "that I set the policy for the campus. . . . You are looking at the man. I set it. . . . Nobody on earth that will come here will be able to change this campus. Whether you like it or dislike it we are going to try to run it like God put it in our heart."[313] There was a righteous possessiveness in Oral which could explode at any moment. In 1980, he told a chapel assembly that had offended him: "You're on my property under God, you're my students. God told me to raise you up. You belong to me as long as you're here and if you don't like belonging to me under God, get up and leave. You're going to be mine while you're here. And so will you faculty. So will you staff. If I have to stand here by myself for awhile God'll send me somebody else."[314]

Democracy was wonderful in the nation, Oral told his faculty in 1974; indeed, it was American democracy which allowed institutions such as Oral Roberts University to exist. But the school was not a democracy. The university was his responsibility before God:

> I see God as the head of the school. I see myself as . . . the appointed head by God . . . and then continuously elected . . . by the Board of Regents. . . . In my heart I attribute to Him the full ownership of the university. In my heart I try to do precisely as I think He wants me to do. I may make mistakes on a day to day level on that, but I have the confidence in the long term that I don't make any mistakes on that. So from that standpoint we are a semi-theocracy in which God is the absolute ruler of this university.[315]

It sounded authoritarian, but to Oral it seemed neither egomaniacal nor repressive. No one on the campus in 1975 would openly challenge his theocratic understanding.

Though Oral's relationship with his faculty and students sometimes turned angry and threatening, and though he did establish and assert his authority with vigor, he was not a tyrant. He conceived of himself as a father figure, and family imagery was frequently evoked by the students and by Oral and Evelyn.[316] When charismatic leader Dennis Bennett visited the campus in 1975, he lectured the students: "I want to tell you that ORU is different. . . . It has something to do with Evelyn and Oral, I think. . . . What I admire about the Robertses . . . is their contact with you. You know it's so obvious that he is Papa around here. . . . I can see that, it's so evident that these two dear people really love you and you love them."[317] In the early years of the university, Oral and Evelyn knew the students by name and frequently visited with them. Even though he no longer knew every student by the mid-1970s, Oral insisted that he did not "feel any less close." "I feel as if I'm very close to the students," he told an *Oracle* reporter, "I think about them day and night. . . . They're my life. They're the only hope I have of multiplying what God's called me to do."[318] Through the years, Oral and Evelyn shared countless hours in public and private with the students—telling them and showing them the blessings of old-fashioned values. Their relationship with the students was not far from that they had with their own children. Even when he turned gruff and authoritarian, Oral genuinely believed he had the student's good at heart: "I'm running around trying to shake your hand and smile and know you better and be part of your life. Do you really believe that? It's the truth if I ever told it. I am concerned about you and I do fight for you and I will fight for you. I'm fighting for you now. I'm trying to keep some of you out of hell."[319] The university was too dear to let it drift. By 1971, Oral could say without equivocation, "The central thing of this ministry is this university."[320]

Oral Roberts University's first decade was another incredible Roberts success story. In the summer of 1975, Oral assured Bob Foresman and Jenkin Lloyd Jones, Jr. that "the school will not fold from a financial or other point of view"—the student body had reached 2,700 and was growing, and they were in "top financial condition."[321] In 1962, as the venture was beginning, Oral had written: "God showed me this several years ago, and He has told me that now is the time. We all know that God has a *time* for everything. I feel I am moving according to God's timetable."[322] It is clear that the timetable was uncannily correct. "Timing has always been one of Oral's strongest points," mused Carl Hamilton in 1983; the university "could not have been started earlier because the partner base wasn't there. . . . Had we waited even two years later, . . . it could not have been started. I'm convinced that the timing was sovereign."[323]

CHAPTER

X

Beyond the Tent

THE CAMPAIGN SEASON began in January 1960 with the same apparent vigor that it had in years past—six days each in Saint Joseph, Missouri and Richmond, Virginia in January and then on to Orlando for a ten-day crusade in February. There were changes—more of the crusades lasted for six days instead of ten, and more were held in rented auditoriums rather than in the tent. Oral conducted eight ten-day campaigns in 1960, along with ten shorter ones; but in 1961, the number of ten-day crusades fell to four, and the last such campaign was held in Yakima, Washington, from September 1-10. No one could have known for sure at the time, but things were winding down.

The fact that the crusades were drawing to an end was not easy to accept; Oral continued to speak bravely about the future. At the end of 1961 he wrote: "Greater things are happening in our crusades. Greater miracles. Larger crowds. More souls saved. Many more healed."[1] Two years later he informed the readers of *Abundant Life* that the crusades would remain the "heartbeat of the ministry"; he planned "to increase the number of crusades both in America and overseas this year so that we can reach more people with God's healing and saving power."[2] Nor was such talk simply fund-raising bravado; there were times when such optimism seemed justified. Questioned about his future plans in November 1962 by the founding regents of the university, Oral replied: "My crusades will go on as long as I have the force."[3] As late as November 1966, he spoke enthusiastically to his staff about his meetings: "This year the crusades have had what I call a new stir in me. . . . I say that the whole team seems to have become more inspired, more aroused. At the same time we notice a quickening among the people. . . . And the crowds have been exceptionally good this year."[4]

In many ways nothing had changed. In 1967, Bob DeWeese told the *Tulsa Tribune* that invitations still came in "every day" and that the meetings were scheduled and planned about a year in advance. The big tent, which still seated 10,000 people, was hauled to five different sites that year by seven trailer trucks. "It's really a lot of hard work and planning," explained DeWeese to newsmen, but he and Collins Steele had honed the procedure to a fine art.[5] At the end of twenty years of crusading, the mishaps had been few—only "two or three meetings" had been canceled because of the weather (including the Amarillo storm), and difficulties in obtaining permits had caused a few last-minute switches.[6]

The crusades of the early 1960s were still sponsored by groups of pentecostal churches, a testimony to Oral's continued personal prestige. The sponsoring pastors of a 1963 Roberts campaign in Miami told a reporter that Oral "probably is the only Pentecostal evangelist that they all would support unreservedly." They listed their reasons: he held crusades only with broad support from "local pastors"; he emphasized soul saving above "other facets stressed in the Pentecostal movement"; he was "denominationally-connected"; he was "on a straight salary from a non-profit organization whose books are publicly audited and local men handle the financial accounts for a local crusade"; "Roberts' advertisements on healing are sedate"; and "the people who make decisions in the crusade would be channeled into their churches in the following weeks."[7]

The crusades became more efficient in the 1960s. Hart Armstrong and Bob DeWeese conducted precrusade training sessions for workers, and the organization produced an instruction manual entitled "Doing the Job Well."[8] Probably most improved were the efforts to follow up on conversions. Oral continued to "highly recommend" that the new converts attend "one of our fine sponsoring churches," because "every born-again Christian should receive the Pentecostal baptism."[9] In Roberts's last American crusade, in Detroit in December 1968, after he had become a Methodist and lost his pentecostal sponsors, Oral still advised his converts to find a local church to attend: "You may be a member of a church. If so, go back and tell your pastor that you've given your life to God and you want to be a real blessing to the church. If you are not a member of a church, join a church and go to the pastor and talk to him and tell him that you are there now as a witness of the Lord."[10] By the 1960s, follow-up techniques included improved methods for supplying sponsoring churches with the names of those answering the altar call. The more aggressive churches developed "intensified follow-up" programs to "give any spiritual guidance necessary" to the converts.[11]

There were few changes in the crusade format. DeWeese still conducted the afternoon service to build faith before the well-rehearsed sequence began at 7:30 in the evening. Everything went like clockwork—selling the books, the singing, Oral's sermon, the altar call, the visit to the invalid tent, and then Oral's return to the healing line. In the area beneath the tent platform, Roberts's aides kept a "supply of chocolate milk and clean white shirts . . . to refresh him during breaks in the service."[12] Novice reporters still wrote wide-eyed accounts of Oral's prayers, "Hee-ul, hee-ul, Lord," and of the occasional eruption of an "unknown tongue."[13] "The service format is thoroughly Pentecostal," wrote a Houston reporter in 1962, "with emphasis on speaking in tongues, 'going on to sanctification,' baptism of the Holy Ghost, personal righteousness and purity, withdrawal from the world and avoidance of alcohol, tobacco and cosmetics."[14] In December 1966, a New York City reporter marveled that with all the "modernization of religion" in America, Oral's crusade remained primitive: "At an Oral Roberts Crusade it's as though none of this had transpired. It's the same presentation that Oral Roberts first saw when he tagged along with his parents, Ellis and Claudius Roberts."[15]

Such assessments were amateurish, of course, but it was true that the campaign services sometimes erupted with the exuberance of the 1950s. Oral's sermons could still stir the faithful to raise their hands amidst "applause and outcries."[16] "I believe in the noisy kind of religion," he told a Minnesota audience in 1960, "it gets annoying sometimes, but I prefer it to the funeral kind."[17] Actually, Oral continued to strive for that delicate balance which allowed controlled enthusiasm. "Oddballs and screwballs" were unceremoniously escorted from the tent, along with saints who became overly expressive. A forty-two-year-old woman who followed Oral's crusades "seeking a double portion of God's spirit" ended up locked in jail after interrupting a service in Dayton, Ohio. She refused to blame Oral, believing rather that his aides "probably don't like me because I smoke."[18] After calling down a spiritual demonstrator in Chattanooga, Oral explained to nonpentecostals in the audience: "I hope people will understand that ours cannot be the usual church service, such as those held in beautiful churches. Some who come to our services don't attend any church and some holler out occasionally. We do our best to keep it under control."[19]

It was the healing line that most resisted change as the crusades ground to an end. The lines became somewhat shorter, but not markedly so, and each evening Oral shed his coat, rolled up his sleeves, and resumed his well-established ritual of chatting with the seekers, laying his right hand on their foreheads, and praying. In 1962, he told a Houston reporter that he still had "an in irresistible urge to touch the sick."[20] In December 1968, Oral spoke introspectively to one of his last crusade audiences about the healing line:

> Once again we start laying our hands on the people that we've done for twenty-one and a half years. And it's, I just have to confess to you, it's as thrilling to me tonight as it was the first night I started. It's thrilling to touch people and to know that something could happen to them. Praise God. It's thrilling, particularly when people will respond and let their faith out. . . . And as we touch you it's a point of contact . . . and when we do it we release our faith and you are expected to release your faith and it's Christ who is the healer. . . . Let's all stretch our hands out and pray together. Dear Father, we thank you tonight for the Holy Spirit and for Jesus, for what He is to us. Oh glory to God. Let your miracles happen tonight to the people, one after another let the deliverances occur. Blessed Lamb of God, heal and deliver. We pray and we believe. And everybody said Amen.[21]

Across the platform they paraded—with "ulcers and hiccups," "broken heart and depression," "demon possession and diabetes," "tumor and goiter."[22]

Oral and his team felt that his healing touch was still powerful in the 1960s, and the ministry published an unending stream of testimonials from those claiming miracles. Perhaps most publicized was the case of Pat Wiggins, a young man who allegedly had been hospitalized for eight years, nine months, and twenty-seven days from a variety of illnesses, including multiple sclerosis, meningitis, and polycythemia vera, before attending Oral's Orlando crusade in 1960. After prayer, Wiggins rose and walked, "with great effort at first"; within a year he had begun a revival ministry of his own.[23] Reporters continued to view the healing line disparately. Some left the meetings feeling that "there was no apparent evidence that anyone was healed," but others reported that "even skeptics admit that seemingly miraculous things happen in the prayer line."[24] The scenes and reactions had the sound of echoes from a decade earlier.

But in the 1960s the crusades did change, in subtle and portentous ways. Already in the late 1950s, the crusades had shortened, and soul saving had replaced healing as the headline in Roberts's promotional material; in the 1960s both trends continued.[25] And there were other symptoms of the revival's flagging energy. Oral's sermons shortened to about thirty minutes, and he preached with noticeably more restraint. Veteran reporters who covered repeat performances in the 1960s noted that Oral was "older this time, and quieter."[26] In March 1959, Bob Daniels joined the team as the "crusade soloist" and song director, the first time Oral had added an entertainment segment in his meetings.[27] In the early 1960s, Daniels was replaced by Vep Ellis, a widely known songwriter, who supervised the "warm-up musical session."[28]

To some extent the content of Oral's sermons changed as well. He sometimes still preached his old crusade sermons, particularly when his audience was predominantly pentecostal, but reporters noted that Oral's sermons "ranged over a variety of topics, stressing the need for faith and repentance," and less time was devoted to healing.[29] Perhaps more important was Oral's decision during a meeting in Dayton in 1961 to preach his first crusade sermon on the "Baptism of the Holy Spirit," a topic which was beginning to catch fire among mainstream Christians. The Holy Spirit and "speaking in tongues" became almost as central to the meetings of the 1960s as healing had been in the 1950s.[30]

Roberts's audiences also changed during the 1960s. The percentage of non-pentecostal people increased markedly; Oral, noted one reporter, made "a special point of emphasizing the religious affiliation of non-Pentecostals who come seeking healing."[31] Although the crusades had been integrated for many years, reporters in the South remarked more frequently on the number of "black faces" in the crowds.[32] But in spite of these changes, the tent still attracted a homogeneous social class; in Oral's words, "the simple, uneducated, uninhibited, with few sidelines, to whom God means all, and who worship with their hands, feet and voices."[33] "We reached a certain plateau," said Lee Braxton years later, "and we saw that we had reached our limit."[34] If Oral's message was ever to reach middle-class America, he would have to meet them outside the tent.

Most ominous was the slow shrinking of the crowds. Some crusades were still large in the 1960s; there were times when the big 10,000-seat tent overflowed and special police were required to handle the traffic.[35] But generally the crowds were smaller; when crusades opened with empty seats, the team

repeatedly and self-consciously told newsmen that they expected a "compara-
tively slow start."[36] The 1967 *Detroit News* headline "Oral Roberts' Crowds
Shrink" told an embarrassing story; Oral's crusade had opened with fewer than
4,000 people, whereas in 1959, "competing with a fireworks display and a visit
by British royalty," he had drawn 10,000 to his opening service.[37]

Oral was never given much to gimmicks to try to bolster his crusade ministry, but he did pay lip service to some of the more powerful fads of the 1960s.
During the surge of Christian anticommunism that brought quick fame to his
fellow Tulsan Billy James Hargis, Roberts flirted with conservative, nationalistic
themes in this meetings.[38] Through 1960 and 1961, he spoke frequently about
the "communist threat," though his message remained a spiritual one: "I believe
personally that the only deterrent to communism is for the American people to
practice their religion, to be active in the faith."[39] "Our battle with Russia is a
spiritual struggle," he told a reporter in Columbia, South Carolina, "it's a struggle that will be decided on a spiritual plane."[40] It would have been unthinkable
for a conservative religious leader to say nothing about the lurking menace of
Communism in the 1960s; Oral made his views clear, but fighting geopolitical
struggles was not his calling. He was soon back about the business of bringing
healing to his generation.

In the late 1960s, in another obvious acknowledgment of current public
interest, Oral spoke frequently about internal American dissent, particularly
about the unrest in black ghettoes. His interest in blacks was unfeigned, but, at
the same time, like most conservative Americans, he believed that the whole
fabric of the nation and "Christianity" was threatened by the urban riots.[41] In
1968, he announced that he would emphasize "ghetto evangelism," because he
had had a "rapport with the black man all through the years."[42] But by the time
he began toying with the idea of bringing healing to urban ghettoes, his crusade
ministry was within months of ending. However sincere his concern for blacks,
such a narrowing of the Roberts ministry would have violated the general pattern of seeking ever-wider audiences. Within months, Oral would find in television a tool which would reach into the ghetto but also into other locales where
the tent had never gone.

One avenue remained to be thoroughly explored before the tent was permanently retired and placed in storage. Oral had still not thoroughly tested the potential of his ministry for foreign evangelism. In 1960 he announced to his partners
that God had once again, for the tenth time, audibly spoken to him, telling him that
he was entering a "new era of my ministry." Among other things, the voice directed
him to "increase my overseas ministry."[43] At least once each year in the 1960s, the
team conducted a campaign outside the country.

Oral's invitations to hold overseas campaigns increased sharply after the
international ministers' seminar which his ministry sponsored shortly after the
opening of the School of Evangelism. He reported that many of the delegates
begged him to conduct crusades in their native lands.[44] In addition, the Berlin
congress "opened many doors."[45] Oral told his staff at the end of 1966 that he
intended to "double or even triple the time we will spend outside this country
in the future."[46]

As it became clearer and clearer that the American crusades were ending,

Roberts repeatedly tested foreign evangelism as a means of stirring his partners. In 1967, he told his partners that Jesus had spoken to him: "Millions are waiting for you. Go to them. Did not I give you your name and your initials to spell GO (Granville Oral)?"[47] The next year, he informed them that May 8, 1968 was "a memorable day," because Jesus had appeared to him again, taking "my hands in His and carrying me across a river deep and wide." Jesus came to show him "the whole human race lost and undone and at the end of its own futile ways." "I knew for certain," Oral reported, "that the call I had received in 1947 to take His healing power to my GENERATION would never be fulfilled unless I spent more time in the far countries of the earth."[48] His staff did a quick check and discovered that there were 146 nations in the world, leaving 94 that Oral had never visited. Whatever happened to the crusades in America, the partners were conditioned by 1968 to the idea that the ministry must continue overseas. The Roberts organization could have survived with that mission, but it would have been much smaller and less influential than other leadings would make it.

To some extent, the interest of American revivalists in world evangelism was a ploy to save their decaying organizations. Overseas campaigns were often little more than fund-raising promotions, with little, if any, evangelistic impact. Oral Roberts's first venture overseas in the 1960s looked much like just such a venture. Accompanied by Hart Armstrong and American businessman W. C. Jones, he spent several days in April 1960 visiting Warsaw and Moscow.[49] He reported to his partners that the "fateful trip" had moved him more deeply than anything since his first trip to Israel, but his activities were severely limited. He was invited to Poland by the United Evangelical Church in Warsaw, and, after assuring the minister of religious affairs that "there are no political overtones to my visit," he was permitted to preach at four services in the church.[50] In Russia, Roberts was even more severely restricted; he was allowed to attend an Easter service in Moscow's Baptist church and to meet with a small group of Protestant ministers, who questioned him closely about his belief in divine healing.[51]

Aside from providing sermon material and a conversation piece for his regular dialogues with reporters, it was difficult to view the trip as more than a fund-raising junket.[52] Ironically, an incident in the Soviet Union the following year seemed to argue the contrary. In May, *Pravda* announced that six Soviet citizens had been given prison sentences for "indulging in illegal gatherings at which 'savage customs' were practiced." Although the story gave no explanation, it indicated that the accused pentecostals had "received guidance from American evangelist Oral Roberts." Oral could only speculate about how his influence had spread in the Soviet Union. He had sponsored short-wave broadcasts reaching the nation for over two years beginning in 1957, but he had discontinued them because they were consistently jammed. Nonetheless, he received about two hundred letters annually from the Soviet Union asking for prayers and Bibles. In retrospect, Oral felt that his meetings with the Soviet ministers during his trip had had an enduring effect.[53]

Oral made several other trips in the 1960s which were exploratory and seemingly cosmetic. In October 1960 he visited Taiwan and Japan. He spoke several times in Taiwan, was impressed with the grave importance of Nationalist

China to the free world, and had a private audience with the Chiangs. Praying for the general, Oral asked that God "guide him to fulfill his destiny to lead his people to victory." He then prayed for the healing of Madame Chiang, who had been ill. Oral reported that his visit was "a great victory for the missionaries in the Orient."[54] He then made a short visit to Japan, where his television program had long been popular, and spoke in Tokyo to "one of the largest Christian audiences ever to assemble in Japan."[55]

In 1961, Roberts held his "first European Crusade." The pentecostal movement was strong in Europe, particularly in Scandinavia, and it had been the scene of some major campaigns by American healing evangelists during the 1950s. It was remarkable that Oral had not campaigned on the Continent until his visit to Helsinki in July 1961. He conducted two days of conferences with 900 pentecostal pastors and then held an eight-day crusade. In the course of the campaign, Oral estimated that he spoke to 50,000 people in the evening services. Never fond of preaching through interpreters, he came away from the Finnish meeting convinced that it was "one of the most effective of my overseas trips." "I hope to go overseas again in a few months," he told his partners, "I feel God has given me a special message and method to help the ministers overseas."[56]

The successful campaign in Finland sparked a series of crusades in Europe. In 1962, Oral and Bob DeWeese conducted seminars for ministers and preached in a brief crusade in Frankfurt, Germany. For the first time, Roberts explained to the Europeans the impact he hoped his new School of Evangelism would have abroad, and, though his crowds were much smaller than those in Finland a year earlier, he reported that the influence "of our German Crusade will be felt for years ahead."[57] In 1963, Oral conducted a three-day crusade in Newport, Wales. He opened his first service with the quip "It's so nice to be home again," paying tribute to his Roberts roots, and closed triumphantly before an audience of over 15,000, which overflowed the local athletic stadium.[58] In October 1964, Oral preached in the last of his European crusades, preaching in a three-day meeting among French Gypsies in Marseilles and then conducting ministers' seminars in Utrecht, Holland.[59]

In 1965, Oral made an extensive tour of Australia, New Zealand, and India. In both New Zealand and Australia, he met in seminars with groups of ministers, mostly explaining Oral Roberts University to his supporters in those countries. He was overwhelmed by the warmth of the New Zealand ministers and promised to "investigate the possibility" of establishing a branch of ORU in New Zealand. In the mid-1960s he was enamored with the idea of overseas branches: "I can see a string of such ORU branches throughout the earth, extending our teaching ministry to additional thousands for the kingdom of God." Oral's return to Australia was his first since his hasty departure nearly twenty years earlier. He was moved when he met several people who had been converted in his fateful campaigns in 1956 and reported that he had a small but "staunch" group of partners there. Several young Australian students expressed a desire to enroll in the inaugural class at the university in the fall.[60]

From Australia the team flew to Trivandrum, India, where Roberts conducted a seminar for about 1,000 Indian pastors before preaching to huge crowds in a local stadium. The three-day crusade climaxed in a dramatic healing service, with about 50,000 people in the audience. Returning to his hotel, Oral "met several prominent Indian families from Calcutta, doctors, planters, former members of Parliament, all thrilled with the service." While in India he also met the maharaja and maharani of Kerala State, having been called to pray for the healing of the maharani. It was one of those incongruous, chance encounters which cluttered Oral Roberts's life. The maharani was a gracious, "beautiful lady," a "high caste Hindu," but she believed in divine healing. Oral prayed for her, "calling upon the name of Jesus of Nazareth"; he reported that "the power of the Lord filled the room as much as I've ever known before." Before taking a friendly leave, Oral asked the maharaja if he had "met Christ," as he had asked the minister of religion in Warsaw and his Communist guide in Moscow; the prince replied politely that he was by birth and persuasion a Hindu.[61]

After 1965, Oral turned his attention wholly to the Third World, in what was to be a final spurt of overseas campaigning. In August 1966 he conducted an impressive five-night campaign in Rio de Janeiro, Brazil. The meetings drew large audiences and received front-page press coverage; Oral reported that "high government officials and prominent citizens" were in the audience each evening.[62] The Brazilian crusade was particularly significant, however, because for the first time the team included twelve students from Oral Roberts University, who sang during the services and "had their first experience with prayer for healing in a Roberts' service."[63] Among those pioneering students was a talented young singer, Patti Holcombe. Patti, later to become Richard Roberts's wife, was ecstatic upon her return: "I have been so stirred that I can never be satisfied until I have completed God's purpose for my life."[64]

In 1967, Oral took another student group to Indonesia and Chile. Enroute to Indonesia, he, Bob DeWeese, and Collins Steele spent a week in Vietnam. Oral spoke at several military installations and once again returned home primed to give newsmen his views on the current world crisis. In Indonesia, he and DeWeese were joined by Chaplain Tommy Tyson and twelve students; thousands flooded into the meetings and healing lines.[65] The Chilean crusade later in the year also attracted huge crowds, but it was marred by the misunderstanding over a Chilean university. Oral became ill with dysentery, and, encouraged by DeWeese and Evelyn to go home, for the first time he abandoned a crusade, and returned to the United States.[66]

Nonetheless, in 1968 Oral renewed his pledge to hold two overseas crusades during the year and began with a tour in June and July which took him to London, Israel, and Nairobi, Kenya. As a result of contacts he had made in Berlin, he was invited to conduct a "mission of renewal" in the historic Methodist Central Hall in Westminster, England. The meeting, sponsored partly by Lord Arthur Rank, was supported by British Methodists.[67] After London, Oral and his team visited Israel, where he again was granted an impromptu interview with Prime Minister Ben-Gurion. In both London and Israel, Oral was accompanied by a thirty-six-member student singing group, the Collegians. The chorus had been trained by "some Tulsa Jewish community members" to sing several songs in Hebrew, and in both countries, particularly in Israel, the youngsters' talent and wholesome appearance won friends. "By personal experience I knew the formidable difficulties of witnessing in Israel," Oral wrote upon his return, but the Collegians were universally welcomed with "good will."[68]

In the Kenya campaign, Oral was aided by another group of eighteen students, four of whom remained in Africa for a year after the campaign was over. He reported that the crusade was the largest in his twenty-one years of ministering; according to his estimates, he sometimes preached to audiences of over 100,000. He felt that the campaign in Africa had "put to a real test God's call to me to go to all nations"; he had once again faced persecution in a variety of forms. In addition to the usual attacks in the press, he was challenged to a "faith healing contest" by a Moslem chief and felt that he had been threatened by Mau Mau tribesmen.[69] But Oral was exhilarated by the Africans' faith in the miraculous; he believed that his healing ministry would explode among the disadvantaged people of the Third World. "Without healing in Africa you really don't reach many people," he told ORU students upon his return. "The black natives in Africa may not be educated, . . . but they have the most terrific discernment. They understand the spirit world and they know when they come up against a supernatural power."[70]

In 1968, Oral Roberts's crusade ministry closed with a whimper; the end, long approaching, became inevitable when Oral announced that he was leaving the Pentecostal Holiness church to become a member of the Methodist church.[71] The summer following his change, he conducted a diminishing number of crusades, for the first time without sponsors.[72]

During the closing months of the year, his crusades wallowed in limbo; he had alienated many of his pentecostal friends and was viewed with courteous curiosity by most Methodists. Speaking to a group of Methodist ministers before a crusade in Washington, D.C. in 1968, Oral confessed that "most Methodist clergy probably wouldn't feel comfortable at his crusades because of the noise": "I'll be myself. We're a lot more noisy than you are. I found this, that when I suppress the power of God and cut out the fanatics that I usually wind up getting things so dead that nobody gets saved. Nobody gets healed. So I just want to sort of let her rip."[73] The three-day campaigns continued through December, ending in Detroit. From December 30 to January 10, 1969, the team campaigned in Jamaica, Trinidad, and Haiti, accompanied by thirty-five students. There Oral met Haitian president Francois Duvalier, announced that he had received "a fresh contact with God" while preaching to large crowds, and then returned home.[74] It was over. For a few months in 1969, Roberts conducted "one day crusades with our partners"; the era of deliverance-tent revivalism had ended.[75]

It is difficult to say when Oral first knew that the crusades must stop. Publicly, he ballyhooed the crusade ministry to the bitter end—he could hardly have told his partners otherwise. And until 1968 he clearly held onto the possibility that foreign crusading would become the core of the ministry. On the other hand, Oral told Bob DeWeese in late 1962, in the midst of a golf match at Santa Anna Country Club: "Bob, the crusades are over. It's gonna be the university now." DeWeese was devastated; he became "so emotional that we had to give up the golf game."[76] In a rare public intimation of his thoughts, in January 1963 Oral told a Miami reporter that he "hoped to retire from the crusade-type ministry he has carried on for 15 years to devote his full time to the university."[77] DeWeese and other members of the team "fought for the crusades." Oral later told his associate evangelist and friend: "You're the only one that's ever changed me." He credited DeWeese with extending the life of the crusades by several years.[78] But the end was inevitable. The dwindling crowds and lagging enthusiasm crushed Oral's tender ego, and he fought depression.[79]

The year 1968 was a virtual midlife crisis for the entire Oral Roberts ministry—it was filled with momentous decisions. The startling series of changes began in 1967, when Oral ended his television series. In the spring of 1968, the university was completely restructured with the departures of Corvin and Messick, and Oral changed churches. It was fitting that he close the year by ending the crusade ministry. In accepting a set of new challenges, Roberts necessarily bade farewell to old friends and old methods.

The reasons for ending the crusade ministry were for the most part obvious. It simply no longer worked. "The country changed the last of the fifties and the beginning of the sixties," Oral told a group of students in 1970, "I sensed it. The prayer line as I used to hold it simply will not work today as it did. . . . I'd change a method tomorrow if I could find a better one."[80] And there were other reasons for changing. Even if a successful crusade ministry could have been sustained overseas, Oral had to face the fact that he had changed. He was physically depleted. The university demanded his attention. Always a poor traveler, he found it harder and harder to endure overseas junkets.[81] In 1967, Oral explained the pressures he was feeling: "You preach and you pray; you wear out. And you have an office, you are building a school and you are doing lots of things and you wear out. . . . I began to get a little impatient. I spoke sharply to people. In the healing line, my wife kept saying, 'Oral, Oral, you were too sharp tonight.' But I said, 'Honey, how can I do it. There's so many of them.' " Oral found his compassion turning to bitterness.[82]

Exhausted and embattled, Roberts struggled through 1968. Years later, he remembered it as walking through "that Netherland, the twilight period." He thought, "God, what are You going to do with my life? Are You through with my life? If You are, thank You for how You've used me." On the other hand, "deep down inside me, the flood of the Spirit was still flowing and I knew that He wasn't through with me."[83] Oral's new call, which would dispel this cloud of uncertainty and melancholy, was a bold new television series, a series conceived in the troubled months in the summer of 1968 and consummated with the beginning of filming in December of that year. Fittingly, the last crusades were held in the same month in which the first new television films were made. "If we wait on God when He changes," reflected Evelyn in 1971, "He will show us something else."[84]

If Oral had conquered his deepest anxieties about the future by the end of 1968, the end of the crusades shocked and disappointed many of his friends and partners. The organization was swamped with mail asking, "Why has Brother

Roberts gone off on the wrong track and quit having crusades?"[85] Whatever lay ahead, an era had ended, and for many of those closest to the ministry, the best was past. For Bob DeWeese, the crusades would always be the "highest point of my life"; he had been atop Mount Everest, and "all other mountains seemed small."[86] Even Oral, having locked his singular mind on grander visions, sometimes looked back nostalgically. He placed one of the tent chairs in the Prayer Tower and struggled to explain its significance to the students:

> It's an old chair, seventeen years old, taken from our crusades. At least hundreds of people have sat on it during the past seventeen years. It's scarred and on the back of it all the paint is worn off because in our crusades as we pray for the sick, people lay their hands on the back of the chair as a point of contact and help me pray for the sick. And you can see where their hands have been, hundreds of hands laid on the back of that chair. And the Lord directed me to take it and put it in the Prayer Tower.[87]

Could those fresh young faces ever really comprehend what had happened during those arduous and ecstatic years? Could they imagine the faith "turned loose" by their hard-handed parents and grandparents as they sat expectant through the heat of twenty summers? Like the heirs of fortunes and cultures, they would have to stretch to comprehend their heritage. And only the grizzled veterans of the war would fully comprehend the meaning of the chair.

THE STUDENTS who best understood were those who had traveled with the team in the 1960s as members of World Action teams. They were the first tentative answer to Oral's haunting question: "If I die, am I going to leave anything?"[88]

The ministry's first effort to use young people to perpetuate and spread its healing message predated the founding of the university. In 1959, Hillard Griffin, director of literature evangelism in the Oral Roberts Evangelistic Association, organized Abundant Life youth teams in Central America to distribute literature and films.[89] The next year, a "Cathedral Cruiser" bus was outfitted with audio-visual equipment to be used by the teams, headed by Donald Spiers, director of the youth team.[90]

In June 1960, the youth team concept blossomed when the association announced that Hillard Griffin and his wife would lead five young people on an eighty-day world tour of sixteen foreign countries. The group included Richard and Evangeline Shakarian, the son and daughter-in-law of FGBMFI founder Demos Shakarian. Also among the young people were a brother and sister from St. Petersburg, Florida, LuWayne and Neil Eskelin, and Mary Ann Hazelton of Tulsa, the pianist for the Abundant Life choir and the reigning Miss Oklahoma. Shakarian was the "youth speaker," the Eskelins were experts at staging "puppet plays based on Biblical happenings," and Hazelton, "who recently turned down a profitable professional career in music for religious work," provided "special music."[91] The group conducted meetings in "churches, auditoriums, penal institutions, orphanages, schools, tents and village squares," leaving behind native youth teams in a number of countries.[92]

The youth team was widely publicized by the ministry. It was launched with the promise that it would be the first of "more than 1,000 teams to be working all over the world to spread the gospel," a prophetic harbinger of the healing teams of the 1980s.[93] More immediately, the team was a transitional step anticipating the founding of the School of Evangelism. Its purposes were loosely defined, but among them was the commission to "spot able young Christians to be brought to Tulsa for a course of training in Roberts' methods of evangelism."[94] The rapid expansion of the university over the next several years sidetracked the youth team experiment, but when World Action teams of students began to be formed in the late 1960s, they were regarded as a renewal of the youth team concept.[95]

The youth team idea resurfaced during Oral's Brazilian crusade in August 1966, when a group of twelve university students, led by Tommy Tyson, accompanied the "regular Crusade Team to preach, sing, witness and help with literature distribution and film showings."[96] It was a natural combination. Oral's new emphasis on world evangelism was refreshingly adorned by the attractive and dedicated young students from the university. The Brazilian experiment was a total success. Upon his return, Oral told his staff that the youth teams seemed to be the link he had been seeking to tie together the university and his evangelistic ministry:

> Out of this Brazilian Crusade may come the bridge between OREA and ORU, between the people who have been blessed by our ministry and their support of the University. For the first time we took students as members of our evangelistic team, and they conducted themselves under the anointing of the Spirit in such a way that it was as if they had been a member of our team for ten or twelve years. Therefore, we plan this coming summer, the Lord willing, to increase the number of students who will be going with us overseas.[97]

In 1967, twelve students, accompanied again by Tommy Tyson, began working in Indonesia a week before Oral and his team arrived, speaking and distributing literature in preparation for the crusade.[98] Oral returned from the Indonesian crusade convinced that "with teams of Holy Spirit-anointed students from ORU traveling with us, we can reach many more than when we went alone."[99] In 1968, for the first time, the groups of students who accompanied him on visits to London, Israel, and Kenya were called World Action teams.[100] One group toured Scandinavia and Bulgaria before joining the Roberts team in London and Israel; another team of students worked in the back country of Kenya (having studied Swahili) before assisting in Oral's campaign in Nairobi.[101]

The World Action team program blossomed in 1968. A World Action committee was established at the university to select students to be "sent to crisis areas around the world—all expenses paid."[102] Oral explained his growing concept to a Greater Tulsa area pastors' seminar in February, projecting that every student at the university would have an opportunity to participate and that some team members would remain abroad for a year.[103] As a pilot experiment, four students had been left in Africa after Oral's crusade in Kenya, training native evangelists, teaching religious education in the schools, and preaching. Roberts had high hopes for the project and promised, "It won't be the last."[104] But when the students returned home in 1969, they reported difficulties which made it clear that their mission would be "the first and the last of the series." Many of the nations of Africa were tightening restrictions on foreign missionaries, and, in addition, the students, who had been enrolled in the university's Graduate School of Theology, returned to find the school closed after Oral's disagreement with R. O. Corvin.[105]

The major shakeups in the Roberts ministry in 1968 forced a total rethinking of the World Action concept. Throughout that turbulent year of change, Oral pondered what role the student teams might play in his new order. In the spring, he informed his partners that "we are still in the early stages of the development of our World Action Teams"; he believed the "evidence" supported a continuation of the idea.[106] In the fall, Oral announced that "the real issue is World Action" and indicated that he was prepared to make the youth teams the major basis of his appeals to his partners. In a special meeting with the students, more than 450 pledged to participate in the program.[107] But several things went awry. In addition to the closing of the theology school, eliminating the most qualified potential team members, the youth team concept apparently did not fire the imagination of the partners, bringing in disappointing returns.[108] Two other changes in the ministry cast the future of the World Action teams in doubt. Once the decision to stop the crusades was firmly made, there was no clear role for the teams to play.[109] Equally disruptive was Oral's switch to the Methodist church. However compelling the idea of sending youth teams abroad, it could not be implemented without somewhere to send them. As Roberts's meetings in America suddenly turned sponsorless when he changed churches, his World Action teams became unwelcome at the far-flung pentecostal mission stations that had hosted them in the past. The Pentecostal Holiness church curtly suggested that Oral send his teams to Methodist missions, if he could find any.[110] The knottiest problems in the World Action program were at the receiving, not the sending, end, as was to be the case later with the ministry's healing teams.

Because of these problems, World Action evolved into a less active and more amorphous program. The hope that someday "one thousand of our graduates will be in a hundred and forty-six nations" gave way to the notion that "World Action is everyone's being a missionary Christian."[111] The term was used to describe the spiritual goals of the university, the belief that all of the students should carry their values into their professional life. "ORU is . . . a tool," explained Oral in 1968. "It's not an end in itself. It's the missionary arm of the ministry. A young man will graduate in business, go out into business but he will be a World Action team member as well as a businessman. Or, he may be called to preach and he will enter into World Action."[112]

The formal World Action program continued after 1968 with diminishing financial support from the ministry. Charles Farah, Jr. was director of the program in the 1970s, and scores of World Action teams did minister in the United States and throughout the world. In the 1970s, however, most of the teams were "self-sponsored," and, although they were still highly visible representatives of the university, they no longer fit the original model of healing mission-ary teams.[113] But the idea of sending teams of young people to take his healing message to the world by no means died in Oral's mind. It was waiting for the evolution of a new methodology.

IN 1968, as Oral thrashed about to find a new showcase for his message, the ministry boiled with new, experimental ideas. Early in the year he told Evelyn that he had the "same stirring in my soul that I felt back in 1947." As he talked, "tears would fill his eyes"; he was in the throes of one of those agonizing per-sonal traumas which presaged precipitous changes in his ministry.[114] The idea which increasingly gained the ascendancy called for a return to television in a bold new format. In the summer and fall of 1968, Oral and his aides mulled over revolutionary concepts for religious programming—discussing ideas which would have been unthinkable a few years earlier. It was an exciting and hectic time to be a part of the ministry.

Oral parted with his old television program (as he parted with the crusades) reluctantly and wistfully. Television remained an important part of the ministry into the mid-1960s. In October 1966, Pat Robertson, who had established his Christian Broadcasting Network in 1959, urged Oral's partners to "pray, sup-port, and tell others about the Oral Roberts Abundant Life telecast"; he be-lieved that Oral had "confronted more Americans with the gospel of Christ than any other living man."[115] In the early 1960s, minor changes of format were made; increasingly Oral taped his sermons in a studio, while the healing line continued to be filmed in the crusades.[116] But he grew more and more dis-satisfied.

Roberts made the decision to discontinue his television series in 1965. About half the stations carrying the program were discontinued in 1966, and the remainder in May 1967.[117] Oral told Lee Braxton of his decision to abandon television while his old friend was driving him to the airport in late 1966. Brax-ton was disconsolate: "I thought the world was coming to an end . . . because that's the way I started with him to promote television and radio." Braxton could not "see the new ministry that was to come out of it"; in fact, neither did Oral see it at the time.[118] "Many people did not understand when we went off television," Oral conceded to his staff at the end of 1968. "I was one of the number. But I knew we had finished that particular course."[119] The time had come to stop and "wait upon the Lord."[120]

The decision to return to television came after "one of the greatest inward struggles" that Oral ever experienced.[121] The scheme that was finally settled on was a high-stakes gamble—a plan to take the program out of the Sunday morn-ing religious ghetto. Television had changed drastically since Oral had first used the medium in 1954; in 1969 an estimated 190 million Americans had access to TV sets. "A whole new generation has come up not knowing God," Oral wrote to his partners, "spitting on the church, and the government, and even on one another."[122] How could those people be reached? Television, he believed, was the answer: "To reach them we have to go where they are, because they are not coming where we are."[123]

There were huge risks. The plan hammered out in the fall of 1968 called for a new weekly series on Sundays and the production of four one-hour specials to be aired in prime time. The cost was staggering. Production costs for the first special at NBC's studio in Burbank were $75,000, and the estimated cost of a 160-station network in prime time was $135,000 per show. The yearly budget for the new television package was projected at $3,000,000.[124] When the time came in December to sign contracts for the first year, Oral wavered. Speaking at a partners' seminar in January 1969, he said: "You will never know in December how close I came to failing the Lord on this television program when I was told by the networks and the people what it would cost. And I staggered along and finally began fasting and the day I said, 'I will do it and I expect a miracle' shook my very soul. I'm committed now. I'm moving now."[125] But contributions began to rise dramatically in anticipation of the new series, even before it was aired, easing somewhat Oral's financial fears.[126]

Cost was only the most obvious of the risks posed by the new television series. A religious special designed for prime time posed novel production and marketing problems. Who would watch such a production? How could television stations be persuaded to air it?

The catalytic figure in assembling the artistic team was Ralph Carmichael, a talented musical writer, director, and arranger, who had scored numerous television specials for some of the nation's most popular singers. Carmichael was widely known for his work in the field of religious music; he had done some work on Oral's radio programs, and in 1968 Oral began discussing with him his ideas about a new approach to religious programming.[127] Oral explained to Carmichael that he wanted to recast his message in a popular, entertaining format, building around the musical talents of the ORU students who would be featured as the World Action Singers. Carmichael listened and told his friend Warren Hultgren: "If they really want what they say they want, they are the pioneers in religious music."[128] It was a dream come true for him, Carmichael told Wayne Robinson; he had "been trying to do music like that all his life and nobody paid any attention to him."[129]

The creative team jelled in the summer and fall of 1968. Carmichael introduced Oral to Dick Ross, who had produced programs for Billy Graham and Kathryn Kuhlman in the past, and who also had directed such nonreligious programs as George Jessel's "Here Come the Stars." To Ross fell the "challenge" of amending "his star's healing, preaching, soul-cleansing image."[130] Wayne Robinson became Oral's interpreter from within the ministry, believing intensely that the time had come for Oral to be "reinterpreted and restated."[131] Al Bush was the manager and facilitator, who coolly and efficiently kept everything on track. And ever-present was Oral, probing, questioning, reminding them of the spiritual import of their mission. At a breakfast meeting in the Roosevelt Hotel in Hollywood, the team made its final commitments; it was agreed to produce the first program in Burbank in December.

Carmichael came to Tulsa in September to begin working with the World Action Singers and with Richard Roberts, who had joined the ministry to be a featured singer on the new programs.[132] While Carmichael worked "day after day" with Richard and the other singers "to produce a new sound in gospel music," Dick Ross created a show which featured not only Richard and the World Action Singers (in modish dress and glamorous stage settings) but also guest star Mahalia Jackson, a "personal friend" of Oral's. Oral preached a short sermon entitled "Touching Someone" and led a prayer. The program was light, upbeat, and innovative.[133] "The show was good," recalled Al Bush. "It was not outstanding, but it was good."[134] Better was on the way.

With a product in hand, the last challenge was to persuade television stations to air the Oral Roberts special in prime time. That job fell to the energetic and efficient Al Bush. The fact that the show had been produced professionally in NBC's studios was enough to get it accepted by some stations, but with others, especially in the major market areas, the selling task was harder. Bush packed a tape of the program in his suitcase and toured the nation's major cities, buying air time on independent stations. He sold them on the quality of the show, and he offered to prepay, anticipating that "they didn't think religionists could have that kind of money." In New York City, Bush presented the owner of a station with a "list of contributors from Manhattan only," about 50,000 names, promising not only to prepay but also "to bring you an audience." Selling the prime-time specials was, for Al Bush, "one of my proudest achievements."[135]

The first "Contact" television special was shown in March 1969, and shortly thereafter Oral inaugurated his Sunday morning half-hour program under the name "Something Good Is Going to Happen to You." Also produced by Dick Ross but filmed at Oral Roberts University, the weekly programs were more conventional than the specials, but they nonetheless introduced an entertainment quality, featuring the World Action Singers and an informal atmosphere. The second special featured guest star Pat Boone. In the third, Oral felt even more comfortable with Dale Evans. The final special of the year featured Anita Bryant in a Christmas theme, and Dick Ross judged it the best of the 1969 productions. Ross told a Los Angeles television writer that Oral had been "uncomfortable" on the first program but that he was much "more relaxed in his role of conversationalist and emcee" with his fellow Oklahoman Bryant. And Ross was delighted with the progress of the supporting cast: "The show has improved in sound and movement. What the kids . . . lack in professional experience they make up for in discipline."[136]

In early 1969, Oral and his television team waited anxiously for the returns on their experiment. When Roberts had first asked Dick Ross to produce his new programs, Ross had been noncommittal. He later explained: "Only when I saw that he was interested in changing his whole approach and was courageous enough to stand up in front of his old constituents, did I respond."[137] How would those old constituents respond? Oral waited, uneasily: "I admit to you when we make changes like this, there are moments when we are frightened, we become extremely nervous."[138]

Oral's fears were well founded. The new programs received a very mixed reaction from traditional religious viewers. *Christianity Today* noted that the program featured the "animated singing and slithering of the World Action

Singers," conceding that it seemed to have "caught on with the younger set."[139] In the eyes of many of Oral's old pentecostal supporters, the new program was the final embarrassing plunge in his fall from grace. "He's gone into orbit," commented one of his former church's leaders; the barrage of epithets which greeted the specials included "Hollywoodizing," "flesh," and "compromise."[140] In November 1969, after it was clear that the programs were a major success, Oral spoke candidly with a group of partners about the initial reaction:

> I've never had as much critical and hate mail in twenty-two years. . . . And I've never seen so many Christian people so mad. . . . All they could think of, we don't do that in our church. I finally wrote one woman, I had to pray over this and get forgiveness after I wrote the letter—I said, 'Mam, I can see you right now. Your dress goes to your ankles, your sleeves are down here, your hair is long, you have no makeup on. Your little church has about 150 in it with about three young people and you are mad they are there because one of the girls has a mini-skirt and you just don't like for her to be in the church because she's defiling it because her dress is not as long as yours is. . . . Where are the young people? They are not in your church, you are not reaching them. . . . What's wrong with their bodies? Their bodies are clean. These young people don't go out and drink and use drugs and smoke and commit adultery. These are clean young people. I like to see them move their bodies. Young people are in movement in this country and if you want to reach one of them you'd better move a little bit."[141]

It did not take long, however, to learn that the television gamble had resulted in a victory of unanticipated proportions. Rating services estimated that nearly 10,000,000 people viewed the first special, and ratings rose steadily for several years.[142] By the end of the first year, the ministry's mail was soaring, setting "all-time highs" month after month.[143] The number of inquiries to the university from prospective students had doubled by January 1970.[144] And the mail turned overwhelmingly favorable. A survey of letters after the Easter special in the spring of 1970 counted 31,000 direct responses to the program in the first week, of which only 114 were critical.[145] Oral was euphoric by the fall of 1970; the most recent special had been followed by over 500,000 letters, most of them, Oral believed, from people who "don't darken the door of a church, don't even know religious terms." The results validated Oral's bold risk. "That's worth something to me," he exuded, "I'm willing to stick my neck out."[146] And the success story continued. In 1973, the spring special attracted an estimated audience of 37,671,921 viewers; in its wake the ministry's mail reached an astonishing all-time monthly high of about 760,000 letters.[147] It had become clear, judged Oral's old friend Rex Humbard, that "Oral Roberts is reaching more non-church people than any man in America. Because he has taken a new approach and he's not afraid of criticism of church people."[148]

Perhaps even more remarkable was the critical acclaim the program won in the early 1970s. The 1969 judgment of a Tulsa television critic that Oral had a "hit on his hands" was true artistically as well as in the ratings.[149] In 1971, the Roberts Valentine special received Emmy nominations in the categories of art direction and scenic design and lighting direction.[150] By the end of 1972, the specials were being broadcast on over four hundred stations. "That means a lot to me," observed Oral, "that . . . after four years we have won the confidence of the television industry."[151] In fact, the programs became a model for religious telecasting. In a conversation with Merv Griffin at the end of 1974, Oral reflected on the religious criticism he had received: "Merv, when we went on television about seven years ago, we had methods of choreography and so on that turned a lot of church people off, but now there are 111 religious shows or programs on television that came on since we went on and most of them have adopted many of our methods."[152] In many ways, the modern electronic church was born with the airing of Oral's first special in March 1969.

In the years from 1969 to 1975, Oral's television specials paraded before the cameras an impressive array of Hollywood talent. The early shows featured stars with recognizable religious connections, such as Mahalia Jackson, Pat Boone, Dale Evans, and Anita Bryant. But the program increasingly took on the character of a "variety show," with commensurately elevating production costs, including among its showcase of stars Jimmy Durante, Jerry Lewis, Lou Rawls, Kay Starr, Roger Williams, the Lennon Sisters, Johnny Cash, Johnny Mathis, Pearl Bailey, Della Reese, Burl Ives, Shari Lewis, Tennessee Ernie Ford, and Jimmie Rodgers. In 1972, a dramatic portrayal of the crucifixion was produced, starring Peter Graves as Luke, Harvey Presnell as a Roman centurion, Jane Powell as Claudia, Pilate's wife, and Richard Roberts as Pilate. The Hollywood talent appearing on Oral's programs was joined by a parade of political figures, who welcomed Oral to their areas for on-location productions, and by Billy Graham, who joined Oral for an interview on a 1972 special.[153]

Oral was conscious of the seeming anomaly of nonreligious stars appearing on the programs—including several non-Christians. But he believed that they were serving his purpose, and he also thought that more and more of them would be won over by his message:

> We will have more and more of the stars of this country who will be willing to give a word for the Lord, which was impossible before, so those others really served a purpose, and some of them that were on before have since accepted Jesus Christ and some of them are coming back on to give their testimony. So it's not all been a failure the way that we've had to work with them, because we introduced some of them to our Lord.[154]

Among the more attractive features of the new television programs—both the weekly shows and the specials—were the wholesome charm of the World Action Singers and the regular appearances of Richard Roberts and his wife, Patti. Richard soloed on the first program, and both he and Patti became celebrity singers as a result of their regular appearances. They were both talented performers. Ralph Carmichael told his friend Warren Hultgren that Richard had enough talent to "be in Las Vegas" or "on any semi-classical platform in the country."[155] In the early 1970s, Richard became "administrator" of the World Action Singers, assuming the responsibility of choosing and managing the students who performed on the program.[156] In the summer of 1970 he acted as host on a youth special aired on prime time.[157]

In spite of the stunning success of the television programs, Roberts was soon fidgety and began making minor changes. The television series remained in a state of creative flux. In December 1972, Oral bought the expensive equipment necessary for the filming of his programs in Mabee Center, including four of the latest RCA color cameras, costing $72,000 each. "My producer told me this morning," he excitedly told the university students, "that when we get through . . . getting the . . . equipment that we would have something equal to NBC."[158] As always, Roberts was committed to going "first-class."[159]

Oral also constantly tinkered with the content and format of the programs. In 1972, he toyed with the idea of telecasting hour services on Sunday mornings because of continued trends toward declining church attendance.[160] In late 1973, Ron Smith reported to the ministry's staff that Oral was "very uneasy about the present format. He keeps wanting to change, but he doesn't always like the change he gets. He is attacking the format. And he doesn't know what he is attacking, and that is always the prelude to seeing something quite a bit different."[161]

In 1974, Oral talked with several producers, seeking new ideas on how to separate himself from the dozens of imitators who were using his new methods of combining religion and entertainment. He brought Merv Griffin to the ORU campus for discussions. "So now," he told Griffin, "we are about to move on into a different . . . plateau. And that's one reason we have you folks to talk to us and to share with us your ideas about America, about the country, about the feelings."[162] Negotiations with Griffin's production company failed, basically because Oral wanted to gain more "creative control," and in 1975 the programs began to be produced by TRACO, a ministry production company headed by Ron Smith. The weekly show was given the new title "Oral Roberts and You" and a format that was "more spontaneous."[163]

As a result of the change, Oral for the first time had creative control over the program, and the films were made in the familiar and friendly environment of the ORU campus. Atmosphere, he explained, was the main reason he wanted to film in Mabee Center:

> Do you know how it feels to be surrounded by people you feel right with? . . . Well you get into a cold television studio with people you don't know and they turn the thing on and tell you to get up there and preach and pray and see how you feel. Folks, its tough. I thank God we've done as well as we have, but I can promise you this morning that we can do a lot better when we are in the place that's God's.[164]

Announcing the changes in *Abundant Life*, Oral wrote: "We do it with our own staff. And with an audience all around us so alive 'in the Spirit' we feel on fire for the Lord. Now I have always felt the anointing of the Spirit on the program, but I definitely feel the Spirit *more* now."[165]

The creative changes in the early 1970s seemed to underline the spiritual nature and objectives of the television programs—a point which had been questioned by much of the religious world. At times it had appeared that Oral's message was almost lost amidst the glitter of the productions, and Oral himself seemed captivated by Hollywood. But he was never completely captured; he remained uncomfortable there, and he was impatient to include more preaching in his programs. He restively preached sermonettes in the most inoffensive language he could summon up, hoping that the world of religious illiterates who listened would want more. He chafed to tell them more.

Oral hoped to use television to reestablish "one-to-one" contact with people—the same relationship he had had under the big tent. The message and intent were the same, he insisted:

> I just simply chose another method here and you will find I'm married to principles but I'm not married to methods. I'd change a method tomorrow if I could find a better one. But I'll never change a principle. I lay on hands to some extent, but not in any degree as I did before, that is physically speaking. But now I lay hands in my view a hundred times more than I did because I've got a hundred times bigger crowds. Television is where it's at, where the people are.[166]

But the entertainment format had seriously limited Oral's time to present his message. "I'll only have eleven minutes in which to preach a major sermon," he complained in 1972, "followed by a prayer which has to be short and has to get inside people. And I admit I worry about that a little."[167]

Beginning in the fall of 1972, when a special was filmed in Mabee Center featuring a conversation between Oral and Billy Graham, the team felt that the program could include more "spiritual emphasis." "We feel that the American public is beginning to accept us for what we are," Richard told a student reporter, "and we're becoming bolder in our witness for Christ. America is more ready now for fewer guests and entertainment and more of the basics of what we believe."[168] In a candid meeting with the student body in December 1972, Oral bared his feelings about the tactics he had used on television. He felt that the ministry had "turned a corner." The early programs "had to be done" because "the news media almost singled me out as if they took their spite out on me." So he played a lesser role in the early productions:

> What we did to get around that is to bring big performers in . . . and now we have won the industry. If I had let out . . . they wouldn't have sold me the time. So I'd rather have half a loaf than no loaf at all. . . . We were scared this last special because each station previews the program and the sermon was so strong and the prayer was longer and stronger. . . . We got it on 416 stations. Now that is a miracle. So what that says to me is, now just go a little deeper.[169]

Oral's intensely pragmatic spirit was never more evident than in his television ministry.

The shifts in the Roberts ministry in the mid-1960s, which included the ending of the crusades and the beginning of the new television programs, were accompanied by sweeping changes in the top level of the ministry's executives. New talents were demanded by the new methods. Oral once again showed an extraordinary aptitude for attracting young, energetic, and talented people to help him capture his vision. Most of the older generation of Roberts lieutenants faded from visibility, although a few continued to play significant roles in the revamped organization of the 1970s.

In the early 1960s, the Oral Roberts Evangelistic Association looked very much as it had in the 1950s. In 1966 the board of trustees listed Oral as chairman, Demos Shakarian as vice-chairman, and Oscar Moore, Nick Timko, John Barton, Carl Wilson, and Evelyn Roberts as members. The association's executive committee included Manford Engel as executive vice-president, young Al Bush, who was manager of the Abundant Life office, and Lee Braxton, whose title was assistant to the president. The directors of the association's World Outreach ministry included Robert F. DeWeese, associate evangelist; Tommy Tyson, associate evangelist; Lee Braxton, director of radio and television; Myron Sackett, director of Hebrew Bible ministry; Collins Steele, manager of crusade equipment; Vep Ellis, minister of music; Robert O. Fraley, director of Christian Stewardship Department; and William Armstrong, director of publications and worldwide literature ministry. Oral Roberts University was headed by a forty-one-member board of regents. Lee Braxton was chairman of the regents; Oral Roberts was president of the university, and John Messick was executive vice-president. It was a tested and loyal organization; most were people with pentecostal backgrounds.[170] Most were also on the verge of leaving or accepting lesser roles in the ministry.

The appointment of Oscar Moore as resident trustee and acting president of the evangelistic association in 1960 was an important administrative move. Oral's extended absences from Tulsa during the early 1960s demanded a more authoritative voice in the Tulsa office. Solid, responsible, and unswervingly loyal, Oscar Moore had Oral's trust and respect. During the hectic years when the university was beginning and the crusades ending, Moore was a stable fixture at the evangelistic association. But in 1969, he resigned; he recognized that the dramatic changes of the late 1960s called for a different style of management and that the leadership of the organization had already passed to a younger and more aggressive set of executives.[171] Oscar Moore and Oral remained fast friends in the years that followed, but their paths separated somewhat. Moore remained a leader in the Pentecostal Holiness church; like many of Oral's friends, he remained loyal but was never really at home in the freewheeling charismatic world which Oral entered full-force in the mid-1960s.

The most traumatic turnover in the Roberts organization in the early 1960s came when G. H. Montgomery was forced to resign as director of the organization's publications. Montgomery's termination, allegedly based on charges of personal misconduct, was one of the rare incidents of a top Roberts executive's being forced out. He left denying the charges against him and deeply resentful. Montgomery had been an extremely competent editor, and he had controlled the ministry's publications more completely than any successor ever did. After leaving Roberts, he joined the Herald of Healing, Inc. of Dallas, the organization founded by Jack Coe and headed by his widow, Juanita. The Coe organization was still quite powerful, and Montgomery used its magazine, which had a circulation of about 100,000, to launch one of the most acid attacks ever aimed at Oral by an informed executive from inside the organization.[172]

A few of the first-generation administrators did survive the changes of the 1960s; the most successful was the ubiquitous Lee Braxton. Braxton's contributions to the organization were so varied and his ability to adjust so remarkable that he remained an important member of the team through the 1970s. He was crushed when the old television series which he had done so much to promote was canceled; he did not play an important role in the development of the new series. But he had already assumed the important position of chairman of the board of regents of the university, a title to which he was reelected for term after term until 1979. In addition, Braxton had a personal acquaintance with the important partners of the ministry rivaled by no other individual, including Oral. His informal role as "Mr. Partner" kept him at the heart of the ministry.[173]

Oral never fired loyal aides when the changes in his methods eliminated their jobs; he found new jobs for them. The university provided jobs for some of his old team members. Collins Steele, Oral's close friend and tent equipment manager through 1968, left the ministry for four years but returned as vice-president for physical plant at the university in 1972. In 1966, Manford Engel became vice-president and director of development at the university in a move that opened the way for Al Bush to assume an executive role at the evangelistic association.[174] Bob DeWeese remained Oral's associate evangelist in title and held partners' rallies throughout the country until the spring of 1973, when he accepted a pastorate in Dayton, Ohio. The end of the crusades had been a traumatic disappointment for DeWeese; it was difficult for him to find "satisfaction" in his new role.[175]

The old management team survived into the mid-1960s because up until 1968 the methods Oral used remained essentially those developed in the 1950s. At the beginning of 1968, the ministry was still described as seven "outreaches": (1) the Abundant Life Prayer Tower, (2) Radio, (3) Bibles for Jews, (4) Crusades, (5) Literature, (6) Overseas Crusades, and (7) Oral Roberts University.[176] Although the university had added a new dimension, the ministry's self-definition had remained remarkably stagnant.

A number of the old "outreaches" continued to be important in the 1960s. Oral's radio program was broadcast weekly on over three hundred stations in the United States and over forty outside the country.[177] The radio was particularly important in expanding his influence overseas. In 1960 he announced plans to build a system of radio stations of his own, including short-wave facilities capable of reaching all over the world. That project was opposed by local radio interests, however, and was soon abandoned.[178] Nevertheless, in the 1960s the radio program continued to be beamed to every continent. When the team conducted a crusade in Jamaica in 1969, one of the members reported: "The Abundant Life radio broadcast has been beamed into Jamaica for nearly 10 years. And it seemed there was not a person in Kingston who did not know the name, Oral Roberts. Everywhere he went his name was a household word. He was that well known and loved."[179]

Oral's most useful tool for communicating with his partners continued to be his publications, particularly *Abundant Life* magazine. The circulation of

Abundant Life stabilized at about 600,000 during the early 1960s, a mailing list which had been built from responses from the crusades and the radio and television programs.[180] G. H. Montgomery exercised almost complete control over the magazine until his departure in the fall of 1961, when Oral again was listed as editor-in-chief.[181] Montgomery was replaced by a young editorial committee, which included Bill Sterne, Bill Armstrong, and Carl Hamilton, but for several years Oral exerted real editorial control. He had always been possessive of the magazine, which he recognized as his lifeline to his supporters. In early 1962 he wrote: "God recently laid it upon my heart to do even more writing in ABUNDANT LIFE magazine. . . . I have resumed my former duties as editor in chief of all Abundant Life Publications. I intend to keep this post in the future. I do not want to lose this close touch with you, my faithful reader and partner.[182]

Oral relinquished control of the magazine again in August 1967, when as a part of the leadership shuffle within the entire organization, he appointed young Wayne A. Robinson editor-in-chief. Robinson, Carl Hamilton's cousin and a recent graduate from Southern Methodist University seminary, lasted less than two years in the job, resigning after a heated confrontation with Oral over the magazine's makeup and design.[183] Once again, Oral announced that he and Evelyn, aided by Richard, would oversee the preparation of the magazine: "Through the years we've had different editors, all of whom gave us great help. Still it is difficult for anyone outside Evelyn and me to put into the magazine what we really feel from the Lord. . . . I am once again the sole editor. It's a thrilling work for me. God is constantly putting new things from His Word into my heart."[184] While Oral's direct involvement in the magazine was limited by other demands on his time, he kept a close eye on it. In 1974, Oral described his continued participation:

> It's brought to me and a lot of times it's laid out very near the way I feel. I'll have to do very little to that issue. But the last one, I sweat blood over it because about two or three times a year, they will goof up. And they don't mean to goof up. . . . And I'm the only guy in this ministry that can do it when it comes to that point, I've got to sit down with it. And this last issue brought to me, I literally, physically tore up, not in a violent way, but just simply said, this won't work. It will not meet people's needs. So I took it and went through it and rewrote it.[185]

Oral's clashes with his more professional journalistic helpers generally focused on his desire to keep the magazine newsy, and filled with testimonials. He believed, correctly, that Wayne Robinson had set out to make the magazine "slick"; that was never what he intended.[186]

While the quality and emphasis of the magazine changed with the editorial shifts, its circulation history was an unbroken success story. The circulation exploded with the return of Oral to television in 1969. By the end of that year, nearly 300,000 new subscribers had been added, bringing the total circulation to over 1,000,000.[187] In the 1970s the magazine was sent without charge to all those who contributed to the ministry, but its amazing growth was nonetheless the most striking success story in religious journalism in the early 1970s.[188] The magazine was widely distributed in all English-speaking areas of the world, and was printed in Spanish and Japanese.[189]

In addition to publishing *Abundant Life*, the Oral Roberts Evangelistic Association circulated huge quantities of other literature. *Daily Blessing*, a quarterly devotional magazine, had reached a stable circulation of 250,000 in the late 1960s.[190] The university spawned numerous publications, including a regular news magazine, *Outreach*. Oral wrote scores of books and tracts on a wide variety of topics, and they were published and distributed by the millions. By 1962, the ministry announced that it was sending a million pieces of literature per week to 105 countries.[191] In 1966, the estimate was "over one-half billion pieces of gospel literature in approximately 79 languages . . . distributed around the world by the Oral Roberts Evangelistic Association. This has been accomplished through the mails, and by the personal contacts of missionaries and our overseas representatives."[192] After his return to television, Oral often offered free books to all those requesting copies, and several of his books surpassed a million in circulation. The saturation of the world with Roberts literature was often accompanied by the circulation of filmstrips, movies, and other visual aids, often dubbed in foreign languages.

The literature and film programs were constantly publicized and apparently stimulated considerable partner support; it is difficult to measure the impact on the recipients. As a result of his experiences overseas, Oral was convinced that the literature was effective. After visiting India, he reported that "every piece we send into this country is read eagerly by at least five different families!"[193] Particularly in the developing nations, the wide distribution of free literature undoubtedly exposed millions to the name Oral Roberts; it seems likely that Oral became one of the most widely read American authors in the 1970s.[194]

A new project which was to have a long and successful life as a part of the Roberts ministry was the Abundant Life Prayer Group. The prayer group was formed by G. H. Montgomery in March 1958, to handle telephone calls coming into the ministry. Volunteer workers manned two telephones in the association's building after taking a "2–3 week training course on public relations, taking into account the concept of Oral Robert's [*sic*] ministry."[195] In 1967, the group moved into the Prayer Tower, where its twenty-four-hour number began receiving an estimated four hundred calls a day "from every corner of the world."[196] The prayer group was a pioneer effort at crisis prevention, counseling alcoholics and their relatives and praying with potential suicides and the desperately ill.[197] It grew steadily through the years.

THE CHANGES in the Roberts organization in the late 1960s were symbolized by the association's move in 1968 to a new building, located just off the Oral Roberts University campus. In the early 1960s, Oral considered adding five stories to the Abundant Life building as the number of employees rose to nearly 550 and overran the building on South Boulder.[198] But an increased use of computers in mail handling in the 1960s diminished the number of employees to around 300 by 1967, and the increasing importance of the university made it desirable to relocate the evangelistic association, bringing "the whole family together."[199]

The revamping of the Oral Roberts Evangelistic Association (which in 1969 significantly changed its name to the Oral Roberts Association) was in part caused by, and was preeminently symbolized by, the rise to power of Albert E. Bush. Bush rose irrepressibly through the organization; he replaced Engel as executive vice-president of the association in 1966 and in January 1970 was named Oral's successor as president of the Oral Roberts Association, an honor no other non-Roberts has ever held.[200] Bush was clean-cut and crisp, with brilliant managerial skills. He helped reshape the image of the Oral Roberts Association in the Tulsa business community; he was a man who would have been at home in the corporate executive suites of any major corporation. Indeed, when he did leave his position with Oral, in August 1972, jaded and drained by the pressures of his job, he began a spectacularly successful career as president and chairman of the board of Mentor Corporation, later becoming an executive in the huge Williams conglomerate in Tulsa.

In the early 1960s, Al Bush computerized the Roberts correspondence department. He negotiated a "joint venture" with IBM which led to the first use of upper- and lower-case computerized printing; the data center at the Abundant Life building became a "showroom as a part of our fee to IBM." Before he left the organization, the ministry was receiving over 500,000 letters a month, and in 1971 Bush led the association into a giant computer conglomerate formed in Tulsa, Mentor Corporation.[201] Bush had an unsurpassed technical grasp of the ministry, an ability to offer accurate profiles of the partners and to pinpoint the sources of the ministry's support. "Because of the automated filing system," recalled Bush, "we were able to segregate the files. If you were a $10,000 giver, I wouldn't ask you for $10. I would approach you at the level of your understanding. . . . We used to shoot rifles. One bullet at one target."[202]

But Al Bush not only handled the mail and partner relations in the late 1960s and early 1970s, his influence permeated the entire Roberts organization. "Everything worked through me, even at the school," recalled Bush, "although I had indirect authorities." In Bush Oral had found the indispensable technician who could turn his ideas into facts: "We were very promotional people. We knew how to turn projects and challenges into money."[203] Bush was universally respected by the other young members of the Roberts team. When he left in 1972, Oral was distraught, but Bush felt that he had been stretched too thin and had become "ineffective."

Wayne Robinson was the second of the team of young executives to join the organization in the 1960s. Robinson seemed a perfect addition to the new leadership. His father had been a Pentecostal Holiness preacher, and Robinson had attended Southwestern College before completing a B.A. degree in journalism at Oklahoma City University and a B.D. degree at Perkins School of Religion at Southern Methodist University. He was a bright student and a talented writer, who upon graduation from Perkins was interviewed for a position with *Christianity and Crisis* magazine. Instead, he joined Oral's ministry and rapidly worked his way up to public relations director and subsequently editor of *Abundant Life* and the writer of much of the ministry's radio and television material.[204]

After leaving Roberts in 1969 because of his clash with Oral on the content of *Abundant Life,* Robinson accepted a position as public relations director of the Oklahoma Conference of the Methodist church and editor of the conference newspaper, continuing to write for Oral's television program as a consultant.[205] In 1971, Robinson returned to the ministry as vice-president for public affairs of Oral Roberts University, occupying an office next to Oral's and acting as a buffer between Roberts and Carl Hamilton.[206] He left permanently in 1972, after having ghostwritten Oral's autobiography *The Call,* this time leaving after a spat with Richard about Robinson's handling of the television programs.[207]

Like all of the young men who served Oral so well during the hectic late 1960s, Robinson was captivated by Oral's personal charisma and threw his life into building the ministry. He served as Oral's theological tutor during the latter's switch to Methodism, and he did much to orchestrate the public remolding of Oral's image. "I really had a drive to help him be understood," recalled Robinson.[208] But of all the young men who shared Oral's dream, Wayne Robinson probably had the most reservations about it. Robinson was painfully ambivalent about his own Pentecostal Holiness roots; he hated the poverty and indignity his upbringing had imposed on him. He had a personal and intimate understanding of the pentecostal soul, its strengths and weaknesses, and shortly after he left the Roberts ministry, he wrote a book entitled *I Once Spoke in Tongues,* which both celebrated and criticized the entire pentecostal experience.[209] "There was a battle going on inside him all the time that is still not resolved," observed Carl Hamilton in 1983. "He has never come to terms with that conflict and Oral was just a chapter."[210]

The third of the triumvirate of talented young men who reshaped the ministry in the late 1960s and 1970s was Ronald R. Smith, who was hired by Al Bush in 1966 to supervise the construction of University Village, a retirement center the ministry built, partly to provide a home for Oral's parents. Smith, like Bush, had been reared in the pentecostal Church of the Open Bible and was serving as chaplain-administrator of a retirement center in Iowa when he was hired by Roberts. Smith became president of University Village, a modern, well-planned retirement center capable of housing about four hundred elderly people in an environment designed to provide for their health and spiritual needs. Located just off the Oral Roberts University campus, the retirement center was the most autonomous of all the Roberts ministries, although it continued to require some subsidy from the evangelistic association into the 1980s. Not only did the village provide a comfortable place for Claudius Roberts to spend her final years, it also helped Oral's image with his partners and in Tulsa.[211]

Although Smith apparently intended to leave the ministry when University Village was completed, his talents brought him a series of rapid promotions. In 1967, he became administrative associate to the president of ORU, and in 1968 he was named vice-president for development. When University Village was completed, Oral asked Smith "to understudy Al Bush," a job which Smith welcomed because of his friendship with and respect for Bush. When Bush left in 1972, Smith was appointed vice-president of the Oral Roberts Association, with Oral resuming the title of president. Smith succeeded somewhat uneasily to the job vacated by Al Bush, feeling that "my talent was a little different from Al's."

He believed that he had never acquired the "range of knowledge" of the complex organization which Bush possessed, having been more accustomed to playing the role of "front man," but it was soon apparent that Smith brought great creative talent to his new responsibilities. His prestige within the organization grew steadily into the late 1970s, when he held the titles of chief executive officer and executive vice-president for finance and endowment.[212]

In 1969, Bush, Robinson, and Smith formed a central management committee, joined by Carl Hamilton and university vice-president for business affairs Bob Eskridge. Eskridge, who had joined the organization in 1965 after serving as mayor of Broken Arrow, a suburb of Tulsa, was, Wayne Robinson felt, a "direct conduit back to Oral."[213] The other four had similar pentecostal roots but had become, Robinson believed, "only in the vaguest sense traditional Christians."[214] They had both the brilliance and the resilience demanded to follow Oral through the transformation of his ministry. Together they projected a new image of the ministry.

Image had always been important to Oral. In 1962, long before the university adopted its controversial aerobics physical fitness program, Oral put all of his employees at the evangelistic association on a "weight reduction program." First, he lost weight himself, and prudent observers did the same. Then came some "judicious prodding," and finally overweight employees were "required to make monthly reports on their progress." Those who failed to make a weight deadline were given three-month leaves of absence without pay; if they still failed to reach a target weight, they were placed on permanent leave.[215] In the mid-1960s, the women in the ministry began wearing makeup, leaving behind the old holiness image.[216]

Probably the most conspicuous example of the ministry's quest for a new image was the civic prominence of the new young executives. Oral had always encouraged his top administrative aides and faculty members to be active in community affairs. The young leaders of the organization were extremely visible in Tulsa in the early 1970s, particularly Al and Marilyn Bush and Ron and Jeanie Smith. When the Bushes were named to head a fund-raising drive for the Arts Council of Tulsa in 1972, the *Tulsa World* listed among Bush's community activities membership on the Tulsa Housing Authority and in the International Young Presidents' Organization, the Kiwanis Club, the Tulsa Chamber of Commerce, the Tulsa Club, the Summit Club, and the Southern Hills Country Club, while Mrs. Bush was a member of the Children's Medical Center Auxiliary, the Women's Alliance of the Arts Council of Tulsa, and the Women's Association of the Tulsa Philharmonic.[217] In 1970, the Smiths were selected the All-American family from Oklahoma, Ron having already become president of the Southside Rotary Club in Tulsa, a member of the mayor's charter revision committee, and a member of the Petroleum Club. His wife, Jeanie, won the title of Mrs. Oklahoma Savings Bond the same year and was also president of the ORU Women's Club and vice-president of Rotary Anns.[218]

The departures of Al Bush and Wayne Robinson in 1972 marked the beginning of another management transition in the Oral Roberts ministry. Ron Smith remained to supply continuity between the old group and the new executives who appeared after 1975, but basic changes began to occur long before he left in 1979. In the long run, the most far-reaching new ingredient in the management team was the growing power of Richard Roberts.

With the beginning of the new television series, Richard became increasingly visible in the ministry. His official position from 1969 to 1973 was director of the World Action Singers, but in 1973 he was named president of the Oral Roberts Evangelistic Association. Explaining the appointment to the evangelistic association staff in December 1973, Ron Smith emphasized that Richard was not "in the line": "I do not report to Richard Roberts. I report to Oral Roberts. But there will be a day when he moves into the line in all probability. That will be the day Oral moves out of the line. I guess that's no secret."[219] While Richard's role remained titular in 1975, his appointment to the presidency of the evangelistic association was a clear message about the future of the ministry.

By the 1960s, the financial lifeblood of the ministry was the direct mail link between Oral and his partners. The partners' list included the names of all the people who had written to Oral through the years—those saved and healed in the campaigns and the hundreds of thousands who deluged the association with responses to the first and second television ventures. The only sales pitch Oral ever made on television was to ask viewers to write to Oral Roberts, Tulsa, Oklahoma. When the letters came, the Oral Roberts Evangelistic Association efficiently opened them, read them, responded to them, and counted the money that the partners contributed to the causes that Oral placed before them.

Roberts repeatedly stated that "the answering of the letters is the most important function of the ministry. . . . When you finally get through to a human being who will take time to sit down and write on a piece of paper the way he feels and what his needs are, that is the high moment of his life." While the volume of mail made it impossible for Oral either to read or to answer personally more than a minute fraction of the letters received (though it is probable that many partners have never understood the workings of mass mail), the Roberts organization developed a sophisticated system which, Oral believed, had integrity and gave him a personal link with his far-flung partners. "This is why we have so little competition," he told a faculty group in 1974. "We have very few people that are concerned with people as we are."[220]

The mail system which was devised in the 1960s was perhaps the most important contribution of Al Bush to the ministry.[221] It was efficient, effective, and probably as personal as any such mass mail system could be. A letter received by the association was considered an invitation both to respond and to present the Oral Roberts program. Every letter written to the association was answered immediately, without discrimination between those making contributions and those not. The response sometimes included free literature, as well as information about the ministry. The correspondent was treated as a potential partner and received monthly letters teaching the "principles of seed-faith" giving. A relatively small percentage ultimately became permanent partners of the ministry.[222]

Oral defended his mail system on two main grounds. First, "every letter that comes to us is read" by some "dedicated person." While Oral did not read the letters, he was sent printouts of the names of those who had requested prayer, with their "needs" broken down into "categories."[223] Second, and more crucial in the ministry's defense of its methods, Oral did indirectly participate in answering the letters. Every two weeks the stenographers at the evangelistic association who read the letters were given sets of paragraphs designed to answer the questions and problems of the writers. The stenographer selected the paragraphs which seemed appropriate, ostensibly making the letter a personal response from Oral. For many years Al Bush composed the letters, drafting paragraphs from notes scribbled by Oral on yellow legal pads. "I would take his words and I would use his construction," recalled Bush, "and I thought I always did that very well."[224] Oral controlled the mail jealously, as he did *Abundant Life,* considering it the most crucial and personal part of the ministry. In 1974, he explained that he and Evelyn had been composing paragraphs around their breakfast table: "I don't feel right unless I do that. As my secretary, Mrs. Rooks, has often reminded me, God has called me. And while I have good associates, I am responsible."[225]

Whatever Oral's connection to the letter writing, the ethics of a direct mail ministry addressing personal letters to millions of people could be defended only by an "extension" theory, which was explored by Evelyn and Al Bush in a conversation in 1971:

> EVELYN: But, wouldn't you say that in most instances, especially if a person has a need that what they get will actually be Oral's words.
> AL: Oh yes.
> EVELYN: He might not have written it that morning, but at some time or another he wrote these down.
> AL: To someone, to an actual person and the answer applied to this other person that had the same problem. . . .
> EVELYN: So in that sense he actually is answering the letter although he's not doing the mechanics of it.
> AL: If you can accept the fact that as a minister you are an extension of Christ in this world, you have to accept the premise that we are establishing here in answering our mail, that we are an extension of Oral Roberts in a sense. The ladies, all the people that work in the mail answering situation are an extension of him. They understand him, they take his answers and they apply them to the needs as they are presented in the letters.
> EVELYN: . . . that's a good answer too that we can give to other people because I know a lot of times Oral says to people you write to me and I will answer your letter. And I've had people say to me, "Now he couldn't possibly do that." . . . But he actually believes, he looks on these two or three or four hundred people, Al, that's working over there as himself.
> AL: We are his extension.[226]

Oral and Evelyn did receive "obvious problem letters" and those "that have important ramifications for one reason or another."[227] At times, such as during the financial crisis of 1968 and 1969, Oral spent considerable amounts of time with the mail.[228] He was repeatedly drawn back to the letters that made the ministry possible. "I have sat down with my mail the past few weeks," he told the university students in 1969, "as I never have before, and I have always paid attention to our mail. I have had the feeling that when we answer a letter, we are not answering on a piece of paper, we are dealing with a human being."[229] Oral and Evelyn always came away from reading the mail filled with personal stories. Some of it was amusing, such as the correspondent who asked Oral to "pray for me to get a girl I met. I have a love for her. It could be puppy love, but she is as cute as a cucumber."[230] But the common denominator that ran through most of the letters was a cry for help from those in need. "What's the tone of the letters?" responded Oral: "The same. It's a funny thing about people crying about the hard times and inflation and you know, I've never had any other time in my life. It's always been hard. And for twenty some years people have written me about their problems. . . . Our mail is no different now than it was in prosperity. . . . It's always been hard." To read his mail, Oral believed, was to know the heartaches of America: "We know what's going on in the country a lot quicker than the President of the United States knows." The answers to those problems, he was convinced, were to be found in the "timeless truths of the Bible," truths he tried to ferret out for his partners.[231]

If Oral was likely never to see the vast majority of his partners face to face, those who were most loyal and generous were invited to Tulsa to attend a seminar. Essentially revisions of the World Outreach conferences begun in the 1950s, the meetings were called laymen's seminars or partners' seminars. Those attending the seminars met their own travel expenses, while the ministry provided the accommodations for their three- or four-day visits to the university campus. The meetings were designed for those "very interested" in Oral's work; generally speaking, those attending were people who had contributed substantially to the ministry over a period of two or three years.[232]

The format of the seminars became fairly standardized. The partners were treated to Oral preaching one or two of his old sermons, as well as to appearances by Richard and other leaders of the ministry and performances by the World Action Singers. The university and its students were on display when the partners came to campus; everyone was alerted to be at his or her best: "This is the week when we have our Laymen's Seminar and it's an opportunity to present not only the university but your own personal witness for Christ. Usually some half of the guests don't know our Lord as a personal Savior. And that may sound strange to some, but many of the people who watch the television program . . . don't know the Lord."[233] In the months after Oral's return to television in 1969, the seminars were jammed with people who had never been in a crusade, or on campus, or to a previous conference.[234] Before they left, they had a sample of how it had been— the old-fashioned sermons, the altar calls, and the healing line with Oral praying and laying on hands. In the midst of this spiritual retreat for the partners, reported Oral, "I really try not to think about what they're going to do for us. We're human and we have to live with that. But I try not to think about it because I get selfish . . . and . . . the Lord lets me down. . . . I've got to think about him and minister to him and be willing for him to come here and leave without giving a dollar and still feel good toward him."[235]

But eventually the subject did turn to money. Even in the seminars, Oral insisted, "we don't ask people for money," but, on the other hand, the seminars were admittedly fund-raisers. Told that rumor had it that those attending the seminars had "better carry your pocketbook because you are going to pledge everything you are going to make from now on," Oral protested that "we invite people to Tulsa to see our work and we explain it to them and they are given an opportunity to pledge, but they know that."[236] In the 1960s, Oral urged his partners to form a Blessing Pact with him; in the 1970s the exhortation was the same—one needed to give to God, and Oral had a project which he believed was worthy of support. Whether a building or a television special, Oral sliced the project into pieces large and small and offered it to the partners: "We take a building and divide it into parts, as low as $180, or as high as $100,000. It might have 3,000 parts. It's amazing how many parts I can find in a building when I start."[237] A typical presentation in 1969 urged those attending a seminar to sponsor a television special:

> Now I want you to help me do it. And if you will, when I enter into a Blessing Pact with you, you will get your needs met. And here's how we will do it. Now the special is far more expensive than the half hour. . . . Have you seen it? Do you agree with me? We can compete with anybody (applause). If you are as tired as I am of God's people doing it second class, I'm ready to do first class for the Lord (applause). Here's what a special cost us, we do it at the NBC studio and the price is fantastic. . . . They charge $75,000 for the studio and the cameramen and all the stuff that you do. . . . We are on 190 stations in Canada and the United States. We are now negotiating for foreign countries. . . . I want you to put down 10, just 10, then put a dash by it, and please everybody do this. Everybody in the room. . . . All right, now, if you don't have something to write, borrow a pen, borrow a piece of paper, put down 10 and dash and put down $7,500. Now that will equal $75,000 which is the mechanical cost of NBC studios for an hour. . . . Now put down under that four, four dash and put down $5,000. The four biggest television markets in the United States beginning with New York and Los Angeles, the average cost for the hour time is $5,000. Now the next big markets, there are ten, like Washington, D.C. and Houston, Texas, Atlanta, Georgia, Detroit, and put down $2,000, the average cost of these ten stations is $2,000 for each one hour time. So put down ten dash $2,000. Under that put down thirty-six. The thirty-six largest markets average cost is $1,000 for one hour. That's what we pay in Oklahoma City. Under that put down 106, the next 106 markets at $300. Those smaller markets, around 800,000 or a million viewers. And then put down 190 at $120 and that's for the duplicate of the video tape. In other words, we make this master tape in color at NBC and then we have to duplicate it. . . . Now in this room there are people chosen of God and you are to do a certain thing. You are to do one of these things. One of them is your depth and there's where you will get your miracle. You don't get it at any other amount.[238]

Once the presentation was completed, the partners began to stream to the front as the sums were called out—$7,500 to $120. Oral encouraged them forward:

Are you number six, my sister? All right, thank you, Lord. Partner, you've been a partner for quite sometime, haven't you? . . . I just hope you folks will see this, feel something in your heart. . . . Let's give her a hand, will you, and all of them a hand (applause). They have been partners, I know then, for quite some time. That touches me very deeply. I've got to do a good job, a better job."[239]

The projects Oral offered to his partners changed through the years with the ebb and flow of the ministry. From 1960 to 1975, the emphasis moved from the crusades to the concept of World Action and overseas evangelism, to the university, and finally to television. He urged his partners to give "where you know beyond any doubt that souls are being won to Christ." Whatever the most visible project at the moment, Oral's job was to describe it to the partners in the most compelling terms.[240] Building his partner base was an imperative he received from God in 1960: "You are to increase the number of your partners immediately! Through them you will be able to do these things."[241]

What did the partners receive in return for supporting the Roberts ministry? Basically, the "very personal" prayers of Oral:

Remember, I want to pray for you and your loved ones. I want to hold your names in my hand and pray. I want to believe for miracles to happen to you. Each time in the past I've felt led to enter into a special time of prayer like this over something definite, God has answered! If you will fill in the names of yourself and your loved ones in the place indicated and mail to me today, I should get them tomorrow or the next day and I shall start to pray at once.[242]

Over and over, Oral assured his partners that God would bless them: "Tell the partners that I will bless and prosper them. I will put money in their hands from new avenues of income and earnings."[243] "Oh God how I want You to help my partners," Oral implored in June 1971, "and You will!"[244]

Oral's fund-raising methods sometimes seemed to grow more sophisticated, but he always continued the use of tokens and symbolism. In the 1960s, regular partners were sent a Blessing Pact Covenant, with the instructions: "Keep your Blessing Pact Covenant inside of the cover of your Bible. As I prayed over it, I felt God's anointing upon me, therefore it is anointed. Use it as a point of contact for the releasing of your faith."[245] Later partners were given Seed-Faith booklets, with monthly coupons to fill in requesting prayer and noting the amount of contribution. The book instructed: "Place this faith book where you keep your important bills like water, gas, electric, etc. The first of each month put God's work first in your life."[246] And there was a constant barrage of special times and mementos designed to draw the partners to the ministry—periods when Oral would spend long hours praying in the Prayer Tower, or place the names of the partners in a Joash Chest to be placed in the chapel, or "lay the name of each partner before the Lord" in the Upper Room in Jerusalem.[247]

Some of the appeals embarrassed Oral's more sophisticated young administrations. It was a heated clash over the inclusion of Seed-Faith testimonials which led to Wayne Robinson's resignation in 1969 as editor of *Abundant Life*.

In late 1968, Robinson was outraged when Oral, beset by deep financial troubles following his move to the Methodist church, hired religious fund-raiser Gene Ewing as a consultant and followed his advice to redesign *Abundant Life* magazine. Ewing, a sometime evangelist and direct mail consultant for a number of independent ministers, including Billy James Hargis, Rex Humbard, and T. L. Osborn, was pictured by Robinson as a bizarre, surrealistic character who traveled with a semiliterate entourage in custom-made limousines. But he was a widely recognized "genius" at devising religious messages to reach the masses; even Robinson grudgingly conceded that Ewing was "one of the world's smartest communicators." While Oral's appeals in the late 1960s were not different in kind from what he had used earlier in his career, the influence of Ewing was clearly visible. In 1968, in return for his help, Oral gave Ewing an airplane, and on more than one occasion afterward he awarded Ewing generous commissions to help him find his bearings back to his supporters.[248]

While Oral Roberts's fund-raising techniques sometimes harked back to the 1950s, during the decade and a half from 1960 to 1975, the organization also developed more sophisticated approaches. In 1965, the evangelistic association established a Christian stewardship department to develop an annuities program and to aid in the preparation of wills. Prospective benefactors were well instructed on the benefits and methods of estate planning.[249] In addition, in 1965 a home ministries department was established, employing several "spirit-filled" ministers as "regional representatives" to contact important partners. By 1978, there were fourteen such representatives in the United States and Canada.[250]

The building of Oral Roberts University made the city of Tulsa another potential source of funds for the Roberts ministry.[251] At the same time, the growth of the university endowment fund, approaching $20,000,000 in the early 1970s, made the university a considerable financial power in the community. The endowment funds were invested in several banks in the Tulsa area and were used for "real estate development on a modest level."[252]

Oral attracted a few substantial supporters through the years. But most of those on the ministry's boards were middle-class people; an individual gift of as much as $100,000 was still a rarity in the mid-1970s. "I don't know many millionaires as friends," Oral told his students in 1971, "but I'm praying for every one I know. And especially if they are graduates and they're on their way to becoming millionaires."[253] In 1976, most of the partners gave contributions in the range of "$5 and $10 and $25." "We have two million families in America," reported Oral, "and I'd rather have two million people who would give a dollar at a time than one person who would give two million. Because if he ever got mad at me, I'd be dead. And these people are really tied to us. . . . They are tied to us because we're interested in them and we're concerned."[254] The amount the partners contributed rose steadily in the 1960s, to over $6,000,000 in 1968 before exploding after the return to television. Annual receipts doubled in 1969 and increased to nearly $25,000,000 by 1972.[255]

By the early 1970s, the Roberts partner family had become, in the words of Al Bush, a "vast church."[256] The most visible members of the family, those who came to the seminars, were jet pilots, businesswomen, morticians, school teachers, auto sales managers, corporate vice-presidents, physicians, chiropractors, farmers, salesmen, engineers, welders, housepainters, and widows.[257] But a profile of the larger body of partners was guesswork. Al Bush felt that the partners were becoming older in the early 1970s, but television may have changed that drift by 1975.[258] It was certain that they were less pentecostal than in earlier years; in fact, Oral was convinced in the 1970s that "the majority . . . don't enter church at all."[259] But all that was certain was that they felt a need, and they believed that Oral Roberts could help them—and would help them— and that they had been inspired to contribute to the vision which Oral had described to them.

CHAPTER

XI

Mainstream

I N 1960, WHEN Episcopalian priest Dennis Bennett announced to his Van Nuys, California congregation that he had spoken in tongues, the widely reported incident was heralded as the beginning of the "neopentecostal" or "charismatic" movement in mainstream American Protestantism.[1] Of couse, the importance of Bennett's experience was partly symbolic; doubtless "untold thousands had received the pentecostal experience and remained in their churches *sub rosa* before this time."[2] But in 1960, speaking in tongues still seemed aberrant and bizarre to most American Christians; by the end of the decade an estimated ten percent of the Episcopal clergy had become charismatic, and there had been outbreaks of tongues speaking at Princeton and Yale. By 1975, nearly every major American denomination had a charismatic wing.[3]

Perhaps even more startling was the news that tongues speaking had erupted on the campus of Notre Dame in 1966. Initially led by American Catholics such as Kevin Ranaghan and Ralph Martin, the charismatic movement blossomed worldwide within the Catholic church under the name of Charismatic Renewal. The espousal of the movement by Leon Joseph Cardinal Suenens, archbishop of Brussels-Malines, Belgium, and his appointment by Pope Paul VI as overseer of the Catholic Charismatic Renewal gave the new movement both added prestige and new power. Estimates of the number of charismatics within the Catholic church in America varied from 200,000 to more than 1,000,000 in the 1970s. They quickly became a powerful, if not dominating, force within the broader charismatic movement. The Catholic movement furnished some of the ablest and most prolific theological spokesmen for the charismatic experience.[4]

Like all revivals in their beginnings, the charismatic revival of the 1960s was ill-defined theologically and institutionally unstructured, blazing outside the confines of the organized denominations with few institutions of its own and without clear leaders. The revival's first leaders were its celebrities, Kathryn Kuhlman, Pat Boone, and, preeminently, Oral Roberts. Unquestionably, the revival's most important promoters were David du Plessis, Demos Shakarian's Full Gospel Business Men's Fellowship International, and Roberts.[5]

No one in the pentecostal world was more aware of or more attuned to the charismatic revival in the mainstream churches than Oral. When he assembled pentecostal leaders in Tulsa in the early 1960s to announce the beginning of the university, he regaled them with stories of what God was doing in the mainstream churches, believing that "this is the hour of the Holy Spirit": "The new tide today is the move of the Holy Spirit. God is stirring up people's hearts. God is invading our churches. There are many unscheduled acts of the Holy Spirit. . . . He's moving into the other churches." Oral sensed an openness in the Roman Catholic church long before the renewal broke out and urged pentecostals to discard their anti-Catholic prejudices: "Faith is where you find it. God comes into people's hearts and when we try to read labels and say well he's labeled this therefore he's a Christian, if he has this label he's not a Christian, then we become judges."[6]

Oral's crusades had kept his healing hand on the pulse of mainstream American Christianity. Over and over he emphasized to the press the high percentage of nonpentecostal people attending his campaigns—by the time the crusades ended, his team estimated that the audience were often eighty-five percent nonpentecostal.[7] Increasingly estranged from the pentecostal denominations, Roberts and the other healing ministers welcomed and promoted the hunger for the Holy Spirit in the older churches.[8] It was Oral's sensing of this hunger which led him to begin preaching on the baptism of the Holy Spirit in his crusades in 1961. In 1963 he reported: "There's a change today. And people in this hour seem to want the Holy Spirit. . . . In our meetings we have as many as a thousand on one night."[9] "There is a time God sweeps in," Oral told his pentecostal friends, "and how happy are the people when they know it is God's time."[10]

The Full Gospel Business Men's Fellowship International proved to be an extraordinarily effective tool for spreading the pentecostal message to the American middle class. By 1975, it had 1,650 chapters, in every state and in fifty-two foreign countries. The average monthly attendance at its meetings included over 500,000 of the world's business and political leaders.[11] The fellowship, like the crusades of the healing evangelists, became less and less pentecostal, until by the 1970s it was a polyglot of denominationalists united only by their experience with the Holy Spirit. The FGBMFI increasingly made use of the gifted charismatic ministers appearing in the mainstream denominations, while the old-time healing revivalists became less visible. But the relationship between Oral Roberts and the FGBMFI remained constant—he was the organization's high priest and most coveted friend.[12] The members of the fellowship were probably the most important reservoir of funds in the building of Oral

Roberts University; Shakarian and Roberts never faltered in their belief that each was specially raised up to spread the baptism of the Holy Spirit to the wider world.[13]

Oral also related cordially and supportively to David du Plessis, a South African minister who after 1960 was the quasi-official pentecostal representative to mainstream Christianity. Dubbed a "World Council of Churches gadfly" by *Christianity Today,* du Plessis came to be known as "Mr. Pentecost" and "Brother Ecumenical."[14] David du Plessis's ecumenism, like that of the healing evangelists, irked the pentecostal denominations; some charged that he was compromising with "modernism and ecumenical apostasy."[15] In 1962, the Assemblies of God revoked du Plessis's ministerial credentials; they were not restored until 1980.[16] Oral and du Plessis worked in common cause during the 1960s to spread the pentecostal experience to mainstream Christians. Wayne Robinson summarized their contributions: "Whereas Roberts was the Pentecostal champion who slew the Goliaths, du Plessis worked quietly behind the scenes. Where Roberts worked with the masses, du Plessis sought to influence the decision-makers."[17] Oral regarded du Plessis as a "warm friend and brother"; in 1964, he commended him to the readers of *Abundant Life:* "David du Plessis is doing an outstanding work among the historical churches in helping their leaders see the baptism with the Holy Spirit, and divine healing. He is a good ambassador for ORU, too. We appreciate him in the Lord."[18]

Perhaps Oral's most direct contribution to the spreading of the charismatic movement in the early 1960s was made by the series of conferences sponsored by the School of Evangelism in the 1960s. The conferences brought together an unprecedented mix of pentecostal and nonpentecostal ministers and laypeople to discuss the Holy Spirit and the meaning of its move into the mainstream churches. The earliest conferences were almost entirely pentecostal, but at the first ministers' seminar in 1963, David du Plessis told the delegates that he had "learned that the Holy Spirit knows how to behave in any kind of church."[19] By the mid-1960s, nonpentecostals had come to dominate the conferences. But it was the blend of the seminars that made them theological hothouses for the budding charismatic movement—bringing together as they did talented people from scores of theological traditions to discuss the meaning of the baptism of the Holy Spirit. The second seminar, held in the spring of 1963, included among its speakers Howard M. Ervin, charismatic Baptist minister, and subsequent conferences presented a roster of important American charismatic ministers, including Episcopalian Dennis Bennett, Presbyterian James Brown, and Methodist Tommy Tyson.[20] Many who attended those conferences reflected in later years that neither Oral nor the other participants "quite understood what he had a hold of"; their meetings were probably the closest thing to planning sessions that the spontaneous revival had.[21]

The most spectacular of the conferences was the international seminar held in November 1963. Over two hundred delegates were flown to Tulsa at the expense of the Oral Roberts Evangelistic Association to participate in the twelve-day meeting. R. O. Corvin, Bob DeWeese, Manford Engel, and Steve Durasoff traveled the globe selecting delegates, bringing to Tulsa representatives from over fifty countries.[22] The delegates, 127 of whom flew to Tulsa on a chartered Air France 707 jet from Paris, were treated to a who's who of speakers from the university and the budding charismatic movement—including R. O. Corvin, Demos Shakarian, David du Plessis, Lutheran Larry Christiansen, and Oral Roberts. Oral issued a welcoming charge: "We called this seminar because God told us to call it. We are all here because God is ready to give a new measure of the Spirit to the world. We need a new breed of men. We need the new wine of the Spirit. We need an invasion of the Holy Ghost upon us."[23]

Once Oral Roberts University opened, it became the centerpiece of the charismatic movement. "The Lord had ORU built," said Episcopalian priest Jerry Schindler after visiting the campus in 1968, "to show that real scholarship and the gift of the Holy Spirit are not contradictory."[24] The faculty soon included representatives from the mainstream churches; among the important early additions to the Graduate School of Theology were Howard M. Ervin, who held a doctorate in theology from Princeton, and Charles Farah, Jr., an ordained Presbyterian minister with a doctorate from Edinburgh University.[25] The faculty and student body of the university became a barometer for measuring the spread of the charismatic movement into American Protestantism and Catholicism. In an interview with the Catholic charismatic magazine *New Covenant* in 1972, ORU chaplain Bob Stamps extolled: "ORU is really ecumenical, and it's a special work of the Lord."[26]

Oral Roberts University provided a platform for speakers from every wing of the charismatic revival. In the years from 1960 to 1975, virtually every important charismatic leader in the world visited the campus, expressed his or her views, and was exposed to the personality and vision of Oral Roberts. The parade was endless—Dr. William Standish Reed, "beloved, Spirit-filled, Episcopalian physician and surgeon," who had befriended Oral in the 1950s; Dennis Bennett and his wife, Rita (the sister of Reed); Lutheran Larry Christiansen; Catholic charismatic Kevin Ranaghan; Charles Blair of Denver; Pat Robertson; Michael Harper, charismatic Anglican priest from London; Ralph Wilkerson; and David Wilkerson, author of *The Cross and the Switchblade* and the founder of Teen Challenge ministries; and scores of others. The university, according to Vinson Synan, "gave a type of intellectual respectability to pentecostalism."[27]

Of those visitors, the one who probably influenced Oral most was Ralph Wilkerson, pastor of the Melodyland Christian Center in Anaheim, California, which in the 1970s became one of the largest churches in the world. He visited the campus several times in the 1960s and 1970s, lecturing to the students and speaking in seminars. Oral acknowledged that Wilkerson "had a great influence on my life in the past several years and is among the men in the world who are really turning the world upside down for the Lord."[28]

In addition to the rising generation of charismatic leaders who visited the campus, older evangelists who, like Oral, had attracted growing followings also spoke at the university. Rex Humbard was a frequent visitor and unabashed supporter of the school. In 1973, the university honored Humbard, Charles Blair, and Ralph Wilkerson by granting them honorary doctorates.[29]

The charismatic personality who most captured Oral's respect in the early

1970s was Kathryn Kuhlman. Kulhman was introduced to Oral by Humbard, and in 1968, after Roberts stopped campaigning, she had the most visible healing ministry in the country. She had long admired Oral; he believed that "she represented the finest of the healing ministry of Jesus."[30] Kuhlman made frequent visits to Tulsa in the last years of her life, giving the baccalaureate address at ORU in 1972 and receiving the university's first honorary doctorate the same year.[31] The flamboyant evangelist signed on as "head cheerleader" for the university and was a warm friend of the Roberts family at the time of her death in 1976.[32]

Roberts's friendship with Billy Graham—highlighted by Oral's presence in Berlin and Graham's dedication address at ORU—did much to lessen tensions between charismatics and evangelicals. The spread of the charismatic movement into the mainstream churches, bringing unexpected acceptance to the pentecostal experience of speaking in tongues, and Oral's discovery of the evangelical world and welcome into it were, in Calvin Thielman's words, "a happy combination of events."[33] While many evangelicals remained reserved about pentecostals and Roberts—the movements still remain "half-sisters" with considerable "sibling rivalry"—Oral's embrace by Graham was sufficient to open many doors.[34] In the afterglow of the dedication day ceremonies, young charismatic Southern Baptist Pat Robertson remarked: "I think this is . . . a world significant moment among evangelical Christians. I think this will mark a great growing together of forces."[35] In the years following the Berlin congress, Oral Roberts University hosted a procession of noncharismatic evangelical speakers, including Leighton Ford, F. F. Bruce, Josh McDowell, and Hal Lindsey.

Of course, Oral had long had good relations with many of the mainstream preachers of Tulsa, frequently attending the Episcopalian, Presbyterian, and Methodist churches of the city and counting Southern Baptist pastor Warren Hultgren among his best friends.[36] But his influence among the mainstream churches mushroomed after the Berlin conference. One of the people he invited to the campus in the wake of that conference was Bob Lamont, pastor of the First Presbyterian Church in Pittsburgh; Lamont insisted that Oral come to preach in his church. Returning from Pittsburgh, Oral spoke excitedly about the visit and its meaning:

> So we went up to Pittsburgh this weekend and his great church which is an old church established in 1778 was packed to the rafters with chairs in the aisles and a big overflow room packed. . . . After preaching yesterday morning, he had the board of his church to take us out for dinner. And after we had eaten, he asked me to stand and share with these people on two things, healing and speaking in tongues, which I did. And last night he asked me to preach again and we had an overflow audience and I made an altar call and some seventy-five people came up to accept the Lord. I felt like pinching myself and saying, "Is this real." . . . I believe the greatest mission field in America is the historic churches. People who are hungry for the Holy Spirit.[37]

In the years following Oral's switch to the Methodist church in 1968, he was inundated with invitations to speak at Methodist conferences and churches, as well as in other denominations. "I've been so well received by these groups," he told his faculty in 1974, "it scared me. . . . I've never had the luxury of being so well received through all the years. . . . I want to tell you there's someting going on today."[38]

Oral was just as elated by the spread of the charismatic experience into the Catholic church, publicly commending the movement and calling ORU to its attention.[39] Leaders of the Catholic Renewal visited the campus to speak, along with other charismatic figures. One of the lecturers in Oral's "Holy Spirit in the Now" course in the mid-1970s was Francis MacNutt, a priest and the most prominent Catholic with a healing ministry in the 1970s.[40]

The role of Oral Roberts and his university in promoting and coordinating the charismatic movements from 1960 to 1975 was no accident. Oral placed himself in the midst of the revival with foresight and calculation—he believed he was fulfilling the prophecy he had announced in Denver in 1948, that he would aid in bringing a "healing for the sick body of the bride of Christ."[41] He was confident that the renewed interest in the Holy Spirit would bring a new fervor and unity to divided Christendom. Through the 1950s, Oral had no inkling of how the healing of the church would come about, but in the mid-1960s he believed a way was opening.

Roberts had never forgotten the message he received in Denver. At the time the prophecy had seemed quixotic and presumptuous for a young man only a year removed from the Pentecostal Holiness parsonage in Enid, Oklahoma. But in the 1960s, Oral launched out to take the Holy Spirit to mainstream Christians, seeing the charismatic revival and himself as forerunners of the second coming of Christ.[42] In 1968, reflecting on his crusades, he claimed a share of credit for the charismatic revival: "There has been a ministry of healing and miracles demonstrated before this nation in these past twenty years, on radio, on television, in the crusades. Something has happened. And in most every denomination today there is at least some degree of new emphasis on healing, on the Holy Spirit. And not all of it can be attributed to our ministry, but some of it can and to God we give the glory."[43] Ten years later, Oral told his faculty with justifiable pride: "We're in the midst of the unfolding of the Charismatic movement. I could have said that part of that new understanding of the Charismatic movement began right out here on this campus in the early 60s, and parts of it began other places on the earth, but that this is one of the centers of the Charismatic movement in the world."[44] The charismatic revival of the 1960s and 1970s in American Protestantism and Catholicism was, of course, a response to a growing hunger for experience in those traditional streams. But no individual more acutely discerned that hunger, or more effectively fed it, than Oral Roberts. It was Roberts, reflected pentecostal historian Vinson Synan, "who made pentecost interesting to professors and churchmen."[45]

Oral's contributions to the charismatic movement were partly social; he informally linked the diverse leaders of the revival. But he also participated in the earliest efforts to buld an intellectual platform from which to launch a charismatic theology. Methodist theologian Albert Outler called Roberts "an important phenomenon," because he brought "a degree of intellectual depth to the revivalist tradition."[46] In the early 1960s, Oral and R. O. Corvin, frequently in consultation with other charismatic leaders, began a concentrated study of speaking in tongues, spending "as high as eighteen hours a day with our Bibles and the Greek."[47] Oral's drift toward mainstream Christianity was accompanied by a change in his theology of the Holy Spirit and the meaning of speaking in tongues. He saw his new theology as a mixture of "second-generation Pentecostal" ideas enlightened by the older theological traditions: "We need each other, and that's what ORU is all about."[48] Roberts's later view discarded the pentecostal notion that speaking in tongues was the "initial evidence" of the baptism of the Holy Spirit, making the experience rather an instrumental tool to be used in the life of every Christian to guide the intellect.[49] Oral boldly floated his new ideas in the early ministerial seminars on the ORU campus, honing them on his pentecostal and charismatic critics. "His theology affected pentecostalism," observed Vinson Synan, forcing pentecostal consideration of the notion that glossolalia was a "prayer language."[50] At the same time, Oral was redefining the pentecostal emphasis on the Holy Spirit and the gifts of the Spirit into an experience that made sense in the traditional churches. "I began to wake up and understand," he said in 1977, "that we can close this gulf between us and we can be a body, we can be one."[51]

THE MOST controversial single act in Oral Roberts's religious life was probably his decision in 1968 to leave the Pentecostal Holiness church to become a Methodist minister. On Sunday morning, March 17, Oral and Evelyn joined four other persons at the chancel rail of the Boston Avenue Methodist Church in Tulsa to be received into the congregation by Dr. Finis A. Crutchfield, the senior minister. Crutchfield spoke warmly of Roberts as "my colleague in Christ"; he acknowledged that Oral had not changed his "fundamental faith" but simply desired "to affiliate himself in Tulsa with an inclusive church that seeks to proclaim the universal Christian gospel."[52] It was a dramatic act, catching the religious world by surprise and gaining attention throughout the nation.[53] One "friend of President Johnson" thanked Oral for "taking this step because they are no longer talking about him in Vietnam."[54]

Oral's change was a thunderclap inside as well as outside his ministry. As always, the move was not so precipitous as it seemed; it was a decision he had "carried for months."[55] In January and February, Roberts told a crusade audience, "the Lord began to deal with" him seriously about the switch.[56] He privately discussed the matter with several members of his organization and family—Mama and Papa Roberts supported the move enthusiastically, as did Bob DeWeese and his wife.[57] In February, two weeks before Oral and Evelyn joined Boston Avenue, Carl Hamilton placed his membership at the church.[58] But others, including Lee Braxton and Oscar Moore, were adamantly against the move, believing it would have "serious repercussions" on the ministry.[59] As the number of people who knew of Oral's discussions with the Methodists grew, he feared that news of the change might leak out. The immediate decision was, therefore, made hastily in March, shocking some of Roberts's closest friends and catching unprepared most of the ORU faculty.[60]

The arrangements for Oral's change in churches were carefully planned and orchestrated. Evelyn had attended Boston Avenue with some regularity for years, and in 1966 she became a member of the Women's Society of Christian Service at the church. Oral attended the congregation occasionally, as he did other churches in Tulsa, and came to know rather well the church's influential minister, Finis Crutchfield. At a Christmas party in 1967, Crutchfield suggested to Oral that he ought to be a Methodist and, Wayne Robinson believed, was somewhat suprised when Oral asked Robinson to pursue the matter.[61] After this initial acknowledgment of the possibility by the two men, Roberts and Crutchfield began to seriously explore the meanings of such a move. Oral later recalled the gist of one of their conversations:

> Finis said, "Oral, I have fine men in my church who are from your university. . . . They are the most effective Christians in my church." I said, "Well, do you all know they speak in tongues. They all believe in healing." He said, "Oh, I'm very much aware of that. . . . They're not carrying this around as a badge of superiority. They're interested in helping people and building the kingdom." "Well," I said, "whoever has this experience should be like that."[62]

After several such discussions, Crutchfield became convinced that the move would be good for his church and arranged for a meeting between Oral and Bishop W. Angie Smith, who presided over the Oklahoma Conference of the Methodist church. In befriending Finis Crutchfield, Oral had allied himself with one of the most respected and powerful Methodist clergymen in the nation, a minister who in the 1980s rose to the position of president of the United Methodist church's council of bishops. Crutchfield's role in the affair was a selfless one that could have stalled his own rise to a bishop's seat; but he was genuinely interested in Oral and the "spiritual formation" of his church.[63]

The timing was right when Oral met with Bishop Smith. On the verge of retirement, Smith was an open-minded, "straight talking guy," who told Oral: "We need you, but we need the Holy Spirit more than we need you and we've got to have the Holy Spirit in the Methodist church." The bishop was ebullient about what Oral could bring to his church, assuring him that it would be "the crowning effort of my ministry if I could take you into the Methodist Church before I retire."[64] Roberts was ready, and the bishop was "so strong," Oral recalled, that he "just took it and ran with it."[65]

Oral was flattered by the reception he received from Crutchfield and Smith, but, at the same time, he made certain that none of his beliefs were compromised by the move. In his discussion with Crutchfield and Smith, Oral emphasized his unwillingness to sacrifice his "calling," reminding them that "if you take me into the Methodist church you can never turn out of the Methodist church anybody who speaks with tongues because I speak in tongues every day."[66] When the news became public, Roberts emphasized that "there will be no change in my standard of the Full Gospel message or of my life, my ministry, or of ORU."[67] "The Methodist church is a roomy church," assured Crutchfield. "It doesn't seek to impose conformity on its members and it encourages every sincere approach to God."[68]

During the discussions preceding Oral's move, it was agreed that he would be ordained into the Methodist clergy, subject to the approval of the Conference Board of Ministerial Training. It was also agreed, however, that Oral would seek ordination as a "local elder" rather than as an "elder-in-full-connection." Methodist ministers were divided into a complicated set of categories, basically designed to set apart those with full-time ministries who participated in the church's pension fund and were annually assigned to their positions by the bishop. Oral did not want an ordination which placed him under the assignment authority of the bishop, and the "local elder" category seemed a good compromise. In 1968, the local elder's ordination carried essentially the same weight and privileges as elder-in-full-connection, but in the 1970s a clearer distinction was made, which would leave Oral dissatisfied with his ordination. Wayne Robinson, who had been Oral's chief advisor on the matter at the time, subsequently admitted that he had been ill-informed and should not have advised Roberts to accept the local-elder ordination.[69]

Oral was assigned a correspondence course to complete before his ordination, and, with the aid of several of his theology professors, he completed it with high marks. There was some tension when the conference committee reviewed Roberts's irregular ordination. Oral reconstructed the dialogue when he appeared before the committee:

> "Dr. Roberts, why do you want to become a Methodist?" I said, "I want to be Christian. My main desire in life is to be a Christian and to be a Holy Ghost minister." "Well, why do you want to do it in the Methodist Church?" I said, "Because I think it has the widest framework and the freest pulpit. . . . And if I can make a contribution to the people in the Methodist Church . . . I want it. And if you feel I can not, you should say so right here in front of me, and we can stop this thing immediately."

The committee unanimously recommended his ordination.[70]

Oral was ordained an elder in the Methodist church on May 27, 1968, at the meeting of the Oklahoma Conference in Oklahoma City, the last meeting presided over by Bishop Angie Smith after twenty-four years as leader of the conference. Although Oral had completed the course of study necessary to qualify him for the ministry, in a magnanimous act that removed any chance of future challenge, Smith declined to reordain Oral, but rather accepted his Pentecostal Holiness ordination. The Methodist church had clear precedent for accepting ministers who did not meet its educational qualifications, because of the church's recent merger with the Evangelical United Brethren, whose ministers had been accepted into the uniting church without additional certification. Oral was among eighteen others who knelt before the bishop for ordination, but when he approached Roberts, Smith stated: "Brother Roberts comes to the Methodist Church from another background. Those who laid their hands upon him whom I do not know, have just as much authority as I, for the real ordination is finally not by human hands but it is of the Holy Spirit. Brother Roberts comes to us an ordained minister and therefore we do not require the laying on of hands."[71] It was over and done; Oral Roberts had formally entered the mainstream of American Protestantism.

Oral's entry into the Methodist church was not without opposition from within; some Methodists compared it to the admission of the pope.[72] Several church officials criticized the move publicly on the grounds that Oral had an "improper educational background," that his healing ministry had not been "proved," and that "immense personal wealth has accrued to his ministry."[73] In Oklahoma, "a rumor persisted of circulation of a petition which would seek to prevent Tulsa evangelist Oral Roberts from being accepted into the Methodist ministry," but such a petition never surfaced.[74] Bishop Smith reportedly received enough hostile mail that he told Wayne Robinson that Oral should grant no interviews at the ordination ceremonies.[75]

In the short run, however, Methodist reaction was quite favorable. The backing of Crutchfield and Smith cut short most criticism. Other Methodist leaders seemed equally enthusiastic about what Oral could bring to the church. Dr. Larry Eisenberg of the General Board of Evangelism of the Methodist church hoped Oral would "bring back the tremendous dynamics that the church once possessed."[76] Oral was pleased by the welcome he received. He was flooded with invitations to speak in Methodist churches and at conferences. "I've got over 400 invitations," he said in 1970. "I can only take a handful. But they all want me to preach on the baptism with the Holy Ghost and divine healing."[77] In 1977, Oral still believed that the move had been a success: "I may not have been a blessing to anybody, but I've been the happiest man these last nine years I have been in the thirty years of my ministry because I am home."[78]

On the other hand, Oral's relationship with his new church remained somewhat distant. Reporter Edward B. Fiske summed up the situation in 1973:

> Roberts' relationship to the Methodist church has been cordial but a bit unusual. . . . The church establishment has by and large played it cool. While virtually no one, even liberals, is willing to criticize him publicly, no one has offered him any major assignment within the denomination. As one well-known Methodist put it, "There just isn't any slot in our structure for someone with his own constituency."[79]

Oral's hope, and that of Bishop Smith and others, had been that he would play an important role in the rejuvenation of the Methodist church.[80] By 1975, it was apparent that he had collected a following among the people of the American Methodist church, but it was not so clear that he would ever become a counselor to the denomination's leaders.

The most forceful immediate reaction to Oral's decision to become a Methodist came from his former pentecostal friends. The announcement stunned and humiliated the pentecostal world. While everyone still remembered the bitter clashes between Oral and the Pentecostal Holiness church in the 1950s, most pentecostals presumed that relations had been improving for years. Bishop J. A. Synan had participated in the dedication of the university, and many Pentecostal Holiness laypeople viewed ORU as a quasi-denominational institution.[81] While a few die-hard Pentecostal Holiness leaders who had long opposed Oral "rejoiced" at his departure, those who had been his friends felt "betrayed" and "hurt."[82] In spite of Oral's insistence that he remained "Pentecostal from my head to my feet," his former friends, thousands of whom had been his partners, were shocked and angry.[83]

There was some irony in the resounding protest from the pentecostal world—many who condemned Oral's move most harshly had always resented his independence. "It was only when they identified that he had deserted them," noted Carl Hamilton, "that they acknowledged he was their leader."[84] In 1970, Oral reminisced about the tensions which had estranged him from his church:

> The heads of the Pentecostal movements never felt free with me. I can under-stand that because they could not control me and to be a member, particularly of a small denomination, it's very difficult to maintain your personal identity. . . . And the leaders have a very special problem because here is a person rising up who has enormous powers . . . over people. . . . People are praising him. It's the old statement back there that Saul has slain his thousands and David has slain his tens of thousands. Here Oral Roberts has done this great work, and what are you doing, brother? . . . The mass of the people related to the ministry. Now on the other hand, I never felt comfortable because I knew how they felt. I knew because they told me. They told me in private letters; they sent word to me. In the early fifties they meant to turn me out of my own church. . . . Now the hated . . . speckled bird is gone. No longer can a pastor visit a home who is outside Pentecost and he wants to win them and he has no entree, he has no way to sit down and relate and he will say, "Do you know Oral Roberts? . . . That's the church I represent!" . . . Because they won tens of thousands of people just through my name. . . . Also, many of them think they've made my ministry and now I've turned and bit the hand that fed me.[85]

As with all divorces, there was bitterness, the remembering of old re-sentments. But this divorce was demanded by the mind and not by the heart. Oral would never forget his debt to pentecostalism; he would not tolerate others' speaking ill of the movement. It was one of those marriages where one of the partners had, through the years, outgrown the other, aspiring to walk in circles the other could not—or would not.

Roberts and his team members tried to forecast the pentecostal reaction. Al Bush urged Oral to issue no public statement, to ride out the furor quietly as he had often done before. But others urged, and Oral agreed, that he should write a letter of explanation to his partners. It did little to ease the impact. Almost overnight the ministry lost between half and two-thirds of its pentecostal partners. Income fell between twenty and twenty-five percent.[86] Construction was halted on the student activities center, "delayed indefinitely" because of the diminishing income.[87] "It was a lonesome ol' time," recalled Oral years later.[88] Twice the ministry was forced to borrow money to meet its payroll, and the word *bankruptcy* was whispered outside Oral's hearing. Ron Smith later dubbed it the "Dark Summer of '68."[89] In 1972, Oral admitted that had he known the ferocity of the reaction against his change of churches, he would have been "tempted never to take the step."[90]

As always when under attack, Oral and Evelyn tried to reply to the hurt friends who wrote to them. "Letters filled with anger, bitterness, and hurt began to pour in by the thousands." Evelyn recalled. "We were accused of being

Communist, turning liberal, and bargaining away ORU."[91] Young Vinson Synan, son of the bishop of the Pentecostal Holiness church, had hoped that ORU would become "an intellectual center for the pentecostal world"; his hopes were shattered by Oral's change of churches. He wrote decrying the "real blow" Roberts had dealt to the "younger generation" of pentecostals, who had considered him "our champion, our hero." He received a handwritten reply from Oral thanking him for his concern, for the love he sensed in Synan's letter, but firmly replying that he felt it was God's will for him to join the Methodist church and that he believed pentecostal people would continue to support him.[92] By 1970, Oral judged that ninety percent of the pentecostal partners he had lost had returned; they had been joined by the tremendous influx of new partners attracted by the television series.[93]

For years after he changed churches, Oral was called on by newsmen to give public explanations. Many imagined that it was a simple bid to attract more affluent supporters. Actually, the motivation was much more complicated. Oral offered a series of different explanations; taken together, they made the choice seem inevitable.

Perhaps most cosmetic was Oral's assertion that he was returning to the church of his youth. Although he apparently had joined the Methodist church in Stratford as a youngster, his earliest religious loyalties were to the Pentecostal Holiness church. It was true, of course, that the Pentecostal Holiness church had strong doctrinal and historic kinship to Methodism; many of its members still looked on Methodism as the mother church.[94] Many of Oral's fellow pentecostals shared his sentiment: "I've been a Methodist and there's never been a time when I was not. It was bred in me and I simply came home."[95] Carl Hamilton spoke in a similar manner about his origins: "As far as I'm concerned there isn't any difference between the Pentecostal Holiness church and the Methodist church. Whether you're a pentecostal Methodist or a Methodist pentecostal, I don't know what the difference is."[96] When Oral discussed his switch with Ellis Roberts, he recalled that his eighty-three-year-old father told him: "Oral, the division should never have happened. God is going to move again. . . . This time people must be united. They must understand. . . . If you go back, go for me also."[97]

If his Methodist heritage inclined him in that direction, it was Oral's Berlin experience which triggered his move toward the mainstream. In Berlin, Oral glimpsed his potential to influence the historic churches. While his change of churches did not grow inevitably out of that insight, the move became an increasingly "logical choice."[98]

The most compelling attraction of the Methodist church was its latitude. Oral was increasingly cramped by pentecostal theology and his church's moral prudishness; both restraints would have hindered his new television format. It was the "unstructured part of Methodism," specifically the autonomy of the Methodist pulpit, which most attracted him. "You talk about feeling free," he explained in September 1968. "I've never been so free in my life. I have a freedom in Christ where you can preach. . . . You don't care what church they go to, just get them saved and let them go. Get them healed and thrust them out into the kingdom of God and not care who gets the credit."[99]

Many of Roberts's critics had never detected his religious openness and were stunned by his union with a church that sheltered some of the nation's most liberal theologians. To some extent, Oral had a limited knowledge of his new church. Asked his feelings about the Methodist church's participation in the Consultation on Church Union discussions, Oral responded: "Personally, I don't think about it. I'm rather naive about it. I don't know the details."[100] In 1972, the editor of the *Texas Methodist* asked Oral if he did not find it "ironic" that someone with his "fundamentalist theology" should choose to join the Methodists. Oral replied: "I don't feel comfortable with labels. I do feel comfortable with the Methodist church. I believe it is the most open church in the world today to the movement of the Holy Spirit."[101] Roberts knew that his new church had a "liberal wing." He did not believe liberalism was the "answer," but he brought with him into the Methodist church a respect for diversity and an irenic spirit which made him ready to listen to anyone.[102]

Unquestionably, Oral also saw in Methodism an opportunity. It appeared to be the major denomination most open to the charismatic movement. "There's a very definite possibility," Oral told a London audience in 1970, "that there will be a renewing in a great many Methodist churches in our country. There's an openness to the Holy Spirit."[103] To some his move seemed a crass power play, the abandoning of the 65,000-member church which had built his empire to exploit the 11,000,000-member Methodist church.[104] Oral was quite conscious that he was joining "one of the largest Protestant churches," a church with millions of potential partners.[105] Both he and his new church hoped to gain from the move. Bishop Smith summarized: "I extend the right hand of fellowship to Dr. Roberts believing the Methodist church has a contribution to make to his ministry, and certain he has a contribution to make to us."[106] But Oral's move was never simply a financial ploy. It was, in fact, a calculated financial gamble. Almost unanimously, his advisors felt that the move would "result in some reduction of financial support." "There are no non-religious reasons for this step," Roberts insisted in his repetitious explanations to the press.[107] His move, he explained, simply allowed "an enlarged opportunity to minister for Christ."[108]

Of course, in Oral's mind, there was a final, overriding explanation: "I tell you, the spirit spoke to me to do this. I can talk all day and that's what happened. I can give you some contributing reasons but without the spirit speaking to my heart, I could not . . . have considered it."[109] He was responding to that familiar gnawing urge:

> Finally it came to a point where I had to make a decision to back away from entering the Methodist ministry which to me was to become a door to the entire historic church world, or I had to run it out to its final course and see if it was God's will. That is, to see if the Methodist hierarchy in Oklahoma felt the way I felt. If they did not, it was obvious that it was just something in my own mind. And you know God always works on both ends of the line.[110]

The confirmation was there; Oral confidently told the press that "I have become a Methodist because it was the will of God."[111] Such statements were inscrutable and puzzling to most reporters. But they were to Oral the ultimate explanation.[112]

THE SWEEPING transformation of Oral Roberts's public image between 1960 and 1975 rested on a growing tolerance among his former adversaries, as well as on his own changes. Roberts began the decade with the same antagonistic relationship with the press. He felt misrepresented ("thrown into the same hopper . . . as everyone else who has ever tried to pray for the sick") and stigmatized by the "faith healer" tag he could not shake.[113] In 1968, Oral reiterated his complaint that "we've not had many good words in this ministry. Only once in a while does the newspaper write an objective report about us. You read it and you would think we were a bunch of bums and murderers and killers and what else?"[114] A reporter from the *Christian Herald* who interviewed Oral in 1968 wrote: "Oral Roberts spent the first five or ten minutes interviewing me. Clearly he wanted to know why I was there; if I planned to follow any preconceived angle . . . whether I was just naturally nasty, mean and destructive."[115]

Roberts's opposition in the early and mid-1960s came from familiar sources. The pentecostal denominations grew increasingly unfriendly to the independent healing ministries, often openly criticizing them, although the Pentecostal Holiness church made no further efforts to expel Oral. In 1964, international pentecostal leader Donald Gee judged that the great revival had "blown itself out," that the "mass healing campaigns have lost their novelty."[116] While Gee and many other pentecostal leaders continued to distinguish Roberts from the less-responsible evangelists, the entire healing movement became a target of pentecostal criticism. Oral was attacked at the World Pentecostal Conference in 1961 and at a similar conference in Toronto in 1968. One speaker charged that "God has not confirmed their [the healing evangelists'] preaching in the last ten years," since "in the healing campaigns, after the first rush of enthusiasm, those who remained healed were only a very small percentage." The address was "suppressed" in the published report because of "violent objections," but it expressed the strongly held conviction of many pentecostal leaders.[117]

Although Oral was often excepted from the most acid attacks made by pentecostal insiders, he was directly implicated, though not named, in the most embarrassing exposé ever written about the healing revival. In 1962, just after he had left the Roberts organization, G. H. Montgomery published a series of six articles indicting the deliverance revival, under the titles "Enemies of the Cross of Christ," "A Lying Spirit in the Mouth of the Prophets," "Their Glory Is Their Shame," "Making Merchandise of You," "Give Me This Power," and "Where Do We Go from Here?"[118] The articles were published in the widely circulated magazine founded by Jack Coe, and those who knew the healing revival's cast of characters could easily identify the salvos fired at Oral. Juanita Coe Hope, Jack Coe's widow, conceded that the articles were "maybe vindictive to Oral," but she also believed that Montgomery had been mistreated and that his charges were documented in a "big thick" book with "dates and everything."[119]

Montgomery's original manuscript apparently named Oral and other evangelists and included charges which did not appear in print—at least some Roberts staff members recollected seeing such an edition. Oral met with his aides to discuss the impending attack; the decision was made to "ignore it," even though attorney Don Moyers believed that the ministry had grounds for a libel suit if Roberts was named.[120] Montgomery and Mrs. Hope reportedly received scores of appeals from Oral's friends, including Demos Shakarian, not to publish the material, but they insisted that "if we don't correct it within ourselves the whole thing's going to be ruined."[121]

As finally published, the articles were a general indictment of the healing ministers. Montgomery claimed that he had been warned that he was "going up against a ruthless group of men" who had "millions of dollars to fight you with." Oral's former editor charged that the healing revival had been genuine in the beginning, but that it had been contaminated by the "pride and glory-seeking" of the evangelists. Their greed led many to become "outright 'con-men' and criminals"—using the revival as "a golden opportunity to practice crime in a new field which was . . . practically out of bounds for law enforcement officers."[122] The evangelists were tyrants, charged Montgomery, and their independent associations were shams.[123] Most of them followed "the lying practice" of padding "their reports to get gain and glory," recklessly claiming miracles without documentation, and they shamelessly misrepresented the "personal attention given the mail they receive."[124] Some of the evangelists had "gained incredible wealth," channeling money to "their own comfort and ease" which had been raised "for God's service."[125]

It would be a mistake to overestimate the impact of the Montgomery attack. Although widely circulated among the hard-core supporters of the revival, the articles never received a broader hearing. Among those who read them, they almost certainly damaged Montgomery more than Roberts. "No man in this world will ever know what it has cost us to tell the people the truth about the existence of sin and crime in present day evangelism," Montgomery wrote in his last article. "Of course, we have not stopped the evil or put crooked evangelists out of business. Poor people will continue to send money to luxury-lined evangelists, while we who have told these people the truth will suffer for the truth we have told."[126] Montgomery's own role in the revival was finished; his attack had little effect on Oral's ministry, or, in fact, on those of the less-savory evangelists who could be identified in the articles.

The Montgomery articles did, however, catalog the pentecostal case against healing evangelists and their independent associations. In his anger, he said in public what many pentecostal leaders believed and said in private. While Oral's formal relationship with his church had stabilized by the mid-1960s, the resentments within the pentecostal movement were deep and bitter.

Oral also continued to receive the same kinds of criticism from other religious leaders in the 1960s that he had become accustomed to in the 1950s. Liberal clergymen often "sneered" at his personal lifestyle and theology, accusing him of "oversimplification," of an abnegation of "social responsibility," of "reducing Christianity to a new form of positive thinking," and of embracing a "new form of heresy—Christianity as entertainment."[127] Fundamentalist editor Noel Smith more caustically judged that "in Oral Roberts' ministerial makeup there are as many principles of a genuine, authentic minister of Jesus Christ as there are magnolias in the Arizona desert."[128] But while all of the same criticisms could still be heard, they were both less frequent and less shrill.

As long as Oral conducted crusades, he could never shake the old perceptions, even though he began each campaign with public disavowals of "faith healing."[129] Reporters continued to be fascinated by the bizarre quirks in the meetings—the occasional deaths, or the escapades of Joseph Lewis, president of the Freethinkers of America, who allegedly pursued Oral, offering rewards to anyone who could "prove himself cured" and threatening to institute a suit against Roberts.[130] These were not new issues, but they seemed to disturb Oral more in the 1960s. Speaking to a group of prospective students in 1963, he revealed a martyr's complex:

> In Miami this year . . . there was a group of men converged upon us in our crusade in an attempt to arrest me for praying for the sick. In the guise that I was practicing medicine without a license. And it was touch and go for several days. And it bothered me. It bothered me a great deal. I'm ashamed to say that but it's the truth. Because I could see that I could be arrested momentarily and that I would be released. . . . But they could come in and arrest me. And that's what they wanted to do so they could embarrass me. They know that it would not stick in this country yet. . . . The Lord came to me and He made a statement. He said, "Do not be afraid to go to jail for your ministry." . . . Then He asked me a question, "When you come before Me, do you want to come and appear before Me with or without scars?"[131]

Local news stories were often critical. Reporters still wanted financial information the ministry would not release; they often felt that Oral "ducked the issue" when the questioning turned to money.[132] Even the building of the university did not convince some that Oral deserved a new image; one writer feared that the school "would be a mill to turn out devotees to the mystic arts of head squeezing, Faginship, and the techniques of cashing in on, and commercializing, religious ignorance."[133]

In August 1962, *Life* magazine published a controversial spread on Oral which he regarded as a blatant betrayal of his confidence.[134] Featuring pictures of a crusade in the Dallas-Fort Worth area and of Roberts's Tulsa headquarters, the article, charged Jenkin Lloyd Jones, was filled with "adroit editorial inferences."[135] The magazine not only questioned the validity of religious healing and speaking in tongues, it cast a glaring spotlight on the opulence of Oral's tastes, including a picture of the "$345 molded plywood chair in his Tulsa office." The article was another in the long list of attacks which caused the ministry endless trouble; it was, in fact, introduced as evidence in one of the ministry's recurrent tax "skirmishes."[136] Oral told the university's regents that "we don't expect people like *Life* magazine . . . to look favorably on the supernatural ministry," but he was stung by the tone of the story.[137] Wayne Robinson estimated that the article caused a loss of over 400,000 partners.[138]

A silver lining appeared after the *Life* article which portended better times. Jenkin Lloyd Jones wrote a ringing defense of Oral in the *Tulsa Tribune*, contesting the explicit and implicit criticisms in *Life*. The Unitarian editor proclaimed himself "agnostic about the efficacy of faith-healing as far as genuine, organic ailments are concerned," but he noted that Catholics and Christian Scientists were likely to take exception to a blanket rejection of religious healing. Furthermore, Jones argued, "even the most coldly-scientific MD's know that attitude of mind has a lot to do with recovery from measurable diseases," and few would argue that Oral did not inspire most of those in his healing lines to "a vastly improved attitude of mind." It was also true that "Roberts lives well" from the offerings given by his supporters, admitted Jones, "but he doesn't live anywhere near as well as the Archbishop of Canterbury or the Pope and he has personal contact with a lot more people." The influential editor gave Oral a needed endorsement:

> When we first began hearing about Brother Oral Roberts we were skeptical. There are plenty of religious racketeers. But we gradually changed our opinion. Whether he really has it or not, Oral Roberts thinks that he has a divine gift for healing. . . . In balance, we think that there are a large number of people on this earth who have found comfort and joy and confidence because of Oral Roberts. He needs no apology. We are proud to have him in Tulsa.[139]

In the late 1960s and early 1970s, Roberts's reputation improved on all fronts. Interest in religious healing grew throughout the 1960s, and hundreds of mainstream ministers came to know Roberts personally through his crusades and the seminars at the university.[140] It was no doubt true, as Bishop Angie Smith told Oral in their discussions in early 1968, that scores of Methodist ministers had suggested to the bishop that Oral would be an asset to their church.[141] By 1970, outside of fundamentalist and sectarian circles, it was difficult to find an outspoken critic of Oral Roberts.

The turnaround by the news media was even more marked. In 1973, Edward B. Fiske, religion editor of the *New York Times,* wrote a major story on "The Oral Roberts Empire" for the *Sunday Magazine.* He noted that Oral had long been the butt of ridicule and an embarrassment to his home town, but then he added: "Now all this has changed. Roberts had, as it were gone straight—and made it in the big time. The tent was folded in 1968 and replaced by a television studio." "It's probably accurate to say," concluded Fiske, "that, in the wake of his plunge into prime-time television, Roberts commands more *personal* loyalty than any other clergyman of the nineteen-seventies. Graham is obviously the dominant figure of the era, but he is a more impersonal force."[142] By the mid-1970s, Oral not only was taken seriously, he had become a media phenomenon, one of the most discussed personalities in the country. Articles about him were often sympathetic and complimentary. Not only did his name appear frequently in the nation's major magazines, but he was "deluged with invitations to appear on network and nationally syndicated radio and television shows."[143] "Everyone was wanting him on television," recalled Wayne Robinson, "I could just call and things just go, go, go." Some months the ministry received between 3,000 and 4,000 "print stories" throughout the world.[144]

The increased media attention, and its positive content, were partly a response to Oral's role change from tent preacher to college president and television personality. The university, while sometimes pictured as an anomaly with a college "drop-out" president, was featured in the 1970s in publications ranging from the *New York Times* to the *Chronicle of Higher Education,* necessarily placing the Roberts ministry in a more favorable light.[145] Oral believed, with some reason, that the ORU basketball program had done more than anything else to mold a new image of respectability for his ministry. "I've been through the fires of Hell with the media," he told his employees in 1972. "One of the things that made it change was last year when we went to New York and played our first game and then went back to the National Invitational Tournament and the media turned around. They were respectful to me as a human being and as a spiritual leader in America."[146]

Oral's new image was not simply a product of his new ventures; he also believed that reporters had come to know him better. Partly, Oral's patent importance made investigators look deeper, digging to find the sources of his charisma. Noting the changed attitudes in 1972, a Tulsa newsman wrote: "The press, which once tended to scoff at his ministry of faith healing and tent revivals, appears to have mellowed, and Roberts believes it is 'because they've taken more time to check us out . . . to see us as we are, rather than what someone says we are.' "[147] Columnist William Willoughby believed, probably correctly, that in earlier years "many reporters of the type who usually are sent out to do a story on Oral Roberts and his healing ministry would be the type who couldn't have been trusted to write a fair account of the baptism of Jesus."[148] Those who persevered, and particularly those who talked personally with Oral, usually went away impressed. *Saturday Evening Post* writer Pete Martin told a reporter that Oral "impressed him more than any personality he had ever interviewed."[149] Edward Fiske found in Oral "a down-to-earth slightly awkward style that produces easy-going credibility."[150] "I have a great deal of respect for Oral Roberts," wrote an Arkansas television critic, "he is cheerful, direct in his preaching, always has a down-to-earth positive message, and is promoting a great university."[151] Oral still appeared "uncertain at times about the motives and intentions of newsmen, particularly those from outside his hometown," but in the early 1970s he had less and less to fear.[152]

The Roberts organization worked furiously to exploit its new image. As he had done at Berlin, Oral admitted to newsmen over and over that during his early ministry he had often exhibited misdirected zeal. "I made a lot of mistakes in my youth," he told a California reporter in 1970. "Now I'm not saying that I was wrong to try to heal people. But I may have gone about it wrong."[153]

In 1972, Doubleday published a new autobiography of Roberts, *The Call.*[154] Written with the aid of Wayne Robinson, the book told Oral's life story sympathetically and in a popular literary style, emphasizing the role of the university in the ministry. *The Call* was widely circulated and reviewed and became the standard source of information for newsmen writing stories about the ministry.

In Tulsa, Oral became one of the most important leaders of the city in the 1960s. Some Tulsans resented his local prestige. When the evangelistic association posted "huge, painted" billboards on the interstate highways entering the city, featuring Oral's countenance and the slogan "Tulsa Is the Home of Oral

Roberts," at least one newsman protested. The city had been hospitable to Roberts when he was "a poverty-stricken evangelist," he wrote, but now it found itself embarrassingly identified with him: "Tulsa discovered itself in the position of having suddenly awakened to find him famous. It hardly mattered when he was an obscure country preacher. But he is not that anymore, and in continuing to revere him this city measures itself for all the world to see."[155]

A majority of Tulsans, however, were captured by Roberts's charm. His friendship with Jenkin Lloyd Jones grew through the years. Even before his editorial defenses of Oral after the *Life* magazine attack, Jones cited Roberts in an editorial on "Our Rudderless Young." Revealing that he and Oral had discussed the rebellion of the nation's youth over dinner, Jones reported that Roberts approved of youthful "visions" but believed that they needed to be directed to "that which is bigger than oneself." "It's not a bad thought," recommended the *Tribune* editor.[156]

More than anything else, Oral Roberts University altered Tulsa's view of the ministry. When the university opened in 1965, publisher Byron V. Boone of the *Tulsa World* wrote: "It takes tremendous desire and enterprise to build a university from scratch. Not many men have followed a lifetime dream so faithfully as has Oral Roberts. . . . Roberts has made a name for himself not only nationally but throughout the world. He has become an institution in Tulsa."[157] Jenkin Lloyd Jones added in the *Tulsa Tribune:* "While Tulsans, generally, have been paying little attention an incredibly brave, expensive and imaginative experiment in higher education has been taking form out of South Lewis Avenue. . . . Oral Roberts University is not a preacher's plaything. . . . You'll be surprised. And delighted."[158]

Oral was thankful for the support of the Tulsa press: "As a general rule . . . particularly in Tulsa, . . . we get a good press. And I can never be thankful enough for the press we have in Tulsa. They have certainly gone beyond even the call of duty."[159] Both of the city's dailies regularly plugged the university and defended Oral against attacks; Bob Foresman, the *Tribune*'s business editor, wrote scores of favorable stories about him, beginning in the 1950s.[160] But it was his friendship with Jones that Oral most treasured. Introducing the distinguished Tulsa editor before Jones's commencement address at the university in 1970, Oral said: "I'm proud he is my friend, my personal friend. He has stood up for us. It's a little more popular to stand up for us now than it was a few years ago. We still have a long way to go on that. . . . But this man stood up in his editorial columns for us and our ministry, for this university, when it was just a little crawling baby."[161] Byron Boone, Jenkin Lloyd Jones, Bob Foresman, and other Tulsa journalists never endorsed Oral's theology, but they were worldly-wise, tolerant men who saw no harm in it; and they liked Oral, admired him, and marveled at his accomplishments.

Furthermore, most of what Oral Roberts said made good sense to Tulsans. He had risen from the same soil as his fellow Oklahomans, and the message of godliness, discipline, and hard work which he preached bore the brand of his homeland. During the rebellious 1960s, Americans looked back nostalgically at older values—nowhere more than in oil-rich Tulsa, which was a haven for conservative politics and conservative religion. In an article featuring Oral and anticommunist preacher Billy James Hargis in 1971, Associated Press journalist Dennis Eckert wrote: "Amid all those oil derricks on the Oklahoma prairie rises an equally formidable forest of steeples. That's Tulsa, fountainhead of faith and fundamentalism where that oldtime religion is one of the city's biggest businesses." Why Tulsa? "It's old-time Americana, the last of the big cities to offer that," answered Billy James Hargis.[162]

As opposed to Hargis, Roberts's message was almost completely apolitical; Oral often joked about his roots in the Democratic "Little Dixie" section of the state, which placed him outside the Republican power structure in Tulsa. But Oral's values were as conservative as those of any Republican. He was appalled by the generation of "beatniks" and rebels who appeared on American campuses in the 1960s.[163] Jenkin Lloyd Jones published a portion of Roberts's inaugural speech to students at the university in 1965 as a "Guest Editorial": "The world doesn't need more college students to wave flags, carry placards, halt traffic, and riot against law and order. What our civilization needs is for you to make your spiritual development a normal part of your education."[164] In the final analysis, it was the clean-cut, neatly dressed, well-mannered young people on the campus who won Tulsa's heart.[165] Jenkin Lloyd Jones looked them over. "I said to myself," he recalled, "these may be simple-minded kids, but they are living a hell of a lot more successfully than the pseudo-sophisticates in Madison."[166]

In addition, Tulsans appreciated Oral Roberts for the sheer economic impact that he had on the city. By 1966, Bob Foresman estimated that "Oral Roberts University has become one of Tulsa's most valuable economic assets, pumping $8 million annually into the city's economy."[167] Four years later, in an article entitled "Oral Roberts Organization Good for Tulsa," Foresman estimated that the "cash flow" of the Roberts organization in its twenty-four years of existence had been about $100,000,000, with the current annual figure being about $15,000,000. In addition to the direct economic impact of the ministry, Oral Roberts University had become the largest tourist site in Tulsa, attracting over 100,000 visitors each year.[168]

Oral's economic conservatism was not doctrinaire, but he saw himself as a product of laissez faire capitalism. Introducing Amway guru Richard M. DeVos to the ORU students in 1976, he said: "He exemplifies a Christian who's operating under a free enterprise system that permits a person who dreams dreams to start with virtually nothing and build. . . . I'm a public enterprise man myself and I'm pretty tired of all the knocks it's getting in the world and the business world is getting. I can see the scars and the flaws too, but I came up under it and without it this school wouldn't be here."[169] It was fitting that by the end of the 1960s, Roberts counted among his best friends in Tulsa some of the richest and most powerful citizens in that rich and conservative city. Whatever his eccentricities, they admired any man who could fight his way to the top.

Oral Roberts's stature in Tulsa was evidenced by a growing list of honors. He was a member of the Rotary Club, and, in the early 1960s, as a result of irresistible pressure from his friend John Williams, he was admitted to the prestigious Southern Hills Country Club.[170] In 1963, Oral was named "Outstanding American Indian of the Year" at Oklahoma's American Indian Exposition, and in 1966 Tulsa's Downtown Civitan Club named him "Outstanding Citizen of the Year."[171] In 1966, he headed a membership drive for the Tulsa Chamber of Commerce; in 1969, he was added to the board of directors of the National Bank of Tulsa; in 1971, he was named a member of the Oklahoma Athletic Hall of Fame board; in 1972, he was inducted into the Oklahoma Hall of Fame; in 1973, he was appointed to the board of the Oklahoma Natural Gas Company; and in 1974, the Oklahoma Broadcasters' Association named him "Oklahoman of the Year."[172] He spoke at high-school commencements, chambers of commerce and other service clubs, and ministerial alliances, and to countless other special groups at the behest of friends—to Tulsa's top insurance salesmen, the national convention of automobile salesmen, the Basketball Hall of Fame, the Fellowship of Christian Athletes camp, the correctional department in Oklahoma City, the Hungry Club of Tulsa, and the Dutch Treat Club in New York City.[173]

Of course, by the 1970s Oral was a national as well as a local celebrity. He continued to evince a kiddish joy and wonder about his fame. In 1972, he gleefully told the ORU students about the treatment he received at NBC's studios:

> This sounds crazy . . . but they have my picture hung up all over the stars in the NBC Studio. . . . There's Flip Wilson and I'm right next to the Killer. Then there's Bob Hope and . . . I'm the only outside one they've ever put up. When I drive up now they have this steel thing that's got my name on it like they have with Dean Martin. . . . Oral Roberts and a star under it. I tell you, they are shrewd people. And when I come out there it's just like rolling the red carpet out. And when I first went out there four years ago, nobody would hardly speak to me. . . . The Lord has given us favor with these people.[174]

Star he was. Almost immediately after the beginning of his specials, Oral became a coveted guest on television talk shows.[175] In 1970 he appeared on Dick Cavett's program, and he and Richard made a guest appearance with Mike Douglas. In 1971 he appeared on a Jerry Lewis telethon, and in February 1972 he was interviewed by Barbara Walters on "Today" and appeared on the "Mike Douglas Show" and Dinah Shore's program. Later that year, he was a guest on Johnny Carson's "Tonight" program and was featured in an NBC "Chronolog" profile, which was quite complimentary. The next year Oral did guest appearances on "Dinah Shore," "Laugh-In," and "Hee Haw," and in 1974 he appeared on Merv Griffin's talk show. Oral performed flawlessly, answering questions with an apparent sincerity and honesty that was disarming. He admitted mistakes freely, confirmed the psychosomatic nature of much religious healing, and was calmly tolerant of contradictory opinions. But he also stuck to his guns. Asked by Cavett if he had "abandoned faith healing," Oral replied, "No, not at all. . . . I am in the home now and can talk to people and stretch forth my hands to minister healing to people in the same way." Oral's openness often blunted the potential hostility of some pretty crusty fellow guests. Asked his thoughts on Oral's answers to Cavett's questions, Henry Morgan responded: "I'm sure if you put me at one side and Mr. Roberts at the other, you'd say there would be violent disagreement. Our backgrounds, our temperaments, our beliefs are entirely different, but somewhere along the line, they're about the same."[176] Merv Griffin described Oral's appearance on his program:

> In case you didn't see the show, Helen Gurley Brown is editor of *Cosmopolitan* . . . and just as Oral was ready to walk out, I turned to her and said, "What denomination are you, Helen?" and she said, "Atheist." And I said, "Oh." . . . And out came Oral. And I said, "Well, your work is cut out for you, Oral, look what I have for you, an atheist. What do you say to an atheist?" And he looked at her and said, "I love her." And she fell to pieces, she collapsed. No one had ever said that to her before. That worked.[177]

Another measure of Oral's rise to celebrity status was the humor associated with his name. When Bob Hope teamed with Oral in a celebrity golf match in Tulsa, he referred to his partner as "star of stage, screen and pulpit" and later instructed Roberts, "We'll call on you when we need something unusual."[178] Oral Roberts jokes became standard fare on television; a Tulsa television critic asked: "If Bob Hope mentions Oral Roberts' name twice in one 60-minute television special, is he a name dropper?"[179] Oral was a notoriously poor joke teller, but he regularly convulsed the ORU student body with lines he had heard in California: "They said, Colonel Sanders and Oral Roberts are making a new movie together and it's entitled 'A Wing and a Prayer.' " After appearing on "Hee Haw," Oral told his students, "I don't mind them laughing at me. . . . I wouldn't have gone on several years ago, but I feel like I have God in my life so strong now that it will be all right."[180]

In fact, Oral developed some pride in his prowess as a comedian. With obvious relish he told the students about his appearance on "Hee Haw":

> They really fixed me up. . . . They put me in the barber chair and this old boy was cutting my hair. . . . Roy Clark was there and they were telling these Oral Roberts jokes. . . . Roy Clark was over there trying to tell him, "Stop, this is Oral Roberts in the barber chair, Archie," and he couldn't get Archie's attention. . . . When he got through . . . Roy Clark said, "Archie, do you know whose hair you were cutting?" "No." "This is Oral Roberts." So Archie throws up his hands and up to now I hadn't said a word. . . . So now my line, and I created my line while I was there. And my line was this, "Archie, during my ministry during the past few years as I've traveled over the world praying for people, I have laid my hands on thousands of people. I can't wait to get my hands on you." So I felt like that the word of knowledge had been given to me.[181]

In spite of Oral's tendency to garble a punch line, he was sometimes quick under pressure. Television writer Troy Gordon told this tale in 1969: "Welborn Hope, Oklahoma's most famous poet, found himself in an elevator with Oral Roberts the other day. 'Reverend,' Welborn said, 'do you remember the four men they hanged in Ada when Sen. Bob Kerr, Oral Roberts and Cal Tinney and I were living there?' He didn't reply, so Welborn added: 'Troy Gordon says they hanged the wrong four men.' 'They'll get around to us,' the evangelist replied."[182] Phillips University president Tom Broce ribbed Oral before an audience at ORU because Roberts's arm was in a sling. "Oral, " he said, "why don't you take care of that shoulder by healing yourself?" After the laughter subsided, Oral retorted, "Tom, why don't you speak in tongues?"[183]

By the 1970s, Oral Roberts's fame had spread throughout the world. In 1968, Carl Albert, Speaker of the House of Representatives, told the ORU student body: "The founder of this school is known the world over. Wherever I have traveled, I have heard of Oral Roberts."[184] Oral had met some of the world's leaders—Chiang Kai-shek, Ben-Gurion, Francois Duvalier—and he was known to others. Demos Shakarian was granted an audience with Fidel Castro shortly after the Cuban revolution, and Castro told him that he listened regularly to both Graham and Roberts on television and thought they "were honest men and what they said were honest things."[185] Oral had many personal friends in the United States Congress; he visited John F. Kennedy in the White House shortly before Kennedy's assassination. At Billy Graham's suggestion, he attended a Henry Kissinger foreign policy briefing in the White House in 1972. Roberts was acquainted with Jimmy Carter, and in 1972 he gave the invocation at the National Democratic Convention in Miami Beach. In Oklahoma, Oral was a recognized political force. Governor David Hall was a "warm personal friend," and other politicians courted Oral's approval. When he ran for governor in 1962, Henry Bellmon revealed, he had an hour-long audience with Oral because "I was told it was the thing to do."[186]

Roberts did not have the same sort of political clout as Billy Graham, nor did he aspire to it. Nonetheless, Oral was honored when political figures noticed him. He was particularly pleased by a personal meeting with Richard Nixon in 1972. Senator Dewey Bartlett of Oklahoma informed Nixon that Roberts would like to meet him, and the president issued Oral three invitations—the first two the evangelist could not accept because of schedule conflicts. When Oral entered the Oval Office, he thanked Nixon for the inspiration he had been to him, recalling that Nixon's struggle to overcome political setbacks had been an encouragement to him in 1968 when it seemed his ministry was near collapse. The two compared television techniques; Oral gave the president a portfolio of materials about ORU, and Nixon gave him a Bible. Then, just before he left, Oral turned to the president and said, "Mr. President, I'm going to pray for you, then I want you to pray for me." Wallis Henley, a young White House aide and a former religion writer from Birmingham, Alabama, bolted to attention, wondering "how the president would react." The small group clasped hands in the middle of the Oval Office, and Oral prayed first. Then Nixon prayed, Henley recalled, "a simple utterance in the straightforward Quaker style."[187] Oral later described his impression of the prayer: "He opened up in a strong voice, 'Our Father,' and I mean he prayed a prayer. He prayed for me. He prayed for my ministry; he prayed for Oral Roberts University; he prayed for the faculty; he prayed for the students. I've been considering adding him to our team ever since. In all seriousness, I was deeply moved by the prayer the man prayed."[188]

Roberts prayed in a variety of places with an anomalous collection of people in the 1960s and 1970s. He made many friends in Hollywood. Jimmie Rodgers "accepted Christ" when Oral prayed in his dressing room, and the evangelist believed that other stars had changed their lives.[189] Flip Wilson stopped Roberts in the television studio one day and told him, "Oral . . . three weeks ago my sister-in-law . . . became very ill, and was rushed to the hospital for an emergency operation and she called me and said, 'Flip I want you to pray.' . . . I told her of course I would. But Oral I didn't, I didn't know how to pray." But the next Sunday, he continued, he had listened as Oral prayed on his program. "The words you said were exactly the words I wanted to say to God about my sister-in-law," he told the evangelist. As tears welled up in his eyes, he pulled Oral close and said, "I love you buddy."[190]

In a 1973 chapel service, Roberts shared with his students "one of the most unique letters" he had ever received. It was a rambling, handwritten note signed "John Lennon." Lennon's cousin, Marilyn McCabe, had written, and Oral had promised to pray for John and Yoko at her request, prompting Lennon to write:

Rev. Roberts,
    This is ex-Beatle, John Lennon. I've been wanting to write you but I guess I didn't really want to face reality. I never do this, this is why I take drugs. Reality frightens me and paranoids me. True, I have a lot of money, being a Beatle, been all around the world, but basically I'm afraid to face the problems of life. Let me begin to say, I regret that I said the Beatles were more popular than Jesus. I don't even like myself anymore, guilt. My cousin, Marilyn McCabe has tried to help me. She told me you were praying for me. Here's my life. . . . Born in Liverpool, my mom died when I was little. My father left me at three. It was rough because just my aunt raised me. I never really liked her. I had an unhappy childhood, depressed a lot. Always missing my mom. Maybe if I'd had a father like you, I would have been a better person. My own father I hate with a passion because he left my mom and me, came to me after we found "A Hard Day's Night" and asked for some money. It made me so mad, Paul had to hold me down. I was going to kill him. I was under the influence of pills at that time. Married Cynthia, had a son John. I had to marry her, I really never loved her. She always embarrassed me walking around pregnant, not married, so I married her. Only one regret, John has had to suffer a lot because recently she's been married again. He and me never get to see each other because Paul and me never got along anymore and that's how the four ended. . . . As the song we wrote, Paul and me, "Money Can't Buy Me Love," it's true. The point is this, I want happiness. I don't want to keep up with drugs. Paul told me once, "you made fun of me for not taking drugs, but you will regret it in the end." . . . Explain to me what Christianity can do for me? Is it phoney? Can He love me? I want out of hell.
P.S. This address staying at the cousin's house. Rev. Roberts, also, I did watch your show until Channel 6 took it off the air. Please try to get it back on. A lot of people I know loved your show. I especially like the World Action Singers, your son Richard is a real good singer. George told me he met you and them when he was at the studio.
Sincerely, John.
P.S. I am, I hate to say, under the influence of pills now. I can't stop. I only wish I could thank you for caring.[191]

Oral also read his answer, which commended to Lennon the peace that comes to the servants of God, introduced him to seed-faith, and invited him to a seminar on campus.[192] It was another of those stray encounters which revealed something of the breadth and power of Roberts's ministry.

A few months earlier, Oral had devoted an entire chapel service to prayer for Governor George Wallace of Alabama. Roberts had flown to the bedside of the wounded governor to pray, and, during that visit, Oral reported, "Wallace experienced a spiritual renewal in his life, and his wife received the baptism of the Holy Spirit."[193] On September 13, 1972, via telephone, Oral and the university student body conversed with the Wallaces. Roberts asked two black students and two white students from Alabama to join him to pray for the governor. Wallace was profusely thankful: "I feel the Holy Spirit is in me, Oral. . . . I feel closer to God than I felt in a long time, especially since your coming to be with me. . . . I feel that a miracle is going to happen myself and I believe as you do . . . that all healing comes through God."[194]

The stories reached out endlessly—of personal encounters, of letters from celebrities, of those moved by the television programs. Oral Roberts had become avant garde. "There is starting to be a move in Tulsa," Oral told the ORU students in 1967. "There is now at least a small definite move among some of the top people—the power structure of our city—toward the Baptism of the Holy Ghost."[195] The move rippled throughout the nation and the world. The small and the great stopped to listen to Oral Roberts. Some of them believed what he said.

CHAPTER

XII

Private Side

A s the crusades dragged to an end in the mid-1960s, Oral Roberts's private life was much as it had been for nearly twenty years. The campaigns grew shorter, and he spent slightly more time in Tulsa, but his visits overseas were more extended than in the 1950s. Oral's crusade routine was nearly the same—he was protected from the "sometimes over-eager public" by his aides; he granted occasional interviews in his room, but otherwise he carefully "watched his diet . . . and his time."[1] He still returned home tired and drained, particularly from the jaunts overseas, and he seemed less "exuberant." "Age has a lot to do with it," explained Evelyn, "and maturity."[2]

The founding of Oral Roberts University seriously altered Oral's lifestyle. When the university opened in 1965, it both demanded and received more and more of his time and attention. He curtailed his outside activities, convinced that "the central thing of this ministry is this university."[3] During the 1960s, Oral was much in evidence on the campus, consulting with Frank Wallace about the design of the buildings, mingling with the students in the dining room, recruiting new faculty members, promoting the basketball team, and, too often, some of his advisors felt, fretting about a plumbing failure in a dormitory.[4] For the first time in his life, he really lived in Tulsa, playing golf and dining with the city's leaders. His presence contributed to his prestige.

Another transition in Oral's personal life came when he began his new television series and became a national celebrity. Once again, he and Evelyn traveled extensively, to California for the production of the programs and for a seemingly endless stream of public appearances. Oral remained highly visible in

Tulsa; he still administered the university, but his job in the 1970s had become much more demanding. In 1970, he told Mike Douglas: "I'm an author. I preach. I write. I travel. I produce a national television program."[5] In pace and movement, Oral's lifestyle came to resemble that of other jet-set celebrities.

There was little time for purposeless social activity in Oral's busy schedule—only the necessary exercise. "The tall, 51-year-old Roberts probably puts in more hours than any other businessman in Tulsa," noted *Tulsa Magazine* in 1969. He slept seven hours a day, Oral told a reporter, and the rest of his time he worked—editing *Abundant Life*, answering the mail, preaching on the radio and television, administering the university, and in civic duties.[6] Her husband was so busy, Evelyn told a reporter, that he had to "pray in the spirit" while shaving in the morning: "Oral talks in tongues, too. Because of his busy schedule he frequently prays very earnestly while he is shaving. It always amuses me when I pass by his bathroom and hear him bathed in the Holy Spirit and speaking in tongues."[7] "Even when I'm playing golf, I'm working," said Oral, "studying God's other book."[8] He played golf as intensely as he worked, and by 1972 his handicap had fallen to six.[9] "Oral is a hell of a golfer," said a "guy in the pro shop" to a reporter in 1972, pointing out that Roberts had just recorded a seventy-three on the difficult Southern Hills course.[10]

Oral Roberts in his late forties and fifties was handsome in countenance and self-assured in presence. While some city-slicker newsmen still thought that "his looks and manner smack of the circus barker or used car salesman," most people found him impressive.[11] *New York Times* reporter Edward Fiske described Oral after a visit to his office in 1973:

> Roberts is just over 6 feet tall, with a stocky build that he drapes in colored shirts and fashionable suits chosen with the advice of the wardrobe people at the National Broadcasting Company and worn with low, Western-style boots. His hair is full and only slightly graying, and his sideburns are long and carefully groomed. His face is a marvel of malleability. When he talks, his eyebrows move up and down, his maw seems to move in circles and his mouth takes a half-moon shape that results in a kind of boyish grin.[12]

Reporters continued to be fascinated by Roberts's prosperity—his expensive suits, the Mercedes he drove in 1972 and the Cadillac he drove in 1975, the president's home he lived in, and his membership in Southern Hills Country Club. Oral continued to explain, somewhat defensively, that God did not intend "for any human being to live in poverty."[13] But in 1962 he erected another defense against the onerous charge that he was profiting off the name of Jesus and at the expense of his partners. When the university began, he and Evelyn divested themselves of most of their personal wealth, and Oral became a salaried employee of ORU. Skeptics pointed out that the move did little to change his lifestyle. "No longer a millionaire," wrote a Chicago journalist, "he merely lives like one."[14] Nonetheless, Roberts's decision to dispose of his personal wealth was a genuine sacrifice.

Oral and Evelyn admitted that their support had been "generous" and that they had "prospered"; in addition to his other earnings, Oral made some profitable investments in "land and property."[15] On the other hand, he insisted that the newspaper estimates that he was a millionaire were wildly exaggerated. When the university began, Oral revealed his plan to divest himself of personal property to his lawyers, R. O. Corvin, and Demos Shakarian; all of them thought the sacrifice was excessive. Evelyn asked her husband to pray about the matter before making a hasty decision. He prayed, "and we felt it, so we did it."[16] Oral and Evelyn divided their estate in half, giving $30,000 to each of their four children (establishing trust funds for the three younger children) and donating $120,000 to the university.[17] At the same time, Oral stopped the practice of receiving "love offerings" during the crusades (a technique long viewed with suspicion by the Internal Revenue Service) and began receiving a salary of $15,000 a year from the evangelistic association. His salary was raised to $24,000 when he became president of the university.[18]

It was difficult for outside observers to believe that he had really done it; Don Moyers remembered the astonishment of Oral's fellow board members at a Bank of Oklahoma meeting when he estimated his private worth at $25,000.[19] It seemed the thing to do; the evangelist decided to die a "poor man" to "vindicate my ministry."[20]

The Roberts family's act genuinely moved their friends. "All I can say," Demos Shakarian told the university regents in 1962, "is Brother Roberts and Sister Roberts are two of the most dedicated people I have ever met."[21] Those closest to Oral always believed him to be honest and generous in financial matters. Even after his original gift, he continued to contribute much of his income to the university.[22] Roberts hoped that his gift would slake the curiosity of the press about his private finances, but that was not to be. Nearly every interview still turned to a ritualistic exchange about his income. "Do you object to discussing your financial affairs?" the newsmen asked. "Do you feel happy talking about *your* money matters with strangers?" replied Oral. "No," admitted his interviewer, "that's a matter between the government and me." "Don't you think I am entitled to the same privacy?" Oral insisted. "I'm not interested in how much money you have," persisted the reporter, "just where it goes."[23] Roberts was distraught that his gift did not stop the questions: "That really didn't change the complexion. I found out the devil just didn't like me. No matter what I did it didn't work."[24]

While Oral's salary as president of the university was never excessive, his lifestyle was more like that of a best-selling author or a television celebrity, two of his other incarnations. In Tulsa, the family lived in the ORU president's home, which overlooked the campus. Built in 1962, the "President's Cottage" was a spacious Spanish-style four-bedroom home with a swimming pool. In 1972, the growth of Oral's celebrity status required the addition of a high fence and sophisticated security equipment to keep intruders off the property.[25]

The president's home was soon surrounded by other houses, including one built within the security compound for Richard and Patti Roberts. Oral's closest advisors and friends—Al Bush, Wayne Robinson, Carl Hamilton, Ron Smith, Howard Ervin, Bill Jernigan, Bob Eskridge, Bob DeWeese, and Ken Trickey—were his closest neighbors. Trickey was a particularly close personal friend; he and Oral played golf together, took walks in the evening, went to the movies, and freely visited in one another's houses. It was a classic man-to-man relationship. "Oral could relax with Ken because Ken talked about athletics and got Oral's mind off his work," recalled Evelyn.[26] Frequently moody and irascible, Oral relaxed while playing golf, and in the early 1970s the university maintained memberships for him in the Southern Hills Country Club and the Meadowbrook Golf and Country Club in Tulsa and in the Santa Anna Country Club in California.[27]

Some of Oral's associates, particularly Al Bush, tried to separate themselves personally from their work, betraying an independence that Oral neither understood nor appreciated.[28] But all of them supplied companionship for Oral, walking with him in the evenings, discussing his dreams and hopes. When they traveled, Oral and Evelyn were usually accompanied by Al and Marilyn Bush, Wayne and Sharon Robinson, or Ron and Jeanie Smith. They dined and golfed around the world, but only occasionally did they attend a western movie or in some other way interrupt the steady flow of business dialogue.[29]

The only significant property that the Roberts family retained in 1962 was their home in Corona del Mar in California, a three-bedroom house where Oral could "go out and rest."[30] His bouts with hay fever in the Oklahoma autumns drove him to California every fall, but when the university opened, Roberts felt obliged to remain in Tulsa, and in 1965 he sold his California home.[31] In 1977, Oral noted that he and Evelyn had not "had a home" for many years: "Now, we've lived in nice places, but we haven't had a home of our own."[32]

THOUGH his sixteen-hour work days, his dreaming and planning, and his ceaseless travel and public appearances devoured most of his time and energy, Oral Roberts remained a loyal family man. He and Evelyn grew closer and closer as her ties to the children diminished, and she was his constant companion. The children, while scattered and sometimes rebellious, remained constantly on their parents' minds. They were a clan—proud, and intensely loyal. Roberts family history had much to do with the functioning of the ministry.

Evelyn played a variety of roles in the ministry. She continued to read testimonies on the radio programs; she frequently spoke to the students and other groups; she was one of the few people who helped answer the partners' mail. Secretary of the board of the evangelistic association, she was Oral's closest confidant. She appeared occasionally on the television programs, but never felt comfortable: "I'm not good at it and I've tried to make Oral see that but I don't think I've convinced him yet."[33] Still trim and attractive as she entered mid-life, Evelyn was "a well-liked civic worker and mother in the city's most affluent circles," ever "the soul of charm" and "spiritual warmth."[34]

Whatever other roles she might play, Evelyn was first and foremost Oral's wife. He bragged shamelessly about her: "I have a wonderful wife, Evelyn. Evelyn is getting prettier every day and sweeter every day. In fact, if I don't hush up I won't even preach, I will get up and go home. And I really love my wife. Evelyn and I have been sweethearts. We have been on our honeymoon for twenty-nine years, . . . and we are very, very close to each other."[35] She reciprocated: "The greatest relaxation of my life is just to be alone with Oral. Sometimes we like to take long walks and just talk."[36]

Evelyn remained basically a "homebody" in spite of a hectic schedule. When Oral traveled without her, he laid out his clothes, and it was Evelyn's job to pack them neatly. She was an "excellent cook," who stressed "hot meals" and "proper nutrition" for the family. When Oral was home, the family routine called for eating dinner together at six o'clock—"one time when we are all together."[37] "I love my home," Evelyn told a reporter. "This is kind of silly I guess, but I don't even like to go out in the evening. I much prefer to spend the evening at home with my family around me."[38]

Oral's parents, Ellis and Claudius, lived their final years in the shadow of their son's imposing vision. Ellis nearly died in 1960 and, according to Claudius, was the first person to learn about the university. Bob Foresman told the story:

> The family had gathered in prayerful silence. There was an expectancy in the air. His famous son, Oral, was rushing home, and the family hoped for a miracle. When Oral Roberts entered the room, he didn't fall on his knees and ask the Lord to heal his father. Instead he sat on the bed, put an arm tenderly under his father's head, and said: "Papa you can't die now. I haven't told you about the university. I want you there when we dedicate it!" The elder Mr. Roberts' eyes brightened and he faintly shouted: "Praise the Lord."[39]

Ellis recovered, and he and Claudius viewed the rising of the university as fulfilled prophecy. After visiting the campus in 1962, Ellis obseved: "The reason I have always said Oral would have the greatest ministry of his day is because God revealed this to us, and the results so far have proved that God is with Oral. I think the new school is going to increase his ministry even more. I think that Oral's ministry is the winding up of the gospel age. The end of it will be in Heaven!"[40] Ellis and Claudius were given the titles "king and queen" by the first seminar class at the University of Evangelism after stirring the group with moving personal testimonies. Ellis's health began to break in the mid-1960s, but Claudius remained a fiery, "pixyish" fixture on the campus, shouting hallelujah with each new accomplishment. Ellis died in November 1967, making a final request that Oral "win souls" in his funeral sermon.[41] Claudius lived until 1974, moving to University Village when it was completed and dying in the infirmary there. At the dedication of the retirement center, Oral ruminated about the influence of his parents:

> The dream of University Village as a retirement center is a part of that belief in practice in my own life of honoring my own parents. My father and mother are . . . extraordinary people. They were hard workers. They were the little people, common people, but who dreamed big dreams, who believed in their children. And when one of them became ill and almost lost his life, stood by him when he could not help himself. And they were the ones who led him to Christ and who helped restore his life and helped instill in him a sense of pride in his parents and a feeling for people.[42]

By the time Claudius Roberts died, all four Roberts children were married, and Oral and Evelyn had become grandparents. Their years as parents had been filled with tensions and heartaches, as well as parental hope. Evelyn often reflected on how much easier their lives would have been without children; they could have avoided the long, lonesome separations. "But I never could have gone through life without children. I am just supposed to be a mother," she told a reporter in 1965, "our children have enriched our lives. . . . Why, we never would have known what parents and grandparents go through if we hadn't had children of our own."[43] Evelyn's words were prophetic. Through their children they would experience many of life's bitterest blows.

The last of the four chilren to leave home was Roberta Jean, who married Ronald Stephen Potts in August 1971. Roberta had just completed her sophomore year at Oral Roberts University and Potts his junior year. Evelyn wanted them to wait until they had completed undergraduate degrees; they would not do it.[44] It was one of the few times Roberta violated her parents' wishes. She had grown tall, dark, and serenely comely like her mother, her high cheekbones justifying Oral's nickname, "my little Cherokee Indian daughter."[45] Quiet as a child, Roberta developed the verve of her mother, combining it with an easy grace which won friends readily.

Roberta also had an early spiritual maturity; she loved her father's ministry and "really believed" in it. During the last years of the crusades, she traveled during the summers to play the organ, first before the meetings began and later, for the first time in North Carolina in 1968, during the service. Oral proudly called her to the platform to speak, and the young teenager gave her testimony with moving simplicity: "I love Jesus today. He's so wonderful to me. He meets my needs. Everything I need He's always given it to me. And when you come in the line today just believe in Him and He will fill everything you want."[46] For Roberta, it was, apparently, that simple. From the "time I was little," she recalled, "I really had an understanding of Jesus my Savior."[47] In 1974, with a sense of awe, Evelyn remembered her as the one "in our family who had the deep, deep, deep spirituality that I can't describe to you. It was difficult for her to express herself out in the public. . . . But when she gets alone with me she tells me her deep, deep feelings about the Lord."[48]

After graduation from Memorial High School in Tulsa, Roberta never considered anything besides attending Oral Roberts University; she loved the spiritual atmosphere of the campus. For the first time she felt perfectly at ease. "I have a real opportunity to witness here. It's just my whole life and I love it," she wrote during her freshman year.[49] After her marriage, Roberta finished her degree at the university with a major in history, and her husband also graduated. They continued to live in Tulsa for five years, Potts working in a savings and loan association and for the ministry. They had two sons, born in 1974 and 1976, Randy and Stephen, before moving to Denver, where Potts became a high school physical education instructor.[50]

Of all the Roberts children, Richard Lee's life was destined to be most intricately interwoven with that of his parents and with the Roberts ministry. It was not always apparent that it would turn out that way. Richard, like all of the Roberts children, loved and admired his parents, but he had no desire to be associated with his father's ministry. In many ways the most straightforward and uncomplicated of the Roberts children, Richard boldly challenged his father's authority. At the same time, Richard's rebellion was a surface one, never plumbing the depths of faithless despair.

During early adolescence, Richard became uneasy about his father's public image. Years later, he told a partners' seminar:

> Have you ever tried being Oral Roberts' son? . . . It was very interesting growing up as his son. Somebody asked me the other day when I first entered the Oral Roberts ministry. I told them about 11:00, on the night of November 12, 1948, when I was born into the world. . . . As I got into school, I was to learn that it was a very controversial ministry. Because of the things that some of the kids in my class would say. And I found myself defending something that I didn't even understand.[51]

But Richard was not deeply scarred by the jibes of his fellow teenagers; he generally felt "oblivious" to them. Nor did he ever have serious "doubts" about the validity of the ministry; because "I had traveled with my father and I knew what was true and what was not true."[52] Asked by Dick Cavett in 1970 if he had ever questioned his Christian faith, Richard replied that he had little interest in such speculation.[53] The singular innocence of his faith and his pragmatic confidence in his father's ministry made Richard's subsequent choices in life seem predetermined.

Richard's rebellion was more earthy and lighthearted. Never a good student, he was "courteous" to his teachers, but no one could persuade him to study.[54] Oral playfully posed his problem with Richard during the first ministers' seminar in 1963:

> I've got a boy, I don't know whether he will get in this school. And he's worried now because he's allergic to books. Well if he don't qualify, he won't get in. . . . My wife just got up. Excuse me just a minute. Well, he's just one of those geniuses that excels in sports. And when he gets in a classroom he's strictly lost. . . . Tell him to study? I'm telling him. It hasn't helped too much yet, but who knows, it may be a miracle.[55]

There was to be no miracle in Richard's case. When he reached his junior year in high school, Oral and Evelyn gave him a Volkswagen in return for a promise to study, but it didn't work. He finished high school without distinction and having demonstrated little inclination to exercise self-discipline.[56]

Richard had also decided that he would have no part of his father's ministry; he wanted to be a "regular person." While in high school he began to distance himself from his family. He became a singer in a Tulsa rock band, "playing dances every weekend on the sly," though forbidden by his parents to dance. His relationship with his father deteriorated rapidly. Richard was probably closer to his father than any of the other chilren, because of his athletic interests. He and Oral played basketball and golf together and went on hunting and fishing trips. During Richard's high school years, Oral "continually pressured" him about his "relationship to Christ," and tried to get him to sing in the crusades. But Richard was going in the opposite direction, and he "put the pressure on right back."[57] His resentment was close to the surface. "He'd say right to Oral's face," Evelyn recalled, "Dad, get off my back." And he warned his mother, "Let me tell you something, I'm not going to put up with Dad much longer."[58]

When Richard graduated from high school in 1966, he refused to attend Oral Roberts University. He defiantly insisted on registering at the University of Kansas. It was a symbolic act. "I had in a sense run away from my parents and run away from God," Richard later confessed.[59] Oral was crushed. He might have forced Richard to attend ORU, but Evelyn prevailed: "Now, Oral, you cannot force a child to go to a college. You can guide him and tell him what you think, but if you force him to go to ORU, he will never be a good student."[60]

Oral and Evelyn fretted through the year that Richard spent in Lawrence, Kansas. Several years later Oral admitted that "we don't know all the things that happened to him and we don't want to know."[61] "We did a lot of praying in those days for the Lord to guide Richard," wrote Evelyn.[62] When Richard came home at the end of his first semester, he and his father had an ugly confrontation on the Southern Hills golf course. Richard described it:

> We went out to the golf course and he was having a meeting at that time there in Tulsa. And he began to pressure me about singing. I hadn't been home for a while and he was really pouring it on. I looked at him and I said, "Dad, get off my back. Leave me alone, I'm not interested. Get out of my life." And, to my shock, he said, "Okay." He said, "I'll never mention God to you again." I said, "That's fine. That's just the way I want it."[63]

Oral backed off. Retreating was not his style, but he left Richard alone. It was the first time, Richard believed, "that God ever had a chance with me." Richard developed a local reputation in Kansas as a singer, working in the coffee houses and nightclubs in the Lawrence area and singing in the Starlight Theater in Kansas City, but he also grew "frustrated and unhappy."[64] His letters home betrayed a growing discontent. Richard's grades were poor, and near the end of his first year he called his parents to ask if he could transfer in the fall to Oral Roberts University. He did not yet know it, but he was returning home never to leave again.

Richard still had little relish for academic life after entering Oral Roberts University, showing more interest in being a disc jockey on the university's radio station, KORU. But he befriended Harold Paul, Oral's old comrade from the Pentecostal Holiness church, who was chairman of the history department, and the two "spent many, many, many hours . . . together that first year sharing and sort of me pouring out my guts to him on how I felt about a lot of things and how even though I was here I really didn't want to be here."[65] And around Thanksgiving of his first year at ORU, Richard met the dynamic personality who was to turn his life dramatically toward his father's ministry, Patti Holcombe.[66]

Patricia Kay Holcombe was from Portland, Oregon, and she was a member of the charter class which enrolled at Oral Roberts University in the fall of 1965. A gifted singer and a statuesque beauty, Patti was a scholarship student and a member of the university's first singing group, the Collegians. A strong-willed, outspoken girl who had come to ORU against the wishes of her father, Patti was enamored with the vision of Oral Roberts. She was in the group of ten university students who traveled with Oral in his crusades in the summer of 1966, including the campaign in Brazil, and she was deeply moved by the experience.[67] Patti nearly got herself expelled when she and several friends threatened to burn publicly copies of the *Abundant Life* which reported the Brazilian campaign, because they thought the story was misleading. They branded the magazine *Abundant Lie*. Years later she vividly recalled her audience with Oral: "I can remember sitting there in a sea of tears and really feeling awful, but out of that verbal—I want to say beating—that fatherly advice, you know, I learned a great deal about our president. His door was open all the time to the students. . . . I can appreciate Oral as a father image. He's done so much for me."[68]

At the time Richard entered ORU, Patti was a junior, who was established as one of the leading musical talents on the campus and as a devotee of the ministry. Richard was first attracted by her talent, but he was also intrigued by two other traits. He liked Patti's fierce independence: "We could go out together and if I didn't call her the next day, she didn't care. She was pretty independent." Richard was also drawn by Patti's spiritual intensity, an intensity which he believed indicated that "she had made a commitment of her life to Christ and she had a peace inside."[69] Patti found Richard "spoiled" and a "real lightweight" when it came to spiritual matters—out of place among "serious believers" like herself. On the other hand, he was handsome, courteous, and well-mannered. "He was such a gentleman, so polite and so sweet," wrote Patti in 1983, "that he took me by surprise.[70]

Richard and Patti dated until the summer of 1968 "off and on"; both remembered the courtship as "basically uneventful." During the summer, Patti went with the Collegians on a summer tour, which took them to Europe and Israel. Richard continued to work at KORU, pined for Patti, and decided that he was in love. He sent her a telegram in Israel saying that he had set the date for their marriage. When Patti arrived home, they talked excitedly about the proposal and decided to marry on Thanksgiving Day 1968. Plans were made, invitations were sent, and then, suddenly, about six weeks before the wedding, Patti told Richard that she was calling it off. She was convinced that his commitment to God was superficial.[71]

Richard was shattered; not only was he losing the girl he loved, but he would be "humiliated." He left his dormitory room and went to the president's home, where he found his mother, who had unexpectedly returned home early from a crusade. Richard tearfully told her that he was going to lose Patti. Evelyn challenged her son: "You know what you've done? You've sort of made a halfway commitment of your life to Christ. And you've said, 'Okay, God, I'll go along with You as long as You give me Patti, as long as You give me this, as long as You give me that, as long as You give me my way.'"[72] She admonished Richard to submit to God's will for his life: "If you lose her, the Lord will give you someone else—the one that's right for you. Honey, if it isn't right for you to have Patti, you wouldn't want it for her either—it just wouldn't work out."

The mother and son knelt and prayed together, until Richard "felt this awful heaviness lift." In that moment of self-examination and passion, Richard later reported, he "received the baptism of the Holy Spirit." He rose with a tranquil spirit, prepared to accept God's judgment about his wedding plans.[73]

Patti also spent a troubled evening after telling Richard she had decided to cancel the wedding. She went to her room to pray and believed she felt a "release" which left her at "peace" with the idea of marrying Richard. Eager to tell him the next morning, she had to listen to his experience first. The two youngsters were sure that God had given His approval to their union.[74]

In the long run, Richard's spiritual crisis led him not to Patti but to Oral. It had been Richard's continued ambivalence about the ministry which had unsettled Patti. Richard was still fighting to maintain his separate identity, and he had steadfastly refused to be involved in his father's work. In retrospect, Patti believed that she had crushed Richard's spirit of independence, pushing him into the ministry when he was "struggling to find the courage to break free."[75] But when Richard rose off his knees in his father and mother's home, the momentous choice was made—he would serve God alongside his father. He and Evelyn called Oral that evening to tell him of Richard's experience and choice. "He had truly come home in every sense of the word," wrote Patti in 1983.[76] Richard immediately joined his father, singing and ministering in a campaign in Dayton, Ohio in September 1968, the first time he had participated in a crusade as an adult. His father proudly announced that Richard had become "a regular member of our Abundant Life radio team" and that he would accompany the World Action Singers in the Caribbean crusades that winter.[77] Richard was talented and subsequently had other career opportunities; in 1971 he was offered a major recording contract, which could have vaulted him to stardom. Oral left the choice open to him, and he chose to stay in the ministry.[78] Richard's spiritual reversal was an unspeakable joy for his parents—they lionized the young woman who had turned his head and heart.[79] It was a tragic irony that Patti was the party who insisted that she and Richard live in an environment where he would blossom and she would suffocate.

On Thanksgiving Day, Richard and Patti were married in Ascension Lutheran Church in a ceremony presided over by Bob DeWeese.[80] They set up housekeeping in a duplex in Tulsa, living on $9,000 a year, both still working as disc jockeys at the university radio station and attending school. But almost immediately after their marriage, the new television programs began, and Richard and Patti became members of the supporting cast.[81] Looking back after their first year of marriage, Richard wrote: "We live in Tulsa, close to the University, but are seldom in town. It seems we are constantly on the go with my father either in partners' meetings, filming television programs and the hour-long specials, or on tour with the World Action Singers."[82] Richard soon decided to drop out of the university, having settled on singing as a career.[83] He and Patti were a talented and attractive couple, and they rose rapidly and naturally to star status on the Roberts programs. Richard soon assumed administrative responsibility for the World Action Singers.

After they had been married for a little over a year, trying unsuccessfully to have a child, in February 1971 Richard and Patti adopted Christine Michelle. Almost immediately after the adoption, Patti discovered that she was pregnant, and in January 1972 a second daughter, Julene Allison, was born. By 1972, Patti was adjusting to the "triple role of wife, mother and career woman."[84]

By the early 1970s, Richard and Patti had become "an important part of the dynasty." Richard was appointed president of the evangelistic association, and he and Patti were stars on the television programs. Their lives had changed commensurately—they became members of Southern Hills Country Club; Richard drove a Mercedes and Patti a Jaguar; they had a new home on the hill and traveled frequently on ministry business.[85] Richard's grasp of the ministry and his influence over the television programming were growing, and Patti seemed to be adjusting to the complicated demands of their marriage. "Three-fourths of me is wife, mother, apple pie, cooking, and washing floors," she told a reporter. "The other fourth is prima donna, and I have to exercise that. I have to sing because it fulfills part of me."[86] Patti was clearly an ambitious young woman, listing her interests as sewing, painting, needlepoint, interior decoration, and horseback riding. She planned to write two books, including an autobiography, and saw "no limits on the future" of her and Richard's singing careers.[87]

It was a fairy-tale marriage. What more could one ask? But the marriage was marred by angry fights, usually centering around Patti's growing resentment of Oral and the way in which the ministry dominated their lives.[88] There were a few public flashes of that resentment. In 1972, Patti told a reporter: "Before Oral became my father-in-law I thought he was a kind, healing, benevolent person. He is all of those, but he is also a volcano."[89] But the public image of the marriage remained untarnished up to 1975. And the Roberts family was hopeful. Evelyn was sure they could work out their problems. In 1974, she confided in a talk with some friends: "I couldn't have asked for a better daughter-in-law, or a sweeter one, than Patti. And they've just been so compatible, and it's just been so beautiful. They've had their problems, you know, we all have our problems. Now when you say you've never had any problems in your home, then you're lying. . . . I don't believe in divorce."[90] Whatever problems Richard and Patti were having, they could work them out.

The rebellion of Ronald David Roberts against his father and the ministry was much profounder and more tortured than that of any other Roberts child. Sensitive, bright, gifted in the study of foreign languages, Ronnie rebelled against the lifestyle associated with the Roberts ministry. Once he left home, he smoked and drank, and, recalled attorney Don Moyers, "anytime he was criticized for that he felt like it was an imposition on his personal freedom and liberty."[91] While he never questioned his father's honesty or his ability to help people, at times he clearly came to question the religious credibility of the ministry.[92] And yet, Ronnie's intellectual odyssey could never blot out his childhood beliefs and experiences. In 1964, he told a crusade audience about the power of the Holy Spirit in his life; in 1967, he called the dedication of the university "one of the most moving experiences in my life"; in 1972, he testified about a healing he had received as a child.[93]

Ronnie's rejection of his father stemmed partly from his feeling that they had not had a close relationship: "My father was aware, too, that we were not having a normal father-son relationship, but he said he had to be away because his work was important. I accepted that."[94] As an adult, Ronnie remembered his father as "a very loving sort of person" but also as "a very commanding and authoritative person." "He is sort of awe inspiring when you're with him," he told a reporter.[95] In later years he was drawn to his loving father, but he would never bend to his authoritative father—he would break instead.

Ronnie distanced himself from his family while still in high school, choosing to attend the First Presbyterian Church in Tulsa because he "could be anonymous" there.[96] But his meandering journey away from home really began when he entered Stanford University as a freshman in the fall of 1962. He was an excellent student, and his mother and father were transparently proud when he was admitted to Stanford. Convinced in later years that Ronnie's stay at Stanford injured him, Evelyn took a part of the blame: "It was not his fault that he went. It was my fault and Oral's. I was really proud that I had a son that was smart enough to go to Stanford, and many times I've asked the Lord to forgive me for that because I think perhaps some of the problems Ronnie came into contact with might not have happened if he'd gone some place here."[97]

Ronnie, judged one friend, had been "rather naive up to that time about his father."[98] His presence on the Stanford campus caused something of a stir. Besieged by questions, he asked his father to come to the West Coast to speak in his dormitory. Oral went, wondering "what in the world I could say" to a "bunch of intellectuals," and spoke on speaking in tongues to an overflow audience. After his speech, a questioner asked Oral how he felt about a group whose prophetic sense led them to commit suicide. Oral responded that "the kind of speaking in tongues I have releases me and makes me bring life." Asked how he knew there was a God, Oral answered: "I feel Him right now." "God just gave me answers right and left," Oral exuded after returning home. Ronnie told him: "Dad, I never was so proud in my life. . . . I know half of them thought you're from Oklahoma, a country preacher, and you'd get up here and you would murder the king's English and you wouldn't know what to do." But he assured his father that he had made no "grammatical errors and the words flowed out." Oral returned home convinced that his son's faith had been stabilized.[99]

But the questions persisted. When Ronnie came home for Christmas vacation, he asked, "Daddy, for the first time in my life I've been asked to prove there's a God. How do you prove to people there's a God?" Evelyn felt that Oral had "explained it all to him," but the intellectual pressures remained intense. "I'm tired of colleges brainwashing our children, aren't you?" Evelyn asked in *Abundant Life* in 1964, reflecting their continued concern about Ronnie.[100] Ronnie increasingly changed his lifestyle, and during his sophomore year, without his parents' knowledge, he dropped out of school. When his parents discovered what he had done, he joined the army. Looking back in 1983, Evelyn believed that Stanford had been the beginning of the end: "He lost contact with the family. He got out there where it was a Godless situation, . . . pure communist professors. . . . This is where his trouble started."[101]

Ronnie's enlistment in the army was a blow to his parents. They feared that he would be sent to Vietnam. Evelyn tried to accept it as God's will, but "I was wanting to help the Lord plan Ronnie's life and my plans didn't include the army."[102] He became a foreign language expert in the service, studying Polish, adding it to the facility he already had in German, French, Spanish, Russian, and Chinese.[103] In many ways it appeared that the army was good for Ronnie. By 1967, his last year in the service, he seemed to be settling down. In March, he married Carol Loy Croskery in a formal wedding ceremony at the First Presbyterian Church in Tulsa.[104] The couple spent the remainder of 1967 at Fort George Mead in Maryland, Ronnie having decided to complete a Ph.D. in linguistics after leaving the service. Evelyn was encouraged: "We want him to finish his education. . . . We have always felt God had something special for Ronnie. He is very open to anything about God and has a mind like his father's."[105]

Ronnie enrolled at Virginia Commonwealth University in Richmond, Virginia, and in 1970 he graduated with a B.A. degree in French. An outstanding student, he won a Woodrow Wilson Fellowship for graduate study at a university of his choice—the first student from Virginia Commonwealth to be so honored.[106] Ronnie reported in *Abundant Life* that he and Carol had just finished the "happiest year of our marriage" and that he was looking forward to beginning his doctoral studies.[107]

The couple spent the next three years at the University of Southern California, where Ronnie worked in a Ph.D. program in foreign languages. Then in 1973, after he had completed the necessary course work, he was asked by a friend to return to Tulsa to teach accelerated language courses in Washington High School. He accepted the job, teaching Chinese, Russian, and German for a year, and then decided to stay. The couple had adopted a daughter; Oral and Evelyn were delighted that they would be living in Tulsa.

Ronnie still would have no part of his father's ministry; his mother explained that when "these kids get away into a Ph.D. program, they have some crazy ideas."[108] He removed himself from the trust fund his father had established for the children, and wore a beard that displeased his parents.[109] But Evelyn could see "such changes" in her son. "He's coming around little-by-little," she told a group of friends. She prayed every day: "Lord, will you help me to keep my mouth shut?"[110] Ronnie was a long way from home in 1975, but he was back in Tulsa, and his life seemed to be stable. His parents still dreamed grand dreams for him. The potential was there.

While Oral and Evelyn struggled with Richard and Ronnie through the years, their oldest daughter, Rebecca, and her husband, Marshall Nash, had been a balm for their spirit. Rebecca, like all of the other children, had resented being a Roberts child; she had confided to her mother that she would "be so glad when I change my name from Roberts."[111] But as she matured, Rebecca held no resentments: "As a child I did not realize the meaning of everything we were doing and sometimes I think Mother and Daddy didn't either. Now that I'm older and can look back on it, I realize the things that happened to us and the sacrifices we had to make were worth it."[112] There was little bitterness in Rebecca.

Evelyn insisted that her daughter complete a two-year college business course at Tulsa University, "because I believe every girl should be prepared to take care of herself."[113] However, Rebecca was well taken care of by her quiet but highly successful husband, Marshall Nash. Marshall left Oral's organization in 1965 to begin a career in building and real estate investment, which by 1975 made him a millionaire and one of the most respected young businessmen in Tulsa. "Quiet and unconventional," he made his fortune building apartments, trading property, and investing in banks. In 1972, the business editor of the *Tulsa World* summarized Nash's accomplishments:

> In addition to his real estate and building activities, Nash is a substantial stock-holder in the proposed Riverside National Bank at Jenks. He also is the youngest director of City Bank & Trust Co., the youngest member of the board of regents at Oral Roberts University, the youngest director of the Home Builders Association of Greater Tulsa, the youngest director of the Tulsa City-County Citizens Bond Advisory Committee, and was the youngest president ever of the Apartment Council of Tulsa. . . . He is chairman of the board of University Village, . . . serves on the executive committee of ORU, and is a junior member of Southern Hills Country Club.[114]

Nash was named to the ORU board of regents in 1970, after he gave $10,000 toward the construction of a chapel at University Village.[115] He had become much more than a son-in-law to Oral; he was a trusted advisor. "Marshall was a great balance wheel," recalled Ron Smith, "he had nothing to gain or lose in telling the truth and, of course, that's the biggest struggle that anyone in a decision making role there has to make."[116]

By 1975, the Nash family had grown to include three "beautiful children." Brenda Ann was born in 1964, and a second daughter, Marcia Elaine, in 1968. In 1972 Jon Oral became the first Roberts grandson. It was a lovely family. In 1974, Marshall told Evelyn: "You know, so many young men that I have business dealings with are having problems in their homes. They're about to get a divorce, and these men come and tell me all about their problems. . . . And sometimes I think that Rebecca and I are the only ones that are happy."[117] A year later, Evelyn asked Rebecca how she and Marshall were doing: "Mother, I just want to tell you the truth. When Marshall walks in that door in the afternoon, I'm just as excited to see him as I was the first day we married." They seemed an island of sanity in the madness of the modern world. Marshall and Rebecca were living proof, Evelyn believed, that "every marriage can be that way."[118]

Oral's encounters with the world in the fifteen years from 1960 to 1975—and even more his struggles with his family—often turned him introspective. By 1975, he was mellower and more subdued; he understood better his inability to impose his own will on others. But more than ever, he knew what he believed. When he returned from Stanford in 1963, he was fired with zeal: "I tell you what I think we should do is stand our ground, and not only stand our ground, make some progress ourselves. If speaking in tongues is real, why don't we do it. If it's not real, quit it. Let's not play around with it. Let's either have it or not have it. Glory to God."[119] When one defends his children, entering mortal combat to save their souls, he must have a bedrock faith to stand upon. By 1975, Oral's war with Satan was global and impersonal, but it also was familial and personal. In the years after 1975, the two streams flowed relentlessly and angrily together—mingling Oral and Evelyn's private and public lives in turbulent and tragic ways.

PART FOUR

MAELSTROM

1975–1985

PROLOGUE

Tulsa and Palm Springs, February 1977

ON FEBRUARY 12, at about six o'clock in the morning, Collins Steele knocked on the door of the president's home and awakened Evelyn. "Mrs. Roberts, can you come to the back door?" he asked through the intercom. Evelyn hurried to the entrance, knowing something was wrong; Steele opened the newspaper to a morning headline reporting an airplane crash in Kansas. "We think it's Marshall and Rebecca," he whispered. Evelyn stepped to the intercom and called her husband: "Oral, put on your bathrobe and come to the kitchen." The hour and Evelyn's tone told Oral that tragedy had struck. "Oral, Marshall and Rebecca are dead," Evelyn told him. "What happened?" he gasped.[1]

Marshall and Rebecca had been returning from a skiing vacation in Colorado, where they had recently purchased a condominium just outside Aspen. Marshall had parlayed his quiet integrity and gambler's instincts into a multimillion-dollar fortune in Tulsa real estate and the ownership of a string of small banks spanning the state of Oklahoma.[2] "I don't think Marshall ever made a bad real estate deal," recalled his bank president brother.[3] The young couple seemed to have everything to live for. Evelyn recalled something Rebecca had said when the Roberts family had gathered on the Christmas before their death: "This has been the best year of my life. At last I know who I am and where I'm going, and I'm excited to see what the New Year will bring."[4]

For several months before the accident, Marshall had been considering the purchase of a private airplane to use in his business. An Oklahoma City dealer offered to fly the Nashes home from Aspen to demonstrate an aircraft to them, and on February 11, the pilot, Marshall, the president of one of Marshall's banks, and the wives of all three men boarded the plane. Flying in hazy but nonturbulent weather over Kansas, the plane crashed. A long lawsuit, finally settled out of court, alleged that the crash was a result of a faulty autopilot, inferior plane design, and pilot error.[5]

It was one of those sudden, razor-sharp amputations which leave their victims stunned and bleeding. "Why?" Evelyn asked as she and Oral dressed and prepared to go to the Nashes' home. But there was little time for immediate reflection; both Oral and Evelyn knew that they must first break the news to their three grandchildren, Brenda, who was thirteen, Marcia, who was eight, and Jon Oral, who was five. "It was our place," said Evelyn. And so, Andy and Munna, as all the grandchildren called them, delivered the message: "Your momma and daddy won't be home; they're dead."[6]

As the news of the tragedy spread on the morning of the twelfth, friends began rallying around to offer support. Roberts's attorney, Don Moyers, drove to the Nashes' home, where he found Oral and Evelyn with "the kids in their arms and . . . terribly broken up." Moyers, whose son had been killed in an air crash, assured them that they would "survive it and God will give you some answers some day."[7] While others comforted, Collins Steele made the morbid trip to Kansas to collect the bodies. Bill Nash, Marshall's brother, and his wife, Edna, hurried home from a visit to Georgia. Nash and Ron Smith selected the caskets. Others made the complicated funeral arrangements.[8]

The return of Bill and Edna Nash solved the most pressing problem, the disposition of the children. On their way home from the St. Louis airport, Bill Nash called to tell Oral that he and Edna had discussed such a tragedy with Marshall and Rebecca and that they felt they should become the parents of the children. It was clearly the best decision; Oral and Evelyn went with the Nashes to tell the children the news. "We had a little prayer service there in the den around the table," recalled Nash, "and Oral was very generous in the type of prayer that he prayed to seal us together as a family. It was a moving and touching experience. . . . And it worked."[9]

The memorial service for Marshall and Rebecca was conducted on February 14 in Mabee Center. The service was sad but expectant; it was labeled a "home-going celebration" for the young couple. James Buskirk eulogized the two, and Bob DeWeese preached a message on the text "Ye shall be sorrowful, but your sorrow shall be turned to joy." "There was some criticism about the style of the funeral," noted one reporter, but most observers were touched by the family's response. A Tulsa television newscaster commented on the funeral service:

> At the services for Oral Roberts' daughter and her husband, Tulsa businessman, Marshall Nash, this afternoon, many people just had to be touched, as I was, watching Dr. Roberts holding his hand high, joyfully responding as the choir offered the "Hallelujah Chorus." It was not unexpected. Oral Roberts has provided inspiration to millions of people throughout the world and today was not an exception, even in his own loss. They say faith can move mountains and that kind of faith was certainly evident at Mabee Center this afternoon, even though we mourned the loss of two of Tulsa's finest people.

... How much happier all of us would be indeed if we could only share the kind of faith Oral Roberts demonstrated this afternoon.[10]

There was, indeed, a national outpouring of sympathy for the Roberts family. James Buskirk read a telegram from Billy Graham: "Beloved Oral, sometimes we have to look at heaven through tears. Those tears sometimes become telescopes that bring heaven so much nearer. Ruth and I will be praying for you and Evelyn and for the family that God's grace will be more than sufficient. We love you in the Lord."[11] The telephones in the Prayer Tower were flooded with calls from all over the world offering "sympathy and support." Roberts's office received sixty-six bushels of telegrams and cards of condolence.[12]

Oral and Evelyn struggled painfully with the tragedy. Evelyn ran the gamut of emotions from disbelief, to anger, to self-pity. Once the public ceremonies were over, she plummeted into depression. Rebecca was gone—thirty-seven years old, "tall, straight and beautiful, with three wonderful children and everything to live for."[13] On the fourth evening after the crash, alone in their Tulsa home, Oral and Evelyn fought back despair. Before retiring, Evelyn said to her husband, "Honey, before I go to bed, will you hold me? This is the worst night. I can't make it through the night. And will you pray with me in the Spirit?"[14] "Only the prayer language of the Spirit kept us sane," recalled Oral.[15] Several months later, after the meaning of the tragedy had begun to become clear to Oral, he related the events of that evening: "I held her and I prayed with this language and I can't explain that to you very well. This language that came out of the depths was not English. It just came up and then came the English words and I found myself praying in English." Oral's prayer that evening contained a message, one that Evelyn resisted but finally acceded to—the two of them should appear on television immediately to let "all our hurting and grieving hang out before millions, many of whom have lost loved ones."[16] "Oral, I can't do that," Evelyn protested, "I can't hang out my grief and hurt for everybody to see." "OK," Oral replied, "I won't ask you to, but I'm going to do it myself."[17]

But Evelyn knew that she could not allow Oral to bear the burden alone, and after several days of planning, the two of them went to the television studio on the Oral Roberts University campus and taped one of the most remarkable programs in the long history of Roberts's television career. Aired on February 27, the show began with Oral standing forlorn and red-eyed before the camera:

This is one of the most difficult times of our lives. We've said to our friends as we've opened our telecast each week, "Something *good* is going to happen to you." And we're going to say it today at a time of tragic loss in our family.

I've faced the sufferings of millions of people around the world and we've tried to sustain people and share our faith, but we've never had the loss of a child.

We've never lost a son or a daughter, and in this moment Evelyn, my darling wife, and I want to say to you, we still believe it, something good is going to happen to you and there will be a breakthrough from *heaven* in '77.

The reason we've come together today, just she and I, is that we didn't want to wait months later and then look back and describe this incident in our lives. We wanted to come to you when we hurt and thank the people who have written and wired and phoned.[18]

It was a paradoxical moment, the television lights harshly examining Oral's theological slogans—is God good, can faith overcome all obstacles? The tragedy was particularly jarring because of the phrase that Oral had used in litany after litany in public appearances aired on television in the preceding months: "There will be a breakthrough from heaven in '77. I believe a breakthrough is coming for your loved ones. I believe it."[19]

If the appearance of Oral and Evelyn on television supplied no theological answers, few could have been unmoved by the bravery of the couple as they struggled to speak, often weeping, reaffirming their faith in God. Their main theme was a word of comfort to others who had lost loved ones—urging them to be sustained by faith in God. A few weeks later, Oral relived the taping:

> Well, we sat there on the television with the cameras on us and we cried like two children and we told about the death. We told how we hurt and then we told what Jesus meant to us. We told them that Rebecca and Marshall were in heaven and some day we're going to heaven. And we told them that we knew they were saved. We also told them that you who have lost loved ones who don't know yours were saved, remember the dying thief, the man on the cross that got saved the last moment.[20]

Like most of Oral's messages, the program was not a philosophical or theological probing, it was a visceral and emotional response to death. In retrospect, Evelyn believed it "proved to be a blessing not only to Oral and me but also to our many friends who had also lost loved ones and were overcome with grief."[21]

Oral and Evelyn's final accommodation of their grief was consistent with the mainstream of Christian thought. They took consolation in the belief that Marshall and Rebecca were alive in heaven. Evelyn wrote a children's book, *Heaven Has a Floor,* as the result of a question from her grandson about the whereabouts of his parents. Assured that they were in heaven after their fatal plane crash, five-year-old Jon Oral asked Evelyn, "Munna, does heaven have a floor?"[22] In the months after the crash, Oral repeatedly asserted: "Rebecca's not out there in the ground. . . . Rebecca is with the Lord Jesus."[23] Beyond the assurance that the Nashes were secure in heaven, some charismatics used the incident to explore the sovereignty of God which allowed (or caused) their death. Some of the messages at the funeral, believed Bill Nash, "inferred if not said, that God killed this young couple."[24] Evelyn specifically repudiated that extreme view when she wrote a short booklet entitled *Coping with Grief* shortly after the tragedy:

> God doesn't take our loved ones away from us. God didn't *take* my daughter away from me. He *accepted* her. He received her when the accident took her life. In no way do I believe my God sent that accident to take my daughter away from me. Yes, He allowed it for some reason. I don't know what that reason is, but I do know that a lot of good things have happened since Rebecca and Marshall went to be with Jesus.[25]

A few days after taping the telecast, Oral and Evelyn went to Palm Springs to rest. Richard accompanied them to play golf with his father. The three of them registered at the Riviera Hotel, still devastated "on the inside."[26] The dry, barren landscape of the desert surrounding Palm Springs seemed symbolic to Oral of his own barren spirit.

One afternoon a friend who was purchasing a home in Palm Springs asked the three of them to visit the house with her. Just as they were about to leave, Oral sat down in a chair in the hotel room and began writing on a yellow legal pad. "You all go ahead," he told Evelyn and Richard, "the Lord is beginning to talk to me and I just have to stay here and see what He says." After visiting for a couple of hours with their friend, Richard and Evelyn returned to get dressed for dinner. Oral excitedly told them to sit down: "Oh, Evelyn, the Lord's just been talking to me since I've been sitting here. . . . Let me sit down and read you what the Lord said." It was a familiar scene. It had "happened many times before," recalled Evelyn, "I'm used to it." But this message was different. This time, "Richard and I sat there and bawled up a storm while he read it." They finally went to dinner, but Oral left in the middle of the meal, because "the Lord's not through talking to me." He returned to his yellow pad, recording the details of the message.[27]

The redoubtable message was revealed by Oral several months later, under the title "I Will Rain upon Your Desert!"[28] Viewing the "twisting gullies and the barren ground" of the desert, Oral's mind had flashed back to a visit to Palm Springs a few months earlier, when a shower had made the desert blossom. The phrase echoed in his grieving mind in February 1977. "In my heart I knew this was a powerful thing God had spoken to me—something very special," he later wrote.[29] The phrase found meaning in the long, detailed message from God about the completion of his healing vision. Several months later, Oral announced what had been outlined on his yellow pad in Palm Springs:

> He said to me: "Son, you cannot put the vision I have given you into a place where My full healing power is not freely accepted. It must not be in a place defeated by a lack of faith in My miraculous power. You must build a new and different medical center for Me. The healing streams of prayer and medicine must merge through what I will have you build. . . .
>
> There rising before me were the details of the buildings. Immediately I was led to read the last two chapters in the Bible, Revelation 21, 22. There I saw the City of God, the New Jerusalem, with its River of Life and its broad avenues. . . .
>
> I saw the City of God as a reflection of God himself bringing healing and health to those who entered there. Suddenly God gave me *a new name* for the Health Care and Research Center I am to build in His name.
>
> "You shall call it THE CITY OF FAITH."
>
> I thought my heart would burst with joy. THE CITY OF FAITH. What a name! I knew only God could give a name like that to the Health Care and Research Center He wanted me to build.[30]

Oral did not announce the building of the City of Faith for over six months after returning from Palm Springs, but he began immediately to plan the medical center. He summoned Jim Winslow, his newly appointed vice-provost for health affairs, along with architect Frank Wallace and his construction chief Bill Roberts. For an afternoon they talked excitedly in the Roberts home about Oral's notes and sketches—Wallace drawing and redrawing buildings to capture the vision. Oral knew that the center would include three buildings—sixty stories, thirty stories, and twenty stories tall. "They finally got the design that he felt God had given him," Evelyn recalled; there were minor changes subsequently but no major ones.[31] Between February and the formal announcement of the project in September, Roberts and his lieutenants hectically learned and planned. It was a scheme that dwarfed Oral's boldest dreams of the past; it would be by far the most difficult financial burden he had ever undertaken.

The desert vision and the building of the City of Faith threw Oral Roberts into a vortex of controversy, reopening old questions about the validity of his communications from God. Jim Winslow averred that "I had no idea that he was even thinking about" building a hospital until Oral returned from Palm Springs.[32] Oral's critics, on the other hand, charged that the project had been conceptualized and planned before the death of Marshall and Rebecca and that Oral had used the tragedy as a means of introducing it.[33]

The two views are not entirely irreconcilable. Like all of Oral's major visions, nothing in the desert message was unthought of, though the language Oral used in reporting it could be taken to imply that. "This was not the first time God had ever talked to him about having a hospital," Evelyn agreed in 1984.[34] For over a year, Oral had been embroiled in a bitter fight to begin a medical school at Oral Roberts University; it appeared that the opening might be delayed because no local hospital would cooperate. In a chapel message exactly one week before the plane crash, Oral unexpectedly began to wander through his dreams. Reflecting on the opposition to the medical school, he stated:

> I dream that the hospitals of Tulsa will affiliate with us. Two have turned us down, one is talking favorably. . . . But I dream far beyond that, for there's no hospital built on this earth that can do what I dream about. I dream about those hundred acres across the street, for a great medical center to be erected. I can see it towering up above the earth now, a single building perhaps, with all the hospital facilities, with all the doctors in the same building. . . . I believe in putting the whole man together through prayer and medicine. I believe in a healing center, spiritual and medical, of bringing doctors, dentists from all over the world. I believe in bringing great researchers from all over the world for cancer, for heart, . . . and putting them under the same roof. . . . I believe in a breakthrough in cancer, . . . I believe, I dream. As I stand here this morning with no money to start that, as I stand here this morning with not many friends in the hospital world who understand what I'm saying and not many friends in the Christian world who understand, . . . I dream of a million people a year coming here into that medical center.[35]

Clearly, much of the City of Faith vision was already on Oral's mind, and had been discussed, though most insiders, including Evelyn and Winslow, did not think it was a serious or desirable alternative.[36] Even the name, the City of Faith, was resurrected from Oral's past—having been proposed in the 1950s for a project which never materialized. Oral closed his chapel speech on February 4 with an allusion to the prophet Elijah praying for rain, which presaged his desert vision. "He knew," Oral concluded, "that through human instrumentality God was going to break the drought and the rain would come. . . . I feel deep down inside this morning that we've crossed over and we're going to do it."[37]

Oral's vision, as always, was a coalescing of insights rather than a flash of revelation. Even more important, the vision began when Oral completely acquiesced to his feelings, when he agreed to listen. After the "tragic death" of Marshall and Rebecca, he told his television audience in November 1981, "I began to listen again."[38] In the grip of personal grief, Oral's mind once again turned back to that source which he had trusted since childhood—that primitive self in the pit of his belly which he identified with the voice of God. He already knew the message; he now decided to obey it.

The funeral, settling the grandchildren with their new parents, and the television program had been cathartic. The desert vision called Roberts furiously back to the world of work and challenge. Oral had always believed in a concept of "equivalent benefit," trusting that every evil in life would bring forth an equivalent good. "Oral and I have done a lot of growing, and we have been able to help a lot of people in their grief," Evelyn wrote. "The Lord is bringing good out of bad."[39] Oral's ministry had always been delicately interwoven with his personal life. It was fitting that the family's greatest personal tragedy would be linked to the ministry's most grandiose monument.

CHAPTER

XIII

Maelstrom

"I T'S LIKE ALL hell's trying to break loose around him," nodded Demos Shakarian in 1983. "The devil's turned loose everything. Can we expect him to do anything else?"[1] Beginning with the deaths of Marshall and Rebecca, the Roberts family entered a time of severe turmoil and tragedy. The personal suffering came during a decade of unprecedented change and controversy in the ministry. As Roberts's external world turned increasingly hostile and threatening, his personal life seemed to be disintegrating. He and Evelyn had entered the maelstrom.

Oral's loyalties to his family seemed to intensify as he grew older. He often reminisced about Ellis and Claudius and the debts he owed to them, and he repeatedly rounded up Elmer, Vaden, and Jewel to thank them and to receive their reassuring testimonies.[2] Ellis and Claudius's children were an odd group in their declining years. Oral's brothers and sister were much like their fellow second-generation children of the Oklahoma soil—modestly successful, provincial, rustic, looking and speaking as befitted their roots. Beside them, Oral seemed polished, refined, cosmopolitan—only his drawl identified him with their common past. But Oral had not forgotten them. In 1982, Orie Roberts, Elmer's wife, attended a devotion at the Oral Roberts Evangelistic Association, and Oral prayed for her:

> My sister-in-law Orie Roberts is here today . . . and she is in need of a great healing. . . . I am going to pray for Orie. . . . They've always been very encouraging and supportive of me in this ministry. My brother Vaden's been

very supportive. My sister Jewel, my parents, of course, while they were living. That doesn't always happen. . . . But my family has been very supportive and very believing, so now I feel like, Orie, that I owe you and Elmer more than I can ever pay you. I owe Jewel. I owe Vaden. I owe my parents more than I could ever pay.[3]

Evelyn and the children were the core of the Roberts family clan. The partners of the ministry were regularly informed about the activities of the Roberts children. In April 1978, Evelyn reported:

Our daughter Rebecca and her husband Marshall are in heaven. . . . Their three young children are with us often and I feel a growing love for Jesus in their hearts as they are being so beautifully nurtured by Bill and Edna. . . . Ronnie and Carol are busy in education and have a small business on the side. They are rearing two beautiful children in Sunday school and church. Ron and Roberta have their two boys in Sunday school and Roberta teaches a class of children. Ron teaches school and coaches. Richard and Patti are heavily involved in ministry—Richard with us and Patti in a calling she feels especially from the Lord for her—and are rearing up two little girls in Sunday school and church.[4]

Evelyn, particularly, worried about the children, ever analyzing and discreetly offering advice, frequently writing and speaking with exceptional candor about the family's successes and failures.[5]

The deaths of Rebecca and Marshall were the first mortal blow to the Roberts family, but that tragedy was both preceded and followed by the slow and painful self-destruction of Ronnie. That calamitous spiral, in hindsight portended since the 1960s by Ronnie's rebellious lifestyle and tortured self-doubts, was relieved occasionally by periods of repentance and reform. Oral and Evelyn retained a parent's hopes—but it was not to be.

The last few years of Ronnie's life were a steady downhill slide. He resigned his high-school teaching job because of the low pay and taught briefly at Tulsa Junior College. Subsequently, he opened a shop in Tulsa, selling Oriental art and antiques, a field in which he had considerable expertise. In the midst of the recession in the early 1980s, his business foundered, and he was forced into bankruptcy. Bill Nash, Ronnie's banker, recognized his creative brilliance but believed that he was "the worst business man I have ever dealt with."[6] Finally, in the "worst thing" that happened to him, Evelyn believed, his marriage collapsed, and he spent his last months living alone in a Tulsa apartment.[7] During these months the family learned that Ronnie had a serious problem with alcohol and drugs. His addiction became public knowledge in the fall of 1981, when he was charged with a felony for forging prescriptions to illegally secure the drug Tussionex at a pharmacy located just a few blocks from the Oral Roberts University campus. He entered a guilty plea, and was placed on probation in February 1982.[8]

Ronnie's deterioration was a nightmare to those who loved him. Everyone who knew him well regarded him as brilliant, a "masterful writer," and an engaging conversationalist. The fact that he smoked, drank, and wore a beard marked him as a rebel and estranged him from his family, but it also betrayed an independence which many admired.[9] But his sparkling wit and independence faded in his final months; he grew fat and slow-witted, addled, his parents believed, by the drugs he depended on.[10] Some close friends were aware that "he had contemplated his own death a number of times."[11]

Ronnie's parents grieved for their eldest son—the son for whom they had always held such great hope. They believed that he had a gift to heal that rivaled Oral's; his academic training could have fitted him to guide the university.[12] They never gave up. In early 1982, after Ronnie's drug problem had been splashed across the nation by the wire services, Oral made several public references to the family trauma. In January, he told a Tulsa audience:

> Most of you know that I have an older son who came out of the Viet Nam War and has never been the same since. That may not have been the reason. All we know is his heartache and our heartache while we love our son and we support our son and we stand up for our son, we have never agreed with some of the practices of our oldest son. . . . But we never give up on him. We've thought we've had enough grief, especially with the press being so nice to hurl whatever I do across America, including my own son when he has a mistake, or any of my sons. . . . Those are moments sometimes you get pretty low.[13]

A few days later, Oral told another group on the ORU campus that God had promised to save his "blood family," and he appealed for their prayers for Ronnie: "My older son . . . loved the Lord all his life, prayed in the Spirit, and prayed for the sick nearly as well as I. Then something happened. He's been in lots of trouble . . . because he did some wrong things. . . . Remember to pray for Ronnie. He's been raised right and still he is right in many ways. He just sort of needs only what God can do."[14]

In Ronnie's final weeks, he and his parents reached out to one another. He was suffering from neuritis in his back and called his parents to pray for him. Evelyn assured him that God would heal him without surgery, and Ronnie replied: "I know He will heal it, Mother, and that's why I want you and Dad to pray." He was still not "living like he should," Evelyn lamented, but "he will."[15] About three months before he died, Oral told Evelyn one afternoon, "Call Ronnie, I have a feeling he needs to come out here tonight." He came. Oral told him, once again, "Ronnie, I think it's time you made a change in your life. . . . Only God can heal you and get you off of the desire for these things." Once again, as he had in the past, he offered his son a job at the university. Ronnie was "touched" and wondered what he could do. Oral proposed to make him an assistant to aid him in writing. His father had offered him many jobs in the past, and the conditions remained the same—he would have to stop smoking and shave off his beard. Evelyn recalled: "Ronnie was very moved and began crying and we got on our knees and had a prayer session with him for about an hour and the Lord really moved in that room. And that boy really committed his life to Jesus Christ. . . . He was a changed person when he left." He promised to pray about the job.[16]

Evelyn visited Ronnie a few days later, on Mother's Day, and he told her that he could never accept a position at the university just because he was a

Roberts. Evelyn left convinced that Ronnie was no longer her "brilliant son." He looked like a "little child," unable to grasp any realistic future for his life. They had reached a final impasse. His father and mother had done all they could—they had aided him, borne criticism because of him, and loved him in his rebellion. They did everything but accept him as he was—that they could not do. He was their son, but he was prodigal. And Ronnie had done all he could for his parents. He honored them, he loved them, and, almost certainly, in his deepest soul, he believed in them, but he could not be what they wanted, and he could not lie. Bill Nash reflected on Ronnie's dilemma: "He was not capable of giving them the answers they wanted to hear because he was too honest. . . . It totally destroyed him."[17] Like all heroic tragedies, the conflict of noble wills demanded that the weaker be sacrificed for the sin of estranging father and son.

On June 9, 1982, Ronald David Roberts was found dead in his automobile, the victim, according to police reports, of a "self-inflicted gunshot wound to the heart."[18] Richard Roberts and George Stovall went to Ronnie's apartment when they received word from the police. In a note he had written, Ronnie said, among other things, that he looked forward to seeing Rebecca again.[19] It was several hours before Richard was able to reach Oral and Evelyn to break the news to them; he solicitously attended his parents through the ordeal that followed.

At the funeral service, Oral delivered a brief eulogy, remembering Ronnie as "a three-year-old singing hymns, as a five-year-old reciting his father's sermons, as a man who was never quite the same after a tour of duty during Vietnam, and as a scholar who mastered five languages and was always willing to share his wealth of knowledge with his father." As Oral and Evelyn rose to leave the chapel, a student stood to say "We love you, brother Roberts." Oral turned, faintly smiled, and raised his hand. In response, the entire audience in the crowded chapel rose "and stretched their arms toward the Robertses in a gesture of love and prayer."[20]

Ronnie's death was in some ways the harshest family misfortune; more than any other act of rejection, noted one family friend, "suicide gets its revenge."[21] But, once again, Oral and Evelyn almost immediately appeared in public, this time speaking in a laymen's conference on campus the evening after Ronnie's funeral. Their closest friends and coworkers watched in awe as the pair performed with broken hearts.[22] The following week James Buskirk introduced Oral in chapel:

> You're aware that very recently sorrow has absolutely invaded the hearts of the Roberts family. And this last weekend was very special. As you know, we had a Lay Seminar on campus. We watched the Robertses as they ministered. It was as though they never believed what they believed more than they believed this weekend. . . . It was as though the Roberts family was seeding for their healing, and they did that exceedingly well.[23]

Oral confessed to the students that he wanted to "fly away": "I wanted not to have to face 2,200 partners. In the minds of many might be the question, 'You are such a preacher of faith, why is this happening to you? What can you do for us?' All those satanic things were trying to find a place in my mind. . . . But do you know what happened? My foundation held. And in retrospect, I wouldn't give away or take back what we gave in that seminar."[24]

Once again there was a national outpouring of sympathy for the Roberts family. Bill Banowsky, Oral's friend and the president of the University of Oklahoma, called from Colorado: "Oral, mothers and fathers of the nation and perhaps of the world are standing with you today, not only for your son but for their children."[25] Among the thousands of letters of condolence was a "precious" note to Evelyn from Ruth Graham, assuring that God could be entrusted with the fate of her son.[26] Oral accepted Ronnie's death with resignation: "My son had a will of his own, and my will cannot cancel out anybody's will." He and Evelyn believed the suicide was the work of the devil. Evelyn wrote a year later, "I was able to accept my son's death a year ago. God doesn't steal your children. The devil steals, kills, and destroys."[27] Oral believed that "something spectacular through this ministry in the healing of people" would come as a result of the tragedy—something which the devil was trying to stop by destroying Ronnie.[28] Shortly after Ronnie's death, Oral returned to Palm Springs, where he received another long message concerning the discovery of a cure for cancer, which he linked with the tragedy.[29]

Theological understanding aside, the Robertses embarked on parental "guilt trips" through the debris of Ronnie's shattered life. When Oral told Evelyn of their son's death, she asked, as any mother would, "Oh, is there something we could have done that we didn't do?" Oral let her "talk herself out." Then he asked: "Let's just think back. Is there anything we could have done?" They searched their memories and "could not recapture one thing that we could have done differently, at least upon the information we had at the time."[30] It was no doubt true—they would never willingly have hurt their beautiful little boy, or their brilliant youngster, or their wayward rebel son. But it was not easy to explore all the possibilities, or to stop retracing the same paths in search of a clue. "I've had to work hard on my dad and mother," remarked Richard, "because you know it's natural that they would say if I had just done this or . . . that. It's not true."[31] But there can be no end of memories—of tender moments or words unspoken, of dreams of what might have been.

Months before the end of Ronnie's life, Richard's marriage had ended in divorce. It was a calamity for the Roberts family which rivaled the deaths of Rebecca and Ronnie; it probably shook the ministry more. And, like Ronnie's self-destruction, it seemed so unnecessary. In 1975, it appeared that Richard and Patti had everything—they were a beautiful and talented young couple with two lovely daughters. Richard's role in his father's ministry was growing rapidly; Patti was featured on the television programs and was known to millions of Americans. The two lived a luxurious and glamorous lifestyle; in 1977 they purchased a home in Palm Springs just a few blocks from Oral and Evelyn's house.

Oral pushed Richard and Patti to the foreground. In 1975, he told the university faculty: "I want you to walk with Evelyn and me, with Richard and Patti and me. I am bringing them in because they are now such a strong part of the whole ministry. . . . And so it's a coming together now of the family, and I thank God for it." Oral sensed that his talented son and daughter-in-law were about to become main cogs in the whole ministry: "Richard and Patti are going to be much more active on campus. . . . I appreciate a son and a daughter who feel the weight of the University and the ministry like this."[32] For a time, it seemed that the formula would work. In 1976, Patti talked enthusiastically with a reporter about her work: "It's not only a job. It's an inspiration for life." The "great thing" about working with Oral and Evelyn, she continued, was that "they live what they profess."[33]

But beneath this glamorous and placid exterior was, in Patti's words "a swirling cauldron of pain and anger."[34] Richard and Patti's marriage came to be marred by "terrible fights," in which she scored her husband for being more loyal to his father's ministry than to his wife.[35] Increasingly, the television portrait of the happily married young Christian couple became a stage creation— hiding a relationship growing more and more strained and distant. Richard was hemmed in, seemingly asked to choose between pleasing his wife (who had led him into his father's ministry) and fulfilling his call.

In hindsight, all parties agreed that the marriage was a mistake. In her 1983 book *Ashes to Gold,* Patti judged that both she and Richard were too young to understand love and that there were symptoms of dissatisfaction from the beginning of their relationship.[36] For instance, she remembered that the two of them were "bored" two days after their honeymoon began and that they returned home early from the trip.[37] Roberta sensed that the two "were not happy" when they returned from their honeymoon: "All those years we knew."[38] But the doubts may well have been one-sided in the early years of the marriage. Evelyn was convinced that "little old innocent Richard was so much in love with her, he didn't know anything else existed but her. He loved the very ground she walked on." Very early in the marriage, however, Oral and Evelyn came to have doubts about Patti's commitment.[39]

The final stage in the deterioration of Richard and Patti's marriage began when she withdrew from the Oral Roberts ministry. In November 1976, she resigned from the television program, and shortly thereafter she formed Patti Roberts International Outreach to sponsor her own "ministry." She gave a series of concerts "at churches, civic programs, fashion shows, and country clubs" and aspired to launch an international ministry.[40] In 1978, Patti undertook the most ambitious of her ministry tours, taking a group of ten musicians and singers with her to Tehran, at a cost of about $22,000. Patti emphasized that her new career was a search for "personal fulfillment"; she had resigned from Oral's program because "I can't be an extension of someone else all of my life." She insisted that she had not rejected Oral's dream, but that she also had "a dream of my own."[41]

In 1977 and 1978, after it became clear to outsiders that Patti had left the television program, rumors persisted that the couple's marriage was in trouble. Patti and Richard vigorously denied the charge. Patti told a reporter that she had "learned to laugh" about such reports and that they had "brought her closer to her husband spiritually." "People have to understand that Rich has his career and I have mine," she insisted. "It is a slap in God's face when any person does not realize his potential."[42] Richard explained in an ORU publication that he and Patti had decided that they would have a "better marital relationship" if they "weren't thrown together 24 hours a day"; he seemed to accept gracefully his wife's pursuit of an independent career.[43] When Patti made her third and largest tour of Iran, in May 1978, Richard joined her team for a week, "not as a singer, but as a companion, and to gain a better understanding of what his wife is doing." Patti told a student reporter: "It's great to have a husband who is just as interested in my work as I am in his."[44] Indeed, Richard had supplied a major part of the money to fund the tour and had written a personal letter urging others to help his wife.[45] All of that was not just a front; Patti was apparently trying to find some way to live within the Roberts orbit and satisfy her own need for independence; Richard was trying to preserve his marriage to a talented and independent woman.

There were strong ties holding the troubled marriage together during the mid-1970s. One was the Roberts family's firm opposition to divorce. Their pentecostal upbringing had countenanced no compromise of the marriage bond. Evelyn was particularly outspoken on the subject, frequently passing on the advice she had given her children:

> I said, "Marshall remember that at our house, we don't get divorces so if you take Rebecca, you'll have to keep her for life and never bring her back." . . . I made them scared for their lives. Now, they may get a divorce tomorrow. . . . You don't know what your children are going to do. But you do know that if you put your trust in God, and tell the children the way you see things before they marry, a lot of times they will go into it a little more seriously.[46]

Evelyn remembered the traumatic impact that her parents' divorce had had on her life, and she sincerely hoped that her children and grandchildren would escape the tragedy.[47] And, at least intuitively, Oral and Evelyn understood that a divorce would injure the image of the ministry. In 1975, Evelyn told the university faculty: "I have not found too many marriages that are helped by a divorce and remarriage. . . . It really grieves me when we at ORU, who are spirit-filled people, cannot sit down together and communicate with each other and keep our marriages intact."[48]

Kathryn Kuhlman also helped hold the marriage together. She became quite attached to the two handsome youngsters, and they spent a good deal of time together—Kathryn urging both of them to try to make their marriage last.[49] Speaking with candor and insight at Kuhlman's funeral in early 1976, Oral expressed gratitude for her influence on the couple:

> My son Richard, and daughter-in-law, Patti, had been married for some time, had been working with me, but there were problems. It's awfully hard today for young people to be married and stay married and overcome the problems of the kind of society we live in. And it's hard to be the son of a preacher, of a well-known man like myself. Hard for a girl to marry into a family like mine. . . . Richard and Patti rode with Kathryn . . . and I don't know what happened

on their way to the airport, but when they got back, a marriage that was in real
danger of breaking up, was cemented and put back together. There was nothing I could do, and my wife, there was nothing we could do. The more we did,
the worse it got. And some way she touched Richard and Patti, and I don't
know what I would have done. . . . There's never been a divorce in my family.
My life stands for something, and yet I was as helpless as a baby.[50]

As in all such personal tragedies, it is impossible to weigh all of the factors
contributing to the final collapse of the marriage, much less to affix blame. In
her book, Patti listed among her specific grievances a moral uneasiness about
the couple's lavish lifestyle and about Oral's teachings on seed-faith. But more
fundamental was her growing obsession with the notion that her husband was
dominated by his father, that he had sold his soul for the power and wealth
which had been bestowed on him.[51] "It was kind of like living with your in-
laws," observed attorney Don Moyers, a friend of both Richard and Patti. "She
wanted a life of her own without them. That put Richard in an awful spot."
After all compromises proved unsatisfactory, Patti's final demand was that
Richard "break away" from his family. "It was a choice," concluded Moyers, "he
couldn't make to the tune of turning down the ministry."[52]

Few people who knew the couple well doubted that Richard did everything
within his power to save the marriage short of leaving his father's ministry. Don
Moyers was convinced that Richard had a "deeper stake" in the marriage up to
its end, if for no other reason than the impact a divorce would have on the
ministry.[53] Richard tried to placate his wife's need for independence. Looking
back, he believed that he had done "everything I could to save it. When from all
corners I was being told to just end it. I don't believe in divorce. And I did
everything in my power to keep it together. Even though quite honestly there
was nothing there."[54] Richard insisted that his wife was forcing him to choose
not between her and his father but "between her and God." He believed that
she wanted to destroy his call.[54] Other members of the Roberts family believed
that Richard lived through years of "hell" trying to save his marriage.[55]

If Patti's prime indictment of Richard was that he sacrificed their marriage
to his father's need for a successor, she was viewed by some inside the Roberts
organization as inordinately "ambitious," as one who "wanted a role that wasn't
available" and had seen "Richard . . . as an avenue."[56] To the Roberts family she
became an enigma, sometimes extroverted and charming and sometimes
threatening and angry.[57] To some extent, both Patti and the Roberts family
traced her demands on Richard to her own unhappy relationship with her father
as a teenager.[58]

On March 10, 1979, the Tulsa newspapers broke the news that Patti had
sued Richard for divorce on the grounds of "incompatibility"; the next day the
divorce was granted.[59] Publicly, the settlement was businesslike and cordial;
Patti received custody of the two children, and Richard was granted "reasonable
visitation rights." Ron Smith spoke briefly with the press on behalf of the
Roberts family: "We wish there was an easy way to do this, but there's not. We
feel bad about the divorce. . . . We really do wish her the best."[60] Smith also

expressed confidence that the divorce would not adversely affect the ministry. Patti also issued a statement:

> Richard and I are both deeply saddened by our divorce. We have agreed upon all of the terms. While I still have custody of our daughters, I will live in Tulsa so that he can meaningfully participate in their lives. We will each separately continue our careers and work. There are no recriminations or controversies but simply a mutual acceptance of the personal tragedy which this divorce represents. I wish him every continued success and have nothing but the highest regard for him, for Oral and Evelyn Roberts and their work.[61]

Actually, the divorce was a relief after the months of tension which had led up to it. The beginning of the end had started in December 1978, when Richard informed Patti that he had discussed a divorce with his father and mother and that they had agreed to it. He told her that she would receive a generous financial settlement, and, apparently by mutual consent, it was decided that Patti would file for the divorce.[62] The conditions were worked out without controversy. In January, Richard sent Patti a letter suggesting final terms for a reconciliation. In it he told her that he still loved her and wanted her if she would agree to give up her career and be a proper wife and mother. She viewed the letter as a "publicity instrument" and agreed to reconcile only if Richard would leave his father's ministry. In Patti's mind, "the attempt at reconciliation had been political on both sides." Nonetheless, there was little overt bitterness at the time of the divorce. Patti recalled that Richard called her on the evening before the divorce was granted, with "gentle concern" in his voice, expressing his final sorrow that they had failed.[63]

Losing Patti was a blow to the Roberts family—not just to the ministry. They had truly loved her and appreciated her role in guiding Richard to the ministry. "Few know what a warmhearted person she is and how much we love her," wrote Evelyn in 1976. "Patti and I are very close. We not only work closely together, we are very compatible and enjoy many of the same things."[64] Patti remembered her last encounter with her mother-in-law as a moment filled with private pain and no bitterness.[65]

The most complicated and crucial family relationship in the collapse of the marriage was between Patti and Oral. She candidly confessed that she had had a "love/hate relationship" with him from their first encounter.[66] Her strong will repeatedly clashed with that of her father-in-law; she was bound to lose. "If you clash with Oral here you've got a problem," observed George Stovall, "I don't care who you are. Because it is his ministry."[67] Oral and Evelyn were baffled by their daughter-in-law's independence and growing hostility. Evelyn recalled a conversation in their home one evening after Oral had refused to help sponsor Patti's trip to Iran because, he said, it was too dangerous. Patti left tearfully. Evelyn followed, reminding Patti that she had "the world at her feet." "Can you tell me what else you want?" she implored. As Evelyn remembered it, Patti looked up and replied: "See that moon up there, I have got to see what's behind it."[68] Oral increasingly seemed an obstacle blocking her own sense of destiny.

Both Oral and Evelyn concluded that the marriage was over long before

Richard and Patti did. After their conversation about Patti's Iranian trip, Evelyn remembered saying to herself, "This girl is never going to make it." But she tried to "keep quiet" for "the children's sake."[69] Patti recollected a conversation with Oral a year before the divorce in which he suggested that they accept the inevitable and end the unhappy union. Oral did not "dislike" her, Patti believed, he was simply a "total realist," and he was prepared to accept the consequences of a divorce.[70] When Patti made a last visit to Oral and Evelyn's Palm Springs home to say goodbye after the divorce, she was shocked by Oral's jaunty greeting and apparent lack of remorse.[71] Actually, he had worried about the divorce as intently as others in the family, but by the time it came, he had accepted it. He had seen the inevitable months earlier; he had weighed the consequences, acknowledged the defeat, and turned to new problems.

Almost inevitably, the reasonable and generous mood surrounding the divorce turned hostile in the months that followed. Patti grew resentful, feeling that the Roberts family was trying to make her the scapegoat for the divorce.[72] Separated from the Roberts empire, her career floundered. While few open attacks were made on her, she faded from public attention. Many felt the decline was inevitable. "She had no idea of the platform Oral was providing for her," surmised ORU professor Charles Farah. "I think she suffered from the feeling that she could do it on her own."[73] In the months after her divorce, Patti's ego became so "battered" that she tottered on the verge of a "nervous breakdown."[74] Finally, she moved to Franklin, Tennessee, where she began working on a book about the marriage, which was published in 1983. While critical of Richard and Oral in her book, Patti also accepted much of the responsibility for the divorce and clearly identified the points of tension which had made it inevitable.

Richard's attitude also turned sour in the months following the divorce. He felt that Patti had broadcast her side of the story "on every television program she can get on," deliberately undermining his efforts to save his career as an evangelist.[75] Richard was extremely vulnerable. No one knew precisely how severely the divorce would wound him. Richard's divorce was a traumatic shock to the pentecostal supporters of the Roberts ministry. Overseas, where pentecostals remained mostly poor and conservative, Richard's divorce eliminated the support of "local churches."[76] In the months following the divorce, ugly rumors surfaced (maliciously spread by his enemies, Richard believed), charging him with sexual indiscretions. He felt helpless to defend his name against scandal.[77]

Nowhere did Richard have to defend himself more than at Oral Roberts University. There was a "move among some of the regents and others right after Richard's divorce" to put him "on the shelf for a while."[78] "I took a lot of heat," Richard later recalled, "but the rewards for doing so have been tremendous."[79] He felt that his experience had drawn him closer to many people in the world who had suffered similar tragedies, and, ultimately, those inside the ministry became less critical. The divorce, Evelyn told a reporter in 1981, was an "eye-opening experience": "It showed me we live in a real world where we have to cope with things that happen."[80] Others concluded the same.

Richard and Patti's divorce rocked the Roberts family and the ministry, but probably less than the announcement ten months later, in January 1980, that Richard had married an ORU law student, Lindsay Ann Salem of Winter Park, Florida. Lindsay was a petite, ravishing beauty of "Lebanese Arab" descent, who met Richard shortly after entering law school in the fall of 1979. The two had a whirlwind romance. "I never clicked with anyone the way I did with Richard," explained Lindsay. "If I had to close my eyes and imagine someone, I never could have come up with someone as good to me as Richard is."[81]

Richard's remarriage, particularly so soon, caused the ministry serious problems. Richard consulted the Oral Roberts Evangelistic Association board before remarrying—as all persons in executive positions in the organization were required to do—and was granted permission. Richard also informed a number of people close to the family, including Bill and Edna Nash, describing Lindsay to them and asking their blessings.[82] But none of that softened the blow. "A lot of people spiritually can live with divorce and they can't with remarriage," noted George Stovall.[83] "Five key members of ORU's administration" held an open forum on campus to answer questions about the remarriage and to quiet student protest. James Buskirk, dean of the theology school at the university, insisted that "divorce in every situation is evil, but divorce, though evil, may be the lesser of two evils." The Roberts family knew that Richard's remarriage would "disturb the students," acknowledged Buskirk, but Oral was "not going to turn his son out. He does not ask us to condone divorce or remarriage, but he asks us not to judge." Regent D. E. Wilkerson explained that Richard had conformed to the organization's regulations about remarriage and avowed that "if there is any discontent among the regents, I am not aware of it." But clearly Richard's reputation—both within and without the organization—had reached its nadir. With regard to Richard's future, Wilkerson observed: "It is in God's hands, and he has to find his own place.[84]

Subsequent events seemed to argue that Lindsay brought to the marriage assets capable of offsetting the liabilities. She seemed to be all she was advertised to be: "a multi-talented, multi-faceted woman. . . . Her captivating poise, charm, and warm friendly attitude make you feel at home and relaxed. Her happy spirit is contagious."[85] Above all, she warmly embraced the role of Richard Roberts's wife. "I just want to be his wife," she told a reporter, "I want to be there when he comes home."[86] Lindsay appeared to admire Oral and Evelyn; she flawlessly "stood beside her husband" as he explained his evangelistic work. By the end of 1980, Lindsay was highly visible in the ministry in a role similar to that which Evelyn had long played.[87]

Richard's new marriage seemed to transform him. He talked excitedly about beginning a new family, revealing that his two daughters had "put in their request for a little brother."[88] When Lindsay became pregnant in 1983, the Roberts men openly hoped that a male Roberts heir would be born. In addition, Richard's marriage seemed to give him a new confidence and a drive to have a healing ministry of his own. "My whole life has opened up," he explained. "I found someone who was not only in love with me but wanted me to succeed. She did not want to be the success; she wanted me to be the success. She wanted to stand by me. . . . I can't tell you that the Lord wouldn't have called me into a healing ministry. All I can tell you is that he didn't until I married Lindsay. . . . My life is totally changed since then."[89] "This is the beginning of what I almost consider the second year of my life," Richard told a group of alumni in February 1981. "The year 1980 has been probably the most exciting year of my life."[90]

Of all of the Roberts children, Roberta was the one most isolated from the family during the turbulent years from 1975 to 1985. She and her minister husband, Ron Potts, were separated from the family in Denver and were somewhat sheltered from the family tragedies. After the deaths of Rebecca and Ronnie, Oral urged Ron and Roberta to return to Tulsa. First Ron agreed that they should make the move, and finally Roberta, who was "harder to convince," agreed to return.[91]

In October 1982, the Potts family arrived, and Roberta was installed as an assistant to Oral. Given a vague charge to familiarize herself with all of the workings of the organization, she occupied an office on the executive floor next to Richard's, and she began a series of interviews with the leaders of the ministry. In the fall of 1983 she began taking classes in the ORU law school.[92] While Roberta's role was still unclear—apparently even to her and Oral—she quickly won friends on the campus with her open and sincere manner. Whatever her future role, it was clear that another Roberts had entered the picture.

At the end of 1983, Oral and Evelyn had nine grandchildren, but in the case of Richard's two daughters and of Ron's two adopted children, Rachel and Damon, the relationship with Andy and Munna had been marred by divorces. By 1984, Marshall and Rebecca's oldest daughter, Brenda, was a student at Tulsa University; Marcia, seemingly more deeply troubled by the deaths of her parents, was living with Ron and Roberta Potts, and Jon Oral had been legally adopted by Bill and Edna Nash. Jon Oral, introduced by Oral in 1978 as "my little crown prince," was precocious and perceptive and particularly adept in computer skills, and more than one insider identified him as a future potential leader in the Roberts empire.[93] Randy and Stevie, the sons of Ron and Roberta Potts, were frequent visitors with their grandparents after their move to Tulsa.

It was no secret that Oral had long craved a namesake grandson. His own sons, as the heirs of the family name, had always been viewed as Oral's potential successors.[94] When Lindsay became pregnant in 1983, Oral and Richard waited expectantly for a male heir. "Richard wanted a son so bad and Oral wanted him to have a son so bad," Evelyn recalled. "They were both putting too much stock in that one baby."[95] On January 17, 1984, their hopes seemed to come true with the birth of Richard Oral Roberts.

Within a few hours after his birth, doctors discovered that the child was having difficulty breathing. The news, Evelyn recalled, "just tore Oral to pieces." For over thirty hours, while doctors fought to save the baby, Oral, Richard, and others prayed. Lindsay was wheeled up to the baby's side to pray; Kenneth Hagin and his wife, and other ministers, came to pray for healing. When Richard Oral finally died, on January 19, it "devastated Oral." He called it the worst tragedy of his scarred life. "I think," Evelyn reflected, "because he felt there was so much healing power in that room that they could have healed a thousand people. . . . But he said there was something in that baby and he got it as far as the head and it would not leave. . . . Some obstacle would not leave. It was stubborn."[96]

The family once again faced misfortune bravely, searching for meanings in the death. They immediately announced the addition of an obstetrics suite in the City of Faith Medical Center in memory of Richard Oral Roberts.[97] At the memorial service, Richard confessed that he had wanted a son so badly that perhaps he had lost perspective. The death of his child made him realize that evangelism must be "first in his life."[98] Richard expressed confidence that "God will give Lindsay and me more sons and daughters" and pledged that "we will serve Him faithfully."[99]

DURING THIS most troubled decade of their lives, Oral and Evelyn grew older with remarkable grace. They were both trim and well groomed, looking much younger than their ages. "My dad," said Richard in 1982, "is sixty-four. . . . He doesn't look it, does he? He looks like he's about fifty and he acts like he's about forty. He's in the best health."[100]

Oral and Evelyn still had a model marriage. In 1977, the editor of *Christian Home* magazine wrote asking for a story about them. "I am particularly impressed by the way you and Evelyn live together in your T.V. appearances," he wrote. "I admire your openness, your honesty, and your sensitivity. I feel you must really love one another."[101] Their common sorrows seemed to push them together even more tightly. Introducing Evelyn to the university's graduates and their families in 1979, Oral went through his familiar spiel: "I want to present the darling of my life, my sweetheart. After 40 years, the woman I love the most, my darling wife Evelyn. Honey, stand. Honey, when you stood then I thought I had introduced the wrong woman because you look so young."[102] And Evelyn remained grateful for Oral's public praise. She told a group of students in 1977: "He bragged on me when we were in the public. He never said anything bad about me, never once. He's not an angel either. But let me tell you what I've tried to do. . . . I have tried to reward him for that. Because I really appreciate hearing a man say beautiful things about his wife."[103] When Evelyn published a best-selling book in 1976 about their marriage, entitled *His Darling Wife, Evelyn*, one reviewer was both charmed and taken aback by the intimacy of the story: "Mrs. Roberts' unabashed admiration for her husband is almost sticky-sweet at times. The reader gets the feeling that he has read things he ought not to have read. But that's to be expected when a man has called his wife 'darling' for 35 years in front of millions of people."[104] Their marriage remained untainted by any hint of infidelity. "That's one of the good things about him," said Al Bush. "He kept his hands clean. He does not have any woman problem."[105]

The most captivating facet of their relationship remained its apparent openness and honesty. "Oral and I often have 'prayer meetings,'" Evelyn wrote, "in which just he and I and the Lord meet and harmonize our thinking and planning. These are precious moments."[106] Most remarkable was their willingness to openly share their feelings with others, most vividly seen in the family tragedies, but also apparent on other occasions. At faculty orientation in 1975, Evelyn quipped: "Believe me, Oral and I have not arrived at the place where our marriage is absolutely perfect. (laughter). . . . There have been times I have really wanted to kick the seat of his pants. (laughter) And I am sure there are many times he has wanted to kick me, too. He hasn't ever kicked me, . . . except with his tongue."[107] While Evelyn was the truest believer in Oral and his ministry, she never let him, or others, forget his human foibles. Oral told of a confrontation in which she accused him of being a "cry baby" and slammed the letters they were reading down on their bed. "Honey, don't slam our letters down on the bed," Oral protested. "No sir, it's your mail today," she replied, "I just feel like taking it and just throwing it away." "Honey, you can't do that," he pleaded. "Then you can't do what you're doing. You can't be a saint on television and a sinner at home." "She got so upset at me and said so many mean things," recalled Oral, that they both finally broke into laughter.[108]

More often, the temperamental outburst came from the other party. "Evelyn and I are opposites, in many ways," Oral wrote in a 1979 article. "She's quiet, steady, the same every time you see her. I'm moody and often irritable, especially if I cannot get the things done that I know God wants me to do. I'm often hard to live with."[109] In 1982, Evelyn discussed Oral's moods:

> If he has had a very particularly strenuous day, he comes in the back door and there's nobody can slam a door like Oral Roberts. Once the door is slammed, I know he's in the house. But he comes in with a particular little whistle and if he is whistling with that whistle, I don't ask him what's happened during the day. I wait and let him tell me. But you know, after you've lived with somebody for forty-three years, you begin to know their little sidelines and things like this.

She candidly confessed that her husband's moods were often frustrating: "There are times he gets on my nerves. I think back, 'Lord, why did I tell you those two years to bring that man to me?' (laughter) . . . But then the Lord says, 'Look, this man has made you run faster than you can run,' which is true. . . . 'This man has broadened your mind,' which is true. And I always say, 'Thank you, Jesus, that I have this man even though he gets on my nerves.'"[110]

If Oral had "broadened" Evelyn, it is difficult to overestimate the strengths Evelyn brought to their marriage and to Oral's ministry. Expressing a commonly held view, Howard Ervin said: "In my opinion, Evelyn has been the strength, the stability, the driving force in all his ministry. . . . She is a very gracious woman, a very intelligent woman, very strong willed."[111] Looking back at the end of his long life, John D. Messick wrote: "President Oral Roberts has the greatest vision and the greatest faith of any man I have ever known. And he's tremendously fortunate in having a wife which to my way of thinking cannot be surpassed in her support in every needed way of her husband and his work. If it were not for her, I'm afraid he could not have succeeded to the extent he has. She's a *great lady*."[112]

As they grew older, Oral got on Evelyn's nerves more and more—partly because they were together almost constantly since the children were gone and

Oral's campaigning days were over. Evelyn recalled an occasion when she offended her husband by asking to be left alone. She salved his wounded ego with a note:

> Oral darling: I want to say to you on paper what I tried to say to you earlier when you were in no condition to listen with your heart. I am sorry I said I wanted to be alone for awhile. I certainly did not mean that I don't enjoy being with you, because I do immensely. . . . Years ago when you traveled in the crusades, I looked forward so much to your coming home. And sometimes it seemed all you wanted the first few days was to be alone to rest and relax. Now in the last three or four years things seem to have reversed. You want to be with me all the time. And now there are times when I want to be alone.[113]

Evelyn was more and more pulled into the ministry. In the midst of the building of the City of Faith, she confided to the news media that "the past summer was the roughest we've ever faced."[114] "It would be so easy now at age 58," she wrote to the ministry's partners in 1979, "if I could sit back, relax, do some needlepoint, enjoy my grandchildren, watch the students of ORU develop into beautiful, worthwhile citizens who will go out and change the world."[115]

Evelyn knew that would not happen. Her husband's dreams became larger and larger as he grew older, and he continued to be a compulsive worker. When not busy writing or performing on television, Oral spent long days in informal conferences with advisors and consultants, discussing new projects. Once plans were made, the details of negotiation would be carried out by a ministry subordinate. Oral himself became less and less accessible—his office was secluded in a secured area on the seventh floor of the John D. Messick Learning Resources Center at the university. "Many have said—especially members of the news media—that they can reach the President of the United States easier and quicker than Roberts," wrote one repoter. "Nobody except members of his immediate family, his secretary or the few who surround him daily can just pick up the phone and call Oral Roberts and get him."[116] Even among ministry officials, the only people with easy access to Roberts were those with the most pressing business—in recent years, for instance, James Winslow, the vice-provost for health affairs.

Frequently Oral worked at home, drafting and redrafting books or directives to his lieutenants. Sometimes he spent hours with his mail, writing answers to the problems posed in the letters. Sometimes he riveted his attention on *Abundant Life*, reasserting his editorial control. He turned out a steady stream of books to be given to anyone who wrote to him. While Roberts always used writing assistants to flesh out his ideas, he was regarded by most within the organization as a "good writer." He labored conscientiously preparing the books which went out under his name, agonizing particularly over the precise phrasing of the final drafts.[117]

In addition to the strain of his work schedule and the family tragedies in the decade after 1975, Oral suffered from a series of minor physical problems. Probably most serious were a delicate surgery to repair a tear on the retina of one eye in December 1981, and an automobile accident which took place just a few weeks later. The surgery on Roberts's eye, done in California, was a complete success, in spite of the fact that the devil had warned him, "I'm going to get you this time."[118] In the automobile accident a few weeks later, Oral and Evelyn demolished a Mercedes in a wreck which left Evelyn unconscious but neither of them seriously injured. Oral reported that his prayers had saved Evelyn's life, and he advised his partners: "Even if the person is unconscious, speak to him or her about Jesus . . . about living . . . about full recovery . . . about health . . . about love."[119]

In spite of their hectic pace, Oral and Evelyn's home life remained amazingly serene. Their lives had always been relatively uncomplicated; Oral worked, and Evelyn cooked and cared for the home. They never employed servants in their house. Oral's tastes were plebeian; he liked "farm food," and Evelyn knew how to cook to suit him.[120] Notoriously incompetent mechanically, Oral couldn't "turn the coffeepot on" by himself. "There are two things he can do," declared Evelyn, "and one of them is preach. And the other one is he knows how to love me. Thank the Lord he does because there are very few other things he knows how to do."[121] Oral's basic recreation remained golf, which he continued to play regularly and well—though his handicap at Southern Hills crept slowly up into double digits in the 1980s.[122] To relax in the evenings, he read western stories. His favorite author was Louis L'Amour, whose scores of books had sold over 100,000,000 copies by 1980.[123] When Oral's eye surgery made it impossible for him to read, he had L'Amour's books recorded on tapes so he could listen to them before going to sleep.[124]

Oral and Evelyn lived a tame social life. By the late 1970s, they no longer held the constant rounds of receptions and dinners in their home for the faculty and students; Carl Hamilton increasingly assumed those responsibilities.[125] Oral liked to be quiet in the evenings, protecting his voice from overuse. Of course, Roberts still had important friends in Tulsa, whose advice he sought and with whom he occasionally dined socially. Jenkin Lloyd Jones recognized that Roberts was a "very private man," but at the same time he marveled at the consummate social skills that Oral had acquired. "He is very gracious at a cocktail party," observed Jones. "If you have people over to dinner with Oral, you have no qualms about getting out the cocktails and serving the wine around the table. Oral and Evelyn just don't drink. There is none of that . . . you would get from a Bible-beating-Baptist. He can melt in very well into almost any group."[126]

Jones was typical of the unlikely friends Oral had in the Tulsa power structure. When the editor first heard of Roberts, he thought Tulsa needed another "faith healer" like it needed a "hole in the head," and through the years he judged each new Roberts revelation as "potentially disastrous." Sometimes, he felt that their friendship was sorely tested by "what you can tolerate in chicanery." But, through it all, Jones watched and listened, and he liked Oral:

> It seemed to me that here was a guy who was much more than just a shouting evangelist. He did have . . . a very great amount of charisma. . . . Some of the greatest rascals in the history of the world have charisma. But it seemed to me

in Oral Roberts' case this was a very benign type of charisma and that he had
the great ability of taking impressionable people and making them stand taller.
Whether they got up off their wheelchair or threw away their crutches, he did
something to them. . . . I think in many cases it was lasting.

Reservations and all, Jones remained faithful through the years: "I like Oral."[127]

In the long run, Oral's most impressive friend in Tulsa was John Williams,
probably the city's most respected businessman and long the head of the
Williams Corporation, a huge conglomerate with holdings in oil, gas, fertilizer,
and real estate. The two met for the first time in the late 1960s, when Williams
was clearly on his way to being one of the city's most influential men and Oral
was blossoming as a world-class evangelist. "I can't remember whether I looked
him up or he looked me up," reminisced Williams. "I rather suspect that . . . he
looked me up." Both men pursued the friendship, however—Oral, Williams
suspected, because he was a "user of people," who was "rather curious as to how
he could use me." And Williams was curious about Oral's success. "It was an
intellectual curiosity, not a religious curiosity," said Williams, "as to how the
devil somebody like Oral operated and became a swayer of people's emotions."[128] Their mutual curiosity led to a genuine friendship. "I think it's one of
those natural things," surmised Al Bush. "They both respect each other. The
best part is, it's not put on, it's not phony."[129] The support of Williams was
"invaluable" to Oral—specifically it gained him membership in Southern Hills
Country Club, generally it gave him access to the city's power structure. Probably more important, Williams was Oral's confidant and advisor. "He ap-
preciates John Williams' judgment," said Don Moyers; Oral knew Williams was
one of the few people who would be absolutely candid with him.[130] John
Williams had a standing that was hard to earn; he had Oral's full respect. "I'm
one of the few people on a peer group basis that he doesn't necessarily think
he's better than," observed the business mogul. "There are not many. . . . You
can count them on one hand."[131] In the rarified atmosphere to which Oral's
success had taken him, a friend such as John Williams, whose tastes, judgments,
and personal devotion were beyond question, was far more valuable than financial contributions.

Of course, Oral had many friends among Tulsa's business and civic leaders;
he "hobnobs with the top men in the city," noted Al Bush.[132] He prized his
personal relationship with Warren Hultgren, vivacious pastor of Tulsa's huge
First Baptist Church and probably the most influential minister in the city. For
years the two played golf regularly on Tuesdays, until in the early 1980s Oral's
long absences from the city broke the pattern.[133] Oral played golf not only with
a variety of influential Tulsans but with a stream of celebrities, ranging from
Bob Hope to Billy Graham. A casual game with Hultgren and their guest Billy
Graham in 1972 produced an oft-told story. As Billy Graham told it:

> I played golf with Oral Roberts and Warren Hultgren, but then something
> good happened to me. Because on the first tee I hit the ball, it went about 25
> yards; I hit a second ball, it went about 35 yards and landed behind a tree. I hit
> a third ball that they offered me and it went about 40 yards. Oral Roberts

stepped up and hit one about 250 yards down the middle. So I was riding in the cart with Oral Roberts. We went over to where my ball was. He picked it up, carried it about 150 yards and laid it down where his was. And when Dr. Hultgren came up in the cart . . . he said, "What happened?" He said, "How did you get up here?" Oral Roberts said, "It was a miracle."[134]

By the mid-1980s, Oral's place in Tulsa society was secure. "I didn't have many friends when I started," he reminisced in 1983. "I've got lots of friends here now."[135]

In spite of the breadth and depth of Roberts's social ties in Tulsa, most of his friendships were functional and superficial. With the exception of a few unusual relationships, such as those with Williams and Hultgren, Oral's associations were cordial but restrained on the part of both parties. Many business leaders who respected Oral's success and his contribution to the city remained convinced that he was a "fraud" and were aghast that the likes of John Williams would associate with him.[136] The feelings were mutual. Oral knew how to survive in high society, but he never liked it. "I'm at parties downtown and various other places that are revolting to my spirit," he told the ORU faculty in 1974. "But when I'm there, I haven't the slightest desire to drink their liquor or use their gutter type language. I'm not there for that purpose. My motivation is different."[137] "How I got in that power structure," he observed in 1981, "is because the spirit of God wanted me in. I'm in it. I'm not of it and that's where the breakage comes. I don't vote their vote or use their language, their four-letter words."[138] These simply were not Oral's people. "He has trouble taking his lofty view of life and bringing it down here and living with it and other men in some ways," concluded Al Bush.[139] Oral's heroes in life were religious figures—Billy Graham and Kathryn Kuhlman—people who shared his ultimates.[140] "When you have the kind of ministry that we have," explained Evelyn, "it's a very lonely, lonely life. Because you can't confer with a lot of people. In the first place, they don't understand what you're doing."[141]

Oral and Evelyn's friendships and their social life were pervasively interwoven with the ministry. They hosted occasional small dinner parties for ministry friends in the neighborhood or visited in their homes. Sometimes Oral spent an evening teaching a new acquaintance about the "prayer language" or praying "for them to be healed."[142] But most evenings were spent casually, eating chili around the kitchen table, with Oral bringing home or calling in one of his top advisors—most of whom lived on the hill next to the president's house. "Our real friends," confided Evelyn, "have been the people who work with us.[143]

The list of associates who had lasted for many years was impressive—the Braxtons, DeWeeses, Steeles, Stovalls, Hamiltons, and Smiths. Oral sadly parted with one of the most loyal of them in 1982. He recalled his last conversation with Lee Braxton:

"Oral, my work is finished." I said, "Yes, your name . . . stands for layman for Christ. You and Demos Shakarian are side by side in my view as the two greatest laymen of this century. Your name is all over the campus in all the

right places." . . . He said, "My part is finished. I want to go." . . . So we
hugged and we prayed and we cried and here were my last words to him and
his to me. "Lee, when you get there, you be sure to locate the eastern gate
because when I come, I want to meet you just inside the eastern gate." He put
his hand on mine and he said, "Oral, I accept that. I'll be there. I'll see you
there."[144]

Of the older crowd, perhaps the DeWeeses were closest to Oral and Evelyn; Oral and Bob DeWeese could laugh and reminisce for hours about their
exploits and trials under the tent. But more often Oral spent the evenings talking over his ideas, honing and polishing them for future use. His closest friend
was likely to be the person in charge of the most pressing project—in recent
years Jim Winslow. "Jim and Oral are very close," said Evelyn. "They talk for
hours sometimes on Oral's plans for the future. . . . A lot of the time we spend
with friends is business."[145] To be Oral's friend was to be totally committed to
him, and to "totally and consummately approve" of his ministry.[146] "I can only
think of three or four who have survived long term by being close," observed
Bill Nash.[147]

No one in the late 1970s filled the void left by Ken Trickey's departure.
Oral and Trickey remained friends, seeing each other occasionally. "Ken still
comes to our house," Evelyn reported, but the wholesome, manly companionship they had enjoyed had been disrupted.[148]

Perhaps Oral's closest friend in the early 1980s was Richard. They played
golf together whenever they could; Richard was a superb golfer, though he had
difficulty beating his father when handicapped by five or six strokes.[149] "He and
Richard are good golf partners," observed Evelyn. "Oral and Richard enjoy
being together . . . because they enjoy the same things. . . . They've always been
buddies. They are, I guess, more so now than ever before. I try to keep them
from talking business every time they get together. It's a little hard. Since
they're both in business together."[150] "We have a fantastic relationship," exuded
Richard, "almost like a brother relationship."[151] Oral and Richard had always
profoundly loved one another; in the 1980s they grew to enjoy each other.

Of course, Oral and Evelyn had friends and acquaintances all over the
country. They were constantly flooded with invitations to visit with their
wealthy benefactors. Such long-time supporters as John Wellons, Demos
Shakarian, Lee Braxton, Henry Krause, Velmer Gardner, William Shrinde,
George Gardner, and Don Locke were successful people with whom the
Robertses felt comfortable.[152] Many of the university's regents were wealthy;
they constantly invited Oral and Evelyn to visit in their homes. But there was
little time for such relaxation, although Oral did occasionally visit friends when
conducting business around the country.[153]

Increasingly in the 1970s and 1980s, Oral and Evelyn had a second set of
friends in California, where they spent nearly half their time in homes in Palm
Springs and Beverly Hills. The Palm Springs home, which they purchased in
1977, was used primarily for golf and relaxation; they did little entertaining
while there. In Palm Springs, Oral "works all morning and about one o'clock he

goes to the golf course. . . . He comes in and we have dinner and watch a little TV and go to bed." In Beverly Hills, Oral and Evelyn had a slightly more active social life. They sometimes visited with old friends such as Demos and Rose Shakarian and Pat and Shirley Boone, or with entertainers they had come to know, such as Buddy Rogers. Among their close friends on the West Coast were two blacks, Rosie Greer, who had become a member of ORU's board of regents, and a black charismatic preacher from Los Angeles, Fred Price. They enjoyed visiting with such friends, Evelyn observed, "because when Oral has written all day, if he hasn't talked, then he can go and have an evening." In addition, while in California, they often entertained their Tulsa friends— particularly when Oral wanted to discuss business with someone such as Jim Winslow or George Stovall.[154]

Roberts's two California homes, partly for security reasons, were not much discussed by the ministry. Oral also remained sensitive about press criticism of his lifestyle.[155] His house in Palm Springs, purchased for $285,000 and financed by a Tulsa bank, was his only privately owned home. In 1982 ORU endowment funds were used to purchase a $2,400,000 house in a high-security development in Beverly Hills. Considered a potentially profitable investment, the house served as Oral's West Coast office and residence.[156]

Oral's flight to California was in part a renewed effort to flee the allergies which had led him to purchase a home in Corona del Mar in 1955. By the mid-1970s, he felt secure enough with the leadership of the university— particularly with Carl Hamilton—that he was not tied to Tulsa. Many of his closest advisors urged him to leave town. "I always used to urge him to get away from the campus and create," recalled Ron Smith. "He cannot be very creative on the campus. Because he's worrying about toilets that may not flush or re-frigerators that are plugged in too long or something like that. That's the wrong level of activity for him."[157] Oral instinctively knew that Smith's assessment was correct. Explaining his absences to the students in 1977, he said: "I fly out for a week . . . because I have lots of work to do. I have books to write. I have thinking to be done. I have dreams to dream. I have praying to be done, and often Evelyn and I go to the desert."[158] "It's different from being here," ex-plained Evelyn, "because you don't feel the pressure right on you." The Roberts family also felt a growing need for privacy and security—both of which were provided by their California houses.[159]

Oral's homes in California inevitably kept alive the old questions about his personal wealth and lifestyle. While probably not as probing as the press had been fifteen years earlier, reporters still took a keen interest in Oral's financial affairs. In 1981, the Associated Press published Roberts's personal income figures for the preceding five years—ranging from $70,000 in 1976 to $178,000 in 1978.[160] In addition to his healthy income, derived mostly from book royalties, Oral continued to enjoy generous expense accounts: "The Robertses wear expensive clothes and jewelry and travel in a company-owned eight-passenger fanjet."[161] Under the heading "O, Dem Golden Slippers," the *Tulsa Tribune* revealed that Oral had purchased fifteen pairs of shoes and boots which retailed for $300 per pair. After a protest from the ministry, a follow-up article lowered the number to "six or seven" and suggested that the cost was "not close to $300."[162] Patti Roberts's book, and an earlier exposé written by Jerry Sholes, renewed curiosity about the family's financial affairs, although Patti confessed that her own "extravagance" while she was Richard's wife had "blunted" her protest.[163]

Roberts's critics sometimes made charges that seemed unlikely. For instance, Fundamentalist minister G. Archer Weniger wrote in 1980: "Sources in Tulsa have informed us that Oral Roberts does not fear financial insecurity since he controls about 17 banks, and has a personal fortune in excess of $10 million it is estimated."[164] Such estimates almost surely mixed indiscriminately Roberts's personal income and wealth and the ministry's income and endowment—funds, to be sure, which Oral controlled and used within the limits set by his legal advisors.

Oral still responded defensively to the interest in his finances. He pointed out that the home in Palm Springs was the "only piece of property we own" and insisted that the house in Beverly Hills "cost no more than a normal, small office."[165] In the late 1970s, he and Evelyn began driving Chevrolets, which were furnished to them without charge by a Tulsa dealer (Richard drove a BMW); they publicized the fact as proof to their partners that they did not spend money frivolously.[166] Oral was perhaps slightly more open about his private finances in the 1980s. He told one reporter that God "doesn't deserve second best" and admitted, "We don't live like paupers."[167]

While the Roberts family's lifestyle spawned continued curiosity and criticism, many of Oral's friends and former friends dismissed the issue. In an article written in 1975, Jenkin Lloyd Jones, Jr. and Bob Foresman argued that "Roberts could be a rich man at this point," but he was still receiving a personal salary of only $29,000 per year, plus a house and car.[168] Demos Shakarian, after decades of close association with the Roberts ministry, insisted: "Oral has been honest." The Roberts empire, noted Shakarian, approached a billion dollars in value by the mid-1980s, and "none of it is Oral's." "He had the business and preaching ability to accumulate a fortune," argued Shakarian, "but he did not."[169] One could argue, observed Ron Smith, that Roberts lived "far beneath the level of living that most people who are in his position have and demand."[170] Many university presidents receive large salaries and have homes and cars at their disposal. And, if one considered Oral a television personality, his lifestyle seemed spartan. "My personal feeling has always been that whatever he has he deserves every stick," said Al Bush in 1983. While the Roberts family lived well, Bush argued, they had accumulated relatively little personal wealth out of the millions of dollars that had been contributed by the partners. They owned the house in Palm Springs, and perhaps a few other investments, but, concluded Bush, "the rest is what you see on the hill."[171]

Actually, in the late 1970s Oral and Evelyn came to feel that they had unnecessarily neglected their own personal finances. When Oral decided to purchase his Palm Springs home in 1977, he discovered that "I'd gotten myself in a position where I didn't receive myself." He reported that he owned a membership in Southern Hills and "one or two other memberships and that's all I have." He called his attorney and said, "You know, I'm upset. I'm hurt." "What's the matter, Oral?" "I've given of myself. I've helped build a university. . . . I really have given and I don't have money even to make a down payment. I don't take private gifts from people. . . . And I've built up this image because people thought I was a crook. . . . I've preached Seed-Faith all these years. Now apparently it's not working in my life."[172] Of course, donors were plentiful once Oral let his need be known. But the general problem remained—there was little "residual wealth" in the Roberts family, certainly not enough to sustain their lifestyle should something happen to the ministry. John Williams discerned in Evelyn and Richard some resentment that "here is the leader of their family who has had this enormous success in life and what have we . . . got to show for it."[173] It could be argued, at least until recent years, that Oral, while enjoying the fringe benefits of a corporate executive, had paid too little attention to his personal finances.

THE PUBLIC achievements of the Roberts ministry after 1975 somewhat obscured the personal maelstrom the family passed through. In the mid-1980s, Oral and Evelyn still "hurt," they were still "picking at themselves." "They are still going through it," said Roberta. "They blamed themselves. . . . They will never show what they have really gone through. Inside they have been hurt a great deal."[174] Occasionally the pain showed through. Preaching to a group of laymen in 1981 about the resurrection of Christ, Oral said:

> We've got to know we are receiving from Jesus and besides that, folks, if I lost all my children, lost my wife and my own body died, there's a resurrection. I'm telling you, the devil isn't going to win this. . . . The resurrection is even going to raise my daughter's body up. . . . Please don't think that I don't live down where you all are and go through all these things. And please don't think I'm preaching to you. I'm preaching to me. You all are just tuning in on what I'm saying to Oral.[175]

Their personal tragedies mellowed Oral and Evelyn. In the repeated crises they faced, both of them returned to the spiritual wells dug in their childhoods. Charles Farah, Oral's long-time friend, observed:

> Spirituality has become reality in his life in a new dimension in the last six or seven years. Mostly because of the things that he has suffered. He has known suffering in a very, very deep dimension. . . . There is something to the suffering of a human being that purifies him. I have never felt that Oral was walking more closely with the Lord that I have in the last year. . . . There is a spirituality there that I think anyone would recognize.[176]

And, in intricate and mysterious ways, the tragedies molded the Oral Roberts ministry. How could it have been otherwise? Because, as Roberta pointed out, they "impacted Dad and Dad and the Lord are the ministry."[177]

XIV

Completing the Healing Vision

"I DON'T BELIEVE the City of Faith would be standing there today if Rebecca and Marshall had not died," said Roberta Roberts Potts in 1983. That is a debated, controversial assessment; it is certain, however, that the City of Faith was a natural outgrowth of Oral Roberts University and of Roberts's dream of bringing healing to his generation. In hindsight, the huge medical complex seems an obvious terminus for Oral's journey, but it came after countless turns which could have led elsewhere. The significance of the undertaking was stated in startling terms by Professor Martin L. Singewald of Johns Hopkins University: "In the last century only one American founded a university and a medical school and teaching hospital, all working together as a unit. That man was Johns Hopkins. In this century, only one American has built a university, a medical school and a hospital all working together, plus a research center. . . . That man is Oral Roberts."[1]

IN ITS second decade of existence, from 1975 to 1985, Oral Roberts University matured and expanded, rightly regarding itself as "the premier *Charismatic* university in the nation." In addition, Carl Hamilton believed, "we are also recognized as a university with an outstanding academic program and faculty."[2] ORU retained its religious character without denominational affiliation, preserving, in the words of Hamilton, "the most beautiful ecumenicity in a group of folk concerned about the Christian faith."[3] On more than one occasion, ORU administrators ran afoul of federal regulations because the school was viewed as "pervasively religious," an accusation which was accepted with pride.[4] Oral still looked on the university as the key to preserving his message. In 1976, he

358

reminded a group of students: "He [God] did say that the work of the students of ORU would go far beyond my work. . . . I don't want it to die when I die. I want it to go beyond myself."[5]

The ORU student body in the second decade was clearly above average— even exceptional. In 1975, the university had about 2,700 full-time students, and an enrollment of around 3,500 including part-time students. By 1978, the number reached 4,000, where it stayed for several years.[6] Fighting the national decline in college enrollments, ORU nonetheless finished the 1983–84 academic year with 4,507 undergraduate and graduate students and projected a growth to over 7,000 by 1990.[7] In 1977, Carl Hamilton noted that the goal of maintaining a "close-knit university community" made rapid growth undesirable.[8] But by 1984 the university family had become so large that the chapel services were being held in Mabee Center, and Hamilton felt that there was "no ideal size" for such a school.[9]

The ORU student body came from all geographical regions of the country and included a sprinkling of foreign students. A majority became familiar with the university through the Roberts television ministry; three-fourths stated that they chose the school because of its "academic reputation." While more of the students were members of the Methodist church than any other denomination by the late 1970s, over forty percent of them in 1978 had Pentecostal backgrounds. The majority had white, Protestant, middle- to upper-middle-class parents, who were better educated and held a higher percentage of white-collar jobs than average. Profiles on the entering classes at ORU indicated that the school was attracting better-than-average students, an exceptional number of whom hoped to pursue professional graduate degrees; neary two-thirds finished in the top twenty percent of their high-school graduating classes. "The academic credentials of the university are being very well documented," wrote Carl Hamilton in 1983. "ORU student teachers regularly make the top scores on the exams mandated by the Oklahoma Department of Education. In a recent *New York Times* survey of colleges, ORU was rated as the highest academic institution in Oklahoma."[10] If ORU had not become all John Messick had set out to build in 1965, it was a solid academic institution with a good student body.

The faculty appeared to be stable and reasonably contented. Of the 35 original faculty members employed in 1965, over half were still at the university in 1984. New faculty members were recruited nationally and were asked to sign "no doctrinal statement of faith," although the faculty handbook demanded that one be "open to the gifts" of the Holy Spirit and conform to the ORU lifestyle—including participation in an aerobics physical fitness program.[11] "We're in the lifestyle business," reminded Hamilton.[12] The size of the faculty in the mid-1980s had swelled to over 325; almost all graduate instructors held Ph.D. degrees, while, "by design," the number holding doctorates among the undergraduate faculty was maintained at about fifty percent.[13] Increasingly, the university had a pool of potential faculty recruits among its own graduates who had gone on to complete advanced degrees at the nation's best universities. In the mid-1980s, about twenty had received funding from the university's "quality program" to complete graduate degrees and return.[14]

Carl Hamilton seemed firmly entrenched as the head of the university in

1983. Although his time with Oral was limited, he felt that their relations were "excellent" and that he had "ready access" when he needed the president's attention. "I essentially function as 'Mr. Inside' for the president," he told a reporter. In a move that shook the ministry, in May 1982, Hamilton suddenly resigned, explaining that he "had accomplished the goals toward which he had been working for more than ten years." More important, apparently, was Hamilton's frustration with the independence of the leaders of the university's medical school and persistent budget problems. After several days of conferences, which resulted in a formal understanding that all university business went to Roberts through Hamilton, the provost withdrew his resignation. Through the difficult days of rapid expansion into graduate education, Hamilton's influence grew. His control of the university seemed virtually uncontested when he suddenly resigned in May 1984.[15]

The departure of Carl Hamilton led to a general reshuffling of the ORU administration. Most of the vice-provost and vice-president titles in the university were eliminated, and two floors of executive offices in the learning resources building were closed. The changes were partly austerity measures, brought on by a new financial crisis in 1984. However, many of the leaders of the ministry, including Oral and Richard Roberts, were convinced that the university had become overstaffed and needed streamlining. Hamilton's replacement was William Jernigan, who assumed the title of dean of the university. Jernigan was the highly respected director of the Learning Resources Center, and his appointment was well received on campus. He defended the scaling down of some of the more ambitious plans framed by Hamilton and viewed his new role as more managerial than policy-making. Perhaps more important, for several years Jernigan had aided in Richard Roberts's crusades, and he consciously sought to link the university more closely with the evangelistic ministry. While all of the administrative shuffling was probably not completed by the end of 1984, the university was clearly back in the hands of the Roberts family.[16]

The university's forty-one-member board of regents continued to be an honor roll of Oral's most affluent and loyal supporters. When Lee Braxton finally resigned as chairman of the board in 1979, having held that position from the university's inception, he was replaced by Donald R. Moyers, one of Tulsa's most respected lawyers and Oral's legal counsel since 1953. Moyers refused to serve more than one term, and in 1981 he was replaced by John McKnight. In 1983, Bob DeWeese was elected to the position.

The university continued to depend heavily for financial support on the Oral Roberts Evangelistic Association. In the late 1970s, the association subsidized as much as fifty percent of the cost of each student's education—even more in the case of some graduate programs. In spite of those subsidies, the university raised its tuition steadily; by the late 1970s, ORU had become the most expensive institution of higher education in the state of Oklahoma. A major jolt came in the midst of a financial crisis caused partly by the huge construction costs of building the City of Faith; all university budgets were reduced by ten percent, and tuition charges in 1980 rose by about forty-five percent. Oral tried to prepare the students a year ahead for the increases: "We shared with you how a year from now we are trusting God with you that your own faith will rise so that you can pick up a larger part of your tuition, but not only pick that up, but to see God put money in your hand far beyond that."[17] Even with the sharp rises in tuition in the early 1980s, Oral Roberts University remained slightly below the national average of costs for private university tuition and below the costs of a number of other private schools in the Southwestern region of the nation.[18]

The percentage of the ORU budget provided by the evangelistic association dropped slightly in the 1980s. The ministry's financial wizard of the 1980s, Fred Van Stone, devised a master plan, based on improved efficiency and outside fund-raising, designed to make the university "fiscally self-sufficient" by 1990. By the 1984–85 academic year, the association's contribution to the university had declined to only $18,000,000 out of a total budget of $55,000,000. The new university administration in 1984 was less intent on gaining financial independence from the evangelistic association. William Jernigan believed that the financial tie was healthy, keeping the university firmly under the control of the association, and he placed Hamilton's plan for financial self-sufficiency "on hold."[19]

While Oral Roberts University gained increasing academic respect through the years, the public often remained most fascinated by the efforts to preserve its lifestyle. In 1975, ORU closed its library to visitors, including students from Tulsa University (which had previously closed its library), at least partly to help preserve its dress code. "Rather than raise a fuss every time a TU student comes out here to have them shave their beards or put on a tie," explained the director of the Learning Resources Center, William Jernigan, "we decided to close our library."[20] When an ORU student reporter, Shelly Lamoureaux, suggested in 1979 that women should be allowd to wear slacks rather than dresses during the cold winter months, the *Tulsa Tribune* ran a feature story suggesting that the "dress code frosts ORU coeds."[21] Newspapers across the nation reran the story, ridiculing the university's dress code under such titles as "College Wants to See Women's Legs in Chapel" and "ORU Women Can't Bare It." The editor of the student newspaper charged the *Tribune* with "irresponsible journalism" for making a national issue out of an innocent suggestion: "The article gave the impression that students at ORU are agitating against the dress code. They are not. . . . ORU has had a dress code since its opening in 1965, and there have always been a few students who have stated that it should be changed. So why is a stated opinion considered news all of a sudden?[22] In fact, while restrictions on dress at ORU still gave the campus a wholesome, almost dressy, atmosphere, there was little evidence of prudishness. The ORU lifestyle had come to accommodate a pom-pon squad at the basketball games, which raised the eyebrows of some of the students. Student Activities Director Tracey Caughell defended the squad's "ministry," admitting that such performances in other places were frequently filled with "vulgarity," but insisting that "our squads offer wholesome, tasteful entertainment."[23] In pom-pon squads, as in other activities, the aim was "to achieve the highest standards possible in accordance with the ORU life style."[24] There was a constant probing, which seemed to extend the lifestyle boundaries through the years.

The most controversial of ORU's lifestyle requirements remained the emphasis on physical fitness. An aerobics program, supported by a system of required physical education courses and computer records of outside activities, was mandated for all students and faculty beginning in 1976. The requirement was one of the most sophisticated physical fitness programs in the country and was supported by most of the students, many of whom reported a continued use of aerobics after graduation.[25] When pressed by Phil Donahue in 1979 to defend the program, Oral retorted: "You don't have to come to ORU. It's not for everybody. Our boys and girls like it. They're beating the doors down to get in."[26] Actually, ORU was riding a wave of support for physical fitness, particularly in the evangelical Christian community, where there was a growing interest in the religious significance of a healthy body.[27]

More specifically, ORU aroused the curiosity of the nation, and the ire of some, because of its restrictions on overweight and handicapped students. Beginning in 1976, prospective students who were "excessively overweight" were required to participate in weight loss programs before entering the university. All students, upon registration, were tested to determine their percentage of body fat. Overweight students were required to commence an individual weight loss program and to "sign a contract with the university to that end": "Female students with more than 35 percent body fat and male students with more than 25 percent body fat are placed on a weight reducing program and must sign a conract promising to lose at least one pound a week until reaching their prescribed weight."[28] Students who failed to make satisfactory progress were placed on "physical probation" for a semester; if one still did not "attain goal weight and does not seem to be making any effort to lose, he will be suspended from classes."[29] The entire campus girded for the campaign against obesity; special meals were available for overweight students in the cafeteria, and, in a move that drew some fire from students, candy bars were replaced in the dormitory vending machines by "health foods."[30]

The program was put to a severe test in 1977 and 1978, when it resulted in the expulsion of four students and a number of others dropped out because they felt the pressure was excessive.[31] The expulsions were partly responsible for a lawsuit filed against the university in late 1977 by the Oklahoma Coalition of Citizens with Disabilities and the American Civil Liberties Union, charging violations of the Rehabiliation Act of 1973. In a seventy-five-page complaint, the groups averred that the ORU weight program was "discriminatory" and pointed toward more far-reaching questions about the university's regulations on the admission of handicapped people.[32]

ORU's weight reduction program was later removed from the complaint, and the obesity policy remained intact, but not before it had been critiqued by the nation's press. The "flab flap" was featured in *Newsweek* and the *New York Times*, and in an Abigail Van Buren column responding to a complaint from the aunt of one of the expelled students.[33] While the policy raised some serious questions, it more often was used to ridicule the school. An Oklahoma newspaper printed a spoof letter to the governor, signed "Oral," which concluded: "I personally have nothing against corpulence. I love all God's children— especially those who look alike and think alike and talk alike and believe alike. Frankly, people wouldn't be fat or handicapped if they had enough faith. I encourage you to move swiftly to meet the Lord's will. (In fact, a lot of people have lost weight initially by sending me their billfolds."[34] The university's policy had some serious defenders, particularly among traditional conservative antagonists of the ACLU. Editorial writer Harry Schwartz argued in the *Wall Street Journal* that society was not bound to capitulate to "medical criminals"; William Buckley's *National Review* charged that the "libertarian position is such as virtually to forbid citizens from banding together to form their own institutions, however idiosyncratic, with independent social purposes, priorities, and standards. Why can't a college discourage gluttony?"[35]

Much more serious was the challenge to the university's regulations on the admission of handicapped students. Once the "obesity issue" was eliminated from the complaint against the university, serious negotiations were begun with officials in the HEW Office of Civil Rights about removing the school's restrictions on the handicapped. ORU had excluded students in wheelchairs since its founding, because, Carl Hamilton explained, when the campus had been built, the needs of the handicapped were not widely recognized, and its buildings made ORU "basically a walking campus."[36] While that formal explanation was correct, it was also true that handicapped students did not fit Oral's vision of building healthy minds, spirits, and bodies.[37] But regardless of past feelings, in 1978 ORU moved quickly to make the changes necessary for the admission of the handicapped, working in cooperation with the Oklahoma Coalition of Citizens with Disabilities. The dispute was resolved "without significant federal intervention."[38]

Aside from such flare-ups, the university's athletic program continued to attract the most public attention—particularly the basketball program. Generally speaking, the news was positive. In 1981, Oral told the students: "The athletic program . . . keeps us on the sports page when they're knocking me and knocking the City of Faith."[39] The basketball team continued to play a schedule of major opponents, and the school competed successfully at the national level in several other sports, including baseball, golf, and tennis.[40] But the success of the sports program faltered a bit after 1975. The university went through a series of four basketball coaches after the departure of Ken Trickey in 1974; its teams were moderately successful but failed to challenge for national prominence.

While the athletic program continued to provide much good publicity for Oral Roberts University, it was also rocked by several negative stories. In 1979, as a result of the publication of Jerry Sholes's book on Roberts, the press uncovered the story that University of Arkansas basketball coach Eddie Sutton had been offered a million-dollar deal to become coach at ORU. Sutton explained that the ORU proposition "was no different than that offered in many other coaching positions" aside from the guarantees it included; expressed the highest regard for Roberts and ORU; and admitted that the offer had been difficult to reject. All in all, the affair seemed to be nothing more scandalous than the public revelation of the market value of basketball coaches; at least, Tulsa sports writers so concluded: "It is difficult to put a dollar value on a coach who can build winning teams, avoid scandal and stay within his budget. He is worth more, perhaps, than a dean. It is not fair. But it is pragmatic."[41]

More serious was an NCAA investigation of the ORU basketball program, which led to a one-year probation in 1980, apparently triggering the resignation of coach Lake Kelly and the offer to Eddie Sutton. Rumors had long persisted that the supporters of the university's athletic program had committed flagrant violations of the NCAA code which restricted gifts to athletes.[42] After a hearing, Oral confessed that the university had unknowingly broken the rules, protesting at the same time that the rules which excluded giving to the athletes were "foreign to us" and violated the spirit of the university. But he pledged that there would be no further violations: "We will send in our charter to play in NCAA or we'll keep the rules."[43]

The program received another jolt in 1982, when popular coach Ken Hayes was fired in mid-season. Hayes had seemed an ideal candidate to rebuild the flagging team when he was hired in 1979. A successful coach at Tulsa University and New Mexico State, Hayes had a clean-cut, religious reputation and was totally in sympathy with the goals of the university. But in his fourth year, Hayes had a lackluster 50–43 win-loss record, although his team in 1981–82 had played in the National Invitational Tournament. On Saturday night, December 18, 1982, shortly after a loss to arch-rival Tulsa University, the fifth loss in the first eight games of the season, Hayes was fired. He was replaced by his assistant coach, Dick Acres, but not before a threatened boycott by the team and a barrage of hostile commentary in the local and national press. One coach in a neighboring state hoped that "no one would take the job" and labeled Oral's goals "unrealistic."[44] There was a furor within the university; it bubbled to the surface in a letter to the *Tulsa World*:

> I am a member of the faculty at ORU and am ashamed of that today. Ashamed and embarrassed. What happened with our Coach Ken Hayes over the weekend is a classic example of the loss of perspective in college athletics; and more so, an example of power running rough shod over character and balanced judgment. This is worrisome in any setting, but is sad and ruinous in an organization once dedicated in practice to right and healing.[45]

Of all those commenting on the Ken Hayes firing, Ken Trickey probably made the shrewdest observations. He knew what was at stake; he understood the aims of the program. "An 18–12 season does not match those buildings on Lewis Street," said Trickey to reporters, "how can a man that built something of that magnitude be happy with an 18–12 team."[46] In the mid-1980s, Oral was still groping for a way to make his basketball team match his ministry.

BY FAR the most significant development in the second decade of Oral Roberts University's existence was the beginning of a number of graduate and professional programs. On April 28, 1975, Oral stunned Tulsa and the nation with the announcement that the university would build medical, dental, and law schools. Those three schools were added to graduate programs announced earlier in business, theology, education, and nursing. "The master plan that God gave me now is coming into fruition," Roberts wrote in *Abundant Life*.[47] The first graduate degrees were granted at the university in 1976, in business administration and theology.[48] When completed, Oral announced, the ORU graduate schools would prepare students for the "four inescapables of life"—medicine, theology, law, and business.[49]

Roberts knew that the graduate programs would be expensive challenges: "The Lord showed me to put ORU together in the eight colleges . . . and build them with the best that we have and God let me start with nothing. He told me He was going to let me build this university out of the same ingredient He used when He made the earth. The Bible says He made it out of nothing."[50] The medical school was the most intimidating of the additions. In the spring of 1974, the ORU board of regents appointed a committee to study the feasibility of beginning a medical college. It was headed by Dr. James Winslow, a member of the board of regents and a prominent Tulsa orthopedic surgeon. After extensive travel and consultation, the committee gave a positive recommendation, and the school was approved by the board in 1975.[51] The decision assured another decade of struggle and controversy for the Roberts ministry. In the midst of the turmoil, in 1979, Oral admitted: "We have bit off probably more than we can chew right now. But we intend to chew it anyway."[52]

The Tulsa newspapers labeled Oral's announcement of the graduate expansion a "breath-taker" and an "amazing plan." There was some reservation; the University of Oklahoma had been studying placing a medical school in Tulsa, and Oral's announcement obviously jeopardized those plans, but by and large the public reaction was favorable. It seemed to be another major contribution to the city, and, as a *Tulsa World* editorial put it, "Oral's record indicates the word 'failure' is not in his vocabulary."[53] "If achieved," added the *Tribune*, "this will outstrip all of Roberts' earlier achievements."[54]

Once again, Roberts's announcement should not have been a total surprise. Like all of his moves, it had been preceded by warnings, but they had not been frequent enough, or loud enough, for outsiders (or even insiders) to take them seriously. When he revealed the graduate expansion in 1975, Oral claimed that the idea had been in his mind "since 1962," since the beginnings of the university.[55] He wrote in *Abundant Life*: "As far back as 1962, God revealed that in taking His healing power to my generation it would include building a medical school. From 1962 until 1974, over 12 years, God was preparing me for this. I often wondered how He intended for me to do it. I never doubted, nor did I question His guidance; I merely wondered how."[56]

Roberts's claim was not merely hindsight. In January 1963, at one of the seminars before the university began, Oral confronted the question of whether ORU would "turn out medical doctors as the Seven Day Adventist people are turning out." It was clearly a subject he had thought about—in his trips abroad he had been impressed by the success of Seventh-Day Adventist "medical missions." "I would answer that question by saying this," he replied, "that God has a magnificient program in the future for this university and He happened to tap on the shoulder some men who aren't scared of anything."[57] In his report to the president's advisory cabinet in 1965, Roberts stated that by 1975 the university would have "six graduate schools," although medicine was not named.[58] In his dissertation, written in the mid-1960s, R. O. Corvin included among the future projections for the university "additional graduate schools in education, engineering, and medicine."[59] While the exact plan for expanding ORU was not in Oral's mind throughout the 1960s, the fact that the university would eventually include graduate education—including a medical school—was contemplated very early.

The issue in the mid-1970s was not whether Oral had ever thought of expanding the university, or of building a medical school, but whether he would do it—and when. In late 1974 and 1975, he felt pressed to make a commitment to expand—realizing that it was a step far larger than the initial act of faith which had launched the university. Speaking in chapel in January 1975, Oral told the students that the plans then in his mind "just scare me spitless. I mean, your mouth gets dry and you can't even spit." He became physically ill:

> What He's told me now to do . . . is far more difficult than building this out of nothing. And it just drove me up the wall and I became ill at the same time. I developed a respiratory problem for a few weeks. . . . I know when it's to be started; I know when it's to be opened; and it can't be done. And I was arguing with God and saying things I shouldn't say and finally I just broke down and cried like a baby. And Evelyn was sitting there by me praying and that wouldn't help because nobody could know what I was going through. . . . And I said, "God, uncall me, take your call off of me because I cannot do this." And then I was so sick trying to breathe, I said, "God, take away my life."[60]

During those traumatic months, James Buskirk, later to become vice-provost for spiritual affairs at Oral Roberts University, came to the campus to preach. At the conclusion of Buskirk's first sermon, Oral came to the altar in tears. He said, "I have not been as close to the Lord in the last thirty days as I am normally and I want the Lord to forgive me." "Everybody froze," Buskirk recalled, and then he and the whole audience began praying for Oral: "I hadn't heard that size group pray in tongues before. It was just like a bubbling fountain." In the final service of the weekend, Oral came forward again. Buskirk described the scene:

> He sat down and shared that the Lord told him to build a graduate school and he said that had some risk for the undergraduate and he said, "I've asked the Lord to take that call away and he hasn't and I've asked the Lord to take my life away." And then he started crying. Just folded up. He said, "I don't have a right to do that and I repent of that. And I need you to pray for me." And a girl next to me said, "My God, he's a five year old with wrinkles." Just so humble and prostrate before them.[61]

While Roberts's announcement of the expansion of the university was startling, the decision was not made without forethought or in reckless disregard of the costs.

The graduate expansion required the building of a huge graduate center addition to the learning resources building. Begun in 1976, it was the only major addition to the university's physical plant during the second decade. The center added 440,000 square feet of floor space to the structure and changed it from a triangle into a diamond-shaped building. When completed in 1978, the huge structure included thirteen acres of floor space and housed the libraries, offices, and most of the classrooms for the entire university.[62]

The new building helped to implement the university's "inter-disciplinary cross-pollination" concept, which called for all undergraduate and graduate students to interact academically, socially, and spiritually. "ORU students exercise together, attend chapel together, live in university housing and develop a relationship that we describe as a 'university family,'" explained Roberts.[63] In the mid-1980s, Carl Hamilton viewed cross-pollination as a "magnificent concept" but confessed that the university was "still implementing it imperfectly." In spite of "formal and informal" efforts to acquaint graduate students in each school with the emphases in other schools, professional education requirements made significant exchange difficult.[64]

In 1984, the university had about 1,000 students enrolled in its graduate programs—all of its schools were accredited by the appropriate agencies. Carl Hamilton projected an enrollment of 2,000 in the graduate schools by the end of the decade and the addition of a number of Ph.D. programs to complement the professional schools. Perhaps the most difficult dilemma in building the graduate programs had been the maintenance of a satisfactory undergraduate enrollment "in the face of declining enrollment on a national scale."[65]

While accreditation did not come easily for any of the graduate programs, there were relatively few problems in the School of Business, which began granting degrees in 1977 under the leadership of Dean R. Henry Migliore, who had a good rapport with the Tulsa business community; in the School of Nursing, which granted its first graduate degrees in 1981 under Dean I. Tomine Tjelta; in the School of Dentistry, which opened in 1978 under Dean Robert G. Hansen; and in the College of Education, which graduated its first advanced class in 1982 under the leadership of Dean Wayne Lee.[66] More controversial were the beginnings of the schools of Theology, Law, and Medicine.

In many ways the most sensitive of the new graduate programs was the School of Theology. Of all intellectuals, theologians had proved to be least compatible with Oral.[67] The closing of the ill-fated, Corvin-led School of Religion was only seven years in the past when the new School of Theology was announced. Leadership and a clear statement of purpose would be the keys to the success of the second venture.

Oral chose his theology dean somewhat impulsively, but he never wavered through a long period of negotiation. James B. Buskirk was a charismatic Methodist evangelist, who held the Arthur Moore Chair of Evangelism at Candler School of Theology at Emory University. Buskirk had met Oral casually at a couple of Methodist retreats, but it was Buskirk's friendship with ORU chaplain Bob Stamps which led to an invitation to speak on the campus in 1974. It was in that series of meetings, attended by Oral in the midst of his soul-searching indecision about beginning graduate education, that he reduced Oral to tears of contrition. As Roberts listened to Buskirk preach, convinced that "Jesus was so real to him," he said to himself: "All right, God, I feel in my heart he's the man, and I am going to prayerfully present it to him."[68]

Oral invited Buskirk to visit in his home the Sunday following his series of sermons. He asked the young preacher what kind of seminary he thought was needed in the Christian world. Buskirk, an evangelical Methodist distressed by the lethargy of his own church, poured out his dreams. Oral asked him to become dean of ORU's projected seminary. Buskirk, who had just received tenure after only four years of teaching, was stunned: "It shook my confidence in him because I didn't know enough about theological education to be a dean." He politely rejected the offer, but after he returned to Atlanta, Oral continued to call occasionally to ask: "What is the Lord saying to you?"[69]

James Buskirk did, indeed, seem the perfect choice to lead Roberts's reentry into theological education. Handsome, dynamic, and a powerful preacher, he came from humble origins only slightly more genteel than Oral's. Buskirk was the son of a Mississippi Methodist minister; he graduated from Millsaps College in Jackson in 1955 and then borrowed money to attend Candler Seminary, where he secured a Master of Divinity degree in 1959. For nearly ten years, he pastored small-town Methodist churches and developed a considerable reputation as an evangelist. In 1969, he decided to return to school, supporting himself by preaching. In 1974, he completed a Doctorate of Sacred Theology degree, granted by Atlanta Inter-Seminary Graduate Institute; two years before his graduation, he began teaching courses in "evangelism" at Candler School of Theology. It was this experienced evangelist and novice theological educator whom Oral accosted in 1974.[70]

One other incident in Buskirk's background prepared him to become the leader of the ORU School of Theology. During a pastorate in Mississippi, he experienced what he believed to be a divine healing through prayer. He was diagnosed to be suffering from "coreoretinis in both eyes" and was told that he would be "totally blind probably in less than six months." Deeply depressed, the young evangelist agreed to pray with one of the members of his congregation, "Miss Virginia," whom he had formerly considered a "kook." After the prayer, he was convinced that he felt a transforming "warmth" in his eyes. When a subsequent examination confirmed that the disease had been arrested, he was certain that he had experienced the healing power of God. He subsequently spoke in tongues and became a leader among charismatic Methodists—though he was not identified with that organized group.[71]

All of that convinced Oral that he had found his man, and when Buskirk returned to the ORU campus in September 1975 for a second speaking engagement, negotiations began in earnest. Roberts told Buskirk that he had still not considered another choice. "I think you're it," he insisted. "If I interview anybody else that's disobedience." "That's crazy," replied his prospective dean, but he found himself seriously thinking about the offer. Though Buskirk was secure at Candler, he felt "uncomfortable" there, a "token evangelical" in a theologically liberal school. He tried to inspire the seminary students with an evangelical zeal and found his work undermined by other faculty members, who

26. Richard Roberts singing at one of his father's last crusades, Dayton, Ohio, 1968. Richard was twenty, and it was the first time he had agreed to sing in a crusade since his teenage rebellion.

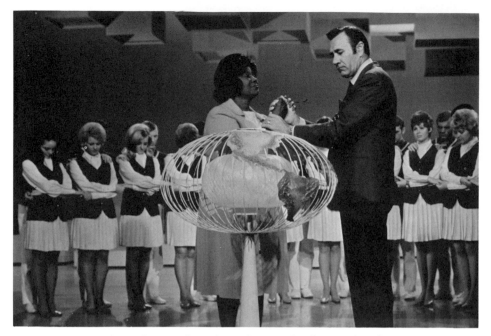

27. Mahalia Jackson and Oral praying on the first Oral Roberts prime-time special, 1968. The attire of the World Action Singers raised Pentecostal eyebrows.

28. Evelyn and Oral reading their mail, October 1971.

29. The Ronald Roberts family. From left to right: Ronnie, Rachel, Carol, and baby Damon, November 1974.

30. Coach Ken Trickey lecturing the Oral Roberts University Titans in a game against Kansas University, March 16, 1974.

31. Oral and Dr. James Winslow at the Medical Building ground-breaking ceremony, January 24, 1976.

32. Members of the Oral Roberts organization. From left to right: Bob DeWeese, Richard Roberts, Oral, Lee Braxton, and Collins Steele. De-Weese, Braxton, and Steele joined the organization when Richard was a baby, and they remained among Oral's closest friends.

33. Oral Roberts University graduation ceremony, 1982. Oral confers an honorary doctorate on his loyal and influential friend John H. Williams. Williams is one of Tulsa's wealthiest and most respected leaders. From left to right: Dale E. Mitchell, John H. Williams, and Oral.

34. Lindsay and Richard Roberts, October 12, 1982.

35. Roberta Roberts's family. Back row: Roberta and Ron Potts. Front row: Randall Potts, Marcia Nash, and Ronald Potts, June 1983.

36. The Hagin Camp Meeting, July 25–29, 1983. Tulsa's three most famous evangelists, T. L. Osborn, Kenneth Hagin, Sr., and Oral, laid their hands on their three sons. Oral has been invigorated by his renewed association with other healing ministries.

37. The Faith and Healing Seminar, June 24–26, 1983. From left to right: James Buskirk (introducing the family); Oral and Evelyn; Roberta; Ronnie, Ron, and Randall Potts; and Richard, Lindsay, Christi, and Juli Roberts. When Ron and Roberta Potts moved back to Tulsa in 1983, it was clear that Oral had pulled his family around him to preserve the ministry.

38. Richard Roberts's healing crusade, Jos, Nigeria, February 1984.

39. The Prayer Tower,
Oral Roberts University.

40. The City of Faith,
Tulsa, Oklahoma.

created "doubt."[72] Buskirk's wife gave him the confirmation he needed—"All of your life you've talked about how you think seminaries ought to be, and now you have your chance of a lifetime."[73] In April 1976 he accepted Roberts's offer and began preparation for the opening of the School of Theology in the fall of 1976.[74] While a novice educator and administrator, Buskirk brought with him to the job a solid reputation in the Methodist church, some experience in theological education, and a sincere commitment to charismatic theology.

The common interest that drew Roberts and Buskirk together was their desire to establish a "Holy Spirit School of Theology."[75] In the mid-1980s, the seminary was the "only fully accredited charismatic graduate school of theology in existence," and Buskirk believed that it was the crucial link in fulfilling Oral's wish to make ORU the "charismatic crossroads of the world."[76] The seminary hosted a series of yearly conferences on the Holy Spirit, which offered the most sophisticated probing of charismatic theology in the 1980s.[77]

The second founding principle of the School of Theology was interdenominationalism. Before the seminary opened, both Roberts and Buskirk paid tribute to its interdenominational commitment. "God is unifying his diversified body," said Buskirk, "and that is modeled here at ORU where all students from virtually all denominations come and find a place to grow, because the Holy Spirit is here." "Yes, this is an interdenominational university," echoed Roberts. "It's private, it's independent. And that includes the theological seminary."[78] In practice, the School of Theology took a strong Methodist turn; by 1982, about forty percent of its students and seventy percent of its faculty were Methodists, and the United Methodist church was the only denomination which had approved the seminary to train its ministers.[79] Although it was not by "design," noted Carl Hamilton, "the seminary . . . is more Methodist than any of the seminaries supported by the United Methodist church."[80] Oral seemed to have no objections to the Methodist drift; at the dedication of the seminary he reported that "the Lord revealed to me in 1968 that there was coming a renewing of the Holy Spirit in the Church, but particularly through a branch of Christ's Body, the United Methodist Church."[81] But Buskirk repeatedly reaffirmed that "the school does not try to make Methodists out of others, but strives to help them effectively relate to their denomination."[82] The theology school grew rapidly, registering nearly three hundred students in 1984, when a Ph.D. program was begun.

Basically, Oral and Buskirk agreed about the seminary's purposes. Roberts intended for it to be a conservative, Bible-based training ground. In 1979, he announced: "And now our seminary is off to a tremendous start and after 200 years of liberalism in many of the seminaries of this world and from which too many were graduated to preach a liberal version of the Gospel, he [Buskirk] has come to build one based upon the Bible and brought alive through Jesus and the Holy Spirit."[83] And yet, the seminary, like Oral, sheltered none of the dogmatism associated with Biblical conservatism—much less fundamentalism. "Oral would expect me as the dean of this seminary to be Biblical," said Buskirk. "He wouldn't ask me to be literalistic."[84] The mix, wrote one observer, "resembles a kind of old-fashioned, nondoctrinal Methodist pietism adapted to the charimatic experience of Spirit baptism and the upwardly mobile atmosphere of Oral Roberts University."[85]

The School of Theology's open theological policy was a matter of concern to some within the university. The "pluralistic" approach could be viewed as a threat to the university's charismatic identity. "This seminary can hardly be called a charismatic seminary," observed one professor. "In fact, it could not very well be called a conservative seminary."[86] Buskirk sharply disagreed. He belived that the seminary would remain charismatic and would always include a faculty at least fifty percent of whom had spoken in tongues, regardless of pressures from outside or in: "That's part of who we are. . . . And that's a statement that some affirmative action people would be upset with. But we are who we are." Nor would the seminary ever swerve to the "left of center" theologically, Buskirk insisted. The school tolerated "diversity," but only within the context of the charismatic experience and evangelical fervor: "I don't have a professor on my faculty who couldn't lead a person to Christ."[87] Nonetheless, when Buskirk unexpectedly resigned in 1984, most insiders felt the seminary would swing to a more independent charismatic stance.

Buskirk's influence reached beyond the seminary. Oral first named him "associate minister," and he later was given the title vice-provost for spiritual affairs. Roberts was captivated by Buskirk's personality, preaching, and vision: "He's one of the few men I have found on earth that I thought God had given the great thoughts that He has given me. . . . I have unlimited confidence in this man. His message touches my life, my heart, my head, my wife, my family, and everything around me."[88] In 1977, Buskirk was placed on the powerful trustees board of the Oral Roberts Evangelistic Association. For a time after his arrival, the theology dean preached on the weekly television programs; some ministry leaders felt that "Oral needed to introduce a newer, sophisticated voice, not as the only voice, but as another aspect of the voice of the healing ministry of Oral Roberts University," but that exposure was short-lived—apparently giving way to the feeling that the partners could identify only with Oral and Richard.[89] Despite that diminution in visibility, in the 1980s Buskirk remained one of the most powerful figures in the ministry. He was Roberts's strongest link to the Methodist church, and his evangelical, charismatic theology pervaded the university. His departure in 1984, along with that of Carl Hamilton, signaled another major change in direction in the ministry.

The opening of the O. W. Coburn School of Law in the fall of 1979 posed a series of constitutional problems which ultimately divided the nation's legal profession. The man hired by Oral in 1976 to found the law school and who led it through a bitter accreditation battle was Tulsa attorney Charles A. Kothe. Kothe, a graduate of the University of Oklahoma School of Law, developed a national reputation as an expert in labor law in the 1950s and first met Oral when consulted about a dispute between the Roberts ministry and the printers' union. Kothe's law firm had a prestigious clientele; he maintained offices in New York City and Washington, D.C., in addition to Tulsa. In the 1960s he served as vice-president and director of the National Association of Manufacturers.[90] Having collected thousands of friends among the wealthiest people in the nation, a commendation from the president, a sizable private fortune, and a valuable art collection, Kothe retired to Tulsa.[91]

Kothe had occasional contacts with Oral through the years; the evangelist visited his office at the National Association of Manufacturers headquarters in New York while preaching in a crusade there, eagerly asking questions about how to conduct his business. When ORU opened, Kothe was invited to conduct seminars on civil rights and business management.[92] Always religious (for thirty years he was a "substitute" Sunday school teacher at the First Presbyterian Church in Tulsa), Kothe became more and more interested in Oral's theology, and, as their friendship grew, Oral led him to experience the prayer language: "In Dean Kothe, I found a man who, like myself, was searching more for God and I remember the day the prayer language burst forth from his lips. I don't think I've ever met a man who was ever more grateful."[93] The garrulous, worldly-wise Kothe was Oral's immediate choice to lead the law school. For Kothe, it seemed a fit challenge for the "due season" of his life, when, at retirement age, he could "put his teaching experience—he's taught at the University of Tulsa, Purdue University and Yale University among other institutions—to use."[94]

The law school seemed to get off to a smooth and auspicious beginning in 1979. Its first class of fifty-four students was greeted by an address by Supreme Court justice Byron White.[95] The school's facilities were excellent, including one of the largest law libraries in the state.[96] The initial funding of the law school was provided by a million-dollar gift from O. W. Coburn, wealthy president of Coburn Optical Industries of Muskogee, Oklahoma. Coburn, who was introduced to Roberts by Kothe, became convinced he should make the gift after one afternoon of discussion with Oral and Kothe. He remained convinced that his seed-faith gift had produced earth-shaking changes in his personal life.[97]

The O. W. Coburn School of Law was established with a clearly articulated, distinctive purpose. Among the missions of the law school was the education of lawyers who would "be a part of a Healing Team ministry." The school emphasized the "whole-person life-style," "cross-pollination" in the curriculum, and the "process of conciliation," or training "lawyers to be healers."[98] In 1978, before the first class arrived, the law school cosponsored the first National Conference on Mediation as a Substitute for Litigation. Kothe outlined the two distinctive goals of the school:

> Our first goal at the O. W. Coburn School of Law is to equip our students with the ability to bring God's healing power to reconcile individuals and to restore community wholeness. That goal requires students not only to become technically competent lawyers with high ethical values but to learn how to integrate their Christian faith into their chosen profession. . . . Our second goal is to restore law to its historic roots in the Bible.[99]

The purposes of the school, Dean Kothe thought, were demanded first by the mission of Oral Roberts University, but they also provided a unique justification for a new law school in the already overcrowded field of legal education.[100] In view of its distinctive mission, the school announced that students would be selected from the "most highly qualified applicants" and "from among those who adhere to the personal and spiritual beliefs of the University."[101]

The law school's stated purposes and student selection guidelines led to a long and bitter accreditation fight with the American Bar Association. The accreditation struggle began innocently enough in 1978, when the university was given authorization to begin the school by the North Central Association of Colleges and Schools, but everyone knew that a more formidable barrier was gaining approval from the American Bar Association. Application was made to the association in September 1980, and the law school received a site visit in October. The initial report raised substantial questions about the school's stated purpose but gave high marks to its financial backing and academic program. The first serious hitch arose in the spring of 1981, when Kothe and Carl Hamilton appeared before the American Bar Association's Committee of Admissions, which was charged with making a recommendation to the association's annual meeting in August. At the beginning of the meeting, Kothe sensed that the committee was "hostile." He recalled that the "first question I asked was, 'Dean, if one of the male members of your faculty wanted to marry another of the male members of your faculty what would you do?'" "At first I didn't think they were serious," recalled Kothe. "I looked and they were all deadpan. And I said, 'Why, I'd fire him.'" Summoned to a second meeting with the committee, Kothe did not appear but rather retained a distinguished Chicago law firm to represent the university. In May 1981, the committee recommended the denial of accreditation.[102]

The issue that disturbed the committee was the religious discrimination implicit in the stated purposes of the O. W. Coburn School of Law, and specifically the requirement that all students sign the code of honor, affirming a belief in Jesus Christ as Lord and Savior.[103] The ABA committee charged that ORU was in violation of the association's Standard 211, which prohibited accredited schools from discrimination on the basis of religion. When questioned by the committee on this point, Kothe insisted that ORU was in compliance if Brigham Young University was, but admitted that the law school was "literally" in violation of the standard, Kothe and his aides had visited over thirty law schools to prepare their case and had found their religious emphasis closest to that of Baylor University, Mississippi College, and Pepperdine University, but they believed that Brigham Young posed the most flagrant challenge to Standard 211. In any case, Kothe believed that the regulation was unconstitutional and so informed the committee. The dean returned to Tulsa from the first meeting shaken, however, and he informed Oral that ORU might have to contest the standard in court. Oral's reaction was predictable: "We're going to go all the way."[104]

Immediately after receiving the committee report, ORU filed suit in the Federal District Court in Chicago, charging the ABA with violating the university's right to freedom of religion. On July 17, the court ruled that the ABA could not deny accreditation to the school solely on religious grounds and delayed further action in the case until after the organization's House of Delegates met in New Orleans.

The Oral Roberts University law school was the most controversial item on the ABA agenda in 1981; the issues it raised were heatedly debated on the floor at the annual meeting. While it was clear that the assembly was overwhelmingly opposed to the admissions standards set by ORU, "nonetheless, the House ultimately decided that Coburn was qualified as a law school and that it had a right to require the oath."[105] ORU's provisional accreditation was assured when the House voted by a slim 147–127 margin to amend Standard 211 to allow schools to have "religious affiliation and purpose."[106] However, the victory in New Orleans did not end the struggle. Almost immediately, bar associations in several states adopted resolutions which demanded rescinding or amending the changes in Standard 211.[107] The midyear meeting of the American Bar Association in January 1982 was once again marked by a "stormy two hour" debate on the issue, but the ORU accreditation was again sustained, by a 176–138 vote.[108] The House of Delegates once again considered the ORU question at its annual meeting in 1982, this time passing by voice vote a compromise amendment to Standard 211, which permitted religious "preference" in hiring and admissions but not at the expense of a "diverse student body." On the thorny issue of constitutionality, the new wording allowed "religious policies as to admission and employment only to the extent that they are protected by the United States Constitution."[109]

The O. W. Coburn School of Law had obviously become ensnared in one of the nation's most perplexing legal mazes. Throughout American history, the courts have interpreted and reinterpreted the religious rights protected by the Constitution. The ORU case raised old issues in particularly poignant ways. Perhaps no group was more offended by the ORU admission standards than Jewish lawyers, and yet, the implication of refusing accreditation to ORU's law school, argued one prominent Jewish attorney, was, "You're telling me I couldn't have a school for Jewish people. I think that's wrong."[110]

Roberts and his associates felt that they had been unfairly singled out by the attack. Oral was indignant when the committee recommended denial of accreditation: "When they start talking about Jesus and about God to us to cut them out, our blood gets stirred up. 'Who by the mouth of thy servant David has said, "Why did the heathen rage?"' That bunch of heathens. . . . Why are they so vain that they think they know it all?" Surely, argued Oral, the ABA could not decide with whom he would have "company": "They don't want us to have our own company here at this school. They don't want us to have people who are chosen because of their faith in God. And they even asked us the question, would we let one of our male professors marry another male in the law school. They actually would like us to bring homosexuality right into our law school. And that's not our company, I want you to know."[111] ORU's leaders were convinced that they were attacked because they were considered vulnerable; Mormon political clout made Brigham Young exempt from similar pressure.[112] Others speculated that had ORU been "one of those high-flying law schools that's soft on Communism, they might not have said so much."[113] Dean Kothe believed that the "eastern press," still remembering Oral's faith healer image, attacked with "an opaque notion of what we were."[114] But, in spite of the opposition, in 1982 the accredited ORU law school graduated its first class, successfully having challenged the most powerful legal association in the nation on the constitutionality of its own rules.

The man groomed by Oral to be his advisor and collaborator in building a medical school—and subsequently an immense medical complex—was a respected Tulsa orthopedic surgeon, Dr. James Winslow. Winslow moved to Tulsa in 1967 as a partner in the Eastern Oklahoma Orthopedic Center and earned a reputation in the medical community as a "good solid citizen."[115] A college athlete himself, he became a fan of the ORU basketball team and the team physician. When Oral twisted his knee playing golf, on the ORU coach's advice he ended up in Winslow's waiting room. Winslow's flustered nurse rushed into the doctor's office and announced, "Oral Roberts is out there." "Well, find out what he wants," replied Winslow. In a moment the nurse returned with the information that Roberts had "hurt his knee." "Good," instructed Winslow, "get the information from him and get him in an examining room and tell him to take off his pants." "Oh," replied the nurse, "we can't tell him to take off his pants." "I haven't got xray eyes," protested the doctor. "If you don't take them off I can't look at his knee." Winslow later learned that Oral had heard most of the exchange, and "instead of leaving he stayed."[116]

Out of that initial encounter began a friendship which was bolstered by occasional golf matches at Southern Hills Country Club. During those times together, Winslow recalled, "we talked about healing in a larger context than I have ever thought about"—they explored Oral's concept that man was mind, body, and spirit. Although Winslow had been reared in a "conservative Methodist" family, his religious ties had become largely nominal; but he enjoyed talking with Oral. It was an intriguing friendship for a young physician.[117]

A series of incidents in Winslow's personal life prepared him for the decision he made in 1975, at age thirty-nine, to become the first dean of the Oral Roberts University medical school. In 1969 and 1970, his wife, Sue, went through extended, and successful, treatment of cancer, and Winslow "had to admit there was no way for her to fully recover without the miraculous touch of God through prayer." During her bout with cancer, Sue Winslow became charismatic and gently urged her husband to investigate the experience. Winslow remained agnostic about speaking in tongues, although he had great confidence in his wife's judgment, and he felt he had witnessed a profound deepening of her character during the months of her illness. One Saturday in the summer of 1972, he impulsively went to Oral's house to discuss the Holy Spirit. The two men talked from ten in the morning until ten in the evening. Oral was a "delightful teacher," taking Winslow painstakingly through his well-rehearsed theology of the Holy Spirit. Actually, the two had discussed the subject many times before, and Winslow had attended the Holy Spirit classes offered at the university. But this time he listened as never before. As he prepared to leave, Oral insisted that the two of them pray. Almost immediately, recalled Winslow, he "prayed in another language."[118]

After Winslow's experience, he and Oral moved inexorably and rapidly together. In January 1973 he consented to become a member of the board of regents of the university, an appointment he had previously resisted. In their more frequent social contacts, Oral began to explore the idea of a medical school with the young physician. Winslow thought the idea was "preposterous" and tried to discourage it at first, but he found it "fun to talk about it" and slowly began to take it seriously.[119] However, in spite of his wife's healing, which he believed had spiritual dimensions, Winslow remained dubious about whether "sudden, supernatural healings took place from visible diseases."[120] Then, in 1974, he seriously injured the fingers on his right hand in a lawn mower accident and suddenly faced the possible end of his career as a surgeon. In the midst of his convalescence, Winslow went to Oral for prayer; he was convinced that his ultimate full recovery was related to Roberts's prayer.[121]

In 1973 and 1974, Winslow and Roberts moved toward acceptance of an ORU medical school; the idea was "growing on" both of them. Winslow headed the committee appointed by the regents in 1974 to study the feasibility of the undertaking; he and Carl Hamilton visited over twenty medical centers to learn and discuss Roberts's ideas. When Oral asked that he become the dean of the school, Winslow balked, feeling unprepared and "uncalled" to undertake such a job, but, on the other hand, he had become infatuated with Oral's vision. He took the job not intending "to stay in it," but, he mused in 1983, "I have never been able to walk away." Winslow had, in fact, been captured by Oral's spiritual mysticism. He no longer doubted the reality of miracles. And he had come to have a strong sense of religious calling: "I may have been conceived at the time Oral was healed. . . . Within a week or two, almost for certain. And I wonder is that just absolute coincidence or not. Who knows."[122]

The appointment of Winslow as the dean of the medical school in January 1976 brought a measure of credibility to the undertaking. Winslow had graduated from the University of Tennessee College of Medicine in 1959 and subsequently completed residencies in general surgery and orthopedic surgery at the Memphis school. His academic experience was limited to one year of lecturing at Tulane University and a brief relationship as an "assistant in orthopedics" with the University of Oklahoma College of Medicine.[123] Winslow regretted that there was no "special school for the training of medical deans," but he announced that he would seek "in-depth orientation" at some of the nation's best medical centers. He began recruiting the twenty full-time faculty members who would be needed to open the school in the fall of 1978.[124]

Most of Roberts's critics presumed that staffing a medical college with physicians sympathetic with Oral's theology would be a formidable task. To some extent that proved to be true. Noting that the influx of physicians into the ministry had tested Oral's "diplomacy," Collins Steele drawled: "If you can deal with them, you can deal with the Lord pretty easily."[125] Sometimes Oral's "diplomacy" failed. He related an incident in 1978:

> Not many weeks ago we were interviewing a potential chairman of a department of our school of medicine. . . . The man had excellent credentials. . . . As we listened to him talk, I soon realized that although he was a great medical

educator . . . he was looking at our medical school from his mind and not from his spirit. He talked about everything but God. Or our mission. Or our healing teams. Or of merging prayer and medicine. So I said to him, "Doctor, do you really know who you are? Do you know who God is? . . . Do you know what Oral Roberts School of Medicine is all about? . . . Doctor, with all respect to you, I suggest that you return home and you get down on your knees. . . . Then come back and let's have another interview."

"That didn't work out," Oral laconically ended the story.[126]

Others did work out. In fact, the school received numerous applications, and, generally speaking, Oral found the applicants not only sympathetic with the aims of the university but also anxious to learn about the baptism of the Holy Spirit.

The doctors only want to know one thing—will it work? Will it help me help a sick person. They are the simplest thinking people of my experience. . . . When they come in here and want me to explain tongues, which I call prayer language, let's see, I led twelve through here in nine days once. And I was in a state of shock because not one of them let me finish. . . . I'm used to dealing with preachers where they'd have to go off and wait three or four months and come back. . . . I met a new breed of man who wants people to get well.[127]

Even the critics of the ORU medical school soon confessed that "Oral has been able to attract some of the best physicians in the country" to Tulsa, but that admission was soon amended with the charge that "they don't stay."[128]

By far the most important early addition to the medical school staff was Dr. Charles B. McCall, who became dean of the school in May 1977; Winslow was promoted to the position of vice-provost of medical affairs. With the arrival of McCall, the academic development of the medical school was in the hands of a seasoned educator. A graduate of Vanderbilt University, he had been serving since 1975 as the dean of the University of Tennessee College of Medicine, having previously been associated with the University of Texas-Southwestern Medical School in Dallas. McCall, who for two years served on a five-person consultant panel advising the ORU medical school, immediately began supervising the school's curriculum and faculty development. Winslow was freed to devote his energies to the larger problems inherent in building a supporting medical complex.[129]

Oral was delighted with McCall's appointment; he commended the new dean as a "good Christian man" who was "strongly involved in the purposes of our school's philosophy of developing the whole man."[130] Winslow was confident that McCall was totally in sympathy with the university's lifestyle, and he knew that McCall brought a degree of academic credibility to the effort which it badly needed. All agreed that McCall "laid a good foundation" for the medical school in the months from May 1977 until his resignation on July 31, 1978.[131]

The issue which put Roberts and McCall on a collision course was the projected opening date for the medical school. Oral's marching orders from the

Lord had clearly instructed him to open his dental and medical schools in 1978, but it very early became apparent that the time schedule was in jeopardy. Not only was the accreditation process for medical schools tedious and demanding, it was absolutely essential that the school negotiate a working agreement with a local hospital before accreditation could be achieved. By the end of 1976, it was apparent that hospital affiliation would not come easily. Oral warned his partners: "We've got to get an affiliation with local hospitals for our medical school. We have not had a breakthrough in this yet. . . . It's got to come in '77, because God told me that I was to open the Medical and Dental Schools in 1978."[132] But the breakthrough did not come in 1977, and once the City of Faith was announced, the negotiations became much more complicated and controversial. By the spring of 1978 it had become clear that the accrediting of the medical school in 1978 was highly unlikely.

In April 1978, McCall frantically maneuvered, trying to arrange the necessary affiliation so that a site visit could be hosted in August and provisional accreditation could be granted in October. If everything worked perfectly, it might be possible to open late in 1978—perhaps even in December. Oral was struggling with the delay within his own spiritual understanding. In a dialogue with McCall in chapel in April, he said:

> When the Lord spoke to me to build Him a medical school, he said to open it in 1978. It never occurred to me that it would not open in the fall of the year. I just never thought about it. And then I've been reminded that 1978 does not necessarily mean a particular month, but it will be in 1978. Now it has placed me in a position of trust and of believing in God. He gave me the statement that He wouldn't be late in '78, and I would say that I have been strained in my faith. . . . Maybe that's one reason that the going has been so tough is to get me back on my knees more.[133]

But by the middle of May the last-hope plans were coming unraveled as opposition to the City of Faith stiffened the resistance of the medical community in Tulsa, and the ORU medical school had still not secured any affiliation agreements with local hospitals.

In early June, the university announced the postponement of the opening of the medical school for "at least a year"; Oral himself made the statement in an interview taped, reported Ron Smith, in "a facing-the-facts moment."[134] McCall was standing firm that the medical school could not open without accreditation, even though the announcement placed Oral in the position of disobeying God. Winslow was caught "in the middle," understanding the imperatives in each man's view.[135] It appeared that reality had prevailed over faith—the school simply could not open in 1978.

Then, in late July, ORU announced that the medical school would open in December, with twenty "provisional" students following a "revised curriculum" composed of "non-medical school courses."[136] McCall's resignation followed immediately; the decision to proceed was made by Oral and Winslow during the dean's absence from the city.[137] McCall's departure was "amicable" in spite of the sharp disagreement; he reasserted that he was "in agreement with the goals and philosophy of the school." His resignation was accepted with "regret" and charged to an "administrative conflict."[138]

The decision to open the medical school without accreditation was, of course, Oral's; it showed, wrote one critic, "who is running the place."[139] Winslow recalled: "He said we're going to open it this year—period. I don't care whether anybody likes it or not. Accreditors or anybody else. They can always turn us down if they don't like it."[140] Oral's faith simply could not tolerate the delay. He had considered the scenario nearly a year earlier and had braced for it. In November 1977, he had told the ORU faculty: "We will open the medical school, accredited or unaccredited, on time. We will do it. And we'll just hold out our bucket and say, 'God, take Your ocean and fill it.' We will get our faculty, we will get the money."[141] When Oral welcomed twenty medical students to the campus in December, he proudly told them that they were "right on time."[142] In hindsight, Winslow believed that Oral's obstinance had saved the school, since its accreditation came just before a virtual moratorium was declared on the building of new medical schools. "I'm convinced," he said, "that one year later we would not have been accredited."[143]

Opposition to the ORU medical school reflected a variety of concerns. Some critics felt that the school was unneeded, since there were already two medical schools in the state. Some doubted, given the "philosophical bent" of the ministry, whether "high standards" could possibly be maintained.[144] But such objections, while important, were minor compared to the question of how the school would relate to Tulsa's hospitals.

In late 1976, ORU began to negotiate with the three major Tulsa hospitals—Saint Francis, Hillcrest, and Saint John—for an affiliation agreement which would allow the school's medical students to train in the hospitals. Winslow had been a member of the staff at Saint Francis, the largest and most prestigious hospital in the state; he was disappointed when that hospital almost immediately turned down the requested affiliation. In the struggle that followed, two of Roberts's most outspoken opponents were Dr. C. T. Thompson, an executive at Saint Francis, and Mr. W. K. Warren, the hospital's wealthy benefactor.[145] The city's other two hospitals expressed some reservations but agreed to negotiate jointly with ORU in early 1977. It was at this delicate juncture in the negotiations—and at this crucially late time in Oral's schedule for the medical school's opening—that the deaths of Rebecca and Marshall occurred and Oral returned from Palm Springs with the full-blown vision of the City of Faith. Clearly, the possibility that ORU would build its own hospital had occurred to all of the parties involved; in fact, it apparently had been suggested to Oral and Winslow on several occasions by the city's other hospital administrators.[146] In August, Hillcrest voted not to affiliate with ORU, and the announcement of the City of Faith in September clouded the negotiations with Saint John. Thus, in the fall of 1978 the medical school was left with little hope of securing the needed affiliation.[147] But, under intense pressure, in late September the medical staff of Saint John Hospital voted 79–66 to establish a "limited affiliation" with the ORU medical school, a crucial victory which allowed the school to press for accreditation.[148]

Once the agreement with Saint John had been completed, the way was open for the visit in November of a five-member, "blue-ribbon" site-visit team representing the Liaison Committee on Medical Education. The team, which was chaired by a member of the Harvard Medical School faculty and cochaired by the chancellor of the Indiana University Medical Center, indicated "unofficially" in November that its report would favor accreditation in February 1979; the battle came to an end when that recommendation was formally approved.[149] The fight over accreditation had lasted to the bitter end. A spokesman for the medical school charged that "the same people who are opposing the City of Faith" made "considerable effort" to keep the "medical school from being accredited."[150] On the other hand, opponents of the school charged that Oral had used his "fairly powerful influence in Washington" to place "considerable pressure" on the accrediting committee. "Can an accrediting body be swayed?" asked C. T. Thompson. "I don't really know. I can tell you that with the slimness of their academic setup at the time to have been accredited was a farce."[151]

Once past the original obstacle of accreditation, the ORU medical school grew, continuing to draw fire from the Tulsa medical community. By 1981, the school was enrolling 48 new students per year and announced plans to expand to 100. The announcement elicited a 150-page report from the Tulsa County Medical Society recommending that no increase in the size of area medical schools be allowed. ORU officials replied that the society had "little or no comprehension of the purpose of the ORU School of Medicine or the City of Faith."[152]

The school also continued to be troubled by internal instability. McCall was replaced in August 1978 by Dr. Sydney A. Garrett, a family practice specialist who had been brought to the university to head the Family Practice Center. "He was available, understood the lifestyle, he believed in the ministry," observed Winslow, and so, after McCall's precipitous departure, Garrett was appointed dean. In June 1982, Garrett left, apparently unable to win the confidence of the "specialists" being attracted to the expanding City of Faith complex, necessitating, according to Winslow, "a change in leadership."[153] The fourth medical dean, appointed in November 1982, was David B. Hinshaw, a "nationally recognized medical educator and administrator," who had formerly served as dean of the Seventh-Day Adventist Loma Linda University School of Medicine in California.[154] Hinshaw once again seemed to bring academic credibility to the medical school, but in 1984 he resigned; he was replaced in July by Larry D. Edwards, who had been chairman of the internal medicine department.[155]

IN THE spring of 1984, for the first time, Oral Roberts University graduated undergraduates and graduates from seven accredited advanced programs. Oral's fears about launching the ambitious scheme in 1974 had been fully justified. The struggle had been bitter. But it was done. There was more to come—the addition of Ph.D. programs and continued growth—but the university vision had become a reality in the second decade.

Of course, the completion of the university did not solve the internal problems of the previous decade; in fact, it tended to exacerbate many of them. Raising endowment funds, attracting students, and maintaining competent faculties became more and more difficult. Even more pressing was the need to protect the distinctive purpose and atmosphere of the university, to keep in perspective its role in the ministry of Oral Roberts. The huge influx of people into the university and the City of Faith medical complex inundated the campus with newcomers who had little understanding of the ministry. It was possible by 1983 for an entire copy of the student body newspaper, the *Oracle,* to be published without a reference to Oral, Richard, or the evangelistic ministry.[156]

Oral could still be thrown into a tirade by an overt expression of disloyalty—by students advocating the right to protest or debate the philosophy of the university, by attacks on the honor code, by disrespect in chapel.[157] Disturbed by a show of dissonance in chapel in 1980, he lectured the audience sternly about the meaning of the university:

> I want you to get an education but this is not an educational institution, it's a ministry from which there is an education. Will you ever learn that? . . . You people in the seminary, while you're teaching about the Bible it's time you taught more faith to yourself and to the rest of us. And you people in the medical school, the same way. And dental school and law school and business school. What have I missed? Nursing school and undergraduate schools, this is a ministry. . . . I was planning to leave town today. I'm not leaving. . . . There may be a bunch of wolves around after this service. Well, the shepherd will be here, friend, to meet the wolf.[158]

During his trials of the 1980s, Oral often felt that he was not getting "enough support from the inside."[159]

Maintaining a sense of family was a constant battle. The honor code and the common chapel services were the chief symbols giving unity to the family, but the university also began holding annual "family seminars," modeled on the partners' seminars conducted by the evangelistic association.[160] Attendance was compulsory for all faculty and students. Despite the growth, the occasional confrontations on campus, and the preoccupation of Oral and Evelyn with other areas in the ministry, Roberts felt that the sense of family had been preserved on campus. "I'm much more aware than I ever was of you and of what's going on," he told the students in 1980, "and conversely I think you're more aware of me." The relationship between him and the students had matured, Oral believed. In the early years it had too often been of the "confrontational-type"; now, as a parent with his later children, he enjoyed the students and felt more at ease with them.[161] In 1982, Evelyn told the students: "I feel like I'm right at home. You're my children, and we're just going to have a little family talk today. . . . I am so glad to be with you because you're a part of me, and I'm a part of you, and I don't feel strange at all standing up here talking to you because I love you. And where there is love, it's easy to talk, right?"[162] There were dissenters in the family, to be sure, perhaps more than in the 1960s, but, by and large, to enter the university grounds was to enter a tribal compound.[163]

THE COMPLETION of the university in the 1980s was overshadowed by the dramatic rise of the City of Faith hospital and medical center. By far the largest financial outlay Roberts had ever attempted, the controversial project completely dominated him and his partners for five years. For a time, it appeared that the City of Faith was the healing vision of Oral Roberts—as in the past it had appeared that the tent crusades and the university were the vision. But as the 1980s wore on, the City of Faith took its place alongside the other institutions and methods as one tool to implement the grander vision.

Plans for the City of Faith were publicly announced in September 1977. Roberts revealed that he would build the entire project immediately—a thirty-story, 777-bed hospital, a sixty-story clinic and diagnostic center, and a twenty-story medical research center. "This is the accepted time," Oral reported the voice of God saying. "People are ready for it. They have not been ready before—neither have you—but they and you are ready now."[164]

The public announcement was preceded by months of frantic consultation and planning. First, Oral had to sell the idea to his own team, although once again, there had been ample warning of what was coming. His critics in Tulsa during the ensuing fight insisted that "he was going to build that damned hospital" all along. C. T. Thompson said: "I will guarantee you that somewhere there is an architect that's got some pretty good sketches of that thing. They did not start that at the last minute."[165]

Roberts's plan, once revealed to the top echelon of ministry administration, did not receive solid support. When Oral sprang the idea on the board of regents, Don Moyers remembered thinking to himself: "Holy Smoke, there's no way in the world we can do that."[166] Oral's top advisors, especially Ron Smith, repeatedly questioned the details of the vision. Evelyn recalled those weeks of discussion: "And when it was getting harder and harder and harder . . . we all went back to him. The men at the office came to him one day and said, 'Now, Oral, you've got so much done. Can't you go back to the Lord and see if we can't stop right there.' So he came home and told me and he just said, 'You know, they just don't believe that God told me sixty, thirty, twenty.'"[167] But Oral persisted; he was determined that the complex would not be a "hodgepodge" of buildings completed over a period of years.[168]

The basic design of the City of Faith was set in the February 1977 meeting in Oral's home, which included Oral, Evelyn, Richard, Winslow, Frank Wallace, and Bill Roberts. Oral knew that he wanted three towers coming out of a common base (first conceived as round towers but later changed to triangular because that shape was more functional), designed so that patients could easily find their way around.[169] He wanted the rooms to "be as much like the bedroom in your home as possible."[170] When completed, the buildings were similar in appearance to others Wallace had designed on the ORU campus, featuring gold-colored reflective glass and fronted with gold-anodized aluminum. The structure enclosed nearly two million square feet of space, more than all of the twenty-one buildings on the ORU campus combined, and the sixty-story clinic was the tallest building in the state of Oklahoma.[171]

Once the design was set, Winslow, Wallace, Bill Roberts, and others went through months of consultation with hospital-design specialists. They had the rare opportunity to plan a complete medical center before construction began.[172] As a result, the City of Faith was a state-of-the-art medical facility. Perhaps the most spectacular innovations were the design of the hospital floors and the widespread use of computers. On each floor, patient rooms were grouped in seven alcoves containing four rooms each. The nurse assigned to each alcove was not more than twelve feet from each patient. Each alcove had a computer terminal connected to a central "hospital patient care information system" capable of reminding the nurse of all patient needs. Most spectacular was a space-age communications center, which jutted out into each open two-floor unit of hospital rooms. Poised midway between the two floors was a platform which had an open view of the fourteen alcoves above and below and which contained a master computer to monitor each nurse's station. "If a nurse doesn't answer her patient's call within a few seconds, the message will transfer to the communications center so someone can see that the patient's needs are met."[173]

While the City of Faith buildings were technologically impressive, they also were loaded with symbolic meaning. The entrance was fronted by an eight-hundred-foot pool, which represented the "River of Life" as pictured in Revelation. Etched on the facing of the buildings were the designs of three prayer towers—looking much like three crosses. The total number of beds proposed for the completed hospital, 777, represented "the perfect number in the Bible."[174] By far most conspicuous was the sixty-foot bronze sculpture of "praying hands" which stood immediately in front of the building. Sculpted by Oklahoma City artist Leonard McMurray, the hands were the world's largest cast-bronze sculpture, cast over a period of two years in a foundry in Mexico City. A ministry brochure explained the meaning of the sculpture: "One hand represents the hand of prayer raised to God, the source of health and healing, and the other the hand of the physician raised in commitment to place all of God's healing power in operation for every patient and against every disease."[175]

From the time of its announcement in September 1977, the City of Faith had a set of clearly articulated purposes. First, the hospital would meet the health needs of the "ORU constituency"; second, the experiment would merge prayer and medicine; third, the hospital would work with the ORU medical school; and fourth, "the center will . . . attempt to show how health care costs can be cut."[176] While all four points reappeared from time to time as justifications for building the center, it was the spiritual motif which set the City of Faith apart. It was, after all, this need which had been central in God's message to Oral: "Son, you cannot put the vision I have given you into a place where My full healing power is not freely accepted. It must not be in a place defeated by a lack of faith in My miraculous power. You must build a new and different medical center for Me. The healing streams of prayer and medicine must merge through what I will have you build."[177]

Merging prayer and medicine was the core purpose of the City of Faith. The combination of a belief in miraculous healing and advanced medical research seemed outlandish to many people—in spite of the long and historic relationship of religion and hospitals. Oral painstakingly and repeatedly explained to his partners his growing interest in medical affairs and how it was consistent with his past behavior and beliefs.[178] Winslow, on the other hand, had to defend his association with "a bunch of people who believe . . . that God supernaturally heals."[179] Over and over in the early months of the project, Oral and Winslow jointly outlined how the City of Faith would bring healing through the best of medical science in a spiritual atmosphere. Roberts remained uncertain about just how the scientific and the spiritual would blend together. "It's going to take ten years after we've opened" to work out the methodology, Oral admitted, "I've never thought it would come quickly."[180] But the desired end was a healing "atmosphere charged with faith and hope."[181]

In addition to the requirement that all doctors in the City of Faith subscribe to the ORU lifestyle and be in sympathy with the aims of the ministry, the care of the patients' spiritual needs was entrusted to "spiritual care-prayer partners" under the direction of Jim Buskirk.[182] The prayer partners were ministers, trained in counseling, and they were considered parts of the patient care system, along with the physicians and nurses. Roberts believed that the prayer partners were a crucial distinctive: "If the prayer partner doesn't do the job, we've just built another fine medical center and we applied to the State of Oklahoma and fought it out in the Oklahoma Supreme Court to build a different medical center, and we will have misrepresented to our partner and to God and to ourselves."[183]

On January 24, 1978, sixty years after the birth of Oral Roberts, groundbreaking ceremonies were held for the City of Faith. It was a joyous celebration. Lee Braxton, a thirty-year veteran with the ministry, declared: "The City of Faith is the crowning jewel of this ministry. It is the capstone which will round out the totality of healing for the whole man as God called Brother Roberts to do." After a service in the chapel, the assembled crowd braved a cold and dreary chill to watch Oral, Evelyn, Richard and Patti, Ron, the three Nash grandchildren, Vaden, and other old friends participate in the ceremonial breaking of the Tulsa sod once again. Seventy-seven white doves were released—"representing the two wings of God's great healing power"—and the scheme was committed into the hands of God and the partners.[184]

It also was submitted to the Oklahoma Health Systems Agency, a review agency which was charged with making recommendations to the Oklahoma Health Planning Commission on the certification of need required for all new hospital construction in the state. On February 8, the agency held open hearings on the City of Faith and received the testimony of about sixty supporters of the project, but it also heard about ten opponents, including a representative of the Tulsa County Medical Society. The medical society had polled its physician members and reported that seventy-eight percent opposed the construction of the City of Faith.[185] On February 27, 1978, the board of trustees of the OHSA voted overwhelmingly to recommend denial of the City of Faith application on four grounds: (1) "The proposed project will offer medical services that will be duplicated or are being offered in existing hospitals in Tulsa"; (2) the City of Faith had not shown it could "obtain affiliation and sharing agreements" with other hospitals in the area; (3) the new hospital could cause rising medical costs

by deflecting users from existing hospitals; and (4) "the applicant has not documented a need for additional hospital beds."[186]

The growing opposition from medical and hospital leaders in Tulsa set the
stage for a showdown meeting of the Oklahoma Health Planning Commission on
April 26, 1978 to vote on the recommendation. Preparing for a full-scale battle,
Oral urged his partners to write to the commission, supporting the City of Faith;
the agency was inundated with between 300,000 and 500,000 letters.[187] The
commission heard statements in opposition to the application from several attorneys representing the Tulsa Hospital Council, as well as presentations by Jim
Winslow, attorney Jack Santee, and several others supporting it. The City of Faith
defense concluded with a brief statement by Oral:

> Members of the Commission, I want to personally thank you for the endless
> hours and the hard work that you have put in in considering our application.
> . . . I am under obligation to three million partner families and their very spe-
> cial health needs. I feel that obligation today in every fiber of my being.
> Likewise, I'm under obligation to my home state, Oklahoma, where I was born
> and raised. . . . And then I feel an obligation to the city of Tulsa, where I have
> lived thirty-one years and expect to live the rest of my life, a city that I love.
> The university and the institutions we have built there were first misun-
> derstood, but I believe that everybody would agree that most people believe
> they have proven to be most beneficial.[188]

The commission opened the floor for comments from the standing-room-only
audience and then voted unanimously to grant the certification of need for the
City of Faith. Construction began on the same day and did not stop until the
hospital opened over three years later.

The basic issue in the fight over certification was "duplication of medical
services" and the negative effect the additional beds would have on Tulsa hospitals. Fearful that the escalation of hospital costs would lead to federal intervention and regulation, hospital administrators insisted that the industry must
control overexpansion. "We have taken a consistent, persistent, and constant
position," said a spokesman for the Tulsa hospitals, "that there is no need for
even one bed in the city of Tulsa."[189] Not only were the occupancy rates in
Tulsa hospitals already below the recommended rates set by the Department of
Health, Education, and Welfare, argued opponents, but the opening of such a
large hospital would create an unrealistic demand for nurses, doctors, and other
employees, which would drive up labor costs.[190]

City of Faith spokesmen contested these claims, arguing that the bed count
used to "frighten the general public" included "phantom beds" which had been
licensed but did not exist, and that, in fact, the occupancy rate in Tulsa was very
high.[191] In addition, they insisted that the hospital would draw both its staff and
its patients from outside the Tulsa community, because of its unique spiritual
emphasis. The peculiar religious identity of the medical center became its chief
defense. "We are not building just another hospital," Winslow told the press,
"but a place where the forces of prayer and medicine can be joined in providing
total health care." The City of Faith would be a "unique national facility," de-

signed to provide "a particular type of holistic medicine advocated by the university," and it would attract "about 45,000 patients annually from Roberts' followers."[192] Winslow estimated that the ministry had 3,100,000 "partner-family units" in the United States and a worldwide following of 94,000,000 people.[193] Furthermore, the defenders of the project insisted that they had never intended to open more than 294 beds in the immediate future, but had applied for the total 777 so that they could build the entire structure rather than add to it later. Critics responded that the hospital was required by law to demonstrate a local and state need—not a supposed national need—and questioned the ability of the Roberts organization to attract patients from outside the area.[194]

Opponents of the City of Faith believed that the ruling of the Oklahoma Health Planning Commission was "decided by . . . political pressure."[195] At the meeting of the commission, one of the attorneys for the Tulsa Hospital Council complained that "we have witnessed an emotional, irrational, religiously oriented campaign the likes of which the United States has probably never witnessed."[196] "The preacher can point a finger," wrote one reporter, "and the telephones start to ring in offices scattered from Oklahoma City to Washington and letters start to pile in so fast they have to assign special secretaries."[197] Roberts did not disguise his willingness to make a political fight for his dream. He began lobbying the Oklahoma legislature in January 1978. Evelyn told the ORU students that Oral, Winslow, and Collins Steele were spending their time in Oklahoma City and that Roberts had told the legislature: "I am here until you pass this application. I'm here. You have me on your hands." "Boy," exclaimed Evelyn, "when you get Oral Roberts on your hands. . . . I haven't a doubt we're going to get that certificate of need."[198] In a show of support in early April, the Oklahoma senate voted 42–5 to "suspend health planning rules" long enough to allow the City of Faith to be approved, if need be, and it was clear that Oral's political clout was sufficient if extraordinary action was needed.[199]

The battle over the City of Faith actually had only begun with the granting of the certification of need. The Tulsa Hospital Council immediately filed a lawsuit in the Tulsa District Court, aimed at overturning the ruling of the commission. District Court Judge Ronald Ricketts refused to issue an injunction halting construction while waiting for the hearing; the Roberts organization agreed that construction would proceed at its own risk. The case was finally heard in November, and Ricketts's decision was based largely on a new issue— the First Amendment separation of church and state. Actually, both sides had recognized the legal potential of that question in the hearings before the commission. City of Faith attorney Jack Santee argued that the religious convictions of the followers of Oral Roberts affected their health, and consequently the religious orientation of the hospital was a health need and a proper concern of the commission.[200] Hospital attorney Earl Sneed argued to the contrary that granting certification "on the basis of a religious philosophy . . . is in direct violation of the honored and revered doctrine of separation of church and state" and that approval by the commission could lead to a "landmark case in the annals of the Supreme Court of the United States concerning separation of church and state."[201] In his decision on December 8, 1978, Judge Ricketts set aside the certification of need and ordered the Oklahoma Health Planning Commission to rehear the case, eliminating from consideration the religious arguments supporting the City of Faith case. The judge ruled that the commission had acted erroneously "in using religion as a basis for granting the certificate of need, violating the U.S. constitution's prohibitions of government involvement in religious matters."[202] The judge still refused, however, to stop construction on the project while the case was pending.

As expected, the City of Faith and the Oklahoma Health Planning Commission appealed the judgment to the Oklahoma Supreme Court, and the Tulsa Hospital Council asked that court to halt construction on the City of Faith. On January 12, 1979, the Supreme Court refused the request to halt construction while the case was being reviewed. In the aftermath of the dispute, spokesmen on both sides believed that the fact that the "Supreme Court was faced with a defacto building" influenced the final outcome of the legal struggle.[203] "If we get that thing built and ready to license," said Winslow in September 1979, "I don't believe this country will stand for it not to be opened." If the state supreme court had the nerve to rule that Roberts had built a "20,000-ton hay barn," the physician added, that was "up to them."[204]

The separation-of-church-and-state ruling threw the City of Faith into that same murky twilight zone that the law school was groping through. Basically, the opposition argued that the City of Faith had been granted certification to provide not just religiously oriented medical care but a "unique version of prayer," and that such special treatment was a violation of the First Amendment.[205] City of Faith defenders responded with a variety of arguments, ranging from the assertion that the hospital was not associated with a "church" and thus was not bound by the amendment, to the claim that the health planning law specifically exempted religious hospitals from First Amendment restrictions.[206]

Whatever the legal merits of the case, Judge Ricketts's ruling did not receive broad public support in Tulsa. "There is a frightening possibility here," protested one journalist, because "it is almost impossible to separate religion from the healing arts."[207] Jenkin Lloyd Jones labeled the "church and state" issue "phonier than a $4 bill." There were legitimate reasons to oppose the City of Faith, Jones argued, but its religious orientation was not one of them: "If prayer is a no-no, how does it happen that so many hospitals are dedicated to saints?"[208] Even if one argued that the City of Faith's religious identity was stronger and more restrictive than in a traditional religious hospital—a point Winslow was willing to concede—a denial of certification would seem to bar such possibilities as a Jewish hospital which served only kosher food. If the ruling was upheld by the Oklahoma Supreme Court, Winslow warned, Oral Roberts University would have "an obligation to the rest of Christianity" to appeal the case to the Supreme Court of the United States. He was confident that "we would have a handful of friendly briefs from almost everybody in that business."[209]

During the interlude before the Oklahoma Supreme Court announced its ruling in April 1981, both sides fought furiously. In January 1979, the Oklahoma legislature, in an impressive show of support for Roberts, passed a "moratorium on further certificates of need" in the Tulsa area—the resolution passed unanimously in the senate and by a vote of 74–15 in the house. The Oklahoma Health Planning Commission immediately enacted the moratorium, effectively stopping all plans for future expansion by Tulsa hospitals in retaliation for their opposition to the City of Faith.[210] The Tulsa hospitals successfully challenged the moratorium in the courts and in March counterattacked by approaching the Department of Health, Education, and Welfare to block federal approval of the City of Faith.[211] When Oral learned of the challenge, he spoke candidly to the students in a special chapel:

> The Federal government of the United States has decided that this ministry must be taken on. We're the only ones in the whole United States who have defeated the Health System Agency. . . . The State of Oklahoma through the legislature and through the state planning commission have spoken in our favor. And have said that there is no right in this town for the local hospitals to have a monopoly. That this is a free country and we have a right to build for our people. The state of Oklahoma has stood up for us. Now the Federal government is coming down on Wednesday to get that changed. And they have said they're going to make the Oral Roberts case a federal case. And that the City of Faith will never open.[212]

But, although the City of Faith did have some nuisance problems with HEW, no major challenge to the certification of the City of Faith was mounted by a federal agency.[213]

Tensions slowly decreased through 1980, after the accreditation of the Oral Roberts University medical school and after it became clear that the City of Faith would be built. Nonetheless, the 6–3 decision of the Oklahoma Supreme Court upholding the certification of need was greeted as a "great day" by the Roberts ministry. The majority of the justices decided that the "controlling" purpose of the hospital was not religious and that therefore the commission had acted correctly.[214] The Tulsa Hospital Council, after consulting its attorneys about appealing to the United States Supreme Court, voted unanimously to end the court battle and extended an invitation to the City of Faith hospital to join the council.[215] Everyone agreed that it was time to get on with business. James Harvey, president of Hillcrest Medical Center, admitted that Oral "has demonstrated an unbelievable ability to raise money"; perhaps he would also be able to attract the thousands of patients that had been predicted.[216]

On the surface, the fierce battle to stop the City of Faith was a straightforward disagreement about health care in Tulsa. Many people, including Saint Francis Hospital's chief benefactor, Bill Warren, were deeply concerned about the impact the huge new hospital would have. Even Jim Winslow acknowledged that there were "purists" among the opponents who believed in the "health planning principle" and fought to preserve it.[217] "I want to tell you how I feel about those people," said Oral in 1978. "I believe they're genuinely sincere. I believe they're good people. They're my brothers and my sisters, and we'll be living here the rest of our lives and so will they."[218]

Naturally, however, the fight against the City of Faith was partly a personal attack on Roberts by those who had long felt he was an embarrassment to Tulsa. The project was another example of Oral's arrogance and his insistence on having his way, a lesson in his brutal use of political power.[219] Jim Winslow was certainly right when he said, "They misunderstand us. They don't want to believe God spoke to Oral."[220] On the other hand, Winslow surmised that some were motivated by sheer jealousy, by the fear that Oral would "build a better mousetrap."[221] More than one Tulsa observer thought that the conflict had Catholic-Protestant connotations—though no such charge ever surfaced in public.[222]

The battle boiled down to a confrontation of strong-willed men. "It was Bill Warren who told him to go build his own hospital," observed Jenkin Lloyd Jones. "Oral did. Well I can't fault Oral. . . . Because they were trying to choke him off and they haven't any right to choke him off. . . . Warren could not abide him. . . . He didn't understand that this man can't be easily squelched. . . . He miscalculated Oral. . . . That was a head-on collision."[223] If it was will that was being tested, Oral was a formidable opponent. He believed he had an advantage:

> The putting together of medicine and prayer in this kind of situation has never been done in history. . . . It's the toughest assignment that I think that God has ever given us. . . . But I have one advantage over all of them. I know the God who spoke to my heart. . . . We're going to obey God. We're going to build the City of Faith. And if they arrest me, I've been told there will be about 4,000 more, and they're going to have to build some new jails.[224]

Though he tried to think the best of his opponents, when cornered Oral talked and acted tough. Faced with opposition from HEW, he told a chapel assembly: "I know in my heart I have no anger toward those people. Cause I know that this is not a people's battle. I know that it's not a thing between me and human beings. I know it's Satan. So if there's anger in my voice, it's not against people. But I sure am mad at the Devil. And I want it known."[225] It was a hard fight, but it barely tested Oral Roberts's staying power.

The legal battle over the building of the City of Faith—ferocious as it was—was probably less traumatic than the financial strain caused by Roberts's determination to build the complex debt-free. The total cost was estimated at about $200,000,000 in 1978, and by the time the center opened, that figure had been raised to $250,000,000; some believed that the finished cost in 1988 would reach $400,000,000.[226] Shortly after the partially finished facility opened in 1982, Oral announced that $140,000,000, "in cash," had been invested up to that point.[227]

From the fall of 1977 through 1982, the financial pressure on the ministry was incredible; Oral remained in constant and fervent communication with his partners, explaining his financial needs. His initial "master plan" for raising the money for the center called for each partner to contribute in multiples of "seven," such as $77 or $777.[228] The response was dramatic; tax records indicated that Oral's partners donated in excess of $38,000,000 in the fiscal year

1977–78, surpassing every other religious association in the nation.[229] Nonetheless, by the summer of 1979 the ministry was out of money, and Oral announced to his national television audience that without an additional $50,000,000, construction would stop. "It was the most awful period I've ever faced in this ministry," Roberts recalled later. "We had built the City of Faith close to halfway on the outside, and we just literally ran out of money. I wrote some of my partners a special letter and went on television. I told the people how I hurt, because we'd never failed to pay God's bills anywhere in the world. He had told me to build the City of Faith debt-free."[230] It was during this crisis that the university's budget was reduced by ten percent and other ministry budgets were cut. During the construction of the City of Faith, budget needs for the ministry grew to an astronomical $10,000,000 a month. There were repeated crises, but somehow Oral's special appeals kept the project going. After one emotional plea, the partners responded with $18,000,000 in one month.[231]

The wrenching financial strain of building the City of Faith, and the fight against its opponents, left scars on Roberts and his organization. Oral had been through many battles in his life, but, he told his faculty, "I know more sufferings today than I've ever known in my life."[232] The ordeal was, Evelyn recalled, "one of the hardest things we've ever gone through."[233] The gigantic costs of the project created inevitable tensions within the organization. Carl Hamilton took the university budget cuts gracefully, but he clearly believed the austerity had been brought on by the City of Faith.[234] Jim Winslow antagonized the university's leaders by declaring in a press conference that "the City of Faith has helped ORU's financial problems, not caused them."[235] Others were quick to point out that the funds contributed to the City of Faith were being sent to Oral Roberts—not to Winslow's project—and that they could and would be diverted into other projects sooner or later.[236] In addition to internal tensions over tight budgets, a few insiders simply did not believe that the grandiose project was justifiable. "One of the few negative voices" was Oral's long-time, most-trusted assistant, Ron Smith. Smith's persistent challenges to the City of Faith contributed to his reluctant decision to resign in 1979.[237]

November 1, 1981 was a proud day for Oral; a gala celebration was held to dedicate the City of Faith. Driven inside Mabee Center by torrential rains, the ceremony attracted over 13,000 people, including many distinguished visitors come to share the moment of triumph. The platform was crowded with Oral's friends and associates; perhaps most obvious were the leaders of the charismatic movement from throughout the nation—Demos Shakarian, Ken Copeland, Kenneth Hagin, Kenneth Hagin, Jr., Pat Robertson, Rex Humbard, Fred Price, Ralph Wilkerson, and scores of others.[238] The national anthem was sung by Oral's friend Barbara Mandrell, "looking stunning in a pink skirt and jacket."[239] Roberts was congratulated by Tulsa mayor Jim Inhofe, Governor George Nigh, and Joseph Kimetto, minister of education from Kenya. Congressman James R. Jones of Tulsa read a letter from President Ronald Reagan, which left Oral gasping: "I just want you all to know I'm no longer the little boy from Tulsa, Oklahoma. President Ronald Reagan. I didn't know this was coming."[240]

After brief remarks by Jim Buskirk and Jim Winslow, Oral spoke on the theme "This Is a New Beginning for the Human Race." "I want to welcome you to something that seems very small in our big world," he began, but then he announced that he believed this occasion to be one of those rare moments in human history when something spectacular was "about to burst forth over the horizon and to touch human life." As at the dedication of the university nearly fifteen years earlier, Oral turned nostalgic, remembering his own roots and his healing ministry. "I want you to look at these two hands," he told the huge, resplendent crowd, many of whom had never seen a tent, "that I have touched more than a million human beings with and prayed for them. I'm proud of the healing ministry. I'll die with it in my heart. It's real to me folks." Turning to the television cameras, Oral thanked his partners for what they had accomplished together and prayed for them:

> Partner, I just want to talk with you for a half minute and tell you this is your moment because you sent your Seed-Faith and you stood up against all those who didn't believe and you helped me. . . . I thank you from the bottom of my heart and I pray for you now. Father, I pray for my partner, that man, that woman, that little boy and that little girl who has sailed on and on with me. Reach out your healing hand and Lord, some way help us to put prayer in medicine.

He alerted his partners that they still had seven years of work to finish the center by 1988 and finally delivered a "prophecy" that "God's going to give a breakthrough in cancer . . . not very far away."[241] It was a vintage Oral Roberts reaction to a moment of triumph—a mixture of nostalgia, pride, and hints of new challenges yet to come.

The dedication ceremony attracted worldwide press attention—reporters from every major wire service attended the event.[242] *Tulsa World* editor Byron Boone wrote an editorial entitled "Miracle on Eighty-first Street." Oral's prediction that the center would open a new chapter in medical history and his comparison of the City of Faith with Mayo Center "may or may not be hyperbole," reflected Boone, but no one could question that the "facility is an enormous accomplishment for Tulsa Evangelist Oral Roberts and his thousands of 'partners' who dreamed about it, fought for it and paid for it."[243] Many news accounts retraced the troubled history of the City of Faith, but in most there was at least a grudging admiration of Oral's dogged, hard-won victory.

In its early years, the City of Faith fell far below the expectations of the Roberts ministry. The complex was successful in recruiting a medical staff from outside the Tulsa area (at the end of 1981 only one physician on the staff, Winslow, was from Tulsa); on the other hand, from the beginning the usage of the hospital fell far behind schedule, particularly the number of people entering the hospital from outside the state of Oklahoma.[244] In 1983 and 1984, widely published syndicated stories suggested that the center resembled a "high-rise medical ghost town." "The concerns and doubts that existed here about the City of Faith have become fulfilled prophecies," said a Tulsa hospital executive.[245]

Jim Winslow acknowledged at the end of 1983 that the hospital had already fallen "one year behind on the calendar."[246] By late 1984 it had still opened only about 130 of its approved 294 beds, and the projected figure of 777 operational beds by 1988 seemed a very remote goal. Low occupancy rates caused a continued need for subsidy from the Oral Roberts Evangelistic Association; in mid-1984 the deficit was running about a million dollars a month. The burden of carrying the City of Faith caused repeated financial crises. In mid-1984, Roberts announced severe curtailments in the ministry, including a reduction of 100 workers in the evangelistic association and 244 at the City of Faith, and the placing of university employees on a four-day work week.[247] In a dramatic announcement in July 1984, he reported that Jesus had once again visited him and an "angel of the Lord" had been placed at his disposal. Oral "dispatched" the angel to bring the "poor, needy and the sick" to the City of Faith, opening the hospital to indigent patients. In the fall of 1984, the occupancy rate at the hospital seemed to be rising.[248]

The City of Faith's most pressing problem was its failure to attract Oral's partners in the numbers anticipated—partly, perhaps, because of exaggerated estimates of the number of "partner-family units." Winslow repeatedly urged the partners to come to the complex for medical care: "You helped build it but you have not used it."[249] In hindsight, there were many reasons to doubt that large numbers of people would travel to Tulsa for medical care, but both Winslow and the City of Faith's critics agreed that the hospital suffered particularly because it was "not an established part of the medical referral system." "You don't find many doctors out there sending patients to the City of Faith," noted C. T. Thompson.[250] In 1983, Winslow urged Roberts's partners to send the names of their local physicians to the City of Faith so that the hospital could establish "a relationship with him or her—so that should you need the services of the City of Faith in the future, the way will already be paved."[251]

"I think the jury is still out on the potential of the City of Faith," said John Williams in late 1983. Winslow remained confident, even jaunty, through the rocky beginning, predicting that the hospital would become financially stable by 1985, and the clinic even sooner.[252] On the other hand, as the hospital's problems deepened, its critics felt vindicated. "You hate to say it," C. T. Thompson told a reporter in 1984, "but almost everything that's happened was totally predictable."[253]

The twenty-story medical research center also developed more slowly than anticipated. In his announcement of the project, Oral promised to build "the most modern Research Center to help find a cure for cancer and other death-dealing diseases."[254] Roberts believed that his researchers would have an advantage: "If the Spirit can get across some knowledge that the researcher hasn't got, we're ahead."[255] By 1984, however, only three floors of the research center were in use. It cost over $1,000,000 to complete and equip each floor of the building, and probably an equal amount per floor to fund the research each year. "We'll have to be willing to pay the tab," commented Winslow about the financial burden the center placed on the Oral Roberts Evangelistic Association.[256]

Oral remained intensely interested in sponsoring cancer research. He had long been fascinated by the disease and believed that he had insights into its demon origins. In 1977, he began to openly speculate that cancer had a "cure" of "spiritual origin" and predicted that "God intends for there to be a medical breakthrough in cancer research."[257] On a number of occasions Oral reiterated his belief that a cure for cancer was near, including at the dedication of the City of Faith, and his comments received some attention in the press, but his prophecy was raised to a new plateau in January 1983.[258]

In his January 1983 letter to his partners, Oral shared the results of hours of "conversation between the Lord and me" after the death of Ronnie. During a seven-hour vision in Palm Springs, he was told that he and his partners must move with dispatch to finish the cancer research center, because "it is later than you think."[259] The revelation once again contained little that was not clearly in Oral's mind already—it represented a firming up of his ideas and a dramatic public announcement of them. For several months Roberts had quizzed Winslow about cancer, listening and refining, and the trauma of Ronnie's death apparently emboldened him to speak.[260]

Oral's revelation made two points. First, cancer was a "Beelzebub disease": "I am convinced that cancer itself is satanic, because it does not obey the normal order of God's creation."[261] He vigorously denied that he had implied that cancer victims were demon-possessed; he simply believed that the disease represented a disorder in God's universe, much like Satan's rebellion against God.[262] More controversial was Oral's prediction that "there will be some kind of major breakthrough in cancer prevention by the end of this century. I'm predicting a major healing coming in the world."[263] While the revelation set no firm deadlines, it was sufficiently stimulating to Oral's partners to bring an immediate outpouring of around $5,000,000 in contributions for the research center.[264]

Oral's cancer revelation kept the cauldron of controversy brewing through 1983. Before making the announcement, he warned Winslow "that this is going to be misunderstood."[265] He was correct. The national news media once again focused on Tulsa—asking if Oral thought he knew the cure for cancer and characterizing his vision as "one of the boldest religious fund-raising appeals yet."[266] "From a medical standpoint," observed his foremost Tulsa critic, C. T. Thompson, "he's a fraud. He's promising to people things that he absolutely cannot produce. . . . How can you get a scientist . . . of any caliber to come in and investigate something where the big leader of the place is talking about it being satanic in origin. . . . The guy needs to be called to task for this."[267] But many insiders believed that their research center would fulfill Oral's prophecy. In 1983, the City of Faith acquired one of the few nuclear magnetic resonance machines in the world, an ultramodern and expensive piece of equipment which Winslow believed "may become a part of God's answer to the disease we call cancer."[268]

THE CITY of Faith complex is owned by Oral Roberts University; the hospital serves as a teaching hospital for the schools of medicine, nursing, dentistry, and theology.[269] In many ways the center was the grand completion of the healing dream. It was the final institution needed to train young people to take healing to the world. Capricious as Oral's actions seemed to his critics, there was an uncanny consistency in the total vision which the City of Faith seemed to fill out. There was not much left to do. "What plans do you have for the future, after the City of Faith is completed?" a student reporter asked Oral in 1980. His reply was direct: "I've built my last building. I'm 90 percent through."[270]

Could it be that the vision was completed? It seemed unlikely in May 1984, when Oral told his partners to get ready for the "greatest announcement in the thirty-seven years since I began."[271] The announcement, coupled with an appeal for support, was of a plan to train and send out "1,000 Healing Teams between now and the beginning of the twenty-first century." The project could be, said Oral, "the biggest thing this ministry has ever been called on by God to do." More than that, it was the culmination, it was the end of the vision: "All things we have done have pointed to this hour."[272]

The healing-team concept was an extension of Roberts's earlier projections that his students would be his successors, taking healing to the world in a way far surpassing his own efforts. They were the family. "Whatever you're in to, stay in touch with us won't you?" asked Evelyn of a group of alumni in 1981. "Because you are ours. You belong to us and we claim you."[273] But the healing teams were the final rallying of those who had imbibed Oral's healing vision. The teams were the resurrection of an idea which had surfaced over and over in the ministry. In 1984, Oral viewed the formation of the teams as the end toward which all the building had led.

The idea of student missionaries was, of course, implicit in Oral Roberts University and had long been manifested in such organizations as the Christian Service Council, through which a large percentage of the undergraduates did volunteer service in Tulsa's religious and benevolent institutions.[274] In addition, the concept was rooted in the youth team experiments of the 1960s and the World Action teams of the 1960s and 1970s. In 1976, a summer missions program was begun as a revised version of student missions. In that program, ORU undergraduate students volunteered for summer tours overseas, working with missionaries in jobs ranging from "person-to-person evangelism, music ministries, teaching, and child evangelism, to construction work, maintenance, first aid, housekeeping, and other practical areas of life."[275] Beginning with fifteen students in 1976, the number in the program grew to nearly two hundred in the early 1980s, ministering in twenty-eight countries.[276] But the student summer missions program was not the kind of organized work that Oral was looking for. University funding for the program was seriously reduced in the financial crunch of 1979, raising some protest from ORU students.[277] By the mid-1980s, the university's funding for the program had dropped from eighty percent to about twenty percent, and ministry leaders were "gravitating toward the understanding" that the university would act only as a "training agency," not as a "mission board."[278]

The healing-team concept was a reformulation of old ideas. In his announcement in 1984, Oral tied his new vision to his perceptions in the 1960s that Africa was closing to missionaries—"they had begun to run the preachers out and close the doors." It was then, he recalled, that he first understood "that

I had to take the doctors and the dentists and the nurses to open a region or a country. Because they all want doctors, I perceived that before the school was open. . . . My old team heard me talking about it before that."[279] Beginning in 1975, when Roberts launched the expansion of the university, he had a vision for the decade beginning in 1985: "As we go into our third decade, our greater emphasis will be not upon the structure of the University, but upon the function of our students. I think the main building program will be behind us. . . . The third decade, as I see it, is a releasing of these mighty forces in a beautiful way upon society."[280] Throughout the late 1970s and the 1980s, amidst the struggles to establish the graduate programs and build the City of Faith, the idea of sending healing teams repeatedly bubbled to the surface.[281] "The time is getting close—down in the deepest part of my calling—to take God's healing power to my generation," Oral wrote to his partners in 1977. "We are getting to that point."[282] In 1979, he told the ORU students that he had a vision of eight hundred healing teams of about twelve persons, covering every nation of the earth by the year 2000.[283] Once again, the plan was falling into place before Oral's announcement in 1984.

In the 1980s, the university was overtly committed to turning out professionals willing to participate in healing teams. In his testimony before the Oklahoma Health Planning Commission in 1978, Jim Winslow had observed that "ORU is dedicated to graduating physicians who will go where there is a medical need: overseas, to the ghettos, to the rural areas of America."[284] While professional students were not obligated legally to perform missionary service, they were asked to make a commitment to "an overseas healing team service for some period of time."[285] The university's students were thoroughly versed in the role they were being groomed to play in the unfolding of Oral Roberts's healing vision.[286]

The most difficult obstacle in the development of a student missions program continued to be placing the healing teams. The independent status of Oral Roberts University made it a training institution without a clientele. The knottiest problem facing Oral in the 1980s was not motivating the youngsters to join the healing teams but finding places for them to go. In 1963, Roberts had announced that the university did not intend to send out missionaries but rather to "work with the churches who do. We will make ourselves available for any service we can render."[287] But those efforts were thwarted, recalled Lee Braxton a decade later, because "we had no base to operate from or no church to tie them to."[288] It was partly those same deficiencies which spelled doom for the later student missions programs.

In the early 1980s, Oral explored a variety of avenues to find openings for healing teams. He considered establishing a "relationship" with a "host of people," including T. L. Osborn, his old Tulsa charismatic friend, who had spent three decades supporting native missionaries throughout the world. "I'm interested in having 475 [the National Council of Churches Mission Board] down and telling them how we can work together," said Jim Buskirk.[289] But by far the most promising connection explored in the early 1980s appeared to be a cautious alliance struck with Bill Bright, founder and leader of Campus Crusade.

After talking to Bright in April 1982, Oral excitedly spoke of the potential of a link with Campus Crusade:

> Right now this very second the global aspects of the outreach of this university are shaping up. I've just got off the phone from one of the most influential men in the world. A spiritual leader who has more people over the world in 150 nations and the Lord spoke to him several months ago that he was to work with us and with our students. While he and I have been friends for thirty years, there was always a difference in the charismatic area and we never fell out or anything like that. . . . We were friends . . . but that was it. Now the charismatic issue is fully settled on both sides. We have a working relationship that will begin this summer and it probably [will be] one of the . . . two or three most important things that has ever happened to this university.[290]

Bright came to the ORU campus in November 1982, received a warm reception, and agreed for a City of Faith physician to spend two months in a Campus Crusade hospital in Swaziland.[291] It was a trial union between two very powerful and independent religious parachurch organizations; the Roberts ministry felt, at least, that there was "a good promising area there."[292]

At the same time, the Roberts organization was exploring the placement of healing teams with government officials in Kenya and Swaziland. In 1981, Jim Winslow and Carl Hamilton visited Kenya to discuss the matter. In negotiations with the nation's president, they agreed to enroll several Kenyan students at the university, including the president's son, and in return "President Moi . . . agreed to take the Healing Teams from ORU into Kenya so that all of God's healing power could be brought to his people."[293] Similar negotiations in Swaziland seemed promising.[294] "I'll be blessed by the time I leave the world to have it working," admitted Oral in 1983, but the healing-team vision was the agenda for the future.[295]

Roberts's May 1984 announcement signaled the beginning—the ministry was ready to "send forth our FIRST FULL PILOT HEALING TEAMS." Each team would include between 12 and 30 "ORU-trained physicians, dentists, nurses, nutritionists, special health workers, evangelists, prayer partners, singers and musicians, teachers, engineers, business and law leaders, and others of special skills and dedication." The first teams were being dispatched, wrote Oral, to Africa, to "the islands in the Caribbean," to Latin America, to "one of the neediest Indian reservations in North America," and to an "impoverished area of the Appalachian Mountains." By the year 2000, Roberts projected that 1,000 such teams, including 21,000 young people, would have been to every one of the "210 nations and/or protectorates on earth." There was much about the plan that was still unclear. Although Oral's announcement indicated that funds were needed to "train and send" the teams, the question of how the teams would be financed was not outlined.[296] Some critics pointed out that most of the funds for previous missions' efforts had been supplied not by the ministry but by the participants.[297]

However incomplete the healing-team plan remained in 1985, it appeared to be, in Oral Roberts's mind, the culmination of his healing vision. It was the end of an arduous journey, he explained to the physicians at the City of Faith:

Now the whole healing team program seems to be falling into place. But, brethren and sisters, without our having built this ministry through the big tent, going in those healing lines and going to forty-five nations, without our taking the praise and the blame, without our standing up when we were doing well and when we were failing, and just preserving, without building the university, without building the School of Medicine and the other graduate schools, without building the City of Faith . . . the healing team concept might have been put back another fifty or 100 years. All I can say is I've obeyed God to the best of my knowledge and I obeyed him in things I didn't know even what I was doing.

Oral's mission was nearing completion—his John the Baptist role fully played out: "This signals a new beginning for the world's salvation and healing. And to me it signals in the most concrete way I know the beginning of an end of the Gospel reach. For when this Gospel of the kingdom is preached . . . to all nations, then shall the end come. Without our healing teams being part of that, I don't think the end can come. . . . So we are part of the biggest thing on God's earth."[298]

CHAPTER

XV

Tightening the Family

IN 1975, TELEVISION remained Oral Roberts's most effective means of communicating his message. Television had supplied the ministry with the names of millions of partners and potential donors, it had recruited students for the university, and it had made Roberts's name a household word throughout the nation. Ten years later, television remained important to the ministry, and Oral still looked for better ways to use the medium, but it was not nearly so central as it had been in the past. The spread of cable systems complicated the religious programming market, as did the proliferation of programs modeled on Roberts's innovative techniques. In the ten years from 1975 to 1985, the Roberts ministry used and discarded a sequence of television formats. Almost certainly, new experiments lay in the future.

From 1975 to 1980, the centerpiece of the television ministry was the prime-time specials, which continued to feature such show business personalities as Jerry Lewis, Robert Goulet, Johnny and June Cash, Minnie Pearl, and "Tennessee" Ernie Ford. Many of the programs were filmed on location, in sites ranging from Alaska to the Grand Ole Opry House in Nashville. The programs were produced by Ron Smith, who replaced Dick Ross in 1975, giving the ministry the creative control which Oral increasingly demanded.[1]

Smith felt that the program made "a great deal of progress" in getting across Roberts's message, particularly when Oral spoke "subtly" rather than "loudly."[2] Oral increasingly preached more directly, however, feeling he had won the right to speak his mind after years of success. "We have won over the television stations for the most part," he told the ORU faculty in 1975, "and they are giving us a great deal of freedom that they denied us."[3] He preached some of his old tent sermons, such as "The Fourth Man" and "Samson and Delilah" (in abbreviated forms), testing his prime-time audiences and the tolerance of his advisors, who preferred a conversational format featuring the Roberts family in informal settings.[4]

At the end of 1979, Oral stopped the production of the hour-long specials. There were no demanding reasons for making the decision; ratings had declined slightly, but not markedly, and they fluctuated depending on the popularity of the guest stars. Costs had not escalated dramatically—although the general austerity measures of 1979 contributed to the decision to curtail television expenses. But, by and large, Oral simply felt, after ten years, that the specials had "run their course"; it was time to experiment with other methods.[5]

The television capabilities of the ministry continued to expand with the construction of a sophisticated production studio adjoining Mabee Center in 1977, which was dubbed "Baby Mabee"; the acquisition of a $700,000 mobile television van in 1979; and the installation of a satellite dish in 1980. The organization was capable of producing and transmitting the most complicated programming. Using these new facilities, the ministry tried several experiments. In 1978, a daily program was announced, designed for showing on the "special networks" and VHF outlets in major cities. Initially, the programs were projected to showcase "the excitement and the spirituality of this campus," perhaps raising the visibility of such figures as Jim Buskirk.[6] But the daily program plan was aborted at the last minute.[7]

There was considerable internal dissension over the plan. Ron Smith felt that the program was a mistake, because "Oral did not have either the stamina or the content to maintain a daily show," and it was judged impractical to allow others "to become visible enough to support that kind of demanding schedule."[8] George Stovall explained the scuttling of the project:

> After talking with several other ministries that have a daily show, such as PTL and 700 Club, we concluded that we could have the same amount of exposure and audience without going on daily. Presently it seems that we would be better off putting our resources into something more beneficial to the partners and ministry as a whole. We are, however, exploring cable television and will of course continue our weekly shows and specials.[9]

However, the idea remained alive. Several other experimental programs were launched, none with marked success. In 1981, a "Sunday Night Live" talk and variety show was aired on a limited network, but it apparently did not live up to expectations.[10] In 1982, the ministry ran programs on the PTL network, featuring the "Holy Spirit in the Now" videotapes, which had been used on the Oral Roberts University campus for a decade, and a series of tapes which featured films of the crusades of the 1950s.[11] Then, in September 1984 Richard Roberts began a five-day-a-week live variety and talk program originating from Mabee Center. The program was a major financial gamble; the ministry committed itself to an eighteen-month trial period. The program was a bold bid to win new supporters in the 1980s.[12]

Another television experiment of the 1980s was Oral's return to prime-time scheduling in November 1981, after an absence of two years. Three specials were filmed and aired monthly, beginning in November. It was an expensive gamble, but Oral believed that he had discovered a format different enough to separate him from his competition. Produced by Sid and Marty Krofft, the specials featured a family of puppets called the Fudge Family in dialogue with the Roberts family. Oral revealed that he had been thinking for months of having a puppet ministry, but the idea coalesced while he was watching a Barbara Mandrell telecast which featured a group of puppets called the Texas Critters.[13] He alerted his partners that he was once again launching out to "attract your unsaved loved ones" and waited for the reaction to the new series.[14]

While the programs won some critical praise, the ministry soon concluded that the series was a "serious mistake."[15] Partly, surmised Richard Roberts, prime-time religious programming simply was "not going over now like it did in the early 1970s."[16] But others believed that the format had not worked. "Talking to puppets was never the answer," observed Ron Smith. "I would not have agreed to the puppets nor Sid and Marty Krofft. They're part of the Hollywood alligator set. They didn't fit Oral Roberts."[17]

Through the years of experimentation, Oral's most important link with his partners remained his half-hour Sunday telecast.[18] Roberts tinkered constantly with the format of the weekly series, turning it into a conversational Bible teaching program in 1979, changing the name to "Oral Roberts and Miracles of Seed Faith" when it was directed by the Kroffts, and returning to an entertainment and preaching format in 1982, when the ministry resumed control of production.[19] The weekly telecast was used to "showcase the ministry," and it featured the Roberts family—Oral, Evelyn, Richard, and Lindsay—as opposed to guest celebrities. The program was pointed to the partners, the people who supported the ministry; it was a calculated narrowing of the television audience.[20]

The changes in the television programs were partly a response to declining ratings. For over a decade, "Oral Roberts and You" was the leading religious telecast in the nation. But its ratings slipped sharply in the 1980s, and on occasion its audience was surpassed by those of other religious programs. Partly, Roberts's ratings problems were related to a general and well-documented decline of interest in religious programming.[21] While the Roberts ministry disputed some of the direst assessments of its television losses, by and large, the news was accepted as a sign of the times.[22] Peggy George, general manager of TRACO, the Roberts production company, pointed out that when Oral began his new program in 1969, there were "only one or two major religious programs. Now, my latest survey shows that there are 96 syndicated in at least five markets."[23] Religious programs were increasingly using cable networks, where they found segregated audiences. At the same time, the traditional Sunday morning "religious ghetto" television slot was being invaded by secular programming.[24]

Oral continued to probe for new ways to use the medium which had served him so well in the past. Many who knew him well, such as Ron Smith, were convinced that he would make his way back to the top of the ratings.[25] Cable television appeared to offer new opportunities; in December 1983, Oral began buying time for his Sunday program on Atlanta's WTBS.[26] He contemplated buying a Tulsa television station from Billy James Hargis in 1983, but then seemed to discard the idea.[27]

In an innovative use of television in February 1984, the ministry broadcast, via satellite, a "healing service" which featured Oral preaching to an audience in Mabee Center and Richard speaking from Africa, where he was conducting crusades. The service was beamed live to nearly two hundred hotels and auditoriums in the United States and Canada, where Oral's partners had been urged to assemble on Sunday afternoon.[28] Roberts had long been fascinated by the potential of satellites to allow a gigantic meeting of his partner family. In 1972, he announced that "we may be called upon to produce a regular church service right here each week and send it across America."[29] The satellite experiment in 1984 was not satisfactory—the links between Africa and America were technically flawed, little time was left for the healing service at the end of the program, and preparations in many of the localities had been "slipshod." No one was ready to predict whether the technique would be used again, but there was no doubt that there would be further experiments to find ways to use television to tie the partner family together.[30]

Oral insisted that his uses of television had two basic aims. First, in spite of the show business trimmings, the major purpose was to broadcast his spiritual message. Roberts performed best in his own studio, surrounded by his partners and friends; his guest stars were frequently touched by the atmosphere. Robert Goulet, who joined a group of students in a "prayer session" just before taking the stage, "confessed he couldn't read the cue cards for the tears in his eyes."[31] The second objective was "intimacy."[32] Roberts was obsessed with making television more and more personal—striving to create that "one-to-one level" where he had few peers.[33] Richard Roberts, who increasingly played a creative role in the television programs, was convinced that the close-up shot could create the feeling: "I watch everybody on television and I seldom see somebody look at me. I seldom see someone come right in on a close-up shot and say 'Now, listen, my friend, I want to talk to you right where you are.' But you watch our program, I'm going to do that to you every week."[34]

In the early 1970s, when the television specials were mushrooming, reshaping Oral's reputation and broadening the partner base, healing crusades seemed a part of Roberts's slightly embarrassing and antiquated past. But to Oral they remained honored memories, and in the 1980s crusading reappeared in the ministry, primarily because of the metamorphosis of Richard Roberts as an evangelist. By the mid-1980s, even Oral was chafing to hit the trail again—in new and less strenuous ways, to be sure. The team of Oral and Richard Roberts was primed and ready in the mid-1980s; it appeared there might be a new audience waiting to be healed.

It was the restlessness of Richard Roberts which refueled the revivalistic zeal of the Roberts ministry. Richard's role in the ministry expanded rapidly after his appointment as president of the Oral Roberts Evangelistic Association

in 1973. He soon held a number of other titles within the organization, including membership on the ORU board of regents and the chairmanship of the
university's executive committee. In the late 1970s, his influence was more
visible at the university, he assumed more responsibility in directing the television programs, and he frequently shared the platform with his father.[35]

The clearest omen of the future came in 1976, when Richard began
scheduling partners' meetings throughout the country. Initially, Patti traveled
with her husband to the one-night meetings, which followed a light and
entertaining format. The services were designed to make personal contact with
the partners, much like those conducted by Bob DeWeese, and included little
preaching.[36]

Patti's withdrawal from the ministry at the end of 1976 interrupted the
schedule of partners' meetings, but Richard began conducting them again in
August 1977, visiting three or four cities each month, accumulating experience
at a dizzying pace. Beginning in 1978, Oral joined his son three or four times a
year for rallies in major cities. The changes in Richard's meetings were quite
perceptible; he continued to use his singing talent to good effect, but he also
preached with increasing force and originality. By the fall of 1979, he reported
to the ORU student newspaper: "I've called them 'partner's meetings' in the
past, but I am doing more than singing. I'm preaching the message and praying
for salvation and healing, and I think that 'crusade service' is a little better
description of what's going on."[37] The ministry advertisement announcing
Richard's appearance in Louisville in 1979 read: "I would like the opportunity
to share God's blessings with you. Come expecting your needs to be met as we
pray for your healing in body, mind and spirit. Join with me as I speak God's
Word and sing His praises. This will be your day."[38]

In the fall of 1979, Richard's meetings began to be referred to as "healing
services." It was a natural ripening, one that Oral and Richard discussed: "My
dad had always said that something would happen when I got around the age of
30. He had always told me how Jesus began his public ministry when he was
thirty; he told me how he himself had begun his public ministry when he was
twenty-nine and a half. He told me there was something special about the age of
thirty, that somehow when you got around thirty, you began to know who you
were."[39] Still reeling from the collapse of his marriage in 1979, Richard felt a
more intense call to preach. But it was not until a year later, in the spring of
1980, after his marriage to Lindsay, that he announced his entry into the healing
ministry. After a successful crusade with his father in Norfolk in April, one
which left Oral ebullient about the resurgence of his own healing ministry,
Richard returned home with ambivalent feelings: "He [Oral] came home terribly excited because he saw his ministry extended and I came home asking questions, 'Lord, isn't it time for me?' "[40] He and Lindsay began praying that Richard
would receive his own healing ministry, and two weeks later, in Albuquerque,
New Mexico, he "stepped out on faith and believed for it."[41] According to
Richard, after the altar call,

before I realized what I was doing, I asked everyone with an arthritis problem
to stand. Well, I was sort of shocked when 200 people stood up. And I began

to speak the word of healing in the name of Jesus whose name is above arthritis. . . . And I began to feel words coming up within me. I knew it was
coming by the Spirit but it was coming so fast. Suddenly I felt that someone
was getting healed and I looked and I saw a woman walking across the front of
the building.[42]

Supported and encouraged by his wife, Richard threw himself wholeheartedly into his new healing ministry, withdrawing from most of his administrative duties in the ministry and at the university.[43] He recognized that it
would take time for the public to perceive him as an evangelist rather than a
singer. "It started out small and it began to grow," Richard said of his ministry
in 1983, "and now it's really starting to move."[44] His crusading was welcomed
by leaders within the ministry, including Oral. "I went to my dad wondering
how he was going to take it because he had had me involved in a lot of different
things," recalled Richard, "and he said, 'I've been waiting for it to come. I knew
the day would come.'"[45]

Beginning in 1982, Richard extended most of his meetings into three-day
crusades. "There is a new fire and fervor in the ministry of Richard Roberts,"
announced *Abundant Life* in October 1982, "to pray for the sick. Richard—
joined by his wife Lindsay, who faithfully stands by his side in the ministry—is
ministering throughout the United States as well as foreign countries praying in
Jesus' name for the thousands of sick and unsaved who are coming in great
numbers to his Healing Crusades."[46] The Roberts organization threw the full
force of its name and resources behind Richard's new call.

Although Richard's crusades by no means attracted the same attention from
the press that his father's had three decades earlier, they usually were attended
by curious, and often respectful, reporters.[47] Most observers in the 1980s were
struck by Richard's use of his father's mannerisms and message. To some he
seemed a clone, a lifeless imitation of his father, mouthing slogans his father had
preached for decades.[48] But as time passed, Richard's sermons began to show
some originality, although they continued to follow closely the major channels
of Oral's theology. They also began to show some acquaintance with the writings of other charismatic preachers, particularly T. L. Osborn, Kenneth Hagin,
and Kenneth Copeland. Perhaps more significant, for illustrations, Richard increasingly called on his own experiences—experiences which accumulated at an
accelerating rate as he expanded his healing ministry.[49]

Of course, Richard's meetings were always somewhat different. His skill as
a singer—he was never rivaled by his father in that area—was a drawing card,
particularly in the early days of his healing ministry; "the show," reported an
Arkansas newsman, was "good, and slick."[50] Richard had to build his crusade
ministry without the cooperation of any organized religious body. While ministry partners supplied a core audience, in the United States, at least, he felt he
attracted mostly "the unchurched and unsaved."[51] Richard knew that he was
outside the established religious order; he neither expected nor received "cooperation" from churches.[52] He also frequently noted that his healing gift worked
in a different way from his father's. While Oral felt the power of God in his
right hand and had been "led to touch people," Richard believed he had been

given a "word of knowledge": "Here is how it operates in me. Many times I will feel something in my own body. Now when it first started happening I didn't know what it was. . . . All of a sudden I will get a pop or a ringing or something in my ear. . . . And I learned over a period of time that that was the Lord giving me an indication that someone was receiving a healing."[53]

Like Oral's crusades decades earlier, Richard's campaigns brought in a deluge of healing and conversion testimonials. In his meetings, Richard combed his audiences, searching for those who felt they had been touched by God:

> Where's that person getting a healing in your shoulder? Wave your hand at me. Step out into the aisle a minute and walk over to where Dr. Winslow or Dr. Buskirk or one of the students are. I want to talk to you a minute. Where's that person who's getting a healing in your knee? I see you waving your hand. Step out into the aisle. Where's that man whose back just went back into place? Some man. Where are you? Where's that woman . . . the left side of your neck as I was praying, it just popped.[54]

The "testimony area" of the ministry editorial department was reactivated to "receive testimonies of physical, spiritual, and financial miracles."[55] The pages of *Abundant Life* once again teemed with accounts of healings of illnesses ranging from cataracts to blindness.[56] "The healing and salvation (healing of the soul) which are taking place are so numerous now," reported *Abundant Life,* "that counting the people who received healings is impossible."[57]

Beginning in 1982, Richard increased his overseas crusades, and by 1984 he had targeted forty countries where he hoped to preach.[58] He was particularly invigorated by campaigns in Jamaica and South Africa, which drew large crowds. "My experience overseas," he reported, "is that people are so hungry to hear what you have to say and they are so grateful that you would take your time and come."[59] Richard's desire to preach overseas, and his glowing reports of successes, impressed many old-timers in the ministry. While he could depend on "Oral's constituency here in the states," overseas "he has to do his own thing," and his apparent success gave new credibility to his evangelistic role.[60]

Richard's assertion of himself in the 1980s fueled an old debate about his personality, ability, and character. Perhaps even more than Oral, Richard bore the brunt of public attacks on the ministry in the 1980s. Few doubted that he could be charming. "Straightforward and instantly likeable," wrote a Tulsa reporter in 1979, "Richard comes off like some guy you went to high school or college with. He's good-looking, friendly, down-to-earth, funny, chatty, quick on his feet and also quick to voice displeasure or disagreement."[61] On the other hand, books written by Wayne Robinson, Jerry Sholes, and Patti Roberts—all people who knew him well—left the combined impression that Richard was spoiled, petulant, devoid of an "inquiring mind," and hedonistic.[62] Wayne Robinson, who left the ministry with a genuine respect for Oral, found Richard's rise to prominence "reprehensible," and doubted the sincerity of his call. Robinson's resentment was so strong, he revealed, that "I had to redo the chapter on Richard three different times at the publisher's recommendation."[63]

Surely some of the criticism of Richard rested on a solid foundation. Too many people spoke harshly of him.[64] His mother described him as "happy-go-lucky," but old friend Don Moyers called him "a spoiled brat."[65] "In the early days he did not work," agreed Bill Nash, "he goofed off and he played golf." But Nash believed, as did other close friends, that he had "seen him change an awful lot" through the years.[66]

One thing Richard could not change was the fact that he was Oral Roberts's son—that he was the heir apparent. "Just because he spelled his name the same way was no reason for that portfolio," argued Robinson. "If he made a 'C' in high school that was probably one of his better grades. He flunked out at Kansas State his first semester. He came there to ORU, took humanities and music, flunked both of them . . . and then is put on the Board of Regents. And made president of the association."[67] Richard's problem, mused John Williams, was "only half dislike"; more important, "he's not respected."[68] There was no way that Richard could escape the fact that he had ridden his father's reputation to prominence. His was a burden that the sons of all successful men carry; it contributed greatly to the maturing of Richard Roberts.

To a remarkable degree, Richard understood his predicament. He knew the resentment that seethed within the organization and at the university because of his rise to prominence. "This is the hardest place in the world for me to minister because I am Joseph's boy," he said in 1983. "The biggest criticism I had over my divorce and remarriage came from right here. It didn't come from the outside world because the outside world has been through it." But he was hopeful in the 1980s that the feeling was changing: "Now that perception is now changing here. Because I've got enough guts and gall that no matter how many people's arms are folded over there at that chapel service, when I go on to preach, I'm going to be myself. I don't really give a hoot. . . . If I feel like praying for the sick, I'm going to pray for the sick. Every time I pray for the sick there are results."[69]

In fact, out of his own crucible of personal trauma and criticism, a new Richard Roberts did appear to be emerging—a more mature, confident, and independent evangelist than might have been predicted. In a sense, he seemed to build on his divorce and the other family tragedies. "I know what broken relationships are about," he told the ORU students in 1982, "I understand how that feels. I have two daughters who live in Nashville."[70] He also came to terms with the call to preach. "On the one hand I had fought it and on the other hand I wanted it," he told an audience in 1981.[71] He remained sensitive to public criticism; since 1980, he revealed, "I've not read a single newspaper article pro or con."[72] While he had by no means received the "knocks that his father had," observed Warren Hultgren, in some ways "the pressure on him is worse than his father." "Tribulation worketh patience," observed Hultgren; he believed the Richard Roberts of the 1980s was much improved by his experiences.[73] Ron Smith felt "great empathy for Richard," because of the "very difficult spot" he occupied.[74] "I think Richard is an unsung hero," said Bill Nash, "he's done remarkably well in taking on this role that's almost been forced upon him."[75]

The reshaping of Richard Roberts's image demanded, above all, that he establish his independence from his father. Oral and Evelyn believed that

Richard had never sacrificed his identity to become "Oral Roberts, Jr." He had, after all, been a "rebellious" son, who had very slowly been drawn to his father's ministry.[76] Richard insisted over and over that he did not want to follow in his father's footsteps, recognizing that "God made each one of us unique, irreplaceable."[77] It could be argued that Richard always had contested his father publicly more successfully than any other individual. Patti recalled that Richard "at times defended me" and once confronted Oral during a television taping about a wrong he believed his father had committed.[78] Bill Nash believed that Richard was "insisting on" being treated as an equal in the ministry and that "Oral is responding to him." He recalled a meeting of the executive council at the university in which Richard challenged his father's tongue-lashing of an employee "as strong as I've seen anybody challenge anybody anywhere in my whole life." Richard's rebuke changed the tone of the meeting and stunned the executives who were present. "I saw something in Richard for the first time," recalled Nash, " and I think I've seen it indirectly through other people's eyes many times since.[79]

Richard's emergence as a formidable evangelist in his own right came mostly after his divorce and remarriage. Supported by his wife, he felt that his whole life had been "revolutionized" by his call to a healing ministry. For the first time, Richard announced, "I knew who I was. . . . I knew what I was supposed to do with my life."[80] It was, he insisted, a genuine spiritual experience, which gave him assurance that he was "God's anointed" and that the world was about to witness a "resurgence of the evangelist."[81]

Richard's new independence was also rooted in a pragmatic realization that he must establish his own identity and credentials. "I'm starting out in the identical way, a different time, but the identical way my dad started out," he said. "If I don't get out as an evangelist and get in the hearts and the minds of the people, then on the day that my dad is no longer here it will disintegrate on its own. So what I must do is what he did. I must get out on the field of evangelism and do what my father did." Such insights came from an older and more secure Richard Roberts. He was "not in a hurry," but he was confident that he had found his place in the healing ministry of Oral and Richard Roberts.[82]

Richard's emergence as an evangelist pleased his father. "My son chomps at the bits at thirty-four the same as I did," Oral said proudly. "He can't stay home now. . . . He's super."[83] Others were pleased as well. "I think he is finding his place now," observed Demos Shakarian.[84]

While Richard's crusades were the primary evangelistic thrust of the ministry in the 1980s, Oral was repeatedly drawn back to the field. Of course, for years he had continued to preach and minister to the sick in the numerous seminars conducted on the campus. Beginning in 1978, he scheduled three or four auditorium meetings in conjunction with Richard's crusades each year. "He's done his part and he's not going to run all over the country doing that again," protested Evelyn in 1983, at the same time admitting that "he'd love to get out there in that sawdust and tent and fill it up."[85] Oral vacillated, sometimes thinking "my crusade days of travelling and preaching are over," but at other times detecting that old feeling in his right hand: "I want to tell you, it's back and it's strong and it's like an electrical current. It gets to feeling like sometimes it's going to take my right arm off."[86]

Roberts was reasonably well pleased with the one-day meetings he conducted from 1978 through 1981. After attracting a crowd of 12,000 in Houston in 1978, he reported that "I felt the anointing as I did in the days when I traveled in the great crusades and then the invitation, nearly 4,000 people stood up to accept Christ."[87] The meetings proved, by and large, that Oral could still draw huge crowds; at Madison Square Garden in June 1979, he preached to the largest audience he had ever attracted in an auditorium, an estimated 21,000 people.[88]

Oral was invigorated by personal contact with audiences, and in 1983 he planned a limited schedule of meetings along with Richard. In July 1983, the two of them were featured speakers in Kenneth Hagin's huge camp meeting in Tulsa; in October they scheduled a four-day healing crusade in Mabee Center in Tulsa.[89] "I believe God wants me to come back face to face with people who are suffering and who have need of healing and wholeness in soul, mind, and body," Oral wrote in *Abundant Life,* announcing that he was going "back on the evangelistic field."[90] Roberts considered his Tulsa crusade his "first full-fledged appearance as an evangelistic healer since 1968."[91]

In 1984, Oral conducted several meetings with Richard, beginning in Phoenix and Baltimore. "God stopped him for fifteen years," while the university and the City of Faith were being built, observed Evelyn, but "now he's gotten back on the trail again." It remained to be seen "how he's going to do," but the new crusade schedule seemed to hold considerable potential for strengthening Roberts's ties with his partners and for broadening the dwindling partner base.[92]

THE EXPANSION and diversification of the Oral Roberts empire after 1975 complicated the ministry's organizational structure. The City of Faith operated under three distinct management boards: the City of Faith Medical Research Center, Inc., which controlled the clinic; the City of Faith Hospital, Inc., which was a nonprofit hospital corporation; and the 8181 Management Company, which provided management services for the entire complex. Jim Winslow held the title vice-provost for health affairs within Oral Roberts University and the title chief executive officer in the City of Faith. On a day-to-day basis, his most influential assistant was Bill Luttrell, hired in 1979 as the chief administrative officer of the City of Faith. Legally, however, the entire medical complex was owned by Oral Roberts University and was controlled by the board of regents of the university. While the educational programs connected with the center were clearly the responsibility of the university, in practice, the medical center enjoyed considerable independence. Nonetheless, ownership and ultimate control of the complex were vested in the university.[93]

Oral Roberts University and the City of Faith were the two major organizational clusters within the Roberts empire in the mid-1980s; in 1983 the two were securely headed by Winslow and Carl Hamilton. "Unless it happened to deal with some policy that would reflect on the mission of the ministry," said

Jim Winslow in 1983, "I'm going to end up with most of the problems of the health care enterprise at my doorstep. More and more, the problems of the university are going to wind up at Carl's doorstep." But neither ORU nor the City of Faith was self-governing. "If you go far enough," continued Winslow, "you'll finally end up in the lap of the members of OREA. And that's where the buck would stop."[94] Ultimate legal control of the ministry rested in the trustees of the Oral Roberts Evangelistic Association. "Now some of the people at the university and the City of Faith don't quite see it that way," observed George Stovall, "but that's the way it is. The leadership in those organizations see it that way."[95]

The Oral Roberts Evangelistic Association, the cockpit of the entire Roberts empire, was headed by Richard as president, but its functioning executive was George Stovall, the association's executive vice-president. Stovall was a solid administrator, one of the few top-level Roberts executives who worked his way up through the organization. He was dependable, efficient, and unerringly loyal. The evangelistic association, housed in a building expanded in 1978 to over 100,000 square feet, employed about five hundred full-time workers, who supervised the mail, television, radio, and the "home ministries" of the sixteen "regional representatives" who maintained contact with Oral's most important partners. In addition, the association maintained offices in England, South Africa, New Zealand, Jamaica, and Canada, supported by gifts from partners in those areas.[96] The board of the Oral Roberts Evangelistic Association not only supervised the functions of the association, however; it controlled the entire ministry. Its members were, in the terminology of lawyer Don Moyers, the ministry's "stockholders."[97] In 1984, that board included eleven people. Four were members of the Roberts family—Oral, Evelyn, Richard, and Roberta. The other seven were James Buskirk, George Stovall, Fred Van Stone, Demos Shakarian, Eleanor Foster, Oscar Moore, and Bob DeWeese.[98]

The lines of real power within the Oral Roberts organization were not always easy to follow (they were obscured by a maze of titles and powerless sinecures), but there was one ultimate source of all authority—the seventh-floor office of Oral Roberts. Oral held two titles: he was president of Oral Roberts University and chairman of the trustees of the Oral Roberts Evangelistic Association. But all titles aside, power was firmly in Oral's grip, and it trickled down to those in the organization who were closest to him. A long line of lieutenants remained for a time in an office near Oral's; everyone understood the status which that honor carried with it.

The first serious shakeup in the Roberts organization after 1975 was the resignation of Ron Smith in August 1979 from his position as "chief of staff." After replacing Al Bush as executive vice-president of the evangelistic association, Smith had worked his way into a position of unprecedented power. "It took Oral a long time to accept me because of the great breadth of experience that Al had," recalled Smith, but after his elevation to the title of chief of staff in 1977, he was Roberts's most powerful administrator.[99] Local wags referred to the seventh-floor office suite as the home of the father, the son, and the holy Smith.

Several factors contributed to Smith's resignation. Some were personal; he had contemplated the move for some time so he could pursue a business career in television production, leading some to charge that he left because of a "love for money."[100] But Smith's resignation was also linked with the publication of Jerry Sholes's exposé book about the ministry. Sholes and Smith were related by marriage, and Smith had been responsible for bringing Sholes into the organization.[101]

Smith insisted, however, that he left because of pressure—pressure so intense that he believed it was responsible for a heart attack he suffered shortly after leaving. That pressure was generated partly by two major shifts taking place within the organization—the emerging institutional influence of the City of Faith and the coming of age of Richard Roberts. Smith persistently questioned the draining financial demands of the City of Faith and came to be viewed as a source of unwelcome negativism. He begrudged the rising influence of the medical administrators, particularly Winslow. Less offensive to him, but just as problematical, was the inexorable rise of Richard to the head of the ministry. "I was too strong to remain in any kind of competitive stance with Richard," recalled Smith, "and too weak to handle my own ego needs in that framework."[102] Ron Smith simply ran afoul of the two most basic changes in the Roberts organization in the decade after 1975.

Smith departed on good terms with Oral. He told the press that their personal relationship had "never been better"; they remained "very warm, close friends."[103] Feelings remained good enough that he returned to work part-time in the production of the ministry's television programs—using his considerable creative talent—in 1984. Smith never wanted to "be a problem to Richard's ascendancy," and while he still chafed about the internal distribution of power within the ministry, he understood, and believed in, Oral Roberts's ministry as few others ever had.[104]

It was remarkable in the mid-1980s how many of Oral's associates from his crusade ministry still held responsible positions in the ministry. Braxton was finally gone, but the membership of Moore, Shakarian, and Bob DeWeese on the trustees board was a symbol of the mutual loyalties between them and Roberts. Of the old group of associates, Collins Steele and Bob DeWeese were the most active in the 1980s. Dependable and loyal, Steele remained a vice-president in the university and Oral's administrative assistant. While not a policy maker, he was Roberts's frequent companion and most trusted emissary.[105] Bob DeWeese returned to the Roberts organization in 1977, after leaving for four years to pastor a church in Dayton, Ohio. DeWeese resumed holding partners' rallies around the country, maintaining contact with many who had been loyal partners since the crusade days. Elected chairman of the board of regents of the university in 1983, DeWeese remained one of Oral's closest personal friends.[106]

Three particularly important new leaders emerged in the organization after 1975. Extremely influential, though not highly visible, was Fred Van Stone, who acted as a consultant during the financial crisis of 1979 and subsequently became the chairman of the executive committe of the board of regents of ORU. Van Stone was hired at the suggestion of Bob Patterson, a Canadian member of the board, and, in the eyes of many insiders, "he saved the whole institution" by "pulling all those loose ends together and getting hold of the checkbooks and putting in some systems and procedures."[107] As a financial administrator, observed bank president Bill Nash, "he is as good as I ever sat down with. He could run anybody's bank in this town."[108] Commanding almost universal respect throughout the organization, Van Stone supplied a managerial expertise that had been missing since the departure of Al Bush in 1972.

Unquestionably the most powerful new leader within the Roberts organization was James Winslow. As the City of Faith came to dominate the Roberts empire, he came to be Oral's closest confidant. In the 1980s, Winslow reported, he spent "a fair amount of my time doing things with Oral"; and for all practical purposes, he functioned as "an untitled administrative assistant."[109] Winslow was probably Oral's best friend; Roberts spent more time with him and probably felt more comfortable with him than with any other administrator in the organization. Bright, articulate, and aggressive, Winslow was a perfect leader for the bloody fight to get the City of Faith built and functioning.

But Winslow also was the source of some internal discontent. Partly, it was caused by the flow of money to the medical complex and by the diversion of Oral's attention in that direction. Winslow did little to assuage the tensions with his straight-shooting managerial style. On several occasions, Oral publicly tried to pour oil on the internal financial feuding.[110] But the resentment seethed just beneath the surface; in 1982 an instructor at the university wrote to the *Tulsa World* charging that the "operations in . . . the University are constantly harassed and intimidated by the unchecked power structure of the City of Faith."[111] "I've had some real fights with Jim Winslow," admitted George Stovall. "He's a very strong-headed person." Winslow's clash with Carl Hamilton in 1983, which triggered the provost's resignation, was resolved only when Oral made it clear that all academic questions came to him through Hamilton. Some of the resentment against Winslow was outspoken. "Winslow is a pawn," said Ron Smith. "I believe that one day Winslow will be back in surgery which is exactly where Winslow belongs. . . . Winslow may be living in some sort of illusion but I guarantee you it is just that. . . . There always has been a fair-haired boy. But fair-haired boys that say yes all the time are very short-lived."[112]

Generally, criticisms were more subdued. Most top administrators recognized that the past decade had been the "City of Faith season." "Oral has spent more time with Jim Winslow in the past five years than he has with me but he's had to do that to build the City of Faith," said Jim Buskirk in 1983. "He's spending a lot less time with him now and he and I are getting together a lot more." Most of Roberts's executives accepted Oral's decree that "whoever is up front is the lead cow."[113]

The other influential new leader in the organization was James Buskirk, dean of the theology school and vice-provost for spiritual affairs. Although the theology school quickly grew to be the largest graduate program at the university, Buskirk's power far exceeded his role as dean. He was Oral's most important link with the Methodist church and, to some extent, with mainstream Protestantism. He was one of the few top-echelon advisors who would argue theologically with Roberts—though he was intensely loyal to Oral's healing vision. Among the ministry administration, Buskirk was best qualified to be Oral's "interpreter in the jargon of theology," a public-relations function Oral seemed less and less concerned about.[114] Roberts repeatedly expressed his confidence in Buskirk's powers as a preacher and leader, but in many ways the ministry had difficulty in finding a suitable use for his considerable talents. Once the decision was made to limit the public preaching sponsored by the ministry to Oral and Richard, Buskirk had to be contented with speaking on campus, developing the prayer partner concept in the City of Faith, and maintaining a limited independent preaching ministry of his own. Many shared the belief of Ron Smith that Oral and Buskirk were "too big for each other": "For Jimmy's sake I hope that he doesn't stay too long."[115] In a move that seemed increasingly inevitable, especially after the departure of Carl Hamilton, Buskirk resigned his position in September 1984 to become minister of the First Methodist Church in Tulsa.[116] His resignation removed the most independent voice from the ministry, as well as its closest link to the mainstream churches. He and Oral remained friends, but for months it had been clear that the drift of the ministry was away from Methodism toward a more independent charismatic stance.[117]

The resignations of Buskirk and Hamilton in 1984 left major gaps in the ministry's power structure. Richard's preoccupation with evangelism and television took him out of the day-to-day administration of the ministry in the 1980s, although he still held several titles. As for the future, it was clear that he would play whatever role he chose. Less clear was the role that Roberta would play. Her return to Tulsa as Oral's administrative assistant and her appointment to the trustees board injected a new ingredient into the administrative formula. Roberta had no "delusions of grandeur" about her role, but she was a perceptive observer.[118] Others watched her development. "She is very quiet," said her cousin Bill Roberts, "but she is strong. She . . . might play a significant role."[119] After Hamilton's resignation, many insiders speculated that Roberta might be named provost of the university. While that idea was clearly premature in 1984, Bill Jernigan agreed that such an appointment would place "the Roberts family where they should be . . . to guarantee the furtherance of the goals" of the ministry.[120]

THE MINISTRY'S increased financial demands after 1975 made it more and more crucial for Roberts to communicate effectively with his partners. That need partly explained his decision to go back on the campaign trail in 1983. His job, Oral believed, was to explain the healing vision to the partners so that they would understand and support it. Analyzing a financial crisis in 1982, he said:

> The income dropped and now it has dropped drastically and we are in financial trouble. And the number one reason is the perception of our partners. They say life is a series of perceptions. Many of our partners perceive that all bills are paid, therefore you don't need us. So I'm having to give them the worst example. It'll just cut their hearts. But sometimes you have to communicate. You have to get people's attention and I've lost theirs the last four months and so I said, "What if this ministry were to go down?"[121]

Roberts's basic approach to his partners remained unchanged from 1975 to 1985, although his methods set off repeated controversies. He continued to ask people to give out of their own need—to practice seed-faith—and he continued to make "covenants" and "pacts" with his partners to encourage consistent support.[122] "What we must have is continuous, continual monthly support," Oral pleaded in 1982. "We need less fluctuation between our high and low months."[123]

The ministry still sponsored seminars, which brought to ORU about 10,000 financial supporters each year. At the conferences, Oral presented the partners a "seed-faith project having various ranges of 'depth.' The partners are encouraged to find their 'depth of giving,' to plant their seeds, and to expect a bountiful crop of blessing."[124] The seminars were models of efficiency; ministry officials gave instructions on estate planning and other tax matters. Partners who opted to place the ministry in their wills were given plaques naming them "Eternal Partners." The ministry's system of "regional representatives" assured that potential donors would be contacted personally and, if necessary, aided with the preparation of wills or other legal matters. A regional representative explained his work in a 1981 seminar:

> This is one more of the areas in which we representatives are happy to help extend Brother Roberts' ministry into your homes and help meet a specific need for we all carry with us a list of lawyers or attorneys and many of them . . . we are acquainted with. . . . And when a partner desires to get to an attorney, we can highly recommend one or more to that person. If they have transportation needs by possibly not having a car available to them on that day, we also help take partners to the lawyers and our time and transportation costs the partners nothing. It is a real privilege for us to be able to do this and to help you get off your shoulders that which is weighing you down.[125]

The lifeblood of the ministry remained its mail. "Our letters are the heartbeat of this ministry," said Richard in 1983, "always have been and always will be."[126] In the mid-1980s, the ministry received over 5,000,000 letters a year, about fifty percent of them including contributions. In return, the organization mailed out around 50,000,000 pieces per year at a cost of over two million dollars. A letter received by the association would probably be answered in three to five days.[127] In 1980 a "telephone ministry" was begun, which established "direct contact" with partners in "unusual situations."[128]

The ministry took pride in its continued record of answering every letter, whether or not the writer had contributed, and in the fact that its answers were "personalized."[129] Even in the most severe financial crises, Oral refused to trim costs by culling nonpaying correspondents from his mailing list.[130] And within the limits of mass mail, Oral worked desperately to maintain a personal touch. "God has singled me out to have a personal relationship with you through our letters, like this letter I'm writing you now," he wrote in a 1983 partner letter. "I can talk to you because I have a personal relationship with you, and you have a personal relationship with me."[131]

In some ways the hyperbole in Roberts's mail became better understood in the 1980s, as "personalized" letters became a pervasive phenomenon. Americans became accustomed to receiving customized letters from potential friends, ranging from Publishers Clearing House to Ronald Reagan. Roberts had simply been using the technique much longer and probably more effectively. Oral and Evelyn continued to "spend a lot of time with the mail," vowed George Stovall, Oral jotting paragraphs on a yellow pad in response to the "symbolic" letters sent to him.[132] Evelyn believed their letters were effective: "I've had a lot of people to tell us that our letters are so personal that they carry them around in their purse for years. They wouldn't throw one of those letters away for anything. Simply because we pray over them and I really do believe the letters are anointed."[133]

In addition to the responses to letters, the ministry mailed to the partners monthly letters composed by Oral, generally outlining the most pressing needs of the ministry. Roberts also remained dependent on his publications to keep his partners informed about the work of the ministry. In the mid-1980s the circulation of *Abundant Life* hovered at about 1,000,000, and *Daily Blessing* had a circulation of about 300,000.[134] While Oral was less involved in the production of *Abundant Life* than in the past, everyone recognized that the magazine remained his "domain."[135] Roberts remained a prolific writer; his books were often offered to his television audiences without charge. In 1981, the ministry estimated that he had written eighty-eight books and that about 14.5 million copies of them were in circulation.[136]

Estimates of the size of the Roberts partner family in the 1980s varied depending on definition. During the debate over the City of Faith, the ministry claimed over 3,000,000 "partner family units."[137] That number was the accumulated total of all persons who had written to the association, and, while it might offer some measure of interest, it was not a count of active supporters. In 1980, George Stovall reported 1,086,867 active partners, a figure which included all who had corresponded within the last year.[138] In the 1980s the circulation of *Abundant Life* ranged between 800,000 and 1,000,000—an indication of the number of people who had contributed during the year. Of that number, Stovall estimated that between 400,000 and 500,000 partners contributed eighty percent of the organization's income.[139] Although recent changes were not well documented or clear, some insiders felt that Oral had a "diminishing partner base," and that it was being "subjected to increased demands."[140] It was clear in the late 1970s and the 1980s that Roberts had aimed at tightening the family, and, perhaps, in the process, had also narrowed it.

The partners certainly were subjected to unprecedented financial pressure, beginning in 1977 with the announcement of the City of Faith. Of course, financial pressure was nothing new for Oral or his partners. "I can't ever remember a year when the finances came easy," said Roberts in 1983, "we used to average eight cents a person in the tent in the offerings. I could barely raise a budget of fifteen to twenty thousand dollars out of eight and ten thousand people a night for fifteen days. . . . It's no tougher now than it was then. It's just that nobody in my partner list has thought this big."[141] But to many observers the repeated and fervent financial appeals since 1977 seemed both more frantic

and more extreme than any Oral Roberts had ever made. He repeatedly returned to Gene Ewing for counsel, and Ewing's garish Midas touch often
showed through in the ministry appeals.

Oral repeatedly pictured himself and his partners in a showdown battle
with Satan. "The truth is," he wrote in *Abundant Life* in 1979, "we believe a
satanic conspiracy is making a last-ditch move against God's work."[142] Over and
over he heard the "devil's roar" and warned his partners of the apocalyptic
battle that approached.[143] Requesting a special gift of twenty-five dollars in
1980, Oral warned that "the devil will be looking at you and telling you not to
send it."[144]

Roberts also filled his communications to his partners with a repetitious
sense of urgency, a stimulus which obviously brought responses. It was true that
the ministry lived on the brink of an emergency, but during the hectic days
when the City of Faith was under construction, desperation pleas were particularly regular. The partners were repeatedly told that "I need you like I have
never needed you before."[145] In February 1982, Oral announced in a news
conference that without immediate help his ministry would fail, the telephones
in the Prayer Tower would be disconnected, and the partners' letters would
receive no answers. Roberts implored his partners to help in the needed
"emergency miracle": "I feel that God is going to lead you concerning where
and how you can get this $25 so you can be a part of this emergency miracle.
Pray and let God lead you. You may have some money put back for something
else. Maybe you have some money saved for something personal. Let God
speak to your heart about planting it as a seed in His work."[146]

The ministry's fund raising emphasized the use of symbols and tokens in a
way reminiscent of the 1950s. In 1976, Roberts sent his partners a "little alabaster box" containing a "precious vial of oil"; he renewed the offer three years
later, reporting that over a million containers had been sent to partners and that
they had resulted in "many healing miracles."[147] Oral repeatedly mailed "prayer
cloths," as he had in the years past. A cloth sent in 1979, along with a letter
asking for a thirty-eight-dollar donation for the City of Faith, included the imprint of Oral's hand and the instruction: "As you place your hand on the imprint
of mine, immediately look to the Healing and Restoring Hand of the Living
Christ."[148] In 1983, Roberts sent to his partners a paper dinner napkin with a
tracing on it of both his hands and the message: "I anoint you, in Jesus' name
with my hands. Be healed! Prosper in all your needs being met. . . . Your partner, Oral Roberts." The gift was inspired by a luncheon meeting with a friend,
who requested that Oral allow him to trace his hands as an aid for his prayers.
The friend's message of thanks to Oral was also printed on the napkin:

> Here is the napkin back that I used to trace your hands while we were having
> lunch on August 8 at 1:15 p.m. and you were explaining what God is leading
> you to do. Thank you. Thank you for doing this for me, my family, and our
> needs. I laid your hands on Duane for that need he has that I explained to you.
> I laid them on my daughter for her new computer school that she is starting. I
> laid them on my bill fold for a financial need I'm feeling, and I touched this

napkin with your hands on it to several others. . . . This tracing of your hands was the next best thing to having you come to our houses in person to pray for us. . . . Here is $100.00 based on II Chronicles 20:20. Thank you for letting us use this simple table napkin in a simple Act of Faith as a point of contact. OUR MIRACLES ARE ON THE WAY!! Bro. James.[149]

The partner letters and *Abundant Life* contained an endless stream of special appeals to the partners. Sometimes the message let partners in on the "confidential" secrets of the ministry; for instance, Oral shared with them a memo from Winslow stating that construction of the City of Faith would have to stop unless more funds were received.[150] Partners were offered honors, such as the registration of their names in the "beautiful, leather-bound, gold-trimmed Oral Roberts Covenant Family Album" or having their names "planted" in Israel by Richard.[151] And there were frequent times when Oral and Richard spent periods in the Prayer Tower making special intercessions for the partners; sometimes the students were rallied to pray for their letters.[152] Frequently, Oral's letters to his partners included a token gift, such as a "little Bible coin" or a piece of cloth, as a seed planted by Roberts.[153] And, always, the letters included explicit, step-by-step instructions about writing in return:

I have enclosed a prayer sheet upon which you are to write your spiritual, physical, and financial needs. The RED area is for your SPIRITUAL healing; the WHITE area is for your PHYSICAL healing; the GREEN area is for your FINANCIAL healing. Check the needs you have and RUSH them back to me. You will have to move quickly on this so I will get your needs *before* May 22. Sometimes the mail moves very slowly. Try to get your answer in the mail to me immediately so I'll be sure to have them in time.[154]

Although Roberts took pride in the fact that the ministry had never sold its services, in early 1983 he recorded forty-eight tapes of reading and commentary on the New Testament and offered them to any partner giving $240.[155] While offering to send tapes in return for a specified gift was a common fund-raising technique among mass evangelists, to some the offer seemed a departure from Oral's old guidelines.[156]

Roberts's financial appeals to his partners quite naturally aroused the interest of the press and opened him to a new round of criticism. "That hot right hand, as healer-preacher Oral Roberts makes plain in his letter," wrote *Newsweek*'s religious editors in September 1979, "is reaching out for his partners' pocketbooks."[157] While the editor of ORU's newspaper, the *Oracle,* charged that the *Newsweek* report was "an opinion which is misleading to the unaware reader," it was mild compared to many of the journalistic reactions to Oral's appeals.[158] One reporter dubbed Oral the "prince of pelf": "Roberts is to evangelical pocket-picking what Walt Disney was to cartoon animation."[159] In perhaps the most indignant attack written in the 1980s, Atlanta columnist Lewis Grizzard warned: "Hold onto your pocketbooks. Oral Roberts is talking to Jesus again. . . . When is somebody going to put a stop to Oral Roberts? The man preys on the old, the sick, and the hopeless. . . . Forget about the rest of us,

Oral, and heal thyself. You're a sick man."[160] Oral simmered under the renewed attacks. Prodded by a hostile reporter during a press conference in 1983, he shot back: "Now you in the news media are trained to be cynical and doubtful. . . . But with us you're dealing with honest, faith-filled, dedicated people."[161]

Roberts's financial appeals of the 1980s were also attacked by a variety of religious leaders. Labeling the ministry's partner letters "hucksterish tactics," a Baptist minister told a newsman: "I have that Oral Roberts appeal on my desk right now. . . . It's unbiblical, unfundamentalist, and un-Christian."[162] A Harvard professor of ethics visiting Tulsa offered a similar judgment to *Tulsa World* religious editor Beth Macklin: "When a man with the power over other people's pocketbooks he [Roberts] exercises proceeds to build against everybody's advice, and offers as his reason 'God told him to,' is he saying that everybody else is separated from God or is God stupid?"[163] Particularly galling to Oral was the criticism he received from Methodists. An Iowa pastor addressed an open letter to him which was featured by the Associated Press: "Now, I understand from very reliable sources that Jesus has been talking with you again, and the theme running through these chats has been money. . . . Oral, you're a United Methodist, and just between us, I would appreciate the benefit of your counsel. . . . Could you please give me the area code and unlisted number to you-know-who? I feel cheated."[164]

The partner letter which triggered the most resounding outburst of public ridicule and criticism was a September 1980 description of Oral's vision of a 900-foot-tall Jesus. Roberts reported that late on the afternoon of May 25, he stood looking at the unfinished skeleton of the City of Faith, distraught over his financial difficulties, when "suddenly an unusual feeling swept over me":

> I felt an overwhelming holy presence all around me. When I opened my eyes, there He stood . . . some 900 feet tall, looking at me. . . . He stood a full 300 feet taller than the 600 foot tall City of Faith. There I was face to face with Jesus Christ, the Son of the Living God. I have only seen Jesus once before, but here I was face to face with the King of Kings. He stared at me without saying a word; Oh! I will never forget those eyes! And then, He reached down, put his Hands under the City of Faith, lifted it, and said to me, "See how easy it is for Me to lift it!"

Oral recalled that his eyes filled with tears, and Jesus assured him that He would speak to the ministry's partners and that the City of Faith would be finished. When the vision was completed, Oral spotted a "young man" standing nearby and told him what he had seen. He later wondered whether the figure was "a man or an angel," but his advice to Oral was "Tell your partners what Jesus said."[165] After several months of consultation, Roberts decided to follow his advice.

The reaction by Roberts's critics to the reported vision was swift and outraged. His old nemesis in Tulsa, C. T. Thompson, labeled the letter "blasphemous" and demanded that Oral "be called to task for this."[166] He addressed a circular letter to the ministers of Tulsa:

Dear Sir:

I am enclosing a copy of a letter which Mr. Oral Roberts sent to his "partners" in September. He describes an event of such over-whelming importance that it must be addressed by the clergy. On May 25, 1980 at precisely 7:00 P.M., Mr. Roberts saw and spoke to a nine hundred foot Jesus Christ who proceeded to lift the City of Faith from its foundation. Ordinary mortals with his access to the media might have trumpeted this across the land immediately, but Mr. Roberts was able to constrain himself until the September letter.

After reading his letter there seems to be only three reasonable alternative conclusions.

1. Jesus Christ *was* here in magnificent proportions.
2. He was not here and Mr. Roberts is a fraud.
3. The appearance was a figment of the imagination.

It would seem reasonable to me that *all* of the communication from Mr. Roberts should be examined for the enormous theological implications. If the institutional church should do so, surely *some* voices would thunder from the pulpit in righteous indignation. The life and spirit of Tulsa is being changed to accommodate economic miracles in the name of God. Can the churches of Tulsa ignore the whole problem?[167]

One Tulsa Unitarian minister reportedly told a Chicago reporter: "Oh boy, Oral has really freaked out this time, he's gone off the wheel, and he's acting out of desperation."[168] Thompson was disappointed with the response to his appeal; the Tulsa clergy was "remarkably silent," with the exception of a "couple of Unitarians and a couple of Lutherans."[169]

If the Tulsa clergy was timid, Roberts's vision unleashed a torrent of criticism from religious spokesmen throughout the nation. S. Duane Bruce, executive director of the South Central Jurisdiction of the United Methodist Church, wrote to Oklahoma's Methodist bishop, charging that the vision was "a fabrication" of a notorious empire builder. He asked that the bishop remind the Methodists of his state that Roberts's ministry was not associated with the Methodist church.[170] Joseph Quillian, Jr., dean of the Perkins School of Theology at Southern Methodist University, who admitted that he "liked Roberts personally," told a reporter: "I wouldn't want to be put into a position of saying Oral Roberts is lying in his teeth, . . . but people are known to have all kinds of hallucinations."[171] Oral's non-Methodist critics were even harsher. Carl McIntire informed the Associated Press that "Oral Roberts, I am afraid, has gone beserk on these visions of his." "No decent Christian," McIntire reportedly said, "believed that Christ was 900 feet tall."[172]

For months after the announcement of the vision, punsters poked fun at Oral. Posters sold in Tulsa for six dollars, depicting the City of Faith with a traffic sign posted in front warning of a "900 ft. Jesus X-ing."[173] Writers speculated about the problems of building a "2000-foot cross," about the "mighty big elevator shoes" which allowed Oral to come "face to face" with a 900-foot tall Jesus, and about the amount of Visine required for Jesus' eyes.[174] The vision had emboldened Oral's old critics; it opened him to the kind of caricature which had been common in the 1950s. One reporter announced that he had recently visited Tulsa but "couldn't get an appointment to see either Oral or Jesus. The best I could do was leave behind a note with Oral Roberts' secretary, asking him if he ever thanks God that his parents didn't name him after the Massachusetts Institute of Technology."[175]

Roberts was not taken completely by surprise by the reaction. Not only had the matter been discussed thoroughly by the leaders of the organization, he had flown Calvin Thielman to Tulsa to get his reaction to the vision. Calvin told Oral that he would "get into trouble on the numbers" and urged him to "soften" the message as much as possible. In a telephone conversation shortly after the debacle, Oral acknowledged to Thielman: "Boy, you were right on that."[176] There is no doubt that the criticisms stung Oral deeply. When the students returned in the fall, Richard talked to them about the "hullabaloo around here": "You let Oral Roberts see a 900-foot Jesus around the City of Faith and everybody gets upset."[177]

The ministry reacted to the criticism in a variety of ways. First, there was some incredulity. After all, this was not the first time that Jesus had appeared or spoken to Oral. "There's nothing new about this," protested Richard, "I've been aware of God speaking to my dad so many times in my lifetime."[178] Second, Oral repeatedly explained and expanded on the vision. Answering pointed questions on the "Phil Donahue Show" in 1982, Oral said: "I saw Jesus with my inner eyes—not my physical eyes." Although some reporters indicated that that was the "first time" Oral had described the vision spiritually, he actually had said exactly the same thing at the dedication of the City of Faith in November 1981. "Yes, I saw him," he had said at that time, but "not with my human eyes." Roberts believed that his critics "understood a lot more than they admitted."[179] Finally, Oral goaded his critics with reminders that the vision came true. The partner letter brought an immediate response from nearly 500,000 people, who contributed almost $5,000,000.[180] Speaking to the convention of National Religious Broadcasters in 1983, Oral took a parting shot at his detractors: "I got a lot of flak nationwide and worldwide over that 900-foot Jesus. But I saw Him, and He finished it. That's the way we'll leave it."[181]

Roberts reasserted his old defenses of the partner system during the years of rising public protest. The basic issue, as he saw it, was his right to communicate with his family. His letters were private, addressed to a select group of people, and their airing in the press violated that private relationship. "I don't like to get mail from anybody that I haven't written to," Oral protested. "All of us get five or six calls a week wanting money." On the other hand, "if I help you, and you write to me, that is a different story." Under those circumstances, Roberts insisted that he had the right to submit his needs to the people who had written to him, along with the other solicitations they received, allowing them to "support the ones that they feel and believe in." Even during his direst financial crises, Oral refused to "prospect" for names for his mailing list with mass mailings (though strongly urged to do so by some of his advisors), insisting that his partner list include only those who had first appealed to him for help.[182] Those names were the product of decades of work and cultivation, and he believed that he had a right to speak frankly to them.

Roberts's second general defense was that he never asked for money. Over and over he insisted, "I can't get on TV and ask for money. Some do, but I can't. I have to concentrate and think on how I can help that person who is discouraged or hurting, who needs to have his needs met."[183] On that score Oral clearly became more vulnerable during the fund-raising campaigns connected with the City of Faith. "He began asking for money on TV," said Al Bush in 1983. "Do you realize that until that occurred that we had never asked for money. . . . He's up front. He talks money. He even sizes it."[184] Oral continued to deny that he was fund raising; when he offered his Bible-reading tapes for a donation of $240, he argued, "the big thing in the letter . . . was that you're going to get forty-eight ninety-minute tapes." "I know the media" perceived the letters as financial appeals, Oral acknowledged, but "I haven't the slightest feeling that I raise money."[185]

The distinction in Roberts's mind, as always, was between fund raising and the presentation of projects which deserved the seed-faith support of others. It was a distinction, many believed, which accounted for the financial success of the ministry. "He developed such a marvelous, powerful formula to implement whatever he deems to be his purpose in life," observed Oral's friend John Williams. That formula was "to always have before him and his partners . . . a series of goals to the glorification of God that are totally unachievable by man, but together we can do them. . . . It's an illustration of pulling together a comprehension of what unites people." Within that framework, Williams continued, the challenges of Oral to his partners, however bizarre, could be viewed as strokes of creative genius: "Some people are totally turned off by 900-foot Jesuses. . . . To me, it's 'how in the world did he ever think of that.' . . . It didn't surprise me. I saluted him for the audacity."[186]

Oral, Williams believed, like all great religious leaders, was "a focal point of rallying for people who have faith that he will solve problems that they cannot solve." "Oral is a one man Catholic church," a prophet for those who "want to be told what to think."[187] While Oral perceived his partner relationship in more spiritual terms than did John Williams, he knew that the partners idolized him and his students: "They really think we're all better than what we are."[188] For decades Oral watched the partners walking the grounds, marveling at the monument they had contributed to that would "extend *beyond* their lives."[189] "All during the ministry they could see what was going on," said Evelyn in 1981, "but even more so now when they come to Tulsa. They see what happens with the money that they give to this ministry."[190]

In a 1982 press conference, Oral "grew testy" when asked if he would allow public inspection of the ministry's financial records, replying that he "satisfies Internal Revenue Service reporting requirements." He curtly added that he made "no apologies" for the use of funds contributed to the ministry: "I think if anyone has a right to take up an offering, I do because of the university and the City of Faith."[191] Oral repeatedly expressed an apparently honest consternation about objections to his appeals for support for education, the City of Faith, and cancer research.[192]

Whatever the criticisms and justifications, Roberts's relationship with his partners was based on several shared beliefs. "Many of them are desperate and they will know the hours that I'm in the Prayer Tower because we write and tell them," he explained, "and so they focus their attention that through prayer they can be helped."[193] Oral's methods and his messages apparently ministered to his partners. "My dad has done some crazy things in his lifetime when you look at it with your mind," acknowledged Richard in 1980.

> He's done a lot of things that have brought controversy right here on this campus by obeying God's word, by students and faculty misunderstanding . . . my dad's heart. I remember several years ago when the Lord told him to make a prayer cloth and to put the imprint of his hand on it and to send it to our partners. . . . Everyone seemed to forget that they took handkerchiefs and aprons from the body of Paul and the sick recovered. . . . But someone tries to do it today to help people and some folks don't understand. . . . It gets in the way of their theology. . . . And when you try to figure it out in your mind you're not ever going to do it.[194]

Oral still believed that his methods, while addressing only certain people, were no different from those of other clergymen. He bristled when he received what he considered self-righteous protests from ministers. Responding to a letter from an irate pastor, he wrote:

> When I go to church, which I do, they take up the offering before I even get to see what the sermon is going to sound like. You know, we have to go on the air and they hear the whole thing, then they decide whether they like it or not. I have to pay mine in before I even hear. . . . Pastor, do you realize that's what you're doing at your church? Plus you go out over your community with your pledge cards before you've ever had the meetings. . . . Under separate cover I'm sending you MIRACLE OF SEED-FAITH, if you get time to read it.[195]

Nonetheless, Richard accurately reported the existence of internal dissension caused by some of the ministry's appeals. The internal criticism was particularly galling to Oral. He told Richard: "What's hard for me is when my own people misunderstand me, when my own people don't support me, when I feel unbelief in my own family."[196] Of course, Oral knew that his advisors did not always agree with him. Al Bush often squirmed to preserve what he believed were the "kernels" of Oral's message amidst the "methods" which sometimes seemed to "contradict" them.[197] When Roberts's vision of Jesus was first discussed, Jim Buskirk felt it was important that Oral make clear that he had seen it in his "mind's eye." The ministry's subsequent wounds, Buskirk believed, were self-inflicted:

> When OREA picked up on it and put it in the magazine, they didn't put that little statement in. . . . We almost invited [criticism] the way the magazine went out. And that's our fault. We make a lot of mistakes like that. . . . We bring on some criticism because of our lack of astuteness and not being as faithful to what Oral really said as we should.[198]

But internal dissatisfaction never reached major proportions. Jim Buskirk had serious objections to the prayer cloths used by the ministry, but he believed that "we've had some fantastic stories and they're as substantial as anything else we've got about people being healed with those prayer cloths."[199] Roberts's old friend and counselor Charles Farah observed that Oral's "methodology . . . has been a great problem" for the faculty, but, he added, "we ask ourselves, if we were in his place, what would we do? I don't happen to have an answer for that."[200] And there was the hard-headed advice of George Stovall to a group of dissident faculty members: "Look, this is paying your salary in case you're interested. You are a part of this ministry. This is the leader of the ministry ministering to his constituency. . . . I can tell you if you came here to change it you are in for a rude awakening. . . . The day I can't be a part of it, I'll walk away."[201]

Above all, Oral argued, his letters helped the partners. "People have trouble" with his letters, he acknowledged, "but my partners don't."[202] Jim Winslow agreed that many of the highly trained scientists connected with the City of Faith experienced culture shock when they read Oral's message to his partners. But, in time, they changed their minds: "After they have been around here for a while and get to know him and know the people, because you see the partners come here to this place, . . . then they begin to perceive that you have got to provide those people some vehicle to express their faith. Then it doesn't seem to bother them any."[203] Oral's supporters—those who found the appeals attractive enough to send him hundreds of millions of dollars—were those same simple, faith-filled people who for centuries had been moved to sacrifice and devotion by relics and incantations and had poured their lives and labors into grander schemes than they themselves could ever have envisioned. "In a way Oral may be a fourteenth century person," observed Jenkin Lloyd Jones.[204] His empire was Tulsa's twentieth-century cathedral. To build it, Oral led his followers with a firm authority: "I had to talk to my partners like I talk to my children and like my father talked to me when I was a child and had to spell it out."[205] "You can talk for hours about his ability to flounder around and come up with the right kind of cornpone that fits his people," marveled John Williams.[206]

There remained no good statistical profile of who "his people" were in the 1980s. Most were probably like Steve Silverheels, a reformed alcoholic who sent his testimony to *Abundant Life,* and Ever Wampler, a Kansas City maintenance man who stood atop the Prayer Tower and told a reporter: "There's nothing else like it in this world. Oral Roberts said he'd build this thing and he did—whether you're for religion or not, you can't argue with this, because there it is."[207] At one of Richard's meetings in Richmond, Virginia, a reporter described the audience as a mixture of "the polyester middle-class" and "the less-well-off."[208] Sociologist William Martin surmised in 1981 that most of those who supported television evangelists were from rural areas in the South and the Midwest and that they were "predominantly middle-aged females of working-class or lower-class backgrounds." He also believed that most were "true believers, mostly members of conservative Protestant churches."[209] Both Oral and Richard were convinced, however, that a majority of their partners were "not church-goers."[210] Both estimates might be partly correct. The Roberts partner family was the church of thousands of lower-middle-class Christians reared in conservative churches but for a variety of reasons alienated from them. Many felt estranged from organized religion—perhaps because of divorce or other problems that created feelings of guilt, or perhaps because sickness or old age had isolated them. The found in Oral a leader whom they perceived to be honest, who shared with them a message of hope, and who gave them worthy exploits to perform for God.

IN MANY ways, Roberts's stature and influence continued to grow through the controversial decade from 1975 to 1985. His political clout was well documented during the fight over the City of Faith. In the midst of the controversy, he was the featured speaker at the Flag Day ceremonies in the United States House of Representatives. "Oral Roberts has great popularity among house members," volunteered Congressman Ted Risenhoover of Oklahoma's Second District.[211]

Oral's political connections were particularly strong in Oklahoma, where he had special friends in Governor David Hall and powerful Speaker of the United States House of Representatives Carl Albert. But his influence extended to Washington and crossed party lines. In 1979 he, along with Billy Graham, was invited to have dinner with Jimmy Carter in the White House. "They just chatted and prayed and had fellowship," reported a Roberts spokesman.[212] Roberts's name was widely recognized. A Gallup survey in 1980 revealed that "some evangelists were as well known as major political figures." Billy Graham's name was recognized by 92.9 percent of the people polled, only slightly fewer than recognized John F. Kennedy and Jimmy Carter; Oral scored 84.1 percent, "which was well ahead of John Anderson" and over forty percentage points more than the next religious figure.[213]

Oral also continued to have many celebrity friends. Some, such as Pat Boone and Ruth Carter Stapleton, had been directly influenced by him.[214] Bob Hope came to Tulsa as the ORU commencement speaker in 1983. Some of Oral's associations still seemed incongruous. He counted among his "warm, devoted friends" seer Jeanne Dixon, whom many charismatics considered "demon-possessed."[215] In another unlikely encounter, Oral's friend Pat Boone, at the request of Elvis Presley, arranged a meeting between Oral and Presley shortly before the singer's death.[216]

Another group which Oral courted with some success in the decade after 1975, particularly with the aid of business dean Henry Migliore and law dean Charles A. Kothe, was business supporters of free-enterprise capitalism. Eugene Swearingen, past president of the University of Tulsa, chairman of the board of regents of Oklahoma State University, and chairman of the board of the Bank of Oklahoma, became a professor of "Free Enterprise" at ORU.[217] "Oral Roberts is a free-enterprise University," declared Kothe in a promotional pamphlet, pointing out that "seed-faith" was a principle that "farmers and successful businessmen know . . . well. What you plant is what you get, be it corn in the ground or dollars wisely invested."[218] A steady stream of business barons received honorary degrees from the university; a number of them, including

Amway founder Rich DeVos, were commencement speakers.[219] While Oral had little time for economic theorizing, many American businessmen perceived, as did Kothe, that "his personal rise from a poverty filled childhood in rural Oklahoma to the crest of a multimillion dollar enterprise . . . is a clear testimony to faith in God, and to the workability of the American economic system."[220]

Most significant, Oral retained, and perhaps expanded, his influence in the charismatic movement. The movement continued to mushroom in the years after 1975; it contributed to a remarkable growth of the pentecostal denominations, an explosion of independent charismatic churches throughout the country, and the continued formation of independent charismatic fellowships within most mainstream churches and the Catholic church. In a Gallup poll conducted for *Christianity Today* magazine in 1980, about nineteen percent of all adult Americans (more than 29,000,000 people) labeled themselves pentecostal or charismatic.[221] The growing visibility of the movement was symbolized by an invitation received by David du Plessis for an audience with the pope.[222] In the 1980s, charismatic leaders made euphoric predictions about the future. "The whole body of Christ is going charismatic," boasted historian Vinson Synan. "That's the trend. It's prophetic. God said he'd pour out His spirit upon all flesh. We're sharing our treasures with the whole body of Christ and other churches have treasures to share with us."[223]

While the charismatic movement continued to mushroom, it also became increasingly diverse and divided.[224] Some of its older divisions were narrowed slightly during the decade; for instance, the older pentecostal denominations became increasingly tolerant of the independent charismatics. In 1980, the Assemblies of God restored the ministerial credentials of David du Plessis.[225] The Assemblies of God particularly, under the leadership of Thomas Zimmerman, showed a willingness to cooperate with charismatics at the local level and experienced a dramatic growth as a result.[226] On the other hand, the revival matured sufficiently for serious theological divisions to surface—some of them erupting into open controversy.[227]

The breadth of the charismatic movement in the 1980s diluted the influence of any one leader, but it highlighted the need for points of common focus, and the movement searched introspectively for its own roots. While Oral Roberts was personally known to an increasingly smaller percentage of charismatics, in many ways he became more and more important to the movement as one of its founding apostles.

While it was impossible for any individual or institution to touch the entire charismatic movement in the mid-1980s—or even to grasp fully its dimension—Oral and his university remained as close as possible to "the center of the present charismatic movement."[228] Roberts remained at the heart of the movement by calculation and intent. Speaking at the City of Faith in 1981, he announced: "I predict and I perceive and I prophesy that this will become the center of the charismatic healing power of God that will flow to the ends of the earth."[229] The centrist position of the university was a direct reflection of Oral's ecumenical spirit, his unwillingness to bicker over the divisive issues which impeded the modern "moving of the Holy Spirit." "I think ORU would impact on probably all of the various facets" of the charismatic movement, surmised theologian Howard Ervin, "and I think that's largely due to Oral's own attitude in which he tries to keep open lines of communication with all of them. I think for that reason they feel that they can touch base with him."[230] In the 1980s, Oral experienced a touching healing with his old friends in the Pentecostal Holiness church, sensing a "real openness" to him on their part. Just before Bishop J. A. Synan died in 1984, Oral telephoned his old friend and antagonist in the hospital and the two emotionally whispered their love for one another.[231]

The ability of the university, and of Roberts, to withstand the divisive pressures within the charismatic movement was severely tested in the 1980s by a controversy over the "faith formula" doctrine. The debate focused on the teachings of evangelist Kenneth Hagin, Sr., who in 1974 established Rhema Bible Training School in Tulsa. Perhaps the two most prominent popularizers of the idea were television teacher Kenneth Copeland and Los Angeles black preacher Fred Price. The "faith message" proclaimed that a Christian through faith could claim healing, good health, and prosperity as an undisputed right. By 1980, the message had been challenged by many charismatics, because it eliminated tragedy from Christian theology and seemed to callously imply faithlessness on the part of all those who suffered.[232]

In effect, the "faith formula" controversy pitted some of the most successful independent preachers against a growing body of teachers and professors in the charismatic movement, many of them trained in historic Christian theology. More than any other charismatic leader, Oral stood astride both camps. His desire to influence and be a part of mainstream Christianity was sincere, but, at the core, he remained an independent evangelist. He knew and admired the bold entrepreneurs who had carved out independent empires outside of denominational structures—as he had done in the 1950s.[233] He would not abandon them under attack.

Roberts's involvement in the controversy began in July 1979, when he attended an evening service of the annual Hagin camp meeting at the Rhema Bible Training Center. The camp meeting had mushroomed since its beginnings in the early 1970s and often attracted over 20,000 people to Tulsa—the most militant vanguard of the charismatic movement—for instruction from prominent faith teachers. Oral was in the midst of his deepest financial trials in the summer of 1979. His friends Pat and Shirley Boone, in town to attend the camp meeting, lunched with Oral on July 27 and urged him to attend the service that evening. Just before the service began, Boone informed Kenneth Hagin, Sr. that Oral would be in the audience and that "he's feeling pretty low."[234] Hagin "felt led" to give the evening's contribution to Roberts, even though "we needed it." When the service began, Oral was seated in the front row, flanked by his good friends Copeland, the Boones, and John Osteen, pastor of a large charismatic church in Houston. Hagin announced that it was not his custom to notice distinguished guests in the audience, but he felt compelled to ask Oral to come to the platform to say a word of greeting. The crowd burst into a standing ovation, which reduced Oral to tears. Roberts spoke briefly of his love and respect for the Hagins, started to his seat, and was asked by his host to remain

on the platform. Hagin announced that he was going to take an offering for
Roberts; Oral protested, and Hagin told him to "sit down and just accept what
the Lord is doing." The Boones, Copeland, and Osteen brought gifts forward.
Fred Price pledged a donation of $25,000 from his Los Angeles church. Oral
was overwhelmed as the huge audience erupted in response to the invitation to
give. He recalled:

> People were standing everywhere. It was a moment of drama such as I have
> not witnessed in my entire Christian experience. They were telling me how
> much they loved us, how they had been touched by our difficulties in this
> ministry and that they felt we should be ministered to by the members of the
> Body of Christ everywhere. I sat with my head in my hands, tears flowing
> down my cheeks, realizing that nothing like this had ever happened in my
> behalf. I certainly had not asked for it, nor even dreamed of it.

The count of the collection on the evening of the meeting was over $100,000;
subsequent payments of pledges brought the total to an estimated $400,000.[235]

Oral welcomed the financial support, and it was followed by other sizable
contributions from churches and independent evangelists, but the money was
far less important than the succor given to his sagging spirit. Under attack in the
press, criticized by many mainstream preachers, including his fellow Methodists,
and worried about his immense financial burdens, Oral's spirit was buoyed. "In
looking back at this service," he later commented, "I can only say that for the
first time in the many years of my ministry I have felt the love of God coming
toward me in this way by groups of people in *other churches and spiritual
groups*."[236] The money was "incidental," surmised Charles Farah, an outspoken
critic of the faith theology; the significance of the evening was that Oral had
found "somebody that believed in him when nobody else did." He had been in
the midst of people of faith, and they "gave Oral the courage to go on
through."[237]

Roberts's contacts with these old and new friends increased in the next few
years. He spoke at the Hagin camp meeting in 1980. Kenneth Hagin preached
in a chapel service at the university, which concluded with his "laying hands" on
Oral to pray for his "healing."[238] In 1983, Oral and Richard joined Kenneth
Hagin, Sr. and Jr., Kenneth Copeland, and Tulsa evangelist T. L. Osborn as the
featured speakers at the annual camp meeting.[239] Beginning in 1980 the faith
teachers were repeatedly invited to the campus of ORU to speak and were
introduced by Oral. Kenneth Copeland, formerly an ORU student and
Roberts's pilot, preached a series in 1980 and was followed in 1981 by John
Osteen, whose son was a medical student at the university.[240] "For two solid
years," commented one of the opponents of the theology, "the heat was on.
These men came in and really strutted their stuff."[241]

The controversy on the ORU campus came to a head in September 1980,
during a visit by Fred Price. Price, who pastored a spectacularly successful
church in Los Angeles of nearly 10,000 members, had contributed about
$175,000 toward the completion of the City of Faith. Price's preaching was
chatty but not emotional, but his message was an extreme version of the faith

formula for health and prosperity.[242] The black minister won over much of the student audience with his colloquial admonitions to faith:

> I won't tolerate any negativism coming into my ears. See, I heard that stuff years back and that's what kept me down there underneath the flood with one nostril above water. (Laughter) And I'm not going down any more. I've been down and I've been up, and up is better. (Laughter) . . . I won't argue with your right to be poor and I'll drive you to the hospital while you have your examination. . . . You know when I preach like this, some folks get all uptight like you're challenging them. I'm not challenging you. If you want to be sick, fine, that's your right to be sick, if you want to. . . . You just be the sick part of the family and I'll be the well.[243]

Price's flights goaded some of his theological opponents on campus beyond toleration—"People were incensed." In the midst of one of his chapel speeches, an ORU theology professor, "a very quiet, meek and passive man," suddenly shouted a one-word protest, "No."[244] Oral perked up in his seat on the platform and began to peer out at the audience to locate the source of the protest. After Price finished his sermon, Roberts took the podium with a rage that surpassed anything in his tempestuous past. He challenged the objector: "I've gone over this earth and preached my guts and life out, here's a man preaching his guts and life out and you, brother, that stood up, you owe an apology. You have no right to be in this building and yell out like that. And embarrass a man of God and embarrass me. You didn't build this school. God told me to build it on His authority and the Holy Ghost. You're sitting here as my guest." "All I said was . . . ," replied the protester. "Are you or are you not going to apologize? If you don't, just check out," interrupted Oral. "I apologize for having yelled out as I did. Since I have done it, sir, I regret it and I apologize," replied the voice. Oral continued: "I accept it and don't do it again on this campus. Don't anybody else. If you don't like the way we do, you go somewhere else." The chapel service dragged on and on. Oral's temper would slowly subside and then flare up again:

> I want to tell you, this man is sent here of God and my life is being changed and your life is being changed if you've got the sense to understand this. If you haven't got the sense to understand it, what are you doing here? (Wild applause) Let me tell you something in the theology school, you didn't build the theology school. I put my life on the line. . . . Just because you haven't heard this somewhere else, give a little time to it. Your dean is doing that, he's giving time to it, he's having patience. . . . I'll tell you one thing, before it's over we'll have a faculty and a student body that'll go with us. . . . Let me tell you something else, if we have to shut the academic program down and turn these buildings over into a Bible school, I'll do it.[245]

"He was Oral the man all the way" in that chapel session, recalled one theology professor—some labeled the occasion "Black Friday."[246] Roberts invited Price for a second visit to the campus only five months later, overriding a specific request made by several faculty members that he not return. Introducing the controversial evangelist, Oral admitted that "I don't understand some of it," but, he said, it's a sad thing to think about if Brother Fred Price never feels led to come back here for there is a group of people who asked me not to bring him back and I felt led to bring him back because I happen to be the head man around here. I'm chief executive officer. (Applause) And the people who asked me are not bad people. They're people who did that because they believed they were doing right. It's not a criticism of them. It just so happens the buck stops right here with this man.[247]

Return visits by Copeland and Price to the campus, Jim Buskirk believed, served mostly to validate Oral's authority: "I don't know whether he was proving that he could invite them back. He's the president; he can do whatever he wants to do."[248] That much was certain.

The opposition on the ORU campus to the faith teachers was formidable, particularly in the theology school. Two of the leaders of the criticism were Oral's close friends of the 1960s Charles Farah and Howard Ervin. Ervin considered the teaching "highly manipulative, . . . a refurbishing of the old Gnosticism," but he was gentle in spirit and soft-spoken in style. He talked calmly, and, he felt, constructively, with Oral about the theological traps in the teaching.[249] Farah was more outspoken, lecturing and writing regularly on the subject, including a book published in 1980. An address Farah delivered before the Society of Pentecostal Studies in 1980 was termed in *Christianity Today* "a veritable declaration of war on the faith formula teaching."[250] Farah's stand made him a "persona non grata" on campus for some time, but he remained convinced that "ultimately I know I did Oral Roberts a favor," because "the school could have been destroyed."[251]

Most charismatics, including Roberts, acknowledged that his theology had never agreed with that of the faith teachers—there had always been more room in Oral's thought for paradox and the inscrutable. Farah believed that Roberts had never perceived God's intervention "in the automatic way that some of them have. . . . He has never said we do not suffer."[252] On the other hand, Oral's beliefs were not far from those of the moderate faith teachers, who admitted that medical science was useful for those with imperfect faith. After preaching at the Hagin camp meeting in 1983, Oral urged his partners, in terminology used by the faith teachers, to make a "Decree List" of their needs: "By definition, DECREE means to determine, to decide, or to MAKE UP YOUR MIND what you want God to do in your life, then set your heart upon it by your faith. . . . When you or I DECREE a thing according to God's word, we have God's AUTHORITY behind that DECREE."[253]

Roberts's attraction to the faith ministries in the 1980s was not primarily a theological one. Partly, he was drawn to them and other successful independent religious leaders because he identified with their struggles. He overlooked their faults. When criticized for making a contribution to help Jim Bakker's PTL network, Oral replied: "I know Jim Bakker. I know that he loves Jesus and Tammy loves Jesus. . . . It matters not if he's not perfect. . . . I'm flawed and everybody is flawed."[254] In introducing Fred Price to the students in January 1981, Oral pointed out that the pastor of Boston Avenue Methodist Church had just spoken at the chapel services and that "the Bishop that is over me in the church" had been invited to speak. Price should also be given a hearing. "There's some things you say that I can't quite agree with, some things I say you can't quite agree with," acknowledged Oral, "but let's harmonize and be brothers and take what we can take."[255] Oral detested anything that smacked of religious bigotry and intolerance. He had suffered from it, and he would not tolerate it at his university. He gave others the right to disagree; he demanded the same.

By 1983, opponents of the faith teachers at ORU believed that they had weathered the storm and won a victory. They were convinced that Oral had seen the danger of the theology. But strong personal ties remained between Roberts and the independent evangelists. He saw them as "men who have had to carve out their own ministry and they have many rough edges about them but they have a deep truth."[256] Roberts wanted his students to be taught "good theology," observed Jim Buskirk, but he also "wanted to expose us to that sort of dynamic Holy Spirit ministry."[257] But the departure of Buskirk in 1984 almost surely signaled a move of the seminary toward the independent ministries.

Oral's identification with the faith teachers was a return to his cultural roots. In the Hagin camp meetings, he was invigorated by the joyous worship and ecstatic moving of the Spirit, an atmosphere much like that in his own meetings in the 1950s. Oral was culturally at home there in a way he would never be in a Methodist church. To some extent, Hagin had reintroduced Roberts to the burgeoning charismatic movement he had done so much to create. In a time when his ties with the Methodist church were shaky, the independent charismatic revivalists showed Oral a whole new constituency that loved and honored him.

The lasting impact of the faith evangelists on the Roberts ministry remains to be seen—particularly their influence on Richard Roberts. Richard established close and personal ties with all of the major leaders of the faith movement.[258] When Richard began his evangelistic ministry, the independent ministers treated him as an equal and a brother; Kenneth Copeland presented him a four-engine Viscount airplane as a gift.[259] Richard echoed his father's view that "if you can accept eighty percent of what somebody says you are very fortunate." But he also observed that the theological critics of the independent ministers were people who had "not been out in the world" to deal with the practical problems of an evangelist.[260] Richard's experience had been much like his father's; he had received scorn from professors and hostility from organized churches while enjoying the camaraderie of those with similar ministries.[261] Richard was clearly on the same centrist theological course that Oral had followed, but his personal affinities and his experience pushed him into the camp of those charismatic preachers who were alienated from the established church.

While Oral's ties with the independent charismatic movement deepened in the 1980s, his relations with the Methodist church weakened. In the 1970s Roberts seemed happy in his new church. He received hundreds of invitations to speak in Methodist churches and conferences, and a parade of Methodist bishops and ministers spoke to the students at ORU.[262] Roberts had a solid relationship with his Methodist pastors in Tulsa, Finis Crutchfield, Bill Thomas, and John Russell—two of whom were elevated to the office of bishop. In 1980, the United Methodist Council on Evangelism held its annual meeting at ORU and featured addresses by Billy Graham and Oral.[263] In 1980, the retiring bishop of the United Methodist Church in Mississippi, Mack B. Stokes, joined the ORU faculty as the head of the theology department in the seminary.

Oral received considerable support from the strong charismatic fellowship within the Methodist church.[264] Many other Methodist leaders became more tolerant of him. In December 1977, the editor of the Methodist magazine *The Christian Home* wrote to him:

> Over the years I spoke negatively about you until more recently. As I have followed your ministry, particularly in these last six to eight years, I have listened to what you were saying and forgot about who you were. I began focusing more on the one whom you serve and discovered that He is the same Jesus I love and serve. I want to thank you for the way your witness has lifted up our Lord.[265]

While the evangelism conference at ORU caused "quite a stir" in the church, one editor believed it had been constructive: "If nothing else, . . . [it] served to break down some unwarranted, outdated stereotypes about Oral Roberts and the independent religious organization he heads. It also serves to illustrate a new breath of 'pluralism' in the UMC."[266] In the late 1970s, Oral still believed that the Methodist church was "the best place in the world I could find."[267]

In spite of these positive signs, Roberts increasingly felt disappointed about his church relationship. He was offended by the frequent criticism voiced by Methodist ministers during the battle to build the City of Faith. And, although Jim Buskirk insisted that it was a result of Oral's busy schedule and not because of a lack of invitations, he preached much less frequently in Methodist churches and conferences in the 1980s. He believed that he had been ostracized by the church's hierarchy.[268] Jim Buskirk thought that "ninety percent" of Oral's dissatisfaction was related to his ministerial ordination. Roberts's local-elder ordination meant that he had no voting rights in the conference; on one embarrassing occasion, he, along with others, was ordered off the floor of a meeting by the presiding officer. "Oral has some feeling that he's not . . . a full Indian," explained Buskirk, and, in fact, it was true. Buskirk admitted that there was "prejudice" against Oral in "the local United Methodist church in Oklahoma"; Roberts's ordination as an elder-in-full-connection had been "successfully blocked" by the church's board of ministry.[269] Oral felt rejected: "I have been extremely aware that the leadership is extremely uncomfortable with me."[270]

Jim Buskirk, Roberts's primary link with Methodism, was distressed by the church's actions and Oral's perceptions. He believed that the church was being short-sighted in overlooking the contributions Oral could make; on the other hand, Roberts had little understanding of the "very connectional" nature of Methodism.[271] In his nearly two decades of membership, the Methodist church had made little use of Oral; he had not served on any committee or church board. "I haven't helped my church very much," Oral said regretfully.[272] Buskirk was forced to agree.[273]

Oral's expectations of his church probably grew through the years. He had received very strong support from Methodist laypeople. He continued to "love the church so much that I would die doing what I believe it would take to renew the church." On the other hand, Oral Roberts could not bear to stay where he was not wanted. "From a logical point of view I would not stay in another day," he said in 1983, "but in my spirit, I cannot move, even if they took my ordination. I'll have to go to the local church and be a United Methodist layman until the spirit told me."[274] His discontent with Methodism was not critical in the mid-1980s; he still did not feel moved to take drastic steps. But there were many hints of change. In the summer of 1984, Oral and Richard associated themselves with the Victory Christian Center in Tulsa, a large independent charismatic church pastored by ORU graduate Billy Joe Daugherty, and the ministry sponsored a huge international ministers' convention for charismatics.[275]

WHILE ROBERTS's reputation within the charismatic movement and the Methodist church ebbed and flowed in the decade from 1975 to 1985, generally speaking, it was a period of public criticism and ridicule which rivaled his trials as a tent evangelist. "Roberts has spent the last nine years molding an image of respectability," wrote a reporter in 1977; that image was destroyed during the City of Faith battle.[276] Another journalist summarized the ministry's difficulties in 1980: "For Roberts, the vision has resulted in law suits by Tulsa area hospitals to halt construction, the demoralization of his donors and resulting destabilization of his cash flow, a handful of media exposes, the flight of a top lieutenant, and a whole raft of questions about the future of his evangelical empire."[277] Once again, the press broke out the old labels of "con man" and "charlatan."[278]

Oral became increasingly uncooperative with the press under the torrent of attacks; one reporter judged him to be "more inaccessible . . . than ever before."[279] Even *Charisma,* one of the leading charismatic magazines, found it impossible to secure an interview with Oral for reporter Sherry Andrews, although she assured the ministry that "we basically wanted to do a nice article."[280] Oral was drawing in for a siege. When Evelyn showed him a front-page story criticizing him in 1975, Oral revealed, "I didn't read it. I was scared to read it because, you know, it might be true. And so I just go along in bliss; ignorance is bliss."[281] He tried to brace the university community for the onslaught that he had been through before: "We're going to suffer a lot this year. We're going to be hit. We're going to be put in a bad light. There may be lots of articles in national magazines. One has just been here. And the man admitted why he was here, that good news is no news and they only print bad news."[282]

The new controversies reawakened all of Roberts's old religious enemies. Many evangelicals had never welcomed the rapprochement with pentecostalism, and they criticized Oral despite his friendship with Billy Graham.[283] Outspoken fundamentalists had always considered Oral one of the "delusion artists of our generation."[284] "We think he is a religious racketeer," wrote Bob Jones, "and feel that Roberts' accounts of God's conversation with him . . . [are] a blasphemous falsehood."[285] Noting the return of Oral to prime time in 1981 along with a puppet show, Baptist Wendell Zimmerman wrote: "Any dumb puppet would be better than past performances."[286] Reviewing the Roberts meeting advertisements of the 1950s and the reward ads run by the Churches of Christ of the period, a minister from that church observed in 1983 that "over the past three decades . . . both he and we have become more 'sophisticated'— 'neutralized' might be a better term."[287] But Oral still received considerable attention in that church's periodicals in the 1980s, including attacks on his "deceptive claims and false teaching" and indictments of his character.[288]

As in the 1950s, attacks on Oral from the right were often reinforced by criticism from liberal religious leaders. In 1980, the National Council of Churches issued a statement condemning television evangelists in general as "slick entertainers" and reasking questions about Oral's personal wealth.[289] On more than one occasion in the 1980s, clergymen visiting the mainstream churches of Tulsa used the occasion to challenge the ministry of Oral Roberts.[290]

To some extent, Oral's reputation was damaged by his general association with the "electronic church." *TV Guide, Saturday Review,* the *Wall Street Journal,* the *Nation,* and scores of other major publications printed critical investigations of that phenomenon in the 1980s.[291] Receiving wide publicity was a book on television evangelists written by sociologists Jeffrey K. Hadden and Charles E. Swann, entitled *Prime Time Preachers.* In Roberts's case, the book depended largely on outdated material and concentrated on Oral's declining television ratings.[292] Attacks on "Bible pounders" were so fashionable in the 1980s that Harold Robbins's 1982 novel *Spellbinder,* "based on his research among such evangelicals as Oral Roberts," was a major success.[293] "I never believed most things I heard about the shenanigans of big evangelist preachers until I began my research," Robbins told reporters. "Now I see them as the ayatollahs of the United States."[294]

Although Oral never supported the Moral Majority, he was frequently lumped indiscriminately with Jerry Falwell and the right-wing political movement of 1979 and 1980.[295] Actually, Oral was sympathetic with the movement, but political agitation was not his style. He studiously avoided formal association with the political movement and tried to duck the barrage of hostile reaction to it.[296] Discriminating television listeners, such as a Mississippi letter-to-the-editor writer, understood the differences: "I think Oral Roberts is a pretty good guy but Bob Jones and Jerry Falwell are dangerous. Of course, I am a whiskey-drinking, sinning Christian but I can't abide Jones and Falwell."[297]

Roberts's most serious problems, however, were caused by a series of widely circulated accounts of his ministry. In 1976, Wayne A. Robinson's book was published: *Oral: The Warm, Intimate, Unauthorized Portrait of a Man of God.* Robinson's book was no hatchet job; he knew Oral well and profoundly admired him. He insisted that it was not a "negative study."[298] But the book did expose in detail the pragmatic underside of the ministry; it reflected Robinson's own loss of faith in its theological supports; and it particularly questioned the mass-mail techniques. Most obvious was Robinson's contempt for Richard. The author later confessed that the book was "done with some anger," particularly the sections about Richard. He also acknowledged that he had "monetary" reasons for writing the book, although insisting that he also "had something to say that needed to be said." Years later he still believed that he had fairly portrayed his "friend, employer, and co-worker."[299]

Robinson's book probably did Roberts little harm with the public. In spite of its critical sections, it was a "warm" story that reflected Robinson's deep respect for his former mentor. But it distressed Oral, to whom disloyalty was the consummate sin. "I knew," said Robinson, "that when someone had been criticized as much as Oral has he tends to lump all critics together."[300] Roberts reportedly refused to read the book; others in the ministry, including Robinson's brother-in-law Carl Hamilton, believed that the book had largely to do with the "battle going on inside Wayne . . . that is still not resolved."[301]

Much more disparaging was a widely circulated book written by Jerry Sholes in 1979, *Give Me That Prime-Time Religion*. Sholes's book was labeled a "pot-boiling paperback" by *Newsweek*, but it received wide attention and supplied Oral's critics with an inexhaustible reservoir of charges.[302] Perhaps most important, it apparently stimulated "Sixty Minutes" to film a segment on the Roberts ministry.

Sholes left virtually no facet of the Roberts ministry unscathed. Ron Smith's brother-in-law, he worked for about three and a half years in the Roberts organization as a writer and associate television producer, and, although he had not been in the top echelon of management, he was close to the policy makers. The impression the book left, wrote one reviewer, was that Oral was "a consummate liar."[303] Sholes's denunciation was so complete, noted the *Tulsa Tribune*, that it included "virtually everything associated with the evangelist's ministry."[304] Much of the criticism was old, including revelations about the Roberts family's lifestyle and the business arrangements which allowed Roberts to profit from the publication of his books. Much of it was no more than judgments others had made somewhat less belligerently—that Oral's pitches to his partners were a "con game" and that "none of them help people."[305] But Sholes's book was filled with sensational charges, including intimations that the Roberts family were "closet sinners."[306] Probably the most heated accusation in 1979 was made in Sholes's final chapter on the City of Faith, which carried the subtitle "The Announcement Lie."[307] The chapter, which Sholes considered the most crucial in the book, argued that Oral had planned the City of Faith long before his desert vision and had deliberately and repeatedly lied about his intentions. While it was clear that Oral had, indeed, considered using the name the City of Faith for a quite different project, and had considered the possibility of building a hospital before the announcement was made, the announcement was, in fact, consistent with the language Roberts, and others in his tradition, had used in the past. Perhaps more damaging in the long run were Sholes's descriptions of the tough-minded conferences in which ministry decisions had been hammered out during the City of Faith fight—conferences which Sholes himself had attended.[308] Those accounts were a serious embarrassment.

It is difficult to fairly assess the Sholes book. "Sholes' critical assessment of personalities is interesting," wrote Jenkin Lloyd Jones, "but there was not much

that was factual in the book which had not been common knowledge. Nevertheless, the book has triggered a new wave of attacks on Roberts, personally, by
people who have been wanting to knock him down. The smell of blood brings
the piranhas."[309] Another Tulsa reporter labeled it "uninhibited mudsling-
ing."[310] The events surrounding the publication of the book took several bizarre
turns. Just before its release, ORU officials announced that they had been approached by a man "claiming to work for the 'opposition' " who offered to sell
them a copy of the manuscript for $12,000.[311] Roberts's supporters believed
that research for the book was funded by the opponents of the City of Faith.
Wayne Robinson reported that he was contacted by a "retired FBI guy who
went around interviewing former employees"; he refused to cooperate.[312]
Sholes countercharged that he was asked by Ron Smith to write a favorable
book about Oral, junking his critical volume, with financial stipulations which
made him consider the offer a "bribe."[313] In an incident shortly after the release
of the book, Sholes was badly beaten in a fight. Though he did not charge that
Roberts was responsible, many concluded that there was a connection.[314]

Roberts ministry officials considered Sholes a "rascal" and a "feather-
weight."[315] Richard thought Sholes was "brilliant," a talented and creative television producer, but believed he "sold his soul for 7500 pieces of silver. . . . For
$7500 he wrote the book."[316] Whatever his arrangements with his publishers,
C. T. Thompson agreed that "Jerry got pretty bitter" when he discovered "you
can't make a living being anti-Oral Roberts."[317]

Whatever the merits of Sholes's book, it probably was the most important
stimulus for the "Sixty Minutes" segment about Oral that was aired on January
27, 1980. Produced by Joseph Wershba and featuring Morley Safer, the program was constructed almost entirely of edited snips of Oral speaking, interview
segments with Jerry Sholes and C. T. Thompson, and editorial commentary by
Safer.[318] The basic issues raised in the program were familiar: the validity of
Oral's claims that he heard God's voice and was a special instrument for healing,
the ministry's fund-raising techniques, the justifications for building the City of
Faith, and Oral's own personal wealth and lifestyle.

In a sense, "Sixty Minutes" was forced to take the tack it did by Roberts's
refusal to cooperate. After first indicating that he would talk with Safer, Oral
subsequently declined an interview and also forbade interviews with other top
administrators. The ban came after a warning from Don Moyers, who advised
that "under no circumstances should he appear, that it would be most inappro-
priate to do so while the City of Faith is still under litigation."[319] Roberts's
friends felt that the producers of the program had not tried to get a balanced
view. Wayne Robinson called the producer and asked to be interviewed. He
was told that the program would not be aired for some time and was disappointed when it was shown almost immediately. The Roberts administrators
were particularly offended by Safer's parting shot, "Oral hunkers down in his
office and speaks only to God and to his flock."[320]

What most infuriated the Roberts organization, however, was a sequence of
shots from an interview with Oral's brother Vaden. Vaden confessed that he did
not understand how God talked to his brother and speculated about the

psychosomatic nature of many of the "healings" he had witnessed. Safer asked, "Do you believe that Oral Roberts' hands can heal?" Vaden replied, "No, sir, hands can heal? No, sir."[321] Vaden later vowed that his sentence had been followed by the statement: "I have seen God heal plenty of people through Oral Roberts, I've seen people walk away from him who appeared to be healed."[322] Most people who knew the family well, including *Tulsa World* religion editor Beth Macklin, believed that the quotation "had to be taken out of context."[323] Oral's attorney, Don Moyers, was incensed by the treatment and believed that it bordered on "slander and libel," but Roberts vetoed any effort to "retaliate."[324]

The "Sixty Minutes" airing pleased Roberts's critics and stirred his supporters. His partners flooded the Prayer Tower with calls and crowded the "Letter to the Editor" columns of newspapers for weeks.[325] "I see no adverse effect in the mail or anywhere else from our partnership," wrote George Stovall. "Often when somebody is fighting you, you gain support from others."[326] Oral tried to dismiss the attack from his mind, but it boiled to the surface:

> I know how the temptation came to me to think about *Sixty Minutes* and what they did and the things they told, that they knew were not true. They didn't dare ask the right person. They wouldn't have liked the answer. Now if that's all I think about is what they did, you know where my mind is and you know it won't take long till I'm destroyed. Yes, I think about them for a few minutes. And I know that when the characters on that program have gone . . . that the children of God will be standing alive, triumphant, serving God, I know that.[327]

As a result of the attacks by Sholes and "Sixty Minutes," ministry employees were required to sign an oath affirming "support of the Oral Roberts Evangelistic Association and all of its ministries" and "promising to keep secret all confidential information about the university and its affiliated organizations." The oath also included the promise "I will not exploit my relationship for personal profit."[328]

The controversy surrounding Oral in the late 1970s and 1980s was most heated in Tulsa. Partly, tensions grew stronger because of Roberts's ever-increasing importance to the city. Any Tulsan traveling outside the city was likely to be asked about Oral. Every article on the city, ranging from newspaper travel articles to a feature story in *National Geographic,* prominently displayed Oral Roberts and his empire.[329] Oral Roberts University remained the top tourist attraction in the state of Oklahoma; the growth of the university and the medical center had a dramatic economic impact on the south side of Tulsa.[330] "He is absolutely one of the most important people in Tulsa," said John Williams. "Just as important as the head of Cities Service. . . . He is our biggest tourist attraction and one of our biggest employers."[331]

Every move that Oral made was likely to trigger an avalanche of protest and defense in Tulsa. It is difficult to tell whether the balance between supporters and opponents changed much during the decade, but both camps became more vocal and shrill. The City of Faith was the last straw. Jenkin Lloyd Jones judged that Oral had not "lost very much," that he remained "an immensely popular

person in the town," but "among certain intellectual groups . . . he is anathema.
. . . He offended the doctors. My own doctor gets livid every time he mentions
him."[332]

The medical community became Oral's most vociferous opponent in Tulsa,
and C. T. Thompson was its most fearless spokesman. Thompson's objections to
Roberts were partly medical: "Whether or not Oral is a fraud, his medical
policies are a fraud. . . . If you promise something superior, and if you promise
it in the name of God, . . . and you don't produce it, then it's fraud." But
Thompson, and others, also objected to the reputation Oral had given Tulsa:
"As a reasonably good Christian I resent the notion that we have to deal with
this brand of Christianity." Too often, Thompson lamented, in Tulsa "if you're
opposed to Oral Roberts, you're opposed to God's will." He found it thoroughly "distasteful" that Tulsa, "which is a neat town," had become an "Oral
Roberts branch."[333]

In the heat of the fight over the City of Faith, Thompson often charged that
other responsible Tulsans cowered at Oral's influence and refused to publicly
express themselves; he was particularly upset that there were not enough "guts
in the clergy" to take Oral on.[334] It was true that few prominent Tulsans joined
in the protests against Roberts, but the letters in the local newspapers made it
apparent that many shared Thompson's views. One Tulsan wrote in 1984: "First
he constructed a major medical facility in Tulsa that is neither warranted,
needed, justified, nor, largely, staffed. Now Oral Roberts has visions of dis-
patching 'healing teams' to solve the medical problems of the world. Amazing.
Simply amazing."[335] And while few powerful voices spoke out against Oral directly, the feeling within the Roberts organization was that several important
local politicians were hostile to the ministry, and they were convinced that Jenkin Lloyd Jones, Jr., the son and successor of Oral's old and important newspaper friend, "has no use for Oral at all."[336]

Every salvo against Oral in the Tulsa newspaper was invariably followed by
a series of defenses. Every time he publicly opposed Oral, recalled C. T.
Thompson, he received a batch of "vitriolic mail" from "all the crazies."[337]
While the evangelistic association revealed that "there is not a greater percentage of partners in Tulsa than in any other city," Tulsa was an international
center of charismatic religion, and defenders were plentiful.[338] One supporter
twitted anti-Roberts correspondents with the gaff: "My husband and I have
found a way to overcome the sadness we feel when we read such letters. We
write a check to ORU for $10 for each derogatory letter, thereby helping the
City of Faith to be built. It makes us feel good."[339]

Some Tulsans believed that all the publicity distorted Roberts's importance
to the city. "We don't pay a lot of attention to Oral in Tulsa," said reporter Beth
Macklin; John Williams agreed that many tried to "pretend that he doesn't
exist."[340] But Roberts was a reality that had to be recognized, and most Tulsans
probably stood somewhere in the middle in their opinions of him. "You don't
have to believe in Roberts' religion to see the positive effects of ORU and the
City of Faith hospital complex," editorialized Byron Boone in the midst of
Oral's financial crisis in 1982. "Just as one doesn't have to accept the religion of

Roman Catholicism to recognize the good works of the Church. . . . This might be the time for Tulsans to invest—not in Oral Roberts, not in his brand of religion—but in institutions that can be much more than even Roberts thought they would be."[341] John Williams pronounced probably the prevailing Tulsa benediction on Oral in 1983: "The endorsement that I gave him was that while he may be a charlatan, he is our charlatan."[342]

If the City of Faith did not destroy the hard-won reputation that Oral had earned as a community asset, it seriously damaged it. In the heat of the controversy, some "fair weather friends" deserted him, and others who had supported him were shaken.[343] Not only had Oral "threatened the establishment," those civic leaders on the hospital boards of the city, but the dimensions of his vision "staggered" his friends.[344] Roberts simply could not be satisfied with a "modest" vision, complained Jenkin Lloyd Jones. "Oral has not only got to ride first class, but he goes through the door into the pilot's compartment."[345] Roberts's unwillingness to compromise, his insistence on marching to God's orders, seemed, even to his friends, unreasonable and selfish. "They felt he was high-handed," reported Warren Hultgren. "They felt that he employed Deity to get his will; that he played a God role. . . . They felt that it evidenced an arrogance and a disregard for the welfare of the city. . . . He has known a dip in popularity."[346]

Roberts understood and regretted the strain in his relations with his home town. Jim Winslow believed that it was Oral's rejection in Tulsa which "hurt him the most" during the City of Faith battles.[347] He played golf less at Southern Hills with his old friends Warren Hultgren and Al Bush.[348] His civic and business activities in the city, Al Bush believed, had become "more and more symbolic."[349] In 1984, Bill and Edna Nash, reflecting on Oral's lengthy absences from the city and his decreasing civic interest, wondered if he had "given up on Tulsa."[350] Tulsa was still home for Oral, and it always would be, but it had also become a battlefield. In July 1984, for the first time in many years, he publicly complained about his treatment from the Tulsa press.[351] Roberts could still work in Tulsa, but he rested and thought better elsewhere.

IN THE mid-1980s, the Roberts ministry had thrown up its defenses and drawn the spiritual family tightly together, ready to fight to the finish for the healing vision. Oral would not compromise his dreams; he persuaded and coaxed and begged his partners, hoping they could see the panorama. He found succor in the support of other independent ministers who were fighting for their own heavenly visions, but he increasingly drew back from the outside world that had received him so well in the 1960s and early 1970s—the media, the Methodist church, and Tulsa.

Conspiratorial themes danced in Oral's mind. Sometimes they burst into the public. "There's been a conspiracy for over ten years for certain forces to take this entire campus away from us," he told a chapel audience in 1978. "Maybe we are overprotective, but you'll feel the same way about your baby."[352] Roberts tried to avoid public argument, as he had in the past, but he could not always suppress his outrage. Stung by attacks on his lifestyle, Oral retorted: "The Devil can take a television, media system and pay a man five million dollars a year to tell dirty jokes and the world calls him a hero. That same system can come against a woman of God or a man of God who is trying to obey God."[353] While taping his commentary on the New Testament, Oral's anger often surfaced. "He was hurting at the time and it came out in these tapes," observed Evelyn, "and I had to go back through it. . . . It must not go down for posterity to hear."[354]

"I don't understand it," said Oral innocently in 1983, "if you go out and build a major university and a medical center in our free enterprise system and don't borrow money and you pay as you go, you pay your bills, . . . people should say, . . . 'that is a fine work.' " How could people oppose a hospital and cancer research? "The spiritual side of me can see it easy," he added, casting the battle into the only terms that made sense to him. "No matter what I do they know I am who I am. That I haven't changed. I'm for the healing Jesus."[355] That probably was the issue. Oral had not changed. He still believed what Ellis and Claudius had taught him in the little churches of southeastern Oklahoma; he believed in miracles and visions and anointed prayer clothes. He was still that marveling, faith-filled little Oklahoma boy who had clamped his hand on thousands of heads. The rub was not that anyone would oppose universities, or hospitals, or cancer research, it was that many people did not like Oral Roberts and his methods and his religion. Oral's cars and homes, even the economic exploitation of his donors, were peripheral questions—questions that could be asked about all such enterprises and their administrators. The irreducible issue was Oral and what he stood for. "One thing I've learned about Oral Roberts' impact on people," wrote Evelyn, "they are either for him 100 percent or against him 100 percent. I don't know *why*."[356] But Oral had known why for many years. Still smarting from his Australian experience in 1957, he told his workers: "I find myself talking to myself. I find myself talking back to the opposition. I find myself saying, 'You just don't understand. If you understood, you wouldn't do this.' And then I know that they understand all right. They are just against it, because they don't want the truth."[357] When the backslapping was over and the vials of vituperation had been emptied, when both friends and foes had had their say, to be a partner with Oral Roberts was to believe he spoke the truth.

PART FIVE

MEANINGS

CHAPTER

XVI

The Message

A T FIRST GLANCE, Oral Roberts's ministry seems a collage of accommodations. "When Oral finds he is not on the right track, he changes right nc w," observed Lee Braxton in 1973. "He's changed a lot of times a way ahead of my thinking."[1] Roberts often left his associates behind, dangling on an atrophied branch, sometimes aghast at Oral's new methods. In the midst of the dramatic changes in the ministry in 1968, Evelyn tried to reassure the workers at the evangelistic association: "I'm sure a lot of you have been upset by the changes we've made and most people can't take change. . . . When he makes a change, he just upsets the whole nation with it and it takes people about a year to get over the change, but we are living in a time of change when we have to change our methods."[2] "Did I agree with all the methods?" asked Al Bush. "No. I didn't even agree with all the theology to be honest with you because it wasn't systematic. That's one of the things that always bothered me. It was so pragmatic. Too often, I thought, the end justified the means."[3] There was a dynamic system of checks and balances in Oral's mind; he chased an idea to its extreme, then returned to "flavor that idea with reality and find a compromise."[4] To many of his critics there seemed to be no absolutes that could not be compromised.

Yet, Oral steadfastly maintained that he had never changed his theology. His methodology changed ceaselessly, sometimes for the better and sometimes for the worse, but never, he insisted, that kernel of truth which God had entrusted to his care. "I haven't changed one iota of the things I believe in," he told a theology class in 1971. "I may use different words. . . . I want to talk in the now, but I want to be saying the same things that the Bible teaches."[5] The changes were always in the window dressing, the words and tools that allowed him to teach old truths to new people. Often Oral reached out to new audiences while pulling his old followers along with him into a new cultural and linguistic experience. "He's smart enough to read his following correctly," observed his friend Edna Nash, "in that they are followers. He didn't get up and verbalize. . . . But he makes a statement in his own lifestyle."[6]

Oral Roberts has been the great popularizer of the central beliefs of the pentecostal revival of the early twentieth century. His theological genius has been his ability to focus, to strip away cultural trappings, to find the pith of the teaching that gave force to the revival, and to concentrate his entire attention on those beliefs. His ministry, he explained in 1962,

> has emphasized the miraculous. It has focused the attention of the world upon the supernatural power of God. We have not tried to be all things to all men. We have tried to operate within the limits of our calling, and that calling, specifically, is to take the message of His healing power to our generation. Now, healing is used by us in its broad term. . . . It means to be made whole in soul, in mind and body.[7]

When Roberts began his independent ministry, he instinctively sensed that "there were many people out there in the denominations who needed what he had to be offered in a new wineskin from the pentecostal mould."[8] The message remained pentecostal; in fact, noted historian Vinson Synan, "he emphasized baptism of the spirit and tongues in a way that was even stronger than most pentecostals in the early sixties."[9] Pentecostals, observed Lee Braxton, deserved the credit for "keeping alive" the idea of miraculous hope through the Holy Spirit, but it was Oral Roberts who sold it to the world.[10]

Although Roberts's practical experience in evangelism and his broad associations with charismatic and evangelical theologians necessarily placed him on the cutting edge of Holy Spirit theology, his call was to explain it to the people. He captured his beliefs in a steady stream of slogans, some borrowed and some "out of my spirit," that came to be inseparably identified with him: "Point of Contact," "God Is a Good God and the Devil Is a Bad Devil," "Turn Your Faith Loose," "Expect a Miracle," "Something Good Is Going to Happen to You," "God Is Greater." "To tell you the truth I don't know where he got them," said Evelyn of his "little slogans."[11]

The "substratum" of Oral's theology, summarized his old friend Howard Ervin, was "pretty largely pentecostal armenianism with an overlay of dispensationalism."[12] Never an "ultrafundamentalist," as sometimes protrayed by casual observers, neither did he abandon his upbringing.[13] In the mid-1980s, Roberts showed a renewed loyalty to his pentecostal roots; Al Bush believed he had always been "more conservative than he appears to be."[14]

Roberts's beliefs were rooted in a conservative, common-sense reading of the Bible, uncritically accepted as the "Word of God." Writing in 1941 in *The Drama of the End-Time*, he counseled, "If we want to know what is going to happen next, we must turn to the precious old book, the book of books, the Bible."[15] Forty years later, in a pamphlet published in 1982, he wrote: "The

Bible is God's Word. In the Word of God you can find the answer to every problem."[16] Oral believed the Bible; he urged his followers to "read it and study it" and to "keep a pen or pencil close by so you can mark the parts you want to memorize or find in a hurry."[17] It was Roberts's uncritical faith in the Scriptures which convinced him that God worked miracles. He not only was perplexed by theological systems which subjected the Bible to scientific criticism, he also was puzzled by doctrinal schemes which placed limits on God's miraculous power:

> You know, for some strange reason, almost the whole Christian world can read the Bible and teach it and think that speaking in tongues was virtually irrelevant and has nothing to do with the Christian world today. I know there's been a lot of brain-washing. But some of it is that people just simply don't believe the Bible and they're willing to let people explain it away. . . . They explain healing away. The Bible is full of healing; it's full of God's power for us to be whole human beings and people can explain that away as though it doesn't exist in the Bible.[18]

Oral made few forays that led him beyond such simple readings of the Bible. He was impatient on such excursions; they made him feel uneasy and faithless. "He is a good Bible student," commented his friend Charles Farah, "but he does not have a theological way of looking at it."[19]

In spite of his literalistic faith in the Bible, it was quite true, as Jim Buskirk observed, that Oral was "not fundamentalist," but rather he spanned "the Bible in his theology. He thinks of it wholistically."[20] Roberts was not rigid or legalistic; he did not, in fact, have a systematic theology. When *Reader's Digest* published a condensed version of the Bible in 1982, fundamentalists uniformly denounced the project, but Oral endorsed it.[21] Whereas the Bible became a static, verbally inspired book to nineteenth-century evangelicals, to pentecostals it was a living revelation to be perceived by experience. Oral tried to place himself theologically in 1967: "I'm basically tied to the revealed Word of God. . . . I stand on that side. However, I don't stand there as much as some of the extreme fundamentalists. I'll try to explain that. As you know, it's hard to explain anything you are trying to say. . . . I think in a sense the Word is still being revealed. You know that theology is really the truth interpreted."[22] To a large extent, Oral's impatience with systematic theology, and with rigid systems of Biblical interpretation, was caused by his emphasis on "the now." "You'll find Oral always has problems with theologians," observed Charles Farah. "It is that he is very action and practical related. He wants to know how does this theology relate to getting the job done, meeting human needs."[23]

It was this immanence of God, a presence which Oral believed he had encountered in his own salvation and healing, that he saw as the genius of his heritage. "A man who accepts God as a personal Being must allow for His present participation in His universe. Deny Him the power to perform miracles and you have imprisoned God the Creator. Deny Him this freedom and He is not omnipotent but rather impotent." God was not "bound to nature," Oral believed; consequently, human history was constantly interrupted by "new mani-

festations" of his power outside natural law. These interruptions were not necessarily "violations" of order; they were rather demonstrations of the "nowness"
of God.[24]

Oral's belief in the immanence of God piqued his interest in Christian existentialism as explained to him by Wayne Robinson. As a result of his own experiences, he told the Tulsa Kiwanis Club in 1956, "I began to realize that God
is not an abstract being as so many people think of Him, . . . but that God
comes to people in the form of their need."[25] Speaking a decade later to a group
of students at ORU, he said: "The baptism of the Holy Spirit is one called
alongside to help. He is the Paraclete. He actually brings Jesus to one's side. For
all practical purposes it's like Jesus walking by your side in the flesh. . . . It's the
'now,' and we are not talking about existentialism from a philosophical standpoint."[26] Oral was intrigued by a philosophy which stressed the primacy of individual perception and experience, of one's present encounter with existence.[27]

Out of his belief in a miraculous and present God grew two of Roberts's
most basic emphases. First was his compulsion to establish a "one on one" relationship with his partners. His audiences, Oral felt, sensed that he talked individually to every person, "possibly because I was led to Christ not through the
church . . . but through my illness and I was converted, healed, on a personal
basis and developed this very deep and personal interest in the individual."[28]
Oral's preaching was intensely practical—ever searching to discover how God
impinged on one's life at the present hour.

A second Roberts trademark was his essentially "upbeat" message of hope.
Few reporters passed over the contrast between Billy Graham's call of sinners to
repentance and Oral's promises of health, happiness, and prosperity. Roberts
frequently acknowledged the difference: "I don't believe in the judgmental gospel that Billy preaches. I ran away from it as a boy. Billy meets the needs of a
lot of people. . . . I reach other needs."[29] Oral never disagreed with Billy's
message. He acknowledged that "if I only live for now, I'm going to miss it too.
I must know there is a judgment. I must know there is a hell."[30] But it was not
his call to preach it. His calling was to tell the world that God is good and He is
in the now.

"The whole thesis of the ministry," said Evelyn in 1971, "has been that
God is a good God."[31] "I think what Oral says to this nation," reflected Charles
Farah, is "'I bring you hope.'"[32] The theme was constant and stated without
equivocation: "God's will for you is always good, because God is a good God."[33]
For decade after decade, Oral clung tenaciously to that precept to find
encouragement in distress, healing for the sick, prosperity for the oppressed—
to find wholeness for man. He wrestled with the paradox of tragedy more than
most independent charismatics and acknowledged its reality, but he would
never renounce his slogan. In tragedy he would find a "seed of an equivalent
benefit," some larger good that grew out of an apparent evil. Good was bound
to be the end result. Because God was here, and God was good.[34]

If the focus of Oral's theology on the present and direct intervention of
God separated him from evangelical Biblical scholarship, as it did to some extent from pentecostals, his tolerance of theological diversity made him an
enigma to many of his friends, as well as to his critics. There is no simple expla-

nation for Oral's willingness to work with a range of American Christians broader than probably any other American religious leader in the twentieth century. In some ways, his extreme doctrinal ecumenism was little more than a continuation of the looseness of pentecostal thought, exacerbated by his role as an evangelist. He was not a trained theologian. He was given to saying "imprecise things," noted one of his professors, which left his faculty "holding our breath."[35] But Oral never became an extremist, as did many of the pentecostal evangelists of the 1950s. One of the older healing revivalists described Roberts's reputation: "Roberts was as the Presbyterians . . . are to the Methodists and the Baptists. I think they are the elite, you know of that group. And that's the way Roberts was amongst the Pentecostals. His belief, his doctrine, you can accept . . . because he wasn't what some term 'overboard.' He was a middle-of-the-road man and still is. He's a gentleman. You can speak Roberts' name and not blush."[36]

Oral's theological tolerance was not simply a self-serving effort to keep his base of support broad, though it was that; it was also an expression of his conviction. Partly, his sense of tolerance grew out of his desire to reach across denominational lines as an evangelist. "My ministry is primarily for the unsaved and the sick," he repeated over and over. "I have never felt led of God to enter into lengthy discussions concerning subjects that do not directly relate to one's . . . salvation or healing. By avoiding these discussions and concentrating on those things that will help the lost and the suffering, I have been able to lead more people to Christ."[37] Roberts agreed that "doctrine has to be preached," but he believed such teaching was the responsibility of the "pastor" rather than the evangelist.[38] And, more and more, Oral became convinced that most doctrinal issues were peripheral, that only Jesus was central: "I'm concerned about their knowing Jesus. I'd rather have a man who knew Jesus and didn't understand the doctrine the way he should, than one who would be perfect on the doctrine and not know Jesus."[39] In the years he spent as a revivalist amidst the doctrinal bickering in American pentecostalism, he came to long for a spirit of toleration and respectful dissent. "Maybe a certain person doesn't subscribe to all we do," he told a crusade audience in Pensacola, Florida in 1957. "Well, that's all right. We don't ask everyone to agree with everything we do. But I would say that he could be respectful because it might be that he would find later that he was wrong. So respect is a wonderful thing to have when you go to some church or some religious meeting that feels strange to you. You would want the respect of others if they came to your church."[40] Oral insisted he would never "fuss at other people about their religion."[41]

Of course, Roberts's association with the wider Christian world beyond the pentecostal churches was an early mark of his crusade ministry. He welcomed everyone to the tent and ministered to all who would receive his message. When the Catholic charismatic movement began, severely testing the theological understanding of old-time pentecostals, Oral was unperturbed: "I can't accept the way they do, but I'm not going to deny an authentic experience with Christ." Every crack in denominational barriers he welcomed as "a wonderful opportunity."[42]

Few things stirred Roberts's ire more than religious intolerance based on denominational loyalty. In 1978, a theology student at the university challenged the use of Mabee Center by the Mormon church to conduct a family seminar. In a chapel confrontation, Oral disagreed with that judgment "one thousand percent" and proceeded to give a rambling lecture on religious tolerance:

> I'm not a Mormon, and I never will be a Mormon, and I don't figure that we're so insecure here that they hurt us. They didn't hurt my faith in God. . . . We have some people who feel that way about the Catholics. They wouldn't want the Catholics to use it. We have some here who wouldn't want the Baptists to use it. You know, you can get pretty narrow. . . . When we attack another religion—I've been attacked in my religion so much, I may be overly sensitive. . . . I didn't want injected here on this campus the attacking of another faith. . . . You can understand why I did because I've been the object of that for thirty-one years. And I know how it feels.[43]

More than anything else, it was the "inclusiveness" of the Methodist church which drew him there in 1968—he was fleeing religious bigotry.[44] Oral's identification with and empathy for "sinners" rested on his belief in tolerance. He mingled easily with the unwashed, dealing nonjudgmentally with them. "I've never been severe with alcoholics," he wrote. "I don't drink. I just don't find any place in my life for alcohol and I notice the closer people get to God and the more of the Holy Spirit they get, the less that they have to have things such as alcohol. But I can't go around preaching against alcohol all the time. I preach Christ."[45] When a reporter asked Roberts if he was "appalled" by the "immoral things" reported in the lives of several former presidents, such as "running around with other women," Oral snapped back that he was "appalled" by "the lack of charity and the willingness of many persons to believe all these stories being written and served up to a public seemingly insatiable for gossip. . . . Being against sin is one thing; jumping to conclusions about a fellow man's morals is another."[46]

Oral's sense of tolerance found expression in his own organization. If one was loyal to the general mission of the ministry, Roberts tolerated great variety in beliefs. A staunch premillennialist, he frequently engaged his coworkers in friendly and indecisive conversations on the subject of Christ's second coming.[47] In fact, he had the profoundest respect for his Jewish friend and lawyer Saul Yager. On the occasion of Yager's retirement, Oral told a story: "We were wrangling over something and Yager spoke up and he had the answer, cooled things down considerably and when it was over he and I walked out and he made an immortal statement. Putting his arm around me, he said, 'Oral, do you know I'm a better Christian than they are?' Don't you think that's a classic?"[48] There were few beliefs more important than personal integrity and honesty. "There's a tremendous power in being an authentic human being," Oral lectured his faculty, "on being honest, according to one's likes."[49] Particularly in the late 1960s, when he was in the final throes of his decision to abandon the Pentecostal Holiness church and the denominational restraints that it represented to him, he came to exalt free inquiry: "One of my concerns is that we develop a spirit of inquiry, where we are free in our search for truth. I'm not afraid of truth."[50] In

1970, he explained to the ORU students that intellectual freedom had been a crucial issue in his change of churches:

> Twenty years ago when I started this ministry I thought I had all the answers. I don't have them all today. But I know my Lord and I know that we will be knowing more tomorrow if we follow and serve Jesus. . . . I reject, in fact I did that by a certain act of mine, I reject anything, any denominational viewpoint that says it's all been revealed. . . . I'll know more truth tomorrow than I know today.[51]

To Oral, openness and tolerance gave meaning to "continual revelation."[52]

The most remarkable facet of Oral's catholicity was his innocent curiosity about modern theology. Culturally at home with religious conservatives (he appreciated Jerry Falwell and the values of the Moral Majority, and he had strong personal ties with the charismatic faith teachers), he also yearned for a healing in the whole body of Christ and stood ready to listen to and learn from anyone. During his studies of modern theology in the 1960s, Oral concluded that theological liberals shared his open-mindedness:

> Can anyone say that he has walked so far and there's no more light? I think that's what's worrying the liberals. I think the liberals have a lot to say to us. . . . They want to know God. . . . I just finished a second reading of Harvey Cox's *The Secular City*. I had a very difficult time with some of his terminology and will never be able to have it otherwise. But after the second reading, I sensed that the man is seeking God.[53]

Asked by a student if theological liberals could be considered genuine Christians, Oral spelled out his sole creedal test: "Henrietta Mears made a very fabulous statement, 'You cannot believe in the Book of Genesis and yet, if you believe in Jesus Christ, He will save your soul.' You can be wrong in doctrine, but you can't be wrong on the Person. You've got to know the Person to be saved."[54] When Oral first announced his intention to build a university, his friend Jenkin Lloyd Jones wondered whether it was possible to build a "respectable university" which was "tied to the first chapter of Genesis." He asked Oral about the possible conflict. "He looked at me with a smile," recalled Jones, "and he said, 'Well, the Lord speaks in many parables.'" "That was a weasel answer," Jones grinned, "but it was a very clever answer too. He didn't want to get himself hung up on anything."[55] It was even more than that. Oral was willing to let every man follow his own path to intellectual honesty if he could reconcile his walk with a personal faith in Jesus.

Roberts hoped that "charismatic theology" would become an alternative to the narrowness of fundamentalism and the experiential emptiness of "liberalism." "The modernists and the liberals," he surmised, "don't know the Person as much as they know the philosophy." Their error, however, was less serious than that of the fundamentalists, "who believe the Bible literally, but can come up to Scriptures such as these on the gifts of the Spirit and just absolutely ignore them." Furthermore, fundamentalists were too often ill-spirited; they "almost preached hate." "It's a ripe and wide open field now for the Charismatic form of theology," Oral believed, going "right straight down the middle of the road . . . to develop a better understanding of the Charismatic methods and moves of the Spirit."[56]

There was a disarming naiveté about Oral's ecumenism. He simply would not label people, nor would he listen to uncharitable preaching. In a North Carolina crusade in 1968, he reported: "I heard a man on the radio the other day and he was fighting the World Council of Churches. . . . I couldn't care less. I'm concerned about the individual that needs Jesus Christ, whether he's in the Council, outside the Council, that's not my affair. . . . I'm determined that I'm going to preach a positive gospel of the power of God and not get into politics and all stuff like that."[57] Calvin Thielman recalled an occasion when he and Oral were riding together in a taxi to a session at Billy Graham's Berlin conference. They passed Carl McIntire standing outside the hall picketing the proceedings. "What's the matter with that man?" asked Oral. "That's Carl McIntire," replied Thielman. "He's got a thing against Billy Graham." Oral apparently did not know McIntire's name. His reply, remembered Thielman, was as "guileless as a child": "Well, why don't he come on in and get the blessing?"[58]

Several minor themes recurred in Oral's thought through the years, occasionally rivaling his more central message for a time. For instance, early in his independent ministry, Oral was forced to confront race prejudice and discrimination, and in the 1960s he elevated the cause of equal rights for blacks into a major theme. Almost from the beginning of the healing revival in the pentecostal subculture, the tents attracted both blacks and whites with messages of hope and miracle help.[59] Oral's tent services were integrated from the beginning, and visiting reporters often noted the presence of blacks at the altar.[60] Sometimes Roberts bent to local customs in the 1950s. In 1956, after an opening service which featured a mingling of the races in Raleigh, North Carolina, local pressure forced segregation in later meetings.[61] Questioned by black leaders about segregation in a Nashville, Tennessee crusade in 1958, Hart Armstrong replied that "Brother Roberts is interested only in healing and salvation, not local customs."[62]

While Oral sometimes capitulated to local pressures in the South during the heat of the integration controversy in the 1950s and, as always, tried to eschew any political involvement which would divert him from his main calling, he left no doubt where his sympathies lay. Over and over in the 1950s, he publicly voiced his support for integration: "I am reaching for the world. I have introduced a novelty in my office. God told me to do it. I am bringing all races to work in my office. We are breaking the color line."[63] He vocally supported President Eisenhower's forcible integration of Central High School in Little Rock, telling reporters: "I have had many meetings in the South for many years. I always insist there be no segregated seating and whites and Negroes can and do sit side by side."[64]

Roberts's respect for blacks was genuine, if sometimes patronizing. He appreciated the "simple faith" they exhibited in his meetings; he shared with them a common background in southern agrarian poverty.[65] Like many southern poor whites, Roberts had no sympathy for the oppressors of the poor. In 1968, he told a chapel audience:

I sat in Rotary the other day and heard one of the Rotarians demean the black people because they were renting his houses and they were leaving the houses almost a wreck. Every word he said was true. At the same time he was collecting the checks. He was despising them. He had never gone down to meet them. He had never said a prayer with one of them, yet he's a first class member of a first class denomination and there was bitterness coming out of him.[66]

When Oral Roberts University opened, it not only accepted blacks as students, but they were often featured in its activities—including membership in the World Action teams, which performed on television and in crusades.[67] During the ghetto riots of the late 1960s, Oral was particularly moved by the plight of American blacks, and he toyed with the idea of directing his ministry especially toward healing that social trauma.[68] But that was not to be. Roberts was not a social reformer, though his message continued to have a broad appeal to American blacks.

A second minor theme that recurred in Roberts's preaching and writing was dispensational premillennialism. An elaborate prophetical theory about the end-time, which pentecostals shared in America with fundamentalists, premillennialism argued that the end was imminent and that a prophesied sequence—the falling away, the rapture, the tribulation, the millennium, and the final judgment—had begun and could be identified by current world events.[69] While Oral was not dogmatic about his prophetic beliefs, and he freely countenanced contrary views among his faculty and friends, he recurrently preached premillennialism. He never really changed the views he had reached when he wrote *The Drama of the End-Time* in 1941.[70] The theory reappeared time after time both in *Abundant Life* magazine and in Oral's preaching.[71] In the 1980s Roberts's premillennialism surfaced in his taped commentary on the Bible and in a televised reaction to the 1984 ABC special "The Day After."[72] Roberts termed the film on nuclear holocaust a "farce," because such a scenario was "not in the Bible!" He urged his partners to listen to his tapes to receive a Biblical understanding of the end-time sequence.[73]

Sometimes, in reaction to some particularly startling development in current events, Oral's eschatology turned heated. Over and over, during his early independent ministry, he sounded the alert that "the Lord is coming soon."[74] Whatever the intent of Oral's prophetic warnings, some who listened to his sermons as pentecostal youngsters in the 1950s went away convinced that they would never reach adulthood.[75] Roberts's anticipation of the second coming of Christ reached its peak in the late 1950s, when he repeatedly advised that "the end is near."[76] "I believe the coming of Christ is so near that if we Christians knew how near it is, that we would all be rejoicing tonight," he told a crusade audience in Trenton, New Jersey in 1957, "and, if the sinners knew how near it is, they would all be frightened tonight."[77] He never fell into the trap of predicting the end; he simply encouraged a feeling of "urgency."[78]

Oral's premillennialism was substantiated by his belief that the healing revival, and particularly his own ministry, was a precursor of the second coming of Christ. "Forerunners of Jesus' second coming are on the earth today," he wrote.

"They are preaching with fire in their bones and with faith in their hearts."[79] While the healing revival of the 1950s did not accomplish all that Oral and the other evangelists had hoped (it did not bring the immediate second coming), he continued to see his role, and that of his university and its students, in a prophetic context.

Premillennial theory also supplied a framework for Roberts's understanding of current events. Like most evangelical Christians, he believed that there was great prophetic meaning in the founding of the nation of Israel; his fascination with Israel and his ministry's work there rested on premillennial assumptions.[80] On occasion, he became more specific, finding prophetic meaning in the launching of Sputnik or the development of the H-bomb or a specific war.[81] But Oral's excursions into prophetic interpretations were always just that—they were brief detours which sometimes seemed no more than necessary bows to public expectation. Generally, he avoided jumping aboard the latest popular religious fad.

Roberts's avoidance of the Moral Majority was predictable, based on his past behavior. He had always been a chest-thumping Oklahoman, a flag-waving American, an outspoken defender of the "free enterprise system," and a critic of Communism.[82] He had no patience with the rebellious youth of the 1960s: "Lots of things in America need to be fixed, but I am for this country. I have been all over the world. There's no place on the earth where you've got freedom like you have right here. I'm for America. I work within the establishment. I don't like some things about the establishment, but I'm not going to tear it down. The alternative is a lot worse."[83]

But saving America was not Oral's mission, nor did he have the temperament for anticommunist crusading. Although in the 1950s he sometimes charged that "communism symbolizes all the bad of unbelief," he mellowed in later years. Before visiting Vietnam in 1968, he reminded his partners that his mission was not political: "I don't dabble in politics—I just preach the Gospel and win souls."[84] After his return, he pronounced himself "unsure" about the merits of the war.[85] Whatever his observations about current events, Roberts consistently argued for a spiritual solution to the world's problems:

> There are millions of people in this country who say they are Christians and they are going to hell. We would be very lucky if there's a million people in the United States who are followers of our Lord. I don't believe America is a Christian country. I don't believe any country in the world is Christian. I quit talking about saving America, saving the world. Christ talked about witnessing to somebody, trying to save a person.[86]

Saving people had always been Oral's call; he never strayed too far away from it.

THE ONE immutable plank in Oral Roberts's thought was his call to bring healing to his generation. His definition of healing grew through the years, but the word remained the hinge of all his thinking. He literally wrung the word out, exhausting it, both theologically and experimentally. In it he found spiritual promises for men's bodies, souls, and spirits and, collectively, for the abolition of sectarian division. All of Roberts's methodologies were pragmatic means to facilitate healing. He was married to none of them; they were simply instruments to bring healing. It was fitting that Oral should pause in his address at the dedication of the City of Faith to announce: "I'm proud of the healing ministry. I'll die with it in my heart. It's real to me folks."[87]

Roberts's early understanding of healing was based on the healing theology which American pentecostals had inherited from nineteenth-century American and European evangelicals.[88] He never read widely in the writings of these earlier advocates of divine healing; he received their ideas, as did most pentecostals, orally, through preaching. When Oral and others began the healing revival in the late 1940s, most pentecostals welcomed their teachings as a "revival of what they had had initially."[89]

Roberts's views on healing depended not so much on an ideological base but on experience. Over and over he traced his passion for healing back to that enchanted moment when he himself had experienced God's touch: "I owe my life, my all to healing. I never wanted to be saved until I found out I could be healed."[90] Speaking in an emotion-filled devotional at the evangelistic association in 1982, in which he prayed for the healing of his sister-in-law, Oral avowed: "The point I'm saying today is they have come too late to tell Oral Roberts that God doesn't heal people. . . . And they've come too late to tell my family. . . . They've never doubted because they were there."[91]

After 1947, Roberts expanded the pentecostal teaching on healing with the addition of ideas and methods that were "unique and controversial."[92] "I could learn very little from the theologians, with all due respect to them, because they more or less deal in theory," reflected Oral in later years. "I had to learn what I've learned in actual combat. Out there in the war that I'm having with the devil over the lives of people. . . . And not many people have been where I've been."[93] Sitting perched above the long lines, viewing every conceivable human illness and perversion, relentlessly studying and preaching Biblical healing texts, Oral honed a theology of healing that was to have a worldwide impact. When the first edition of *If You Need Healing—Do These Things!* was published, he wrote: "So far as I know the Lord gave [these sermons] to me directly and [they] have never been preached in this form by other preachers."[94] As in all of Oral's thought, his theology of healing was not a product of systematic study or borrowed ideas. He read popular magazines and newspapers, and his writings were littered with illustrations from those sources; he discussed and asked questions incessantly, but the assimilation was his own.

Oral's first departure from conventional pentecostal thought was his assertion that he had "God-anointed hands."[95] Many pentecostals questioned all claims of "a special call"; Roberts's sensation in his right hand was quite controversial.[96] "When the Lord's presence came in my hand," he told a crusade audience in 1968, "I was really concerned about myself, whether I was just thinking I felt it. And I talked to brethren about it, and they warned me. But the fact was it was there."[97] Throughout his life, Oral remained fascinated by the healing potential of hands, a subject which has also engrossed others interested in spiritual healing. Physician William Standish Reed saw the "laying on of hands" as an "act of love" that had great symbolic meaning.[98] Oral believed that

"somehow the power of God was transmitted through the hands of the followers of Christ"; his own hands came to symbolize his healing ministry. In one of
his early crusade sermons, he memorialized hands:

> The hand of man is a healing instrument—your doctor's hand, your mother's
> hand, the hand of a friend, the hand of a beloved person, the hand of your
> little child—especially if the spirit of the person whose hand is outreached is
> filled with love. If the person is the "right" kind of person inside he communi-
> cates through his hands. The very emotion of the inner man is expressed
> through his hands. Don't you remember when your mother put her hands on
> you? . . . Isn't there a healing influence in your hands?[99]

Although Oral's own right hand was so intensely attuned to God's healing
power that it pulsated as if charged with electricity, he did not claim a miraculous touch, only that his hands were an "extension of the hands of Christ" and
that they became the point of contact for the release of healing faith.[100] The
huge bronze praying hands before the City of Faith were fitting symbols of the
Roberts ministry.

While Roberts's early trademark was the gift in his right hand, he called on
all of the methods used by other healing evangelists. Bob DeWeese remembered that Oral had "fantastic discerning qualities," using the "word knowledge"
to discern diseases and pronounce them healed in a manner made famous by
William Branham and Kathryn Kuhlman.[101] He sometimes ceremonially
anointed the sick with oil, and in the 1960s he emphasized more sacramental
means of receiving healing, such as "confession" and the "Holy Communion."[102] In 1983, Oral sent a packet of wafers to his partners so that they could
take communion together at an appointed time for healing: "Now, Partner, I
have enclosed this packet containing the bread, the symbolic element of His
body, for our Holy Communion service on May 22 at 2 p.m. CDT. . . . As we
join our faith together through the Spirit and in a very personal way according
to God's Word (I Corinthians 11: 23–28), I want you to get into faith that
God's WHOLE HEALING will begin for you right there as you take it."[103]
Roberts's formula for healing was always syncretistic; he believed God worked
in a great variety of ways to bring healing to those who had faith. Over and over
he returned to his belief that some unknown word might trigger a mass miracle
of healing for all believers.[104]

The mixture of old pentecostal notions and Oral's own creative healing
ideas was illustrated in the list of thirteen instructions given in the initial version
of *If You Need Healing—Do These Things!*:

1. Stand on the Atonement (Matthew 8:17; Isaiah 53:5).
2. Understand that sickness is Satan's oppression (Acts 10:38).
3. Jesus is your Great Physician (John 10:10; Luke 9:56).
4. Take Jesus as your Complete Savior (Isaiah 53:5; 43:11; Galatians 3:13).
5. Know that God's perfect will is to heal you now (Acts 10:38; Hebrews
   13:12).
6. Come for healing as you are (James 5:14, 15).
7. Remember that James 5: 14–16 is your promise, too.

8. Recognize the authority of those praying for your healing (Luke 9:1–6; 10:17; Matthew 10:1–8; 8:5–13).
9. Secure a point of contact (James 2:20).
10. Turn your faith loose—Now!
11. Close the case for Victory.
12. Change your outlook on life.
13. Help others receive deliverance through your faith in God.[105]

Most of the proof-texting was orthodox pentecostal theology, but the concluding points embodied Roberts's practical formula for physical healing.

The first key was "turning your faith loose." For decade after decade, Oral urged his partners to "release your faith in order to receive healing."[106] Through the years he fleshed out his understanding of faith. He was convinced that "everyone has faith," citing Romans 12:3, "God hath dealt to every man the measure of faith." Some simply misplaced their faith.[107] All faith, Roberts believed, began in doubt ("Some of the greatest faith I've ever had began in honest doubt"), but healing faith must end in a full assurance: "Faith is simply right believing—believing that God is a good God and that He loves and cares for you, that He is a God of all power and that He wishes to use His power on your behalf."[108] When one was filled with the supernatural "gift of faith," he was "supernaturally emptied of doubt."[109] Oral's methods were directed toward activating the power of faith.

Roberts often referred to the "point of contact" as the "greatest discovery I ever made."[110] The point of contact was "something you do" to help release faith. While Oral's point of contact was his right hand, which he placed on a person or the radio microphone or some other physical object, he also asked the recipient of his prayer to perform some physical act to concentrate his or her faith. He pointed out that Biblical miracles often required just such acts of faith from those receiving healing.[111] " 'Any-time faith' won't work," he warned, "but faith that sets the time is your most powerful weapon to secure deliverance."[112]

If one turned his faith loose through a point of contact, he then could "close the case for victory."[113] "Burn every bridge between you and the old affliction," Oral urged. "Don't talk about the affliction except when God especially impresses you to give your testimony."[114] In his early preaching, Roberts proclaimed that it was "God's will to heal everybody." In 1957, he was asked: "Do you believe that everyone can be healed by faith in God?" He answered: "I'm going to get you out of your suspense. I'll give you my answer. Yes!"[115] Such bold assertions resounded through the pentecostal world like a "clap of thunder," recalled Harold Paul; to outsiders it often appeared that Oral was giving a "command to God."[116] In later years, Roberts came to leave more room for paradox, but still, in 1971, he defended his old belief:

People often would accuse me of manipulating God. They would say, "You put your hands on the person and say, 'Heal.' " Well they didn't understand that I believe the Bible teaches that it's the will of God to heal. Now there may be exceptions when God will sovereignly say yes or no, but I was simply

operating in a positive way upon something that I believe the Bible teaches.
. . . And when I said, "God heal," I was not trying to manipulate God, I was
simply being positive in my own faith.[117]

He did acknowledge, however, that it had been a "mistake" to presume that
everyone he touched would be healed:

> I used to think everyone I prayed for would be healed. If I had died at that
> hour, I would have been sincere, because when I felt the power go through
> me, I thought that was equivalent to a miracle. What I was not reckoning with
> was the free moral agency of the person I was praying for. Nor was I reckon-
> ing with the sovereignty of God, nor the degrees of power that I might feel.
> There were a lot of things I was not reckoning with, because no one had ever
> told me and it wasn't in a book. You could only find it out by trial and error.[118]

From the very beginning of his healing ministry, Oral placed great stress on
the mental and emotional foundation of good health. He repeatedly told his
audiences that "eighty-five percent of diseases come from emotional distur-
bances."[119] He warned in his sermons about the debilitating side effects of fear,
loneliness, and depression. Speaking in 1955, in Florence, South Carolina, he
advised:

> I read an article recently by the medical profession that fear touches the vital
> part of your body. It touches every vital organ. It touches your heart. It
> touches your nervous system . . . it devastates, it degenerates, it weakens and it
> makes the body susceptible to germs that ordinarily it would throw off. . . . I
> believe that fear is the thing that keeps us from controlling our emotions. I
> think we go to pieces because we get scared. . . . When I am strong in my faith
> . . . I'm on top of the world.[120]

In 1949, he observed in *Healing Waters* that the "greatest protection from
cancer . . . is to live a life free of tensions, fears, frustrations."[121] The cure for
emotional distress was a "positive and joyous mental attitude," and Oral
endlessly dispensed that elixir.[122] In June 1984, in a special note to his partners,
he wrote: "My child, I want you to start feeling good about yourself."[123]

Oral was keenly aware of the emotional and psychosomatic nature of much
of the healing under his tent. He conceded that in the "excitement of a given
moment" it was difficult to "know all that has or has not happened."[124] He
unashamedly laid claim to psychosomatic healings.[125] In 1981, he told a group
of physicians: "One of the things that I've had to fight against was that everybody I prayed for and if they were healed they were emotionally healed. There
was nothing of a physical nature healed. Then I read a report where eighty to
eighty-five percent of all illnesses are emotionally induced. I thought they ought
to have me on their payroll if I was out helping people get healed emotionally."[126] In later years, when Roberts developed a full-blown philosophy of
"whole man healing," he linked body and soul and physical and spiritual well-
being so closely together that it was difficult to distinguish illness and healing in
one area from the other. While he understood and accepted naturalistic expla-

nations of healing, he was also convinced that God healed miraculously: "I was healed of both an organic and a functional disease. My stuttering was emotional. There is no doubt about that. But the death germs of tuberculosis in my lungs that caused my hemorrhages was an organic disease."[127] Oral believed that he had witnessed in his campaigns the healing of cancers, tuberculosis, fractured and displaced bones, and other "organic illnesses"; indeed, he once touched a "little baby" which had "died" during a service and brought it back to life.[128] His healing ministry was built on hundreds of thousands of testimonies of "miracles"—"incredible, wonderful, unaccountable."[129]

Roberts's belief in the miraculous was nowhere better illustrated than in his discussions of demon possession. In the earliest years of his healing ministry, Oral, and his audiences, seemed spellbound by demons and their relation to human sickness. He thought his sermon on demon possession usually turned "the tide of the meeting"; his audiences marveled at Oral's command over the evil spirits. Roberts believed that he had a unique gift for discerning the presence of demons in people; he explained the three ways the gift worked in him:

> First of all, I discern demon spirits by the eyes of the person. The eyes, as you know, are the windows of the soul. And personally, when I'm in the presence of a person with demons, I can see the leering and gleaming in the eye of the individual. That's one of the first things I do when I'm near a person who's abnormal, is to look in their eyes. . . . Second, I can tell by the breath or the odor of the body. . . . It is a living stench in one's nostrils. If I get a whiff of it, if a person is five or six people away . . . I know the person is coming toward me. But in the final analysis I tell by the Spirit of God which I feel in my hand when I touch that person. Now every living thing has a vibration. . . . And a demon has a vibration. . . . If I'm near them, I will feel it to some extent. But if I fail there, I put my hand upon a person.[130]

Through the years, Roberts developed an elaborate theory about evil spirits, although he confessed that there "is so little knowledge about demons."[131] Essentially, he believed that demons were "fallen angels" who were cast out of heaven at the time of the fall of Lucifer, who was one of the three "great arch-angels" and the "most beautiful of the angels."[132] "A demon is a strange, abnormal personality of evil," Oral wrote in 1954. "He lost his celestial body, spiritual illumination, godly knowledge and balance. He is now a miserable, disfranchised, homeless, psychopathic creature."[133] Fallen angels roamed the earth seeking sinful souls who would permit them to take up residence in human bodies. In 1948, Oral announced that demon possession was "very real and widely prevalent"; in later years he came to believe that "there are not a great many people in the world possessed of the devil."[134]

Roberts believed that demons were responsible for all sorts of moral deficiencies, as well as sicknesses. Demons caused lying and were particularly linked to epilepsy (although he never taught that all liars or epileptics were demon-possessed).[135] He early associated demon possession with mental illness, noting that it was frequently called "dementia praecox" or "schizophrenia."[136] Oral's announcement in 1983 that he believed cancer was spiritual in nature rested firmly on his long-held convictions about Beelzebub, "the chief demon."[137] As early as 1949, he had written: "The disease itself stems from the oppression of the devil. His chief name is, Beelzebub."[138] Oral made a clear distinction between demon "oppression" and "possession," but nonetheless he very early associated certain diseases, including cancer, with the active influence of the fallen angels.

In a remarkable dialogue with Bob DeWeese, Roberts presented to the medical and pastoral staff of the City of Faith in 1981 a long and full explanation of his theory of demons and his practical experiences with them. In a wildly incongruous scene, he told stories of spiritual diagnoses and remedies in the midst of one of the most modern medical research centers ever built; it was a stark confrontation of old-fashioned healing faith with the sterile world of scientific medicine. The presentation was followed by a disjointed question-and-answer period. Would some of the patients at the City of Faith be demon-possessed? Oral was guarded about the faddish interest in exorcism, but, yes, he answered, the City of Faith would receive demon-possessed people. "Brother Roberts," asked one staff member, "should there be any mechanism for casting out demons in a hospital ministry?" Replied Oral,

> I'd say there should be, but I don't think we've arrived at that place yet. The City of Faith Hospital is certainly designed for the Spirit of God to work, but I believe you doctors would agree that the average hospital is not engaged in that sort of thing whatsoever. I would say the first few months and years here, we should be extraordinarily careful about even trying to cast them out. . . . You can't just indiscriminately think you can cast out demons.

Would there be a "definitive policy statement . . . on who has the authority and responsibility to attempt exorcism?" Oral believed that the answer to those questions would come only with time. Jim Winslow took the floor to assert the authority of the physician:

> If a patient is admitted to the City of Faith Hospital, the authority is . . . clear. . . . The physician admits the patient to the hospital and he's responsible. . . . If you nurses see somebody you think is demon possessed, you just see all these gold coats around here, I can guarantee you they're better equipped. I don't know if the anointing is on them, but they're better equipped to take care of that problem. . . . Get in the chain of authority and stay there. . . . When you get out of the authority, you're guaranteed to get in trouble, anointing or no anointing.

Oral brought the meeting to a soothing end with the assurance that they would not be faced with many cases of demon possession until "this place really is large enough and begins to make a dent upon the devil's kingdom," and he expressed his confidence in "these two Jimmys here [Winslow and Buskirk] and others in authority." But it was clear that putting modern medical research together with the discerning of demons was not going to be easy.[139]

If combining scientific medicine with a miraculous faith was to prove difficult, an older and more central probelm in any theology of divine healing was the presence of failure. If divine healing was provided for in the atonement of Christ, why were some not healed who seemingly had faith? It was this dilemma which had so sharply divided the charismatic movement in the 1970s over the doctrine of the faith teachers. Was failure always a matter of human imperfection, or was there an overarching "sovereignty of God" which in some paradoxical way overruled the provisions of the atonement?[140]

Roberts's thinking on this question softened through the years. His intensely practical and experimental faith forced him to examine failure. He confessed to his crusade audiences repreatedly that he felt "terrible" when he prayed and a person was not healed. Such experiences shook his faith:

> As I began to pray for the sick and saw some healed and others not, I was the most embarrassed person you ever saw. . . . And finally you come to a point sometimes when you don't know, but you have the feeling you have to do it. You have to do it whether they get healed or not, whether they get saved or not. And I began to pray to the Lord, "Lord, what if I fail?" And the Lord really put me in my place. He said, . . . "You've already done that." And I'm one preacher that can only go up. . . . I've already failed in many ways.[141]

Early in his ministry, Oral prayed for the healing of Harold Paul's father-in-law, who was critically ill with cancer. When Paul told Oral some time later that his relative had died, "a cloud came over" Oral, but he then replied, "Harold, I don't attribute my success to my failures."[142] Asked in 1956, "Are all the people you pray for healed?" Oral replied, "Apparently they are not."[143]

The question of why healing did not occur was pentecostalism's knottiest dilemma. For many years Oral held precariously to the belief that it was God's will to heal everyone—failures were charged to his own lack of "perfect power," or to the subjects' need for "perfect faith" and freedom "from the sins of life."[144] "It may be too hard for my faith," wrote Oral in 1968. "It may be too great for your faith. But we know that when men are in reciprocity with God, when they have faith in Him, God can do anything!" "Go to the bottom of each success or defeat," he insisted, "and you will find that faith or doubt is present."[145] Of course, pentecostals had developed, and Oral depended on, a catalog of reasons for healing failures. Sometimes healing was "progressive" rather than instant and might not be immediately visible. One's healing could be lost: "If a violation of the law of nature brought on the sickness, even though God may heal the person, a continuation of that violation will bring the sickness back."[146] While all sickness was not related to sin, "it is possible many times to look back and see how in small animosities, in little sins we commit without even thinking about them, we may indeed let in the devil's invisible forces."[147] Finally, Oral accepted the fact that there was a "death time" for everyone and that death was "a form of healing too."[148]

In the 1970s, Roberts's thinking came to accommodate a much stronger sense of "mystery" and "sovereignty," a posture undoubtedly reenforced by his growing association with mainstream Protestant and Catholic charismatics.[149] "Generally it is God's will to heal," he told a group of students in 1971, "but you cannot take away from God his sovereignty. When I use the word sovereignty I mean that God is God and He reserves to Himself the power to do what He will do, even if it sets aside one of His own rules. . . . There are those sovereign cases . . . that God may decide . . . not to heal."[150]

There were experimental reasons for mellowing, as well. In 1971, Evelyn and Bob DeWeese discussed the crusades. "Do you believe that we have actually left a lot of people hopeless and disappointed . . . over the years simply because of the way Oral has preached?" she asked. "That's a strange thing," answered DeWeese, "I've seen people come with great faith and hope that they would be healed and they were not, but they went right on maintaining that faith and hope because there's something within the human heart, we don't give up easily."[151] As Oral looked back in the 1980s, he also saw mixed results:

> I've probably had more failures in praying for the sick than any man who ever lived. And I probably had a lot of successes. However, you seldom ever find anyone I've prayed for who doesn't love me. Who doesn't respect me. Even though my prayers may not have gotten through for them. Why do they respect and love me? Because I tried. And they know I tried. The greatest failure is not to try. I try and sometimes fail. . . . But in God's eyes, that in itself is a success as far as I'm concerned.[152]

In the autumn of his life, looking back over the thousands who "remained ill, some of them . . . died before their time," Oral confessed, "I've had to live with that."[153] He could only accept the mystery and keep trying.

Estimates of the effectiveness of Oral's healing techniques vary widely. He admitted that sometimes "person after person came by with apparently no miraculous results."[154] Roberts told a reporter in 1955 that he would be the "happiest man in the world" if he "could bring healing to 25 percent of those who ask for it."[155] Tommy Tyson, Oral's associate evangelist in the 1960s, "estimated that two to three percent of the persons for whom Roberts prayed were healed instantly, like a miracle," although many others seemed to be "gradually helped."[156] Bob DeWeese, on the other hand, was the truest believer: "Oral is the only person that I have ever worked with that could consistently, when he touched people, bring something to happen in that person's life. . . . I would watch the faces of the people. . . . Some would say, 'What did you do to me?' "[157] There were no empirical measures; all that remained were millions of subjective experiences.

An important change in Roberts's healing concept occurred when he came to broaden his definition of healing in the late 1950s to mean "wholeness." Actually, from the beginning of his ministry, Oral taught that man was composed of body, soul, and mind, but that "we are a unit." "Life is a whole," he preached to his radio audience in 1949, and the "miracle of your healing begins within."[158] The quest for wholeness meant that "healing is not an end in itself but a means to that infinitely greater miracle, the conversion of the soul. It leads people to understand that God is concerned about their whole being—the spiritual AND the physical."[159] But Oral used the words long before he developed his full-blown philosophy of wholeness: "I used the terms, 'be made whole,' but I didn't know what I was saying because I was thinking about praying for an arm or an ear or some part of the body. I began to realize that people had to be healed in their spirit as well as the body. This was a transformation of my own thinking."[160]

In the 1960s, before the founding of the university, Roberts was clearly preaching not physical healing but "wholeness": "It is the recognition that one is a spirit, mind and body. . . . And we must move simultaneously and harmoniously in one direction, spiritually, intellectually, physically, moving toward wholeness. Now that becomes a way of life. . . . Otherwise, you are just part of a human being."[161] "Through the years I learned that whole-man healing is really what Jesus is talking about when He uses the term, 'Be made whole.' "[162] Year after year, Oral instructed those in his healing lines to reach out for more than a physical cure: "Some person says it will be great to be healed in my body but I can tell you people who have strong bodies, without a pain, who are absolutely miserable. So we know healing of the body, however precious, can not be an end in itself. I know people who are right with God but who have problems in their families, and they become ill. What I think we need this morning is to begin to be made whole."[163]

What human beings needed were lives that were full and rewarding in every way—they needed wholeness.

It was the quest for wholeness which led Roberts relentlessly toward the merging of prayer and medicine in the 1980s. That unlikely wedding of modern science and religious supernaturalism became increasingly plausible to a wide variety of people in the mid-twentieth century, but no one sought the union more dramatically than Oral Roberts. Curious though the combination seemed, it was consistent with Oral's long-held beliefs.

Roberts's affirmation of medical science was well documented. In the first volume of *Healing Waters,* he wrote: "I have the highest respect for the highly skilled men and women who are devoting their lives for a healthier world. There is no conflict between God's healing power wrought through faith and prayer and the doctors' efforts to bring a cure through earthly means."[164] Over and over Oral counseled his partners not to refuse medical treatment lest they be considered "queer, odd, eccentric, unintelligent."[165]

Roberts's endorsement of medical science disturbed some of his supporters. Pentecostal extremists "took offense," but Oral believed he led many to accept his view. Years later, he speculated that his public announcement that his children had taken Salk vaccine had "changed the tide" in an area where "thousands of people would not take it."[166] Even in the 1980s, Oral thought that many of his active partners were "people who don't go to doctors, who need to go to doctors."[167]

All healing comes from God, Roberts believed; anything which assisted it was God-ordained. In 1951, he thought that divine healing went beyond medical science: "My work begins where medical science ends. . . . I alone cannot heal a person, but God working through me has healed many."[168] In later years, however, he saw medicine and prayer as complementary. In 1963, Oral outlined three forms of healing—"medical healing," which was concerned with eliminating sickness; "psychiatry and psychology," which "assists the person in accenting the positive"; and "healing by faith," in which the "total man" was healed.[169] "Oral Roberts has always believed in prayer and medicine," declared the advertisements announcing the opening of the City of Faith. "He knows he cannot heal, just as physicians know they cannot heal. . . . According to Oral Roberts, medicine and surgery are God's instruments, and prayer and faith are God's instruments as well."[170]

Early in his healing ministry, Oral coveted the recognition of physicians; he advertised the endorsement of some with dubious credentials.[171] In later years, he was more reserved in claiming support, noting in 1957 that "some have attended our meetings and in rare instances have even come in the prayer line with the patients." By the late 1950s, Roberts recognized that most physicians were "reluctant to have their names publicly associated with healing by faith."[172] His admiration for physicians remained genuine, however; he believed they were working against a common foe: "I've never been turned away by a doctor. In the height of my ministry when it seemed like the whole world was against me, . . . and I'd get sick right in the middle of a crusade, I'd call a doctor . . . and he'd receive me, treat me courteously. He treated me better than some of my fellow pastors treated me. . . . They are against disease and they are for health."[173]

With the passage of time, Oral believed that he "began to win a little with the doctors," but "they had no way to express themselves in my favor."[174] In 1968, he told a class at ORU: "The relationship I have with doctors is on a growing scale. The more they know about me, the more they appreciate us. The less they know about us, the less they appreciate us. When they learn that I use medicine and I use doctors, they are impressed by that. When they know that we have a doctor on campus, they are impressed by that."[175] In 1964, Oral spoke before about twenty members of the Tulsa Christian Medical Society, concluding that "you and I agree on 95% of our work. Let's not let the 5% stand between us."[176]

Two developments opened the way for Roberts to explore his vision of combining medical science with religious healing. First, the charismatic movement attracted reputable physicians to spirit-filled religion. Most important of Roberts's charismatic physician friends was William Standish Reed, a prominent Michigan surgeon who was a devout Episcopal layman and a member of the administrative committee of the Order of Saint Luke, a historic Episcopalian organization devoted to prayer for healing. Reed gave a powerful boost in credibility to Roberts: "There is only one Oral Roberts. And I don't see too many people going out and preaching this Word and healing the multitudes, being seized by Christ's compassion and healing them all."[177] Reed skillfully placed the charismatic concept of wholeness in a medical framework. He summarized his ideas in a speech at ORU in 1964:

> Wholeness, what is it? The extraordinary attribute of unusual men who have left the world and come to Jesus. . . . We need to open the field of the logo-psychosomatic. The logos is the spirit of man, the psychi is the mind of man, and the somatic is the body of man. . . . We need someone who has the syn-

thetic mind, who can take all of these various aspects of man and put us back together again. . . . The only kind of doctors that can fill this particular bill are those who are baptized with the Holy Ghost because they do not know otherwise what the spirit is.[178]

Oral's call and Reed's vision had much in common; in 1964 the Episcopalian physician joined Roberts in a crusade and ministered with him in the "invalid tent," forming, reported *Abundant Life*, a "unique combination of medical science and healing through faith."[179] By the 1970s, physicians had become increasingly visible in the Roberts ministry; some were included on the ORU board of regents.[180] When the ORU medical school was begun, William S. Reed heralded it as the natural culmination of the charismatic revival: "The new medical school is seen as a natural evolutionary outcome resulting from the American spiritual revolution of the last two decades. America is beginning to insist upon Christian care and Christian physicians and nurses. Hundreds of thousands of charismatic and evangelical Christians across America are beginning to request compassionate Christian care."[181]

Outside the charismatic movement, there was a growing awareness among physicians that modern medical science, for all its accomplishments, had fallen far short of introducing a millennium of health and well-being. The Christian Medical Commission of the World Council of Churches, spurred on by the writings of distinguished Swiss physician and author Paul Tournier, turned its attention increasingly to discovering a "medicine for the whole man." The commission's reports in the 1980s not only endorsed "wholistic medicine," including the need to minister to man's spirit as well as his body, but also explored the values of nonwestern medical systems and entertained the possibility of miracles.[182] The explorations of the Christian Medical Commission in the 1980s were remarkably akin to those of Roberts, though William S. Reed supplied the only tenuous contact between the two.

Equally visible in the United States in the 1980s was the wholistic medical philosophy of Granger Westberg. Westberg sponsored the establishment of a number of health centers designed to promote "wellness" as a result of spiritual and physical counseling, arguing that the drift of medical science had been too much toward the curing of illness rather than the preservation of health by ministering to the whole man.[183] Westberg's ideas had considerable impact on American hospitals in the 1980s; among those incorporating his ideas was the Hillcrest Medical Center in Tulsa. When the City of Faith opened, the *Tulsa World* noted that Westberg's centers had received the endorsement of the American Medical Association and pointed out that Roberts's approach to healing was similar.[184] Hillcrest hospital administrator James D. Harvey took exception to the comparison, noting that Westberg made a distinction between his "wholistic" system, which was "distinctly religious and frankly in the Judaeo-Christian tradition," and the health movement generally known by the name "holistic," which was "a mixture of occultism and Eastern philosophies, including Hindu, Buddhism, and others."[185] The editor replied with some indignation that Harvey had apparently dismissed "the evangelist (and, presumably, those who share his beliefs) from the Judaeo-Christian tradition," adding that both Westberg and Roberts were examples of the growing willingness to mix religion and medicine. The issue was not "what kind of medical and religious treatment people choose for themselves."[186]

Although many people questioned the way in which Oral Roberts combined medicine and prayer in the 1980s, the idea of combining the two had become avant garde. In 1958, Oral told a reporter visiting one of his crusades: "I hope God lets me live another 30 years, for I think by then we'll see an unbelievably close alliance between science and the kind of healing I encourage. The doctors are finding out that their medicines don't always help."[187] The statement had an eerily prophetic ring in the 1980s.[188]

In the mid-1980s, Roberts was still searching for the full meaning of combining prayer and medicine. He wanted more than the ordinary ministerial comfort by hospital chaplains. Oral had never liked to visit hospitals; in a lecture in 1967, he frankly explained:

> Most doctors I know will accept your comfort for his patient, but he does not want your healing for his patients. . . . Hospitals are not designed for the healing of sick by prayer. They just aren't. I suppose the hardest thing in the world for me is to pray for a sick person in a hospital, unless I come to give him comfort rather than healing. He doesn't expect to be healed. I could number on my hand the people who I thought wanted to be healed when I prayed for them in a hospital. They want to get well, but they are not necessarily interested in getting healed through your prayer.[189]

The concept that slowly germinated in Oral's mind, honed during a decade of discussion and friendship with Jim Winslow, was to train physicians who could treat mind, body, and spirit, and, finally, to build a hospital where prayer was not only allowed but where it was considered an equal partner in the healing of the sick. Prayer and medicine, estranged by the domineering ascendancy of modern science, were going to be joined together—"The bridge is being built, and the gulf is being closed."[190] Oral's old friend and teacher William Standish Reed, having become head of an organization of 3,500 charismatic physicians and a world-renowned lecturer on "holistic medicine," visited Tulsa in 1979 to pronounce his benediction on the new hospital. He pronounced the City of Faith a milestone in moving "vital Pentecostal holiness Christianity out of the periphery."[191]

It was a herculean task. "Oral Roberts isn't kidding himself," he told a Tulsa audience in 1981. "I understand the struggle we're in. We need the kind of physician who will pioneer, who will stick, who will go through this type of thing with us, deal with people who are so divided in the way they've been taught about their health."[192] The City of Faith experiment was still in its early stages in 1984, but the theory of healing behind it had been refined for decades and would, no doubt, survive.

ROBERTS'S theology of healing contained several minor planks. Perhaps most controversial was his teaching of seed-faith, a concept which blossomed in the

1970s and became Oral's major fund-raising message. Seed-faith was rooted, however, in Roberts's early discovery that personal prosperity was endorsed by God in III John: 1, 2, and it grew with his increasing feeling that poverty was an oppression which needed healing as much as a physical disease. In another striking confluence with liberal theology, though independently arrived at, Oral came to conclude that sickness was generally related to poverty and social oppression.

Although the theme was more muted during the early days of Oral's healing ministry, almost from the beginning he told his working-class audiences, many of whom had lionized poverty as they had rejected medical science, that "I think it's God's will for us to prosper materially. . . . God will see to it if we have faith that we have our proper share."[193] By the mid-1950s, the message had become clearer:

> God changed my thinking and I'll preach it across America. Many of our preachers have had no homes . . . and they've heard me preach and gone out and believed this thing and God gave them a home and a better church . . . and supplied their needs, and they deserved their needs to be met. And some of you people out there have better jobs because you've heard this preached and you deserve a better job. . . . Use your faith and get what you need and use the rest for the glory of God. . . . Pay your debts. . . . He will help to supply the money to pay them.[194]

"Gradually," wrote Oral in 1974, "the Spirit began to show me that in the Bible healing is for the whole man. It's for the body, it's for the soul, it's for the mind, for finances. It's for any problem that needs to be healed."[195]

Most of the principles of Roberts's teaching on seed-faith were visible in the 1950s and 1960s, when he developed the "Blessing Pact" and "Prayer Pact" covenants with his partners, promising to pray for their prosperity.[196] The full development of the idea came in 1970, however, with the publication of *The Miracle of Seed-Faith,* a book that quickly surpassed one million copies in distribution.[197] According to Evelyn, "the controversy and turmoil" surrounding Oral's move to the Methodist church drove him "back to the Bible," and he emerged with the "three spiritual laws of Seed-Faith."[198] Roberts believed that he had discovered the true New Testament principle of giving, replacing the Old Testament concept of tithing. "In the Old Testament, you gave because you owed it," he explained. "It was a DEBT. You didn't give your tithe or your ten percent—you PAID it." In the New Testament, mankind's debt had been paid by Jesus, and people should expect "a great blessing."[199]

The first "key principle" of seed-faith was that "God is your source." Oral cited Phillippians 4:19: "My God shall supply all your need according to his riches in glory by Christ Jesus."[200] The promise meant that God would supply "abundantly" the "material" needs of His children, not just the "bare essentials of existence." There were no limits to the riches of God. More important, however, one depended not on man but on God to supply his needs. "If you can grasp the three key principles of seed-faith, and joyously apply them in your personal life," Oral told the ORU students in 1971, "they'll be dynamite. You won't have to worry about the money for next semester or the summer. You won't have to worry about a job. . . . You won't have to worry about whether you should or should not marry, or what girl or what boy. . . . Because you'll be taking it out of man's hands, and putting it in God's. And you'll come to know Him as your source."[201]

The second "key principle" was "Give that it may be given to you." The proof-text was Luke 6:38: "Give, and it shall be given unto you; good measure, pressed down, shaken together, and running over, shall men give into your bosom. For with the same measure that ye mete withal it shall be measured to you again."[202] In a wide variety of ways, Oral argued that giving was the key to receiving. Harvesting resulted from sowing seed. In a novel interpretation of the atonement, he argued that God sowed the seed of his son, Jesus, in order to receive the harvest of redeemed mankind. Seed-faith, he believed, was "the microcosm of the gospel."[203] "So we never ask anyone to give to us because we need it," Roberts avowed in 1976. "I know our churches do it every Sunday. But that's really not the Bible way. God's way is to meet a need in another person's life. . . . So I say, don't give to me because I have a need. You give because you have a need."[204] He extolled selfless giving as God's road to abundance, whether the gift was money, effort, time, talent, love, compassion, or forgiveness—planting a seed led to a harvest.[205] "You take a marriage that's in trouble and you get those partners to giving to each other and giving first," he explained, "it solves the marriage problem overnight. It solves the problem between a parent and children. It solves problems in the city. The moment we start giving, expressing our love through our gifts, then we start receiving."[206]

The third "key principle" was "Expect a miracle."[207] Many of Roberts's associates considered the third principle the "breakthrough," because people had been taught to give, but they had not expected to receive in return.[208] The return might not be immediate, Oral warned, but it would come: "Now in seed-faith God is going to meet your need, but no one knows when and no one knows how."[209] At that point he returned to his old exhortation, "Release your faith, God will send the miracle."[210]

In the early 1970s, seed-faith became the dominant theme in Roberts's teaching; seed-faith testimonials far outweighed healing testimonials in *Abundant Life,* and Oral spoke repeatedly on the subject to Methodist pastors. In one month in 1970, testimonials in *Abundant Life* announced: "A Raise, Plus a Bonus"; "New Job as General Manager"; "A Bonus Surprise from Day to Day"; and "Sales Have Tripled."[211] Oral believed the concept could rejuvenate his new church. It clearly provided a boost for his own ministry. As he "shared his message with Methodists in many cities," Evelyn wrote, "his ministry took on a new vitality. New partners began to warmly receive Oral and his messages."[212] Seed-faith theology was the financial message which allowed the huge expansion of the Roberts ministry in the late 1970s.

Seed-faith was, of course, controversial. However explained, it had the sound of a "gimmick" to raise funds, and it offended people inside and outside the ministry.[213] Oral insisted that he was not asking for contributions when he taught seed-faith: "If you don't do it with us, do it with somebody who's doing

God's work."[214] He simply claimed an equal right to present his claims in the open market for seed-planting. "If I were a Methodist pastor," he told a group of clergymen in a brisk confrontation on seed-faith in 1977, "I know what I'd do. . . . There's Oklahoma City University . . . and there's missions. . . . I'd buy them, or I'd get out of the church. . . . Then I'd say, which of these projects is yours?"[215] Roberts was disappointed that he never made much headway in getting his concept accepted in Methodist churches.[216]

Others questioned seed-faith because it sounded like "bribing God."[217] Oral was repeatedly pressed by questioners about "bargaining" with God. Did he believe divine love could be won through a crass materialistic manipulation? He returned over and over to Biblical texts that commended giving and receiving, and to his theory that God planted Jesus Christ in hope of a harvest. Perhaps most telling, Oral insisted that seed-faith was nothing more or less than the natural principle of planting and harvesting. "What do you do as a farmer when you put the seed in the ground?" he asked a questioner. "Are you bargaining? . . . If you plant your wheat you're doing a secular but a spiritual thing too. And why are you planting it? Without a question, you're planting it for a harvest. . . . Seedtime and harvest will not cease."[218] The genius of seed-faith was that it seemed to capture a self-evident "principle of life."[219] Oral recognized that: "I think that there is a seed-faith concept outside of Christianity. . . . I see it as people stumbling on to that much of the truth. I know businessmen who practice having good merchandise . . . who'll return your money without question. They're practicing that much of the seed-faith concept. And they've built a great business on it."[220] Charles Farah agreed that the principle of sowing and reaping had been used by evangelists to satisfy their own "incredible human greed," but, although he had participated in many partners' seminars on the ORU campus, he insisted that "I've never seen that in Oral," even though he may sometimes be "heard that way."[221]

ROBERTS'S "secondary call . . . to help bring healing to the sick body of the bride of Christ" proved to be the most elusive of all his healing goals.[222] He always tried to be respectful of organized religion, of the institutional church, but he had little success with them in his John the Baptist role. "He sees institutional churches as poor models," acknowledged Jim Buskirk, "they are often structures that won't move."[223]

Increasingly in the 1980s, Roberts seemed ready to bypass the organized church to bring healing to the "body of Christ." He insisted that he, his students, and his partners were "as much a church as anybody in the world if not more so."[224] The church was Christians, wherever they might be, within or without the boundaries of organized religion.[225] "He sees the church more for her *kerygma,* what she teaches, than he does for the *koinonia,* the fellowship. . . . His fellowship is in a group of people here," observed Buskirk.[226] Oral told his ORU family in 1980: "This place right here where we open our Bibles and read and study together, sing together, pray together, we assemble together as the Body of Christ. This is the church as much as there is any church upon this earth."[227]

James Buskirk still hoped in the mid-1980s that Oral's call to bring healing to the body of Christ would come through the renewal of the institutional church, by producing dedicated pastors, "for which the church is bleeding and dying."[228] But it became increasingly clear that Roberts was prepared to act outside the denominational system through his healing teams and the independent charismatic movement.

ORAL'S healing message was based on a broader theology of the Holy Spirit. Christians, he believed, were sick "to the extent that they are divided, they are sick to the extent that they don't know about the gifts of the Spirit. They don't know about God's great healing power."[229] Individual healing and the healing of the Christian world must come through a restoration of the New Testament spiritual gifts. Explaining and activating the gifts of the Holy Spirit, the central legacy of modern pentecostalism, became for Oral Roberts a means of bringing healing to the body of Christ.

Oral's early views of the Holy Spirit were purely pentecostal; they remained so until the early 1960s. His writing and preaching echoed orthodox pentecostal views; speaking in tongues was the "sign" of the baptism which "every true Christian must receive." He boasted that the "full-gospel" churches which preached "true pentecost" were "God's last outposts between you and modernism." While Roberts taught that "the Baptism of the Holy Ghost brings resistless power," he deemphasized speaking in tongues, a gift which he "rarely" used. Roberts's views remained conventional through the 1950s, though he said remarkably little about the baptism with the Holy Spirit in his crusades.[230]

In the early 1960s, Oral began to radically revise his teaching on the Holy Spirit. He became increasingly impatient with pentecostal bickering over minor theological distinctions, but even more with what he regarded as a symbolic rather than a functional understanding of the baptism.[231] Asked in 1967 if he considered "tongues speaking . . . the initial experience," the cardinal test of pentecostal orthodoxy, Oral replied: "I never use that term myself. . . . I've been raised on that. I accept it, but I don't like to use that term because it suggests that you don't speak in tongues continuously the rest of your life. And I was injured by that."[232]

In later years, Oral frequently expressed resentment about pentecostal misuse of the Holy Spirit. He felt that pentecostals had suppressed the power they had discovered. Among the benefits he gained by changing churches in 1968 was getting "out from under this denominationalizing the baptism with the Holy Ghost to where I could be a free man."[233] Usually, however, Oral expressed gratitude for his pentecostal upbringing; he believed that his new views were the result of natural growth:

> I'll never cease to thank God that I was raised by Pentecostal parents. But the Pentecostal parents did not have the dimension of the Charismatic outworkings of the baptism of the Holy Ghost. Maybe they weren't raised up for that purpose. They were, as a general group, an unlearned people. But they had an experience. And the church owes them a debt. But they were not theologians.

They were not able to apply the workings of the baptism beyond an ecstatic emotional experience of reality in their own lives and helping the other person get the same thing he had. . . . I feel that the Lord has been merciful to me and allowed me to have more of a revelation, which I should have as a second-generation Pentecostal.[234]

The general source of Oral's new understanding of the baptism with the Holy Spirit was the emerging charismatic movement in the mainstream churches. "Now the historical people who have come in have added great strength to us," he told a group of students in 1967, "because they are more Charismatic than the Pentecostals are. That is, they dwell upon the application of the Holy Spirit through the gifts of the Spirit to a particular need."[235] In the swirling debates over the Holy Spirit in the 1960s, Roberts was in his element. His restless and curious mind was receptive to new ideas. Reacting to questions from students in 1967, he admitted: "I don't have the answers for you today. I can't feed you out of a spoon, and you can't feed me out of a spoon. We are going to have to hammer out some of these answers."[236] A few months later, he asked: "Where in history has there been a seminary class that reached out and pulled in the Charismatic men (people like myself) and we sit down and talk frankly. When has there ever been a studied effort to discover the Charismatic theology? Oh, I'm expecting mighty things to come out of here. It's going to shed light on all theology."[237] Through the years, especially in his class on "The Holy Spirit in the Now," Roberts came as near as possible to "hammering out" a consensus charismatic view of the Holy Spirit.

The chief charismatic revision of pentecostal theology held that speaking in tongues was a "prayer language" with a practical use, as opposed to a symbolic evidence of the baptism with the Holy Spirit. The new theology also made clear the distinction between the use of tongues for "personal edification" and the "gift of tongues." In 1969, the Oral Roberts University *Bulletin* summarized the charismatic view:

> The baptism with the Holy Spirit is an experience which brings an enduement of Christ's power to the Christian, the ability of speaking in tongues for personal edification, and enables him to be a more effective witness of Jesus Christ, the Son of God (Acts 1:8; 2:1–4; I Corinthians 14: 2, 4, 14; Ephesians 6:18).
>
> The nine gifts are resident in the Holy Spirit and are manifested by Him through the believer to meet special needs. (I Corinthians 12: 7–11) . . .
>
> The Gift of the Word of Wisdom—for making decisions in harmony with the highest will of God. The Gift of the Word of Knowledge—for a clearer perception of knowledge and a deeper insight into truth beyond sense perception. The Gift of Faith—to be rid of doubt and to bring an inner certainty, a knowing that God will intervene and act. The Gift of Healing—for the emergence of compassion and inner compulsion, using faith, in cooperation with the natural and supernatural, to bring healing to the whole man. The Gift of Working of Miracles—for the releasing of divine power that settles an issue, that breaks through the humanly impossible. The Gift of Prophecy—for inspired utterance that interprets hidden meanings of truth. The Gift of Discern-

ing of Spirits—to identify correctly and understand how to deal with various spirits which manifest themselves through man. The Gift of Tongues—for personal and corporate edification of the intellect through the revelation of the hidden meaning of the message spoken, bringing understanding to the mind as well as the spirit.[238]

During the decade of the 1970s, Oral fleshed out his new undertaking of the Holy Spirit in several ways. Some of his new beliefs were reflected in the statement in the ORU *Bulletin* in 1983. First, the difference between the "baptism in the Holy Spirit" and the "nine gifts resident in the Holy Spirit" was emphasized: "The baptism in the Holy Spirit with the Spirit-given ability to pray and praise God in tongues in one's private or personal devotions IS NOT THE GIFT OF TONGUES. . . . Not all believers exercise the GIFT OF TONGUES, JUST AS ALL WOULD NOT MANIFEST A GIFT OF HEALING (I. Cor. 12:30)." While the university "enthusiastically and officially accepts the work of the Holy Spirit in the operation of these gifts," it also recognized that they were granted by the Holy Spirit "as He wills" and were not a part of the experience of all Christians.[239] The gifts were particularly subject to abuse by those who claimed the leading of the Holy Spirit. Oral had never tolerated tongues speaking in his meetings, and in later years he still believed "from years of practical experience that it is seldom beneficial to have a message in tongues in a large gathering."[240] Roberts, and other veteran pentecostals, considered the use of the "gifts" by the new charismatics dangerously antinomian, and they sought to establish boundaries. Generally speaking, they concluded that the prophetic gifts were "more confirmational than . . . directional" and that they "must always be judged by the Word of God."[241]

Central to Oral's new view of the Holy Spirit was his awakening to the "prayer language" which was available to every Christian. In the late 1960s and 1970s, he began teaching that the "baptism of the Holy Spirit" had an "extra dimension," or a "second stage," which had a number of practical uses for early Christians:

> *First,* they received a new language of prayer and praise in which they could release their inner selves (Acts 2:30–32).
> *Second,* they understood the Person of Christ, that He is not dead; He's alive in the now—alive forevermore! (Acts 2:30–32).
> *Third,* they understood that the Spirit would convict people of their sins, that if they would preach under the anointing of God people would be convicted and would come to Christ (Acts 2:37).
> *Fourth,* they developed a holy boldness which they had not had before. (Remember, they fled at the death of Christ.) (Acts 4:13).
> *Finally,* they moved into a supernatural level that seemed almost completely foreign to them during the 3 years when Jesus's physical presence had been on the earth (Acts 3).[242]

While the belief that "power" came from the baptism of the Holy Spirit was not new, some of Roberts's other ideas were.[243] His notion that the baptism of the Holy Spirit corresponded with a kind of personal indwelling of Christ was novel: "We seek the invisible, unlimited form, the Holy Spirit, who is the

Christ raised from the dead, alive forevermore and in our hearts and in Him resides all of the gifts and all the fruit of the Spirit. If I'll just seek Christ, He's got them all."[244] That view was reflected in an addition to the university *Bulletin,* which read: "It is the work of the Holy Spirit to reproduce our Lord's life in each one of us."[245]

Most important, however, was Oral's exploration of the prayer language, "the rivers of the Holy Spirit flowing up out of your belly—out of your innermost being (John 7:39, 39)."[246] He developed a concrete method for teaching others how to receive the experience: "First you have to stop speaking in your own language for a moment. . . . You simply stop praying and praising God in English. . . . Second, you have to open your mouth."[247] Then, out of the "deepest depths of our being—down in our belly," bypassing the intellect, would come a "prayer language" speaking to God, an utterance freed from "inhibitions, hidden resentments, repressions and scars that are embedded in the human spirit."[248] After praying to God in tongues, Roberts believed he could "interpret back to my mind," enabling him to pray with "understanding." "This sounds simplistic," Oral observed in his "Holy Spirit in the Now" class, "but this is really the way it is—praying in the Spirit (tongues) opens up your mind more keenly to the will of God and to a clearer understanding of what is in His mind for you (Romans 8: 26, 27)."[249] After he discovered the use of the prayer language, Oral reported, the whole world "looked different"; it was the release his burdened soul had been craving during the early years of the university.[250] Oral's lectures about the "therapeutic value" of tongues were a "major breakthrough" in pentecostal theology. According to Robert Voight, "It took the infilling of the spirit and speaking in tongues out of the emotional and put it over into the intellectual."[251]

Roberts's later view of the baptism of the Holy Spirit and the prayer language meshed easily with mainstream and Catholic charismatic theology. The baptism was not a badge of superiority, it was a tool of "inner healing" available to all Christians. One additional step was required, however, to ease tensions between charismatics and non-tongues-speaking evangelicals. Did the "enduement" of the Spirit enjoyed by charismatics differ in kind from that vested in other Christians? Oral increasingly moved toward the Catholic view that in every Christian "the Holy Spirit has already come in and you have an open door to a deeper level of communication with God."[252]

In the 1960s, Oral had publicly worried about a theology which denied the baptism with the Holy Spirit to all nonpentecostals. His admiration of Billy Graham and other evangelical Christians made him unwilling to question their spirituality. In a 1967 class at the university, he confessed: "I believe that Billy has a measure of baptism with the Holy Spirit. At this point I will get in all kinds of opposition with theologians. I often say, which comes first, tongues or the baptism of the Holy Ghost. The baptism of the Holy Spirit comes first. Now at what time does one start speaking in tongues? This is an unresolved question."[253] Like Catholic charismatics, Roberts came to believe that the gifts of the Holy Spirit resided dormant in the whole Christian church, ready to be reemphasized and resurrected by the charismatic movement.[254]

Charismatic theology remains in its formative stage—still "fluid" and fragmented.[255] Charles Farah believed that Oral's migration had kept him in "a centrist position from the very beginning. I have never seen him in any excess."[256] Jim Buskirk found Oral in the same position, in the very center of the charismatic thought—not by design, believed Buskirk; "he just happens to be there."[257] As always he stood poised, ready to move, asking questions, refining and polishing his teachings. All that remained inviolate was the message that God offered healing to man.

CHAPTER

XVII

The Man

"ORAL IS NOT A PERSON. He is not an evangelist. He is a phenomenon," conjectured his friend John Williams.[1] Roberts played so many different roles that he once told Bob Foresman and Jenkin Lloyd Jones that he had "worn thirty-two different hats in his life including author, television personality, educator, developer, publisher, civic leader, and a man who knows his way through the thorniest financial thickets."[2] "Is he a fraud? Is he a con artist? Or is he the messiah?" acerbically asked one of his critics.[3] Was there an answer to such pointed questions?

Most observers agree that Roberts is a bright human being. "Oral Roberts is a man of great intellect," wrote Demos Shakarian in 1951, "he is a learned man."[4] While Oral's learning was clearly practical and not scholarly, in native ability Wayne Robinson judged him to be "incredibly brilliant," and Tulsa reporter Bob Foresman considered him "highly intelligent."[5] "He's a man of the earth," observed Al Bush, "a very gut level man who understands basic primal emotions."[6] Calvin Thielman compared Roberts to Lyndon Johnson, whom he also knew: "Oral . . . has a huge amount of native brains. He's got a lot of crudeness, a lot of earthiness . . . and a lot of things that are sort of dumb."[7]

Oral's powerful mind depended on two almost contradictory gifts—an extraordinary ability to focus and a capacity to conceptualize in sweeping generalizations and theories. "One on one he's awfully good," said his nephew Bill Roberts of Oral's capacity to lock his attention on one person.[8] His attention to an idea was just as vicelike—he would pursue an idea relentlessly, perhaps for months on end, thinking of little else, grinding and wearing on those around him. On the other hand, James Buskirk marveled at Oral's "comprehensive sweeping vision," which frequently clashed with the "specialized" learning of scholars. He was a theological "generalist," who roamed fearlessly in areas where specialists feared to venture.[9]

Roberts was a vociferous reader. Collins Steele remembered him reading every evening after his crusade services; Wayne Robinson often sat silently beside him on long airplane flights while Oral read for hours.[10] "I study books all the time," he told a group of students in 1976, "I read thirty magazines a month. I finish one to two big books a week while carrying on my work."[11] By and large, his reading was popular rather than scholarly; his excursion into theology in the 1960s was burdensome to him. Reporting to an early advisory council at the university, Oral acknowledged that he "must be informed, knowledgeable." He listed among the magazines that he read regularly *Life, Look, Time, Newsweek, U.S. News and World Report, Fortune, Atlantic Monthly, Harper's, Reader's Digest,* and *Nation's Business.*[12]

More important than his intellectual ability, and certainly more so than his learning, Roberts had, in the words of John Williams, "command presence." Williams often pleased Oral by telling him that if he had not been an evangelist, he could have been the "head salesman" for Williams's mammoth corporation.[13] Few of the successful Tulsans who knew Oral best doubted that he would have been a leader in any field. Jenkin Lloyd Jones, Jr., not one of Oral's great admirers, told Chicago reporter Bruce Buursma in 1982: "I really think that if Oral hadn't made a good living off God, he'd be president of General Motors. He can reduce a $500,000-a-year corporate executive to jelly. We call him the fastest tambourine in the West."[14]

Roberts's influence over people who knew him well rested on his ability to communicate utter sincerity and honesty. Some critics believed that he was "self-deluded, having obscured in his own mind the distinction between himself and God."[15] But, by and large, beginning with his fellow pentecostals in the late 1940s, Oral told people that he was "sincere and honest and they believed me."[16] No one believed it more than the bright young men who passed through the upper echelons of the Roberts ministry. Those who left—Bush, Robinson, Smith, Hamilton, Buskirk—were the keenest observers of Oral's character, and the truest believers. "There's not a fraudulent bone in his body," observed Ron Smith.[17] While many of his friends questioned Oral's methods and agreed that he had a large capacity to "rationalize," all agreed with Warren Hultgren: "He believes in what he is doing deeply."[18]

Oral thought he deserved that much from his critics, and his latent persecution complex flared when his personal integrity was questioned. He had been a good citizen of Tulsa, an honest businessman; he had been discreet in his private and public conduct: "I had to prove myself before my message could be heard and I went around trying to show them that I'm real."[19] His public behavior had always been moral, courteous, and controlled. Warren Hultgren judged him to be "one of the most even-tempered and self-controlled people I have ever known"; he had often witnessed Oral shed personal abuse and ridicule without retaliation. Bob DeWeese believed that there was "not one man in a million that has the strength of character . . . that could have withstood the temptations . . . and the testings of all this time."[20] Oral and Evelyn tried to live by their convictions, and they had taught them to their children.[21] What more could they do to prove their sincerity, Roberts wondered:

> I remember through the years of traveling this nation and the world when I was called a crook and a charlatan and everything that they could think of that the devil helped them think of some new [names] that man hadn't thought of . . . and it was so bad I wanted to shoot myself. . . . I knew I was honest. I knew I never cheated anybody. I knew I didn't lie. I knew I never desired another woman except my wife. I knew it. They didn't know it, but I knew it.[22]

If Oral's public life did not convince everyone that he was honest, his personal presence frequently did persuade doubters. Face-to-face he was disarmingly straightforward, admitting weaknesses, tolerant of disagreement, and firm in his own convictions.[23] It was his transparent sincerity which reporter Beth Macklin observed win over a Tulsa Ministerial Alliance meeting which had opened "full of animosity," and which stirred Billy Graham's Berlin conference and pushed Oral into the evangelical world. Over and over again, in conversations with reporters and academic leaders, in speeches to his family at the university and to audiences in person and on television, Oral opened his heart with childlike candor—exposing his weaknesses and problems, repenting and asking for help. It was easy to question what Oral Roberts did; it was difficult to impugn what he felt.

Nothing neutralized Roberts's critics more than his candid confessions of his own faults. Of course, those faults were visible enough to those who knew him best. "Evelyn is a jewel to have lived with him," observed Oral's attorney and friend Don Moyers. "I love him very much, but I don't know whether I could take him on a daily basis at all."[24] Oral's "foibles and weaknesses," observed John Williams, "bother a tremendous number of people," keeping them from appreciating the "total phenomenon."[25]

Most visible of those "foibles" was, to use Oral's term, his "irritability."[26] Roberts repeatedly confessed that he had been irritable with his mother during his childhood illness, with the sick in his healing lines, with his employees in the association. "I was born with a short trigger and I've been working on lengthening it and haven't got it lengthened much," he told the ORU students in 1977.[27] His temper sometimes exploded into angry harangues, in which he slowly talked out his anger. After some of the memorable displays of the Roberts temper in chapel services, Evelyn rose to try to smooth things over. "I know some of you don't like him and you don't have to," she told the students in 1972, "sometimes I don't like him either, but I love him."[28] Oral's anger could turn abusive and unreasoning; it often made him a difficult taskmaster. It was a burden some capable people within the ministry ultimately rebelled against.

Roberts also has often been accused of lacking personal warmth.[29] "I remember that while touching people was important," said Al Bush, "yet people never thought he was warm."[30] Oral's aloofness was partly a product of his celebrity status. When not ministering, explained Demos Shakarian, "he likes to be left alone. He's tired."[31] Drained by public performance, he had little emotion left for personal encounters. But there were other reasons. Oral found it impossible to have a close relationship with any woman besides Evelyn; Patti remembered that his greeting for her was not a hug but a pat on the back.[32] More than anything else, Oral's call virtually precluded deep personal relationships. While his call was to minister to people, his obsession was not the people but the call. Everyone he came into contact with became an actor in that larger drama.

In his ministering, Roberts always made a distinction between compassion and sympathy. Compassion, which he believed was a desire to help one in need, was the heart of his call; sympathy, which was comforting the suffering, he had little time for. After leaving the ministry, Al Bush suffered an automobile accident in Los Angeles which nearly took his life and seriously interrupted his business career. Returned to a Tulsa hospital in a serious condition, Bush received a visit from Oral. "Al, I didn't want to come, but Evelyn said I ought to," Oral began. After a few words, he concluded, "I'm here and I want to tell you . . . to get over it and get up." Then, he turned and left.[33] There was no sympathy, only compassion. As well as he knew Oral, Al Bush was stunned; but he was also moved, "it just revolutionized him."[34]

ALL OF Oral Roberts's life was controlled by two primal drives—a relentless restlessness and a sense of divine calling. They were perhaps the same drive in secular and religious versions. They were powerful, unquenchable motivations. Oral searched endlessly for explanations of the spiritual drive, surrounding it with a theology for intuition. He knew less about the general sources of his discontent, though he was not completely naive about them.

The fact that Roberts had an immense drive was obvious. To recognize that her husband was a "funny person," quipped Evelyn, all one had to do was notice "the way ORU looks."[35] "There is a name that you can put to my husband," she observed in 1981, "it is c-h-a-n-g-e . . . Oral c-h-a-n-g-e Roberts."[36] A favorite line on campus, which Oral repeated about himself, was that "when I die and they bury me that I'll put up one finger . . . above the dirt and say, 'Let me build one more building.' "[37] He could not stop; he could not be satisfied. Asked in 1976 if he felt a sense of satisfaction looking out across the ORU campus, he replied: "I've never been satisfied in my life. I'm not satisfied with what we've got, or with my own performance. I entered this ministry because I was dissatisfied . . . and I'm dissatisfied today. . . . I want to build the best thing the world's ever had."[38]

Roberts's insatiable appetite for accomplishment and recognition lent intensity to his whole life. "He takes golf seriously," observed Warren Hultgren. "When he and Richard play you'd think they were playing for the U.S. Open. He is an intense man. Which is one of his strengths and one of his weaknesses." Oral's earnestness, Hultgren believed, made him pay "a bigger price than he has to" for his success.[39] Coupled with his drive were the stormy Roberts temper and a notorious lack of a sense of humor.[40] Of course, it was intensity which built the Roberts empire. "I have never seen him back down," said his friend Demos Shakarian. "I have seen him slowed down. . . . But it got finished."[41] The price of his success was high, so high, observed Warren Hultgren, that "any normal person would have cracked."[42] Oral was far from normal.

The causes of Roberts's powerful psychological drive were visible from childhood and seem reasonably conventional. From his deprived adolescence he inherited a vivid and abiding hatred of poverty. In 1974, he said: "I began to hate poverty at about the age of three. And from there on up to seventeen, as long as I stayed home, I hated it worse. And I haven't loved poverty any better since. . . . I've had all of that I can stand. I like to prosper."[43] Oral resented the squalor of his youth, as Evelyn did her early deprivation; they both resented the poverty of their early years of marriage. They embraced prosperity both theologically and experientially, with a relief common to those who escape desperation.

Roberts was scarred by his deprived childhood. He carried through his life feelings of inadequacy born in the consciousness of a poor, stammering child who early learned that "this world can sometimes be a cruel and lonesome place in which to live."[44] Sensitive to others' feelings and to his own, Oral overcame his sense of rejection by appropriating the iron will and unquenchable spirit of Claudius. It was Claudius who was the prod in the family.[45] The Roberts home, as so often was the case with the poor, centered around Claudius. It was she who passed on to her son an indomitable will to be more than others, or he himself, judged he could be.

Roberts confessed that he had fought an "inferiority complex" throughout his life. "Every human being I am convinced has an inferiority complex," he observed in 1959. "The more I talk to people, even great men, the more I am convinced that each of us is lonely, we feel we have very few friends."[46] In a speech in chapel in 1976, Oral ruminated about his childhood. He remembered his "terribly low-esteem of myself," which "grew worse as I grew older." At times "I could not say my name." Yet, "inside" that little boy was an "understanding that if God were with him he was to expect miracles."[47] In later years both perceptions—low self-esteem and spiritual drive—would repeatedly reappear.

Oral's fear of rejection made him detest intrusions where he might not be wanted. He avoided embarrassing confrontations and preferred for his subordinates to conduct negotiations. He drew back quickly when rebuffed and was careful not to take advantage of important friendships, such as those with Billy Graham and John Williams. Roberts was frequently compelled to fight for his causes, but he despised asking for favors.

Oral's continued insecurity had ample opportunities to resurface in his dealings with professional educators. His feelings about higher education remained ambivalent in the extreme. To some extent, he carried through his life the pentecostal antiintellectualism which he had reacted against: "I don't trust education *per se*. I never have and I never will. I trust God."[48] He sometimes turned defensive about his credentials to head the university; he knew his accomplishments went down "tough with the academic community."[49] Occasionally, he felt called on to defend his abilities: "It wouldn't be a great problem for me to soon have a doctor's degree, because I have really applied myself. . . . I'm a student."[50]

The emphasis on quality in the Roberts ministry was clearly related to Oral's deprived past. From the beginning, he wanted the best tent and the best equipment. When he announced plans for the Abundant Life headquarters building in 1957, he said: "I would like to have the best building ever made. . . . For that I have to pay a price, because many people do not believe that the people of God should have anything nice. But here's one who does."[51] "Gold. He loves gold," smiled architect Frank Wallace, describing Oral's tastes. The campus glittered, and it was the best money could buy: "We don't intend for anybody to have in our field better than what we've got."[52] It was all a part, Ron Smith believed, of "his immense desire to be accepted. Not necessarily as a personality, but more as a concept."[53]

Escape from poverty also explained Oral's open embrace of a comfortable lifestyle. Like many poor boys, his personal tastes remained simple, but he liked quality "hardware," and he liked comfort.[54] While in the 1950s Oral often tried to play down his own good fortune, in the 1980s his emphasis on seed-faith made that seem unnecessary. "In addition to being something of a hedonist himself," quipped Jenkin Lloyd Jones, "maybe he's on the right track."[55]

The most recurrent manifestation of Oral's lingering childhood insecurities was his persecution complex. Roberts's feelings of persecution probably diminished some in the 1960s, but they returned in the mid-1980s. "The more my needs are met, the more I'm persecuted," he told his partners in his Bible commentary tapes.[56] While Oral's persecution complex was tied to his early deprivation, it was, of course, firmly based on reality. Whether justly or not, Roberts has probably received more criticism than any modern religious leader. The insults have sometimes been crude and personal. A basketball fan in Madison Square Garden walked over to Oral's seat to say, "You're a stiff." Roberts reportedly replied: "That's alright. God bless you."[57] "I have known him in situations in which people have been publicly unkind in his presence," said Warren Hultgren. "He has never said anything derogatory in my presence about anyone at any time. Now, I know he feels hurt and he ought to feel angry . . . but he internalizes whatever feelings he has."[58] After years of observation, Edna Nash believed that Oral handled criticism with "as much grace as anyone I have ever seen."[59]

Roberts apparently genuinely believed that he had profited from the years of scrutiny and criticism. "It's wrong in the long run not to be hit," he said in 1983. "Because you have got to know who you are."[60] Controversy and struggle were God's way to make one spiritually tough. Reflecting on the bitter fight to build the City of Faith, Oral observed: "These problems and struggles were exactly what should have been thrown against me and against those who were with me at that time. It touched us. There's no way we could have built what we have built here unless people had opposed us."[61] But the criticism pricked him; it fed the smoldering temper imprisoned inside him and the brooding self-doubts that would never be exorcised.

From his youth, Oral's spirit vacillated between euphoric highs and deep depressions. His youthful emotions ran from dreams of glory far surpassing any reasonable expectation to periods of despair, bitterness, and sickness. It was a pattern of emotions to be repeated many times in his life. "I have mountaintop and valley experiences," he wrote in 1979. "Evelyn says I am thunder one moment and quietness the next."[62]

When Roberts was feeling high, he often became playful and self-consciously boastful. Informing the students that Billy Graham intended to tape an interview with him for one of his television specials, Oral exuded: "He and I will have an interview together on the stage and I don't know exactly what will happen when Mr. Number One gets here with Mr. Number Two."[63] On another occasion, he excitedly told the students of an invitation to speak at Emory University: "And they're having not only the student body but a thousand Methodist pastors and have asked me to come and preach on tongues, interpretation of tongues, and divine healing. I hope I can get familiar with that subject before I go down there. And I believe I can! So we are considering that invitation and we have several more like it."[64] He readily acknowledged that his confidence sometimes turned into cockiness.[65]

Roberts's sense of self-importance, his ego, was tied up in the sweeping mission God had given him. "You can imagine," he declared in 1982, "how I . . . felt almost overwhelmed by God reminding me that He had set me in the Body of Christ to be a forerunner of that healing and health He is going to bring to His people."[66] In the eyes of his critics, his entire ministry was a "golden egoistic monument."[67] Oral's ego did pervade the ministry. His office in the Abundant Life building featured spotlighting on his chair, because, explained architect Cecil Stanfield, "Roberts feels he should be the center of interest here."[68] His later offices featured raised platforms which placed him above the level of his visitors.

If Roberts sometimes seemed to revel in his status and triumphs, at other times he was seized by spells of melancholia, often marked by weeping and open confessions of his faults. "Get me when I'm low," he told the ORU students in 1982. "I tell you, I was so low when I reached up I couldn't even touch down. Have you ever been that low in self worth? . . . That's been a problem with me; it's a problem to me this very day."[69] Oral was sometimes moved to contrition about his own spiritual condition, penitent of the anger and bitterness he had harbored. In the midst of a 1959 devotional sermon at the evangelistic association, he began "preaching to me today":

> I want to apologize. . . . I want you to forgive me. . . . As I look over this room I scarcely see a one that I have not had bitterness toward on some small matter or some strong matter. I will tell the truth. . . . I want to get this out of me. . . . Evidently I am self-centered. I am selfish by nature. But I know I am not humble. I have always wanted to be, but that is one thing I know I am not. If I could only be, God help me. . . . I do not want to skip over this and have it in me, because it will corrode.[70]

Over and over, Oral confessed his faults and asked his spiritual family members to "breathe a prayer for me."[71] Oral could be "so stubborn," complained Evelyn, that he thought "what he says is law and gospel." "There is only one person who can handle Oral Roberts," she believed, "and that's the Lord."[72] Oral's own conscience could bring him low.

Roberts's deepest depressions were not caused by his character flaws—flaws that he, Evelyn, and everyone else associated with the ministry learned to live with—they were caused by forebodings that he had been disobedient to his heavenly calling. It was running from God's call that struck him down at age seventeen; fleeing from God would bring him to tears and repentance time after time in his life. When that strong compulsion came welling up in his belly to launch out in faith, he often offered agonizing resistance: "My back is to the wall today. . . . God has been dealing with me to where I've been getting up at night. I've been in tears . . . over myself that I haven't been aware like I should be aware."[73] The ego left in those low times: "I always dislike myself when I am not sensitive to Him."[74] In those painful, brooding moments, he reached out for sustenance and support.[75] But relief came only with obedience.

ALL OTHER insights into Roberts's character pale, however, compared to his spiritual calling. In the diverse incarnations required by his huge ministry, only one came naturally—that of preacher. "I'm an evangelist first and last," he said in 1972. "I try to be an educator, the best I know how, . . . but I'm really a God-called evangelist, God-called preacher."[76] The meaning of the phrase "God-called evangelist" contained the most recondite explanation of Oral Roberts, both as a man and as a phenomenon.

Roberts was a natural preacher. His style, like his beliefs, was more a product of experience than of theory or the emulation of others. He did study homiletics at Oklahoma Baptist University; he perhaps learned to structure his sermons more than was common in pentecostal circles. He genuinely admired and respected his fellow evangelists, particularly Billy Graham and Kathryn Kuhlman, but he had close associations with none of them. He borrowed freely—"He picked up things everywhere," observed Gordon Lindsay—but primarily Roberts sensed what worked with his audiences, and he constantly experimented to find a better way.[77]

Oral's preaching never appealed to everyone, especially to those accustomed to more scholarly and closely reasoned presentations. Many observers left his meetings disappointed by what they felt were long, rambling, and shallow lessons delivered in an incurable Oklahoma drawl.[78] But most pentecostals avowed that "no one could touch him."[79] Nor was the admiration always confined to the faithful. A poetry critic found in Oral's sermons an earthy lyrical quality: "There is also a great persuasiveness in the way he talks. His language is simple, his speech is not bombastic. It is good language. If you had never been inside a schoolroom, but had mingled with men and listened as they talked, you could understand him."[80] Oral's style changed through the years, becoming, like his dress, less gaudy and flamboyant. But it retained its natural poetic quality:

> This is your appointment.
> This is your moment to get saved and know it.
> This is your hour to be healed from the crown of your head to the soles of
>   your feet.

This is your hour to meet God and for God to meet you.
This is your hour to be changed.
This is your hour for miraculous visitation from God.
This is your appointment with God.[81]

Roberts's tutors were the King James Bible and the songlike flights of the spirit-filled preachers of camp-meeting days. In style, Oral began his career as a second-generation pentecostal preacher—fervent, ecstatic, and given to spiritual rhapsody. In later years he was calmer, but the old ingredients were still present.[82]

The quality which first thrust Oral to the fore of the healing revival and gained the respect of the pentecostal subculture, however, was not his skill in pentecostal oratory but the order and content of his sermons. He studied and carefully prepared his lessons; he was the foremost teacher of the great healing revival of the 1950s. The pentecostal movement was not totally devoid of substantive preaching, but the movement's antiintellectualism and dependence on the leading of the Spirit generally produced sermons more notable for fervor than content. In later years, Oral told ORU students that he spent "100 hours minimum to preach one sermon on a TV special"; he had always carefully prepared his lessons.[83] With the beginning of his independent ministry, Roberts entered a period of intensive sermon preparation, filling his Bibles with three- and four-point outlines typed on the stationery of scores of scattered hotels. The outlines were orderly examinations of nearly every text in the Bible that implicated healing or the miraculous, and they left Oral's pentecostal audience with the indelible impression that they had sat at the feet of a scholar.[84]

Although Roberts's sermons reflected study and preparation, they were models of simplicity. Completely devoid of theological complexities, they were uncritical expositions of Biblical passages.[85] In 1977, he explained to ORU seminary students his preaching style: "We learned in the homiletics class to divide a sermon into seven parts, and for years I did that. Now then I'd have three or four points, because I've found the human mind couldn't contain the seven and it made me a slave to my outline, because it's hard to remember seven points."[86]

Oral's commitment to practical, simple preaching was illustrated by his practice of using sermons over and over again. His classic lessons—"The Fourth Man," "Holding the Rope," "You Can't Go Under for Going Over," "Samson and Delilah"—spanned from the early crusade days to the prime-time specials. The sermons must have become like old favorite songs to Oral's partners, tried and true, full of assurance and hope. "A sermon isn't really powerful until you preach it fifty times," he observed. "You know why? Because you can't know it. And you can't preach well something you don't know well."[87] Oral's sermons never wandered far from those sure truths that he knew, that core message that God had committed to him for his generation. He rehearsed them again and again; he asked his audiences to repeat the key phrases; the result was a twentieth-century litany in celebration of the Holy Spirit.

Roberts insisted that his old sermons were always laced with new insights and illustrations. In many ways, his illustrations were what gripped his audiences and made his points. He believed that an evangelist's stories should come from his own life and experiences, that they should be "in the now." "I don't like 18th century and 17th century illustrations," he told a group of students, "I want something that I myself feel in my gut." Sermons were built on experience, which was why, he explained, "I was in my thirties before I could really preach . . . because you have to live."[88] His sermons became, in fact, personal commentaries on his vast experience. Handwritten additions covered his outlines—"72 yr. old man," "Woman at Minneapolis deliv. fr. unclean spirit," "Florida woman," "Lee Braxton," "Bro. Branham."[89] If sermons were built on experience, the crusades offered enough for a lifetime of preaching.

The ultimate aim of Oral's preaching was communication with his listeners. He refused to preach from notes, because "when I walk up there I don't want anything but you on my mind. I want to preach to you, with your need, because I want my needs met. . . . It's an act of love."[90] "I don't like any preacher that thinks about what he's saying instead of me," he insisted. "If I'm sitting in his audience, he ought to be thinking about me. . . . In the name of God, what's he up there for?"[91] Roberts's intimacy with his crusade audiences, magnified by his personal contact with hundreds each service in the prayer line and thousands at the altars, was probably unparalleled in the history of mass evangelism in America. It was a craving for intimacy which drew him back to evangelism in the 1980s. He had an insatiable need to feel his audiences in personal encounter.

In all Roberts did, including his preaching, the gyroscope that kept him on course was his "call." He stood in that long tradition of Christian vocation which believed that man did not choose God but God chose man. His sense of calling, observed Wayne Robinson, was the "transcendent referent to his life." He might "get tired of it and react against it, but then, eventually, he'll come back."[92] Nothing in Roberts's life could be explained outside that call. It was fitting that his autobiography published in 1972 was entitled *The Call.* In a very real sense, Oral Roberts was the call. His confrontation with God was not that polite glow of confirmation which urged more normal men toward Christian servitude—it was surer and hotter.

There is no doubt that Oral had felt the call from the time Ellis and Claudius had told him he was "to be specially used of God."[93] The suggestion was etched so deeply into the psyche of that bright little farm boy that it could not be removed. He felt it "very definitely" when he wrote his plaintive letter to the *Pentecostal Holiness Advocate* from his sickbed in Stratford in 1935.[94] He almost surely never entertained a serious doubt that he was a "God-called preacher" through the next half-century of his tumultuous career.

Portions of Oral's call fit easily into the model he inherited from evangelical Protestantism through pentecostalism. When he preached, he felt the "anointing of God on me."[95] Evelyn believed the anointing completely transformed her husband: "When he's preaching and praying, I don't know him as my husband; he is God's man then."[96] In 1963, Oral tried to explain "the anointing" he felt to a group of his partners:

The anointing of the Holy Ghost is an energy—it's pure energy. It is an invisible spiritual force that comes upon you and you feel it. It separates you from yourself. Suddenly you're not yourself. . . . Thoughts go through your mind that you did not think of, the Holy Spirit put that thought in your mind. You feel, sometimes you say it felt like electricity because we don't know the words to describe it. . . . But we'll use all kinds of phrases because it's difficult to explain that which can't be seen and that which is not known very well by us.[97]

Difficult as it was to describe, Oral was certain that he knew when he had the anointing of the Holy Spirit; when he did, "it is like God talking."[98]

While the concept of a God-called, anointed minister was a part of American evangelical history, especially spread through Methodism to pentecostalism, Oral also defined his calling in uniquely pentecostal terms. Beginning in 1947, he asserted that the gift of healing worked through him. In later years, Roberts believed that he possessed a number of the nine gifts of the Spirit: "I know the gift of healing works through me; it doesn't work all the time. I know the gift of faith stands out in me. I know the gift of wisdom and knowledge works in me at times."[99] Furthermore, he was certain that he had been set apart for some very special works. "There's a lot I can do for you that's never been done," he told the ORU faculty in 1971, "don't underestimate what I can do in your life because I'm a God-called man. I have something in me that's not of Oral Roberts, it's a gift of God. I can't lay credit for it because God gave it to me, but I can help you."[100]

ORAL'S summary call, to take healing to his generation, was revealed to him, he repeatedly testified, at the time of his healing in 1935. The call was announced in 1947 and progressively unfolded to him throughout his lifetime. "After my conversion and healing the whole thing was revealed to me expect for the specifics," he said in 1983. "God was merciful, I couldn't have stood it. But when the time came, He revealed it."[101] Roberts's pursuit of healing ran straight as an arrow through the meandering history of his ministry. The crusades, the television programs, the university, the City of Faith, the healing teams, they were all strands in the whole cloth—they were methods to implement the call. That was the inner truth that Oral knew which his critics could never get straight—it was not he that made the decisions, it was God: "It's not my healing ministry. It's God's ministry. It isn't my school; its God's university. It isn't my City of Faith; it's God's City of Faith."[102]

Roberts's answer to the call was dogged and determined, though the way was often hard. He counseled his seminary graduates not to "try to get a big church" but to "ask for the hardest spot."[103] He repeatedly reaffirmed his own determination to "serve Him under a shade tree if we have to."[104] But his response to God was also bold. "I'm not frightened of God if I'm sincere," he told the ORU students, because nothing could sway him from his call—"God would have to rub me out. He couldn't handle me at all unless He had rubbed me out."[105] In the midst of the struggle over the City of Faith, Oral challenged God:

When that bunch of people who can't tell their left hand from their right, when they don't know down from up, ... I say, "God, I can't handle that bunch. I've been up there trying to handle them. I sit down, and I stretch my hand out to shake theirs. I pray. I talk nice. I smile. And it doesn't get anywhere. . . . Look, God, they say You're mighty busy, but don't forget me in the process. This is Yours. You'd better come down here and take care of Your business on South Lewis where we are. . . . We ask You, don't You care for us?" If you don't think I tell Him that, you ought to be around when I pray. And a man heard me say that, and he said, "That would scare me to death." Well, I get more scared if I don't talk to Him.[106]

The ultimate expression of Oral's acceptance of his call was obedience. He could talk to God, and for God, and with God because he was a consummately receptive vessel: "If there's one thing that characterizes my life it's obedience."[107] "When you press him to the wall," said Jim Winslow, "one hundred percent of the time he tries to do what God has led him to do. If you use one word to characterize the man, you'd have to use obedience."[108] Regardless of how impossible it seemed—to build a university when he did not know how, or to found a medical center, or to discover the cure for cancer—Oral would do it, and he would do it on time. "I think Oral would sacrifice anything he had," said Don Moyers, "clear down to his family, to try to carry out what he regards as God's direction."[109] Indeed, he did precisely that.

Oral's intransigence, his impatience, and his intolerance of sensible questions about his plans were the reactions of an obedient son. He detested bad news; even from his most trusted advisors, he accepted it reluctantly: "The information has to come to me. But I want them to say it quick. I don't want my mind to dwell on that because I'll get scared, I'll start worrying, and then we'll all have just one problem with the school, we won't have any."[110] Once he was certain that he had heard the voice of God, Oral's aim was obedience; contrary voices, however practical and well-intended, were standing in the way of his call.

Bound as he was to obeying the instruction of God, Roberts was compelled to pursue the mystery of private revelation. He recognized, as did those who recoiled at each new revelation, that the whole of his life and work hung on the validity of his divine encounters. In probing that question, Oral did his most creative thinking.

The most controversial, most frequent, and least clear of all of Oral's explanations for his decisions was "God told me." While he repeatedly denied that "I'm special," in truth, the whole of the Roberts ministry hung on his unique relationship with God. He heard God's direction in a special way, perhaps because "God wants somebody that's ignorant enough that will do what He says."[111] In a 1979 interview with University of Oklahoma president Bill Banowsky, the discussion moved toward that core question. Banowsky asked: "Oral, do you feel that you've been set apart by Almighty God?" "I don't know how he feels, but I know," interjected Evelyn. Oral replied that in the Bible God spoke to a number of people and that "He speaks to every body." But Banowsky pressed the point; did God "choose some people above all others," and was Oral one of those chosen? "You're asking a hard question," said

Roberts hesitantly. They sparred for a moment, and Banowsky started to move on, but Oral returned. "You've got to the question," he told Banowsky, and slowly began to answer:

> I doubted God. I doubted He had spoken to me. I went for a long time with His voice ringing in my ears wondering whose voice it was. Was it Oral Roberts? Was it somebody else? And then God has a way of cornering you and giving you such evidence that now you have to obey or disobey. And I reached the ultimate moment of my life that my soul was at stake. And that's what I was careful to answer you. . . . Yes, brother, he did speak to me.[112]

Oral's direct messages from God were what most alienated him from the outside world. "After a while it doesn't take much imagination to figure out that Oral and God are rather synonymous," said one critic. "I think either what he writes is crazy or he's crazy."[113] His revelations were a problem for his friends, as well. Roberts's communication with God imposed a tyranny, however benevolent, within his organization. "If you'd walk in" to his office, recalled Al Bush, "he'd say, 'Oh, God just told me.' . . . That was his favorite line—'God just told me.' Well, God speaks to me too and he hasn't told me that. . . . That was my rub. I just wish he wouldn't use that."[114] Oral's best friends in Tulsa cowered when he began to speak words from God. Warren Hultgren found it a "pretty heavy" theology which "ultimately breaks down."[115] It was tolerable to employ poetic license to describe one's inner feelings, but to actually believe that God was speaking was fanatical. Bob Foresman remembered an occasion when he and Jenkin Lloyd Jones visited Oral in the midst of the 900-foot-Jesus debacle. Jones finally blurted out: "It's all well and good to say that sort of thing, but . . . what do you really think?"[116] Oral flushed. They parted politely but worlds apart. Roberts could sell his projects to Tulsa, but he would never convince the rational world that his directions came from God.

Oral's belief that he heard the voice of God was, of course, by no means a novel experience in the Christian tradition. Throughout Christian history, many of the foremost leaders of the faith have been led by visions and divine voices. Nowhere was that tradition better preserved than in the American pentecostal subculture. Oral's father and mother had conversed with God and Jesus on such intimate terms that his own messages from God were a part of his birthright. When he told his parents of his initial charge from God, they believed it without questioning.[117] His visions were received by his pentecostal peers in the 1950s as predictable and reliable.[118] As his own theology developed, it demanded an active, existential God of the "now," who "does speak to His people today."[119] The queer thing was not so much that the Christian tradition had bred another prophet, or that a belief in direct revelation was still alive in the twentieth century, but that such a visionary had succeeded, that he had aroused a nation, and that he sat in the boardrooms of Tulsa's most prestigious companies. The paradox was that he seemed to be able to do what he said.

The mechanics of God's communications with Oral remain shrouded in mystery, as all such transcendental experiences must remain subjective and existential. There was a devotional quality in Oral's personality, made evident in his frequent praying. "Jesus Christ is more familiar to me than my father or mother or my wife or my children," he said in 1963. "I know Jesus, I know him as a person, I know this man and yet I want to know him so much better than I know him because to know him as I know him is to want to know more of him."[120] Out of such spiritual cravings, honestly professed, come visions.

More mysterious was the voice of God, which repeatedly and precisely, "in clear, crisp terms," gave Roberts marching orders.[121] While Oral firmly believed that God talked to everyone, he knew He did not talk to everyone in an "audible voice."[122] Through the years, he believed that he had come to recognize God's voice speaking to him, whether in short, pithy phrases or in intervals so long that "I asked him to stop because my body wouldn't take it."[123] He believed that the language was distinctive and foreign to him; he would write it down furiously to report and obey: "When he talks to me it's the clearest language I've ever heard. There is no way that I could misunderstand. The very phrasing or the words are so different from humans. . . . It always fills me clear to my head. . . . I immediately know that it's not me, because I can't think of those terms. I can't turn a phrase like that."[124]

WHILE Roberts understood his leading from God in the supernaturalistic framework of Christian mysticism, he, and those around him, explored "feeling" and "intuition" to explain his experiences. Oral's willingness to change and his loose and tolerant theology were consciously tied to a desire to remain open to God's leading. "I have kept my life totally open to God." he wrote in 1964. "Also my mind is totally open to new ideas and expressions of God as He manifests Himself in our lives today."[125] His openness, his sensitive listening for God, made him uncannily conscious of his own feelings. "I believe he was telling me exactly what he felt," said Al Bush of Oral's reportings of God's voice. "When he says that, he means he is terribly pressed to do something."[126] Roberts frequently discussed ideas for months and years with his assistants before finally encasing them in the words of God.[127] The voice of God was not the beginning of the revelation, it was the end; it came at that "moment of crisis" when Oral was overwhelmed by a "compelling urge" to act on what was festering inside him. Then the voice spoke. It was at that moment of release that Roberts's depression was broken and he became "revitalized by the Spirit of God" by articulating the truth within him.[128]

That source of truth which Roberts was tapping into was the "capacity for deep feelings" which resided in every human being.[129] If one had "sincerely sought God's will in a situation, then follow whatever leading you feel in your heart. Act upon it, even though you may not understand everything about it."[130] Over and over, Oral asserted that intuitive insight had worked in his life and ministry: "I have feelings, I get it down here in the pit of my stomach, that I can't explain but I understand them. Some may call that intuition, some may call it the guidance of God, but whatever it is I know I have it. . . . When I am really in tune, I can walk across this campus . . . and I can pick up eighty percent of what's going on."[131] He had unswerving confidence in his feelings: "Since Jesus Christ came into my life in 1935, I have never made a serious mistake when I followed my deep feelings. This does not mean that I haven't made full use of investigation, counsel and planning."[132] The secret was to "trust Him."[133] In later years, Oral connected trust in one's private leadings with the prayer language of the Holy Spirit. "When you believe on the Man Jesus, something happens in your belly or the inner man. Right down in the solar plexus something happens." In that innermost receptacle of life, the "rivers of living water" began to flow up, being released by the prayer language, to enlighten the mind to the most primal understandings of the spirit.[134]

Oral was aware, after decades of celebrating feeling and dealing with the erratic prophets of the pentecostal subculture, that such a view raised serious confirmational questions. In his class on "The Holy Spirit in the Now," he established guidelines to distinguish between "directional" and "confirmatory" uses of the gifts of the Holy Spirit—although such dividing was by no means an exact science.[135] He confessed that "once in a while we go off the deep end," although he and his supporters insisted that his "batting average" was exceptional.[136] His general guidelines were:

1. Be receptive to God's direction.
2. Consider the question of God's will in the light of His goodness.
3. Listen to the voice of God.
4. Study the Bible under the guidance of the Holy Spirit.
5. Trust God.
6. Act upon God's directions.[137]

The system of checks and balances worked in Roberts's mind when he tried out his new ideas: "In God's dealing with me, I always wait until a pattern forms. Until it becomes something I cannot shake out of my mind and that is when I begin to move in that particular direction. If it will leave my mind quickly, I don't pay much attention to it."[138]

The consummate test of God's leading, however, and the ultimate vindication of Oral's prophetic role in the minds of his supporters, was pragmatic. Roberts knew that God talked to him, because something "clicks inside you, and you just know it," but if others wanted proof, they would have to observe the fulfilled vision.[139] Answering a hostile reporter who wanted proof that God had spoken, Oral replied, "I'd say your best proof is in the results."[140] He repeatedly returned to his life's work as the verification of his message. How else could it have happened? He could not have built the vision, or even conceived it. How often had he flown into the face of reason and prudence? "There's only one way it's possible and that's by faith."[141]

In the 1960s and 1970s, Oral developed a novel theory about the fall of man. He believed that the curse of death placed on Adam and Eve in the Garden of Eden had to do with "the death of something inside him, the image of God in him, the spiritual dominance. . . . The mind got up in the saddle and from that day to this man has lived as if he never had a soul. . . . He has lived in the flesh." The result, Roberts thought, was a tyranny of rationalism, magnified in modern times by a "generation of pseudo-intellectuals, . . . people who really believe that they *know*." Their sin was the transgression of the fall, "trying to live completely on the sense level, denying the intuitive, denying the supernatural—either good or evil." Man still had his subjective connection to God, submerged in his belly, if only he would tap it through spiritual awakening.[142]

In a very real sense, Oral Roberts was an ultimate romantic, a prophet of the intuitive, speaking out of a tradition of Christian mysticism and pentecostal ecstasy. He was a spokesman for "right-brained" thinking; Oral Roberts University professors were fittingly interested in psychological studies of the brain.[143] Oral recognized that the cause he was defending could be defined in nonreligious terms: "You see flashes of intuition from people who don't even know God. On the other hand, there doesn't seem to be much difference between the secular and spiritual gifts."[144]

Roberts not only defended feeling, emotion, and subjectivism; like a modern Thoreau, he lived by his creed. There was an unerring pragmatism about his listening; he tested, drew back, and fought against the leadings. But, finally, he succumbed, regardless of the cost. "I am an emotional person," he said in 1957. "For that reason I think I'm normal. . . . Jesus was electric with emotion."[145] Oral was the quintessential pentecostal, capturing the ability to feel, and to pull those feelings to the surface and trust them. "To me he's a poet," said ORU dean Robert Voight. "The poet is a person who feels the groundswell coming out of the people and . . . gives form to the idea. . . . He expresses then what he feels coming out."[146] The personality of Oral Roberts was totally subsumed in that poetic calling. He was a conduit taking messages back and forth—smelling the earth beneath and breathing in from heights other men could not climb. He could feel men, and he could feel God. It was an awesome call. "I have absolutely no envy for the man," said Ron Smith, "I would absolutely rather be dead than to be in his shoes."[147] On more than one occasion, Oral expressed the same wish.

CHAPTER

XVIII

The Ministry

ORAL ROBERTS was a "businessman not by choice" but because "I have to be."[1] By the mid-1980s, he had come to be the chief executive officer of an organization that employed about 2,300 people and did an annual business of about 110 million dollars, about sixty percent of which was raised through contributions.[2] Understandably, Roberts showed some pride in his administrative skills. *Tulsa Tribune* business editor Bob Foresman marveled at his "acumen as a businessman." In 1971 he wrote: "He cuts through details and red tape, goes straight to the point, like a computer."[3]

Whether or not Roberts was a good executive was a complicated question. In some important ways, he was ineffective. "Detail wise," said Bill Nash, "he's not a good businessman. . . . He could not run a bank. . . . Because he does not plan properly."[4] Oral frustrated the businessmen on his boards, often moving with indefensible haste and without planning, refusing to measure the consequences.[5] Those indiscretions grew out of who he was and his sense of calling. On the other hand, "in an undisciplined way," observed Al Bush, he was a brilliant businessman. Bush, one of Tulsa's more talented executives, believed that he learned much during his apprenticeship with Oral—"How to view the world and how to act in it and how to interact with the people was probably the greatest group of lessons that I learned."[6]

The successes and the failures of the Oral Roberts ministry, and the strengths and weaknesses of Oral as an administrator, were clearest in the complex interfacing of Roberts and "his men." From the beginning he aspired to bring "the finest young executives to Tulsa"; generally, Tulsans were impressed by the quality of his top administrators.[7] Wayne Robinson believed that "the kind of people he would choose to work with him on the executive level you would feel comfortable with going to any . . . professional meeting. They would never be wild-eyed enthusiasts that would embarrass you."[8] In Oral's ministry, as in other large institutions, there was some tendency for conventional administrators to stay and for the brilliant and the creative to leave, but few would question Roberts's commitment to competence, or the presence of considerable talent within his organization at any given time.

The first thing Oral demanded of "his men" was work. "You will produce for him or you won't be around," observed his nephew Bill Roberts.[9] He asked no more or less than he himself gave; his own schedule was grinding and demanding. George Stovall thought Oral was "the greatest motivator of people that I know": "He made me better than I would have been. Being associated with him has helped me to know that I can do things that I wouldn't have been able to do before. He does stretch people."[10] Working with Oral, particularly at the top executive levels, where one was in constant contact with him, was exhilarating. But it was also exhausting. When Al Bush left the organization, he felt that he was completely "out of gas. . . . The decision was made in absolute complete fatigue. . . . You don't keep hours, you do what is required."[11] Ron Smith, who suffered a near-fatal heart attack shortly after leaving the ministry, believed that he had to "leave ORU and that management relationship or die."[12]

A few of Roberts's most talented subordinates left because there was no room to assert their own identity—in Al Bush's words, to earn an "equity" in the business.[13] While Oral paid his executives "adequately," it was no doubt true, as Bill Roberts observed, that "when you're working for Oral you're not going to make a lot of money."[14] George Stovall believed that "generally speaking the people who leave are those who don't see a significant role for themselves. . . . If you want to be rich, if you want to make a big name for yourself, this probably isn't the place to be."[15]

The second important quality that Oral required of his associates was loyalty. Oral liked spirituality; he prayed with his associates at every stormy meeting. But he did not demand it. Although almost all of his top executives were charismatic, some were not, including Bill Roberts, and Oral worked well with outside advisors who did not share his religious views. But loyalty he demanded.

Loyalty was the key to the preservation of the vision. Though he believed it was "nonsense," Bill Roberts understood why Oral "can't afford not to believe that everybody that's in a key position is not with him a hundred percent."[16] Loyalty was a theme he preached over and over in his speeches at the university: "You do carry in your heart a conviction that I am called of God. I want to reaffirm to you that this University was raised up under God's authority to be based on the Holy Spirit. We have had lots of talks about this and we will be having others. It seems to be a battle that is never won."[17] Within the context of personal loyalty to him and to his vision, Oral would protect his subordinates. "You could disagree with him if you were personally loyal to him," said Wayne Robinson. "That could cover a multitude of sins."[18] If one questioned Oral's call, he would have to leave.

Those who survived for long periods of time in the Roberts organization were the loyalists. Oscar Moore made suggestions to Oral, but he never tried to "alter him."[19] At Lee Braxton's funeral, Oral's eulogy was "He was as loyal to me as is possible for a human being to be to another one in this world."[20] Of Bob DeWeese he said, "He's been faithful. . . . He's never, never turned to the right or the left. He's stood by us through thick and thin."[21] For the most part, the top administrators still exhibited such loyalty. George Stovall felt "fulfilled" as a manager under Oral's guidance. Jim Winslow found Roberts's demand for loyalty a "very effective way of managing."[22] Carl Hamilton said in 1974: "I'm a team player, and I enjoy being on this team and working with each of you and with President Roberts. What I'll say, he has this pair of football shoes he runs up and down your back with cleats, but he has a can of salve that he carries with it."[23]

"Oral's modus operandi is quite simple, quite direct and quite forceful," observed business mogul John Williams. "He is a user of people." His antennae constantly scanned the landscape to identify anyone on the horizon who might further his mission. A long parade of people passed through the inner chambers of his seventh-floor offices as his most favored advisors of the moment, only to be moved downstairs when their work was done. Most knew what had happened; some were relieved, others viewed it as a betrayal. But Ron Smith expressed what everyone that reached the top echelons of the Roberts ministry needed to know: "Oral has absolutely no . . . ultimates. He is not loyal to anyone [except] . . . God as he perceives Him."[24] There was nothing novel or sinister about Oral's administrative style, remarked John Williams. "You have to use people. How else are you going to accomplish your end. . . . I spent all of my life using people because that's how you run a company. . . . It is not necessarily a bad thing to use people unless you are using them for an evil purpose."[25] Oral did not callously discard those he had used. He rarely fired a high-ranking employee; he offered them secure and comfortable sinecures.

Roberts believed that others were called into his ministry in the same way that he was; he appealed to that sense of calling to convince them to join him. He never offered a "job," he offered a calling.[26] Jim Buskirk found it an "infuriating" technique, though he eventually capitulated to it.[27] Oral chided both Al Bush and Ron Smith for being "out of God's will" when they told him they were leaving the organization—both men insisted that Oral was not "the interpreter of that."[28]

Roberts has not always used his talented helpers effectively. Al Bush considered him the "world's worst delegator."[29] Too often, his hand was in everything, the trivial competing for his attention along with major concerns. As the empire expanded in the 1980s, the problem of delegating authority became critical, however, and by necessity, areas of delegated authority became clear. When Roberts's attention was absorbed by the City of Faith in the late 1970s, Carl Hamilton and the university gained a degree of independence. The medical complex demanded such specialized talents that Jim Winslow's management was uncontested. Oral's attention focused only on the hottest project of the moment; other phases of the ministry operated relatively autonomously. To some extent it had always been that way, but, more than ever, in the 1980s the Oral

Roberts ministry was not a one-man operation, no matter how much it depended for survival on Oral.[30] Even so, when crises came, such as the reorganization of the university in 1984, Roberts's personal leadership was forcefully reasserted.

If the ministry was bigger than Oral, it was still difficult to tell "how much bigger."[31] Oral had long argued that his ministry was a composite. In 1962, he said:

> We have surrounded ourselves with men and women who feel the same thing, and in that sense, we have become a composite—the individual, like myself, is no longer an individual. Neither are you, but those of us in this ministry, who are part of the mission, who are dedicated to this cause of deliverance by the supernatural power of God, those of us who have joined together are an entity; we are a composite person.[32]

Roberts had subsumed his entire identity in the mission of the ministry; he never really understood when others continued to view it as his and demanded a "dignified autonomy" of their own. There was no room for autonomy in the composite ministry.[33]

Roberts repeatedly said that he needed and wanted people in his organization who would criticize him. Ministry staff meetings always featured open exchange; during his crusades and in chapel, Oral's speeches were often followed by question-and-answer sessions that sometimes turned candid and heated. Evelyn had "always been very faithful to remind" him of his "shortcomings," Oral revealed, and he "trained my men" to "be very open and frank with me."[34] He knew that "flattery is disastrous."[35] "Once he knows somebody is up front with him," said Jim Winslow, "he does not mind one bit for you to disagree, it's fair game to argue it out."[36] But in the final analysis Oral made the decisions. Outlining his administrative policy to the president's advisory cabinet in 1965, he stated: "I shall listen carefully, weigh the council's thought and even their vote but I shall try to remember that I'm president; the buck stops here."[37] Ron Smith was convinced that Oral had the capacity to simply tune out alternate views he did not want to hear: "He said to me more than once, 'Why didn't you tell me.' And I said, 'I did, but you wouldn't listen.'"[38]

The "biggest decision" that anyone in a "decision making role" in the Roberts organization ever faced, concluded Ron Smith, was whether to tell Oral the truth.[39] Very few stood up to him under pressure. "I was disappointed in my co-workers," said Al Bush. "They would capitulate in front of him. There was a time to stand up and be counted and they wouldn't do it."[40] There were many reasons for the capitulations. George Stovall admitted that his protests were tempered by his belief in Roberts's call—by the fact that he had seen him do the impossible. But mostly it was the "very mesmerizing" presence of the man, and the desire to protect one's place near him.[41] One after another of those close to Oral confessed, as Jim Winslow did in 1975, "I love President Roberts and the relationship that he and I have had has been a highlight in my life."[42] Roberts also ruled by intimidation, though most insiders believed that stormy confrontations became less frequent in the 1980s.[43] Every administrator in the Roberts ministry knew the feel of "spikes up and down his back."[44] In 1974, Oral asked Ron Smith if he remembered their recent clash when he "read your pedigree and told you exactly what I thought, and when I was through, I thought, 'Well, I've lost him.' " Smith responded, "Which one?"[45] To work for Roberts, reflected Al Bush, was "to fight every day of your life for something that seems so obvious to you. . . . Would you like to have to defend everything you did? He wore me out." Bush believed "that I was probably one man who was able to say no and that I would say what had to be said." But the price was high: "One of the things I had to do sometimes at night was to go home, take off my clothes, stand in front of the mirror to check to see whether I still had all my parts. Figuratively speaking, he would emasculate you."[46]

It was unclear in the 1980s who the most independent voices were within the ministry. Jim Winslow had the independent spirit of a successful physician who was not dependent on the ministry for his livelihood. Carl Hamilton insisted that all Oral asked was that his team "follow me as I follow Christ."[47] Hamilton's abortive resignation in 1983 indicated an unexpected independence, which was confirmed by his departure in August 1984. Jim Buskirk was probably the most independent voice in the ministry up until 1984; he remained a preacher with a substantial ministry of his own and a sense of personal integrity: "If you've got the stuff to be your own person here, that's great. If you don't have the stuff to be your own person, you can be tempted to compromise."[48]

The difficulty of maintaining autonomy and critical honesty from within the Roberts organization greatly increased the importance of Oral's outside advisors—particularly his attorneys, Saul Yager and Don Moyers. "Saul," said Evelyn at a banquet honoring Yager, "came along and taught Oral how . . . to stay out of jail, and that's the truth."[49] Oral often fought tooth and nail with his attorneys, but he "bowed to their opinion" when he would to no one else's.[50] When Roberts tried to retain Don Moyers as his "general counsel," Moyers refused: "I don't want to get to the point that I can't tell you no and give a hoot whether you take it or you don't. I don't owe you a thing."[51] Outsiders gave Oral the kind of advice he could probably never get from inside.

Many astute outside observers believed that the Roberts organization "gobbled everybody" associated with it.[52] It was a Catch-22; to work for Oral was to allow one's "own ego to be subservient," but that act of homage was easily seen as "weakness."[53] John Williams saw the dilemma as Oral's most glaring managerial flaw: "He has no respect for the people that are willing to work for him. Anybody that's willing to work for Oral, . . . he owns him."[54] Al Bush struggled introspectively with the self-sacrifice he made: "I must tell you it was a terrible strain. . . . As a matter of fact, I think it's perceived as a weakness in a man who can submerge himself in another man's personality and life." But he understood it, and he accepted it: "I always accepted the right because he had a mission. He had given up everything, including his family, in a sense. It was hard for him to countenance anyone who couldn't give as much."[55] But it was emptying. "He literally burnt Al up," said John Williams, "it was like putting him in a flame and consuming him to where Al was totally useless to him."[56]

And yet, for all the tension and struggle within the ministry, for all Oral's authoritarian rule and tempestuous outbursts, for all the reservations of those who left him, not one important administrator (save G. H. Montgomery) has ever attacked either Oral or his mission.[57] Nor could they ever escape Oral's aura. "I'm still on staff without payroll," said Wayne Robinson in 1983, "I'm constantly introduced and referred to as formerly. . . ."[58] Al Bush, smiled John Williams, was still Oral's "peon," despite the fact that he was fifty-two years old and headed a large Tulsa corporation.[59] Bush, remembering how Oral had told him how to get his hair cut when he was his chief executive officer, told of a recent encounter at Southern Hills when Oral, after a friendly chat, gave his hair a little jerk to let him know "my hair's too long." It was all right. Bush loved Oral, deeply enough to give him anything he had. If he believed Oral needed him, he softly and pensively whispered, he would return.[60]

Whatever the price, those who served in Oral's army loved him. Even Patti Roberts could say after her divorce that she was "still desperately in love with Oral's dream."[61] "When you get that close to someone," reflected Wayne Robinson, "he invades your psyche and your self-identity."[62] Oral had taken them all high on the mountaintop; he had prayed with them and dreamed with them, and they had caught glimpses of the God that spoke to him. "I nearly lost my life because of what I think happened to me there," said Ron Smith, "but I wouldn't go back and change a minute of it. . . . I mean the lessons are fabulous. If I had died on September 19th, I would have lived through an awful lot more than I had the right to experience."[63]

ALMOST from the beginning of his public ministry, from the time when he began to accumulate a noticeable amount of property, people asked whether Oral Roberts's ministry could survive his death. Jenkin Lloyd Jones began thinking about the question in the 1960s, he recalled, and in 1979, in the midst of the squabble over building the City of Faith, he editorially asked, what "after Oral Roberts?" "The trouble with a one-man show," he wrote, "is that when the man goes the show is over." Since the survival of the Roberts ministry was a question of importance to Tulsa, Jones publicly wondered why the organization had not begun to groom a "wisely chosen" successor.[64]

The succession question never escaped the attention of the Roberts organization; in fact, sometimes it consumed it. Oral insisted that he would be "immortal" until his work was finished, but over and over in private conversations within the ministry, and occasionally in public meetings, the "unforgivable question" would surface: "What is your opinion of how this organization would function now if something should happen to *the man?*"[65] When the university was founded, Oral felt compelled to react to the question:

> Many have been concerned with how to perpetuate this ministry after we are gone. I believe there is no way this can be done through legalism, or theology, or denominationalism, or rules and regulations. It is in our choice of men who feel this same calling, men who will be the faculty and staff. They will choose the students who in the final analysis will receive this message as God gave it to us, or they will not receive it. We cannot guarantee it any more than Christ

could when He left the earth. He had to sow the seed, to believe God for the miracle to multiply it many times.[66]

Pondering the question in 1983, Oral's answer was the same:

I don't know. I just have to go one day at a time. I know I will have no debt. They carry a large policy on my life. The university does. It would carry them probably a year. But if my men learn to live by faith, there won't be a great problem. If they don't, I believe there will be a serious problem. . . . I think you do it through the right people, . . . Jimmy [Winslow] and Jim Buskirk and Richard and Carl Hamilton and then these students.[67]

Although there clearly was no legalistic way to assure the continuation of the ministry after Roberts's death, the succession issue reappeared frequently in Oral's thinking. He acknowledged that "success without a successor is failure." In the 1960s he viewed the university as his lasting heritage: "Through this University, I believe that this ministry and this concept will not only live for a hundred years, or a thousand years, but I believe it will leave its stamp on the souls of men for eternity."[68] While building the City of Faith, Roberts added the medical complex to his legacy: "You've heard the opposing council say that Oral Roberts will die, and that's a true statement, I could have added, unless Jesus comes first. . . . My ministry has been and is a ministry of healing. It will continue far beyond my lifetime, through my son, through the men and women who work with me and my students and the City of Faith."[69] Radiating out from these institutions were the hundreds of healing teams that Oral envisioned would perpetuate his work. More than most American evangelists—Graham, Moody, Finney, or Edwards—Roberts had spent much of his life building institutions which would survive him.

Roberts protected the institutions by two devices. First, his life was insured for millions of dollars, enough, Oral believed, to sustain the ministry for a year. Second, he built physical facilities which far exceeded the needs of the ministry, both at the university and at the City of Faith, and the entire investment was virtually debt-free. The controversial construction of the entire shell of the City of Faith was at least partly a recognition of the succession question. Oral believed that the project must be completed "while I'm in the prime of my life and most able to raise the funds and to pay for it."[70] Everyone assumed that the ministry's income would drop when Roberts died; he was determined not to leave the institutions saddled with debt.

It has always been clear that the Roberts ministry was a family enterprise as well as a set of institutions. Oral was open about his hopes for his sons. Asked in 1975 by Bob Foresman and Jenkin Lloyd Jones, Jr. about his successor, Oral replied: "I have two fine sons: I can't predict what they can do. I couldn't lay my hand on anybody today. I wouldn't try."[71] In the decade after 1975, the family tragedies that removed two of the Roberts children narrowed the options. On the other hand, the tragedies pushed the family together. When Roberta returned to Tulsa, John Williams observed: "It's the clan closing in and girding

their loins for the future."[72] Roberta acknowledged that the future of the ministry "depends on a great deal of strength on the part of our family."[73]

By the mid-1980s, the central figure in the succession drama was Richard
Roberts. Some doubters, both within and without the ministry, still did not
believe that Richard could be Oral's successor—they questioned his depth, his
commitment, and his lack of "a recognizable kind of authority."[74] On the other
hand, by the mid-1980s almost everyone acknowledged that "he'll have to do
it," however difficult the transition might be for him and the ministry.[75] The
only question seemed to be about the precise role Richard would play. "I don't
know whether Richard will ever be president of ORU," opined George Stovall,
"I don't think he has to be. But I do expect to see the day when the president of
ORU reports to Richard. Or it will be obvious who is the head of the ministry."[76] Realism placed the choice in Richard's hands. "Richard will have the
place he wants," judged Howard Ervin. "That's a question that the young man
will have to decide himself."[77]

Richard seemed singularly unperturbed by the succession question in the
mid-1980s. He knew, as others knew, that there would be no successor until
Oral was gone, and Richard's priority in the 1980s was to establish his own
reputation as an evangelist, to earn public respect, and to validate his independence. He and Oral were "a father-son team," Richard insisted, and ministry
publicity increasingly was calculated to project that image. Richard knew that
his position was solid. Only he could relate to the partners of the ministry: "Do
you want to receive a letter from Rev. Roberts or do you want to receive a
letter from Rev. Smith?" He had the support of the leaders of the ministry: "I
would say that the leadership of this campus—the Jim Winslows, the Carl
Hamiltons, the Jim Buskirks, the Bill Roberts, the Fred Van Stones . . . are on
their knees praying, believing that I am the one . . . when my dad is gone. And
the only way I know is because they tell me." But more than all of that, the
certainty of Richard's succession seemed to be assured by his own growing
depth and confidence. His healing ministry seemed to give him a new self-
assurance: "There's a lot more in me than people realize. When the time comes,
I'll be there if that's what God's will is. I have no fear concerning the future of
the ministry. I do not believe that God raised up this ministry for it to go under
when Oral Roberts dies."[78]

The ministry which Oral had built and which Richard was heir to in the
mid-1980s was immensely complex and shot through with deep internal tensions. "Oral is always conscious of those tensions," observed Ron Smith, "right
now Oral is operating in a permissive will context, simply because that is a
vehicle to get him where he wants to go."[79] Actually, there were several clear
fault lines running through the ministry; some were more dangerous than
others. Protecting the charismatic commitment of the institutions remained a
problem; only a "very few persons in the whole undergraduate school" teaching
staff were "experientially" charismatic in the mid-1980s, although all, insisted
Dean Robert Voight, were supposedly "in harmony with the goals and purposes" of the institution.[80] The administration, of course, was solid, and the
evangelistic association's control of the university was clearly established. But

there was theological tension on the campus between the essentially evangelical character of much of the university, symbolized by its Methodist leanings, and the increasing identification of Oral and Richard with the independent healing evangelists and the charismatic movement. Those tensions seemed harmless enough in view of Oral's theological tolerance, but it was by no means certain that they could coexist in his absence. Perhaps most threatening was the immense power of the medical complex and its leaders. Some insiders felt that the medical leadership neither understood nor was committed to the healing vision of Oral Roberts. At least one ministry leader believed that "the battle lines are pretty clearly drawn."[81]

No one could know the future, but "my prediction," said Bill Roberts, "is . . . that there's going to be a dogfight."[82] Ron Smith believed that there would be another major shakeup before Oral died, unless he had lost the "energy to fight."[83] But whatever shakeups lay in the future, either in Oral's lifetime or after, they would not be far different from those in other large corporations— neither bloodier nor more unnatural. Richard took a remarkably sophisticated and confident view of the ministry's present complexity and cloudy future: "I think that it is normal. If there's not some struggle there's not any growth. . . . All I can tell you is that I'm committed to be here. And I'm not only strong, but I'm a lot stronger than most people think."[84]

"I DON'T know anybody in the world in the Christian realm that has accomplished in a lifetime what this man has accomplished," said Demos Shakarian, introducing Oral to the World Convention of the Full Gospel Business Men's Fellowship International in 1981.[85] As Oral neared the end of his life, he sensed his historical significance. He had been told that he would someday be recognized as an eminent Christian, that his importance might even surpass that of Billy Graham: "Charles Allen . . . told me about Billy's great ministry and impact on him. But he said, 'When the records are written at the end of the century, it will be your ministry that has touched the people and touched the body of Christ.'"[86] It was still too early to make such judgments. But Oral had been faithful to his vision. In 1983, he told his partners, probably without overstatement, "Throughout the world my name, Oral Roberts, is synonymous with healing."[87]

Roberts's worldwide influence was the harvest of a life of sowing. First and foremost, it was a product of his preaching. Many people looked at the buildings he had built and read the ministry's income and marveled, "How can this be?" "But they don't know all of those hundreds and hundreds of great crusades of thousands and thousands, when people were really pulled towards heaven."[88] Scattered all over the world were the hundreds of thousands who had felt his touch. They helped him build his university, they sent their children to be educated there, and they built the City of Faith. Furthermore, their number was increased mightily by television. In 1973, *New York Times* reporter Edward B. Fiske asked the question: "How significant will Oral Roberts turn out to be?" Admitting that there was no quantitative answer to the question, he added: "It's probably accurate to say that, in the wake of his plunge into prime-time television, Roberts commands more *personal* loyalty than any other clergyman in the nineteen-seventies. Graham is obviously the dominant figure of the era, but he is a more impersonal force. . . . Roberts, on the other hand, is a personally significant figure to thousands of people in middle America."[89] In the 1980s, Richard began extending that personal ministry to thousands of additional individuals.

Oral's legacy was also inextricably linked to his message. Although he had never claimed complete originality for his healing ideas, he was a popularizer with few rivals. His concept of merging prayer and medicine, the scientific and the spiritual, institutionalized in the City of Faith, was a bold experiment, and potentially an important one. "Let's say that in fact the hypothesis under which we are operating proves to be a valid hypothesis," conjectured Jim Winslow, "and when the story is written of what we have done is, in fact, that providing whole person health care—mind, body and spirit—putting prayer and medicine together, results in better health care. That might be the most significant thing anybody ever did in . . . health care."[90]

Hundreds of other independent ministries have been touched by Oral and his methods. "I don't know one minister," observed Demos Shakarian, "Catholics, Protestants, that doesn't love Oral. They just respect him."[91] And the flood was mounting. After two decades of existence, the university had influenced a number of young men who had established powerful ministries of their own—Billy Joe Daugherty, Bill Basansky, Doug Mobley, Terry Law, Carlton Pearson, Jonathan Gainsburgh. "They're in positions of leadership all over the place," said Oral proudly of the ORU students. "We think they are outstanding."[92] The vision of thousands of students carrying the healing message to the world seemed possible, even probable. It was a considerable legacy.

In spite of his troubles in recent years, the world seemed poised to accept Roberts's leading in the 1980s. The pentecostal and charismatic movements continued to mushroom in the United States—the Assemblies of God were the fastest-growing denomination in the nation in the 1980s.[93] As the battles of the past faded into memories, many pentecostals saw Oral in heroic terms. "I think pentecostal people still have a kind of nostalgic place in their heart for Oral," said Vinson Synan, "because they remember the crusades."[94] No one had done more to bring the pentecostal message to respectability and visibility in America; Roberts was the most important artifact of the great revival which had taken the Holy Spirit from the ghetto into the nation's plushest hotels.

Perhaps even more staggering were the outlines of Roberts's past and potential influence outside the United States. Pentecostal and charismatic religion was exploding in the Third World nations. In many countries, pentecostals had come to be the largest Protestant group; some recent estimates judged that the pentecostal "family" was the largest Protestant body in the world and projected that by the year 2000, half of the world's Protestants would be pentecostal.[95] Many of the nations of Africa, Asia, and Latin America were in the midst of the great modern rural-to-urban migration which the United States experienced in the 1890s. In that uprooting in America, pentecostalism was born and flourished. For nearly forty years, Oral, and more recently Richard, tried to influence the developing nations—drawn by the response of the expectant multitudes. Roberts's vision of sending healing teams throughout the world seemed to be coming to fruition at precisely the proper moment in the demographic development of the Third World. Timing had always been Oral's supreme gift. It seemed possible that he might be right on time again.

EPILOGUE

IN 1984, AT AGE sixty-seven, Oral Roberts was in many ways mellower and more subdued. "Why is he giving . . . support to your effort," Ron Smith challenged me in our discussion of Oral, "because it's not his nature."[1] But it was time for reflecting. Speaking at a chapel service in 1982, Oral glanced back, as one must when he sees the end approaching: "As I stand here today, I would do it all over again. I'd take every step. I'd make every journey. I'd fly every mile. I'd try to climb every mountain. I'd do it all over again. I wouldn't (applause) . . . change a thing. . . . I'd lay it upon me and upon you and upon everybody who will listen. I'd tell everybody to listen to God's voice."[2] It would be fitting for Oral to retire; it might even be productive. "He deserves rest," said his friend Demos Shakarian. "I'd like to see him get to the place where he will be under no more pressure. It's going to be harder each year from here on out to sustain that tremendous drive." Oral could become the "senior statesman of the Christian church," sharing his "forty years of experience" with the world. He was, Shakarian believed, the "focal point" of the charismatic movement, and, by extension, the cutting edge of modern Christianity.[3]

But most people who knew Oral well could not picture him as an elder statesman. "Oral's greatest achievements have been in the midst of rage," observed Ron Smith. "The rage at incompetence, the rage at inactivity. . . . Oral is non-productive when he is not in a rage."[4] Few doubted that the rage would return, a righteous indignation against anything that thwarted the completion of his call. John Williams and Jenkin Lloyd Jones, two of the most astute Roberts watchers in the world, agreed that Oral would never be finished. Williams, who perceived that he was losing his own drive, becoming "a conservator rather than a buccaneer," and resigned his executive position in his early sixties, believed that Oral could never make that decision: "He will have an inventory of grander schemes the day he dies. He has to. It's the only way he can operate. He's got to run faster and faster and faster until he burns out."[5] Jones believed the same:

> I've always looked at Oral Roberts as one looks at the motorcycle rider at the carnival in the bowl. He rides around and around going faster and faster and I've always wondered when you go past that red line. . . . Just like the motorcycle rider in the bowl, he is being kept alive by the centrifugal force of his speed. And so it is not the kind of thing that you prefer to put the brakes on very much.[6]

It was true. Oral would not quit. "I've got a lot more to do," he admitted in 1983.[7] But it was not altogether that he could not quit. The partners did need goading and new and loftier goals to achieve, but it was not just cash that made Oral run. It was his calling.

The vision was not finished. It would not be finished when the university became financially self-sufficient. It would not be finished when the City of Faith was fully operative. Because the university was not the vision, and the City of Faith was not the vision. "To understand Oral Roberts there is one key," Roberts explained, "and that is that I think in wholes. I never think in parts. . . . I don't consider doing something in addition to. This is the whole."[8]

In the mid-1980s, all of the parts were there. It seemed unlikely that any new institutions would be built. The mission that lay ahead was to find out how to use them to bring healing to Oral's generation, to make men and mankind whole. Only when that was accomplished would John the Baptist be done, and the Lord could get on with His final business.

BIBLIOGRAPHICAL
ESSAY

There is plentiful source material for a study of Oral Roberts. The Holy Spirit Room in the Oral Roberts University Library houses a collection of literature on pentecostalism, including much material on the Pentecostal Holiness church. More important is the large collection in the Oral Roberts University Archives. Archivist Lannae Graham is still in the early stages of organizing and preserving the materials, but I was fortunate to be able to use most of the collection. The notes in this book cite hundreds of specific items in the archives; this essay will outline the most important general sources of information on Roberts.

In November 1947, Oral Roberts began publishing the first magazine heralding the healing revival which spawned hundreds of independent ministries. His monthly periodical went through several name changes; Roberts consistently regarded it as his most important tie to his supporters. Its titles were: *Healing Waters* (November 1947–August 1953), *America's Healing Magazine* (September 1953–December 1955), *Healing* (January 1956–July 1956), and *Abundant Life* (July 1956–). The ministry has published a variety of other periodicals. *Daily Blessing* (1959–) is a widely circulated devotional magazine. In the 1950s, several specialized publications were begun. A comic book series was published under the titles *Oral Roberts' True Stories* (1956–1959) and *Junior Partners* (1959–1961). A small quarterly featuring Roberts's radio and television programs was *Air Waves* (1956–1957). An informative mimeographed newsletter distributed to evangelistic association employees was *OREA Partners* (1958–1959).

With the opening of the university in the 1960s, a new generation of regular publications was begun. For historical purposes, the most important is probably the student newspaper, the *Oracle* (1966–). In addition to the catalogs published biannually by the university (which contain carefully framed theological statements), ORU published a promotional quarterly for several years. The first two issues were named the *ORU Witness* (April-May 1964–Summer 1964), and subsequent issues were called *Outreach* (Fall 1964–Winter 1968). *Communiqué* is an alumni quarterly begun in the summer of 1975. Since 1980, the O. W. Coburn School of Law has published a yearly volume under the title *Journal of Christian Jurisprudence*. The City of Faith publishes a newsletter under the title *Lifeline* (1982–), and the Oral Roberts Evangelistic Association has a similar monthly publication entitled *OREA Today* (1980–).

While these ministry publications furnish a public account of Roberts's ministry after 1947, his earlier years are not so well documented. An indispensable source for those years is the *Pentecostal Holiness Advocate* (1917–), the official publication of the Pentecostal Holiness church. Oral wrote a letter to his church's newspaper during his illness in 1935, and beginning in 1937 his name appeared regularly in notices of his evangelistic meetings and in a long list of articles he wrote for the journal. By the 1950s the denominational pentecostal journals in the United States had fallen silent about the independent evangelists, and the general pentecostal periodical which followed Oral's career most closely was Donald Gee's *Pentecost* (1947–1966), published in London under the auspices of the World Conference of Pentecostal Churches.

Oral Roberts is the author of many books. Of considerable interest are his earliest works which were written before he began his independent ministry: *Salvation by the Blood* (Franklin Springs, Ga.: Pentecostal Holiness Publishing House [1938]) and *The Drama of the End-Time* (Franklin Springs, Ga.: Publishing House of the Pentecostal Holiness Church [1941]). Probably the most important book ever written by Roberts was the small volume which he used to launch his healing ministry: *If You Need Healing—Do These Things!* (2d ed.; Tulsa: Standard Printing Co. [1947]). The first printing of 3,000 books in May 1947 was quickly followed by a "second edition" of 10,000 in September. The text was substantially revised for the first time in 1949, and it subsequently has been changed many times. Several million copies of the book have been printed through the years.

The ministry has published a number of autobiographical treatments of Roberts's life. Not only do they record many details, they also show the ministry's understanding of itself at various points in its history. The most important are: *Oral Roberts' Life Story* (Tulsa: Oral Roberts [1952]); *My Story* (Tulsa and New York: Summit Book Co., 1961); *My Twenty Years of a Miracle Ministry* (Tulsa: Oral Roberts, 1967); *My Personal Diary of Our Worldwide Ministry* (Tulsa: Oral Roberts, 1968); and *The Call* (Garden City, N.Y.: Doubleday and Co., 1972).

Roberts's books and tracts have been reprinted over and over through the years, frequently slightly revised and sometimes under different titles. His basic ideas appear over and over again. Some of his more important books on healing are: *Deliverance from Fear and from Sickness* (4th printing; Tulsa: Oral Roberts [1954]); *Seven Divine Aids for Your Health* (Tulsa: Oral Roberts, 1960); *Turn Your Faith Loose!* (Tulsa: Oral Roberts Tract Society, n.d.); *What Is a Miracle?* (Tulsa: Oral Roberts [1964]); *Twelve Greatest Miracles of My Ministry* (Tulsa: Pinoak Publications, 1974); *The Miracles of Christ* (Tulsa: Oral Roberts Evangelistic Association, 1975); *Oral Roberts' Favorite Healing Scriptures* (Tulsa: Oral Roberts Evangelistic Association, 1976); and *Flood Stage* (Tulsa: Oral Roberts, 1981). Several books illustrate Roberts's changing views on the baptism of the Holy Spirit. A tract published for the first time in the 1950s set out a basically pentecostal understanding: *Why You Must Receive the Baptism of the Holy Ghost* (Tulsa: Oral Roberts Tract Society, n.d.). The tract was reprinted several times through the years, and later editions showed marked changes. For other later statements of Oral's views on the Holy Spirit, see *The Baptism with the Holy Spirit* (Tulsa: Oral Roberts [1964]) and *The Holy Spirit in the Now* (3 vols; Tulsa: Oral Roberts University, 1974). Two publications which document Roberts's continued interest in premillennialism are a 1950s tract, *It Is Later Than You Think* (Tulsa: Oral Roberts Tract Society, n.d.), and *God's Timetable for the End of Time* (Tulsa: Heliotrope Publications [1969]).

In the 1970s, the ministry emphasized the doctrine of seed-faith. The basic principles of that teaching may be found in *Miracle of Seed-Faith* (Charlotte, N.C.: Commission Press [1970]); *The Miracle Book* (Tulsa: Pinoak Publications, 1973); *How to Live above Your Problems* (Tulsa: Pinoak Publications, 1974); *Better Health and Miracle Living* (Tulsa: Oral Roberts Evangelistic Association, 1976); *Seed-Faith Commentary on the Holy Bible* (Tulsa: Pinoak Publications, 1975); and *How to Get through Your Struggles* (Tulsa: Oral Roberts Evangelistic Association, 1977).

Some other particularly useful books and tracts written by Roberts are: *The Diary of a Hollywood Visitor* (Tulsa: Healing Waters Tract Society, 1951); *Questions and Answers on Doctrine* (Tulsa: Oral Roberts Evangelistic Association, n.d.); *You Are What Your Believ-*

ing Is (Tulsa: Oral Roberts Tract Society, n.d.); *Questions and Answers about His Life and Ministry* (Tulsa: Committee on Information, Oral Roberts' Million Soul Crusade, n.d.); *Oral Roberts' Best Sermons and Stories* (Tulsa: Oral Roberts, 1956); *The Oral Roberts Reader* (Rockville Center, N.Y.: Zenith Books, 1958); *God Is a Good God* (Indianapolis and New York: Bobbs-Merrill Co., 1960); *How God Speaks to Me* (Tulsa: Oral Roberts [1964]); *101 Questions and Answers* (Tulsa: Oral Roberts [1968]); *The Teen-Age Rebel* (Tulsa: Oral Roberts, 1968); and *How to Know God's Will* (Tulsa: Oral Roberts Evangelistic Association [1982]).

The Bibles which Roberts used for preaching and studying from the early 1940s to the mid-1950s are in the archives collection. They are filled with sermon outlines which chronicle the changing emphasis in his preaching. Oral frequently jotted notes in his Bibles and made comments on specific texts.

A number of useful books have been written by members of the Roberts family. Valuable for Oral's early life is E. M. and Claudius Roberts, *Our Ministry and Our Son Oral* (Tulsa: Oral Roberts, 1960). Largely the recollections of Oral's mother, the book is a crucial source on his early life. Evelyn Roberts wrote an early account of her life with Oral, *I Married Oral Roberts* (Tulsa: Oral Roberts Evangelistic Association, 1956). She later revised and expanded that work into a best-selling book, *His Darling Wife, Evelyn* (New York: Dell Publishing Co. [1976]). Another useful book written by Evelyn is *Coping with Grief* (Tulsa: Oral Roberts Evangelistic Association [1979]). In recent years the evangelistic association has released a flood of booklets and tracts under the name of Richard Roberts. They are generally restatements of Oral's primary teachings and are designed for use in Richard's meetings. See Richard Roberts, *If You Need Healing Do These Things* (Tulsa: Richard Roberts, 1982); *How to Overcome Our Fear with Faith* (Tulsa: Richard Roberts, 1982); *The Authority You Have in Jesus' Name* (Tulsa: Richard Roberts, 1983); *Your Miracle and Blessing Plan with God* (Tulsa: Richard Roberts, 1984).

The Oral Roberts ministry publishes an enormous amount of promotional literature in the form of tracts, brochures, and booklets. That material ranges from instructional booklets for those in the crusade healing lines to brochures about the university and the City of Faith. Many of them have been preserved in the Oral Roberts University Archives. Roberts's dealings with his partners are documented by a variety of coupon booklets and "gifts" sent out by the ministry through the years. Another important source of information about that relationship and about the ministry is the monthly partner letter which is mailed to several million people. Those letters not only reveal Oral's dealings with his partners, they also provide a running account of the ministry's perception of its current status.

Probably the most important documentary source of information on the Roberts ministry is the huge collection of tapes, films, and transcripts located in the archives. Almost from the beginning of his ministry, Oral's crusade sermons were taped, as were most of his radio and television programs. Beginning in the early 1950s, recordings were made of most of the public meetings sponsored by the ministry and many of the organization's internal meetings. Most of this material has been transcribed, and the transcripts have been catalogued by the archives staff. The transcripts are unedited and are filled with grammatical and spelling errors, but they are an invaluable record of the public and private development of the ministry. They are particularly revealing because of the testimonial nature of pentecostalism. Oral, Evelyn, and the other actors in the ministry drama have repeatedly told their experiences and speculated about their meaning. In addition, Oral and Evelyn have always viewed the ministry, including the university, as their family, and they repeatedly speak with unexpected candor about their problems and hopes in the transcripts. The changes in Oral's thought, as well as the continuity in it, are preserved on tape beginning with the Healing Water radio broadcasts of 1947 and ending with his taped commentary on the New Testament, which was finished in 1983.

A large part of the writing about Oral Roberts and his ministry has been done by journalists. Soon after Oral began his healing ministry in 1947, he began to attract attention in the nation's newspapers and magazines. By 1950 his crusades almost always triggered articles in local newspapers, leaving behind hundreds of individual impressions. Roberts first attracted the attention of national magazines in 1951, when both *Life* and *Look* published articles about his ministry: "A New Revivalist," *Life*, May 30, 1951, pp. 73–78; Lewis W. Gillenson, "The Summer Sawdust Trail," *Look*, July 31, 1951, pp. 84–87. The Oral Roberts University Archives has an extensive collection of newspaper and magazine articles. Beginning in the mid-1950s, the ministry subscribed to a professional clipping service; during earlier years, local supporters generally sent copies of articles to Roberts. The archives have cataloged thousands of clippings in a chronological file. Several hundred are cited in the notes of this book.

Two extensive and favorable journalistic assessments of Roberts written in the 1950s were Will Oursler, "Healing—with Faith," *American Weekly*, February 17, 1957, pp. 22, 25–26 (an expansion of this article was published in Will Oursler, *The Healing Power of Faith* [New York: Hawthorn Books, 1957], pp. 150–64); and Emily Gardner Neal, *God Can Heal You Now* (Englewood Cliffs, N.J.: Prentice-Hall [1958]), pp. 194–200. Many of the articles on Roberts showed little knowledge of either his ministry or the pentecostal subculture. An exception was John Kobler, "Oral Roberts: King of the Faith Healers," *American Magazine*, May 1956, pp. 20–21, 88–90. Kobler's research included an interview with Oral. A good photographic essay from the 1950s is Eve Arnold, "The Laying On of Hands," *Cosmopolitan*, February 1956, pp. 78–83. Several other useful journalistic treatments from the 1950s are Phil Dessauer, "'God Heals—I Don't,'" *Coronet*, October 1955, pp. 52–61; Joseph Andrews, "Oral Roberts Can Save You!", *Suppressed*, September 1956, pp. 45–46, 56; Henry Lee, "Brother Roberts—Salvation's Salesman," *Pageant*, June 1957, pp. 86–91; and T. F. James, "The Miracle of Faith Healing," *Cosmopolitan*, December 1958, pp. 34–41.

Several articles in the 1960s illustrated the improved public image of Roberts. Pete Martin wrote a two-part series on the ministry: "Oral Roberts," *Christian Herald*, February 1966, pp. 37–39, 95–114; and March 1966, pp. 20–24, 73–81. An objective popular treatment was Hayes B. Jacobs, "Oral Roberts: High Priest of Faith Healing," *Harper's Magazine*, February 1962, pp. 37–43.

Perhaps the best journalistic article about the ministry since the building of the City of Faith is Bruce Buursma, "Oral Roberts and His Skeptics," *Chicago Tribune Magazine*, January 3, 1982, section 9, pp. 8–10, 14. For a sampling of the critical articles about the hospital, see David Fritze, "The Gold and the Glory," *Oklahoma Monthly*, October 1977, pp. 10–16, 98, 101–103; "Miracle or Mistake?", *Tulsa Home and Garden*, March 1978, pp. 32–35; "When God Talks, Oral Listens," *Time*, November 16, 1981, p. 64; and William J. Broad, "And God Said to Oral: Build a Hospital," *Science*, April 18, 1980, pp. 267–68, 270–72.

Some of the most critical assessments of the Roberts ministry have been made by religious opponents. Some have attacked him personally, while others simply question speaking in tongues and divine healing. See John R. Rice, *Four Great Heresies* ([Murfreesboro, Tenn.]: Sword of the Lord Publishers, 1975); James M. Tolle, *Have Miracles Ceased?* (Beaumont, Tex.: Tolle Publications, n.d.); A. G. Hobbs, *Have Miracles Ceased?* (Fort Worth: Hobbs Publications, 1953); V. E. Howard, *Fake Healers Exposed* (sixth printing, rev.; West Monroe, La.: Central Printers and Publishers, 1970). In 1953, Hobbs's tract was in its forty-second printing and claimed a circulation of over 325,000.

Two doctoral dissertations have been written by leaders within the ministry which throw some light on its growth. Particularly important is Raymond Othel Corvin, "Religious and Educational Backgrounds in the Founding of Oral Roberts University," Ph.D. dissertation, University of Oklahoma, 1967. Invaluable background material on the Pentecostal Holiness church in Oklahoma is supplied by George Harold Paul, "The Religious Frontier in Oklahoma: Dan T. Muse and the Pentecostal Holiness Church," Ph.D. dissertation, University of Oklahoma, 1965.

There is a large body of literature about American pentecostalism which should be consulted for information about Roberts's pentecostal roots. For a bibliography of that literature, see Charles Edwin Jones, *A Guide to the Study of the Pentecostal Movement* (2 vols.; Metuchen, N.J., and London: Scarecrow Press and American Theological Library Association [1983]). Roberts also has been described in the stream of popular and scholarly books published in the 1970s and 1980s dealing with American revivalism. By far the most satisfactory treatments of Roberts within this general context are David Edwin Harrell, Jr., *All Things Are Possible* (Bloomington: Indiana University Press [1975]), and Richard Quebedeaux, *The New Charismatics* (Garden City, N.Y.: Doubleday and Co. [1976]).

Three important books have been written about Roberts by people with considerable inside information. Most friendly is Wayne A. Robinson, *Oral: The Warm, Intimate, Unauthorized Portrait of a Man of God* (Los Angeles: Acton House [1976]). The most sweeping exposé ever published about the ministry was Jerry Sholes, *Give Me That Prime-Time Religion* (New York: Hawthorn Books [1979]). Patti Roberts gave her assessment of her marriage to Richard and her life in the ministry in Patti Roberts with Sherry Andrews, *Ashes to Gold* (Waco, Tex.: Word Books [1983]).

Second to the transcripts in the ORU archives, personal interviews have been the most important source for this book. I have talked with hundreds of people who have had personal dealings with Oral (surely every other person I have encountered in recent years has had an Oral Roberts story to tell). I recorded interviews with over fifty people; in some cases the interviews were several hours long. Some of the interviews were recorded over ten years ago, but the majority were conducted in 1983 and 1984. The following are the most important: Connie Adams, January 26, 1978; Lee Braxton, December 18, 1973; Albert E. Bush, February 11, 1983; James Buskirk, January 28, 1983, February 11, 1983, February 16, 1983, February 18, 1983, and August 17, 1984; W. R. Corvin, June 30, 1983; Bob DeWeese, January 19, 1983; Howard Ervin, January 25, 1983; Charles Farah, January 25, 1983; Jewel Faust, January 17, 1983; Bob Foresman, December 13, 1983; Kenneth Hagin, Jr., December 12, 1983; Kenneth Hagin, Sr., April 24, 1973 and December 12, 1983; Carl H. Hamilton, January 13, 1983 and January 17, 1983; Juanita Coe Hope, December 6, 1973; Warren Hultgren, March 30, 1983; Bill Jernigan, August 17, 1984; Jenkin Lloyd Jones, Sr., March 31, 1983; Charles Kothe, February 23, 1983; Freda Lindsay, December 7, 1973; Gordon Lindsay, July 27, 1972; Beth Macklin, December 14, 1983; Oscar Moore, January 20, 1983; Donald Moyers, December 13, 1983; Bill Nash, April 2, 1984; Edna Nash, April 2, 1984; Idell Northcutt, June 29, 1983; David Nunn, September 2, 1972; Harold Paul, January 28, 1983; Roberta Roberts Potts, December 13, 1983; Derek Prince, January 31, 1974; Bill Roberts, February 23, 1983; Evelyn Roberts, February 16, 1983, April 3, 1983, and November 1, 1983; Oral Roberts, February 16, 1983, August 17, 1984, and September 3, 1984; Richard Roberts, March 31, 1983 and September 5, 1984; Wayne Robinson, April 4, 1983; Demos Shakarian, January 27, 1983; Boyce Carson Simpkins, June 29, 1983; Ron Smith, February 24, 1983; Collins Steele, January 13, 1983; George Stovall, January 27, 1983; J. A. Synan, April 16, 1983; L. C. Synan, April 16, 1983; Vinson

Synan, May 22, 1983; Calvin Thielman, April 8, 1983; C. Thomas Thompson, February 2, 1983; Okemah Van Ness, June 29, 1983; Robert Voight, January 25, 1983; Frank Wallace, February 18, 1983; John Williams, March 30, 1983; James Winslow, February 4, 1983; Thomas Zimmerman, October 18, 1980. Copies of all of these taped interviews are in the possession of the author.

NOTES

Explanation of Citations

ABBREVIATIONS:

AHM   *America's Healing Magazine*
AL   *Abundant Life*
HW   *Healing Waters*
OREA   Oral Roberts Evangelistic Association
ORU   Oral Roberts University
PHA   *Pentecostal Holiness Advocate*

GENERAL:

The Oral Roberts University Archives maintains a large newspaper clipping file. Often the clippings are not identified by page number. In cases where I have cited such materials, I have noted the name of the newspaper and the date, and placed ORU at the conclusion of the citation.

All transcripts cited are located in the Oral Roberts University Archives. Many of the transcriptions are filled with typographical, spelling, and grammatical errors. I have corrected the texts unless I thought the error originated with the speaker.

All interview citations are taken from tapes in the possession of the author.

Part I

PROLOGUE
Ada, Oklahoma, July 1935

1. Map, State of Oklahoma, Dept. of Highways, Jan. 1, 1935, Oklahoma Historical Society.

2. See Gaston Litton, *History of Oklahoma* (2 vols.; New York: Lewis Historical Publishing Co., 1957), vol. 2, pp. 23–24.

3. Oral Roberts, Speech to Graduate and Theology Students Transcript, Oral Roberts University Archives, Jan. 13, 1977, p. 8. Little documentary evidence exists about Oral Roberts's early life. The reconstruction of his childhood is necessarily dependent upon his memory and that of others who knew him. Fortunately, the pentecostal movement is a rich testimonial tradition, given to endless reflection on the meaning of one's experiences. Of course, in the 1950s the stories Oral told of his childhood in repeated sermons became a sort of hagiography for his followers. While the accuracy of his recollections is open to question, in the cases where it is possible to test his recall of dates and names, his memory seems remarkably good.

4. The account of Oral Roberts's healing became the centerpiece of his later ministry. He told the story countless times in his meetings. In addition to his family, a number of other residents of Ada recalled the events of the evening, and there is general agree-

ment among them. No documentary evidence of the Moncey meeting remains. The Ada newspaper was filled with accounts of local revivals, but it is not remarkable that a pentecostal tent crusade was overlooked. For general accounts of the healing, see Oral Roberts, *My Story* (Tulsa and New York: Summit Book Co., 1961), pp. 25–35; E. M. and Claudius Roberts, *Our Ministry and Our Son Oral* (Tulsa: Oral Roberts, 1960), pp. 57–59; Evelyn Roberts, Evangelism of Oral Roberts Class Transcript, 1971, p. 16; OREA Devotion Transcript, Mar. 25, 1982, p. 4; Oral Roberts Interview, Feb. 16, 1983; Jewel Faust Interview, Jan. 17, 1983.

5. E. M. and C. Roberts, *Our Ministry,* p. 57.

6. O. Roberts, OREA Devotion Transcript, Mar. 25, 1982, p. 4.

7. "Letter," *PHA,* July 11, 1935, p. 14.

8. Oral Roberts, *How God Speaks to Me* (Tulsa: Oral Roberts, 1964), pp. 8–9.

9. O. Roberts Interview, Feb. 16, 1983.

10. O. Roberts, *How God Speaks to Me,* p. 9.

11. For Oral's limited understanding of the message, see O. Roberts, OREA Devotion Transcript, Mar. 25, 1982, pp. 4–6.

12. Moncey Business Card, Oral Roberts University Archives, Tulsa, Oklahoma.

13. Faust Interview; Boyce Carson Simpkins, Okemah Lawson Van Ness, and Idell Northcutt Interviews, June 29, 1983.

14. Moncey Business Card, ORU Archives.

15. O. Roberts, OREA Devotion Transcript, Mar. 25, 1982, p. 5. Estimates of the number of people present at the revival range from several hundred, which seems most likely, to over two thousand.

16. Haskell Rogers, "I Saw Oral Roberts Healed!" *Full Gospel Business Men's Voice,* Oct. 1959, pp. 3–5. Rogers was an Assembly of God pastor, and his presence was evidence of the crossdenominational nature of the crusade. He recollected that it was a "chilly . . . spring evening." That clearly was incorrect. He also remembered the year as 1934 instead of 1935. If Rogers was correct about the weather, however, the most likely date of the incident was during the week of July 12, 1935. Ada experienced an unusual period of "coolness" during that week. See "Coolness Holds for Week Here," *Ada Evening News,* July 19, 1935, p. 1.

17. O. Roberts, Speech to Graduate and Theology Students Transcript, Jan. 31, 1977, p. 18; OREA Devotion Transcript, Mar. 25, 1982, p. 6.

18. Rogers, "I Saw Oral Roberts Healed!" p. 4.

19. O. Roberts, OREA Devotion Transcript, Mar. 25, 1982, p. 8.

20. E. M. and C. Roberts, *Our Ministry,* pp. 58–59; O. Roberts, Life Story Transcript, undated, p. 7.

21. O. Roberts, OREA Devotion Transcript, Mar. 25, 1982, p. 8; O. Roberts, Healing Waters Broadcast, Apr. 24, 1949, Tape, ORU.

22. Evelyn Roberts, Evangelism of Oral Roberts Class Transcript, 1971, p. 14.

23. O. Roberts, Life Story Transcript, undated, p. 6.

24. O. Roberts, OREA Devotion Transcript, Mar. 25, 1982, p. 8.

25. Rogers, "I Saw Oral Roberts Healed!" p. 8.

26. Ibid. However, Oral had often taken a leading role in school plays. See Simpkins, Van Ness, and Northcutt Inverviews.

27. Evelyn Roberts, Evangelism of Oral Roberts Class Transcript, 1971, p. 14.

28. O. Roberts, Life Story Transcript, undated, p. 6.

29. Ibid. Elmer "bent over and wept." See George Stovall, "For the First Time," *AL,* June 1979, p. 13.

1. ROOTS

1. Oral Roberts, *My Story* (Tulsa and New York: Summit Book Co., 1961), p. 33.

2. Ibid., p. 13; "Oral Roberts University," *Ada News,* Apr. 4, 1967, ORU Archives; O. Roberts, Banquet Transcript, July 8, 1981, p. 8; Jewel Faust Interview, Jan. 17, 1983.

3. See Julius Lester Medlock, *When Swallows Fly Home* (Oklahoma City: Northwest Publishing Co., 1962), p. 1.

4. Ibid., p. 2.

5. See O. Roberts, *My Story,* p. 13; E. M. and Claudius Roberts, *Our Ministry and Our Son Oral Roberts* (Tulsa: Oral Roberts, 1960), pp. 11–12; Faust Interview.

6. George H. Shirk, *Oklahoma Place Names* (New ed.; Norman: University of Oklahoma Press, 1974), p. 195.

7. Medlock, *When Swallows Fly Home,* pp. 42–43.

8. Shirk, *Oklahoma Place Names,* p. 20.

9. Medlock, *When Swallows Fly Home,* p. 29.

10. Ibid., pp. 30–32.

11. See O. Roberts, *My Story,* p. 13; E. M. and C. Roberts, *Our Ministry,* p. 17.

12. O. Roberts, *My Story,* p. 13; Faust Interview.

13. "Oral Roberts University," *Ada News,* Apr. 4, 1967, ORU.

14. Bessie M. Hatchett, "Court Dockett, Sixth District, Center, Indian Territory," Typed Manuscript, Oklahoma Historical Society, p. 93.

15. O. Roberts, *My Story,* p. 13.

16. See Edwin C. McReynolds, *Oklahoma: A History of the Sooner State* (Norman: University of Oklahoma Press, 1954), p. 396.

17. The year 1936 was very harsh. See "Farm Situation in Pontotoc County," *Ada Evening News,* Jan. 3, 1937, p. 13; Angie Debo, *Oklahoma: Foot-Loose and Fancy Free* (Norman: University of Oklahoma Press, 1949), pp. 9, 76–78.

18. Debo, *Oklahoma,* p. 119. For the origins of Ada's settlers, see J. Hugh Biles, *The Early History of Ada* (Ada, Oklahoma: State Bank of Ada, Oklahoma, 1954), pp. 148–55. Predominantly, they were from Texas, Tennessee, and Arkansas.

19. For information on the Indians of the region, see Arrell Morgan Gibson, *Oklahoma* (2d ed.; Norman: University of Oklahoma Press, 1981).

20. A local historian of Ada, Oklahoma, listing the "pioneers of Ada," found fewer than two hundred residents who had arrived before 1903. Biles, *Early History,* pp. 148–55.

21. See Gaston Litton, *History of Oklahoma* (2 vols.; New York: Lewis Historical Publishing Co., 1957), vol. 2, pp. 21–23.

22. Litton, *Oklahoma,* vol. 1, p. 31. By 1900 the white residents in Indian Territory "vastly outnumbered the Indians." Ibid., vol. 2, p. 22.

23. One Pontotoc County resident remembered being invited as a young girl in the 1890s to a square dance at the home of Will Hays, "the Indian man from whom we leased our land." "The house was full of Indians," she recalled, "and they really enjoyed the evening square dancing, and I enjoyed seeing them." Lillie Reed Smith, "Early Days in Ada, Indian Territory," Typed Manuscript, Daughters of the American Revolution Collection (hereafter DAR), Oklahoma Historical Society, p. 14.

24. Roy S. McKeown, *Cabin in the Blackjacks* (N.p.: Roy S. McKeown [1980]), p. 34.

25. *History of Pontotoc County, Oklahoma* (2 vols; Ada: Pontotoc County, Historical and Genealogical Society, 1976), vol. 1, p. 263.

26. B. M. Hatchett, "Maxwell Records," Typed Manuscript, DAR, Oklahoma Historical Society, p. 14.

27. For a good description of life in Indian Territory, see Smith, "Early Days in Ada," Oklahoma Historical Society.

28. Shirk, *Oklahoma Place Names,* p. 47.

29. Biles, *Early History,* pp. 5–6; Shirk, *Oklahoma Place Names,* pp. 3–4.

30. "Lucky Pontotoc County," *Ada Evening News,* Aug. 2, 1935, p. 4.

31. McKeown, *Cabin,* pp. 78–96; *Ada, Oklahoma City Directory, 1934–35* (Springfield, Mo.: Interstate Directory, 1935), p. 2.

32. [Editorial,] *Ada Evening News,* May 12, 1935, p. 13. While the local news was still peculiarly laden with violence, the churches were flourishing. W. D. Little, editor of

the *Ada Evening News,* was a God-fearing man who frequently included religious instruction in his editorials. See, for instance, "The Church," *Ada Evening News,* May 10, 1935, p. 10.

33. Debo, *Oklahoma,* p. 84.

34. Ibid., p. 98; McReynolds, *Oklahoma,* p. 401.

35. See Evelyn Roberts, *His Darling Wife, Evelyn* (New York: Dell Publishing Co., 1976), p. 32; Faust Interview; *Ada City Directory, 1917* (Ada, Oklahoma: News Publishing and Printing Co. Publishers, 1917), p. 158; O. Roberts, A Memorial Service for E. M. Roberts Transcript, Nov. 20, 1967; O. Roberts, "A Tribute to Ellis M. Roberts," *AL,* Feb. 1968, p. 19; B. M. Hatchett, "Maxwell Township, School District 5, Maxwell Records," Typed Manuscript, Oklahoma Historical Society.

36. E. M. and C. Roberts, *Our Ministry,* pp. 9–11.

37. Ibid., pp. 12–13.

38. O. Roberts, Banquet Transcript, July 8, 1981, p. 8.

39. E. M. and C. Roberts, *Our Ministry,* p. 13.

40. Ibid.

41. Ellis Roberts, "Oral Roberts' Father's Own Story," *HW,* Aug. 1951, p. 6.

42. Carl Hamilton, "Tribute to Ellis M. Roberts," *AL,* Feb. 1968, p. 22; Carl Hamilton Interview, Jan. 13, 1983.

43. Ellis Roberts, "Oral Roberts' Father's Own Story," p. 6.

44. Bill Dryden became conference superintendent. Both he and York long lived in the Ada area. See *Yearbook of the Pentecostal Holiness Church, 1931* (Franklin Springs, Ga.: Publishing House of the P.H.C., n.d.), p. 10. See also George Harold Paul, "The Religious Frontier in Oklahoma," Ph.D. dissertation, University of Oklahoma, 1965, p. 68.

45. E. M. and C. Roberts, *Our Ministry,* p. 14.

46. See Ellis Roberts, "Oral Roberts' Father's Own Story," p. 6.

47. Thurnae York, "Honoring Our Elders," *PHA,* Oct. 9, 1952, pp. 5, 8.

48. G. H. Montgomery, "Camp Meeting Reflections," *PHA,* Aug. 24, 1939, p. 2.

49. Ellis Roberts, "Oral Roberts' Father's Own Story," p. 6; E. M. and C. Roberts, *Our Ministry,* p. 14.

50. E. M. and C. Roberts, *Our Ministry,* pp. 14–15; Ellis Roberts, "Oral Roberts' Father's Own Story," p. 6.

51 E. M. and C. Roberts, *Our Ministry,* pp. 18–23.

52. Ibid., p. 27.

53. Ibid.; O. Roberts, *My Story,* p. 9.

54. Ellis Roberts, "Oral Roberts' Father's Own Story," p. 7.

55. O. Roberts, *My Story,* p. 26.

56. E. M. and C. Roberts, *Our Ministry,* p. 10; O. Roberts, *My Story,* pp. 9, 26; Faust Interview.

57. For general accounts of the origins of American pentecostalism, see Robert Mapes Anderson, *Vision of the Disinherited* (New York and Oxford: Oxford University Press, 1979), and Vinson Synan, *The Holiness-Pentecostal Movement in the United States* (Grand Rapids: William B. Eerdmans Publishing Co., 1971).

58. For a particularly good description of early pentecostal beliefs, see Anderson, *Vision,* pp. 79–97.

59. For a discussion of the pentecostal debt to the holiness movement, see Synan, *The Holiness-Pentecostal Movement.*

60. See Medlock, *When Swallows Fly Home,* pp. 32–33.

61. Ellis Roberts, "Oral Roberts' Father's Own Story," p. 11.

62. Irwin recruited J. H. King, a Methodist minister, and by 1900 King had assumed leadership of the Fire-Baptized Association. A complicated series of mergers in the early twentieth century brought together the Fire-Baptized Holiness church, the Pentecostal Holiness church, and the Tabernacle Pentecostal church. In 1917 the united group organized into conferences along Methodist lines and began publication of a regular periodical, the *Pentecostal Holiness Advocate.* See *Discipline of the Pentecostal Holiness*

Church, 1937 (Franklin Springs, Ga.: Publishing House of the Pentecostal Holiness Church, 1937), p. 5; Paul, "Religious Frontier," pp. 5, 32–33.

63. U.S. Bureau of the Census, *Religious Bodies: 1916* (2 vols.; Washington: Government Printing Office, 1919), vol. 2, p. 147.

64. R. H. Lee, "Associate Editor's Notes," *PHA*, Mar. 11, 1937, p. 8. The census listed only 12,955. U.S. Bureau of the Census, *Religious Bodies: 1936* (2 vols.; Washington: Government Printing Office, 1941), vol. 2, part 2, p. 1313.

65. See Paul, "Religious Frontier," for a general discussion of the growth of the church in the West.

66. A "Free Methodist" church sponsored a meeting near Billings in 1905 in which one of the people spoke in tongues. It "scared the people out of the meeting house," and the ministers "did not know what it was ourselves." Paul, "Religious Frontier," p. 66.

67. Ibid., p. 67.

68. See "Editorial Comment," *PHA*, May 19, 1938, p. 2.

69. Debo, *Oklahoma*, pp. 126–27. As late as 1957, the pentecostals were not mentioned in the chapter on religion in a major two-volume state history. Litton, *Oklahoma*, vol. 2, pp. 443–81.

70. Duncan Aikman, "The Holy Rollers," *American Mercury* 15, no. 58 (1928): p. 183.

71. See Anderson, *Vision*, pp. 101, 165.

72. By the late 1940s, some of the church's leaders were seriously interested in establishing a seminary, though that move was never taken. G. H. Montgomery, "Do We Need A Seminary?" *PHA*, Feb. 15, 1945, pp. 2-3. For general discussions of the church's attitude toward the establishment of educational institutions, see Paul, "Religious Frontier," and Raymond Othel Corvin, "Religious and Educational Backgrounds in the Founding of Oral Roberts University," Ph.D. dissertation, University of Oklahoma, 1967. For the church's interest in interdenominational organizations, see "National Association of Evangelicals," *PHA*, Nov. 26, 1942, pp. 2-3; "General Board Votes for Evangelicals," *PHA*, Oct. 14, 1943, p. 3.

73. "Added unto Them," *PHA*, Dec. 15, 1938, p. 4.

74. See W. Eddie Morris, *The Vine and Branches John 15:5* (N.p.: W. Eddie Morris, 1981), p. 50.

75. L. C. Synan Interview, Apr. 16, 1983.

76. G. H. Montgomery, "Bible Evangelism," *PHA*, Apr. 14, 1938, pp. 2-3; Oscar Moore Interview, Jan. 20, 1983; Corvin, "Religious and Educational Background," pp. 142–43.

77. "A Good Confession," *PHA*, Dec. 1, 1938, p. 4.

78. *Discipline, 1937*, p. 12.

79. Ibid.

80. See Paul, "Religious Frontier," pp. 46–47. See Paul G. Chappell, "The Divine Healing Movement in America," Ph.D. dissertation, Drew University, 1982.

81. Morris, *Vine and Branches*, pp. 61–62; George Floyd Taylor, "Divine Healing," *PHA*, May 1, 1947, p. 7.

82. Morris, *Vine and Branches*, pp. 54–62. See "Divine Healing—Fact or Fad," *PHA*, May 13, 1943, p. 4.

83. *Discipline, 1937*, p. 12.

84. G. H. Montgomery, "The Pentecostal Holiness Stand on Sanctification," *PHA*, June 20, 1940, pp. 2-3. For a good summary of the church's position on sanctification, see W. H. Turner, *The Difference Between Regeneration, Sanctification, and the Pentecostal Baptism* (Franklin Springs, Ga.: Publishing House of the Pentecostal Holiness Church, 1947).

85. Morris, *Vine and Branches*, p. 48.

86. See, for instance, G. H. Montgomery, "Does the Russo-German Alliance Seal Civilization's Doom?" *PHA*, Oct. 26, 1939, pp. 2-3. Montgomery's answer to the question was "If this war continues, civilization as we know it now is doomed."

87. Vinson Synan, Speech, Indiana University, May 13, 1983.

88. Morris, *Vine and Branches,* p. 49; *Discipline, 1937,* p. 42.

89. Montgomery, "Camp Meeting Reflections," p. 3.

90. *Discipline, 1937,* p. 41.

91. Morris, *Vine and Branches,* pp. 58–59.

92. *Discipline, 1937,* p. 42.

93. Ibid., p. 41.

94. Ibid., p. 43.

95. See Paul, "Religious Frontier," pp. 115–16.

96. Ibid., p. 122.

97. Ibid., p. 79.

98. O. E. Sproull, "Christ and the Common People," *PHA,* Sept. 29, 1938, p. 4.

99. See Paul, "Religious Frontier," p. 69. Oklahoma had a strong socialist movement in the 1930s. See McReynolds, *Oklahoma,* pp. 345–47.

100. "What Is Education?" *PHA,* July 8, 1943, p. 2.

101. Anderson, *Vision,* pp. 98–113.

102. Paul, "Religious Frontier," p. 122.

103. Mr. and Mrs. E. M. Roberts, Minister's Seminar Transcript, Apr. 29, 1963, pp. 1–2.

104. Ellis Roberts, "Oral Roberts' Father's Own Story," p. 7. For a picture, see O. Roberts, "Tribute to Ellis M. Roberts," *AL,* Feb. 1968, p. 19.

105. E. M. and C. Roberts, *Our Ministry,* pp. 29–30; O. Roberts, "Tribute to Ellis M. Roberts," p. 19.

106. Ellis Roberts, "Oral Roberts' Father's Own Story," p. 10.

107. Faust Interview.

108. Mr. and Mrs. E. M. Roberts, Laymen's Seminar Transcript, Apr. 24, 1966, p. 4.

109. Mr. and Mrs. E. M. Roberts, Minister's Seminar Transcript, Apr. 29, 1963, p. 6.

110. Evelyn Roberts, *His Darling Wife,* p. 34.

111. O. Roberts, Contemporary Methods in Evangelism Class Transcript, Oct. 11, 1967, p. 36; Chapel Transcript, Oct. 26, 1973, p. 7.

112. E. M. and C. Roberts, *Our Ministry,* pp. 43, 48.

113. O. Roberts, Chapel Transcript, Oct. 26, 1973, p. 6.

114. G. H. Montgomery, "Attention Evangelists," *PHA,* Feb. 12, 1942, p. 3.

115. Evelyn Roberts, *His Darling Wife,* p. 34; Faust Interview; O. Roberts, Church Sermon Transcripts, Feb. 6, 1975, p. 5. Ellis was an ordained minister in the frontier Pentecostal Holiness church; his friend and mentor M. L. Dryden was his conference superintendent. But he was not careful to keep his ministerial papers in order—his ministerial commission, he believed, came from the Lord and the people who accepted his ministry. See *Yearbook, 1931* (Franklin Springs, Ga.: Publishing House of the Pentecostal Holiness Church, n.d.), pp. 10, 16. In 1931 he was "reinstated as ordained." He appeared irregularly at the annual conferences and rarely sent in reports. When he did appear, however, he was recognized as a minister, and reordination was a formality.

116. See E. M. and C. Roberts, *Our Ministry,* p. 39; O. Roberts, Chapel Transcript, Oct. 26, 1973, p. 7; Faust Interview; *Ada, Oklahoma City Directory, 1934–35,* p. 178.

117. Ellis Roberts, "Oral Roberts' Father's Own Story," p. 11; E. M. and C. Roberts, *Our Ministry,* p. 32.

118. Mr. and Mrs. E. M. Roberts, Laymen's Seminar Transcript, Apr. 24, 1966, p. 7.

119. Faust Interview; E. M. and C. Roberts, *Our Ministry,* pp. 46–47.

120. E. M. and C. Roberts, *Our Ministry,* p. 42.

121. O. Roberts, Church Sermon Transcript, Feb. 6, 1975, p. 6.

122. E. M. and C. Roberts, *Our Ministry,* pp. 44–45; Mr. and Mrs. E. M. Roberts, Minister's Seminar Transcript, Apr. 29, 1963, p. 8.

123. Ibid.

124. E. M. and C. Roberts, *Our Ministry,* p. 42.

125. Ibid., p. 47.

126. Mr. and Mrs. E. M. Roberts, Minister's Seminar Transcript, Apr. 29, 1963, p. 7.

127. E. M. and C. Roberts, *Our Ministry,* pp. 31–32.

128. Ibid., p. 32.

129. Ellis Roberts, "Oral Roberts' Father's Own Story," p. 10.

130. E. M. and C. Roberts, *Our Ministry,* p. 38.

131. Minister's Seminar Transcript, Jan. 18, 1963, pp. 25–26.

132. E. M. and C. Roberts, *Our Ministry,* pp. 38–39; Ellis Roberts, "Oral Roberts' Father's Own Story," p. 10.

2. THE MOLD

1. See "The New Year." *Ada Weekly News,* Jan. 3, 1918, p. 4; "Week's Death List from Pneumonia," *Ada Weekly News,* Oct. 31, 1918, p. 4.

2. Mr. and Mrs. E. M. Roberts, Minister's Seminar Transcript, Apr. 29, 1963, pp. 3–4; E. M. and Claudius Roberts, *Our Ministry and Our Son Oral* (Tulsa: Oral Roberts, 1960), pp. 33–35; Oral Roberts, Life Story Sermon Transcript, n.d., pp. 1–2.

3. E. M. and C. Roberts, *Our Ministry,* p. 35; Yvonne Nance, "A Mother Talks about Her Son," *AL,* May 1960, p. 10.

4. See, for instance, W. T. Jeffers, *What I Know about Oral Roberts* (Tulsa: Frontiers of Faith, n.d.), p. 11.

5. Mr. and Mrs. E. M. Roberts, Minister's Seminar Transcript. Apr. 29, 1963, p. 2.

6. Ibid., p. 5.

7. G. H. Montgomery, "She Named Him Oral," *AHM,* Feb. 1954, p. 5.

8. Ibid.; Oral Roberts, *My Story* (Tulsa: Summit Book Co., 1961), p. 191.

9. W. D. Little Interview, June 29, 1983.

10. Montgomery, "She Named Him Oral" p. 5. Cousin Minnie appears in the early court records as the oldest of the grandchildren. See B. M. Hatchett, "Maxwell Records, Maxwell Township, School District 5," Typed Manuscript, Oklahoma Historical Society.

11. E. M. and C. Roberts, *Our Ministry,* p. 26.

12. O. Roberts, Memorial Service for E. M. Roberts Transcript, Nov. 20, 1967, p. 2; O. Roberts, *My Story,* pp. 26–27.

13. Mr. and Mrs. E. M. Roberts, Laymen's Seminar Transcript, Apr. 24, 1966, pp. 5–6. When Ellis got home, he told Oral about his experience, and Oral said: "Papa, what if you hadn't a knew God?" Ellis replied: "You wouldn't have no Mama."

14. George Stovall, "For the First Time Here Is the Personal Account of Oral Roberts' Healing," *AL,* June 1979, p. 12.

15. E. M. and C. Roberts, *Our Ministry,* p. 45.

16. Oral Roberts, *Oral Roberts' Life Story* (Tulsa: Oral Roberts, 1952), p. 23.

17. Ibid.; O. Roberts, Chapel Tape, Nov. 14, 1967.

18. Boyce Carson Simpkins Interview, June 29, 1983.

19. Evelyn Roberts, Miscellaneous Speech Transcript, Mar. 2, 1974, p. 10.

20. O. Roberts, "Giving off the Top," *AL,* Feb. 1975, p. 3; O. Roberts, Faculty Meeting Transcript, Feb. 4, 1971, p. 4.

21. Jewel Faust Interview, Jan. 17, 1983.

22. Gilbert Bond, "I Made Oral Roberts Tough by Throwing Rocks in Front of Him," *AL,* May 1979, p. 20.

23. Montgomery, "She Named Him Oral," p. 6.

24. E. M. and C. Roberts, *Our Ministry,* p. 51.

25. O. Roberts, *Life Story,* pp. 7–38.

26. Ibid., p. 35.

27. Oral and his friends long remembered his traumatic efforts to ask Boyce's par-

ents for permission to take her to a movie. O. Roberts, *Life Story*, p. 29; Simpkins Interview.

28. Montgomery, "She Named Him Oral," p. 6. See also O. Roberts, *Life Story*, pp. 29–38.

29. O. Roberts, Crusade Transcript, Dec. 13, 1957, p. 3; O. Roberts, Church Sermon Transcript, Feb. 29, 1976, pp. 6–7.

30. O. Roberts, Chapel Transcript, Oct. 6, 1982, p. 6.

31. E. M. and C. Roberts, *Our Ministry*, p. 47.

32. Montgomery, "She Named Him Oral," p. 6.

33. Ibid.; W. R. Corvin Interview, June 30, 1983; Faust Interview.

34. See O. Roberts, *Life Story*, p. 29.

35. Faust Interview; E. M. and C. Roberts, *Our Ministry*, p. 74.

36. O. Roberts, Faculty Chapel Transcript, Sept. 5, 1967, p. 2.

37. Simpkins Interview; Okemah Lawson Van Ness and Idell Northcutt Interviews, June 29, 1983.

38. E. M. and C. Roberts, *Our Ministry*, p. 51; Simpkins, Van Ness, and Northcutt Interviews.

39. E. M. and C. Roberts, *Our Ministry*, p. 52; Faust Interview.

40. "Roberts' Mother Chose Career Before He Was Born," *Tulsa Tribune*, undated clipping, ORU Archives.

41. E. M. and C. Roberts, *Our Ministry*, p. 53.

42. E. M. and Claudius Roberts, "Our Son Oral and His Ministry," *AL*, Sept. 1965, p. 18.

43. E. M. and C. Roberts, *Our Ministry*, pp. 39, 47–48.

44. Ibid., p. 46; O. Roberts, Faculty Orientation Transcript, Aug. 14, 1978, p. 8.

45. O. Roberts, "How God's Healing Power Came to Me," *HW*, May 1948, p. 1.

46. O. Roberts, OREA Devotion Transcript, Mar. 25, 1982, p. 7.

47. O. Roberts, "How God's Healing Power Came to Me," p. 1.

48. O. Roberts, *My Story*, p. 26.

49. O. Roberts, "The Scribes and Pharisees," *PHA*, May 21, 1945, p. 4.

50. O. Roberts, Church Sermon Transcript, Feb. 29, 1976, p. 6.

51. Nance, "A Mother Talks about Her Son," p. 10.

52. Glenn Shetton, "Big Bread," *Wichita Falls Times*, Mar. 9, 1960, p. 2A.

53. Simpkins, Van Ness, and Northcutt Interviews.

54. O. Roberts, "How God's Healing Power Came to Me," p. 1.

55. George H. Shirk, *Oklahoma Place Names* (Norman: University of Oklahoma Press, 1974). pp. 13–14.

56. Bertha Teague, Telephone Interview, June 29, 1983.

57. E. M. and C. Roberts, *Our Ministry*, p. 54.

58. O. Roberts, *My Story*, p. 4.

59. O. Roberts, Chapel Tape, Nov. 14, 1967; Nance, "A Mother Talks about Her Son," pp. 10–11.

60. Evelyn Roberts, *His Darling Wife, Evelyn* (New York: Dell Publishing Co., 1976), p. 34; O. Roberts, Church Sermon Transcript, Feb. 29, 1976, p. 6.

61. O. Roberts, Crusade Transcript, Nov. 1956, p. 23.

62. O. Roberts, "How God's Healing Power Came to Me," p. 1.

63. O. Roberts, Crusade Transcript, Nov. 1956, p. 23. For general descriptions of his rebellious spirit, see O. Roberts, Banquet Transcript, July 8, 1981, pp. 9–10; O. Roberts, Speech to Graduate and Theology Students Transcript, Jan. 31, 1977, p. 10; Evelyn Roberts, Miscellaneous Speech Transcript, Mar. 2, 1974, p. 10.

64. O. Roberts, Speech to Graduate and Theology Students Transcript, Jan. 31, 1977, p. 10.

65. Evelyn Roberts, Miscellaneous Speech Transcript, Mar. 2, 1974, p. 10.

66. O. Roberts, Church Sermon Transcript, Feb. 6, 1975, p. 6.

67. Wayne A. Robinson, *I Once Spoke in Tongues* (Old Tappan, N.J.: Fleming H. Revell Co., Spire Books, 1975), pp. 17–19, 32.

68. Ibid., p. 19.

69. Thomas Zimmerman Interview, Oct. 18, 1980.

70. Donald Gee, "Persecution," *Pentecost*, Mar. 1951, p. 17.

71. Tommy Logue, "Synan Provides Historical Perspetive," *Oracle*, Oct. 10, 1980, p. 7; Vinson Synan Interview, May 22, 1983.

72. Bob Foresman and Jenk Jones, Jr., "Oral Roberts: What Makes Him Tick," *Tulsa Tribune*, June 11, 1975, pp. 1B–2B.

73. Evelyn Roberts, *His Darling Wife*, pp. 37–38; O. Roberts, *My Story*, p. 5; E. M. and C. Roberts, *Our Ministry*, p. 54.

74. O. Roberts, *My Story*, p. 5.

75. Ibid. While Oral made little money from these jobs, and did little more than send occasional reports to his hometown paper as a "stringer," he was clearly ambitious and busy. See O. Roberts, *Life Story*, p. 43; O. Roberts, Crusade Transcript, Nov. 1956, p. 23; Little Interview. While Little did not remember Oral's being a "stringer" for the newspaper, he noted that it was common to use such out-of-town people to cover local news for the paper. Oral showed an ability to write and a penchant for making contact with the local press when he became a preacher.

76. See O. Roberts, *My Story*, pp. 4–5; O. Roberts, Crusade Transcript, Nov. 1956, pp. 23–24; O. Roberts, Crusade Transcript, Mar. 12, 1959, p. 18.

77. O. Roberts, Church Sermon Transcript, Feb. 6, 1975, p. 6.

78. O. Roberts, *Life Story*, p. 44.

79. O. Roberts, Church Sermon Transcript, Feb. 6, 1975, p. 7.

80. O. Roberts, *Life Story*, p. 44.

81. E. M. and C. Roberts, *Our Ministry*, p. 54.

82. O. Roberts, My Own Personal Story Transcript, Oct. 21, 1970, p. 7.

83. O. Roberts, *Life Story*, p. 43.

84. Peter Martin, "Oral Roberts," *Christian Herald*, Mar. 1966, p. 77.

85. O. Roberts, *Life Story*, p. 13; O. Roberts, *My Story*, pp. 2–3.

86. O. Roberts, Banquet Transcript, July 8, 1981, p. 9.

87. See Simpkins, Van Ness, and Northcutt Interviews.

88. O. Roberts, "How God's Healing Power Came to Me," p. 1–2.

89. See O. Roberts, Chapel Tape, Nov. 14, 1967.

90. O. Roberts, Crusade Transcript, Nov. 1956, p. 26.

91. O. Roberts, Chapel Tape, Nov. 14, 1967.

92. E. M. and C. Roberts, *Our Ministry*, p. 56.

93. O. Roberts, Banquet Transcript, July 8, 1981, p. 12; Evangelism of Oral Roberts Class Transcript, 1971, p. 2.

94. See O. Roberts, *My Story*, p. 15.

95. Evangelism of Oral Roberts Class Transcript, 1971, p. 3.

96. See O. Roberts, *My Story*, pp. 15–16; O. Roberts, Chapel Transcript, Oct. 26, 1973, pp. 4–5; O. Roberts, Banquet Transcript, July 8, 1981, p. 8; O. Roberts, Chapel Tape, Nov. 14, 1981; E. M. and C. Roberts, *Our Ministry*, p. 56; O. Roberts, *Life Story*, pp. 13–14.

97. O. Roberts, Church Sermon Transcript, Feb. 6, 1975, p. 7; George Stovall, "For the First Time Here Is the Personal Account of Oral Roberts' Healing, *AL*, June 1979, p. 12.

98. O. Roberts, Chapel Transcript, June 16, 1982, p. 5.

99. Claudius Roberts, Chapel Transcript, Oct. 26, 1973, p. 4.

100. O. Roberts, Crusade Transcript, May 26, 1955, pp. 9–10.

101. O. Roberts, *My Story*, p. 19; Oral Roberts, *My Twenty Years of a Miracle Ministry* (Tulsa: Oral Roberts, 1967), p. 7.

102. O. Roberts, "The Growth of a Miracle," *AL*, Feb. 1963, p. 2; O. Roberts, *My Story*, p. 18.

103. O. Roberts, *My Story*, p. 18.

104. Ibid., p. 20.

105. O. Roberts, Life Story Sermon Transcript, undated, p. 6.

106. Ibid., p. 21. For general descriptions of this story, see O. Roberts, Chapel Transcript, Oct. 6, 1982, p. 11; O. Roberts, Crusade Transcript, Nov. 1956, p. 9; E. M. and C. Roberts, *Our Ministry*, p. 56; O. Roberts, Chapel Tape, Nov. 14, 1967; O. Roberts, "How God's Healing Power Came to Me," p. 2.

107. Ibid.

108. O. Roberts, Chapel Tape, Nov. 14, 1967; O. Roberts, "How God's Healing Power Came to Me," p. 2.

109. O. Roberts, Chapel Transcript, Oct. 26, 1973, pp. 8–9.

110. O. Roberts, Church Sermon Transcript, Feb. 6, 1975, p. 8.

111. O. Roberts, OREA Devotion Transcript, Mar. 25, 1982, p. 4.

112. O. Roberts, *My Story*, p. 20; O. Roberts, Church Sermon Transcript, Feb. 26, 1976, p. 7.

3. EVANGELIST

1. Oral Roberts, *Oral Roberts' Life Story* (Tulsa: Oral Roberts, 1952), p. 51. Sugg Clinic was organized two years earlier; it was Ada's first medical center. See *Ada. Oklahoma City Directory 1934–35* (Springfield, Mo.: Interstate Directory, 1935), p. 211.

2. O. Roberts, Laymen's Seminar Transcript, Dec. 6, 1963, p. 13.

3. O. Roberts, Banquet Transcript, July 8, 1981, p. 17.

4. E. M. and Claudius Roberts, *Our Ministry and Our Son Oral* (Tulsa: Oral Roberts, 1960), p. 62.

5. Yvonne Nance, "A Mother Talks about Her Son," *AL,* May 1960, p. 11.

6. O. Roberts, Banquet Transcript, July 8, 1981, p. 17.

7. Nance, "A Mother Talks about Her Son," p. 11.

8. O. Roberts, Speech to Graduate and Theology Students Transcript, Jan. 31, 1977, p. 18; Chapel Transcript, Nov. 24, 1979, pp. 4–5.

9. O. Roberts, *Life Story,* pp. 52–53; O. Roberts, OREA Devotion Transcript, July 26, 1962, p. 5; R. O. Corvin, Room Sponsors Seminar Transcript, May 20, 1963, p. 4; Oral Roberts, *My Story* (Tulsa and New York: Summit Book Co., 1961), pp. 38–39.

10. O. Roberts, *My Story,* p. 39.

11. Okemah Lawson Van Ness Interview, June 29, 1983.

12. Haskell Rogers, "I Saw Oral Roberts Healed!" *AL,* Dec. 1958, p. 11.

13. Idell Northcutt Interview, June 29, 1983.

14. George Stovall, "For the First Time Here Is the Personal Account of Oral Robert's Healing," *AL,* June 1979, p. 13.

15. G. H. Montgomery, "She Named Him Oral," *AHM,* Feb. 1954, p. 6.

16. O. Roberts, *My Story,* p. 39.

17. E. M. and C. Roberts, *Our Ministry,* p. 68; O. Roberts, Chapel Transcript, Oct. 6, 1982, p. 10; Carl H. Hamilton Interview, Jan. 13, 1983.

18. "Reports," *PHA,* May 28, 1936, p. 12.

19. "Reports," *PHA,* Oct. 15, 1936, p. 7.

20. O. Roberts, Chapel Transcript, Oct. 6, 1982, p. 9.

21. Stovall, "For the First Time Here Is the Personal Account of Oral Roberts' Healing," p. 13.

22. Evelyn Roberts, *His Darling Wife, Evelyn* (New York: Dell Publishing Co., 1976), p. 22.

23. O. Roberts, Chapel Transcript, Nov. 14, 1967, p. 2; "Oral Roberts, You Are Born for a Purpose," *AL,* Sept. 1965, p. 7.

24. R. H. Lee, ed., *Yearbook of the Pentecostal Holiness Church, 1936* (Franklin Springs, Ga.: Publishing House of the Pentecostal Holiness Church, 1936), pp. 18–19. See also the *Yearbooks* of 1937 and 1938. Oral was secretary-treasurer of the organization.

25. O. Roberts, "Is the World Overtaking You?" *PHA,* July 1, 1937, p. 13.

26. Lee, *Yearbook, 1936,* p. 42.

27. Boyce Carson Simpkins Interview, June 29, 1983.

28. *PHA,* July 20, 1939, p. 11.

29. E. M. and C. Roberts, *Our Ministry,* p. 30. See Harold Paul, "The Religious Frontier in Oklahoma," Ph.D dissertation, University of Oklahoma, 1965, pp. 100–101.

30. G. H. Montgomery, "Camp Meeting Reflections," *PHA,* Aug. 24, 1939, pp. 2–3.

31. "East Oklahoma Conference Camp Meeting," *PHA,* Sept. 26, 1940, p. 9.

32. W. Eddie Morris, *The Vine and Branches* (N.p.: W. Eddie Morris, 1981), pp. 94–95.

33. "Oklahoma," *PHA,* Aug. 26, 1937, p. 2.

34. O. Roberts, "Why You Must Receive the Holy Ghost," *HW,* May 1950, p. 15.

35. O. Roberts, Chapel Transcript, Nov. 14, 1967, p. 3.

36. Evelyn Roberts, Miscellaneous Speech Transcript, Mar. 2, 1974, pp. 10–11; Evelyn Roberts, Chapel Transcript, Feb. 3. 1982, p. 5; Evelyn Roberts, *His Darling Wife,* pp. 10–11. Oral remembered rushing in himself. He also remembered Evelyn singing. O. Roberts, *My Story,* pp. 43–44.

37. O. Roberts, *My Story,* p. 43.

38. Evelyn Roberts, Chapel Transcript, Feb. 3, 1982, p. 6.

39. Evelyn Roberts, *His Darling Wife,* pp. 20–30. Perhaps the fullest account of the early years of Evelyn's life is in Evelyn Roberts, Miscellaneous Speech Transcript, Mar. 2, 1974, pp. 4–9.

40. Fahnestock was "admitted" to the ministry of the Pentecostal Holiness church in 1919 in Oklahoma City. Lee, *Yearbook, 1935,* p. 22. That would make him a Christian at the time of his marriage, although he might not have yet received the baptism of the Holy Spirit.

41. Oscar Moore Interview, Jan. 20, 1983.

42. Evelyn Roberts, Miscellaneous Speech Transcript, Mar. 2, 1974, p. 7.

43. Ibid.

44. Evelyn Roberts, *His Darling Wife,* p. 24.

45. Beverly Shields, "Evelyn's Sister Works as ORU Operator," *Oracle,* Feb. 1, 1980, p. 12.

46. Evelyn Roberts, *His Darling Wife,* p. 30.

47. Evelyn Roberts, Miscellaneous Speech Transcript, Mar. 2, 1974, p. 9.

48. Evelyn Roberts, *His Darling Wife,* p. 29.

49. Evelyn Roberts, Miscellaneous Speech Transcript, Mar. 2, 1974, p. 9.

50. Evelyn Roberts, *His Darling Wife,* p. 30.

51. Evelyn Roberts, Miscellaneous Speech Transcript, Mar. 2, 1974, p. 9.

52. E. M. and C. Roberts, *Our Ministry,* p. 64.

53. "Oral Roberts, You Are Born for a Purpose," p. 7.

54. In 1937 Ellis accepted a position as pastor of the church in Westville. See O. Roberts, Chapel Transcript, Nov. 14, 1967, pp. 2–3; O. Roberts, Chapel Transcript, Oct. 6, 1982, pp. 9–10; O. Roberts, Speech to Graduate and Theology Students Transcript, Jan. 31, 1977, p. 18. Ellis placated Oral, and Claudius took care of the objecting pastor.

55. Moore Interview; E. M. and C. Roberts, *Our Ministry,* p. 64.

56. E. M. and C. Roberts, *Our Ministry,* p. 64.

57. Chapel Transcript, Mar. 26, 1970, p. 3.

58. O. Roberts, "Here's How It All Began," *AL,* Feb. 1979, pp. 5–6.

59. O. Roberts, *My Story,* pp. 1–2; Bob Foresman and Jenk Jones, Jr., "Oral Roberts: What Makes Him Tick," *Tulsa Tribune,* June 11, 1975, pp. 1B–2B; Harold Paul Interview, Jan. 28, 1983.

60. W. O. Moore, "Fifty-Two Saved in Sand Springs Revival," *PHA,* Apr. 21, 1938, p. 13.

61. "A Church Catches Fire!", *PHA,* Apr. 21, 1938, p. 2.

62. "From Evangelist Oral Roberts East Oklahoma Conference," *PHA,* Nov. 17, 1938, p. 11.

63. Ibid.

64. G. H. Montgomery, "New Blood for the Body," *PHA*, Nov. 17, 1938, p. 4.

65. O. Roberts, "Character Building," *PHA*, Aug. 26, 1937, p. 5. It was a feather in the cap of an aspiring young evangelist to publish in the paper. Oral later had the article published as a tract and listed it as his first publication. The article appears in the same issue as Montgomery's report on the camp meeting; he probably brought it back with him from Oklahoma.

66. See O. Roberts, "Jesus over against the Treasury," *PHA*, Dec. 16, 1937, pp. 4–5, 10.

67. O. Roberts, "Lord, Come and Teach Us to Pray," *PHA*, Mar. 10, 1938, p. 4.

68. O. Roberts, "Relationship of Pastor and Evangelist," *PHA*, Apr. 21, 1938, pp. 5, 10; Moore Interview.

69. O. Roberts, "Pessimism versus Optimism," *PHA*, June 30, 1938, p. 5.

70. O. Roberts, "Lord, Come and Teach Us to Pray," p. 5.

71. O. Roberts, *Salvation By the Blood* (Franklin Springs, Ga.: Pentecostal Holiness Publishing House, 1938), p. 5.

72. Ibid., p. 6.

73. Ibid., p. 8.

74. "Books That Are Available Written by Members of the Pentecostal Holiness Church," *PHA*, July 7, 1938, p. 15.

75. Moore Interview.

76. Evelyn Roberts, "I Married Oral Roberts," *HW*, Nov. 1952, p. 14.

77. O. Roberts, Speech to Student Meeting Transcript, Aug. 20, 1975, p. 15; O. Roberts, Chapel Transcript, Nov. 14, 1967, p. 5; Evelyn Roberts, Chapel Transcript, Feb. 3, 1982, p. 8.

78. Evelyn Roberts, Miscellaneous Speech Transcript, Mar. 2, 1974, p. 12.

79. Evelyn Roberts, Chapel Transcript, Feb. 3, 1982, p. 7.

80. "Devoted to Oral's Ministry She's Constantly by His Side," *Oracle*, Sept. 20, 1974, p. 5. See also Yvonne Litchfield, "This Is Mrs. Oral Roberts, Believer in Love at First Sight," *Tulsa World*, Feb. 15, 1967, ORU.

81. Evelyn Roberts, "I Married Oral Roberts," p. 7.

82. O. Roberts, Chapel Transcript, Nov. 14, 1967, p. 5.

83. Yvonne Litchfield, "This Is Mrs. Oral Roberts . . . ," *Tulsa World*, Feb. 15, 1967, ORU; Moore Interview.

84. "Devoted to Oral's Ministry She's Constantly by His Side," p. 5.

85. Evelyn Roberts, "I Married Oral Roberts," p. 7.

86. O. Roberts, Chapel Transcript, Nov. 14, 1967, p. 6.

87. Ibid.

88. See E. M. and C. Roberts, *Our Ministry*, p. 64; Evelyn Roberts, *His Darling Wife*, pp. 14–15.

89. Evelyn Roberts, "I Married Oral Roberts," p. 7.

90. O. Roberts, Life Story Sermon Transcript, n.d., p. 7.

91. Evelyn Roberts, "I Married Oral Roberts," p. 7.

92. O. Roberts, Life Story Sermon Transcript, n.d., pp. 7–8.

93. Evelyn Roberts, Speech to ORU Students Transcript, Feb. 11, 1975, n.p.; Evelyn Roberts, Chapel Transcript, Feb. 3, 1982, p. 8.

94. "Devoted to Oral's Ministry She's Constantly by His Side," p. 5.

95. Evelyn Roberts, Minister's Seminar Transcript, Jan. 19, 1963, p. 39.

96. O. Roberts, *My Story*, p. 47.

97. Evelyn Roberts, Chapel Transcript, Feb. 3, 1982, p. 7; Evelyn Roberts, "I Married Oral Roberts," p. 14.

98. Evelyn Roberts, *His Darling Wife*, p. 21; Evelyn Roberts, "I Married Oral Roberts," p. 14.

99. O. Roberts, Chapel Transcript, Nov. 14, 1967, pp. 7–8; Moore Interview.

100. O. Roberts, *My Story*, p. 47.

101. Evelyn Roberts, "I Married Oral Roberts," p. 14.

102. Ibid.

103. Evelyn Roberts, Chapel Transcripts, Feb. 3, 1982, pp. 9–10.

104. O. Roberts, *My Story*, p. 48.

105. Evelyn Roberts, Chapel Transcript, Feb. 3, 1982, pp. 9–10.

106. Lee, *Yearbook, 1939*, pp. 14, 22.

107. See "Meetings and Conferences," *PHA*, Jan. 26, 1939, p. 4; "Native of East Oklahoma P.Y.P.S.," *PHA*, June 15, 1939, p. 15.

108. "Forty-Two Experiences in Athens Revival," *PHA*, June 27, 1940, p. 13.

109. "From Brother Oral Roberts," *PHA*, May 30, 1940, p. 13.

110. "Forty-Two Experiences in Athens Revival," p. 13.

111. "Evangelists' Reports," *PHA*, Oct. 17, 1940, p. 9.

112. "The East Oklahoma Conference," *PHA*, Nov. 21, 1940, p. 9.

113. "The Evangelistic Album," *PHA*, Nov. 28, 1940, p. 11.

114. O. Roberts, Crusade Transcript, May 26, 1955, p. 12.

115. "The Evangelist Album," p. 11.

116. O. Roberts, Crusade Transcript, May 26, 1955, p. 12.

117. Ibid.

118. "Oral Roberts Reports," *PHA*, Feb. 20, 1941, pp. 9–11. See also "Meetings and Conferences," *PHA*, Jan. 2, 1941, p. 15.

119. "The Revival in Washington, D.C.," *PHA*, May 15, 1941, p. 9.

120. "In a Tight Spot in Washingon, D.C.," *PHA*, Apr. 17, 1941, pp. 3, 8.

121. Lee, *Yearbook, 1941*, p. 3; "General Conference Directory," *PHA*, Jan. 30, 1941, p. 4.

122. "From the Field," *PHA*, Aug. 14, 1941, p. 11.

123. G. Oral Roberts, "Temptations of the Evangelist," *PHA*, Nov. 25, 1943, pp. 5, 9.

124. "The Revival in Washington, D.C.," p. 9.

125. L. C. Synan Interview, Apr. 16, 1983.

126. O. Roberts, Chapel Transcript, Nov. 14, 1967, p. 8.

127. Oral Roberts, *The Drama of the End-Time* (Franklin Springs, Ga.: Publishing House of the Pentecostal Holiness Church, 1941), p. 7.

128. Evelyn Roberts, Student Meeting Transcript, Mar. 19, 1975, pp. 10–12.

129. O. Roberts, Chapel Transcript, Nov. 14, 1967, p. 8.

130. Evelyn Roberts, Student Meeting Transcript, Mar. 19, 1975, p. 12.

131. Evelyn Roberts, Chapel Transcript, Feb. 3, 1982, p. 10.

132. "Evangelists' Reports," *PHA*, May 29, 1941, p. 11.

133. O. Roberts, *The Drama of the End-Time*, p. 6.

134. See Bible inscribed "Oral Roberts, Ada, Oklahoma, Route 2, April-37," ORU.

135. "Evangelists' Reports," *PHA*, May 29, 1941, p. 11. See also Eve Arnold, "The Laying On of Hands," *Cosmopolitan*, Feb. 1956, p. 82.

136. Tract (no publication information), Anna Bell Campbell Arnold Scrapbook, Pentecostal Holiness Church Archives, Oklahoma City.

137. O. Roberts, Chapel Transcript, Nov. 15, 1967, pp. 6–7.

138. For a good analysis of the pentecostal clergy, see Robert Mapes Anderson, *Vision of the Disinherited* (New York and Oxford: Oxford University Press, 1979), pp. 98–113.

139. G. H. Montgomery, "Rugged Individualism in Religious Progress," *PHA*, Jan. 7, 1943, p. 2.

140. G. H. Montgomery, "Attention Evangelists," *PHA*, Feb. 12, 1942, p. 3.

141. "Preparing for the Revival," *PHA*, Feb. 20, 1941, p. 5.

142. "With the Editor," *PHA*, May 4, 1939, p. 2.

143. Lee, *Yearbook, 1940*, pp. 10–11, 6.

144. Lee, *Yearbook, 1940*, pp. 10–11; Vinson Synan, *Emmanuel College* (Franklin Springs, Ga.: Emmanuel College Library, 1968), p. 93.

145. "God Is with Emmanuel College," *PHA*, Dec. 5, 1940, p. 3.

146. O. Roberts, Chapel Transcript, Nov. 14, 1967, pp. 8–9.

147. O. Roberts, *Salvation by the Blood*, pp. 24–26.

148. O. Roberts, "Sin Is Mankind's Worst Enemy," *PHA*, June 1, 1937, p. 97.

149. O. Roberts, "The Scribes and the Pharisees," *PHA*, May 21, 1942, pp. 4–5.

150. O. Roberts, *Salvation by the Blood*, p. 21.

151. O. Roberts, Chapel Transcript, Nov. 14, 1967, p. 9. See also O. Roberts, Speech at Seminary Transcript, Feb. 9, 1976, p. 7; O. Roberts, *Life Story*, pp. 54–55.

152. Paul Interview; O. Roberts, *The Drama of the End-Time*, p. 4.

153. Angie Debo, *Oklahoma: Foot-Loose and Fancy Free* (Norman: University of Oklahoma Press, 1949), p. 120.

154. Paul Interview.

155. Ibid.

156. Ibid.

157. O. Roberts, Faculty Retreat Transcript, Aug. 25, 1970, p. 9.

4. PASTOR

1. Oral received a much higher salary in Fuquay Springs than in his subsequent pastorates in Pentecostal Holiness churches.

2. Joe E. Campbell, "New Tabernacle Built at Fuquay Springs, N.C.," *PHA*, Jan. 1, 1942, p. 12.

3. Ibid. See Oral Roberts, "Great Revival at Fuquay Springs," *PHA*, Apr. 16, 1942, pp. 13–14.

4. Shirley Hayes, "Fuquay Folks Knew Oral Roberts Way Back When," *Independent* (Fuquay-Varina, N.C.), Nov. 17, 1982, p. 1.

5. Shirley Hayes, "When Oral Roberts Came, He Hit the Ground Running," *Independent*, Nov. 24, 1982, pp. 1–2.

6. Ibid.

7. Hayes, "Fuquay Folks Knew Oral Roberts Way Back When," p. 1.

8. O. Roberts, "Great Revival at Fuquay Springs," p. 13.

9. "Revival at Fuquay Springs," *PHA*, Aug. 20, 1942, p. 9.

10. See Shirley Hayes, "Evelyn Roberts Talks about Her Year in Fuquay Springs," *Independent*, Dec. 1, 1982, pp. 1–3.

11. G. H. Montgomery, "Shawnee," *PHA*, Mar. 20, 1941, p. 5.

12. Hayes, "Fuquay Folks Knew Oral Roberts Way Back When," p. 1.

13. Angie Debo, *Oklahoma: Foot-Loose and Fancy Free* (Norman: University of Oklahoma Press, 1949), p. 101.

14. "Oral Roberts' Broadcast," *PHA*, Nov. 5, 1942, p. 16; B. B. Scrivner, "201 Experiences in Shawnee in Three Years," *PHA*, Aug. 23, 1945, p. 13.

15. Scrivner, "201 Experiences in Shawnee in Three Years," p. 13.

16. R. H. Lee, ed., *Yearbook of the Pentecostal Holiness Church, 1942* (Franklin Springs, Ga.: Publishing House of the Pentecostal Holiness Church, 1941), p. 23.

17. Dan T. Muse, T. T. Lindsey, and L. J. Oliver, eds., *Yearbook of the Pentecostal Holiness Church, 1945* (Franklin Springs, Ga.: Board of Publishers of the Pentecostal Holiness Church, n.d.), p. 32.

18. Hayes, "Fuquay Folks Knew Oral Roberts Way Back When," p. 1.

19. Evelyn Roberts, Student Meeting Transcript, Mar. 19, 1975, p. 15.

20. Hayes, "Fuquay Folks Knew Oral Roberts Way Back When," p. 1.

21. Evelyn Roberts, *His Darling Wife, Evelyn* (New York: Dell Publishing Co., 1976), p. 146.

22. Evelyn Roberts, Speech to ORU Students Transcript, Feb. 11, 1975, p. 17.

23. Hayes, "Evelyn Roberts Talks about Her Year in Fuquay Springs," p. 1; Scrivner, "201 Experiences in Shawnee in Three Years," p. 13.

24. Oral Roberts, *My Story* (Tulsa and New York: Summit Book Co., 1961), p. 49.

25. Hayes, "Evelyn Roberts Talks about Her Year in Fuquay Springs," p. 1.

26. Evelyn Roberts, Speech to ORU Students Transcript, Feb. 11, 1975, p. 15.

27. Lee, *Yearbook, 1942*, p. 10; *Yearbook, 1943*, p. 5.

28. Lee, *Yearbook, 1943*, p. 6; *Yearbook, 1944*, p. 6. He must have been disappointed not to be elected a delegate to the General Conference.

29. Oral Roberts, "We Need," *PHA*, Jan. 28, 1943, p. 3.

30. Lee, *Yearbook, 1944*, p. 5; "East Oklahoma Plans Minister's Conference," *PHA*, Jan. 27, 1944, p. 9.

31. Oscar Moore Interview, Jan. 20, 1983.

32. [Advertisement,] *PHA*, July 17, 1941, p. 16.

33. Oral Roberts, *The Drama of the End-Time* (Franklin Springs, Ga.: Publishing House of the Pentecostal Holiness Church, 1941), p. 65.

34. Oral Roberts, "Is Hitler the Anti-Christ?" *PHA*, Jan. 16, 1941, p. 7.

35. Oral Roberts, "By-Passing the Holy Ghost," *PHA*, Jan. 27, 1944, p. 6. See also his articles "Some Facts about Hell," *PHA*, July 11, 1946, p. 3; "Getting People to Jesus," *PHA*, Oct. 11, 1945, pp. 3–4.

36. See notations in Bibles, ORU.

37. Granville Oral Roberts, "Temptations of the Pastor," *PHA*, Nov. 4, 1943, pp. 5, 10–11.

38. See "Our Sleeping Giant," *PHA*, Nov. 15, 1945, pp. 3, 15–16; "History of the Sunday School," *PHA*, Nov. 22, 1945, pp. 6–7; "How to Prepare to Teach the Sunday School Lesson," *PHA*, Dec. 20, 1945, pp. 5, 13; "Teaching Little Children," *PHA*, Jan. 3, 1946, pp. 4, 11; "Handling Difficult Situations in the Sunday School," *PHA*, Feb. 7, 1946, pp. 6, 15; "Vacation Bible School," *PHA*, Mar. 28, 1946, pp. 6–7, 10.

39. O. Roberts, "Teaching Little Children," p. 4.

40. O. Roberts, "Handling Difficult Situations in the Sunday School," p. 6.

41. Harold Paul Interview, Jan. 28, 1983.

42. Oral Roberts, "Educational Activities," *PHA*, Feb. 24, 1944, p. 10. It is significant that in 1943 the East Oklahoma Conference discontinued its special collection for Emmanuel College. Oral was chairman of the Education and Publication Committee. Lee, *Yearbook, 1943*, p. 5.

43. "The Western School," *PHA*, Apr. 13, 1944, p. 2.

44. O. Roberts, "Educational Activities," p. 10; "Roberts and Turpin to Tour East Oklahoma Conference in Behalf of School," *PHA*, Feb. 17, 1944, p. 8; Paul Interview; Carl Hamilton Interview, Jan. 13, 1983.

45. O. Roberts, "Educational Activities," p. 10.

46. O. Roberts, Faculty Retreat Transcript, Aug. 25, 1970, p. 9.

47. O. Roberts, Chapel Transcript, Jan. 22, 1975, p. 14.

48. "Roberts Began Healing Ministry in Toccoa Church," *Toccoa (Georgia) Record*, May 11, 1978, pp. 1–2. Oral was offered, and apparently accepted, the pastorate in Radford, Virginia. But he changed his mind before moving. See "Roberts to Radford," *PHA*, Jan. 24, 1946, p. 15.

49. "Roberts Began Healing Ministry in Toccoa Church," p. 2.

50. O. Roberts, *My Story*, p. 71.

51. See O. Roberts, *My Story*, p. 71; O. Roberts, Chapel Transcript, Nov. 15, 1967, pp. 1–2; Lawson remained alive for many years to testify to the healing.

52. "Roberts Began Healing Ministry in Toccoa Church," p. 2. For an earlier healing experience, see O. Roberts, *My Story*, pp. 65–66.

53. *The Yahnseh, 1946* (OBU Yearbook, no publication information), n.p.

54. See O. Roberts, Miscellaneous Speech Transcript, Apr. 3, 1957, p. 10; O. Roberts, Chapel Transcript, Nov. 15, 1967, pp. 2–3; O. Roberts, Speech at Seminary at ORU Transcript, Feb. 9, 1976, pp. 3–4.

55. O. Roberts, Speech at Seminary at ORU Transcript, Feb. 9, 1976, p. 9.

56. O. Roberts, Faculty Retreat Transcript, Nov. 25, 1970, p. 9. Oral understood their reservations, because he knew that some who "went away, for a great education,

came back denying the power of God." O. Roberts, Chapel Transcript, Nov. 14, 1967, p. 10.

57. Joseph A. Synan, "Editor Speaks at O.B.U.," *PHA*, Apr. 4, 1946, p. 10. He was introduced by Oral.

58. G. H. Montgomery, "Rev. R. L. Rex to Enter Evangelistic Field," *PHA*, July 8, 1943, p. 11.

59. Dan T. Muse et al., eds., *Yearbook of the Pentecostal Holiness Church, 1946* (Franklin Springs, Ga.: Publishing House of the Pentecostal Holiness Church, n.d.), pp. 32, 37. See also G. H. Montgomery, "And It Came to Pass," *PHA*, Oct. 23, 1947, p. 3; Muse et al., *Yearbook, 1947*, p. 45. The average in 1947 fell to $1,350.92. Wayne Robinson remembered that when his father retired from the Pentecostal Holiness ministry at age seventy-two, the highest salary he had ever received was $60 a week. Wayne A. Robinson, *I Once Spoke in Tongues* (Old Tappan, N.J.: Fleming H. Revell Co., Spire Books, 1975), p. 17.

60. "Visitor's Card," Enid Pentecostal Holiness Church, ORU Archives.

61. G. H. Montgomery, "Seven Secrets of America's Greatest Soul-Winner," *HW*, June 1950, p. 12.

62. See J. A. Synan, "Bulletin of Southwestern Pentecostal Holiness College," *PHA*, Aug. 22, 1946, p. 13.

63. See "Educational Activities," *PHA*, Sept. 27, 1947, p. 7.

64. See Harold Paul, "The Religious Frontier in Oklahoma," Ph.D. dissertation, University of Oklahoma, 1965, pp. 192–94; *The Southwestern, 1947* (Yearbook of Southwestern Pentecostal Holiness Church, no publication information), pp. 4–5.

65. *The Southwestern, 1947*, pp. 4–5. See also "The Advocate Goes to School," *PHA*, Jan. 2, 1947, p. 7. Although Oral soon lost personal contact with the school, he long considered it one of the fruits of his labor.

66. "Preacher's Convention in Oklahoma City," *PHA*, Feb. 27, 1947, p. 11.

67. Mrs. Oral Roberts, "Loyal Women of the Pentecostal Holiness Church in the West," *PHA*, May 8, 1947, pp. 6, 9.

68. Montgomery, "Seven Secrets of America's Greatest Soul-Winner," p. 12.

69. Raymond W. McLaughlin, "Intensional-Extensional Language as a Measure of Semantic Orientation," *Bulletin of the Evangelical Theological Society* (Summer 1967), p. 144. McLaughlin cited a letter from the registrar at Phillips which stated that Oral had "above average grades." See also O. Roberts, Chapel Transcript, Nov. 14, 1967, pp. 10–11; O. Roberts, Chapel Transcript, Aug. 29, 1980, p. 11.

70. R. O. Corvin, "Night Classes for Southwestern Preachers," *PHA*, Sept. 5, 1946, p. 11. "Those taking this course," wrote Corvin, "will be expected to keep accurate, up-to-date records and engage in extensive Sunday School work."

71. See Oral Roberts, *Oral Roberts' Life Story* (Tulsa: Oral Roberts, 1952), pp. 62–69; O. Roberts, *My Story*, pp. 72–73.

72. "Why the Revival Doesn't Last," *PHA*, Apr. 3, 1941, p. 2.

73. O. Roberts, "The Revival We Must Have—Now!", *PHA*, Mar. 27, 1947, p. 4.

74. O. Roberts, Crusade Transcript, Aug. 9, 1968, p. 13.

75. O. Roberts, *Life Story*, p. 62.

76. O. Roberts, Chapel Transcript, Nov. 14, 1967, pp. 9–10; Oral Roberts, *My Twenty Years of a Miracle Ministry* (Tulsa: Oral Roberts, 1967), p. 7.

77. O. Roberts, *My Twenty Years of a Miracle Ministry*, p. 7.

78. O. Roberts, *My Story*, p. 40.

79. Ibid.; O. Roberts, *Life Story*, pp. 54–55.

80. O. Roberts, *My Twenty Years of a Miracle Ministry*, p. 9.

81. Bob Foresman and Jenk Jones, Jr., "Oral Roberts: What Makes Him Tick," *Tulsa Tribune*, June 11, 1975, p. 12.

82. Ibid.; Richard Roberts Interview, Mar. 31, 1983.

83. O. Roberts, *Life Story*, p. 62.

84. O. Roberts, Speech to Young Couples Transcript, Nov. 22, 1969, n.p.

85. O. Roberts, *My Story*, p. 73; Evelyn Roberts, Student Meeting Transcript, Feb. 11, 1975, pp. 30–31; Oral Roberts and Evelyn Roberts, Evangelism of Oral Roberts Class Transcript, 1971, p. 4.

86. O. Roberts, Faculty Chapel Transcript, Sept. 5, 1967, p. 2.

87. O. Roberts, Chapel Transcript, Nov. 14, 1967, pp. 10–11.

88. O. Roberts, *My Story*, p. 73.

89. O. Roberts, Chapel Transcript, Nov. 15, 1967, p. 10.

90. O. Roberts, Chapel Transcript, Nov. 14, 1967, p. 9; Gilbert "Gib" Bond, "I Made Oral Roberts Tough by Throwing Rocks in Front of Him," *AL*, May 1979, p. 20.

91. Bond, "I Made Oral Roberts Tough," p. 20.

92. O. Roberts, Speech to Graduate and Theology Students Transcript, Jan. 31, 1977, p. 10.

93. Oral Roberts, *Oral Roberts' Best Sermons and Stories* (Tulsa: Oral Roberts, 1956), p. 92.

94. Evelyn Roberts, Chapel Transcript, Feb. 3, 1982, p. 10.

95. O. Roberts, *Life Story*, p. 63; O. Roberts, "To the Partners . . . ," *AL*, May 1964, p. 22.

96. O. Roberts, Chapel Transcript, Nov. 14, 1967, p. 12.

97. O. Roberts, Laymen's Seminar Transcript, Nov. 7, 1969, p. 15.

98. O. Roberts, Contemporary Methods of Evangelism Class Transcript, Oct. 11, 1967, p. 26.

99. Evelyn Roberts, Student Meeting Transcript, Feb. 11, 1975, p. 31.

100. O. Roberts, Contemporary Methods of Evangelism Class Transcript, Oct. 11, 1967, p. 26; Evelyn Roberts, Student Meeting Transcript, Feb. 11, 1975, p. 31.

101. Evelyn Roberts, Evangelism of Oral Roberts Class Transcript, 1971, p. 9.

102. O. Roberts, *My Story*, p. 76.

103. Evelyn Roberts, Student Meeting Transcript, Feb. 11, 1975, pp. 33–34.

104. O. Roberts, Evangelism of Oral Roberts Class Transcript, 1971, p. 6.

105. O. Roberts, *My Story*, p. 80; O. Roberts, *Best Sermons*, p. 47.

106. O. Roberts, *My Story*, p. 94.

107. O. Roberts, Chapel Transcript, Nov. 14, 1967, p. 14.

108. O. Roberts, *My Story*, p. 95.

109. O. Roberts, Chapel Transcript, Nov. 14, 1967, p. 4; O. Roberts, *My Story*, p. 95; O. Roberts, "God's Hand on His Servants," *HW*, May 1949, p. 10.

110. O. Roberts, *My Story*, p. 78.

111. O. Roberts, Chapel Transcript, Nov. 15, 1967, p. 6; O. Roberts, *My Story*, p. 93; O. Roberts, "To Touch neither the Gold nor the Glory," *HW*, Mar. 1956, pp. 3–5.

112. O. Roberts, "Partners for Deliverance," *PHA*, May 29, 1947, p. 14.

113. O. Roberts, "The City-Wide Healing Revival," *PHA*, May 22, 1947, p. 6.

114. Ibid., p. 7.

115. O. Roberts, *My Story*, p. 42.

116. O. Roberts, "Partners for Deliverance," p. 15.

117. O. Roberts, Chapel Transcript, Nov. 14, 1967, p. 15. For general descriptions, see O. Roberts, *My Story*, pp. 96–97; O. Roberts, Speech to Graduate and Theology Students Transcript, Jan. 31, 1977, pp. 13–14; Bond, "I Made Oral Roberts Tough," pp. 20–21.

118. O. Roberts, Chapel Transcript, Nov. 14, 1967, p. 15.

119. O. Roberts, *My Story*, p. 96.

120. Bond, "I Made Oral Roberts Tough," pp. 20–21.

121. O. Roberts, Chapel Transcript, Nov. 14, 1967, p. 15.

122. O. Roberts, Speech to Graduate and Theology Students Transcript, Jan. 31, 1977, pp. 13–14.

123. O. Roberts, Chapel Transcript, Nov. 14, 1967, p. 15.

124. Oral Roberts, "1000 Attend Healing Service," *PHA*, June 12, 1947, p. 2.

125. O. Roberts, Chapel Transcript, Nov. 14, 1967, p. 11.

126. Bond, "I Made Oral Roberts Tough," pp. 20–21; O. Roberts, *My Story*, p. 93.

127. O. Roberts, *Life Story*, p. 82. See also O. Roberts, Faculty Orientation Transcript, Aug. 14, 1978, p. 8.

128. O. Roberts, "1000 Attend Healing Service," p. 2.

129. Moore Interview; Evelyn Roberts, "I Married Oral Roberts," *HW*, Jan. 1953, p. 10.

130. E. M. and Claudius Roberts, *Our Ministry and Our Son Oral* (Tulsa: Oral Roberts, 1960), pp. 67–68.

131. Evelyn Roberts, "I Married Oral Roberts," p. 10.

Part II

PROLOGUE
Australia, January 20–February 10, 1956

1. Yvonne Nance, "The Woman behind the Man," *AL*, June 1957, p. 16.

2. "A Faith Healer's Million Souls," *People* (Australia), Jan. 11, 1956, ORU.

3. G. H. Montgomery, "Looking Forward with Oral Roberts in 1953," *HW*, Feb. 1953, p. 10.

4. "Oral Roberts Goal for 1956: A Million Souls for Christ," *Tulsa Tribune*, Dec. 10, 1955, ORU.

5. "Oral Roberts for Australia," *Commonwealth Revivalist*, Mar. 1955, ORU.

6. "Tent Cathedral Goes Overseas," *Healing*, Jan. 1956, pp. 9–10.

7. "Oral Roberts Goal for 1956: A Million Souls for Christ"; *Sydney Morning Herald*, Jan. 19, 1956, p. 9; Jan. 20, 1956, p. 7.

8. Bob DeWeese Interview, Jan. 19, 1983.

9. Hart R. Armstrong, "Facts and Proofs concerning the False Press Reports in Australia," *Healing*, April 1956, p. 15.

10. Armstrong, "Facts and Proofs," p. 15. See also Dan L. Thrapp, "Evangelist Recalls Australia Terror," *Los Angeles Times*, Sept. 28, 1957, p. 10.

11. DeWeese Interview; O. Roberts, Youth Seminar Transcript, June 19, 1963, p. 47.

12. Basil D. Tyson, "What 'New Life' Had to Say about Oral Roberts," *Evidence* (Australia), Mar. 1956, ORU; Jay Nelson Tuck, "He Spends $2,500,000 a Year Advertising His 'Faith Healing,'" *Confidential*, Oct. 1959, p. 65.

13. Bill Lamkin, "Graham's Six-Month Tour Like a World Travelogue," *Charlotte (N.C.) Observer*, July 6, 1959, ORU.

14. "Sunday Show," *The Bulletins* (Sydney), Feb. 1, 1956, p. 19.

15. Noel McDonald, "Oral Calls the Tune; Fans Pay the Piper," *Sydney Sun*, Jan. 21, 1956, pp. 1–2.

16. See "Cleric Quits amid Hoots," *Tulsa Tribune*, Feb. 17, 1956, ORU; "Trouble for Oral," *Time*, Feb. 13, 1956, ORU.

17. Philip Duncan, "The Story of the Australian Campaigns," *Healing*, April 1956, p. 6; Collins Steele Interview, Jan. 13, 1983.

18. Armstrong, "Facts and Proofs," p. 15.

19. Oral Roberts, "My Personal Story about the Melbourne Campaign," *Healing*, Apr. 8, 1956, p. 14. For a general account by Roberts, see Oral Roberts, *The Call* (New York: Doubleday & Co., 1972), pp. 74–92.

20. Oral Roberts, *My Story* (Tulsa and New York: Summit Book Co., 1961), p. 174; the *Argus* attack began before Roberts arrived, in an article by Michael Reece, "Bible, Ballyhoo in the Big Top," Feb. 4, 1956, p. 9.

21. O. Roberts, *The Call*, p. 77.

22. O. Roberts, "My Personal Story about the Melbourne Campaign," p. 14.

23. "Crowd Chases Faith Healer," *Argus,* Feb. 9, 1956, ORU.

24. G. H. Montgomery, "The Truth about the Melbourne Campaign," *Healing,* April 1956, pp. 16–18; "An Oral Examination," *Argus*, Feb. 7, 1956, p. 9.

25. Ibid.; Steele Interview.

26. "Not-So-Verbal Oral Quits Sinful Sydney," *Sun-Herald* (Sydney), Feb. 12, 1956, ORU.

27. Steele, DeWeese Interviews.

28. Montgomery, "The Truth about the Melbourne Campaign," p. 17.

29. Steele Interview.

30. "Team Profiles," *AL,* July 1973, p. 16.

31. DeWeese Interview.

32. Montgomery, "The Truth about the Melbourne Campaign," p. 17.

33. Norman Banks, "Melbourne Diary," *Healing,* April 1956, pp. 19–20.

34. Montgomery, "The Truth about the Melbourne Campaign," p. 17.

35. Norman Banks, "Melbourne Diary," pp. 19–20.

36. Montgomery, "The Truth about the Melbourne Campaign," pp. 17–18.

37. J. H. K., "What 'New Life' Had to Say about Oral Roberts," *Evidence,* Mar. 1956, ORU.

38. O. Roberts, *My Story,* p. 186; Steele Interview.

39. *Argus,* Feb. 10, 1956, ORU.

40. O. Roberts, *The Call,* pp. 77–81.

41. "Not-So-Verbal Oral Quits Sinful Sydney."

42. Ibid. See also "Disgusted with Australians," *Age* (Sydney), Feb. 13, 1956, ORU.

43. See ORU Clipping Collection, Feb. 12, 1956.

44. "The Back of Mr. Roberts," *Sunday Telegraph,* Feb. 12, 1956.

45. "Not-So-Verbal Oral Quites Sinful Sydney."

46. "Australia Reds Broke Up Meetings, States Roberts," *Tulsa Tribune,* Mar. 1, 1956, p. 22.

47. Montgomery, "The Truth about the Melbourne Campaign," p. 18.

48. Oral Roberts, *My Twenty Years of a Miracle Ministry* (Tulsa: Oral Roberts, 1967), p. 34.

49. Norman Banks, "Melbourne Diary," p. 19.

50. Steele Interview.

51. "We Should Be Ashamed," *Argus,* Feb. 13, 1956, ORU; "Disgusted with Australians," *Age* (Sydney), Feb. 13, 1956, ORU.

52. J. H. K., "What 'New Life' Had to Say about Oral Roberts."

53. Gordon Powell, "The Boomerang," *Sydney Morning Herald,* Aug. 18, 1956, ORU. See also "Sympathy for Oral Roberts," *Age,* Apr. 11, 1956, ORU.

54. Evelyn Roberts, *His Darling Wife, Evelyn* (New York: Dell Publishing Co., 1976), p. 119.

55. See "Trouble for Oral," *Time,* Feb. 13, 1956, ORU; "Australians Take Slap at Oral Roberts," *Tulsa Tribune,* Feb. 9, 1956, ORU; Robert C. Ruark, "Tastes for Talent Down Under," *Tulsa Tribune,* Feb. 17, 1956, ORU; "Oral Roberts Flayed for 'Luxury Living,' " *Tulsa Tribune,* Feb. 24, 1956, ORU; "A Question for Oral Roberts," *Tulsa World,* Mar. 3, 1956, ORU.

56. "Australia Boots Out Religious Racketeer!" *Flash* (Hamilton, Canada), Aug. 14, 1956, p. 7.

57. See Thrapp, "Evangelist Recalls Australia Terror," p. 10.

58. "Oral Roberts Home Again; Takes a Rest," *Tulsa Tribune,* Feb. 14, 1956, ORU.

59. O. Roberts, *The Call,* p. 82.

60. Evelyn Roberts, *His Darling Wife,* pp. 118–19.

61. Ibid.; O. Roberts, Chapel Transcript, Oct. 13, 1972, p. 9.

62. Nance, "The Woman behind the Man," pp. 16–17.

63. Thrapp, "Evangelist Recalls Australia Terror," p. 10.

5. HEALING REVIVALISM

1. Angie Debo, *Tulsa: From Creek Town to Oil Capital* (Norman: University of Oklahoma Press, 1943), p. 3.

2. Ibid.; George H. Shirk, *Oklahoma Place Names* (Norman: University of Oklahoma Press, 1974), p. 279.

3. Oral Roberts, *My Story* (Tulsa and New York: Summit Book Co., 1961), p. 130.

4. Robert Freeland, "Air Crossroads of the Nation," *Tulsa World*, Aug. 3, 1947, Magazine Section, p. 1.

5. O. Roberts, *My Story*, p. 130.

6. Oral Roberts, "What Faith Means to My Family and Me," *HW*, Sept. 1949, p. 10.

7. O. Roberts, *My Story*, p. 130.

8. O. Roberts, Chapel Transcript, Jan. 30, 1976, p. 12.

9. O. Roberts, Chapel Transcript, Jan. 30, 1976, pp. 12–13; O. Roberts, *My Story*, pp. 130–33; Evelyn Roberts Interview, Apr. 3, 1984.

10. O. Roberts, Chapel Transcript, Nov. 15, 1967, pp. 3–4; O. Roberts, Evangelism of Oral Roberts Class Transcript, 1971, p. 4.

11. O. Roberts, Chapel Transcript, Nov. 15, 1967, pp. 4–5.

12. Roy Smith, "Pastor Says Many Healed in Athens," *PHA*, July 10, 1947, p. 10.

13. "Healing Revival in Newman Church," *PHA*, July 17, 1947, pp. 10–11; Oral Roberts, "How God's Healing Power Came to Me," *HW*, May 1948, pp. 2–3.

14. "Healing Revival in Newman Church," p. 10.

15. "Hear," *Tulsa World*, June 8, 1947, Sports Section, p. 4.

16. "Bridgeman Evangelistic Party," *Tulsa World*, July 6, 1947, sec. 1, part 2, p. 6.

17. O. Roberts, My Personal Testimony Transcript, Oct. 21, 1970, p. 15; O. Roberts, *My Story*, p. 133.

18. O. Roberts, Chapel Transcript, Nov. 15, 1967, p. 11.

19. O. Roberts, *My Story*, p. 133.

20. Carl Hamilton Interview, Jan. 17, 1983.

21. Oral Roberts, *Oral Roberts' Life Story* (Tulsa: Oral Roberts, 1952), p. 100. See also "Oral Roberts' Genesis Revealed," *Duncan (Okla.) Banner*, May 22, 1981, ORU; O. Roberts, *My Story*, pp. 133–34.

22. O. Roberts, *My Story*, p. 134.

23. "Church Noise Curb Asked," *Tulsa World*, Aug. 2, 1947, sec. 2, p. 1.

24. "Revival Feud Charge Filed," *Tulsa World*, Aug. 6, 1947, p. 10.

25. "Church Shots Case Dropped," *Tulsa World*, Aug. 9, 1947, sec. 2, p. 1.

26. At one point he recalled that "we never learned the identity of the man who shot at me," but in another account he reported that the man arrested stated that "I do not know why I did it." See O. Roberts, *Life Story*, p. 102, and O. Roberts, *My Story*, p. 134. See also Oral Roberts, *The Call* (New York: Doubleday & Co., 1972), pp. 73–74.

27. O. Roberts, *My Story*, p. 134; Oral Roberts and You, Television Tape, Dec. 6, 1981.

28. O. Roberts, Chapel Transcript, Nov. 15, 1967, p. 5.

29. O. Roberts, *Life Story*, p. 102.

30. Hamilton Interview, Jan. 13, 1983.

31. Oral Roberts, *My Twenty Years of a Miracle Ministry* (Tulsa: Oral Roberts, 1967), p. 10.

32. O. Roberts, *Life Story*, p. 121.

33. O. Roberts, *My Story*, p. 135.

34. Ibid., p. 134.

35. O. Roberts, Chapel Transcript, Nov. 15, 1967, pp. 5–6.

36. "Girl Healed of Infantile Paralysis" and "Pastors Praise Brother Roberts Healing Revival in Muskogee, Oklahoma," *HW*, Nov. and Dec. 1947, p. 3.

37. O. Roberts, Chapel Transcript, Nov. 15, 1967, p. 14.

38. O. Roberts, *My Twenty Years of a Miracle Ministry*, p. 11.

39. O. Roberts, Chapel Transcript, Nov. 15, 1967, p. 14.

40. Ibid., p. 15.

41. O. Roberts, *My Story*, pp. 51–55.

42. See "Oral Roberts," *PHA*, Jan. 1, 1948, p. 16.

43. "Pastor Reports Great Meeting in Minneapolis," *HW*, April 1948, p. 2.

44. "The Roberts Healing Campaigns after May 1," *HW*, May 1948, p. 9.

45. O. Roberts, Chapel Transcript, Nov. 15, 1967, p. 6; "Bethel Temple Campaign," *HW*, Jan. and Feb. 1948, p. 8. Pastor Henry Hoar reported: "I received a touch of healing in my own body. I am now a new man, feeling a new courage and fire for my work as a pastor; my daughter, also a minister of the Gospel, was wondrously healed after a nervous breakdown; my son was touched by God's power also."

46. O. Roberts, "Tent Cathedral," *HW*, Jan. and Feb. 1948, p. 6; Evelyn Roberts, Chapel Transcript, Feb. 3, 1982, pp. 13–14.

47. O. Roberts, Crusade Transcript, Apr. 22, 1955, pp. 20–21; O. Roberts, *My Story*, pp. 136–37.

48. Oral Roberts Bible, ORU Archives.

49. "Under the Big Tent," *HW*, April 1948, p. 6.

50. "Oral Roberts Purchases Hammond and Steinway for Use in Meetings," *HW*, June 1948, p. 11.

51. "The Finest Gospel Equipment in America," *HW*, August 1948, p. 2.

52. O. Roberts, Crusade Transcript, Apr. 22, 1955, p. 21.

53. See O. Roberts, Chapel Transcript, Nov. 15, 1967, p. 10; O. Roberts, Evangelism of Oral Roberts Class Transcript, 1971, pp. 6–7; Oral Roberts Interview, Feb. 16, 1983.

54. "3,342 Come for Salvation during Roberts Healing Campaign in Durham, N.C.," *HW*, Aug. 1948, p. 1.

55. Ibid.

56. O. Roberts Interview, Feb. 16, 1983.

57. "3,342 Come for Salvation during Roberts Healing Campaign in Durham, N.C.," pp. 1–9.

58. O. Roberts, Evangelism of Oral Roberts Class Transcript, 1971, pp. 6–7; O. Roberts Interview, Feb. 16, 1983.

59. Dan Brennan, "Crippled Child Stirs," *Minneapolis Tribune*, Aug. 23, 1948, p. 1.

60. O. Roberts, OREA Devotion Transcript, Mar. 25, 1982, p. 12.

61. George W. Wasson, "Roberts' Healing Campaign a Great Success," *PHA*, Nov. 18, 1948, p. 14. Ironically, the local paper did cover a Baptist revival conducted at the same time. See "Baptists Open Simultaneous Association Revivals Sunday," *Ada Evening News*, Sept. 17, 1948, p. 3

62. O. Roberts, *Life Story*, p. 39.

63. Roberts' Meeting a Great Success," *PHA*, Oct. 21, 1948, p. 10. Oral never lost his loyalty to Ada. He returned to preach for an evening in 1949 to help raise funds for a new building. George W. Wasson, "Roberts in Ada, Oklahoma for One Night Service," *HW*, May 1949, p. 5.

64. See Charles E. Blair, "From the Ministers," *HW*, Dec. 1949, p. 10.

65. O. Roberts, Speech at Seminary at ORU Transcript, Feb. 9, 1976, p. 11.

66. O. Roberts, Chapel Transcript, Jan. 1968, pp. 6–7.

67. O. Roberts, Chapel Transcript, Jan. 22, 1975, p. 7.

68. O. Roberts, Chapel Transcript, Nov. 15, 1967, p. 15.

69. See [advertisement,] *Florida Times Union* (Jacksonville), Mar. 5, 1949, p. 12. For support from Florida church leaders, see L. J. Oliver, "Roberts' Meetings," *PHA*, Mar. 17, 1949, pp. 2, 9; O. Roberts Interview, Feb. 16, 1983.

70. See Fred Sanders, "Salvation Sought by 3,000," *PHA*, Mar. 10, 1949, p. 4; Bert E. Parmer, "Estimated 5,000 Converted in Jacksonville," *PHA*, Apr. 14, 1949, p. 6; Jake Till, "Over 6,000 Saved in Tallahassee Revival," *PHA*, May 12, 1949, p. 6; V. W. Callahan, "85,000 People Attend," *HW*, Feb. 1950, p. 1.

71. Charlton Price, "Faith Healing, Science Agree, Says Roberts," *Houston Post*, Oct. 16, 1949, ORU.

72. O. Roberts, Chapel Transcript, Nov. 15, 1967, p. 9.

73. W. J. Anderson, "Oral Roberts Campaign in Bakersfield, California," *PHA*, Oct. 6, 1949, p. 12.

74. Dan Brennan, "Crippled Child Stirs," p. 1.

75. *HW*, April 1948, p. 6.

76. Till, "Over 6,000 Saved in Tallahassee Revival," p. 6.

77. Oral Roberts, *101 Questions and Answers* (Tulsa: Oral Roberts, 1968), p. 18.

78. O. Roberts, "How God's Healing Power Works through Me," *HW*, June 1948, pp. 1–2; G. H. Montgomery, "God's Seven Messages to Oral Roberts," *AL*, April 1958, p. 25.

79. Oral Roberts, *If You Need Healing—Do These Things!* (2d ed.; Tulsa: Standard Printing Co., 1947).

80. Callahan, "85,000 People Attend," p. 1.

81. O. Roberts, *Life Story*, pp. 143–46.

82. "Roberts' Genesis Revealed," *Duncan (Okla.) Banner*, May 22, 1981, ORU.

83. See *Houston Post*, Oct. 8, 1949, sec.1, p. 2.

84. O. Roberts, My Own Personal Testimony Transcript, Oct. 21, 1970, p. 9.

85. Anderson, "Oral Roberts Campaign in Bakersfield, California," p. 12; O. Roberts, My Own Personal Testimony Transcript, Oct. 21, 1970, p. 9.

86. "Whither Thou Goest," *AL*, Dec. 1982, p. 21.

87. Oral Roberts, *Oral Roberts' Best Sermons and Stories* (Tulsa: Oral Roberts, 1956), p. 37.

88. O. Roberts, Chapel Transcript, Nov. 15, 1967, pp. 12–13.

89. O. Roberts, My Own Personal Testimony Transcript, Nov. 21, 1970, pp. 9–10; O. Roberts, Chapel Transcript, Nov. 15, 1967, p. 12.

90. O. E. Sproull, "The Largest Tent Ever Constructed for the Gospel Ministry," *HW*, Jan. 1950, p. 15; [advertisement,] *Florida Times Union* (Jacksonville), Mar. 4, 1950, p. 16.

91. Vaden Roberts, "News about the 'Tent Cathedral,' " *HW*, Jan. 1951, p. 14; G. H. Montgomery, "Looking Forward with Oral Roberts," *HW*, Jan. 1952, p. 13; "Oral Roberts' 'Big Top' Can Seat 18,000," *The Oregon Statesman* (Salem), Aug. 14, 1957, ORU.

92. "Anniversary," *AL*, June 1957, p. 2.

93. O. Roberts, OREA Devotion Transcript, Feb. 4, 1957, p. 18; Dan L. Thrapp, "Evangelist Recalls Australia Terror," *Los Angeles Times*, Sept. 28, 1957, part 1, p. 10.

94. See G. H. Montgomery, "The March of Deliverance," *AHM*, May 1954, p. 4.

95. "Roberts Says Last Crusade Big Success," *Tulsa Tribune*, Apr. 5, 1958, ORU. See lists of meeting schedules in *Healing Waters*.

96. "Report to Pensacola," *Pensacola Journal*, Apr. 21, 1957, p. 4A.

97. O. Roberts, Chapel Transcript, Nov. 15, 1967, pp. 11–12.

98. Bob DeWeese Interview, Jan. 19, 1983.

99. See, for instance, L. J. Oliver, "Oral Roberts Campaign in Tampa," *PHA*, May 10, 1951; "Sponsoring Pastors in Miami Campaign," *HW*, March 1950, p. 3; and *Healing Waters* generally.

100. DeWeese Interview. See also *Washington Star*, May 30, 1953, ORU.

101. DeWeese Interview.

102. Ed Harrill, "Volunteer Workers Aid Evangelist in Conducting Crusade," *Charleston (S.C.) Evening Post News*, Apr. 22, 1958, p. 1-B.

103. Oliver, "Oral Roberts Campaign in Tampa," p. 12; see also Till, "Over 6,000 Saved in Tallahassee Revival," p. 12.

104. Horace Sams, "161 Attend Ministers Banquet," *HW*, April 1981, p. 8.

105. DeWeese Interview.

106. Evelyn Roberts, Miscellaneous Speech Transcript, June 8, 1981, p. 3.

107. Collins Steele Interview, Jan. 13, 1983.

108. John Meek, "Evangelist Oral Much Like Billy," *Post-Standard* (Syracuse, N.Y.), June 9, 1958, ORU; Mike Gildea, "Estimated 13,000 Listen to Sermon by Oral Roberts," *Charleston (S.C.) Evening Post,* Apr. 25, 1953, ORU.

109. Marty Papo, "Solitude Helps Prepare Oral Roberts," *Pueblo (Colo.) Chieftan,* Aug. 30, 1958, ORU.

110. Bernard W. Wynn, "Afflicted Entreat Evangelist's Help," *Indianapolis Times,* Nov. 14, 1956, ORU. See also Bill Rose, "7,000 Are Expected at 'Healing Campaign,' " *Oakland Tribune,* Oct. 1, 1954, p. 4; Juanita Coe Hope Interview, Dec. 6, 1973. Coe's crusades were much more boisterous. Mrs. Hope recalled that Oral told her husband, "There'll be no shouting in my tent or speaking in tongues."

111. DeWeese Interview.

112. Steele Interview; DeWeese Interview.

113. See "Oral Roberts Refused Permit in City Limits," *St. Petersburg Times,* Dec. 8, 1953, ORU; "Temple Seeks 25,000 Signers to City Protest," *St. Petersburg Times,* Dec. 14, 1953, ORU.

114. Steele Interview.

115. DeWeese Interview.

116. Anthony Harrigan, "Standing in Need of Hope," *News and Courier* (Charleston, S.C.), Apr. 27, 1958, ORU.

117. V. E. Howard, *Fake Healers Exposed* (Sixth printing, rev.; West Monroe, La.: Central Printers and Publishers, 1970), p. 41. After 1956, many of the services were filmed for television, and the "cyclopean eye of the camera" dominated the service, though it did not seem to detract from the appreciation of those present. See "Roberts Packs an Evangelistic Wallop," *Trenton Evening Times,* June 12, 1957, ORU; Tom Perry, "Boy's Case Stirs 10,000 at Crusade," *News and Courier* (Charleston, S.C.), Apr. 23, 1958, ORU.

118. See Ora Spaid, "About 3,000 Hear the Rev. Oral Roberts," *Louisville Courier-Journal,* Mar. 7, 1959, sec. 2, p. 1; Steele Interview.

119. DeWeese and Steele Interviews. There are countless accounts of the meetings in the newspapers.

120. DeWeese Interview; "Information for Those Who Wish Prayer and Healing" (Tract, no pub. info., ORU).

121. "Information for Those Who Wish Prayer and Healing."

122. "Roberts Aide Denies Rumors of Partiality," *Elkhart (Ind.) Truth,* Apr. 14, 1956, p. 2.

123. "TV Newscaster Meets Ministers on Retraction," *Albuquerque Journal,* Mar. 11, 1957, ORU; "Roberts Aide Denies Rumor of Partiality," *Elkhart (Ind.) Truth,* p. 2. The organization's literature emphasized that "no charge is made for prayer cards." "Important Information," *Healing,* June 1956, p. 21.

124. "Information for Those Who Wish Prayer and Healing"; DeWeese Interview.

125. Ibid.

126. Ibid.

127. "Demos Shakarian Reports the Oral Roberts Campaign in Los Angeles," *HW,* Dec. 1951, p. 11.

128. Gildea, "Estimated 13,000 Listen to Sermon by Oral Roberts."

129. O. Roberts, Evangelism Unit No. 1 Transcript, n.d., p. 9.

130. "They Stand in Hope," *Milwaukee Sentinel,* Nov. 15, 1958, ORU.

131. Dan Brennan, "Crippled Child Stirs," p. 13.

132. Bernard W. Wynn, "Afflicted Entreat Evangelist's Help," *Indianapolis Times,* Nov. 14, 1956, ORU.

133. See crusade tapes. Whereas Oral often preached for over an hour in his early campaigns, "long for an evangelist" even by pentecostal standards, by the end of the

decade his lessons were frequently no more than thirty minutes and had been visibly manicured for television. G. H. Montgomery, "Oral Roberts in Action," *HW*, Sept. 1951. Sometimes he preached a "double header," a sermon that could be easily divided for television. "Roberts Packs an Evangelistic Wallop," *Trenton Evening Times*, June 12, 1957, ORU. It was evident to everyone that Oral's preaching became less exuberant in the 1960s. See Evangelism of Oral Roberts Class Transcript, 1971, passim.

134. "Rev. Roberts Revival Drew 45,000 Persons," *Albuquerque (N.M.) Journal*, Mar. 11, 1957, ORU; "Roberts Calls Tent Crusade Here His Best," *Trenton Evening Times*, June 17, 1967, ORU.

135. James Buchanan, "Roberts Revival Quiet, Businesslike," *Miami Herald*, Jan. 22, 1958, ORU.

136. O. Roberts, Crusade Transcript, Apr. 23, 1955, pp. 24–25.

137. Clark Porteous, "Evangelist Sways Thousands in Tent Campaign," *Memphis Press Scimitar*, June 23, 1950, p. 1.

138. O. Roberts, Crusade Transcript, June 27, 1956, pp. 8–9.

139. Ibid., pp. 13–14.

140. Clark Porteous, "Evangelist Sways Thousands," p. 1.

141. "Evangelist to Open Crusade," *Oakland Tribune*, Jan. 1, 1959, p. 24D; Dan Thrapp, "Evangelist Recalls Australia Terror," p. 10. Oral prided himself on the low-key financial appeals in his campaigns, but on occasion the parsimony of his audience prompted him to "get rough with the people." He recalled an audience in a San Bernardino, California campaign that had been contributing only about "5¢ a piece" until he told them one evening: "You have rejected me and my ministry and you know I am sent of God, you rejected God." O. Roberts, Chapel Transcript, Nov. 15, 1967, p. 16. Usually, however, taking the offering was left in the hands of Bob DeWeese, who insisted that he "never spoke more than a minute." DeWeese Interview.

142. DeWeese Interview. See "2,000 'Touched' by Evangelist," *Charleston (W. Va.) Daily Mail*, Nov. 9, 1959, ORU; Porteous, "Evangelist Sways Thousands," p. 1; James Buchanan, "Roberts Revival Quiet, Businesslike."

143. DeWeese Interview, " 'Poor Man's Billy Graham' Packs 'em in at Auditorium," *Oklahoma City North Star*, Feb. 20, 1958, ORU.

144. See Dan Brennan, "Crippled Child Stirs," pp. 1, 13.

145. Montgomery, "Oral Roberts in Action," p. 7.

146. "10,000 Hear Faith Healer at N.Y. Town," *Springfield (Mass.) News*, Mar. 26, 1958, ORU.

147. O. Roberts Interview, Feb. 16, 1983.

148. DeWeese Interview.

149. O. Roberts, Regents Seminar Transcript, Nov. 9, 1963, n.p.

150. See Bill Rose, "5,500 Are Expected at Roberts Evangelist Rally," *Oakland Tribune*, Oct. 2, 1954, p. E14.

151. James A. Haught, "Faith-Healer Electrifying," *Charleston (W. Va.) Sunday Gazette Mail*, Mar. 9, 1958, p. 25.

152. H. Richard Hall Interview, May 31, 1972.

153. "A Round Table Discussion," *AL*, Jan. 1973, p. 9.

154. Rev. and Mrs. James V. Fordyce, "Missionaries Report on Rev. Oral Roberts Healing Campaign," *PHA*, Feb. 10, 1949, p. 5.

155. Dan L. Thrapp, "Evangelist Oral Roberts Thrashing Devil in Tent," *Los Angeles Times*, Oct. 7, 1951, part 1, p. 44.

156. Oral and Evelyn Roberts, Evangelism of Oral Roberts Class Transcript, 1971, pp. 12–13.

157. O. Roberts Interview, Feb. 16, 1983.

158. Hoover Adams, "Wellons Had Big Role in Oral Roberts' Rise," *Daily Record* (Dunn, N.C.), Dec. 23 and 24, 1982, p. 12.

159. Robert DeWeese, "Roberts Campaign in Tampa-St. Petersburg Tremendous Success," *HW*, May 1951, p. 2.

160. Ora Spaid, "About 3,000 Hear the Rev. Oral Roberts," p. 1.

161. Clark Porteous, "Evangelist Sways Thousands," p. 1.

162. G. H. Montgomery, "Oral Roberts in Action," p. 11.

163. Ora Spaid, "About 3,000 Hear the Rev. Oral Roberts," p. 1.

164. O. Roberts, Crusade Transcript, Mar. 22, 1956, pp. 14–15.

165. Reporters frequently noted Oral's harsh manner. See Clark Porteous, "Evangelist Sways Thousands," p. 1; Charlie Conner, "Evangelist Draws Overflow Crowd," *Charleston (W. Va.) Daily Mail,* Nov. 6, 1959, ORU.

166. Steve Durasoff and Evelyn Roberts, Evangelism of Oral Roberts Class Transcript, 1971, p. 15.

167. Oral and Evelyn Roberts, Evangelism of Oral Roberts Class Transcript, 1971, p. 15.

168. O. Roberts, Crusade Transcript, Apr. 21, 1957, p. 7.

169. O. Roberts, *Best Sermons,* p. 106.

170. "What God Hath Wrought by Faith," *HW,* April 1950, p. 11.

171. John Meek, "Don't Park in Sin," *Syracuse (N.Y.) Post-Standard,* June 13, 1958, ORU.

172. O. Roberts, Crusade Transcript, Sept. 2, 1958, pp. 23–25.

173. O. Roberts, Crusade Transcript, Apr. 23, 1981, p. 7.

174. Wade H. Mosley, "Evangelist Ends Stand," *Milwaukee Journal,* Nov. 17, 1958, ORU.

175. O. Roberts, *Best Sermons,* p. 110.

176. O. Roberts, Crusade Transcript, Apr. 21, 1957, p. 16.

177. Ibid.

178. O. Roberts, Crusade Transcript, Apr. 20, 1957, p. 18.

179. R. DeWeese, "Roberts Campaign in Tampa-St. Petersburg Tremendous Success," p. 14.

180. Oral Roberts, *The Holy Spirit in the Now* (3 vols.; Tulsa: Oral Roberts University, 1974), vol. 2, p. 28.

181. O. Roberts, Crusade Transcript, July 10, 1957, pp. 8–9; "Roberts Says Mass Miracle Still Possible," *Ohio State Journal,* July 11, 1957, ORU.

182. O. Roberts, Chapel Transcript, Nov. 15, 1967, p. 24.

183. Steele Interview.

184. George R. Harris, "609 Saved in Shawnee," *HW,* Dec. 1950, p. 16; Ray Bridgeman, "Roberts Ministry Stirs Enid," *HW,* Dec. 1950, p. 16; "Three-Day Roberts Meetings Sweep Enid and Shawnee," *HW,* Dec. 1950, p. 1.

185. John Meek, "Evangelist Oral Much Like Billy"; Doris Miller, "Roberts Draws 8,000 at Close," *Herald-Dispatch* (Huntington, West Virginia), Mar. 10, 1958, ORU; "Over 20,000 Brave Heat to Hear Roberts," *Columbus (Ohio) Evening News,* July 15, 1957, ORU.

186. W. T. Jeffers, "The Climax in Hollywood Bowl," *AL,* Dec. 1957, p. 43.

187. DeWeese Interview.

188. Louise Evans, "Tent Revival Attracting Thousands Here Nightly," *Amarillo Daily News,* Sept. 6, 1950, p. 1.

189. Ibid., p. 7.

190. "Rains Soak Plains Area," *Amarillo Daily News,* Sept. 6, 1950, p. 1.

191. See "Flash Storm Pelts Seagraves Vicinity," *Amarillo Daily News,* Sept. 9, 1950, p. 4.

192. "Man Dies after Dash in Rain When Wind Grabs Revival Tent," *Amarillo Daily News,* Sept. 9, 1950, p. 1.

193. "U.S. Weather Bureau Map," *Amarillo Daily News,* Sept. 9, 1950, p. 8.

194. Oral Roberts, "Flash," *HW,* Oct. 1950, pp. 1, 15; "Treating Forty Tent Victims," *Amarillo Globe,* Sept. 11, 1950, pp. 1–2.

195. O. Roberts, "Flash," p. 1.

196. See "Fifty Hurt As Tent Falls," *Amarillo Daily News,* Sept. 11, 1950, pp. 1–2, 4, 7, 18.

197. " 'Few Injuries Are Miracle,' Roberts," *Amarillo Daily News,* Sept. 11, 1950, p. 1.

198. "Revival Is Closed," *Amarillo Globe,* Sept. 11, 1950, p. 2.

199. Howard, *Fake Healers,* pp. 43–44.

200. "From A to Izzard," *Amarillo Daily News,* Sept. 12 1950, p. 1. The title of the editorial was "There's a Lesson in the Gospel Tent," Oral liked it enough to reprint it. "Escape of 7,000 Called 'Miracle,'" *HW,* Nov. 1950, p. 14.

201. O. Roberts, *My Twenty Years of a Miracle Ministry,* n.p.

202. Oral Roberts, "My Plans for the Future," *HW,* Nov. 1950, pp. 4–5.

203. Ibid.

204. Ibid. See also V. Roberts, "News about the 'Tent Cathedral,'" pp. 14–15.

205. Mike Gildea, "Crusade Continues," *Charleston (S.C.) Evening Post,* Apr. 25, 1958, ORU.

206. Colbert B. Bigby, "Oral Roberts in Columbia," *PHA,* May 18, 1950, p. 6; W. E. Mann, "An Evaluation of Oral Roberts," *Toronto Telegram,* June 27, 1956, ORU.

207. Donald Bishoff, Jr., "'Healing' Is Not So Simple," *Richmond Times Dispatch,* Jan. 23, 1960, ORU; Ora Spaid, "About 3,000 Hear the Rev. Oral Roberts," p. 1.

208. Richard Carter, "That Old-Time Religion Comes Back," *Coronet,* Feb. 1958, p. 126; Hayes B. Jacobs, "Oral Roberts: High Priest of Faith Healing," *Harper's Magazine,* Feb. 1962, p. 43.

209. "What about the 'Faith Healers'?" (Reprint from *Presbyterian Outlook,* no pub. info., ORU).

210. Ora Spaid, "About 3,000 Hear the Rev. Oral Roberts," p. 1.

211. O. Roberts, *My Story,* p. 148.

212. See O. Roberts, "Divine Ammunition in the Book of Acts," *PHA,* July 17, 1947, p. 4; O. Roberts, My Own Personal Testimony Transcript, Oct. 21, 1970 pp. 9–10.

213. Jack Coe, *Apostles and Prophets* (Dallas: Herald of Healing, 1954), p. 30.

214. O. Roberts, Crusade Transcript, June 12, 1957, pp. 16–18.

215. "Six-Day Crusade by Evangelist to Open on LI," *Newsday,* Mar. 24, 1958, p. 4. For a general statement on this subject, see O. Roberts, *My Story,* pp. 147–48.

216. "Oral Roberts Takes Positive Approach to Help Audience," *Pueblo (Colo.) Star-Journal,* Aug. 29, 1958, ORU.

6. MINISTRY

1. Yvonne Nance, "The Woman behind the Man," *AL,* June 1957, p. 15.

2. Evelyn Roberts, Miscellaneous Speech Transcript, June 8, 1981, p. 5.

3. Ibid., O. Roberts, Chapel Transcript, Nov. 16, 1967, p. 4; Nance, "The Woman behind the Man," p. 15; O. Roberts, Miscellaneous Speech Transcript, Apr. 3, 1957, p. 10.

4. "A Personal Report from Bro. Roberts," *HW,* Oct. 1948, pp. 2, 9.

5. "Team Profiles," *AL,* July 1973, p. 17; O. Roberts, Chapel Transcript, p. 4; "Honored," *Tulsa Tribune,* Aug. 8, 1967, ORU.

6. Nance, "The Woman behind the Man," p. 15. During the earliest crusades, Evelyn went along and "helped Oral on the platform," but by 1948 she had been relieved of that responsibility. Yvonne Litchfield, "This Is Mrs. Oral Roberts," *Tulsa World,* Feb. 15, 1967, ORU.

7. Nance, "The Woman behind the Man," p. 15.

8. George M. Engel, "Healing Waters Is Four Years Old," *HW,* Nov. 1951, p. 18.

9. Gilbert Asher, "Pastor Realizes Dreams Far beyond Expectations," *Tulsa World,* Sept. 8, 1949, sec. 2, p. 1.

10. G. H. Montgomery, "Looking Back over Ten Years of Deliverance Ministry," *AL,* June 1957, pp. 3–9.

11. Oral Roberts, "Oral Roberts Tells How the Founding of the Magazine Was Based on a Great Healing and the Amazing Results," *AL,* Nov. 1969, p. 3.

12. See W. B. Lee, "About Healing Waters, Inc.," *HW*, Oct. 1949, p. 14; [picture caption,] *HW*, July 1950, p. 14; Jake Till, "Over 6,000 Saved In Tallahassee Revival," *PHA*, May 12, 1949, p. 6; Gilbert Asher, "Pastor Realizes Dream Far beyond Expectations," p. 1.

13. "Healing Waters Office Workers," *HW*, May 1948, p. 10.

14. Ruby White, "Healing Waters Employees Banquet," *HW*, Feb. 1949, p. 15.

15. "The Vaden Roberts Story," *HW*, Nov. 1950, p. 6; Oral Roberts, *My Story* (Tulsa and New York: Summit Book Co., 1961) pp. 143–44.

16. Nance, "The Woman behind the Man," p. 16.

17. Generally local pastors handled the preliminary work in the services, such as taking the offerings, and assisted Oral in the healing line. See "Roberts' Healing Campaign a Great Success," *PHA*, Nov. 18, 1948, p. 14.

18. "Reg G. Hanson Manager Roberts Healing Campaigns," *HW*, August 1948, p. 11; "Roberts' Healing Campaign a Great Success," p. 14.

19. [Masthead,] *HW*, Dec. 1949, p. 3. Lee was the former office manager of the Tourneau Company in Toccoa. George Hitt, "Roberts, The Healing Evangelist, In State," *Independent* (Anderson, S.C.), Apr. 17, 1950, ORU.

20. O. Roberts, OREA Staff Meeting Transcript, Oct. 20, 1966, pp. 5–6; W. T. Jeffers, *What I Know about Oral Roberts* (Tulsa: Frontiers of Faith n.d.), p. 24; Oral Roberts, *My Twenty Years of a Miracle Ministry* (Tulsa: Oral Roberts, 1967), passim; Evelyn Roberts Interview, Nov. 1, 1983.

21. "Dr. O. E. Sproull Joins Roberts' Party," *HW*, Jan. 1949, p. 16.

22. Oral Roberts, *Oral Roberts' Life Story* (Tulsa: Oral Roberts, 1952), p. 148.

23. Harold Paul Interview, Jan. 28, 1983.

24. Ibid.; "Dr. O. E. Sproull Joins Roberts' Party," p. 16; "Resigns Church," *PHA*, Jan. 20, 1949, p. 14.

25. "The Lee Braxton Story As Told by Himself," *HW*, June 1951, pp. 6–7, 10–12; Lee Braxton, "Holmes Bible and Missionary Institute," *PHA*, Aug. 21, 1941, p. 10; J. A. Synan, "Home Missions," *PHA*, June 3, 1943, p. 7; Oscar Moore Interview, Jan. 20, 1983.

26. Lee Braxton, "N.C. Business Man Flies to Miami Meeting — Writes His Impressions," *HW*, March 1949, p. 1; "The Lee Braxton Story As Told by Himself," p. 11.

27. O. Roberts, Miscellaneous Speech Transcript, Nov. 20, 1982, p. 7.

28. "The Lee Braxton Story As Told by Himself," p. 11.

29. Lee Braxton Interview, Dec. 18, 1973; W. Kevin Armstrong, "Braxton Banks on Books," *Oracle*, Dec. 1981, p. 9.

30. Braxton Interview.

31. O. Roberts, Miscellaneous Speech Transcript, Nov. 20, 1982, p. 7.

32. Ibid., p. 8.

33. "Lee Braxton Reports Amazing Progress and Problems of Healing Waters," *HW*, August 1950, pp. 10–11; Bob Foresman, "He Joined Roberts for $1 a Year," *Tulsa Tribune*, Jan. 8, 1964, p. 37.

34. Gilbert Asher, "Pastor Realizes Dream Far beyond Expectations," pp. 1, 39.

35. "The Beautiful Healing Waters Office in Tulsa, Oklahoma," *HW*, Nov. 1951, p. 1; O. Roberts, *Life Story*, p. 108.

36. Charles Kohte Interview, Feb. 23, 1983. See "Tour of the New Healing Waters Office in Tulsa," *HW*, Nov. 1949, pp. 12–13.

37. "They've Served the Lord Together for over Thirty Years," *Daily Record* (Dunn, N.C.), Dec. 23 and 24, 1982, p. 12; O. Roberts, Chapel Transcript, Nov. 16, 1967, p. 4. Oral apparently called Wellons to solicit the loan, although he later recollected that Wellons called him. O. Roberts, Chapel Transcript, Jan. 30, 1976, pp. 13–14.

38. "Miracle of Seed-Faith, Part III," *AL*, Dec. 1971, p. 10.

39. Ibid.; O. Roberts, *My Story*, pp. 137–39; Armstrong, "Braxton Banks on Books," p. 9.

40. Oral Roberts, "The Story behind Healing Waters," *HW*, June 1952, p. 15.

41. See "Healing Waters Radio Log," *PHA,* Aug. 14, 1947, p. 15; *HW,* Nov. and Dec. 1947, p. 3.

42. Healing Waters Broadcast Tape, June 5, 1949, ORU. See also Apr. 24, 1949; May 22, 1949; June 12, 1949; June 29, 1949; O. Roberts, "The Story behind Healing Waters," p. 15; "Oral Roberts and Healing Waters Male Trio," *HW,* April 1948, p. 4.

43. Oral Roberts, "100 Radio Stations for Healing Waters Broadcast in Twelve Months," *HW,* Sept. 1949, p. 12.

44. See Lee Braxton, "Interest in Healing Waters Radio Programs Increasing," *HW,* Feb. 1950, p. 11; "The Lee Braxton Story As Told by Himself," p. 12; "Lee Braxton, National Radio Director Calls Special Radio Meeting in Tulsa," *HW,* July 1951, p. 15.

45. See L. J. Oliver, "Florida Roberts' Meetings," *PHA,* Mar. 17, 1949, p. 9; "Pastors Praise Brother Roberts Healing Revival in Muskogee, Oklahoma," *HW,* Nov.-Dec. 1947, p. 3.

46. Evelyn Roberts, Miscellaneous Speech Transcript, June 8, 1981, p. 3.

47. "Partners for Deliverance," *HW,* Nov.-Dec. 1947, p. 6.

48. *HW,* Jan. 1950, p. 12; Sept. 1950, p. 11.

49. Oral Roberts, *If You Need Healing—Do These Things!* (2d ed.; Tulsa: Standard Publishing Co., [1949]), p. 129.

50. Reg G. Hanson, "How to Secure Anointed Handkerchiefs," *HW,* June 1948, p. 9.

51. "From Mrs. Oral Roberts," *HW,* July 1950, p. 16.

52. Prayer Cloth, ORU Archives.

53. Healing Waters Broadcast, Apr. 24, 1949, ORU.

54. Hanson, "How to Secure Anointed Handkerchiefs," p. 9.

55. "Facts and Figures," *HW,* Feb. 1951, p. 15. See "Summary of Oral Roberts Ministry During 1951," *HW,* Feb. 1952, p. 3; "Summary of the Oral Roberts Ministry in 1952," *HW,* Feb. 1953, p. 13; G. H. Montgomery, "The March of Deliverance," *AHM,* Feb. 1954, p. 4; G. H. Montgomery, "Anniversary," *AL,* June 1957, p. 2.

56. "Summary of Brother Roberts' Ministry for Year 1954," *AHM,* Feb. 1955, p. 10.

57. Ibid.

58. "Fourth Million Souls Won to Christ," *AL,* April 1959, p. 2.

59. *Oakland Tribune,* Aug. 25, 1951, p. D3.

60. O. Roberts, Crusade Transcript, Apr. 22, 1955, p. 9. Bob DeWeese recalled that for years "the newspapers would come to him here in Tulsa and say, 'What are your plans, Oral?' and Oral's reply would be 'to win a million souls to Christ this year!' " He offered "nothing after that; his whole energy was devoted to the crusades." Bob De-Weese Interview, Jan. 19, 1983. For an example of the changed emphasis, see Oral Roberts, "A Master Plan," *AL,* Oct. 1956, pp. 3-5, 18-22.

61. George W. Cornell, "Preaching Powerhouse Denies Faith Healing," *Democrat and Chronicle* (Rochester, N.Y.), Mar. 30, 1958, ORU.

62. G. H. Montgomery, "Ten Men and a Million Souls," *HW,* May 1953, p. 5.

63. Montgomery, "The March of Deliverance," *AHM,* Feb. 1954, p. 4; and *AHM,* Dec. 1953, p. 4.

64. O. Roberts, "Second Call to Action," *AHM,* Jan. 1955, pp. 6-7, 9.

65. Manford Engel, "Mission Accomplished Second Million Soul Crusade Completed," *AL,* March 1957, p. 13. Sometimes the campaigns were overlapping. In 1956, Oral launched a campaign to win one million in one year.

66. "The Third Million Souls Won to Christ!", *AL,* April 1959, p. 2.

67. Oral Roberts, "Souls Unlimited," *AL,* May 1959, pp. 4-7.

68. Engel, "Mission Accomplished Second Million Soul Crusade Completed," p. 13.

69. "The Third Million Souls Won to Christ!", p. 2.

70. Bush and Evelyn Roberts, Evangelism of Oral Roberts Class Transcript, 1971, p. 18.

71. "Flagpole Sitter Finds God While Reading Oral Roberts Story," *AHM,* June 1954, p. 17.

72. See "Only Two More Months to Reach Radio Goal," *HW*, April 1950, p. 9; "Wanted: 20,000 Radio Partners," *HW*, June 1950, pp. 10–11; "Lee Braxton Reports Amazing Progress," *HW*, August 1950, p. 10; Lee Braxton, "Healing Waters Radio Meeting Success," *HW*, August 1951, pp. 14–15; G. H. Montgomery, "The March of Deliverance," *HW*, May 1953, p. 4.

73. Lee Braxton, "Oral Roberts Goes on ABC Network October 4," *AHM*, Oct. 1953, p. 13.

74. "Oral Roberts' Worldwide Radio Guide," *AL*, Nov. 1956, pp. 12–14.

75. See Oral Roberts, "Second Call to Action," *AHM*, Jan. 1955, p. 7.

76. Montgomery, "The March of Deliverance," p. 4.

77. "Overseas Radio Stations," *AL*, Nov. 1956, p. 13.

78. Oral Roberts, "Help Me Win Souls in Russia," *AL*, Jan. 1957, p. 2.

79. See "Evangelist Aiming Gospel toward Russia," *Grand Rapids (Mich.) Herald*, Apr. 21, 1957, ORU.

80. O. Roberts, "Souls Unlimited," pp. 4–5.

81. "Only Two More Months," *HW*, April 1950, p. 9.

82. "Lee Braxton Reports Amazing Progress," p. 10.

83. Ibid., "Healing Waters Radio Meeting Success," pp. 14–15.

84. Oral Roberts, "Healing Waters," *HW*, Nov. 1950, p. 10.

85. "Healing Waters to Be Heard on 100 Stations," *HW*, August 1951, pp. 14–15.

86. "Radio to Play Big Role in Oral Roberts' Plans," *Tulsa Tribune*, Dec. 11, 1959, ORU.

87. Pete White, "About the New Film," *HW*, August 1952, p. 11.

88. "Venture into Faith," *HW*, August 1952, pp. 8–9; Lee Braxton, "Bible Deliverance Film Being Made," *HW*, August 1952, p. 10.

89. Ibid.

90. "Looking Forward with Oral Roberts in 1953," *HW*, Feb. 1953, p. 10.

91. Lee Braxton, "Venture into Faith," *AHM*, Jan. 1954, p. 18.

92. "Thousands Saved through 'Venture into Faith,'" *AHM*, Nov. 1953, p. 11.

93. "Summary of Brother Roberts' Ministry for Year 1954," p. 10.

94. G. H. Montgomery, "Looking Forward with Oral Roberts," *HW*, Jan. 1952, p. 13.

95. Braxton, "Oral Roberts Goes on ABC Network October 4," p. 13; G. H. Montgomery, "Looking into a New Year," *AHM*, Feb. 1954, p. 4.

96. Oral Roberts, "My Plans for Television," *AHM*, Jan. 1954, p. 12.

97. Ibid.

98. "Previewing the Oral Roberts TV Program," *AHM*, Jan. 1954, p. 4.

99. "Oral Roberts on the World's Air Waves," *Air Waves* 2, no. 1, no date, p. 10.

100. Evelyn Roberts, *His Darling Wife, Evelyn* (New York: Dell Publishing Co., 1976), p. 228.

101. "TV News," *AHM*, June 1954, p. 12.

102. Wayne Robinson recalled that Oral always liked to pray for an individual when he taped his prayers for radio. Interview, Apr. 4, 1983.

103. See Rex Humbard, Chapel Transcript, Oct. 13, 1971, p. 5.

104. Evelyn Roberts, Miscellaneous Speech Transcript, June 8, 1981, p. 10; O. Roberts, Chapel Transcript, Nov. 15, 1967, p. 15.

105. G. H. Montgomery, "The March of Deliverance," *AHM*, Sept. 1954, p. 4.

106. Oral Roberts, "A Call to Action," *AHM*, June 1954, p. 12.

107. Lee Braxton, "Millions See the First Oral Roberts Telecast," *AHM*, March 1955, p. 22.

108. O. Roberts, Evangelism Unit #1 Transcript, n.d., p. 9. See also pp. 1, 10.

109. Braxton, "Millions See the First Oral Roberts Telecast," p. 22.

110. O. Roberts, Crusade Transcript, July 10, 1957, p. 14.

111. O. Roberts, *My Story*, p. 159.

112. G. H. Montgomery, "The March of Deliverance," *AHM*, Sept. 1954, p. 4. See O. Roberts, Crusade Transcript, July 10, 1957, p. 14.

113. *Wichita Falls Record News,* p. 1.

114. Anita Synder, "Here Is the Story of the Wichita Falls Miracle," *AHM,* July 1955, pp. 3–4, 14.

115. "The Growth of a Miracle," *AL,* Feb. 1963, p. 5.

116. "New Television Schedule," *AHM,* Jan 1955, p. 8.

117. "The Oral Roberts TV Network," *AHM,* March 1955, p. 24.

118. See O. Roberts, *My Story,* p. 157; G. H. Montgomery, "Looking into a New Year," *AHM,* Feb. 1954, p. 4.

119. "The Oral Roberts TV Network," p. 3.

120. Lee Braxton, "Man's Greatest Miracle — Our Greatest Opportunity," *AL,* Nov. 1957, p. 20.

121. Braxton, "Millions See the First Oral Roberts Telecast," p. 22.

122. "Oral Roberts on the World's Air Waves," p. 10; George Stovall Interview, Jan. 27, 1983.

123. O. Roberts, Kiwanis Speech Transcript, 1956, p. 5. See O. Roberts, *My Story,* pp. 157, 169–70; O. Roberts *My Twenty Years of a Miracle Ministry,* p. 20.

124. "Canvas Cathedral Evangelist," *Gilbert (Ariz.) Enterprise,* Jan. 1957, ORU. This article was a part of a syndicated series of twelve articles. Oral's television success clearly set him apart from the other healing evangelists and was duly noted in the pentecostal community. See "News From North America," *Pentecost,* June 1955, p. 3. From the beginning the organization also envisioned its television films as a means of foreign influence. See O. Roberts, Crusade Transcript, Dec. 14, 1957, pp. 8–9.

125. Lee Braxton, "TV Enthusiasm in Fresno and Amarillo," *AHM,* Jan. 1954, p. 18; O. Roberts, "My Plans for Television," pp. 12–14.

126. See O. Roberts, "Who Will Sponsor TV in New York City?" *AHM,* April 1954, p. 12.

127. See "Outstanding Offerings for the Television Ministry," *AHM,* April 1954, p. 12.

128. O. Roberts, Chapel Transcript, Nov. 15, 1967, p. 15.

129. O. Roberts, "A Call to Action," *AHM,* June 1954, pp. 12–13; Montgomery, "The March of Deliverance," *AHM,* July 1954, p. 4.

130. See "Your New Magazine," *AL,* July 1956, p. 2.

131. See [Advertisement,] *AL,* Sept. 1956, p. 11; "Religion Books Roll off Presses at Printing Plant," *Sparta News-Plaindealer,* Dec. 23, 1955, ORU.

132. See "Does Your Newspaper Carry This Column?" *AL,* Nov. 1959, p. 6.

133. "Oral Roberts," *Publisher's Weekly,* Mar. 23, 1959, ORU. See G. H. Montgomery, "A 'Daily Blessing' Is Coming Your Way!", *AL,* Feb. 1959, p. 23.

134. Montgomery, "The March of Deliverance," *HW,* August 1953, p. 4. See also O. Roberts and E. Roberts, Evangelism of Oral Roberts Class Transcript, 1971, p. 9; O. Roberts, Kiwanis Speech Transcript, 1956, p. 3.

135. O. Roberts, "At Last . . . the Right Name," *Healing,* June 1956, p. 3.

136. See G. H. Montgomery, "Ruminations of One Waiting for the Whistle to Blow," *PHA,* Oct. 13, 1949, p. 2; J. A. Synan Interview, Apr. 16, 1983; Paul Interview; Moore Interview.

137. W. T. Jeffers, *What I Know about Oral Roberts,* p. 25.

138. G. H. Montgomery, "Bob DeWeese Host of the Campaigns," *Healing,* March 1956, p. 8.

139. O. Roberts, *Life Story,* p. 148.

140. DeWeese Interview.

141. Paul Interview.

142. DeWeese Interview.

143. Ibid.

144. Montgomery, "Bob DeWeese Host of the Campaigns," p. 7.

145. "Team Profiles," *AL,* July 1973, p. 16.

146. Montgomery, "Bob DeWeese Host of the Campaigns," p. 9.

147. Ibid.

148. Ibid., p. 18.

149. DeWeese Interview.

150. Collins Steele Interview, Jan. 13, 1983; G. H. Montgomery, "Collins Steele," *AL*, July 1956, pp. 22-23.

151. See Hart R. Armstrong, "Gather Them Up," *Healing*, March 1956, pp. 19-20.

152. "You Should Know That," *HW*, Dec. 1950, p. 3.

153. Oscar Moore, "Oral Roberts' Offer Accepted by Board," *PHA*, Feb. 22, 1951, pp. 9-10; [picture caption,] *HW*, July 1950, p. 14.

154. See "Announcement of Name Change for Healing Waters, Inc.," *AL*, May 1957, p. 16; Braxton Interview. Like the change of the title of the magazine to *Abundant Life*, the organizational change reflected the revised self-image of the Roberts ministry.

155. See "Romantic Development of Oral Roberts' Ministry," *Pentecost*, Sept. 1959, p. 11; "Trustees Hold Meeting in Tulsa," *AL*, Nov. 1961, p. 15.

156. Albert E. Bush Interview, Feb. 11, 1983.

157. O. Roberts, "Second Call to Action," *AHM*, Jan. 1955, pp. 6-7.

158. O. Roberts, "Third Call to Action," *Healing*, Feb. 1956, pp. 12-13.

159. See O. Roberts, "Souls Unlimited," pp. 4-7.

160. G. H. Montgomery, "Deliverance Is Brought to Crow Indian Reservation," *AHM*, Nov. 1955, p. 6; "Indian Tribes Honor Oral Roberts," *Billings (Mont.) Gazette*, Aug. 27, 1955, ORU.

161. O. Roberts, "A Call to Action for Our Third Million Soul Crusade," *AL*, March 1957, p. 18.

162. Hilliard Griffin, "Missionary to American Indians," *AL*, Nov. 1959, pp. 7-9.

163. Nance, "The Woman behind the Man," p. 17.

164. O. Roberts, "My Trip to the Holy Land," *AHM*, March 1954, p. 12; see pp. 2-3, 12-17; see also "Tulsa Evangelist Back from Holy Land," *Tulsa Tribune*, Dec. 19, 1953, ORU.

165. G. H. Montgomery, "Looking into a New Year," *AHM*, Feb. 1954, p. 4.

166. O. Roberts, "The Spell of Israel over Me!", *AL*, July 1959, p. 3.

167. Oral Roberts, *Oral Roberts' Best Sermons and Stories* (Tulsa: Oral Roberts, 1956), p. 53.

168. See "Heart Attack Fatal to Oral Roberts Associate," *Tulsa Tribune*, Aug. 8, 1967, ORU.

169. "Christian Friends of Israel, Inc.," *Christian Friends of Israel Messenger*, Nov. 1951, p. 2.

170. Oral Roberts, "How I Remember Myron Sackett," *AL*, Nov. 1967, p. 23; see pp. 22-25; "Israel Sees the Gospel!", *Christian Friends of Israel Messenger*, Feb. 1954, p. 8.

171. See Myron Sackett, "Three Reasons Why I Came to Brother Roberts," *Christian Friends of Israel Messenger*, June-July 1955, p. 2.

172. "A Call to Action for Our Third Million Soul Crusade," *AL*, March 1957, p. 18.

173. O. Roberts, "How I Remember Myron Sackett," p. 24.

174. See Evelyn Roberts, Miscellaneous Speech Transcript, June 8, 1981, p. 5.

175. O. Roberts, "The Spell of Israel over Me!", p. 7.

176. O. Roberts, "I Am a Christian Friend of Israel," *Christian Friends of Israel Messenger*, Feb., Mar., Apr. 1956, p. 4.

177. "A Call to Action for Our Third Million Soul Crusade," pp. 14-21.

178. Engel, "Mission Accomplished Second Million Souls Crusade Completed," p. 13.

179. O. Roberts, "Souls Unlimited," p. 5. See also G. H. Montgomery, World Action Conference Transcript, June 4, 1957, p. 8.

180. *Life Crusade* (Tulsa: Oral Roberts, n.d.).

181. Al Bush and Evelyn Roberts, Evangelism of Oral Roberts Class Transcript, 1971, p. 18.

182. "Diary of Our Trip," *AHM*, March 1955, p. 5.

183. "Overseas Offices," *AHM*, August 1954, p. 13; "Radio Luxembourg Listeners," *AHM*, March 1955, p. 5.

184. Oral Roberts, "The Lord Told Me to Go on Radio and TV," *Air Waves* 2, no. 1, no date, p. 7.

185. Tommy Hicks, "I Saw Three Million People Bow before God," *AHM*, Nov. 1954, p. 13. See pp. 12–13, 17.

186. Charlton Price, "Faith Healing, Science Agree, Says Roberts," *Houston Post*, Oct. 16, 1949, ORU.

187. G. H. Montgomery, "Looking Forward with Oral Roberts," *HW*, Jan. 1952, p. 13.

188. "Looking Forward with Oral Roberts in 1953," *HW*, Feb. 1953, p. 10.

189. "Diary of Our Trip," p. 2.

190. A. J. Schoeman, "The South African Campaign Report," *AHM*, March 1955, pp. 8–10.

191. "Oral Roberts Says 30,000 Converted on Africa Trip." *Tulsa World*, Jan. 16, 1955, ORU.

192. See Bob Foresman, "Amid Traffic Jams and Charges of Mass Hysteria—Oral Roberts Cuts a Swath in South Africa," *Tulsa Tribune*, Feb. 1, 1955, sec. 2, p. 21; "U.S. Evangelist Has Collected 13,000 in City," *Rand Daily Mail* (Johannesburg), Jan. 11, 1955, ORU.

193. DeWeese Interview.

194. "Diary of Our Trip," p. 5.

195. O. Roberts, *Best Sermons*, p. 93.

196. "Expect Great Things from God," *AHM*, March 1955, n.p.

197. O. Roberts, "A Master Plan," *AL*, Oct. 1956, pp. 3–5, 18–22; O. Roberts, "It's Great to be Back in America," *Healing*, March 1956, p. 23.

198. O. Roberts, "The Lord Told Me to Go on Radio and TV," p. 7; Evelyn Roberts, Evangelism of Oral Roberts Class Transcript, 1971, p. 10.

199. O. Roberts, Devotion Transcript, Feb. 4, 1957, p. 1.

200. " 'We Were Cured,' People Tell Oral Roberts Meeting," *Rand Daily Mail* (Johannesburg), Jan. 17, 1957, p. 9.

201. O. Roberts, "I Went to Africa in Your Place," *AL*, April 1957, p. 8; Evelyn Roberts, Evangelism of Oral Roberts Class Transcript, 1971, p. 10.

202. "Hot Gospeller Calls 12,000 to Turn to God," *Rand Daily Mail* (Johannesburg), Jan. 14, 1957, p. 1.

203. Evelyn Roberts Interview, Apr. 3, 1984. See "South Africa Customs Agents Search Tulsan," *Tulsa Tribune*, Feb. 20, 1957, ORU; "Oral Roberts Explains African Diamond Mixup," *Tulsa Tribune*, Feb. 21, 1957, ORU.

204. "Rev. Oral Roberts Invited to Japan," *Syracuse (N.Y.) Post Standard*, June 8, 1958, ORU.

205. "Crusade by Oral Roberts through Russia Proposed," *Tulsa World*, Jan. 19, 1959, ORU.

206. Telegram copy, ORU Archives.

207. See "A One-Man Religious Industry," *Rand Daily Mail* (Johannesburg), Jan. 23, 1957, p. 7.

208. O. Roberts, "It's Great to Be Back in America," p. 23.

209. Ibid. See "Straight from the Heart," *Healing*, Jan. 1956, p. 19.

210. "World Evangelist Oral Roberts to Dedicate Tulsa Headquarters," *Lawton (Okla.) Constitution*, May 1, 1959, ORU.

211. L. J. Oliver, "Oral Roberts Campaign in Tampa," *PHA*, May 10, 1951, p. 12; Oral Roberts, "The Burden of a Million Souls," *HW*, July 1953, pp. 12–14.

212. Oral Roberts, "Announcing an Emergency," *AL*, Sept. 1956, p. 31.

213. A. A. Allen, *Your Christian Dollar* (Dallas: A. A. Allen, 1958), p. 28.

214. See Oral Roberts, Crusade Transcript, Dec. 14, 1957, p. 9; O. Roberts, "A Call to Action," *AHM*, June 1954, pp. 12–13.

215. O. Roberts, "Announcing an Emergency," p. 31.

216. See, for instance, Myron Sackett, "Deliverance from Poverty," *AL*, April 1958, pp. 18–19.

217. Oral Roberts, "Do You Want God to Return Your Money Seven Times?" *AHM*, April 1954, p. 10.

218. O. Roberts, *My Twenty Years of a Miracle Ministry*, p. 23.

219. O. Roberts, *My Story*, p. 161.

220. Evelyn Roberts, *His Darling Wife*, p. 159.

221. "Finds Blessing Pact," *AL*, May 1958, p. 23.

222. [Advertisement,] *HW*, July 1950, p. 16.

223. Brochure, no pub. info., ORU Archives.

224. "Healing Waters to Be Heard on 100 Stations," *HW*, March 1951, p. 13.

225. Braxton, "Healing Waters Radio Meeting Success," pp. 14–15.

226. G. H. Montgomery, "Million Souls Crusade Draws Businessmen to Tulsa," *AHM*, Oct. 1954, p. 14.

227. Montgomery, "The March of Deliverance," *AHM*, Sept. 1955, p. 14.

228. Anita Snyder, "Master Soul Winners Meet for Conference," *AL*, Oct. 1956, pp. 6–7.

229. Yvonne Nance, "Record Crowd Meets for Fourth Conference," *AL*, Aug. 1957, pp. 26–27.

230. "Aides to Hear Evangelist," *Tulsa Tribune*, May 9, 1959, ORU.

231. Nance, "Record Crowd Meets for Fourth Conference," p. 27.

232. Evelyn Roberts, Miscellaneous Speech Transcript, June 8, 1982, p. 9.

233. Montgomery, "The March of Deliverance," *HW*, June 1953, p. 4.

234. "A Miracle in Masonry," *AHM*, Nov. 1954, p. 5.

235. Eve Arnold, "The Laying On of Hands," *Cosmopolitan*, Feb. 1956, p. 80; "Evangelist Lists Plans," unidentified Tulsa newspaper clipping, ORU.

236. "Gary Praises Oral Roberts at Ceremony," *Tulsa Tribune*, May 23, 1957, ORU. See "God's Answer to the Impossible," *AL*, August 1957, p. 22.

237. "Evangelist Shops Here for Marble," *Rutland (Vt.) Daily Herald*, May 3, 1957, p. 1.

238. For a description of the building, see "Seven Story Pulpit," *Cablegram*, no. 2, 1959, pp. 12–16; "Oral Roberts Purchases Marble for New Building," *Tulsa Tribune*, May 5, 1967, ORU.

239. See "Abundant Life," *AL*, Jan. 1958, p. 7; "The Abundant Life Building Takes Shape," *AL*, March 1958, p. 27; Oral Roberts, "The Lord Told Me to Build," *AL*, April 1959, pp. 4–6.

240. O. Roberts, *My Twenty Years of a Miracle Ministry*, p. 36.

241. O. Roberts, Chapel Transcript, Jan. 30, 1976, p. 1; "New Building Work Stops," *Tulsa World*, Apr. 6, 1958, ORU.

242. Ibid.

243. OREA Devotion Transcript, Nov. 1957, pp. 11–12.

244. O. Roberts, OREA Devotion Transcript, July 20, 1962, p. 10.

245. See letter from W. E. Bender, Jr. to Oral Roberts, Mar. 14, 1958, ORU Archives.

246. O. Roberts, OREA Devotion Transcript, July 20, 1962, p. 10.

247. See "Oral Roberts Building Sold to Risk Firm," *Tulsa World*, Apr. 5, 1959, ORU; Pete Martin, "Oral Roberts," *Christian Herald*, Mar. 1966, p. 80.

248. See letter from W. E. Bender, Jr. to Oral Roberts.

249. Elaine Dittman, "Abundant Life Mural," *Oracle*, Oct. 7, 1977, p. 12; "Modern Lighting," *Tulsa World*, June 10, 1960, ORU; *The Redemptorama* (Tulsa: OREA, n.d.).

250. "Dedicated to the Glory of God," *AL*, July 1959, pp. 14–15; Margaret Muse Oden, "A Great House for God," *PHA*, Dec. 1959, pp. 6, 14; "Summerfield Cancels Dedication Here," *Tulsa Tribune*, Apr. 17, 1959, ORU.

251. "Does Sacred History Repeat Itself?" *OREA Partners*, Mar. 13, 1959, pp. 1–2, 7–8.

252. See O. Roberts, OREA Devotion Transcript, Nov. 1957, p. 10.

7. THE PRICE OF GLORY

1. For a general survey of the revival, see David Edwin Harrell, Jr., *All Things Are Possible* (Bloomington: Indiana University Press, 1975).

2. See "The Lord Doeth This," *PHA*, May 27, 1948, p. 3.

3. Demos Shakarian Interview, Jan. 27, 1983.

4. G. H. Montgomery, "The Demos Shakarian Story," *HW*, Mar. 1953, p. 11.

5. "Looking Forward with Oral Roberts in 1953," *HW*, Feb. 1953, p. 10.

6. "United Pentecost," *PHA*, June 2, 1938, p. 3.

7. See "Corvin Speaker in City-Wide Campaign," *PHA*, Jan. 24, 1946, p. 15; V. V. Pate, "Birmingham Rally a Success," *PHA*, June 27, 1946, p. 14.

8. Harold C. Herman, "Christ Came to Hollywood Boulevard," *Pentecost*, Dec. 1948, pp. 6-7.

9. "Will the Revival Come This Year?" *PHA*, Jan. 1, 1948, p. 2.

10. David J. du Plessis, "Pentecostal Leader at National Association of Evangelicals," *Pentecost*, June 1949, p. 16.

11. See John Thomas Nichol, *Pentecostalism* (New York: Harper and Row [1966]), pp. 208-45; Walter J. Hollenweger, *The Pentecostals* (1st U.S. ed.; Minneapolis: Augsburg Publishing House, 1972), pp. 29-46.

12. "Brother Roberts to Preach in Des Moines, Iowa," *HW*, Oct. 28, 1948, p. 8.

13. "Constitutional Convention of the Pentecostal Fellowship of North America," *PHA*, Nov. 11, 1948, p. 4.

14. Oral Roberts, "Elisha, the Double Portion Man," *PHA*, Jan. 27, 1949, p. 5.

15. Cline Halsey, "Report of International Pentecostal Convention, Des Moines, Iowa," *HW*, Dec. 1948, p. 16.

16. "The Historic Convention," *Voice of Healing*, Jan. 1949, p. 7.

17. George Harold Paul, "The Religious Frontier in Oklahoma," Ph.D. dissertation, University of Oklahoma, 1965, p. 277. It is interesting that Donald Gee, the foremost publicist of worldwide Pentecostalism, made a tour of the United States in 1947 and did not mention the healing revivalists in his reports. See *Pentecost*, 1947.

18. "Great Healing Campaign in America," *Pentecost*, June 1950, p. 9.

19. "Renewed Emphasis upon Divine Healing," *Pentecost*, Sept. 1949, p. 14.

20. "World-Wide Pentecostal Revivals, 1906-1956," *Voice of Healing*, July 1956, p. 13.

21. "The Sign-Gift Ministries — God's Way of Deliverance for the Last Days," *HW*, Aug. 1948, p. 10.

22. Oral Roberts, *Oral Roberts' Best Sermons and Stories* (Tulsa: Oral Roberts, 1956), p. 123.

23. Oral Roberts, "What God Has Shown to Me," *AHM*, Oct. 1954, pp. 4-5; Bill Rose, "Preaching Mission to Hear Tale of 'Miracle Healing,'" *Oakland Tribune*, Oct. 7, 1954, p. E32.

24. "Transferred Power," Sermon Tape, June 13, 1952, ORU Archives.

25. "F. F. Bosworth Rejoices over Roberts Meeting in Miami," *HW*, Feb. 1949, p. 4.

26. See Harrell, *All Things Are Possible*, pp. 53-58.

27. See "Visit to Great Oral Roberts Tent Meeting at Granite City, Ill.," *Voice of Healing*, Sept. 1948, p. 7; "Address Directory," *Voice of Healing*, Apr.-May 1951, p. 6; "News of Last Days Revivals," *HW*, Oct. 1950, p. 14; "Great Crowds Throng Union Full Gospel Meetings across America," *HW*, Jan. 1951, p. 12.

28. Manford Engel, "Healing Ministry Convention Conducted in Tulsa," *HW*, Jan. 1952, p. 15.

29. See Harrell, *All Things Are Possible*, pp. 27-41; Gordon Lindsay Interview, July 27, 1972; Oscar Moore Interview, Jan. 20, 1983. See also David Nunn and W. V. Grant, *The Coming World-Wide Revival* (Dallas: W. V. Grant, n.d.), pp. 22-24; David Nunn Interview, Sept. 2, 1972.

30. Gordon Lindsay, "The Story of the Great Restoration Revival," *World-Wide Revival*, Apr. 1958, p. 18.

31. Ibid.; "Bro. Roberts with Rev. Branham and Party," *HW*, May 1948, p. 3; Lindsay Interview.

32. Lindsay Interview.

33. "The Branham Meetings," *HW*, June 1948, p. 10.

34. Oral Roberts Interview, Feb. 16, 1983.

35. "Program for Rev. Wm. Branham," *HW*, July 1948, p. 8. See also "Rev. Lindsay Visits Rev. Roberts," *HW*, Oct. 1948, p. 9.

36. "Wm. Branham Attends Roberts Campaign in Tampa, Florida," *HW*, Mar. 1949, p. 6.

37. "Branham Visits Roberts Campaign," *Voice of Healing*, Apr. 1949, p. 16. For an example of Roberts's continued support of Branham, see "Branham Holds Campaign in Kansas City," *HW*, Nov. 1950, p. 15.

38. See "Oral Roberts Preaches to a Great Congregation in New York City," *Pentecost*, June 1951, p. 6; "Among the Healing Campaigns," *Pentecost*, Dec. 1954, p. 14; Nunn Interview; Donald Gee, *Wind and Flame* (rev. and enl. ed.; Croydon, G.B.: Heath Press, 1967), pp. 242–45.

39. For instance, Bishop Joseph A. Synan brought his mother, ill with cancer, to one of Oral's early meetings. The Synan brothers were disillusioned when she died. Interviews with J. A. Synan and L. C. Synan, Apr. 16, 1983.

40. Oral Roberts, "What Faith Means to My Family and Me," *HW*, Sept. 1949, p. 10; "Preacher Enters Healing Ministry after Hearing Brother Roberts Preach," *HW*, Nov.-Dec. 1947, p. 5.

41. "Pictures and Report on Minneapolis Campaign," *HW*, Apr. 1948, p. 2.

42. Oral Roberts, "Mildred Wicks," *HW*, May 1949, p. 5.

43. "3,342 Come for Salvation during Roberts Healing Campaign in Durham, N.C.," *HW*, Aug. 1948, p. 9; see *Voice of Healing*, 1950.

44. "Brother Turpin Healed, Enters Evangelistic Work," *PHA*, June 9, 1949, p. 2.

45. Nunn Interview.

46. Kenneth Hagin Interviews, Apr. 24, 1973, Dec. 12, 1983.

47. Lexie Allen, *God's Man of Faith and Power* (Dallas: A. A. Allen, 1954), pp. 16–161; see Harrell, *All Things Are Possible*, pp. 66–75.

48. "Steve Pringle's Personal Testimony," *HW*, Nov. 1949, p. 3.

49. Velmer Gardner, Layman's Seminar Transcript, Nov. 19, 1966, p. 3.

50. Velmer Gardner, "A Miracle-Working God," *AL*, June 1965, pp. 6–9.

51. "Evangelistic Party from New York," *HW*, Jan. 1950, p. 7.

52. Rex Humbard, "Man with A Vision," *Answer*, March 1956, p. 6; Rex Humbard, Chapel Transcript, Oct. 13, 1971, p. 4.

53. Oral Roberts Interview, Feb. 16, 1983.

54. Lindsay Interview.

55. "Great Crowds Attend Jack Coe Meeting in Tulsa," *HW*, Nov. 1950, p. 15.

56. Lee Braxton Interview, Dec. 18, 1973.

57. "Our Cover Picture," *Voice of Healing*, July 1951, p. 3.

58. Lindsay Interview.

59. Jack Coe, "Which Evangelist Has the World's Largest Tent?" *International Healing Magazine*, July 1956, pp. 5, 16.

60. See "Publicity-Minded Newspaper Prints Many Slurs and Distorted Facts about Oral Roberts," *International Healing Magazine*, May 1956, p. 14; "War Is Declared," *Miracle Magazine*, May 1956, pp. 14–15.

61. Demos Shakarian, "How Our Fellowship Came into Being," *Full Gospel Business Men's Voice*, Feb. 1953, pp. 3–5; R. F. DeWeese, "Tacoma Business Men's Luncheon," *HW*, Oct. 1949, p. 15.

62. Demos Shakarian Interview, Jan. 27, 1983; Shakarian, "How Our Fellowship Came into Being," pp. 3–4; John and Elizabeth Sherrill, *The Happiest People on Earth* (Waco, Texas: Chosen Books, 1975), pp. 118–19.

63. Sherrill, *The Happiest People on Earth*, pp. 19, 121; Shakarian Interview.

64. "Full Gospel Business Men's Fellowship of America Start New National Association," *HW,* Jan. 1952, p. 12.

65. Shakarian Interview; "Full Gospel Business Men's Fellowship of America Start New National Association," p. 12; "Full Gospel Business Men," *HW,* Jan. 1953, p. 13.

66. Thomas R. Nickel, "Full Gospel Business Men's Convention," *AHM,* Dec. 1953, p. 13.

67. "Full Gospel Business Men's Convention in Washington, D.C. Inspiring," *Voice of Healing,* Aug. 1954, p. 18; Demos Shakarian, "We Want You in Our Midst," *Full Gospel Business Men's Voice,* June 1954, pp. 5–7.

68. Shakarian Interview; Nunn Interview.

69. Braxton Interview.

70. Oral Roberts, *The Holy Spirit in the Now* (3 vols.; Tulsa: Oral Roberts University, 1974), vol. 2, pp. 24–25.

71. Chapel Transcript, Dec. 10, 1982, p. 28.

72. Oral Roberts, Crusade Transcript, July 10, 1957.

73. Oral Roberts, "This Will Be Our Greatest Year," *AL,* Jan 1959, p. 12. See also Velmer Gardner, "Will This Recent Healing Revival Taper Off?" *World-Wide Revival,* June 1958, p. 9.

74. Shakarian Interview.

75. See Harrell, *All Things Are Possible,* pp. 107–116.

76. "Ten Rules We Must Obey If We Are to See a World-Shaking Revival," *Voice of Healing,* Nov. 1949, pp. 12–13.

77. C. B. Hollis Interview, July 28, 1972.

78. "The Deliverance Campaigns," *Pentecost,* June 1956, p. 17.

79. Gardner, "Will This Present Healing Revival Taper Off?" p. 9.

80. "From the Ministers," *HW,* Dec. 1949, p. 10; "Bishop Muse Lauds Roberts' Ministry," *HW,* Oct. 1948, p. 10; Harold Paul Interview, Jan. 28, 1983.

81. Joseph A. Synan, ed., *Yearbook of the Pentecostal Holiness Church,* 1950 (Franklin Springs, Ga.: Publishing House of the Pentecostal Holiness Church, n.d.) p. 7.

82. J. A. Synan Interview; "Bishop Lauds Roberts Meetings," *HW,* July 1948, p. 9.

83. "My Trip Out West," *PHA,* Apr. 7, 1949, p. 6.

84. "Conference Supt. Reports Campaign in Tampa," *PHA,* May 10, 1951, p. 12.

85. See Stanley Howard Frodsham, "Greater Things Shall Ye Do," *HW,* July 1949, pp. 2, 15; "High Official of Church of God," *HW,* June 1950, p. 15.

86. Oscar Moore, "Roberts' Meeting a Great Success," *PHA,* Oct. 21, 1948, p. 10; Bert E. Parmer, "Estimated 5,000 Connected in Jacksonville Meeting," *PHA,* Apr. 14, 1949, p. 6; "Roberts Campaign in Jacksonville," *PHA,* May 11, 1950, p. 10; see *Healing Waters.*

87. "3,300 Souls Reported to Seek God in Durham Meeting," *PHA,* Aug, 19, 1948, p. 5.

88. Healing Waters Broadcast, Tape, May 29, 1949.

89. "What's the Secret behind Oral Roberts Success," *HW,* Nov. 1951, p. 16; Paul Interview.

90. Crusade Transcript, May 26, 1955, p. 10.

91. Oral Roberts, Crusade Transcript, Mar. 24, 1957, pp. 3–5.

92. Oral Roberts, "Faith for Healing," *PHA,* Oct. 2, 1947, p. 5.

93. "North Carolina Business Man Reports Observations of Roberts Meeting," *PHA,* Feb. 24, 1949, p. 4.

94. "Oral Roberts' Campaign in Tacoma," *PHA,* Sept. 15, 1949, p. 4; W. J. Anderson, "Oral Roberts in Los Angeles," *PHA,* Nov. 18, 1951, p. 13. Pentecostal Holiness leaders would have approved of Roberts's publication of an article entitled "John Wesley's Message to This Generation," *HW,* Oct. 1949, pp. 1, 4–5.

95. "The March of Deliverance," *HW,* July 1953, p. 4.

96. See Oral Roberts, "Divine Ammunition," *PHA,* July 17, 1947, pp. 4–5; Oral Roberts, "God's Divine Power to Heal," *PHA,* Jan, 29, 1948, pp. 5–6; Oral Roberts,

"Deliverance from Demon Power," *PHA*, Jan. 6, 1949, pp. 8, 10; Oral Roberts, "Turning the Commonplace into the Miraculous," *PHA*, Aug. 10, 1950, pp. 4–5. For a listing of his schedule, see "Oral Roberts," *PHA*, Jan. 1, 1948, p. 16. His meetings were listed as "healing campaigns" and were separated from those of other evangelists. The paper soon stopped listing his revival schedule. His father, of course, continued to pastor through 1949. In 1948 he was stationed on Konawa; Dan T. Muse, T. T. Lindsey, and L. J. Oliver, eds., *Yearbook of the Pentecostal Holiness Church, 1948* (Franklin Springs, Ga.: Board of Publication of the Pentecostal Holiness Church, n.d.), n.p.

97. G. H. Montgomery, "The Camp Meeting at Ada," *PHA*, Aug. 19, 1948, p. 3; Muse et al., eds., *Yearbook of the Pentecostal Holiness Church, 1949*, pp. 4–10; Joseph A. Synan, ed., *Yearbook of the Pentecostal Holiness Church, 1950*, pp. 7, 19.

98. "Laymen's Association News," *PHA*, Oct. 16, 1952, p. 4.

99. See Lee Braxton, "The Pentecostal Holiness National Broadcast," *PHA*, June 5, 1952, p. 4.

100. See Lee Braxton, "I Visited Southwestern Bible College," *PHA*, Feb. 26, 1953, p. 8; "Personal and Pentecostal," *Pentecost*, June 1955, p. 11; Paul, "Religious Frontier," p. 194.

101. Moore Interview; Evelyn Roberts, *His Darling Wife, Evelyn* (New York: Dell Publishing Co., 1976), p. 113.

102. "Healing," *PHA*, Aug. 7, 1947, p. 7.

103. *The Pentecostal Holiness Church, 1898–1948* (Franklin Springs, Ga.: Publishing House of the Pentecostal Holiness Church, 1951), pp. 557–58.

104. Braxton Interview.

105. Paul Interview.

106. H. T. Spence, "To Our Conference Superintendents, Pastors, and Laymen," *PHA*, Mar. 29, 1951. p. 2.

107. Bob DeWeese Interview, Jan. 19, 1983.

108. G. H. Montgomery, "Divine Healing According to the Scriptures," *PHA*, June 3, 1948, pp. 3–4.

109. Paul Interview.

110. J. A. Synan Interview; L. C. Synan Interview; Vinson Synan Interview, May 22, 1983.

111. "Evangelist Roberts Is Invited to Return Soon," *Houston Post*, Oct. 28, 1949, sec. 1, p. 1.

112. Thomas Zimmerman Interview, Oct. 18, 1980.

113. "A Word of Explanation," *PHA*, Oct. 12, 1950, p. 2.

114. J. A. Synan Interview; Paul Interview; Moore Interview.

115. J. A. Synan Interview; Moore Interview.

116. Paul Interview.

117. Moore Interview.

118. Oral Roberts Interview, Feb. 16, 1983.

119. Evelyn Roberts, Chapel Transcript, Feb. 3, 1982, p. 13.

120. See Benjamin B. Warfield, *Counterfeit Miracles* (New York: Charles Scribner's Sons, 1913). For more recent fundamentalist statements, see John R. Rice, *False Doctrines* (Murfreesboro, Tenn.: Sword of the Lord Publishers, 1970), pp. 197–248, and Loyd Kalland, "Are Miracles Possible Today?" *Christian Life*, Apr. 1955, p. 47.

121. See "Are So-Called Healing Campaigns Scriptural?" *Toronto Globe and Mail*, June 28, 1952, p. 11. That was the title of a sermon preached by T. T. Shields at the large Jarvis Street Church.

122. Oct. 7, 1955, p. 13; see also, for examples, *Florida Times Union* (Jacksonville), Apr. 7, 1955, ORU; *Twin-City Sentinel* (Winston Salem, N.C.), May 21, 1955, p. 5; *Pensacola Journal*, Apr. 21, 1957, p. 8.

123. *Florida Times Union* (Jacksonville), Apr. 15, 1955, ORU.

124. [Advertisement,] *Florida Times Union* (Jacksonville), Apr. 7, 1955, ORU.

125. See V. E. Howard, *Fake Healers Exposed* (6th printing, rev.; West Monroe, La.:

Central Printers and Publishers, 1970) pp. 3, 29, 38–39; "The Truth about Faith Healing," *Odessa American,* Feb. 21, 1957, ORU.

126. "The Truth about Faith Healing," *Odessa American*, Feb. 21, 1957, ORU.

127. Howard, *Fake Healers,* p. 38.

128. "About a Certain Minister," *HW,* Dec. 1950, p. 5.

129. Evelyn Roberts, Evangelism of Oral Roberts Class Transcript, 1971, p. 17.

130. Connie Adams Interview, Jan. 28, 1980; Harold Dowdy Interview, Feb. 22, 1981; Joseph Andrews, "Religion Is Big Business for This Huckstering Evangelist," *Suppressed,* Sept. 1956, p. 44.

131. "Healing as the Center of Life Called Idolatry," *(Louisville) Courier Journal,* Mar. 7, 1959, sec. 2, p. 1; Charles Connor, "City Clergymen Skeptical of Oral Roberts' Methods," *Charleston (W. Va.) Daily Mail,* Oct. 29, 1959, ORU; "Problems," *Christian Century,* Feb. 4, 1959, ORU.

132. "Oral Roberts," (Milwaukee) *Catholic Herald Citizen,* Nov. 15, 1958, ORU; "Evangelist Forbidden to Catholics," *Milwaukee Journal,* Nov. 12, 1958, ORU.

133. Titus Cranny, "Catholics and Oral Roberts," *Lamp,* July 1958, p. 18. See also Raymond J. Neufield, "The Question Box," *Brooklyn Tablet,* Apr. 5, 1958, ORU.

134. See *HW,* Mar. 1952, p. 1.

135. Bob Considine, "Minister Explodes with Eloquence about So-Called 'Faith Healers,' " Sept. 21, 1955, INS Clipping, ORU.

136. Ibid.; Carroll R. Stegall, Jr., "What about Faith Healers?" *Presbyterian Outlook,* reprint, ORU.

137. Ibid.

138. Alexander Benton, "The Faith Healer and His Crowds," *Priest,* Feb. 1957, p. 111; Henry Erffmeyer, "The Problem of Suffering," *Listener's Digest,* pp. 13–14, ORU (reprint from *Banner*).

139. W. E. Mann, "What about Oral Roberts?" *Christian Century,* Sept. 5, 1956, p. 1018; Mary Moore Mason, "Great Controversy," *Richmond News Leader,* Jan. 1960, ORU.

140. J. C. Wynn, "Seen and Heard," *Presbyterian Life,* Oct. 13, 1956, ORU.

141. Harland G. Lewis, "Implications for the Churches," *Christian Century,* Sept. 5, 1956, p. 1020.

142. Wynn, "Seen and Heard", see also Cranny, "Catholics and Oral Roberts," p. 8; "Sideglances," *Ligourian,* Feb. 1956, pp. 114–15.

143. Mann, "What about Oral Roberts?" p. 1018.

144. John Kobler, "Oral Roberts: King of the Faith Healers," *American Magazine,* May 1956, p. 90.

145. W. E. Mann, "The Big Come-On," *Toronto Telegram,* June 25, 1956, ORU.

146. Mann, "What about Oral Roberts?" p. 1019; Andrews, "Religion Is Big Business for This Huckstering Evangelist," p. 56; "Bob's Illness 'Suspicion,' Doctor Says," *Charleston (W. Va.) Gazette,* Nov. 7, 1959, ORU.

147. "Alabamian Dies at Lakewood Revival Service," *Atlanta Journal,* Apr. 19, 1951, p. 20.

148. "Faith Fails to Save Indian," *Calgary Herald,* Aug. 8, 1955, p. 1; "Death Triumphant over Faith Healer," *Albertan,* Aug. 8, 1955, p. 1.

149. "Woman Dies of Cancer after 'Cure,' " *Indianapolis Star,* Jan. 31, 1956, p. 21.

150. "Man Dies at Crusade," *Oakland Tribune,* Jan. 7, 1959, p. 10-D.

151. Bill Shaw, "Little Girl Dies in Oral Roberts Tent," *Fayetteville (N.C.) Observer,* May 21, 1959, ORU.

152. "Death First in 'Cathedral Tent,' " *Fayetteville (N.C.) Observer,* May 21, 1959, ORU.

153. Jim Pharr, "Doctor Criticizes Moving Serious Sick," *Fayetteville (N.C.) Observer,* May 22, 1959, ORU.

154. "Faith Cure Believer Dies after Discarding Insulin," *Indianapolis News,* July 6, 1959, ORU.

155. Ibid. See also Jay Nelson Tuck, "He Spends $2,500,000 a Year," *Confidential*, Oct. 1959, p. 25.

156. " 'I Got Saved,' " *Newsweek*, July 29, 1959, p. 60; see also Harvey Taylor, "Be Certain You're Cured, Oral Warns," *Detroit Times*, July 8, 1959, ORU; "Faith 'Cure' Spells Death For Diabetic," *Detroit Times*, July 6, 1959, pp. 1, 4.

157. Roma Rudd Turkel, "Faith Healing," *Information*, Feb. 1957, p. 54.

158. Ono Rio, "Divine Healing," *Saint Anthony's Messenger*, Nov. 1956, ORU.

159. James W. Collison, "Signs and Wonders, Inc.," *The Voice of Saint Jude*, July 1960, p. 45.

160. "The March of Deliverance," *AHM*, May 1955, p. 2.

161. Oral Roberts, *Best Sermons*, p. 106.

162. Ibid.

163. Phil Dessauer, "God Heals—I Don't," *Coronet*, Oct. 1955, p. 61.

164. "The March of Deliverance," *AHM*, May 1955, p. 4.

165. Mike Beaudoin, "Oral Roberts Crusade Opens at Fairgrounds," *Tallahassee Democrat*, Apr. 18, 1959, ORU.

166. "Faith Healers and Their Miracles," *Our Sunday Visitor*, Feb. 1956, p. 2; see also G. H. Montgomery, "No Doctors Present," *AL*, Feb. 1957, p. 20.

167. Evelyn Roberts, Miscellaneous Speech Transcript, June 8, 1981, p. 7.

168. For examples of local followup efforts, see "Revival Follow Up," *Miami Herald*, Jan. 25, 1958, ORU; [Advertisement,] *Detroit Times*, June 25, 1956, ORU.

169. [Editorial,] *Herald of Faith*, Aug. 1957, p. 3.

170. Healing Waters Broadcast, no. 73, tape, June 19, 1949, ORU.

171. "The Man on Fire—The Story of Oral Roberts," *Success Unlimited*, Sept. 1958, p. 6.

172. "Healing—with Faith," *American Weekly*, Feb. 17, 1957, p. 22.

173. World Action Conference Transcript, June 4, 1957, p. 5.

174. Evelyn Roberts, Evangelism of Oral Roberts Class Transcript, 1971, pp. 5–6.

175. Mann, "What about Oral Roberts?" p. 1019.

176. Oral Roberts, *God Is a Good God* (Indianapolis and New York: Bobbs-Merrill Co., 1960), p. 81.

177. Oral Roberts, "A Dynamic Report," *AL*, June 1957, p. 12.

178. See chapter 15, "The Message," for a fuller discussion of this point.

179. Oral Roberts, Evangelism of Oral Roberts Class Transcript, 1971, pp. 10–11.

180. Daniel J. O'Hanlon, "The Pentecostals and Pope John's 'New Pentecost,' " *America*, May 4, 1963, p. 634.

181. Collinson, "Signs and Wonders, Inc." p. 40.

182. Oursler, "Healing—with Faith," p. 25.

183. Richard Carter, "That Old Time Religion Comes Back," *Coronet*, Feb. 1958, p. 126.

184. "The Big Come-On," *Toronto Telegram*, June 25, 1956, ORU; see also June 26, 1956; "Faith Healer's 'Cures' Cause Dispute," *Christian Advocate*, Apr. 19, 1956, ORU; Conner, "City Clergymen Skeptical of Oral Roberts' Methods."

185. W. E. Mann, "Healer's Methods Like Production Line," *Toronto Telegram*, June 26, 1956, ORU.

186. Mann, "What about Oral Roberts?" p. 1019.

187. Quoted in Bob Considine, "Television Paradox," *Vallejo Times-Herald*, Sept. 21, 1955, p. 6.

188. Rio, "Divine Healing," ORU.

189. Andrews, "Religion Is Big Business for This Huckstering Evangelist," p. 44.

190. Wynn, "Seen and Heard," ORU.

191. "Oral Roberts," *Milwaukee Catholic Herald-Citizen*, Nov. 15, 1958, ORU.

192. Hayes B. Jacobs, "Oral Roberts: High Priest of Faith Healing," *Harper's Magazine*, Feb. 1962, p. 43.

193. Roberts, *God Is a Good God*, p. 64.

194. Oral Roberts, "An Open Letter to Magazine and Newspaper Editors," *AL*, Feb. 1957, pp. 16–17, 28–29.

195. DeWeese Interview.

196. "Australian Boots Out Religious Racketeer!" *Flash*, Apr. 14, 1956, p. 7.

197. "Witch-Doctors, Faith Healers, Psychosomatics," *Easton (Pa.) Express*, July 15, 1958, ORU.

198. "A New Revivalist," *Life*, May 30, 1951, pp. 73-78.

199. Lewis W. Gillenson, "The Summer Sawdust Trail," *Look*, July 31, 1951, p. 84.

200. "Oral Roberts Reported in Life Magazine," *HW*, July 1951, p. 3.

201. Oral Roberts, *Oral Roberts' Life Story* (Tulsa: Oral Roberts [1952]), p. 139.

202. Chester Morrison, "Faith Healer at Work," *Look*, June 29, 1954, pp. 88–94.

203. Oral Roberts, "In the Clouds with God," *HW*, Mar. 1950, pp. 2, 12. Oral's postal problems in latter years centered on the theft of his mail. See "Roberts Takes Mail Problem to Washington," *Tulsa Tribune*, Mar. 14, 1957, ORU; Lit Roper, "Suspect Says $8,000 in Roberts' Mail Bag," *Tulsa Tribune*, Mar. 19, 1957, ORU; "Two Mailmen Face Counts," *Tulsa World*, May 22, 1959, ORU.

204. See G. H. Montgomery, "Lawmakers and Healers," *PHA*, Aug. 1949, p. 3.

205. Jack Roberts, "$10,000 Dares Oral Roberts to Prove Faith Healing," *Miami News*, Jan. 19, 1958, ORU; "Drops Plan to Accuse Oral Roberts," *Long Island Daily Press*, June 12, 1959, ORU; O. Roberts, Ministers Seminar Transcript, Jan. 20, 1963, pp. 9–10.

206. See O. Roberts, Chapel Transcript, Nov. 15, 1967, p. 14; Lee Braxton, OREA Devotion Transcript, Dec. 22, 1977, pp. 19–20; O. Roberts Miscellaneous Speech Transcript, Nov. 20, 1982, pp. 9–10.

207. "Miracles for the Multitude," *New York Herald Tribune*, June 29, 1955, ORU.

208. "Tele Follow-up Comment," *Variety*, July 27, 1955, ORU.

209. "Preacher on TV and His 'Miracles,'" unidentified wire service clipping in ORU archives dated Aug. 1955. Attorney Donald Moyers considered this the most ominous crisis in the early history of the ministry. Moyers Interview, Dec. 13, 1983.

210. "Preacher's Timely TV Miracles Raise Question of Stations' Standards," *New York Times Magazine*, undated clipping, ORU.

211. "Roberts' Circular Letter," *New York Times*, Mar. 4, 1956, ORU.

212. "Letters Commenting on Oral Roberts and the Article by Times' Critic," *New York Times*, Mar. 4, 1956, ORU.

213. Ibid.

214. "Oklahoma Faith Healer Draws a Following," *Christian Century*, June 29, 1955, pp. 749–50.

215. See Wambly Bald, "Churchmen Defend Wide Use of Television," *New Haven (Conn.) Register*, Apr. 26, 1958, ORU; Wambly Bald, "Series Uses Top Writers and Stars," *Louisville Times*, Apr. 16, 1958, ORU; "Do Religion, Television Mix?" *Denver Post*, Apr. 20, 1958, ORU; "New Menace on TV," *Catholic Preview of Entertainment*, June 1957, ORU; David A. Runge, "Protestant Clergymen Are Urged to Speak Up," *Milwaukee Journal*, Apr. 19, 1959, ORU.

216. "NAFBRAT Asks FCC to Revoke KCOP (TV)," *Broadcasting-Telecasting Magazine*, Sept. 16, 1957, ORU; Adon Taft, "Stormy Preacher to Campaign Here," *Miami Herald*, Jan. 17, 1958, ORU.

217. See Ben Armstrong, *The Electric Church* (Nashville: Thomas Nelson Publishers, 1979), pp. 44–52.

218. See "Baptists Condemn NCC Radio Policy," *Official Newsletter of the National Religious Broadcasters*, Dec. 1957, p. 1. Lee Braxton sent Oral a copy of Hultgren's article with the note inscribed: "Dr. Hultgren has taken a strong stand on broadcasting which is in our favor, just thought you might like to drop him a line of commendation and encouragement and appreciation." ORU Archives.

219. O. Roberts, Baccalaureate Address Transcript, May 14, 1974, pp. 3–4.

220. O. Roberts, *Best Sermons*, pp. 50–52.

221. Moyers Interview.

222. T. F. James, "The Miracles of Faith Healing," *Cosmopolitan*, Dec. 1958, p. 38.

223. "The Faith Healer," *Journal of the American Medical Association*, Jan. 28, 1956, p. 292.

224. Turkel, "Faith Healing," p. 53.

225. Book Review, *Review and Expositer*, Oct. 1955, pp. 548–49.

226. Wade H. Boggs, Jr., *Faith Healing and the Christian Faith* (Richmond: John Knox Press [1956]), pp. 11–19; Wilfred Backelman, "Leading Denominations Study Healing," *Lutheran Standard*, Oct. 17, 1959, p. 3.

227. "The Man on Fire—The Story of Oral Roberts," p. 2.

228. "Seven-Story Pulpit," *Kabelgram*, no. 2, 1959, p. 12; see also T. F. James, "The Miracles of Faith Healing," pp. 34–41; Jacobs, "Oral Roberts: High Priest of Faith Healing," pp. 37-43.

229. Mann, "Healer's Methods Like Production Line."

230. W. E. Mann, "An Evaluation of Oral Roberts," *Toronto Telegram*, June 27, 1956, ORU.

231. John Pitts, "Spiritual Healing," *Religion in Life*, Spring 1956, p. 163; see pp. 163-204. Pitts knew little about pentecostalism. He wrote that Oral was "a minister of a Church known as the Assemblies of God," p. 163. See Henry Lee, "Brother Roberts—SALVATION'S SALESMAN," *Pageant*, June 1957, p. 90.

232. Pitts, "Spiritual Healing," p. 165.

233. Mike Gildea, "Crusade Continues," *Charleston (S.C.) Evening Post*, Apr. 25, 1958, ORU.

234. "Roberts Revival Stirs Emotions," *Danville (Va.) Register*, May 10, 1956, p. 6.

235. "Faith Healing Claimed," *Pueblo (Colo.) Star-Journal and Chieftan*, Sept. 7, 1958, ORU.

236. See "City Woman Claims 'Faith Cure,' " *Burlington (Vt.) News*, Mar. 28, 1958, ORU; "Evangelist Cured Child, Hellertown Family Insists," *Bethlehem (Pa.) Globe-Times*, July 9, 1958, ORU; "Wheelchair to Evangelism," *Tulsa Tribune*, Nov. 12, 1960, ORU.

237. "Let's Follow Christ's Example," *Northern Illinois Farmer*, July 1958, Second Issue, ORU; Doral Chenoweth, "Foe Blasts Evangelist," *Columbus Citizen*, July 15, 1957, ORU.

238. "Letters to the Editor," *Charleston (S.C.) Post*, May 6, 1958, ORU; "Roberts Appreciative," *Bethlehem (Pa.) Globe Times*, July 23, 1958, ORU.

239. Bob Foresman Interview, Dec. 13, 1983.

240. "Healing—with Faith," pp. 25–26; Will Oursler, *The Healing Power of Faith* (New York: Hawthorne Books, 1957). pp. 150–64.

241. Oursler, *The Healing Power of Faith*, p. 150.

242. (Englewood Cliffs, N.J.: Prentice-Hall [1958]), pp. 194–200.

243. O. Roberts, OREA Devotion Transcript, Feb. 13, 1958, pp. 7–8.

244. Neal, *God Can Heal You Now*, pp. 194–95; "Literary Corner," *Athens (Ga.) Banner-Herald*, Apr. 10, 1959, ORU.

245. "City Clergyman Skeptical of Oral Roberts' Methods"; see also Franklin L. Artley, "Sounding Board," *Presbyterian Life*, Nov. 24, 1956, p. 3.

246. See Richard Rettig, "How I Was Led into a Healing Ministry," *AL*, Jan. 1957, pp. 24–25.

247. See Lee Braxton, "The New Ministry of Oral Roberts," *Healing*, June 1956, p. 15; Ken Neal, "Oral Roberts Explains His Doctrine to Tulsa Clerics," *Tulsa World*, Mar. 13, 1958, ORU.

248. Neal, "Oral Roberts Explains His Doctrine to Tulsa Clerics."

249. "A Famous Tulsan," *Tulsa Tribune*, May 4, 1959, ORU.

250. "From the Ministers," *HW*, Dec. 1949, p. 10.

251. Clark Porteous, "Evangelist Sways Thousands in Tent Campaign," *Memphis Press Scimitar*, June 30, 1950, p. 1.

252. Jack Hutton, "Faith Can Heal, Evangelist Says." *Albertan*, Aug. 1, 1955, p. 3.

253. "Oral Roberts Sees Reporters," *Arkansas Gazette* (Little Rock), Mar. 29, 1958; "Oral Roberts Takes 'A New Approach,'" *Muskogee (Okla.) Sunday Phoenix,* May 4, 1958, ORU.

254. Mary P. McGuire, "Voice of the Eastside," *Indianapolis Recorder,* Feb. 14, 1959, ORU; Basil Hall, "Keeping Posted," *Charleston (S.C.) Evening News,* Apr. 25, 1958. p. 1-B,

255. Ruth Carter Stapleton, Chapel Transcript, Nov. 15, 1978, p. 2.

256. Paul E. Gustafson, "Chapter and Verse," *Milwaukee Sentinel,* Nov. 22, 1958, ORU; "City's Friendliness Impresses Roberts," *Johnstown (Pa.) Tribune-Democrat,* July 26, 1957, ORU.

257. Jim Pharr, "The Word Is 'Sincerity,' " *The Fayetteville (N.C.) Observer,* May 16, 1959, ORU.

258. See Oral Roberts, *My Story* (Tulsa and New York: Summit Book Co., 1961), p. 171. For other examples, see Bert E. Parmer, "Estimated 5,000 Converted in Jacksonville Meeting," *PHA,* Apr. 14, 1949, p. 6; "Governor of Georgia Welcomes Oral Roberts to Atlanta," *HW,* June 1951, p. 1; "May Equal Graham, Revival Opens," *Atlanta Constitution,* Apr. 7, 1951, p. 6.

259. Oral Roberts, "A Dynamic Report on . . . Spiritual Healing," *AL,* June 1957, pp. 12–13.

260. Oral Roberts, *The Diary of a Hollywood Visitor* (Tulsa: Healing Water Tract Society, n.d.) p. 5.

261. Gil Rowland, "Christ's Coming Is Near," *Greenville (S.C.) News,* Apr. 13, 1953, p. 5; "President's Wife Sends 'Thank You' to Wahrens," *Carrington (N.D.) Independent,* Feb. 19, 1953, ORU.

262. See "Des Moines Campaign Scenes," *HW,* Sept. 1952, p. 7; O. Roberts, "A Dynamic Report on . . . Spiritual Healing," p. 12.

263. O. Roberts, OREA Devotion Transcript, Mar. 19, 1958. p. 9; Otis Perkins, "Oral Roberts Crusade Ends As Thousands Crowd Tent," *Charleston (S.C.) News and Courier,* Apr. 28, 1958, ORU; "Tallest Church Draws Visitors," *Holdrege (Neb.) Citizen,* Feb. 19, 1959, ORU; Dr. W. George Crane, "Jealousy in High Places," *Uniontown (Pa.) Standard,* Feb. 6, 1959, ORU.'

264. "Oral Roberts Entertained in Washington," *Tulsa Tribune,* June 26, 1958, ORU.

265. Evelyn Roberts, OREA Partners Transcript, Dec. 19, 1958, p. 3.

266. "From the Pen of Oral Roberts," *AL,* Oct. 1958, p. 3.

267. Evelyn Roberts, OREA Partners Transcript, Dec. 19, 1958, p. 3.

268. *AL,* Jan. 1957, p. 21.

269. Dan L. Thrapp, "Evangelist Recalls Australia Terror," *Los Angeles Times,* Sept. 28, 1957, part 1, p. 10. See Charles Jones, "I've No Secrets to Hide," *Miami News,* Jan. 21, 1958, ORU.

270. Bob Foresman, "Canvas Cathedral Evangelist, Part V," *Gilbert (Ariz.) Enterprise,* Jan. 18, 1957, ORU.

271. George Dugan, "Evangelist Opens 6-Day L. I. Crusade," *New York Times,* Mar. 26, 1958, p. 39. See also Joanne Braunberns, "Roberts Says Full Gospel Churches Are Major Religious Movement," *Register-Guard* (Eugene, Ore.), Sept. 25, 1958, ORU; Paul, "Religious Frontier," pp. 276–77.

272. Henry Cauthen, "Columbia's Two Big Religious Revivals and Their Processes," *Columbia (S.C.) Record,* May 11, 1950, p. 10A. Roberts's supporters felt that they were ignored by the press in Columbia compared to Graham. Paul Interview.

273. "Has Billy Graham's Racket Been Stolen?" *Hamilton (Ontario) Flash,* Apr. 7, 1956, p. 20.

274. Dan L. Thrapp, "Evangelist Oral Roberts Thrashing Devil in Tent," *Los Angeles Times,* Oct. 7, 1951, part 1, p. 44.

275. Dugan, "Evangelist Opens 6-Day L.I. Crusade"; ORU; Albin Krebs, "Oral Roberts 'Second' Only to Billy Graham," *Tulsa Tribune,* Feb. 11, 1958, p. 5. Articles also tended to become more discriminating, seeing beyond the pentecostal exuberance.

276. Bill Rose, "Oral Roberts, Billy Graham," *Oakland Tribune,* Jan. 6, 1959, p. 12E.

277. See O. Roberts Interview, Feb. 16, 1983; Calvin Thielman Interview, Apr. 8, 1983; O. Roberts, Chapel Transcript, Oct. 13, 1972, pp. 8–9.

278. It is interesting that Roberts's first public hint about beginning a television program took notice of Graham's use of the media. "To Whom It May Concern," *HW,* Oct. 1951, p. 11.

279. Oral Roberts, *The Holy Spirit in the Now* (3 vols.; Tulsa: Oral Roberts University, 1974), vol. 2, p. 28; O. Roberts Interview, Feb. 16, 1983.

280. O. Roberts Interview, Feb. 16, 1983; O. Roberts, Chapel Transcript, Nov. 15, 1967, pp. 20–21.

281. O. Roberts, Chapel Transcript, Oct. 13, 1972, p. 8.

282. See Donald Gee, "Billy Graham in London," *Pentecost,* March 1954, p. 17.

283. Paul Gustafson, "Evangelist Fervent Disciple of Faith," *Milwaukee Sentinel,* Nov. 12, 1958, ORU; O. Roberts, *The Holy Spirit in the Now,*, vol. 2, p. 78.

284. "The Man on Fire—The Story of Oral Roberts," p. 3.

285. Thrapp, "Evangelist Recalls Australia Terror"; Florence Patton, "Cure of Stuttering Led Evangelist to Preach," *Corpus Christi (Tex.) Times,* Jan. 8, 1959, ORU.

286. Dessauer, "God Heals—I Don't," p. 60; Harry Golden, Jr., "Roberts Expects 100,000 Converts," *Detroit Free Press,* Jun 2, 1956, p. 4.

287. O. Roberts, *Best Sermons,* p. 12.

288. See W. T. Jeffers, *What I Know about Oral Roberts* (Tulsa: Frontiers of Faith, n.d.), p. 20, for the maturing effect of the financial crisis.

289. O. Roberts, OREA Devotion Transcript, Feb. 4, 1957, pp. 13, 18, 20.

290. See "Oral Roberts Aides Open Ad Agency," *Tulsa Tribune,* Sept. 9, 1959, p. 4; "Geyer, Morel Agencies Merge," *Advertising Age* (Chicago), Dec. 15, 1958, ORU; Doris Willens, "Big Agency Seems to Be Fading," *New York Journal American,* Feb. 9, 1959, ORU.

291. "The Evangelical Life," *New Yorker,* Feb. 7, 1959, ORU.

292. George W. Cornell, "Preaching Powerhouse Denies Faith Healing," *Democrat and Chronicle* (Rochester, N.Y.), Mar. 20, 1958, ORU. Actually, the emphasis on soul saving had been highly visible in Oral's internal publications for some time, but it was difficult for reporters to ignore the healing line. See "Important Information," *Healing,* June 1956, p. 21.

293. Harold Schachern, " 'Different' Roberts Will Crusade Here," *Detroit News,* July 2, 1959, ORU.

294. See Jan Gerard, "A Million Souls a Year," *Garden City (N.Y.) Newsday,* Mar. 28, 1959, ORU; Bill Rose, "Oral Roberts to Open 'Drive for Souls,' " *Oakland Tribune,* Jan. 2, 1959, p. 1A.

295. *National Enquirer,* Oct. 15, 1961, p. 7.

296. O. Roberts, Crusade Transcript, Apr. 22, 1956, p. 23.

297. O. Roberts, Miscellaneous Speech Transcript, 1956, pp. 4–5.

298. Dan Thrapp, "Evangelist Recalls Australia Terror."

299. Albin Krebs, "Misunderstood, Flamboyant, Controversial," *Gilbert (Ariz.) Enterprise,* Dec. 7, 1956, ORU; O. Roberts, Evangelism of Oral Roberts Class Transcript, 1971, p. 16.

300. Adon Taft, "Life Just Beginning for Oral," *Miami Herald,* Jan. 25, 1958, ORU.

301. O. Roberts, Evangelism of Oral Roberts Class Transcript, 1971, p. 18; Cornell, "Preaching Powerhouse Denies Faith Healing."

302. Oral Roberts, "A Dynamic Report on Spiritual Healing," *AL,* June 1957, p. 12.

303. Oral Roberts, "This Will Be Our Greatest Year," *AL,* Jan. 1959, p. 12.

304. O. Roberts, OREA Devotion Transcript, Nov. 1957, p. 10.

305. O. Roberts, "This Will Be Our Greatest Year," p. 12.

306. Oral Roberts, "Souls Unlimited," *AL,* May 1959, p. 5.

8. PRIVATE SIDE

1. Evelyn Roberts, "I Married Oral Roberts," *HW,* Jan. 1953, p. 10.

2. See Basil W. Hall, "Keeping Posted," *Charleston (S.C.) Evening Post,* Apr. 25, 1958, p. 1-B.

3. Evelyn Roberts, "I Married Oral Roberts," p. 11.

4. Collins Steele Interview, Jan. 13, 1983.

5. Ibid.; Bob DeWeese Interview, Jan. 19, 1983.

6. Hazel A. Smith, "Oral Roberts Takes Positive Approach to Help Audiences," *Pueblo (Colo.) Star-Journal,* Aug. 29, 1958, ORU.

7. Marty Pago, "Solitude Helps Prepare Oral Roberts," *Pueblo (Colo.) Chieftan,* Aug. 30, 1958, ORU.

8. See Sean Sound, "County Lines," *New York Daily News,* Apr. 6, 1958, ORU; Steele and DeWeese Interviews.

9. Bill McGrotha, "Activity a Must," *Tallahassee (Fla.) Democrat,* Apr. 21, 1959, ORU.

10. Steele Interview. See "Four Hour Stint of Study and Prayer Aids Oral Roberts in Preparing Campaign Sermons," *Pueblo (Colo.) Star-Journal,* Aug. 30, 1958, ORU.

11. Phil Dessauer, " 'God Heals—I Don't,' " *Coronet,* Oct. 1955, pp. 52–61.

12. "Four Hour Stint."

130. Dessauer, " 'God Heals—I Don't,' " pp. 52–61.

14. Hall, "Keeping Posted."

15. Hoover Adams, "Wellons Had Big Role in Oral Roberts' Rise," *Daily Record* (Dunn, N.C.), Dec. 23 and 24, 1982, p. 13.

16. Steele and DeWeese Interviews; Evelyn Roberts Interview, Nov. 1, 1983.

17. Evelyn Roberts Interview, Nov. 1, 1983.

18. Granville Oral Roberts, *My Story,* (Tulsa and New York: Summit Book Co., 1961), p. 63.

19. Evelyn Roberts, Student Meeting Transcript, Mar. 19, 1975, p. 18; Evelyn Roberts, "I Married Oral Roberts," p. 11.

20. Evelyn Roberts, "I Married Oral Roberts," p. 11.

21. Evelyn Roberts Interview, Nov. 1, 1983; Yvonne Litchfield, "This Is Mrs. Oral Roberts," *Tulsa World,* Feb. 15, 1967, ORU.

22. Oral Roberts, Faculty Retreat Transcript, Aug. 25, 1970, p. 9.

23. Charles Kothe Interview, Feb. 23, 1983; "The Lee Braxton Story As Told by Himself," *HW,* June 1951, pp. 11–12; "Miracle of Seed-Faith, Part III," *AL,* Dec. 1971, pp. 9–11.

24. "Demos Shakarian Reports the Oral Roberts Campaign in Los Angeles," *HW,* Dec. 1951, p. 11.

25. John Kobler, "Oral Roberts: King of the Faith Healers," *American Magazine,* May 1956, p. 88.

26. Daniel M. Burnham, "Rise of Rev. Roberts," *Wall Street Journal* (Midwest Edition), May 1, 1959, pp. 1, 6.

27. Ibid., p. 6. See also Oral Roberts, "A Dynamic Report on . . . Spiritual Healing," *AL,* June 1957, p. 13.

28. Manford Engel, "Important Notice," *HW,* Jan. 1953, p. 15; see also G. H. Montgomery, "The March of Deliverance," *AHM,* May 1955, p. 4.

29. Evelyn Roberts, *His Darling Wife, Evelyn* (New York: Dell Publishing Co., 1976), p. 111.

30. Evelyn Roberts, "I Married Oral Roberts," p. 14.

31. "Mrs. Oral Roberts Fills Father's Shoes," *Tulsa Tribune,* May 1958, p. 8, ORU.

32. "Evangelist Hero to Wife, Kiddies," *Johnstown (Pa.) Tribune-Democrat,* Nov. 8, 1958, ORU.

33. "Mrs. Oral Roberts Fills Father's Shoes."

34. Beverly Paulson, "I'm His Escape Valve," *Miami Herald,* n.d., ORU.

35. Diane B. Webster, " 'Whither Thou Goest' Vow Is Echoed by Mrs. Roberts," *Fresno Bee*, Oct. 25, 1958, p. 3-B.

36. See O. Roberts, *My Story*, pp. 63–64; Evelyn Roberts, "Whither Thou Goest," *AL*, Dec. 1982, pp. 20–21.

37. Kobler, "Oral Roberts: King of the Faith Healers," p. 89.

38. Ibid.

39. Yvonne Nance, "The Woman behind the Man," *AL*, June 1957, p. 17.

40. "Evangelist's Wife Cites Her Multiple Problems," *Shenandoah (Pa.) Herald*, June 28, 1958, ORU.

41. Marty Pago, "Preaching of Evangelist Awes Mrs. Oral Roberts," *Pueblo (Colo.) Star-Journal*, Sept. 3, 1958, ORU.

42. Nance, "The Woman behind the Man," p. 17.

43. Evelyn Roberts, Miscellaneous Speech Transcript, Mar. 17, 1973, p. 5.

44. Evelyn Roberts, Student Meeting Transcript, Feb. 11, 1975, pp. 27–28.

45. Evelyn Roberts, Chapel Transcript, Feb. 3, 1982, p. 15.

46. O. Roberts, Crusade Transcript, Indianapolis, Nov. 1956, p. 22.

47. Evelyn Roberts, Student Meeting Transcript, Feb. 11, 1975, pp. 28–29.

48. Bob Foresman, "A Room of Oral Roberts Residence Built by Indian Family Long Ago," *Tulsa Tribune*, Dec. 24, 1958, ORU.

49. O. Roberts, *My Story*, p. 56.

50. O. Roberts, Crusade Transcript, Indianapolis, Nov. 1956, pp. 21–22.

51. Evelyn Roberts, *His Darling Wife*, p. 105.

52. Chapel Transcript, Oct. 16, 1970, p. 1.

53. Oral Roberts, "The Roberts Children Tell It Like It Is!" *AL*, Sept. 1972, p. 13; Evelyn Roberts, *His Darling Wife*, p. 105; Evelyn Roberts Interview, Nov. 1, 1983.

54. O. Roberts, *My Story*, pp. 60–61.

55. Oral Roberts, "My Children and I," *HW*, Jan. 1955, p. 4.

56. O. Roberts, Crusade Transcript, Mar. 24, 1957, p. 2.

57. O. Roberts, *My Story*, p. 62.

58. Kobler, "Oral Roberts: King of the Faith Healers," p. 89.

59. "Evangelist Plays Golf to Relax and Keep Fit," *Star* (Johannesburg), Jan. 14, 1957, p. 11.

60. O. Roberts, Speech at Seminary Transcript, Feb. 9, 1976, p. 7.

61. Ernestine Graveley, "The Quiet Half of the Team," *Daily Oklahoma Magazine*, Sept. 11, 1955, p. 5.

62. O. Roberts, *My Story*, pp. 61–62.

63. "Evangelist's Wife Cites Her Multiple Problems," *Shenandoah (Pa.) Herald*, June 28, 1958, ORU.

64. O. Roberts, "My Children and I," p. 4.

65. "Evangelist Hero to Wife, Kiddies."

66. Evelyn Roberts, "Letters to My Children," *AHM*, April 1955, p. 18.

67. Nance, "The Woman behind the Man," p. 17.

68. Yvonne Nance, "The Church Triumphant," *AL*, June 1975, p. 10; O. Roberts, Speech at Seminary Transcript, Feb. 9, 1976, pp. 6–7.

69 Evelyn Roberts, "Letters to My Children," pp. 17–19.

70. Marty Pago, "Preaching of Evangelist Awes Mrs. Oral Roberts."

71. Evelyn Roberts, *His Darling Wife*, p. 114.

72. Webster, " 'Whither Thou Goest' Vow is Echoed by Mrs. Roberts."

73. O. Roberts, "The Roberts Children Tell It Like It Is!", p. 13.

74. Evelyn Roberts, *His Darling Wife*, p. 114.

75. Ibid., p. 122.

76. Richard Roberts Interview, Mar. 31, 1983. In 1956, Oral told a reporter that he did not "go to dances, circuses or fairs, nor permit his family to do so." He "shuns theaters" and considered most movies "unclean." Kobler, "Oral Roberts: King of the Faith Healers," p. 89.

77. "Rebecca Ann Roberts," *HW,* June 1948, p. 9.

78. Evelyn Roberts Interview, Nov. 1, 1983.

79. George Stovall Interview, Jan. 27, 1983.

80. "There Is an Amazing Difference," *AL,* Sept. 1958, p. 12.

81. See Don Bachelder, "Business World," *Tulsa World,* Jan. 2, 1972, ORU.

82. "Future Circuit Rider?" *HW,* Jan.-Feb. 1948, p. 3.

83. O. Roberts, "My Children and I," p. 4.

84. Foresman, "A Room of Oral Roberts Residence Built by Indian Family Long Ago."

85. Evelyn Roberts, Miscellaneous Speech Transcript, Mar. 2, 1974; Evelyn Roberts Interview, Nov. 1, 1983.

86. "Des Moines Campaign Scenes," *HW,* Sept. 1952, p. 7.

87. Stovall Interview.

88. OREA Partners Transcript, Aug. 15, 1958, p. 2.

89. E. M. and Claudius Roberts, *Our Ministry and Our Son Oral* (Tulsa: Oral Roberts, 1960), pp. 76-77.

90. Evelyn Roberts, Miscellaneous Speech Transcript, Mar. 2, 1974, p. 23; Evelyn Roberts Interview, Nov. 1, 1983; "Mrs. Oral Roberts Fills Father's Shoes."

91. Foresman, "A Room of Oral Roberts Residence Built by Indian Family Long Ago."

92. "Some Rules May Be Bent," *Tulsa Tribune,* May 6, 1976, ORU; Wayne Robinson Interview, Apr. 4, 1983; Richard Roberts Interview, Mar. 31, 1983.

93. Oral Roberts Interview, Feb. 16, 1983; Evelyn Roberts Interview, Nov. 1, 1983; "Mrs. Oral Roberts Fills Father's Shoes"; Foresman, "A Room of Oral Roberts Residence Built by Indian Family Long Ago."

94. Evelyn Roberts, "I Married Oral Roberts," p. 11.

95. Kobler, "Oral Roberts: King of the Faith Healers," p. 90.

96. Burnham, "Rise of Rev. Roberts," p. 1.

97. O. Roberts, University Village Seminar Transcript, June 9, 1970, p. 5; Ellis Roberts, "Oral Roberts' Father's Own Story," *HW,* August 1951, p. 11.

98. O. Roberts, *My Story,* p. 11.

99. Evelyn Roberts Interview, Nov. 1, 1983. See "Mr. and Mrs. Ira Fahnestock," *Tulsa World,* Oct. 10, 1971, ORU.

100. Evelyn Roberts Interview, Nov. 1, 1983; Bob Foresman, "Busy Reverend Roberts 'Revives' at His Farm," *Tulsa Tribune,* Jan. 17, 1953, sec. 2, p. 13.

101. Evelyn Roberts Interview, Nov. 1. 1983.

102. Foresman, "Busy Reverend Roberts 'Revives' at His Farm."

103. Bob Foresman Interview, Dec. 13, 1983; Foresman, "Busy Reverend Roberts 'Revives' at His Farm"; Kobler, "Oral Roberts: King of the Faith Healers," p. 90.

104. Foresman, "Busy Reverend Roberts 'Revives' at His Farm."

105. Evelyn Roberts Interview, Nov. 1, 1983.

106. Foresman, "Busy Reverend Roberts 'Revives' at His Farm." See "Noted Evangelist Exhibits Cattle in Stock Show," *Sulphur Springs (Tex.) News-Telegram,* Mar. 5, 1957, ORU.

107. Evelyn Roberts Interview, Nov. 1, 1983.

108. "Oral Roberts 'Trades' Ranch Home for Town House," *Tulsa Tribune,* Dec. 21, 1957, sec. 2, p. 11.

109. See Will Oursler, *The Healing Power of Faith* (New York: Hawthorne Books [1957]), p. 163; see also Pete Martin, "Oral Roberts," *Christian Herald,* Feb. 1966, part 1, pp. 76-77.

110. Burnham, "Rise of Rev. Roberts," p. 1.

111. Foresman, "A Room of Oral Roberts Residence Built by Indian Family Long Ago."

112. Robinson Interview. See "Home of Evangelist Entered by Prowler," *Fullerton (Cal.) News Tribune,* Nov. 21, 1958, ORU.

113. Kobler, "Oral Roberts: King of the Faith Healers," p. 90.

114. Hayes D. Jacobs, "High Priest of Faith Healing," *Harpers Magazine*, Feb. 1962, p. 42.

115. "The Man on Fire—The Story of Oral Roberts," *Success Unlimited*, Sept. 1958, reprint, p. 7.

116. Oursler, *The Healing Power of Faith*, p. 164.

117. O. Roberts, Kiwanis Speech, 1956, p. 4.

118. See V. E. Howard, *Fake Healers Exposed* (6th printing, rev.; West Monroe, La.: Central Printers and Publishers, 1970), pp. 44–45; Douglas J. Firesen, "A Remarkable Incident," *HW*, July 1950, p. 12; Oral Roberts, "An Open Letter to Magazine and Newspaper Editors," *AL*, Feb. 1957, p. 29.

119. Burnham, "Rise of Rev. Roberts," p. 1.

120. David Fritze, "The Gold and the Glory," *Oklahoma Monthly*, Oct. 1977, p. 98.

121. Burnham, "Rise of Rev. Roberts," p. 1; Oral Roberts, "An Open Letter to Magazine and Newspaper Editors," p. 29.

122. "The Man on Fire—The Story of Oral Roberts," p. 7.

123. W. George Crane, "Jealousy in High Places," *Uniontown (Pa.) Standard*, Feb. 5, 1959, ORU; Oursler, *The Healing Power of Faith*, p. 163.

124. Graveley, "The Quiet Half of the Team," p. 3.

125. "The Man on Fire—The Story of Oral Roberts," p. 7.

126. The *Journal* described Roberts's wealth: "There's no doubt the evangelist has achieved material rewards. These include: Membership in the swank Tulsa Country Club; election by the Tulsa Chamber of Commerce to its list of 50 top executives in the area; a private twin-engine plane (donated by followers) and ownership of a 10-room, ranch-style house centered in five acres of tree-studded lawn in one of the more expensive suburban areas of Tulsa." Burnham, "Rise of Rev. Roberts," p. 1.

127. Kobler, "Oral Roberts: King of the Faith Healers," pp. 88–89.

128. Dessauer, " 'God Heals—I Don't,' " p. 60.

129. O. Roberts, Chapel Transcript, Nov. 15, 1967, p. 16.

130. Dan Brennan, "Crippled Child Stirs," *Minneapolis Tribune*, Aug. 23, 1948, p. 13.

131. Jim Pharr, "The Word Is 'Sincerity,' " *Fayetteville (N.C) Observer*, May 16, 1959, ORU; Charles Zaimes, "Oral Roberts—Crusader for Christ," *Allentown (Pa.) Call*, July 5, 1958, ORU.

132. "Canvas Cathedral Evangelist," *Gilbert (Ariz.) Enterprise*, Jan. 1957, ORU.

133. Bill Rose, "Oral Roberts to Open 'Drive for Souls,' " *Oakland Tribune*, June 2, 1959, p. 1–A.

134. O. Roberts, Chapel Transcript, Nov. 15, 1967, pp. 17, 16.

135. OREA Partners Transcript, Jan. 10, 1959, p. 3.

136. Bob Bell, Jr., "Oral Roberts Winds Up Crusade," *Nashville Banner*, Nov. 29, 1958, p. 6.

137. O. Roberts, Chapel Transcript, Nov. 15, 1967, p. 24.

Part III

PROLOGUE
Berlin, October 26–November 4, 1966

1. "World Evangelism Congress Is Underway Wednesday in Berlin," *Riverside (Cal.) Press*, Oct. 16, 1966, ORU; Carl F. H. Henry and W. Stanley Mooneyham, eds., *One Race, One Gospel, One Task* (2 vols.; Minneapolis: World Wide Publications [1967]).

2. "World Congress: Springboard for Evangelical Revival," *Christianity Today*, Nov. 25, 1966, p. 226.

3. Carl F. H. Henry to Oral Roberts, May 17, 1965, ORU; Calvin Thielman Interview, Apr. 8, 1983.

4. R. O. Corvin, "Oral Roberts and R. O. Corvin Attend World Congress on Evangelism in Berlin," *AL,* Jan. 1967, p. 16; Oral Roberts, OREA Staff Meeting Transcript, Jan. 20, 1966, p. 2; Oral Roberts Interview, Feb. 16, 1983.

5. Oral Roberts, "My Personal Impressions of the World Congress on Evangelism," *AL,* Jan. 1967, p. 28.

6. Warren Hultgren Interview, Mar. 30, 1983.

7. O. Roberts, OREA Staff Meeting Transcript, Oct. 20, 1966, p. 2.

8. O. Roberts Interview, Feb. 16, 1983.

9. Hultgren Interview.

10. Corvin, "Oral Roberts and R. O. Corvin Attend World Congress on Evangelism," p. 20. Oral was uncomfortable, knowing that "somehow I wasn't in the mainstream." O. Roberts Interview, Feb. 16, 1983.

11. Thielman Interview; O. Roberts Interview, Feb. 16, 1983.

12. Ibid.

13. Thielman Interview. See George W. Dollar, *A History of Fundamentalism in America* (Greenville, S.C.: Bob Jones University Press [1973]), p. 210.

14. O. Roberts Interview, Feb. 16, 1983; Thielman Interview; O. Roberts, Laymen's Seminar Transcript, Nov. 18, 1966, p. 2.

15. Henry and Mooneyham, *One Race, One Gospel, One Task,* vol. 2, p. 488.

16. Calvin Thielman, Chapel Transcript, Nov. 21, 1966, p. 3.

17. Ibid.; Thielman Interview.

18. Corvin, "Oral Roberts and R. O. Corvin Attend World Congress on Evangelism," pp. 20–21.

19. "Overflow Crowd of Delegates Bombards Panel with Questions on Healing," *AL,* Feb. 1967, p. 21.

20. Ibid., pp. 21–22.

21. Thielman Interview; Thielman, Chapel Transcript, Nov. 21, 1966, pp. 1–3.

22. "Overflow Crowd of Delegates Bombards Panel With Questions on Healing," p. 20.

23. Corvin, "Oral Roberts and R. O. Corvin Attend World Congress on Evangelism," p. 22.

24. O. Roberts, Laymen's Seminar Transcript, Oct. 18, 1966, p. 3; Corvin, "Oral Roberts and R. O. Corvin Attend World Congress on Evangelism," p. 22; Oral Roberts, *The Holy Spirit in the Now* (3 vols.; Tulsa: Oral Roberts University, 1974), vol. 2, p. 20.

25. Oral Roberts, "We Have Been Conquered by Love," *AL,* Feb. 1967, p. 23.

26. Thielman Interview.

27. Ibid.

28. Oral Roberts, "We Have Been Conquered by Love," p. 23.

29. Thielman Interview; Billy Graham, Oral Roberts University Dedication Press Conference Transcript, 1967, n.p.

30. Corvin, "Oral Roberts and R. O. Corvin Attend World Conference on Evangelism," p. 22.

31. O. Roberts, "We Have Been Conquered by Love," p. 23.

32. Corvin, "Oral Roberts and R. O. Corvin Attend World Conference on Evangelism," p. 24. Thielman Interview.

33. Chapel Transcript, Nov. 21, 1966, p. 1.

34. "World Congress: Springboard for Evangelical Revival," p. 227.

35. Thielman Interview.

36. O. Roberts, "My Personal Impressions of the World Congress on Evangelism," p. 30; O. Roberts, Chapel Transcript, Jan. 1968. p. 8

37. Thielman Interview.

38. O. Roberts, Chapel Transcript, Jan. 1968, pp. 7–8; Oral Roberts, "The Challenge of Chile," *AL,* Apr. 1968, p. 8.

39. O. Roberts, Laymen's Seminar Transcript, Nov. 18, 1966, p. 2.

40. Edward B. Fiske, "The Oral Roberts Empire," *New York Times Magazine,* Apr. 23, 1973, p. 17.

41. Hultgren Interview.

42. Thielman Interview.

9. ORAL ROBERTS UNIVERSITY

1. Oral Roberts Interview, Feb. 16, 1983; Oral Roberts, "Here's How It All Began," *AL,* Feb. 1976, p. 5.

2. O. Roberts Interview, Feb. 16, 1983.

3. Lee Braxton, Partners Seminar Transcript, May 9, 1965, pp. 10–11.

4. Melvin Steakley, "Lines to Faith-Healing Form on Revival Trail," *Houston Chronicle,* Aug. 4, 1962, p. 8.

5. Carl H. Hamilton Interview, Jan. 13, 1983; O. Roberts, Regent Seminar Transcript, Nov. 1962, p. 4, O. Roberts, Faculty Orientation Transcript, Aug. 24, 1971, p. 60.

6. Lee Braxton, "ORU Today," *AL,* Feb. 1970, p. 21; O. Roberts, Graduation Transcript, May 25, 1969, pp. 1–2.

7. Evelyn Roberts, *His Darling Wife, Evelyn* (New York: Dell Publishing Co., 1976), p. 211.

8. Devotion Transcript, July 20, 1962, p. 3.

9. Bob DeWeese Interview, Jan. 19, 1983.

10. Raymond Othel Corvin, "Religious and Educational Backgrounds in the Founding of Oral Roberts University," Ph.D. dissertation, University of Oklahoma, 1967, p. 15.

11. DeWeese Interview.

12. O. Roberts, Miscellaneous Speech Transcript, Jan. 22, 1973, p. 11.

13. DeWeese Interview.

14. Corvin, "Religious and Educational Backgrounds," p. 152.

15. O. Roberts, Graduation Transcript, May 25, 1969, p. 1.

16. O. Roberts, Partners Seminars Transcript, May 9, 1965, p. 1. See "Oral Roberts Sewage Plant Hotly Opposed," *Tulsa World,* Sept. 20, 1962, ORU.

17. O. Roberts, "Spiritual Responsibility of ORU," Speech Transcript, Nov. 1962, pp. 5–6; Donald Moyers Interview, Dec. 13, 1983; Corvin, "Religious and Educational Backgrounds," p. 153; Oral Roberts, *The Holy Spirit in the Now* (3 vols.; Tulsa: Oral Roberts University, 1974), vol. 2, p. 18.

18. Corvin, "Religious and Educational Backgrounds," pp. 151–52; "ORU: The Roberts Reflect on Past, Present, and Future," *Oracle,* Dec. 12, 1980, n.p.

19. As late as December 5, the organization reported that "three possible locations" were under consideration. "Religious School Planned," *Tulsa Tribune,* Dec. 5, 1961, ORU.

20. See Bob Foresman, "Evangelist School Due," *Tulsa Tribune,* Dec. 22, 1961, p. 26; Corvin, "Religious and Educational Backgrounds," pp. 152–53.

21. Oral Roberts University of Evangelism, Brochure, ORU Archives, no pub. info.

22. O. Roberts, Partners Letter, Jan. 15, 1962, ORU.

23. Bob Foresman, "Evangelist School Due"; Corvin, "Religious and Educational Backgrounds," p. 153.

24. O. Roberts, Partners Letter, Jan. 15, 1962. See also Oral Roberts, "A Spiritual Revolution throughout the Earth," *AL,* May 1962, pp. 6–10.

25. Corvin, "Religious and Educational Backgrounds," p. 151.

26. O. Roberts, Devotion Transcript, July 20, 1962, p. 8.

27. O. Roberts, Faculty Chapel Transcript, Aug. 19, 1974, p. 9.

28. O. Roberts, Devotion Transcript, July 20, 1962, p. 8.

29. O. Roberts, Chapel Transcript, Jan. 11, 1966, p. 4.

30. Hamilton Interview, Jan. 13, 1983.

31. Oral Roberts, *My Twenty Years of a Miracle Ministry* (Tulsa: Oral Roberts, 1967), p. 84.

32. O. Roberts, Devotion Transcript, July 20, 1962, pp. 5–6; Hamilton Interview, Jan. 13, 1983. The concern remained. In 1964, Evelyn told a partners' meeting: "Our son's gone through this and over the Christmas holidays he told us of the atheistic pressures and frustrations that caused three of his colleagues to take their own lives." Yvonne Nance, "A Life from the Lord," *AL,* May 1964, p. 22.

33. O. Roberts, Devotion Transcript, July 20, 1962, pp. 5–6.

34. O. Roberts, President's Advisory Cabinet Transcript, May 29, 1965, p. 10.

35. "OC College Official to Be President of Oral Roberts School," *Tulsa Tribune,* June 7, 1962, ORU; Oral Roberts, "The R.O. Corvin Story," *AL,* Jan. 1963, pp. 7–11. See *Oral Roberts University Bulletin for 1967–69* (no pub. info.), p. 16.

36. O. Roberts, "The R. O. Corvin Story," pp. 10–11; Room Sponsors Seminar Transcript, May 20, 1963, p. 4; Partners Seminar Transcript, May 9, 1965, p. 8; O. Roberts, OREA Devotion Transcript, July 26, 1962, p. 5.

37. O. Roberts, "The R. O. Corvin Story," p. 11.

38. Room Sponsors Seminar Transcript, May 20, 1963, p. 4.

39. Hamilton Interview, Jan. 13, 1983; Harold Paul Interview, Jan. 28, 1983.

40. See William C. Armstrong, "Divine Moment," *AL,* Feb. 1963, pp. 2–7; Bob Foresman, "Roberts Details 4-Year University Plans," *Tulsa Tribune,* Nov. 28, 1962, ORU.

41. Armstrong, "Divine Moment," p. 3.

42. Foresman, "Roberts Details 4-Year University Plans"; O. Roberts, Graduation Transcript, May 25, 1969, p. 2.

43. *Oral Roberts University Bulletin, June, 1969* (Tulsa: Oral Roberts University, 1969), p. 108.

44. O. Roberts, Regents Seminar Transcript, Nov. 25, 1962, p. 10; O. Roberts, President's Advisory Cabinet Transcript, May 29, 1965, p. 7; George Stovall Interview, Jan. 27, 1983.

45. Regents Seminar Transcript, Nov. 25, 1962, p. 6; O. Roberts, Regents Seminar Transcript, Nov., 1962, p. 4.

46. Doyle Helbling, "34 Regents Accept Challenge," *AL,* March 1964, p. 18; O. Roberts, Regents Seminar Transcript, Nov. 9, 1963, n.p.

47. Evangelism of Oral Roberts Class Transcript, 1971, p. 18.

48. Hamilton Interview, Jan. 13, 1983.

49. Partners Letter, Feb. 27, 1962, ORU.

50. O. Roberts, OREA Devotion Transcript, July 20, 1962, p. 9. See also Oral Roberts, "A Personal Letter concerning the Oral Roberts University," *AL,* Sept. 1962, pp. 15–16.

51. O. Roberts, Regents Seminar Transcript, Nov. 1962, pp. 6–7; O. Roberts, Chapel Transcript, Aug. 24, 1977, p. 18.

52. O. Roberts, Chapel Transcript, Jan. 30, 1976, pp. 17–18; O. Roberts, Chapel Transcript, Aug. 24, 1977, p. 18.

53. O. Roberts, OREA Devotion Transcript, July 26, 1962, p. 1.

54. O. Roberts, Regents Seminar Transcript, Nov. 25, 1962, p. 20.

55. Letter from John D. Messick to David E. Harrell, Jan. 27, 1983.

56. Partners Seminar Transcript, May 9, 1965, p. 2.

57. *Who's Who in America, 1968–69* (Chicago: Marquis Who's Who [1969]), vol. 35, p. 1506.

58. Messick to Harrell, Jan. 27, 1983. See also Bob Foresman, "Dr. Messick Planning Faculty," *Tulsa Tribune,* Mar. 16, 1964, ORU; Bob Foresman, "The Academic Wheelhorse of ORU," *Tulsa Tribune,* Apr. 19, 1967, ORU.

59. Bob Foresman, "Dr. Messick Planning Faculty."

60. George Harold Paul, "The Religious Frontier in Oklahoma," Ph.D. dissertation, University of Oklahoma, 1965, p. 169.

61. John D. Messick, "The Challenge of Christian Youth," *PHA,* Nov. 23, 1939, p. 5.

62. Messick to Harrell, Jan. 27, 1983; Hamilton Interview, Jan. 13, 1983.

63. Messick, Regents Seminar Transcript, Nov. 25, 1962, p. 20; Messick to Harrell, Jan. 27, 1983.

64. Bill Sampson, "ORU Works Steadily toward Its Next Goal—Accreditation," *Tulsa Tribune,* June 18, 1966, ORU; Messick to Harrell, Jan. 27, 1983; Messick, Partners Seminar Transcript, May 9, 1965, p. 3; Carol Tyler, "Dr. John D. Messick Cannot Retire," *Greenville (N.C.) Reflector,* Jan. 12, 1969. ORU.

65. Messick to Harrell, Jan. 27, 1983.

66. Foresman, "The Academic Wheelhorse of ORU."

67. Ibid.; *Oral Roberts University Bulletin for 1965–66* (no pub. info.), p. 9.

68. Granville Oral Roberts, *Oral Roberts University, 1965–1983* (New York: Newcomen Society of the United States, 1983), p. 13.

69. *Oral Roberts University Bulletin for 1965–66,* p. 10.

70. See *Oral Roberts University Bulletin for 1967–69,* p. 10.

71. Ministers Seminar Transcript, Jan. 20, 1963, p. 19.

72. Raymond O. Corvin, "Graduate School of Theology to Open Concurrently with the College of Liberal Arts," *ORU Outreach,* Winter 1965, p. 4; Corvin, "Religious and Educational Backgrounds," p. 160.

73. "Minister's Seminar," *AL,* April 1963, pp. 2–10; Paul Interview.

74. William C. Armstrong, "Released for Service," *AL,* July 1963, pp. 14–17.

75. Yvonne Nance, "Youth Set on Fire," *AL,* Sept. 1963, pp. 2–7.

76. Doyle Helbling, "International Seminar," *AL,* Feb. 1964, pp. 10–11.

77. Nance, "Youth Set on Fire," p. 6.

78. Oral Roberts, "The President's Report," *AL,* Feb. 1970, p. 5.

79. See "A Time of Sharing," *AL,* June 1966, pp. 12–17; "What Does the Ministry of Oral Roberts Mean to You as a Denominational Pastor?" *AL,* Oct. 1965, pp. 6–9.

80. Kathryn P. Ingley and Yvonne Nance, "God Is Moving by His Spirit," *AL,* June 1968, p. 19.

81. Evelyn Roberts, Miscellaneous Speech Transcript, June 8, 1981, p. 11. See also, Derek Prince Interview, Jan. 31, 1974.

82. O. Roberts, Ministers Seminar Transcript, Jan. 18, 1963, p. 3.

83. Vinson Synan Interview, May 22, 1983.

84. O. Roberts, Ministers Seminar Transcript, Apr. 28, 1963, p. 4; see also Ministers Seminar Transcript, Jan. 20, 1963, p. 1; Corvin, "Religious and Educational Backgrounds," pp. 136–43.

85. See Ministers Seminar Transcript, Jan. 20, 1963, p. 3.

86. Ministers Seminar Transcript, Apr. 28, 1963, pp. 1–2.

87. Lee Braxton Interview, Dec. 18, 1973.

88. Wayne A. Robinson, *I Once Spoke in Tongues* (Old Tappan, N.J.: Fleming H. Revell Co., Spire Books, 1975), p. 114; Albert E. Bush Interview, Feb. 11, 1983; Robert Voight Interview, Jan. 25, 1983.

89. O. Roberts, Ministers Seminar Transcript, Apr. 28, 1963, pp. 6–7.

90. *Oral Roberts University Bulletin, June, 1969,* p. 109.

91. "Eight Major Goals of the Oral Roberts University," *ORU Witness,* July 1964, pp. 2–5.

92. Oral Roberts, "Quest for the Whole Man," *AL,* Nov. 1965, pp. 13–25.

93. Wayne A. Robinson, *Oral: The Warm, Intimate, Unauthorized Portrait of a Man of God* (Los Angeles: Acton House, 1976), pp. 70–71.

94. Oral Roberts and Lee Braxton, "How You Can Light AN ETERNAL FLAME at Oral Roberts University," Brochure, no pub. info., p. 1.

95. Professional and Businessmen's Seminar Transcript, Nov. 27, 1964, n.p.

96. O. Roberts, Banquet Transcript, Dec. 5, 1970, p. 8.

97. Charles Farah Interview, Jan. 25, 1983. See also Regents Seminar Transcript, Jan. 20, 1963, pp. 15, 13.

98. John D. Messick, "Executive Vice President Asks Students and Parents a Question," *ORU Outreach,* Winter 1965, p. 13.

99. Oral Roberts University Dedication Transcript, Apr. 1967, n.p.

100. "I Am Reaffirming Our Commitment," *AL,* July 1970, p. 7.

101. O. Roberts, Faculty Chapel Transcript, Aug. 19, 1974, p. 16.

102. "For Such a Time As This," *ORU Outreach,* Winter 1965, p. 25.

103. Chapel Transcript, Feb. 22, 1974, p. 3.

104. Evangelism of Oral Roberts Class Transcript, 1971, p. 19.

105. Jan Dargatz, "An Exclusive *Oracle* Interview," *Oracle,* May 22, 1971, pp. 2–3. See also Evangelism of Oral Roberts Class Transcript, 1971, p. 19.

106. "I Am Reaffirming Our Commitment," p. 7.

107. Miscellaneous Speech Transcript, Jan. 22, 1973, pp. 9–10.

108. Regents Seminar Transcript, Nov. 25, 1962, p. 22.

109. *Oral Roberts University Bulletin, June, 1961,* pp. 108–109.

110. Beth Macklin, "First Endowed Chair Established at ORU," *Tulsa World,* Aug. 12, 1972, ORU; "Over 1,200 Attend Holy Spirit Class," *Oracle,* Sept. 22, 1972, p. 1.

111. Cathy Sanco, "1965–1975: A Decade of Dedication," *Communique,* Summer 1975, pp. 8-9. For an earlier estimate, see O. Roberts, President's Advisory Cabinet Transcript, May 29, 1965, p. 14.

112. Patti Roberts with Sherry Andrews, *Ashes to Gold* (Waco, Texas: Word Books [1983]), p. 41.

113. "Quest for the Whole Man," *AL,* Nov. 1965, p. 25.

114. *Bulletin* for the 1965–66 Academic Year, p. 8.

115. The early faculty at Oral Roberts University who had formerly taught at Southwestern included historians Harold Paul and Frank Sexton and English instructor Carl Hamilton.

116. Corvin, "Religious and Educational Backgrounds," p. 156; Hamilton Interview, Jan. 17, 1983; Messick to Harrell, Jan. 27, 1983.

117. Sampson, "ORU Works Steadily toward Its Next Goal—Accreditation"; Foresman, "The Academic Wheelhorse of ORU."

118. Voight Interview.

119. "ORU," *Oracle,* Dec. 12, 1980, n.p.; "Student Body Composition Melting Pot," *Oracle,* Oct. 25, 1968, p. 1.

120. See Bob Stamps, "God's Work at Oral Roberts University," *New Covenant,* May 1972, pp. 10–11; "ORU's Denominational Melting Pot Boasts 194 Unknowns," *Oracle,* Nov. 15, 1974, p. 8.

121. O. Roberts, President's Advisory Cabinet Transcript, May 29, 1965, p. 12; "ORU," *Oracle.*

122. Sanco, "1965–1975: A Decade of Dedication," pp. 8–9.

123. Messick to Harrell, Jan. 27, 1983; Frank Wallace Interview, Feb. 18, 1983; O. Roberts and Braxton, "How You Can Light AN ETERNAL FLAME at Oral Roberts University."

124. Messick to Harrell, Jan. 27, 1983.

125. O. Roberts, *Oral Roberts University, 1965–1983,* p. 13.

126. See, for descriptions of the system, William Jernigan, "Dial Access at Oral Roberts University," *Educational Product Report,* June 1971, pp. 13–20; "ORU Buys 'Dial-A-Lesson,'" *Tulsa World,* June 5, 1965, ORU; William W. Jernigan, "Oral Roberts Favors 'Futuristic,'" *Library Journal,* Dec. 1, 1966, pp. 5889–5891; "Director of ORU Center Is Appointed," *Tulsa Tribune,* Sept. 16, 1964, ORU; Bob Foresman, "Electronic Teaching at Roberts U," *Tulsa Tribune,* Mar. 16, 1964, ORU.

127. See John W. Abernathy and Clarence H. Dollmeyer, "ORU—Nation's First GES-Powered University," *Gas Energy Systems,* May 1965, pp. 3-6.

128. See Lee Braxton, "The Prayer Tower Goes Up," *AL,* May 1966, pp. 18–19; O. Roberts, Chapel Transcript, Jan. 11, 1966, pp. 6–9; Wallace Interview; "The Prayer Tower," *Alton (Ill.) Evening Telegraph,* Sept. 8, 1972, p. 12-A.

129. Ministers Seminar Transcript, Jan. 20, 1963, p. 22.

130. O. Roberts, Banquet Transcript, Apr. 23, 1973, p. 20. See also O. Roberts, Chapel Transcript, Jan. 22, 1975, p. 14.

131. See "Quick Facts about ORU," Pamphlet, no pub. info.

132. See Robert Eskridge, "We Are Moving the Earth Again at ORU," *AL*, Nov. 1970, pp. 16–17; "ORU's Mabee Center," *Tulsa Tribune*, June 14, 1972, p. 1-B; Wallace Interview; Troy Gordon, "Round the Clock," *Tulsa World*, Dec. 6, 1972, ORU; Oral Roberts Interview, Sept. 3, 1984.

133. "Smoking Lamp Lighted at ORU," *Tulsa Tribune*, Dec. 26, 1970, ORU.

134. Faculty Meeting Transcript, Nov. 9, 1971, p. 13.

135. See *School of Arts and Science Catolog* (Oral Roberts University, 1981–83), p. 47; O. Roberts, Chapel Transcript, Mar. 17, 1971, pp. 8–9; Oral Roberts, "FLASH!" *AL*, Apr. 1972, pp. 16–19.

136. See "Quick Facts about ORU"; Kenneth Cooper, Dedication Transcript, Sept. 29, 1974, passim.

137. Larry Van Dyne, "God and Man at Oral Roberts," *Chronicle of Higher Education*, Dec. 8, 1975, p. 3.

138. O. Roberts, *The Holy Spirit in the Now*, Vol. 2, pp. 78–79.

139. O. Roberts, Evangelism of Oral Roberts Class Transcript, 1971, p. 9.

140. Bob Foresman, "ORU's Architect Gaining Repute," *Tulsa Tribune*, March 1979, ORU; Dargatz, "An Exclusive *Oracle* Interview," pp. 2–3; Wallace Interview.

141. O. Roberts, "Speech to Sub-Contractors," Miscellaneous Speech Transcript, 1974, p. 1.

142. Wallace Interview.

143. Ibid.; Bill Roberts Interview, Feb. 23, 1983.

144. Wallace Interview.

145. Ibid.

146. See Suzanne Keith, "ORU Buildings Abound in Symbolism," *Oracle*, Oct. 5, 1979, p. 11; Gordon Lyons, "ORU Architect Comments on His Work," *Oracle*, Oct. 5, 1979, p. 10.

147. Carl Albert, "ORU Is an Unfolding Miracle of Almighty God," *AL*, July 1972, p. 22; "Technology Must Be Used for Mankind," *Tulsa World*, May 29, 1972, ORU.

148. John Williams Interview, Mar. 30, 1983.

149. See Wallace Interview; Bill Roberts Interview; Corvin, "Religious and Educational Backgrounds," p. 153.

150. See O. Roberts, Evangelism of Oral Roberts Class Transcript, 1971, pp. 8–9.

151. Braxton Interview; Edward Fiske, "Oral Roberts' College Has Grown in 7 Years," *New York Times*, June 13, 1972, sec. 2, p. 1.

152. See *Oral Roberts University Bulletin for 1965–66 Academic Year*, p. 14; Van Dyne, "God and Man at Oral Roberts"; O. Roberts, Ministers Seminar Transcript, Jan. 20, 1963, pp. 8–9.

153. Messick to Harrell, Jan. 27, 1983; Frank Leslie, "Goals and Methods at Roberts U. Outlined," *Tulsa World*, Sept. 5, 1965, ORU.

154. "ORU on the Move," Brochure, Apr. 15, 1968, no pub. info., p. 1; see "Tulsa and ORU," Brochure, no pub. info.; "Large Tulsa Gifts Help ORU Expansion Program," *Tulsa Tribune*, Nov. 8, 1967, ORU.

155. Ronald E. Butler, "ORU Opens Special Events Center Drive," *Tulsa World*, Dec. 9, 1970, p. 1-B.

156. Calvin Thielman Interview, Apr. 8, 1983.

157. Calvin Thielman Telephone Interview, Feb. 9, 1984.

158. Beth Macklin, "Dr. Billy Graham Coming to Tulsa," *Tulsa World*, Nov. 10, 1966, p. 1.

159. O. Roberts Interview, Feb. 16, 1983.

160. "Graham Calls for Putting Christ Back in College at ORU Rites," *Tulsa Tribune*, Apr. 3, 1967, p. 1. See also Jim Henderson, "Graham and ORU Draw Multitude," *Tulsa World*, Apr. 3, 1967, ORU.

161. ORU Dedication Transcript, Apr. 2, 1967, n.p.

162. "Symbolic Fire Glows As ORU Speakers Heard," *Tulsa World,* Apr. 3, 1967, ORU.

163. Ibid.

164. See ORU Dedication Transcript, Apr. 2, 1967, n.p.

165. Ibid.

166. See Macklin, "Dr. Billy Graham Coming to Tulsa."

167. "ORU to Fill Education Gap," *Tulsa Tribune,* Apr. 1, 1967, ORU.

168. "ORU Needs Our Help," *Tulsa World,* Apr. 4, 1967, p. 6.

169. "School for Squares," *Tulsa Tribune,* Apr. 4, 1967, ORU.

170. ORU Dedication Press Conference Transcript, 1967, n.p.

171. "State Board Accredits Roberts U," *Tulsa World,* Jan. 20, 1967, ORU; Messick to Harrell, Jan. 27, 1983.

172. See Ronald E. Butler, "ORU Eyes New Era with Accreditation," *Tulsa World,* Apr. 1, 1971, p. 1–E.

173. O. Roberts, Chapel Transcript, Nov. 15, 1967, p. 8.

174. O. Roberts, Miscellaneous Speech Transcript, Jan. 22, 1973, pp. 9–10.

175. O. Roberts, Faculty Chapel Transcript, Aug. 19, 1974, p. 6.

176. Ibid.

177. O. Roberts, Faculty Retreat Transcript, Aug. 25, 1983, p. 10.

178. Banquet Transcript, Apr. 23, 1973, p. 18.

179. Ibid.

180. O. Roberts, Chapel Transcript, Mar. 31, 1971, p. 1.

181. Butler, "ORU Eyes New Era with Accreditation"; Carol Langston, "ORU Given Full Accreditation," *Tulsa Tribune,* Mar. 31, 1971, p. D-1.

182. "ORU Leaps Ahead," *Tulsa World,* Apr. 2, 1971, ORU.

183. "Big Day for ORU," *Tulsa Tribune,* Apr. 1, 1971, ORU.

184. Messick to Harrell, Jan. 27, 1983; "Hamilton Is ORU Assistant Dean," *Tulsa Tribune,* June 8, 1967, ORU; Oral Roberts Interview, Sept. 3, 1984.

185. Bob Foresman, "ORU's Dr. Messick Retiring," *Tulsa Tribune,* Jan. 19, 1968, pp. 31, 36; O. Roberts, Graduate Baccalaureate Transcript, May 25, 1969, p. 3.

186. See "ORU Center Is Named for Dr. Messick," *Tulsa Tribune,* Feb. 1, 1968, ORU.

187. Hamilton Interview, Jan. 13, 1983.

188. Ron Smith Interview, Feb. 24, 1983.

189. Messick to Harrell, Jan. 27, 1983.

190. See O. Roberts, Faculty Retreat Transcript, Aug. 25, 1983, p. 10.

191. Robinson, *Oral,* pp. 120–22.

192. Smith Interview.

193. Oral had prayed for Hamilton's daughter, Carla Jo, when she was stricken with pneumonia, and all believed a miraculous healing followed. Oral Roberts, *The Call* (Garden City, N.Y.: Doubleday and Co., 1972), pp. 207–9.

194. Hamilton Interview, Jan. 13, 1983.

195. See Debbie Titus, "Time Waits for No Man," *Communique,* Fall 1982, pp. 5–8.

196. Kyle Goddard, "Faculty Endorsement Key to Naming of ORU's Dean," *Tulsa Tribune,* Jan. 26, 1968, ORU.

197. Messick to Harrell, Jan. 27, 1983.

198. Goddard, "Faculty Endorsement Key to Naming of ORU's Dean."

199. Titus, "Time Waits for No Man," pp. 5–8.

200. O. Roberts, Chapel Transcript, Mar. 31, 1971, p. 2.

201. Robinson, *Oral,* pp. 122–24.

202. Oscar Moore Interview, Jan. 20, 1983.

203. Nell Boggs, "Dean of ORU Theology Out in Policy Dispute," *Tulsa Tribune,* Mar. 19, 1968, pp. 17, 21.

204. Nell Jean Boggs, "ORU Dean: 'I Was Fired,'" *Tulsa Tribune,* Mar. 22, 1968, pp. 37, 42.

205. Braxton Interview; Paul Interview; Hamilton Interviews, Jan. 13, 1983 and Jan. 17, 1983.

206. Hamilton Interview, Jan. 13, 1983.

207. Hamilton Interview, Jan. 17, 1983.

208. "Ervin Nominated for Post at ORU," *Tulsa World,* Mar. 20, 1968, ORU.

209. "Oral Removes Dean," *Oklahoma City Journal,* Mar. 22, 1968, ORU; V. Synan Interview.

210. Boggs, "ORU Dean: 'I Was Fired,' " p. 37.

211. Hamilton Interview, Jan. 17, 1983.

212. James Buskirk Interview, Jan. 28, 1983.

213. Contemporary Methods in Evangelism Class Transcript, Oct. 11, 1967, p. 5. See also Contemporary Methods in Evangelism Class Transcript, Nov. 29, 1967, passim.

214. Wayne Robinson Interview, Apr. 4, 1983; Robinson, *Oral,* pp. 92–95.

215. Robinson, *Oral,* pp. 92–97. Robinson recalled that several regents resigned when Oral refused to fire him, but Roberts insists there was no such defection. Robinson Interview; Oral Roberts Interview, Sept. 3, 1984.

216. Contemporary Methods in Evangelism Class Transcript, Oct. 11, 1967, p. 22.

217. Farah Interview.

218. Contemporary Methods in Evangelism Class Transcript, Nov. 29, 1967, n.p.

219. Howard Ervin Interview, Jan. 25, 1983.

220. Darlen Ulseth, "Nichols Organizes Crusade," *Oracle,* Dec. 11, 1967, p. 1.

221. V. Synan Interview.

222. Beth Macklin, "ORU Eyes Role in Chile College," *Tulsa World,* Dec. 3, 1967, ORU.

223. Farah Interview.

224. V. Synan Interview.

225. Hamilton Interview, Jan. 13, 1983; Roberts, *The Call,* p. 130.

226. Moore Interview.

227. Hamilton Interview, Jan. 13, 1983.

228. Paul Interview.

229. "Oral Removes Dean," *Oklahoma City Journal,* Mar. 22, 1968, ORU.

230. Robinson, *Oral,* p. 93.

231. "Tulsan Elected to Church Job," *Tulsa Tribune,* Aug. 27, 1968, ORU.

232. See Delores Boyd, "Regents Integrate Seminary," *Oracle,* Mar. 14, 1969, p. 1.

233. Moore Interview.

234. Evelyn Roberts, "How Obedience to God's Call Changed Our Lives," *AL,* Jan. 1969, p. 10.

235. Ministers Seminar Transcript, Jan. 20, 1963, pp. 6–7.

236. Hamilton Interview, Jan. 13, 1983.

237. *Oral Roberts University Student Handbook, 1967–68* (Tulsa: Oral Roberts University, n.d.), n.p.

238. *Oral Roberts University School of Arts and Sciences Catalog, 1981–82* (Tulsa: Oral Roberts University, n.d.), p. 35.

239. O. Roberts, Chapel Transcript, May 12, 1971, p. 6.

240. Banquet Transcript, Aug. 21, 1972, p. 8.

241. *Student Handbook, 1967–68,* p. 13; *Student Handbook, 1965–66,* no pub. info., p. 24. It is an interesting commentary on the early student body that they were also instructed in the "social graces": "Remember that Oral Roberts University students should have social graces equivalent to those of any other institution and these include proper use of eating utensils with the spoon always going away from your body when dipping soups. . . . A spoon is never to be left in a cup after stirring the contents but put on the saucer. . . . Finally, study your book of etiquette to see that you do the proper things at all times." "ORU Bulletin Board," May 19, 1966, no. 35, p. 3 (mimeographed sheet).

242. *Student Handbook, 1965–66,* p. 26.

243. *Student Handbook,* 1967–68, p. 56.

244. *Oral Roberts University School of Arts and Sciences Catalog,* 1981–83, pp. 53–54.

245. "ORU Develops from Dream," *Oracle,* undated [1978], p. 2; Voight Interview.

246. Chapel Transcript, Sept. 23, 1970, p. 12; "ORU's Rules Strict," *Tulsa World,* Aug. 20, 1972, pp. 1-H, 2-H.

247. O. Roberts, Chapel Transcript, Apr. 14, 1972, p. 25.

248. Faculty Orientation Transcript, Aug. 24, 1971, p. 3.

249. Evangelism of Oral Roberts Class Transcript, 1971, p. 15.

250. O. Roberts, Chapel Transcript, Sept. 23, 1970, p. 13.

251. Hamilton Interview, Jan. 13, 1983.

252. Evangelism of Oral Roberts Class Transcript, 1971, p. 14.

253. Hamilton Interview, Jan. 13, 1983.

254. See "P. E. Requirements Get More Rugged," *Oracle,* Dec. 15, 1972, p. 1; "Computer Records Aerobics," *Oracle,* Jan. 31, 1975, p. 1; Kenneth Cooper, Aerobics Building Dedication Transcription, Sept. 29, 1974, pp. 3–4; Steve Love, "Aerobics," *Tulsa Magazine,* Feb. 6, 1975, pp. 25–29.

255. O. Roberts, Faculty Meeting Transcript, May 5, 1970, p. 10.

256. Faculty Orientation Transcript, Aug. 24, 1971, p. 4.

257. O. Roberts, Chapel Transcript, Feb. 11, 1970, pp. 10–11.

258. O. Roberts, Chapel Transcript, Apr. 14, 1972, p. 17.

259. O. Roberts, Faculty Meeting Transcript, Feb. 4, 1971, pp. 6–7.

260. [O. Roberts,] "A Guest Editorial," *Tulsa Tribune,* Sept. 9, 1965, ORU.

261. See *Congressional Record,* 91st Cong., 1st Sess., Nov. 18, 1969 (reprint, ORU).

262. O. Roberts, Faculty Chapel Transcript, Aug. 19, 1974, p. 20. See also Oral Roberts, "Miracle of ORU," *AL,* Jan. 1972, pp. 2–3.

263. "School for Squares," *Tulsa Tribune,* Apr. 4, 1967, ORU.

264. Evangelism of Oral Roberts Class Transcript, 1971, p. 7.

265. Ibid.

266. See "Getting Us Together and Getting Us Out," *AL,* Jan. 1971, pp. 12–15.

267. See chapter 10 for a discussion of student evangelistic efforts.

268. See Ken Trickey, "ORU Today," *AL,* Feb. 1970, pp. 11–13.

269. See Gene Dennison, "Trickey Beams over ORU Year," *Tulsa Tribune,* Feb. 25, 1971, p. 2-C.

270. See "Fuqua Receives Nod of Writers," *Tulsa Tribune,* Mar. 25, 1972, ORU.

271. Dennis Eckert, "Roberts' Evangelistic Fervor Propelling ORU Cagers," *Tulsa Tribune,* Oct. 27, 1971, p. 2-C.

272. Sam Godaper, "Oral Roberts," *Middletown (N.Y.) Times Herald-Record,* Dec. 7, 1971, ORU.

273. O. Roberts, OREA Devotion Transcript, Dec. 1, 1972, n.p.

274. O. Roberts, *My Twenty Years of a Miracle Ministry,* p. 77. See also "Editor's Note," *Outreach,* Winter 1967, p. 27.

275. O. Roberts, Church Sermon Transcript, First Methodist Church, Feb. 6, 1975, p. 14.

276. O. Roberts, Banquet Transcript, Jan. 28, 1972, p. 5.

277. See Fred Landard, "ORU Stands Tall in Recruiting," *Tulsa Tribune,* May 15, 1967, ORU.

278. Gene Dennison, "National Image of ORU Is Pointed Up by Recruiting," *Tulsa Tribune,* Feb. 10, 1971, ORU.

279. O. Roberts, OREA Devotion Transcript, Dec. 1, 1972, n.p.; see also Bill Connors [sports editorial], *Tulsa World,* Mar. 14, 1984, p. 2-D.

280. O. Roberts, Faculty Orientation Transcript, Aug. 24, 1971, pp. 8–12.

281. Ibid. Oral tied the World Action Singers to the athletes as students who were contributing in unusual ways to the ministry and urged special treatment for them as well.

282. Robinson Interview.

283. Pat Putnam, "Don't Send My Boy to Harvard," *Sports Illustrated,* Nov. 4, 1974, p. 20. The story had been previously printed in the *New York Times.*

284. Bill Connors, "Sports of the World," *Tulsa World,* Nov. 10, 1974, pp. 5-S, 10-S.

285. O. Roberts, Faculty Chapel Transcript, Nov. 11, 1974, p. 23.

286. O. Roberts, Faculty Orientation Transcript, Aug. 24, 1971, p. 7.

287. O. Roberts, Faculty Meeting Transcript, Nov. 9, 1971, p. 12.

288. O. Roberts, OREA Devotion Transcript, Dec. 1, 1972, n.p.

289. See Jeff Pugh, "Oral Roberts U.—High Scorers for the Gospel," *Los Angeles Times,* Mar. 6, 1972, pp. 1, 13–14.

290. Dave Kindied, "Image-Keeping at Oral Roberts Forces Trickey to Pack His Bags," *Louisville Courier-Journal,* Mar. 14, 1974, pp. 1-C, 6-C. See also Robinson Interview; "Oral Roberts," *Monroe (La.) Morning World,* Mar. 17, 1974, p. 10-B.

291. "Trickey to Leave ORU," *Oracle,* Feb. 8, 1974, p. 1.

292. O. Roberts, Banquet Transcript, Aug. 21, 1972, p. 8.

293. "Prayer Tower Still Stands," *Oracle,* Mar. 12, 1974, p. 1.

294. Corvin, "Religious and Educational Backgrounds," p. 187; Bush Interview.

295. O. Roberts, Miscellaneous Speech Transcript, Jan. 22, 1973, pp. 7–8.

296. O. Roberts, Faculty Meeting Transcript, Apr. 20, 1972, p. 4.

297. O. Roberts, Chapel Transcript, Apr. 14, 1972, p. 32.

298. O. Roberts, Miscellaneous Speech Transcript, Jan. 22, 1973, p. 3.

299. Michael Brown, "Guest Editorial," *Oracle,* Dec. 12, 1968, p. 2.

300. "Hamilton Speaks to *Oracle* of Purpose," *Oracle,* Jan. 14, 1983, p. 6.

301. Michael D. Miller, "No Mediocrity at Oral Roberts University," *Tulsa Tribune,* June 18, 1966, ORU; see also Sampson, "ORU Works Steadily toward Its Next Goal—Accreditation"; *Kansas City Star,* Feb. 19, 1967, ORU.

302. Voight Interview.

303. O. Roberts, President's Advisory Cabinet Transcript, May 29, 1965, pp. 5–6.

304. O. Roberts, Chapel Transcript, Apr. 14, 1972, pp. 16–17.

305. O. Roberts, Faculty Meeting Transcript, Apr. 20, 1972, pp. 8–9.

306. Robinson Interview; Smith Interview.

307. "ORU Policy Calls for Annual Faculty Review," *Tulsa Tribune,* May 22, 1972, p. 2-C; "Faculty Advances, Tenures Disclosed," *Oracle,* Dec. 6, 1974, p. 1.

308. Smith Interview.

309. Faculty Orientation Transcript, Aug. 24, 1971, p. 5.

310. O. Roberts, Chapel Transcript, Sept. 23, 1970, p. 11.

311. O. Roberts, Faculty Meeting Transcript, May 5, 1970, pp. 12–13.

312. Ministers Seminar Transcript, Apr. 28, 1963, p. 7.

313. O. Roberts, Chapel Transcript, Sept. 23, 1970, p. 11.

314. O. Roberts, Chapel Transcript, pt. 2, Sept. 19, 1980, pp. 39–40.

315. O. Roberts, Faculty Chapel Transcript, Aug. 19, 1974, pp. 5-6.

316. O. Roberts, Chapel Transcript, Apr. 14, 1972, p. 27.

317. Chapel Transcript, Oct. 19, 1975, pp. 5–6.

318. Randy Day, "President Shares, Cares," *Oracle,* Aug. 24, 1974, p. 3. See also, O. Roberts, Chapel Transcript, Apr. 14, 1972, p. 15.

319. O. Roberts, Chapel Transcript, Apr. 14, 1972, p. 18.

320. O. Roberts, Faculty Meeting Transcript, Feb. 4, 1971, p. 4.

321. Bob Foresman and Jenk Jones, Jr., "Oral Roberts: What Makes Him Tick," *Tulsa Tribune,* June 11, 1975, pp. 1B–2B.

322. "A Spiritual Revolution throughout the Earth," *AL,* May 1962, p. 8.

323. Hamilton Interview, Jan. 13, 1983.

10. BEYOND THE TENT

1. Speaking Personally," *AL,* Jan. 1962, p. 2.

2. "A Look at the New Year," *AL,* Jan. 1964, p. 2. See also Yvonne Nance, "A Life from the Lord," *AL,* May 1964, p. 22.

3. O. Roberts, Regents Seminar Transcript, Nov. 1962, p. 5.

4. O. Roberts, OREA Staff Meeting Transcript, Oct. 20, 1966, pp. 2–3.

5. See "Roberts Crusades Set Up by Hard Work, Planning," *Tulsa Tribune,* July 25, 1967, p. 14.

6. Ibid.; Jack McNamara, "Oral Roberts Wins Crusade Approval," *Pittsburgh Press,* June 15, 1960, ORU.

7. "Pentecostals Here Hail Roberts," *Miami Herald,* Jan. 5, 1963, ORU.

8. "Training Set for Crusade," *Chattanooga (Tenn.) News-Free Press,* Mar. 21, 1961, ORU.

9. Ann Hitch, "Sick, Infirm Offer Prayers As Roberts Grasps Them," *Dayton (Ohio) Journal Herald,* Aug. 3, 1961, p. 41.

10. O. Roberts, Crusade Transcript, Dec. 13, 1968, p. 15.

11. See "Rev. Roberts Opens 6-Day Life Crusade," *Houston Post,* Aug. 1, 1962, sec. 1, p. 6; "Intensified Follow-Up of Roberts Crusade Planned Next Week," *Memphis Mirror,* Feb. 3, 1967, ORU.

12. Anne Hitch, "5,000 Pack Tent to Hear Roberts," *Dayton (Ohio) Journal Herald,* Aug. 2, 1961, p. 12.

13. Wayne Woodlief, " 'Thankya, Jesus' Echoes throughout Tent," *Norfolk (Va.) Ledger-Star,* July 20, 1966, ORU.

14. Melvin Steakley, "Lines to Faith-Healing Form on Revival Trail," *Houston Chronicle,* Aug. 4, 1962, p. 8.

15. Mike McGrady, "An Evening with Oral Roberts," *Garden City (N.Y.) Newsday,* Dec. 17, 1966, ORU.

16. Melvin Steakley, "500 Heed Oral Roberts," *Houston Chronicle,* Aug. 1, 1962, sec. 1, p. 11.

17. Don Morrison, "Oral Roberts Opens 5-Day Crusade in City," *Minneapolis Tribune,* Nov. 23, 1960, ORU.

18. See "Oral Roberts Denounces 'Oddballs and Screwballs,' " *Vancouver (B.C.) Province,* Oct. 11, 1961, ORU; Al Pikora, "Tempest under Revival Tent," *Dayton (Ohio) Daily News,* Aug. 4, 1961, p. 1; see also Don Ore, "Oral Roberts Does Battle with Devil and Heckler," *Vancouver (B.C.) Sun,* Oct. 11, 1961, p. 1.

19. George Burnham, "Oral Roberts Warns 6,000 'Rising Tide of Fear' in U.S.," *Chattanooga (Tenn.) News-Free Press,* Mar. 30, 1961, ORU.

20. Steakley, "500 Heed Oral Roberts." Touch them he did, sometimes fifty, sometimes eighty, and sometimes, "near the end of the physically gruelling performance," when "the spirit weakens," Oral, "obviously tiring, hustles the hopeful through with assembly-line dispatch." Van Hetherly and Melvin Steakley, " 'Jesus Heal!' " *Houston Chronicle, Texas Magazine,* Oct. 7, 1962, p. 6.

21. Crusade Transcript, Dec. 13, 1968, pp. 16–17.

22. Ibid., p. 17ff. The audience reached out to touch the backs of the well-worn metal chairs as a point of contact, or they "slid to their knees on the cement floor and prayed audibly." See Sue Titcomb, "Emotions Flow As Oral Roberts Preaches, Heals," *Charlotte (N.C.) News,* Mar. 20, 1964, p. 5-A.

23. "Recipient of 'Miracle' Ends Revival Sunday," *Jacksonville (Fla.) Journal,* June 3, 1961, ORU; see Pat Wiggins, *The Pat Wiggins Story* (Tulsa: Abundant Life Publications, 1962).

24. "800 Seek Help from Roberts As Crusade Ends," *Toronto Globe and Mail,* Aug. 12, 1963, p. 5; Hetherly and Steakley, " 'Jesus Heal!' " p. 12.

25. See, for instance, Billie Cheney Lovell, "Only God Heals, Evangelist Says," *Atlanta Journal,* May 19, 1966, ORU.

26. Jerry Edgerton, "2,000 in W. Hempstead Hear Oral Roberts Open Crusade," *Garden City (N.Y.) Newsday,* Dec. 9, 1966, p. 29.

27. "Bob Daniels," *AL,* Sept. 1959, p. 3; Bob DeWeese Interview, Jan. 19, 1983.

28. "Roberts Crusade Set Up by Hard Work, Planning." In a portentous moment in a crusade in Dayton, Ohio in September 1967, Richard Roberts "stood to sing about Jesus." "Richard Roberts," *AL,* Dec. 1968, p. 6.

29. Nancy Gregorik, "Oral Roberts Crowds Shrink," *Detroit News,* July 12, 1967, ORU.

30. See O. Roberts, Youth Seminar Transcript, July 24, 1965, p. 3; Edmund Willingham, "Roberts Preaches to 3,500," *Nashville Tennessean,* Apr. 24, 1964, ORU.

31. Steakley, "Lines to Faith-Healing Form on Revival Trail"; see also Larry Agee, "8,500 Hear Oral Roberts," *Columbus (Ga.) Enquirer,* May 4, 1961, ORU.

32. John S. DeMott, "Oral Roberts Talks Here, Seeks Pledge," *Charlotte (N.C.) Obsever,* Nov. [n.d.], 1962, ORU.

33. Hetherly and Steakley, " 'Jesus Heal!' " p. 12.

34. Lee Braxton Interview, Dec. 18, 1973.

35. See Letitia Gray, "Thousands Hear Evangelist," *Tampa (Fla.) Times,* Jan. 31, 1962, p. 1. See also "Anaheim Crusade's 'Canvas Cathedral,'" *Los Angeles Herald-Examiner,* Oct. 14, 1967, ORU.

36. "700 Answer Faith Healer's Call in Toronto," *Toronto Mail and Globe,* Aug. 7, 1963, p. 4.

37. Gregorik, "Oral Roberts' Crowds Shrink."

38. See Evangelism of Oral Roberts Class Transcript, 1971, pp. 16–18.

39. "Evangelist Begins Crusade," *Yakima (Wash.) Herald,* Sept. 2, 1961, p. 5.

40. Mont Morton, "Roberts Says Reds Afraid of Bible," *Columbia (S.C.) Record,* May 20, 1960, ORU. Anywhere "there is a live, red-hot Christian," Oral told a Georgia reporter, "Communism is licked." "Evangelist Says Christians Hold Answer to Threat of Communism," *Columbus (Ga.) Ledger,* May 6, 1961, ORU.

41. "Evangelist Sees Peril in Internal Problems," *Anaheim (Cal.) Register,* Oct. 26, 1967, ORU.

42. O. Roberts, Chapel Transcript, Sept. 1, 1968, p. 9.

43. Oral Roberts, "God Has Spoken to Me Again," *AL,* June 1960, p. 6. See also Oral Roberts, *My Story,* (Tulsa: Summit Book Co., 1961), pp. 192–93.

44. Oral Roberts, "A Look at the New Year," *AL,* Jan. 1964, p. 3.

45. Oral Roberts, "A Special Message to My Partners," *AL,* May 1967, p. 28.

46. O. Roberts, OREA Staff Meeting Transcript, Oct. 20, 1966, p. 1.

47. O. Roberts, "A Special Message to My Partners," p. 28.

48. Oral Roberts, "I Have Seen Jesus Again!" *AL,* July 1968, pp. 3–4.

49. See Oral Roberts, "My Fateful Journey inside the Iron Curtain," *AL,* July 1960, pp. 2–7; Oral Roberts, "My Trip to Russia for Christ," *AL,* Aug. 1960, pp. 9–14.

50. O. Roberts, "My Fateful Journey inside the Iron Curtain," pp. 3, 5.

51. O. Roberts, "My Trip to Russia for Christ," pp. 9–14; Bill Sampson, "Oral Roberts Tells of Russ Religion," *Tulsa World,* May 6, 1960, ORU.

52. See Donald Merrick, "Oral Roberts Tells of Soviet Trip," *State* (Columbia, S.C.), May 28, 1960, ORU.

53. "Roberts Urges Prayer for Russian Followers," *Tulsa Tribune,* May 8, 1961, ORU.

54. "Tulsan Prayed for Chiangs," *Tulsa Tribune,* Nov. 10, 1960, p. 16; Oral Roberts, "The Healing Power of Christ in the Orient, Part I," *AL,* Jan. 1961, pp. 2–5.

55. Ibid.; see O. Roberts, *My Story,* p. 202; Oral Roberts, "The Healing Power of Christ in the Orient, Part II," *AL,* Mar. 1961, pp. 2–5, 14.

56. Oral Roberts, "My First European Crusade," *AL,* Oct. 1961, pp. 2–5; "Finns Responsive to Roberts," *Tulsa Tribune,* July 27, 1961, p. 3.

57. Hart R. Armstrong, "Oral Roberts' Visit to Germany," *AL,* Oct. 1962, pp. 5–7.

58. Alice Duncombe, "Wales Crusade," *AL,* Oct. 1963, pp. 3–9.

59. Oral Roberts, "My World Trip for Souls," *AL*, Feb. 1965, pp. 7–12.

60. Oral Roberts, "My World Trip for Souls," *AL*, Apr. 1965, pp. 2–7.

61. Oral Roberts, "Great Harvest of Souls in India," *AL*, May 1965, pp. 5–13.

62. See Oral Roberts, "The Brazil Story," *AL*, Nov. 1966, pp. 2–14.

63. "Oral Roberts Returns from Brazilian Crusade," *Tulsa Tribune*, Aug. 19, 1966, ORU.

64. "What Has the Brazil Crusade Meant to You Personally," *AL*, Dec. 1966, p. 21.

65. See Oral Roberts, "Mission to Vietnam," *AL*, Oct. 1967, pp. 5–14; Nell Jean Boggs, "Oral Roberts Finds Journey to South Vietnam 'Sobering,'" *Tulsa Tribune*, July 22, 1967, ORU; see Oral Roberts, "God's Time for Indonesia," *AL*, Nov. 1967, pp. 5–12.

66. See Oral Roberts, "The Challenge of Chile," *AL*, Apr. 1968, pp. 8–17; Evelyn Roberts Interview, Nov. 1, 1983.

67. See "Mission of Renewal," *AL*, Sept. 1970, pp. 20–21.

68. See Oral Roberts, "God Opened the Door for World Action in London and Israel," *AL*, Nov. 1968, pp. 2–15; Beth Macklin, "Roberts Hopes Next Trip Overseas to Include Cuba," *Tulsa World*, Aug. 7, 1968, ORU; Nell Jean Boggs, "Ben Gurion Interview Gained with Ingenuity," *Tulsa Tribune*, Aug. 6, 1968, ORU.

69. See Oral Roberts, "Our Largest Crusade in 21 Years in Africa," *AL*, Oct. 1968, pp. 2–10; "Kenya Paper Criticizes Oral Roberts," *Tulsa Tribune*, July 17, 1968, ORU; "Roberts Turns Down Bid for Faith Healing Contest," *Tulsa World*, July 20, 1968, ORU.

70. O. Roberts, Chapel Transcript, Sept. 1, 1968, pp. 9–10.

71. DeWeese Interview.

72. O. Roberts, Chapel Transcript, Sept. 1, 1968, p. 12.

73. O. Roberts, Crusade Transcript, Aug. 9, 1968, p. 19; Russell Chandler, "Roberts' Rules," *Washington (D.C.) Star*, Aug. 10, 1968, ORU.

74. See Phil Rounds, "Jesus Happens . . . ," *AL*, Apr. 1969, pp. 7–14; "Hope for the Hopeless," *(Kingston, Jamaica) Gleaner*, Nov. 30, 1968, ORU.

75. See "One-Day Crusades with Our Partners," *AL*, July 1969, p. 15. Actually, Oral had scheduled such one-day partner meetings from the early 1960s. See Hayes B. Jacobs, "Oral Roberts: High Priest of Faith Healing," *Harpers Magazine*, Feb. 1962, p. 37.

76. DeWeese Interview.

77. "Secularism a Threat, Evangelist Says," *Miami Herald*, Jan. 5, 1963, ORU.

78. DeWeese Interview.

79. Evangelism of Oral Roberts Class Transcript, 1971, pp. 14–16.

80. Oral Roberts, My Own Personal Testimony Transcript, Oct. 1970, p. 14.

81. Evelyn Roberts Interview, Nov. 1, 1983.

82. O. Roberts, Chapel Transcript, Nov. 15, 1967, p. 24.

83. Kathryn Kuhlman Funeral Service Transcript, Feb. 23, 1976, pp. 1–2.

84. Evelyn Roberts, Evangelism of Oral Roberts Class Transcript, 1971, p. 16.

85. Evangelism of Oral Roberts Class Transcript, 1971, p. 13.

86. Ibid., p. 18.

87. O. Roberts, Chapel Transcript, Sept. 1, 1968, p. 17.

88. Evangelism of Oral Roberts Class Transcript, 1971, p. 12.

89. "Abundant Life Youth Teams," *AL*, Mar. 1959, pp. 10–11.

90. Manford Engel, "Cathedral Cruiser to Carry Gospel," *AL*, Apr. 1960, p. 11.

91. See "American Youth Teams to Leave on World Mission for Christ!" *AL*, July 1960, pp. 15–16; "Abundant Life World Tour to Begin July 5," *Tulsa Tribune*, June 10, 1960, ORU; Richard Shakarian, "In 80 Days around the World Campaign," *Los Angeles Herald and Express*, June 4, 1960, p. 4-B.

92. "Around the World for Christ," *AL*, Nov. 1960, pp. 4–6.

93. James H. Kerby, "Youth Time," *AL*, May 1960, p. 19. See also O. Roberts, "God Has Spoken to Me Again," p. 6.

94. "Abundant Life World Tour to Begin July 5"; see also "American Youth Team

to Leave on World Mission for Christ!" p. 15; "Global Objective: Religion," *Tulsa Tribune*, July 2, 1960, ORU.

95. Evangelism of Oral Roberts Class Transcript, 1971, p. 12.

96. Tommy Tyson, "Mission to Brazil," *Outreach*, Summer 1966, p. 13.

97. O. Roberts, OREA Staff Meeting Transcript, Oct. 20, 1966, p. 1.

98. See "Friendship Tour to Indonesia," *Outreach*, Summer 1967, pp. 6–7.

99. Beth Macklin, "ORU Students Learn 'Laying On of Hands,'" *Tulsa World*, Aug. 3, 1967, ORU.

100. See Oral Roberts, "I Can Hear the Cry of Lost Souls," *AL*, May 1968, p. 23.

101. See Oral Roberts, "God Opened the Doors for World Action in London and Israel," *AL*, Nov. 1968, pp. 2–15; Oral Roberts, "Our Largest Crusade in 21 Years," *AL*, Oct. 1968, pp. 2–10.

102. "ORU World Action Students," Brochure, no pub. info., p. 3.

103. "Students at ORU to Visit Israel with Action Team," *Tulsa Tribune*, Feb. 27, 1968, ORU.

104. "Four Man World Action Team," *AL*, Oct. 1968, pp. 12–13.

105. "ORU Missionaries Return from Africa, Find Change," *Tulsa World*, [undated clipping,] ORU.

106. Oral Roberts, "The Challenge of Chile," p. 23.

107. O. Roberts, Chapel Transcript, Sept. 1, 1968, pp. 3–4.

108. Charles Farah Interview, telephone, Feb. 17, 1984.

109. In the summer of 1968, students participated in Oral's American crusades, as well as those overseas, but in January 1969 that avenue of service came to a close. See Oral Roberts, Crusade Transcript, Aug. 9, 1968, p. 13.

110. Chapel Transcript, Oct. 9, 1968, p. 12; Vinson Synan Interview, May 22, 1983.

111. O. Roberts, Chapel Transcript, Sept. 1, 1968, p. 15; Oral Roberts, "Put On a Bigger Coat," *AL*, Sept. 1968, p. 4.

112. O. Roberts, Chapel Transcript, Sept. 1, 1968, p. 13. The term came to mean, explained Carl Hamilton, "that wherever a student or a group of students or a group of faculty are, they are a healing team." Carl Hamilton Interview, Jan. 13, 1983.

113. See Farah Telephone Interview; "Where (World) Action Is," *Tulsa World*, Dec. 15, 1968, ORU; Yvonne Nance, "World Action Teams Sent to the Orient, Africa, and America," *AL*, Aug. 1969, pp. 12–13.

114. Evelyn Roberts, "How Obedience to God's Call Has Changed Our Lives," *AL*, Jan. 1969, p. 10.

115. "We Must use Television to Communicate the Gospel to This Generation," *AL*, Oct. 1966, p. 23; William C. Armstrong, "Reaching Out to Souls in a Ministry of Total Evangelism," *AL*, Aug. 1966, p. 19.

116. "New TV Program," *AL*, Apr. 1965, pp. 22–23.

117. Oral Roberts, *The Call* (Garden City, N.Y.: Doubleday and Co., 1972), p. 186.

118. Braxton Interview.

119. O. Roberts, Devotion Transcript, Dec. 24, 1968, p. 9.

120. Oral Roberts, "Back on Television," *AL*, Mar. 1969, p. 3.

121. Yvonne Nance, "Television—Our Greatest Outreach to Meet People's Needs," *AL*, Nov. 1972, p. 6.

122. O. Roberts, "Back on Television," p. 3.

123. O. Roberts, Chapel Transcript, Mar. 14, 1969, p. 17.

124. Ibid., p. 16; Oral Roberts, "We Are Returning to Television," *AL*, Feb. 1969, p. 7.

125. O. Roberts, Partners Seminar Transcript, Jan. 25, 1969, p. 11.

126. O. Roberts, Chapel Transcript, Mar. 14, 1969, p. 16.

127. Ron Smith Interview, Feb. 24, 1983; "Carmichael to Conduct ORU Concert," *Tulsa Tribune*, Sept. 13, 1968, p. 38; O. Roberts, *The Call*, pp. 192–93.

128. Warren Hultgren Interview, Mar. 30, 1983.

129. Wayne Robinson Interview, Apr. 14, 1983.

130. Mary Begley, "Christmas Show Next," *Los Angeles Times*, Dec. 18, 1969, ORU.

131. Robinson Interview.

132. O. Roberts, Chapel Transcript, Sept. 1, 1968, p. 8.

133. O. Roberts, "We Are Returning to Television," pp. 2–6. Richard pressed his father to put the young singers in a modish format, which Oral reluctantly accepted. O. Roberts, *The Call*, p. 193. Tulsa television critic Bill Donaldson previewed the program and judged that it was done with "great professionalism" and that, while "essentially religious in tone," it had "considerable entertainment value as well." Bill Donaldson, "Showcase," *Tulsa Tribune*, Mar. 22, 1969, ORU.

134. Albert E. Bush Interview, Feb. 11, 1983.

135. Bush Interview; Al Bush and Evelyn Roberts, Evangelism of Oral Roberts Class Transcript, 1971, pp. 8–9.

136. Begley, "Christmas Show Next."

137. Ibid.

138. O. Roberts, Devotion Transcript, Dec. 24, 1968, p. 10.

139. "Roberts Ratings: Rising," *Christianity Today*, Jan. 16, 1970, p. 36.

140. J. A. Synan Interview and L. C. Synan Interview, Apr. 16, 1983; Juanita Coe Hope Interview, Dec. 6, 1973; Hoyt Elkins, "It's a Show of Faith," *Sacramento (Calif.) Union*, Aug. 3, 1970, ORU; Evelyn Roberts, *His Darling Wife, Evelyn* (New York: Dell Publishing Co., 1976), p. 230.

141. O. Roberts, Laymen's Seminar Transcript, Nov 7, 1969, p. 14. Oral had long chafed under the narrowness of his pentecostal upbringing. His television program was a public renunciation of the lifestyle, as his change of churches had been a renunciation of the myopia of pentecostal denominationalism.

142. O. Roberts, Banquet Transcript, May 5, 1973, p. 4.

143. Oral Roberts, "The President's Report," *AL*, Feb. 1970, p. 8.

144. "Roberts Ratings: Rising," p. 36.

145. Evelyn Roberts, Chapel Transcript, Apr. 15, 1970, p. 8.

146. O. Roberts, Chapel Transcript, Sept. 23, 1970, p. 12.

147. O. Roberts, Banquet Transcript, May 5, 1973, pp. 3–4.

148. Chapel Transcript, Oct. 13, 1971, p. 11.

149. John Hamill, "Evangelist Roberts Has Hit in 'Contact,'" *Tulsa Tribune*, Aug. 27, 1969, p. 18-D.

150. Bill Donaldson, "Showcase," *Tulsa Tribune*, Apr. 20, 1971, ORU.

151. O. Roberts, OREA Devotion Transcript, Dec. 1, 1972, n.p.

152. O. Roberts and Merv Griffin, Chapel Transcript, Nov. 14, 1974, p. 18.

153. See *Abundant Life* for regular advertisements of the specials—all were widely advertised.

154. O. Roberts, Chapel Transcript, Oct. 13, 1972, p. 6.

155. Hultgren Interview.

156. That move was a significant extension of Richard's visibility in the Roberts ministry. See Yvonne Nance, "ORU World Action Singers," *AL*, May 1970, pp. 2–3; Yvonne Nance, "Behind the Television Camera," *AL*, Nov. 1970, pp. 12–15; Yvonne Nance, "Television—Our Greatest Outreach," pp. 6–9; Patti Roberts with Sherry Andrews, *Ashes to Gold* (Waco, Texas: Word Books [1983]), p. 76; Bill Donaldson, "Showcase," *Tulsa Tribune*, May 25, 1970, p. 14-A.

157. See Bill Donaldson, "Showcase," *Tulsa Tribune*, May 27, 1970, ORU.

158. O. Roberts, Chapel Transcript, Nov. 10, 1972, p. 7.

159. O. Roberts, Chapel Transcript, Dec. 6, 1972, p. 11. One of the cameras was purchased by the university students and was named "Evelyn II." See "$72,827.37 Pledged to Pay for Television Equipment," *Oracle*, Dec. 8, 1972, p. 2; Beth Macklin, "Roberts to Produce TV Shows at ORU," *Tulsa World*, Dec. 28, 1972, ORU.

160. O. Roberts, Chapel Transcript, Nov. 10, 1972, p. 6.

161. OREA Staff Meeting Transcript, Dec. 28, 1973, p. 14.

162. O. Roberts and M. Griffin, Chapel Transcript, Oct. 14, 1974, p. 18.

163. Lowell Noel, "'Oral Roberts and You' Changes Image and Crew," *Oracle*, Jan. 17, 1975, p. 1; Oral Roberts, "February 9th Was a New Day for Us on Television," *AL*, Mar. 1975, pp. 2–3; Smith Interview.

164. O. Roberts, Chapel Transcript, Dec. 6, 1972, p. 4.

165. O. Roberts, "February 9th Was a New Day for Us on Television," pp. 2–3.

166. O. Roberts, My Own Personal Testimony Transcript, Oct. 1970, p. 14.

167. O. Roberts, Chapel Transcript, Oct. 13, 1972, p. 4.

168. Renee Colwill, "Television Special Uses Mabee Center Setting," *Oracle*, Oct. 13, 1972, p. 1.

169. O. Roberts, Chapel Transcript, Dec. 6, 1972, pp. 6–7.

170. See "The Oral Roberts Evangelistic Association, Inc.," *AL*, Apr. 1966, p. 15; "Trustees Hold Meeting in Tulsa," *AL*, Nov. 1961, p. 15; "Here Are Our Trustees," *AL*, Mar. 1962, pp. 20–21.

171. "Oscar Moore Named Administrator," *AL*, May 1960, p. 5; Oscar Moore Interview, Jan. 20, 1983.

172. See "Roberts Aide Resigns," *Tulsa Tribune*, Aug. 23, 1961, ORU; Braxton Interview; Moore Interview; Hope Interview; Hamilton Interview, Jan. 17, 1983; "PR Man Gets Job in Texas," *Tulsa World*, Aug. 15, 1961, ORU.

173. See Lee Braxton and Evelyn Roberts, Evangelism of Oral Roberts Class, 1971, pp. 15–16; Bob Foresman, "He Joined Roberts for $1 a Year," *Tulsa Tribune*, Jan. 8, 1964, p. 37; W. Kevin Armstrong, "Braxton Banks on Books," *Oracle*, Dec. 1981, p. 9.

174. See "Joins ORU," *Tulsa Tribune*, Dec. 12, 1971, p. 18-A; "Engel Given ORU Office," *Tulsa World*, Nov. 16, 1966, ORU.

175. "Team Profiles," *AL*, July 1973, pp. 16–17; Braxton Interview; DeWeese Interview.

176. Oral Roberts, *My Personal Diary of Our Worldwide Ministry* (Tulsa: Oral Roberts, 1968). See William C. Armstrong, "Reaching Out to Souls in a Ministry of Total Evangelism," *AL*, Aug. 1966, pp. 18–23.

177. Armstrong, "Reaching Out to Souls in a Ministry of Total Evangelism," p. 19.

178. See "Roberts Radio Fight Grows," *Tulsa Tribune*, July [n.d.], 1961, ORU; "Oral Roberts Group Drops License Bid," *Tulsa Tribune*, July [n.d.], 1961, ORU; "Radio to Play Big Role in Oral Roberts' Plans," *Tulsa Tribune*, Dec. 11, 1959, ORU.

179. Phil Rounds, "Jesus Happens," *AL*, Apr. 1969, pp. 8–9. See also O. Roberts, "My World Trip for Souls, Part One," p. 7; "The Miracle of Jesus in the Now," *AL*, June 1972, pp. 18–20.

180. See Oral Roberts, "A Personal Statement," *AL*, Nov. 1962, p. 7; Armstrong, "Reaching Out to Souls in a Ministry of Total Evangelism," p. 21.

181. See [Masthead,] *AL*, Oct. 1961, p. 4.

182. Oral Roberts, "The 'New Shape' of Abundant Life Magazine," *AL*, Feb. 1962, p. 2; Robinson Interview.

183. See Wayne A. Robinson, *Oral: The Warm, Intimate, Unauthorized Portrait of a Man of God* (Los Angeles: Acton House [1976]), pp. 99–109; Robinson Interview; Beth Macklin, "State Methodists to Pick District Superintendents," *Tulsa World*, May 13, 1969, ORU.

184. Oral Roberts, "Oral Roberts Tells How the Founding of This Magazine Was Based on a Great Healing," *AL*, Nov. 1969, p. 3.

185. O. Roberts, Faculty Chapel Transcript, Oct. 11, 1974, p. 14.

186. Robinson Interview.

187. O. Roberts, "Oral Roberts Tells How the Founding of This Magazine Was Based on a Great Healing," p. 3.

188. Ken Briggs, "Religious Periodicals Lose Readers," *Tulsa World*, Aug. 6, 1971, ORU.

189. W. P. Sterne, "Meeting the People's Needs in 1960," *AL*, Dec. 1960, p. 16; Al Bush and Evelyn Roberts, Evangelism of Oral Roberts Class Transcript, 1971, pp. 18–19.

190. Robinson, *Oral,* p. 56.

191. "Keeping Posted," *AL*, Mar. 1962, p. 11.

192. Armstrong, "Reaching Out to Souls in a Ministry of Total Evangelism," p. 21.

193. Oral Roberts, "Great Harvest of Souls in India," *AL*, May 1965, p. 11.

194. See O. Roberts, Chapel Transcript, Sept. 1, 1968, p. 9.

195. George Fisher, "Abundant Life Prayer Groups," *OREA Partners,* Mar. 28, 1958, p. 3.

196. "Prayer," *AL*, Apr. 1967, p. 3.

197. See Jo Ann Green, "Prayer Partners Have Secret Place," *Tulsa Tribune*, Jan. 7, 1961, ORU. At least one suicide was prevented by the group in 1969, and thousands of people sent letters of appreciation for assistance received. See "Phone Call Saves California Woman," *Tulsa World,* Oct. 26, 1969, p. 1-B. By 1971, Al Bush estimated that the prayer group was averaging over 700 calls a day. A. Bush and Evelyn Roberts, Evangelism of Oral Roberts Class Transcript, 1971, p. 14.

198. See "Abundant Life Home to Get Five More Stories," unidentified clipping, ORU.

199. Walt Radmilovich, "Abundant Life Building Here Sold," *Tulsa World,* Apr. 8, 1967, ORU; O. Roberts, OREA Staff Meeting Transcript, Oct. 20, 1966, p. 4; "New OREA Building Due," *Tulsa Tribune,* Aug. 3, 1967, ORU.

200. See "ORU Promotions," *Tulsa Tribune,* Nov. 17, 1966, p. 23; "Bush Succeeds Roberts as Head of ORA Board," *Tulsa Tribune,* Jan. 17, 1970, ORU.

201. "Agreements Signed to Form Computer Service Combine," *Tulsa World,* Sept. 21, 1971, p. 1-B.

202. Bush Interview; A. Bush and Evelyn Roberts, Evangelism of Oral Roberts Class Transcript, 1971, p. 4; Robinson Interview.

203. Bush Interview. Others felt that Bush wanted to use his considerable skills to accumulate a personal fortune—a goal which was clearly impossible within the Roberts organization. George Stovall Interview, Jan. 27, 1983.

204. Robinson Interview.

205. Robinson, *Oral,* pp. 120–25; Robinson Interview.

206. Robinson, *Oral,* pp. 120–25.

207. Robinson Interview.

208. Ibid.

209. Wayne A. Robinson, *I Once Spoke in Tongues* (Old Tappan, N.J.: Fleming H. Revell Co., Spire Books, 1975). In the book Robinson spoke well of Oral.

210. Hamilton Interview, Jan. 17, 1983.

211. See Greg Broadd, "New Housing Project Here Unusual," *Tulsa World,* Dec. 21, 1969, ORU; Smith Interview; O. Roberts, University Village Seminar Transcript, June 9, 1970, p. 6.

212. Smith Interview.

213. "ORU Vice President," *Tulsa World,* Dec. 8, 1966, p. 32; Robinson Interview.

214. Robinson Interview.

215. Richard White, "Lose Fat or Job, Staff Told," *Tulsa Tribune,* Mar. 26, 1962, ORU; "Weight Control Program Fair?" *Tulsa Tribune,* Apr. 3, 1962, ORU.

216. Pete Martin, "Oral Roberts," *Christian Herald,* part 2, Mar. 1966, p. 23; V. Synan Interview; Oral Roberts Interview, Sept. 3, 1984.

217. "Bushes Will Lead Kanchi Fund Effort," *Tulsa World,* Mar. 8, 1972, ORU.

218. See Mary Margaret Fallis, "Smiths Vie for National Honors," *Tulsa Tribune,* Aug. 12, 1970, ORU; "Mrs. U.S. Savings Bond Takes Oath," *Tulsa Tribune,* Sept. 16, 1970, ORU.

219. Ronald R. Smith, OREA Staff Meeting Transcript, Dec. 28, 1973, pp. 9–10.

220. O. Roberts, Faculty Chapel Transcript, Nov. 11, 1974, p. 11.

221. See Robinson, *Oral,* pp. 20–28, for a description of the system.

222. A. Bush and Evelyn Roberts, Evangelism of Oral Roberts Class Transcript, 1971, pp. 15–20.

223. Ibid.

224. Bush Interview.

225. O. Roberts, Faculty Chapel Transcript, Nov. 11, 1974, p. 12.

226. A. Bush and Evelyn Roberts, Evangelism of Oral Roberts Class Transcript, 1971, pp. 15–16.

227. Ibid., p. 15.

228. Robinson, *Oral,* pp. 26–27.

229. O. Roberts, Chapel Transcript, Feb. 28, 1969, p. 3.

230. Evelyn Roberts, Chapel Transcript, Apr. 15, 1970, p. 3.

231. O. Roberts, Faculty Chapel Transcript, Nov. 11, 1974, p. 15; O. Roberts, Chapel Transcript, Feb. 28, 1969, p. 3; Robinson, *Oral,* pp. 20–28.

232. Faculty Chapel Transcript, Nov. 11, 1974, p. 20.

233. O. Roberts, Chapel Transcript, Oct. 13, 1971, p. 1.

234. Evelyn Roberts, Chapel Transcript, Apr. 15, 1970, p. 5.

235. O. Roberts, Faculty Chapel Transcript, Nov. 11, 1974, p. 21.

236. O. Roberts, Laymen's Seminar Transcript, Dec. 9, 1963, pp. 91–92.

237. Faculty Chapel Transcript, Nov. 11, 1974, p. 21.

238. O. Roberts, Partners Seminar Transcript, June 14, 1969, pp. 16–18.

239. O. Roberts, Partners Seminar Transcript, Jan. 25, 1969, p. 8.

240. Oral Roberts, "Happy Is the Tither," *AL,* June 1960, p. 4.

241. O. Roberts, "God Has Spoken to Me Again," p. 7.

242. O. Roberts, "Back on Television," p. 5; "Very Personal," *AL,* June 1971, p. 7.

243. O. Roberts, "God Has Spoken to Me Again," p. 7.

244. "Very Personal," p. 7.

245. Oral Roberts, "My Blessing Pact Covenant with God," Booklet (no pub. info.).

246. Oral Roberts, "My Spiritual, Physical, and Financial Blessing-Pact with God," Booklet (no pub. info.).

247. See Oral Roberts, "God's Voice to Me," *AL,* May 1964, pp. 8–11; "Work Has Begun on the Joash Chest!" *AL,* Oct. 1973, p. 21.

248. Robinson, *Oral,* pp. 99–109; David Fritze, "Oral Roberts' Past Is the Reason He Wants a Huge Hospital Built," *Oklahoma Monthly,* Oct. 1977, p. 102; Robinson Interview.

249. See "An Exciting, New Confidential Service for Consecrated Christians," *AL,* May 1965, pp. 20–21; O. Roberts, President's Advisory Cabinet Transcript, May 29, 1965; O. Roberts, Partners Seminar Transcript, Jan. 25, 1969, pp. 1–2.

250. Family Seminar Transcript, Aug. 27, 1978, pp. 7–8.

251. See "Tulsa and ORU" (promotional booklet, no pub. info.); during 1968 and 1969, the Tulsa newspapers frequently printed ads urging people to buy annuities to support ORU.

252. See O. Roberts, Faculty Meeting Transcript, Nov. 9, 1971, pp. 15–16; O. Roberts, Chapel Transcript, Mar. 17, 1971, pp. 3–4; O. Roberts, Chapel Transcript, Apr. 14, 1972, p. 17.

253. O. Roberts, Chapel Transcript, Mar. 17, 1971, p. 5.

254. Oral Roberts, Miscellaneous Speech Transcript, Oct. 3, 1976, pp. 9–10.

255. Robinson, *I Once Spoke in Tongues,* pp. 111–12; Braxton Interview.

256. A. Bush and Evelyn Roberts, Evangelism of Oral Roberts Class Transcript, 1971, p. 20.

257. "The Happy Builders," *AL,* Mar. 1967, pp. 17–20.

258. A. Bush and Evelyn Roberts, Evangelism of Oral Roberts Class Transcript, 1971, p. 21.

259. O. Roberts, Evangelism Unit No. 1 Transcript, 1971, p. 11.

11. MAINSTREAM

1. Charles Farah Interview, Jan. 25, 1983; Larry Douglas Hart, "A Critique of American Pentecostal Theology," Ph.D. dissertation, Southern Baptist Theological Seminary, 1978, p. 157.

2. Vinson Synan, ed., *Aspects of Pentecostal-Charismatic Origins* (Plainfield, N.J.: Logos International, 1975), p. 3; Derek Prince Interview, Jan. 31, 1974.

3. "Fanning the Charismatic Fire," *Christianity Today*, Nov. 24, 1967, ORU.

4. Hart, "A Critique of American Pentecostal Theology," pp. 184–217; Synan, *Pentecostal-Charismatic Origins*, p. 3.

5. See Richard Quebedeaux, *The New Charismatics* (Garden City, N.Y.: Doubleday and Co., 1976), pp. 77–78.

6. Oral Roberts, Room Sponsors Seminar Transcript, May 20, 1963, p. 2; O. Roberts, Ministers Seminar Transcript, Apr. 28, 1963, pp. 6–17.

7. O. Roberts, My Own Personal Testimony Transcript, Oct. 21, 1970, pp. 8–9.

8. See Gordon Lindsay and David du Plessis, "The Astounding Move of God in the Denominational Churches," *Voice of Healing*, Jan. 1960, pp. 4–5, 14–15.

9. O. Roberts, Ministers Seminar Transcript, Jan. 18, 1963, p. 4.

10. O. Roberts, Room Sponsors Seminar Transcript, May 20, 1963, p. 1.

11. John and Elizabeth Sherrill, *The Happiest People on Earth* (Waco, Texas: Chosen Books, 1975).

12. Demos Shakarian Interview, Jan. 27, 1983.

13. See *Ecumenical Education Voice*, May 1967, pp. 8–10; W. J. Hollenweger, *The Pentecostals* (1st U.S. ed.; Minneapolis: Augsburg Publishing House, 1972), pp. 6–7.

14. See "Fanning the Charismatic Fire."

15. Gordon Lindsay, "The Truth about the Present Move of God in the Historical Churches," *Voice of Healing*, Nov. 1961, p. 4.

16. John Maust, "Charismatic Leaders Seeking Faith for Their Own Healing," *Christianity Today*, Apr. 4, 1980, p. 44.

17. Wayne A. Robinson, *I Once Spoke in Tongues* (Old Tappan, N.J.: Fleming H. Revell Co., Spire Books, 1975), p. 112.

18. Oral Roberts, "My World Trip for Souls, Part One," *AL*, Mar. 1965, p. 19; see Doyle Helbling, "International Seminar," *AL*, Feb. 1964, p. 12.

19. William P. Sterne et al., "Ministers' Seminar," *AL*, Apr. 1963, p. 6.

20. See "What Does the Ministry of Oral Roberts Mean to You as a Denominational Pastor?" *AL*, Oct. 1965, pp. 6–9.

21. Robert Voight Interview, Jan. 25, 1983.

22. R. O. Corvin, International Seminar Transcript, Nov. 11, 1963, p. 1; Raymond Othel Corvin, "Religious and Educational Backgrounds in the Founding of Oral Roberts University," Ph.D. dissertation, University of Oklahoma, 1967, pp. 154–55.

23. Helbling, "International Seminar," p. 12; see "Oral Roberts Flying 212 Foreign Delegates Here," *Tulsa Tribune*, Nov. 6, 1963, ORU; "Oral Roberts University," *Pentecost*, Dec. 1963–Feb. 1964, p. 11.

24. "Lord Had ORU Built, Priest Believes," *Tulsa Tribune*, Jan. 13, 1968, ORU.

25. When Oral began teaching his class "The Holy Spirit in the Now," he was assisted by Ervin and Farah. Beth Macklin, "First Endowed Chair Established at ORU," *Tulsa World*, Aug. 12, 1971, p. 1.

26. "God's Work at Oral Roberts University," *New Covenant*, May 1972, p. 11.

27. Vinson Synan Interview, May 22, 1983.

28. Oral Roberts, *The Holy Spirit in the Now* (3 vols.; Tulsa: Oral Roberts University, 1974), vol. 1, p. 49; O. Roberts, Graduate Baccalaureate Transcript, May 30, 1971, n.p.

29. See O. Roberts, Chapel Transcript, Feb. 28, 1969, p. 1.

30. O. Roberts, Kathryn Kuhlman Funeral Service Transcript, Feb. 23, 1976, pp. 4–5.

31. Kathryn Kuhlman, Baccalaureate Address Transcript, May 28, 1972, p. 4.

32. Ibid.; O. Roberts, Kathryn Kuhlman Funeral Service Transcript, Feb. 23, 1976, pp. 4–5; Oral Roberts Interview, Feb. 16, 1983.

33. Calvin Thielman Interview, Apr. 8, 1983.

34. See "Oral Roberts University," *Christianity Today*, Sept. 24, 1965, p. 47; J. I. Packer, "Charismatic Renewal," *Christianity Today*, Mar. 7, 1980, p. 16.

35. Oral Roberts University Dedication Press Conference Transcript, 1967, n.p.

36. For an example of that influence, see O. Roberts, Fifth Avenue Presbyterian Church Transcript, Dec. 9, 1973.

37. O. Roberts, Chapel Transcript, Dec. 5, 1967, pp. 1–2.

38. O. Roberts, Faculty Chapel Transcript, Oct. 28, 1974, p. 11.

39. See Willard Clapton, Jr., "Oral Roberts Calls Evangelists the Leathernecks of the Clergy," (Washington, D.C.) *Post-Times Herald*, Feb. 27, 1967, ORU; "God's Work at Oral Roberts University," *New Covenant*, May 1972, pp. 1–11, 28.

40. O. Roberts, *The Holy Spirit in the Now*, vol. 2, p. 30.

41. See Oral Roberts, "God's Voice to Me," *AL*, May 1964, p. 8.

42. O. Roberts, *The Holy Spirit in the Now*, vol. 2, p. 48.

43. O. Roberts, Crusade Transcript, Aug. 25, 1968, p. 10.

44. O. Roberts, Faculty Orientation Transcript, Aug. 14, 1978, p. 17.

45. V. Synan Interview.

46. Edward B. Fiske, "Oral Roberts and His Skeptics," *New York Times Magazine*, Jan. 3, 1973, p. 26.

47. O. Roberts, Youth Seminar Transcript, July 24, 1965, p. 4.

48. O. Roberts, Contemporary Methods of Evangelism Class Transcript, Oct. 11, 1967, pp. 34–35. See chapter 16 for a fuller discussion of Roberts's theology of the Holy Spirit.

49. Voight Interview; V. Synan Interview; O. Roberts, Contemporary Methods of Evangelism Class Transcript, Oct. 11, 1967, pp. 34–35.

50. V. Synan Interview.

51. O. Roberts, Miscellaneous Speech Transcript, June 6, 1977, p. 11. Charismatic theology remains in flux, searching for the meaning of the pentecostal experience. See Hart, "A Critique of American Pentecostal Theology." While Oral did not formulate a systematic theology in the 1960s and 1970s, he provided an atmosphere of openness for discussion, and he boldly and publicly sought new explanations for what he had inherited.

52. "Oral Roberts Received by City Church," *Tulsa World*, Mar. 18, 1969, ORU.

53. See, for instance, "New Church, Old Voice," *Newsweek*, Apr. 1, 1968, ORU.

54. O. Roberts, Chapel Transcript, Jan. 1968, p. 12.

55. O. Roberts Interview, Feb. 16, 1983. See Wayne A. Robinson, *Oral: The Warm, Intimate, Unauthorized Portrait of a Man of God* (Los Angeles: Acton House [1976]), pp. 72–80.

56. O. Roberts, Crusade Transcript, Aug. 9, 1968, p. 15.

57. Evelyn Roberts, *His Darling Wife, Evelyn* (New York: Dell Publishing Co., 1976), p. 175.

58. "College Dean Fired in Theology Dispute," *Daily Oklahoman* (Oklahoma City), Mar. 23, 1968, ORU.

59. Lee Braxton Interview, Dec. 18, 1973.

60. Harold Paul Interview, Jan. 28, 1983; Evelyn Roberts, *His Darling Wife*, p. 175.

61. Robinson, *Oral*, pp. 80–83.

62. O. Roberts, Crusade Transcript, Aug. 9, 1968, p. 15.

63. See Beth Macklin, "Denomination Bankrupt without Spiritual Formation, Crutchfield Asserts," *Tulsa World*, Dec. 19, 1982, p. 2-B; Robinson, *Oral*, pp. 80–83.

64. See Evelyn Roberts, *His Darling Wife*, p. 170; O. Roberts, Miscellaneous Speech Transcript, June 6, 1977, pp. 18–19; O. Roberts Interview, Feb. 16, 1983.

65. O. Roberts Interview, Feb. 16, 1983.

66. O. Roberts, My Own Personal Testimony Transcript, Oct. 21, 1970, p. 13; O. Roberts, Crusade Transcript, Aug. 9, 1968, pp. 15–16.

67. "ORU to Remain As It Is," *Tulsa Tribune,* Mar. 19, 1968, ORU.

68. Joanne Gordon, "Roberts Explains Church Decision," *Tulsa World,* Mar. 24, 1968, ORU.

69. Ibid.; James Buskirk Interview, Feb. 18, 1983; Farah Interview; Robinson, *Oral,* pp. 84–86.

70. O. Roberts, Crusade Transcript, Aug. 9, 1968, p. 18.

71. Beth Macklin, "Methodist Leaders Urge Closer Ties with Council," *Tulsa World,* May 29, 1968, ORU; Buskirk Interview, Feb. 18, 1983.

72. Nell Jean Boggs, "Roberts May Set Methodists 'On Fire,' Cleric Says," *Tulsa Tribune,* Apr. 6, 1968, ORU.

73. "Methodist Oral Roberts Visits Dallas," *Rockford (Ill.) Star,* May 11, 1968, ORU.

74. "State Methodism's Growth Emphasized," *Tulsa World,* May 28, 1968, ORU.

75. Robinson, *Oral,* p. 87.

76. Boggs, "Roberts May Set Methodists 'On Fire,' Cleric Says."

77. O. Roberts, My Own Personal Testimony Transcript, Oct. 21, 1970, p. 14.

78. O. Roberts, Miscellaneous Speech Transcript, June 6, 1977, p. 7.

79. Edward B. Fiske, "The Oral Roberts Empire," *New York Times Magazine,* Apr. 23, 1973, p. 24.

80. O. Roberts, Chapel Transcript, Jan., 1968, p. 11.

81. See V. Synan Interview.

82. Ibid.; Paul Interview.

83. O. Roberts, Crusade Transcript, Aug. 9, 1968, p. 17.

84. Carl Hamilton Interview, Jan. 13, 1983.

85. O. Roberts, My Own Personal Testimony Transcript, Oct. 21, 1970, pp. 11–13.

86. O. Roberts Interview, Feb. 16, 1983; Albert E. Bush Interview, Feb. 11, 1983. Hamilton Interview, Jan. 13, 1983; O. Roberts, Address to Law Students Transcript, Apr. 5, 1982; Evelyn Roberts, *His Darling Wife,* p. 167.

87. "ORU Building Fund Lack Halts Work," *Tulsa World,* June 7, 1968, ORU.

88. O. Roberts, Address to Law Students Transcript, Apr. 5, 1982, p. 6.

89. Ronald R. Smith, OREA Staff Meeting Transcript. Dec. 28, 1973, p. 3; Evelyn Roberts, *His Darling Wife,* p. 167; Bush Interview.

90 Oral Roberts, *The Call* (New York: Doubleday and Co., 1972), p. 126.

91. Evelyn Roberts, *His Darling Wife,* p. 167.

92. V. Synan Interview.

93. O. Roberts, My Own Personal Testimony Transcript, Oct. 21, 1970, p. 13.

94. Historian Vinson Synan has noted both the strong historical ties of the Pentecostal Holiness church to Methodist theology and the tendency of those leaving the denomination to go into the Methodist church. See V. Synan, *Pentecostal-Charismatic Origins;* V. Synan Interview.

95. O. Roberts, Miscellaneous Speech Transcript, Feb. 17, 1970, n.p.

96. Hamilton Interview, Jan. 17, 1983.

97. O. Roberts, Miscellaneous Speech Transcript, June 6, 1977, p. 16; Oral Roberts Interview, Feb. 16, 1983.

98. Fiske, "The Oral Roberts Empire," p. 17; Evelyn Roberts, *His Darling Wife,* p. 171; "Oklahoma's Orbit," *Magazine of the Sunday Oklahoman* (Oklahoma City), May 5, 1968, pp. 4, 6.

99. O. Roberts, Chapel Transcript, Sept. 1, 1968, p. 13.

100. John Dart, "Freer Views on Charisma," *Los Angeles Times,* [unidentified clipping,] ORU.

101. "God Is in the Now," *Texas Methodist,* Mar. 24, 1972, ORU.

102. O. Roberts, Chapel Transcript, Jan. 1968, p. 5.

103. O. Roberts, Miscellaneous Speech Transcript, Feb. 17, 1970, n.p.

104. See "Oklahoma's Orbit," p. 5.

105. O. Roberts, My Own Personal Testimony Transcript, Oct, 2, 1970, p. 11.

106. "Oral Roberts to Become Methodist Minister," *Texas Methodist,* Mar. 29, 1968. ORU.

107. Joanne Gordon, "Roberts Explains Church Decision," p. 27.

108. "Roberts to Be Methodist Pastor," *Tulsa Tribune,* Mar. 18, 1968, ORU.

109. O. Roberts, Miscellaneous Speech Transcript, Feb. 17, 1970, n.p.

110. O. Roberts, Crusade Transcript, Aug. 9, 1968, p. 15.

111. "Methodists Act on Oral Today," *Daily Oklahoman* (Oklahoma City), May 28, 1968, ORU.

112. See chapter 16 for further discussion of Roberts's understanding of God's supernatural leadings.

113. O. Roberts, Laymen's Seminar Transcript, Dec. 6, 1963, p. 16.

114. O. Roberts, Crusade Transcript, Aug. 25, 1968, p. 14.

115. Pete Martin, "Oral Roberts, Part II," *Christian Herald,* Mar. 1966, p. 24.

116. "Pentecostal Winds of Change," *Pentecost,* Mar.-May 1964, p. 17.

117. Carl F. H. Henry, "Pentecostal Meeting Makes Holy Land History," *Christianity Today,* May 22, 1961, p. 30; Hollenweger, *The Pentecostals,* pp. 357–58.

118. See *International Healing Magazine,* Feb. 1962, to *Christian Challenge,* July 1962. The magazine changed names in June 1962.

119. Juanita Coe Hope Interview, Dec. 6, 1973.

120. Oscar Moore Interview, Jan. 20, 1983; Donald Moyers Interview, Dec. 13, 1983. The articles were allegedly sent to several popular magazines, which rejected them as too controversial. Bob Foresman Interview, Dec. 13, 1983; Robinson, *Oral,* p. 56.

121. Hope Interview.

122. G. H. Montgomery, "Enemies of the Cross of Christ," *International Healing Magazine,* Feb. 1962, p. 3.

123. G. H. Montgomery, "Their Glory Is Their Shame," *International Healing Magazine,* Mar. 1962, pp. 3, 10.

124. G. H. Montgomery, "A Lying Spirit in the Mouth of the Prophets," *International Healing Magazine,* Apr. 1962, pp. 6–7, 14.

125. G. H. Montgomery, "Making Merchandise of You," *International Healing Magazine,* May 1962, pp. 14–15.

126. G. H. Montgomery, "Where Do We Go from Here?" *Christian Challenge,* July 1962, p. 14.

127. Pete Martin, "Oral Roberts," *Christian Herald,* Feb. 1966, p. 110; Fiske, "The Oral Roberts Empire," p. 24.

128. Noel Smith, "What Noel Thinks of Oral," *Missouri Leader and Press* (Springfield), Feb. 6, 1972, ORU.

129. "Evangelist Begins Crusade," *Yakima (Wash.) Herald,* Sept. 2, 1961, p. 5.

130. See "Youth Dies Waiting for Evangelist 'Cure,'" *Las Vegas Review-Journal,* May 5, 1961, ORU; Lester Kinsolving, "Inside Religion," *Davis (Calif.) Enterprise,* Oct. 9, 1973, ORU; Joseph Lewis, "Faith Healing Is a Big Fraud!" *National Insider,* Aug. 7, 1966, p. 7.

131. O. Roberts, Youth Seminar Transcript, June 19, 1963, p. 45; O. Roberts, *The Call,* pp. 57–61.

132. Marvin D. Callaway, "Oral Roberts Ducks Issue," *Portland Oregonian,* Sept. 7, 1966, ORU.

133. "People's Forum," *Tulsa Tribune,* June 11, 1963, ORU. There was little doubt in the early 1960s that the "evangelism of Oral Roberts involves controversy and big money." Fred Kiewit, "Evangelism of Oral Roberts Involves Controversy and Big Money," *Kansas City (Mo.) Star,* July 2, 1961, ORU.

134. "Frenzy of Faith in a Man's Touch," *Life,* Aug. 3, 1962, pp. 12–21.

135. Jenkin Lloyd Jones, "On Brother Roberts," *Tulsa Tribune,* Aug. 2, 1962, ORU.

136. Moyers Interview.

137. O. Roberts, Regents Seminar Transcript, Nov. 26, 1962, n.p.

138. Robinson, *Oral,* p. 69.

139. Jenkin Lloyd Jones, "On Brother Roberts." For Oral's private reaction to the editorial, see O. Roberts, Regents Seminar Transcript, Nov. 26, 1962, n.p.

140. See "8,000 Attend Second Session of Oral Roberts Crusade Here," *Kokomo (Ind.) Tribune,* Aug. 18, 1966, ORU; "An Episcopal Rector Attends His First Crusade," *AL,* Apr. 1967, pp. 12–13.

141. Oral Roberts Interview, Feb. 16, 1983.

142. Fiske, "The Oral Roberts Empire," pp. 15, 16.

143. Jim Henderson, "Oral Roberts Hit by Media 'Boom,' " *Tulsa World,* Feb. 12, 1972, ORU.

144. Wayne Robinson Interview, Apr. 4, 1983; Robinson, *Oral,* pp. 138–46.

145. See "Oral Roberts University Has Grown in 7 Years," *New York Times,* June 13, 1972, sec. 2, p. 1; Larry Van Dyne, "God and Man at Oral Roberts," *Chronicle of Higher Education,* Dec. 8, 1975, pp. 3–4.

146. O. Roberts, OREA Devotion Transcript, Dec. 1, 1972, n.p.

147. Henderson, "Oral Roberts Hit by Media 'Boom.' "

148. William Willoughby, "Oral Roberts: Rousing Return to TV," *Christianity Today,* Mar. 28, 1969, p. 40.

149. "Oral Roberts Praised Highly in Magazine Article," *Tulsa Tribune,* Jan. 31, 1966, ORU.

150. Fiske, "The Oral Roberts Empire," p. 15.

151. Lonnie Meachum, "Pull Up a Chair," *Batesville (Ark.) Guard,* Jan. 27, 1972, ORU.

152. Henderson, "Oral Roberts Hit by Media 'Boom.' "

153. Tom Tiede, "Faith Healing, 1970 Style," *Alameda (Calif.) Times Star,* Sept. 10, 1970, ORU.

154. See note 57.

155. "Who's Proud of Whom?" *Southside Times* (Tulsa), [unidentified clipping, 1963,] ORU.

156. "Our Rudderless Youth," *Tulsa Tribune,* May 13, 1961, ORU.

157. "Good Luck to ORU!" *Tulsa World,* Sept. 7, 1965, p. 14.

158. "Our New University," *Tulsa Tribune,* Mar. 16, 1965, ORU.

159. O. Roberts Chapel Transcript, Nov. 15, 1967, pp. 18–19. For a notice of Roberts's speech before the Oklahoma Press Association, see Robert V. Peterson, "Speech by Tulsa's Oral Roberts Impresses Newsmen," *Durant (Okla.) Democrat,* Feb. 4, 1966, ORU.

160. See Bob Foresman, "Oral Roberts Organization Good for Tulsa," *Tulsa Tribune,* July 18, 1970, p. 2-B.

161. O. Roberts, Commencement Address Transcript, May 24, 1970, p. 3.

162. "Tulsa 'Mecca' for Conservative Folks," *Wichita (Kan.) Beacon,* Oct. 1, 1971, ORU. See also "Conservative Religions Find Refuge in Southwestern City," *Grit,* Apr. 30, 1972, p. 7.

163. Beth Macklin, "America Faces Crisis, Roberts Warns," *Tulsa World,* May 3, 1967, ORU.

164. "A Guest Editorial," *Tulsa Tribune,* Sept. 9, 1965, ORU.

165. Warren Hultgren Interview, Mar. 30, 1983.

166. Jenkin Lloyd Jones Interview, Mar. 31, 1983.

167. Bob Foresman, "Economic Value of ORU Is Told," *Tulsa Tribune,* Dec. 8, 1966, ORU. See also "Financial Impact Is Seen in ORU's Dedication Rites," *Tulsa World,* Apr. 4, 1967, ORU; "ORU's Value to Community Stressed," *Tulsa Tribune,* Aug. 2, 1967, ORU.

168. Bob Foresman, "Oral Roberts Organization Good for Tulsa."

169. O. Roberts, Commencement Address Transcript, May 2, 1976, p. 3.

170. John Williams Interview, Mar. 30, 1983.

171. "A Contribution to His People," *AL,* Oct. 1963, pp. 21–23; "Civitans Name Oral 'Citizen of the Year,' " *Tulsa World,* June 3, 1966, ORU.

172. See "Oral Roberts to Chair Membership Drive Aimed at Adding 500 to C-C List," *Tulsa Magazine,* May 12, 1966, p. 1; "Roberts Gets Seat on Board of NBT," *Tulsa World,* Nov. 15, 1969; ORU; "Oral Roberts Is Named to 'Hall' Board," *Tulsa Tribune,* Jan. 13, 1971, ORU; "Seven Sooners Due Hall of Fame Induction," *Oklahoma City Oklahoman,* Apr. 30, 1972, ORU; Denise Gaither, "Roberts Named Top Oklahoman," *Oracle,* Jan. 25, 1974, p. 1.

173. The transcripts of Roberts's speeches during these years are evidence of the diverse invitations he received.

174. O. Roberts, Chapel Transcript, Nov. 10, 1972, p. 7.

175. The World Action Singers, directed by Ralph Carmichael, appeared on the "Joey Bishop Show" in December 1968, before the specials were aired.

176. "Dick Cavett's Tough Questions," *AL,* June 1970, pp. 10–12.

177. Merv Griffin, Chapel Transcript, Nov. 14, 1974, pp. 4–5.

178. Jim Henderson, "Bob Hope Tees Off on Agnew," *Tulsa World,* May 16, 1972, pp. 1-B, 6-B.

179. "Round the Clock," *Tulsa World,* Sept. 24, 1969, ORU.

180. O. Roberts, Chapel Transcript, Dec. 6, 1972, p. 12.

181. Ibid., p. 11.

182. "Round the Clock."

183. "Over the Coffee Cup," *Enid (Okla.) Morning News,* Sept. 25, 1975, ORU.

184. Carl Albert, Chapel Transcript, Nov. 13, 1967, p. 2.

185. Sherrill, *The Happiest People on Earth,* p. 177.

186. O. Roberts, Graduation Address Transcript, May 30, 1971, p. 1; "Henry Bellmon Speaks on Moral Majority Issue," *Sapulpa (Okla.) Herald,* Oct. 10, 1980, ORU.

187. Wallis Henley, "President Prays in His Office during Visit by Oral Roberts," *Birmingham (Ala.) News,* Mar. 2, 1973, p. 10.

188. O. Roberts, Faculty Luncheon Transcript, Aug. 22, 1972, pp. 8–12; see also "Roberts Offers Nixon Invitation," *Oracle,* Sept. 15, 1972, pp. 1, 3.

189. O. Roberts, Chapel Transcript, Oct. 13, 1972, p. 6; O. Roberts, OREA Devotion Transcript, Dec. 1, 1972, n.p.

190. O. Roberts, Faculty Chapel Transcript, Oct. 28, 1974, p. 12.

191. O. Roberts, Chapel Transcript, Jan. 26, 1973, pp. 1–2.

192. Ibid., pp. 2–5.

193. "George Wallace Receives Special Prayer during Chapel," *Oracle,* Sept. 22, 1972, p. 2.

194. O. Roberts, Chapel Transcript, Sept. 13, 1972, pp. 6–7.

195. O. Roberts, Chapel Transcript, Dec. 5, 1967, p. 3.

12. PRIVATE SIDE

1. Bill Leonard, "Roberts Resents 'Faith Healer' Label," *Hutchinson (Kan.) News,* Nov. 25, 1961, ORU.

2. Steve Durasoff and Evelyn Roberts, Evangelism of Oral Roberts Class Transcript, 1971, p. 13.

3. O. Roberts, Faculty Meeting Transcript, Feb. 4, 1971, p. 4.

4. Ron Smith Interview, Feb. 24, 1983.

5. "Mike Douglas Show," *AL,* Dec. 1970, p. 10.

6. Nell Boggs, "Oral Roberts," *Tulsa Magazine,* June 1969, pp. 21–22.

7. Yvonne Litchfield, "This Is Mrs. Oral Roberts, Believer in Love at First Sight," *Tulsa World,* Feb. 15, 1967, ORU.

8. Boggs, "Oral Roberts," pp. 21–22.

9. Bob Hartzell, "12-Handicapper Draws Big Gallery," *Tulsa Tribune*, May 16, 1972, ORU.

10. Paul Galloway, "The Healer as Teacher and Golfer," *Chicago Sun Times*, Nov. 5, 1972, p. 36.

11. Jerry Le Blanc, "Oral (Whrr, Beep) Roberts," *Chicago Tribune*, Apr. 9, 1972, p. 50.

12. Edward B. Fiske, "The Oral Roberts Empire," *New York Times Magazine*, Apr. 22, 1973, ORU.

13. Fred Kiewit, "Evangelism of Oral Roberts Involves Controversy and Big Money," *Kansas City (Mo.) Star*, July 2, 1961, ORU.

14. Le Blanc, "Oral (Whrr, Beep) Roberts."

15. O. Roberts, Chapel Transcript, Nov. 15, 1967; Evelyn Roberts, *His Darling Wife, Evelyn* (New York: Dell Publishing Co., 1976), p. 150.

16. Donald Moyers Interview, Dec. 13, 1983.

17. O. Roberts, Chapel Transcript, Nov. 15, 1967, p. 22; Oral Roberts Interview, Sept. 3, 1984.

18. Oral Roberts, *The Call* (New York: Doubleday and Co., 1972), p. 159; Moyers Interview.

19. Moyers Interview.

20. See Evelyn Roberts, *His Darling Wife*, pp. 150–52; O. Roberts, Chapel Transcript, Nov. 15, 1967, pp. 21–22; Edmund Willingham, "Oral Roberts Plans to Die a 'Poor Man,'" *Nashville Tennessean*, May 3, 1964, p. 6–F; David Fritze, "The Gold and the Glory," *Oklahoma Monthly*, Oct. 1977, p. 98.

21. Demos Shakarian, Regents Seminar Transcript, Nov. 28, 1962, p. 9.

22. Wayne A. Robinson, *Oral: The Warm, Intimate, Unauthorized Portrait of a Man of God*, (Los Angeles: Acton House, [1976]), pp. 46–48.

23. Pete Martin, "Oral Roberts," *Christian Herald*, Feb. 1966, pp. 95–96.

24. O. Roberts, Chapel Transcript, Nov. 15, 1967, p. 22.

25. See O. Roberts, Banquet Transcript, Aug. 21, 1972, p. 7; O. Roberts, Chapel Transcript, Aug. 24, 1977, pp. 18–19.

26. Evelyn Roberts Interview, Apr. 3, 1984.

27. Robinson, *Oral*, pp. 46–47, 111–14; O. Roberts Interview, Sept. 3, 1984.

28. Wayne Robinson Interview, Apr. 4, 1983; Smith Interview; Albert E. Bush Interview, Feb. 11, 1983.

29. Robinson, *Oral*, pp. 14–18.

30. O. Roberts, Regents Seminar Transcript, Nov. 1962, pp. 9–10.

31. Evelyn Roberts Interview, Apr. 3, 1984; O. Roberts, Chapel Transcript, Aug. 24, 1977, p. 18.

32. O. Roberts, Chapel Transcript, Aug. 24, 1977, p. 18.

33. Yvonne Nance, "Evelyn Roberts," *AL*, May 1965, p. 23.

34. Ibid.; Litchfield, "This Is Mrs. Oral Roberts."

35. O. Roberts, Crusade Transcript, Aug. 25, 1968, pp. 1–2.

36. Nance, "Evelyn Roberts," p. 23.

37. Ibid.

38. Ibid.

39. "Oral Roberts Organization Good for Tulsa," *Tulsa Tribune*, July 18, 1970, p. 2–B.

40. "The New Oral Roberts University of Evangelism Is Part of What God Told Us Would Come to Pass," *AL*, June 1962, p. 4.

41. O. Roberts, Memorial Service for E. M. Roberts Transcript, Nov. 20, 1967, p. 11.

42. O. Roberts, University Village Seminar Transcript, June 9, 1970, p. 4.

43. Nance, "Evelyn Roberts," p. 23.

44. Evelyn Roberts, *His Darling Wife*, p. 143.

45. O. Roberts, Crusade Transcript, Aug. 25, 1968, p. 1.

46. Ibid.

47. Roberta Roberts Potts Interview, Dec. 13, 1983.

48. Evelyn Roberts, Miscellaneous Speech Transcript, Mar. 2, 1974, p. 24.

49. "Greetings from Our Growing Family to Yours This New Year," *AL*, Jan. 1970, p. 14.

50. Roberta Roberts Potts Interview, Mar. 5, 1984, telephone.

51. Richard Roberts, Partners Seminar Transcript, Oct. 1, 1976, p. 4.

52. Richard Roberts Interview, Mar. 31, 1983.

53. See "Dick Cavett's Tough Questions," *AL*, June 1970, p. 12.

54. Evelyn Roberts Interview, Nov. 1, 1983.

55. O. Roberts, Ministers Seminar Transcript, Jan. 20, 1963, p. 13.

56. Evelyn Roberts Interview, Nov. 1, 1983.

57. Richard Roberts Interview, Mar. 31, 1983.

58. Evelyn Roberts, *His Darling Wife*, p. 130.

59. Richard Roberts, Chapel Transcript, Apr. 25, 1979, n.p.

60. Evelyn Roberts, *His Darling Wife*, pp. 131–32.

61. O. Roberts, Chapel Transcript, Sept. 23, 1970, p. 6.

62. Evelyn Roberts, *His Darling Wife*, p. 132.

63. Richard Roberts, Partners Seminar Transcript, Oct. 1, 1976, p. 5.

64. Ibid.; Evelyn Roberts, *His Darling Wife*, p. 132; Elviretta Walker, "Evangelist's Wife Shuns Limelight," *Oklahoma City Journal*, July 29, 1967, ORU.

65. Richard Roberts, Faculty Orientation Transcript, Aug. 20, 1974, p. 37.

66. Yvonne Nance, "We Are Learning We Can Count on God," *AL*, Aug. 1969, p. 14.

67. Yvonne Nance, "From Broadway to Christ," *AL*, Sept. 1966, p. 20; Oral Roberts, "The Brazil Story," *AL*, Nov. 1966, pp. 2–14.

68. Faculty Orientation Transcript, Aug. 20, 1974, pp. 36–37.

69. Richard Roberts, Partners Seminar Transcript, Oct. 1, 1976, pp. 5–6.

70. Patti Roberts with Sherry Andrews, *Ashes to Gold* (Waco, Texas: Word Books [1983]), pp. 52–53.

71. Ibid.

72. Partners Seminar Transcript, Oct. 1, 1976, pp. 5–6.

73. Nance, "We Are Learning We Can Count on God," pp. 14–16.

74. Ibid., p. 16; Patti Roberts, *Ashes to Gold*, pp. 61–63.

75. Patti Roberts, *Ashes to Gold*, p. 55.

76. Ibid., p. 62.

77. "Richard Roberts," *AL*, Dec. 1969, pp. 6–8.

78. Robinson, *Oral*, pp. 132–33.

79. See Evelyn Roberts, *His Darling Wife*, pp. 133–35.

80. "ORU Coed Engaged to Richard Roberts," *Tulsa Tribune*, Oct. 18, 1968, ORU.

81. Patti Roberts, *Ashes to Gold*, pp. 73–76.

82. "Greetings from Our Growing Family to Yours This New Year," p. 15.

83. Evelyn Roberts Interview, Nov. 1, 1983.

84. "Patti Roberts," *Oracle*, Nov. 17, 1972, p. 5.

85. Patti Roberts, *Ashes to Gold*, pp. 82–83.

86. "Patti Roberts."

87. Ibid.

88. Patti Roberts, *Ashes to Gold*, p. 97.

89. Genelle Richards, "Patty's Life Exciting," *Tulsa Tribune*, Oct. 5, 1972, p. 1-B.

90. Evelyn Roberts, Miscellaneous Speech Transcript, Mar. 2, 1974, p. 24.

91. Moyers Interview.

92. See David D. Ryan, "Oral Roberts' Son Says His Father's Power Is Prayer," *Richmond (Va.) Times Dispatch*, Feb. 7, 1970, ORU.

93. Phil Clark, "Arena of Love," *AL*, Mar. 1964, p. 11; "To My Wife and Children," *AL*, June 1967, p. 21; Oral Roberts, "The Roberts Children Really Tell It Like It Js," Sept. 1972, p. 14.

94. Ryan, "Oral Roberts' Son Says His Father's Power Is Prayer."

95. Ibid.

96. Ibid.

97. Evelyn Roberts, Miscellaneous Speech Transcript, Mar. 2, 1972, pp. 21–22; Evelyn Roberts Interview, Nov. 1, 1983.

98. Robinson Interview.

99. See O. Roberts, Ministers Seminar Transcript, Jan. 19, 1963, pp. 39–41; O. Roberts, *The Call*, pp. 17–20.

100. Yvonne Nance, "To the Partners," *AL*, May 1964, p. 22.

101. Evelyn Roberts Interview, Nov. 1, 1983.

102. Nance, "Evelyn Roberts," p. 24.

103. Robinson, *Oral*, p. 133.

104. "Miss Carol Croskery Marries R. D. Roberts," *Tulsa World*, March [n.d.] 1967, ORU.

105. Walker, "Evangelist's Wife Shuns Limelight."

106. "Wins Scholarship," *Tulsa Tribune*, Feb. 27, 1970, ORU.

107. "Greetings from Our Growing Family to Yours This New Year," p. 15.

108. Evelyn Roberts, Miscellaneous Speech Transcript, Mar. 2, 1974, pp. 22–23.

109. Robinson, *Oral*, pp. 133–34.

110. Evelyn Roberts, Miscellaneous Speech Transcript, Mar. 2, 1974, pp. 22–23; Evelyn Roberts Interview, Nov. 1, 1983.

111. Evelyn Roberts, Salvation Army Meeting Transcript, Mar. 17, 1973, p. 3.

112. "To My Wife and Children," p. 21.

113. Walker, "Evangelist's Wife Shuns Limelight."

114. Don Bachelder, "Business World," *Tulsa World*, Jan. 2, 1972, ORU.

115. "$10,000 Chapel Gift Announced," *Tulsa Tribune*, Mar. 26, 1970, ORU.

116. Smith Interview.

117. Evelyn Roberts, Miscellaneous Speech Transcript, Mar. 2, 1974, p. 21.

118. Evelyn Roberts, Faculty Orientation Transcript, Aug. 18, 1975, p. 37.

119. O. Roberts, Ministers Seminar Transcript, Jan. 19, 1963, p. 42.

Part IV

PROLOGUE
Tulsa and Palm Springs, February 1977

1. "In Loving Memory of Our Daughter and Son-In-Law," *AL*, Apr. 1977, pp. 3–9; Collins Steele Interview, Jan. 13, 1983; Oral Roberts Interview, Feb. 16, 1983.

2. Bill Nash Interview, Apr. 2, 1984; "Order Issued on Nash Estate Distribution," *Tulsa Tribune*, May 8, 1979, ORU.

3. B. Nash Interview.

4. Evelyn Roberts, *Coping with Grief* (Tulsa: Oral Roberts Evangelistic Association, 1979), p. 12.

5. B. Nash Interview.

6. "In Loving Memory of Our Daughter and Son-In-Law," pp. 5–6.

7. Donald Moyers Interview, Dec. 13, 1983.

8. B. Nash Interview.

9. Oral Roberts, Family Seminar Transcript, Feb. 19, 1977, pp. 11–12; B. Nash Interview.

10. "In Loving Memory of Our Daughter and Son-In-Law," p. 9; see also p. 3; "Nash's 'Home Coming' Is Celebrated Feb. 14," *Oracle*, Feb. 18, 1977, p. 2; Nicki Van Deventer, "No Miracle Cure for Grief," *Tulsa Tribune*, Aug. 4, 1977, pp. 1-A, 4-A.

11. "In Loving Memory of Our Daughter and Son-In-Law," p. 4.

12. Van Deventer, "No Miracle Cure for Grief," p. 1-A.

13. Evelyn Roberts, *Coping with Grief,* p. 1.

14. O. Roberts, Miscellaneous Speech Transcript, June 6, 1977, p. 12.

15. Oral Roberts Interview, Feb. 16, 1983.

16. Ibid.; O. Roberts, Miscellaneous Speech Transcript, June 6, 1977, p. 12; Oral Roberts, " 'I Will Rain upon Your Desert,' " *AL,* Oct. 1977, p. 3.

17. Evelyn Roberts, *Coping with Grief,* pp. 3–4.

18. "In Loving Memory of Our Daughter and Son-In-Law," p. 5.

19. O. Roberts, Church Sermon Transcript, Dec. 17, 1976, p. 7; O. Roberts, Chapel Transcript, Dec. 3, 1976, pp. 6–8.

20. O. Roberts, Miscellaneous Speech Transcript, June 6, 1977, p. 13.

21. Evelyn Roberts, *Coping with Grief,* p. 4.

22. Bernadette Pruitt, "Child's Question Spins Heavenly Book," *Tulsa World,* Apr. 15, 1979, ORU.

23. O. Roberts, Laymen's Seminar Transcript, June 19, 1981. p. 29.

24. B. Nash Interview.

25. Evelyn Roberts, *Coping with Grief,* p. 11.

26. Evelyn Roberts Interview, Apr. 3, 1984.

27. Ibid.

28. O. Roberts, " 'I Will Rain upon Your Desert,' " pp. 2–5, 7–13.

29. Ibid., p. 4; O. Roberts, Dedication Transcript, Nov. 1, 1981, pp. 13–14.

30. O. Roberts, " 'I Will Rain upon Your Desert,' " p. 5.

31. Evelyn Roberts Interview, Apr. 3, 1983; James Winslow Interview, Feb. 4, 1983; Frank Wallace Interview, Feb. 18, 1983.

32. Winslow Interview.

33. C. Thomas Thompson Interview, Feb. 2, 1983; Jerry Sholes, *Give Me That Prime-Time Religion* (New York: Hawthorn Books [1979]), pp. 191–207.

34. Evelyn Roberts Interview, Apr. 3, 1984.

35. O. Roberts, Chapel Transcript, Feb. 4, 1977, pp. 9–12.

36. Evelyn Roberts Interview, Apr. 3, 1984; Winslow Interview.

37. O. Roberts, Chapel Transcript, Feb. 4, 1977, pp. 16–17.

38. "Oral Roberts and You" Telecast, Nov. 15, 1981.

39. Evelyn Roberts, *Coping with Grief,* p. 11.

13. MAELSTROM

1. Demos Shakarian Interview, Jan. 27, 1983.

2. See George Stovall, "For the First Time Here Is the Personal Account of Oral Roberts' Healing," *AL,* June 1979, pp. 12–13.

3. Oral Roberts, OREA Devotion Transcript, Mar. 25, 1982, pp. 11–12; see also E. M. and Claudius Roberts, *Our Ministry and Our Son Oral* (Tulsa: Oral Roberts, 1960), p. 70; Oral Roberts, *My Personal Diary of Our Worldwide Ministry* (Tulsa: Oral Roberts, 1968), p. 52.

4. Evelyn Roberts, "Bloom Where You're Planted," *AL,* Apr. 1978, p. 16.

5. See Evelyn Roberts, *How to Raise Your Children in God's Love* (Tulsa: Oral Roberts Evangelistic Association, 1982).

6. Bill Nash Interview, Apr. 2, 1984.

7. Evelyn Roberts Interview, Nov. 1, 1983.

8. "R. D. Roberts Pleads Guilty to Drug Count," *Tulsa World,* Dec. 19, 1981, p. 2-A; Evelyn Roberts Interview, Nov. 1, 1983.

9. Wayne Robinson Interview, Apr. 4, 1983.

10. B. Nash Interview; Evelyn Roberts Interview, Nov. 1, 1983.

11. Richard Roberts Interview, Mar. 31, 1983.

12. O. Roberts, Chapel Transcript, Sept. 23, 1970, pp. 7–9; Robinson Interview.

13. O. Roberts Miscellaneous Speech Transcript, Jan. 11, 1982, pp. 2–3.

14. O. Roberts Banquet Transcript, Feb. 6, 1982, p. 24.

15. Evelyn Roberts, OREA Devotion Transcript, Mar. 25, 1982, p. 15.

16. Evelyn Roberts Interview, Nov. 1, 1983.

17. B. Nash Interview.

18. "Memorial Service Held for Roberts," *Communique,* Summer 1982, p. 7.

19. Richard Roberts Interview, Mar. 31 1983; George Stovall Interview, Jan. 27, 1983.

20. "Memorial Service Held for Roberts," p. 7.

21. Charles Farah Interview, Jan. 25, 1983.

22. Ibid.; Howard Ervin Interview, Jan. 25, 1983.

23. O. Roberts, Chapel Transcript, June 16, 1982, p. 3.

24. Ibid., p. 15.

25. Ibid., p. 17.

26. Evelyn Roberts Interview, Feb. 16, 1983.

27. Evelyn Roberts, "Life Changing Experiences," *AL,* Aug. 1983, p. 4.

28. O. Roberts, Chapel Transcript, pp. 12–13.

29. Evelyn Roberts Interview, Feb. 16, 1983.

30. O. Roberts, Chapel Transcript, pp. 11–12.

31. Richard Roberts Interview, Mar. 31, 1983.

32. O. Roberts, Faculty Orientation Transcript, Aug. 18, 1975, pp. 31–33.

33. Janelle Hirchert, "Busy Patti Roberts Thinks Positive," (Champaign, Ill.) *News Gazette,* Aug. 24, 1976, p. 10-A.

34. Patti Roberts with Sherry Andrews, *Ashes to Gold* (Waco, Texas: Word Books [1983]), p. 20.

35. Ibid., pp. 96–97.

36. Ibid., pp. 20–21, 57.

37. Ibid., p. 72.

38. Roberta Roberts Potts Interview, Dec. 13, 1983.

39. Evelyn Roberts Interview, Nov. 1, 1983.

40. "Patti to Spice Spring Banquet," *Oracle,* Apr. 7, 1978, p. 1.

41. Jacquelyn Boucher, "Exploring Her Potential Is a New Goal for Patti Roberts," *Tulsa Tribune,* Apr. 13, 1978, ORU.

42. Ibid.

43. "Richard Discusses ORU," *Communique,* Winter 1978, p. 4.

44. "Patti Ready for Concert Ministry in Middle East," *Oracle,* Apr. 14, 1978, pp. 1, 5.

45. Patti Roberts, *Ashes to Gold,* pp. 124–25, 127; Richard Roberts Interview, Sept. 5, 1984.

46. Evelyn Roberts, Salvation Army Speech Transcript, Mar. 17, 1973, p. 8.

47. See Evelyn Roberts, *His Darling Wife, Evelyn* (New York: Dell Publishing Co. [1976]), p. 236.

48. Evelyn Roberts, Faculty Orientation Transcript, Aug. 18, 1975, p. 35.

49. Patti Roberts, *Ashes to Gold,* pp. 101–102.

50. O. Roberts, Kathryn Kuhlman Funeral Service Transcript, Feb. 23, 1976, pp. 8–9; see also Oral Roberts, "A Tribute to Kathryn Kuhlman," *AL,* May 1976, pp. 2–5.

51. Patti Roberts, *Ashes to Gold,* pp. 87, 93, 119.

52. Donald Moyers Interview, Dec. 13, 1983.

53. Ibid.

54. Richard Roberts Interviews, Mar. 31, 1983; Sept. 5, 1984.

55. Potts Interview; Evelyn Roberts Interview, Nov. 1, 1983.

56. Stovall Interview; Potts Interview; Farah Interview.

57. Potts Interview; Evelyn Roberts Interview, Nov. 1, 1983.

58. See Patti Roberts, *Ashes to Gold,* p. 93; Evelyn Roberts Interview, Nov. 1, 1983.

59. "Evangelist's Son Sued for Divorce," *Tulsa World,* Mar. 9, 1979, ORU; "Patti

Roberts Seeks Divorce," *Tulsa Tribune,* Mar. 9, 1979, ORU; "Patti, Richard Roberts Divorce Granted," *Tulsa World,* Mar. 10, 1979, ORU; "Roberts Divorce Granted," *Tulsa Tribune,* Mar. 10, 1979, ORU.

60. "Evangelist's Son Sued for Divorce."

61. "Patti, Richard Roberts Divorce Granted."

62. Patti Roberts, *Ashes to Gold,* pp. 135–36; Richard Roberts Interview, Mar. 31, 1983.

63. Patti Roberts, *Ashes to Gold,* pp. 22–23, 143–45.

64. Evelyn Roberts, *His Darling Wife,* p. 235; see also Evelyn Roberts, "1976," *AL,* Jan. 1976, p. 10.

65. Patti Roberts, *Ashes to Gold,* p. 139.

66. Ibid., p. 86; see pp. 162–63.

67. Stovall Interview.

68. Evelyn Roberts Interview, Nov. 1, 1983.

69. Ibid.

70. Patti Roberts, *Ashes to Gold,* pp. 128–29, 140.

71. Ibid., p. 140.

72. Ibid., p. 142.

73. Farah Interview.

74. Patti Roberts, *Ashes to Gold,* pp. 146–51.

75. Richard Roberts Interviews, Mar. 31, 1983; Sept. 5, 1984.

76. Farah Interview.

77. Richard Roberts Interview, Sept. 5, 1984.

78. Stovall Interview.

79. Richard Roberts Interview, Mar. 31, 1983.

80. Elaine Osborn, "Evangelist's Wife Survives Public Controversies, Private Tragedies," *Santa Ana (Calif.) Register,* Apr. 25, 1981, ORU.

81. "Getting to Know Lindsay Roberts," *OREA Today,* Aug. 1980, pp. 1–2.

82. B. Nash Interview.

83. Stovall Interview.

84. Ruth Miller, "Israel Trip Highlight Forum," *Oracle,* Jan. 25, 1980, p. 1.

85. "Getting to Know Lindsay Roberts," p. 1.

86. Ibid.; Ann Shurts, "Roberts' Ministry Enhanced by Wife," *Oracle,* Feb. 15, 1980, p. 1.

87. See "Richard and Lindsay Roberts Join Together," *AL,* Nov. 1982, p. 19; Lindsay Roberts, "My Miracle Harvest," *Daily Blessing,* Jan., Feb., Mar. 1983, pp. 67–68.

88. Shurts, "Roberts' Ministry Enhanced by Wife," p. 1.

89. Richard Roberts Interview, Mar. 31, 1983.

90. Richard Roberts, Banquet Transcript, Feb. 7, 1981, p. 5.

91. Potts Interview.

92. Ibid.

93. B. Nash Interview; Ron Smith Interview, Feb. 24, 1983.

94. Potts Interview; Robinson Interview.

95. Evelyn Roberts Interview, Apr. 3, 1984.

96. Ibid.

97. Beth Macklin, "City of Faith Plans OB Suite in Memory of Roberts Infant," *Tulsa World,* Feb. 13, 1984, p. 8-B.

98. Evelyn Roberts Interview, Apr. 3, 1984.

99. Macklin, "City of Faith Plans OB Suite in Memory of Roberts Infant."

100. Richard Roberts, Crusade Service Transcript, Nov. 20, 1982, p. 15.

101. David I. Bradley to Oral Roberts, Dec. 28, 1977, ORU Archives.

102. O. Roberts, Baccalaureate Address Transcript, May 6, 1979, p. 4.

103. Evelyn Roberts, Student Meeting Transcript, Mar. 19, 1975, p. 17.

104. Vicki Chandler, "Darling Evelyn Just a Love Story with Oral," *National Courier,* Dec. 24, 1976, p. 17.

105. Albert E. Bush Interview, Feb. 11, 1983; Evelyn Roberts, *His Darling Wife,* p. 185.

106. Evelyn Roberts, *His Darling Wife,* p. 110.

107. Evelyn Roberts, Faculty Orientation Transcript, Aug. 18, 1975, p. 35.

108. O. Roberts, Miscellaneous Speech Transcript, July 29, 1977, p. 18.

109. "Oral Roberts," *Christian Home,* Mar. 1979, p. 16.

110. Evelyn Roberts, Chapel Transcript, Feb. 3, 1982, p. 15.

111. Ervin Interview.

112. Letter from John D. Messick to David E. Harrell, Jan. 27, 1983.

113. Evelyn Roberts, *His Darling Wife,* p. 111.

114. Eileen Keerdoja and Joan Gordon, "Roberts: The Lord Told Me to Build," *Newsweek,* Dec. 10, 1979, p. 24.

115. Evelyn Roberts, "Here's How It All Began," *AL,* Feb. 1979, p. 12.

116. "They've Served the Lord Together for Over Thirty Years," *Daily Record* (Dunn, N.C.), Dec. 23 and 24, 1982, p. 12.

117. O. Roberts Interview, Feb. 16, 1983; Evelyn Roberts Interview, Apr. 3, 1984.

118. Evelyn Roberts, Chapel Transcript, Feb. 3, 1982, pp. 19–20.

119. O. Roberts, "What to Do When an Accident Strikes," *AL,* Sept. 1983, p. 23; see O. Roberts, Banquet Transcript, Feb. 6, 1982, pp. 19–22; Evelyn Roberts, Chapel Transcript, Feb. 3, 1982, pp. 19–20.

120. Evelyn Roberts Interview, Apr. 3, 1984.

121. Evelyn Roberts, Chapel Transcript, Feb. 3, 1982, pp. 15–16.

122. Bob Foresman and Jenk Jones, Jr., "Oral Roberts: What Makes Him Tick," *Tulsa Tribune,* June 11, 1975, p. 1-B; O. Roberts Interview, Feb. 16, 1983.

123. See Norma Lee Browing, "The Real-Life Romance of Louis L'Amour," *Success Unlimited,* Oct. 1980, pp. 12–15.

124. Evelyn Roberts Interview, Apr. 3, 1984.

125. Ibid.

126. Jenkin Lloyd Jones Interview, Mar. 31, 1983.

127. Jones Interview; see also Bush Interview, Moyers Interview.

128. John Williams Interview, Mar. 30, 1983.

129. Bush Interview.

130. Moyers Interview.

131. Williams Interview.

132. Bush Interview.

133. Warren Hultgren Interview, Mar. 30, 1983; Messick to Harrell, Jan. 27, 1983.

134. Billy Graham, Miscellaneous Speech Transcript, Oct. 18, 1972, pp. 5–6.

135. O. Roberts Interview, Feb. 16, 1983.

136. Williams Interview.

137. O. Roberts, Faculty Chapel Transcript, Aug. 19, 1974, p. 14.

138. O. Roberts, Faculty Meeting Transcript, Aug. 17, 1981, p. 10.

139. Bush Interview.

140. Patti Roberts, *Ashes to Gold,* p. 91.

141. Evelyn Roberts Interview, Apr. 3, 1984.

142. Ibid.; O. Roberts, Banquet Transcript, Feb. 7, 1981, pp. 9–10.

143. Evelyn Roberts Interview, Apr. 3, 1984.

144. O. Roberts, S. Lee Braxton Memorial Service Transcript, Nov. 20, 1982, pp. 16–17.

145. Evelyn Roberts Interview, Apr. 3, 1984.

146. Smith Interview.

147. B. Nash Interview.

148. Evelyn Roberts Interview, Apr. 3, 1984; B. Nash Interview; Robinson Interview.

149. O. Roberts Interview, Feb. 16, 1983; Richard Roberts Interview, Mar. 31, 1983.

150. Evelyn Roberts Interview, Apr. 3, 1984.

151. Richard Roberts Interview, Mar. 31, 1983.

152. Hoover Adams, "Wellons Had Big Role in Oral Roberts' Rise," *Daily Record* (Dunn, N.C.), Dec. 23 and 24, 1982, p. 13; O. Roberts Interview, Sept. 3, 1984.

153. Evelyn Roberts Interview, Apr. 3, 1984; B. Nash Interview.

154. Evelyn Roberts Interview, Apr. 3, 1984.

155. See Russell Chandler, "Oral Roberts: Old Time Religion—with a Twist," *Los Angeles Times,* Feb. 27, 1984, pp. 1, 3, 11.

156. Evelyn Roberts Interview, Apr. 3, 1984; O. Roberts Interview, Sept. 3, 1984.

157. Smith Interview.

158. O. Roberts, Chapel Transcript, Aug. 24, 1977, p. 19.

159. Evelyn Roberts Interview, Apr. 3, 1984.

160. See "Roberts Income Reported," *Phoenix and Times Democrat,* (Muskogee, Okla.) Nov. 8, 1981, ORU.

161. Chandler, "Oral Roberts: Old Time Religion—with a Twist," pp. 1, 3, 11.

162. "O, Dem Golden Slippers," *Tulsa Tribune,* Sept. 8, 1979, ORU; "Oral Roberts' Shoes Not Close to $300," *Tulsa Tribune,* Sept. 10, 1979, ORU.

163. Patti Roberts, *Ashes to Gold,* pp. 109, 123; see Chandler, "Oral Roberts: Old Time Religion—with a Twist," p. 11.

164. "Give Me that Prime Time Religion," *Fundamental Baptist Fellowship of America News Bulletin,* Jan.-Feb. 1980, p. 2; Jerry Sholes, *Give Me That Prime-Time Religion* (New York: Hawthorn Books [1979], pp. 118–24; Thompson Interview.

165. Evelyn Roberts Interview, Apr. 3, 1984; Chandler, "Oral Roberts: Old Time Religion—with a Twist," p. 11.

166. "It's Time For the Truth to Be Told," *AL,* Aug, 1980, p. 9.

167. Chandler, "Oral Roberts: Old Time Religion—with a Twist," p. 11.

168. Foresman and Jones, "Oral Roberts: What Makes Him Tick."

169. Shakarian Interview.

170. Smith Interview.

171. Bush Interview.

172. O. Roberts, Chapel Transcript, Aug. 24, 1977, pp. 20–21.

173. Williams Interview; O. Roberts Interview, Sept. 3, 1984; Richard Roberts Interview, Sept. 5, 1984.

174. Potts Interview.

175. O. Roberts, Laymen's Seminar Transcript, June 19, 1981, p. 30.

176. Farah Interview.

177. Potts Interview.

14. COMPLETING THE HEALING VISION

1. Byron Hirst, "Introduction," in Granville Oral Roberts, *Oral Roberts University, 1965–1983* (New York: Newcomen Society of the United States, 1983), p. 6; Roberta Roberts Potts Interview, Dec. 13, 1983.

2. "The Ten Most Frequently Asked Questions about ORU," *AL,* Oct. 1983, p. 21. See also "Education in the Spirit," *Logos,* Nov.-Dec. 1977, pp. 7–8.

3. Carl Hamilton Interview, Jan. 17, 1983.

4. Oral Roberts, Chapel Transcript, Feb. 8, 1980, pp. 10–11.

5. O. Roberts, Speech at ORU Seminary Transcript, Feb. 9, 1980, pp. 10–11.

6. Star Jauff, "Projected Enrollment Announced," *Oracle,* Nov. 5, 1982, p. 3.

7. Hamilton Telephone Interview, May 14, 1984.

8. See Dennis Johnson, "Provost Ponders Plans, Predictions," *Oracle,* Sept. 30, 1977, pp. 1, 7.

9. Hamilton Telephone Interview, May 14, 1984.

10. "The Ten Most Frequently Asked Questions about ORU," p. 21; "Teachers Get

a 'B,'" *Tulsa World*, May 3, 1984, p. 8-A. For information on students, see Rick Olivito, "Freshmen Compare with National Profile," *Oracle*, Nov. 10, 1978, pp. 1, 10; "Survey Reveals ORU Frosh Profile," *Communique*, Fall 1978, p. 4; "ORU Gets High Rating in Recent National Survey," *Oracle*, Mar. 26, 1982, p. 1; Hamilton Interview, Jan. 17, 1983.

11. Hamilton Interview, Jan. 17, 1983.

12. Katha McSweeney, "Newbriefs," *Quincy (Mass.) Patriot Ledger*, Jan. 26, 1979, p. 8.

13. Hamilton Telephone Interview, May 14, 1984.

14. Hamilton Interview, Jan. 17, 1983; O. Roberts, *Oral Roberts University, 1965–1983*, p. 13.

15. Debbie Titus, "Time Waits for No Man," *Communique*, Fall 1982, pp. 5–8; Hamilton Interview, Jan. 17, 1983; James Winslow Interview, Feb. 4, 1983.

16. Oral Roberts Interview, Aug. 17, 1984; Richard Roberts Interview, Sept. 5, 1984; William Jernigan Interview, Aug. 17, 1984.

17. O. Roberts, Chapel Transcript, Nov. 9, 1979, p. 2.

18. See Jelleta Fryman, "University Departments Make Ten Percent Cut," *Oracle*, Feb. 23, 1979, p. 8; Rose Ann Pearce, "ORU Tightens Financial Belt," *Tulsa Tribune*, June 7, 1979, ORU; Julie Del Cour, "ORU to Hike 1980 Tuition 43.9 Percent," *Tulsa World*, Aug. 31, 1979, ORU; Marjorie Waltrip, "1981–82 Tuition Increase Announced," *Oracle*, Feb. 20, 1981, p. 1; W. Kevin Armstrong, "Cost of Education to Increase Next Year," *Oracle*, Feb. 26, 1982, p. 1.

19. Hamilton Telephone Interview, May 14, 1984; Jernigan Interview.

20. "ORU and TU Agree: No Visitors in Libraries," *Oracle*, Aug. 29, 1975, p. 1.

21. Yvonne Rehg, "Dress Code Frosts ORU Coeds," *Tulsa Tribune*, Feb. 1, 1978, pp. 1-A, 4-A.

22. Kathlyn Auten, "'Dress Code' Front Page News?" *Tulsa Tribune*, Feb. 6, 1978, ORU.

23. "Caughell Defends Her Squads," *Oracle*, Jan. 21, 1983, p. 5.

24. "Drill and Cheer Joined in Newly Formed Pom-pon Squad," *Oracle*, Jan. 21, 1983, p. 8.

25. Paul Brynteson, "Fitness for Life," *Journal of Physical Education and Recreation*, Jan. 1978, pp. 37–39.

26. "Roberts Defends ORU Rules on Weight Control, Curfew," *Tulsa Tribune*, Apr. 4, 1979, ORU.

27. See William Proctor, "Aerobics: "Why It's Good for the Christian Heart," *Christian Herald*, May 1983, pp. 30–31, 34; Susan Richardson, "Getting Fit for a Better Life," *Christian Life*, June 1983, pp. 24–30.

28. "Fat Teachers Might Lose Jobs at Oral Roberts U.," *Washington (D.C.) Star*, Mar. 12, 1978, ORU.

29. Lenora Marsh, "Pounds-Off Program Emphasizes Progress," *Communique*, Winter 1978, p. 5.

30. Mark Filbert and Lenora Marsh, "Administration Strives for Food Improvements," *Oracle*, Jan. 28, 1977, p. 1.

31. See Brenda Stockton-Hiss, "Students Feel Vicitimized by Mandatory Weight Program," *Oklahoma City Oklahoman*, Mar. 24, 1978, ORU; Micki Van Deventer, "Suspended Coed to Finish Degree at OSU," *Stillwater (Okla.) News-Press*, Dec. 20, 1977, ORU; "Extra Weight May Cost ORU Students Diplomas," *Atlanta Journal*, Oct. 6, 1977, ORU.

32. See "Oral Roberts University Accused of Bias," *Chronicle of Higher Education*, Nov. 21, 1977, p. 12; "Extra Weight May Cost ORU Students Diplomas"; "The ORU Fat Fetish," *New York Times*, Apr. 13, 1980, ORU.

33. "F Is For Fat," *Newsweek*, Oct. 24, 1977, p. 112; "College Criticized for Get-Thin Policy," *New York Times*, Dec. 4, 1977, ORU; "Coed Suspended," *West Palm Beach (Fla.) Times*, May 26, 1978, ORU.

34. "Forgive Us Our Lard," *Oklahoma Observer* (Tulsa), Oct. 25, 1977, ORU.

35. *National Review*, Nov. 11, 1977, p. 1280; "Why Should We Pay for Medical

Criminals?" *Wall Street Journal*, Oct. 5, 1978, ORU; Mark Bricklin, "Things Here and There," *Prevention*, Apr. 1978, pp. 78–83.

36. "Oklahomans Request HEW Review of University," *Paraplegia News* (Seal Beach, Calif.), Feb. 1978, ORU.

37. See Paul Wenski, "Obesity Issue Holding Up HEW Probe," *Oklahoma City Oklahoman*, June 11, 1978, ORU; Albert E. Bush Interview, Feb. 11, 1983.

38. See "ORU Architectural Barriers to Handicapped Due Removal," *Tulsa World*, Nov. 10, 1978, ORU; Laurie Mower, "ORU to Modify Tower Dormitories, Accept Disabled," *Tulsa Tribune*, Nov. 10, 1978, ORU; "ORU Makes Itself Accessible to the Handicapped," *Oracle*, Nov. 18, 1977, p. 1.

39. O. Roberts, Chapel Transcript, Jan. 7, 1981, p. 14.

40. See Keith Skrzypczak and Marshall Upjohn, Jr., "Oklahoma Business," *Oklahoma Sports*, Nov. 1982, p. 17.

41. Bill Connors, "Sports Editor," *Tulsa World*, July 6, 1979, ORU; see also "Sutton Confirms Offer, Defends Roberts," *Tulsa World*, July 6, 1979, ORU; Bob Hartzell, "Honorable Intentions Don't Stop Criticism," *Tulsa Tribune*, July 6, 1979, ORU.

42. Wayne Robinson Interview, Apr. 4, 1983; Jerry Sholes, *Give Me That Prime-Time Religion* (New York: Hawthorn Books [1979]), pp. 109–117.

43. O. Roberts, Chapel Transcript, Jan. 7, 1981, p. 10.

44. Clay Henry, "Firing of Hayes Stuns Killingsworth, Others," *Tulsa World*, Dec. 22, 1982, p. 2-E.

45. "The People's Voice," *Tulsa World*, Dec. 22, 1982, p. 8-A. See also A. C. Griffith, "Hayes Dismissal Leads to Attempted Boycott," *Oracle*, Jan. 7, 1983, p. 8; "Rumors, Miscalculations Twist Current Judgments," *Oracle*, Jan. 7, 1983, p. 4; Bill Connors, "Firing Makes Coaches Wary of ORU Post," *Tulsa World*, Dec. 21, 1983, p. 2-C.

46. Henry, "Firing of Hayes Stuns Killingsworth, Others."

47. Oral Roberts, "The Vision of God and of Oral Roberts," *AL*, Mar. 1976, p. 4.

48. Oral Roberts, "I Am Happy to Announce the Opening of Two Fully Accredited Graduate Schools at Oral Roberts University," *AL*, June 1975, p. 20.

49. O. Roberts, Address to Law Students Transcript, Apr. 5, 1982, p. 2.

50. O. Roberts, Miscellaneous Speech Transcript, Oct. 3, 1976, p. 12; O. Roberts, Speech to Student Meeting Transcript, Aug. 20, 1975, p. 9.

51. O. Roberts, Chapel Transcript, Apr. 28, 1975, pp. 3–4.

52. O. Roberts, Chapel Transcript, Aug. 24, 1979, p. 11.

53. "Breath-Taker at ORU," *Tulsa World*, Apr. 30, 1975, p. 8-A.

54. "An Amazing Plan," *Tulsa Tribune*, Apr. 29, 1975, ORU.

55. O. Roberts, Chapel Transcript, Jan. 22, 1975, p. 18.

56. Oral Roberts, "Here's How It All Began," *AL*, Feb. 1979, p. 5; Hamilton Interview, Jan. 17, 1983.

57. O. Roberts, Ministers Seminar Transcript, Jan. 20, 1963, p. 6.

58. O. Roberts, President's Advisory Cabinet Transcript, May 29, 1965, pp. 13–14.

59. Raymond Othel Corvin, "Religious and Educational Backgrounds in the Founding of Oral Roberts University," Ph.D. dissertation, University of Oklahoma, 1967, p. 188.

60. O. Roberts, Chapel Transcript, Jan. 22, 1975, pp. 18–20. See also O. Roberts, "Here's How It All Began," pp. 7–13.

61. James Buskirk Interview, Feb. 18, 1983.

62. O. Roberts, Chapel Transcript, Apr. 28, 1975, p. 4; Bob Roller, "ORU Breaks Ground Tomorrow for New Addition to the LRC," *Oracle*, Jan. 23, 1976, p. 1; Oral Roberts, "Oral Roberts University Medical School," *AL*, Oct. 1976, p. 13; Shelly Lamoreaux, "Grad Center Nears Completion," *Oracle*, Mar. 4, 1977, p. 7.

63. O. Roberts, *Oral Roberts University, 1965–1983*, p. 21; see also O. Roberts, Chapel Transcript, Apr. 28, 1975, p. 7. Graduate and undergraduate student interaction was originally called "cross-fertilization." See "ORU Plans Medical, Law, Dental Colleges by 1980," *Tulsa World*, Apr. 29, 1975, p. 1.

64. Hamilton Interview, Jan. 17, 1983.

65. Titus, "Time Waits for No Man," pp. 5-8; Hamilton Telephone Interview, May 14, 1984; Robert Voight Interview, Jan. 25, 1983.

66. Oral Roberts, "Dr. Jim Winslow and Dr. Robert G. Hansen Discuss ORU's Medical and Dental Schools," *AL*, Mar. 1976, p. 11.

67. O. Roberts Interview, Feb. 16, 1983.

68. Oral and Evelyn Roberts and James Buskirk, "The Spiritual Awakening in America," *AL*, July 1976, pp. 8-13; Buskirk Interview, Feb. 11, 1983.

69. Buskirk Interview, Feb. 11, 1983; James Buskirk, Youth Seminar Transcript, Nov. 28, 1982, pp. 39-40.

70. See Beth Macklin, "Evangelist to Be Theology Dean," *Tulsa World*, Apr. 28, 1976, p. 1-D; "Buskirk Returns to ORU," *Oracle*, Sept. 26, 1975, p. 1.

71. James Buskirk, untitled typed manuscript, June 17, 1983; Buskirk Interview, Feb. 11, 1983.

72. Buskirk Interviews, Feb. 11, 1983; Feb. 18, 1983.

73. Brett Hoffman, "Buskirk Affirms Seminary and Church Life," *Oracle*, Jan. 21, 1983, p. 7.

74. Macklin, "Evangelist to Be Theology Dean."

75. James Buskirk, Youth Seminar Transcript, Nov. 28, 1982, p. 40.

76. "Theology School Hosts Seminary Days for Interested," *Oracle*, Jan. 21, 1983, p. 1; Buskirk Interview, Feb. 18, 1983.

77. See "Conference on the Holy Spirit," Brochure, Nov. 2-5, 1983, ORU. Whatever other directions the seminary might take, Oral insisted that it would remain "frankly, unashamedly charismatic." O. Roberts, Speech at ORU Seminary Transcript, Feb. 9, 1976, p 13; Richard Roberts Interview, Mar. 31, 1983.

78. Oral and Evelyn Roberts and James Buskirk, "The Spiritual Awakening in America," p. 9.

79. "Grad Theology Approved by Methodist Body," *Oracle*, Jan. 22, 1982, p. 1.

80. Hamilton Interview, Jan. 17, 1983.

81. Oral and Evelyn Roberts and J. Buskirk, "The Spiritual Awakening in America," p. 9.

82. Howard Ervin Interview, Jan. 25, 1983; Ruth Robinson, "Helping People Become Whole Is Buskirk's Aim," *Chattanooga (Tenn.) Daily Times*, Nov. 21, 1981, ORU.

83. O. Roberts, Baccalaureate Address Transcript, May 6, 1979, p. 5.

84. Buskirk Interview, Feb. 18, 1983.

85. Richard Quebedeaux, *The New Charismatics* (Garden City, N.Y.: Doubleday and Co., 1976), p. 92.

86. Charles Farah Interview, Jan. 25, 1983; see Ervin Interview.

87. Buskirk Interview, Feb. 18, 1983.

88. O. Roberts, Baccalaureate Address Transcript, May 1, 1977, p. 4.

89. Ron Smith Interview, Feb. 24, 1983; Buskirk Interview, Feb. 18, 1983.

90. Charles A. Kothe, "Not Just Another Law School," *Oklahoma Bar Journal*, July 28, 1979, p. 1614.

91. Julie Del Cour, "Law Dean Confesses to Varied Career," *Tulsa World*, Aug. 26, 1979, pp. 1-B, 4-B; "O. W. Coburn School of Law," Brochure, ORU; Charles Kothe Interview, Feb. 23, 1983.

92. Kothe Interview.

93. O. Roberts, Address to Law Students Transcript, Apr. 5, 1982, p. 4; Kothe Interview.

94. Del Cour, "Law Dean Confesses to Varied Career," p. 4-B.

95. Julie Del Cour, "ORU Law School Dedicated," *Tulsa World*, Sept. 20, 1979, p. 1-F.

96. Kothe Interview; "O. W. Coburn School of Law," Brochure, ORU.

97. O. Roberts, Address to Law Students Transcript, Apr. 5, 1982, p. 2; Kothe Interview.

98. "O. W. Coburn School of Law," Brochure, ORU; "Harmonizing Ethics and

Law," Pamphlet, ORU; Keith Skrzypczak, "Christian Conciliation," *Tulsa Tribune*, Sept. 18, 1979, ORU.

99. Charles A. Kothe, "Preface," *Journal of Christian Jurisprudence*, 1980, pp. 1–3.

100. Kothe Interview.

101. "O. W. Coburn School of Law," Brochure, ORU.

102. Kothe Interview.

103. Majorie Waltrip, "Road To ABA Accreditation Completed," *Oracle*, Aug. 28, 1981, p. 1.

104. Kothe Interview.

105. Charles T. Hvass, "Report of ABA Annual Meeting," *Hennepin Lawyer*, Sept.-Oct. 1981, p. 18.

106. Waltrip, "Road to ABA Accreditation Completed," p. 1.

107. "ABA Challenged for Easing Its Ban on Religious Bias," *Chronicle of Higher Education*, Nov. 25, 1981, ORU.

108. Marjorie Waltrip, "Law School Survives ABA Rejection Attempt," *Oracle*, Jan. 29, 1982, p. 1; Kothe Interview.

109. Bill Winter, "ABA Fine Tunes Religious Bias Rule," *American Bar Association Journal*, Oct. 1982, ORU.

110. Kothe Interview.

111. O. Roberts, Laymen's Seminar Transcript, June 21, 1981, pp. 5, 6.

112. Kothe Interview.

113. O. Roberts, Miscellaneous Speech Transcript, Aug. 16, 1982, pp. 5–6.

114. Kothe Interview.

115. Thomas C. Thompson Interview, Feb. 2, 1983.

116. James Winslow, Chapel Transcript, Jan. 26, 1976, pp. 4–5.

117. Winslow Interview.

118. O. Roberts, "Dr. Jim Winslow and Dr. Robert G. Hansen Discuss ORU's Medical and Dental Schools," p. 11; Winslow Interview.

119. Ibid.; James Winslow, Chapel Transcript, Jan. 26, 1976, p. 6.

120. Winslow Interview.

121. James Winslow, "Why I Believe in Miracles," *AL*, May 1978, pp. 15–19; Oral Roberts, "God's Medicine, *AL*, Sept. 1977, pp. 3–8.

122. Winslow Interview.

123. "James Winslow, Jr.," *Tulsa World*, Nov. 1, 1981, p. 3; "Winslow Appointed Dean of New Medical School," *Oracle*, Dec. 12, 1975, p. 2; Pat Atkinson, "Tulsan Named Dean of ORU Med School," *Tulsa World*, Dec. 2, 1975, p. 1.

124. Atkinson, "Tulsan Named Dean of ORU Med School."

125. Collins Steele Interview, Jan. 13, 1983.

126. O. Roberts, Chapel Transcript, Nov. 17, 1978, pp. 9–10.

127. O. Roberts Interview, Feb. 16, 1983.

128. Esther Fritz Kuntz, "Tulsa Hospitals Withdraw Opposition, Remain Wary," *Modern Health Care*, Dec. 1981, p. 66; Thompson Interview.

129. Kathlyn Auten, "McCall Named New Med Dean," *Oracle*, Mar. 4, 1977, p. 1; Kathlyn Auten and Rick Barney, "Winslow Comments on Promotion," *Oracle*, Mar. 10, 1977, p. 1.

130. Ibid.

131. Winslow Interview; Thompson Interview.

132. Oral Roberts, "A Breakthrough from Heaven in '77," *AL*, Jan. 1977, p.7.

133. O. Roberts, Chapel Transcript, Apr. 19, 1978, pp. 6–7.

134. "Opening Delayed," *Norman (Okla.) Daily*, June 6, 1978, ORU.

135. Winslow Interview.

136. "Medical School at ORU Will Have Initial Class," *Oklahoma City Oklahoman*, July 30, 1978, ORU; "Evangelist's Medical School to Open without Accreditation," *Medical World News*, Sept. 18, 1978, ORU.

137. Thompson Interview.

138. See Dave Seldon, "Med School Dean Resigns ORU Spot," *Oklahoma City Oklahoman*, Aug. 1, 1978, ORU; "Dean of Med School Resigns Position," *Oracle*, Aug. 25, 1978, p. 1; "Oral Roberts Dean Resigns in Dispute," *American Medical News*, Aug. 11, 1978, ORU; Winslow Interview.

139. Helen Parmley, "Oral Roberts' Medical School: God's Will versus Tulsa's," *Dallas Morning News*, Aug. 6, 1978, ORU.

140. Winslow Interview.

141. O. Roberts, "Faculty Luncheon Transcript," Nov. 16, 1977, p. 3.

142. Richard Lewis, "Evangelist Urges MDs to Call on 'Man Upstairs,'" *American Medical News*, Dec. 22/29, 1978, ORU.

143. Winslow Interview.

144. There were also strong objections to the dental school on the basis of lack of need. Thompson Interview.

145. Winslow Interview; Thompson Interview.

146. Winslow Interview; O. Roberts, Chapel Transcript, Feb. 14, 1978, pp. 14–15; Jenkin Lloyd Jones, Sr. Interview, Mar. 31, 1983.

147. See Parmley, "Oral Roberts' Medical School: God's Will versus Tulsa's"; "Miracle or Mistake?" *Tulsa Home and Garden,* Mar. 1978, pp. 34–35.

148. Janet Pearson, "St. John Votes ORU Affiliation," *Tulsa World*, Sept. 29, 1978, ORU.

149. See Janet Pearson, "ORU's Med School Gets Unofficial Yes on Accreditation," *Tulsa World,* Nov. 30, 1978, p. 1; "Site Team Visits ORU, St. John," *Oracle*, Dec. 8, 1978, pp. 1–6; Janet Pearson, "ORU Med School Wins Accreditation," *Tulsa World*, Feb. 17, 1979 p. 1.

150. "ORU Grad School of Medicine to Develop Programs at St. John," *Oracle*, Feb. 23, 1979, p. 1.

151. Thompson Interview.

152. "City of Faith Encounters Further Opposition," *Oracle*, Dec. 11, 1981, p. 1.

153. Winslow Interview.

154. "New Dean Joins Med School," *Oracle*, Oct. 1, 1982, p. 1; "Ministry News," *AL,* Dec. 1982, p. 8; Winslow Interview.

155. "ORU Appoints Dean for School of Medicine," *Tulsa World*, July 6, 1984, p. 2-A.

156. See *Oracle*, Dec. 9, 1983.

157. O. Roberts, Chapel Transcript, Aug. 19, 1978, pp. 14–24; O. Roberts, Chapel Transcript, Aug. 29, 1980, pp. 5–8; "ORU: The Roberts Reflect on Past, Present, and Future," *Oracle,* Dec. 12, 1980, p. 1.

158. O. Roberts, Chapel Transcript, Sept. 19, 1980, pp. 40–41.

159. "ORU: The Roberts Reflect on Past, Present, and Future," p. 1.

160. Rick Barney, "Seminar Schedule Is Outlined," *Oracle,* Feb. 4, 1977, pp. 1, 6; "Family Seminar Begins Tonight," *Oracle,* Aug. 25, 1978, p. 1.

161. "ORU: The Roberts Reflect on Past, Present, and Future."

162. Evelyn Roberts, Chapel Transcript, Feb. 3, 1982, p. 3.

163. See "Students Stand Up for President against Biased Coverage," *Oracle,* Jan. 28, 1983, p. 5.

164. Oral Roberts, "'I Will Rain upon Your Desert!'" *AL,* Oct. 1977, p. 9; Rick Barney, "ORU Pioneers $100 Million Medical Complex," *Oracle,* Sept. 9, 1977, p. 1.

165. Thompson Interview; see Sholes, *Prime-Time Religion,* pp. 191–207.

166. Donald Moyers Interview, Dec. 13, 1983.

167. Evelyn Roberts, Miscellaneous Speech Transcript, June 8, 1981, p. 14.

168. O. Roberts Interview, Feb. 16, 1983.

169. Frank Wallace Interview, Feb. 18, 1983; Esther Fritz Kuntz, "Design, Religion, Medicine Join Hands at Oral Roberts' City of Faith," *Modern Health Care,* Dec. 1981, p. 64.

170. Wallace Interview.

171. "Oral Roberts' Vision," *Logos,* Jan.-Feb. 1979, p. 11; O. Roberts, Dedication Transcript, Nov. 1, 1981, n.p.; Gordon Lyons, "ORU Architect Comments on His Work," *Oracle,* Oct. 5, 1979, p. 10.

172. Wallace Interview; David Westerfield, "Drafts Precede Digging in Raising City of Faith," *Oracle,* Oct. 21, 1977, p. 1; Winslow Interview.

173. Kuntz, "Design, Religion, Medicine Join Hands at Oral Roberts' City of Faith," pp. 62–63.

174. Mary Beth Thibeau, "Buildings in City of Faith Represent Biblical Concepts," *Oracle,* Oct. 5, 1979, pp. 10–11; Wallace Interview.

175. "The Healing Hands," Brochure, no pub. info.; Cecil Peaden, "Praying Hands," *Tulsa Tribune,* Oct. 1, 1979, pp. 1-B, 3-B.

176. Barney, "ORU Pioneers $100 Million Medical Complex."

177. O. Roberts, " 'I Will Rain upon Your Desert!' ", p. 5.

178. Oral Roberts, "God Has Spoken to Me Again," *AL,* Feb. 1978, pp. 2–8.

179. O. Roberts, Dedication Transcript, Nov. 1, 1981, p. 21.

180. Oral Roberts Interview, Feb. 16, 1983.

181. O. Roberts, " 'I Will Rain upon Your Desert!' ", p. 5.

182. See Jim Winslow, "Meet Your Health Care Team at the City of Faith," *AL,* Dec. 1979, pp. 20–21; Oral Roberts, "Jesus Tells You Five Steps You Can Take to Receive Your Healing," *AL,* July-Aug. 1978, p. 13.

183. O. Roberts, Banquet Transcript, July 8, 1981, p. 22.

184. "City of Faith," *AL,* Mar. 1978, pp. 8–10; O. Roberts, Dedication Transcript, Jan. 24, 1978, n.p.

185. "City of Faith Still on Hold," *Oracle,* Feb. 17, 1978, pp. 1, 13; Oklahoma Health Planning Commission Transcript, Apr. 26, 1978, p. 34.

186. Oklahoma Health Planning Commission Transcript, Apr. 26, 1978, p. 18.

187. Ibid., pp. 28, 36–37; "The City of Faith," *Logos,* Jan.-Feb. 1979, p. 11.

188. Oklahoma Health Planning Commission Transcript, Apr. 26, 1978, p. 43.

189. Ibid., p. 27.

190. See David Fritze, "The Gold and the Glory," *Oklahoma Monthly,* Oct. 1977, p. 14.

191. Oklahoma Health Planning Commission Transcript, Apr. 26, 1978, pp. 12–13.

192. "Evangelist's Medical School to Open without Accreditation," *Medical World News,* Sept. 18, 1978, ORU.

193. Ibid.; "City of Faith Still on Hold," p. 1.

194. See Oklahoma Health Planning Commission Transcript, Apr. 26, 1978, pp. 19–28; Thompson Interview.

195. Thompson Interview.

196. Oklahoma Health Planning Commission Transcript, Apr. 26, 1978, p. 28.

197. Ralph Marsh, "A Story of Medicine, Power, Prayer," *Tulsa Tribune,* Apr. 12, 1978, pp. 1-A, 4-A.

198. Evelyn Roberts, Chapel Transcript, Jan. 13, 1978, pp. 5–7.

199. Ben Blackstock, "Politicians, Hospitals, Banks Mix It Up in ORU Hospital Fight," *Okemah (Okla.) News Letter,* Apr. 6, 1978, ORU.

200. Oklahoma Health Planning Commission Transcript, Apr. 26, 1978, pp. 14–15.

201. Ibid., p. 31.

202. "State Supreme Court Considers City of Faith," *Communique,* Winter 1979, pp. 1, 4.

203. Thompson Interview.

204. David Culp, "Dr. James Winslow Outlines Development and Status of City of Faith Complex," *Oracle,* Sept. 21, 1979, p. 1.

205. Thompson Interview.

206. Culp, "Dr. James Winslow Outlines Development and Status of City of Faith Complex," p. 1; Winslow Interview.

207. David Westerfield, "Court Rules against the City of Faith," *Oracle,* Dec. 8, 1978, p. 1.

208. Jenkin Lloyd Jones, "Phony Religious Issue," *Tulsa Tribune,* Dec. 18, 1979, ORU.

209. Culp, "Dr. James Winslow Outlines Development and Status of City of Faith Complex," p. 1; Winslow Interview.

210. See "City of Faith Compromise May Be Proposed," *Oracle,* Feb. 23, 1979, pp. 1, 3.

211. "City of Faith Contested by Attorneys," *Oracle,* Apr. 27, 1979, p. 1.

212. O. Roberts, Chapel Transcript, Mar. 5, 1979, pp. 14–16.

213. See Cecil Peaden, "Grant to ORU Blocked," *Tulsa Tribune,* Dec. 12, 1979, ORU.

214. Kevin Armstrong, "COF Ruling 'Great Day' for ORU," *Oracle,* Mar. 27, 1981, pp. 1, 3.

215. "Hospital Council Not to Appeal COF," *Oracle,* Apr. 17, 1981, p. 1; "Tulsa Hospital Approved," *Hospitals,* May 1, 1981, ORU.

216. Kuntz, "Tulsa Hospitals Withdraw Opposition, Remain Wary," p. 63.

217. Winslow Interview; John Williams Interview, Mar. 30, 1983.

218. O. Roberts, Chapel Transcript, Feb. 24, 1978, p. 18.

219. Thompson Interview; Moyers Interview; "Miracle or Mistake?", p. 34.

220. David Westerfield, "City of Faith Rises, Opposition Continues," unidentified newspaper clipping, ORU.

221. Winslow Interview.

222. Ibid.; Jones Interview.

223. Jones Interview.

224. O. Roberts, Chapel Transcript, Aug. 19, 1978, p. 9.

225. O. Roberts, Chapel Transcript, Mar. 5, 1979, p. 20.

226. "Miracle or Mistake?", p. 33; Kuntz, "Design, Religion, Medicine Join Hands at Roberts' City of Faith," p. 62.

227. Oral Roberts Press Conference Transcript, Feb. 25, 1982, p. 1.

228. O. Roberts, " 'I Will Rain upon Your Desert!'", pp. 10–11.

229. "Appeal to the Flock," *Newsweek,* Sept. 10, 1979, p. 29.

230. Oral Roberts, "A Miracle Has to Take Place," *AL,* Oct. 1980, p. 6.

231. Evelyn Roberts Interview, Apr. 3, 1984; "Roberts Tells Senate of Financing Woes," *Tulsa World,* Apr. 7, 1982, p. 2-A.

232. O. Roberts, Faculty Luncheon Transcript, Nov. 16, 1977, p. 5.

233. Evelyn Roberts Interview, Apr. 3, 1984.

234. See "Provost Sees 'Positive Results' in University Budget Cutbacks," *Oracle,* Aug. 24, 1979, pp. 1, 2.

235. Culp, "Dr. James Winslow Outlines Development and Status of City of Faith Complex," p. 1.

236. George Stovall Interview, Jan. 27, 1983; Buskirk Interview, Feb. 18, 1983.

237. Smith Interview.

238. City of Faith Dedication Transcript, Nov. 1, 1981, pp. 4–5.

239. Pat Upton, "Oral Roberts Opens City of Faith Center," *Tulsa World,* Nov. 2, 1981, p. 1-A.

240. O. Roberts, City of Faith Dedication Transcript, Nov. 1, 1981, p. 28.

241. Ibid., pp. 3–19.

242. See Upton, "Oral Roberts Opens City of Faith Center " pp. 1-A, 2-A; see also ORU clipping file.

243. Byron Boone, "Miracle on Eighty-First Street," *Tulsa World,* Nov. 2, 1981, p. 4-A.

244. Kuntz, "Tulsa Hospitals Withdraw Opposition," pp. 63, 66.

245. Bruce Buursma, "Oral's 'City' A Ghost Town?" *Tulsa World,* June 19, 1983, p. 1-B; Paul Taylor, "City of Faith Is Ailing," *Tulsa World,* July 8, 1984, pp. 2-B, 4-B.

246. Winslow Interview.

247. See Oral Roberts Press Conference Transcript, Feb. 25, 1982; Russel Chan-

dler, "Oral Roberts: Old-Time Religion—with a Twist," *Los Angeles Times,* Feb. 27, 1984, p. 1; Oral Roberts, Partner Letter, June 1984; Paul Taylor, "City of Faith Is Ailing," *Tulsa World,* July 8, 1984, pp. 2-B, 4-B.

248. Oral Roberts Interview, Aug. 17, 1984; Beth Macklin, "City of Faith Says the Poor Are Coming," *Tulsa World,* Aug. 21, 1984, p. 9-A; Beth Macklin, "City of Faith Seeking Indigent Patients to Save Accreditation," *Tulsa World,* July 16, 1984, pp. 1-A, 2-A; Rusty Lang, "City of Faith Move Queried, Praised," *Tulsa World,* July 18, 1984, p. 9-C.

249. James Winslow, "We Are Two Years Old," *AL,* Nov. 1983, p. 17.

250. Thompson Interview.

251. Winslow, "We Are Two Years Old," p. 17.

252. Winslow Interview.

253. Taylor, "City of Faith Is Ailing," p. 2-B; see also R. Claire, "City of Faith Falls Short," *Oklahoma City Oklahoman,* Oct. 31, 1982, ORU.

254. O. Roberts " 'I Will Rain upon Your Desert!' ", p. 7.

255. O. Roberts, Banquet Transcript, July 8, 1981, pp. 28–29.

256. Winslow Interview.

257. Oral Roberts, "I Believe the Cure for Cancer Has a Spiritual Origin," *AL,* Jan. 1977, pp. 2–4.

258. See O. Roberts, " 'I Will Rain upon Your Desert!' ", p. 7; City of Faith Dedication Transcript, Nov. 1, 1981, p. 17; Fritze, "The Gold and the Glory," pp. 14–15.

259. O. Roberts, Chapel Transcript, Dec. 10, 1982, p. 9; Oral Roberts Interview, Feb. 16, 1983.

260. Winslow Interview.

261. Oral Roberts Interview, Feb. 16, 1983; O. Roberts, Chapel Transcript, Dec. 10, 1982, p. 11.

262. See Oral Roberts, "Answers to the Tough Questions," *AL,* Apr. 1983, p. 14.

263. Margaret Hall, "Doing the Impossible," *Religious Broadcasting,* Mar. 1983, p. 35; O. Roberts, Chapel Transcript, Dec. 10, 1982, p. 11.

264. Bart Ziegler, "Donations Exceed $5 Million in Roberts' Cancer Research," *Tulsa World,* May 28, 1983, p. 16-A.

265. Winslow Interview.

266. "Jesus to Oral Roberts: 'Find a Cure for Cancer,' " *Atlanta Journal,* Jan. 18, 1983, pp. 1-A, 7-A; O. Roberts, "Answers to Tough Questions," p. 13.

267. Thompson Interview.

268. James Winslow, "NMR," *AL,* July 1983, p. 22.

269. "Questions Commonly Asked about the City of Faith," *Tulsa World,* Nov. 1, 1981, p. 5.

270. "ORU: The Roberts Reflect on Past, Present, and Future," p. 1.

271. Beth Macklin, "Roberts Wants to Circle Globe with 1,000 Medical Teams," *Tulsa World,* May 7, 1984.

272. Oral Roberts, Partner Letter, May 1984.

273. Evelyn Roberts, Banquet Transcript, Feb. 7, 1981, p. 10.

274. See "Christian Service Council," Brochure, ORU; "Oral Roberts University," *AL,* Oct. 1982, p. 14.

275. "Christian Service Council," Brochure, ORU.

276. "Oral Roberts University," *AL,* Aug. 1982, pp. 22–23.

277. See David Westerfield, "Missions Cuts Raise Questions," *Oracle,* Mar. 9, 1979, p. 2; "Funds Not Sufficient for Missions Program," *Oracle,* Feb. 23, 1979, pp. 1, 7.

278. Buskirk Interview, Feb. 18, 1983. After the founding of the graduate schools, Oral began projecting healing teams of fifteen to twenty persons surrounding a core of professional graduates.

279. O. Roberts Interview, Feb. 16, 1983.

280. Ken Irby, "ORU As It Might Have Been," *Oracle,* Apr. 30, 1975, p. 6.

281. See "A New Television Production Center under Construction," *AL,* June

1977, pp. 14–15; O. Roberts, Chapel Transcript, Aug. 24, 1979, p. 10; James Buskirk, Baccalaureate Address Transcript, May 6, 1979, pp. 11–12; City of Faith Dedication Transcript, Nov. 1, 1981, p. 21.

282. Oral Roberts, "'Go . . . Where My Voice Is Heard Small . . . ,'" *AL,* Apr. 1977, p. 22.

283. O. Roberts, Chapel Transcript, Aug. 20, 1979, p. 9.

284. Oklahoma Health Planning Commission Transcript, Apr. 26, 1978, p. 6.

285. Winslow Interview.

286. O. Roberts, Chapel Transcript, Aug. 29, 1980, p. 9.

287. O. Roberts, Ministers Seminar Transcript, Apr. 28, 1963, p. 10.

288. Lee Braxton Interview, Dec. 18, 1973.

289. Buskirk Interview, Feb. 11, 1983.

290. O. Roberts, Address to Law Students Transcript, Apr. 5, 1982, p. 3.

291. See Bill Bright, Chapel Transcript, Nov. 12, 1982, n.p.; Bill Bright, Miscellaneous Speech Transcript, Nov. 11, 1982, n.p.; Winslow Interview.

292. Winslow Interview.

293. James Winslow, "Kenya," *AL,* Aug. 1981, p. 15.

294. O. Roberts, Laymen's Seminar Transcript, June 21, 1983, p. 7; James Winslow, "Please Bring Us That Same Healing Power in Our Country," *AL,* Aug. 1982, pp. 20–21.

295. O. Roberts Interview, Feb. 16, 1983.

296. O. Roberts, Partner Letter, May 1984.

297. Macklin, "Roberts Wants to Circle Globe with 1,000 Medical Teams." There was a clear drift in the organization toward the view that "we don't want to be senders as such." Buskirk Interview, Feb. 18, 1983.

298. O. Roberts, City of Faith Transcript, June 5, 1981, pp. 6–9.

15. TIGHTENING THE FAMILY

1. Ron Smith Interview, Feb. 24, 1983. Jerry Lewis directed several specials. Most insiders felt Smith was Roberts's most talented producer. Wayne Robinson Interview, Apr. 4, 1983; Albert E. Bush Interview, Feb. 11, 1983; Richard Roberts Interview, Mar. 31, 1983.

2. "Designs in Steel," *Oracle,* Sept. 3, 1976, p. 7.

3. Oral Roberts, Faculty Orientation Transcript, Aug. 18, 1975, p. 31.

4. See Beth Thornton, "Van, Daily Show Coming Soon," *Oracle,* Oct. 20, 1978, p. 4.

5. Ron Smith Interview, telephone, May 24, 1984.

6. Thornton, "Van, Daily Show Coming Soon"; David Westerfield, "Something Good Comes to TV," *Oracle,* Sept. 1, 1978, p. 1; Smith Interview.

7. O. Roberts, Chapel Transcript, Nov. 9, 1979, p. 2.

8. Smith Interview.

9. "Answers from George Stovall," *OREA Today,* Apr. 1980, p. 2.

10. "Sunday Night Live," *AL,* Mar. 1981, p. 14; Smith Interview.

11. See Regina Stone, "ORU TV Comes Home," *Oracle,* Sept. 17, 1982, pp. 1, 7.

12. Richard Roberts Interview, Sept. 5, 1984; Oral Roberts Interview, Aug. 17, 1984.

13. O. Roberts, Faculty Chapel Transcript, Sept. 14, 1981, pp. 11–14.

14. O. Roberts, "Why Prime Time," *AL,* Dec. 1981, p. 7; Richard Roberts, Chapel Transcript, Oct. 7, 1981, p. 3.

15. Robert A. McLean, "Churches Waning TV Program May Be Born Again," *Dallas Times Herald,* Nov. 5, 1981, p. 10-B.

16. Richard Roberts Interview, Mar. 31, 1983.

17. Smith Interview.

18. See "Go into the World and Preach the Gospel," *AL,* Mar. 1980, pp. 14–17

19. See Jan Franzen, "TV Ministry Changes Format," *Christian Life*, Aug. 1979, pp. 14, 60; "Tulsa Studios Used despite ORTV Move," *Oracle*, Feb. 1982, p. 1; Richard Roberts Interview, Mar. 31, 1984.

20. Richard Roberts Interview, Mar. 31, 1984.

21. Jeffrey Hadden and Charles E. Swann, *Prime Time Preachers* (Reading, Mass.: Addison Wesley Publishing Co. [1981]), pp. 22–24 and passim; William C. Martin, "Birth of a Media Myth," *Atlantic*, June 1981, pp. 7, 10–11, 16; "TIO Disputes Evangelists' Audience Claims," *Broadcasting*, Oct. 19, 1981, p. 12.

22. See "Oral Roberts Ratings Slip Sixteen Percent," *Ada (Okla.) News*, Nov. 27, 1981, ORU.

23. "Oral Roberts Lost Sixteen Percent of TV Audience, Spokesman Admits," *Tulsa World*, Nov. 26, 1981, p. 5-G.

24. Jim Galloway, "Religious Programming Being Edged Out on Sunday Morning," *Atlanta Journal*, Apr. 30, 1983, pp. 1-A, 5-A.

25. Smith Interview.

26. See Partner Letter, Dec. 1983; Richard Roberts Interview, Mar 31, 1983.

27. See *Tulsa Tribune*, Nov. 3, 1983, ORU.

28. See "Worldwide Healing Service," *AL*, Feb. 1984, pp. 2–6; Partner Letter, Feb. 1984.

29. O. Roberts, Chapel Transcript, Dec. 6, 1972, p. 4; see also O. Roberts, Chapel Transcript, Nov. 10, 1972, p. 6.

30. Evelyn Roberts Interview, Apr. 3, 1984.

31. Troy Gordon, "Round the Clock," *Tulsa World*, Jan. 5, 1976, ORU.

32. "Designs in Steel," *Oracle*, Sept. 3, 1976, p. 7.

33. Richard Roberts Interview, Mar. 31, 1983.

34. Ibid.

35. See Ruth Miller, "Richard Roberts Expands Ministry," *Oracle*, Oct. 26, 1979, pp. 1, 3; Jim Lewis, "OREA Expands to Meet Partners' Families Needs," *Oracle*, Sept. 15, 1978, p. 1; "Answers From George Stovall," *OREA Today*, Apr. 1981, p. 2.

36. Yvonne Nance, "A New Generation Taking God's Healing Power," *AL*, Nov. 1976, p. 8; see also Richard Roberts, Partners Meeting Transcript, Oct. 1, 1976, p. 7.

37. Ruth Miller, "Richard Roberts Expands Ministry," p. 1; see Richard Roberts, Crusade Transcripts, 1979, passim.

38. [Advertisement,] *Louisville Courier-Journal*, Apr. 28, 1979, p. 2-B.

39. Richard Roberts, Chapel Transcript, Sept. 9, 1981, p. 5.

40. O. Roberts, Banquet Transcript, Feb. 7, 1981, p. 5.

41. "Informative Meeting Held for Employees," *OREA Today*, Dec. 1980, p. 2.

42. Richard Roberts, Banquet Transcript, Feb. 7, 1981, p 6.

43. Richard Roberts, Crusade Transcript, Nov. 20, 1982, p. 11.

44. Richard Roberts Interview, Mar. 31, 1983.

45. Richard Roberts, Crusade Transcript, Nov. 20, 1982, p. 11; Demos Shakarian Interview, Jan. 27, 1983; O. Roberts, Laymen's Seminar Transcript, June 18, 1981, p. 3.

46. "Richard Reports," *AL*, Oct. 1982, p. 22.

47. See Ward Morgan, "Full House Hears Famous Evangelist," *Bluefield (W. Va.) Telegraph*, Nov. 14, 1981, ORU.

48. Robinson Interview; Bill Nash Interview, Apr. 2, 1984.

49. See Richard Roberts, Crusade Transcript, June 6, 1982.

50. Doug Smith, "Small Crowd Finds Unspoken Maladies Miraculously Cured at Faith-Healing Show," *Arkansas (Little Rock) Gazette*, Mar. 31, 1982, p. 1-B.

51. Richard Roberts Interview, Mar. 31, 1983.

52. Richard Roberts, Miscellaneous Speech Transcript, Dec. 9, 1982, pp. 21–22.

53. Ibid., pp. 10, 16; Ed Briggs, "Roberts' Heir Apparent Preaches, Croons, Heals at Mosque," *Richmond (Va.) Times-Dispatch*, Apr. 10, 1981, p. 6-B.

54. Laymen's Seminar Transcript, June 21, 1981, p. 22.

55. "Editorial Department Produces Publications," *OREA Today*, May 11, 1981, p. 7.

56. "People Jammed the Aisles with Healings Too Numerous to Count," *AL*, June 1982, pp. 10–16.

57. "Richard Roberts," p. 22.

58. Partner Letter, Mar. 1984.

59. Richard Roberts, Miscellaneous Speech Transcript, Dec. 9, 1982, p. 21.

60. Charles Farah Interview, Jan. 25, 1983.

61. Janet Pearson, "Richard Roberts," *Tulsa World*, Dec. 2, 1979, p. 1-H.

62. See Robinson Interview; Wayne Robinson, *Oral: The Warm, Intimate, Unauthorized Portrait of a Man of God* (Los Angeles: Acton House [1976]); Patti Roberts with Sherry Andrews, *Ashes to Gold* (Waco, Texas: Word Books [1983]); Jerry Sholes, *Give Me that Prime-Time Religion* (New York: Hawthorn Books, 1979).

63. Robinson Interview.

64. John Williams Interview, Mar. 30, 1983.

65. Evelyn Roberts Interview, Nov. 1, 1983; Donald Moyers Interview, Dec. 13, 1983.

66. B. Nash Interview.

67. Robinson Interview.

68. Williams Interview.

69. Richard Roberts Interview, Mar. 31, 1983.

70. Richard Roberts, Chapel Transcript, Mar. 3, 1982, pp. 15–16.

71. Richard Roberts, Banquet Transcript, Feb. 7, 1981, p. 5.

72. Richard Roberts Interviews, Mar. 31, 1983; Sept. 5, 1984.

73. Warren Hultgren Interview, Mar. 30, 1983.

74. Smith Interview.

75. B. Nash Interview.

76. Evelyn Roberts Interview, Nov. 1, 1983.

77. Richard Roberts Interview, Mar. 31, 1983.

78. Patti Roberts, *Ashes to Gold*, p. 92.

79. B. Nash Interview.

80. "Richard Roberts Ministers to the Needs of Others," *Oracle*, Apr. 24, 1981, p. 10.

81. Richard Roberts Interview, Mar. 31, 1983.

82. Ibid.

83. O. Roberts Interview, Feb. 16, 1983.

84. Shakarian Interview.

85. Evelyn Roberts Interview, Feb. 16, 1983.

86. Richard Roberts, Crusade Transcript, Nov. 20, 1982, p. 16; O. Roberts, OREA Employees Meeting Transcript, Feb. 3, 1982, p. 8.

87. O. Roberts, Chapel Transcript, Apr. 19, 1978, p. 5.

88. "21,000 Hear Oral Roberts," *Tulsa World*, June 18, 1979, ORU.

89. See "Campmeeting '83 Guest Speakers Include Well-Known Home-Folks," *Tulsa World*, June 27, 1983, p. 12-A; Oral Roberts, "Back on the Evangelistic Field!" *AL*, Oct. 1983, p. 3.

90. O. Roberts, "Back on the Evangelistic Field!", p. 3.

91. Grant Williams, "Roberts Returns to Roots," *Tulsa Tribune*, Oct. 21, 1983, pp. 1-E, 2-E.

92. Evelyn Roberts Interview, Nov. 1, 1983.

93. O. Roberts Interview, Sept. 3, 1984; George Stovall Interview, Jan. 27, 1983; James Winslow Interview, Feb. 4, 1983; "Questions Commonly Asked about the City of Faith," *Tulsa World*, Nov. 1, 1981, p. 5; "Dr. Winslow Answers Questions on City of Faith," *Oracle*, Mar. 9, 1979, p. 5.

94. Winslow Interview.

95. Stovall Interview.

96. Stovall Interview; Beth Thornton, "OREA to Move into New Quarters," *Oracle*, Nov. 17, 1978, pp. 1, 3; "Answers from George Stovall," *OREA Today*, July 1980, p. 7.

97. Moyers Interview.

98. Stovall Interview.

99. Smith Interview.

100. Richard Roberts Interview, Mar. 31, 1983; see Janet Pearson, "Ron Smith, Oral Roberts' Top Aide, Resigns," *Tulsa World*, Aug. 3, 1979, ORU.

101. Robinson Interview; see "Roberts' Aide Says He Will Stay," *Tulsa Tribune*, Aug. 2, 1979, p. 15-A.

102. Smith Interview.

103. Pearson, "Ron Smith, Oral Roberts' Top Aide, Resigns."

104. Smith Interview.

105. See "Collins Steele," *AL*, June 1979, pp. 19–20.

106. See "Rev. Robert F. DeWeese," *AL*, June 1979, pp. 18–19; "Rev. Bob DeWeese," *AL*, Jan. 1984, pp. 26–27; Robert DeWeese Interview, Jan. 19, 1983.

107. B. Nash Interview; Stovall Interview; O. Roberts Interview, Aug. 17, 1984.

108. B. Nash Interview.

109. Winslow Interview.

110. O. Roberts, Chapel Transcript, Sept. 14, 1981, pp. 8–10; Oral Roberts Press Conference Transcript, Feb. 25, 1982, pp. 1–15.

111. "The People's Voice," *Tulsa World*, Dec. 22, 1982, p. 8-A.

112. Smith Interview.

113. James Buskirk Interview, Feb. 11, 1983.

114. Ibid.

115. Smith Interview.

116. Beth Macklin, "ORU Theology Dean to Be Senior Minister of First Methodist," *Tulsa World*, Aug. 13, 1984, p. 3-A.

117. O Roberts Interview, Aug. 17, 1984; Buskirk Interview, Aug. 17, 1984.

118. Roberta Roberts Potts Interview, Dec. 13, 1983.

119. Bill Roberts Interview, Feb. 23, 1983.

120. William Jernigan Interview. Aug. 17, 1984.

121. O. Roberts, Chapel Transcript, Feb. 26, 1982, p. 21.

122. See "Why It Is So Important for You to Be Faithful Each Month with Your Blessing Pact with God!" (pamphlet, no pub. info.), n.p.; O. Roberts, "Here Are the Things God Is Saying to Me," *AL*, Sept. 1979, pp. 2–4.

123. "University Faces Financial Crisis," *Communique*, Spring 1982, n.p.; "Answers from George Stovall," *OREA Today*, Apr. 1982, p. 2.

124. "Laymen's Seminar Planned," *Oracle*, Oct. 10, 1975, p. 1; see also Evelyn Roberts, *His Darling Wife, Evelyn* (New York: Dell Publishing Co. [1976]), p. 209; Evelyn Roberts, Miscellaneous Speech Transcript, June 8, 1981, pp. 17–18; Ronald Smith, Interview Transcript, Mar. 16, 1977, pp. 3–37.

125. Financial Planning Session, Seminar Transcript, June 20, 1981, pp. 8–10, 23.

126. Richard Roberts Interview, Mar. 31, 1983.

127. Stovall Interview. Roberts had a recurrent problem with the theft of his mail. See "Mail 'Crime' Puts Drain on Roberts," *Tulsa World*, May 20, 1982, p. 1-F; Mike Kimbrell, "Postal Employee Arrested in Theft of Mail from Oral Roberts," *Tulsa World*, Feb. 17, 1984, p. 10-A; "Massengale Pleads Guilty," *Okmulgee (Okla.) Times*, Dec. 11, 1981, ORU.

128. "Telephone Ministry Directly Calls Partners," *OREA Today*, Mar. 1980, p. 2.

129. Stovall Interview,

130. Bush Interview; Stovall Interview.

131. Partner Letter, June 1983.

132. Stovall Interview.

133. Evelyn Roberts, Miscellaneous Speech Transcript, June 8, 1981, p. 6.

134. "Editorial Department Produces Publications," *OREA Today*, May 1981, p. 7; Stovall Interview.

135. Carl Hamilton Interview, Jan. 7, 1983; Stovall Interview.

136. "Editorial Department Produces Publications," p. 7.

137. "The City of Faith," *Logos*, Jan.-Feb. 1979, p. 11; Lewis, "OREA Expands to Meet Partners' Families Needs," p. 1.

138. "Answers from George Stovall," *OREA Today*, July 1980, p. 7.

139. Stovall Interview.

140. Smith Interview.

141. O. Roberts Interview, Feb. 16, 1983.

142. Oral Roberts, "I'm Sounding an Alert," *AL*, Oct. 1979, p. 4.

143. Partner Letters, Dec. 1981; Dec. 1983.

144. "Letters from Roberts," *Johnson City (Tenn.) Evening Press-Chronicle*, Nov. 20, 1980, ORU.

145. Oral Roberts, "My Back's against the Wall," *AL*, July 1981, p. 7.

146. "Tel-A-Gram," Tulsa, Oklahoma, Feb. 1981, ORU Archives; "Oral Roberts Calls on Prayer Partners to Keep Ministry Alive," *Tulsa World*, Mar. 6, 1982, pp. 1-A, 4-A.

147. "The Alabaster Box and the Oil of Anointing for Your Healing," *AL*, May 1976, pp. 20–21; "Healing and Gladness of Heart," *AL*, Apr. 1979, p. 11.

148. George Stovall curtly denied that the prayer cloths were being sold for a set price. "City of Faith Prayer Cloth Sales Denied," *Tulsa Tribune*, Feb. 16, 1979, ORU; "My Personal Letter to You," *AL*, Feb. 1979, pp. 14–15; "I Want You to Have a Breakthrough to Healing," *AL*, Mar. 1979, p. 16.

149. Partner Letter and Napkin, Sept. 1983; see Kenneth L. Woodward with Sylvester Monroe and Joane Gordon, "Appeal to the Flock," *Newsweek*, Sept. 10, 1979, p. 79.

150. "Special Roberts Appeal Nets Hospital Millions," *Tulsa World*, Oct. 31, 1981, p. 9-D.

151. Oral Roberts, "God Is Your Total Source," *AL*, Feb. 1980, p. 13; Oral Roberts, "Who Is This Person in Your Family," *AL*, Feb. 1980, p. 6; Richard Roberts, "Get Yourself Ready for a Miracle," *AL*, Feb. 1968, p. 6.

152. "Keeping You Informed," *OREA Today*, Dec. 1980, p. 1; "ORU to Pray for Partners," *Oracle*, Apr. 18, 1980, p. 1.

153. See Partner Letter, Nov. 1983.

154. Partner Letter, May 1983.

155. See Oral Roberts, "A Breakthrough for Cancer Is Coming," *AL*, Feb. 1983, pp. 3–8; Beth Macklin, "Request by Oral Roberts Draws National Attention," *Tulsa World*, Feb. 6, 1983, p. 2-A; Stovall Interview.

156. Bush Interview.

157. Woodward et al., "Appeal to the Flock," p. 79.

158. David Westerfield, "Newsweek Gets Response," *Oracle*, Sept. 14, 1979, p. 4.

159. David Rossie, "Keeping Up with the Reverends," *Binghamton (N.Y.) Press*, Mar. 1, 1981, ORU.

160. "Why Oral Roberts Talks Cash to the Son of God," *Atlanta Constitution*, Jan. 21, 1983, p. 2-A.

161. "Answers to the Tough Questions," *AL*, Apr. 1983, p. 13.

162. Jack Mobley, "Pastor Isn't Buying Religious Hard-Sell on Radio, TV," *Chicago Tribune*, Oct. 7, 1980, ORU.

163. Beth Macklin, "Roberts Supporters Worry Ethics Prof," *Tulsa World,* Oct. 28, 1979, ORU.

164. "Share Jesus' Area Code, Oral Urged," *Tulsa World,* Feb. 13, 1983, p. 12-A.

165. "Oral Meets Big Jesus Christ," *Oklahoma Observer* (Tulsa), Nov. 10, 1980, p. 10; Oral Roberts, "I Must Tell Somebody," *AL,* Sept. 1980, pp. 10–13.

166. C. Thomas Thompson Interview, Feb. 2, 1983.

167. C. Thomas Thompson, mimeographed letter in possession of author.

168. Bruce Buursma, "Oral Roberts and His Skeptics," *Chicago Tribune Magazine,* Jan. 3, 1982, sec. 9, pp. 8–10.

169. Thompson Interview.

170. "The Hospital That Oral Roberts Built," *Seattle (Wash.) Times,* Nov. 4, 1981, ORU.

171. Helen Parmley, "SMU Official Suggests Oral Roberts Saw Hallucination," *Dallas Morning News,* Dec. 14, 1980, p. 35-A.

172. "Fundamentalist Terms Roberts' Vision a 'Hoax,'" *Southwest Times Record* (Fort Smith, Ark.), Nov. 29, 1980, p. 2-A; "Giant Jesus Image Draws Fire," *Los Angeles Times,* Dec. 6, 1980, ORU; J. D. Tant, "Oral's 900 Foot Tall Jesus," *Vanguard,* Dec. 1980, p. 12.

173. "A Cross to Bear," *Saturday Oklahoman and Times*(Oklahoma City), Dec. 19, 1981, ORU.

174. Henry Gay, "More Questions from Our Readers," *Poulsbo (Wash.) Herald,* Nov. 5, 1980, ORU; "Oral's Encounter," *Oklahoma Observer* (Tulsa), Nov. 10, 1980, p. 10.

175. Jim Fitzgerald, "Who Would Want to Argue with a 900-Foot-Tall Christ," *Detroit Free Press,* May 16, 1981, ORU.

176. Calvin Thielman Interview, Apr. 8, 1983.

177. Richard Roberts, Chapel Transcript, Oct. 20, 1980, p. 5.

178. Ibid., p. 7.

179. O. Roberts, Dedication Transcript, Nov. 1, 1981, p. 16.

180. "Donations Pour In After Vision Described," *Tulsa World,* Nov. 1, 1980, p. 2-C.

181. Margaret Hall, "Doing the Impossible," *Religious Broadcasting,* Mar. 1983 p. 35.

182. O. Roberts Interview, Feb. 16, 1984.

183. "Oral Roberts Man to Man," *Midland (Tex.) Reporter Telegram,* Oct. 8, 1978, ORU.

184. Bush Interview.

185. O. Roberts Interview, Feb. 16, 1984.

186. Williams Interview.

187. Ibid.

188. O. Roberts, Chapel Transcript, Aug. 24, 1979, p. 8.

189. Charles A. Kothe, "Oral Roberts University: Promoting Free Enterprise" (brochure, no pub. info.).

190. Evelyn Roberts, Miscellaneous Speech Transcript, June 8, 1981, p. 3.

191. "Roberts Tells Senate of Financing Woes," *Tulsa World,* Apr. 7, 1982, p. 2-A.

192. O. Roberts, Chapel Transcript, Nov. 9, 1979, p. 7.

193. O. Roberts, Chapel Transcript, Sept. 24, 1979, n.p.

194. Richard Roberts, Chapel Transcript, Oct. 20, 1980, pp. 12–13.

195. O. Roberts, Chapel Transcript, Nov. 9, 1979, pp. 5–6.

196. Richard Roberts, Chapel Transcript, Oct. 20, 1980, p. 14.

197. Bush Interview.

198. Buskirk Interview, Feb. 18, 1983.

199. Ibid.

200. Farah Interview.

201. Stovall Interview.

202. O. Roberts Interview, Feb. 16, 1983.

203. Winslow Interview.

204. Jenkin Lloyd Jones Interview, Mar. 31, 1983.

205. O. Roberts, Address to Law Students Transcript, Apr. 5, 1982, p. 7.

206. Williams Interview.

207. Elaine Vitt and Andelia Herrin, "City of Faith Hospital Stirs Controversy," *Jackson (Miss.) Daily News,* Nov. 17, 1981, ORU.

208. Briggs, "Roberts' Heir Apparent Preaches, Croons, Heals at Mosque."

209. "TIO Disputes Evangelists' Audience Claims," *Broadcasting,* Oct. 19, 1981, ORU.

210. Richard Roberts, Miscellaneous Speech Transcript, Dec. 9, 1982, p. 19; O. Roberts Interview, Feb. 16, 1983.

211. "Roberts to Be Speaker," *Vanita (Okla.) Journal,* May 30, 1978, ORU.

212. Phil Gailey, "Noted Evangelists Wooed by Carter," *Washington (D.C.) Star,* Nov. 4, 1979, p. 5-A.

213. John Dart, "Survey Bolsters TV Evangelists," *Los Angeles Times,* July 5, 1980, p. 24.

214. Beth Macklin, "Ruth Carter Stapleton Explains Experiences of Inner Healing," *Tulsa World,* Nov. 16, 1978, ORU; Ruth Carter Stapleton, Chapel Transcript, Nov. 15, 1978, pp. 1–2.

215. O. Roberts, Miscellaneous Speech Transcript, Jan. 22, 1973, p. 9.

216. Joe Edwards, "Nashville Notes," *Memphis Commercial Appeal,* Dec. 11, 1981, ORU.

217. Bob Foresman, "Tulsan Sees Signs of Upturn," *Tulsa Tribune,* Jan. 7, 1983, ORU.

218. "Oral Roberts University: Promoting Free Enterprise."

219. See various Commencement Transcripts.

220. "Oral Roberts University: Promoting Free Enterprise."

221. Bettye Anderson, "Charismatics Seek Fellowship," *Jackson (Tenn.) Sun,* Oct. 22, 1982, ORU.

222. Beth Macklin, " 'Mr. Pentecost' Says Charismatic Movement Growing," *Tulsa World,* Mar. 10, 1979, p. 3-C.

223. Tammy Logue, "Synan Provides Historical Perspective," *Oracle,* Oct. 10, 1980, p. 7.

224. Thomas Zimmerman Interview, Oct. 18, 1980.

225. See John Maust, "Charismatic Leaders Seeking Faith for Their Own Healing," *Christianity Today,* Apr. 4, 1980, pp. 44–46.

226. Zimmerman Interview.

227. See Maust, "Charismatic Leaders Seeking Faith for Their Own Healing," pp. 44–46.

228. Farah Interview.

229. O. Roberts, City of Faith Dedication Transcript, June 5, 1981, p. 5.

230. Howard Ervin Interview, Jan. 25, 1983.

231. Vinson Synan Telephone Interview, Apr. 16, 1984; Harold Paul Interview, Jan. 28, 1983; B. Nash Interview; O. Roberts, Address to Law Students Transcript, Apr. 5, 1982, p. 6.

232. See Vinson Synan, "Faith Formula Fuels Charismatic Controversy," *Christianity Today,* Dec. 12, 1980, pp. 65–66; Brett Hoffman, "City-Wide Range of Views on Faith," *Oracle,* Dec. 4, 1981, p. 6.

233. In 1980 and 1981, Roberts strongly supported Jim Bakker. See "Ministries Rally to PTL's Aid," *Charisma,* Dec. 1981, ORU.

234. Kenneth Hagin, Sr. Interview, Dec. 12, 1983; Kenneth Hagin, Jr. Interview, Dec. 12, 1983.

235. Oral Roberts, "The Night I Found That God Hadn't Forgotten Me in Our Struggle," *AL,* Oct. 1979, pp. 6–13; "Hagin Collection for ORU May Exceed $100,000," *Tulsa Tribune,* July 28, 1979, ORU; K. Hagin, Sr. and K. Hagin, Jr. Interviews.

236. O. Roberts, "The Night I Found That God Hadn't Forgotten Me in Our Struggle," p. 11.

237. Farah Interview.

238. See Chapel Transcript, Nov. 28, 1979; O. Roberts, Rhema Campmeeting Transcript, July 24, 1980; K. Hagin, Sr. Interview.

239. "Campmeeting '83 Guest Speakers Include Well-Known 'Home-Folks.' "

240. See Chapel Transcript, Jan. 16, 1980; Brett Hoffman, "Osteen Highly Esteems Roberts Lifestyle," *Oracle,* Oct. 23, 1981, p. 7.

241. Farah Interview.

242. See John Dart, "Low-Key Pastor Reaches Big Time," *Los Angeles Times,* Dec. 7, 1981, ORU; Brett Hoffman, "Price Talks on Living Faith," *Oracle,* Feb. 13, 1981, p. 7.

243. Fred Price, Campus Address Transcript, Feb. 5, 1981, p. 8.

244. Farah Interview.

245. Chapel Transcript, part 2, Sept. 9, 1980, pp. 38–39.

246. Farah Interview.

247. Fred Price, Chapel Transcript, Feb. 6, 1981, p. 25.

248. Buskirk Interview, Feb. 18, 1983.

249. Ervin Interview.

250. Synan, "Faith Formula Fuels Charismatic Controversy," p. 65; see Charles Farah, Jr., *From the Pinnacle of the Temple* (Plainfield, N.J.: Logos International, n.d.); Charles Farah, Jr., "Toward a Theology of Healing," *Acts,* May-June 1977, pp. 23–29.

251. Farah Interview.

252. Ibid.

253. O. Roberts, Partner Letter, Aug. 1983.

254. O. Roberts, Family Seminar Transcript, Aug. 30, 1981, pp. 14–15.

255. O. Roberts, Chapel Transcript, Jan. 30, 1981, pp. 23–24.

256. Ibid., p. 23.

257. Buskirk Interview, Feb. 18, 1983.

258. See Richard Roberts, Crusade Transcript, May 8, 1982; Richard Roberts, Miscellaneous Speech Transcript, Dec. 9, 1982; K. Hagin, Sr. Interview.

259. Richard Roberts, Chapel Transcript, Oct. 20, 1980.

260. Richard Roberts Interview, Mar. 31, 1983.

261. Richard Roberts, Miscellaneous Speech Transcript, Dec. 9, 1982, pp. 10, 22.

262. See Miscellaneous Speech Transcript, Oct. 2, 1976.

263. See John Maust, "Evangelism's Revival in Mainline Denominations," *Christianity Today,* Jan. 25, 1980, pp. 44–46; "Billy Graham to Speak at ORU Meeting," *Tulsa World,* July 10, 1979, ORU.

264. Buskirk Interview, Feb. 18, 1983.

265. Letter from David I. Bradley to Oral Roberts, Dec. 28, 1977, ORU Archives.

266. Spurgeon M. Dunnam III, "Evangelism Congress at ORU," *United Methodist Reporter,* Jan. 25, 1980, ORU.

267. O. Roberts, Miscellaneous Speech Transcript, June 6, 1977, p. 7.

268. O. Roberts Interview, Feb. 16, 1983.

269. Buskirk Interview, Feb. 18, 1983.

270. O. Roberts Interview, Feb. 16, 1983.

271. Buskirk Interview, Feb. 18, 1983.

272. O. Roberts Interviews, Feb. 16, 1983; Aug. 17, 1984.

273. Buskirk Interview, Feb. 18, 1983.

274. O. Roberts Interview, Feb. 16, 1983.

275. Beth Macklin, "City of Faith Seeking Indigent Patients to Save Accreditation," *Tulsa World,* July 16, 1984, pp. 1-A, 2-A.

276. David Fritze, "The Gold and the Glory," *Oklahoma Monthly,* Oct. 1977, p. 14.

277. William J. Broad, "And God Said to Oral: Build a Hospital," *Science,* Apr. 18, 1980, p. 267.

278. See "When God Talks, Oral Listens," *Time,* Nov. 16, 1981, p. 16; "A Reporter at Large," *New Yorker,* Apr. 2, 1979, p. 41; "Playboy Looks at the Electronic Chruch," *Cleveland (Ohio) Press,* Sept. 6, 1980, ORU, "More Letters," *Bluefield (W. Va.) Telegraph,* Dec. 6, 1981, ORU.

279. Fritze, "The Gold and the Glory," p. 102.

280. Stephen Strang, "A Christian Journalist's Dilemma," *Charisma,* Mar. 1981, p. 6.

281. O. Roberts, Church Sermon Transcript, Jan. 26, 1975, p. 6.

282. O. Roberts, Chapel Transcript, Aug. 24, 1979, p. 10; O. Roberts Interviews, Feb. 16, 1983; Aug. 17, 1984.

283. See J. I. Packer, "Charismatic Renewal," *Christianity Today,* Mar. 7, 1980, pp.

16–20; Curtis Hutson, *The Fullness of the Holy Spirit* (Murfreesboro, Tenn.: Sword of the Lord Publishers, 1981).

284. George W. Dollar, *A History of Fundamentalism in America* (Greenville, S.C.: Bob Jones University Press [1973]), p. 281.

285. "Editorial," *Faith for the Family,* Nov. 1978, ORU.

286. "Oral Roberts Upgrades His TV Specials," *Baptist Bible Tribune,* Sept. 4, 1981, p. 2.

287. Letter from Don Alexander to D. E. Harrell, Jan. 27, 1983.

288. [Eugene Britnell,] "Oral Roberts Exploits Death of Son for More Money!" *Sower,* Oct. 1982, p. 3; Lewis Willis, "Oral Roberts Said He Talked with Jesus," *Guardian of Truth,* Mar. 3, 1983, p. 15; J. D. Tant, "Oral Roberts," *Vanguard,* Nov. 1980, p. 13.

289. Richard Mortlock, "Churches Lash 'Worship-by-Tube' TV Evangelists," *New York Star,* June 24, 1980, ORU.

290. Beth Macklin, "Church Historian Critical of TV Preachers," *Tulsa World,* Apr. 3, 1982, p. A-6; Beth Macklin, "Scottish Clergyman Raps TV Preaching," *Tulsa World,* Mar. 4, 1982, p. 9-A.

291. See, for instance, Paul Hemphill, "Praise the Lord—and Cue the Cameraman," *TV Guide,* Aug. 12, 1978, pp. 4–8; John Mariani, "Television Evangelism," *Saturday Review,* Feb. 1979, pp. 22–25; Jim Montgomery, "The Electric Church," *Wall Street Journal,* May 19, 1978, ORU; Carey McWilliams, "Second Thoughts," *Nation,* Dec. 1, 1979, p. 552.

292. Hadden and Swann, *Prime Time Preachers,* pp. 51–55 and passim.

293. "Robbins Tackles Bible Pounders," *Dyersburg (Tenn.) State Gazette,* Nov. 10, 1982, ORU.

294. Vernon Scott, "Robbins Tackles Bible Pounders," *Virginia (Minn.) Mesabi News,* Nov. 8, 1982, ORU.

295. See "The Hallelujah Radicals," *Review,* June 20, 1982, p. 5.

296. See "Evangelist Oral Roberts Supports Moral Majority," *Maine Press Herald* (Portland), May 9, 1981, ORU.

297. D. R. Segal, "Laugh unto the Second Generation," *Delta Democrat-Times* (Greenville, Miss.), Nov. 19, 1981, ORU.

298. Robinson, *Oral,* p. xi.

299. Robinson Interview.

300. Ibid.

301. Hamilton Interview, Jan. 13, 1983.

302. See Woodward et al., "Appeal to the Flock," p. 79; see also George R. Plagenz, "Evangelist Probed As Never Before," *Santa Maria (Calif.) Times,* Apr. 12, 1980, ORU; Arthur S. Brisbane, "Peddling a Man of God," *Kansas City Times,* Jan. 4, 1980, ORU; G. Archer Weniger, "Give Me That Prime Time Religion," *Fundamental Baptist Fellowship of America News Bulletin,* Mar.-Apr. 1980, p. 1.

303. Brisbane, "Peddling a Man of God."

304. "Ex-Employee's Book Fires Salvo at Roberts," *Tulsa Tribune,* July 4, 1979, ORU.

305. See Sholes, *Give Me That Prime-Time Religion,* p. xv.

306. Ibid., p. 153.

307. Ibid., pp. 191–208.

308. See "Ex-Employee's Book Fires Salvo at Roberts."

309. "After Oral Roberts," *Tulsa Tribune,* July 20, 1979, ORU.

310. "Ex-Employee's Book Fires Salvo at Roberts."

311. "ORU Officials Offered 'Information' on Book," July 7, 1979, ORU.

312. Robinson Interview.

313. "Ex-Employee's Book Fires Salvo at Roberts."

314. "Sixty Minutes," vol. 12, no. 20, Transcript, pp. 7–10; see Hadden and Swann, *Prime Time Preachers,* p. 58.

315. Hamilton Interview, Jan. 17, 1983; Farah Interview.

316. Richard Roberts Interview, Mar. 31, 1983.

317. Thompson Interview.

318. See "Sixty Minutes," pp. 7–12.

319. "Regents Chairman Blasts 'Sixty Minutes,' " *Oracle,* Feb. 1, 1980, p. 3; Moyers Interview.

320. "Sixty Minutes," p. 12.

321. Ibid., p. 8.

322. William Willoughby, "If You Hear Good News, You'll Be a Better Person," *New York News World,* July 20, 1980, ORU; "It's Time for the Truth to Be Told," *AL,* Aug. 1980, p. 9.

323. Beth Macklin Interview, Dec. 14, 1983.

324. Moyers Interview.

325. "Prayer Tower Receives Positive Calls during 'Sixty Minutes' Program," *OREA Today,* Mar. 1980, p. 8; see "Letters to the Editor," *Venice (Fla.) Gondolier,* Feb. 28, 1980, ORU; and ORU clippings file in general.

326. "Answers from George Stovall," *OREA Today,* Aug. 1980, p. 6.

327. Chapel Transcript, Feb. 8, 1980, pp. 14–15.

328. "ORU Employees Asked to Sign Loyalty Oath," *Nowata (Okla.) Star,* Jan. 11, 1980, ORU.

329. See Christiane Bird, "Look at Tulsa," *Arkansas Gazette* (Little Rock), Oct. 2, 1983, p. 5-C; Robert Paul Jordan, "High-Flying Tulsa," *National Geographic,* Sept. 1983, pp. 393-98.

330. See "ORU Tops Attractions List," *Pauls Valley (Okla.) Democrat,* Apr. 12, 1981, ORU; "The Roads District," *Tulsa World,* Feb. 22, 1979, ORU.

331. Williams Interview.

332. Jones Interview.

333. Thompson Interview.

334. Ibid.

335. R. D. Stathem, "Roberts' Critic," *Tulsa World,* May 12, 1984, p. 8-A; for some typical exchanges in the letter-to-the-editor section of the *Tulsa World,* see "The People's Voice," Mar. 17, 1982, p. 15-A; June 26, 1983, p. 8-I.

336. Moyers Interview; Winslow Interview.

337. Thompson Interview.

338. "Answers from George Stovall, *OREA Today,* Dec. 1980, p. 6.

339. "The People's Voice," *Tulsa World,* Sept. 21, 1979, ORU.

340. Macklin Interview; Williams Interview.

341. "Oral's New Appeal," *Tulsa World,* Mar. 9, 1982, p. 6-A.

342. Williams Interview.

343. Jones Interview.

344. Hultgren Interview; Jones Interview; Bush Interview.

345. Jones Interview.

346. Hultgren Interview.

347. Winslow Interview.

348. Hultgren Interview; Bush Interview.

349. Bush Interview; Williams Interview.

350. Edna Nash Interview, Apr. 2, 1984.

351. See Macklin, "City of Faith Seeking Indigent Patients to Save Accreditation," p. 1-A.

352. O. Roberts, Chapel Transcript, Aug. 19, 1978, p. 25; see also Chapel Transcript, Aug. 29, 1980, p. 5.

353. Chapel Transcript, Feb. 8, 1980, p. 8.

354. Evelyn Roberts Interview, Feb. 16, 1983.

355. O. Roberts Interview, Feb. 16, 1983.

356. Evelyn Roberts, *His Darling Wife,* p. 113.

357. O. Roberts, OREA Devotion Transcript, Feb. 4, 1957, p. 19.

16. THE MESSAGE

1. Lee Braxton Interview, Dec. 18, 1973.
2 Evelyn Roberts, OREA Devotion Transcript, Dec. 24, 1968, p. 2.
3. Albert E. Bush Interview, Feb. 11, 1983.
4. Oscar Moore Interview, Jan. 20, 1983.
5. Oral and Evelyn Roberts, Evangelism of Oral Roberts Class Transcript, 1971, pp. 14-15.
6. Bill and Edna Nash Interviews, Apr. 2, 1984.
7. O. Roberts, OREA Devotion Transcript, July 20, 1962, p. 1.
8. Charles Farah Interview, Jan. 25, 1983.
9. Vinson Synan Interview, May 22, 1983.
10. Braxton Interview.
11. Evelyn Roberts, Evangelism of Oral Roberts Class Transcript, 1971, p. 8.
12. Howard Ervin Interview, Jan. 25, 1983.
13. See John Pitts, "Spiritual Healing," *Religion in Life*, Spring 1956, p. 164.
14. Bush Interview; Beth Macklin Interview, Dec. 14, 1983.
15. Oral Roberts, *The Drama of the End Time* (Franklin Springs, Ga.: Publishing House of the Pentecostal Church [1941]), p. 10.
16. Oral Roberts, *How to Know God's Will* (Tulsa: Oral Roberts Evangelistic Association, 1982), p. 9.
17. Oral Roberts, "God's Prescription for You for the New Year," *Daily Blessing*, Jan., Feb., Mar. 1983, p. 4.
18. O. Roberts, Faculty Meeting Transcript, Apr. 20, 1972, pp. 3-4.
19. Farah Interview.
20. James Buskirk Interview, Feb. 18, 1983.
21. Suzanne Trimel, "The Bible," *Lebanon (Ind.) Reporter*, Sept. 22, 1982, ORU.
22. O. Roberts, Class Transcript, Nov. 29, 1967, pp. 9-11.
23. Farah Interview.
24. Oral Roberts, *What Is a Miracle?* (Tulsa: Oral Roberts, 1964), pp. 6-7.
25. O. Roberts, Kiwanis Club Speech Transcript, 1956, pp. 9-10.
26. O. Roberts, Class Transcript, Oct. 11, 1967, p. 7.
27. See O. Roberts, Faculty Chapel Transcript, Sept. 5, 1967, p. 4.
28. O. Roberts, My Own Personal Testimony Transcript, Oct. 21, 1970, pp. 2-3.
29. Paul Galloway, "The Healer as Teacher and Golfer," *Chicago Sun Times Midwest Magazine*, Nov. 5, 1972, p. 31; see also Pete Martin, "Oral Roberts, Part I," *Christian Herald*, Feb. 1966, p. 95.
30. O. Roberts, Speech to Graduate and Theology Students Transcript, Jan. 31, 1977, p. 8.
31. Evelyn Roberts, Evangelism of Oral Roberts Class Transcript, 1971, p. 10.
32. Farah Interview.
33. O. Roberts *How to Know God's Will*, p. 6.
34. O. Roberts, Evangelism of Oral Roberts Class Transcript, 1971, p. 16.
35. Farah Interview.
36. H. Richard Hall Interview, May 31, 1972.
37. Oral Roberts, *Questions and Answers on Doctrine* (Tulsa: Oral Roberts Evangelistic Association, n.d.), pp. 1-2.
38. O. Roberts, Evangelism Class Transcript, Jan. 3, 1968, pp. 30-32.
39. Karl E. Lutze, "Oral Roberts of Tulsa," *American Lutheran*, Sept. 1955, pp. 18-19.
40. O. Roberts, Crusade Transcript, Apr. 20, 1957, p. 16.
41. O. Roberts, Banquet Transcript, Apr. 23, 1973, p. 11.
42. O. Roberts, Evangelism Class Transcript, Jan. 3, 1968, pp. 20, 33.
43. O. Roberts, Chapel Transcript, Aug. 19, 1978, pp. 12-20.
44. See O. Roberts, Miscellaneous Speech Transcript, Oct. 2, 1976, pp. 8-9.

45. Oral Roberts, *The Holy Spirit in the Now* (3 vols.; Tulsa: Oral Roberts University, 1974), vol. 1, p. 33.

46. Oral Roberts, "Is Something Bothering You?" *Carefree Enterprise*, July 1976, p. 24.

47. O. Roberts, Contemporary Methods in Evangelism Class Transcript, Oct. 11, 1967, p. 29; Wayne Robinson Interview, Apr. 4, 1983.

48. O. Roberts, Banquet Transcript, Apr. 23, 1973, p. 20.

49. O. Roberts, Faculty Chapel Transcript, Aug. 19, 1974, p. 10.

50. O. Roberts, Faculty Chapel Transcript, Sept. 5, 1967, p. 3.

51. O. Roberts, Chapel Transcript, Mar. 26, 1970, p. 9.

52. O. Roberts, Contemporary Methods of Evangelism Class Transcript, Oct. 11, 1967, p. 6.

53. O. Roberts, Evangelism 501 Class Transcript, Jan. 3, 1968, pp. 3–4.

54. Ibid., p. 18.

55. Jenkin Lloyd Jones Interview, Mar. 31, 1983.

56. O. Roberts, Evangelism 501 Class Transcript, Jan. 3, 1968, p. 2.

57. O. Roberts, Crusade Transcript, Aug. 25, 1968, p. 9.

58. Calvin Thielman Interview, Apr. 8, 1983.

59. See David Edwin Harrell, Jr., *All Things Are Possible* (Bloomington: Indiana University Press [1975]), pp. 98–99.

60. See J. M. McLean, "Oral Roberts' Campaign in Tacoma," *PHA*, Sept. 15, 1949, p. 4; Louise Evans, "Tent Revival Attracting Thousands Here Nightly," *Amarillo (Tex.) Daily News*, Sept. 6, 1950, p. 7.

61. See "Oral Roberts in Raleigh," *Raleigh (N.C.) Carolinian*, Dec. 8, 1956, ORU.

62. K. M. Smith, "Nashville Ministers, Refusing to Be Segregated, Threatened with Expulsion from Oral Roberts Meet Here," *Nashville (Tenn.) National Baptist Union Review*, Dec. 13, 1958, ORU.

63. Oral Roberts, *Oral Roberts' Best Sermons and Stories* (Tulsa: Oral Roberts, 1956), p. 50.

64. "God's Best Weapon on Reds," *Los Angeles Herald Examiner*, Sept. 26, 1957, ORU.

65. Oral Roberts, *Oral Roberts' Life Story* (Tulsa: Oral Roberts [1952]), p. 128. For a discussion of the racial attitudes of Roberts and other evangelists, see David Edwin Harrell, Jr., *White Sects and Black Men in the Recent South* (Nashville: Vanderbilt University Press, 1971).

66. O. Roberts, Chapel Transcript, Oct. 6, 1968, p. 11.

67. See O. Roberts, All-Sports Awards Banquet Transcript, May 4, 1972, n.p.; Oral Roberts, "Hate, Love, and the Christian," *AL*, Mar. 1968, pp. 12–13.

68. See O. Roberts, Chapel Transcript, Sept. 1, 1968, pp. 11–12; John Dart, "Freer Views on Charisma," *Los Angeles Times* [unidentified clipping], ORU; O. Roberts, "Hate, Love, and the Christian," p. 11.

69. See George M. Marsden, *Fundamentalism and American Culture* (New York and Oxford: Oxford University Press, 1980).

70. See O. Roberts, *The Drama of the End Time*.

71. See "The H Bomb," *AHM*, Aug. 1955, pp. 2–3; "The Second Coming of Christ," *AL*, Oct. 1967, pp. 23–27; O. Roberts, Chapel Transcript, Oct. 20, 1971.

72. See Bible Tape, no. 6.

73. O. Roberts, Partner Letter, Dec. 1983.

74. See Healing Waters Broadcast Tape, May 1, 1949; Healing Waters Broadcast Tape, Apr. 24, 1949.

75. V. Synan Interview.

76. O. Roberts, *Best Sermons*, p. 123.

77. O. Roberts, Crusade Transcript, June 12, 1957, p. 20; see Bob Wilson, "World's End Near, Declares Roberts," *Fayetteville (N.C.) Observer*, May 17, 1959, ORU; George Burnham, "Oral Roberts Says Second Coming of Jesus Christ Now Draws Near," *Chattanooga News—Free Press*, Mar. 28, 1961, ORU.

78. G. H. M[ontgomery]., "Looking Forward with Oral Roberts in 1953," *HW*, Feb. 1953, p. 10; O. Roberts, "A Look at the New Year," *AL*, Jan. 1964, p. 2.

79. Oral Roberts, *It Is Later Than You Think* (Tulsa: Oral Roberts Tract Society, n.d.), p. 11.

80. See Youth Seminar Transcript, June 9, 1967, p. 9; O. Roberts, My Own Personal Testimony Transcript, Oct. 21, 1970, pp. 1–2; O. Roberts, Chapel Transcript, June 12, 1982, p. 16.

81. Ibid.; "Oral Roberts Talks about the Lord's Return," *AL*, Feb. 1958, pp. 20–24.

82. See Evangelism of Oral Roberts Class Transcript, 1971, pp. 11–15; Miscellaneous Speech Transcript, Oct. 3, 1976, pp. 13–14.

83. O. Roberts, Chapel Transcript, Sept. 23, 1970.

84. O. Roberts, "A Special Message to My Partners," *AL*, May 1967, p. 29.

85. "Oral Roberts Unsure about Vietnam War," *Tulsa Tribune*, Feb. 29, 1968, ORU.

86. O. Roberts, Chapel Transcript, May 12, 1971, p. 6.

87. "Oral Roberts and You" Telecast, Nov. 15, 1981.

88. See Paul G. Chappell, "The Divine Healing Movement in America," Ph.D. dissertation, Drew University, 1982; Donald W. Dayton, "The Rise of the Evangelical Healing Movement in Nineteenth-Century America" (unpublished paper presented at the Society for Pentecostal Studies, Oral Roberts University, Nov. 13, 1980).

89. Harold Paul Interview, Jan. 28, 1983.

90. O. Roberts, *Life Story*, p. 158.

91. O. Roberts, OREA Devotion Transcript, Mar. 25, 1982, p. 10; see Laymen's Seminar Transcript, Dec. 6, 1963, p. 13.

92. Moore Interview.

93. O. Roberts, Evangelism of Oral Roberts Class Transcript, 1971, p. 16.

94. Oral Roberts, *If You Need Healing—Do These Things!* (2d ed.; Tulsa: Standard Printing Co. [1947]), p. 3.

95. See Mary Moore Mason, "Roberts Says He Hates Devil and His Sickness," *Richmond (Va.) News Leader*, Jan. 21, 1960, p. 13.

96. Oral Roberts, *101 Questions and Answers* (Tulsa: Oral Roberts, 1968), p. 85.

97. O. Roberts, Crusade Transcript, Aug. 9, 1968, p. 13.

98. "Divine Healing," *AL*, Aug. 1964, p. 22.

99. O. Roberts, *Best Sermons*, pp. 101–102.

100. Graduation Baccalaureate Transcript, May 26, 1968, p. 9.

101. DeWeese Interview; see O. Roberts, *Life Story*, p. 145; O. Roberts, "How God's Healing Power Works through Me," *HW*, June 1948, p. 1.

102. Oral Roberts, *Seven Divine Aids for Your Health* (Tulsa: Oral Roberts, 1960), pp. 29, 38, 54.

103. Oral Roberts, Partner Letter, May 1983.

104. Oral Roberts, "The Mass Miracle," *AL*, Nov. 1957, pp. 5–6.

105. O. Roberts, *If You Need Healing*, pp. 45–46.

106. Oral Roberts, *God Is a Good God: Believe It and Come Alive* (Indianapolis and New York: Bobbs-Merrill Co., 1960), p. 42; R. F. DeWeese, "If I Were Coming to the Crusade for Healing," *AL*, Sept. 1966, p. 9.

107. O. Roberts, *101 Questions and Answers*, p. 14; O. Roberts, *God Is a Good God*, p. 36.

108. O. Roberts, *The Holy Spirit in the Now*, vol. 1, p. 33; O. Roberts, *101 Questions and Answers*, p. 13; O. Roberts, Banquet Transcript, Oct. 22, 1969, p 7.

109. O. Roberts, *The Holy Spirit in the Now*, vol. 2, p. 18.

110. O. Roberts, *Best Sermons*, p. 46; O. Roberts, *101 Questions and Answers*, p. 18.

111. See Bible Tape no. 8.

112. Oral Roberts, *Turn Your Faith Loose!* (Tulsa: Oral Roberts Tract Society, n.d.), p. 3.

113. Ibid., p. 4.

114. O. Roberts, *If You Need Healing*, pp. 43-44.

115. O. Roberts, Crusade Transcript, June 12, 1957, p. 18.

116. Paul Interview; Macklin Interview.

117. O. Roberts, Evangelism of Oral Roberts Class Transcript, 1971, p. 14.

118. O. Roberts, Contemporary Methods in Evangelism Class Transcript, Nov. 29, 1967, pp. 12-13.

119. O. Roberts, Healing Waters Broadcast Tape, June 5, 1949; [advertisement,] *HW*, Mar. 1948, p. 2.

120. O. Roberts, Crusade Transcript, Apr. 23, 1955, p. 6.

121. Oral Roberts, "The Healing of Cancer," *HW*, Feb. 1949, p. 2.

122. O. Roberts, *Seven Divine Aids for Your Health*, p. 70.

123. Oral Roberts, Partner Letter, June 1984.

124. O. Roberts, *101 Questions and Answers*, p. 24.

125. See Albin Krebs, "Misunderstood, Flamboyant, Controversial," *Gilbert (Ariz.) Enterprise*, Dec. 7, 1956, ORU.

126. O. Roberts, Banquet Transcript, July 8, 1981, pp. 25-26.

127. O. Roberts, *101 Questions and Answers*, p. 71.

128. O. Roberts, *God Is a Good God*, pp. 133-34; O. Roberts, *The Holy Spirit in the Now*, vol. 2, p. 50.

129. O. Roberts, *What Is a Miracle?*, p. 45.

130. O. Roberts, Crusade Transcript, Sept , 1958, p. 23; Oral Roberts, "Demons," *AHM*, Sept. 1954, pp. 2-3, 5-6; O. Roberts, *The Holy Spirit in the Now*, vol. 2, pp. 49, 70.

131. O. Roberts, *Best Sermons*, p. 61.

132. O. Roberts, Evangelism of Oral Roberts Class Transcript, 1971, p. 12.

133. O. Roberts, "Demons," p. 2.

134. Oral Roberts, "The Ministry of Casting Out Demons," *HW*, Aug. 1948, p. 8; Evangelism of Oral Roberts Class Transcript, 1971, p. 13.

135. See O. Roberts, City of Faith Address Transcript, Dec. 3, 1981.

136. O. Roberts, "The Ministry of Casting Out Demons," p. 8.

137. Oral Roberts, "I Believe the Cure for Cancer Has a Spiritual Origin," *AL*, Jan. 1977, pp. 3-4.

138. Oral Roberts, "The Healing of Cancer," *HW*, Feb. 1949, p. 2.

139. See City of Faith Transcript, Dec. 3, 1981, pp. 23-39.

140. See John Thomas Nichol, *Pentecostalism* (New York: Harper and Row [1966]), pp. 16-17.

141. O. Roberts, Crusade Transcript, Aug. 9, 1968, pp. 12-13; O. Roberts, Crusade Transcript, Apr. 21, 1957, p. 16.

142. Paul Interview.

143. O. Roberts, *Best Sermons*, p. 106.

144. Ibid.; see also Bill Rose, "Rev. Roberts to Conduct Ten-Day Healing Mission," *Oakland Tribune*, Sept. 30, 1954, p. 6-D.

145. O. Roberts, *101 Questions and Answers*, pp. 30-31, 43.

146. O. Roberts, *What Is a Miracle?*, p. 35.

147. O. Roberts, *God Is a Good God*, p. 154.

148. O. Roberts, *101 Questions and Answers,* p. 39; Evangelism of Oral Roberts Class Transcript, 1971, p. 18.

149. See *The Holy Spirit in the Now,* vol. 2, p. 33; Evangelism of Oral Roberts Class Transcript, 1971, p. 5.

150. Evangelism of Oral Roberts Class Transcript, 1971, p. 17.

151. Ibid., p. 12.

152. O. Roberts, City of Faith Transcript, June 5, 1981, p. 3.

153. O. Roberts, Banquet Transcript, July 8, 1981, p. 11.

154. O. Roberts, *Life Story*, p. 154.

155. Phil Dessauer, " 'God Heals—I Don't,' " *Coronet,* Oct. 1955, p. 57.

156. Betty Brenner, "Oral Roberts Lauded by Evangelists," *Flint Michigan Journal,* Mar. 21, 1971, ORU.

157. DeWeese Interview.

158. O. Roberts, Healing Waters Broadcast Tape, Apr. 24, 1949.

159. Oral Roberts, "A Dynamic Report on . . . Spiritual Healing," *AL,* June 1957, p. 12.

160. O. Roberts, Evangelism of Oral Roberts Class Transcript, 1971, p. 16.

161. Ibid., p. 20.

162. O. Roberts, *The Holy Spirit in the Now,* vol. 2, p. 22.

163. O. Roberts, World Outreach Conference Transcript, Mar. 11, 1968, n.p.

164. Oral Roberts, "Your Healing in the Roberts Meeting," *HW,* Sept. 1948, p. 2.

165. O. Roberts, *What Is a Miracle?,* p. 54; see Pete Martin, "Oral Roberts," *Christian Herald,* Mar. 1966, p. 24.

166. O. Roberts, *What Is a Miracle?,* p. 54.

167. O. Roberts, Banquet Transcript, July 8, 1981, pp. 23–24.

168. "Talmadge Talks As Oral Roberts Opens Revival," *Atlanta Journal,* Apr. 7, 1951, p. 12.

169. O. Roberts, Laymen's Seminar Transcript, Dec. 6, 1963, pp. 15–16.

170. "Questions Commonly Asked about the City of Faith," *Tulsa World,* Nov. 1, 1981, p. 5.

171. See "Des Moines Campaign Scenes," *HW,* Sept. 1952, p. 7.

172. O. Roberts, "A Dynamic Report on . . . Spiritual Healing," p. 12.

173. O. Roberts, Banquet Transcript, July 8, 1981, p. 12.

174. O. Roberts Interview, Feb. 16, 1983.

175. O. Roberts, Contemporary Methods of Evangelism Class Transcript, Nov. 29, 1967, p. 15.

176. Bob Foresman, "Oral Roberts Tells Doctors Divine Healing Takes Varied Forms," *Tulsa Tribune,* Dec. 16, 1964, ORU.

177. William S. Reed, "We Must Save the Sick to Save Souls," *AL,* Feb. 1961, p. 9; see also "Surgeon Urges: 'Pray with Patient,' " *Tulsa Tribune,* Oct. 19, 1960, ORU. The Order of Saint Luke remained aloof from the charismatic movement, but its official publication recommended books by Roberts and Kathryn Kuhlman. See "Ministry of Healing Literature," *Sharing,* Aug. 1968, p. 16.

178. O. Roberts, Professional and Businessmen's Seminar Transcript, Nov. 27, 1964, n.p.

179. Doyle Helbling, "Moment of Truth," *AL,* May 1964, p. 4.

180. Fannie Lou Leney, "I Discovered What a Physician Could Learn about Healing," *AL,* Aug. 1970, p. 19. Dr. Leney testified that she had made many "wonderful friends in Christ, many of whom were also physicians."

181. "ORU City of Faith," *Tulsa World,* Feb. 11, 1979, p. 2-B.

182. See, for instance, *The Search for a Christian Understanding of Health, Healing, and Wholeness* (Geneva, Switzerland: Christian Medical Commission, 1982); Stuart J. Kingma, "A Unified View of Healing," *Contact,* Dec. 1982, pp. 11–15.

183. See Granger Westberg, ed., *Theological Roots of Wholistic Health Care* ([Hinsdale, Ill.]: Wholistic Health Centers, 1979). See also Edmund D. Pellegrina, "Educating the Christian Physician," *Hospital Progress,* Aug. 1979, pp. 46–53.

184. "Whole Person Therapy," *Tulsa World,* Sept. 4, 1979, ORU.

185. " 'Wholistic' or 'Holistic'?" *Tulsa World,* Sept. 15, 1979, ORU.

186. "The 'Holistic' Facts," *Tulsa World,* Sept. 15, 1979, ORU.

187. "Oral Roberts Despises 'Faith-Healer' Label," *Wilkes-Barre (Pa.) Sunday Independent,* Feb. 23, 1958, ORU.

188. For a very early reference by Oral to bringing together medicine and religion, see an article printed in *Healing Waters* written by Norman Vincent Peale, "Christ's Healing Power," Dec. 1949, pp. 6–7.

189. Contemporary Methods of Evangelism Class Transcript, Nov. 29, 1967, pp. 14–15.

190. "God's Medicine," *AL,* Sept. 1977, p. 4.

191. Chapel Transcript, Feb. 14, 1979, p. 11.

192. Banquet Transcript, July 8, 1981, p. 24.

193. O. Roberts, Healing Waters Broadcast Tape, June 5, 1949.

194. O. Roberts, Crusade Transcript, Apr. 22, 1955, pp. 21–22; see Crusade Transcript, July 10, 1957, p. 16.

195. O. Roberts, *The Holy Spirit in the Now,* vol. 2, p. 22.

196. See "The Blessing Pact," *AL,* Nov. 1969, p. 20; "My Impression," *AL,* June 1969, pp. 9–14.

197. "How I Discovered the Miracle of Seed-Faith," *AL,* Oct. 1971, pp. 2–17; Oral Roberts, *The Miracle of Seed-Faith* (Charlotte, N.C.: Commission Press, 1970).

198. Evelyn Roberts, *His Darling Wife, Evelyn* (New York: Dell Publishing Co., 1976), p. 177.

199. Oral Roberts, "Giving Off the Top," *AL,* Feb. 1975, pp. 2–7.

200. O. Roberts, *The Miracle of Seed-Faith,* pp. 13–17.

201. O. Roberts, Chapel Transcript, May 21, 1971, pp. 3–4; see also Banquet Transcript, Oct. 22, 1969, p. 5; O. Roberts, *God Is a Good God,* p. 63; Chapel Transcript, Aug. 29, 1980, p. 9.

202. O. Roberts, *The Miracle of Seed-Faith,* pp. 17–29.

203. See ibid., pp. 6–8; O. Roberts Interview, Feb. 16, 1983.

204. O. Roberts, Miscellaneous Speech Transcript, Oct. 3, 1976, p. 9.

205. O. Roberts, Chapel Transcript, Feb. 11, 1970, p. 10.

206. O. Roberts, Miscellaneous Speech Transcript, Oct. 3, 1976, p. 9.

207. O. Roberts, *The Miracle of Seed-Faith,* pp. 29–34.

208. Robert Voight Interview, Jan. 25, 1983.

209. O. Roberts, Evangelism of Oral Roberts Class Transcript, 1971, p. 17.

210. O. Roberts, *The Miracle of Seed-Faith,* p. 32.

211. "Do You Need a Beginning of Miracles in Your Life?" *AL,* Feb. 1970, pp. 23–27.

212. Evelyn Roberts, *His Darling Wife,* p. 177.

213. Robinson Interview; Voight Interview.

214. O. Roberts, Chapel Transcript, Mar. 14, 1969, p. 19.

215. O. Roberts, Church Sermon Transcript, Apr. 20, 1977, pp. 48–49.

216. James Buskirk Interview, Feb. 11, 1983.

217. Charles Kothe Interview, Feb. 23, 1983; Patti Roberts with Sherry Andrews, *Ashes to Gold* (Waco, Texas: Word Books [1983]), p. 119.

218. O. Roberts, Church Sermon Transcript, Apr. 20, 1977, pp. 38–39.

219. Bush Interview; Farah Interview.

220. O. Roberts, Faculty Chapel Transcript, Oct. 11, 1974, p. 21.

221. Farah Interview.

222. O. Roberts, Speech at Seminary Transcript, Feb. 9, 1976, p. 11.

223. Buskirk Interview, Feb. 11, 1983.

224. O. Roberts, Family Seminar Transcript, Aug. 28, 1982, p. 16.

225. Bible Reading Tape no. 8.

226. Buskirk Interview, Feb. 11, 1983.

227. O. Roberts, Chapel Transcript, Aug. 29, 1980, p. 8.

228. Buskirk Interview, Feb. 18, 1983.

229. O. Roberts, Speech at Seminary Transcript, Feb. 9, 1976, p. 11.

230. For early statements on the subject, see Oral Roberts, "Why You Must Receive the Holy Ghost," *HW,* May 1950, pp. 6–7; Oral Roberts, *Why You Must Receive the Baptism of the Holy Ghost* (Tract, no pub. info.).

231. See Youth Seminar Transcript, July 24, 1965, p. 9; Professional and Businessmen's Seminar Transcript, Nov. 29, 1964, p. 10.

232. O. Roberts, Contemporary Methods of Evangelism Class Transcript, Oct. 4, 1967, p. 30.

233. O. Roberts, Laymen's Seminar Transcript, Nov. 7, 1969, p. 15.

234. O. Roberts, Contemporary Methods of Evangelism Class Transcript, Oct. 11, 1967, p. 34.

235. Ibid., p. 35.

236. O. Roberts, Contemporary Methods of Evangelism Class Transcript, Oct. 4, 1967, p. 25.

237. O. Roberts, Evangelism 501 Class Transcript, Jan. 3, 1968, p. 6.

238. *ORU Bulletin, June, 1969* (Tulsa: Oral Roberts University, 1969), p. 109.

239. *Oral Roberts University School of Arts and Sciences, 1981–1983* (Tulsa: Oral Roberts University, n.d.), p. 36.

240. O. Roberts, *The Holy Spirit in the Now,* vol. 1, p. 42.

241. Ibid., vol. 2, p. 60; see Professional and Businessmen's Seminar Transcript, p. 12.

242. O. Roberts, *The Holy Spirit in the Now,* vol. 1, p. 25.

243. Oral Roberts, *The Baptism with the Holy Spirit* (Tulsa: Oral Roberts [1964]), pp. 6–7, 14–15.

244. O. Roberts, Miscellaneous Speech Transcript, June 6, 1977, pp. 10–11.

245. *Oral Roberts University School of Arts and Sciences, 1981–83,* p. 36.

246. O. Roberts, *The Holy Spirit in the Now,* vol. 1, p. 46.

247. Ibid., vol. 2, p. 10.

248. Ibid., vol. 1, pp. 23, 46.

249. Ibid., p. 30.

250. O. Roberts Interview, Feb. 16, 1983.

251. Voight Interview.

252. O. Roberts, *The Holy Spirit in the Now,* vol. 1, p. 35.

253. O. Roberts, Contemporary Methods of Evangelism Class Transcript, Oct. 4, 1967, p. 25.

254. See Kilian McDonnell, *Catholic Pentecostalism: Problems in Evaluation* (Pecos, N.M.: Dowe Publications [1970]).

255. Ervin Interview.

256. Farah Interview.

257. Buskirk Interview, Feb. 18, 1983.

17. THE MAN

1. John Williams Interview, Mar. 30, 1983.

2. "Oral Roberts: What Makes Him Tick?" *Tulsa Tribune,* June 11, 1975, p. 1-B.

3. C. Thomas Thompson Interview, Feb. 2, 1983.

4. Demos Shakarian, "Demos Shakarian Reports the Oral Roberts Campaign in Los Angeles," *HW,* Dec. 1951, p. 11.

5. Bob Foresman Interview, Dec. 13, 1983.

6. Albert E. Bush Interview, Feb. 11, 1983.

7. Calvin Thielman Interview, Apr. 8, 1983.

8. Bill Roberts Interview, Feb. 23, 1983; Collins Steele Interview, Jan. 13, 1983; "Oral Roberts Man to Man," *Midland (Tex.) Reporter-Telegram,* Oct. 8, 1978, ORU.

9. James Buskirk Interview, Feb. 11, 1983.

10. Wayne Robinson Interview, Apr. 4, 1983.

11. O. Roberts, Speech at Seminary at ORU Transcript, Feb. 9, 1976, p. 12.

12. O. Roberts, President's Advisory Cabinet Transcript, May 29, 1965, p. 3.

13. Williams Interview.

14. Bruce Buursma, "Oral Roberts and His Skeptics," *Chicago Tribune Magazine,* Jan. 3, 1982, Sec. 9, pp. 10–11.

15. Thompson Interview.

16. Oral Roberts, *Oral Roberts' Life Story* (Tulsa: Oral Roberts [1951]), p. 121.

17. Ron Smith Interview, Feb. 24, 1983; Robinson Interview; Bush Interview.

18. Warren Hultgren Interview, Mar. 30, 1983.

19. O. Roberts, Chapel Transcript, Jan. 1968, p. 6.

20. Bob DeWeese, Evangelism of Oral Roberts Class Transcript, 1971, p. 19.

21. See Foresman Interview; OREA Devotion Transcript, Mar. 25, 1982, p. 15.

22. O. Roberts, Miscellaneous Speech Transcript, Oct. 2, 1976, p. 10.

23. See Patti Roberts with Sherry Andrews, *Ashes to Gold* (Waco, Texas: Word Books [1983]), p. 89; Pete Martin, "Oral Roberts," *Christian Herald,* Feb. 1966, p. 108.

24. Donald Moyers Interview, Dec. 13, 1983.

25. Williams Interview.

26. See O. Roberts, "A Spiritual Revolution," Crusade Transcript, Nov. 1956, pp. 25–26.

27. O. Roberts, Speech to Graduate and Theology Students Transcript, Jan. 31, 1977, p. 12.

28. Evelyn Roberts, Chapel Transcript, Apr. 24, 1972, p. 24.

29. See P. Roberts, *Ashes to Gold,* p. 90.

30. Bush Interview.

31. Demos Shakarian Interview, Jan. 27, 1983.

32. P. Roberts, *Ashes to Gold,* p. 90.

33. Robinson Interview.

34. Ibid.

35. Evelyn Roberts, Student Meeting Transcript, Feb. 11, 1975, p. 27.

36. Evelyn Roberts, Miscellaneous Transcript, June 8, 1981, p. 11.

37. O. Roberts, Speech to Sub-Contractors Transcript, 1974, p. 4.

38. O. Roberts, Speech at Seminary at ORU Transcript, Feb. 9, 1976, pp. 12–13.

39. Hultgren Interview.

40. Robinson Interview; Bill Roberts Interview.

41. Shakarian Interview.

42. Hultgren Interview.

43. O. Roberts, Speech to Sub-Contractors Transcript, 1974, p. 2.

44. O. Roberts, Crusade Transcript, Dec. 13, 1957, n.p.

45. O. Roberts, Chapel Transcript, Oct. 26, 1973, p. 7.

46. O. Roberts, OREA Devotion Transcript, Jan. 27, 1959, p. 10.

47. O. Roberts, Chapel Transcript, Jan. 14, 1976, p. 6.

48. O. Roberts, Faculty Chapel Transcript, Apr. 19, 1974, p. 10.

49. O. Roberts, Chapel Transcript, Apr. 14, 1972, n.p.

50. O. Roberts, Speech at Seminary at ORU Transcript, Feb. 9, 1976, p. 6.

51. O. Roberts, Miscellaneous Speech Transcript, Apr. 3, 1957, p. 10.

52. O. Roberts, Speech at Seminary at ORU Transcript, Feb. 9, 1976, p. 12.

53. Smith Interview.

54. See P. Roberts, *Ashes to Gold,* p. 90.

55. Jenkin Lloyd Jones, Sr. Interview, Mar. 31, 1983.

56. Bible Reading Tape no. 8.

57. "Evangelist Heal Thyself," *Crawdaddy New York,* May 14, 1972, ORU.

58. Hultgren Interview.

59. Edna Nash Interview, Apr. 2, 1984.

60. O. Roberts Interview, Feb. 16, 1983.

61. O. Roberts, Faculty Retreat Transcript, Aug. 25, 1983, pp. 11–12.

62. "Oral Roberts," *Christian Home,* Mar. 1979, p. 16.

63. O. Roberts, Chapel Transcript, Oct. 13, 1972, p. 3.

64. O. Roberts, Faculty Chapel Transcript, Feb. 19, 1973, p. 1.

65. O. Roberts, Chapel Transcript, Nov. 15, 1967, p. 4.

66. O. Roberts, Chapel Transcript, Dec. 10, 1982, p. 15.

67. Thomas Zimmerman Interview, Oct. 18, 1980; David Fritze, "The Gold and the Glory," *Oklahoma Monthly,* Oct. 1977, p. 15.

68. "Modern Horatio Alger Success Story," *Springfield (Mo.) Leader and Press,* May 14, 1959, ORU.

69. O. Roberts, Chapel Transcript, Oct. 6, 1982, p. 7.

70. O. Roberts, OREA Devotion Transcript, Jan. 27, 1959, pp. 18–19.

71. O. Roberts, Chapel Transcript, Sept. 1, 1968, p. 18.

72. Evelyn Roberts, Faculty Orientation Transcript, Aug. 18, 1975, p. 36.

73. O. Roberts, Faculty Meeting Transcript, Apr. 20, 1972, p. 3.

74. O. Roberts, Faculty Chapel Transcript, Aug. 19, 1974, p. 19.

75. Buskirk Interview, Feb. 11, 1983.

76. O. Roberts, Chapel Transcript, Dec. 6, 1972, p. 3.

77. Gordon Lindsay Interview, July 27, 1972.

78. See Dan L. Thrapp, "Evangelist Oral Roberts Thrashing Devil in Tent," *Los Angeles Times,* Oct. 7, 1951, p. 44.

79. Shakarian Interview.

80. Doris Miller, "Poetry Today," *Huntington (W. Va.) Herald-Advertiser,* Mar. 9, 1958, ORU.

81. Ibid.

82. See Evangelism of Oral Roberts Class Transcript, 1971, for a series of inside discussions of the changes in Oral's style.

83. O. Roberts, Speech at Seminary at ORU Transcript, Feb. 9, 1976, p. 8.

84. See Bible Reading Tape no. 3.

85. See W. T. Jeffers, *What I Know about Oral Roberts* (Tulsa: Frontiers of Faith, n.d.), p. 21; Jan Franzen, "TV Ministry Changes Format," *Christian Life,* Aug. 1979, p. 60.

86. O. Roberts, Speech to Graduate and Theology Students Transcript, Jan. 31, 1977, p. 16.

87. Ibid., p. 15.

88. Ibid., pp. 1, 17, 10.

89. Bible Reading Tape no. 3.

90. O. Roberts, Speech to Graduate and Theology Students Transcript, Jan. 31, 1977, p. 16.

91. Ibid., p. 17.

92. Robinson Interview.

93. Oral Roberts, "How God's Healing Power Came to Me," *HW,* May 1948, p. 1.

94. Oral Roberts, "Letter," *PHA,* July 11, 1935, p. 14.

95. Oral Roberts, *101 Questions and Answers* (Tulsa: Oral Roberts, 1968), p. 50.

96. Evelyn Roberts, "I Married Oral Roberts," *HW,* Jan. 1953, p. 11.

97. O. Roberts, Room Sponsors Seminar Transcript, May 20, 1963, p. 3.

98. O. Roberts, *101 Questions and Answers,* p. 50.

99. O. Roberts, Miscellaneous Speech Transcript, Jan. 22, 1973, p. 9.

100. O. Roberts, Faculty Orientation Transcript, Aug. 24, 1971, p. 5.

101. O. Roberts Interview, Feb. 16, 1983.

102. O. Roberts, Chapel Transcript, Jan. 24, 1979, n.p.

103. O. Roberts, Speech to Graduate and Theology Students Transcript, Jan. 31, 1977, p. 13.

104. O. Roberts, Miscellaneous Speech Transcript, Apr. 3, 1957, p. 10.

105. O. Roberts, Speech to Graduate and Theology Students Transcript, Jan. 31, 1977, p. 23.

106. O. Roberts, Chapel Transcript, Jan. 24, 1979, n.p.

107. O. Roberts, Speech to Student Meeting Transcript, Aug. 20, 1975, p. 9.

108. James Winslow Interview, Feb. 4, 1983.

109. Moyers Interview.

110. O. Roberts, Faculty Chapel Transcript, Aug. 19, 1974, p. 25.

111. O. Roberts, Chapel Transcript, Jan. 22, 1975, p. 14.

112. O. Roberts, Interview Transcript, Aug. 17, 1979, pp. 19–22.

113. Thompson Interview.

114. Bush Interview.

115. Hultgren Interview.

116. Foresman Interview.

117. O. Roberts, Dedication Transcript, City of Faith, Nov. 1, 1981, p. 13.

118. Harold Paul Interview, Jan. 28, 1983.

119. "The Vision of God and of Oral Roberts," *AL,* Mar. 1976, p. 4.

120. O. Roberts, Room Sponsors Seminar Transcript, May 20, 1963, p. 3.

121. Oral Roberts, *How God Speaks to Me* (Tulsa: Oral Roberts, 1964), pp. 38–39.

122. Oral Roberts, *How to Know God's Will* (Tulsa: Oral Roberts Evangelistic Association, 1982), p. 8.

123. O. Roberts Interview, Feb. 16, 1983.

124. Ibid.

125. O. Roberts, *How God Speaks to Me,* p. 22.

126. Bush Interview.

127. Buskirk Interview, Feb. 18, 1983.

128. O. Roberts, *How God Speaks to Me,* p. 13.

129. O. Roberts, Crusade Sermon Tape, June 13, 1952, ORU Archives.

130. O. Roberts, *How to Know God's Will,* p. 11.

131. O. Roberts, Speech to Sub-Contractors Transcript, 1974, p. 2.

132. Oral Roberts, *My Story* (Tulsa and New York: Summit Books, 1961), p. 158.

133. O. Roberts, *How to Know God's Will,* p. 11.

134. Oral Roberts, *The Holy Spirit in the Now* (3 vols.; Tulsa: Oral Roberts University, 1974), vol. 1, pp. 28, 48; O. Roberts Interview, Feb. 16, 1983.

135. See O. Roberts, *The Holy Spirit in the Now,* vol. 2, pp. 50–52.

136. O. Roberts, Dedication Transcript, City of Faith, Nov. 1, 1981, p. 16; O. Roberts Interview, Feb. 16, 1983.

137. O. Roberts, *How to Know God's Will,* p. 4.

138. O. Roberts, Miscellaneous Speech Transcript, Jan. 22, 1973, p. 2.

139. O. Roberts, Banquet Transcript, July 8, 1981, p. 15.

140. "Answers to the Tough Questions," *AL,* Apr. 1983, p. 14.

141. O. Roberts, My Own Personal Testimony Transcript, Oct. 21, 1970, p. 1; see Interview Transcript, Aug. 17, 1979, pp. 20–22.

142. O. Roberts, *The Holy Spirit in the Now,* vol. 2, pp. 65–68.

143. See Bernadette Pruitt, "Know Your Right from Your Left-Brain," *Tulsa World,* May 14, 1974, p. 7-A.

144. O. Roberts, Miscellaneous Speech Transcript, Jan. 22, 1973, p. 1.

145. O. Roberts, Miscellaneous Speech Transcript, Apr. 3, 1957, p. 9.

146. Robert Voight Interview, Jan. 25, 1983.

147. Smith Interview.

18. THE MINISTRY

1. Oral Roberts, Church Sermon Transcript, Feb. 6, 1975, p. 10.

2. George Stovall, Telephone Interview, Oct. 23, 1984.

3. Bob Foresman, "Business Acumen of Roberts Unquestioned," *Tulsa Tribune,* Dec. 25, 1971, ORU. See O. Roberts, Speech at Graduate School Transcript, Apr. 4, 1976, pp. 5–6; O. Roberts, Commencement Address Transcript, May 1, 1977, p. 3.

4. Bill and Edna Nash Interviews, Apr. 2, 1984.

5. See Faculty Meeting Transcript, Nov. 9, 1971, pp. 5–6; Bill Roberts Interview, Feb. 23, 1983; Frank Wallace Interview, Feb. 18, 1983.

6. Albert E. Bush Interview, Feb. 11, 1983.

7. See Bob Foresman, "Australia Reds Broke Up Meetings, States Roberts," *Tulsa Tribune,* Mar. 1, 1956, ORU; Pete Martin, "Oral Roberts," *Christian Herald,* Feb. 1966, p. 39.

8. Wayne Robinson Interview, Apr. 4, 1983.

9. Bill Roberts Interview.

10. George Stovall Interview, Jan. 27, 1983.

11. Bush Interview.

12. Ron Smith Interview, Feb. 24, 1983.

13. Bush Interview.

14. Bill Roberts Interview.

15. Stovall Interview.

16. Bill Roberts Interview.

17. O. Roberts, Miscellaneous Speech Transcript, Jan. 22, 1973, p. 3.

18. Robinson Interview.

19. Oscar Moore Interview, Jan. 20, 1983.

20. O. Roberts, Miscellaneous Speech Transcript, Nov. 20, 1982, n.p.

21. OREA Devotion Transcript, Mar. 25, 1982, p. 17.

22. James Winslow Interview, Feb. 4, 1983; Stovall Interview.

23. Carl Hamilton, Faculty Orientation Transcript, Aug. 20, 1974, p. 34.

24. Smith Interview.

25. John Williams Interview, Mar. 30, 1983.

26. OREA Devotion Transcript, Jan. 27, 1959, p. 26.

27. James Buskirk Interview, Feb. 11, 1983.

28. Bush Interview; Smith Interview.

29. Bush Interview.

30. Bob DeWeese Interview, Jan. 19, 1983; Bill Roberts Interview; Carl H. Hamilton Interview, Jan. 13, 1983; Buskirk Interview, Feb. 11, 1983.

31. Stovall Interview.

32. OREA Devotion Transcript, July 20, 1962, pp. 2–3.

33. Smith Interview; Bush Interview.

34. O. Roberts, University Village Seminar Transcript, June 9, 1970, p. 4.

35. OREA Devotion Transcript, Jan. 27, 1959, p. 20.

36. Winslow Interview.

37. O. Roberts, President's Advisory Cabinet Transcript, May 29, 1965, p. 3.

38. Smith Interview.

39. Ibid.

40. Bush Interview.

41. Stovall Interview; Smith Interview.

42. Chapel Transcript, Dec. 5, 1975, p. 3.

43. Stovall Interview.

44. Chapel Transcript, Apr. 14, 1972, p. 15.

45. Faculty Orientation Transcript, Aug. 20, 1974, p. 33.

46. Bush Interview.

47. Carl H. Hamilton Interview, Jan. 13, 1983.

48. Buskirk Interview, Feb. 11, 1983.

49. Evelyn Roberts, Banquet Transcript, Apr. 23, 1973, p. 9.

50. Moore Interview.

51. Donald Moyers Interview, Dec. 13, 1983.

52. Jenkin Lloyd Jones, Sr. Interview, Mar. 31, 1983.

53. Smith Interview.

54. Williams Interview.

55. Bush Interview.

56. Williams Interview.

57. Jerry Sholes cannot be accounted a major figure.

58. Robinson Interview.

59. Williams Interview.

60. Bush Interview.

61. Patti Roberts with Sherry Andrews, *Ashes to Gold* (Waco, Texas: Word Books [1983]), p. 49.

62. Robinson Interview.

63. Smith Interview.

64. Jenkin Lloyd Jones, "After Oral Roberts?" *Tulsa Tribune,* July 20, 1979, ORU; Jones Interview.

65. See Charles Price, "Faith Healing, Science Agree, Says Roberts," *Houston Post,* Oct. 16, 1949, ORU; Ronald R. Smith, OREA Staff Meeting Transcript, Dec. 28, 1973, p. 13.

66. Oral Roberts, "President's Report," *AL,* Feb. 1970, p. 8.

67. O. Roberts Interview, Feb. 16, 1983.

68. O. Roberts, Partner's Seminar Transcript, May 9, 1965, p. 11.

69. O. Roberts, Chapel Transcript, Feb. 24, 1978, p. 16.

70. Ibid., p. 14; O. Roberts Interview, Feb. 16, 1983.

71. "Oral Roberts, What Makes Him Tick?" *Tulsa Tribune,* June 11, 1975, p. 1-B; see Evelyn Roberts, Miscellaneous Speech Transcript, Mar. 2, 1974, p. 25.

72. Williams Interview.

73. Roberta Roberts Potts Interview, Dec. 13, 1983.

74. Jones Interview; Bush Interview; Smith Interview.

75. Bill Roberts Interview.

76. Stovall Interview.

77. Howard Ervin Interview, Jan. 25, 1983.

78. Richard Roberts Interview, Mar. 31, 1983.

79. Smith Interview.

80. Robert Voight Interview, Jan. 25, 1983.

81. Smith Interview.

82. Bill Roberts Interview.

83. Smith Interview.

84. Richard Roberts Interview, Mar. 31, 1983.

85. Demos Shakarian, Full Gospel Business Men's Fellowship 1981 World Convention Transcript, July 3, 1981, p. 1.

86. O. Roberts, My Own Personal Testimony Transcript, Oct. 21, 1970, p. 16.

87. Oral Roberts, Partner Letter, May 1983.

88. O. Roberts, Evangelism of Oral Roberts Class Transcript, 1971, p. 19.

89. Edward B. Fiske, "The Oral Roberts Empire," *New York Times Magazine,* Apr. 23, 1973, p. 24.

90. Winslow Interview.

91. Demos Shakarian Interview, Jan. 27, 1983.

92. O. Roberts Interview, Feb. 16, 1983.

93. "Happenings," *Christian Life,* June 1983, p. 17.

94. Vinson Synan Interview, May 22, 1983.

95. Vinson Synan, Speech, Indiana University, May 13, 1983; David B. Barrett, ed., *World Christian Encyclopedia* (Nairobi, Oxford, and New York: Oxford University Press, 1982), p. 14; Vinson Synan, ed., *Aspects of Pentecostal-Charismatic Origins* (Plainfield, N.J.: Logos International, 1975), p. 1.

EPILOGUE

1. Ron Smith Interview, Feb. 24, 1983.

2. O. Roberts, Chapel Transcript, Apr. 17, 1982, p. 12.

3. Demos Shakarian Interview, Jan. 27, 1983.

4. Smith Interview.

5. John Williams Interview, Mar. 30, 1983.

6. Jenkin Lloyd Jones, Sr. Interview, Mar. 31, 1983.

7. Oral Roberts Interview, Feb. 16, 1983.

8. Ibid.

INDEX

Abundant Life, 130, 134, 142, 217, 223, 253, 271, 274–278, 281, 284–285, 289, 313, 350, 365, 402–403, 406, 412, 414, 447, 459, 462, 499
"Abundant Life concept," 209
Abundant Life Crusade, 203
Abundant Life Prayer Group, 224, 276
Abundant Life youth teams, 263–264
Acres, Dick, 364
Ada (Oklahoma), 3–7, 11
Ada Evening News, 32
Ada revival, 4–7
Advocate, 48–49
African campaign, 260–261
Ahlstrom, Sydney E., viii
Air Waves, 499
Albert, Carl, 227, 309
Allen, Asa Alonzo (A. A.), 141, 149, 152–153
Alton revival, 83
Amarillo Daily News, 109
Amarillo disaster, 91, 106–109
American Bar Association, 372–373
American Broadcasting Company (ABC), 123
American Indian ministry, 136
American Magazine, 173, 502
American Weekly, 175, 502
America's Healing Magazine, 130, 142, 499
Anderson, Robert, 20
Andrews, Joseph, 502
Andrews, Sherry, 429
Anointed cloths, 111, 119–120. *See also* Prayer cloths
Argus, 75, 77
Armstrong, Hart R., 74, 133, 165, 168, 175, 179, 184, 254, 258, 446
Armstrong, William, 273, 275
Arnold, Eve, 502
Ashes to Gold, 341, 503
Assemblies of God, 16, 31, 112, 153, 155, 160, 218, 223, 422, 494
Associated Press, 355, 416
Athens (Georgia) revivals, 48–81
Australian Crusades, 73–79, 180–183, 259
Azusa Street meeting, 15

Bakker, Jim, 426
Banks, Norman, 78
Banowsky, Bill, 340, 480–481
Barnhouse, Donald Grey, 163
Barton, John, 134, 273
Bebee, Frank, 9

Belcher, Page, 145
Beller, Dan, 216
Ben-Gurion, David, 137
Bender, W. E., Jr., 144
Bennett, Dennis, 287
Benson, C. Irving, 78
Bible, distribution of in Israel, 137–138
Bible Deliverance films, 124–125
Blair, Charles, 87, 216
Blessing Pact, 129–130, 141–143, 283–284, 461
Bond, Gilbert "Gib," 68
Boone, Byron V., 305, 390, 434
Boone, Pat, 421, 424
Boone, Shirley, 423–424
Boston Avenue Methodist Church, 426
Bosworth, B. B., 5
Bosworth, Fred F., 149
Branham, William, 109, 148, 150–151, 154, 450
Braxton, Lee, 74, 154, 171, 184, 205, 224, 235, 383, 394, 439–440, 487; assistant to the president, 270; chairman of the board of regents of ORU, 212–213, 274; early life, 114–116; friendship with Oral Roberts, 184, 191, 353; Healing Waters building construction, 115–116; OREA leader, 131, 133, 205, 210; radio network, 115, 118, 123, 128–129, 142; resignation of, 360; support of healing revivals, 157–159; television producer, 266; vice president of FGBMFI, 154
Brazilian Crusade, 264
Brens, W. J., 76–77
"Bridgeman Evangelistic Party," 82
Bright, Bill, 394–395
British medical commission, 173
Broad, William J., 502
Broadcast Training, Broadcasting, and Film Commission of the National Council of Churches of Christ, 172
Bruce, S. Duane, 416
Buck Horn revival, 14
Bulletin, 465–467
Burchell, C. D., 49
Bush, Albert E. (Al), 122, 134, 138, 218, 268, 274, 277, 279–280, 353, 418–419, 435, 439, 469, 471–472, 482, 486–490
Buskirk, James B., 330, 339, 346, 366–370, 389, 394, 398, 407, 409–410, 419–420, 426–427, 441, 463, 467, 470, 487
Buursma, Bruce, 502

The Call, 278, 304, 478, 500
Campaign audiences, changes in, 110, 256
Campaigns, overseas, 257–258
Campbell, Joe E., 56, 159
Campus Crusade, 394–395
Canadian revivals, 48
Cardone, Mike, 212
Cardone, Nick, 212
Carmichael, Ralph, 267
Carnegie, Dale, 115
Carter, Jimmy, 421
"Cathedral Cruiser," 263
Catholic opposition to Roberts, 164, 169
Catholic Renewal, 287–288, 292
Caughell, Tracy, 361
Cavett, Dick, 318
Center (Oklahoma), 9, 11
Center (Oklahoma) revival, 22
Central Assembly of God Church (Denver), 87
Charisma magazine, 429
Charismatic movement, vii, 278, 287, 289–290, 293, 422–423, 428–429, 494–495
Charismatic Renewal, 287–288, 292
Charismatic theology, 465–466
Chickasaw Nation, 9–11
Chilean fiasco, 237
Christian Broadcasting Network, 266
Christian Century, 164, 172, 174
Christian existentialism, 442
Christian Friends of Israel, Inc., 136
Christian Home, 348, 428
Christian Medical Commission of the World Council of Churches, 459
Christianity and Crisis, 277
Christianity Today, 199, 289, 422, 426
Chronicle of Higher Education, 255, 304
Churches of Christ, 108, 161–163
Churches of God, 16, 112
City of Faith Hospital, Inc. 406
City of Faith medical center, viii, xi, 143–145, 333–355, 358, 378–379, 381, 406, 408, 412, 418, 421, 428, 431–433, 435, 454; cancer research, 391–392; certification of need, OHSA denial of, 383–387; cost of, 388; dedication ceremony, 389–390; design of, 382; financial crisis, 360–361, 413–418, 435; fundraising techniques, 389; groundbreaking ceremonies, 383; healing-team concept, 393; occupancy problems, 391; opposition to, 423–424, 431–435
City of Faith Medical Research Center, Inc., 406
Coburn, O. W., 370
Coe, Jack, 149, 152, 153–154, 273; Florida arraignment, 171
Communique, 499
Conference News, 59
Conference Stationing Committee, 58
"Contact" television special, 268
Cooper, Kenneth, 242
Copeland, Kenneth, 389, 423–424, 426
Coping with Grief, 332, 501

Cornell, George W., 121, 176
Corvin, Raymond Othel, 23, 36, 60, 62, 158, 160, 200, 204, 207, 211–212, 216, 222, 232, 234–239, 293, 366–367, 503
Crane, George, 194
Crosby, John, 171
Croskery, Carol Loy, 324
Crutchfield, Finis A., 293–294, 427

Daily Blessing, 130, 276, 412, 499
Daily World, 82
Daniels, Bob, 256
"Dark Summer of '68," 297
Daugherty, Billy Joe, 429
"The Day After" television special, 447
Debo, Angie, 17
Dessauer, Phil, 502
DeVos, Richard M., 306, 422
DeWeese, Robert F. (Bob), 170, 321, 330, 454, 456, 470–471, 487; associate evangelist, 92–96, 100, 127, 259–260, 273–274; campaign manager, 74, 76–77, 132, 165, 254; chairman of the board of ORU, 360; friendship with Oral Roberts, 184, 354; OREA leader, 131, 210, 407–408; preaching career, 132–133, 254
Dial access information retrieval system (DAIRS), 223
Direct mail system, 280–282
Dispensational premillennialism, 19, 50, 59, 162. *See also* Premillennialism
Dixon, Jeanne, 421
Documented Healings of the Twentieth Century, 168
Donahue, Phil, 362
Doyle, Bill, 82–83
The Drama of the End-Time, 50, 440, 447, 500
Dryden, Bill, 13, 16, 24, 26
Dryden, Dewey, 13, 16
Dryden, Luther, 13, 16
Du Plessis, David, vii, 146, 148, 216, 289, 422
Durham tent crusade, 85–86

East Oklahoma Conference, 23, 37–38, 49, 52, 60, 155, 160
Ebenezer Pentecostal Holiness Church, 114
Eckert, Dennis, 306
Edmondson, Howard, 145
Education and Publication Committee of the East Oklahoma Conference, 58
Edwards, Larry D., 379
8181 Management Company, 406
Eisenberg, Larry, 296
Ellis, Vep, 212, 256, 273
Emmanuel Junior College, 17, 52–53, 58, 60, 158, 222
"Empty Tomb in Jerusalem," 50
Engel, Manford, 113–114, 120, 122, 131, 133, 144, 184, 193, 210, 273–274
Engle, Charlie, 25–26
Engle, Mattie, 25–26
Enid pastorate, 62–68

Entire sanctification, 18–19
Ervin, Howard M., 217, 220, 235, 237, 289, 423, 426, 492
Eskridge, Bob, 228, 279
"Eternal Partners" system, 411
European Crusade, 259
Evangel College, 218
Evangelical United Brethren, 295
Evangelism, 120–121, 441
Evangelistic campaigns: Ada (Oklahoma), 87; Athens (Georgia), 48, 81; Australia, 73–79, 180–183, 259; Canada, 48; Denver (Colorado), 85–86; Durham (North Carolina), 85–86; ending of, 261–263; India, 259–260; Okmulgee (Oklahoma), 42–43; overseas, 73–79, 258–261; profits, 100; South Africa, 138–140; Soviet arrests, 258; urban ghettoes, 257
Ewing, Gene, 285, 413

Fahnestock, Evelyn Lutman, 39–41, 44
Fahnestock, Ira A., 39–41
Faith evangelists, 425–428
"Faith formula" controversy, 423
Faith healing, 121–122
Falwell, Jerry, 430, 445
Farah, Charles, Jr., 219, 236, 265, 357, 420, 426, 441, 463, 468
Federal Communications Commission, 171
Fire-Baptized Holiness Association, 16
Fire-Baptized Pentecostal Holiness Church, 17
First million soul crusade, 121
First World Outreach Conference, 143
Fiske, Edward B., 303, 313, 493
Flag Day ceremonies, 421
Foglio, Frank, 212
Ford, Leighton, 200, 205
Foresman, Bob, 129, 175–176, 193, 305–306, 469, 481, 485, 491
Foster, Eleanor, 407
Foursquare Gospel Church, 16
Fourth Annual Preachers' Convention, 62
Fourth Million Soul Crusade, 120–121
Fraley, Robert O., 273
Freeman, William, 148
Freethinkers of America, 171, 302
Fritze, David, 502
Frodsham, Stanley H., 155
Fudge Family, 399
Full Gospel Business Men's Fellowship International (FGBMFI), vii, 97, 140, 153–155, 288–289, 493
"Full-gospel" revivals, 15–16
Full Gospel Tabernacle, 55
Fuller Theological Seminary, 202
Fundamentalism, 161–164, 445
Fuquay Springs pastorate, 55

Gardner, George, 154
Gardner, Velmer, 152, 212
Garrett, Sydney A., 379
Gary, Raymond, 143

Gates, Wayne E., 174
Gee, Donald, 148, 156, 300, 500
General Conference, 49, 52, 54, 58, 161
General Presbytery of the Assemblies of God, 155
George, Peggy, 399
Give Me That Prime-Time Religion, 431, 503
Glossolalia, 16, 465–467
God Can Heal You Now, 175, 502
Goddard, Kyle, 234
Gordon, Troy, 308
"The Gospel of the Cross," 57
Gould, Jack, 172
Graduate School of Theology, 216, 221, 234–235, 238, 367, 369–370
Graham, Billy, viii, 74, 78, 94, 125, 130, 170, 178–180, 199, 201, 204, 206, 228, 230, 291, 331, 352, 421, 428, 442, 446
Graham, Ruth, 200, 340
Green, Aline, 83
Greensboro revival, 48–49
Griffin, Merv, 271

Hagin, Kenneth, Jr., 389
Hagin, Kenneth, Sr., 152, 389, 406, 423–424, 426–427
Haile Selassie, Emperor, 199
Hale, Jerry, 247
Hamilton, Carl, 82, 213, 232–236, 238, 250, 275, 358–360, 363, 367, 389, 395, 406, 409–410, 431, 487, 489
Hansen, Robert G., 367
Hanson, Reg G., 113, 119
Hargis, Billy James, 257, 306, 400
Harvey, James, 387, 459
Harvey, Paul, 128
Hayes, Ken, 364
Healing, 130, 499
Healing line, 102–106, 255–256
Healing ministry, 91, 120, 448–451; deaths during, 164–165; in Enid (Oklahoma), 67–69; invalid tent, 98, 101–102; positive accounts by reporters, 174–175; religion and health, relationship of, 173–174; research, 175; severely ill persons, 100–104; testimonials, 167–168; verification question, 127, 166
The Healing Power of Faith, 175, 502
Healing revivalism, 152–161
Healing teams, 393–396
Healing Waters, 85, 88–102, 112, 118–120, 130, 133, 148, 157, 163, 191, 452, 457, 499
Healing Waters, Inc., 112–120, 133, 143
Healing Waters Radio Log, 123
Healing Waters radio network, 81–82, 115–118
Healing Waters Trio, 118
Heaven Has a Floor, 332
Heneke, Ben, 145
Henry, Carl F. H., 199, 204
Herald of Healing, Inc., 273
Hicks, Tommy, 138, 154

Hinshaw, David B., 379
His Darling Wife, Evelyn, 348, 501
Hobbs, A. G., 502
Holcombe, Patricia Kay (Patti). *See* Roberts, Patti
Holiday, Bud, 14
Hollis, Ernest, 223
Hollywood Bowl youth rally, 146–147
Holmes Bible School, 36
"Holy Rollers," 17, 178, 181
Howard, V.E., 108
Hultgren, Warren G., 173, 200, 206, 228, 267, 352, 435, 470, 472–473, 481
Humbard, Rex, 126, 152, 216, 219, 230, 290, 389
"Humbard Musical Evangelistic Party," 152
Hutchinson, Forney, 176

I Once Spoke in Tongues, 278
If You Need Healing—Do These Things, 68, 89–99, 115, 119–120, 158, 174, 449–451, 500–501
India crusade, 259–260
Indian Territory, 8, 10–11
Inhofe, Jim, 389
Internal Revenue Service, 173
Irwin, B. H., 16
Irwin, Claudius, 12. *See also* Roberts, Claudius
Izzard, Wes, 109

Jackson, Gayle, 149, 170
Jackson, Lige, 12
Jacobs, Hayes B., 502
James, T. F., 502
Jeffers, W. T., 131
Jernigan, William, 224, 360–361, 410
"Jesus Only" movement, 149
Jewish ministry, 135–137
John Mabee Foundation of Tulsa, 225
Jones, Bob, 429–430
Jones, Byon A., 59, 212
Jones, Charles Edwin, 503
Jones, James R., 389
Jones, Jenkin Lloyd, Jr., 434, 470, 490–491
Jones, Jenkin Lloyd, Sr., xi, 176, 230, 232, 244, 302, 305–306, 351–352, 386, 388, 420, 431, 433, 435, 445, 469, 474, 481, 497–498
Jones, Jerry, 117–118
Jones, Shirley, 73
Jones, W. C., 258
Jordon, Jesse Lee, 48
Journal of Christian Jurisprudence, 499
Journal of the American Medical Association, 173
Junior Partners, 499

KCRC, 117
Kelly, Lake, 364
Kenneth H. Cooper Aerobics Center, 225
Kerr, Aubry, 42
Kerr, Robert S. (Bob), 42, 171
Kimetto, Joseph, 389

King, Joseph H., 16–17
King, R. O. C., 202
Kobler, John, 164, 173, 194, 502
Kothe, Charles A., 370–371, 421–422
Krofft, Marty, 399
Krofft, Sid, 399
Kuhlman, Kathryn, 291, 342, 450

Lamont, Bob, 291
Lawson, Clyde, 61
Learning Resources Center, 361
Lee, Henry, 502
Lee, Robert E. "Daddy," 61
Lee, W. B., 113
Lee, Wayne, 367
Lennon, John, 310–311
Lewis, Joseph, 171, 302
Lewis, Minnie, 26
Life magazine, 170, 223, 302, 305, 502
Life Story, 170
Lifeline, 499
Lightman, Herb A., 124
Lindsey, Gordon, 148–149, 151–152, 154–155
Literature Saturation Crusades, 138
Look magazine, 170, 223, 502
Luttrell, Bill, 406

McArdle, Mrs. Sadie R., 129
McBroom, W. Ralph, 49
McCall, Charles B., 376–377
McClendon, Paul I., 224
McClintock, F. G., 228
McIntire, Carl, 416, 446
McKechnie, Bill, 104
Macklin, Beth, 433–434
MacLean, J. M., 158
McMurray, Leonard, 382
MacNutt, Francis, 292
McPherson, Aimee Semple, 5, 16, 132, 136
Maddox, Mary Jane, 8
Mail ministry, 111–112, 411–418
Malone, Moses, 246
Mann, W. E., 164, 168–169, 174
Martin, Pete, 304, 502
Martin, Ralph, 287
Martin, Tony, 123
Martin, William, 420
Mason, Willard, 180
Mayo, John D., 193
Maxwell, James, 145
Media attention, 303–304
Melton, T. A., 156
Merritt, Simpson, 36
Messick, John D., 213–214, 216, 219, 222, 232–233, 238, 273
Methodist church, 15–17, 19, 296–299, 369, 410
Miami Herald, 181
Migliore, R. Henry, 367
Millard, Geneva, 113

Millard, Roberta, 113
Millennialism, 16. *See also* Premillennialism
Million Soul campaign, 122, 142–143
Million Souls Stand, 133
The Miracle of Seed-Faith, 419, 461, 500
Missionary Alliance, 18
"The Modern Tongues and Healing Movement," 74
Moncey, George W., 5–7, 67
Montgomery, G., H., 17–18, 38, 42–43, 48–49, 52–53, 63, 77, 91, 126, 129–132, 136, 147, 158–159, 165–166, 214, 273, 275–276, 300–301
Moore, Oscar, 47, 56, 81, 87, 133–134, 160–161, 273, 407, 487
Moral Majority, 430, 445, 448
Morrison, Chester, 171
Mt. Gap, Georgia, camp meeting, 49
Moyers, Donald R., 173, 301, 322, 343, 360, 404, 407, 432–433, 471, 480, 489
Muse, Dan T., 20–21, 26, 53, 69, 156, 159, 503
Muskogee revival, 83

Nance, Yvonne, 143, 145
Nash, Bill, 191, 330, 332, 405, 435, 485
Nash, Brenda Ann, 325
Nash, Edna, 330, 435, 440, 474
Nash, Marcia Elaine, 325
Nash, Marshall Everett, 192, 324–325, 329–334
Nash, Rebecca. *See* Roberts, Rebecca
Nash, W. J., 61
Nation, 430
National Association for Better Radio and Television, 172
National Association of Evangelicals, 17, 147, 172
National Catholic Welfare Conference, 165
National Council of Churches, 430
National Enquirer 181
National Geographic, 433
National Religious Broadcasters, 173
Navajo Tribal Council, 135
Neal, Emily Gardiner, 175, 502
Neopentecostal movement, 287–289
New York Times, 172, 178, 303–304, 313, 359, 362, 493
New Yorker magazine, 180
Newsweek, 171, 362, 414, 431
Nichols, John, 237
Nigh, George, 389
Nixon, Richard, 154, 309
Noble, Vaden, 33
Nunn, David, 152

O. W. Coburn School of Law, 370–374
Oakland Tribune, 174, 178
Ockenga, Harold, 202–203
O'Dell, Fred, 167
Oklahoma Baptist University, 59

Oklahoma Coalition of Citizens with Disabilities, 362–363
Oklahoma General Board of Education, 62
Oklahoma Health Planning Commission, 383–387, 394
Oklahoma Health Systems Agency, 383
Oklahoma Pentecostal Holiness subculture, 39
Oklahoma Territory, 11
Oliver, L. J., 157
Olsen, Pastor Russell H., 84
Open Bible Church, 132
Oracle, 380, 414, 499
Oral Roberts Association, 277
Oral Roberts Evangelistic Association, Inc. (OREA), 114, 118, 120, 133–134, 141–145, 194, 212, 227, 273, 277, 346, 360, 391, 400, 407, 412–416, 433, 499
Oral Roberts' Life Story, 123, 500
Oral Roberts publications, statistics, 130–131
Oral Roberts' True Stories, 130, 499
Oral Roberts University, viii, 199, 208–213; academic-spiritual tensions, 248–250; accreditation, 230–232; ACLU suit, 362–363; acquisition of land, 208; aerobics program, 279, 362; athletic program, 363–364; basketball team, 244–248; budget, 361; building construction, 223–228; Christian Service Council, 244; City of Faith medical center, 382–396 (*see also* City of Faith medical center); code of honor pledge, 239–240; dedication ceremony, 228; dental school, 377; dress code, 361–362; faculty, 222, 290, 359; family seminars, 380; finances, 213, 306, 360–361, 413–418, 435; graduate expansion, 364–396; Graduate School of Theology, 216, 221, 234–235, 238, 367, 369–370; handicapped students, restrictions on, 362–363; "interdisciplinary cross-pollination" concept, 367; Learning Resources Center, 223–224; library, closing of, 361; Mabee Center, 224–225; major goals of, 219–221, 248–249; medical school, 365, 374–379; NCAA investigation of, 364; OREA, relationship with, 212; overweight students, restrictions on, 279, 362–363; O. W. Coburn School of Law, 371–374; partner conferences, 216–217; pentecostal opposition to, 218; School of Evangelism, 257, 264, 289–290; School of Theology, 367, 369; seminars, 216–217; student body, composition of, 223, 359; tenure, abolishment of, 250; university codes, 239–244
Oral Roberts University Archives, 499
Oral Roberts University Library, 499
Oral Roberts University of Evangelism, 209, 211
Oral: The Warm, Intimate, Unauthorized Portrait of a Man of God, 430–431, 503
Order of Saint Luke, 174
OREA Partners, 499
OREA Today, 499
ORU Witness, 499

Osborn, T. L., 138, 149, 394, 424
Osteen, John, 423–424
Oursler, Will, 167, 175, 502
Outler, Albert, 292
Outreach, 276, 499

Pan American Broadcasting Company, 123
Pardue, Austin, 175
Parham, Charles G., 15
Paris Chapel, 26
Partner conferences, 142–143
Partner system, 282–286, 412–415, 417–418, 420–421
Partners' seminars, 282–283
Pathescope Productions of New York City, 126
Patti Roberts International Outreach, 341
Paul, George Harold, 53, 60, 131, 238, 319
Pentecost, 148, 500
Pentecostal churches: hostility toward healing revivalists, 155–161, 300; opposition to healing revivalism, 300–301; opposition to Oral Roberts University, 218; sponsorship of evangelistic campaigns, 92–93, 254
Pentecostal Fellowship of North America, 17, 147–148
Pentecostal Holiness Advocate, 4, 17, 34, 37, 42–44, 47–48, 51–52, 59, 62, 68, 87, 131, 147, 157, 214, 478, 499
Pentecostal Holiness church, 16–21, 36, 49, 51–52, 54, 58, 112, 158–161, 503
Pentecostal Holiness *Discipline*, 18
Pentecostal Holiness Florida Conference, 157
Pentecostal partners, 297–298
Pentecostal Young People's Society, 37, 48
Pentecostalism, viii, 15–16, 20, 63, 146–150, 155, 494–495
Phillips, Leon C. (Red), 42
Pitts, John, 174
Plenty-crossed churches, 156
Pontotoc County, 3, 9, 12
Pope, J. M., 55
Potts, Roberta. *See* Roberts, Roberta Jean
Potts, Ronald Stephen, 317, 347
Powell, Gordon, 78–79
Pravda, 258
Prayer card system, 96–97, 100
Prayer cloths, 111–112, 119, 413, 419–420
Prayer language, 465–467
"Prayer Pact," 461
Prayer partners, 383
Prayer Tower, 224
Premillennialism, 136, 149, 444, 447, 500. *See also* Dispensational premillennialism
Presbyterian Outlook, 163
Presley, Elvis, 421
Price, Charles, 5, 132
Price, Fred, 389, 423–427
Prime Time Preachers, 430
Pringle, Steve, 82–83, 151
Protestant opposition to Roberts, 164
Protestantism, 19

Pryor, J.P., 13
Pryor, Martha, 13
PTL network, 426
Public relations campaign, 180–181
Publications, translation of, 138

Quebedeaux, Richard, 503
Quillian, Joseph, Jr., 416

Radio ministry, 57, 120, 123, 142, 274
Ranaghan, Kevin, 287
Randolph, Jennings, 243
Rank, Arthur, 221
Ray, Chandu, 199
Reader's Digest condensed version of the Bible, 441
Reagan, Ronald, 389
Redemptorama, 144–145
Reed, William Jeff, 11
Reed, William Standish, 219, 449, 458–460
Register, 174
Religion in Life, 174
A Religious History of the American People, viii
Review and Expositer, 174
Rhema Bible Training School, 423
Rice, John R., 502
Richey, Raymond T., 5, 82, 154
Ricketts, Ronald, 385–386
Rider, Jonas, 165
Robbins, Harold, 430
Roberts, Amos Pleasant, 8–10, 12, 16
Roberts, Bill, 215, 223, 227, 334, 381, 486, 493
Roberts, Christine Michelle, 322
Roberts, Claudius, 3, 12–15, 25–26, 316, 473, 501
Roberts, Ed, 9
Roberts, Ellis Melvin, 3, 12–17, 21–24, 27, 36, 316
Roberts, Elmer, 3–7, 13
Roberts, Evelyn, 41–50, 184–188, 273, 281, 314–317, 337–344, 348–351, 353–356, 456, 480, 501
Roberts, Granville Oral, 25; anticommunism, 447; autobiography, 278; baptism, 36; belief in demons, 453–454; Billy Graham, comparison with, 178–179; campaign routine, 183–185; Catholic opposition to, 164, 169; civil rights, position on, 446–447; conversion to Methodism, 261, 293–299; crusade ministry, ending of, 261–263; "dedication" of, 26; Denver prophecy, 87, 292; early sermons, 36; ecumenism, 443, 446; Enid (Oklahoma) pastorship, 62, 64–65, 68; evangelistic career, beginning of, 36–37, 42, 55–57; eye surgery, 350–351; family, 183–196, 314–317, 337–340, 348–353; father and son revival team, 36, 42–43; finances, 170, 192–195, 313–315, 355–357, 424; first healing experience, 61; healing of by Ellis, 34; healing of fellow ministers, 151–152; high school,

30–33; licensing of as a minister, 37; marriage of, 44–48; move to Tulsa, 80–81; naming of, 26; Oral Roberts University, message from God, 207; as *Pentecostal Holiness Advocate* staff writer, 62; Pentecostal Holiness Church, discontent with, 63–66; pentecostal opposition to, 155–161, 218, 300–301; personal characteristics, 469–470; personal wealth, divestment of, 313–314; physicians, relationship with, 458; political clout, 309, 420; Protestant opposition to, 164; preaching style, 98, 476–478; public image, 170–178, 300, 304–311; stuttering, 7, 28; theology, 53, 66, 90, 166, 168, 181, 229, 293, 299, 426, 439–468, 483–484; tolerance of other religions, 444–445; tuberculosis, 3–7, 32–35, 453; Tulsa honors, 306–307; visions of Jesus, 415–417
Roberts, J. Willis, 12
Roberts, Jewel, 4
Roberts, John, 12
Roberts, Julene Allison, 322
Roberts, L. V., 113, 131
Roberts, Lindsay Ann (née Salem), 346–347, 401–402
Roberts, Ora, 3
Roberts, Oral. *See* Roberts, Granville Oral
Roberts, Orrie, 336–337
Roberts, Patti (née Holcombe), 221, 260, 319–322, 340–345, 401, 490, 503
Roberts, Rebecca Ann, 48, 189–191, 324–325, 329–334
Roberts, Richard Lee, 88, 188, 192, 267, 280, 317–322, 340–345, 354, 400–406, 492
Roberts, Richard Oral, 347–348
Roberts, Roberta Jean, 188, 192, 317, 347, 357–358, 410, 491–492
Roberts, Ronald David, 58, 190–192, 322–324, 337–341
Roberts, Vaden, 17, 432–433
Roberts, Velma, 13–14, 22, 24
Roberts, Willis, 27–28
Roberts Jewish Outreach, 135–137
Robertson, Pat, 207, 266, 389
Robin Hood Ranch, 193
Robinson, A. E., 48
Robinson, Wayne A., 31, 236, 267, 275, 277–278, 284, 430–432, 442, 469–470, 486, 490, 503
Rooks, Ruth, 112, 191
Roosevelt, Theodore, 9
Rose, Bill, 174, 178
Ross, Dick, 267
Rotary Club, 306
Russell, John, 428

Sackett, Myron, 136, 273
Safer, Morley, 432
Salem, Lindsay Ann. *See* Roberts, Lindsay Ann
Salvation by the Blood, 43–44, 500
Sand Springs revival, 42

Santee, Jack, 384–385
Saturday Evening Post, 175, 304
Saturday Review, 430
Schmitz, Charles H., 172
Schwartz, Harry, 363
Scofield Reference Bibles, 50
Seed-faith, 284, 357, 411, 421, 460–462, 500
Seven World Outreaches, 134–141, 274
Seventeen, 223
Seventh Day Adventists, 365
Shakarian, Demos, 97, 134, 140, 153–155, 185, 273, 336, 389, 407, 469, 472–473, 493–494, 497
Shakarian, Evangeline, 263
Shakarian, Richard, 263
Shelton Brothers, 57
Sholes, Jerry, 363, 408, 431–433, 503
Singewald, Martin L., 358
"Sixty Minutes," 431, 433
Smith, Noel, 301–302
Smith, Ronald R., 278–280, 381, 397–398, 407–408, 410, 431–432, 484, 488–493
Smith, W. Angie, 294–295, 299, 303
Sneed, Earl, 385
Society of Pentecostal Studies, 426
"Something Good Is Going to Happen to You," 268
Souls Unlimited campaign, 122
South African campaigns, 138–140
South Central Jurisdiction of the United Methodist Church, 416
Southwestern Bible College, 208, 211
Southwestern Board of Education, 62
Spalding, James C., 219
Spellbinder, 430
Spence, Hubert T., 49, 156, 160
Spiers, Donald, 263
Sponsoring pastors, 92–93
Sports Illustrated, 223, 245
Sproull, O. E., 53, 113–114, 131, 158
Stamps, Bob, 243, 367–369
Stanfield, A. G., 113
Stanfield, Cecil, 144, 209, 226
Stapleton, Ruth Carter, 176, 421
Stark, S.E., 26
Steele, Collins, 75–76, 78, 93–94, 131, 133, 184, 273–274, 329–330, 408, 470
Stegall, Carroll, Jr., 74, 163, 169
Stephenson, George, 81
Sterne, Bill, 275
Stevenson, Hugh, 9
Stokes, Mack B., 428
Stott, John, 199
Stovall, George, 346, 399, 407, 409, 412, 420, 433, 486–488, 492
Straton, John Roach, 145
Straton, Warren, 145
Student missions program, 393–396
Suenens, Leon Joseph Cardinal, 287
Sulphur (Oklahoma), 23, 37–38
Summerfield, Arthur E., 145

Sunday Magazine, 303
Suppressed, 502
Sutton, Eddie, 363–364
Sutton, Ernest, 15
Swan and Mason Advertising, Inc., 180
Swann, Charles E., 430
Swearingen, Eugene, 421
Sydney Bulletin, 75
Sydney Morning Herald, 78
Sydney Sun, 75
Sydney Sunday Truth, 77
Synan, J.A., 53, 61–62, 156, 160–161, 230, 296, 423
Synan, L.C., 50, 160
Synan, Vinson, 19, 237, 298, 422, 440, 494

Television ministry, 96–97, 122–123, 125–130, 397–400; Billy Graham special, 272; "Contact" television special, 268–270; cost of, 128–129; critical acclaim, 269–270; Federal Communications Commission investigation, 171–172; format, 271–273; healing line, 171–172; Hollywood celebrities, 270–272; prime time specials, 267; production studio, 400; satellite broadcasting, 400; temporary ending of, 266
Temple, Paul L., 193–194
Tents, 74, 85, 107
Texas Methodist, 299
Thielman, Calvin, 200–201, 203, 205, 228, 417, 446, 469
Third World Crusades, 260
Thomas, Bill, 427
Thompson, C.T., 378–379, 391, 415–416, 432, 434
Till, Jake, 89
Time, 171, 502
Timko, Nick, 134, 273
Titans, 244
Tjelta, I. Tomine, 367
Tokyo visit, 259
Tolle, James M., 502
Tomlinson, A. J., 16
TRACO, 271, 399
Trickey, Ken, 244, 247, 314–315, 354, 363–364
Tulsa County Medical Society, 383
Tulsa Evangelistic Center, 236
Tulsa Hospital Council, 384–387
Tulsa Ministerial Alliance, 176
Tulsa press, 304–306
Tulsa Tribune, 79, 129, 175–176, 230, 234, 243, 302, 305, 355, 361, 365, 431, 485
Tulsa World, 116, 230, 232, 279, 305, 364–365, 390, 415, 433, 459
Turpin, L. E., 60, 151
TV Guide, 430
Tyson, Tommy, 219, 243, 260, 264, 273, 456
"Twentieth Century Evangelism," 202–203

United Methodist Church, 428
United Methodist Council on Evangelism, 428
University of Evangelism, 211–212
University Village Retirement Center, 278

Valdez, A. C., Jr., 154
Van Horne, Harriet, 172
Van Stone, Fred, 360, 408–409
Variety, 171
Venture into Faith, 124–125, 137
Victory Christian Center, 429
The Voice of Healing, 149–150
Voight, Robert G., 241, 249, 492
Volunteer help, 111–112
Vonderscher, Mary Ida Buddington, 165

WABC-TV, 129
Wall Street Journal, 185–186, 192, 194–195, 363, 430
Wallace, Frank, 215, 223, 225–227, 334, 381, 474
Wallace, George, 311
Warfield, Benjamin B., 162
Warren, W. K., 378, 387–388
Wicks, Mildred, 56, 81, 151
Wiggins, Pat, 256
Wilkerson, D. E., 346
Wilkerson, David, 290
Wilkerson, Ralph, 216, 389
Williams, Carl, 212
Williams, J. Floyd, 218
Williams, John H., 228, 306, 352, 357, 404, 418, 420, 434, 469–470, 487, 489, 497
Williams Corporation, 352
Willoughby, William, 304
Wilson, Carl, 273
Wings of Healing Temple, 84
Winslow, James, 334, 365, 374, 377, 381, 384, 387, 389–390, 394–395, 406–407, 409, 435, 460, 487–489, 494
Winslow, Sue, 374–375
World Action Singers, 267, 270, 280, 321
World Action teams, 263–265
World Conference of Pentecostal Churches, 500
World Congress on Evangelism, 199–206
World Council of Churches, 237, 446
World Outreach ministry, 74, 140, 273
World War II, vii, ix
WRAL, 56
Wyatt, Thomas, 84

Xenoglossy, 16

Yager, Saul, 208, 444, 489
York, Dan, 13–14, 16, 26
York, Dolly, 13–14, 16
"Your Faith Is Power," 125

Zachary, Doyle, 151, 157
Zimmerman, Thomas, 31, 160, 218, 422
Zimmerman, Wendell, 430